email
total.23@total.sem.com
total,123@total.sem.com

1-800-446-6004

Test Vouchers
save 100.00

Request New Test
Engine

over email

A+ Certification Exam Guide

Other Certification Exam Guides from Computing McGraw-Hill

BOONE • *Java 1.1 Certification Exam Guide*

THOMAS & PEASLEY • *Lotus Notes Certification Exam Guide*

MEZICK & HILLIER • *Visual Basic Certification Exam Guide*

NET GURU TECHNOLOGIES, INC. • *Webmaster Administrator Certification Exam Guide*

MUELLER & WILLIAMS • *The CNA/CNE Study Guide, Intranetware Edition*

A+ Certification Exam Guide

Michael Meyers

McGraw-Hill

New York San Francisco Washington, D.C. Auckland Bogotá
Caracas Lisbon London Madrid Mexico City Milan
Montreal New Delhi San Juan Singapore
Sydney Tokyo Toronto

Library of Congress Cataloging-in-Publication Data

Meyers, Michael, date.
A+ certification exam guide / Michael Meyers.
p. cm.
Includes index.
ISBN 0-07-913765-2 (book/CD-rom)
1. Computer technicians—Certification. 2. Microcomputers—Maintenance and repair—Examinations—Study guides. 3. Computing Technology Industry Association—Examinations—Study guides.
I. Title.
TK7885.54.M48 1998
621.36'16'076—dc21 98-7472
CIP

McGraw-Hill

*A Division of The **McGraw-Hill** Companies*

5 6 7 8 9 0 DOC/DOC 9 0 3 2 1 0 9

P/N 044463-3
PART OF ISBN 0-07-913765-2

The sponsoring editor for this book was Scott Grillo, and the production supervisor was Pamela Pelton. It was set in Vendome ICG by Jana Fisher through the services of Barry E. Brown (Broker—Editing, Design and Production).

Printed and bound by R. R. Donnelley & Sons Company.

This book is printed on recycled, acid-free paper containing a minimum of 50% recycled de-inked fiber.

This book is dedicated to the core of Total Seminars.

To Brian Schwarz—for holding the laptop at Discovery Zone.

To Dudley Lehmer—for keeping cool when the rest of us of freaked out.

To Janelle Meyers—for keeping us organized and paid.

CONTENTS

ACKNOWLEDGMENTS

To seriously maul the quote from Winston Churchill "Never has one person, ever owed so much to so many different people". If any of these folks ever need help moving a piano or paying for bail, they know they can call me first.

I have to start with Scott Grillo, my editor at McGraw-Hill, for being the cool-headed and patient human that I never will. Next is Barry Brown for explaining the 43,231 things that new authors shouldn't do-after I did every one of them.

I also want to say thanks to all the folks at Total Seminars who put up with me over the last nine months. Thanks for the extra hours, the insight, the constructive criticism and laughing at most of my bad jokes.

Last, and most, thanks to "The World's Most Understanding Family", my wife Alison and my daughter Emily. I'll be home for dinner tonight—for a change.

INTRODUCTION

The A+ Certification

In the Introduction to this book, you will:

- Understand the importance of A+ Certification.
- Discover the structure and goals of the exam.
- Discover the "where," "when," and "how much" of the exam.
- Plan a strategy to pass.

Every profession requires specialized skills. If you want to get or keep a job that requires those specialized skills, you often need some type of certification or license. If you want to be paid to fix cars, you get the ASE (Automotive Service Excellence) certification. If you want to be paid to do someone's accounting, you become a CPA (certified public accountant). If you want to be paid to rub the back, cut the hair, or polish the nails of your fellow human beings, there are different certifications that you need.

Yup, most professions have some method that allows you to show that you are competent and capable of performing at a certain level. You pass some type of test to prove that you have the necessary skills and have received some piece of paper or pin or membership card that you can show to potential clients or employers. This certification gives those clients or employers at least a level of confidence that you can do what you say you are going to do for them. Without this certification, either you won't be allowed to work in your profession or nobody will trust you to do the work. PC technicians, however, are an exception.

Since the inception of microcomputers in the late '70s, there has been no agreed-upon way for PC technicians to show clients or employers that they know what they are doing under the hood of a personal computer. Sure, there have been vendor-specific certifications, but the only way to get them was to first get a job at an authorized warranty or repair facility and then get the certification. Not that there's anything wrong with vendor-specific training, it's just that no one manufacturer has taken enough market share to make that IBM or Compaq training something that works for any job. Then there's always the little detail of getting the job first before you can get certified.

The software/networking side of the computer business doesn't suffer from the same lack of certification. Due to the monopolistic aspect of certain companies at one time or another (Microsoft, Novell, etc.), vendor-specific certifications are a great inroad to getting and keeping a job. For example, Microsoft's MCP (Microsoft Certified Professional) and MCSE (Microsoft Certified System Engineer), Novell's CNA (Certified Novell Administrator) and CNE (Certified Novell Engineer), and Cisco's CCIE (Cisco Certified Internetwork Expert) have opened the doors for many who have decided to pursue certification.

But what about the person who runs around all day replacing floppies, repartitioning hard drives, upgrading device drivers, and building systems? What about PC hobbyists who decide to make the jump and want to start to get paid for their skills? What about those who, because they had the audacity to show that they knew the difference between CMOS and a C: prompt, find themselves with a new title like PC Support Technician or Electronic Services Specialist? Or how about the person who ends up being "the person who doesn't get a nickel extra, but fixes the computers?"

Until now there has been no nationally recognized certification for PC technicians that they can use to show a certain level of competence. Technicians haven't had a piece of paper to put on their wall or pin to stick on their chest to show they knew their stuff. Until now. Welcome to A+ Certification!

What Is A+ Certification?

A+ is a certification sponsored by CompTIA, the Computing Technology Industry Association. A+ Certification shows that you have a basic competence in supporting microcomputers. The goal is to test what is generally assumed to be the knowledge held by a technician with six months of full-time PC support experience. You achieve this certification by taking two computer-based, multiple-choice examinations. The certification is widely recognized throughout the computer industry, and significantly improves a technician's ability to secure and keep employment.

CompTIA is a nonprofit, industry trade association based out of Lombard, Illinois. It consists of over 7,500 computer resellers, value-added resellers (VARs), distributors, manufacturers, and training companies all over the U.S. and Canada. Only companies and organizations can be members of CompTIA; there are no individual memberships. The cost to join CompTIA is based on sales or the number of employees, and ranges from $150 to $10,000 annually.

The goal of CompTIA is to provide a forum for networking (as in meeting people), to represent the interests of its members in government, and to provide certifications for many different aspects of the computer industry. Currently, their only significant certification is A+. Check out the CompTIA Web site at http://www.comptia.org, for details on the other certifications that you can obtain from CompTIA.

Virtually every company of consequence is a member of CompTIA. Here's a few of the biggies:

- 3COM
- Adobe
- Apple
- AST
- ATT
- Black Box
- Canon
- Compaq
- Digital
- Epson
- Fujitsu
- Hayes
- Hewlett Packard
- IBM
- Intel
- Iomega
- Lexmark
- Lotus
- Microhouse
- Microsoft
- Minolta
- NEC
- Netgear
- Netscape
- Novell
- Okidata
- Oracle
- Panasonic
- Peachtree
- Rockwell
- Sun Microsystems
- Sybex
- Symantec
- Toshiba

CompTIA began offering A+ Certification back in 1993. When it was first started, it was largely ignored. However, over the course of the last few years, CompTIA has managed to position A+ Certification to the point where it is considered to be the de-facto requirement for entrance into the PC industry. Many companies require A+ Certification for all their PC support technicians, and A+ Certification is becoming widely recognized both in the U.S. and internationally.

How Do I Become A+ Certified?

First of all, there are no prerequisites for A+ Certification. You pay the testing fee and take two exams. You will immediately know whether you have passed or failed. If you pass both exams, you are an A+ Certified technician. There are no requirements for professional experience, you don't have to go through an "authorized training center," there are no annual dues, and there are no continuing education requirements. If you pass, you're in. That's it. You must first pass the "Core" exam (CompTIA calls each test an *exam*). After passing the Core exam, you then take the Microsoft Windows/DOS exam.

A major rewrite of the A+ exam was released in July of 1998. Prior to the 1998 exam revision there was a third "Macintosh OS" exam and a very few basic Mac questions on the Core exam. Due to a joint decision of Apple Computer and CompTIA, the A+ Macintosh OS exam as well as the Macintosh-specific questions in the Core are removed in the new version of the A+ exam.

The new exam covers several topics that were not in the earlier exam; Windows 95, networking/internet and laptops. *This book covers all the new topics and will prepare you to pass the new 1998 revision of the A+ Certification exam.*

What Are the Tests Like and How Are They Structured?

Both the exams are extremely practical, with little or no interest in theory. All questions are multiple choice. You should schedule to take both exams at the same time.

Core Exam

The Core exam tests you on basic hardware knowledge. You should be able to recognize; know how to clean, handle, install, and diagnose; understand the function of; and know the different types of each of these components:

- CPUs
- RAM

- ROM/CMOS
- Expansion busses
- Floppy drives
- IDE drives
- SCSI devices
- CD-ROM drives
- Video cards
- Monitors
- Modems
- Printers
- Cables and connectors

In addition, the core exam tests for a solid understanding of operating systems. You should be comfortable with both DOS, Windows 3.1 and Windows 95." In particular, you should understand the function, optimization, and proper use of:

- Boot files
- Disk caching
- Virtual memory
- Device drivers
- TSRs
- Basic system errors

The core exam expects that you are comfortable with basic troubleshooting. You should be able to pick an obvious "first step" for a broad cross-section of symptoms linked to the previously listed hardware and software. For example, you should be able to answer a question such as: A dot-matrix printer is printing blank pages. The first item to check is: A) the printer drivers, B) the platen, C) the print head, or D) the ribbon. The correct answer is D) the ribbon. You can make an argument for any of the others, but common sense tells you to check the simplest possibility first.

You should be very comfortable with very basic electrical components and the proper use of volt-ohm-meters (VOMs) to test them. You should be able to identify basic electrical components and their electronic symbols. The A+ core exam also requires you to be comfortable with the control of electrostatic discharge (ESD) and electromagnetic interference (EMI).

Last, the core exam assumes that you are comfortable with both binary and hexadecimal, in the context of practical use in PC configuration.

Windows/DOS Exam

The Windows/DOS exam adds on to the Core exam, assuming all the same hardware and software knowledge you needed to pass the core module. However, the Windows/DOS exam takes a very strong slant towards understanding DOS and Windows.

From a hardware standpoint, you will be expected to know how to install and configure all the hardware devices listed in the Core exam into a DOS or Windows PC.

The Windows/DOS exam aggressively tests your knowledge of DOS, Windows 3.1 and Windows 95. If it is in the \DOS or \WINDOWS\COMMAND directory, know it. You should be very comfortable with the proper configuration of all boot files: AUTOEXEC.BAT, CONFIG.SYS, SYSTEM.INI, and WIN.INI.

The exam asks a number of questions regarding system optimization. This includes DOS memory management, caching, and power management. You will be tested on your ability to configure hardware, CMOS, boot files, and TSRs to properly optimize a system.

How Do I Take the Tests?

The tests are administered by Sylvan Prometric. There are thousands of Sylvan Prometric testing centers across the U.S. and Canada. You can take the exams at any testing center. Call Sylvan Prometric at 1-800-77MICRO to schedule the exams and to locate the nearest testing center. You must pay for the exams when you call to schedule. Be prepared to sit on hold for a while, and have your social security number and a credit card ready when you call. Sylvan Prometric will be glad to invoice, but you won't be able to take the tests until they receive full payment.

How Much Does It Cost?

The cost of the tests varies. If you work for a CompTIA member, there are some significant discounts. You can also save money by taking more than one exam at a time.

You must pass both exams within 90 days in order to be A+ Certified. You don't have to pass the Core exam before you can take the Win/DOS exam. If you pass one exam and fail another, you must repay and retake the other exam within 90 days. You must pay for every exam you take, whether you pass or fail. If you fail both exams in the assigned time, you will have to pay for and retake *both* exams.

Say, for example, you sign up to take both exams at the same time. You fail the Core but pass the Win/DOS. You must then reschedule and repay to take the Core exam within 90 days, or you will have to pay for and retake both exams!

How to Pass the A+ Exams

The single most important aspect to remember about A+ Certification is that the exams are designed to test the knowledge of a new technician with only six months of experience. So keep it simple! The tests aren't interested in your ability to manually set DRAM timings in the CMOS or explaining the difference between the Intel 430TX and 430VX chipset. Don't bother with a lot of theory; being able to do hex-to-binary conversions in your head won't help a bit. Think in terms of simple, practical knowledge and you'll pass.

Is it safe to assume that it's probably been a while since you've had to take an exam? Is it also safe to assume that it's been a while since you've had to study for an exam? If these statements are true, then you're probably going to want to read the next several sections. They will provide you with a proven strategy to get you through and to pass the A+ exams. Try it. It works.

Obligate Yourself

The very first step you should take is to schedule the exams. Have you ever heard the old adage "heat and pressure make diamonds?" If you don't give yourself a little "heat," you'll end up procrastinating and unnecessarily delaying taking the exams. Even worse, you might not take them at all. Do yourself a favor. Determine the amount of time you need to study (see the next section) and then call Sylvan Prometric to schedule the exams. When you know they are coming up, it makes it a lot easier to turn off the TV and crack open the book.

Set Aside the Right Amount of Study Time

After helping thousands of technicians get their A+ Certification, Total Seminars has developed a pretty good "feel" as to the amount of study time to pass the A+. This time has been quantified in Table 1-1. Keep in mind that these are averages; if you're not a great student or if you're a little on the nervous side, add another 10 percent. Or if you're the type who can learn an entire semester of geometry in one night, reduce the numbers by 10 percent. To use this table, just circle the values that are most accurate for you and add them up to get the number of study hours. To that value, add the number of months of direct, professional experience supporting PCs:

0: Add 50 hours
Up to 6: Add 20 hours
6 to 12: Add 10 hours
Over 12: Add 0 hours

A total neophyte should need around 200 hours of study, and an experienced technician shouldn't need more than 40.

Amount of Experience . . .	None	Once or Twice	Every Now & Then	Quite a Bit
Installing any type of card	16	14	8	2
Installing hard drives	6	3	2	1
Installing SCSI devices	8	6	4	2
Installing modems	6	6	4	2
Installing printers	4	3	2	1
Installing RAM	8	6	4	2
Installing CPUs	6	6	4	3
Fixing printers	5	5	3	3
Fixing monitors	5	5	3	3
Complete system builds	12	10	8	4
Using DOS	8	8	6	2
DOS memory management (EMM386, PIF files)	10	10	6	4
Using Windows 3.1 or Windows for Workgroups	8	6	4	2

Amount of Experience . . .	None	Once or Twice	Every Now & Then	Quite a Bit
Installing Windows 3.1 or WFW	4	3	1	1
Using Windows 95	4	4	2	1
Installing Windows 95	6	5	4	3
Creating tape backups	4	4	3	1
Accessing an electronic BBS (not Internet)	6	6	3	2
INI files	2	2	2	1
Installing a Network Card	12	8	4	1
Using a volt ohmmeter	4	3	2	1
Electrical wiring	4	2	2	1

Studying for the Test

Now that you have a feel for how long it's going to take, you should have a strategy for studying. The strategy outlined in this section has proven itself to be an excellent "game plan" for getting the knowledge of the study materials into your head.

First, read the book—the whole book. Read it as though you were reading a novel, starting on page one and going all the way through. Don't skip around on the first read-through, even if you are a highly experienced technician. There are terms and concepts that build on each other; skipping around will simply confuse you, and you'll just end up turning on the TV.

Your goal on this first read is to understand concepts, to understand the "whys" and not just the "hows." It is very helpful to have a PC nearby as you read, so you can stop and inspect the PC to see and try out a particular concept. For example, as you read about floppy drives, inspect the cables. Do they look like what is shown in the book? Is there a variation? Why? It is imperative that you understand *why* you are doing something; don't let yourself be limited to just knowing *how* to do it.

One of the greatest secrets in the computer business is that "everything old is new again." Sure, technology continues to get faster, with wider data paths, but the underlying technology—the core of what makes your PC, your printer, and your modem operate—has changed very little since its inception 15 years ago. This leads to the last point for the initial read-through. You will notice a lot of historical data—old stuff—that you might be tempted to skip over. Don't! The A+ exams take a strong interest in older equipment. Equally important, by understanding how some of the older stuff works, you can appreciate the need for and function of most components on current PCs.

After you've completed the first read-through, go through the book again. This time, try to knock out one chapter at a sitting. Get a highlighter and mark the phrases and sentences that bring out major points. Really take a hard look at the pictures and tables, noting how they elaborate the concepts. When you get to the end of each chapter, create some questions for yourself. If you really want to burn in the information, try changing some of the questions and then try to answer them again.

Practice Tests

The absolute last step is to take the tests on the enclosed CD-ROM. These tests are your "final exams" to give you an accurate feel for how well prepared you are for the exams. Don't try them until you think you can pass the real exams. When you think you're ready, go for the practice exams. Use the results to see where you need to "bone up," and try them again. After two or three passes, you should be in the 85 to 90 percent range. When you get there, you are ready to pass the A+ Certification exams! If you have any problems or questions, or if you just want to argue about something, feel free to send me an e-mail, at michaelm@totalsem.com.

Test Updates

Our industry is constantly changing. In keeping with this ongoing change, CompTIA recognizes the need for ongoing question updates, as well as occasional changes to the testing procedure. 1998 promises to be such a year.

CHAPTER 1

The Visible PC

In this chapter, you will:

- See the major components of a PC.
- Understand the different connectors in a PC.
- Recognize the most common cards in a PC.
- Learn how to set jumpers and switches.

Sometimes, in order to understand the details, you first need to understand the big picture. This chapter's job is to allow you to understand the function and recognize the main components of the CPU. You will also see all the major connectors, plugs, and sockets, and be able to recognize a particular part by simply seeing what type of connectors are attached to that part. Even if you are an expert, don't skip this chapter! It introduces a large number of terms that will be used throughout the rest of the book. Many of these terms you will know but some you won't, so take some time and read it.

It is handy, although certainly not required, to have a PC that you can take the lid off and inspect as you progress. So get thee to a screwdriver, grab your PC, take off the lid, and see if you can recognize the various components as they are discussed.

CPU

The CPU (central processing unit, also called the microprocessor) is where all the calculations take place in a PC. CPUs come in a variety of shapes and sizes (Figure 1.1). The most common in today's PCs are the PGA (Pin Grid Array) and SEC (Single Edge Cartridge).

> Modern CPUs generate a lot of heat. To cool the CPU, a cooling fan or a heatsink is attached (Figure 1.2). This cooling device is usually removable, although some CPU manufacturers sell the CPU with a fan permanently attached.

CPUs have a make and model, just like an automobile. When talking about a particular car, most people speak in terms of a Ford Taurus or a Toyota Camry. When they talk about CPUs, its an Intel 486 or an AMD K6. Some of the more common makes are AMD, Cyrix, and Intel. Some of the more common models are 8088, 286, 386, 486, Pentium, Pentium Pro, K5, K6, and 6x86. In the early years of CPUs, makers would sometime make the exact same model, so you could get an AMD 486 or an Intel 486

Figure 1.1
Typical CPUs

Figure 1.2
Installed CPU under a fan

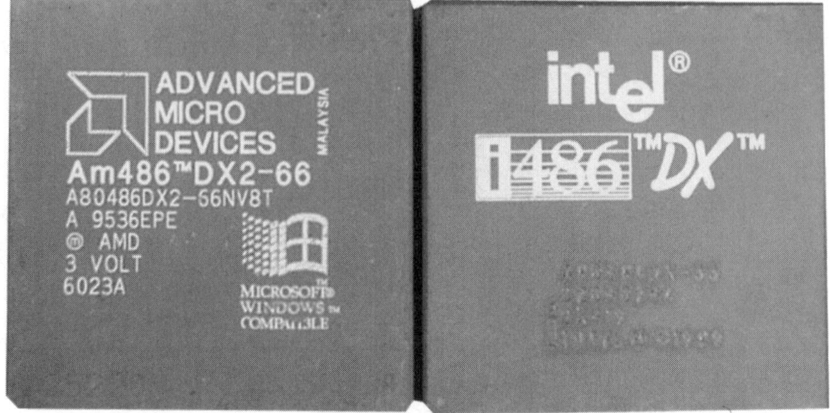

Figure 1.3
The AMD 486 and Intel 486

(Figure 1.3). This is no longer true, although some models are very similar, such as the Intel Pentium and the Cyrix 6x86.

CPUs have a "top speed," which is determined at the factory. It is called the *clock speed* and is measured in megaHertz (MHz). The first CPU used in PCs had a clock speed in the range of 4.77 MHz. Today's CPUs have clock speeds up to 500 MHz. When talking about a CPU, people often cite the make, model, and clock speed, for example, an 180-MHz Intel Pentium Pro. CPUs of the same make and model are produced with many different clock speeds (Figure 1.4). For example, the Intel Pentium Pro comes in three different speeds: 166, 180, and 200 MHz. The main reason for picking one speed over another is primarily the thickness of your wallet.

RAM

RAM (random-access memory) is where the CPU stores programs and data it is currently using. RAM is measured in units called *bytes*. Modern PCs have many millions of bytes of RAM, so RAM is measured in units called *Megabytes*. An average PC will usually have anywhere from 8 Megabytes to 64 Megabytes of RAM, although it can easily be more or less. RAM has been packaged in many different ways over the years. The two most current packages are called SIMMs (single inline memory module) and DIMMs (dual inline memory module). See Figure 1.5.

There are many different sizes of SIMMs and DIMMs. The two most common sizes of SIMMs are 30-pin and 72-pin (Figure 1.6). It's easy to tell the difference between them, as the 72-pin SIMM is much larger than the 30-pin SIMM. 72-pin SIMMs are more modern and are designed to hold

Figure 1.4
Same CPUs, different speeds

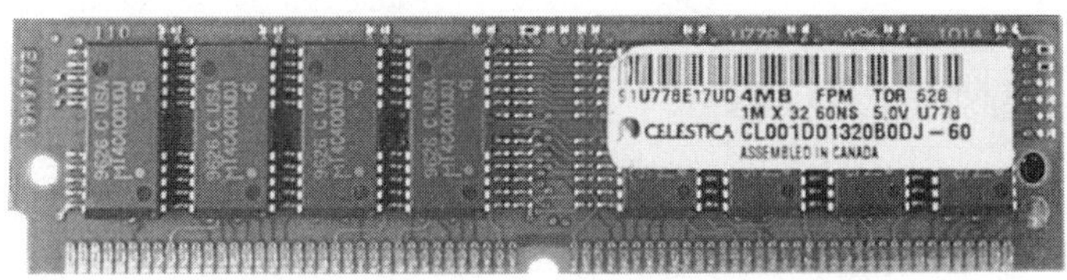

Figure 1.5
SIMM and DIMM RAM packages

Figure 1.6
30- and 72-pin SIMM

Figure 1.7
168-pin DIMM and SO-DIMM

more RAM than 30-pin SIMMs. 72-pin SIMMs can also transfer information to and from the CPU faster than 30-pin SIMMs. There are also two different sizes of DIMMs used by PCs: a 168-pin DIMM and a 72-pin SO DIMM (Figure 1.7). The SO DIMM is very small, and its small size makes it very popular in laptops. Only the 168-pin DIMMs are commonly used in desktop PCs.

Motherboard

The motherboard is like a car chassis. In a car, everything is connected to the chassis either directly or indirectly. In a PC, everything is connected to the motherboard, either directly or indirectly. A motherboard is a thin, flat piece of circuit board, usually of green or gold color, usually slightly larger than a piece of paper (Figure 1.8).

A motherboard has a number of special sockets that accept various PC components. There are sockets for the microprocessor (Figure 1.9), sockets

Figure 1.8
Photo of bare motherboard

Figure 1.9
Socket for a CPU

for RAM (Figure 1.10), sockets to provide power (Figure 1.11), connectors for floppy drives and hard drives (Figure 1.12), and connectors for external devices such as mice, printers, joysticks, and keyboards (Figure 1.13). A few components are soldered directly to the motherboard (Figure 1.14). Between the various devices, the motherboard is filled with tiny wires, called "traces," which electrically link the various components of the PC together (Figure 1.15).

All motherboards also have multipurpose *expansion slots* that allow the addition of optional components. There are thousands of different types of optional devices that can be added to a PC, including scanners,

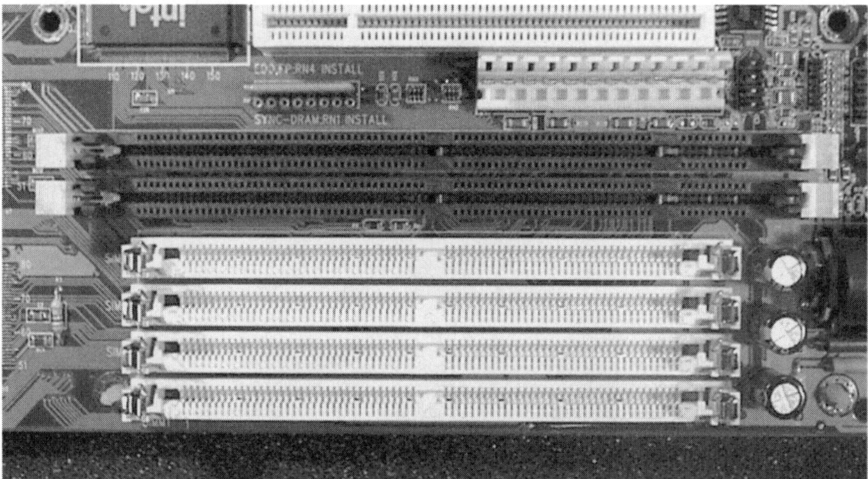

Figure 1.10
Sockets for RAM

Figure 1.11
Sockets for power plugs

Figure 1.12
Floppy- and hard-drive connectors

Figure 1.13
Various external connectors

Figure 1.14 Soldered components

Figure 1.15 Traces

Figure 1.16
Expansion slots—one slot has a card inserted

modems, network cards, sound cards, and tape backups. The expansion slots allow optional devices to communicate with the PC. The device that connects to the expansion slot is generically called an *expansion card* or just a *card*. There are different types of expansion slots for different types of cards (Figure 1.16).

The position of the expansion slots and external components is very standardized. They have to be. The motherboard is mounted to the box or case, the part of the PC that you actually see (Figure 1.17). The box

Figure 1.17
Motherboard in box

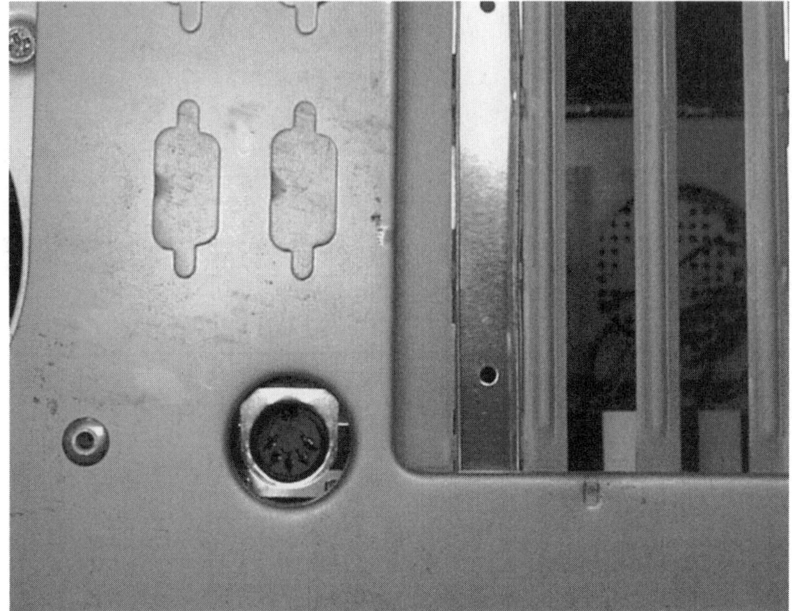

Figure 1.18
Keyboard socket visible through a hole in the box

needs to have holes that allow devices to access the external connectors. For example, if the motherboard has a connector for a keyboard, there needs to be a hole in the box though which the keyboard plug can be inserted. See Figure 1.18.

Equally important, if the expansion slots allow you to add cards to the PC, then there must also be holes that allow different devices to connect to their cards (Figure 1.19). Clearly, there must be a certain type of box to

Figure 1.19
Inserted card from the back of the PC

go with a certain type, or layout, of motherboard. Fortunately, there are very few different layouts of motherboard, requiring only a few different types of boxes. We'll visit this in more detail later.

Power Supply

The *power supply*, as its name implies, provides the necessary electrical power to make the PC operate. The power supply takes standard 110-volt AC power and converts it into 12-, 5-, and sometimes 3.3-volt DC power. The vast majority of power supplies are about the size of a shoe box cut in half, and are usually gray or metallic (see Figure 1.20).

Leading out of the power supply are a number of connectors. There is one set of connectors for the motherboard (Figure 1.21), and a number of other "general-use" connectors that provide power to any device that needs electricity (Figure 1.22). On most PCs, the back of the power supply is visible, with a connection for the power plug. There is always a fan that keeps the interior of the PC cool (Figure 1.23).

Figure 1.20
Typical power supply

Figure 1.21 Power connectors for the motherboard

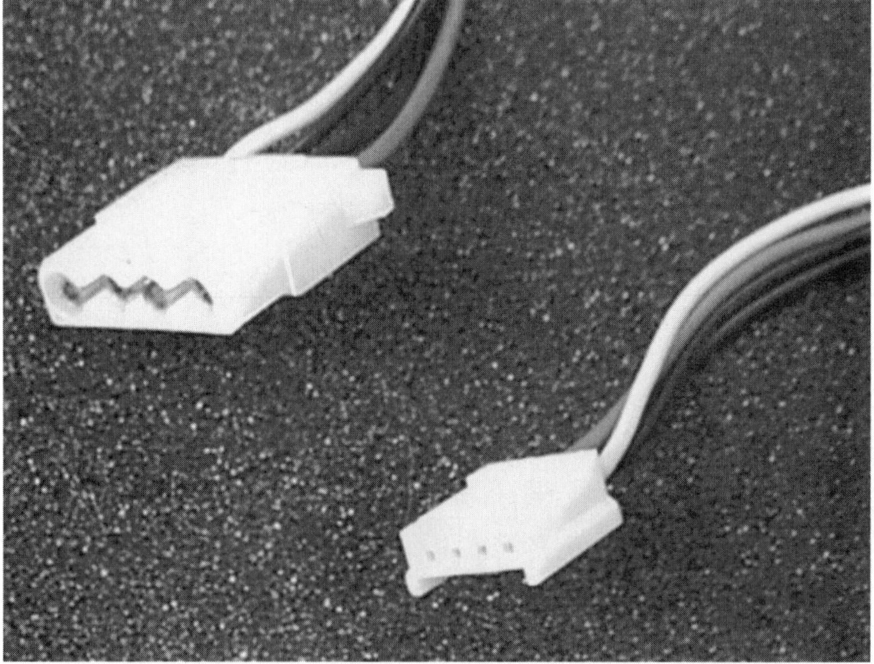

Figure 1.22 General-use power connectors

Figure 1.23
Power supply fan

Floppy Drive

The floppy drive allows you to access floppy diskettes. There are two types of floppy drives; one is 3.5 inches in diameter, and the other is 5.25 inches in diameter (Figure 1.24). The 5.25-inch drive is completely obsolete, but is still encountered on older PCs. The floppy drive is connected

Figure 1.24
3.5- and 5.25-inch floppy drives

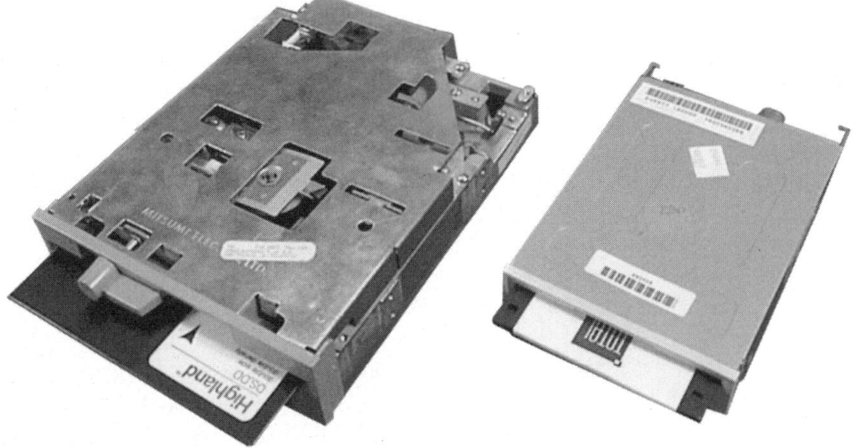

Figure 1.25
On-board floppy controller

to the computer via a 34-pin ribbon cable, which in turn is connected to the floppy controller. In early PCs, the floppy controller was a special card that was inserted into an expansion slot. Today's PCs all have the floppy controller built into the motherboard (Figure 1.25).

Floppy ribbon cables (Figure 1.26) are different than any other type of cable, in two ways. First, they are the narrowest ribbon cable, only slightly more than 1-inch wide. Second, there is a twist in the cable, usually close to where the floppy cable is connected to the floppy drive.

A PC can support up to two floppy drives. If it has two, they will be connected to the same ribbon cable (Figure 1.27). Since floppy drives need power, one of the power connectors must be attached to supply power to the floppy (Figure 1.28).

Hard Drive

Hard drives store programs and data that are not currently being used by the CPU (Figure 1.29). Like RAM, hard-drive capacity is measured in megabytes. Unlike RAM, however, hard-drive capacity is also measured in

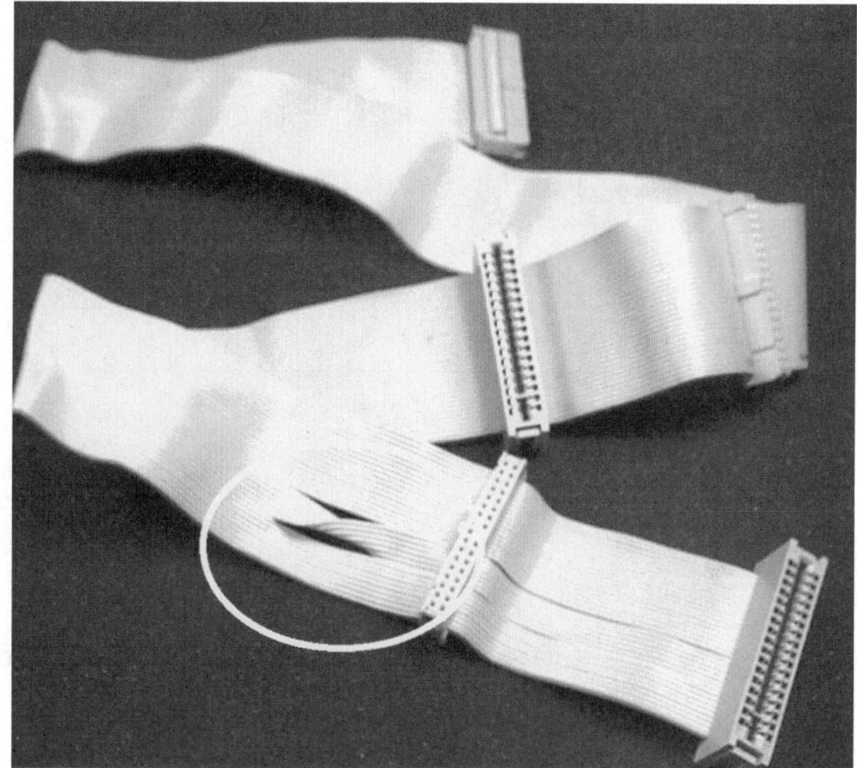

Figure 1.26
Floppy-drive cable

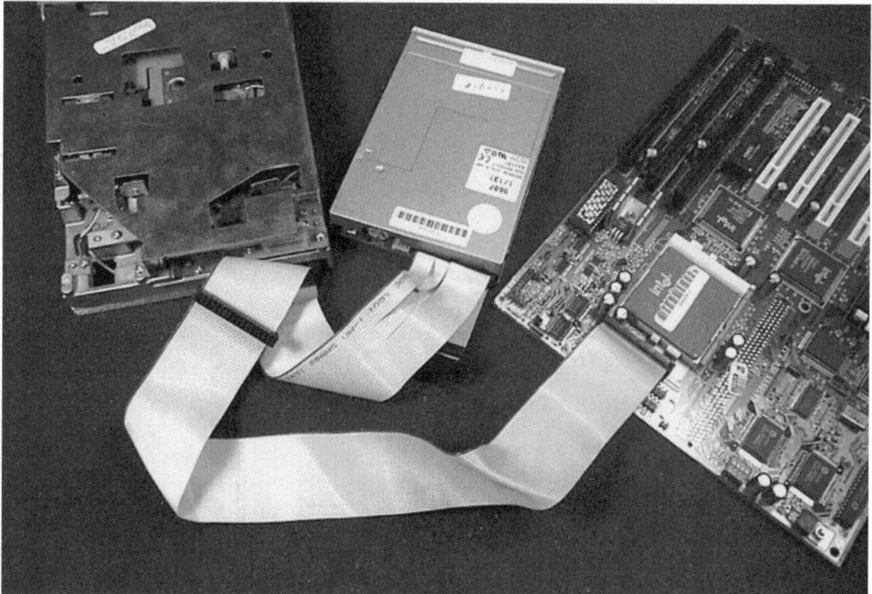

Figure 1.27
Two floppy drives

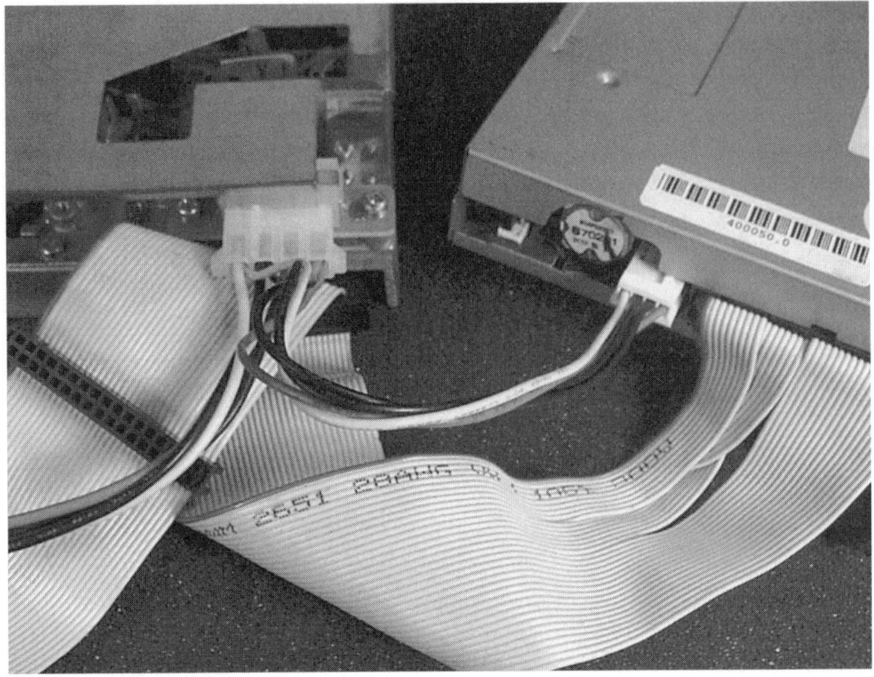

Figure 1.28
Floppy-drive power connectors

Figure 1.29
Typical hard drive

hundreds or thousands of megabytes. Since most new hard drives have capacities of over 1000 megabytes, the capacities are measured in *gigabytes*, equaling roughly 1000 megabytes. An average PC will have at least one hard drive. The capacity of a single hard drive can vary from as low as 10 megabytes (on very old systems) up to tens of gigabytes. The average size of a hard drive in a new system is slightly over two gigabytes.

There are two common types of hard drives: IDE and SCSI (Figure 1.30). IDE drives are far more common in the average PC. SCSI drives tend to be more common in high-end PCs such as network servers or graphics workstations. Any PC might have an IDE, SCSI, or both installed. SCSI and IDE drives look quire similar. They are both about the same size as a floppy drive, but with wider ribbon cables. These cables have no twist. IDE drives use a roughly 1.5-inch-wide, 40-pin ribbon cable, while SCSI drives use a roughly 2-inch-wide, 50-pin cable.

Since IDE drives are so common, they usually have the controller built into the motherboard (Figure 1.31). Years ago, there was only one controller, although today's motherboards have two controllers. Some older systems have the controllers on a card. IDE supports up to two hard drives per controller (Figure 1.32). Each ribbon cable, therefore, has two connectors for hard drives. With two controllers, each controlling two drives, a PC can support up to four IDE drives.

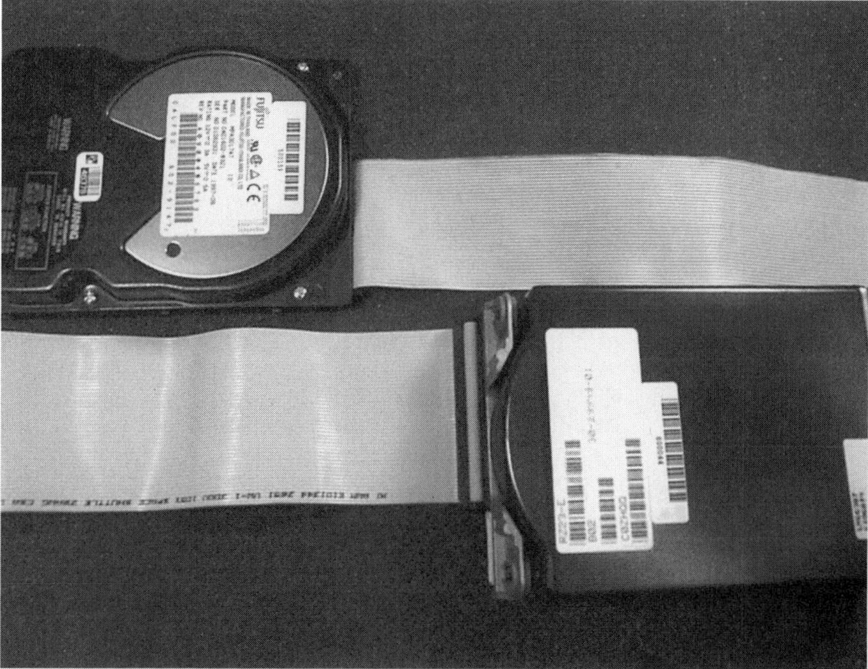

Figure 1.30
IDE and SCSI hard drives with cables

Figure 1.31 On-board IDE controllers

Figure 1.32 Two IDE drives on one controller

SCSI drives might look like IDE drives, but they are quite different on the inside. First, very few motherboards have SCSI controllers. You usually need to buy a special card called a *SCSI host adapter.* Also, you can put more than two SCSI drives on the same ribbon. It's not at all uncommon to see CD-ROM drives, tape backups, and other devices connected to the

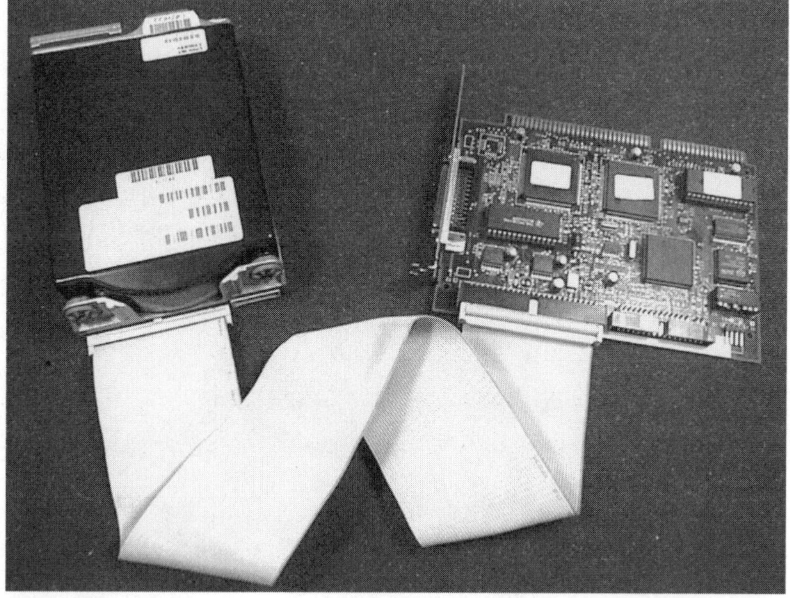

Figure 1.33
SCSI chain

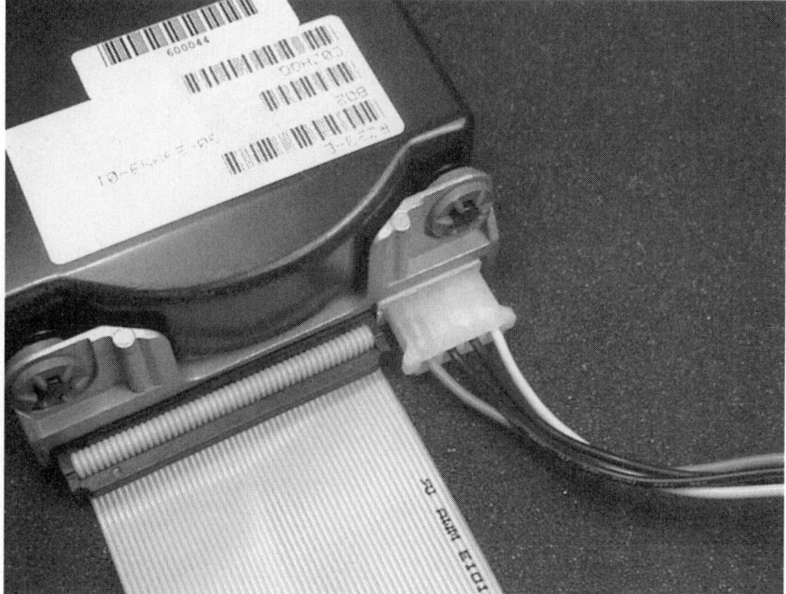

Figure 1.34
Hard-drive power connector

same ribbon cable as the SCSI hard drive (Figure 1.33). One thing that IDE and SCSI share is the need for electricity. Every drive needs a power connector (Figure 1.34).

CD-ROM Drive

CD-ROM drives allow the system to access CD-ROMs. CD-ROM drives are quite large, usually the single largest component inside the PC. With the front of the CD-ROM drive visible in the front of the PC, as well as its boxy shape and metallic appearance, the CD-ROM drive is hard to miss (Figure 1.35). When CD-ROM drives were first developed, they had their own special controllers. Sound-card makers then began to add those special controllers to their sound cards (Figure 1.36).

Figure 1.35
Typical CD-ROM drive

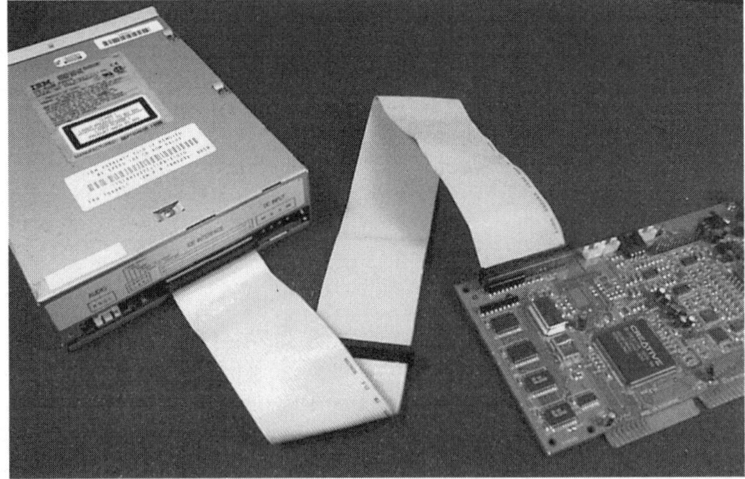

Figure 1.36
CD-ROM drive controlled by a sound card

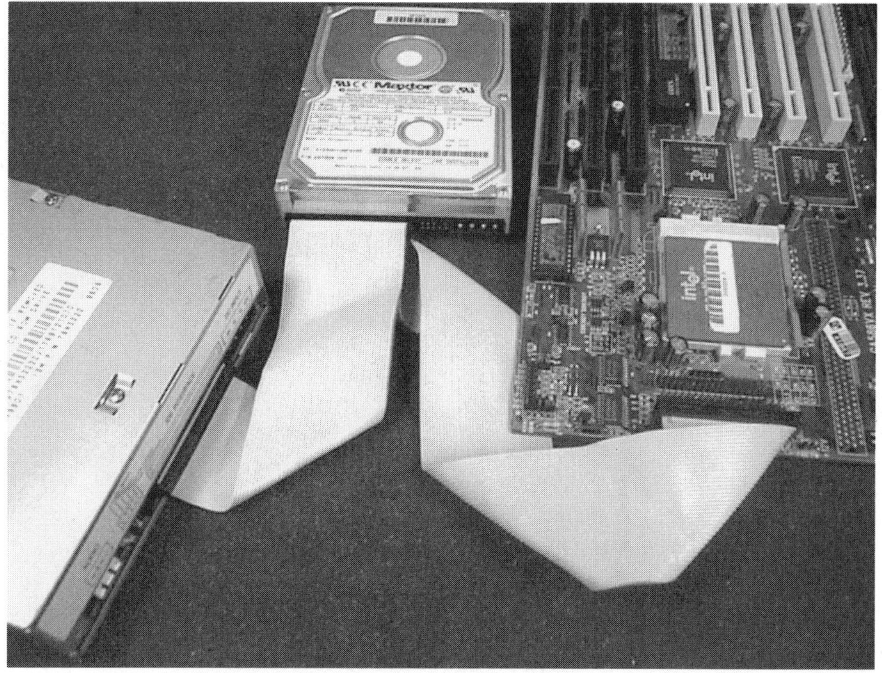

Figure 1.37
Hard drive and CD-ROM drive

These special controllers are now pretty much obsolete and have been replaced by CD-ROM drives that run on either IDE or SCSI controllers, just like hard drives. So there are now basically two type of CD-ROM drives: IDE and SCSI. On most PCs, it is common to have an IDE hard drive and an IDE CD-ROM drive on one controller (Figure 1.37).

SCSI CD-ROM drives go on the same ribbon cable as the SCSI hard drives. One nice aspect to SCSI is that, since you can have up to seven devices on one ribbon cable, you can set up systems with a large number of CD-ROM drives. Of course, CD-ROM drives, like hard and floppy drives, also need power cables (Figure 1.38).

Connectors

The next several sections are going to deal with a number of different devices that are commonly seen in PCs. But before we dive into the realm of sound cards, modems, network card, and mice, you need to understand that there are many types of connectors (often called *ports*) used by these different devices, and these connectors have there own naming conven-

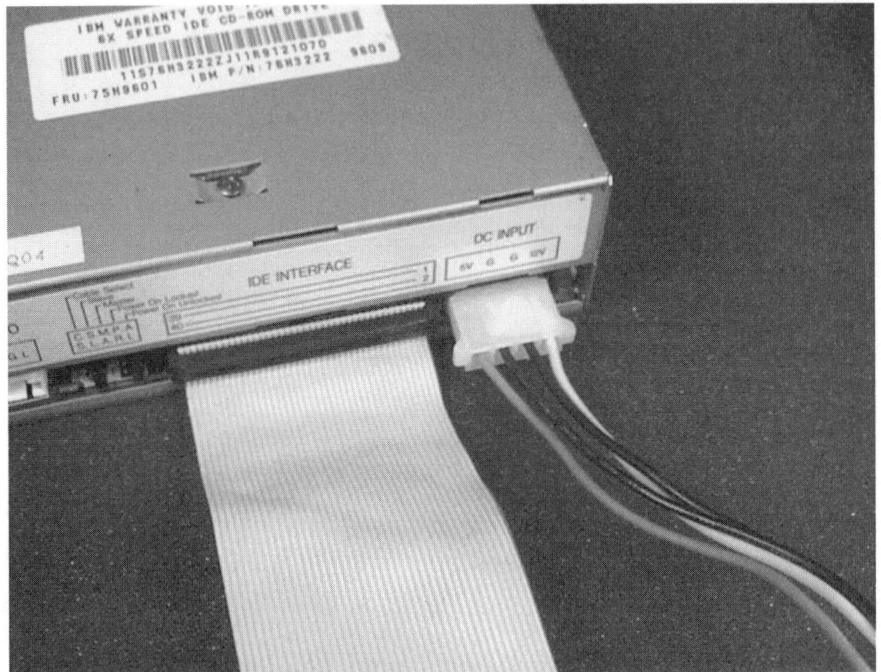

Figure 1.38
CD-ROM drive power connector

tions. It's not acceptable to go around saying things like "that's a printer port" or "that's a joystick connector." You need to be comfortable with the more commonly used naming conventions, so you can say "that's a male DB-25" or "that's a mini-DIN."

Although there are close to 50 different connectors used with PCs, almost all connectors can all be broken down into six types: DB, DIN, Centronics, RJ, BNC, and audio.

DB type connectors are one of the oldest and most common type of connectors used in the back of PCs. They are distinct due to their slight D shape, designed to allow only one proper way of inserting the plug into the socket. Each DB connector has groups of small pins and sockets (male/female) that insert as a group. DB connectors in the PC world and can have from 9 to 37 pins, although a DB connector with more than 25 pins is now quite rare. Sockets can be either male or female. Figure 1.39 shows some examples.

DIN connectors are of a European design that is also common on PCs. These connectors are round and come in only two sizes: DIN and mini-DIN. The sockets are always female. See Figure 1.40.

Centronics connectors are similar to DB connectors, having the same D shape to ensure proper insertion. Unlike DBs, however, Centronics connectors use one large central tab, covered with contacts instead of pins. Even though the Centronics have flat contacts instead of pins, the word *pins* is still used to describe the number of contacts. For example, a Centronics connector with 36 contacts is still called a 36-pin connector. Centronics connectors are also distinct in that the sockets have wire "wings"

Figure 1.39
DB connectors

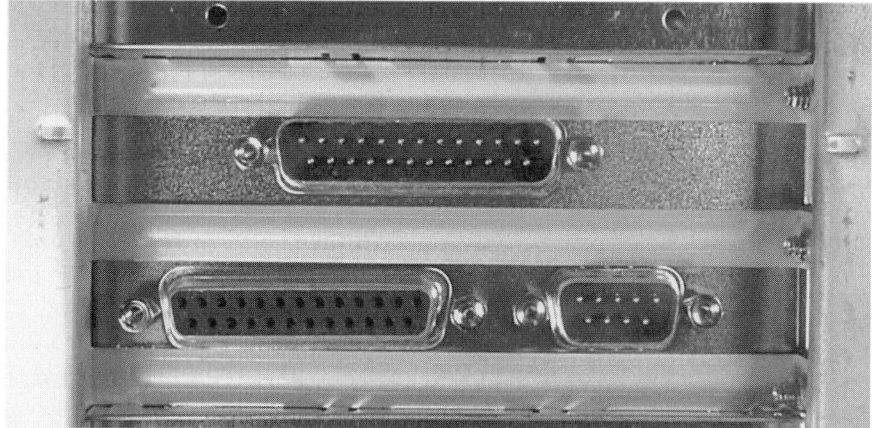

Figure 1.40
DIN and mini-DIN

that lock the plug to the socket to reduce the chance of accidental removal. Sockets are always female. With the exception of some obsolete SCSI host adapters, Centronics sockets are rarely seen sticking out of the back of a PC. However, almost every printer in existence has a 36-pin Centronics socket. See Figure 1.41.

Everyone has seen an RJ type connector. The little plastic plug used to connect your telephone wire to the jack is a classic example of an RJ plug. Fortunately, there are only two types of RJ jacks used in PCs: the RJ-11 and the RJ-45. The phone jack is the RJ-11. It is used almost exclusively for modems. The RJ-45 jack is slightly wider than the RJ-11. RJ-45 is used for one very popular type of network cabling, and most network cards have an RJ-45 socket (Figure 1.42).

BNC connectors, also (though incorrectly) known as coaxial or "coax" connectors, are beginning to fade from common PC use, but there is still a large number of PCs with coax connectors hanging out the back. (See Figure 1.43.) The coax cable used with PCs looks exactly like the one that runs into the back of your TV. The connectors, however, are different in that they don't screw in the way the TV coax connectors do. The connectors use a twist-type connection, which is really what BNC means. Two types of cards can use a BNC connector: network cards that need to link to coax network cables, and old terminal emulation cards. The emulation cards were direct links to mainframes and are rare. The older coax networks are fading away, but still have a large presence. There is one new way that screw-type connectors might show up in the back of a PC. There are

Figure 1.41
Centronics port

Figure 1.42
RJ jacks

Figure 1.43
BNC connector

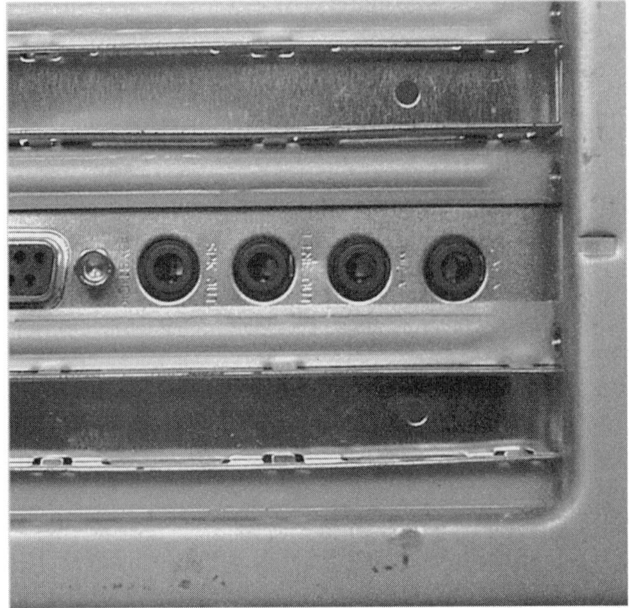

Figure 1.44
Mini-audio connector

now cards that you can purchase to allow your PC to be used as a television. They have a screw-type coax connector for, you guessed it, your TV cable! Hmm . . . Microsoft Word and MSNBC on the same screen at the same time! Can life get any better?

Audio connectors are perhaps the simplest of all, and there is really only one type of audio connector that sees popular use: the "mini audio" connector (Figure 1.44). These small connectors have been around for years; they're what you use to plug a set of headphones into a Walkman. Audio connectors are used almost exclusively on sound cards.

Keep in mind that there is a virtually endless number of connectors. These six types of connectors cover the vast majority, but there are others. There's no law or standard that requires the makers of particular devices to use a particular connector, especially if they have no interest in making that device interchangeable with similar devices from other manufacturers.

Sound cards

Sound cards perform two functions. First, they take digital information and turn it into sound, outputting the sound through speakers. Second, they take sound that is input through a microphone and turn it into digital data. Sound cards are well named; they are cards that deal with sound (Figure 1.45).

In order to play and record sounds, a sound card needs to connect to at least a set of speakers and a microphone. Virtually all sound cards have four sockets for miniature audio jacks: microphone, speaker, line in, and line out. Many sound cards will also have a female 15-pin DB socket that allows you to directly connect to electronic musical instruments.

The microphone and speaker sockets are for connecting to a microphone and speakers. Line in allows a sound card to record from a stereo, tape recorder, etc, and line out allows the sound card to output to those same type of devices. On most systems, only the speaker and microphone sockets are used. Most PCs also have a small cable running between the sound card and the CD-ROM drive, which allows the CD-ROM drive to play audio CD-ROMs through the sound card, in essence turning your PC into a stereo system (Figure 1.46).

Figure 1.45 Typical sound-card connectors

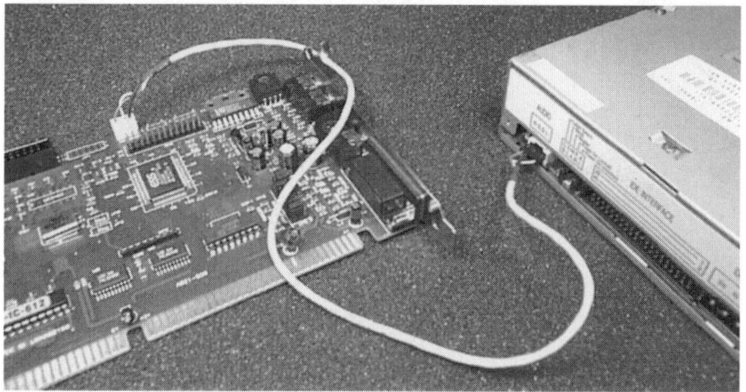

Figure 1.46 CD-ROM on sound-card cable

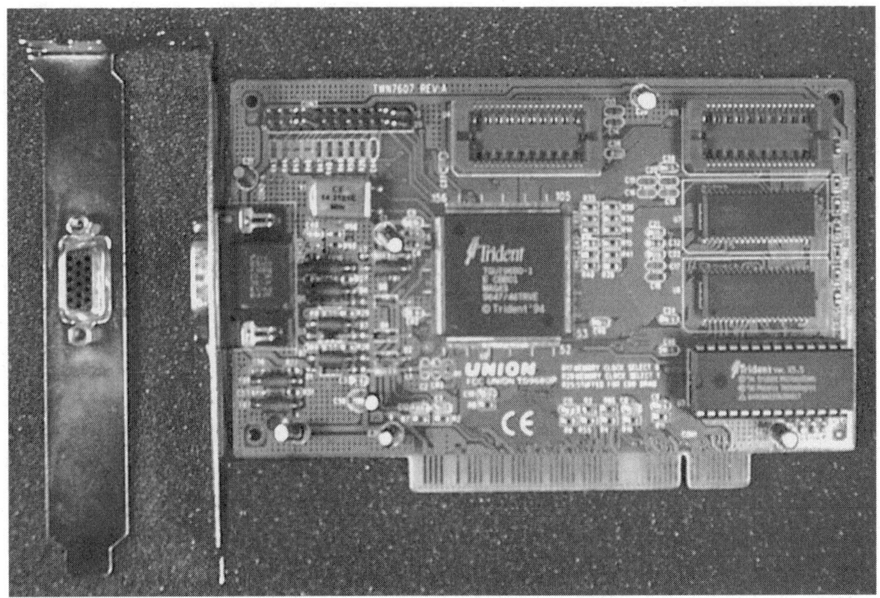

Figure 1.47
Typical video card

Video

Of all the cards in a PC, the video card is by far the easiest to identify. Unless the PC is very old and has a 9-pin female DB connector, the video card will have a distinct 15-pin female DB connector. And while most DB connectors have only two rows of pins, the video card has three. There's nothing else like it in the back of a PC (Figure 1.47).

Network Card

Networks are connected PCs that share information. The PCs are usually connected by some type of cabling, usually an advanced type of phone cable or coax. Network cards (NICs) provide the interface between the network and PCs. A NIC will be distinguished by one or more of the following types of connectors: an RJ-45, BNC, 15-pin female DB, or 9-pin female DB (Figure 1.48). It is very common to see NICs with more than one type of connector. Probably the most common combination NIC has an RJ-45 and a BNC.

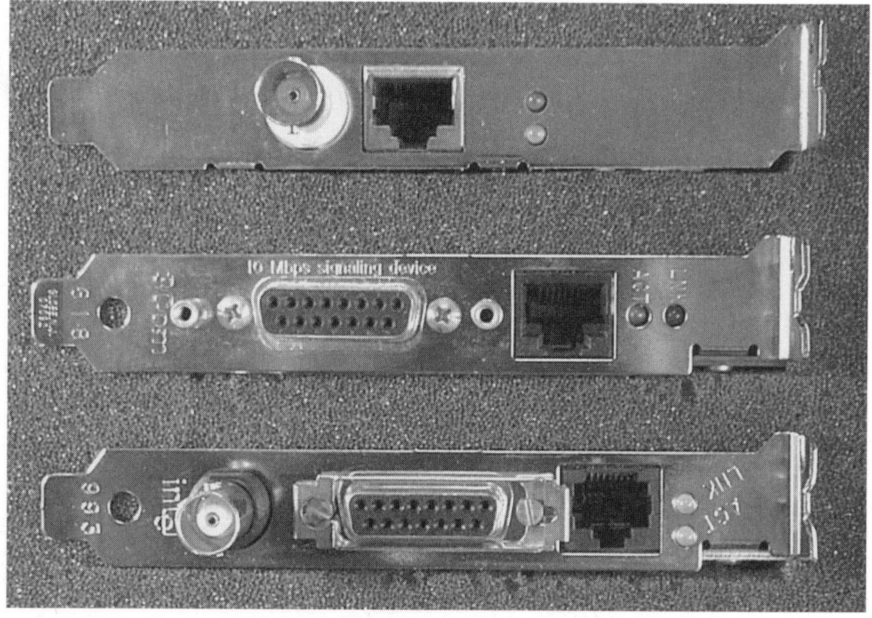

Figure 1.48
Typical network card connectors

Keyboard

All PCs have a keyboard port connected directly to the motherboard. There are two types of keyboard connectors. The oldest, but still quite common type, is a special DIN-type connector popularly known as the *AT-style*. It was the keyboard connector on the original IBM PC, and is still used in the most modern PCs today. However, the AT-style keyboard connector is quickly beginning to disappear, being overshadowed by the smaller *PS/2-style mini-DIN* (Figure 1.49). You can use an AT-style keyboard with a PS/2-style socket (or the other way around) by using a converter. While the AT connector is unique in PCs (Figure 1.50), the PS/2-style mini-DIN is also used in more modern PCs for the mouse. Fortunately, all PCs that use the mini-DIN for both the keyboard and mouse clearly mark each mini-DIN socket as to its correct use.

Mouse

A better name for this section might be "What's a serial port, what does it look like, and what does a mouse have to do with it?" It's hard to believe, but there was a time, long ago and far away, when PCs worked just fine

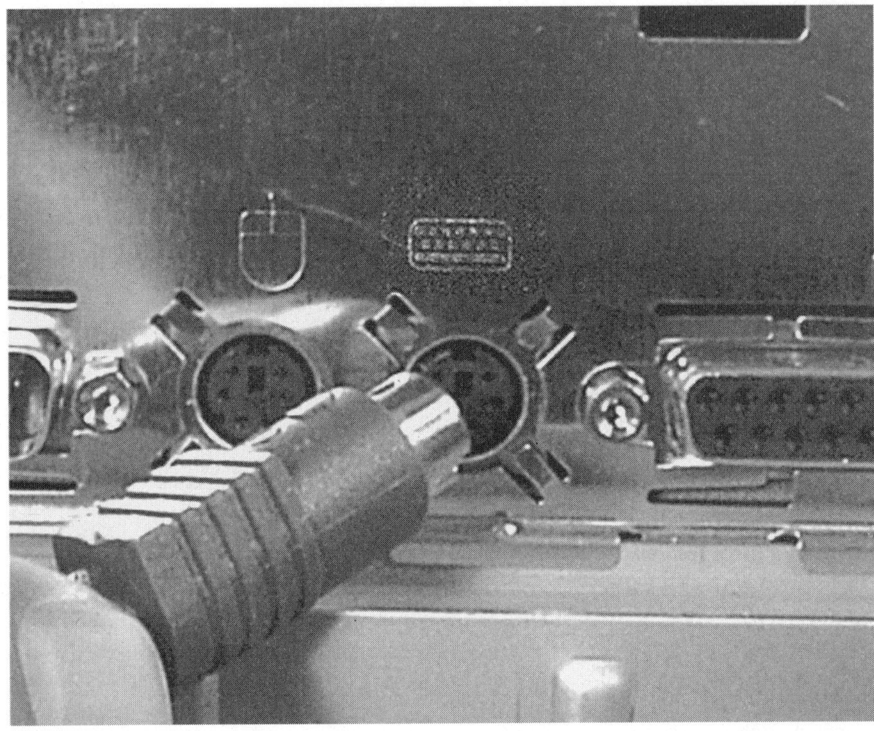

Figure 1.49 Mini-DIN keyboard connector

Figure 1.50 AT-style keyboard connector

without mice. When the PC was being created by IBM, mice were not part of the picture. But IBM did something very smart that allowed mice, as well as a lot of other devices that were invented after the PC was first introduced, to easily become part of the PC.

IBM wanted the PC to be easily customized. To that end, the company added a number of ways to add components. First were the expansion slots. IBM added a lot of unused slots to which anyone (anyone with the technical know-how, at least) could add special cards in order to add functions. The original PC had only two cards: the video card and the floppy-drive controller. Hard-drive controller cards, network cards, sound cards, modems, and a few thousand other devices were all created because IBM had the foresight to add an expansion bus.

The second way that IBM allowed the PC to be easily customized was through the adoption of standardized ports that allowed people to add devices without even opening the case. The first of these standardized ports was (and still is) called a *serial port*. Now please understand that IBM didn't invent serial ports, which had been around for a long time, but they made sure that every IBM PC came with two serial ports, ready to use.

A serial port is a direct link to the PC. It does only one thing: it takes a stream of serial data (which runs on only one wire) and converts it into a format that is easily understood by the CPU. Equally, a serial port takes data from the CPU and outputs it in serial format. Think of serial data as a telegraph wire sending Morse code, but instead of sending "dots" and "dahs" it sends ones and zeros. Not only did IBM put serial ports in all its PCs, it told everyone how to write software that could talk to the serial port and manipulate the incoming or outgoing data. To top it all off, IBM standardized the serial connector, defining the size, shape, and number and function of all the pins. That way you knew if you invented a device that worked in one IBM PC, it would also work in all the others.

The super-standard IBM serial connector is either a 25- or a 9-pin male DB connector. No other connector in the back of a PC looks like these serial connectors. The 25-pin connector was the first of the two sizes, but over time it became obvious that only about nine of the pins were needed by most devices. As a result, the 25-pin serial port, although still made, is rarely used. You can get an adapter that allows you to convert 9 to 25 or 25 to 9. You would be hard-pressed to find a PC without at least one 9-pin serial port. See Figures 1.51 and 1.52.

Most of the people reading this book have some PC experience. Somebody out there right now is reading this and asking the question: "Where do COM ports fit into this?" Well, they don't. A COM port is not a physical thing. A COM port is comprised of two values, called I/O address and

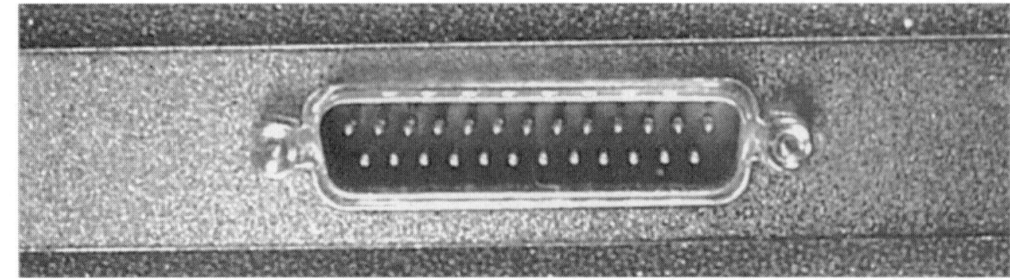

Figure 1.51
25-pin serial port

Figure 1.52
9-pin serial port

the IRQ, which are assigned to a serial port. If you don't know what an IRQ or I/O address is, don't worry. They are covered in detail later. Calling a serial port a COM port is like looking at the White House and saying "That's 1600 Pennsylvania Avenue!" No; it's the White House. Its *address* is 1600 Pennsylvania Ave! Get the difference? Now back to serial ports and mice.

Now that you understand and can identify serial ports, we can turn our attention back to mice. For many years, there was no such thing as a mouse port. The mouse was connected into serial ports, either 9- or 25-pin. However, as mice become more common, a demand was created for the mouse to have its own connector, just as the keyboard had its own connector. In the mid-'80s, a new type of mouse connection was created. Although still a serial port, it was a mini-DIN connector. This special serial port, just for the mouse, was called a *PS/2 mouse port,* in deference to the first PC that used it, the IBM PS/2 (Figure 1.53).

In older days, serial ports were on a card, usually called an I/O card. Modern motherboard now have built-in serial ports. The serial ports are connected either directly to the back of the motherboard or to the motherboard via a small ribbon cable. This bit of cable is rather ingloriously referred to as a "dongle" (Figure 1.54).

Figure 1.53
PS/2 mouse port

Figure 1.54
Typical dongle

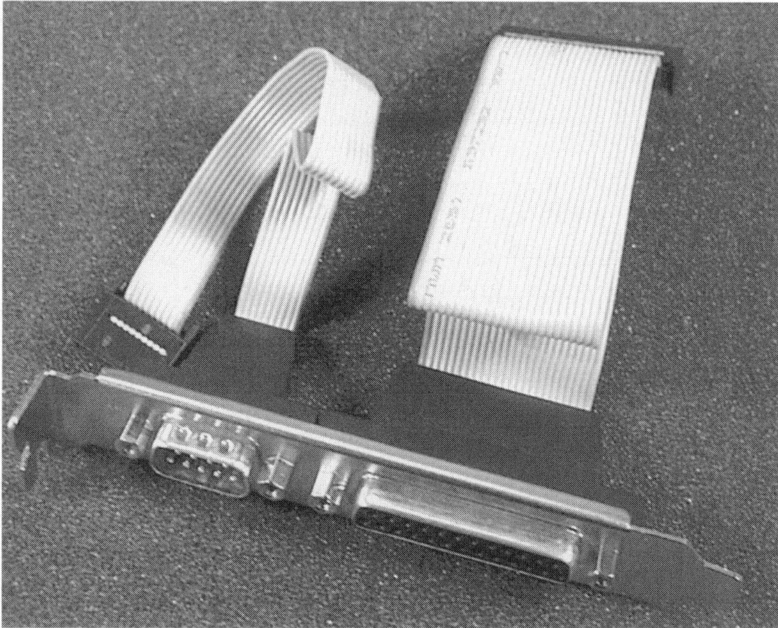

Figure 1.55 Typical modem connections

Modem

A modem works with your telephone line, and is designed to translate analog telephone signals into digital serial data. Modems can also translate digital serial data into analog telephone signals. There are two types of modems, internal and external. An external modem sits outside the PC and is plugged into a serial port. An internal modem is a card that snaps into an expansion slot. Internal modems carry their own onboard serial port. A modem is another device that is easy to identify in PCs. All modems, internal or external, have two RJ-11 sockets. One connects the modem to the telephone jack on the wall, and the other is for an optional telephone so you can use the phone line when the modem isn't (Figure 1.55).

Printer

The vast majority of printers use a special connector called a *parallel port*. Parallel ports carry data on more than one wire, as opposed to the serial port, which used only uses one wire. Parallel ports are distinct in the PC world. They are 25-pin female DB connectors (Figure 1.56). There are some

SCSI host adapters with an identical 25-pin female DB type connector, but they are rare in PCs.

Like serial ports, parallel ports on earlier PC were mounted on a card, usually the same card with the serial ports. Parallel ports today are directly supported by the motherboard via a direct connection or "dongle" (Figure 1.57).

Figure 1.56
Parallel port

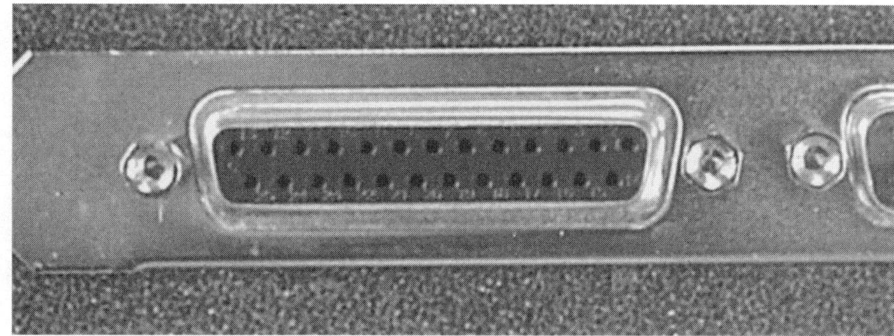

Figure 1.57
Parallel port connected to a motherboard

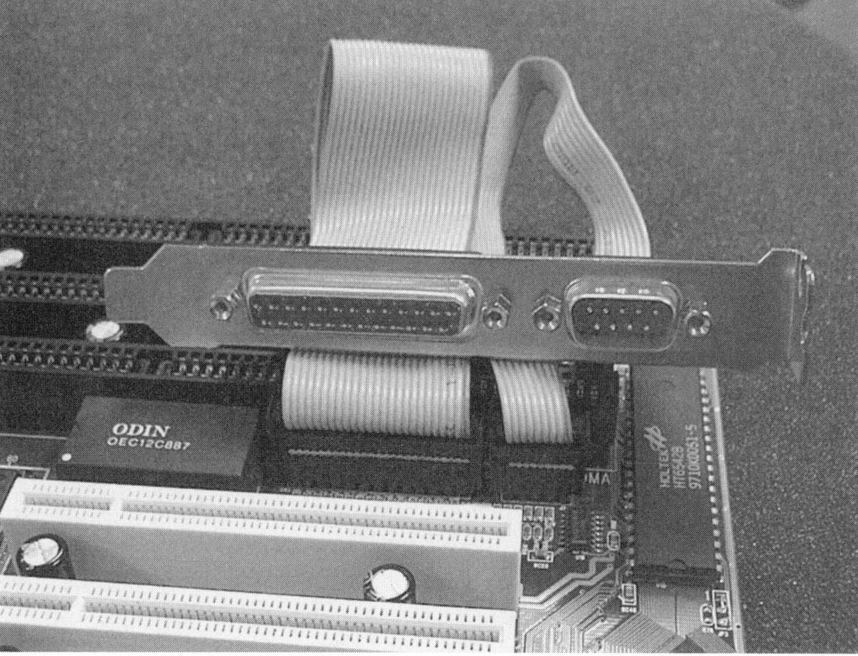

Figure 1.58
Joystick port

Joystick

Joysticks weren't supposed to be just for games. When IBM began to add the 15-pin female DB joystick connector to PCs, they were supposed to be a hard-working input device, just as the mouse is today. Nevertheless, that just wasn't to be. Except in the most rare circumstances, the only thing joysticks do today is allow you to play a $1500 game machine. (See Figure 1.58.) But, really, is there any more gratifying feeling than easing that joystick over, pressing the fire button, and watching a Russian SU-27 fighter get blasted by a well-placed Sidewinder? I think not.

Jumpers and Switches

All motherboards and cards need to be set up in one way or another. Entire chapters of this book are devoted to the "hows" and "whys" of setting up these devices, but I want to take a moment to look at the primary tools of hardware setup: jumpers and switches. All motherboards and most cards have circuitry that must be turned on or off for some reason or another. Jumpers and switches are what allows you to perform this turning on and off. This section will teach you how to recognize jumpers and switches and how to use them properly.

Switches, more accurately called *DIP switches,* have been in many PCs since the original IBM PC. DIP switches look like a tiny, Lego-sized block, usually brightly colored (although black is not uncommon) that has a neat row of tiny rocker-arm or slide switches across its top (Figure 1.59). You can turn a switch on or off by flipping the tiny switches. The best way to flip these switches is by using a small screwdriver or a mechanical pencil with the lead removed (Figure 1.60). Don't use a pen or pencil. They leave marks, making it harder to read next time. Worse, they can leave ink or lead residue inside the PC, a potential problem if it gets in the wrong component. Using your fingers or fingernails is fine, but might be difficult, especially if there are a lot of cards and cables in the way.

You will usually determine how to set these switches by reading documentation that came with the device you are configuring. Unfortunately, this documentation can sometime be a little confusing. One problem is if you have more than one set of DIP switches. How can you tell which one to set? You must read the numbers on the board next to the switch. Switches are always numbered with the nomenclature S1, S2, etc., or SW1, SW2, etc. By looking for the S or SW, you can identify one switch from another.

It can often be challenging to determine which way is "on" and which way is "off." The first problem is that there are a number of ways to specify "on" and "off." In DIP switches, the terms *on, closed,* and *shorted* are synonymous. Equally, *off* and *open* also mean the same thing. Second, most DIP switches have a word printed on the switch to give you a clue. If there

Figure 1.59
DIP switches

Figure 1.60
Flipping a DIP switch

Figure 1.61
Switch-state identifier

isn't a word, look for a small dot, which usually points to the closed or on position. This will identify the state of the switch. See Figure 1.61.

Jumpers are tiny pins, usually about half a centimeter long, that are closely grouped together in twos or threes. A tiny piece called a *shunt* is slid down between two pins to create a circuit. Jumpers without a connected shunt are considered "open" or "off," while jumpers with a shunt are considered "shorted," "closed," or "on" (Figure 1.62).

When there are only two pins, this is relatively easy. But when three or more pins are involved, it might not be as obvious. Let's use an example with three pins. The documentation says only "2-3," meaning you are to

A

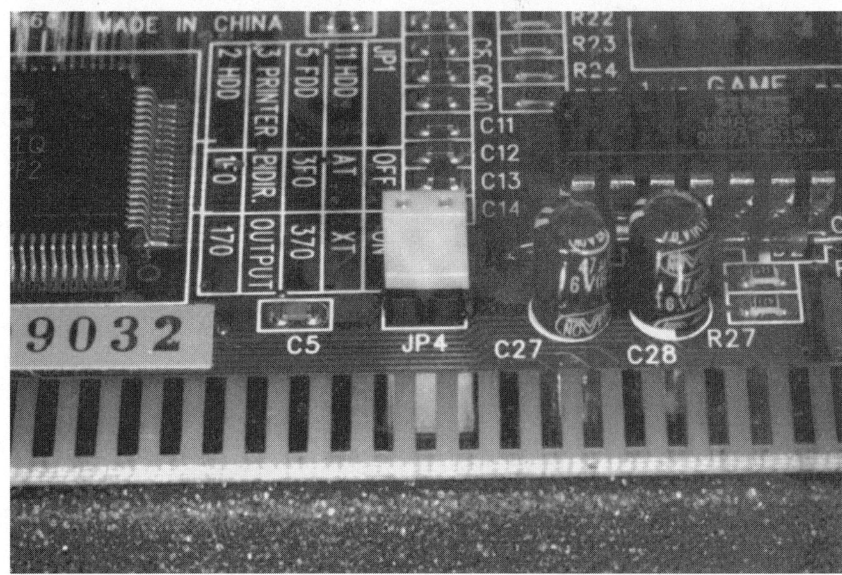

B

Figure 1.62
Open and closed jumpers

Figure 1.63
Jumper labeling

place a jumper on the second and third pins. But which two of the three are the second and third pins? If you look closely at the board upon which the jumpers are mounted, you should be able to see a small number 1 on one side or the other, identifying the first pin. You would then short the other two pins.

Each group of jumpers is identified by the nomenclature JP1, JP2, JP3, etc. Use this to identify the jumpers you want to set (Figure 1.63). It is common to see a shunt on only one jumper pin, called a *parked jumper* (Figure 1.64). This is done to keep the shunt handy should you ever need to later

Figure 1.64
Parked jumper

Figure 1.65
Jumpers

Figure 1.66
Graphics representing jumpers

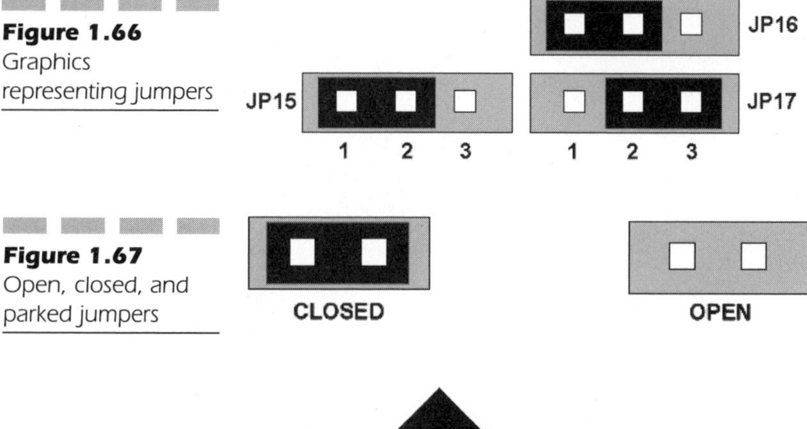

Figure 1.67
Open, closed, and parked jumpers

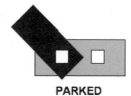

short that jumper. This book uses a special diagram when discussing jumpers that looks straight down at them. For example, a set of jumpers that looks like Figure 1.65 will be represented by a diagram that looks like Figure 1.66. If a jumper is shorted, the shunt will be represented by a black rectangle; otherwise, it will be considered open (Figure 1.67).

Documentation

Let's close this chapter with a short mention of documentation. Every modem, every sound card, and especially every motherboard comes with a booklet describing the proper setting for switches and jumpers. Without this book, you would not know how to set the jumpers and switches. This is particularly important with motherboards. Every motherboard has jumper and/or DIP switches. Every motherboard should also come with documentation, called the "motherboard book," to tell you how to set them. If you don't have that book, you are in for serious frustration and pain. Luckily, the Internet has alleviated that pain somewhat by making it relatively easy, if a bit time-consuming, to replace a lost or never-received motherboard book. Motherboard books are crucial, so store them away in a safe place.

Keep in mind that this chapter is important. Decent technicians should be able to recognize the main parts of a PC. They should be able to properly name the different types of connectors, and they should definitely be able to say what types of devices connect to those ports. Make sure you know the difference between types of cards. Good technicians can tell the difference by simply running their fingers along the back of a PC—which sure beats pulling it out from under the desk!

CHAPTER 2

Microprocessors

In this chapter you will:

- Understand the concepts of buses, and the functions of the data bus and the address bus.
- Understand the clock, clock speed, and concept of clock doubling.
- Understand the relationship of RAM to the CPU and RAM caching.
- Inspect the different type of processors available in the past and today.
- Learn how to install and upgrade processors.

For all practical purposes, the terms *microprocessor* and *CPU* (central processing unit) mean the same thing: it's that big chip inside your computer that is often described as the "brain" of the system. CPUs have names like 486 or Pentium, and are invariably covered up with some huge fan or heatsink, so they're often quite easy to locate inside the computer.

Although the computer might seem to act quite intelligently, calling the CPU a *brain* is a huge overstatement of its capabilities. The CPU is really nothing more than a very powerful calculator—but, oh, what a calculator! Today's CPUs can add, subtract, multiply, and divide millions of numbers per second. When you can process that much information that quickly, it is easy to look intelligent! It's simply the speed of the CPU, rather than actual intelligence, that makes computers capable of performing feats such as accessing the Internet and drawing pictures.

A good PC technician needs to understand some basic CPU functions in order to be able to support PCs, so let's start by choosing an example CPU. If you were going to teach someone how an automobile engine works, you would want to use an example engine that was relatively simple, so we're going to do the same thing with CPUs. The CPU we're going to look at is the famous Intel 8088 that was invented in the late '70s.

Let's begin by visualizing the CPU as a man in a box (Figure 2.1). This is one clever guy in this box. He can perform virtually any mathemati-

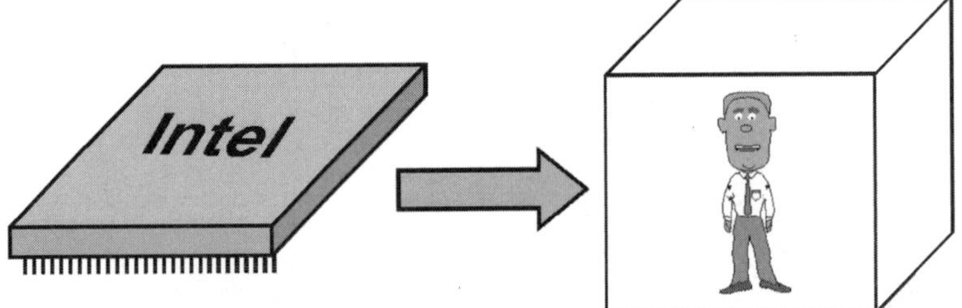

Figure 2.1 Imagine the CPU as a "man in a box"

Figure 2.2
How can you talk to the man in the box?

cal function, manipulate data, provide answers to questions, and do it *fast.* You want to use this guy to get work done, but there's a catch. This man cannot see outside the box. He cannot hear anything outside the box. There is no way for him to communicate with the outside world, and there is no way that we can communicate with him. If we want to take advantage of this guy's skills, we need a way to talk to him (see Figure 2.2).

External Data Bus

Fortunately, this box comes with a communication device. This device consists of 16 light bulbs, 8 inside the box and 8 outside the box. Each light bulb on the inside of the box is connected to one on the outside, creating a pair of lights. Each pair of lights must be either on or off. Also, each connected pair of light bulbs has two switches, one switch on each side. This setup means that the man inside the box or someone outside the box can turn any one of the eight pairs of light bulbs on or off. This light-bulb communication device is called the *external data bus.*

Figure 2.3 is a cut-away view of the external data bus. Understand that if you flip a switch, both light bulbs go on and the switch on the other side is flipped. If you turn a switch off, both light bulbs on each side are turned off and the other switch is turned off.

By creating different patterns of lights, you can communicate with the guy in the box. You must, however, come up with a sort of "code book" so you can understand the patterns of lights. We'll come back to the external data bus in a moment. Now you can see that the CPU looks like this from the outside (Figure 2.4).

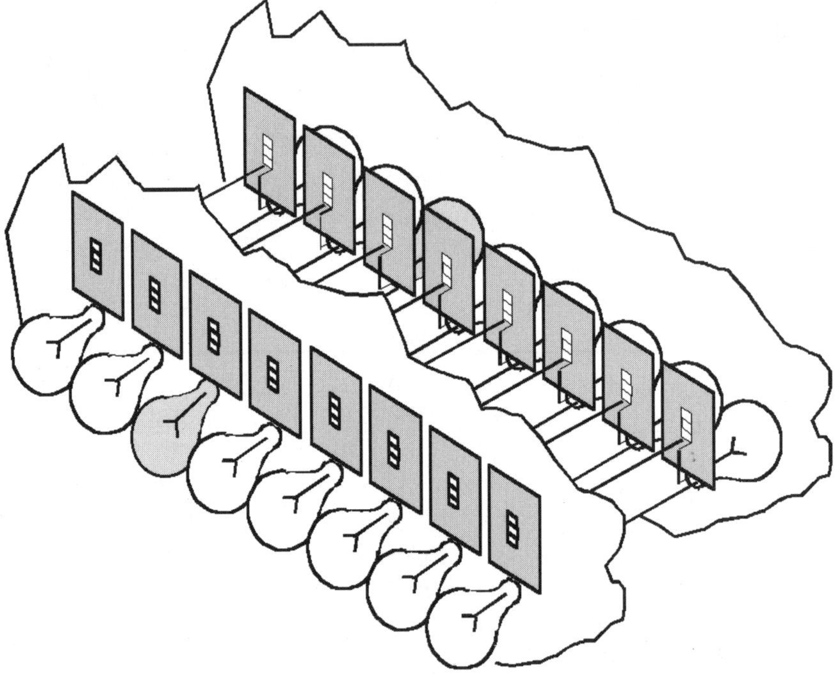

Figure 2.3
Cut-away of the external data bus—note one light is on

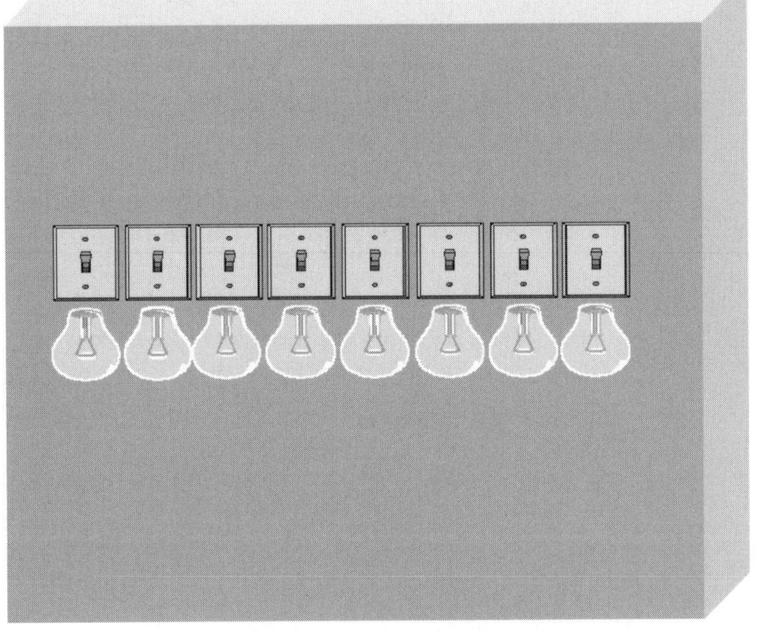

Figure 2.4
The CPU from the outside

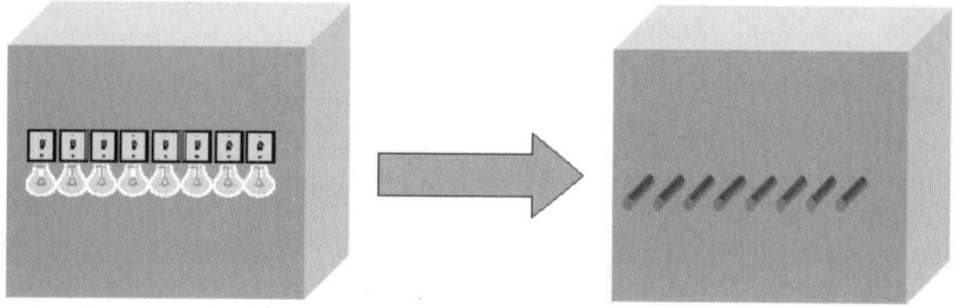

Figure 2.5
Analogy and reality, side by side

Before we go any further, I want to make sure you're clear on the fact that this is an analogy, not reality. There really is an external data bus, but there are no light bulbs or switches (Figure 2.5). There are, however, little wires sticking out of the CPU. If you apply voltage to one of these wires, you are in essence "flipping the switch." Get the idea? So if there is voltage on that wire, and if a tiny light bulb *were* on this wire, that light bulb would be shining, wouldn't it? By the same token, if there was no power on the wire, then the light bulb wouldn't be shining. That is why I use the "switch and light-bulb" analogy—to help you appreciate that these little wires are "flashing" on and off at a phenomenal rate.

Rather than saying that one of the external data bus wires is "on" or "off," I'll just use the number 1 to represent "on" and the number 0 to represent "off" (Figure 2.6). That way, if I want to describe the state of the lights at any given moment, instead of saying something like "on-off-off-off-on-on-off-off," I can just say "10001100".

In the world of computers, we are constantly turning wires on and off. As a result, this "1 and 0" or *binary system* is used to describe the state of these wires at any given moment. We will revisit this binary numbering system in greater detail later in the book.

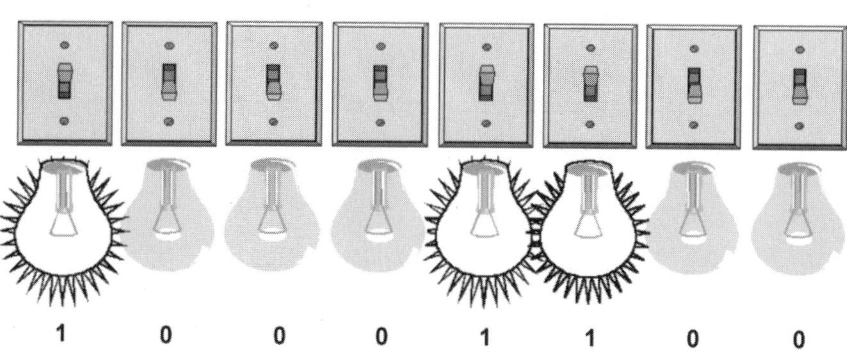

Figure 2.6
1 means on and 0 means off

Registers

Let's go inside the box for a moment and give the guy in the box four "work tables" to use. These are not tables in the classic sense; you can't eat a pizza on them. They simply hold light bulbs. Each table has 16 light bulbs with switches that the guy in the box can turn on and off. This setup, however, is substantially different from the external data bus. Here the light bulbs are not in pairs, just 16 light bulbs straight across with one switch for each bulb, and *you have no access to the light bulbs. Only the guy in the box can manipulate them.* These tables are called *registers* (Figure 2.7).

The function of these registers is to provide the man with a workplace for the problems you're going to give him. You need to be able to identify each register, so let's give them names: AX, BX, CX, and DX (Figure 2.8). Now, there are more registers than just these four, but these are called the *data* or *general-purpose registers.* You'll see more registers later, but for now these four are enough.

Before you close the lid on the box, you have to give the man one more tool. Remember the code book we talked about earlier? Let's make one for the external data bus so we can communicate. This code book would contain information such as "10000111 (light bulbs 8-3-2-1 on) means move the number 7 into the AX register." There are some rules here. Counting from right to left, commands start in the last four light bulbs 8-7-6-5 (in technical lingo, the *high-order bits*). Data is in the first four light bulbs 4-3-2-1 (the *low-order bits*). See Figure 2.9.

These commands are the microprocessor's machine language. The commands described here are not actual commands; they've been simplified somewhat to clarify the concept. The 8088, however, has commands

Figure 2.7
A register

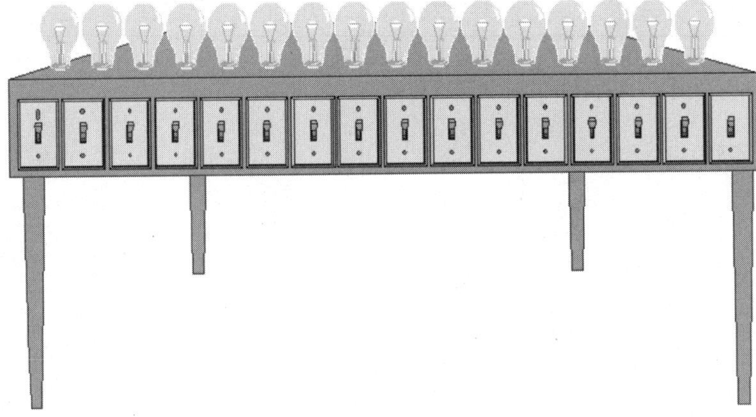

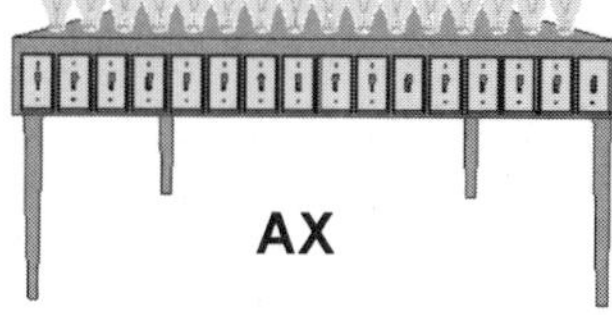

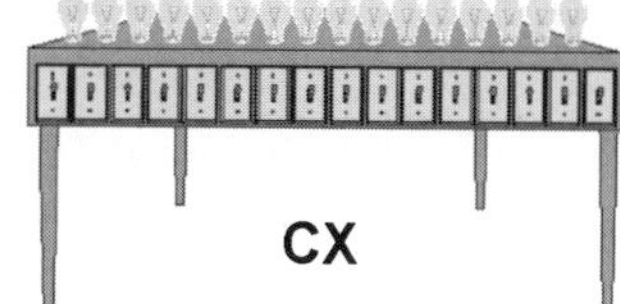

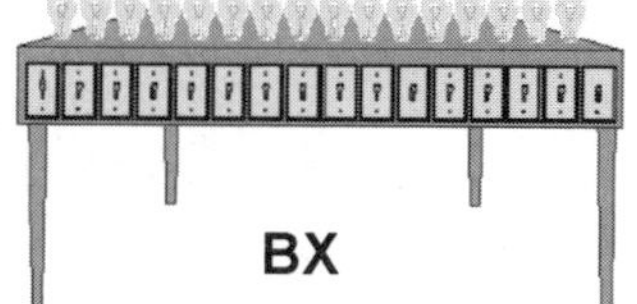

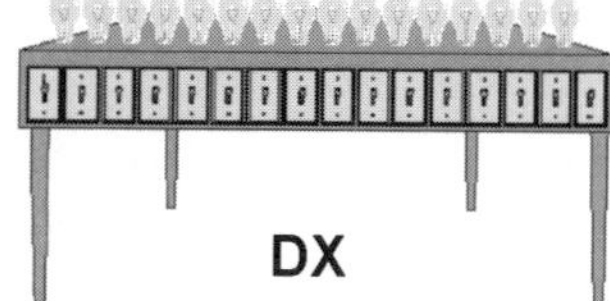

Figure 2.8 The four data registers

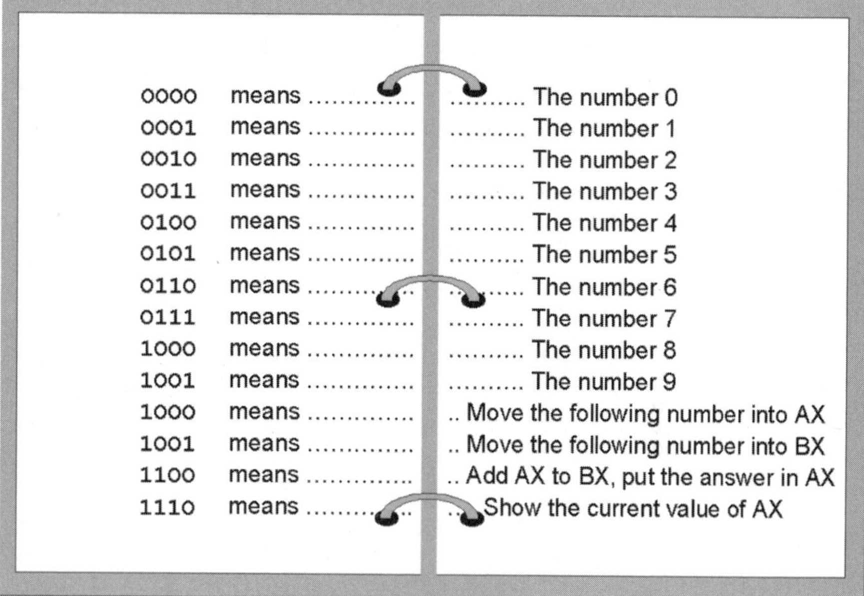

0000 means .... The number 0
0001 means .... The number 1
0010 means .... The number 2
0011 means .... The number 3
0100 means .... The number 4
0101 means .... The number 5
0110 means .... The number 6
0111 means .... The number 7
1000 means .... The number 8
1001 means .... The number 9
1000 means .... Move the following number into AX
1001 means .... Move the following number into BX
1100 means .... Add AX to BX, put the answer in AX
1110 means .... Show the current value of AX

Figure 2.9 The CPU's code book

very similar to these—plus a few hundred more! Here are some examples of real machine language for the Intel 8088:

10111010 The next line of code is a number. Put that number into the DX register.

01000001 Add 1 to the number already in the CX register.

00111100 Compare the value in the AX register with the next line of code.

So here is our CPU so far: the guy can communicate with the outside world via the external data bus, there are four registers with him, and he

Figure 2.10
Our CPU so far

has a code book so he can understand the different patterns on the external data bus (Figure 2.10).

Clock

Just because you switch the lights on and off doesn't mean the guy inside is going to look at his code book and act on it. Have you ever seen an old-time manual calculator—the ones with the big crank on one side? You pressed the numbers you want to deal with, then the + key, but that wasn't good enough—you then had to *pull the crank* on the side of the calculator to get your answer (Figure 2.11). Well, the CPU also has a "crank." You "pressed the buttons" by lighting the correct light bulbs on the external data bus; now you need to "pull the crank." The crank of the CPU is a special wire called the *clock* (most diagrams show the clock wire as CLK).

Figure 2.11
Nothing happens until you pull the crank!

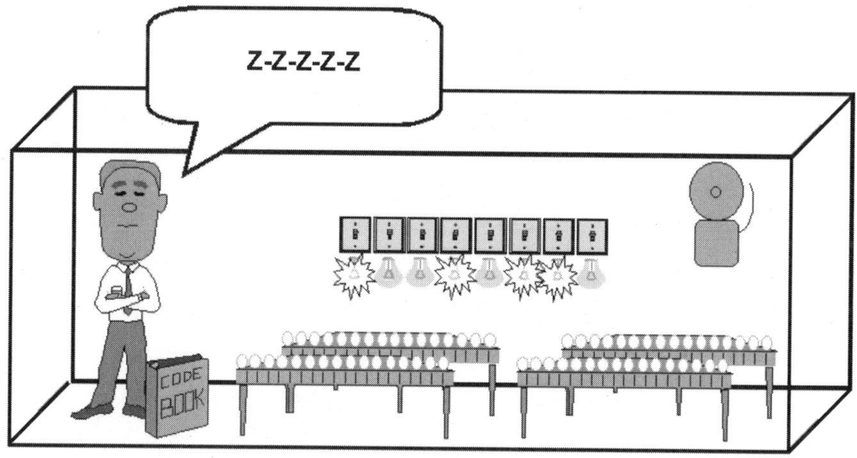

Figure 2.12 The CPU does nothing unless activated by the clock

To continue the analogy, let's put a buzzer inside the box with an activation button outside the box. Once you have the light bulbs on the external data bus set up, press the button to activate the buzzer and the guy will act on the lights (Figure 2.12). Each time the CLK wire is charged is called a *clock cycle*. Once a command has been placed on the external data bus, the clock wire must be raised to a given voltage—a clock cycle—in order for the CPU to process the command.

The CPU needs at least two clock cycles to act on each command. Using the manual-calculator image, you need to pull the crank *at least twice* before anything happens. Some commands require hundreds of clock cycles to be processed (Figure 2.13).

Let's look at the old-time manual calculator one more time. If you tried to pull the crank too quickly, like maybe 30 times per second, the cal-

Figure 2.13 The CPU needs more than one CLK to do anything!

culator would break; it was not designed to operate that quickly. CPUs have the same problem. If you place too many clock cycles on a CPU, it will overheat and stop working. The maximum number of clock cycles that your CPU can handle is called the *clock speed.* A CPU's clock speed is determined by the CPU manufacturer, and is the fastest speed at which the CPU can operate. The Intel 8088 processor had a clock speed of 4.77 MHz (millions of cycles per second).

1 Hertz (1 Hz) = 1 cycle per second
1 MegaHertz (1 MHz) = 1 million cycles per second

Understand that a CPU's clock speed is its *maximum* speed, not the speed at which it is running! A CPU can be run at any speed, as long as that speed is slower or equal to its clock speed. The system crystal determines the speed at which a CPU operates. The system crystal is usually a quartz oscillator, very similar to the one in a wristwatch, which is soldered to the motherboard (Figure 2.14). You should never run the CPU above its rated clock speed (Figure 2.15). The clock speed is always marked somewhere on the CPU itself.

Figure 2.14 One of many types of system crystals

Figure 2.15 A CPU's clock speed is its top speed

Figure 2.16
The speed of the CPU is determined by the crystal

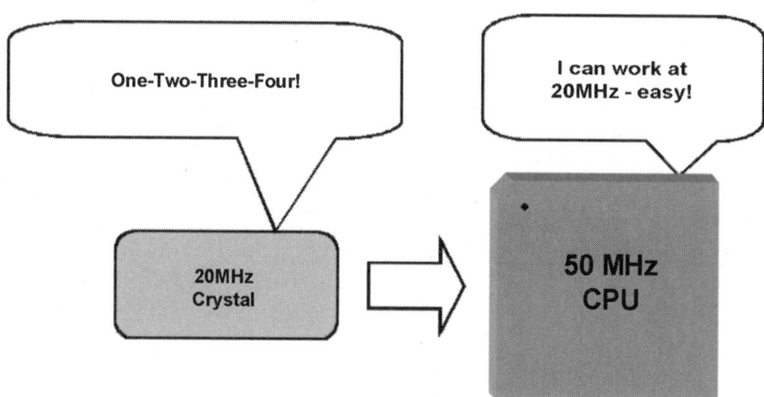

Figure 2.17
Slow crystal, fast CPU

It is crucial to understand the relationship of the system crystal to the clock speed of the CPU (see Figure 2.16). It makes sense to visualize the system crystal as a metronome for the CPU. A CPU can be pushed by a crystal with a lower clock speed than its own, but it will operate at the speed of the crystal (see Figure 2.17). Don't try to run a CPU faster than its clock speed or it will overheat and then lock up (Figure 2.18). Running a CPU slower than its clock speed is called *underclocking*, and running a CPU faster than its clock speed is called *overclocking*. If you underclock, you are not taking advantage of all of the power of the CPU. If you overclock, the CPU won't work. We will go into more detail on this later in the chapter.

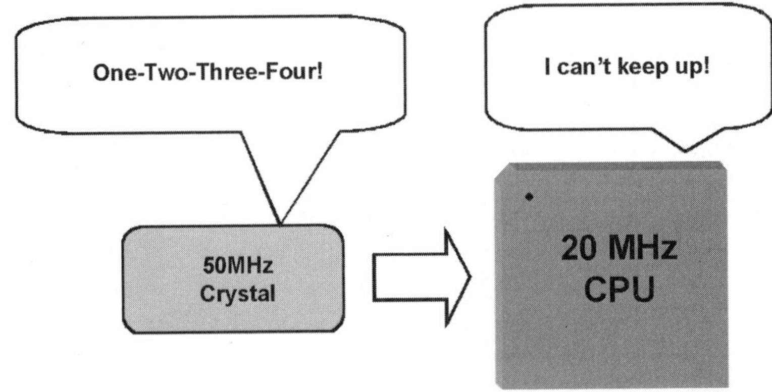
One-Two-Three-Four!
I can't keep up!
50MHz Crystal
20 MHz CPU

Figure 2.18
Fast crystal, slow CPU

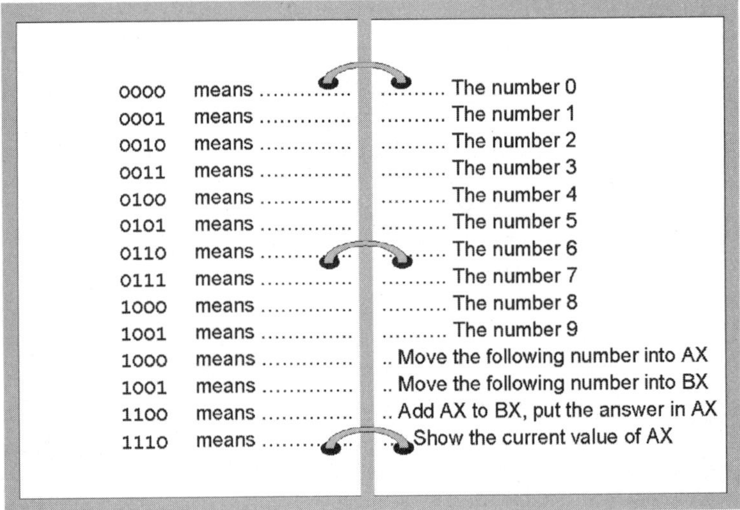
0000 means .... The number 0
0001 means .... The number 1
0010 means .... The number 2
0011 means .... The number 3
0100 means .... The number 4
0101 means .... The number 5
0110 means .... The number 6
0111 means .... The number 7
1000 means .... The number 8
1001 means .... The number 9
1000 means .... Move the following number into AX
1001 means .... Move the following number into BX
1100 means .... Add AX to BX, put the answer in AX
1110 means .... Show the current value of AX

Figure 2.19
The CPU's code book again (to reference commands)

Back to the External Data Bus

Now that you have all the necessary components, let's watch how this setup allows a microprocessor to get work done. To do this, you are going to add 2 to 3 and receive the answer. You will keep sending commands to the microprocessor until you get the result. Let's refer back to the code book to tell the guy in the box what to do (Figure 2.19). Using the code book, here are the steps for 2 + 3:

1. Send the command 10000010 (move 2 into AX).
2. Send 10010011 (move 3 into BX).
3. Send 11000000 (add BX into AX).
4. Send 11100000 (show the value in AX).

This set of commands is known as a *program,* which is a series of commands sent to a CPU in a specific order for the CPU to perform work. Each discrete setting of the external data bus is a *line of code.* This program, therefore, has four lines of code.

Running the Program

Let's watch each step as the program is executed:

1. Flip external data bus switches to 10000010.
2. Repeatedly add voltage to the clock until the switches on the external data bus suddenly all turn off (that means the guy in the box has acted on the command).
3. Flip external data bus switches to 10010011.
4. Repeat step 2.
5. Flip external data bus switches to 11000000.
6. Repeat step 2.
7. Flip external data bus switches to 11100000.
8. Repeat step 2, except you will see the value 00000101 (5) suddenly appear on the external data bus.

Congratulations! You have just added 2 to 3 and received the answer 5! You are a programmer! One more reality check—think about the registers again. Clearly, there are no "tables" or "racks of light bulbs." The four registers are tiny storage areas on the CPU. They are microscopic semiconductor circuits called TTL logic (not light bulbs); if they are holding a charge they are "on," and if they are not holding a charge they are "off."

Figure 2.20 shows a diagram of a real 8088 CPU, showing the actual wires that compose the external data bus and the single clock wire.

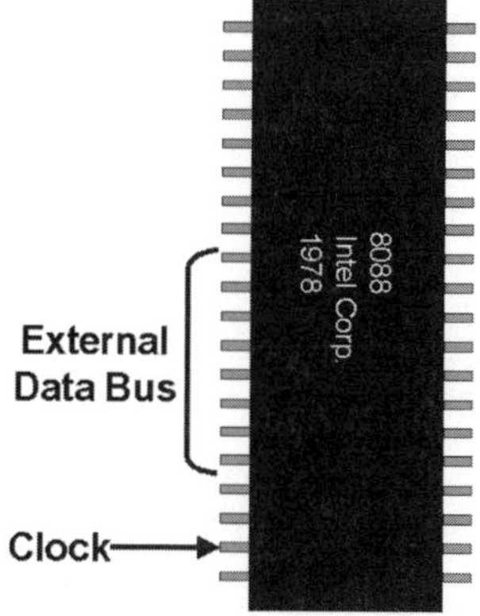

Figure 2.20 Diagram of 8088, showing the clock and external data bus

Since the registers are inside the CPU, they can't be shown in this figure.

Memory

By using the program described in the previous section, you can add 2 to 3. Because you are manually setting the voltages on the external data bus and clock wire, however, it is a very slow way to add 2 to 3. Keep in mind that the 8088 has a clock speed of 4.77 MHz, so you need some way to store the programs on something that will feed each line of the program to the CPU at a high rate of speed. That way the processor reads the data as fast as it can process it, or at least a lot faster than you can flip switches!

What can you use to store programs? Since each line of code is nothing more than a pattern of eight ones and zeros, any device that can store ones and zeros, eight across, will do the trick.

Memory Storage Options

Why not store each line of code on a paper card? You could use one card for each line of code, stack the cards in the right order, and then run them through a "card reader." The card reader would then feed the cards sending the lines of code to the CPU at a high rate of speed! Sounds great, right? (See Figure 2.21.)

Paper cards were used in the early days of computing. Back when CPUs had clock speeds in the kHz (thousands of cycles per second) range, paper cards could feed programs into the CPU at sufficient speed to keep up with the processor, but today they would be horribly slow. Plus, there is a small problem. Programs generate data. When a computer adds 2 to 3, the answer of 5 is generated on the external data bus. Cards are okay for storing programs, but what about data? You need some type of storage that the CPU can write data to.

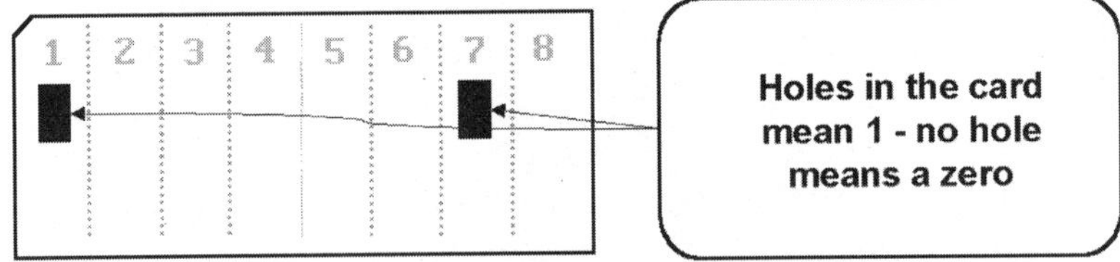
1
2
3
4
5
6
7
8
Holes in the card mean 1 - no hole means a zero

Figure 2.21
Paper cards can hold programs

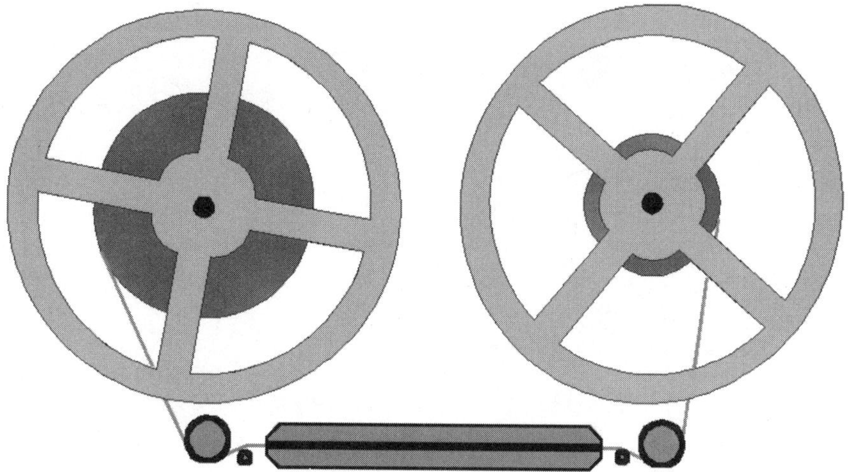

Figure 2.22
Streaming tape is not random access

One early way of handling this problem was to place data on magnetic tape. Unlike paper cards, the CPU could write data on magnetic tape fairly easily. Magnetic tape, however, could not be randomly accessed (see Figure 2.22). Every CPU has the ability to jump from one place in a program to another. If the CPU has to jump to a new line of code a lot, the tape will be constantly rewinding and fast-forwarding to get to the line of code the CPU needs!

RAM: Random-Access Memory

You need a storage system that can store not only programs, but also data. This system must be able to jump to *any* line of code as easily as any other. The ultimate device to do this is RAM (random-access memory). In the chapter of this book dedicated to RAM, I will develop the concept of RAM in detail, but at this point let's look at RAM as an electronic spreadsheet. Each cell in this spreadsheet can store only a one or a zero, and each cell is called a *bit*. Each row in the spreadsheet is eight bits across to match the external data bus of the 8088, and each eight bits is called a *byte*. So each row is one byte wide. Physically, RAM is groups of semiconductor chips on small cards that snap into your computer (see Figure 2.23).

Electronically, RAM looks like a spreadsheet (Figure 2.24). In the PC world, RAM transfers and stores data to and from the CPU in byte-sized chunks (pardon the pun). RAM is therefore arranged in byte-sized rows. The number of rows of RAM varies from PC to PC, and RAM can have hundreds of thousands of rows (later you will see millions, but for the moment just think in terms of thousands).

Figure 2.23
Typical RAM (30-pin SIMM)

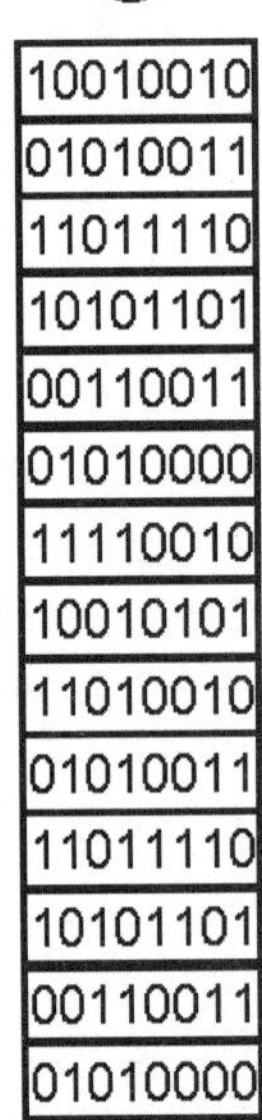

Figure 2.24
To the CPU, RAM looks like a spreadsheet

Any one row of RAM can be accessed as easily and as fast as any other row, which is the "random access" part of RAM. Not only is RAM randomly accessible; it's also fast. By storing programs on RAM, the CPU can access and run programs very quickly. RAM is also used to store data that is actively being used by whatever program is currently running.

Don't confuse RAM with mass storage devices like hard and floppy drives! You use hard drives and floppy drives to permanently store programs and data that are not currently needed.

Any individual 1 or 0 = a *bit*
4 bits = a *nibble*
8 bits = a *byte*
16 bits = a *word*
32 bits = a *double word*
64 bits = a *paragraph* or *quad word*

Address Bus

So far, you have a CPU and RAM. Now what you need is some connection between the CPU and the RAM so they can talk to each other. To do so, let's extend the external data bus (Figure 2.25). Wait a minute! How can you connect the RAM to the external data bus? (See Figure 2.26.) This is not a matter of just plugging it in! RAM is a spreadsheet with thousands and thousands of discrete rows, and you only need to look at the contents of one row of the spreadsheet at a time, right? What are you going to do?

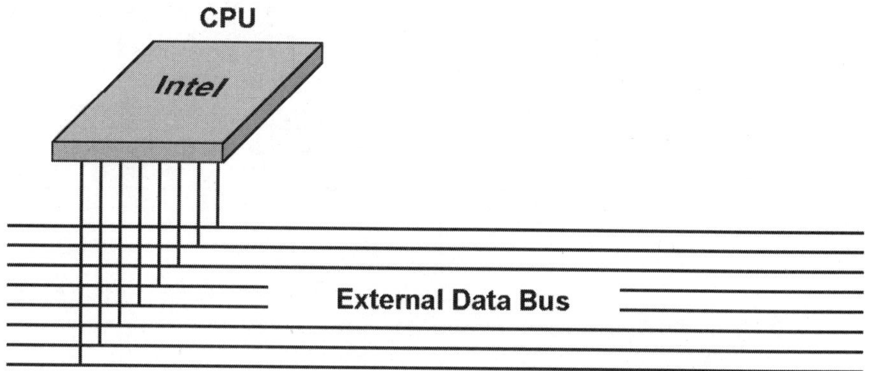

Figure 2.25 Extending the external data bus

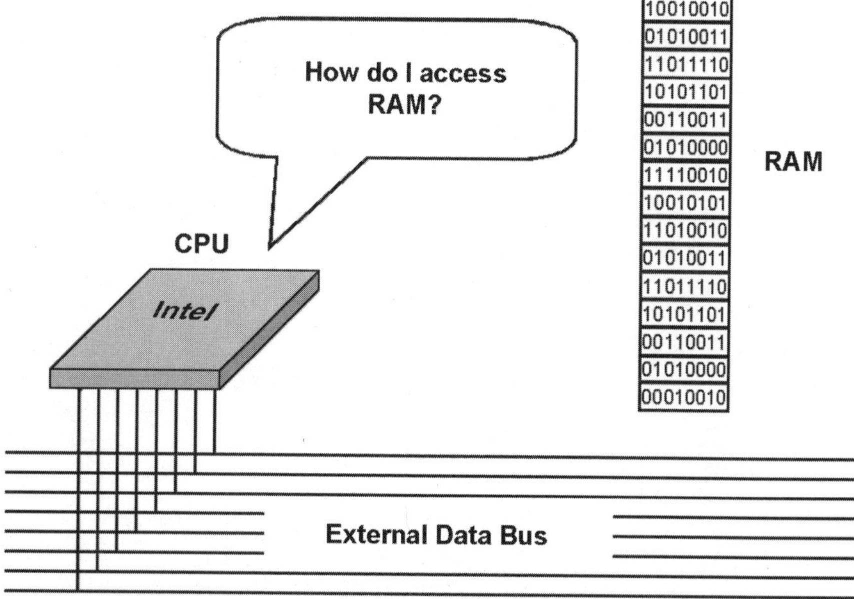

Figure 2.26 How do you connect RAM to the CPU?

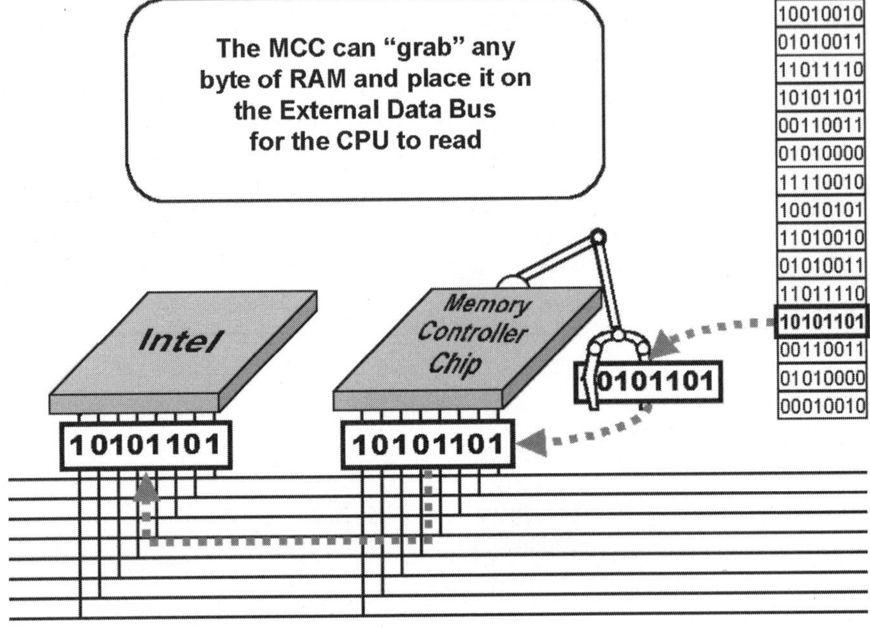

Figure 2.27 The MCC grabbing a byte of RAM

In order to allow the CPU to access a row of RAM whenever necessary, you need to add an entirely new set of circuitry that allows the CPU to "grab" one row of RAM. Let's see how this is done. You give the CPU access to RAM by adding a new chip to the system, called a *memory-control chip* or *MCC*. The MCC has circuitry to electronically "grab" any single line of RAM and place that data on the external data bus, thus allowing the CPU to act on that code (Figure 2.27).

This is great, but you need to give the CPU the ability to tell the MCC *which line of code* it needs! (Figure 2.28) You have to provide the CPU with a way to talk to the MCC—a new type of data bus called the *address bus*. The address bus is a set of wires that runs from the CPU and allows the CPU to control the MCC. Different CPUs have different numbers of wires (which you will soon see is very significant). The 8088 has 20 wires in its address bus (Figure 2.29).

By turning wires on and off in different patterns, the CPU can tell the MCC which line of RAM it wants at any given moment. Let's consider these 20 wires. There are two big questions here: "How many different patterns of "on" and "off" wires can there be in 20 wires?" and "Which pattern goes to which row of RAM?"

The answer to the first question is fairly easy. Each wire can be only on or off; they can be in only one of two different states. If there were only one wire on the address bus, it could be either on or off or 2^1 different

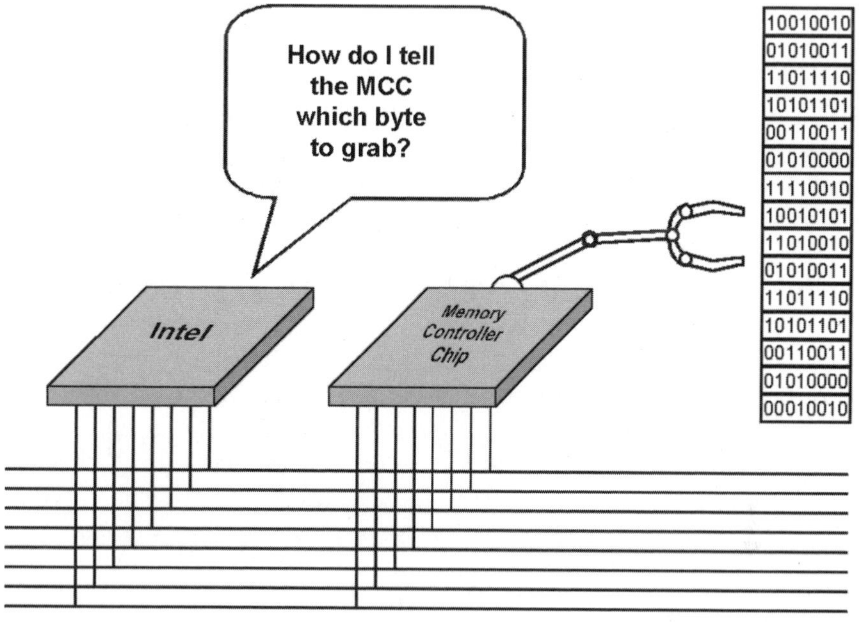

Figure 2.28
How does the CPU control the MCC?

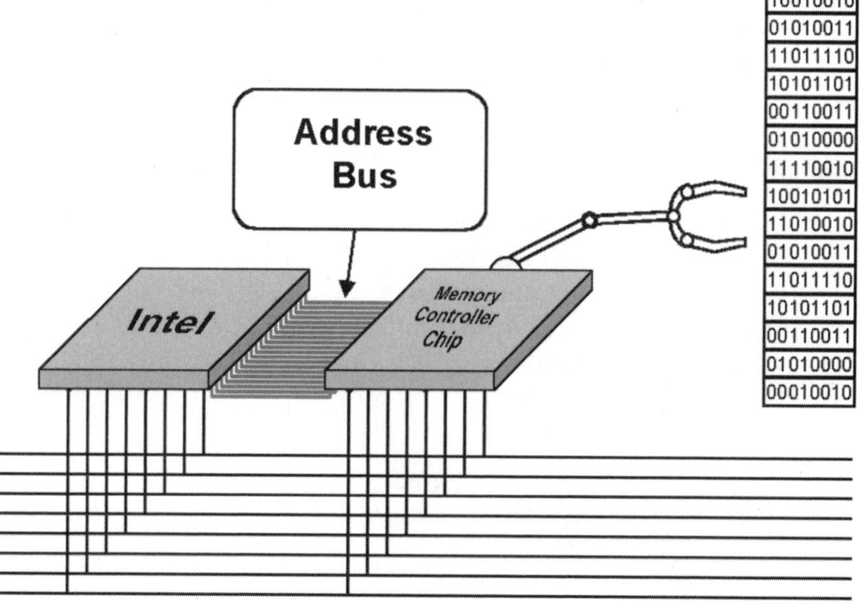

Figure 2.29
The address bus

combinations. If you had two address bus wires, there would be four different combinations, or 2^2. If you had 20 wires, you would have 1,048,576 (2^{20}) combinations. Since each pattern points to one line of code and since each line of RAM is one byte, *if you know the number of wires in the address bus, you know the maximum amount of RAM that a particular CPU can handle.* Since the 8088 has a 20-wire address bus, the most RAM it can handle is 2^{20} or 1,048,576 bytes. The 8088, therefore, has an address space of 1,048,576 bytes.

Remember that everything in the CPU boils down to ones and zeros. In regards to the address bus, you are interested in the maximum number of patterns it can generate (how much RAM it can take). You know that the 8088 has 20 address wires and the total address space is 1,048,576 bytes. Although this is accurate, no one uses such an exact term to discuss the address space of the 8088. What you say is that the 8088 has 1 megabyte (1 meg or 1MB) of address space. The base value used in computing is 210, or 1024, which is called a *kilobyte* (1K). If someone says he has one kilobyte (1K), he really has 1024 bytes. A *megabyte* is 1K × 1K or 1024 × 1024, which equals 1,048,576 bytes. So don't confuse one million (1,000,000) with 1MB (1,048,576), or one thousand (1000) with 1K (1024).

1 kilobyte = 2^{10} = 1024
1 megabyte = 2^{20} = 1,048,576
1 gigabyte = 2^{30} = 1,073,741,824

1 kilobyte is not equal to 1,000 (one thousand)
1 megabyte is not equal to 1,000,000 (one million)
1 gigabyte is not equal to 1,000,000,000 (one billion)

Now, the second question is a little harder: "Which pattern goes to which line of RAM?" To understand this, let's take a moment to discuss binary counting. In binary, there are only two numbers, 0 and 1, which makes binary a darned handy way to work with wires that are being turned on and off. Let's try to count in binary: 0, 1, . . . what's next? It's not 2! Now let's count to 1000: 0, 1, 10, 11, 100, 101, 110, 11, 1000. Think about good old base 10 (regular numbers) for a moment. If you have the number 365, can you put zeros in front of the 365, like this: 000365? Sure you can—it doesn't change the value. Same thing in binary, but in this case we will add enough zeros to make 20 places:

00000000000000000000
00000000000000000001
00000000000000000010
00000000000000000011

00000000000000000100
00000000000000000101
00000000000000000110
00000000000000000111
00000000000000001000

This would be a great way to represent each line of RAM. The last RAM row would be 11111111111111111111. When the CPU turns off all the address bus wires, it wants the first line of RAM; when it turns on all of the wires, it wants the 1,048,576th line of RAM.

Now for another reality check. Figure 2.30 shows a diagram of an Intel 8088 microprocessor, with the location of the address wires. If you look at the earlier diagram of the location of the 8088's external data bus wires (Figure 2.29), you'll notice that some of the external data bus and address bus wires overlap. That's okay—some of the wires do both! It's called *multiplexing*.

The original IBM PC used an Intel 8088 CPU. Intel's presence from the beginning has allowed them a virtual monopoly on supply of CPUs for IBM-compatible PCs. Although there are serious competitors, Intel also controls the standards that allow CPUs to be IBM compatible. As technology has progressed from the 8088 to the most current CPU, the size of the external data bus, address bus, CPU registers, and amount of RAM storage has also grown. This progression from 8-bit technology to 16-bit, 32-bit, and finally 64-bit technology has allowed systems to communicate and process more information faster and more efficiently.

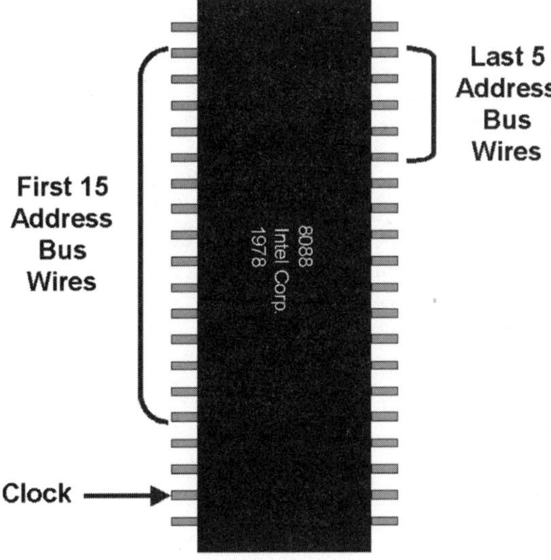

Figure 2.30
Location of address bus wires on an 8088

Although Intel definitely has the largest share of the CPU market, a number of other companies, led by Advanced Micro Devices (AMD) and Cyrix Corporation, continue to grow in technology and sophistication. As I discuss the different CPUs, you will see that the early processors were dominated by Intel. As we move forward, however, you will see other brands of CPUs begin to appear. In today's CPUs, you have a real choice in CPUs.

Now that you have a basic understanding of registers, external data buses, and address buses, let's take a tour of the family of Intel processors, as well as some of its more famous competitors.

CPU Packages

DIPP (DUAL INLINE PIN PACKAGE): 8088, 8086, 80286 DIPPs were the first generation of packaging for microprocessors. They are distinct, with two rows of pins on either side of the processor (Figure 2.31).

PGA (PIN GRID ARRRAY): 80286, 80386, 486 PGAs are very popular for desktop machines, as their relative size allows for easy heat dissipation. The pins are evenly distributed along the bottom of the chip. PGA chips go into regular PGA or the popular ZIF (zero insertion force) sockets. See Figure 2.32.

SPGA (STAGGERED PIN GRID ARRAY): Pentium, K5, K6, 6x86, P6 SPGAs have some or all of their pins organized in a diagonal pattern. This allows the CPU to have more closely packed pins, thereby keeping

Figure 2.31
DIPP chip

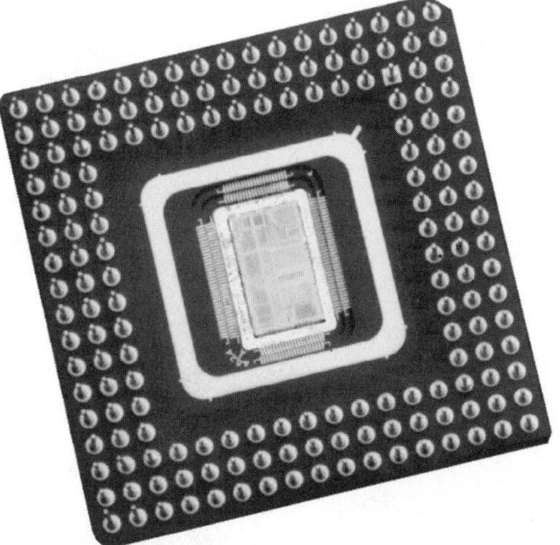

Figure 2.32
PGA chip

Figure 2.33
SPGA chip

the overall package smaller. Like PGA chips, SPGA CPUs also have special ZIF sockets. See Figure 2.33.

PQFP/CQFP (PLASTIC/CERAMIC QUAD FLAT PACK): 80286, 80386, 486 Because of their small size, PQFPs are used primarily on laptop machines. They also have strong mounts, which are difficult to jar loose. PQFPs are easy to remove, as long as one has the special tool. They are inserted into a special mount known as a *carrier ring*. See Figure 2.34.

PLCC/CLCC (Plastic/Ceramic Leaderless Chip Carrier): 80286, 80386 PLCCs are popular for machines that are designed for upgradability, since they can be easily removed. They have no leads (pins), which makes them difficult to damage during removal or installation. They are identifiable by their restraining clips (Figure 2.35).

SEC Cartridge (SINGLE EDGE CONTACT): Pentium II With the size of CPUs getting larger and larger, Intel has developed the single-edge contact cartridge for Pentium II CPUs. They stand on edge, so the CPU

Figure 2.34
PQFP chip

Figure 2.35
PLCC chip

Figure 2.36
SEC cartridge

takes up less space on the motherboard and can be more easily cooled (Figure 2.36).

The 8086 CPU Family

When IBM decided to enter the small-computer business, they decided that they would need a more powerful processor than the 8-bit microprocessors that were popular at the time. IBM wanted a chip that was not going to be too hard to integrate into their systems, they wanted a chip based on addressing concepts and machine language that programmers would easily understand, and they wanted a chip with flexibility and expandability. Mostly, they wanted a chip that would allow existing applications on CPM-based machines to be easily recompiled for the new chip.

Intel Corporation invented an improved version of their very popular 8080 processor, called the 8086 (Figure 2.37). The 8086 chip was a full 16-bit chip. Although 16-bit chips were also being produced by some of Intel's competitors, the 8086 had the ability to address up to 1 megabyte (1MB) of memory when everyone else was still addressing only 64 kilobytes (64K). This addressability was achieved by combining two 16-bit registers (2^{16} = 64K) into one 20-bit (2^{20} = 1MB) register. This addressing scheme sliced the

TABLE 2.1

The 8086 CPU

Chip Type	Clock Speed (MHz)	Register Size	External Bus	Address Bus
Intel 8088	4.77—10	16-bit	8-bit	20-bit
Intel 8086	4.77—10	16-bit	16-bit	20-bit

Figure 2.37
Intel 8086 chip

1 megabyte into 64K chunks, which also made integrating programs written for earlier computers easier.

There was one problem with the 8086 chip: it was too powerful. The problem was in the 8086's 16-bit external bus. There were no devices invented that could send or receive the 16-bit data to and from the 8086. In order to get an 8086 to speak to an 8-bit device, the 8086 had to chop its data into two pieces and send each piece separately. Intel was aware of this and created the 8088 processor. The 8088 was identical to the 8086 except it had only an 8-bit external bus. The 8088 was the chip that IBM decided to use in its first microcomputer, the IBM PC. The 8088 was also used in the "upscale" PC, the IBM XT. The 8086 was rarely used in comparison to the 8088.

The 80286 CPU Family

In 1983, Intel introduced its next generation of chip, the 80286. (There was an interim chip, the 80186, which was little more than a slightly enhanced 8086. It died quickly due to the appearance of the 80286.) The 80286, or as it was more popularly known, the 286, was a significant leap in technology from the 8086. The 286 first appeared in the IBM model AT (Advanced Technology) computer. See Figure 2.38.

Modes

When Intel made the 8086/8088, they promised to make every subsequent chip backwardly compatible. The 80286 had a number of major enhancements that made it far superior to the 8088/8086 chip. In order to take advantage of these functions, it needed programs that could use them. But what if all the programs were designed to run on the 8088? In this case, you wouldn't want the extra features of the 286; you'd just want the 286 to run like an 8088. The answer that Intel came up with was simple and elegant: starting with the 286 (and this is still true in today's CPUs), all CPUs would begin by acting like an 8088. In order to take advantage of the higher functions, you would then have to run special programs to "shift" the CPU into a higher mode. The 286 had two modes: the first mode was 8086 compatible, and was called *real mode*; the second, more powerful mode was called *protected mode*.

Protected Mode

When the 286 was shifted into protected mode, it had the ability to use up to 16 megabytes of memory and run more than one program at a time. This could happen only if you had an operating system designed to handle these advanced functions. DOS was designed to run on an 8086, so if you ran DOS on a 286 you were in real mode. In order to take advantage

Figure 2.38
Intel 286

TABLE 2.2
The 80286 CPU

Chip Type	Clock Speed (MHz)	Register Size	External Bus	Address Bus
Intel 80286	8—20	16-bit	16-bit	24-bit

of the 286 protected mode, you needed a special operating system. In protected mode, multiple programs are stored in memory. An operating system designed to run in protected mode creates a "focus," running a few lines of one of the programs stored in memory. After some amount of time, the operating system can then switch its focus to one of the other programs in memory. Technically speaking, this is not multitasking, but if the operating system can switch back and forth between the programs very rapidly, it would certainly look as though multitasking were taking place.

Did anyone write an operating system to take advantage of this power? Well, some people did. Certain flavors of UNIX were created to run on 286s. Novell NetWare 2.2 needed a 286, as did the first versions of OS/2. These were all very special situations. Also, once you switched into protected mode, the only way to go back to regular 8086 mode was to reboot the computer! For the most part, everyone ran DOS on 286s in those days, which meant that the 286 computers were little more than fast 8086s.

The 80386 CPU: the 386DX Family

In 1985, Intel unveiled its next-generation chip, the 80386, 386 for short (Figure 2.39). The 386 was Intel's first true 32-bit chip; the registers, address

Figure 2.39
Intel 386DX-33

TABLE 2.3

The 80386DX CPU

Chip Type	Clock Speed (MHz)	Register Size	External Bus	Address Bus	Internal Cache
Intel 80386DX	16—33	32-bit	32-bit	32-bit	None
AMD AM386DX	20—40	32-bit	32-bit	32-bit	None
AMD AM386DXL	20—33	32-bit	32-bit	32-bit	None
AMD AM386DXLV	25—33	32-bit	32-bit	32-bit	8K

bus, and external bus were all 32 bits wide. The 386 also included a number of new registers for debugging and memory management. The 386 could run in three different modes: real mode, 286 protected mode, and its own very powerful 386 protected mode. Once the 386 was switched to 386 protected mode, it had two functions that set it apart from earlier CPUs: virtual memory and a mode called virtual 8086.

Virtual Memory

The 386's 32-bit address bus allowed for up to four gigabytes of addressable memory, far more than any PC currently needs (2^{32} = 4,294,967,296 = 4GB). However, today's PCs can often use more RAM than they have installed. Programs are run in RAM. If you try to load more programs than your RAM can store, you'll get some kind of "out of memory" error. With the right operating system, the 386 chip can create "pretend RAM," better known as *virtual memory,* by electronically changing a part of permanent storage—in particular hard drives—into memory. This virtual memory looks like regular RAM to the operating system. The part of your hard drive that acts like virtual memory is called a *swap file,* and is used by all of today's operating systems.

Virtual 8086

386s also had a more advanced protected mode known as *virtual 8086.* In 286 protected mode, it was impossible to run 8086-mode DOS programs. With virtual 8086, the operating system created virtual 8086 "bubbles"—memory areas completely separated and virtually addressed within the 1MB 8086 limit. In other words, a DOS program could run within an 8086 bubble while the CPU stayed in protected mode. The operating system created "virtual registers" whenever the program wanted to use to them.

The operating system would then inspect what the program was trying to do and verify that it wasn't trying to do something dangerous.

The 80386SX CPU Family

In order to increase the popularity of the 386 chip, Intel recognized the need for a 386 processor that could operate easily on 16-bit motherboards. This need was fulfilled with the 80386SX (Figure 2.40).

Figure 2.40
Intel 80386SL (courtesy of Intel)

TABLE 2.4
The 80386SX CPU

Chip Type	Clock (MHz)	Register Size	External Bus	Address Bus	Cache	Voltage*	SMM*
Intel 80386SX	16—25	32-bit	16-bit	24-bit	None	5 V	No
Intel 80386SL	16—25	32-bit	16-bit	24-bit	None	3.33 V	Yes
AMD AM386SX	20—40	32-bit	16-bit	24-bit	None	5 V	No
AMD AM386SXL	16—40	32-bit	16-bit	24-bit	None	5 V	Yes*
AMD AM386SXLV	33	32-bit	16-bit	24-bit	8K	3.3 V	Yes
IBM 386SLC	20	32-bit	16-bit	24-bit	8K	3.3 V	Yes

*See Power-Saving Strategies

The 386SX differed from the standard 386 (now known as the 386DX) in two ways. First, the external data bus was reduced to 16 bits to match the 286's external data bus. Second, the address bus was reduced to 24 bits. This limited the address range of the 386SX to 16 megabytes (2^{24} = 16 Megs).

Although the 386SX looked like a 286 on the outside, it was a full 386DX on the inside. The 386SX could handle all of the modes and functions of the DX - 386 Protected Mode, Virtual Memory and Virtual 8086. Many people believe that the "SX" stands for "Single Channel" and the "DX" stands for "Dual Channel." There is no proof to this and Intel has never made any statement to that effect. "SX" and "DX" are not acronyms.

Power-Saving Strategies

CPUs, like all other electrical components, need electricity. Also like all other electrical devices, CPUs require a certain voltage of electricity. During the realm of the 8086s, 80286s, and 80386s, all CPUs needed five volts to operate. During the realm of the 80386s, however, a new type of PC started to become popular: the laptop. There were 80286 laptops, but it wasn't until the 386s that they became truly common. Earlier portable computers derived their power from AC outlets. You turned off the PC, unplugged it, moved to another location, and then plugged it in again. Laptops were designed from the start to derive their power from built-in batteries. As we all can attest, batteries work for only a relatively short time. The first laptops had batteries that lasted less than half an hour—hardly acceptable for any serious work!

It quickly became obvious that if laptops were to become a mainstream product, they would have to have battery lives in the multiple-hour range. To do that, either the batteries would have to be made better or the laptops would have to use less power. On the "better battery" side, battery makers began to develop longer-lasting battery technologies with names like Nickel-Cadmium and Lithium-Ion. Intel decided to attack the power problem by making lower-voltage CPUs that required less power. Additionally, Intel forwarded a new function for CPUs, called SMM (system management mode), which could shut down unused, power-draining peripherals.

LOWER VOLTAGE Up to this point, all CPUs ran on 5 volts of DC power. Intel invented a special 386SX designed to run in laptops that ran at 3.3 volts instead of 5 volts. This CPU was called the 386SL. By reducing the voltage usage from 5 to 3.3 volts, the 386SL used roughly half the power of an equivalent 386SX. By reducing the CPU's voltage, Intel led the way for reducing the voltage in every other chip in the laptop. All of the support chips in the laptop were also reduced to 3.3 volts, resulting in a laptop that would use far less power.

Lower voltages have totally taken over the PC world. Although many 486s and even a few of the very first Pentium CPUs used 5 volts, all current CPUs, whether they are in a laptop or on your desk, use 3.3 or even less volts.

On a few late-generation 386 and all 486 systems, you have two voltage issues. First, you need to determine the voltage of the CPU. Second, you need to make sure that the motherboard supplies the proper voltage to the CPU. Let's look first at determining CPU voltage.

DETERMINING CPU VOLTAGE ON 386/486 SYSTEMS Non-Intel CPU voltages can be determined by the model of microprocessor. For example, all AMD AM386DLs are 5 volts and all AMD AM386DLVs are 3.3 volts. The tables in this and previous sections contain all of the voltage information for the most common CPUs.

There are a few exceptions to this rule. Certain non-Intel microprocessors are 3.3 volts, but only up to a certain clock speed. Any chips running at a faster clock speed will use 5 volts. One such chip is the AM386DLV. The 25-MHz system is a 3.3-volt chip, while the 33-MHz version is a 5-volt chip. Intel sold the exact same model of chips in both 3.3- and 5-volt versions. Intel's rules are as follows:

- The only 3.3-volt 386 is the 386SL; all other 386s are 5 volts.
- On 486s, look for the "SL-enhanced" backwards ampersand (&). After this symbol, there will be a 3 or a 5. A 3 stands for 3.3 volts, while a 5 means 5 volts.
- On 486s, almost all non-PGA-packaged chips are low voltage. All PGA chips without the backwards & are 5 volts.

When in doubt, call your supplier or reference this book, but get it right if you want the system to work!

WHAT VOLTAGE IS YOUR MOTHERBOARD? Once you know the voltage your CPU needs, you must then begin to verify that the motherboard can give that voltage to the CPU. From a voltage standpoint, there are three different types of 386/486 motherboards: 5 volts, 3.3 volts, or switchable between 3.3 and 5 volts.

Figure 2.41
A 5-volt motherboard

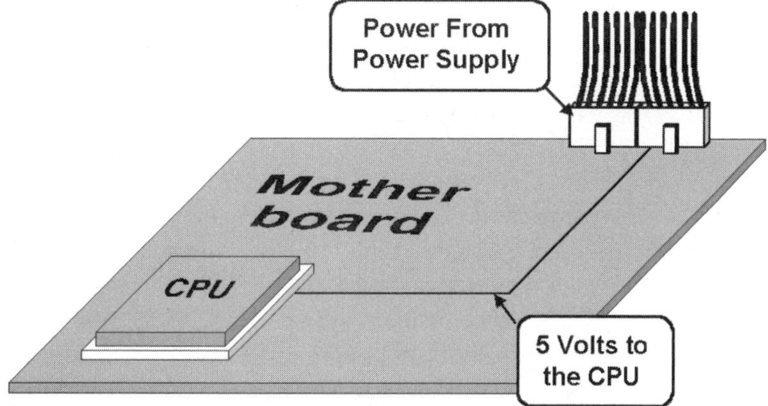

At first glance, this might seem confusing. Doesn't the power supply give the power to the CPU? Yes, but the voltage moves from the power supply through the motherboard and then to the CPU. As you will see in the chapter on power, the power supplies output in two voltages, 5 volts and 12 volts. The 5-volt power is for electrical components like the CPU. Early motherboards simply passed the 5 volts straight to the CPU (Figure 2.41).

When the 3.3-volt CPUs came along (Figure 2.42), there was clearly a need to provide 3.3 volts to those CPUs. There were a couple of ways to do this. First, the manufacturers could have simply created a new power supply that generated 3.3 volts. This was done in many laptops. Well, 3.3-volt CPUs quickly moved from the laptop world to the desktop world. Now 3.3-volt desktop machines were a problem. First, motherboard makers wanted to keep their systems cheap. With the exception of a few specialized (and expensive) laptops, nobody was making 3.3-volt power supplies. If someone

Figure 2.42
A 3.3-volt motherboard

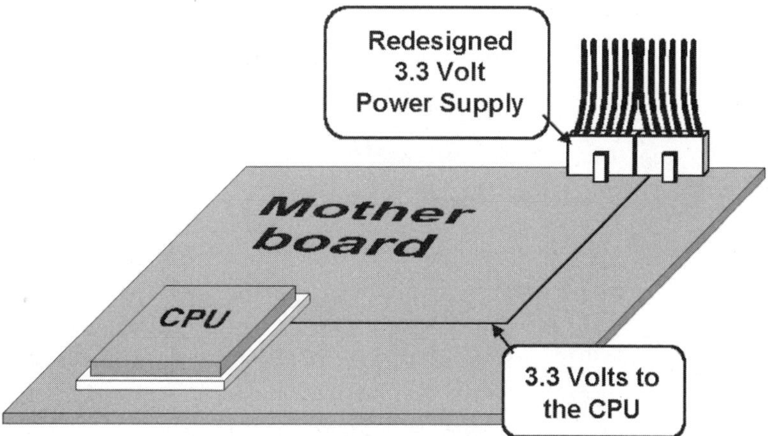

started making 3.3-volt motherboards, it would be nice if the motherboard could take a standard 5-volt power supply and convert the 5 volts to 3.3 volts.

The second possible solution is making variable-voltage CPUs. As you get into 486s, you will see that certain CPUs are identical, with the exception of their voltages. Motherboard makers don't want to make two versions of the exact same motherboard with different voltages. What they would like to do is make *one* motherboard on which you can change the voltage, depending on what type of 486 you install.

In the short time frame of 3.3-volt 386s, most motherboards were either one voltage or the other, which was fine since there was little or no interchanging of CPUs in the 386 world. In fact, almost all low-power 386 CPUs were soldered to the motherboard. Since the CPUs were soldered to the motherboard, you were never going to change the CPU. The motherboard would therefore provide either 3.3 or 5 volts, depending on the CPU, and would not be interchangeable.

The CPU voltage was never an issue for 386 systems due to the fact that the 3.3-volt 386s were invariably soldered to the motherboard.

The 486s changed this. During their reign, CPUs began to have a high degree of interchangeability. I'll go into this in more detail in the 486 section, but the bottom line is that there was a tremendous demand for single motherboards that could support both 5- and 3.3-volt CPUs. Fortunately, the answer was both simple and inexpensive.

VOLTAGE REGULATORS TO THE RESCUE! There is a wonderful, cheap, little electric component called a *voltage regulator* that does one thing well: it can convert one voltage of electricity into another voltage. Voltage regulators were not invented for the PC industry. They've been around for a long time and have millions of applications in our world. They come in a myriad of shapes and sizes, but the ones used in PCs are relatively common in appearance. They are roughly ¾ to 1 inch long and have three wires (electricians call them *leads*) that are soldered to the motherboard. These devices tend to generate a lot of heat, so they are almost always mounted on some type of cooling fins. Figure 2.43 shows an example. By adding a voltage regulator to the motherboard, manufacturers could make systems that supported either a 3.3-volt or a 5-volt CPU (Figure 2.44).

This is by far the most common type of 486 motherboard, so it's very important to make sure the jumper is properly set for the type of CPU installed. Once you know the correct voltage for the CPU, you then have to take the time to find the jumper(s) or switch(es) to flip for the correct voltage. Figure 2.45 is a nice example. It's usually easy to set this type of

Figure 2.43 Typical PC voltage regulator

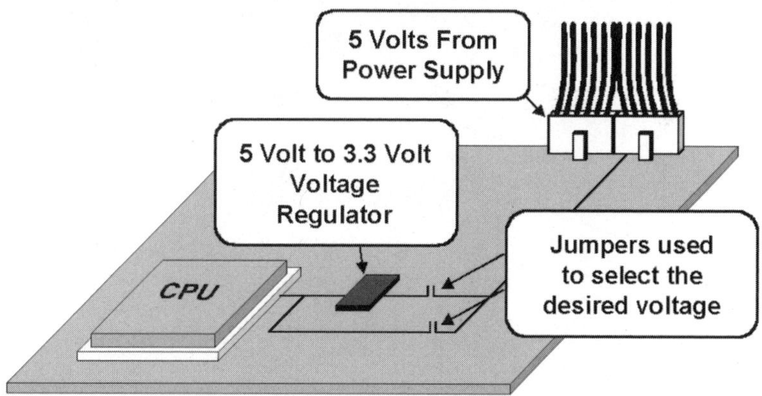

Figure 2.44 A two-voltage motherboard

motherboard for either 3.3- or 5-volt operation, but not always. Figure 2.46 shows the jumper layout of a particularly difficult 486 system.

Which set of jumpers is for voltage settings, and what is the function of all the other jumpers? It's a good thing you have your motherboard book! There are many different ways a 486 system can be configured for 3.3 or 5 volts. Be sure to take the time necessary to verify that the system has the proper voltage.

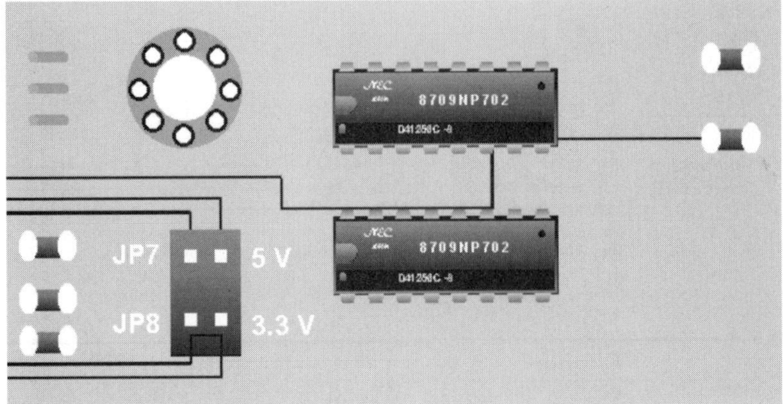

Figure 2.45 Voltage-select jumpers

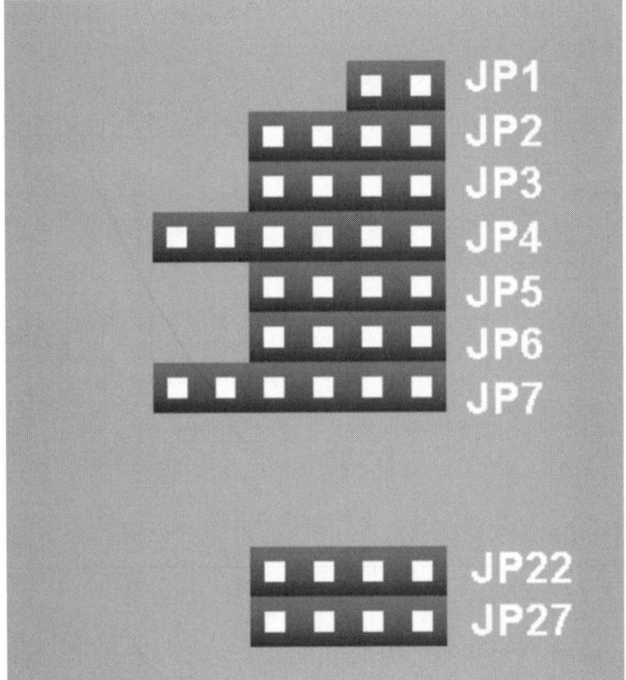

Figure 2.46 Overly complex set of jumpers

SMM (SYSTEM MANAGEMENT MODE) The other way to save power is to turn off devices not being used by the system. For example, if you walk away from your PC, wouldn't it be nice to have the monitor turn itself off after a set amount of time? How about telling the hard drive to stop spinning if it hasn't been accessed after a few minutes? System Management Mode is a hardware-based function, designed by Intel, that allows the CPU to selectively shut down the monitor, hard drives, and any other peripheral not in use in order to save power.

The 486 CPU Family

In 1989, Intel released the i486. The i486 has 32-bit registers, a 32-bit external data bus, and a 32-bit memory address bus, exactly like the 386DX. However, the i486 is far more than the 386DX. It is actually the combination of a slightly improved 386DX, a built-in (and also improved) 387 math coprocessor, and most importantly a built-in 8K write-through cache, all on the same chip (Figure 2.47).

No New Modes!

The 486 runs the exact same modes as a 80386. None of the new features of a 486 (math coprocessor and cache) are tied to a specific 486 mode. The most advanced mode the 486 can run is 80386 protected mode, with vir-

Figure 2.47
Intel 486DX-50.
(courtesy of Intel)

TABLE 2.5
The 486 CPU

Chip Type	CPU Speed	Clock Multiplier	External Bus	Internal Cache	Math Unit	Volts	SMM
Intel 80486DX	25, 33, 50	1×	32-bit	8K	Yes	3.3/5	Yes*
Intel 80486DX/2	25/50, 33/66	2×	32-bit	8K	Yes	3.3/5 V	Yes*
Intel 80486DX/4	25/75, 33/100	3×	32-bit	16K	Yes	5 V	Yes*
Intel 80486SX	16, 20, 25	1×	32-bit	8K	None	5	Yes*
Intel 80486SL	16, 20, 25	1×	32-bit	8K	None	3.3 V	Yes
AMD AM486DX	33, 40	1×	32-bit	8K	Yes	5 V	No
AMD AM486DXLV	33	1×	32-bit	8K	Yes	33 V	Yes
AMD AM486DX2	25/50, 40/80	2×	32-bit	8K	Yes	3.3/5 V	No
AMD AM486DX4 "Ehanced"	40/120, 33/133	3× 4×	32-bit	16K W/B	Yes	3.3 V	Yes
AMD AM486DXL2	25/50, 40/80	2×	32-bit	8K	Yes	5 V	No
AMD AM486SX	33, 40	1×	32-bit	8K	None	5 V	No
AMD AM486SXLV	33	1×	32-bit	8K	None	3.3 V	Yes
AMD AM486SX2	25/50	2×	32-bit	8K	None	5 V	No
CYRIX CX486DX	33	1×	32-bit	89K W/B	Yes	3.3/5 V	Yes
CYRIX CX486DX2	25/50, 40/80	2×	32-bit	8K W/B	Yes	3.3/5	Yes
CYRIX CX486DLC	33—40	1×	32-bit	1K W/T	Yes	5 V	Yes*
CYRIX SLC	20—33	1×	16-bit	1K W/T	No	3.3/5 V	Yes
CYRIX CS486SLC2	25/50	2×	32-bit	1K W/T	No	3.3/5	Yes

*See SMM

tual memory and virtual 8086, just like an 80386. From a program's point of view, there is no difference between an 80386 with a math coprocessor and a 486!

Improved Instruction Set

The 486's instruction set includes new functions for optimizing the 486's ability to work in multitasking environments, as well as allowing control over new cache functions. Also, some of the 486's machine-language commands act as RISC (Reduced Instruction Set Computing) instructions. This means that machine-language commands do not have to be "decoded" inside the chip. The computer sees and immediately executes about 20 percent of the 486's most common commands. The other commands still have to be decoded. Since decoding takes at least one clock cycle, removing decoding from the processor's functions, whenever possible, is a tremendous asset.

NOTE: *The 486 is not a RISC chip! It is considered a CISC (Complex Instruction Set Computing) chip with a few RISC functions.*

Math Coprocessor

All CPUs can add, subtract, multiply, and divide. Remember when you added 2 to 3? There are basic mathematical commands built into every CPU's instruction set. What if you wanted to determine the cosine of a number? There are no built-in commands to perform higher mathematical functions such as trigonometrics (sine, cosine, tangent), logrithmatics (e^x, log10x, ln x), or large floating-point numbers (3.027×10^{24}). In order to perform high math functions like these in the past, programmers had to write code using approximation formulas. These took hundreds, maybe thousands, of lines of code to get an answer for something like a log (34.2321).

When Intel designed the 8088, it sold a supplementary CPU called the 8087 that could perform these calculations. Why not design the 8088 with all these functions built in? Well, they could have—but it would have increased the cost of the 8088 by at least a factor of two. Plus, very few people needed these extra functions unless they were doing heavily math-intensive calculations. So Intel felt that if you wanted to do extra calculations, you would be willing to pay more. The IBM PC had an extra slot on the motherboard designed for the optional math coprocessor.

When the 80286 was created, an improved 8087 called the 80287 was developed. The IBM 286 AT had an optional 80287 slot, and the same with the 80386—the 80387.

The 486 has a 387 math coprocessor built into the CPU. The built-in 387 math coprocessor is substantially more powerful than its external 80387 brother. Because it is on board the CPU, it depends much less on clock cycles. Also, the internal math coprocessor is able to take advantage of the cache, as needed, to store data and code. Lastly, there are two different 32-bit pathways to the math unit that can work at the same time, effectively providing a 64-bit program and data path between the math unit and the rest of the 486.

On-Board Cache

The 8K on-board write-through RAM cache allows the 486 to store upcoming lines of instructions as well as data. Although an 8K cache seems small, it can allow for tremendous speed improvements. Let's see how caching works.

Webster's defines *cache* as follows: "to set something aside, or to store nearby for anticipated use." The word *cache* first became popular in the 18th century when French trappers would bury food and supplies in strategic areas in case they were ever stranded by the weather. In the computer world, cache means to set aside data you've used in the past in a special, fast storage area. Then if you need the data again, it can be more easily (and much more quickly) accessed.

To understand caching, you need to understand that speed is everything in the PC world. If you look at any type of data (programs, documents, fonts, whatever), it almost always starts on a hard, floppy, or CD-ROM drive (collectively known as *mass storage*), is first read into RAM, and is then read into the CPU. The data then returns through the same process: the CPU writes to RAM and RAM writes to mass storage (Figure 2.48).

The problem is that mass storage is much slower than RAM, and RAM is much slower than the CPU. Caching allows you to speed up the system by creating special storage areas for data that is being moved from the hard drive, RAM, and CPU. Based on the diagram in Figure 2.49, you can see that there are two distinct types of caches: one for mass storage and another for RAM. At this point, I will concentrate on the RAM cache. For an in-depth discussion of hard-drive caches, see the chapter on DOS.

DRAM (AND WHY IT IS CACHED) Dynamic RAM, or DRAM, is the RAM of choice for the PC world. DRAM is cheap, small, and relatively

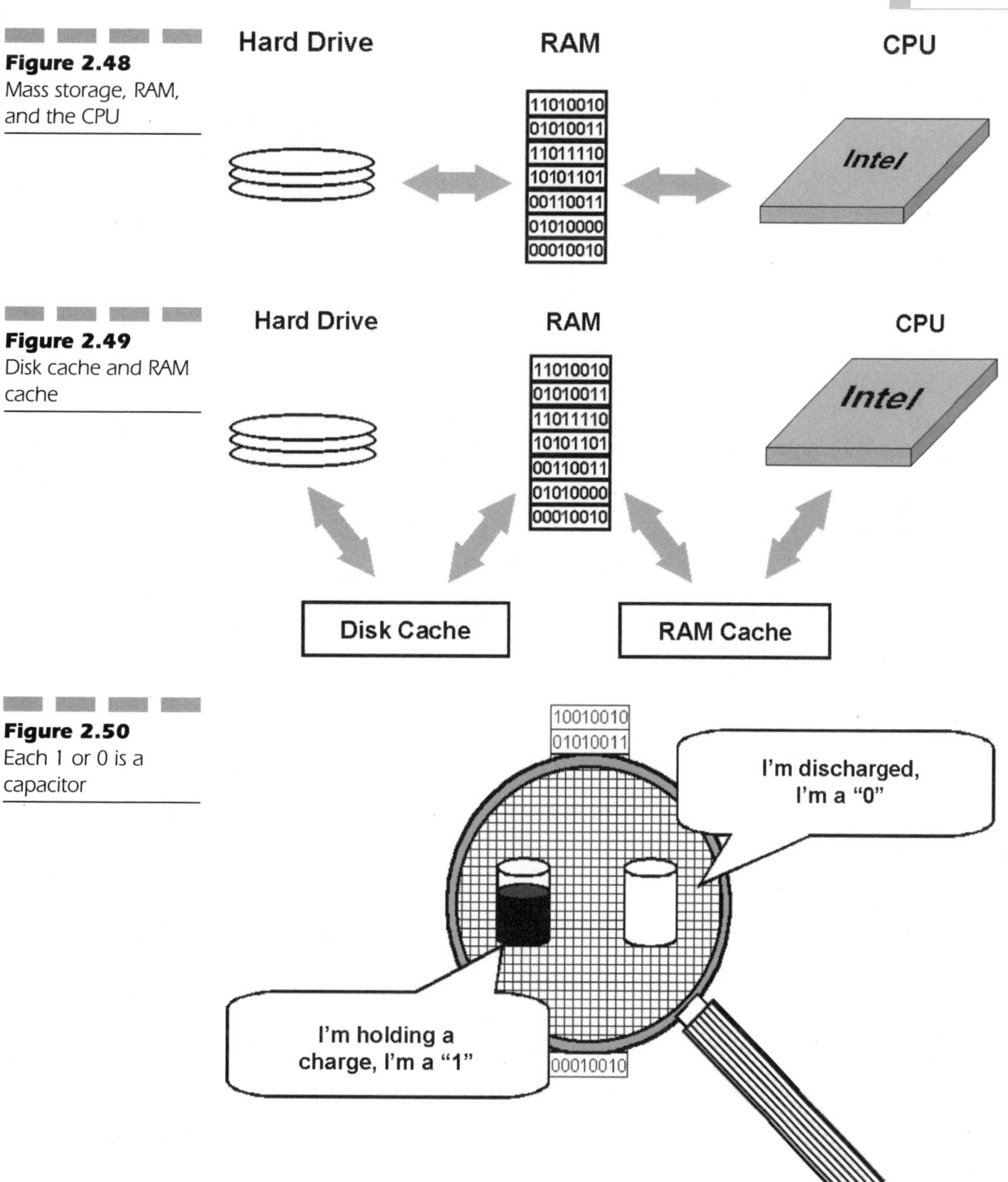

Figure 2.48
Mass storage, RAM, and the CPU

Figure 2.49
Disk cache and RAM cache

Figure 2.50
Each 1 or 0 is a capacitor

fast, although not as fast as today's CPUs. DRAM works by making each storage bit a microscopic capacitor and transistor. A charged capacitor is a 1 and a discharged capacitor is a 0 (Figure 2.50).

DRAM has a small problem, however: the capacitors. A capacitor resembles a battery in that it holds a charge and then discharges it. Unlike a battery that holds a charge for months, the tiny capacitors in the DRAM hold their charges for about 16 milliseconds. Therefore, the DRAM needs an entire set of circuitry to keep the capacitors charged. The process of recharging these capacitors is called *refresh*. Without refresh, data added to RAM would disappear after 16 milliseconds, which is why DRAM is considered "volatile" RAM (Figure 2.51).

The memory-controller chip (MCC) tells the refresh circuitry on the DRAM chip when to refresh. Every few milliseconds, the MCC sends a refresh signal to the RAM, and the RAM chips begin their refresh. Unfortunately, if the CPU decides to access the RAM at this point, the MCC creates a "wait state" (Figure 2.52). The other problem with DRAM is that it is not as fast as the CPU. The CPU often has wait states, not because the RAM is refreshing, but simply because it has to wait for the DRAM to get the values it needs.

SRAM Wait states cause the computer to slow down. By getting around wait states, you could significantly increase computer speed. You can do this by adding special SRAM chips to the computer. SRAM (static RAM) is another type of RAM that doesn't use tiny capacitors to store ones and zeros. Instead, SRAM uses a special circuit called a "flip-flop." Using flip-flops instead of capacitors means that SRAM doesn't have to be refreshed. SRAM is almost as fast as the fastest CPU.

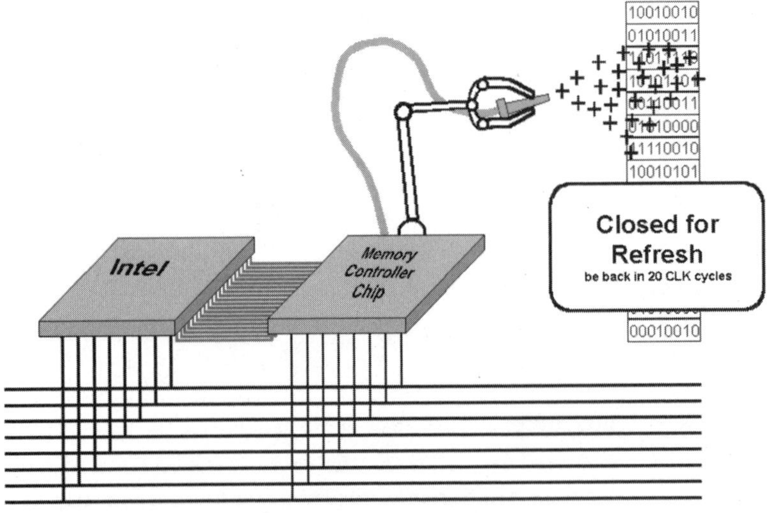

Figure 2.51
The DRAM must be refreshed

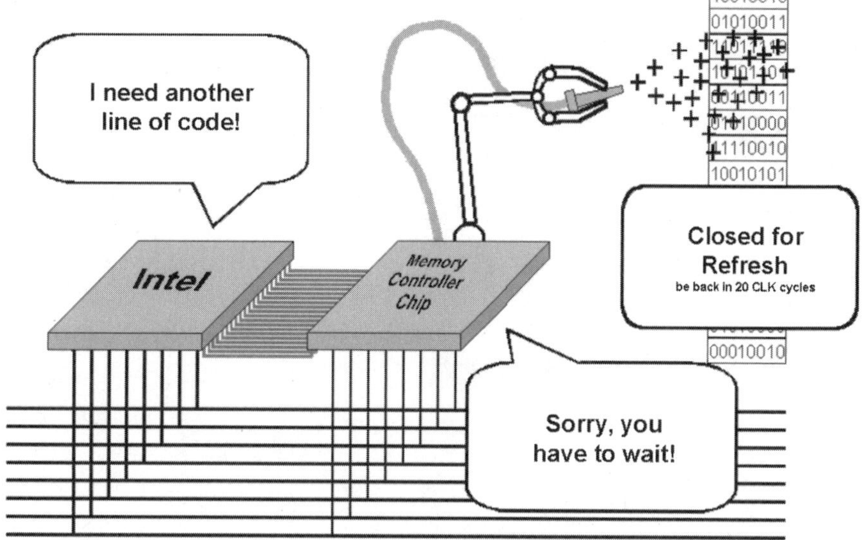

Figure 2.52
Hitting a wait state

Now that you have this SRAM, how do you use it? Why not get rid of the DRAM and replace it with SRAM? Because SRAM is at least 10 times more expensive than DRAM, that's why! However, you can afford a small amount of SRAM as a cache.

DRAM is fast, cheap, and must be refreshed; SRAM is very fast, very expensive, and has no refresh.

INTERNAL CACHE The main difference between a 486 and 386 chip is that a 486 has a small (8192 bytes) SRAM cache built into the chip. All commands for the 486 go through the cache. The 486 stores a backlog of commands in the cache, so if a wait state is encountered, the 486 keeps processing from the cache. This is called an *internal cache* or *level-one (L1) cache* (see Figure 2.53).

Caching stores any code that has been read in the past. That way if the CPU asks for the same code again, it's already be in the cache and the CPU doesn't have to wait for DRAM to get it. All CPUs from the 486 on have internal caches.

EXTERNAL CACHE Although an internal cache on the CPU is very helpful, sometimes more cache would be useful. Therefore, many MCCs are designed to work with an *external* or *L2 cache*. An L2 cache contains the same good stuff that's in an L1 cache, just more of it. An L2 cache is usually around 64K to 1MB, depending mainly on the size of your wallet.

This memory manifests itself with special SRAM chips that sit on the motherboard. Many motherboards have an L2 cache soldered permanently to the motherboard (Figure 2.54).

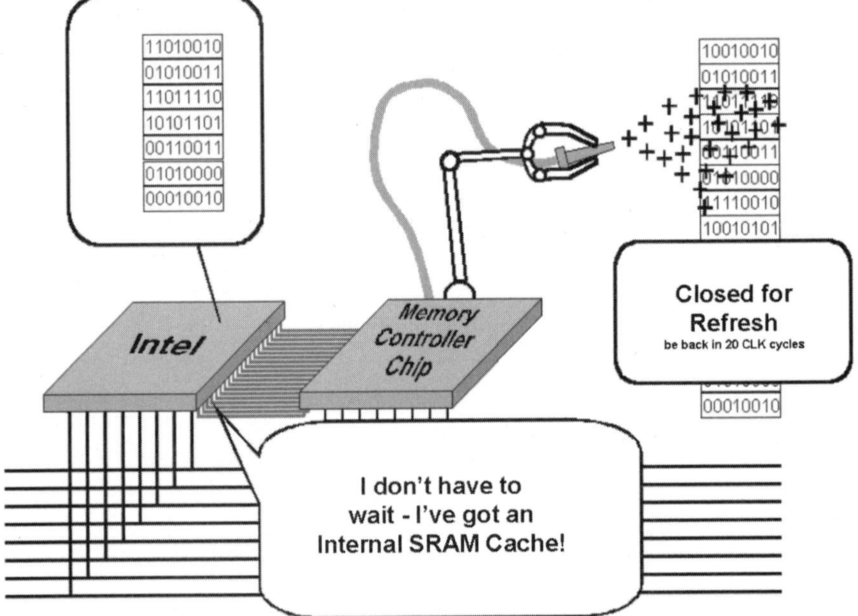

Figure 2.53
Internal cache

Figure 2.54
Typical external (L2) cache

WRITE-BACK VS. WRITE-THROUGH Everything discussed so far is based only on *reading* from the RAM chips to the CPU. What would happen if you *wrote* data to the RAM? What should the cache do with this data? Some caches immediately send all data writes directly to RAM, even if it means hitting a wait state. This is called *write-through*. However, some caches store the write data in the cache and write it to RAM later. These caches are called *write-back*. Write-back caches are harder to implement, but are much more powerful than write-through caches. Write-through caches are cheaper to use, but not as powerful. See Figure 2.55.

DIFFERENT CACHES FOR DIFFERENT CHIPS Different makers of 486s had different ways of caching. Check the tables in this chapter to see the differences between chip makers as to the size of caches and write-through vs. write-back. Cyrix, AMD, and Intel were constantly one-upping each other, touting their respective caches and sizes.

Clock Doubling

Once 486s got up to a 33-MHz clock speed, the PC industry found itself with a bit of a problem. CPU makers wanted to increase their CPU speeds greater than 33 MHz, but the motherboards at the time couldn't go faster than that! This was due to radio frequency interference (RFI), among

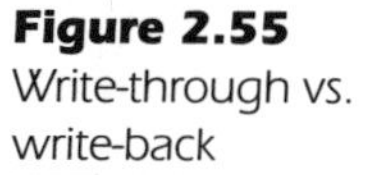

Figure 2.55
Write-through vs. write-back

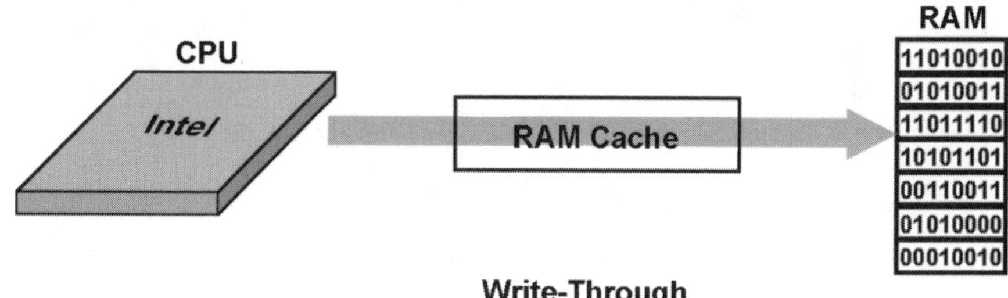

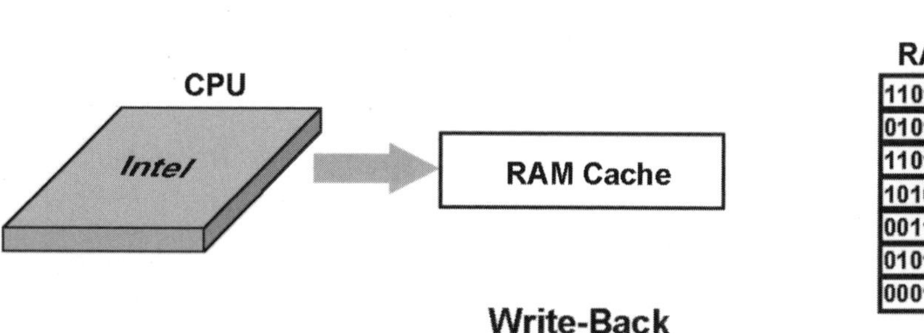

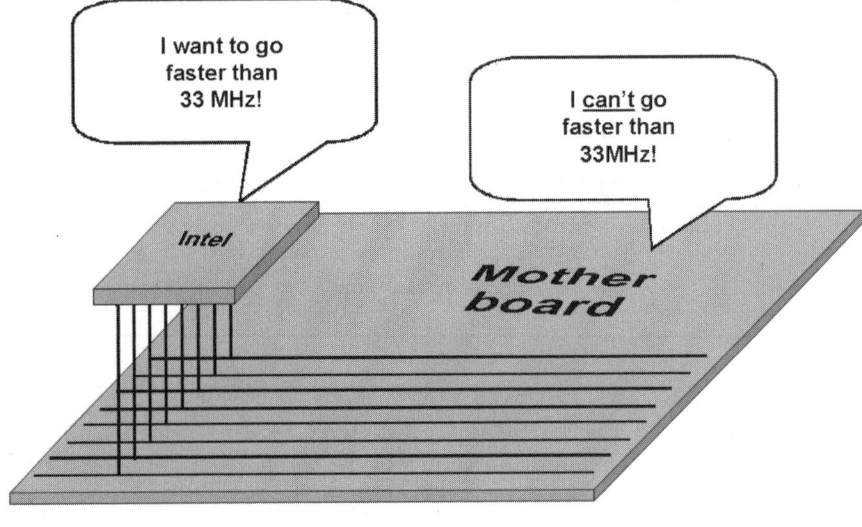

Figure 2.56
CPUs could be made to break 33 MHz, but not motherboards

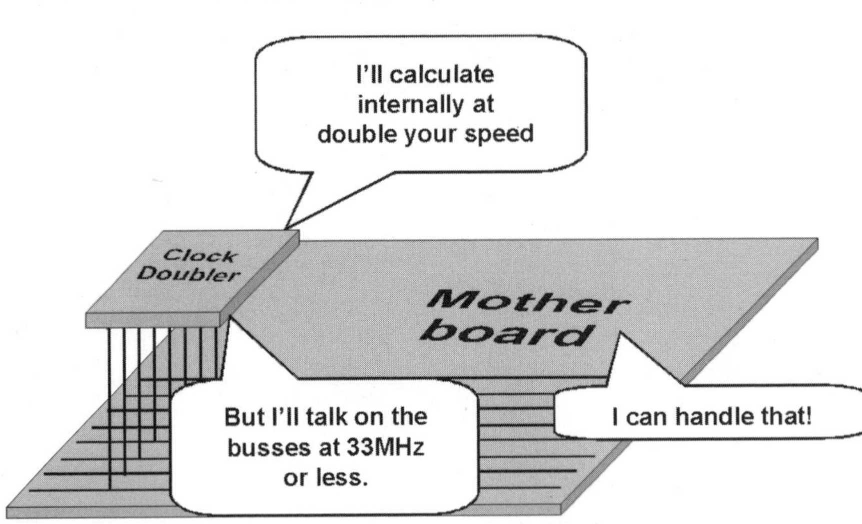

Figure 2.57
The relation of clock doubling between the CPU and motherboard

other problems. Oh sure, you could get a motherboard to go faster, but they would be too expensive, so "cheap technology" was locked at 33 MHz. See Figure 2.56.

To circumvent this problem, Intel came up with the idea of a clock-doubling CPU. Clock doubling means to run the internals of a CPU at one clock speed, and the external data bus and address bus at another, slower speed. CPUs that have internal caches spend the majority of the clock cycles inside themselves, not sending any data on the external buses. These chips can run at some multiplier of the system clock while they are inside. This allows faster processing without having to speed up the entire computer (Figure 2.57).

Clock-doubling chips always have two speeds: an internal speed and an external speed. The first clock doubler was the Intel 486DX/2 (Figure 2.58), and it came in two different speeds: 25/50 MHz and 33/66 MHz. The first speed is the external or system bus speed, and the second value represents the internal speed of the CPU.

In the 486 world, the multiplier is built-in at the factory. For example, the 486DX/2 multiplies the system crystal's clock speed by two. So if you have a 486DX/2 33/66 being pushed by a 33-MHz crystal, it runs at an internal speed of 66 MHz. But remember that the clock speed is a *maximum* speed; you can run a CPU slower than its clock speed by pushing it with a slower crystal. If you decide to run the 486DX/2 with a 25-MHz crystal, the 486DX/2 33/66 will double the clock speed to 50 MHz (Figure 2.59).

Clock doubling has come to mean *any multiplier*. For example, the 486DX/4 actually triples the clock speed, but is still called a doubler. Just because someone says "doubler," don't assume "times two."

Upgrading 486 CPUs

A CPU is useless until you place it in a motherboard. The device into which you insert the CPU is classically called a *socket*. During the reign of the 8088s, 286s, and 386s, there was little interest in sockets, as the concept of upgrading a CPU was an extremely rare occurrence. However, towards the end of the 386s, a number of standards, driven by customer demand, created the desire and the ability to upgrade CPUs.

Figure 2.58
A clock-doubled 486: the DX/2

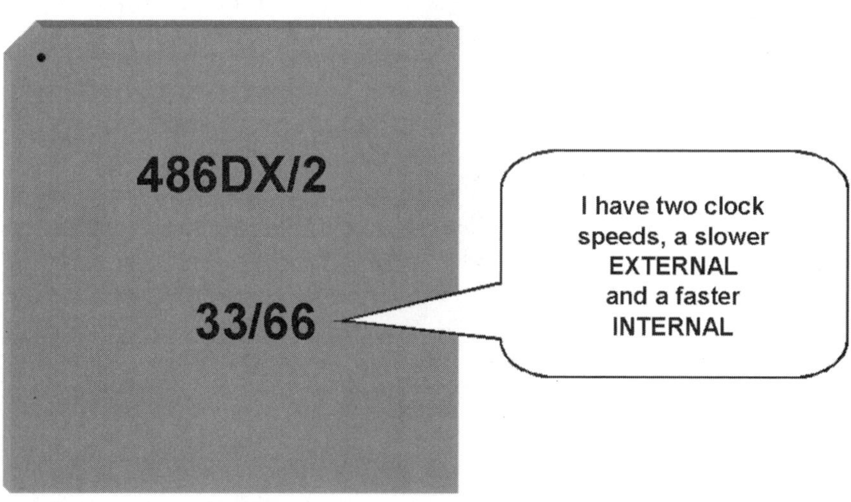

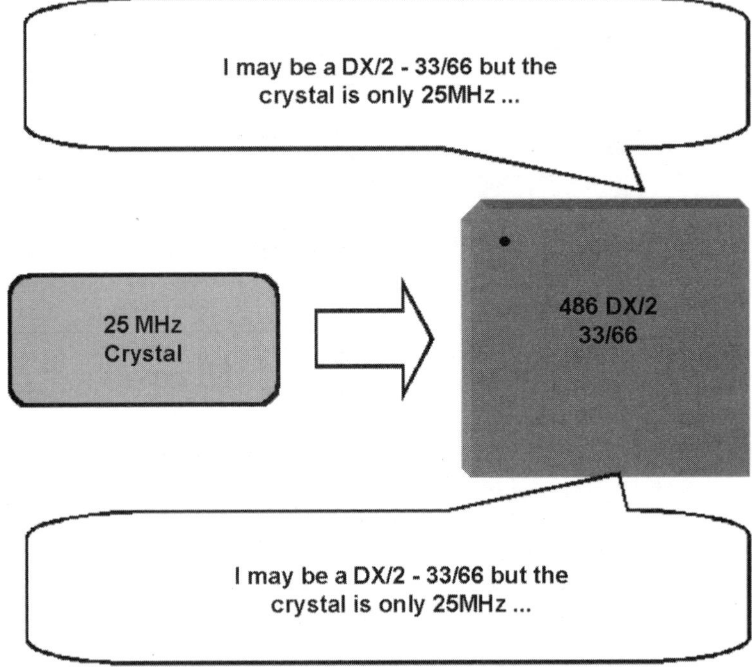

Figure 2.59
Underclocking a clock doubler

The first concept that made upgradability practical was motherboards that had more than one clock speed. Remember that the system crystal is on the motherboard. If you remove a 25-MHz CPU and insert a 33-MHz CPU, the 33-MHz CPU would still run at only 25 MHz. Starting with a few 386 motherboards and becoming mainstream in the 486 motherboards, we began to see the ability to change the system crystal speed via jumpers on the motherboard (Figure 2.60).

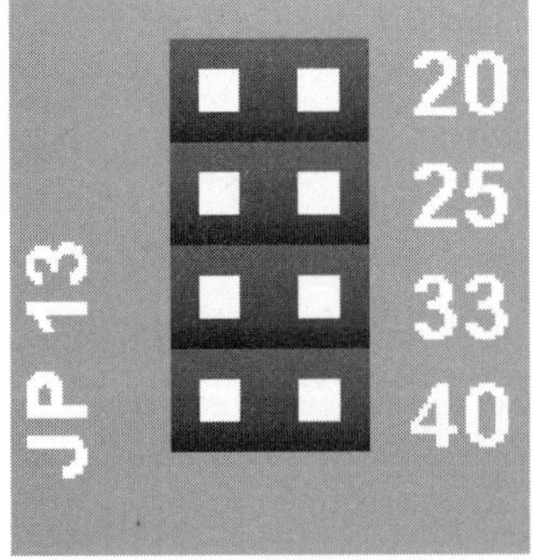

Figure 2.60
Jumpers to adjust motherboard speed

The second concept was the strong adoption of the PGA-type CPU package. There were (and still are) many types of CPU packages, but by the time of the 486s, the vast majority of CPUs made were in the PGA package. Since the CPUs were all PGA, the motherboards all had PGA sockets. As long as the motherboard had adjustable voltage and motherboard speed, you could easily change the CPU in the system.

The third way to improve the ease of upgradability was the ZIF (zero insertion force) socket. ZIF sockets have a lever arm that allows for simple removal and installation of CPUs. Before ZIF sockets came along, you had to use a special removal tool to take the CPU off the motherboard (Figure 2.61a). ZIF sockets allowed for a much easier and safer removal (Figure 2.61b). There are many types of ZIF sockets; Table 2.6 and Figure 2.62 show the different types of 486 ZIF sockets.

Overdrive CPUs for 486s

When the 486 chip was first released, a number of computer manufacturers began to make "upgradeable" systems. These had proprietary CPU cards (often called *daughter cards*) that could be removed and replaced with a daughter card that had a more powerful CPU. As more powerful 486s came into the market, Intel realized that first-generation 486s running at 25 MHz would be good candidates for upgrading. Intel unveiled the 486 "overdrive" chips to take advantage of this anticipated market. 486 overdrive chips were nothing more than a 486DX/2 or DX/4 with an extra pin. In order to take advantage of an overdrive processor, you normally needed a special, 169-pin PGA/ZIF socket designed especially for the overdrive chip.

Although overdrives were a simple, effective upgrade for systems that were prepared for their use, there were some major downsides. First, if you plugged in an overdrive CPU, the old processor was disabled—*but you couldn't remove it!* This was frustrating considering that you could have sold your old 486SX or DX. Second, most 486 motherboards could accept multiple types of regular processors, which negated the need for an overdrive chip. However, if you already had an overdrive-ready motherboard, it was often a cost-effective option.

The term *overdrive* is now used by Intel to describe a broad family of replacement processors, not only for 486 systems, but also for older Pentium systems. Table 2.7 lists Intel 486 overdrive processors. The 486 overdrive CPUs are no longer produced. Intel now sells a series of overdrive CPUs that can convert a 486 system to the Pentium level. These 486-to-Pentium overdrive CPUs are covered in the Pentium section later in the chapter.

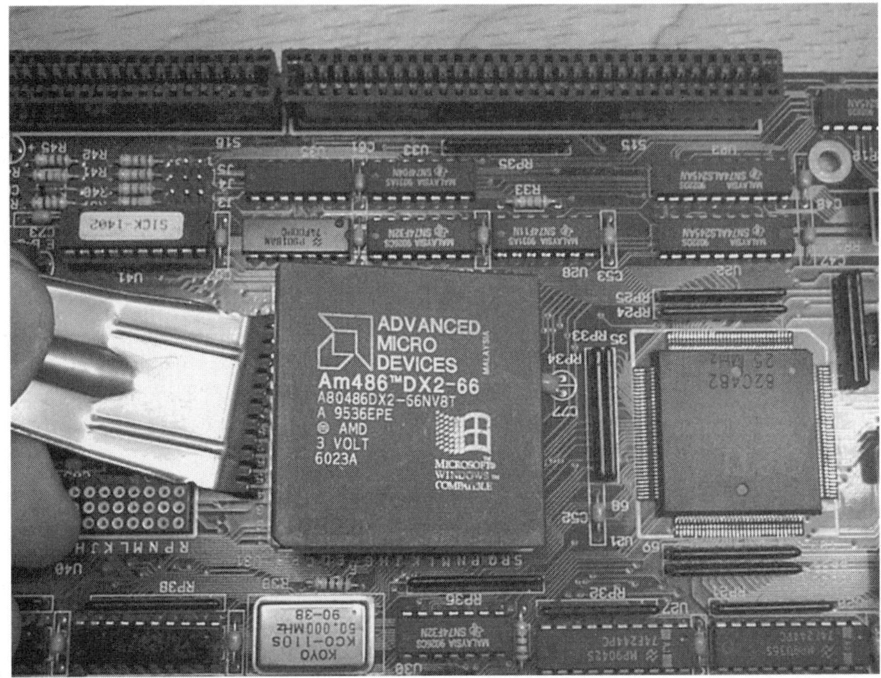

Figure 2.61a
CPU removal tool

Figure 2.61b
ZIF socket

TABLE 2.6

486 ZIF sockets

Socket	No. of Pins	Pin Layout	Voltage	CPU Type
1	169	17 × 17 PGA	5 V	486SX/SX2, DX/DX2, 486 overdrive
2	238	19 × 19 PGA	5 V	SX/SX2, DX/DX2, DX4, Pentium overdrive
3	237	19 × 19 PGA	5 V/3.3	SX/SX2, DX/DX2, DX4, Pentium overdrive
6	235	19 × 19 PGA	3.3 V	486 DX4, Pentium overdrive

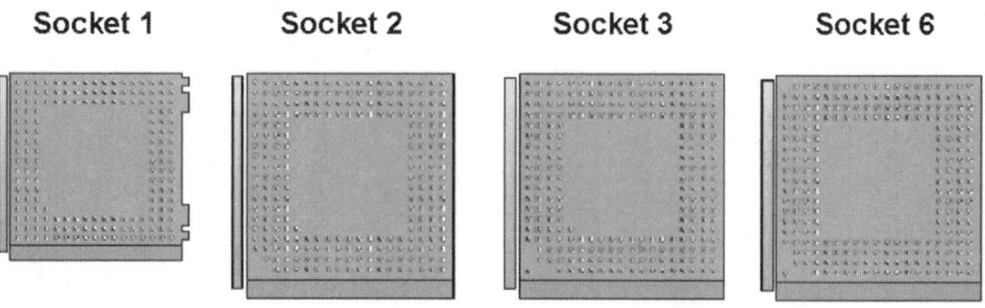

Figure 2.62
486 ZIF sockets

TABLE 2.7

Intel 486 overdrive CPUs

Chip	Speed (MHz)	Recommended Upgrades
486DX/2	25/50	486SX-25 486DX-25
486DX/2	33/66	486SX-33 486DX-33
486DX/4	25/75	486SX-25 486DX-25 486DX/2 25/50
486DX/4	33/100	486SX-33 486DX-33 486DX/2 33/66

Upgrading 386s: the Cyrix CX486DRx^2 / CX486SRx^2

To say that no one upgraded before 486s is not exactly true. Motherboard manufacturers began to create upgradeable systems as early as the 286 era. As mentioned earlier, these systems usually had a CPU-on-a-board type of strategy that allowed the replacement of the CPU, crystal, and a few other support chips all in one.

There were some attempts at replacement CPUs for 286 and 386 systems, but the 286-to-386 replacement chips were universally buggy and generally rejected by end users. 386-to-486 replacement chips had more success,

Figure 2.63
Cyrix DRx^2 (courtesy of Cyrix)

due to the fact that the 386 and 486 shared the same size address and external data bus, and it was a lot easier to create upgrade CPUs.

By far the most popular of all 386-to-486 replacement CPUs was the Cyrix DRx^2 and the SRx^2 for 80386DX and 80386SX systems, respectively. The upgrade was performed by replacing the 386 with a Cyrix chip. The Rx^2 chips were clock-doubled versions of the Cyrix DLC and SLC chips. These chips were extremely dependable and were an excellent alternative to motherboard replacement for older 386 computers. With the upgrade, you received all the benefits of a 486DX/2, a 1K write-back cache, and clock doubling (Figure 2.63).

The Pentium CPU: The Early Years

The Pentium processor was introduced in 1993. It was a major technological leap forward from the 486, and included many new functions. The Pentium has a 64-bit external data bus that splits internally as two "dual-pipelined" 32-bit data buses. They allow the chip to process two separate lines of code simultaneously. The Pentium also sports an 8K write-back cache for data and an 8K write-through cache for programs. The program cache is capable of *branch prediction,* where the program cache attempts to anticipate branching within the program it's running. The CPU stores a few lines of code from each branch, so when the code reaches the branch, the Pentium already has the lines of code stored within the cache (Figure 2. 64).

Dual Pipeline

All CPUs have a *pipeline,* which is all of the discrete steps each command must go through to be processed. If you were to look at the steps of a 486, for example, you would see Figure 2.65. The problem is the execution stage. Inside the CPU are different sets of circuitry to handle different types of commands. There are four main circuits inside the CPU for different commands (see Figure 2.66), so a command passes through some or all of these circuits as it is processed (Figure 2.67).

Think of pipelining as washing clothes. You don't sort, wash, dry, fold, and iron one load at a time. You get it all sorted, then you start one load in

Figure 2.64
Pentium CPU

Figure 2.65
Simplified CPU pipeline

Pre-fetch	Grabs data from the internal cache
Decode	Determines the type of command
Execute	Processes the command
Write back	Updates the proper register(s)

Figure 2.66
Four main processes in a CPU

ALU (Arithmetic Logic Unit)	Handles simple math commands
FPU (Floating Point Unit)	Handles complicated math commands
Address	Handles where to place command/data
Control	Controls the other three

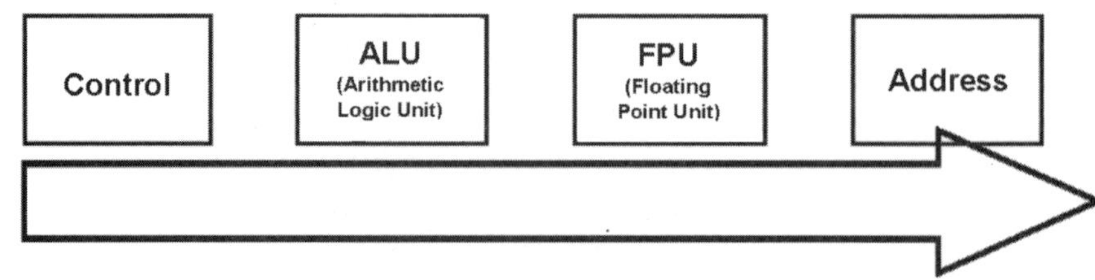

Figure 2.67
Possible pipeline

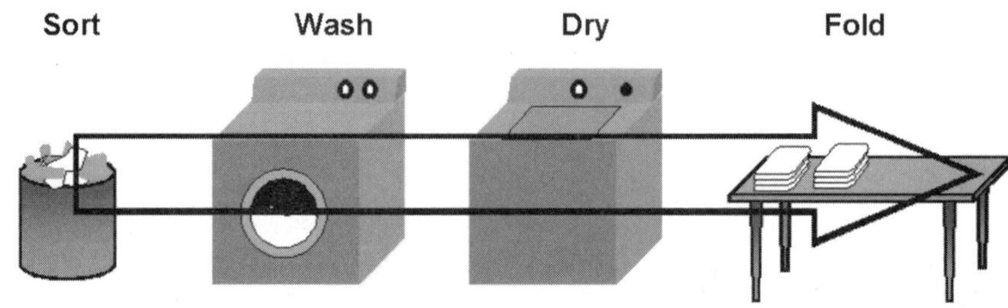

Figure 2.68
Pipelines are like washing clothes

the washer. After that load is finished, you put it in the dryer and start another load in the washer so the washer and dryer are running at the same time. You keep this up until you are washing, drying, folding and maybe even ironing at the same time. This is far more efficient. See Figure 2.68.

Having an extra washing machine and an extra dryer would certainly speed up the process, wouldn't it? Sure, you would sometimes have to wait on some of the other steps in the pipeline, but it would help (Figure 2.69). Well, a Pentium has a second, separate set of circuitry that allows more

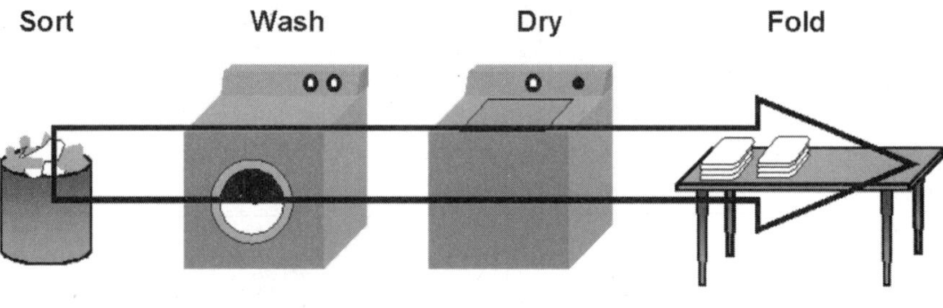

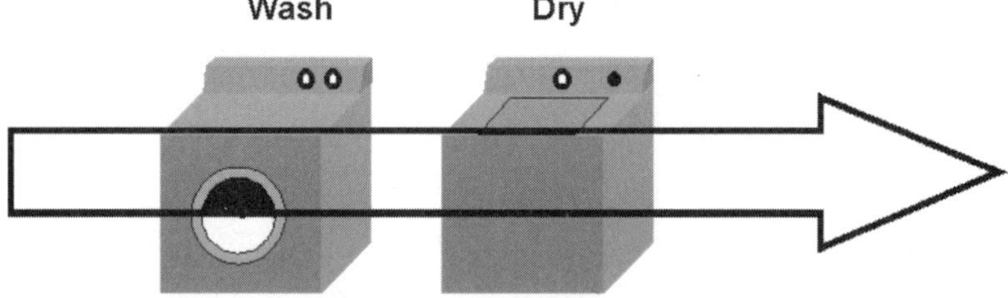

Figure 2.69
Not all stages are required

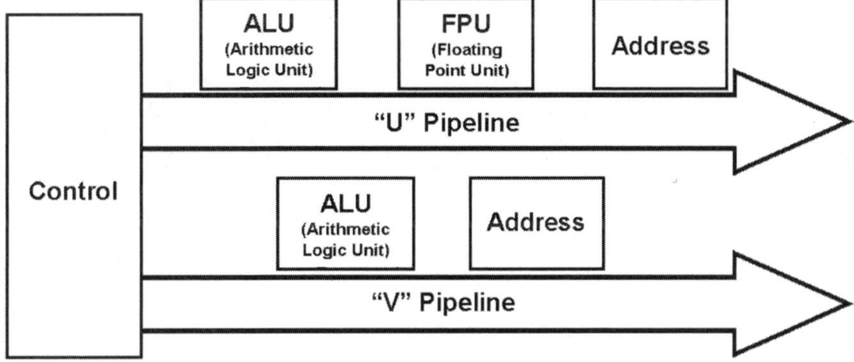

Figure 2.70 Dual pipelining, Pentium style

than one command (of certain types) to be processed at a time. This is called *dual pipelining* (Figure 2.70).

The names of the pipelines are U and V. The U pipeline is the main one that can do anything; the V pipeline can handle only simple commands, such as integer addition.

CPU Voltages

A CPU is little more than a huge conglomeration of millions of tiny transistors. All transistors create heat, and the faster you make a transistor work, the more heat it generates. The tiny transistors in a CPU generate a trivial amount of heat individually, but as you add more and more transistors to faster and faster generations of CPUs, the amount of heat becomes significant. If a CPU gets too hot, it locks up and does not operate.

When you look at a CPU, what you are looking at is a plastic or ceramic outer case. The electronics of the CPU are much smaller than the case (Figure 2.71). Why? The case is used to dissipate the heat generated by the

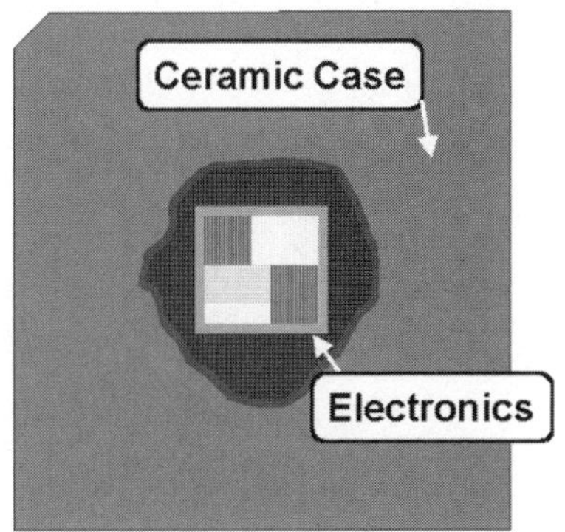

Figure 2.71 Relative size of the CPU case to electronics

CPU. The heat from 8088, 286, and 386 systems was relatively low due to the relatively low speeds and low number of transistors. The outer case could easily handle the necessary dissipation. By the time of the 486, however, plastic cases were no longer acceptable and ceramic cases became standard. Heat first became a serious problem in late-generation 486 CPUs. This was easily resolved for the most part by using cooling fans that could be attached to the CPU. However, the Pentium created some very serious heat problems that simply adding a fan could not repair. The first two Pentium CPUs, the 60-MHz and 66-MHz, needed 5 volts for operation, and they were very hot.

If you can make a CPU that will run at a lower voltage, usually by making the tiny transistors even tinier, the CPU will generate much less heat. So why didn't Intel make the first Pentiums 3.3 volts instead of 5 volts? Intel simply didn't have the technology at the time to make a 3.3-volt CPU with that many transistors. Consequently, the original 5-volt Pentiums had much larger cases than the later 3.3-volt versions (Figure 2.72). As Intel developed the technology to make lower-power CPUs, the Pentium shrunk down to the common size seen today.

LOW-VOLTAGE CPU'S IN THE EARLY PENTIUMS CPU voltage in the early Pentium world is relatively simple. With the exception of the Pentium 60 and 66, which operated at 5 volts, all the early Pentiums ran universally at 3.3 volts.

WHAT VOLTAGE IS YOUR MOTHERBOARD? Even as 3.3-volt CPUs began to dominate the early Pentiums, there was talk of lower-voltage CPUs. The potential of even lower voltage CPUs made it hard for motherboard makers to sleep. How could they make a motherboard that supports both 3.3 and lower voltages? How could they keep the motherboards they make today from being obsolete tomorrow? People don't want to buy computer parts—especially hard-to-replace motherboards—that have a high potential of being obsolesced too quickly.

The first way to support lower-voltage CPUs was by adding more than one voltage regulator to the motherboard. The motherboard makers

Pentium 60,66

All other Pentiums

Figure 2.72 Relative size difference between Pentiums

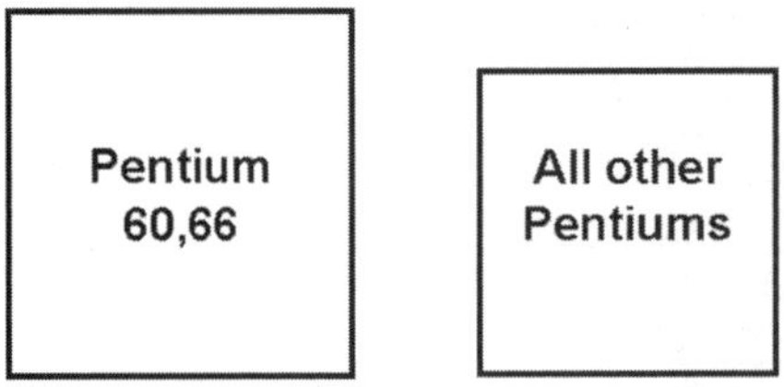

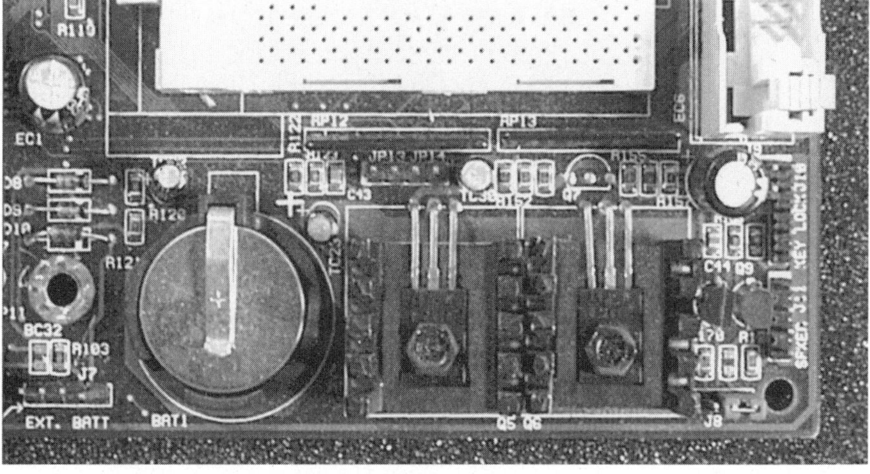

Figure 2.73
Two voltage regulators

knew that the lower voltage was going to be in the range of 2.9 volts. Taking a chance, many motherboard makers simply added a second voltage regulator that dropped the voltage from 5 to 2.9 volts. Figure 2.73 is an example of a motherboard with two voltage regulators. You could activate the proper voltage regulator by moving the four jumpers located directly below the voltage regulators.

The second concept, proposed by Intel, was to have CPUs that came with their own standardized voltage regulators. Whatever voltage regulator was needed was soldered to a small card, called a *voltage regulator module* (VRM). The VRM would fit into a special VRM slot next to the CPU.

The example in Figure 2.74 has both a VRM as well as soldered voltage regulators. The jumpers inside the VRM slot control the voltage regulators, and when a VRM is installed, the jumpers are first removed. This disables the voltage regulators and gives the VRM control.

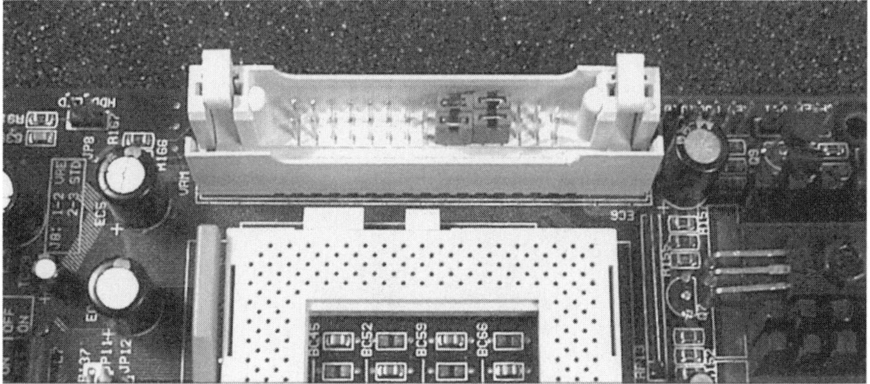

Figure 2.74
VRM slot

Pentium Clock Doubling

Remember the 33-MHz motherboard speed limit in the 486 world? Well, this limit was soundly crushed with the Pentium. All Pentium motherboards run at speeds of at least 66 MHz. However, early Pentium CPUs had clock speeds up to 200 MHz. How could they do that on motherboards that ran only at 66 MHz? Simple—they were all clock doublers (Figure 2.75). Plus, Pentium clock doubling (better known as the "multiplier" of the Pentium world) isn't limited to whole numbers like 2 or 3 times the motherboard speed. An early Pentium could have multipliers of 1, 1.5, 2, 2.5, and 3.

Equally interesting is the fact that you have to configure the multiplier on a Pentium. With 486s, if you bought, say, a 33/66 486DX/2, the multiplier was 2 and there was no way to change it. Sure, you could use different-speed motherboards, but you couldn't change the multiplier from times two to something like times three. The 486 multiplier was built in by the CPU manufacturer.

Pentium CPUs don't have a built-in multiplier. All Pentium motherboards come with a set of jumpers or switches that allow you to set the proper multiplier. So when you install a Pentium, not only do you have to set the motherboard speed, but you also need to set the multiplier. Figure 2.76 is a Pentium motherboard that clearly shows both the motherboard speed and the multiplier jumpers.

Figure 2.75 Pentiums are clock doublers

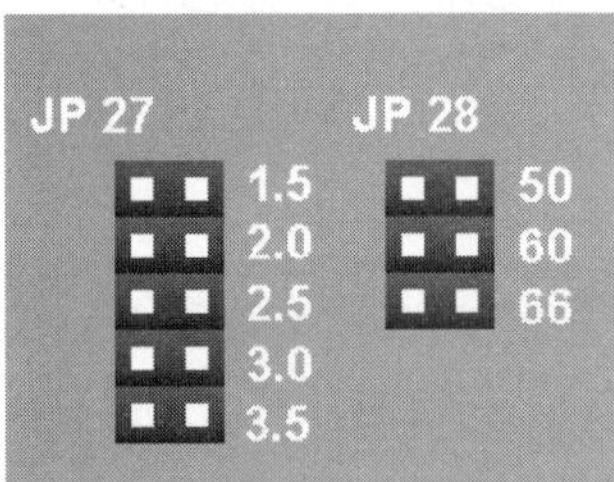

Figure 2.76 Pentium motherboard clock and multiplier jumpers

TABLE 2.8

Early Pentium CPUs

CPU	Maker	Core Speed	External Speed	Multiplier	Cache	Voltage	Package[2]
Pentium-P5	Intel	60	60	1×	8T/8W	5 V	Socket 4
Pentium-P5	Intel	66	66	1×	8T/8W	5 V	Socket 4
Pentium-P54C	Intel	75	50	1.5×	8T/8W	3.3 V	Socket 7
Pentium-P54C	Intel	90	60	1.5×	8T/8W	3.3 V	Socket 7
Pentium-P54C	Intel	100	66	1.5×	8T/8W	3.3	Socket 7
Pentium-P54C	Intel	120	60	2×	8T/8W	3.3 V	Socket 7
Pentium-P54C	Intel	133	66	2×	8T/8W	3.3 V	Socket 7
Pentium-P54C	Intel	150	60	2.5×	8T/8W	3.3 V	Socket 7
Pentium-P54C	Intel	166	66	2.5×	8T/8W	3.3 V	Socket 7
Pentium-P54C	Intel	200	66	3×	8T/8W	3.3 V	Socket 7
K5 - PR75[1]	AMD	75	50	1.5×	8T/8W	3.3 V	Socket 7
K5 - PR90[1]	AMD	90	60	1.5×	8T/8W	3.3 V	Socket 7
K5 - PR100[1]	AMD	100	66	1.5×	8T/8W	3.3 V	Socket 7
K5 - PR120[1]	AMD	90	60	1.5×	8T/8W	3.3 V	Socket 7
K5 - PR133[1]	AMD	100	66	1.5×	8T/8W	3.3 V	Socket 7
K5 - PR166[1]	AMD	116	66	1.75×	8T/8W	3.3 V	Socket 7
6x86/6x86L - P120[1]	Cyrix	100	50	2×	8T/8W	3.3 V[3]	Socket 7
6x86/6x86L - P150[1]	Cyrix	120	60	2×	8T/8W	3.3 V[3]	Socket 7
6x86/6x86L - P166[1]	Cyrix	133	66	2×	8T/8W	3.3 V[3]	Socket 7
6x86/6x86L - P200[1]	Cyrix	150	75	2×	8T/8W	3.3 V[3]	Socket 7

1 See P - Rating

2 See Pentium Socket Types

3 The 6x86L used 2.9 volts

So how do you know the correct clock speed and multiplier? Simple—the manufacturer tells you and you do what they say! For example, if you buy a Pentium 200, you set the clock speed to 66 and the multiplier to 3. When you buy a Pentium, the first question you should ask is "What is the clock speed and multiplier?" If the supplier can't give you a quick answer, run away! Table 2.8 lists early Pentium CPUs.

Early Pentium Competitors

Because *Pentium* is a copyrighted product name, competitors have chosen to call their chips by a variety of names, each intended to imply compatibility with the Intel x86 family of processors. Unlike some of their later CPUs, early Pentium competitors had little success against the true Intel Pentium.

AMD K5 The AMD K5 was pin-compatible to the Pentium, but it was a different animal on the inside. It was basically a RISC (Reduced Instruction Set Computing) CPU designed to be compatible with the Pentium (see Figure 2.77). AMD sold them cheap and they made some serious sales in the low-end area. The K5, however, was quickly eclipsed by other CPUs.

CYRIX 6x86/6x86L The Cyrix 6x86 delivered true Pentium-level performance at a very low price (Figure 2.78). Early in this chapter you saw how the 486 offered improved performance over the 386 by streamlining the operating instructions within the processor. Because similar improvements were made within the architecture of the 6x86, it could process instructions as quickly as a Pentium at a lower clock rate. The 6x86 CPU ran at a clock rate substantially slower than the Pentium chip it was designed to replace, yet delivered comparable performance. Unfortunately, the first 6x86 CPUs were very hot and had a few small bugs. The 6x86L eliminated these early problems and was a powerful, inexpensive CPU.

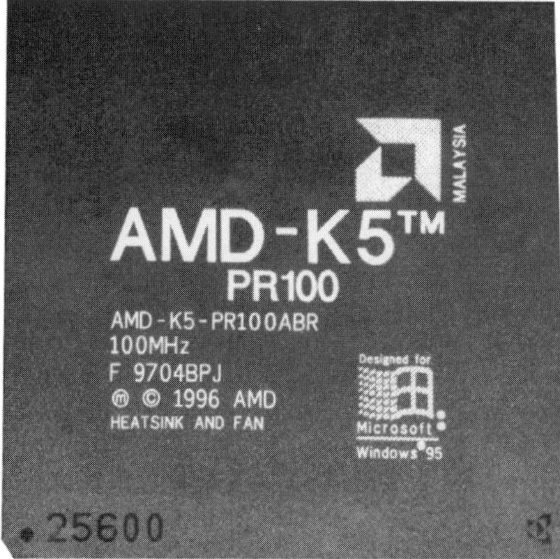

Figure 2.77
AMD K5

Figure 2.78
IBM/Cyrix 6x86

P-RATING Intel's competitors have a problem; they can't compare apples and oranges. Let's say Cyrix makes the 6x86, which runs at 100 MHz. Now, Cyrix knows that their 100-MHz 6x86 can handle more calculations per second than an Intel 100-MHz Pentium due to improvements in caching, pipelining, and program execution. In fact, the 100-MHz 6x86 runs as fast as a 120-MHz Pentium. In order to show this improvement, Cyrix, IBM Microelectronics, SGS-Thomson, and AMD developed the P-rating, which allows you to quickly compare a Cyrix or AMD CPU against Intel chips.

The problem with P-ratings is that they can cause some confusion. For example, if a person buys a Cyrix P-120, they are really getting a 100-MHz CPU. Therefore, when purchasing AMD and Cyrix CPUs, be prepared to install the CPU using different values than the ones printed on the CPU! Table 2.9 lists a few examples. There is, however, nothing wrong with P-ratings! In fact, they are an excellent way to compare AMD and Cyrix CPUs to Intel processors. However, it is not an absolute, perfect gauge. Use it as a rough guideline only.

Pentium Socket Types

The Pentium CPU had significantly more pins and therefore needed a larger case than the 486. The original Pentium 60 and 66 simply used a larger PGA-type package. All other Pentiums used a totally different type of case, called a Staggered Pin Grid Array (SPGA). The SPGA, as its name describes, staggers the pins, allowing a higher pin density and a smaller

TABLE 2.9

P-ratings for two example CPUs.

CPU	P-Rating	External Speed	Multiplier	Internal Speed
Cyrix 6x86 - P200+	200	75 MHz	×2	150 MHz
AMD K5 - 166	166	66 MHz	×1.75	116.5 MHz

Figure 2.79 Early Pentium socket types. (courtesy of Intel)

TABLE 2.10 Pentium socket types.

Socket Number	No. of Pins	Pin Layout	Voltage	CPU Type
4	273	21 × 21 PGA	5	Pentium 60/66
5	320	37 × 37 SPGA	3.3 V	Pentium 75/90/100/120
7	321	21 × 21 SPGA	2.5/3.3 V	Pentium 75 - 233

case. The SPGA package continues to be the most popular package for many Pentium CPUs. See Figure 2.79.

Pentium Overdrive CPUs for 486 Systems

Known as the P24T before its release in early 1995, the Pentium overdrive was touted as a plug-in upgrade for 486 systems. The Pentium overdrive is a Pentium with a 32-bit external data bus and two 16K caches instead of two 8K caches. A more realistic name for the Pentium overdrive might be something like a Pentium SX. Intel specifies a special 238-pin PGA ZIF socket for Pentium overdrive that most motherboard manufacturers integrated into their 486 boards. However, the price of true Pentium motherboards has dropped so dramatically that there is now relatively little demand for the Pentium overdrive. You can simply purchase a real Pentium processor with a superior motherboard tuned to run a true Pentium 64-bit expansion bus for little more than the price of the Pentium overdrive. Nevertheless, the Pentium overdrive is a convenient and easy upgrade that many end users find attractive.

TABLE 2.11

Pentium overdrive CPUs for 486s

Chip Speed (MHz)	Recommended Upgrades
Pentium 25/63	486SX-25, 486DX-25, 486DX/3-25/50, 486DX/4-25/75
Pentium 33/83	486SX-33, 486DX-33, 486DX/2-33/66, 486DX/4-33/100

Figure 2.80
Drawing of an AMD 5x86

First on the list is the AMD 5x86. Despite the eye-catching name, this processor is simply a pin-compatible 486 that runs at a clock-quadrupled 133 MHz (Figure 2.80). At this clock speed, it offers performance comparable to a 75-MHz Pentium. Before you say "no way," remember that the 75-MHz Pentium runs on a 50-MHz system bus, compared to 60/66 MHz for its faster siblings.

Pentium Overdrive CPUs for Pentium Systems

The Pentium overdrives for Pentium systems are still being sold by Intel, although the "writing is on the wall" for Intel to stop producing these processors. Like their earlier overdrive brothers, these CPUs are a bit pricey for most people, although many motherboards can be upgraded only with these chips.

TABLE 2.12

Pentium overdrive CPUs for Pentiums

Chip	Speed (MHz)	Recommended Upgrades
Pentium	180	Pentium 75 to 150
Pentium	200	Pentium 100 to 166

Figure 2.81
Pentium Pro.

In 1995, Intel released the next generation of CPU, the Pentium Pro, often called the P6. The P6 has the same bus and register sizes as the Pentium. What makes the P6 so powerful are three new items: quad pipelining, dynamic processing, and an on-chip L2 cache. However, the P6 is optimized for true 32-bit code and is often slower than a Pentium when running 16-bit code (DOS and Windows 3.*x*). The Pentium Pro has a distinct, rectangular SPGA package (see Figure 2.81).

Quad Pipelining

The Pentium is a dual-pipelined CPU, but the P6 can handle four separate pipelines simultaneously. On average, this allows the equivalent of three simultaneous processes.

Dynamic Processing

From time to time, all CPUs must go to DRAM to access code, no matter how good its cache. When a RAM access takes place, the CPU must wait a few clock cycles before processing. Sometimes the wait can be 10 or 20 clock cycles. When the P6 is forced into wait states, it looks at the pipeline to see if any commands can be run while the wait states are active. If it finds commands it can process (that are not dependent on the data being fetched from DRAM), then it will run these commands *out of order!* After the DRAM fetch is given to the P6, it rearranges the commands and continues processing.

On-Chip L2 Cache

The P6 has both an L1 and L2 cache on the CPU. Since the L2 cache is on the chip, it will probably be almost as fast as the L1 cache. You can even see this cache in Figure 2.13; it's the interior square on the right.

The Pentium Pro has a unique SPGA case that fits into a special socket, called *Socket 8*. No other CPU uses this type of socket (Figure 2.82). The Pentium Pro has made strong inroads in the high-end server market, but its poor performance running DOS and Windows 3.*x* programs, combined with its high cost, has made it unacceptable as most people's desktop computer.

TABLE 2.13

On-chip L2 cache for P6s

Chip Type	CPU Speed (MHz)	Clock Multiplier	External Bus	L2 Cache
Pentium Pro	166	2.5×	64-bit	512K
Pentium Pro	180	3×	64-bit	256K
Pentium Pro	200	3×	64-bit	256K, 512K, 1MB

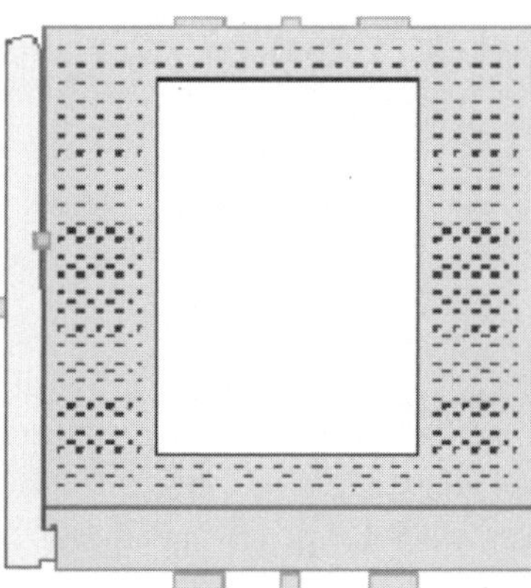

Figure 2.82
Socket 8

Later Pentiums

Intel's usual game plan in the nasty business of chip-making is to introduce a new CPU and simultaneously declare all previous CPUs obsolete. However, the Pentium Pro was never really developed for most users. It was to be the CPU for powerful, higher-end systems. This kept the Pentium as the CPU of choice for all but the most power-hungry systems. After the development of the Pentium Pro, a new generation of Pentium CPUs were developed by Intel, AMD, and Cyrix that incorporated a series of powerful improvements, some of which were taken from the Pentium Pro. These improvements require that they be regarded as a new family of CPUs, which I'll call the "later Pentiums." Although there are certainly some profound differences between these CPUs, they all carry four groups of similar improvements: MMX, split voltage, increased multipliers/clocks, and improved processing.

This group of CPUs marks a major shift in Intel's control of CPUs. Both AMD and Cyrix have produced CPUs that are considered by many to be superior to Intel's Pentium. In particular, AMD's K6 (Figure 2.83) is so good that most consider it to be on par with the latest generation of CPUs: the Pentium II.

MMX

In 1996, Intel forwarded a new enhancement to its Pentium CPU, called multimedia extensions and better known as MMX. MMX is manifested

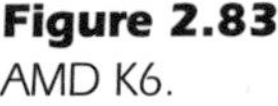

Figure 2.83
AMD K6.

TABLE 2.14

Later Pentium CPUs

CPU	Make	Internal Speed	External Speed	Multiplier	Cache	External Voltage	Core Voltage	Package
Pentium-P55C	Intel	166	66	2.5×	16T/16W	3.3 V	2.8 V	Socket 7
Pentium-P55C	Intel	200	66	3×	16T/16W	3.3 V	2.8 V	Socket 7
Pentium-P55C	Intel	233	66	3.5×	16T/16W	3.3 V	2.8 V	Socket 7
Pentium-P55C	Intel	266	66	4×	16T/16W	3.3 V	2.8 V	Socket 7
Pentium-P55C	Intel	300	66	4.5×	16T/16W	3.3 V	2.8 V	Socket 7
Pentium-P55C	Intel	333	75	4.5×	16T/16W	3.3 V	2.8 V	Socket 7
K6	AMD	166	66	2.5×	32T/32W	3.3 V	2.9 V	Socket 7
K6	AMD	200	66	3×	32T/32W	3.3 V	2.9 V	Socket 7
K6	AMD	233	66	3.5×	32T/32W	3.3 V	3.2 V	Socket 7
K6	AMD	266	66	4×	32T/32W	3.3 V	3.2 V	Socket 7
6x86MX - PR166	Cyrix	133	66	2×	64W	3.3 V	2.9 V	Socket 7
6x86MX - PR166	Cyrix	150	60	2.5×	64 W	3.3 V	2.9 V	Socket 7
6x86MX - PR200	Cyrix	150	75	2×	64W	3.3 V	2.9 V	Socket 7
6x86MX - PR200	Cyrix	166	66	2.5×	64 W	3.3 V	2.9 V	Socket 7
6x86MX - PR233	Cyrix	188	75	2.5×	64W	3.3 V	2.9 V	Socket 7

as four new registers and 57 new commands added to the Pentium code book. These commands can be used to move and manipulate large chunks of data. This ability is particularly helpful (and was designed) for graphical applications such as games. Both Cyrix and AMD have copied the MMX extensions in their CPUs. The downside to MMX is that applications need to be written to take advantage of MMX. Although few such applications have been written, the number is growing.

MMX is kind of like the built-in math coprocessor. You get it whether you need it or not. All new CPUs from all manufacturers are MMX enabled. You can't save money by trying to buy a non-MMX CPU.

Split Voltage

Improvements in CPU manufacturing have continued, resulting in Pentium CPUs that run at even lower than 3.3 volts. Yet these CPUs still need 3.3 volts in order to communicate with other chips on the motherboard. To fulfill both needs, all later Pentiums now have "split voltage." They literally need two different voltages to operate properly. Yet once again a whole new family of motherboards has to be created to take advantage of split-voltage CPUs. Even though later Pentiums use the exact same Socket 7 used by most earlier Pentiums, you can't install a later Pentium into these motherboards because they can't provide the proper voltage.

Increased Clocks and Multipliers

Later Pentiums all have vastly increased multipliers, resulting in higher speeds. Most early Pentiums used 2.5 multipliers at best, but later Pentiums are up to 4.5 multipliers. By the time you read this, it will be even higher.

Intel has recently created a very fast series of Pentium II CPUs that can run with an external speed of 100 MHz. These Pentium IIs are physically identical to their slower siblings. The first Pentium II of this new group has a 4x multiplier giving it a 4x100—400 MHz clock speed with even faster clock speeds imminent.

Improved Processing

All later Pentiums have some improvement in plain old Pentium branch prediction. The Intel Pentium has made a slight improvement by making the branch prediction a little smarter, allowing it a better chance of getting the correct code. The Cyrix 6x86MX and the AMD K6 have incorporated the Pentium Pro features of speculative execution and out-of-order execution, making them more like the Pentium Pro and Pentium II than the Pentium.

Pentium II

Intel's current "hot" CPU is the Pentium II. In reality, the Pentium II is little more than a faster Pentium Pro with MMX. The Pentium II is distinct with the new SEC cartridge, replacing the older-style SPGA socket of the Pentium Pro and allowing more room on the motherboard (Figure 2.84).

Figure 2.84 Pentium II. (courtesy of Intel)

TABLE 2.15 Pentium II CPUs

Chip Type	CPU Speed	CLK Mult	External Speed	EXT'L Bus	Address Bus	L1 Cache	L2 Cache
Pentium II	233	3.5×	66 MHz	64-bit	32-bit	16K W/B & 16K W/T	512K
Pentium II	266	4×	66 MHz	64-bit	32-bit	16K W/B & 16K W/T	512K
Pentium II	300	4.5×	66 MHz	64-bit	32-bit	16K W/B & 16K W/T	512K
Pentium II	333	5.0x	66 MHz	64-bit	32-bit	16K W/B & 16K W/T	512K
Pentium II	400	4.0x	100 MHz	64-Bit	32-Bit	16 K W/B & 16K W/T	512K

Although the Pentium II is an excellent CPU, it has some limitations that might cause trouble in the future. For example, it generates the greater-than 200-MHz speeds by using large multipliers of a 66-MHz bus clock, while Cyrix and AMD CPUs currently handle bus speeds approaching 100 MHz. This points to easier upgradability for non-Intel chips in the future.

The SEC cartridge might also be a problem in that it is licensed by Intel. This prevents other CPU manufacturers from making CPUs that fit in the SEC's special "slot 1" connection. While this might be a big opportunity for Intel to take even more market share, it virtually guarantees that many systems will continue to use the older SPGA-type Socket 7.

Inserting a CPU

Inserting and removing CPUs is a relatively simple process; just don't touch the pins or you might destroy the CPU. In Figure 2.85, note the notch and black dot in the upper left-hand corner on the inside square of the CPU. This "orientation notch" or "index corner" is designed to help you align the CPU correctly. It must line up with the notch on the socket. Be careful! Improperly installing your CPU will almost certainly destroy the CPU and/or the motherboard.

Installing a CPU into a ZIF socket is as simple as making sure that the orientation notches line up on the CPU and ZIF socket. Table 2.16 lists all the ZIF sockets from previous sections, combined to help verify the type of socket you are using, and Figure 2.86 is a diagram of the ZIF socket and CPU. Figure 2.87 shows how they go together.

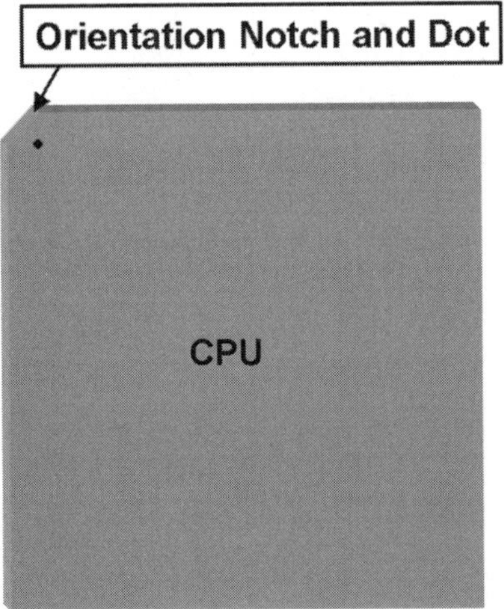

Figure 2.85 Location of orientation notch.

TABLE 2.16

ZIF sockets

Socket Number	No. of Pins	Pin Layout	Voltage	CPU Type
1	169	17 × 17 PGA	5	486SX/SX2, DX/DX2
2*	238	19 × 19 PGA	5 V	SX/SX2, DX/DX2, DX4, Pentium overdrive
3	237	19 × 19 PGA	5 V/3.3 V	SX/SX2, DX/DX2, DX4, Pentium overdrive
4	273	21 × 21 PGA	5 V	Pentium 60/66
5	320	37 × 37 SPGA	3.3 V	Pentium 75/90/100/120
6	235	19 × 19 PGA	3.3 V	486 DX4, Pentium overdrive
7	321	21 × 21 SPGA	2.5/3.3 V	Pentium 75 - 233
8	387	21 × 24 SPGA	2.5 V	Pentium Pro

*ODPR = Overdrive processor with voltage regulator
PGA = Pin grid array
SPGA = Staggered pin grid array
VRM = Voltage regulator module

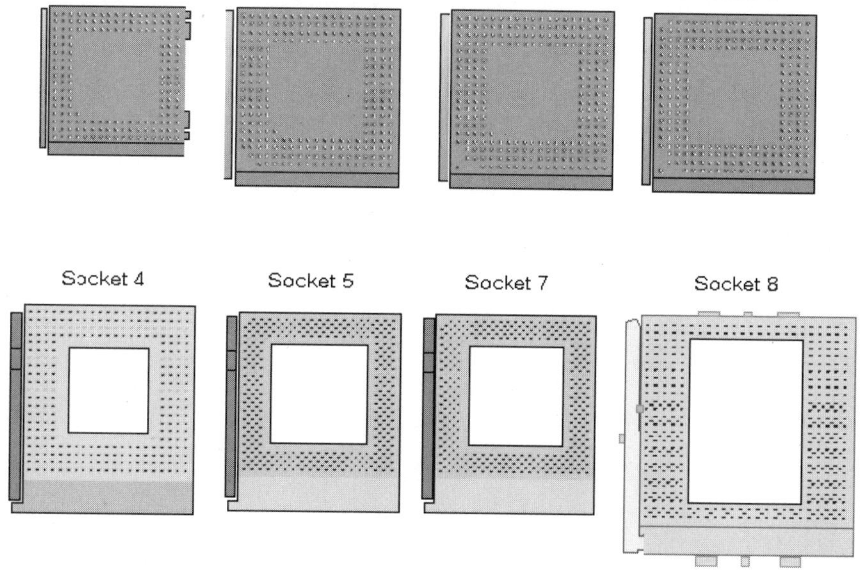

Figure 2.86
Socket diagrams. (courtesy of Intel)

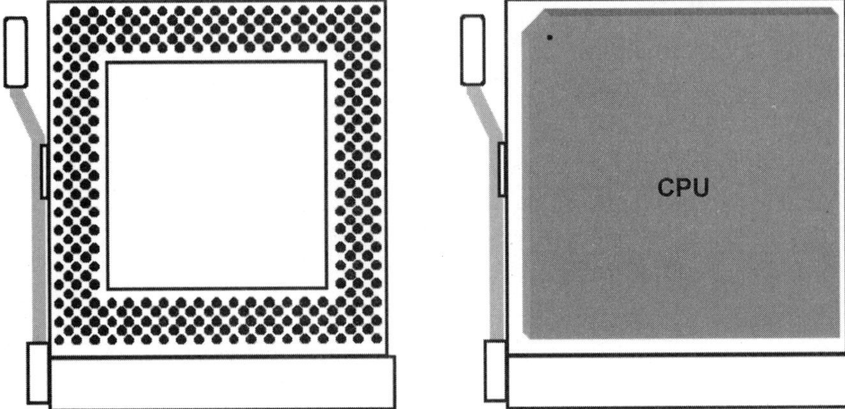

Figure 2.87
Proper insertion of CPU.

In this chapter, you have seen the basic components and functions of a PC's CPU. I have provided a historical view to help you better understand the amazing evolution of CPUs in the less-than-20-year lifespan of the personal computer.

The information in this chapter will be referred to again and again throughout the book. Take the time to memorize certain facts, such as the size of the external data buses and clock-doubling features. These are things that good technicians can spout off without having to refer to a book.

CHAPTER 3

Power Supplies

In this chapter you will:

- Be introduced to the standards of PC-compatible power supplies.
- Inspect different types of power connectors and their different functions.
- Learn how to properly install a power switch.
- Learn how to use a voltmeter to perform a basic test of a power supply.

In a break from traditional computer marketing, IBM allowed the development of an "open architecture" for the IBM PC. What constitutes an "IBM-compatible PC" has often been more a matter of opinion than fact. To be classified as an IBM-compatible PC, a computer must comply with a very loosely enforced set of standards. This loose enforcement has been a mixed blessing.

It has fostered an environment of constant innovation and creativity. If PC manufacturers develop new and better ways of doing things, they need no approval from anyone to begin production. Consumers judge the merits of a new PC technology. This has led to wonderful innovations that have been embraced by the entire industry (e.g., Sound Blaster sound cards, enhanced IDE, Iomega ZIP drives, and scanners) and some notable failures (e.g., Micro Channel, light pens, and 2.88MB floppies). It has also led to the nightmare of hardware incompatibility. While not as much of a problem as it once was, you will occasionally run into two devices that either require special configuration to work together or simply will not work together. With the possible exception of floppy drives, the power supply is the only truly standard piece of equipment in a PC (see Figure 3.1).

The power supply does not supply the power. After all, the electricity comes out of the wall socket, and ultimately from the Power Company. The "power supply" in a PC actually acts as a step-down transformer, converting 115V AC (volts of alternating current) into voltages of DC (direct current). The PC uses the 12-volt current to power motors on devices like hard drives and CD-ROMs and for support of on-board electronics. However, manufacturers are free to use the voltages any way they wish, and may deviate from these assumptions.

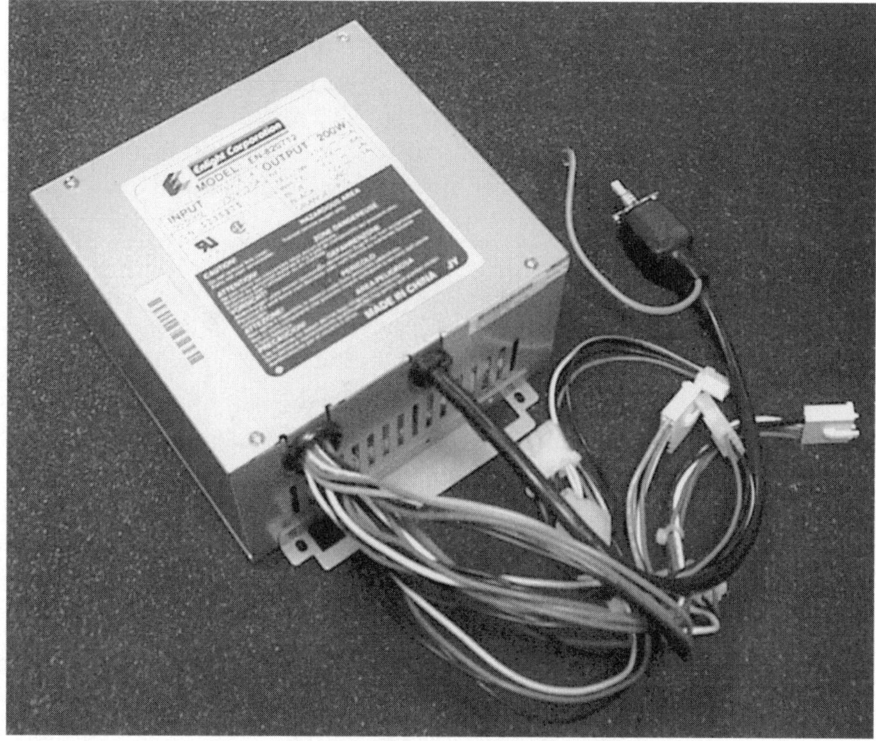

Figure 3.1
Typical power supply

Motherboard Connections

The most popular type of power supply used today is known as the "AT" power supply. This chapter will focus on the AT power supply. However, the AT has been around for almost twenty years and is beginning to show its age. A new type of power supply, called ATX power supply, is quickly supplanting AT as the power supply of choice. See the Motherboards and BIOS Chapter for a discussion of ATX—including the ATX power supplies.

A pair of connectors—P8 and P9—link the power supply to the motherboard. These connectors can be easily recognized because of the row of "teeth" along one side and a small guide on the opposite side that help to hold the connection in place (see Figure 3.2). Because the connectors are "faced" (they have a front and a back), they cannot be installed backward. However, they can be reversed. When connecting P8 and P9 to the motherboard, keep the black ground wires next to each other. All motherboards and power supplies follow this rule. Be careful; incorrectly inserting P8 and P9 can damage both the power supply and other components in a PC. Figure 3.3 shows the plug on the motherboard.

A few PC makers today do not use these standard connections. Dell, IBM, and Compaq have proprietary connections on some models. If the power supply needs to be replaced, you must go to the manufacturer and pay their prices. Figure 3.4 shows how P8 and P9 should be installed. You must install them so the two black grounds on each connector are together. Installing them backwards can damage your motherboard and/or the power supply (see Figure 3.5).

Figure 3.2 P8 and P9 connectors

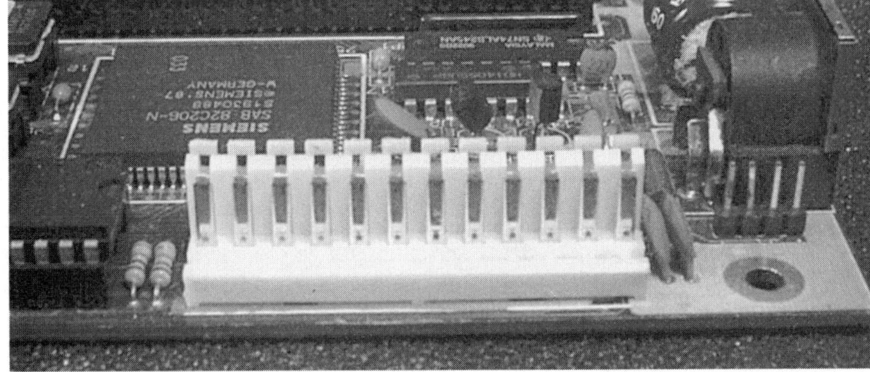

Figure 3.3 A standard P8 and P9 connection

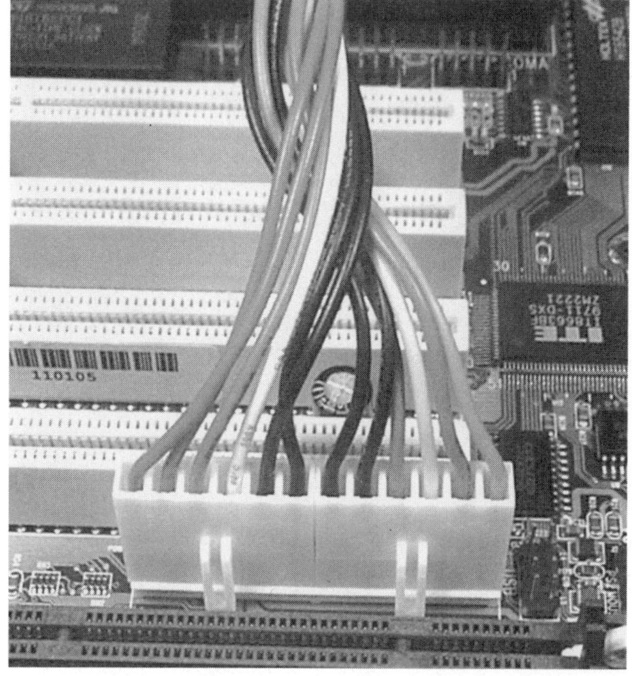

Figure 3.4
Installed P8 and P9—Note that the black grounds on each connector are together

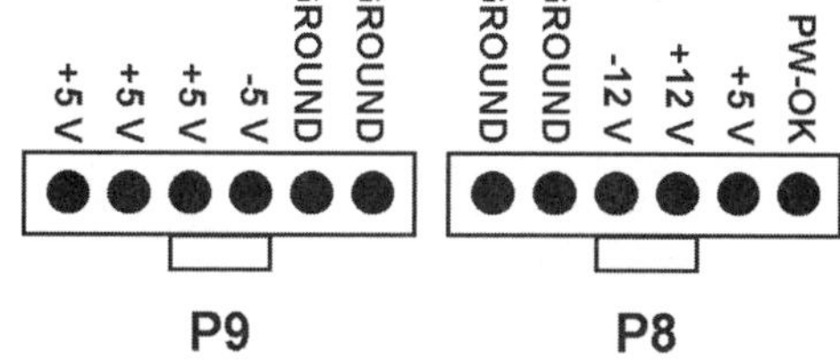

Figure 3.5
Diagram of P8 and P9

Connections to Peripherals

Many different devices inside a PC require power, including hard drives, floppy drives, CD-ROM drives, ZIP drives, and fans. Your power supply has two or possibly three different types of connectors to which you can install your peripherals. Let's take a look at each of these power connections.

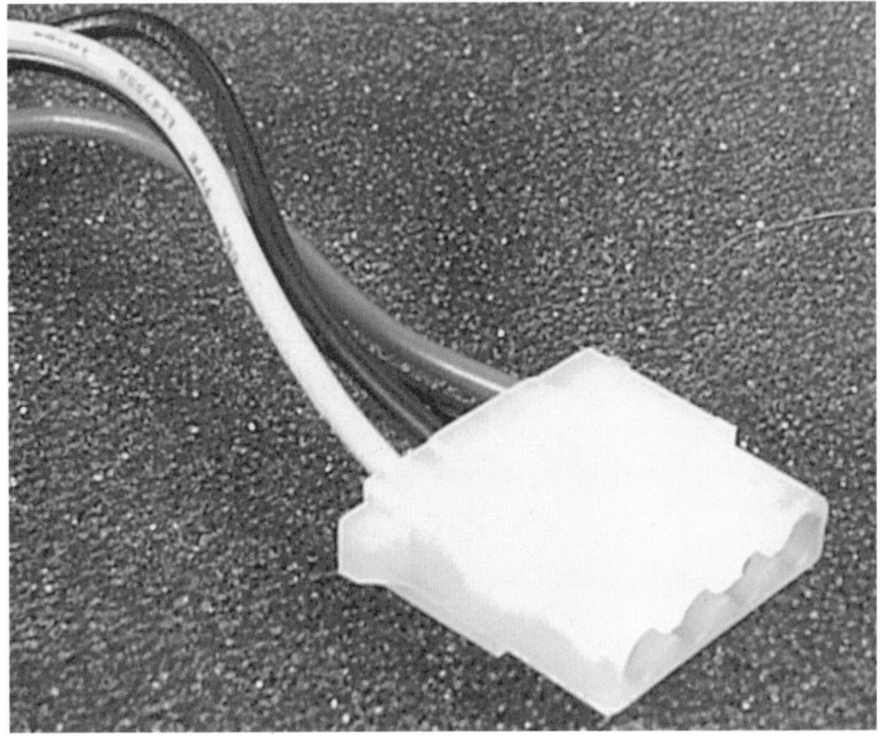

Figure 3.6
Standard molex connector

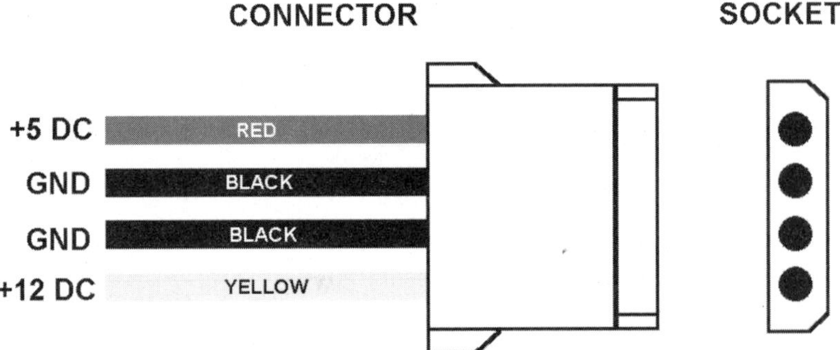

Figure 3.7
Diagram of molex connector and socket

Molex Connectors

The first and most common type of connection is called the *molex*, which is primarily used for devices that need both 12 volts and 5 volts of power (Figure 3.6). A molex connector has chamfers (notches), which make for easy installation. These chamfers can be defeated if you push hard enough, so always inspect the molex connection to ensure proper orientation before you install. Installing a molex backwards will almost certainly destroy the device into which the molex is connected (Figure 3.7).

Mini-Connectors

Most systems also provide a "mini" connector. The mini is used primarily on 3.5-inch floppy drives because floppy-drive makers have adopted the mini connector for that use (Figure 3.8). Be careful about installing these connectors! Whereas molex connectors are extremely difficult (but not impossible) to install incorrectly because of the notches (chamfers) on the socket, minis can be inserted upside down with very little effort. Installing a mini incorrectly will almost certainly destroy the device (Figure 3.9). Figure 3.10 depicts a correctly oriented mini connection.

Submini Connectors

Most power supplies also provide a small, two-hole connector, known most commonly as a submini (see Figure 3.11). Although the main purpose of these small connectors is to provide 5-volt power to the LED lights in the front of some computers, they can be used in other rather unique ways. One of these uses is providing power to the floppy drive since floppy drives need only a ground wire and a +5-volt DC wire (Figure 3.12).

Be careful! It is even easier to install a connector backwards on a floppy drive because it has no guides for proper orientation. The only way to properly orient the connector is by the color of the wires: the red +5-volt DC wire to the extreme outside of the floppy, and the black ground wire

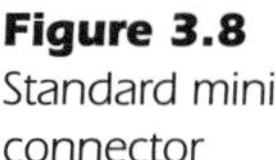

Figure 3.8 Standard mini connector

SOCKET

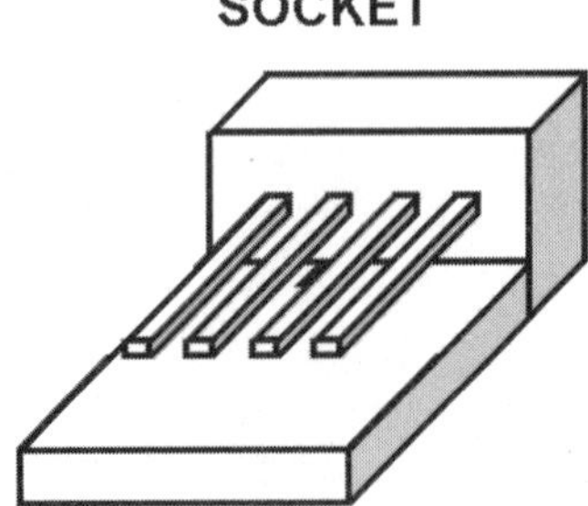

CONNECTOR

+5 DC RED
GND BLACK
GND BLACK
+12 DC YELLOW

Figure 3.9
Mini connector with plug

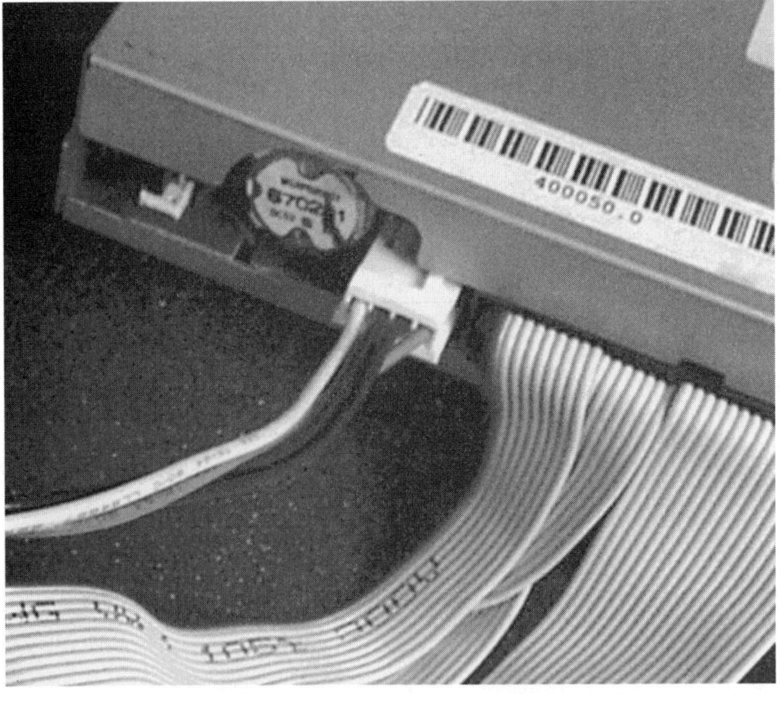

Figure 3.10
Correct orientation of a mini connector

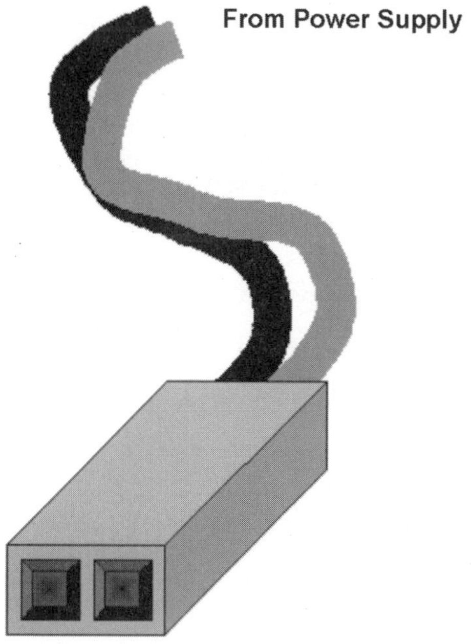
From Power Supply

Figure 3.11
A submini

I Need the sub-mini
for power

Figure 3.12
A submini is used to power front displays

to the inside (Figure 3.13). The floppy drive might not work, will get warm to the touch, and will then eventually smoke if you inadvertently reverse the connection.

Splitters and Converters

You might occasionally find yourself not having enough connectors to power all the devices inside your PC. In this case, you can purchase splitters to create more connections (Figure 3.14).

Wattage

Power supplies are rated in watts. A PC requires sufficient wattage for the machine to run properly. The average desktop PC with two hard drives and a CD-ROM drive will need an average of 115 to 130 watts while running, and up to 200 watts when booting up. Play it safe and buy 200- to 230-watt power supplies. They are by far the most common wattage, and will give you plenty of extra power for booting up, as well additional functionality in the future.

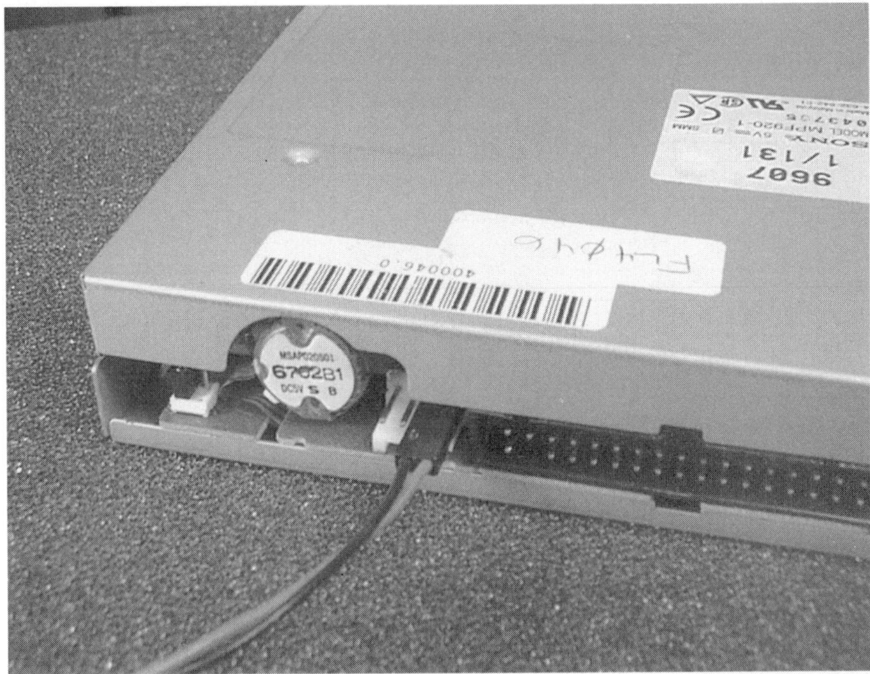

Figure 3.13
A submini connector on 3.5-inch floppy—the red wire on the far right

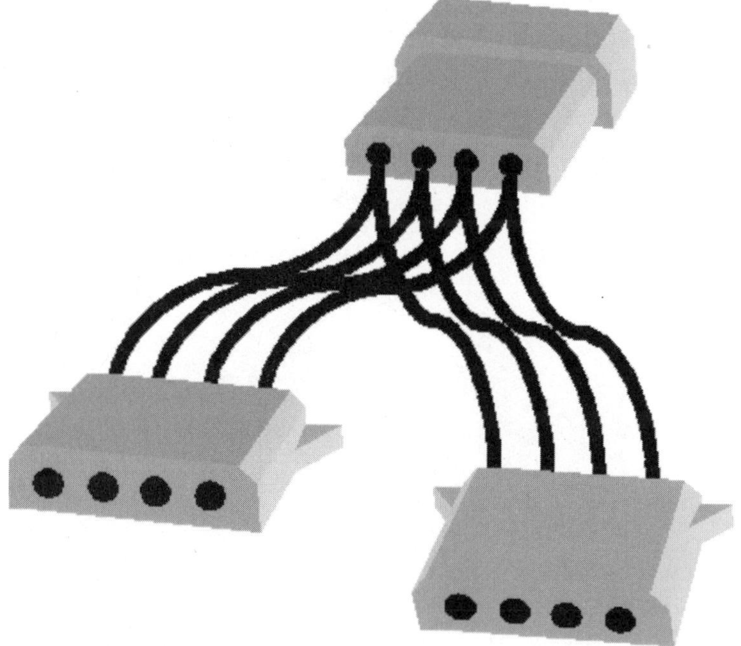

Figure 3.14
Molex splitter

Sizes

Power supplies are available in a variety of shapes and sizes. Although the sizes are very standard, the names for the sizes are not. For most desktop or mini-tower PCs, the power supply is an "AT mini" power supply in the 200- to 230-watt rating. To save time and repeat visits to your friendly neighborhood electronics shop, do yourself a favor: remove the suspect power supply and take it in with you to guarantee that you choose the correct replacement.

When Power Supplies Die

Power supplies fail in two ways, easily and hard. When they die easily, the computer will not start and the fan in the power supply will not turn. In this case, verify that electricity is getting to the power supply before you do anything! Avoid the embarrassment of trying to repair a power supply when the only problem is a bad outlet or an extension cord that is unplugged. Assuming that the system has electricity, the best way to absolutely verify that a power supply is working or not working is to check

Figure 3.15 Testing one of the +12.volt DC connections (it looks okay)

the voltages coming out of the power supply with a voltmeter (Figure 3.15).

Do not panic if your power supply puts out slightly more or less voltage than its nominal value. The voltages supplied by most PC power supplies can vary by as much as –10 percent to +8 percent of their stated values. This means that a 12-volt line can vary from 10.8 to 12.9 volts without exceeding the tolerance of various systems in a PC.

Be sure to test every connection on the power supply! That means P8 and P9, as well as every molex, mini, and submini. Since all voltages are between –20 and +20 DC, simply set the voltmeter to the 20-volt DC range for everything. Figure 3.16 shows how I set my voltmeter.

If the power supply does not provide any power, be sure to check the fuse within the power supply. Open the power supply and locate the fuse; it looks like a tiny glass cylinder with silver metal caps on each end. Look closely at the fuse; if it has blown, then you should see a dark smoky spot on the glass. It is a simple matter to unsolder the fuse from the printed circuit board, test it for continuity with a volt-ohm-meter (VOM), and replace the fuse if needed (Figure 3.17).

Another indication of power supply failure is a dead fan. If you turn on the computer and it boots up just fine, but you notice that it seems

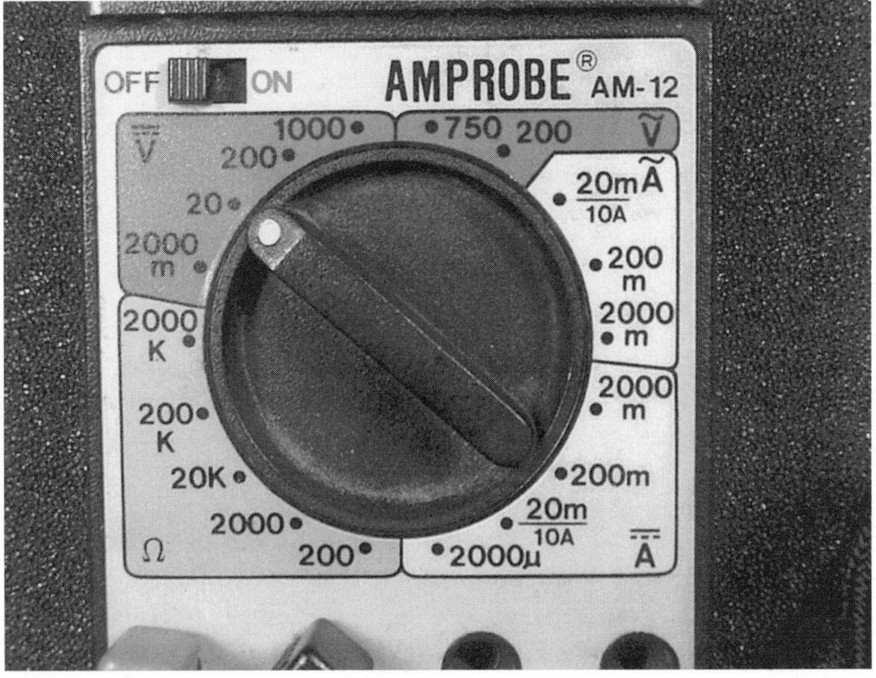

Figure 3.16
Voltmeter set to a 20-volt dc range

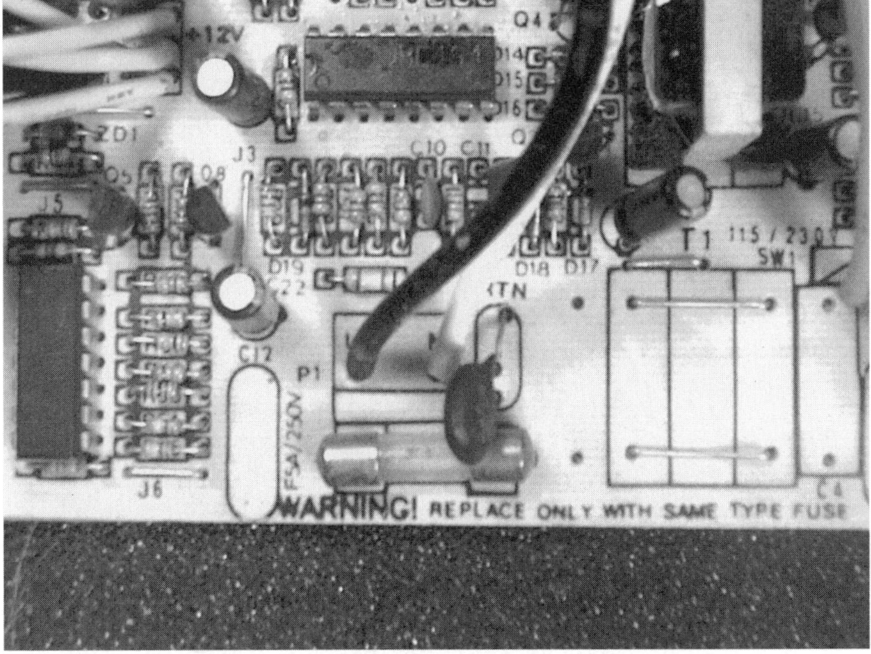

Figure 3.17
Fuse within the power supply

Figure 3.18 Fan removed from power supply

unusually quiet, the power supply fan is bad and needs to be replaced as quickly as possible. This fan not only keeps the voltage regulator circuits cool within the power supply, it also provides a constant flow of outside cool air through the computer's interior. Without this airflow, the CPU can quickly overheat and destroy itself. Replacement fans are inexpensive and easy to come by at any electronic parts outlet. As you can see in Figure 3.18, there are only four easy to remove screws holding the fan in the power supply. Note also the connector on the fans' power cord. It might be necessary to cut off the connector from the old fan and solder it onto the power leads of the replacement fan.

Switches

The power switch is behind the on/off button on every PC. It is usually secured to the front cover or inside front frame on your PC, making it a rather challenging part to access (see Figure 3.19). Familiarity with the power switch is important for two reasons. First, a broken power switch is a common source of problems for power supplies that will not start. Second, when replacing a power supply, you will usually plug the new power into the original switch.

Fortunately, there are only two common types of switches: "rockers" and "plungers." Both of these switches have four tab connectors that attach to four color-coded wires leading from the power supply. These switches handle 120-volt current and are interchangeable. The type of computer box determines the type of switch used in a system (Figure 3.20).

Figure 3.19
Typical location of power switch

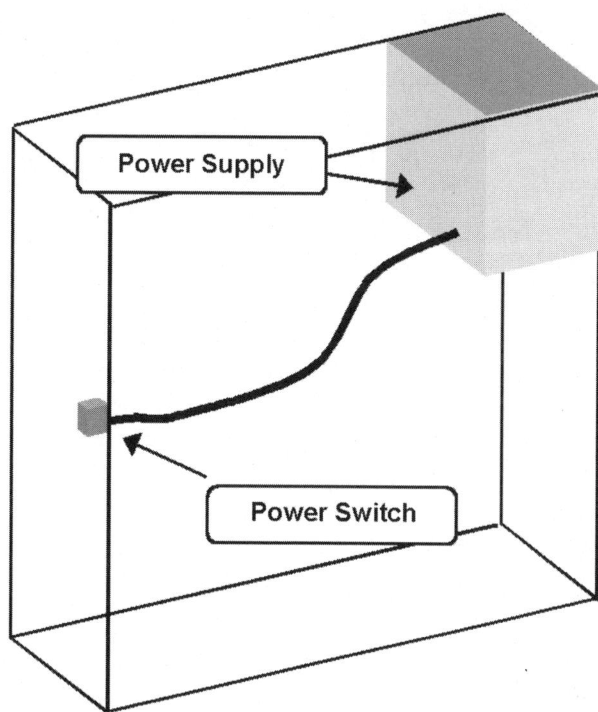

Figure 3.20
Types of switches

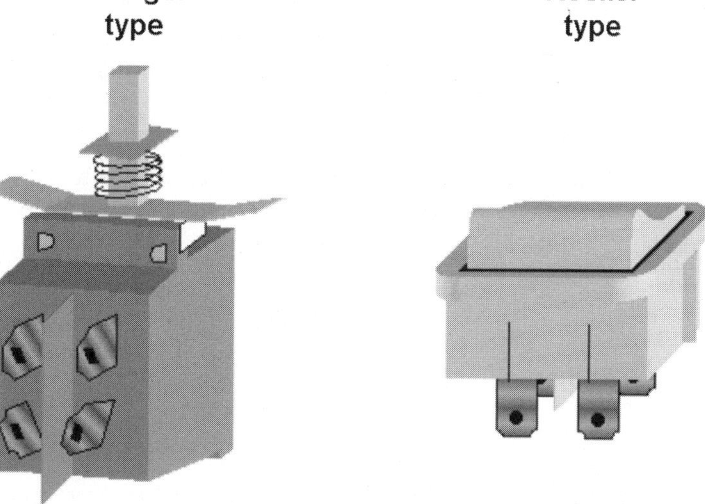

Figure 3.21
Correct wire placement

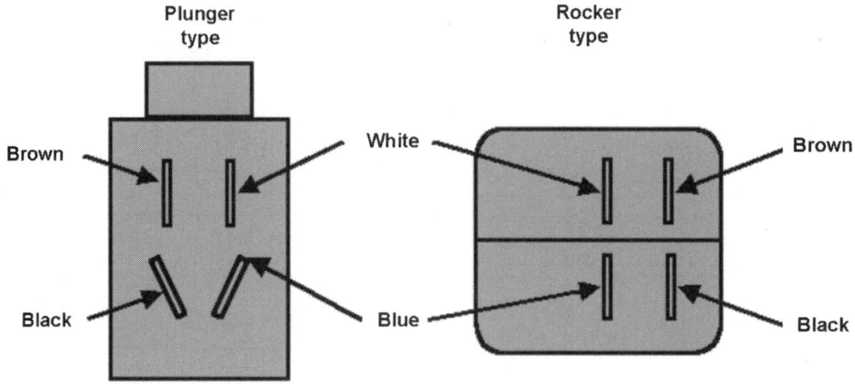

Replacement switches are cheap and readily available at any electronics store, but when replacing a switch, remember "black to brown and blue to white." All power supplies have these four colors, and they must be properly matched; if not, when you turn on the power supply, you will be in the dark—literally—since you will blow a circuit breaker.

The diagram in Figure 3.21 shows the proper placement of the power wires into the switch. The four plugs that go into the PC are 115 volts, so be careful! Make sure the power supply is unplugged.

When Power Supplies Die Hard

If all power supplies died easily, this would be a much shorter chapter. Unfortunately, the majority of PC problems occur when power supplies die "hard." This means that one of the internal electronics of the power supply has begun to fail. The failures are *always* intermittent and tend to cause some of the most difficult-to-diagnose problems that exist in PC repair. The one secret to discovering that a power supply is dying is the word *intermittent.* Whenever I have intermittent problems, my first guess is that the power supply is bad. Here are some other clues:

- "Whenever I start my computer in the morning, it starts to boot and then locks up. If I hit Ctrl—Alt—Del two or three times, it boots up fine."
- "Sometimes when I start my PC, I get an error code. If I reboot, it goes away. Sometimes I get different errors."
- "My computer runs fine for an hour or so, then it locks up—sometimes at often as once or twice an hour."

Sometimes bad things happen, and sometimes they don't. That's the clue for replacing the power supply. And don't bother with the voltmeter, since the voltages will be within tolerances except for every so often, when they will spike and sag—far more quickly than your voltmeter can measure. When in doubt, change the power supply. Power supplies break in computers more often than any other part of the PC, second to the floppy drives. I keep power supplies in stock for swapping and testing.

Danger!

Electricity can kill you, especially electricity from the wall outlet. A power supply might appear innocuous, but if you do not unplug the power supply before you open it, you could end up as a baked potato. While a power supply is closed, it is safe, but once you get access to the 115-volt VAC lines on the inside, you must be very careful not to touch anything unless the power supply is unplugged.

CHAPTER 

RAM

In this chapter, you will:

- See the different types of RAM packaging.
- Understand RAM banking.
- Understand different types of DRAM.
- See how to properly install RAM.
- Understand RAM access speed.

RAM (random-access memory) is the "working memory" of your PC. Although this was touched on in Chapter 1, let's review RAM's function in the PC. When not in use, programs are held in mass storage, which usually means a hard drive but could also mean floppies, a CD-ROM, or some other device that can hold values when the computer is turned off (Figure 4.1). When you load a program by typing its name in DOS or by clicking an icon in Windows, the program is copied from the mass storage device to RAM and then run (Figure 4.2).

Any device that can hold data is memory. *Random access* means that any part of the memory can be accessed with equal ease. A single sheet of paper with a list of names could be called random access since you can see any one name as easily as another. A cassette tape would not be random access since you would have to rewind or fast-forward the tape to access a particular piece of information. The term *random-access memory* in the PC world, however, refers to a specific type of electronic storage device known as *dynamic random-access memory* (DRAM).

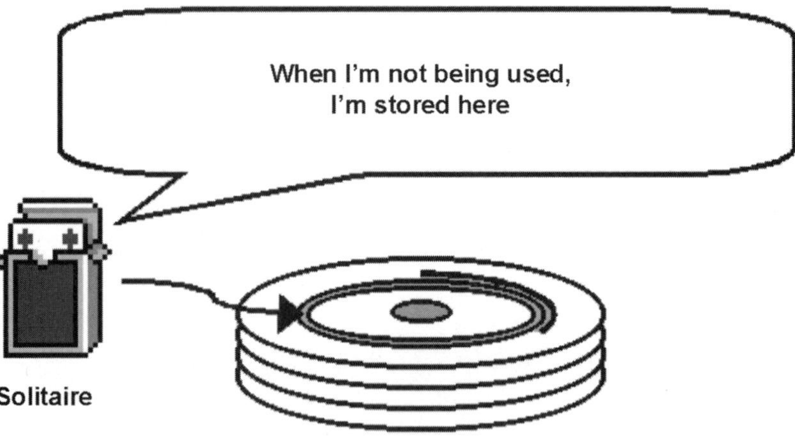
When I'm not being used,
I'm stored here
Solitaire

Figure 4.1 Unused programs are stored on mass storage

When I'm "run", a copy of
me is sent to RAM
11010010
01010011
11011110
10101101
00110011
01010000
00010010

Figure 4.2
When a program is running, it is in RAM

DRAM

DRAM is the most popular type of electronic memory in the PC world. As mentioned in the previous chapter, DRAM is a special type of semiconductor that stores individual ones and zeros using a microscopic capacitor and transistor (Figure 4.3). It comes to us in many different ways, usually soldered onto a card of some type (Figure 4.4). I will talk about these different cards later in the chapter, but for the moment, I'm going to concentrate on the individual chips on the card (see Figure 4.5). Once you understand how the individual chips are organized, I will return to the cards and describe how they work together.

Organizing DRAM

Due to its low cost and ability to contain a lot of data in a relatively small package, DRAM is the de-facto RAM used in all computers today. Even Macintoshes and mainframes use DRAM. In fact, DRAM can be found in just about everything today, from automobiles to automatic bread makers (Figure 4.6).

So what kind of DRAM do you need for PCs? Remember that the original 8088 processor had an eight-bit external data bus. All the commands

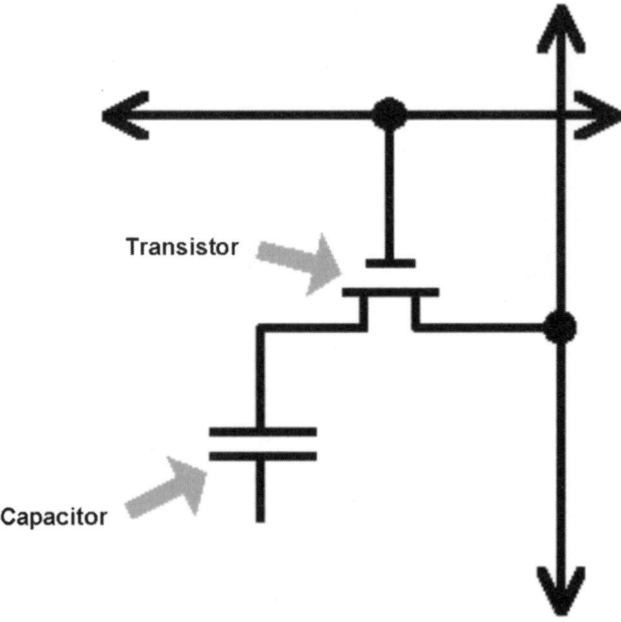

Figure 4.3 Schematic of a one-bit DRAM storage

Figure 4.4 Typical DRAM

given to an 8088 processor were in discrete, 8-bit chunks. (Refer back to Chapter 2 if this is not clear!) Therefore, you need RAM that can store data in 8-bit chunks. Even today's most modern CPUs can still run 8088 commands, so the necessary RAM "width" is still eight bits. When people talk about PC memory, they say things like "32 megabytes," "8 megabytes," or, if your computer is really old, "640 kilobytes." You'd never say something like "16 megawords" or "32 megabits." That's because memory is always eight bits or one byte across. So when discussing memory in PCs, you're always talking about "byte-wide" memory (Figure 4.7). But DRAM is not manufactured just for the PC industry. Many devices that use DRAM don't use byte-wide memory, so DRAM manufacturers sell their chips in a broad range of sizes that wouldn't be familiar to PC people (Figure 4.8).

Let's take some time to understand how DRAM manufacturers sell chips, and then we'll fit that into the byte-wide PC world. When referring to individual DRAM chips, you will primarily be interested in two values:

Figure 4.5
Close-up of DRAM

Figure 4.6
Lots of things need DRAM

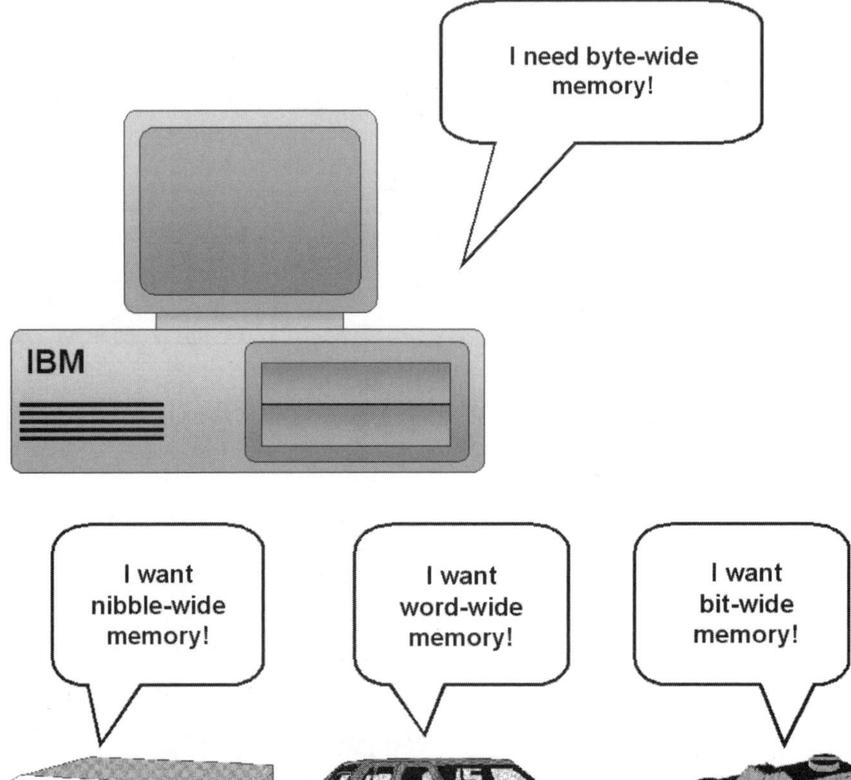

Figure 4.7 PCs need byte-wide DRAM

Figure 4.8 We need many widths of DRAM

the depth and the width. To explain this, I'll use a couple of analogies. Have you ever taken film in to be developed? You can usually select how large you want the photographs to be, right? You can usually get them in either 3 × 5 or 4 × 6 format, or if you're willing to pay more you can even get them in the 6 × 8 size (Figure 4.9).

When you say "3 × 5," what does that mean? Of course, it means three inches high by five inches wide. You do the same thing when discussing lumber, saying things like "2 × 4" or "1 × 12" (Figure 4.10).

Well, DRAM works exactly the same way. DRAM has a depth and a width that are measured in units of bits. Some common depths are 256K, 1MB, 4MB, and 16MB, and some common widths are 1 bit, 4 bits, 8 bits, and 16 bits. When you combine the depth and the width, you get the size of the DRAM chip. When talking about individual DRAM chips, then, you'd say something like 256K × 1 or 1MB × 4 (Figure 4.11).

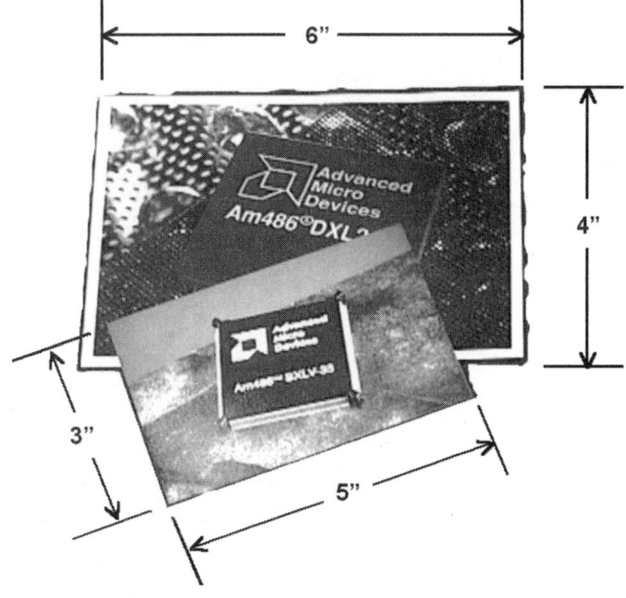

Figure 4.9
Height and width of photos

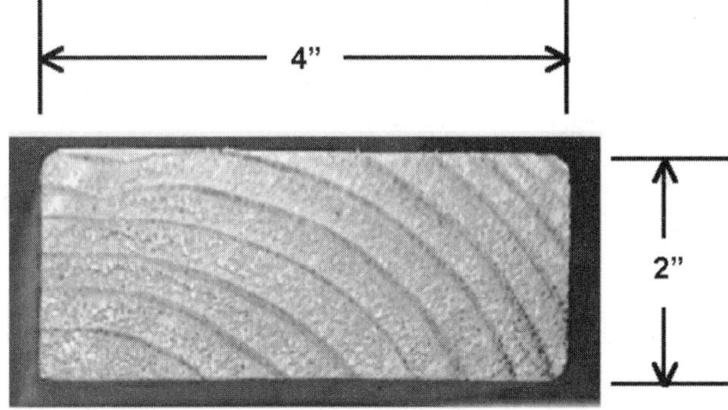

Figure 4.10
Height and width of lumber

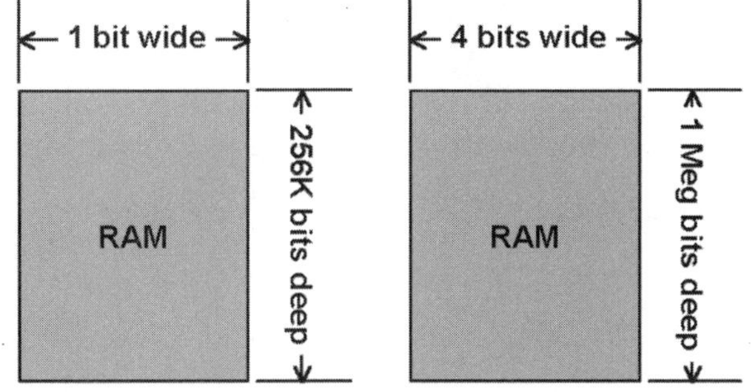

Figure 4.11
Height and width of DRAM

Figure 4.12 Different DRAM may look identical

If someone held up a 3 × 5 photo and asked you, "How large of a photo am I holding?" You could probably "eyeball" it and say: "That's a 3 × 5 photo." Unfortunately, it is virtually impossible to do that with DRAM. Two chips that look identical can be very different on the inside! The only way you can tell one DRAM from another is by reading the information printed on the chip itself. There is no direct correlation between physical size and the internal organization of the chip (see Figure 4.12). The following are some current common DRAM sizes (there are more):

Remember that 1K = 1024 and 1MB = 1,048,576.

So if you were to go up to a DRAM salesman and say: "I'd like 32 megabytes of RAM, please!" He would look at a bit strangely. DRAM makers don't think in terms of bytes. DRAM is sold in depth-by-width units such as "256K × 4." Now we need to put the DRAM world into the PC world and understand how the two work together!

A Historical Look

Before we get started, I need to warn you about something. You're going back in time here, when the first DRAMs were used in PCs. I know how most folks hate to talk about old stuff—I do, too—but if you want to understand how DRAM works today, you have to talk about how DRAM worked a long time ago. You'd be surprised how much of the original technology is still used today!

In the original IBM PC, the most DRAM that the PC could use was 640K (655,360 bytes). Later in the book, I'll explain this limitation—but for now I need you to trust me. I promise to completely clarify this limit later.

The single greatest truism of the PC business is "Everything old is new again!"

PCs need byte-wide RAM. Although today's DRAM chips can have widths of greater than one bit, back in the old days all DRAMS were one bit wide. That means you only had sizes like 64K × 1 or 256K × 1—always one bit wide. So how was one-bit-wide DRAM turned into eight-bit-wide memory? To help you understand what was done, visualize RAM as an "electronic spreadsheet." You've probably used a spreadsheet such Excel, Lotus 123, or Quattro Pro. Imagine a spreadsheet where the only values you can enter are 0 and 1. The number of columns is the width and the number of rows is the depth. This spreadsheet concept is exactly how the CPU sees RAM, so 640K of RAM would look like Figure 4.13 to the CPU.

The goal is taking a bunch of one-bit-wide DRAM chips and turning them into eight-bit-wide RAM (see Figure 4.14). The answer is quite simple; just take eight one-bit-wide chips and electronically organize them with the memory controller chip. First, put eight one-bit-wide chips in a row on the motherboard (Figure 4.15), then wire up this row of DRAM chips to the memory controller chip (which has to be designed to handle this) to make byte-wide memory (see Figure 4.16). You just made eight one-bit-wide DRAMs look like one eight-bit-wide DRAM (Figure 4.17). This row of chips has to add up to eight bits, and each chip has to be the same depth. You couldn't use seven 256K × 1 chips and one 64K × 1 chip; it wouldn't add up to 256 kilobytes (Figure 4.18).

Figure 4.13
RAM spreadsheet

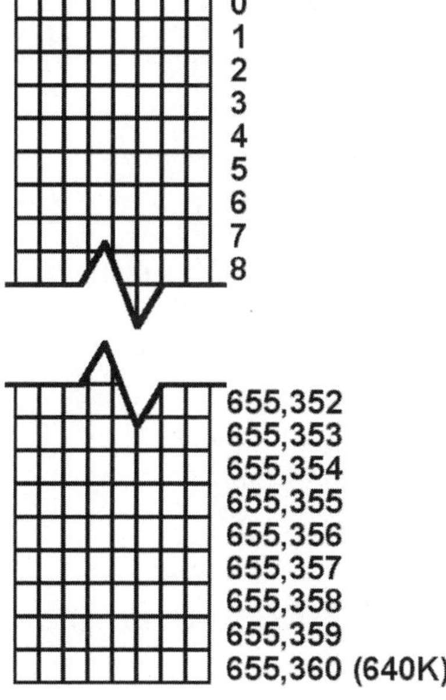

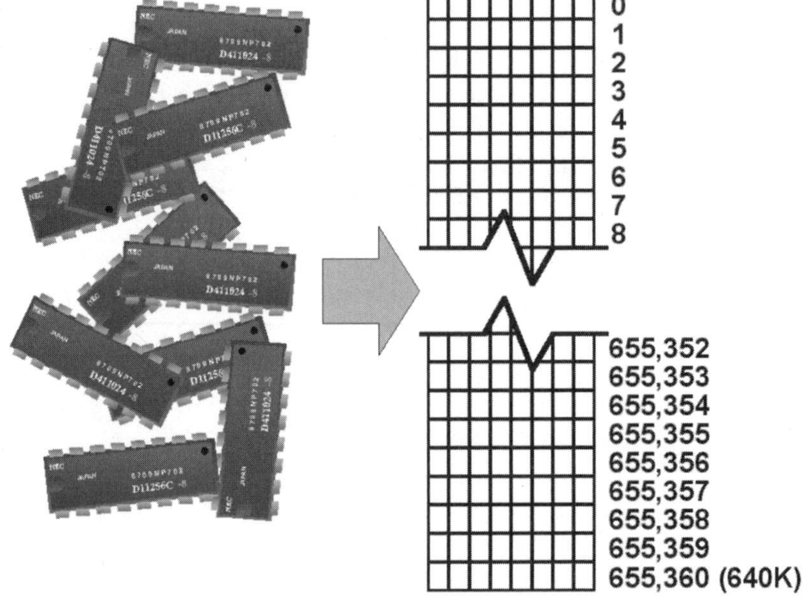

Figure 4.14
How do we turn chips into a spreadsheet?

Figure 4.15
One row of DRAM

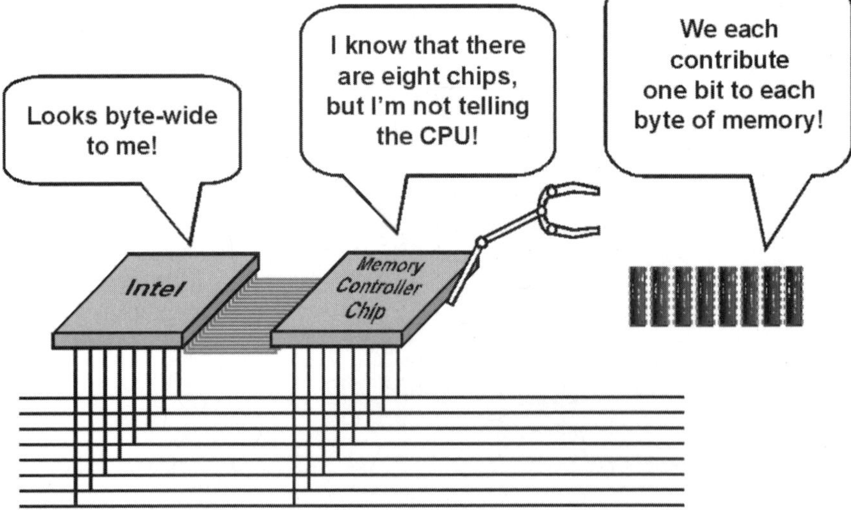

Figure 4.16
The MCC in action

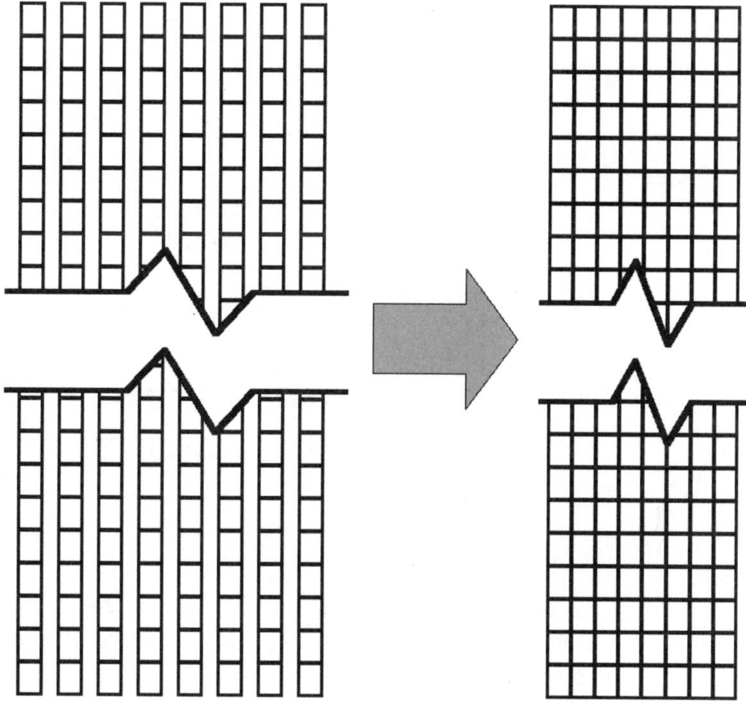

Figure 4.17
Eight one-wides make one eight-wide

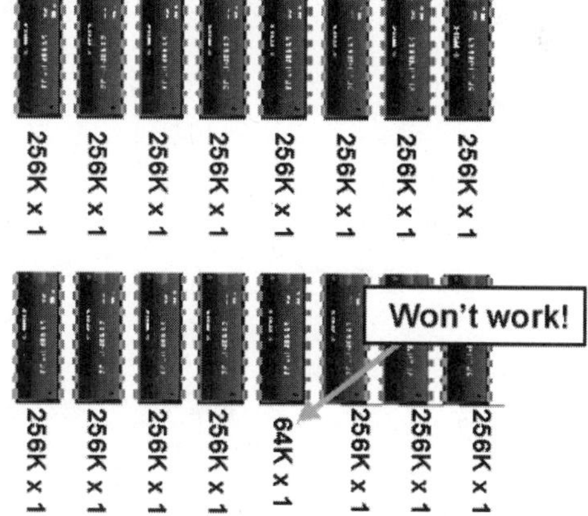

Figure 4.18
All DRAM must be the same depth in a row

Multiple Rows

You can use multiple DRAMs to create byte-wide memory, but there's a little problem. Back in the days of the 8088 processor, the biggest DRAM chip you could get was 256K × 1. With eight of these, the biggest row you could have was 256 kilobytes—but computers needed more RAM. Since

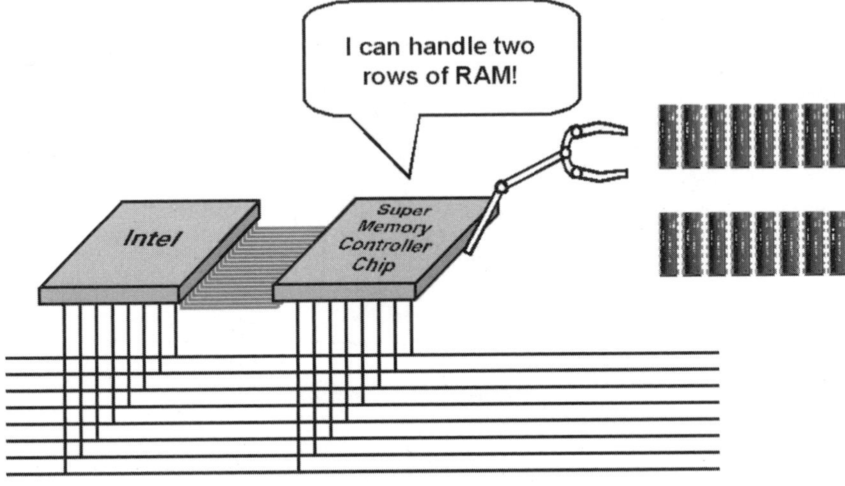

Figure 4.19
MCC with two rows of DRAM

the biggest row was 256 kilobytes, the only way to get more RAM was to add more rows! Adding more rows required an improved memory chip that could control more than one row of chips, so new types of memory controller chips (MCC) were created that could handle two or more rows of RAM (Figure 4.19).

Now, when the CPU needs a certain byte of memory, the CPU requests that byte via the address bus. The CPU has no idea where the byte of RAM is physically located. The MCC keeps track of this and just gives the CPU whatever byte it requests (Figure 4.20). It is easy to determine if your

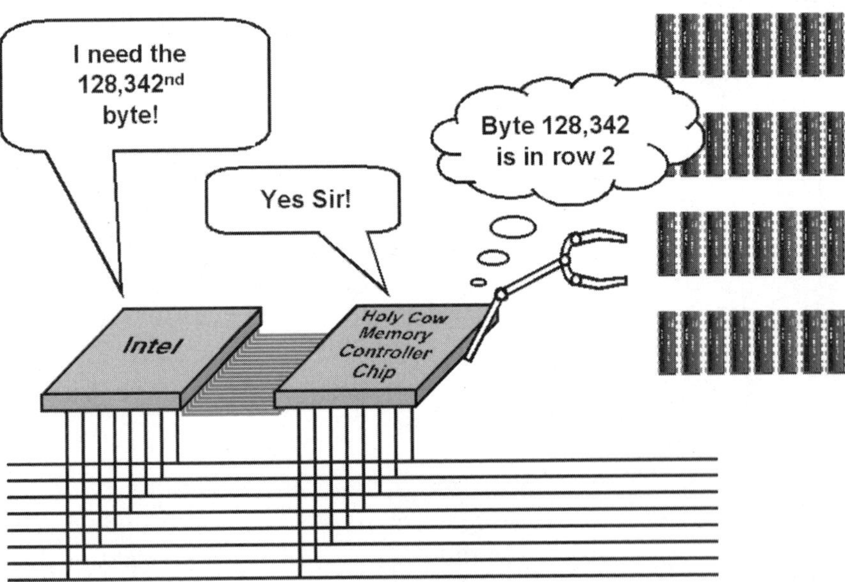

Figure 4.20
Only the MCC knows the real location of the DRAM

Figure 4.21
Empty rows, ready for DRAM to be added

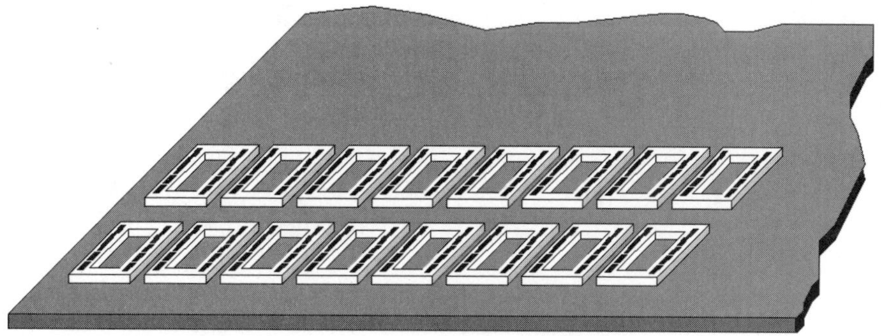

CPU can handle more than one row of RAM. All you have to do is to look at the motherboard. You can see rows of sockets ready for you to add RAM (Figure 4.21). You don't have to use all the rows, but if you use a row, it has to be completely filled with chips of the same depth.

"Populated" means a row with DRAM inserted; "unpopulated" means a row that has no DRAM.

You can have different sizes of DRAM in different rows (Figure 4.22); just remember that the DRAM chips have to be the same size in the same rows (Figure 4.23). The total amount of RAM is the sum of all the rows (Figure 4.24).

Parity

Parity is for error detection. It is usually manifested through an extra chip that is one bit wide and as deep as all the other chips in the row. This ninth bit allows the MCC to compare the number of ones stored in a byte with the number of ones found when the byte is accessed. In order for parity to work, you must have an MCC that is designed to use the parity chip.

Figure 4.22
One populated and one unpopulated row

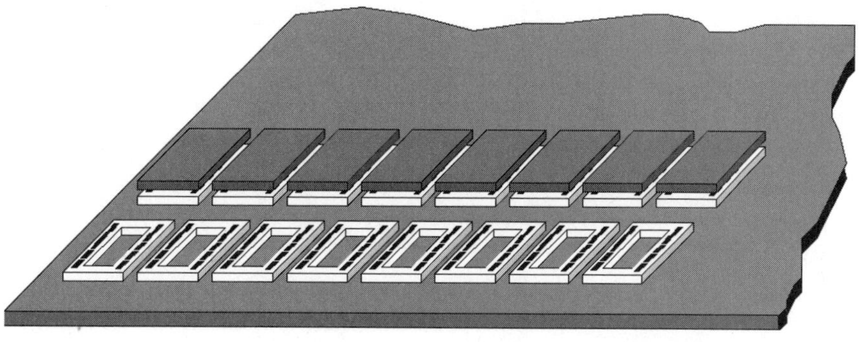

Every time data is placed in RAM, the parity bit is set. Every time you access that byte of RAM, the parity bit is checked. If something has happened between data storage and retrieval to change one of the bits, then you will get the infamous "Parity error, system halted" message. Parity checking was useful in the early days of desktop computers when DRAM had a relatively high failure rate, but today's DRAMs are much more dependable, so much so that very few PCs still support parity (see Figure 4.25).

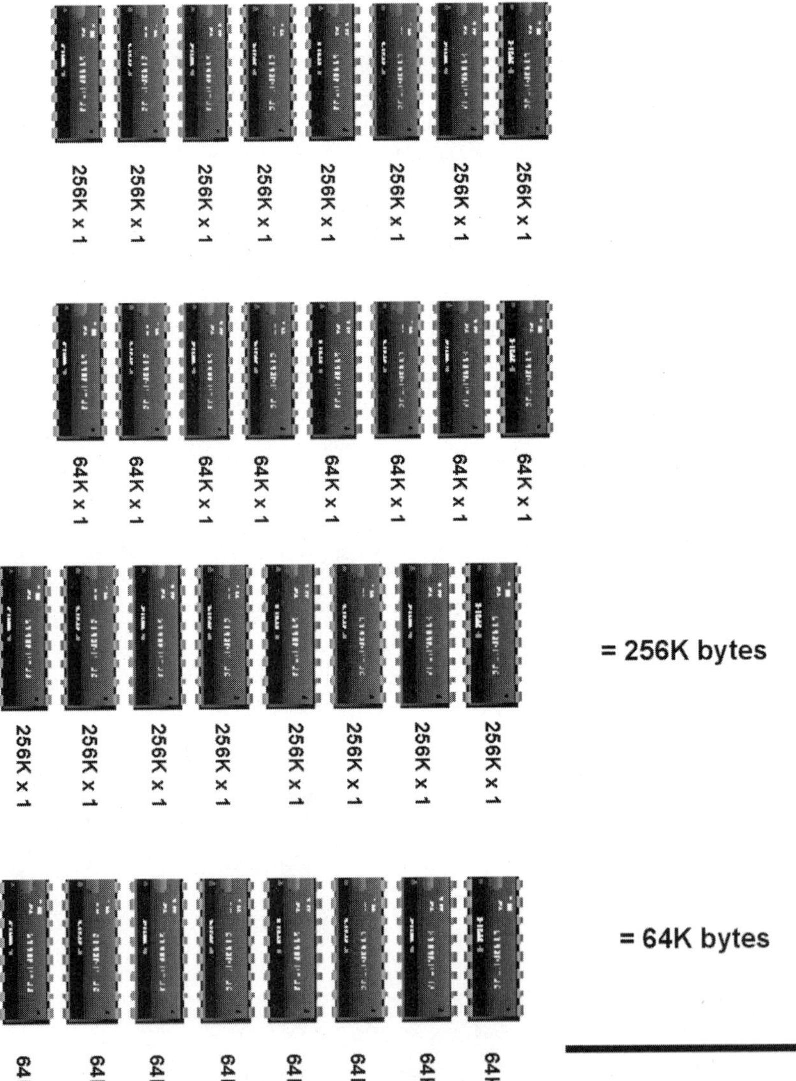

Figure 4.23 Different rows can have different depths

Figure 4.24 All DRAM is cumulative

Figure 4.25
Here's a close-up of older style DIPP DRAM. Note that the 9 chips show that it is parity

RAM Packaging, Part 1

There have been many popular types of RAM packages over the years. In this section, you'll take a quick look at the more common ones used in the early part of the PC industry. After a short diversion, you'll return to the RAM packages used in modern machines.

DIPPs

The first-generation DRAM chips used a DIPP (dual in-line pin package). These types of chips are distinguished by two rows of pins extending from either side of the package (Figure 4.26). Installing DIPPs was, at best, a hassle. It was easy to break a pin or to improperly insert the DRAM into its socket. Plus, as RAM chips began to drop in price during the late '80s and early '90s, it became obvious that, when dealing with DRAM, you were dealing more with complete rows than with individual chips. Think about it. When you want to add RAM, you have to populate an entire row, right? If you want to remove RAM, again you must remove an entire row. So why mess with individual chips when 99 percent of the time you are going to be dealing with entire rows?

This demand created a new type of DRAM package. Instead of individual chips inserted into individual sockets, the RAM was soldered to a small board that could be inserted into the motherboard. This type of package was called a SIPP (single in-line pin package).

30-Pin SIPPs

The SIPP used a standardized set of pins that mounted into the motherboard, which eliminated the need for individual mounts for each

Figure 4.26
Classic DIPP package

DRAM. The SIPPs board revolutionized the way DRAM was used in a PC. For example, by the time SIPPs had been invented, new DRAM chips were available that were more than one bit wide—so you could find 256K × 4 chips. The rule is that each row must equal eight bits, which used to mean that you had to use eight one-bit chips. But now you could use two four-bit chips to do the same thing. With DIPPs, you had to use whatever chips were designed to use the sockets soldered to the motherboard. If you had eight little sockets on the motherboard, that was what you had to use—period. But with SIPPs, the 30-pin connectors were independent of the type of chips soldered onto it. So you could take out a 30-pin SIPP with eight 256K × 1 chips and replace it with a 30-pin SIPP with two 256K × 4 chips, and the system wouldn't know the difference! The SIPP package really made installing and removing RAM much simpler (Figure 4.27).

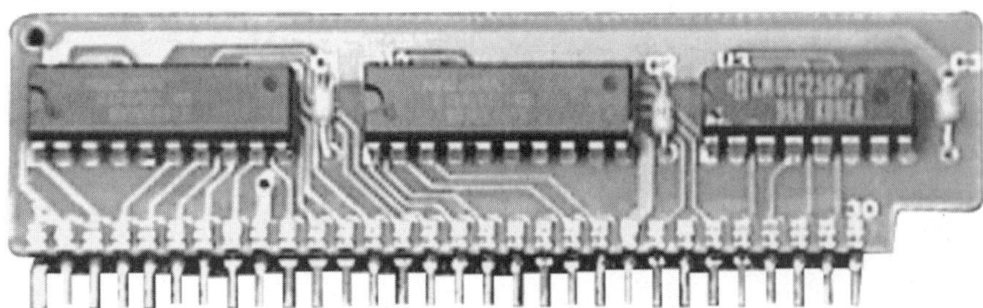

Figure 4.27
30-pin SIPP

SIPP packages plugged directly into the motherboard via their own special socket. They were relatively easy to install; all you had to do was push down. Unfortunately, SIPPs also had a rather nasty Achilles heel. The 30 pins that connected the package to the motherboard were just as delicate as the pins on the DIPP chips. Like the DIPP chips, it was just too easy to accidentally break off one of the pins—which made the whole SIPP garbage. So, although SIPPs were revolutionary, they were quickly replaced by their much more robust successor, the 30-pin SIMM.

30-Pin SIMMs

SIMMs (single in-line memory modules) are the next rung on memory's evolutionary ladder. Physically, they look very similar to SIPPs, with one exception: no pins. There is nothing to bend and no way to inflict serious bodily harm to you or the chips (Figure 4.28).

SIMMs are inserted into a special SIMM socket. It is virtually impossible to install SIMMs improperly due to the notch on one side of the card. Electronically, 30-pin SIMMs are identical to 30-pin SIPPs. You can even purchase a simple converter that allows SIPPs to be inserted into SIMM sockets and vice versa (Figure 4.29).

In 30-pin SIMMs, each printed circuit card has 30 pins or contacts along the edge. The most important thing to remember about 30-pin SIMMs is that, although their depths might vary, they are always 8 data bits (one byte) wide. Although a SIMM chip is always 8 bits wide, the chips on the package can differ widely. Figure 4.30 shows some examples of different chip layouts for a 30-pin SIMM.

KEEPING TRACK OF YOUR SIMM CHIPS One unfortunate aspect of 30-pin SIMMs (you will see this is true for all DRAM) is that you can't tell how deep a SIMMs chip is simply by looking at it. Figure 4.31 shows a

Figure 4.28
30-pin SIMM

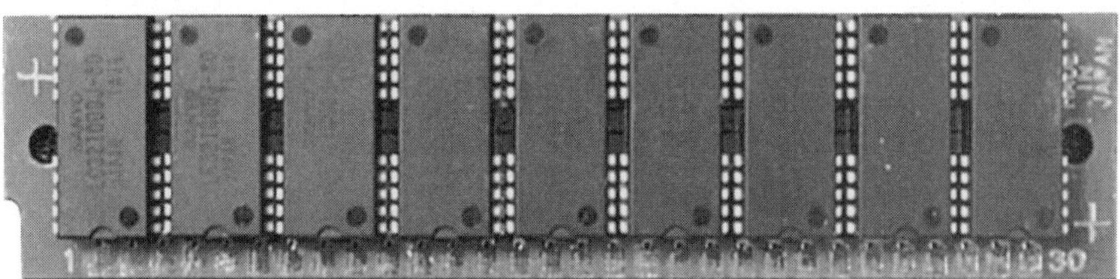

Figure 4.29 Eight rows for 30-pin SIMMs

Figure 4.30 Different chip layout on SIMMs

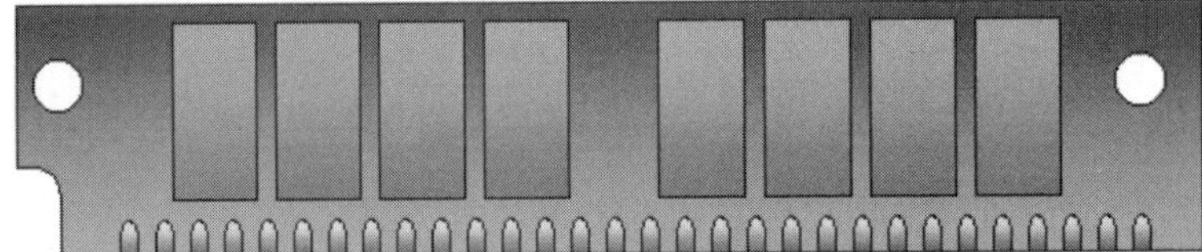

Eight x1 chips - “x 8” SIMM

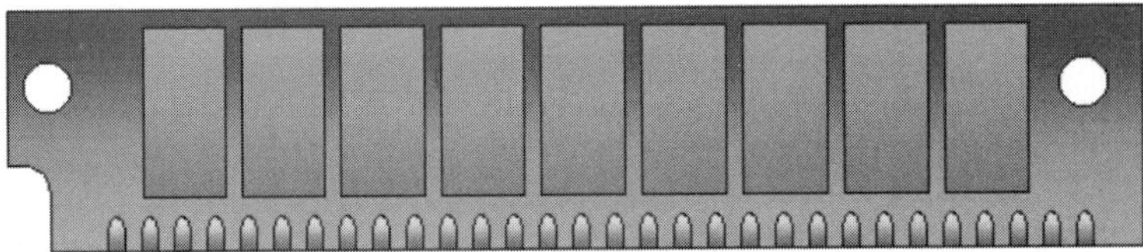

Nine x1 chips - “x 9” SIMM

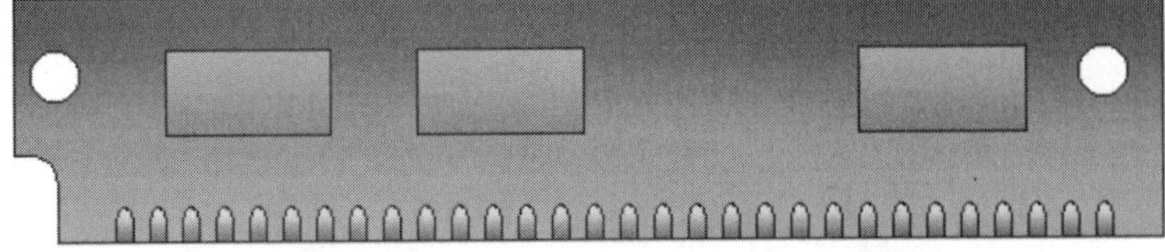

Two x4 chips & one x1 - “x 3” SIMM

Figure 4.31
Identical looking, but very different SIMMs

Figure 4.32
How to be sure of the size of SIMM-labeled 1 × 9

4 × 3 SIMM and a 1 × 3 SIMM. Notice that they look almost identical. The best way to know what depth SIMM you have is to label it when you buy it. Every SIMM I own has a small label on it that tells me its size—that way there's never any guessing (Figure 4.32). It's easy to tell a parity from a nonparity SIMM. All nonparity 30-pin SIMMs have an even number of chips. All parity 30-pin SIMMs have an odd number of chips.

SIMM CHIPS AND PARITY When purchasing SIMM chips, the question is: "Do I need parity or nonparity?" This is decided exclusively by the motherboard. Refer to your motherboard book to determine whether your machine requires parity or nonparity chips. Another way is to look at the chips currently in your PC—are there an odd (parity) or even (nonparity) number of chips? Some PCs allow you to turn off the parity; look at Figure 4.33, which shows a screen from a PC's advanced CMOS (see CMOS) settings. On these machines, you can mix parity with nonparity chips, as long as the parity is turned off.

ACCESS SPEED It takes a certain amount of time for the DRAM chip to supply the MCC with the requested data. This is called the *access speed,* and it is typically given in nanoseconds (commonly abbreviated as ns). The faster the chip, the shorter the delay, and the smaller the access-speed number. Therefore, a 100-ns chip is slower than a 60-ns chip.

A lower access-speed number means faster access.

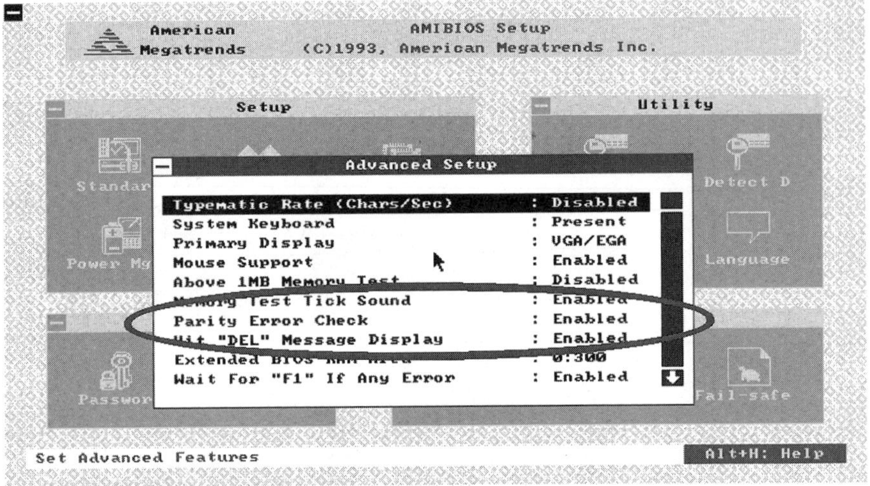

Figure 4.33 Parity option on older CMOS

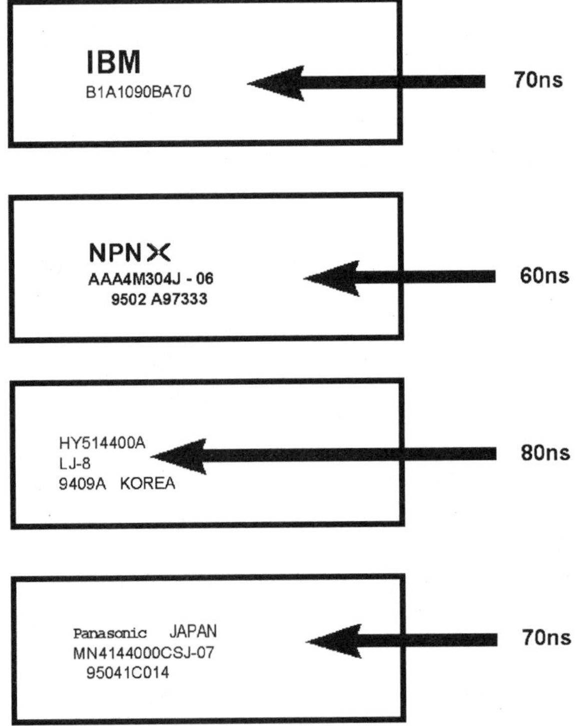

Figure 4.34 Determining access rates

Every motherboard requires a certain speed of DRAM, so it is crucial for you to be able to "eyeball" a DRAM chip to determine its access speed. Access speeds range from as slow as 200 ns on ancient 8088s, up to 50 ns for the newest DRAMs. Figure 4.34 shows some examples of chips and determines their access speeds.

Although there are some exceptions, which you will visit later, the easiest guideline is to simply use the proper-speed DRAM, based on your motherboard book, and to make sure that every piece of DRAM is that speed.

TALKING THE TALK If you want to purchase DRAM at a cheap wholesale place, it is imperative to be able to speak the language of DRAM. For example, each individual package of SIMM or SIPP is called a "stick," so if you want four SIMM packages, you would say: "Give me four sticks of RAM." Never ask for parity or nonparity. There are only three widths of DRAM in 30-pin SIMMs or SIPPs: × 8, which is by definition nonparity, × 9, which is by definition parity, and × 3, which is simply a × 9 SIMM in a three-chip package—also parity. So by saying "× 8" or "× 3," you are specifying whether or not you want parity.

There are only three common sizes in 30-pin SIMMs or SIPPs: 256K, 1MB, and 4MB. These three sizes make up 95 percent of all 30-pin SIMMs, so when describing these sizes, you want to drop the unit values and just use the number. When talking about a 30-pin SIMM or SIPP, therefore, you'd just say "4 × 8" or "1 × 3."

If you say "× 3," "× 8," or "× 9," you are talking about 30-pin SIMMs or SIPPs.

Always specify "SIMMs" or "SIPPs" so you get the right package. Finally, when you specify an access speed, don't say "50 nanoseconds." Just say "fifties" or "eighties." If you're buying just one stick, say "50" or "60." So if you were going to order some SIMMs, the conversation would go something like this: "I'd like 16 sticks of 1 × 8 sixties SIMMs, and 4 sticks of 256 × 9 eighties SIPPs, please."

Banking

The 8088 processor inside the original IBM PC defined many of the rules still in force today as to how RAM is accessed, but RAM access functions have not stood still. The first major improvement to RAM access from the IBM PC was a concept known as *banking*. Simply put, banking means to access more than one row of DRAM at a time. Every PC since the 286 performs this banking function. Let's see how banking came to be and how it is used today.

One concept I must clarify is that not every command in the 8088 CPU's machine language is one byte wide. Many commands are 16 or even 32 bits wide. So how can the 8088, with only an 8-bit external data bus, handle commands that are more than one byte wide? The answer is simple; it chops the commands up into one-byte chunks.

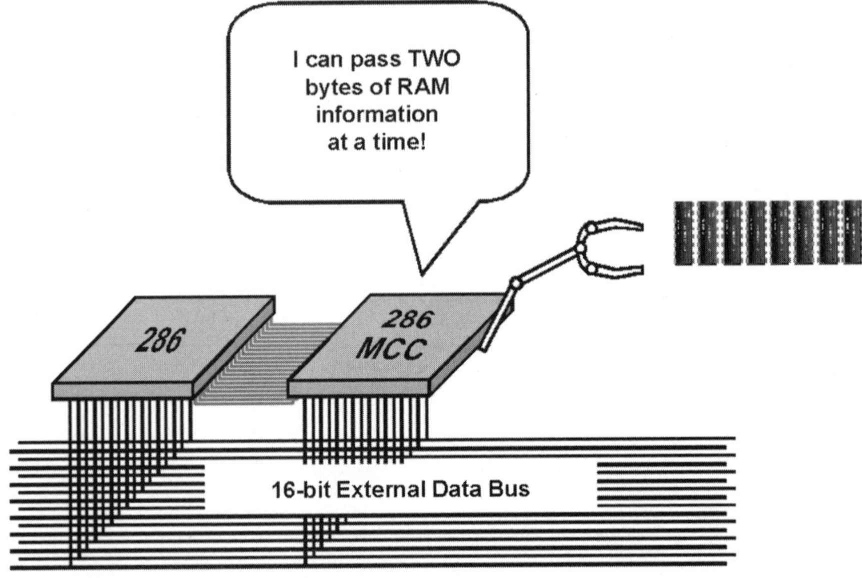

Figure 4.35 Most MCCs can pass more than eight bits at a time

So every time the 8088 CPU runs into commands like these, it must access RAM at least twice before it can act on the command, due to its 8-bit external data bus. When the 286 CPUs arrived, an opportunity arose. Do you remember from Chapter 2 that a 286 has a 16-bit external data bus? With the right MCC, a 286 can access 16 bits every time memory is accessed. It would be much faster to access two bytes every time you went to RAM instead of just one (Figure 4.35). The only problem with this was that one row (or one SIMM) could give only one byte each time it was accessed, because that's all it was designed to do (Figure 4.36). A new type of 16-bit wide DRAM would have to be invented (which nobody wanted to do back then), or you could just install DRAM in pairs that worked together as a team (Figure 4.37).

When the 386s and 486s with their 32-bit external data buses came out, two more rows or two more SIMMs were simply added to the two existing ones to make four 8-bit rows. The RAM had to be wide enough to match the size of the external data bus. Combining the widths of DRAM to match the width of the external data bus is called *banking*. The number of SIMMs that make up a bank depends on the MCC, which in turn depends on the CPU's external data bus size.

> The number of rows of SIMMs that can be simultaneously accessed by the MCC is a bank.

Figure 4.38 lists some "rules of thumb" for banking with 30-pin SIMMs. The most important rule of banking is that all SIMMs in the same bank

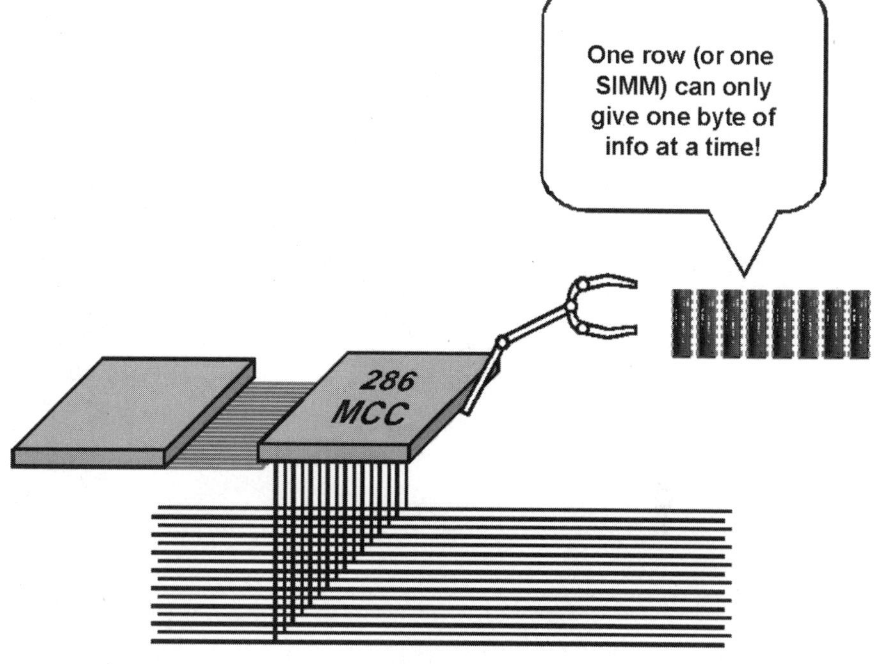

Figure 4.36
One eight bit row can only pass one byte

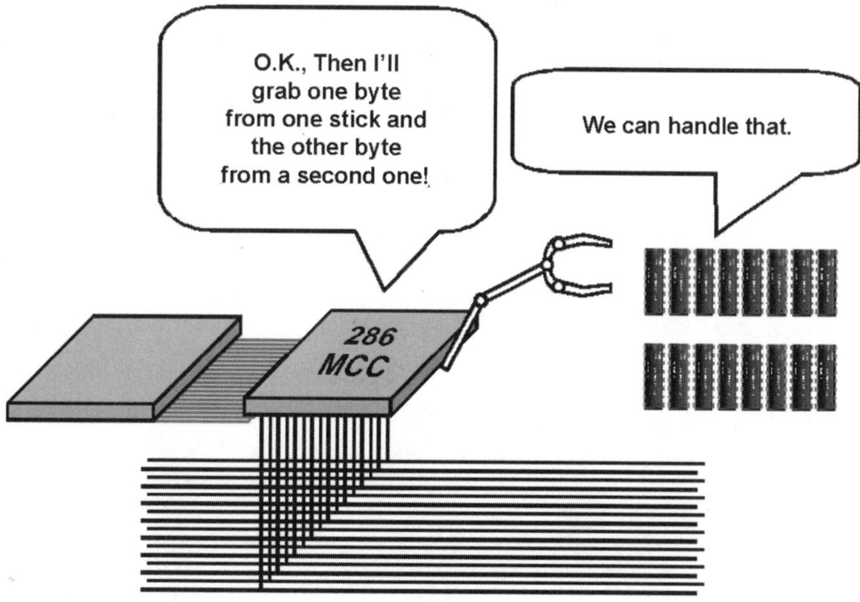

Figure 4.37
Passing more than eight bits with two rows

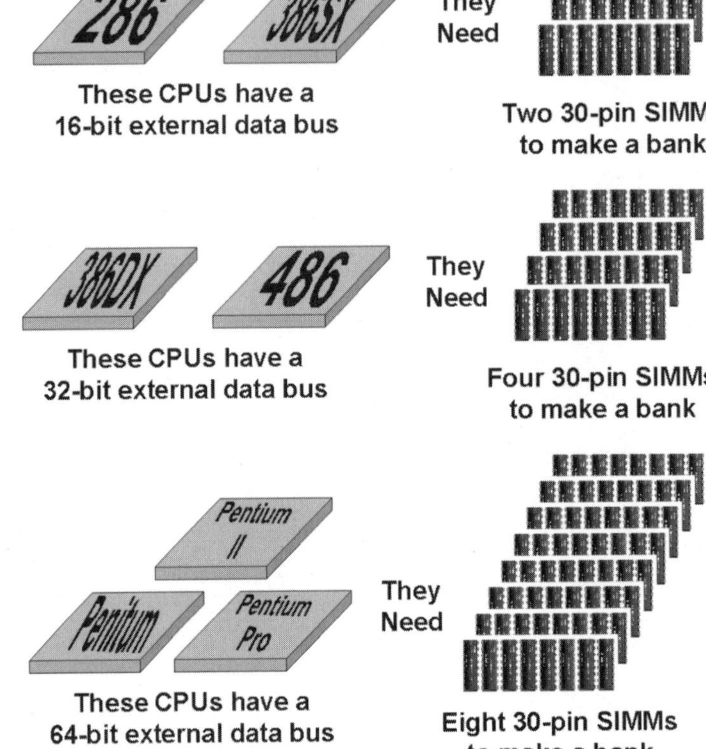

Figure 4.38 Banking rules

must be identical. For example, if you have a 486 (32-bit external data bus) and 30-pin SIMMs (8 bits wide), you must have four identical 30-pin SIMMs to make a bank. You can have four 1 × 8s, four 4 × 3s, or four 256 × 9s—it doesn't matter as long as they are identical. They also should be the same speed. See Figure 4.39.

The amount of RAM in each bank is totaled for the actual amount of RAM. Using the earlier example of a 486, if you have four 1 × 8 SIMMs, you have four times one megabyte, or four megabytes of RAM. If you

Figure 4.39 All ROWS in the bank must be identical

Figure 4.40 Eight 30-pin SIMM slots in a 486 make two banks

have a 286 with two 256 × 9 SIMMs, you have 512K of RAM. Almost all PCs have more than one bank. Figure 4.40 shows an old 486 system with connectors for up to eight rows of 30-pin SIMMs.

Since you know that you need four 30-pin SIMMs to make a bank, the fact that there are eight connectors on this motherboard tells you that it is designed for two banks. Having more than one bank on a motherboard allows for flexibility in the amount of RAM in your system. You can have different sized SIMMs *in different banks*. For example, assuming you have a 486 system with two banks, you can install 4 × 8 SIMMs in one bank (16MB) and 1 × 8 SIMMs in another (4MB), for a total RAM amount of 20MB. Imagine how limited RAM installation would be like if you didn't have multiple banks! Virtually all systems today have multiple banks for RAM. (See Figure 4.41.)

The connectors where you install a bank are also collectively called a *bank*. Therefore, a bank without any SIMMs is called an "unpopulated" bank and a bank filled with SIMMs is called a "populated" bank.

A bank must be either completely populated or completely unpopulated. This is fairly obvious, but I want to be completely clear. Let's say you have a 486 system that needs four sticks to make a bank. You have two banks. You will have either four or eight sticks in the system—not three and not five—since that's the only way to properly fill four-stick banks.

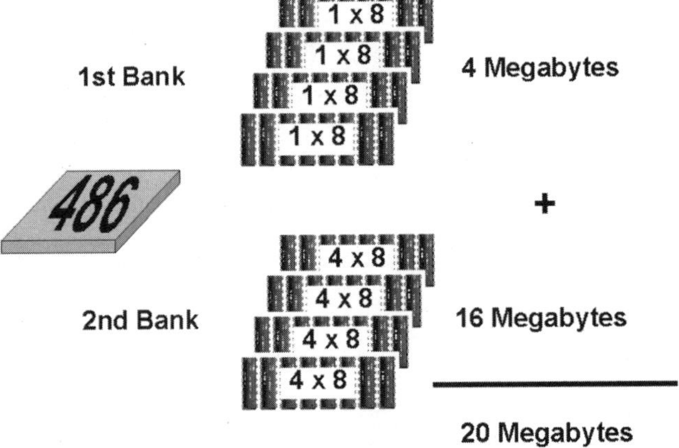

Figure 4.41 Banks are cumulative

RAM Packaging, Part 2

Now that you have a basic understanding of the different types of earlier DRAM packages, you can now move forward into the more modern types of DRAM with the necessary conceptual tools to appreciate why they're used in today's machines.

72-Pin SIMMs

Most of the examples in the previous section used 486 CPUs. Why didn't I use Pentiums? Well, Pentium motherboards don't use 30-pin SIMMs—for a very good reason. You would need eight 30-pin SIMMs to make a bank to match the 64-bit external data bus of the Pentium. Although this is no problem electronically, it takes up a massive amount of physical space on the motherboard. You would need 16 slots just to create two banks! What was needed was a new type of DRAM packaging that was more than 8 bits wide.

Enter the 72-pin SIMM. Like its little brother, the 72-pin SIMM has the same number of pins on each stick as its name—72 in this case. Unlike 30-pin SIMMs, however, each 72-pin SIMM is 32-bits wide. This means that for a 386DX or a 486 motherboard, you can replace four rows of 30-pin SIMMs with one row of 72-pin SIMMs. For a Pentium, you would need only two 72-pin SIMMs (Figure 4.42). Although similar to the 30-pin SIMM, the 72-pin SIMM is about an inch longer and has a distinct notch in the middle of the pins to assist in inserting the stick (Figure 4.43).

Since 72-pin SIMMs are 32 bits wide, the term "× 32" is used for non-parity and "× 36" is used for parity when describing them. If you hear about a "1MB × 32 SIMM," you might be inclined to think it was 1 megabyte, but that is incorrect. A 1MB × 32 SIMM has 1 megabyte of 32 bits, which means that SIMM holds four megabytes of RAM (1,048,576 × 32 = 4 megabytes). Here are some common 72-pin SIMMs and their sizes:

1 × 32 = 4 megabytes, no parity

1 × 36 = 4 megabytes, parity

2 × 32 = 8 megabytes, no parity

2 × 36 = 8 megabytes, parity

4 × 32 = 16 megabytes, no parity

4 × 36 = 16 megabytes, parity

8 × 32 = 32 megabytes, no parity

8 × 36 = 32 megabytes, parity

16 × 32 = 64 megabytes, no parity

16 × 36 = 64 megabytes, parity

Figure 4.42
72-pin SIMM

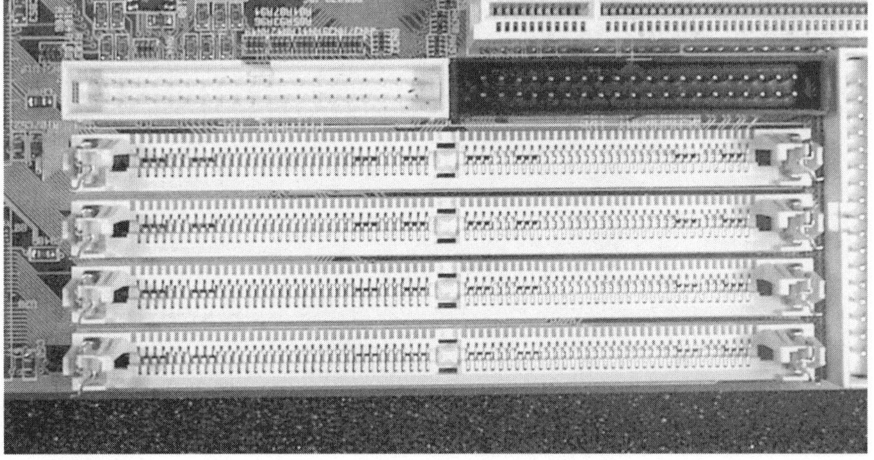

Figure 4.43
72-pin SIMM slots

Figure 4.44 Labeling is the secret to identification

Since 72-pin SIMMs are 32 bits wide, you need only one 72-pin SIMM to make a bank in a 386 or 486. You need two 72-pin SIMMs to make a bank on a Pentium or Pentium Pro. Other than the width, 72-pin SIMMs are just like the older 30-pin SIMMs. They have an access speed, the choice of parity or nonparity, and are used in banking. Like 30-pin SIMMs, it is virtually impossible to install a 72-pin SIMM incorrectly since it is also notched.

If you say "× 32" or "× 36," you are talking about 72-pin SIMMs.

Unlike the 30-pin SIMMs, there is no definite way to tell a parity 72-pin SIMM from a nonparity 72-pin SIMM. Just make sure you write the type of SIMM on the back of the stick and you'll never have a problem. In fact, many DRAM makers and distributors print this information right on the SIMM, as shown in Figure 4.44. (They're not being nice, they just don't want you to bother them with stupid questions.)

Interestingly, there are two types of parity SIMMs available: true and TTL parity. True parity is just as it sounds: a real parity chip for every eight data bits. TTL parity emulates parity and costs less. The few systems that use parity will tell you which one to use.

168-Pin DIMM

The most popular new package in use today is the 168-pin DIMM. A DIMM (dual in-line memory module) is more than just a bigger, wider SIMM. The *dual* in DIMM comes from the fact that each side of each pin has a separate function, while each side of each pin is the same on a SIMM. DIMMs have the extra pins necessary to enable rather interesting options, such as buffering, ECC, and SDRAM (discussed later). A DIMM stick is 64 bits wide, which means you need only one to create a bank in a Pentium-class motherboard (Figure 4.45).

Another type of DIMM is most commonly used in laptops: SO-DIMM. SO-DIMMs are much shorter than 168-pin DIMMs. They have only 72 pins (pure coincidence) and a 32-bit data path (Figure 4.46). However, their convenient size has made them extremely popular for use with laptops.

Figure 4.45
168-pin DIMM

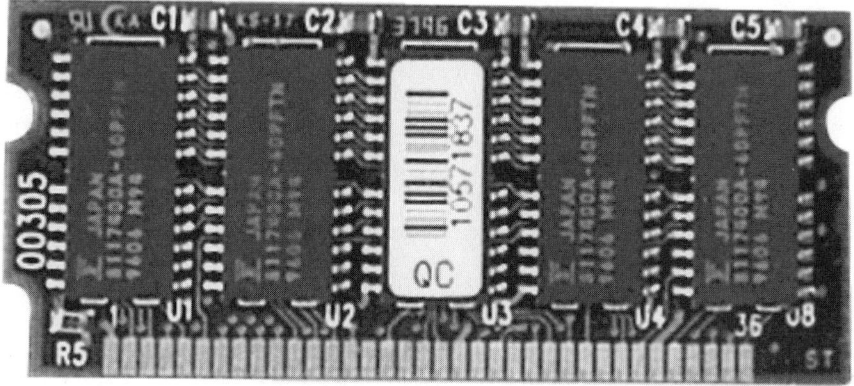

Figure 4.46
72-pin SO-DIMM

Since a 168-pin DIMM is 64 bits wide, a 1 × 64 DIMM is 1MB of 64 bits wide, or 8 megabytes. Here are some common 168-pin DIMMs and their sizes:

1 × 64 = 8 megabytes

2 × 64 = 16 megabytes

4 × 64 = 32 megabytes

8 × 64 = 64 megabytes

16 × 64 = 128 megabytes

Although 168-pin DIMMs are officially "× 64" wide chips, many technicians just say "16-megabyte 168-pin DIMMs." Be ready to "talk the talk" either way.

The Magic Banking Formula

With 30-pin SIMMs, 72-pin SIMMs, SO-DIMMs, and 168-pin DIMMs, it can get a little challenging to remember how many sticks of each type of

DRAM are needed to make a bank on different systems. Don't bother trying to memorize them; the powers that be are just gonna come out with wider SIMMs/DIMMs and wider external data buses, and you'll be right back where you started. Instead, I have a formula you can use to determine the number of SIMM/DIMM sticks needed to make one bank; I call it my "magic banking formula."

$$\text{One Bank} = \frac{\text{Width of External Data Bus}}{\text{Width of the SIMM chip}}$$

So a 32-bit external data bus and 30-pin SIMMs (8 bit wide data) = 32 ÷ 8 = 4 30-pin SIMMs per bank for a 486, and a 64-bit EDB and 168-pin DIMM (64-bit wide data) = 64 ÷ 64 = 1 168-pin DIMM per bank for a Pentium II. Stick with this formula, no matter what they throw at you in the future. It will always tell you the number of sticks to make a bank.

Mixing DRAM Packages

Many motherboards have slots for more than one type of DRAM. This is done to add more flexibility to motherboards, and to allow you to move from an older type of DRAM to a newer type without losing your investment in the older type of DRAM. For example, Figure 4.47 shows an old 486 motherboard that can handle both 30-pin and 72-pin SIMMs.

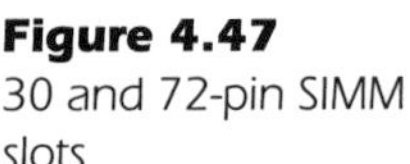

Figure 4.47
30 and 72-pin SIMM slots

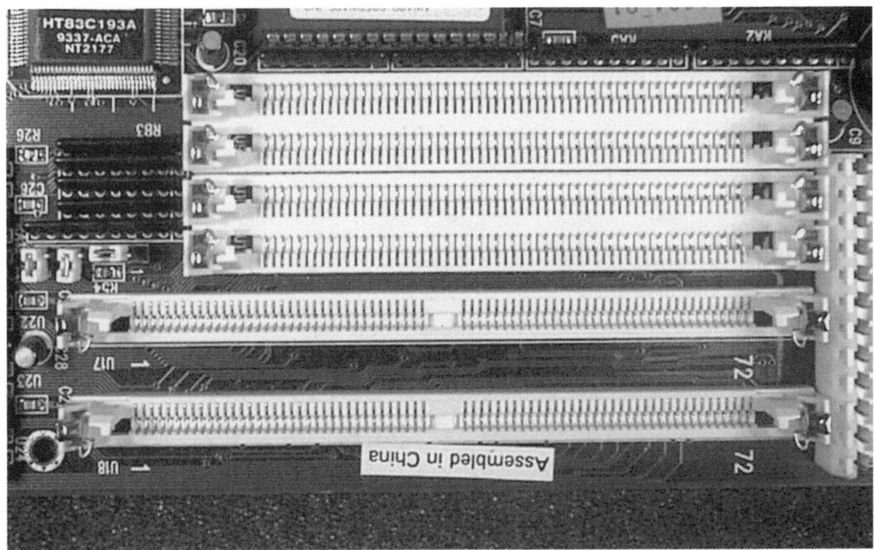

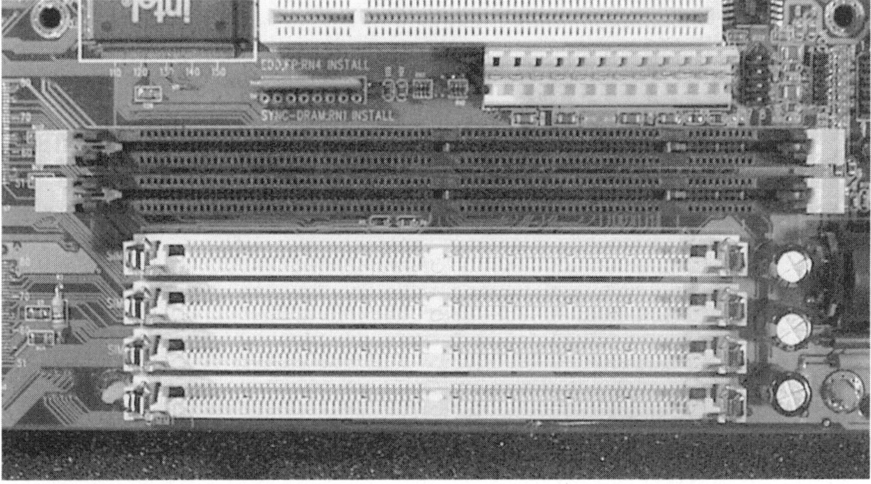

Figure 4.48
SIMMs and DIMMs

There is nothing wrong with this at all; just be aware that you might have to move a jumper or two around to get them to work. Also be aware that some types of SIMMs take precedence over others. On this particular board, if you populate both of the 72-pin banks and the 30-pin bank, one of the 72-pin banks will be ignored—I have no idea why! Figure 4.48 shows a modern motherboard that can take both 72-pin SIMMs and 168-pin DIMMs. In this case, you can install only SIMMs or DIMMs. I have another virtually identical motherboard that allows them to work together; go figure.

Improvements in DRAM

As we look at RAM, you'll need to understand some of the improvements on the classic FPM DRAM of the original 8088 days. When I say improvements, I'm talking about functional technology improvements, not just widening the RAM via a new type of stick as you saw in the previous sections. My goal here is not to go into great depth on these improvements, but rather to allow you to recognize these improvements and take advantage of them when they are available.

EDO

As described in Chapter 2, all DRAM needs to be refreshed in order to keep the data and programs it stores valid. The process of refresh creates a

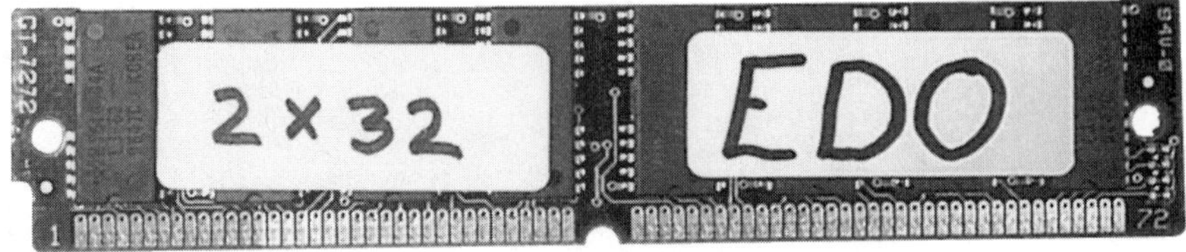

Figure 4.49 How to tell EDO from FPM - another label

big bottleneck in RAM access. Sure, things like SRAM caches certainly reduce the impact, but any way to minimize the frequency of refresh will improve the overall speed of the computer—thus EDO (extended data out) FPM DRAM. EDO DRAM is nothing more than a moderate improvement on old-style FPM DRAM. EDO needs to be refreshed much less often, thereby providing an extended period where data can be taken out of RAM. EDO RAM is on either a 72-pin SIMM or a DIMM (168 or SO), and looks exactly like regular DRAM. There is no standard way to tell EDO from FPM DRAM, so be sure to label your EDO RAM as such (Figure 4.49).

You want to use EDO whenever possible. Unfortunately, you can't just put EDO RAM in any computer. In order to take advantage of EDO, you need a motherboard that is designed to handle it. The majority of today's Pentium systems can use EDO RAM; refer to your motherboard book to see if your system can use it.

Mixing EDO and FPM RAM is not a good idea. Most systems that use EDO will run with FPM RAM, but you are losing the benefits of EDO. Equally, most systems that need FPM RAM will also work with EDO, but the EDO will be treated as regular FPM RAM and your computer won't run any faster. Some systems simply won't work unless the proper type of RAM is installed.

SDRAM

The "hot" RAM that everyone is using today is called SDRAM (synchronous dynamic random-access memory). SDRAM is still DRAM, but it is synchronous—tied to the system clock. Let me explain. Regular DRAM (EDO or FPM) is not tied to any clock. If the CPU wants some data from RAM, the MCC sends the necessary signals to the DRAM, waits a certain number of clock ticks, then accesses the RAM again to get the data. The number of clicks of the clock is either set through CMOS or determined by the MCC every time the system boots up. The number of clicks is not exact, and is rounded up to ensure that the MCC won't access DRAM before the necessary data is ready. This is wasteful of system time, but until recently DRAM was too slow to be handled any other way.

SDRAM is tied to the system clock, so the MCC knows when data is ready to be grabbed from SDRAM, resulting in little wasted time. Plus, SDRAM is quite a bit faster than DRAM. Last, SDRAM pipelines instructions from the MCC that allow commands to be ready as soon as the previous one is taken by the MCC. Collectively, these improvements make SDRAM four to six times faster than regular DRAM.

Currently, SDRAM is available only on 168-pin DIMMs, so many people think that every time they see a 168-pin DIMM it's SDRAM. This is wrong. 168-pin DIMMs can also be regular DRAM, although that is pretty rare.

SDRAM is always a DIMM, but a DIMM isn't always SDRAM.

In order to take advantage of SDRAM, you must have a system that is designed to use it. Chances are that if you have a system with a slot for 168-pin DIMMs, your system can handle SDRAM. Since SDRAM is tied to the system clock, it doesn't have an access speed; it has a clock speed just like a CPU. There are four clock speeds that are commonly found: 66, 75, 83, and 100 MHz. These speeds are marked on the DIMM. You need to get a clock speed that is faster or equal to the motherboard speed. If you have a 66-MHz Pentium 200, for example, 66-MHz SDRAM would be fine.

Although most motherboards still run at 66 MHz or less, those times are changing. I always get 83- or 100-MHz SDRAM not because I need it today, but because I want some RAM that will last for a while.

A lot of people say that SDRAM provides little speed improvement over regular/EDO DRAM. That is true. However, both FPM and EDO have a lot of trouble running on motherboards faster than 66 MHz, and SDRAM can easily handle speeds up to 100 MHz. Get SDRAM.

ECC

ECC (error correction code) DRAM is becoming very popular in higher-end systems. ECC is a major advancement in error checking on DRAM. As mentioned earlier, DRAM rarely goes bad anymore, but it is still prone to occasional "hiccups" that can cause data loss while not destroying hardware. Parity is virtually useless for these types of occasional problems, but ECC is excellent at detecting problems in RAM and *fixing most of them on the fly*. ECC DRAM can be in any form, although it is most common as 168-pin DIMMs. In order to take advantage of ECC RAM, you need a motherboard that is designed to use ECC. Check you motherboard book. You will rarely see ECC RAM in the standard home or office system.

Working with RAM

All DRAM chips are extremely sensitive to static, so be extremely cautious when working with DRAM. When I install DRAM, I always use an anti-static wrist pad, available at any electronics store. Always handle SIMMs and DIMMs like a piece of film, keeping you fingers on the edges. There is no worse feeling than destroying a 16MB DIMM chip because of static discharge.

A Word on Speed

There is often a temptation to mix speeds of DRAM in the same system and there are some situations where you can get away with mixing speeds on a system, but the safest, easiest rule is to always use the speed of DRAM specified in the motherboard book and to make sure that every piece of DRAM is that speed! Unacceptable mixing of DRAM speeds will almost always manifest itself in the system locking up every few seconds to every few minutes. You might also get some data corruption, so don't do your income tax on a machine with mixed DRAM speeds until the system has proven itself to be stable for a few days. The important thing to note here is that you won't break anything, other than possibly data, by experimenting.

Okay, enough disclaimers. First, you can use RAM that is faster than what the motherboard specifies. For example, if the system needs 70-ns DRAM, you can put in 60-ns DRAM and it will work fine. Faster DRAM is not going to make the systems run any faster, however, so don't look for any system improvement.

You can usually get away with putting one speed of DRAM in one bank and another speed in another bank, as long as all the speeds are as fast or faster than the speed specified by the motherboard. Don't bother trying to put different-speed DRAMs in the same bank. Yes, it works once in a while, but it's too chancy. I avoid it.

A Word on Banks

Although banks are generally straightforward and rarely cause problems, you need to be aware of a few situations that might cause trouble. All systems number their banks, usually starting with the number 0. Some systems require you to populate bank 0 before you populate any other bank. Most systems don't care. So if you install some RAM and the system doesn't boot up, always try the RAM in another bank to be sure that your system isn't "bank-sensitive."

Not all banks take all sizes of DRAM. For example, I have some older Pentium motherboards that take 72-pin SIMMs, but won't use any SIMMs bigger than 4 × 32. So the biggest DRAM sticks I can put in there are 16 megabytes. There's no way around it.

Watch out for interleaved banks. It is usually a safe assumption that the connectors are grouped together by banks. In a Pentium system with four rows of 72-pin SIMMs, the first two rows are usually one bank and the second two rows are another. However, you might occasionally run into a system where the banks are "interleaved." Using the same example, the first and third rows are one bank while the second and fourth rows are the other bank.

Last, be aware that not everybody banks according the "magic banking formula." Many Pentium systems will run with just one 72-pin SIMM. In many of these systems you will end up with a serious system slowdown, however; so on the rare occasion where I stumble onto one of these systems, I still bank the way I know to be correct.

Installing SIMMs

All SIMMs have a notch on one side that prevents them from being installed improperly. When installing SIMMs, be sure to insert the SIMMs at the angle shown in Figure 4.50. When I install SIMMs, I visualize the same motion as a chip shot in golf. If you're not a golfer, visualize scooping ice cream out of a container.

After the SIMM is securely seated into the slot, push it upright until the holding clamps on either side are secured. Make sure that the holes on either side show the small retaining tabs coming through (Figure 4.51). If the SIMM does not insert relatively easily, it's probably backwards. Also, most SIMMs will stand up vertically when properly installed, so if it isn't vertical, it's probably backwards.

Take advantage of installing more than one SIMM to see how they line up across their tops. An improperly installed SIMM will almost always give itself away by not having a nice uniform appearance across the top, as compared to the other SIMMs (Figure 4.52).

Installing DIMMs

DIMMs are far easier to install than SIMMs. A good hard push down is usually all you need to ensure a solid connection. Make sure that the DIMM snaps into position to show it is completely seated. You will also notice that the two side tabs will move in to reflect a tight connection (Figure 4.53).

Figure 4.50
Inserting a SIMM

Figure 4.51
SIMM not all the way in

Figure 4.52 Improperly inserted SIMM

Figure 4.53 Inserting a DIMM

CMOS

After the SIMMs are installed, turn on the PC. If the DRAM is installed correctly, you will notice that the RAM count on the PC will reflect the new value. If the RAM value stays the same, you probably have a disabled bank or the SIMM is not properly installed. Check the motherboard book to see if a jumper needs to be changed to turn it on. If the computer does not boot and there is nothing on the screen, you probably have not installed all the RAM sticks correctly. Usually a good second look is all you need to see if that's the problem.

Once the RAM is installed and the RAM count reflects the new value, your CMOS needs to be updated to show the new amount of RAM installed. On most machines, this is done automatically. However, if your machine says something like "CMOS memory mismatch, Press F1 to continue," you'll have to use your CMOS setup program, then simply save and exit. Your CMOS will be reset. Reboot again and your RAM is installed. (See CMOS.)

All RAM counts listed when your PC is booting are based on units of 1024 bytes (1K). So 4MB will show as 4096, 8MB as 8192, 16MB as 16384, etc., most RAM counts will stop before they get to the value you expect, however. For example, a machine with 8MB might count to only 7808. This is acceptable; some of your memory is simply "skipped" during the count, but it's all there.

Troubleshooting RAM

Today's DRAM chips are tough—the MTBF (mean time between failure) rate for 16MB of RAM in a post-1995 computer is something like 30 to 35 years! The overwhelming majority of errors that look like bad RAM are usually something else.

Bad RAM chips manifest themselves in only two ways: parity errors and lockups/page faults. Parity errors are simply errors that the MCC detects from the parity chips (if you have them). These errors are reported by the operating system if you are using DOS, OS/2, or Windows 95—Windows will intercept the error and report it in a window. They look something like "Parity error at *xxxx:xxxx*," where *xxxx:xxxx* is a hexadecimal value. If you get an error like this, write down the value! The secret to parity errors is that they always happen at the same place. If you get another parity error and it shows a different value, then it's a bogus error. If the error shows up at the same place every time, you probably have a bad SIMM chip. My favorite SIMM tester is Troubleshooter by Forefront (813-724-8994). Although Troubleshooter does a lot of things other than just checking RAM, the RAM checker is all I use. My second choice would be Norton Diagnostics, part of Norton Utilities.

There is another product that's for only the most serious users: QAPlus/FE from Diagsoft (813-207-7000). The RAM testing functions of QAPlus work best if you use them on your RAM before something goes wrong. It will literally draw a picture of your RAM and give you a snapshot of your memory layout. Then when you use the RAM tester, it will tell you which SIMM is bad!

If you are using DOS 6.20 or higher, you already have a very good RAM checker in HIMEM.SYS. HIMEM.SYS by default checks all the RAM in your system every time it runs. It's accurate, but if it finds bad RAM, all it will say is that you have "unreliable" memory. Then you're reduced to finding the bad SIMM with the "replace and pray" method—which is opening the system case and replacing each SIMM, one at a time, with a known good replacement SIMM. (You've got one of those lying around, don't you?) This is certainly a valid method for troubleshooting, but it requires you to open the case and have an extra SIMM.

If you get parity errors that are intermittent, it's almost certainly a bad power supply.

The last place that bad RAM tends to manifest itself is within Windows. Whenever Windows 3.1 gives a "general protection fault" or Windows 95 gives a "page fault," they always provide a long string of hexadecimal digits, for example "KRNL386 caused a page fault at 03F2:25A003BC." When I get these, I document that crazy string of letters and numbers. If I keep getting the same error at the same value, there is a good chance that I have a bad RAM chip. I then again use the "replace and pray" method to determine which DRAM stick is the bad one.

CHAPTER 5

Motherboards and BIOS

In this chapter, you will:

- Understand the function of BIOS.
- See different types of BIOS.
- Examine various CMOS setups.
- Learn to properly configure and maintain CMOS.

In Chapter 2, you saw how the address bus and external data bus connect RAM to the CPU in order to run programs and transfer data. However, the computer needs more than just a CPU and RAM. It needs input devices such as keyboards and mice to accept input from users. The computer needs output devices like monitors and sound cards to display the current state of the programs being run. A computer also needs permanent storage devices, such as floppy drives and hard drives, in which to store data when you turn off the computer. The external data bus joins together all of these parts of the computer (Figure 5.1).

The external data bus is not the only bus that connects all the parts of the PC. The address bus is also connected to the different parts of the PC (Figure 5.2). Knowing this, two big questions come to mind. The first is, "Where are these buses, and how are they physically organized?" The second question is, "How do these wires allow communication between the CPU and the different components of the PC?" In this chapter, I will answer these questions through an examination of BIOS and motherboards. Let's begin with BIOS.

Figure 5.1 Everything is connected to the EDB

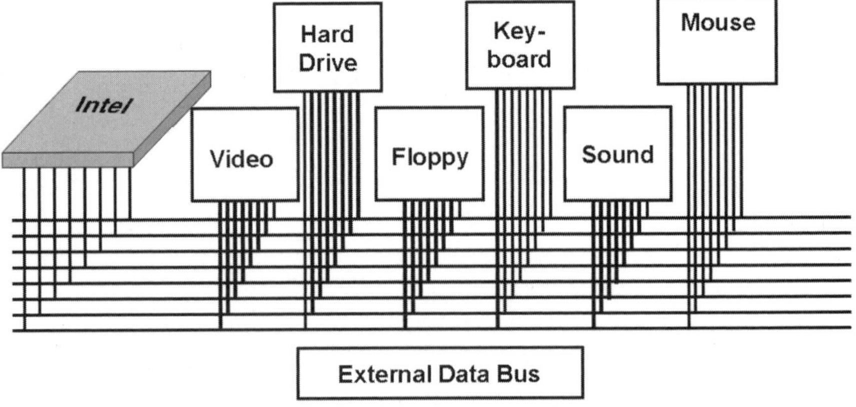

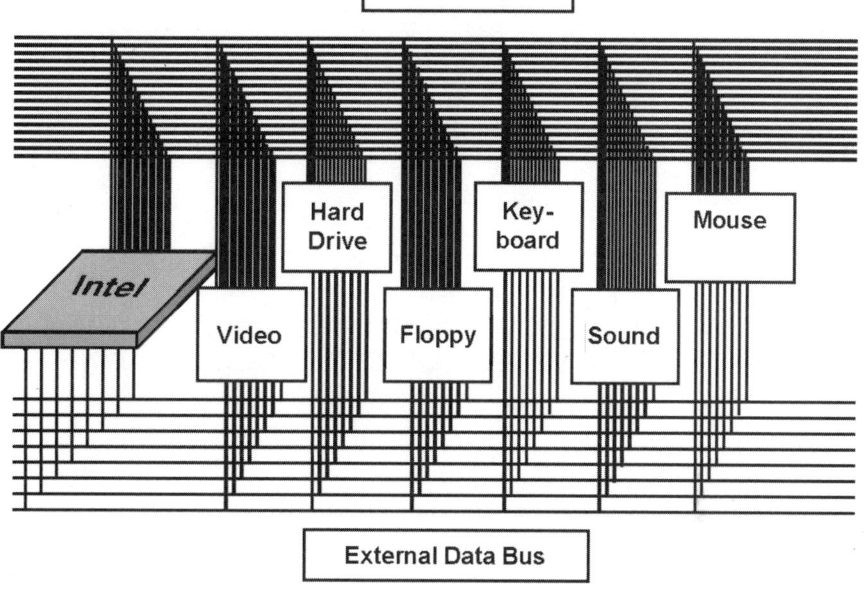

Figure 5.2
Everything is also connected to the address bus

BIOS

So far, you understand how programs can be written to accomplish simple work like adding 2 to 3. Now you see that all these devices are attached to the CPU. How is data placed on the screen? How does the hard drive know to retrieve a file? How does the computer know the mouse is being moved? The buses are used to communicate with all these devices.

Let's use the keyboard as an example. The keyboard connects to the external data bus via a special chip known as the *keyboard controller*. An early keyboard controller was the Intel 8042 (Figure 5.3). The 8042 has long since been obsolesced by more advanced keyboard controllers, but the name stuck. All keyboard controllers are generally called "an 8042." Although the 8042 and the CPU exchange data through the external data bus, they need some type of programming to allow them to speak to each other.

Every time you press a key, a scanning chip in the keyboard notices which key has been pressed. Then the scanner sends a coded pattern of ones and zeros to the 8042 chip, called the *scan code*. Every key on your keyboard has a unique scan code. The 8042 chip stores the scan code in its own memory registers.

How does the CPU get the scan code out of the 8042? (See Figure 5.4.) Well, the 8042 chip accepts commands exactly like the 8088 CPU. Remem-

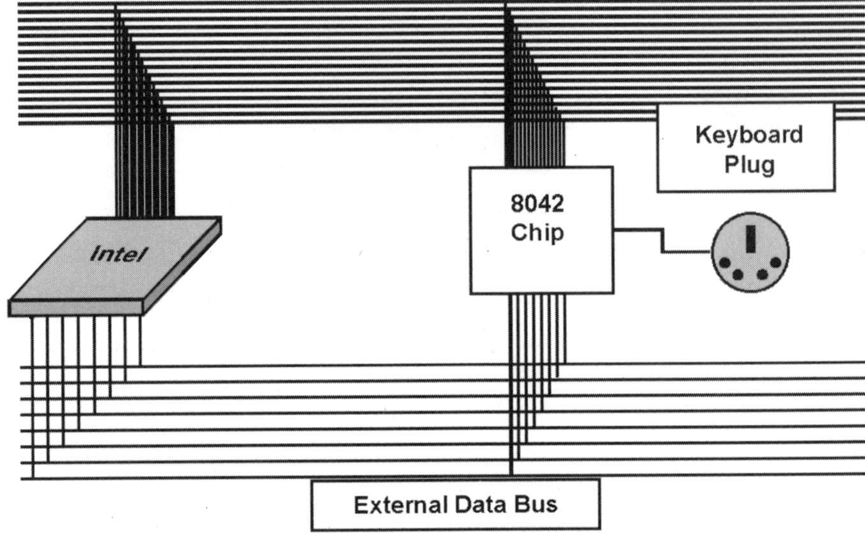

Figure 5.3
The 8042 chip

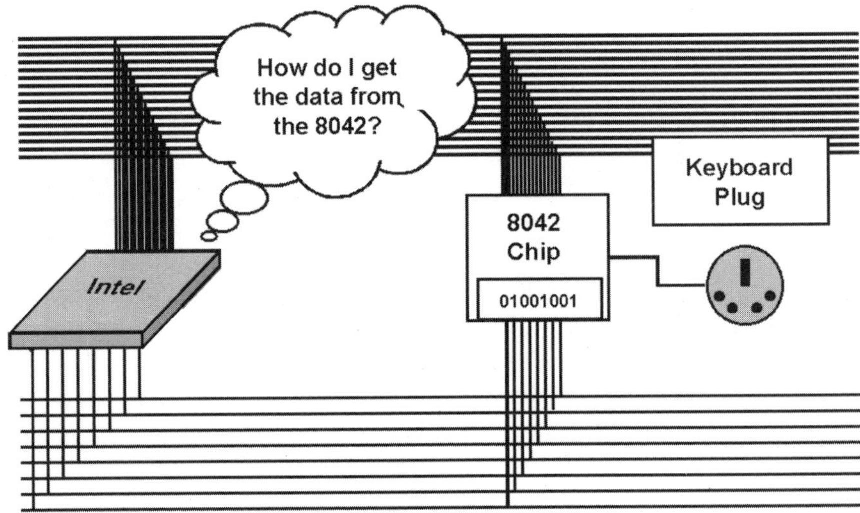

Figure 5.4
How does the CPU communicate with the 8042?

ber when you added 2 to 3 with the 8088? Remember the command that told the 8088 to provide the value stored in the AX register and put it on the external data bus? The 8042 has its own code book, much simpler than the CPU but conceptually the same. In order to determine the scan code stored inside the 8042, you need to know the command (or series of commands) to make the 8042 put the scan code of the letter on the external data bus so the CPU can read it.

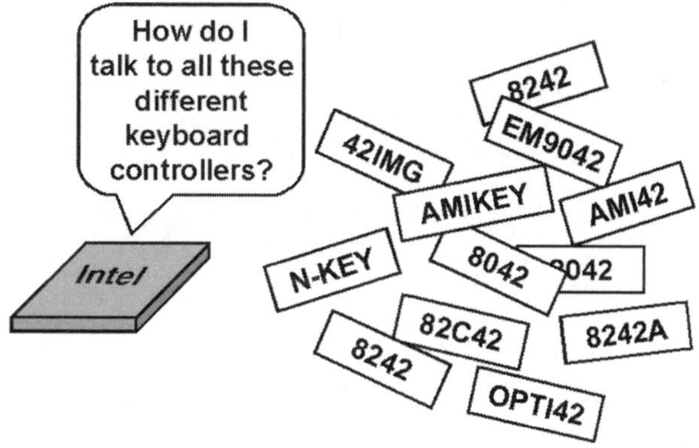

Figure 5.5
So many different keyboard controllers

You need a program to allow the CPU to talk to the 8042, which creates two major issues. First, there is the problem of different 8042 chips (Figure 5.5). You see, the original 8042 chip, designed in 1978, has been redesigned and improved upon many times over the years, and with each redesign the code book of the 8042 has been expanded and/or changed. Second, where is this program stored? You can't store the program on a hard or floppy drive. As you will see later in this chapter, the keyboard needs to be installed and working before you can install a storage device.

So how do you handle these issues? There are lots of different 8042 chips out there, but your motherboard will have a particular 8042 chip soldered on it. You're not going to be changing the 8042 chip, so what you need to do is put the program that knows how to talk to the specific 8042 chip *on the motherboard with the 8042 chip*. Now, where is this program stored? On DRAM? No, it would be erased every time the computer was turned off. You need some type of program storage device that is *permanent* and doesn't depend on other peripherals in order to work.

The program is stored on a special type of device called a ROM (read-only memory) chip. ROM chips can store programs exactly like RAM chips, with two major differences. First, ROM chips are nonvolatile, meaning that the program(s) stored on ROM aren't erased, even when the computer is turned off. Second, ROM chips are read-only, meaning that once the program(s) are stored, they can't be changed. See Figure 5.6.

When the CPU wants to talk to the 8042, it goes to the ROM chip to access the proper program. Understand that there are *many* programs on the ROM chip. For example, more than one program needs to talk to the 8042. The program described in the previous paragraph accesses the scan code, but there are other programs for procedures such as changing the typematic buffer rate (when you hold down a key and the letter is repeated). There are programs on the ROM chip to talk to the keyboard (via the

Figure 5.6
Typical ROM BIOS

8042), the floppy drive(s), the hard drive(s), the monitor, and a few other devices on your computer. So clearly there is not just one program on that ROM chip! To talk to all that basic hardware requires hundreds of little programs (2 to 30 lines of code each). These hundreds of little programs stored on the ROM chip are called, collectively, the *BIOS* (basic input/output services). Each tiny program is called a *service*. See Figure 5.7.

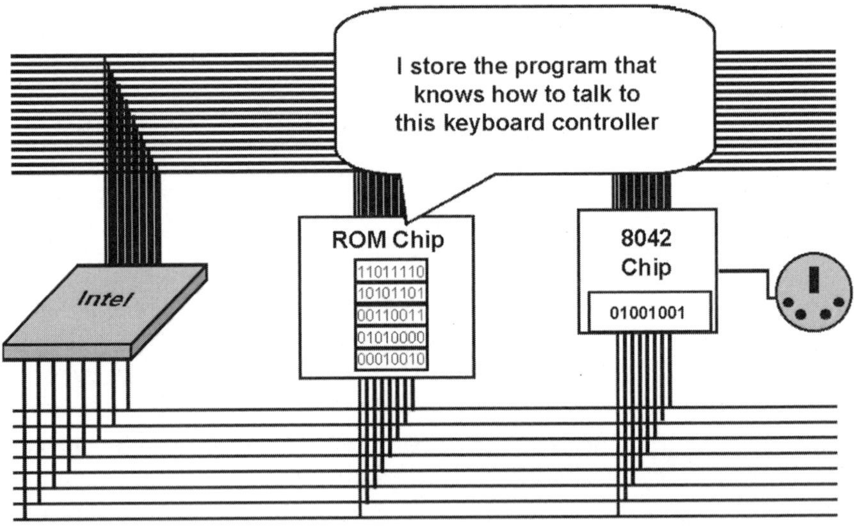

Figure 5.7
Function of the ROM chip

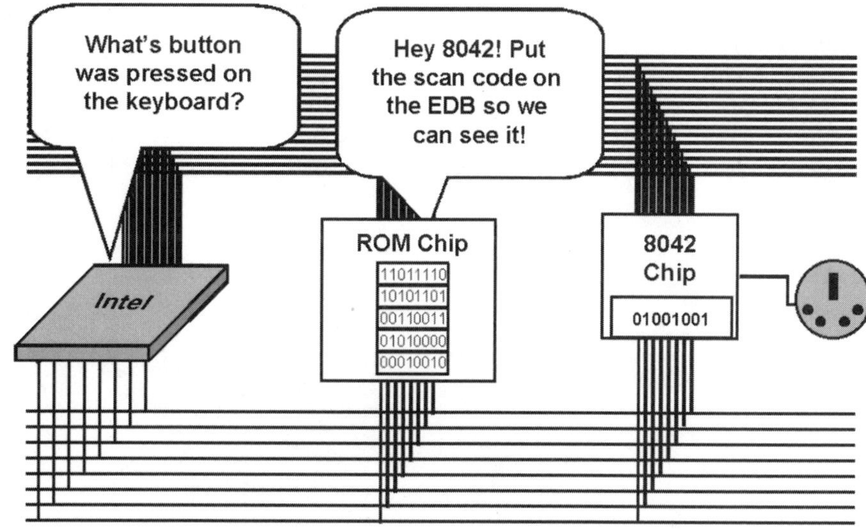

Figure 5.8 CPU running BIOS routine

Please say the following sentence out loud: "BIOS is software." BIOS is hundreds of little programs designed to talk to the most basic parts of your computer. The programs are stored on a ROM chip because it can hold the programs even when you turn off the computer (Figure 5.8). Although there is some variance, most ROM chips store around 65,536 lines of BIOS programming.

BIOS and Its Relation to Memory Addressing

BIOS is software, right? So how does the CPU run software? Well, if the software is in RAM, the address bus specifies which byte of RAM to run. On the original 8088 chip, the address bus consisted of 20 wires. These 20 wires could be turned on and off in 1,048,576 (1MB) different combinations, and each combination was like the "phone number" for every byte of RAM. Turning wires on and off on the address bus tells the memory controller chip which byte of RAM to access. However, now your ROM chip is loaded with 65,536 bytes of BIOS code. How is the correct code accessed? The same way RAM is accessed—through the address bus.

All the patterns generated by the address bus are called the *address space*. A good analogy would be your local phone company. In the 713 area code, the phone numbers from 713-000-0000 to 713-999-9999 are all the numbers that our phones can generate, right? That's exactly 10,000,000 different telephone numbers. You could say that the address space of the 713 area code is 10,000,000. The address space for an 8088 processor is 1,048,576.

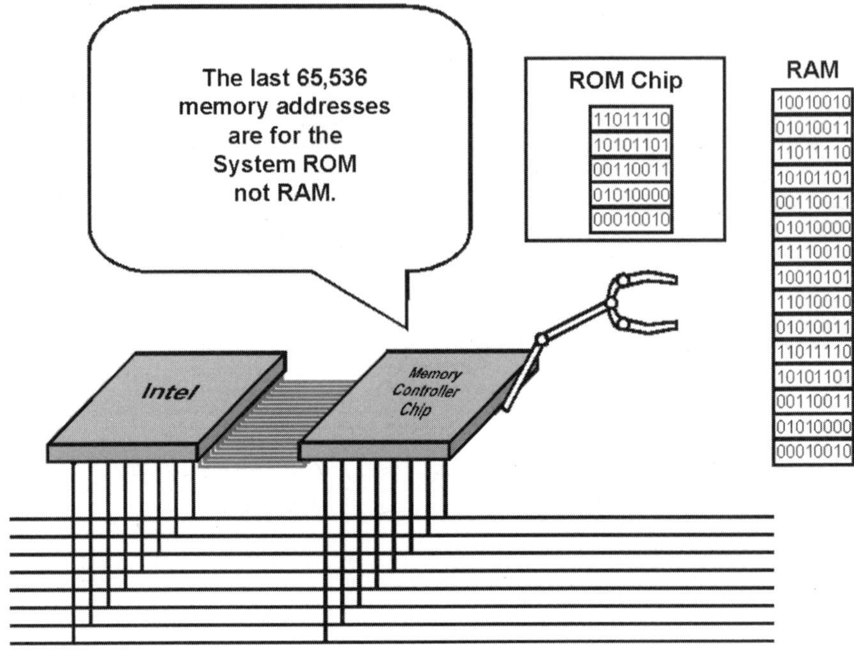

Figure 5.9 Reserving address space for ROM

When IBM invented the IBM PC, they declared that the last 65,536 patterns on the address bus would be "reserved" for the BIOS on the ROM chip (Figure 5.9). That means that you could not add 1MB of RAM to a computer with an 8088 chip. At this point it looks as if the most RAM you could add is about 1MB minus 65,536 bytes. Using the telephone analogy, it would like the phone company keeping all the phone numbers from 777-7777 up to 999-9999 for its own use.

The CPU must be able to communicate with every piece of hardware in your computer. You have to be able to tell the sound card to play a song, or tell the video card to put graphics on the monitor. There must be some kind of software to talk to all the hardware of your computer.

All hardware needs BIOS.

The BIOS stored on the ROM chip attached to the motherboard is officially known as the *system BIOS*. The reason the "on-board" BIOS is called the system BIOS is to differentiate it from other forms of BIOS that might be on the computer.

When IBM designed the original IBM PC back in 1981, they knew that other devices would be invented in the future that would need BIOS support. IBM did not want to get into a game where every time you added a device, you had to replace the system ROM, so they decided the easiest way to handle the problem was to have devices with their own ROM chip. In the original 8088, therefore, IBM decided to reserve 384K out of the 1024K (1MB) of memory addresses for ROM. That leaves 640K of memory addresses for RAM.

What if you have a 286, 386, 486, or Pentium? They have much larger address buses, as big as 32 wires, which means they can put a lot more RAM on their PCs. However, they must still reserve the last 384K of the first megabyte of memory space for their BIOS to be backwardly compatible to the 8088. I will go into this concept in more detail later in the book.

The Many Faces of BIOS

A computer's hardware breaks down into three groups. The first group is hardware that is common, is necessary, and never changes. The BIOS for these devices is stored on the system BIOS ROM chip. An example of this type of device would be the keyboard. I'll call this the "core group." The second group is hardware that is also common and necessary, but that might change from time to time. This group includes RAM (you can add RAM), hard drives (you can add a larger or a second hard drive), and floppy drives (same as hard drives). The BIOS for these devices is also stored on the system BIOS chip. This second group of hardware requires BIOS information that changes, so it must be stored on a separate, special RAM chip called a *CMOS* (complementary metal-oxide semiconductor) *chip*. I'll call this group of devices the "CMOS group." The last group is composed of noncore devices such as mice, sound cards, tape backup units, and CD-ROM drives. I'll call this the "everything else group."

Core Group: The System ROM

You have seen an example of a core device with the keyboard/8042 chip. Other examples of core devices are:

- Parallel ports
- Serial ports
- Speaker
- Support chips

Look at the ROM chip a little more closely. The ROM chip, which stores the system BIOS, resides on the motherboard. ROM chips are distinctive in that they are in DIPP packages and almost always have a label on them.

Although you can buy ROM chips that can store megabytes of programming, the ROM chips on the majority of IBM-compatible PCs store around 64K of programming. Because they are nonvolatile, ROM chips are the best way to store BIOS. *Nonvolatile* means that the chip does not need electricity to store programs. You can turn off the computer on Friday and back on the following Monday, and the BIOS programs will still be there. It is easy to see the importance of nonvolatility. The downside to ROM is that you cannot change the BIOS routines once they are stored on the chip. ROM is also very slow compared to other types of memory, like DRAM.

Fortunately, the system BIOS is rarely dealt with by the majority of technicians. Like a good hot-water heater, the system BIOS almost never fails. It works year after year, quietly and efficiently doing its work in the background. However, like a good hot-water heater, on those rare occasions when it does break, the result can be catastrophic. I will discuss the failure of system BIOS later in this chapter.

Once again—do not confuse ROM and BIOS! BIOS is *software*. ROM is the hardware chips where BIOS is stored.

CMOS Group: The Changeable Ones

Some BIOS routines talk to other common devices that are more likely to change. These changeable hardware devices include things such as:

- RAM
- Hard drives
- Floppy drives
- Video

The BIOS routines for these devices are also stored on the ROM chip. However, if you change one of these items, such as upgrading a hard drive or adding a second hard drive, certain parameters must be changed to reflect the modifications to the hardware. You cannot change the BIOS routines on the ROM, so you need another type of storage chip that can be modified to reflect these changes. This changeable chip is called the CMOS (complementary metal-oxide semiconductor) chip. In the PC world, CMOS chips do not store programs; they store only data that is read by BIOS to complete the programs needed to talk to changeable hardware. The CMOS chip also acts as a clock to keep the date and time.

At this point, don't worry about what parameters are stored on the CMOS chip; I will go into these parameters in minute detail when discussing the different types of hardware. For now, simply appreciate that there is a system BIOS chip and a CMOS chip in your computer (Figure 5.10).

Figure 5.10
Typical CMOS chip

Although CMOS chips can store up to 64K of data, the PC usually needs only a very small amount—about 128 bytes—to store all the necessary information on the changeable hardware. If the data referencing a particular piece of hardware stored on the CMOS is different from the actual hardware, the computer will not be able to access that particular piece of hardware. It is crucial that this information be correct. If you change any of the previously mentioned hardware, you must update the CMOS to reflect those changes. So you will need to know how to change the data on the CMOS chip.

UPDATING CMOS: THE SETUP PROGRAM Since the CMOS must be changed when you make certain hardware changes, you need to be able to access and update the data on the CMOS chip. This is the function of the CMOS setup program. CMOS setup is a special program that allows you to make changes on the CMOS chip. It is stored on the system ROM. There are many ways to start the CMOS setup program, depending on the brand of BIOS you have on your computer. When you fire up your computer in the morning, the first thing you will likely see is the BIOS information, for example:

```
AMIBIOS (C) 1998 American Megatrends Inc.
Press <DEL> if you want to run setup
(C) American Megatrends Inc.,
40-0100-006259-00101111-060692-SYMP-F
```

Or maybe something like this:

```
Phoenix BIOS(TM) Pentium Version 1.03 (2.25B)
Copyright (C) 1985-1998 Phoenix Technologies Ltd.
All Rights Reserved
```

Who or what is American Megatrends, and who or what is Phoenix Technologies? These are brand names of BIOS companies. They write BIOS and sell them to computer manufacturers. In the bad old days, the days of XTs and 286s, when a company made a motherboard they usually hired a few programmers to write the BIOS. In today's world, almost nobody writes their own BIOS. Instead, they buy their BIOS from third-party BIOS makers like American Megatrends and Phoenix Technologies. Although there are about ten different companies that write BIOS, three big companies control 99 percent of the BIOS business: American Megatrends (AMI), Award Software (Award), and Phoenix Technologies (Phoenix). AMI, Award, and Phoenix pretty much control the entire BIOS market these days, and they each have different ways to access the CMOS setup program.

For AMI and Award, press the Delete key when the machine first begins to boot. For Phoenix, press Ctrl-Alt-Esc. Watch your screen as your computer boots up. Most BIOS manufacturers will tell you how to access the CMOS setup right on the screen, for example:

```
Award Modular BIOS v4.51PG, An Energy Star Ally
Copyright (C) 1984-97, Award Software, Inc.
Intel 430VX CHIPS, AUTO CPU VOLTAGE DETECT START Ver. 2.3
Award Plug and Play BIOS Extension v1.0A
Copyright (C) 1996, Award Software, Inc.
Press DEL to enter Setup
12/30/96 - i430VX - 8663-2A59GG0BC-00
```

Note that you simply press the Delete key to access the CMOS setup. Motherboard manufacturers can change the key combinations to access the CMOS setup. If these do not work, try one of the following key combinations: Ctrl-Alt-Ins, Ctrl-A, Ctrl-S, Ctrl-F1, or F10.

AMI, Award, and Phoenix are not the only BIOS makers in the world. Watch your computer when it boots to determine your manufacturer. You can also take the cover off your PC and see whose name is on the system ROM chip. Read your motherboard book to determine the process to access the CMOS setup program.

If you are not sure how to access your CMOS setup, there are a number of good third-party utilities to let you edit your CMOS. Try Touchstone's Checkit Pro, available at almost any software store. Another way is to reboot the PC and hold down several keys. That will often cause an error and prompt you with something like:

```
Keyboard Error
Press F1 to enter Setup
```

You can often generate the same error by simply unplugging the keyboard. After you get the error, plug the keyboard back in and press whatever key the machine tells you to press.

A QUICK TOUR THROUGH CMOS SETUP (AWARD) Every maker of BIOS has a different CMOS setup program, but don't let the different screens confuse you! They all say basically the same thing; you just have to be comfortable poking around. The only secret is to not save anything unless you know it is right. Due to its popularity, for your first exposure to CMOS we'll concentrate on Award. When you boot a machine with Award BIOS, you will see something like this:

```
Award Modular BIOS v4.51PG, An Energy Star Ally
Copyright (C) 1984-97, Award Software, Inc.
Intel 430VX Chips, Auto CPU Voltage Detect Start - Ver. 2.3

Award Plug and Play BIOS Extension v1.0A
Copyright (C) 1996, Award Software, Inc.

Press DEL to enter Setup
1/30/98 - i430LX - 8663-2A59GG0BC-00
```

Press the Delete key and the screen in Figure 5.11 will appear. You are now in the CMOS setup program. This program is stored on the ROM chip, but all it does is edit the data on the CMOS chip. Although I will describe the contents of the CMOS setup program, concentrate on the most basic part, the standard CMOS setup. Select Standard CMOS Setup, and the standard CMOS screen will appear (see Figure 5.12). Here you can change floppy drive, hard drive, and date/time settings. You will learn how to properly set up the CMOS for these devices in later chapters.

Figure 5.11
CMOS screen

```
ROM PCI/ISA BIOS (2A69HQ1A)
CMOS SETUP UTILITY
AWARD SOFTWARE, INC.

STANDARD CMOS SETUP          INTEGRATED PERIPHERALS
BIOS FEATURES SETUP          SUPERVISOR PASSWORD
CHIPSET FEATURES SETUP       USER PASSWORD
POWER MANAGEMENT SETUP       IDE HDD AUTO DETECTION
PNP/PCI CONFIGURATION        HDD LOW LEVEL FORMAT
LOAD BIOS DEFAULTS           SAVE & EXIT SETUP
LOAD SETUP DEFAULTS          EXIT WITHOUT SAVING

Esc : Quit                   ↑ ↓ → ←    : Select Item
F10 : Save & Exit Setup      (Shift)F2 : Change Color
```

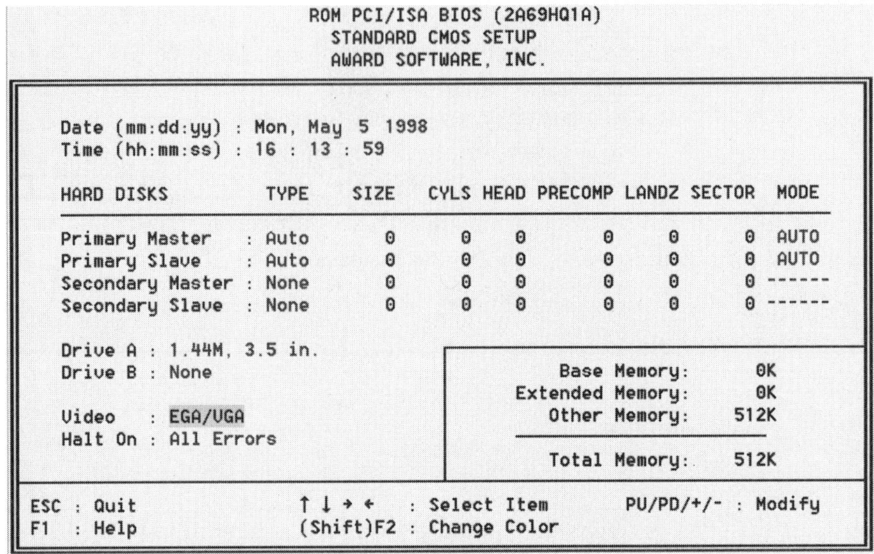

Figure 5.12 Typical standard CMOS screen

The first BIOS was nothing more than a standard CMOS setup. Today, virtually all computers have many extra CMOS settings. They control items such as memory management, password and booting options, diagnostic and error handling, and power management. At this point, my goal is only for you to be aware of the *existence* of CMOS setup and know how to access the CMOS setup on a PC. As you understand more and more of the computer, we will return to CMOS many times to properly set up whatever device is being discussed.

Award has virtually cornered the desktop PC BIOS market with its Award Modular BIOS. You will know if you have Award BIOS when you run the CMOS setup program. If you see a screen like the one displayed in Figure 5.11, you have the Award Modular BIOS. Because of the overwhelming popularity of this brand of BIOS, it deserves special attention.

Motherboard makers buy a basic BIOS from Award and can add options based on the needs of the motherboard. This can cause problems, as seemingly identical CMOS setups can be extremely different. Options that show up on one computer might be missing from another.

PHOENIX BIOS Phoenix BIOS is the "Mercedes Benz" of BIOSes (Figure 5.13). Phoenix creates a custom BIOS for optimal use in the machine for which it is designed. As a result, Phoenix BIOSes have fewer options. You will usually see Phoenix BIOSes in machines with proprietary motherboards, such as laptops.

AMI BIOS American Megatrends competes directly with Award, providing highly flexible BIOSes (Figure 5.14). AMI was the most used BIOS for many years until Award became more predominant, starting around 1994 to 1995. Although AMI no longer holds the virtual monopoly it once had in BIOSes, it is still quite popular.

Figure 5.13
Phoenix BIOS

```
        PhoenixBIOS Setup - Copyright 1992-97 Phoenix Technologies Ltd.
    Main    Advanced    Security    Power    Exit

                                                       Item Specific Help
    System Time:                    [16:19:20]
    System Date:                    [03/02/1994]

    Legacy Diskette A:              [1.2 MB, 5¼"]      <Tab>, <Shift-Tab>, or
    Legacy Diskette B:              [Not Installed]    <Enter> selects field.

  ▶ Primary Master:                 C:  121 MB
  ▶ Primary Slave:                  None
  ▶ Secondary Master:               None
  ▶ Secondary Slave:                None

  ▶ Memory Cache
  ▶ System Shadow                   [Enabled]
  ▶ Video Shadow                    [Enabled]

    System Memory:                     640 KB
    Extended Memory:                  1024 KB

  F1  Help    ↑↓ Select Item    -/+   Change Values        F9  Setup Defaults
  ESC Exit    ↔ Select Menu     Enter Select ▶ Sub-Menu    F10 Save and Exit
```

Figure 5.14
AMI BIOS

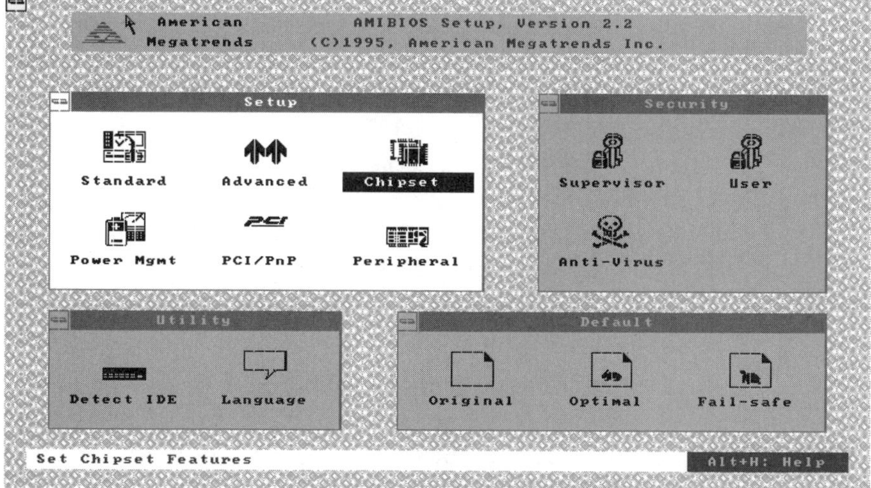

CARE AND FEEDING OF YOUR CMOS Losing CMOS information is a common problem. If the information on the CMOS chips is erased, the computer will not be able to boot up and/or you will get nasty looking errors. Unfortunately, it is easy to lose CMOS information. Some of the more common reasons for losing CMOS data are:

- The on-board battery runs out
- Pulling and inserting cards
- Touching the motherboard
- Dropping something on the motherboard
- Dirt on the motherboard
- Faulty power supplies
- Electrical surges

Losing the CMOS just happens, and is accepted as "one of those things" in the world of computing. The errors that point to lost CMOS information usually take place while the computer is booting. Watch for errors like:

- CMOS configuration mismatch
- CMOS date/time not set
- No boot device available
- CMOS battery state low

Although these errors sometimes point to other problems, when they show up at boot, the first place to check is the CMOS settings. In order to check the CMOS settings, you need to have all of your CMOS settings memorized or you need to compare the current CMOS settings to a backup copy. Since it is impossible to prevent, the correct course of action is to prepare for losing the CMOS by keeping backups. The best way to do this is to use the CMOS save and restore program, CMOSSAVE, found on the accompanying CD-ROM.

CMOSSAVE is stored in ZIP format as CMOS1.ZIP.

RUNNING CMOSSAVE Run CMOSSAVE by inserting a blank diskette into the A: drive and typing:

```
CMOSSAVE a:filename
```

The *filename* is anything you want, preferably something that describes the computer whose CMOS is being saved. The CMOS information for hundreds of computers can be placed on one diskette. You can lose your CMOS information by inserting or removing cards at an angle, by not using a good surge suppressor, or by letting the computer get dirty. So be careful.

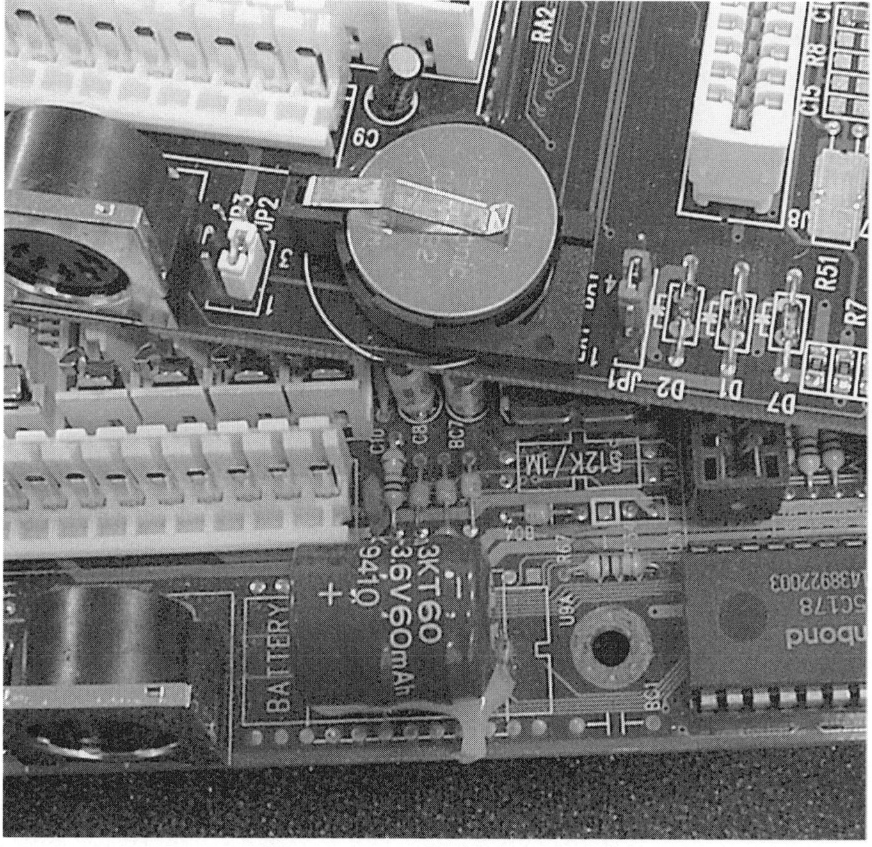

Figure 5.15
Typical batteries

THE BATTERY The beauty of CMOS chips is that the data stored on them can be changed. The trade-off for this ability is that the CMOS chip needs a trickle voltage whether the computer is turned on or not. To provide the CMOS with power when the computer is turned off, all motherboards come with a battery (see Figure 5.15). These batteries are mounted in two ways: on-board and external. On-board batteries are mounted directly to the motherboard, where external batteries are not.

Many PCs today no longer need a battery as the CMOS chip itself has enough battery power to keep itself running. The voltage for this battery is approximately 3.6 or 6 volts, depending on whether you have a low-power (3.3 volts) or standard (5 volts) motherboard. Most low-power motherboards will work with either voltage, but you should always check the motherboard documentation to verify the correct voltage. On-board batteries are usually rechargeable (NiCd) or lithium metal-hydride (LiMH), and will last for an average of five to seven years. External batteries (Figure 5.16) are usually nonrechargeable AA alkaline batteries, and tend to last for two to four years.

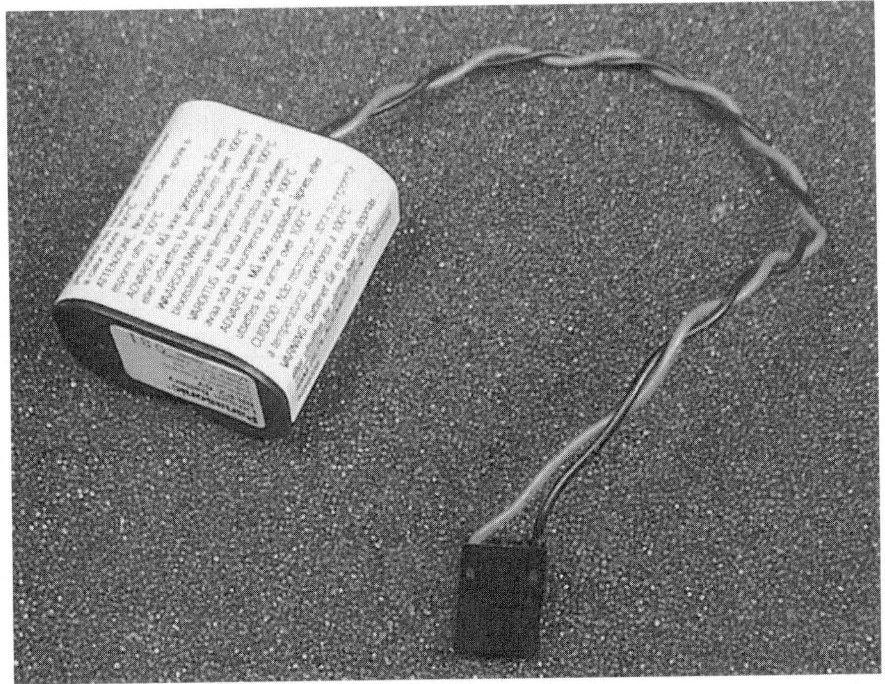

Figure 5.16
External battery pack

It's usually pretty clear when the battery needs to be replaced. The first clue is that the CMOS clock begins to slow down. Go to the C:\> prompt and type "time." If you notice that you are losing time, then you need to change the battery. However, remember that if you are on a DOS machine (this includes Windows 95), DOS uses the CMOS clock to get the date only on boot. Once the PC is running, DOS uses the memory refresh timer on the memory controller to keep time. This is fine, except that the refresh timer does not do seconds very well and, as a result, you will lose one or two seconds a day. Many people never turn off their computers, so their clocks lose time. Do not confuse this with a bad battery. If you reboot, the computer will update itself from the CMOS and show the correct time. If the CMOS battery is low, it will still be incorrect.

When the CMOS battery really dies, the effect is painfully clear. The scenario is something like this: you get lost CMOS errors as previously discussed, so you reconfigure the CMOS settings. You reboot and the errors return. It's definitely time to change the battery. Sometimes the PC will hold the CMOS information during the week, but over the weekend, when the PC is off for two days, the CMOS data will be lost. Do not let these seemingly "intermittent" problems fool you. Anytime a PC loses its CMOS information more than once in a week, replace the battery immediately just to eliminate it as a possible problem.

The CMOS chip contains a capacitor that allows you to replace the battery without losing data. For motherboards with welded on-board batteries, a connection is usually provided to add an external battery to replace a worn-out on-board one. Remember that the external battery must have the same voltage as the on-board battery you are replacing.

If you have a motherboard that doesn't have a battery, you're in luck. The latest motherboards have CMOS chips with very long-lasting batteries. These batteries virtually never go out. Unfortunately, the machines almost never have an external battery connector. I've had only one go on me and I just replaced the motherboard. Sure, you could get a new CMOS chip, but it's not worth the time or the price.

FLASH ROM Using ROM chips for the BIOS has a huge shortcoming. The problem is that you can't change the BIOS without physically removing the ROM. A few years ago, a new type of ROM chip, called *flash ROM*, was developed, and it has now become the primary type of system ROM used in PCs. Flash ROMs look exactly like regulars ROM chips; you can't tell whether you have a flash or not just by looking at the system BIOS chip. See Figure 5.17.

The major difference in flash ROM is that you can reprogram it without removing the chip! This is a major advantage for today's systems, since every time some new type of technology comes out there is invariably a need to update the BIOS to take advantage of this technology. Let's use MMX as an example. If you buy an MMX CPU, you might not be able to take full advantage of it unless your BIOS can be updated to handle the

Figure 5.17
Flash ROM and clock

new features of MMX. If you have a regular ROM, you can either physically yank out the ROM chip or buy a new motherboard. This can be a little expensive—and difficult. But with flash ROM, all you have to do is run a small DOS program combined with an "update file" to change your BIOS. Although the exact process varies from one BIOS maker to another, it usually entails booting off a floppy diskette and running a command such as:

```
AW P55T2.BIN
```

It's really that simple! Most of these utilities allow you to make a backup of your BIOS in case the update causes trouble, so always make the backup! If for some reason a flash update messes up your computer, you might end up throwing the motherboard away without a good backup.

As a rule, don't update your BIOS unless you have a strong compelling reason to do so. If it ain't broke . . .

It's actually fairly easy to determine if you have flash ROM. Peel back the little sticker on the chip, and if you see a small, round glass "window," you don't have flash ROM. If you see the number 28 or 29 in the chip's number (something like "29*xxxxx*" or "*x*28*xxxxxx*"), then you have flash ROM!

"Everything Else" Group

The last group of hardware contains "everything else." IBM could not possibly add all the necessary BIOS routines for every conceivable piece of hardware. When programmers wrote the first BIOS, network cards, mice, and sound cards did not exist. Early PC designers at IBM understood that they could not anticipate every new type of hardware, so they gave us a few ways to BYOB (Bring Your Own BIOS).

OPTION ROM The first way to BYOB is to put the BIOS on the hardware device itself. Look at a popular card, an Adaptec 2940 SCSI host adapter. There is a chip on the card that looks a lot like the ROM chip on a motherboard, because it *is* a ROM chip, and there is a BIOS on it! (See Figure 5.18.) The system BIOS does not have a clue about how to talk to this card, so the card has to bring its own BIOS with it.

DRIVERS Installing BIOS on a ROM is extremely inflexible, and is rarely done for most devices. Far more popular is adding special programs called *device drivers* to the system. All PCs have a "list" of device drivers

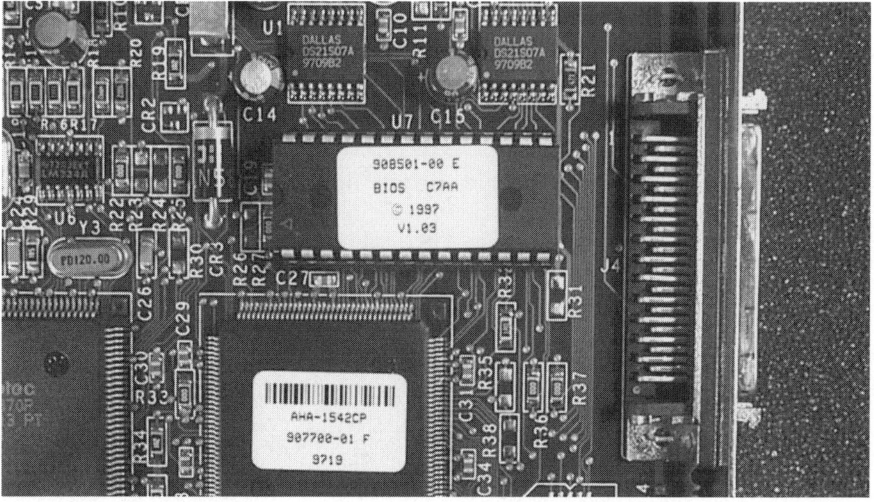

Figure 5.18
ROM on adapter

loaded into RAM every time the computer starts. This list can be one text file, many text files, or, in the case of Windows 95/98, a special database. If you're uncomfortable with the concept of text files, directories (folders), or file extensions, jump ahead to the chapter on DOS for clarification.

CONFIG.SYS The most popular way to add BIOS for DOS PCs is through a special file called CONFIG.SYS, which is a text file in the root directory of your C: drive. It can be changed with a text editor like EDIT.COM. The main (but not the only) reason CONFIG.SYS exists is for you to load extra BIOS for hardware that your system BIOS does not support. This is where the BIOS for "everything else" is initialized in DOS. BIOS routines that are initialized by CONFIG.SYS are stored on the hard drive in special device-driver programs. These files usually end with a .SYS or .EXE extension.

These device drivers come with the device when you buy it. When you buy a sound card, for example, it comes with a diskette or CD-ROM that holds all the necessary device drivers. There is usually some installation program that automatically installs the necessary drivers and updates the CONFIG.SYS file. Device-driver files can be easily identified in CONFIG.SYS. Any line that begins with DEVICE= or DEVICEHIGH= loads a device driver. Let's look at a few lines of a typical CONFIG.SYS and identify the device drivers:

```
DEVICE=C:\DOS\HIMEM.SYS (BIOS)
DEVICE=C:\DOS\EMM386.EXE noems highscan (BIOS)
BUFFERS=30 (not BIOS)
DOS=UMB (not BIOS)
```

```
LASTDRIVE=m (not BIOS)
DEVICEHIGH =C:\SCSI\ASPI2DOS.SYS /D /Z (BIOS)
DEVICEHIGH =C:\SCSI\ASPICD.SYS /D:ASPICD0 (BIOS)
```

When the computer is booted up, the CONFIG.SYS file is read and the device drivers are loaded from the hard drive to RAM. I will return to CONFIG.SYS when discussing memory, and cover these lines in detail.

SYSTEM.INI Device drivers that are run through CONFIG.SYS have certain limitations. DOS can use only 640K of RAM, and every device driver in your CONFIG.SYS takes up some of this precious 640K. Also, DOS is a single-tasking operating system, and is therefore incapable of running more than one program simultaneously.

Windows 3.*x* runs in protected mode, which Microsoft calls "386 enhanced mode." Although Windows 3.*x* can use the device drivers from CONFIG.SYS, it would be beneficial for it to use device drivers that can run in extended memory and therefore accessed by more than one program at a time. Therefore, Windows has its own drivers for accessing hardware in protected mode. These drivers are loaded in the SYSTEM.INI file. The SYSTEM.INI file is located in the \Windows directory and, like CONFIG.SYS, it is a text file. SYSTEM.INI is broken up into groups, and each group can be identified by the name in square brackets that start the section. The standard sections are [boot], [keyboard], [boot description], [386Enh], and [drivers]. The majority of drivers that are loaded after the installation of Windows 3.*x* are located in the [386Enh] section. They are distinguished by their drivers= line, just like in CONFIG.SYS. Here's a part of an example [386Enh] section from a SYSTEM.INI file:

```
[386Enh]
device=vwpd.386 (BIOS)
device=dva.386 (BIOS)
device=*vmcpd (BIOS)
SystemROMBreakPoint=false (not BIOS)
device=mach.386 (BIOS)
DebugLocalReboot=TRUE (not BIOS)
device=vshare.386 (BIOS)
device=lpt.386 (BIOS)
device=serial.386 (BIOS)
VirtualHDIrq=OFF (not BIOS)
```

This begs the question: "If I have a device driver in CONFIG.SYS, do I also need a device driver in SYSTEM.INI?" The fast answer is "No," but there are some major exceptions. First, Windows programs can use CONFIG.SYS drivers, but DOS programs can't use Windows protected-mode drivers. Second, many devices can have a device driver in only CONFIG.SYS or SYSTEM.INI—not both. I usually just let the installa-

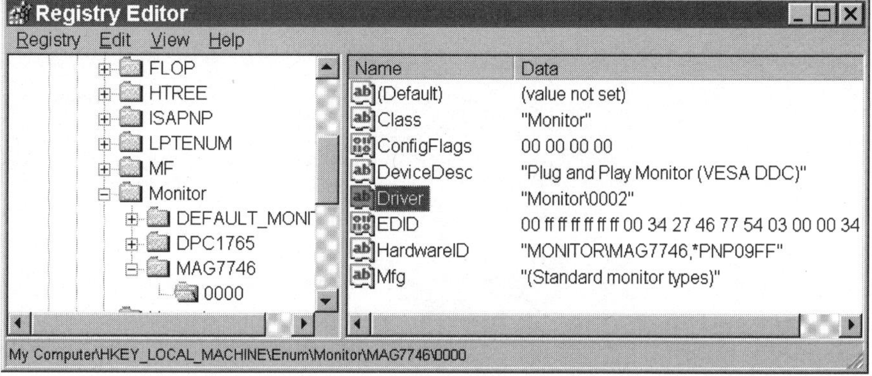

Figure 5.19
Registry

tion program do what it wants to do, and worry about the details only if something goes wrong.

Also, Windows will add device drivers that completely take over the function of the system BIOS. These device drivers are often generically called "32-bit drivers" and are indistinguishable from any other driver in the SYSTEM.INI file.

REGISTRY One of the big problems of a DOS/Windows 3.*x* combination is that you can have device drivers installed in more than one location. One of the more powerful features of Windows 95 is the consolidation of all of these files into a new type of configuration file called the *registry* (Figure 5.19). Every configuration setting in Windows 95 is stored in the registry, including all device-driver information.

Unlike CONFIG.SYS and SYSTEM.INI, the registry is not a text file. It can be edited only with a special program called the *registry editor* (REGEDIT). Even though you can directly access the registry through REGEDIT, there is no reason to edit it manually in order to add or delete device drivers.

In the overwhelming majority of situations, you would use two programs, the Add New Hardware Wizard (Figure 5.20) and Device Manager (Figure 5.21) to edit the registry. These two programs provide a far more intuitive interface for installing hardware and necessary drivers. The Add New Hardware Wizard is used to install new devices. The Device Manager is used to change or remove the drivers for any particular device.

The only downside to the Windows 95 system is the fact that it is backwardly compatible with SYSTEM.INI and CONFIG.SYS. So you could install a sound card into SYSTEM.INI or CONFIG.SYS and it would work

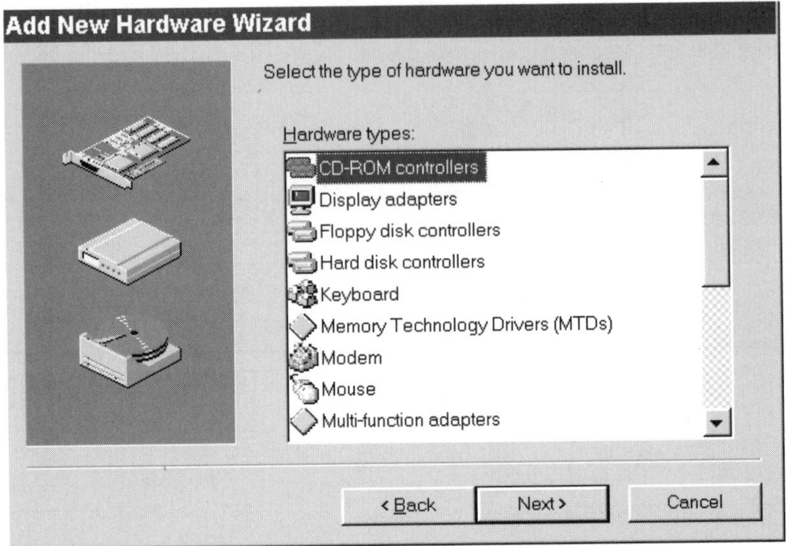

Figure 5.20 Add New Hardware Wizard

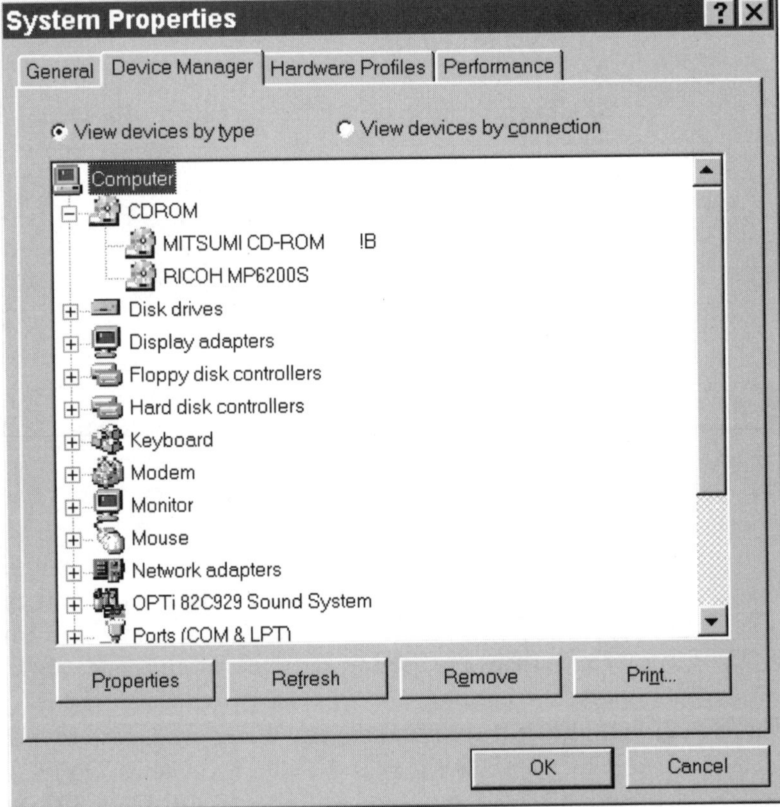

Figure 5.21 Device Manager

perfectly. Unfortunately, if you go into the Device Manager, you won't see any information about a sound card. This isn't good because most newer technicians only know to look in the Device Manager; if they don't see any information on the sound card, they will immediately assume that there is some kind of witchcraft going on inside the PC.

DEVICE DRIVERS VS. ROM Using device drivers is the most popular way to provide BIOS support for hardware, and the main reason for this is flexibility. Imagine the difficulty of only using ROM chips. Say you discovered that your Adaptec SCSI card would not work under Windows. We could call the company that sold you the card, and they would tell you the reason it didn't work is because the BIOS routines are not designed to run under Windows. How could you upgrade the BIOS? Since the BIOS is stored on an on-board ROM chip, you would have to open the computer, remove the card, and replace the chip with a new ROM chip that had the new BIOS. It is much easier to use device drivers. If an upgrade is necessary, the card maker can send you a diskette with the new device driver, and you don't need to open the PC or replace ROM chips. However, as you delve further into different devices, you will see that ROMs are still alive and well, and being used on a broad cross-section of devices.

You now know that there are two different sets of programs on the system ROM: the BIOS routines and the CMOS setup program. Let's take a look at the third and last aspect of the system ROM: the POST.

POST (power-on self test)

When the computer is turned on or reset, it initiates a special program, also stored on the ROM chip, called the *power-on self test* or *POST*. The function of the POST is to allow the system to be "checked out" every time the computer is turned on. To perform this check, the POST sends out a standard command that says to all the devices "check yourselves out!" All the devices in the computer then run their own internal diagnostic—the POST doesn't specify what to check. The quality of the diagnostic is up to the people who made that particular device.

Let's consider the POST for a moment. Some device, let's say the 8042 chip, runs its diagnostic and determines that it is not working properly. What will the POST do about it? There's only one thing to do—tell the human being in front of the PC! So how does the computer tell the human? The first thought is to put some information on the monitor. That's fine, but what if the video card is faulty? What if some really low-level device (there's still a ton of devices I haven't even covered yet) isn't operational? Well, all POSTs first test all the most basic devices. If anything goes wrong on this first group of devices, the computer will beep using its built-in speaker. But what if the speaker doesn't work? Trouble! The POST assumes it always works. In order to know whether the speaker is working or not, all PCs beep on start up to let the user know whether the speaker is working. Now you know why every computer always beeps when it first starts!

The POST can therefore be divided into two parts. First is the test of the most basic devices—up to and including the video. If anything goes wrong, the computer will beep. Second is a test of the rest of the devices. If anything goes wrong here, a text error message will appear on screen.

Before and During the Video Test: the Beep Codes

The computer tests the most basic parts of the computer first. If anything goes wrong, the computer will send a series of beeps. The meaning of these beeps varies from one BIOS manufacturer to another. Tables 5.1 and 5.2 list the beep codes for the AMI and Phoenix BIOSes.

TABLE 5.1

AMI Beep Codes

# of Beeps	Problem
1	The memory controller is not refreshing DRAM
2	654K RAM parity error.
3	64K RAM error.
4	System timer doesn't work
5	The CPU is generating an error
6	Keyboard controller is bad
7	A Card mounted CPU generated an error.
8	Video card is missing or bad
9	ROM Chip is bad
10	CMOS chip is bad
11	Cache memory is bad

TABLE 5.2

Table of Post Beep Codes for Phoenix BIOS

Code	Description
1-1-3	CMOS write/read test in-progress or failure
1-1-4	BIOS ROM checksum in-progress or failure
1-2-1	Programmable Interval Timer test failure
1-2-2	DMA initialization in-progress or failure
1-2-3	DMA page register write/read test fail
1-3-1	RAM refresh verification in-progress or failure
1-3-3	1st 64K RAM chip or data line failure - mullet-bit
1-3-4	1st 64K RAM odd/even logic failure.
1-4-1	1st 64K RAM address line failure
1-4-2	1st RAM parity test in progress or failure
2-1-1	1st 64K RAM chip or data line failure - bit 0
2-1-2	1st 64K RAM chip or data line failure - bit 1
2-1-3	1st 64K RAM chip or data line failure - bit 2
2-1-4	1st 64K RAM chip or data line failure - bit 3
2-2-1	1st 64K RAM chip or data line failure - bit 4
2-2-2	1st 64K RAM chip or data line failure- bit 5
2-2-3	1st 64K RAM chip or data line failure- bit 6
2-2-4	1st 64K RAM chip or data line failure- bit 7
2-3-1	1st 64K RAM chip or data line failure - bit 8
2-3-2	1st 64K RAM chip or data line failure - bit 9
2-3-3	1st 64K RAM chip or data line failure - bit A
2-3-4	1st 64K RAM chip or data line failure - bit B
2-4-1	1st 64K RAM chip or data line failure - bit C
2-4-2	1st 64K RAM chip or data line failure - bit D
2-4-3	1st 64K RAM chip or data line failure - bit E
2-4-4	1st 64K RAM chip or data line failure - bit F
3-1-1	Master DMA register test in-progress or failure.
3-1-2	Slave DMA register test in-progress or failure.
3-1-3	Master interrupt mask register test fail
3-1-4	Slave interrupt mask register test fail
3-2-4	Keyboard controller test in-progress or failure
3-3-4	Screen memory test in-progress or failure
3-4-1	Screen initialization in-progress or failure
3-4-2	Screen retrace tests in-progress or failure
4-2-1	Timer tick interrupt test in progress or failure
4-2-2	Shutdown test in progress or failure
4-2-3	Gate A20 failure
4-2-4	Unexpected interrupt in protected mode
4-3-1	RAM test i failure above address 0FFFFh
4-3-3	Interval timer channel 2 test failure
4-3-4	Time-Of-Day clock test in progress or failure
4-4-1	Serial port test in progress or failure
4-4-2	Parallel port test in progress or failure
4-4-3	Math Coprocessor test in progress or failure

TABLE 5.3

Common POST Beep Errors and Solutions

Problem	Solution
RAM refresh failure Parity error	1) Reseat and clean the RAM chips 2) Replace individual chips until the problem is corrected. RAM BIT error Base 64K error
8042 error Gate A20 error	1) Reseat and clean keyboard chip. 2) Replace keyboard. 3) Replace motherboard.
BIOS checksum Error	1) Reseat and clean ROM chip 2) Replace BIOS chip
Video Errors	1) Reseat video card 2) Replace video card
Cache memory error	1) Reseat and clean cache chips 2) Verify cache jumper settings are correct 3) Replace cache chips
Everything else	1) Clean motherboard 2) Cache memory is bad

Some error codes are chip-set or platform-specific, and vary from system to system. However, these codes are basically constant. Refer to your motherboard book for details. Table 5.3 lists the most common POST problems and how to deal with them.

Many computers generate beep codes when the only problem is a bad power supply! The secret to determining if you have a bad power supply is to turn the computer on and off three or four times, and see if you generate the same beep code every time. If you get the same beep code, it's probably legitimate. If the beep codes are different, if the machine stops working, or if the computer seems to heal itself, check the power supply.

After the Video Test: the Error Messages

Once the video has been tested, the POST will display any error messages on the screen. These POST error messages are displayed in one of two different ways: old-style numeric error codes or more modern text error messages.

NUMERIC ERROR CODES When a computer generates a numeric error code, the machine will lock up and the error code will appear in the upper left-hand corner of the screen. For example, Figure 5.22 indicates that the keyboard is not responding. There are hundreds of error codes, but Table 5.4 lists the five most common codes and the probable causes of the problem.

TEXT ERRORS BIOSes no longer use numeric error codes. Because the overwhelming majority of numeric error codes are never used, AMI reduced the number of error codes to about 30, and substituted text to describe the problem. Instead of mysterious numbers, you get text that is usually, but not always, self-explanatory.

Figure 5.22
Old style numeric error code

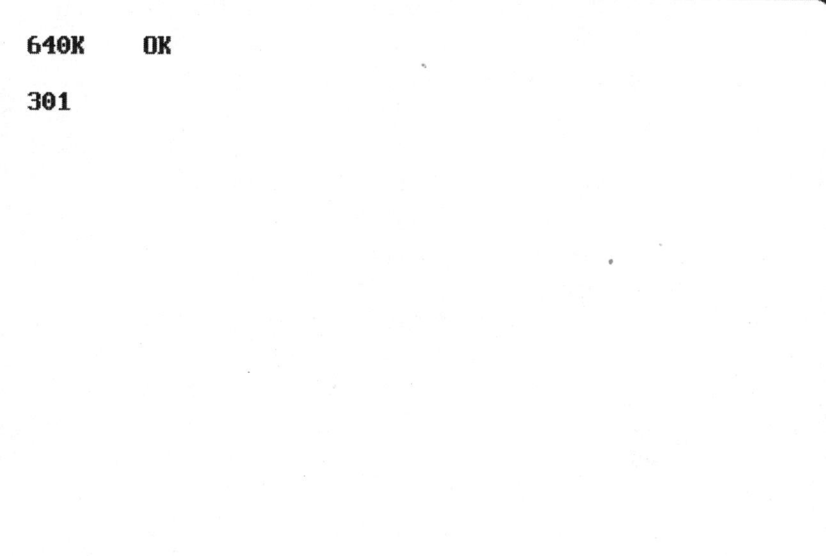

TABLE 5.4

Common Numeric Error Code

Error Code	Problem
301	The keyboard is broken or not plugged in
1701	The hard drive controller is bad
7301	Floppy drive controller bad
161	Dead battery
1101	Bad serial card

```
AMIBIOS (C) 1997 American Megatrends Inc.
Press <DEL> if you want to run setup

HDD Controller Failure
Press <F1> to continue

(C) American Megatrends Inc.,
40-0100-006259-00101111-060692-SYMP-F
```

Text errors are far more useful since one can simply read the screen to determine the bad device.

POST Cards

Beep codes, numeric codes, and text error codes, although helpful, can sometimes be misleading. Worse than that, an inoperative device can sometimes disrupt the POST, forcing the machine into an endless loop. This causes the PC to act "dead"—no beeps and nothing on the screen. In this case, you need a device to monitor the POST and report which piece of hardware is causing the trouble.

The devices designed for this are known as *POST cards*. Manufacturers make POST cards for all types of PCs. They will work with any BIOS, but you need to know the type of BIOS you have in order to use them properly. When a computer provides an error code that doesn't make sense, or if your machine is locking up and not rebooting, turn off the computer, install the POST card in any expansion slot, and restart the PC. All POST cards have some type of display, usually a two-digit hexadecimal display that a technician must decode by referring to a manual that comes with the POST card.

A lot of people sell POST cards today, with prices ranging from $50 up to $1500. Spend the absolute least amount of money you can. The more expensive cards add bells and whistles that you do not need, like diagnostic software and voltmeters. Try JDR Microdevices (800-538-5000) for a good, cheap POST card. Ask for wholesale, mention Total Seminars, and they should sell it to you for about $30. In addition, they have a JDR-PDI card, a combination POST Card and DMA/IRQ tester card (I'll explain IRQ/DMA later) for under $100 that is an excellent value.

Turn off the PC, install the POST card in any unused slot, and turn on the PC. As you watch the display, notice the different hexadecimal readouts and refer to them as your POST progresses (Figure 5.23). You will recognize many of them! Good technicians will often memorize 50 to 100 different POST codes. Memorizing them is faster than looking them up in a book.

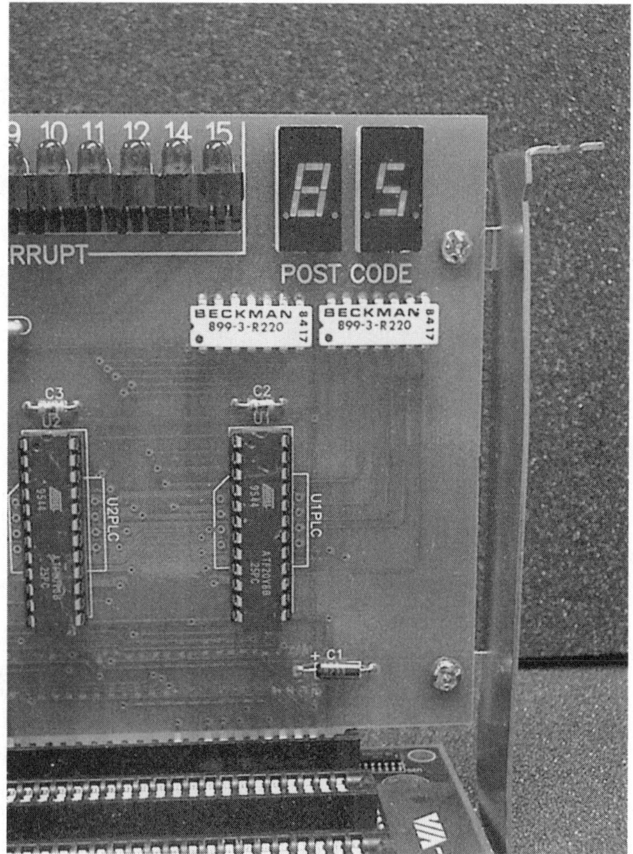

Figure 5.23
POST card in action

So you got a beep code, a text error code, or a POST error. Now what do you do with that knowledge? I explained beep code problems earlier, but what about text or POST errors? The important thing to remember is that a POST error does not fix the computer; it only tells you where to look. You then have to know how to deal with that bad or misconfigured component.

The Boot Process

All PCs need a process to begin their operations. Unfortunately, there is no "start" button on the front of the PC. Instead, IBM decided when the first PCs were developed to create a process where all the user has to do is provide electricity to the computer (flipping the on/off switch). Once power was fed to the PC, the tight interrelation of hardware, firmware, and software would allow the PC to start itself, to "pull itself up by the bootstraps" or "boot" itself. All PCs still follow the original boot process as described by IBM for the original IBM 286 AT computer.

The first electrical component to "wake up" when the computer is turned on is the CPU itself. As soon as the power supply provides the proper voltage, a special wire called "voltage good" is read by the CPU, telling it that it can safely start. Every Intel and clone CPU has a built-in memory address that it immediately sends via its address bus. This special address is the first line of POST programming on the system ROM! The POST is then run.

After the POST has finished, there must be a way for the computer to find the programs on the hard drive in order to start the main program called the *operating system*. BIOS begins to look for the operating system by first checking to see if a diskette is in the floppy drive. If there is a floppy diskette inserted, the PC assumes that the operating system is on the floppy. If there is no floppy, the system then looks for an operating system on the hard drive. All floppy and hard disks have a very specific location on them called the *boot sector*. If the disk is bootable, it will contain special programming designed to tell the system where to locate the operating system. A disk that has a functional operating system is called a bootable disk or a system disk. The term *bootable disk* is usually associated with hard drives, while the term *system disk* is more commonly used by floppy drives. Either way, if there is no bootable disk, you will get the error:

```
Non-system disk or disk error
Replace and press any key when ready
```

Many CMOSes have settings that allow you change the order in which devices are searched for an operating system. This system has a reversed standard, so first it checks the hard drive (C:) and then the floppy disk (A:), as shown in Figure 5.24. This is commonly done to prevent a hacker from inserting a bootable floppy and accessing the system.

Motherboard Layouts

The particular way components are positioned on a motherboard is called the motherboard's *form factor*. There are currently two standard form factors used by most motherboards: AT and ATX. The AT form fac-

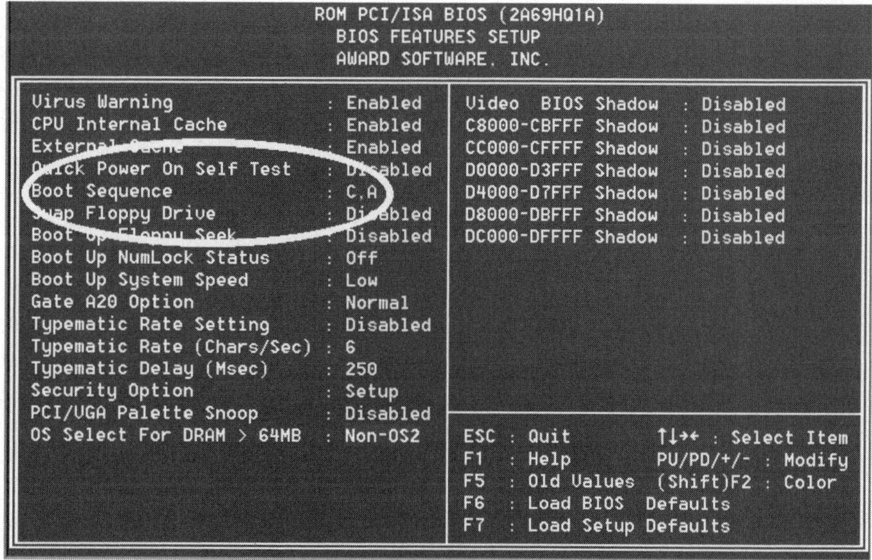

Figure 5.24 CMOS changing boot sequence

tor, invented by IBM in the early '80s, has been the predominant form factor for motherboards. The AT-type motherboard can be distinguished by the position of the keyboard plug and its power socket (Figure 5.25).

The AT motherboard has a few size variations (Figure 5.26). The original size of the AT motherboard was almost the same size as two pieces of paper laid side by side. It needed to be quite large since the first PCs carried a lot of individual chips. As technology improved, there was a strong demand for a smaller AT motherboard. A smaller size was created and dubbed "baby AT." The original-size AT motherboard was then called a "full AT," "regular AT," or sometimes just "AT." The baby AT has been and continues to be the most common size of AT form factor. There is even some variation in size within baby ATs! One motherboard might be slightly larger or smaller than another, which is okay as long as the keyboard and expansion slots stick to the form-factor specifications (Figure 5.27).

Even though the AT form factor has predominated for many years, there have been a number of problems with the AT motherboards. The single greatest problem is the connectors. Clearly, PCs are going to have quite a few cables hanging out their backs. When PCs were first invented, the only devices plugged into the average PC were a monitor and a keyboard. That's what the AT was designed to handle. The only dedicated connector on an AT motherboard is the keyboard plug. If you want to add connectors for anything else, you have to do it through the expansion slots.

Over the years, the number of devices plugged into the back of the PC has grown tremendously. Your average PC today has a keyboard, a mouse,

Figure 5.25
AT motherboard

Figure 5.26
Different sizes of AT motherboards

Figure 5.27 Commonality between AT motherboards

a printer, some speakers, a monitor, and a phone line connected to it. These added components have created a demand for a new type of form factor, one that would have more dedicated connectors for more devices. There were many attempts to create a new standard form factor. Invariably, these new form factors integrated dedicated connectors for at least the mouse and printer, and many even added connectors for video, sound, and phone lines. Although many excellent designs were created by motherboard manufacturers, no one new form factor become very popular. One new form factor that did have a small degree of success, however, was known as LBX (Figure 5.28).

Figure 5.28 LBX motherboard

Figure 5.29
ATX motherboard

The main problem with form factors like LBX was their inflexibility. Certainly, there was no problem with dedicated connections for devices like mice or printers, but the new form factors also added connectors for devices like video and sound— devices that were prone to obsolescence, making the motherboard useless the moment a new type of video or sound card came into popularity.

Yet there continued to be a tremendous demand for a new form factor—a form factor that had more standard connectors, but that would also be flexible for possible changes in technology. This demand led to the creation of ATX (Figure 5.29).

Although relatively new, ATX has taken a strong position in motherboard form factors and today is quite common—easily as popular as AT. ATX is exactly the same size as a baby AT, but is turned 90 degrees relative to the computer's box. ATX is distinct from the AT in the lack of an AT keyboard port, which is replaced with a rear plate that allows access to all necessary ports (Figure 5.30). ATX also uses a P1 power connector instead of P8 and P9 (Figure 5.31).

The ATX form factor includes many improvements over AT. The position of the power supply allows for better air movement. The CPU and RAM are placed in such a way to allow easier access.

Unlike AT power supplies, ATX uses a feature called soft power. This means that it uses software to actually turn the PC on and off. The physical manifestation of soft power is the power switch. Instead of the thick

Figure 5.30
ATX ports

Figure 5.31
P1 connector

power cord used in AT systems, and ATX power switch is little more than a pair on small wires leading to the motherboard.

There is no performance enhancement in using ATX over AT. The motherboard you choose should be based on another factor, such as price, cache, or the motherboard's top speed. The form factor is secondary. Keep in mind that AT uses a different box than an ATX. You cannot upgrade an AT system with an ATX motherboard, as well as the other way around. ATX has definitely made some inroads and is bound to continue to take market share over the next few years.

Motherboard Installation and Replacement

To most techs, the concept of adding or replacing a motherboard can be extremely intimidating. It really shouldn't be—motherboard installation is a common and necessary part of PC repair. It is inexpensive and easy, although it can sometimes be a little tedious and messy due to the large number of parts involved. This section covers the process of installation/replacement and will show some of the tricks that makes this necessary process easy to handle.

Choosing the Motherboard and Case First, determine what motherboard you need. What CPU are you using? Will the motherboard work with that CPU? Since most of us buy the CPU and the motherboard at the same time, make the seller guarantee that the CPU will work with the motherboard. How much RAM do you intend to install? Are there extra RAM sockets available for future upgrades? There are a number of excellent motherboard manufacturers available today. Some of the more popular brands are Tyan, Asus, Shuttle and Gigabyte. Your supplier may also have some lesser known but perfectly acceptable brands of motherboards—as long as there is an easy return policy it's perfectly fine to try one of these.

Second, do not worry about size. Virtually any motherboard will fit into any case made today. Usually a quick visual inspection will be sufficient to see if it will fit. Keep form factor with form factor—AT motherboards for AT boxes and ATX motherboards with ATX boxes.

Third, all motherboards come with a technical manual, better known as the "motherboard book." You must have this book! This book is your only source for all of the critical information about the motherboard! For example, if you have an on-board battery and that battery decides to die, where would you install a replacement external battery? Where do you plug in the speaker? Even if you are letting someone else install the motherboard, insist on the motherboard book—you will need it.

Fourth, pick your case carefully. Cases come in four basic sizes: Slimline, Desktop, Mini-Tower, and Tower. The Desktop and Mini-Tower are the most popular choices but as mentioned earlier, pretty much any motherboard will fit in any case. Power supplies come with the case. Watch out for very inexpensive cases—they often have very poor quality power supplies that can stop working, or worse, damage your new motherboard. Cases come with many different options but there are two more common options that point to a better case. One option is a removable face—many cheaper cases will screw the face into the metal frame using wood screws. A removable face makes disassembly much easier! Another is a detachable motherboard mount. Clearly, the motherboard will have to be attached to the case in some fashion. In better cases, this is handled by a removable tray or plate, allowing you to physically attach the motherboard to the case separately, saving the difficult chore of sticking your arms into the case to turn screws.

Installing the Motherboard If replacing a motherboard, first remove the old motherboard. Begin by removing all the cards. Also remove anything else that might impede removal or installation of the motherboard such as hard or floppy drives. Keep track of your screws—the best idea is to temporarily return the screws to their mounting holes until the part is to be reinstalled. Sometimes even the power supply has to be removed temporarily to allow access to the motherboard. Document the position of the little wires for the speaker, turbo switch, turbo light, and reset button in case you need to reinstall them.

Unscrew the motherboard. IT WILL NOT SIMPLY LIFT OUT. The motherboard is also mounted to the case with plastic connectors called "standouts" that slide into keyed slots at the bottom of the box. Screws hold the motherboard in place. If the CPU, or RAM has been removed, be sure to replace them before installing the new motherboard. Don't forget to set the motherboard speed, voltage and clock multiplier if necessary—chedk the motherboard book.

When you put in the new motherboard, do not assume that you will put the screws and standouts in the same place as they were in your old motherboard. When it comes to the placement of screws and standouts, there is only one rule: anywhere it fits. Do not be afraid to be a little tough here! Installing motherboards can be a wiggly, twisty, scraped knuckle process.

Once the motherboard, with CPU and RAM properly installed, is mounted in the case, it's time to insert the power connections and test. A POST card can be a real help here as you won't have to add a video card, monitor and keyboard to verify that the system is booting. If you have a POST card, start the system, and watch if the POST is taking place—you should see a number of POST codes before the POST stops. If you don't have a POST card, install a keyboard, video card and monitor. Boot the system and see if the BIOS information shows up on the screen. If it does, you're probably O.K. If it doesn't it's time to refer to the motherboard book to see where you messed up.

Wires, Wires, Wires: The last and often the most frustrating, part of motherboard installation is connecting the lights and buttons on the front of the box. These usually include, but not always, the following:

Soft power
Turbo switch
Turbo light
Reset button
Keylock
Speaker
Hard drive active light

These wires have specific pin connections to the motherboard. Although you can refer to the motherboard book for their location, usually a quick inspection of the motherboard is sufficient.

There are a few rules to follow when installing these wires. The first rule is: "The lights are LED's (Light Emitting Diodes) not lightbulbs—they have a positive and negative side. If they don't work one way, turn the connector around and try it the other". The second rule is: "When in doubt, guess." **Incorrect installation will not result in damage to the computer.** The device that was incorrectly wired simply will not work. Refer to the motherboard book for the correct installation. The third and last rule is" "With the exception of the soft power switch on an ATX system, you do not need any of these wires for the computer to run!" The only possible downside is that the PC will only run in non-turbo (slow) mode, but it will run.

There is no hard and fast rule for determining the function of each wire. Often the function of each wire is printed on the connector. If not, track each wire to the light or switch to determine its function.

The Next Step We have described the motherboard's function as providing easy access to the wires of the external data bus and the address bus for all of its devices. This chapter has described the devices (ROM chips, CMOS chips, keyboard controllers, etc.) that mount directly onto the motherboard. What if we want to add other devices? For other optional devices, and additional bridge is required: the expansion bus.

CHAPTER 6

Expansion Bus

In this chapter, you will:

- Understand the function of an external data bus.
- See how I/O addressing works.
- See how IRQs and DMAs work.
- Understand COM and LPT ports.
- Look at some common installation issues.
- Understand the different types of expansion buses.

This chapter dwells on a fairly broad, but closely linked set of topics that I have decided to call "the expansion bus." A better title might be something like "How do I add cards and motherboards to an existing system," but I might have a little trouble getting all that on the title page! The function of an expansion slot is to allow flexibility in configuration when adding devices to your PC. Expansion slots are standardized connections that provide a common access point for any device to be installed.

In today's world of Plug-n-Play (PnP) devices, many people would say that this topic isn't very important, but they would be wrong. Granted, the ability of a new device to be snapped in and then automatically work is wonderful, but it is also very problematic—in other words, it doesn't always work. As you will see, many PnP devices today have some rather nasty habits and don't work properly. I might also add that quite a few devices that are being sold today are still not able to configure themselves. Understanding how motherboards and the expansion cards soldered to them work together in order to allow a sound card or modem to run properly is absolutely vital. You need to understand the expansion bus and motherboard, so we'll start with something you already know—the external data bus.

It's the Crystals!

Considering what this book has described up to this point, there should be only one data bus on the PC: the external data bus. Everything in the computer is connected to everything else in the computer via the external data bus (Figure 6.1). Whether a device is welded to the motherboard or snapped into a socket should make no difference. Every device in the computer—RAM, keyboard, network card, sound card, etc.,—is connected to the external data bus.

Figure 6.1
The CPU and two cards tied to the external data bus

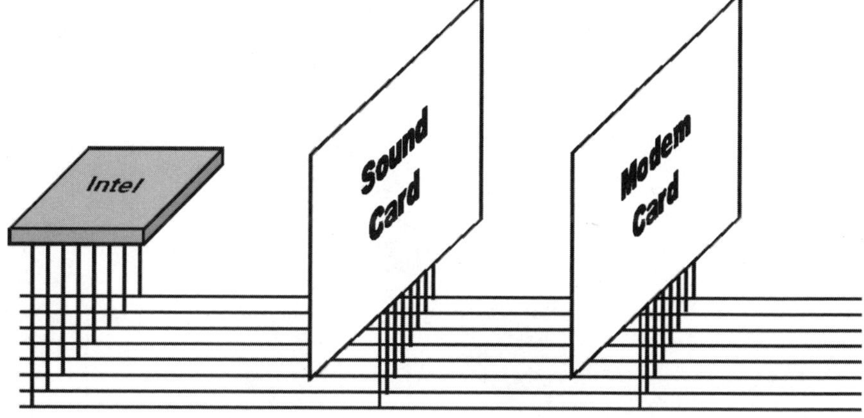

All integrated circuits are regulated by a quartz crystal oscillator, just like the one that runs a watch. The crystal acts like a drill sergeant calling a cadence, setting the pace of activity in the computer. Every device welded to the motherboard is designed to run at the speed of the system crystal. If there is a 66-MHz keyboard chip, there is also a 66-MHz memory controller chip and 66-MHz everything else, all timed by a 66-MHz crystal.

Now consider what happens if you buy a device that did not come with your computer. Take a sound card as an example. Like most every other electronic device, the chips on a sound card need to be pushed by a crystal. At what speed should these chips run? 25 MHz? 33 MHz? 66 MHz? If you used the system crystal, that would mean you would need to have sound cards for every possible computer speed. You would not be able to just buy a sound card. You would have to find one that ran at the same speed as your motherboard. That also means that if you make sound cards for a living, you would have to make them for every possible speed.

This is ridiculous, and IBM knew it when they designed the PC. They had to make an extension to the external data bus that *ran at its own standardized speed.* This part of the external data bus would be used for devices to be snapped into the PC. That was achieved by adding a different crystal that controlled the part of the external data bus connected to the expansion slots (Figure 6.2). This way, no matter what speed CPU you have, the expansion slots all run at a standard speed. In the original IBM PC, that speed was about 14.31818 MHz ÷ 2, or about 7.16 MHz. See Figure 6.3.

So now you have, in essence, two different buses. The first bus is the external data bus running at the speed of the CPU. The second bus is the expansion bus, running at the speed of the expansion bus crystal. How can this work? Wouldn't data being moved from the faster bus overrun

Figure 6.2 Function of System and expansion crystal

Figure 6.3 Typical expansion bus crystal

the other? No. Expansion devices can tell the CPU that they are not ready by generating a wait state, just like DRAM. Also, most expansion devices have buffer areas to store extra data coming from the CPU (or vice versa).

The external data bus is the primary data path for the entire computer. All devices on the external data bus run at the speed of the system crystal.

> The expansion bus is an extension of the external data bus that runs at the speed of the expansion bus crystal.

The two buses have different names: the part of the external data bus that supports the expansion slots is the *expansion bus,* and the part of the external data bus that is timed by the system crystal and supports the CPU, RAM, and other important components on the motherboard is the *system bus.*

History of PC Expansion Buses: Part 1

8-Bit ISA

On first-generation IBM XTs, the 8088 processor had an 8-bit external data bus and ran at a top speed of 4.77 MHz. Therefore, IBM made the expansion slots on the XT with an 8-bit external bus connection. IBM settled on a standard expansion bus speed of 8.33 MHz (maximum), although most machines ran their expansion buses at around 7 mHz. And 7 MHz was fast enough—at the time it was faster than the CPU! This expansion bus was called the *PC bus,* and the slots looked like Figure 6.4.

The address bus wires also go out to the expansion slots. The connections that start with the letter A are the 20 address bus wires, and the connections that start with the letter D are the eight external data bus wires. I will discuss the function of most of the other connections as you progress through this chapter.

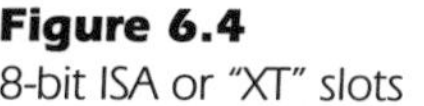

Figure 6.4
8-bit ISA or "XT" slots

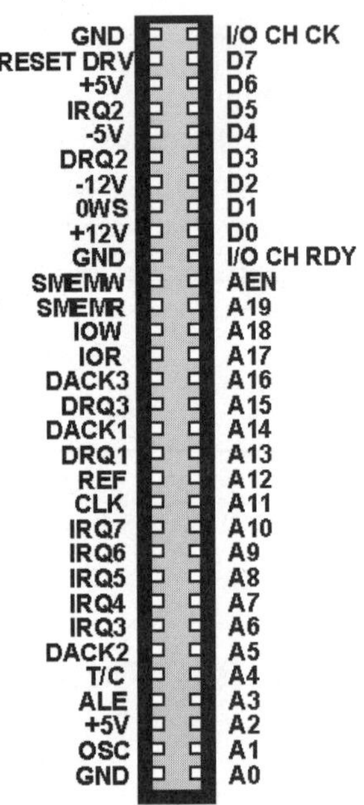

Figure 6.5 Pinout for 8-bit ISA slot

IBM did something no one had ever done before. They allowed competitors to copy the PC bus. They also allowed third parties to make cards that would snap into their PC bus. Remember that IBM invented the PC expansion bus. It was (and still is) a patented product of IBM Corporation. By allowing everyone to copy the PC expansion bus technology, IBM established the industry standard and created the clone market. See Figure 6.5.

16-Bit ISA

When the 286 was invented by Intel, IBM wanted to create a new expansion bus that would take advantage of the 286's 16-bit external data bus, yet still be backwardly compatible with older 8-bit cards. This was achieved by simply adding an extra slot to the PC bus, creating a new 16-bit bus (Figure 6.6). This was called the *AT bus* because IBM used it in their 286-based IBM AT computer.

Notice that the connectors add eight more external data bus wires and four more address wires. This new 16-bit bus also ran at a top speed of 8.33 MHz, but just about every motherboard maker used the same crystal as on the 8-bit ISA bus to ensure total compatibility. See Figure 6.7.

IBM, while retaining the patent rights, allowed third parties to copy their bus architecture, but they never released the complete specifications

Figure 6.6
16-bit ISA or "AT" slots

Figure 6.7
Pinout for 16-bit ISA or "AT" slot

GND	I/O CH CK
RESET DRV	D7
+5V	D6
IRQ2	D5
-5V	D4
DRQ2	D3
-12V	D2
0WS	D1
+12V	D0
GND	I/O CH RDY
SMEMW	AEN
SMEMR	A19
IOW	A18
IOR	A17
DACK3	A16
DRQ3	A15
DACK1	A14
DRQ1	A13
REF	A12
CLK	A11
IRQ7	A10
IRQ6	A9
IRQ5	A8
IRQ4	A7
IRQ3	A6
DACK2	A5
T/C	A4
ALE	A3
+5V	A2
OSC	A1
GND	A0
MEM CS16	SBHE
I/O CS16	LA23
IRQ10	LA22
IRQ11	LA21
IRQ12	LA20
IRQ15	LA19
IRQ14	LA18
DACK0	LA17
DRQ0	MEMR
DACK5	MEMW
DRQ5	SD08
DACK6	SD09
DRQ6	SD10
DACK7	SD11
DRQ7	SD12
Vcc	SD13
MASTER	SD14
GND	SD15

for these two types of expansion buses. Today we call these buses 8-bit and 16-bit ISA slots. Because the term ISA (Industry Standard Architecture) did not become official until 1990, these buses are often referred to as the XT or AT buses.

So there are two types of standardized expansion slots—the 8-bit ISA and the 16-bit ISA. These slots are extensions of the external data bus, yet they run at only around 7 MHz, regardless of the speed of the system. So the best throughput you can have is 16 bits wide at 7 MHz. This is fine as long as the external data bus on the CPU is 16 bits or less (8088 and 80286). The 7-MHz speed is only slightly slower than the 12 MHz of the fastest 286.

The 8-bit and 16-bit ISA buses were for many years the only serious option for PC users. It was these expansion buses upon which the PC industry was built. Although other expansion buses are now coming into the forefront of PC use, I need to describe some generic features of card installation, while focusing on the ISA bus. Once you understand these concepts, you can move on to the more advanced expansion buses with a solid, clear understanding of their benefits.

Over the next few sections, we will delve deeply into the "big three" of card installation: I/O addresses, IRQs, and DMA. These three topics are together probably the single greatest headache confronting PC technicians. I will go over each of these in detail, starting with I/O addresses.

I/O Addresses

The external data bus is used to transfer lines of programs between memory (RAM and ROM) and the CPU. The external data bus also allows data to travel back and forth from peripherals such as the keyboard, hard drives, and CD-ROM drives to the CPU. You can run BIOS routines from ROM to tell peripherals to do whatever it is they are supposed to do, but the question is: "If everything is plugged into the external data bus, how does the CPU know how to talk to a particular device, and how do particular devices know the CPU is talking to them?" See Figure 6.8.

Remember the other bus used in a PC: the address bus. You communicate with devices by assigning them unique I/O addresses, which are patterns of ones and zeros transmitted across the address bus by the CPU to address memory. The CPU uses an extra wire, called the *IO/MEM* (input/output or memory) wire to notify devices that the address bus is not being used to specify an address in memory (Figure 6.9). Instead, it is being used to read to or write from a particular device. The address bus has

Figure 6.8
How can the CPU talk to one device?

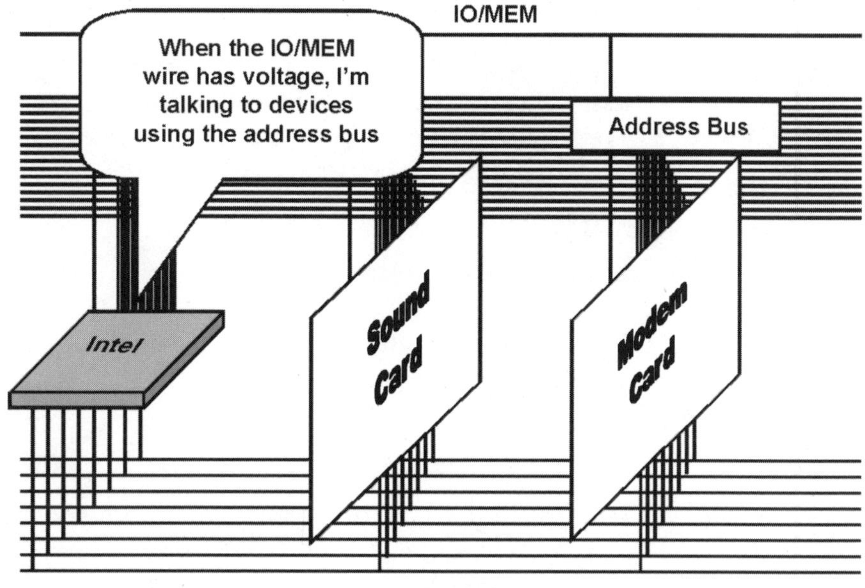

Figure 6.9
Function of IO/MEM wire

at least 20 wires, but when the IO/MEM wire has voltage, only the first 16 wires are monitored.

All devices, both those embedded on the motherboard (like the 8042 keyboard controller) and those inserted into expansion slots (like a video card), respond to special, unique patterns built into them. For example, the hard-drive controller responds to 16 unique commands. If the CPU lights

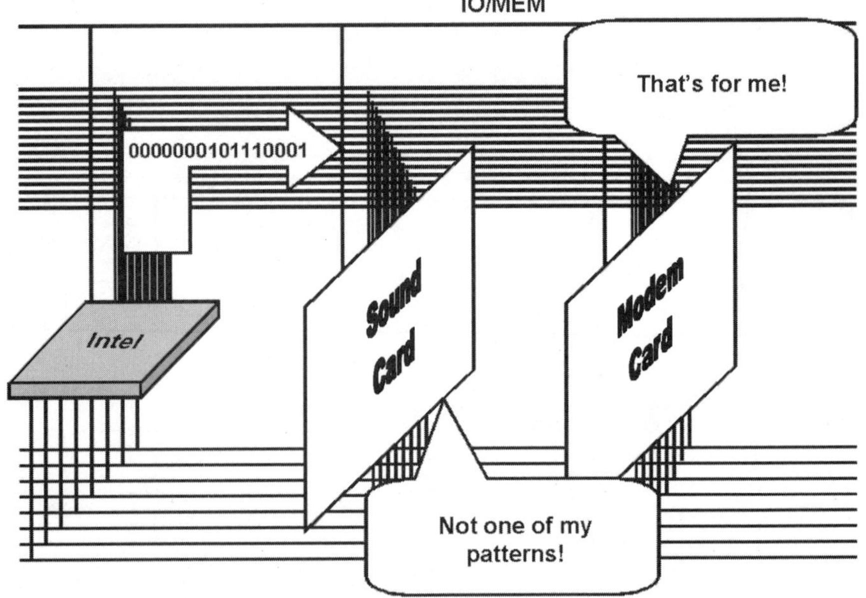

Figure 6.10 Sending an I/O address

up the IO/MEM wire and puts the pattern 0000 0001 1111 0000 onto the address bus, the hard-drive controller will send back a message describing its error status. All the different patterns used by the CPU to talk to the devices inside your computer are known as the *I/O addresses.* See Figure 6.10.

Hexadecimal

Sorry, but before I go any further, we will have to talk about hexadecimal numbers. I know that most of us hate the thought, but if you are going to fix computers, you are going to have to know how to talk *the dreaded hex!*

This entire section is repeated in the chapter on memory!

Don't panic. Hex is really almost trivial once you understand the secret. Hexadecimal, also known as base-16 mathematics, is a complete numbering system based on 16 instead of 10 digits. You can add, subtract, even do trigonometry with hex. I don't care. The only part of hex you need to know for the purposes of this book is how it is used in the PC world. To help you understand hex, I will use the address bus. When the IO/MEM wire is asserted, it uses the first 16 wires to talk to the devices in the computer. These wires can have either voltage or no voltage on them. A wire with voltage is represented by 1, and a wire with no voltage is 0. With 16 wires, there are 65,536 different combinations of ones and zeros, from 0000000000000000 to 1111111111111111.

Each different combination of charged and uncharged wires represents one pattern that the CPU can send down the address bus to talk to some device. The problem here is that it is a real pain to say things like, "The command to tell the hard-drive controller to show its error status is 0000000111110000." Think how difficult it would be to try to talk to someone about these different patterns of ones and zeros! For example, try telling another person to write down the following series of ones and zeros as you dictate them:

```
0010010001001001001000100100100100100001001111111010101010101000010
1011100
```

I guarantee that they will mess up somewhere as they try to write them down. Forget it! Although your computer is good at talking in ones and zeros, human beings find it very difficult.

What you need is some kind of shorthand, some way to talk about ones and zeros so human beings can understand it. This is where hexadecimal becomes very useful. Hex is a shorthand description of the state of wires. In the PC world, hexadecimal is nothing more than a shorthand method of describing a series of binary values.

Pretend that you have a computer with a four-wire address bus. How many different patterns can you create? Well, look at all the possibilities of ones and zeros you can make with four wires: 0000, 0001, 0010, 0011, 0100, 0101, 0110, 0111, 1000, 1001, 1010, 1011, 1100, 1101, 1110, and 1111.

So there are 16 different possibilities. There are no computers with only a four-wire address bus, but just about every processor ever built has an address bus with a multiple of four wires (8, 16, 20, 24, or 32). The largest common denominator of all these address bus sizes is four, so you can use this four binary digit grouping to create a shorthand by *representing any combination of four ones and zeros with a single character.* Since there are 16 different combinations, the 16 unique characters of the base-16 numbering system called hexadecimal are the natural choice. The hex shorthand is shown in Table 6.1.

So when you talk about a particular pattern being sent to a device on the address bus, you would not specify 0000000111110000. First, you would mentally break these 16 digits into four sets of four: 0000, 0001, 1111, and 0000.

Then you would give each four-character set its own hex shorthand: 00 (0), 0001 (1), 1111 (F), and 0000 (0). So instead of a bunch of ones and zeros, you could say something like "01F0."

To represent all the possible I/O addresses, we will always have four digits, from all zeros—0000 (0), 0000 (0), 0000 (0), and 0000 (0)—to all ones—1111 (F), 1111 (F), 1111 (F), and 1111 (F). All the possible I/O addresses can be rep-

TABLE 6.1

Possible Permutations for Four Wire

Binary Number		Hexadecimal Value
0000	all wires off	0
0001	only 4th wire on	1
0010	only 3rd wire on	2
0011	3rd and 4th on	3
0100	only 2nd wire on	4
0101	2nd and 4th wire on	5
0110	2nd and 3rd wire on	6
0111	only 1st wire off	7
1000	only 1st wire on	8
1001	1st and 4th on	9
1010	1st and 3rd on	A
1011	only 2nd off	B
1100	1st and 2nd on	C
1101	only 3rd off	D
1110	only 4th off	E
1111	all wires on	F

resented by four-digit hexadecimal values, starting at 0000 and ending at FFFF.

This explanation of hexadecimal is heavily slanted to the concept of I/O addresses, but hex is used in many other areas of the PC. We'll revisit this entire concept during the discussion of memory management.

The Rules of I/O Addresses

All devices respond to more than one pattern. The I/O address is a *range* of patterns. The pattern of ones and zeros that represent each address is used to give various commands to each device or for the device to talk to the CPU. For example, the hard drive's I/O address range is 01F0-01FF. If the CPU sends a 01F0 pattern, it is asking the hard-drive controller if there is an error anywhere. The command 01F1 is a totally separate command. No device has only one I/O address.

ALL DEVICES MUST HAVE AN I/O ADDRESS This is how the CPU talks to everything in your computer and there is no exception. Every device in your computer either has a preset I/O address or you must give it one. Basic devices in the computer have preset I/O addresses. For example, if you buy a hard-drive controller, it will have preset I/O address of 01F0-01FF. A sound card has to configure its own I/O address when you install it into a system.

ONCE A DEVICE IS USING AN I/O ADDRESS, NO OTHER DEVICE CAN USE IT. When you install that new sound card in your system, you have to know what I/O addresses are being used, and you must be sure that the sound card uses I/O addresses that no other device is currently using.

Every device in your computer has an I/O address. No two devices can share any I/O addresses or the device(s) won't work.

So the big question here is: "How do I know what I/O addresses are being used in my computer?" Fortunately, most of the I/O addresses were set up by IBM a long time ago. When IBM released the PC to the public domain, they provided a list of I/O addresses that you must use in order to be "IBM compatible." This list, shown in Table 6.2, is still followed by every PC in the world today.

Talking the Talk

I/O addresses are 16-bit addresses, which are always displayed in four hexadecimal numbers, such as 01F0. However, when discussing I/O addresses, most people drop the leading zeros, so 01F0 is usually referred to as 1F0. Also, almost no one talks about the I/O address. What is usually discussed is the I/O base address, which is the first pattern of ones and zeros. If the I/O address for a hard drive is 1F0-1FF, the I/O base address is just 1F0. When discussing any hex value, many people put a lowercase *h* on the end to show you it is a hex value. For example, some people will show the I/O base address for the floppy controller as 3F0h.

When talking about I/O addresses, always drop the leading zeros.

The I/O address is a range of addresses; the I/O address for the joystick is 200-207.

The I/O base address is the first I/O address for a device; the I/O base address for the joystick is 200.

Many people put an *h* on the end of a hex value to show that it is hex; the I/O base address for the floppy is 3F0h.

TABLE 6.2

The Original IBM I/O Address List

I/O Address Range	Usage
0000-000F	DMA controller
0020-002F	Master IRQ controller
0030-003F	Master IRQ controller
0040-0043	System timer
0060-0063	Keyboard
0070-0071	CMOS clock
0080-008F	DMA page registers
0090-009F	DMA page registers
00A0-00AF	Slave IRQ controller
00B0-00BF	Slave IRQ controller
00C0-00CF	DMA controller
00E0-00EF	Reserved
00F0-00FF	Math coprocessor
0170-0177	Secondary hard drive controller
01F0-01FF	Primary hard drive controller
0200-0207	Joystick
0278-027F	LPT2
0210-0217	Reserved
02B0-02DF	Secondary EGA
02E8-02EF	COM4
02F8-02FF	COM2
0378-037F	LPT1
03B0-03BF	Mono video
03C0-03CF	Primary EGA
03D0-03DF	CGA video
03E8-03EF	COM3
03F0-03F7	Floppy controller
03F8-03FF	COM1

Armed with this knowledge, you can show the I/O address map, as shown in Table 6.3. Take a close look at the I/O address map one more time. Notice that there are no I/O addresses for sound cards, and no I/O addresses for network cards. In fact, IBM mapped out the I/O addresses for only the most common devices. So if you want to install a sound card, what I/O addresses are available? Well, look at I/O base address 210h, then look at the next I/O base address—it's 278h, isn't it? All the I/O base addresses between these two are open for use, so there are plenty of unused addresses! By the way, you'll notice that the last address is 3F8h, so couldn't you use all the addresses from 3F8 all the way to FFFF? Unfortunately, you can't due to a limitation of both DOS and Windows. (Okay, there is a way, but bear with me for a moment and assume that you can't; I promise to explain later!)

You can now see that I/O addresses provide a two-way communication pathway between peripherals and the CPU. If the CPU wants to talk to a device, BIOS routines or device drivers can use I/O addresses to initiate conversations over the external data bus. Later in this chapter, I will help you put this theory into practice.

Interrupts

The CPU can now communicate with all of the devices inside the computer, but there's still a small problem. I/O addressing is a two-way communication, but it must be started by the CPU. A device, such as mouse, can't send its own I/O address to the CPU to get the CPU's attention. So how does a device initiate a conversation with the CPU? For example, how does the mouse tell the CPU that it has moved? How does the keyboard tell the CPU that somebody just pressed the J key? You need some kind of mechanism to tell the CPU to stop doing whatever it is doing and talk to a particular device. (See Figure 6.11.)

This mechanism is called *interruption*. Every CPU in the PC world has an INT (interrupt) wire, shown in Figure 6.12. If this wire is charged, the CPU will stop what it is doing and deal with the device. Say you have a PC with only one peripheral, a keyboard, the CPU is running WordPerfect, and the user presses the J key. The keyboard is connected to the CPU's INT wire and charges the wire. The CPU temporarily stops running WordPerfect and runs the necessary BIOS routine to query the keyboard.

This would be fine if there was only one device in the computer. However, as we all know, there are a lot of devices and almost all of them will

TABLE 6.3

Updated I/O Address Map

I/O Base Address	Usage
0h	DMA controller
20h	Master IRQ controller
30h	Master IRQ controller
40h	System timer
60h	Keyboard
70h	CMOS clock
80h	DMA page registers
90h	DMA page registers
A0h	Slave IRQ controller
B0h	Slave IRQ controller
C0h	DMA controller
E0h	Reserved
F0h	Math coprocessor
170h	Secondary hard drive controller
1F0h	Primary hard drive controller
200h	Joystick
210h	Reserved
278h	LPT2
2B0h	Secondary EGA
2E8h	COM4
2F8h	COM2
378h	LPT1
3B0h	Mono video
3C0h	Primary EGA
3D0h	CGA video
3E8h	COM3
3F0h	Floppy controller
3F8h	COM1

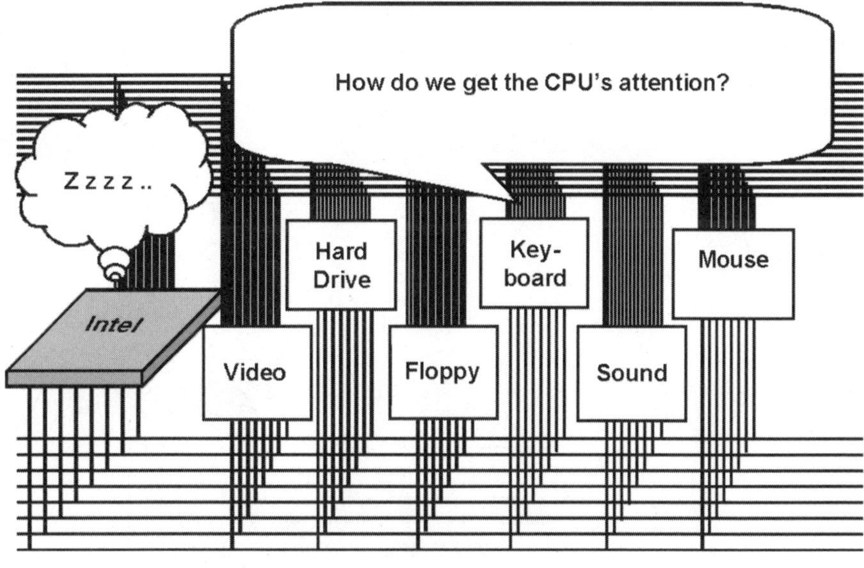

Figure 6.11 How do devices tell the CPU they need attention?

Figure 6.12 The INT wire

need to interrupt the CPU at some point. So you need some kind of "traffic cop" chip to act as an intermediary between all the devices and the CPU's INT wire. In the original IBM PC, a chip known as the 8259 was added to the system.

The 8259 was hooked to the INT wire of the CPU on one side, and had other eight wires called IRQs (interrupt requests) that extended out from the chip into the motherboard (Figure 6.14). Every device that needed to interrupt the CPU got an IRQ. If a device needed to interrupt the CPU, it lit its IRQ and the 8259 then lit the INT wire on the CPU. Whenever the INT wire was lit, the CPU talked to the 8259 via its I/O address to determine which device was interrupting. The 8259 told the CPU which IRQ was lit and this allowed the CPU to know which BIOS to run.

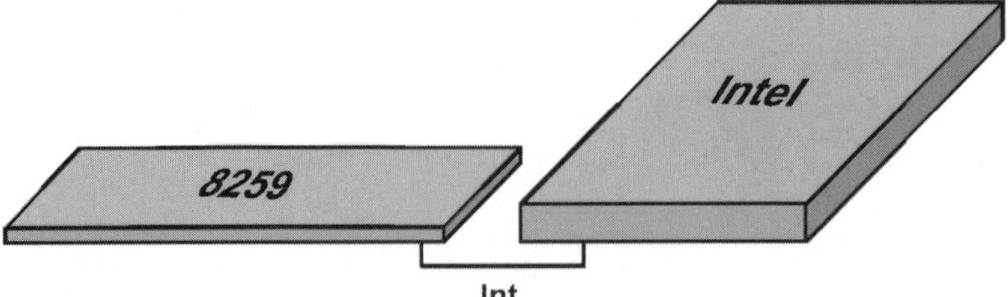

Figure 6.13
8259 with CPU

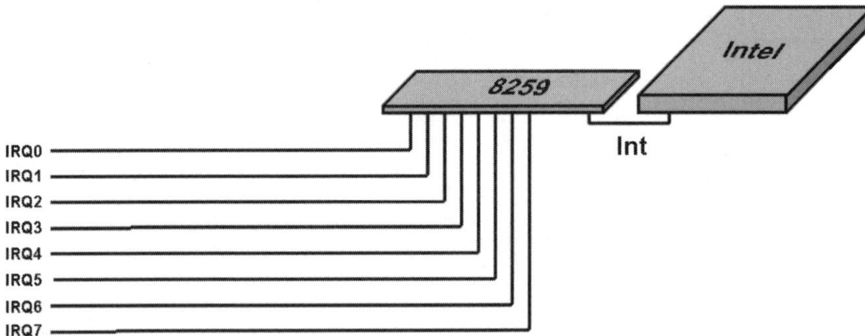

Figure 6.14
The eight IRQs from the 8259

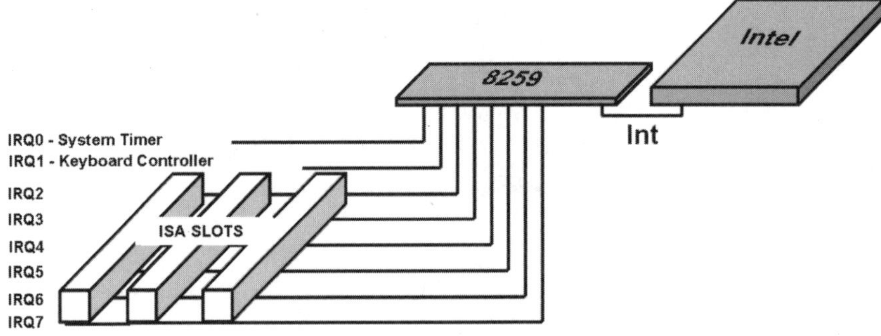

Figure 6.15
IBM PC - Function of IRQs

Most of the IRQ wires were dedicated to certain devices. IRQ 0 went to a device called the *system timer* that told the RAM when to refresh. IRQ 1 went to the keyboard, and the other six wires ran straight to the ISA expansion bus. (See Figure 6.15.) So any ISA card could use IRQs 2 through 6. This system of IRQ usage, although developed way back in the early '80s, is still used on today's most modern PCs.

Now there are some important rules here. The first rule is that no two devices can share an IRQ. So if one device is using IRQ 3, no other device can use that IRQ.

Under almost all circumstances, no two devices can share an IRQ.

TABLE 6.4

IRQs Assignments on IBM PC and XT

IRQ	Default Function
IRQ 0	System timer
IRQ 1	Keyboard
IRQ 2	Reserved
IRQ 3	COM2
IRQ 4	COM1
IRQ 5	LPT2
IRQ 6	Floppy Drive
IRQ 7	LPT1

To prevent devices from sharing IRQs, IBM gave an IRQ map to card manufacturers so they knew which IRQs to use for certain types of devices, just like they did for I/O addresses (see Table 6.4).

So where's the IRQ for the hard drive, or sound cards? Unfortunately, the original IRQ map was produced before either of these devices were invented! You might notice that IRQ2 is "reserved." IBM didn't want anyone to use IRQ2; they were going to use it for something special, a mainframe card called the 3270. You see, IBM thought that most PCs would be hooked to mainframes, so they wanted to keep IRQ2 just for these 3270 cards.

Virtually every device in your computer needs an IRQ, although there are a few exceptions. A joystick, for example, doesn't use an IRQ. If you write a program to use a joystick, you have to write it to constantly check the joystick to see if a button has been pressed or the stick has been moved.

If you install something in your computer, it will have an I/O address, and it will almost certainly have an IRQ.

You might notice items called COM1, COM2, and LPT1. Let's take a moment to discuss what they are and how they function in the PC.

COM and LPT Ports

IRQs and I/O addresses were not invented for the IBM PC. Mainframes, minis, and pre-PC microcomputers all used IRQs and I/O addresses. When IBM was designing the PC, they wanted to simplify the installa-

TABLE 6.5

COM and LPT Assignments

Port	I/O Address	IRQ
COM1	3F8	4
COM2	2F8	3
LPT1	378	7
LPT2	278	5

tion, programming, and operation of devices. Since virtually every peripheral needs both an IRQ and I/O address, IBM created *standard preset combinations* of IRQs and I/O addresses. For serial devices, the preset combinations are called COM ports. For parallel devices, they are called LPT ports. The word *port* is used to describe a "portal" or two-way access. Table 6.5 lists the preset combinations of I/O addresses and IRQs.

Ports do make installation easier. Look at modems. They do not have any setting for IRQs or I/O addresses. Instead, you set their COM port. Most people do not realize that they are really setting the IRQ and I/O address when they select a COM port. If you set a modem to COM1, what you are really doing is setting the modem's IRQ to 4 and the modem's I/O address to 3F8 (see Table 6.5).

A COM and an LPT port is nothing more than a preset combination of an IRQ and I/O address.

Programmers also enjoy the benefits of ports. All ports are built into the system BIOS, so programmers do not have to know the I/O address for a modem. They simply run the BIOS routine to output data or commands to the appropriate COM port, and the BIOS routine translates and sends the command or data to the correct I/O address. Even operating systems understand ports. That is why you can type commands like DIR>LPT1 and DOS will know which BIOS routine to activate so the directory will output to the printer instead of the monitor.

COM3 and COM4

Back in the original PCs, IBM dedicated two IRQs to serial ports: IRQ4 for COM1 and IRQ3 for COM2. Many systems needed more than two serial devices, however, and there was a lot of complaining about the lack of COM ports. IBM then established two more COM port standards, COM3 and COM4, and assigned two previously unused I/O addresses (3E8-3EF for COM3 and 2E8-2EF for COM4) to these ports. See Table 6.6.

Remember, this was in the days when there was only one 8259, so there were no extra IRQs. So IBM just doubled them up. COM3 used IRQ4 and COM4 used IRQ3. Hey, wait a minute! The number-one rule of setting IRQs is to never let two devices share the same IRQ. Well, there is an exception to that rule. Two (or more) devices can share the same IRQ *as long as they never talk at the same time!*

Back in the old days, there were a lot of devices that could share IRQs. For example, you could have a dedicated fax card and a modem on the same IRQ. Neither device had a device driver and the fax would never run at the same time as the modem (this was before Windows). So these two devices could be set to COM1 and COM3. In today's computers, you can no longer set one device as COM1 and another device as COM3, or one device as COM2 and another as COM4. If you do, the computer will lock up.

If you accidentally have two devices sharing the same IRQ, the computer will eventually lock up. However, you won't destroy anything—just correct the problem and try again.

LPT Ports

LPT ports are for parallel connections. In the old days, parallel ports were used only for high-speed printers, so when IBM standardized ports for parallel devices, they were called LPT ports, LPT being an abbreviation of *line printer.* LPT ports work well. Because IBM standardized the LPT port to not talk back, IRQ7 for LPT1 and IRQ5 for LPT2 are never used by the LPT port. IRQ5 and IRQ7 can therefore be used for other devices.

Of course, there is also an exception for this. Many devices are being made today to plug into the parallel plug in the back of your PC. Many devices that plug into a parallel port (for example, tape backups and modems) use an interrupt. So if you use IRQ7 for another device, do not

TABLE 6.6

COM Port Assignments

COM Port	IRQ	I/O Base Address
COM 1	4	3F8H
COM 2	3	2F8H
COM 3	4	3E8H
COM 4	3	2E8H

plug anything other than your printer into LPT1. Buy a new LPT2 parallel-port card. Also, many printers now interrupt, so be careful.

Physical vs. I/O Ports

I need to clarify something right away. A serial port is a physical item, a 9- or 15-pin male DB connector in the back of your PC, but a COM port is just the I/O address and IRQ assigned to it. A parallel port is a 25-pin female DB connector on the back of your PC, but an LPT is just the I/O address and IRQ assigned to it. Think of a telephone. If someone pointed to your phone and said, "that is a 324-5444," you would correct them: "No, that's a telephone. The number assigned to it is 324-5444." Same with serial and parallel ports. You would not look at a serial port and say "That's COM1." See Figure 6.16.

Back to the 8259

With the original PC, IBM discovered that six IRQs were not enough for most systems, so when the 286 AT was invented, they added another 8259. The 8259 was designed to run in a "cascade" (Figure 6.17), which means that you can hook another 8259 to the first 8259, but the INT connection

That's COM 1!
No, it's a serial port set to COM 1!

Figure 6.16 Physical vs. I/O ports

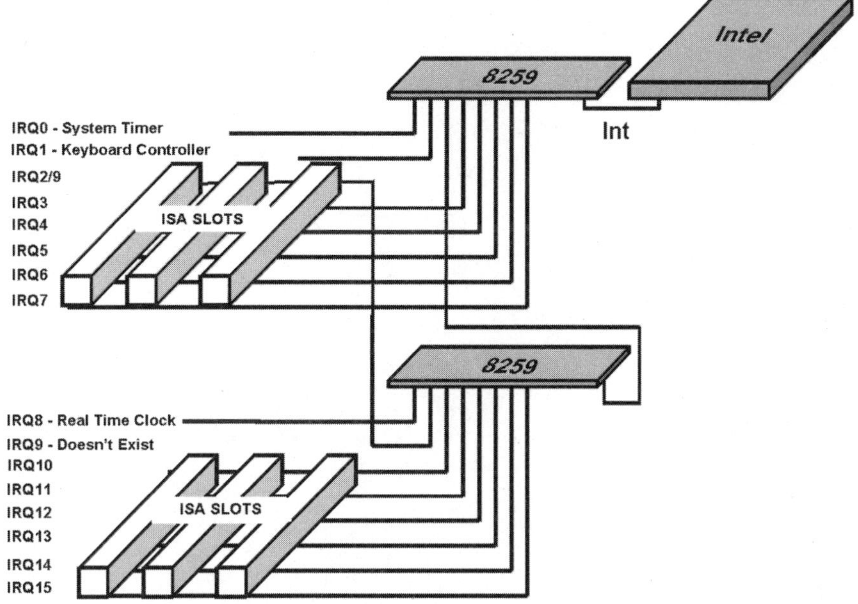

Figure 6.17
Dual 8259 cascade

on the second 8259 has to take one of the IRQs from the first 8259. IBM decided to take the INT wire from the first 8259 and hook it into the IRQ2 of the first. However, this created a problem in that a lot of cards were already using IRQ2. So IBM ran the IRQ9 wire over to the IRQ2 position on the ISA slot, allowing older cards to still work. This cascading procedure adds eight more IRQs, but you lose one in the process. The eight new wires run to the extension on the 16-bit ISA expansion slot. See Table 6.7.

Refer back to the ISA slot pinouts to see the IRQ positions.

Table 6.7 lists the IRQ map as designed for the two 8259s in the original IBM AT computer. Again, notice that the cascade removes IRQ 2. IRQ 9 is hooked to the old IRQ 2 wire, so if a device is designed to run on IRQ 2, it will run on IRQ 9. In essence, IRQ 2 and IRQ 9 are the same IRQ. Three IRQs are hard-wired (0, 1, and 8). Four IRQs are so common that no PC or device maker dares change them for fear that their devices will not be compatible (6, 13, 14, and 15). Four IRQs default to specific types of devices but are very changeable—as long as the hardware device allows it (IRQ 3, 4, 5, and 7). The rest (IRQ 2/9, 10, 11, and 12) are not specific and are open for use.

There is no IRQ2 or IRQ9. It is called IRQ 2/9.

TABLE 6.7

IRQ Assignments with COM3 and COM4

IRQ	Default Function
IRQ 0	System timer
IRQ 1	Keyboard
IRQ 2/9	Open for use
IRQ 3	Default COM2, COM4
IRQ 4	Default COM1, COM3
IRQ 5	LPT2
IRQ 6	Floppy Drive
IRQ 7	LPT1
IRQ 8	Real-time clock
IRQ 10	Open for use
IRQ 11	Open for use
IRQ 12	Open for use
IRQ 13	Math-coprocessor
IRQ 14	Primary hard drive controller
IRQ15	Secondary hard drive controller

These settings are somewhat flexible. If a device that uses a certain IRQ is not present, that IRQ is available. For example, if you do not have a secondary hard-drive controller, IRQ 15 can be used by another device.

I/O Ports Today

There's a lot of confusion about I/O ports, but now you understand what they are, I can eliminate that confusion. First, even though IBM dictated what the I/O address and IRQ for a particular COM or LPT port might be, the IRQ can be changed as long as the device can actually do it and the software that talks to that device knows about the change. So you can change, say, COM1's IRQ from 4 to 5 if the hardware and software allows it. Let's use my motherboard as an example. Like most computers today, I have two built-in serial ports. You can change the COM port settings by accessing the CMOS. (See Figure 6.18.)

Note that serial port 1 is set to I/O address 3F8 and IRQ4. What COM port is that? It's COM1, but I could change the COM port to any of the following settings:

3F8/IRQ4: standard COM1
2F8/IRQ3: standard COM2
3F8/IRQ5: COM1 but with the nonstandard IRQ5
2F8/IRQ5: COM2 but with the nonstandard IRQ5

It is also important to know that if a standard device isn't using the IRQ assigned to it or if you don't have that device, the IRQ is open for use. The most common example of this is LPT2, which uses IRQ5. Most PCs today don't have a second parallel port, so it is common for devices to use IRQ5. A good example of this is sound cards. When a sound card is installed, it will almost always want to be set to IRQ5.

Don't forget that if you set a device to a COM/LPT port, you are using an IRQ. This is always a big problem for new technicians who don't understand IRQs and their relationship to COM/LPT. Most people have already heard that you don't let more than one device use an IRQ. But because they don't know that a COM/LPT port is by definition an I/O address and an IRQ, they get into trouble. If someone has a COM1 and then tries to install some other device to IRQ4, the system will lock up. But they don't see the error, because they don't realize that COM1 is IRQ4!

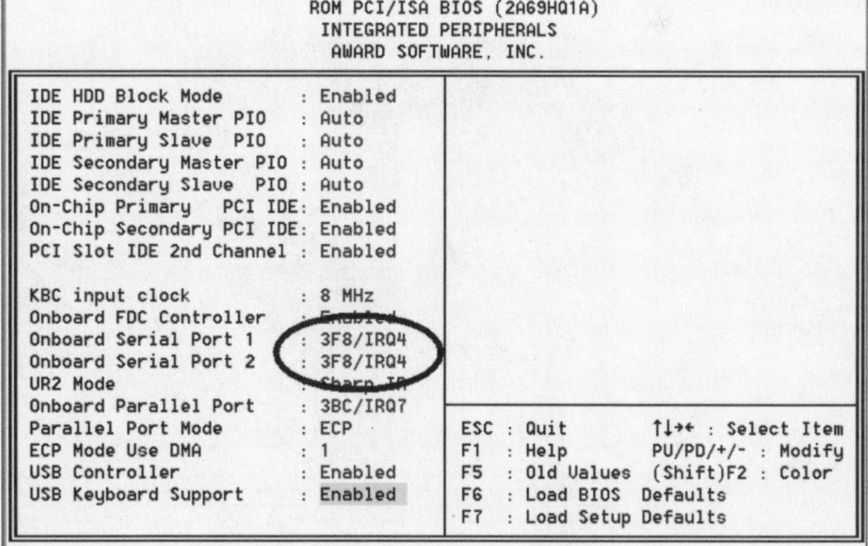

Figure 6.18 Port settings for an onboard serial port

The combination of I/O address and IRQ is the cornerstone of CPU-device communication. But there is one more aspect of the this communication I must discuss—the badly misunderstood concept of DMA.

DMA

CPUs do a lot of work. They run the BIOS, operating system, and applications. CPUs handle interrupts and access I/O addresses. They are busy little chips. CPUs also deal with one other item—data. Data is constantly being manipulated, such as being moved. CPUs move data from one place in RAM to another. Peripherals send data to RAM (for example, a scanner) via the CPU, and the CPU sends data from RAM to peripherals (for example, a laser printer).

All of this data moving is obviously necessary, but it is also very simple to do. Moving data is a waste of the CPU's power and time. Moreover, with all of the caches and such on today's CPUs, most of the time the system is doing nothing while the CPU is handling some internal calculation. See Figure 6.19.

So, why not make devices that can access memory directly, without involving the CPU? (See Figure 6.20.) The process of accessing memory without using the CPU is called *Direct Memory Access*, or DMA. DMA allows

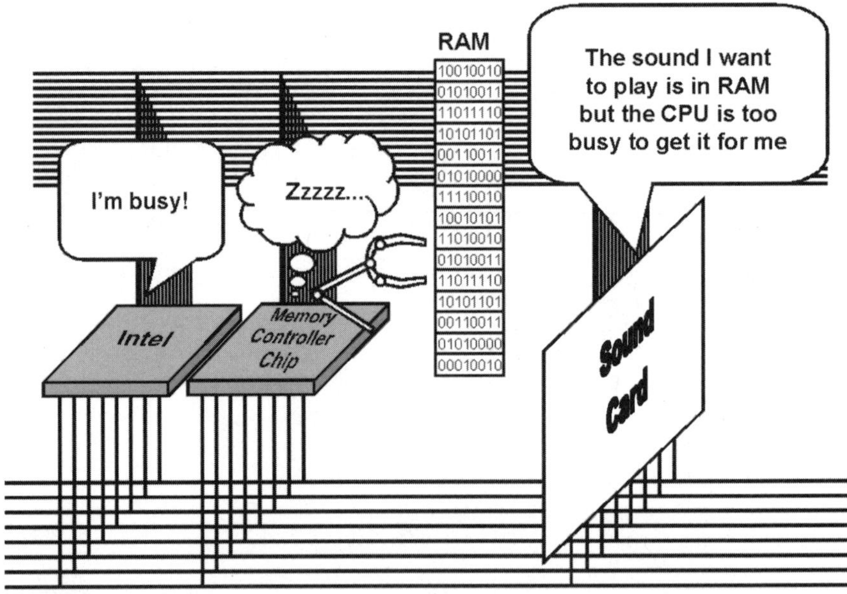

Figure 6.19 The need for DMA

Figure 6.20
Why not talk to the MCC directly?

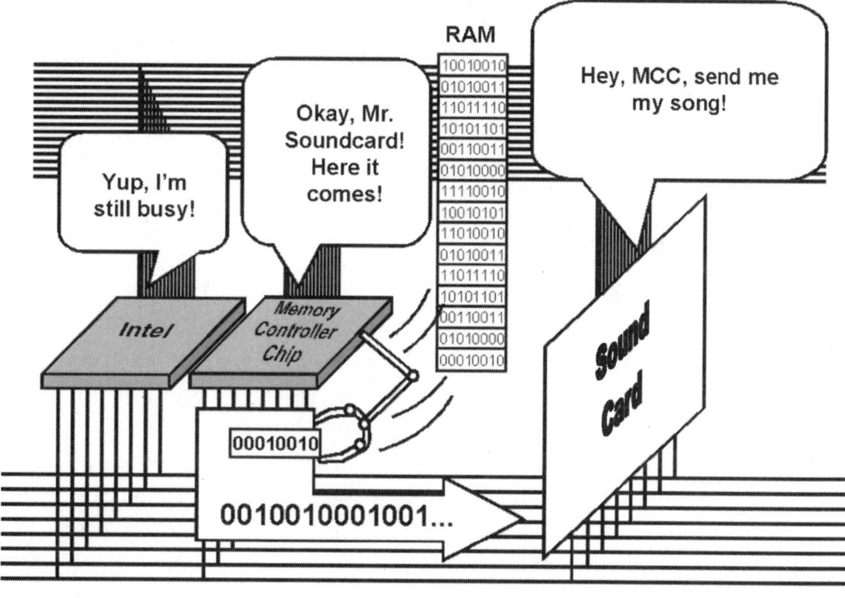

Figure 6.21
DMA in action

the system to run background applications without interfering with the CPU (Figure 6.21). This is excellent for creating background sounds in games, and accessing floppy and hard drives.

However, the concept of DMA as described here has a problem. What if more than one device wants to use DMA? Who is to keep these devices

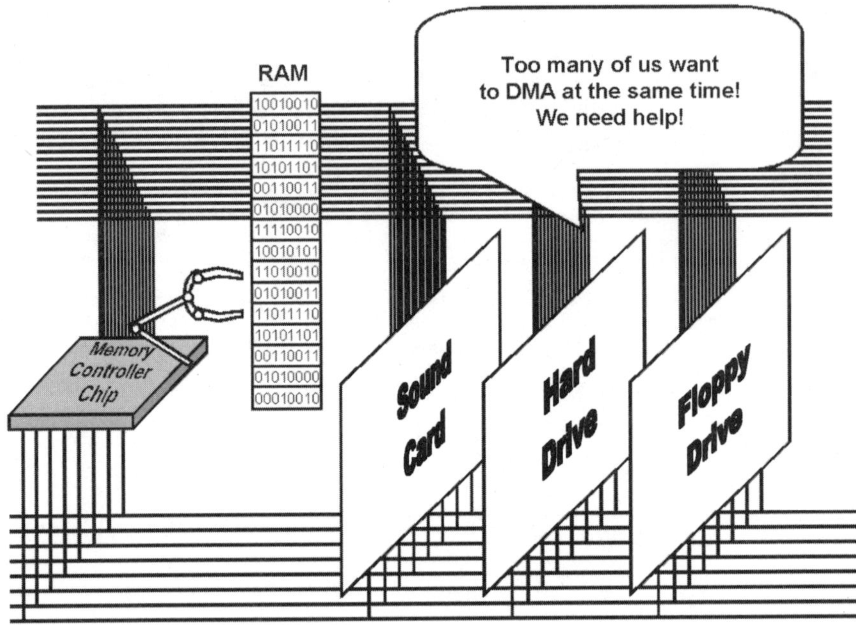

Figure 6.22 DMA needs a controlling chip

from stomping on the external data bus at the same time? Plus, what if the CPU suddenly needs the data bus? How can you stop the device using DMA so the CPU, which should have priority, can access the bus? (See Figure 6.22.)

Knowing this, IBM installed *another, very simple CPU* called the 8237 chip to control all DMA functions (Figure 6.23). This primitive CPU can handle all the data passing from peripherals to RAM and vice versa. This takes necessary but simple work away from the CPU, so the CPU can spend time doing more productive work. The DMA chip passes data along the external data bus when the CPU is busy and not using the external data bus. This is perfectly acceptable since the CPU accesses the external data bus only a small percentage of the time: 20 percent of the time on a 486, and 5 percent of the time with a Pentium.

The 8237 chip is linked to the CPU via the HRQ wire, which informs the CPU that the data is was going to be busy. The 8237 has four wires, called DRQs (DMA requests), which lead to the DRAM refresh circuitry and ISA slots. DRQs were, and still are, more commonly known as DMA channels. If a device wants to perform a DMA data transfer, it must activate its assigned DMA channel. See Figure 6.24.

DRQs work exactly like IRQs, with all the same rules—such as no two devices being able to share the same DMA channel.

DMA channel and *DRQ* are identical terms. No two devices can share DRQs.

In 286s on up, there are two cascaded DMA chips, for a total of seven DRQs; DRQ0 and DRQ4 are the same, just as IRQ2 and IRQ9 are the same (Figure 6.25). However, you never say DRQ 0/4—just DRQ0.

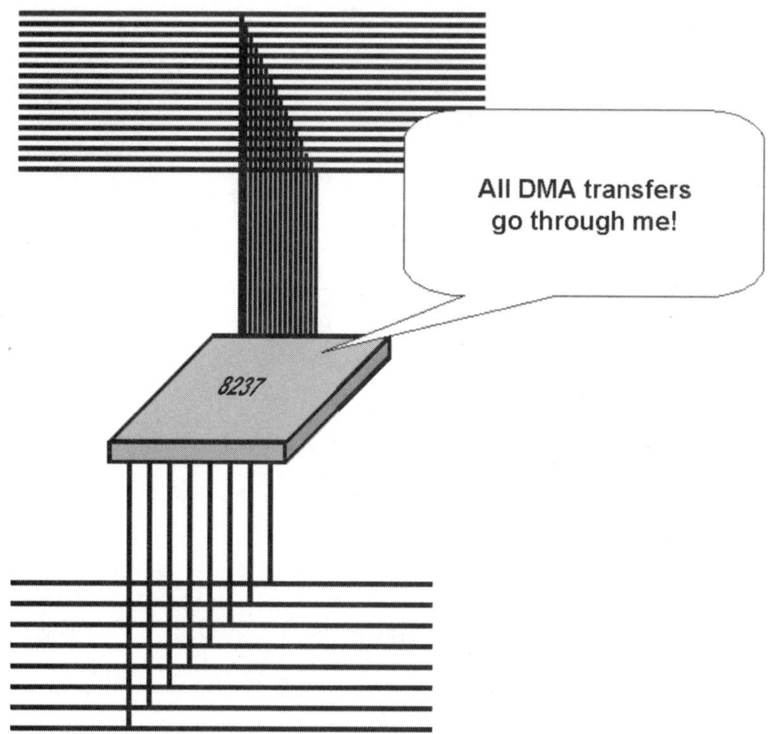

Figure 6.23
The 8237

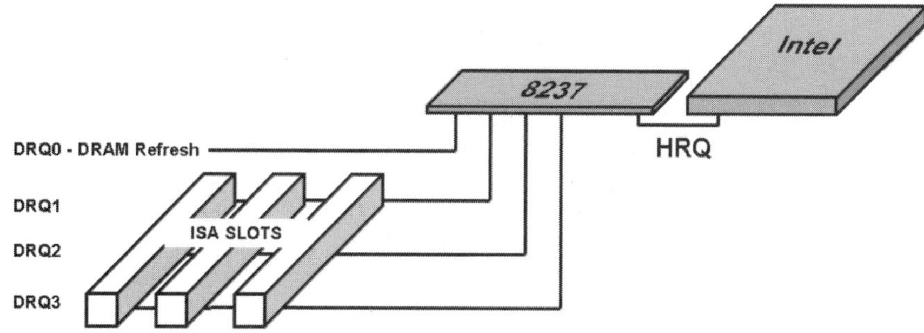

Figure 6.24
8237 in the original IBM PC

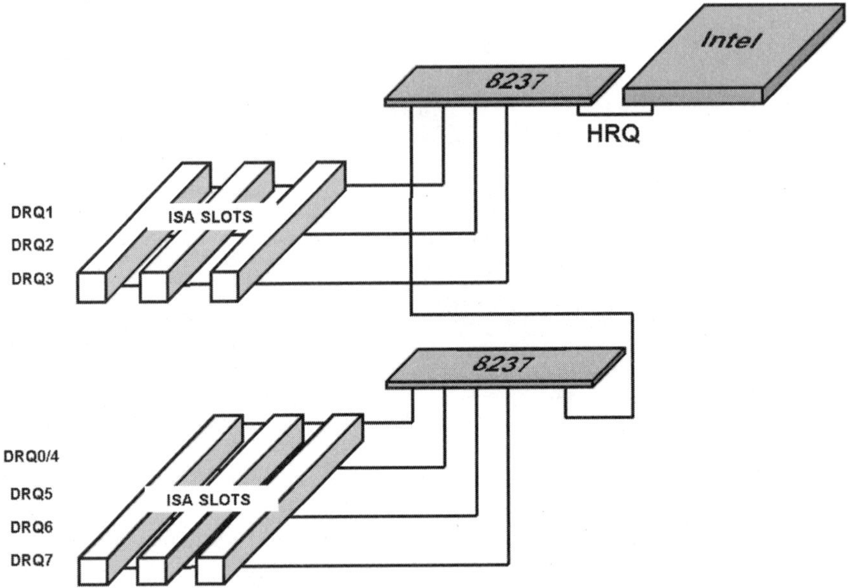

Figure 6.25
Cascaded 8237s

DMA Limitations

DMA, as originally designed by IBM, has some serious limitations. First, DMA is designed to run from cards installed on the ISA bus. As a result, DMA is limited to a maximum speed of roughly 8 MHz. Second, each 8237 can handle only byte-wide data. Although this wasn't a problem in the first IBM PC, as PCs moved from 8088s through 286s, 386s, and 486s, it was faster to skip DMA and just wait for the CPU to move data. DMA can be moved in two-byte chunks in 286s and up with dual 8237s by using 8 bits from each 8237. But even 16-bit data is too slow for more modern systems. This slowness has relegated DMA to low-speed, background jobs like floppy access, sound creation, and tape backup. However, there has been a bit of a resurgence in the use of DMA through the use of bus mastering.

There are two types of DMA transfers: 8-bit and 16-bit. If a device wants to use 8-bit transfers, it should use a lower DMA channel: 0 through 3. If a device wants to use 16-bit transfers, it should use a high DMA channel: 5 through 7.

Bus Mastering

Some devices can use DMA without accessing the 8237s or the CPU. These devices are known as *bus masters*. Bus-mastering devices are usually created for high-speed data transfers—they are doing something "weird" to the system that would confuse the 8237s or the CPU. Bus mastering is powerful, but not too common. You will revisit bus mastering later in this chapter when I discuss a few special installation issues.

Who Uses DMA?

Not very many devices use DMA. The only devices that commonly use it are sound cards and floppy drives. However, virtually any device can be designed to use DMA. See Table 6.8.

Although it is important to understand the *why* of I/O address, IRQ, and DMA, we need to discuss the *how* of installation, configuration, and troubleshooting the "big three." The following sections are designed to give you a solid methodology to ensure that you can set up any device in any PC with a minimum of effort and a maximum of speed.

Chipsets

Before we dive into device installation, I want to make a quick diversion. I've been talking about a lot of different chips in your PC. Take a look at the motherboard in Figure 6.26; you can see the CPU and RAM, but can you see the 8259 chips? Can you find the 8237s? How about the memory controller chip? You can't, can you! But you might notice two (sometimes three or even one) chips. They are distinct in that they names such as *Intel, Opti,* or *VIA* on them.

This is the *chipset,* which are specialized chips that have consolidated *all* the functions of these many chips we've discussed. All chipsets act exactly

TABLE 6.8

DMA Assignments

DMA Channel	Type	Function
0	8-Bit	None
1	8-Bit	Open for use
2	8-Bit	Floppy drive controller
3	8-Bit	Open for use
5	16-Bit	Open for use
6	16-Bit	Open for use
7	16-Bit	Open for use

Figure 6.26
Typical chipset

like the original chips they have replaced. Even though you don't have an 8259, all the IRQs are there. The same applies to the DMA and memory-management functions.

A Better Bus

The first-generation expansion buses, 8- and 16-bit ISA, were both excellent buses for their time. In fact, the 16-bit ISA (which is often referred to as just *ISA*) continues to soldier on in even the most modern PCs available today. Yet the ISA bus suffers from some tremendous limitations. It is slow, running at up to only 8.33 MHz. It is narrow and unable to handle the 32- and 64-bit external data buses of more modern processors. Last, it is stupid. If you add a device to the system, you have to manually, or at best semimanually, configure the I/O address, IRQ, and DMA to allow that device to work correctly. When the 386 was introduced, there was tremendous demand to improve or even replace the ISA bus to correct these deficiencies. Let's look at this evolution of later-generation expansion buses, in order to bring you up to date with the systems of today.

History of Expansion Buses: Part 2

So far I have talked about only two types of expansion buses: 8-bit ISA and 16-bit ISA. The ISA buses run at a maximum of 8.33 MHz, although most run at around 7 MHz. The buses require users to configure I/O addresses, IRQs, and DMAs manually. The technology is free, however, because IBM released the design to the public domain.

MCA

When the 386 started to appear in 1986, IBM decided to create a new type of expansion bus, called Micro-Channel Architecture (MCA), as shown in Figure 6.27. This bus is 32-bit to match the 386's (and the 486's) 32-bit external data bus. It is also faster than the ISA bus, running at about 12 MHz. What really makes the MCA bus different, however, is its ability to self-configure devices. When you buy a Micro-Channel device, it always comes with an "option disk." You simply install a new device in the Micro-Channel computer, insert the option disk when prompted, and the IRQs, I/O addresses, and DMA channels will be automatically configured. MCA is an excellent bus.

MCA has some major drawbacks, however. First, the slots are different, so MCA cards are incompatible with ISA. Second, MCA is licensed by IBM, meaning that they did not release it to the public domain, so it is expensive. Also, MCA devices are much more sophisticated than ISA devices, making them two to three times more expensive than the equivalent ISA device.

MCA is now a dead technology. Virtually no manufacturers other than IBM made MCA computers, primarily because of licensing and manufacturing costs. Today, there are newer buses that perform all the functions

Figure 6.27
Microchannel slots

Figure 6.28
MCA is dead

of MCA at a fraction of the cost. Although you can still purchase MCA cards, the cold fact that the technology is no longer supported by new systems virtually guarantees that you are wasting your money (Figure 6.28).

EISA

When MCA came out in the mid-'80s, it created quite a stir. IBM was trying not only to regain control of bus standards, but also to charge for licensing that standard. An industry group of clone makers created a competitor to MCA called Enhanced ISA (EISA, pronounced "ee-suh") in 1988. Basically, EISA does everything that MCA does: it is a faster, 32-bit, self-configuring expansion bus (Figure 6.29). EISA has two aspects that make it an attractive option to MCA. First, it is much cheaper than MCA, although not nearly as cheap as ISA. Second, EISA uses a double-slot connector that is compatible with ISA devices.

Although considered the high-end expansion bus for years, EISA also seems to be a dying technology for many of the same reasons mentioned for MCA. However, EISA still has a strong installed base of machines and you can still find new systems today that support EISA. Although EISA will certainly be around for at least a few more years, I'd recommend staying away and stick to newer buses.

VESA VL-BUS

Although MCA and EISA were fine buses, neither gained any significant following. Before Windows, the expansion bus speed of the ISA slots (7 MHz) was sufficient for most tasks. As a result, virtually all 386 and early 486 systems were a strange combination of a 32-bit external data and address bus, running at the speed of the CPU, connected to a 7-MHz, 16-bit expansion bus. In essence, you had two data buses: a fast, wide local bus and a slow, narrow expansion bus (Figure 6.30).

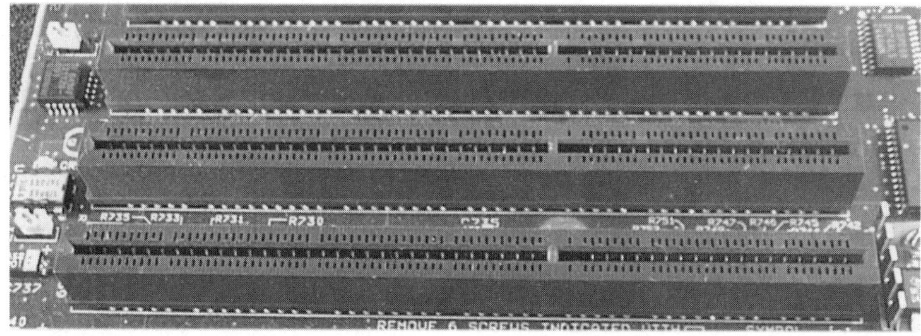

Figure 6.29 EISA slots

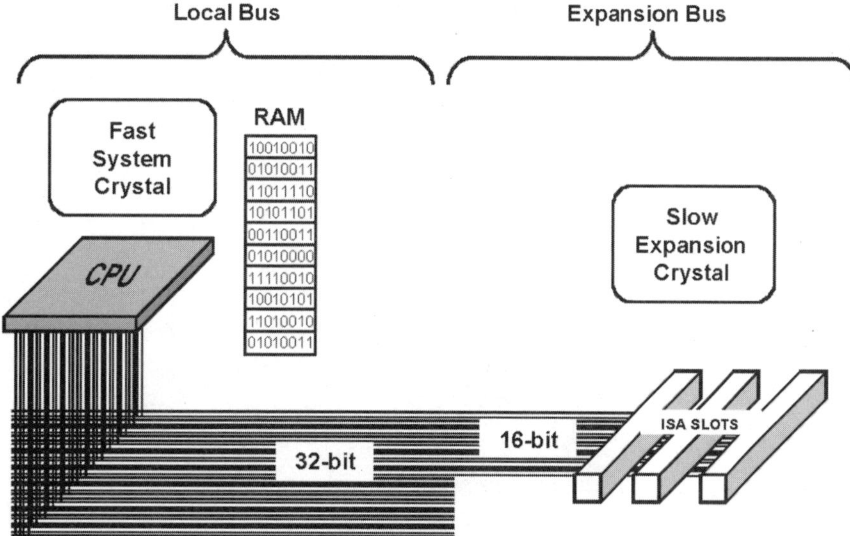

Figure 6.30 Local vs. expansion bus

Microsoft Windows changed that. The graphical user interface (GUI) of Windows put huge new demands on video. The 16-bit data path and 7-MHz top speed of the ISA video cards could not keep up with these new demands. Two solutions presented themselves. The first was the creation of coprocessed video cards. These video cards were preprogrammed with Windows objects such as scroll bars and menus. The video BIOS of all VGA video cards have similar programming for the ASCII character set. On a standard VGA card, if the video card receives instruction to output the letter J to the monitor, it does not specify each pixel. It is preprogrammed with the ASCII character set, and will output a predefined J.

The new Windows coprocessed video cards were preprogrammed with common Windows GUI features such as scroll bars, title bars, and mouse cursors. Instead of having to draw each feature of the interface, these new video cards could pop out a scroll bar the same way that earlier cards could pop out a J. These cards could probably have kept the average computer user happy for a time, avoiding the need for a new, faster expansion bus. One problem remained, however: the new, Windows-ready coprocessing video cards would not be available for more than a year after the introduction of Windows 3.0.

The other way to increase throughput was to tap back into the local bus, so the Video Electronics Standards Association (VESA) created the VL (VESA local) bus. The VL-bus solution to both of these problems was to tap back into the local bus (Figure 6.31). Remember that while there is only one external data bus that connects everything in the PC, the external data bus is divided into two parts: the system bus and the expansion bus. The system bus ran at the speed (or half the speed) of the system crystal, usually between 25 and 33 MHz on a 386 or 486. The expansion bus, into which ISA cards are snapped, ran off a different crystal at a standard 7 MHz in order to ensure backward compatibility.

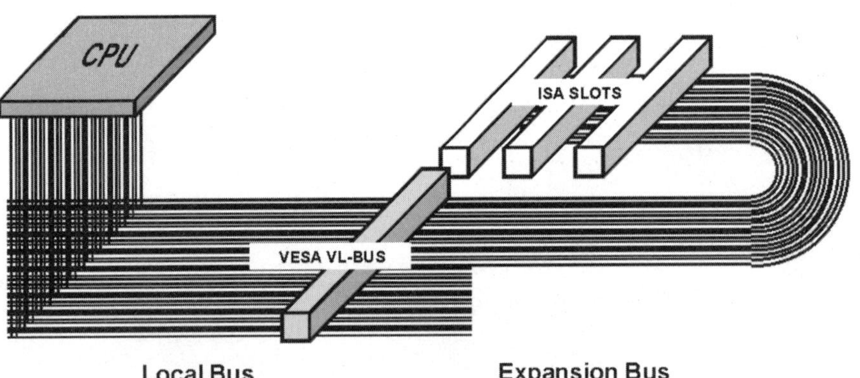

Figure 6.31
VESA VL-BUS

Figure 6.32
VESA VL-BUS slots

By tapping directly into the local bus, VL-bus devices could use the full 32-bit data bus available on 386 and 486 machines. In addition, VL-bus devices could run at either the speed of the system bus (synchronously) or at the speed of a crystal on the VL-bus itself (asynchronously). VL-buses have a top practical speed of 33 MHz. Most CMOS setup programs on motherboards with a VL-bus allow you to set the speed of the VL-bus to either synchronous or asynchronous. While either will work, for optimum performance you should set it to run at whichever speed is faster.

VL-bus slots are *parasitic slots* (Figure 6.32). The reason VL-buses must work with another bus is that each VL-bus slot is paired with another bus slot, usually a 16-bit ISA slot (the specifications allow for the VL-bus to work with MCA and EISA slots, but in practice this is not done). VL-buses rely on the ISA slot for all basic control functions (I/O addressing, IRQs, DMA, etc.). The VL-bus slot controls only those functions specific to VL-bus devices, including burst mode, bus mastering, and 32-bit data transfers.

VL-bus devices are capable of bus mastering. You have already seen two other bus-mastering devices: the CPU itself and the 8237 DMA chip. Remember that the 8237 can take control of the external data bus if the CPU is not currently using it. Each VL-bus device can act in the same fashion, taking control of the external data bus if the CPU is not using it. The VL-bus can *arbitrate* among up to three VL-bus devices that want to use the external data bus at the same time, assigning different priorities to each device.

VL-bus devices are capable of a limited *burst mode*. The VL-bus device can take control of the external data bus for up to four bus cycles. By doing so, it can pass up to 16 bytes (128 bits) of data in a single burst. This significantly reduces the number of clock cycles needed to pass that data by sending the addressing information only once. Because the VL-bus can arbitrate among only three bus-mastering devices, the practical maximum number of VL-bus slots is three.

A VL-bus is a cheap, simple way to get a fast, wide data path. Except for the extra slot connection, installing VL-bus devices is identical to the installation of any ISA device. Plug the card in, set the IRQ, I/O address, and DMA (if applicable), and you are ready to go.

While VL-buses present a huge advantage over ISA technology, it has one severe limitation in that it is designed to run with a 486 CPU. With 64-bit Pentium systems, VL-buses are rather limited by their 32-bit data path. As a result, virtually no Pentium systems use VL-buses, and they have quickly died—although there is still a solid market for VL-bus devices.

PCI

The latest type of expansion bus is Peripheral Component Interconnect (PCI). Designed by Intel and released to the public domain, PCI provides a stronger, more flexible alternative to any other expansion bus (see Figures 6.33a and 6. 33b). As a result of this great power and flexibility, com-

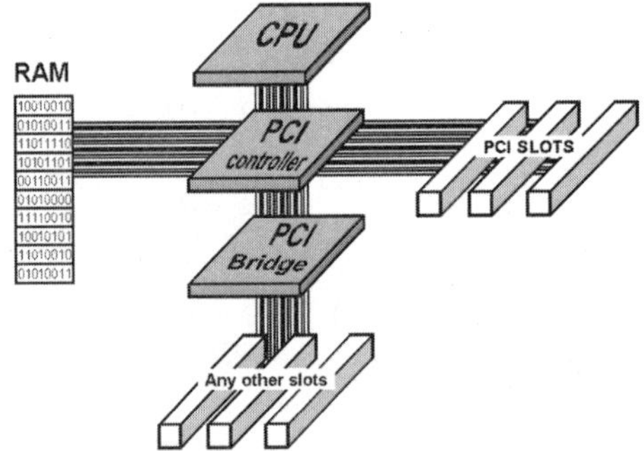

Figure 6.33a PCI bus

Figure 6.33b PCI bus slots

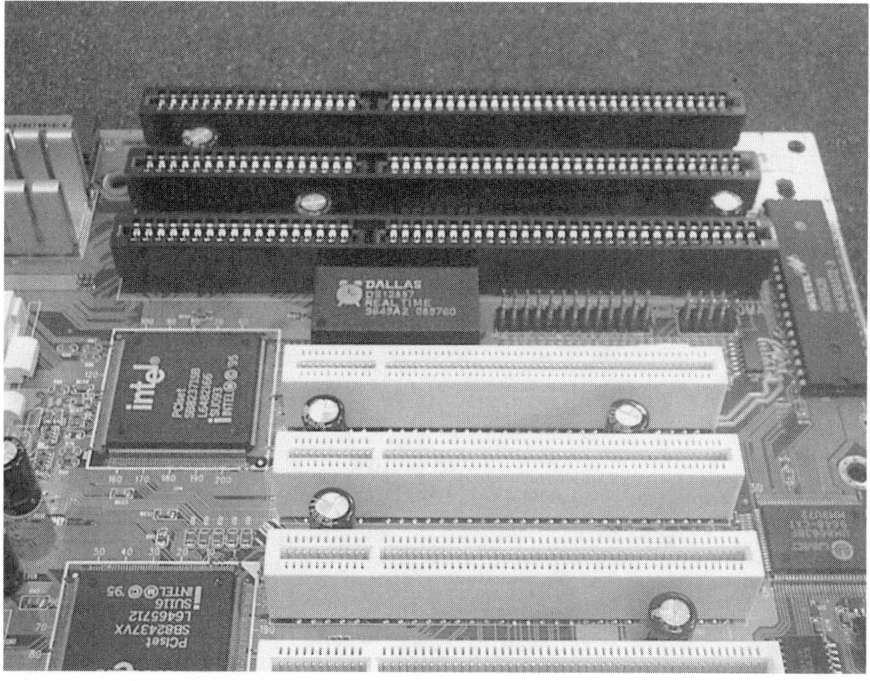

Figure 6.34 Motherboard showing PCI and ISA slots

bined with low price, PCI is now the predominant expansion bus in the PC world.

PCI is far more than the VL-bus. While the VL-bus is limited to 486s, PCI is independent of the CPU. Even Apple is using PCI. PCI can exist by itself on the motherboard or it can exist with any other expansion bus, such as VL-bus, MCA, and EISA (Figure 6.34). Because of this flexibility, PCI offers motherboard manufacturers great flexibility in the creation of "transitional motherboards" that allow you to use both the newest, most advanced bus and any and all previously purchased equipment.

PCI is known as a "mezzanine" bus since it actually sits between the system (local) bus and the expansion bus. PCI expansion slots do not connect devices to the same expansion bus used by ISA and VL-bus slots. Instead, they connect to a PCI bus, which acts as an intermediary between PCI devices and the system bus. The PCI bus acts as a *bus master*, taking full control of the external data bus when it can, in order to pass data more quickly. You have already met two other bus-mastering devices: the CPU itself and the 8237 DMA chip. As you recall, the 8237 can take control of the external data bus if the CPU is not currently using it. The PCI bus acts in the same fashion, taking control of the external data bus in order to transfer data.

PCI's bus-mastering capabilities are much more powerful than those of the 8237 DMA chip. For example, while DMA is limited to either 8- or 16-bit data transfers, PCI devices can use 32 bits of the external data bus for data transfers. In a Pentium system, the 64-bit external data bus is used only for transfers between the CPU and the main memory or level-2 cache. PCI-2 takes advantage of the full 64-bit external data bus. Better yet, two PCI devices can transfer data between themselves while the CPU uses the external data bus, provided the CPU is not communicating with another PCI device. If the CPU uses the external data bus to communicate with a PCI device, the CPU must also use the PCI mezzanine bus. However, if the CPU uses the external data bus to talk to some non-PCI device, such as the main memory or an ISA modem or network card, the PCI bus remains dormant.

The PCI mezzanine bus is sufficiently separate from the system bus that two PCI devices (for example, a hard-drive controller and a video card) can exchange data at the same time the CPU uses the system bus to access a non-PCI device. PCI devices do not have to wait for the system bus to become available before they can transfer data among themselves, provided there is no activity on the PCI bus itself.

The PCI bus uses the same wires for both addresses and data. While this clearly saves money for the motherboard manufacturers, it also seems inefficient. The PCI bus more than makes up for this limitation on its speed, through the use of its powerful *burst mode*. The PCI bus recognizes when the reads or writes in its buffer have consecutive addresses. Instead of addressing each byte individually, the PCI bus groups them into packets and sends them to the PCI devices as a single burst. The receiving unit assumes that consecutive bytes are to be written to consecutive addresses, eliminating the need to use up a clock cycle to relay addressing information. The PCI bus employs this burst mode completely independently of the CPU. Data sent by the CPU hit the PCI bus as individually addressed bytes and are converted by the PCI bus into bursts.

Unlike the VL-bus, which is limited to bursts of four clock cycles, the PCI bus possesses great flexibility with regard to the length of its bursts. Because the PCI bus remains functionally separate from the system bus, the PCI controller can use longer bursts than the VL-bus or a DMA chip, which must check much more frequently for CPU activity on the external data bus. Remember that the expansion bus and the system bus are directly linked, while the PCI bus (a mezzanine bus) is not *directly* linked with either. The separation of the PCI mezzanine bus from the system and expansion buses creates the opportunity for these long bursts.

The PCI mezzanine bus can support more than just expansion slots. On-board I/O controllers and video controllers can also hook into the

PCI bus. With the first PCs and their ISA expansion buses, the external data bus was divided into the system bus and the expansion bus. PCI adds a third player: the PCI mezzanine bus.

PCI devices are self-configuring. While they still need interrupts and I/O addresses, these are set by the PCI bus. Remember when you installed a hard drive controller? Did you set its I/O address and interrupt (IRQ)? No. Why not? Because ISA (the Industry Standard Architecture) had already defined the I/O address and IRQ for that device, as well as for video cards, keyboard controllers, etc. These were considered *assumed hardware.* The reason you had to assign I/O addresses and IRQs for devices such as sound cards and network cards is because those devices did not exist when the ISA specifications were written. PCI SIG (the organization that defines the PCI standard) *assumes* that you will have a sound card, a network card, SCSI controller, etc. In fact, they assumed that you might have multiple sound cards, network cards, SCSI controllers, etc. PCI SIG defined the I/O addresses and interrupts for multiple occurrences of virtually every device commonly in use today, as well as some not-yet-common devices. The intelligent PCI mezzanine bus interrogates PCI cards as they are installed, and assigns them to preset I/O addresses.

PCI handles interruption differently as well. Instead of setting a device to an IRQ, the PCI bus assigns each device an interrupt channel. Each PCI device has four interrupt channels, A through D. The PCI bus has its own registers that keep track of the IRQs in use by the system and *channel* the interrupt requests of PCI devices onto unused IRQ wires on a case-by-case basis. The only restriction appears to be that Interrupt A for a PCI hard-drive controller must access IRQ14 for backward compatibility reasons. (Remember that IRQ14 was preset in the ISA/VL-bus specifications for the primary hard-drive controller.) Because the PCI bus can arbitrate between devices, multiple devices can share the same interrupt channel.

PCI is currently 32 bits, but the latest generation of PCI, PCI-2.1, is either 32 or 64 bits to take advantage of the Pentium and P6 external data buses. PCI-2.1 has optional SCSI connections as standard equipment, just like a Macintosh. PCI also supports the use of multiple processors.

It is impossible to purchase a new motherboard today that is not PCI. The only real option you can get in expansion slots is PCI and ISA or PCI and EISA slots. No doubt about it; PCI is king.

PC Cards

The PC card bus, once known as PCMCIA (Personal Computer Memory Card International Association), was designed to give laptop computers a

Figure 6.35
PC card

measure of flexibility. The PC card bus manifests itself through the use of small, flat cards that are inserted into holes in the side laptops (Figure 6.35). PC cards can be any type of device. Some of the more common PC card devices are modems, network cards, hard drives, and SCSI host adapters.

There are three standard thicknesses for PC cards. The first, Type I, is 3.3 mm thick. These cards are rarely used today. The second, Type II, is slightly thicker than the Type I card at 5 mm. Type II is the most common PC card in use today. The last standard thickness is Type III, which is 10.5 mm thick. The Type III card is used primarily for hard drives.

Plug-n-Play

While not a type of expansion bus, I need to take a moment to explain the concept of Plug-n-Play before moving into real device installation. Plug-n-Play (PnP) is a series of standards designed to allow devices to be self-configured. PnP is a broad standard, crossing over ISA, VL-bus, EISA, and PCI. In theory, all you have to do is install a device and it will automatically configure its I/O address, IRQ, and DMA with no user intervention. Unfortunately, given the broad cross-section of devices currently used in PCs all over the world, PnP has yet to reach this worthy goal. But it is getting closer every day. Until that day is reached, however, PnP can be a very confusing, challenging way to install devices into your PC.

In order for PnP to work properly, three separate items are required. First you need a PnP BIOS. If you have a Pentium computer, you almost certainly have a PnP BIOS. You can verify this by watching the boot process and see if it is advertised, for example:

```
Award Modular BIOS v4.51PG, An Energy Star Ally
Copyright (C) 1984-96, Award Software, Inc.
Intel 430VX CHIPS, AUTO CPU VOLTAGE DETECT START Ver. 2.3

Award Plug and Play BIOS Extension v1.0A
Copyright (C) 1996, Award Software, Inc.

Press DEL to enter Setup

12/30/96–i430VX–8663-2A59GG0BC-00
```

A PnP BIOS will also have a reference in the CMOS, as shown in Figure 6.36.

The second item necessary for PnP is a PnP operating system such as Windows 95 or Windows NT 5.0. Last, you need a PnP device. If you have a PCI device, then it is by default PnP. ISA devices will usually advertise the fact that they are PnP on the box as well as in the documentation.

Figure 6.36
PnP BIOS

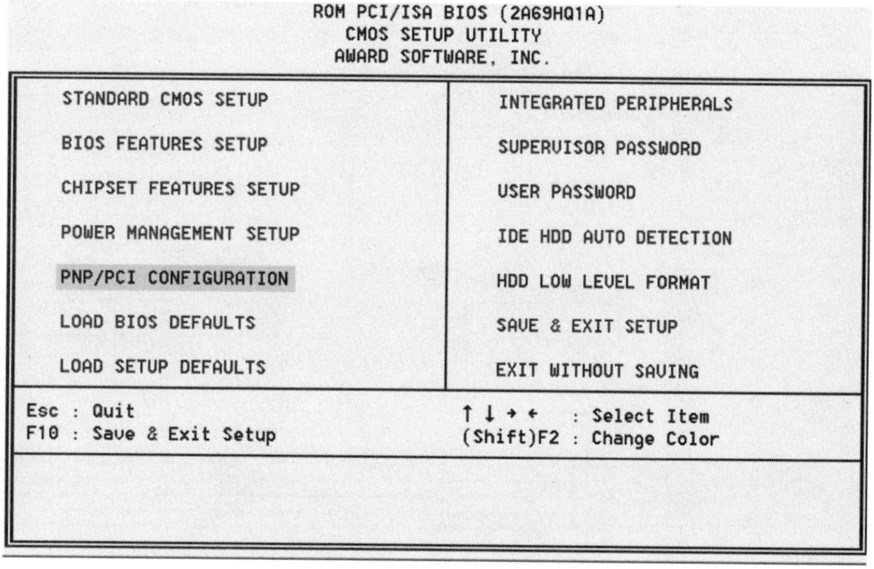

```
ROM PCI/ISA BIOS (2A69HQ1A)
CMOS SETUP UTILITY
AWARD SOFTWARE, INC.

STANDARD CMOS SETUP          INTEGRATED PERIPHERALS
BIOS FEATURES SETUP          SUPERVISOR PASSWORD
CHIPSET FEATURES SETUP       USER PASSWORD
POWER MANAGEMENT SETUP       IDE HDD AUTO DETECTION
PNP/PCI CONFIGURATION        HDD LOW LEVEL FORMAT
LOAD BIOS DEFAULTS           SAVE & EXIT SETUP
LOAD SETUP DEFAULTS          EXIT WITHOUT SAVING

Esc : Quit                   ↑ ↓ → ←    : Select Item
F10 : Save & Exit Setup      (Shift)F2 : Change Color
```

Non-PnP devices are considered to be *legacy equipment*. For example, if you have a non-PnP sound card, it will be called a legacy card. If you have a non-PnP BIOS, it would be called a legacy BIOS.

The PnP standard lumps I/O address, IRQ, and DMA together under the term *system resources*. For example, the system resources for the floppy drive are I/O address 3F0-3F7, IRQ 6, and DMA 2.

Let's look at a hypothetical scenario to learn how PnP works. To do this, assume that you have a machine with PnP BIOS, a PnP operating system (Windows 95), and a mix of PnP and legacy devices. The majority of the work done by PnP is during the boot process. Let's watch as the PnP boots, allocating system resources to devices in the system.

The PnP BIOS takes over immediately after the POST, first telling all PnP devices to "be quiet," which is done so the BIOS can find any legacy ISA devices (Figure 6.37). The next step is to determine what system resources are being used by legacy devices. At this point, the process differs between different BIOS companies. Basically, there are two ways to go; the BIOS can try to find the ISA devices, or you can tell the BIOS what system resources are being used and the BIOS will work around those resources.

This brings to light a rather interesting point. It is relatively easy to write a BIOS routine to find what I/O addresses are being used by legacy devices, but impossible to write one that can reliably find the IRQs and DMAs on those same devices. As a result, most PnP BIOS will automatically find I/O addresses, but give you the choice of indicating which IRQs and DMAs are used—or they will pass off the responsibility of detecting legacy IRQs and DMAs to the operating system. You can usually see this in the CMOS setup.

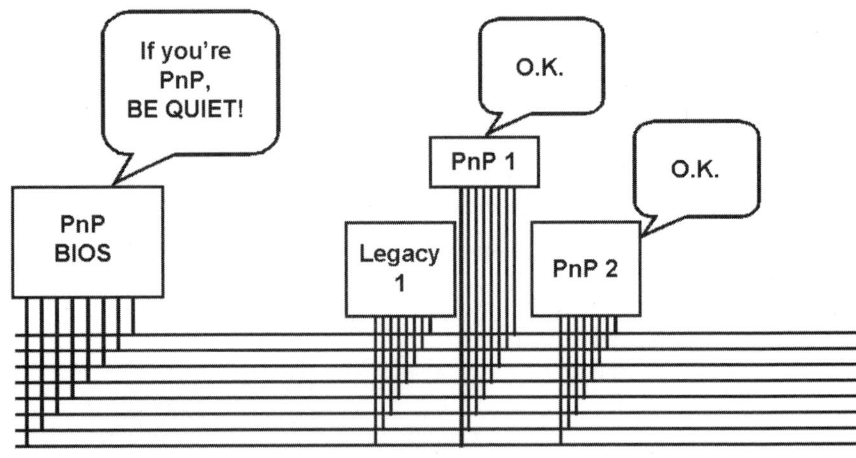

Figure 6.37 Initial PnP configuration - PnP devices go "quiet"

Figure 6.38
Award BIOS PnP screen

```
                    ROM PCI/ISA BIOS (2A69HQ1A)
                      PNP/PCI CONFIGURATION
                       AWARD SOFTWARE, INC.

Resources Controlled By   : Manual    PCI IRQ Actived By    : Edge
Reset Configuration Data  : Enabled   PCI IDE IRQ Map To    : PCI-AUTO
                                       Primary   IDE INT#   : A
IRQ-3  assigned to : PCI/ISA PnP       Secondary IDE INT#   : A
IRQ-4  assigned to : PCI/ISA PnP
IRQ-5  assigned to : PCI/ISA PnP      Used MEM base addr    : C800
IRQ-7  assigned to : PCI/ISA PnP      Used MEM Length       : 8K
IRQ-9  assigned to : PCI/ISA PnP
IRQ-10 assigned to : PCI/ISA PnP
IRQ-11 assigned to : PCI/ISA PnP
IRQ-12 assigned to : PCI/ISA PnP
IRQ-14 assigned to : PCI/ISA PnP
IRQ-15 assigned to : PCI/ISA PnP
DMA-0  assigned to : PCI/ISA PnP
DMA-1  assigned to : PCI/ISA PnP
DMA-3  assigned to : PCI/ISA PnP      ESC : Quit        ↑↓→← : Select Item
DMA-5  assigned to : PCI/ISA PnP      F1  : Help        PU/PD/+/- : Modify
DMA-6  assigned to : PCI/ISA PnP      F5  : Old Values  (Shift)F2 : Color
DMA-7  assigned to : PCI/ISA PnP      F6  : Load BIOS  Defaults
                                      F7  : Load Setup Defaults
```

Figure 6.38 shows the PnP screen from a typical Award BIOS. The left-hand side of the screen contains the PnP settings. There are two things to note here. First is the Resource Controlled By setting. Your choices are Auto and Manual. If you set this to Auto, the BIOS will defer all system resource determination to the operating system. If you set it to Manual, you must manually set all the IRQ and DMA information to either PnP/PCI ISA or legacy ISA. From experience, I find the manual setting easier to use since I know what legacy devices are using what IRQs and DMAs. The second item is Reset Configuration Data, but you need to look at the next step in the boot process to understand this option.

Every PnP BIOS keeps a list of all system resources used, usually on the CMOS or flash ROM, although on some early PnP systems it was kept on the hard drive. Interestingly, there is no official name for this storage area—although it is often incorrectly called the *ESCD*—and it is up to the BIOS makers as to its physical location. However, the BIOS routines are very standardized. In other words, the PnP standard doesn't care where the information is stored, but it must respond correctly when the BIOS is queried. I will call this storage area the *device list* (Figure 6.39). In the example, assume that the IRQ and DMA resources are manually configured in CMOS. The PnP BIOS then refers to this list to determine which resources are already used.

Now that the BIOS knows which resources are available, it can "wake up" each PnP device, asking the device which system resources it needs (Figure 6.40). You can't give just any available system resource to a PnP de-

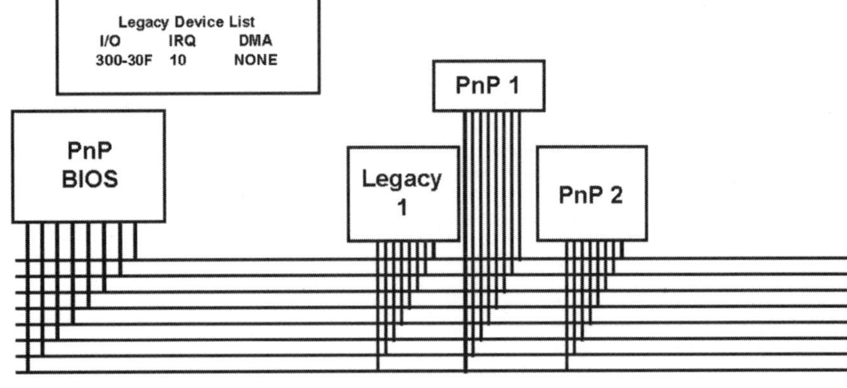

Figure 6.39 BIOS referencing device list

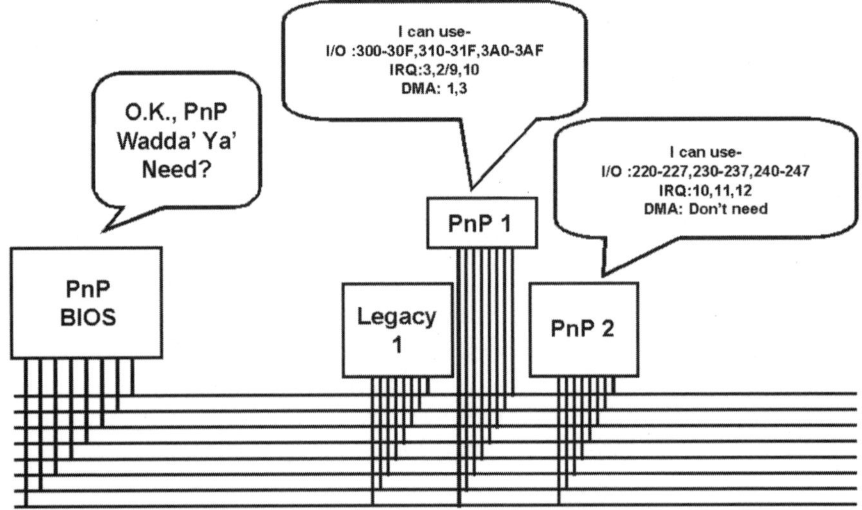

Figure 6.40 BIOS querying PnP for system resources

vice. Each PnP device has an internal "list" of acceptable system resources from which the BIOS must choose. If a device can use only IRQs 3, 5, or 7, then the BIOS can't allocate IRQ 10 to the device; it must choose from the "list." As each PnP device calls for certain resources, the BIOS allocates those resources to the PnP device (Figure 6.41) and adds them to the device list (Figure 6.42).

Sometimes adding another piece of equipment can confuse the PnP settings. For example, if you have a PnP device that needs a resource that is already taken by another device, you need to make the system reallocate the resources. That's where the Reset Configuration Data option comes into play, by making the PnP BIOS reconfigure all the devices. This is most often done when you install a device and it just doesn't seem to be recognized by the system. The device list can also be edited by the operating system. Unlike the BIOS, Windows makes a strong attempt to find the IRQs and DMAs for legacy devices through its own system information program. This program runs automatically at boot and when the Add New Hardware Wizard is run from the Control Panel (Figure 6.43).

The Windows 95 Device Manager allows you to accept the installation as defined by the PnP by accepting the default "Use Automatic Settings" option (Figure 6.44), or you can manually change the PnP settings by clicking the Change Setting button (Figure 6.45). The only downside to manually changing a resource is that Windows then "locks" that resource out of the PnP and permanently dedicates the resource to that device—effectively making that particular device no longer PnP (Figure 6.46).

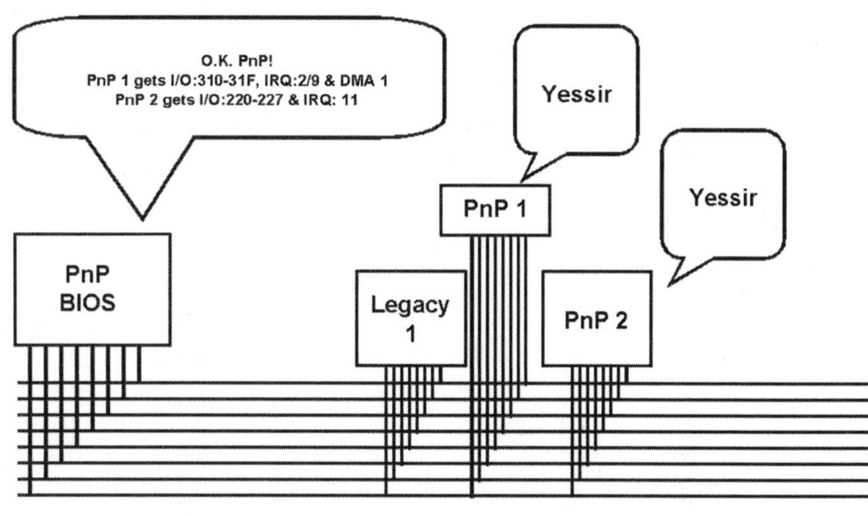

Figure 6.41 BIOS allocating system resources

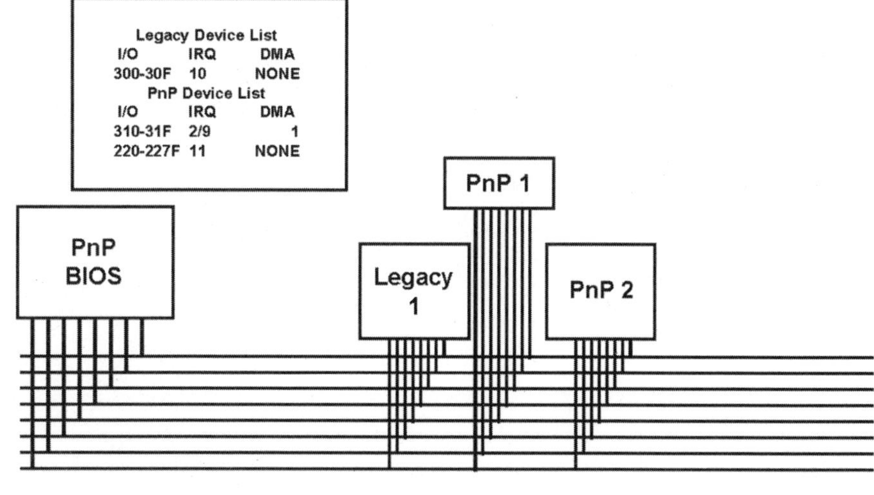

Figure 6.42 Updated device list

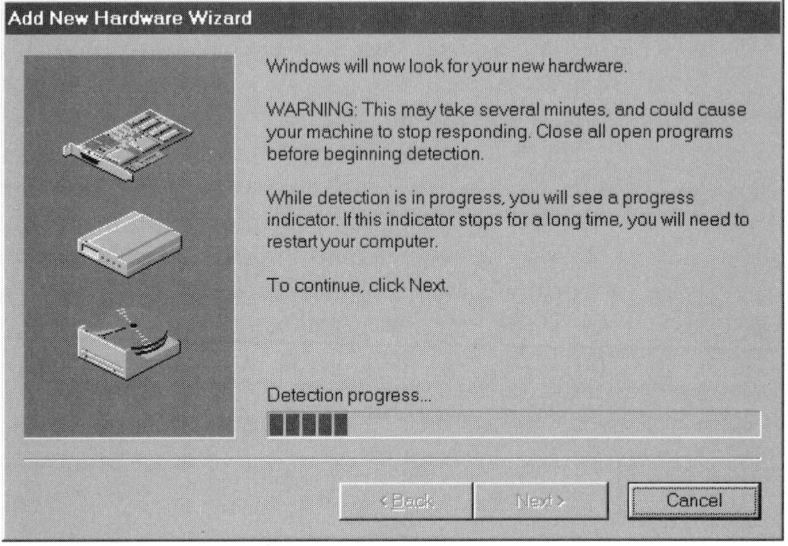

Figure 6.43 Windows 95 hardware wizard

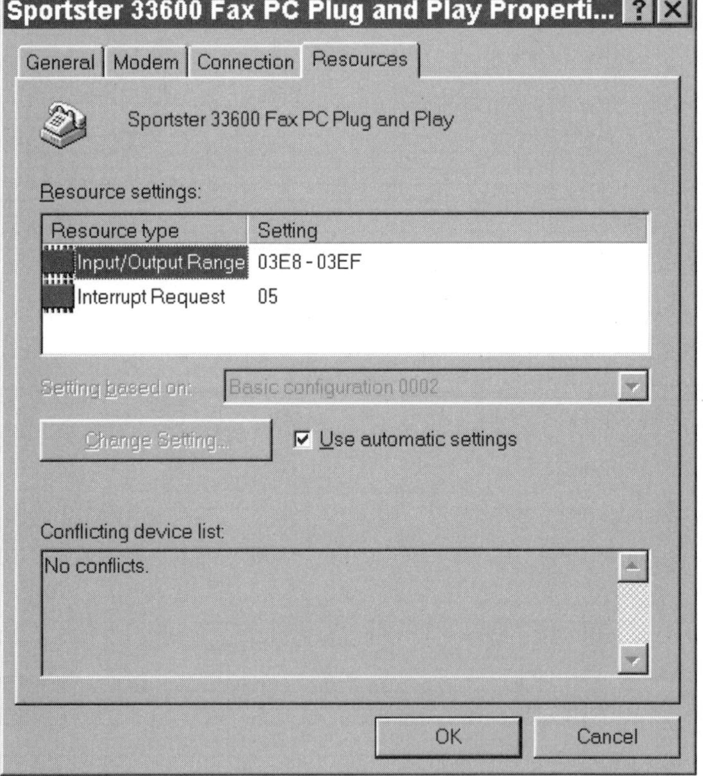

Figure 6.44 Device Manager set to Automatic

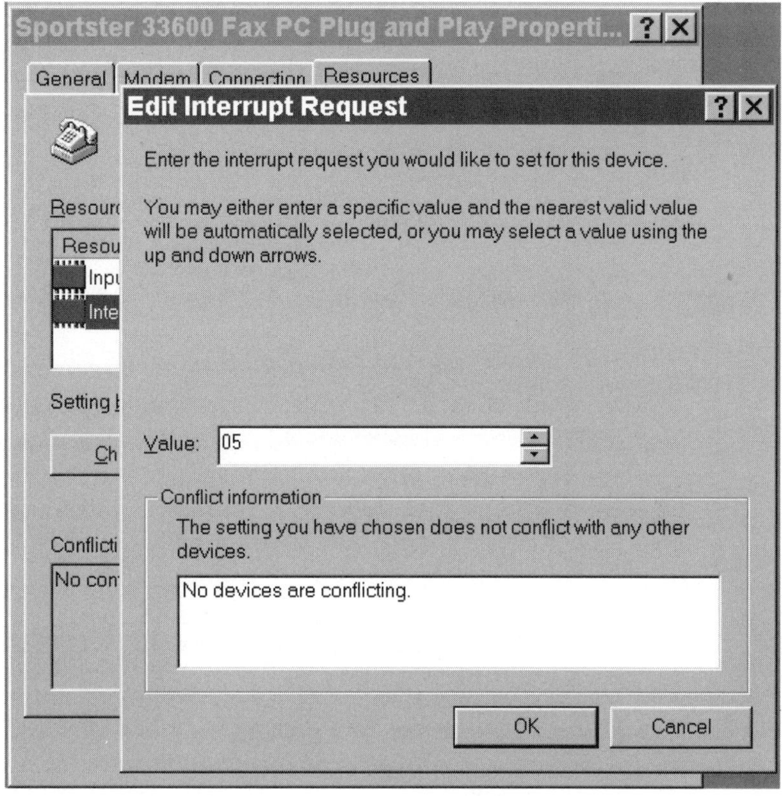

Figure 6.45
Manually changing a resource

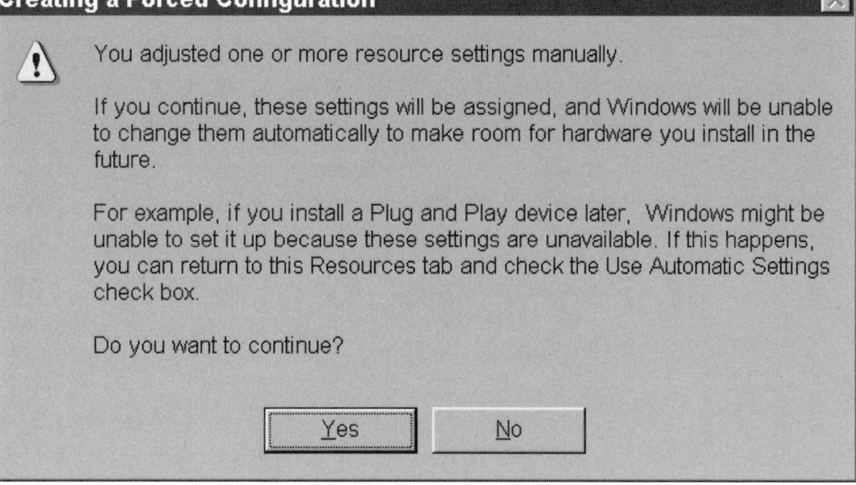

Figure 6.46
Manual configuration warning

The secret to PnP is not to look at it as a totally automatic system for self-configuring devices. Rather, think of it as a "helper" function that allows you to more quickly set up devices in your PC. The goal of the next section is to develop a method for fast and efficient device installation and resource conflict resolution.

The Rules of Device Installation

Too many technicians find the concept of device installation intimidating. Invariably, this intimidation (maybe *trepidation* is a better word) is due to two factors—lack of knowledge and lack of documentation. Whether you are building an entirely new system or just installing a new card into an existing system, there are certain steps you must understand and document if you want to set up your system quickly and easily:

1. Know what you already have. Use programs, knowledge, and horse sense to determine all the system resources used in the system. I'll call this the "inventory."
2. Install the device, first determining how the device will configure its system resources, which system resources to give the device, and what the device needs for installation: programs, jumpers, etc. Then actually install the device.
3. Inspect the results of the installation and verify that either the device took the system resources you wanted it to use or it took resources that aren't being used by other devices. Also correct any resource conflicts by "tweaking" whatever settings are necessary to ensure that the device does not conflict. I call this step "the tweak."
4. Actually run the device to ensure that it is in good working order. You need to check every aspect of the device to completely verify that there are no system conflicts.
5. After the device is running, update your inventory so it will be accurate the next time you need it. Again, this is the "inventory." If it's done properly, you won't have to do the first inventory the next time you need to install a device in this system!

So there are five discrete steps to deal with for every installation: inventory, installation, tweak, check, and inventory. Let's start installing!

Inventory

Before anything else happens, you need to determine what system resources are being used by the PC. The most powerful tool you can use, more powerful than some fancy "system information" program and far more reliable, is a piece of paper. Get a piece of paper, any paper, and write the following information along the left-hand margin:

```
IRQ 2/9
IRQ 3
IRQ 4
IRQ 5
IRQ 6
IRQ 7
IRQ 10
IRQ 11
IRQ 12
IRQ 14
IRQ 15
```

Why didn't I write down IRQ 0, 1, 8, or 13? Because they are dedicated to the system timer, keyboard, real-time clock, and math coprocessor and are not available for devices. You will never find a device that allows you to set its IRQ to 0, 1, 8, or 13, so I don't even bother writing them down.

Why do I write IRQ 2/9? Because IRQ 2 and IRQ 9 don't exist. Maybe it would be more correct to say that they are combined onto the same wire. There is no IRQ 2, and there is no IRQ 9; there is only IRQ 2/9.

Now look in the PC. Do you have a floppy drive? What IRQ does it use? IRQ 6. Does it use a DMA? Sure it does: DMA 2. Floppy drives have their own I/O address (see the I/O address map), so I don't write it down as there is no risk that anything else will use that I/O address. Let's inventory the floppy drive by writing it down:

```
IRQ 2/9
IRQ 3
IRQ 4
IRQ 5
IRQ 6 (floppy drive, DMA 2)
IRQ 7
IRQ 10
IRQ 11
IRQ 12
IRQ 14
IRQ 15
```

Do you have hard drives or any ATAPI devices like CD-ROM drives using the hard-drive controllers? Document them, as follows:

```
IRQ 2/9
IRQ 3
```

```
IRQ 4
IRQ 5
IRQ 6 (floppy drive, DMA 2)
IRQ 7
IRQ 10
IRQ 11
IRQ 12
IRQ 14 (primary HDC, two drives)
IRQ 15 (secondary HDC, CD-ROM and ZIP drives)
```

Okay, how about COM ports? How many serial ports do you have? To what COM port are they assigned? You need to write down every active COM port on your system. Virtually any serial port can be disabled—in CMOS if it is an on-board port, or by moving jumpers if it is on a card. Disabled serial ports aren't documented; if you have serial ports to which a COM port has been assigned, you have an active port.

What if the serial port is active, but nothing is installed on it? Disable the port! Although most systems will allow you to use the system resources of an active but unused port, don't get into the habit! I've been confused too many times. Just disable the unused port so there is no question about it if a problem arises later.

My system has two serial ports that I call Serial 1 and Serial 2. Serial 2 has been disabled in my CMOS. I have a serial mouse plugged into the serial port set to COM1. Again, I won't write down the I/O address since each COM port has a dedicated I/O address assigned to it:

```
IRQ 2/9
IRQ 3
IRQ 4 (COM1, mouse)
IRQ 5
IRQ 6 (floppy drive, DMA 2)
IRQ 7
IRQ 10
IRQ 11
IRQ 12
IRQ 14 (primary HDC, two drives)
IRQ 15 (secondary HDC, CD-ROM and ZIP drives)
```

Why did I put the COM1 next to IRQ 4? Because COM1 is, by definition, IRQ 4 and the I/O address 3F8-3FF. You should have all of the COM and LPT port resources memorized; it sure makes inventory faster.

Many older parallel ports don't use their assigned LPT port IRQs. As mentioned earlier, if a device doesn't use its assigned IRQ, that IRQ can be used by another device. However, most parallel ports today not only use their assigned IRQ, but many will also use a DMA channel. Figure 6.47 shows the CMOS for my parallel port. This parallel port uses a more advanced mode called ECP (enhanced capabilities port). These ports can be set to use IRQ and DMA, and are the most common LPT ports available today.

Figure 6.47
Parallel port settings

```
                ROM PCI/ISA BIOS (2A69HQ1A)
                 INTEGRATED PERIPHERALS
                  AWARD SOFTWARE, INC.

IDE HDD Block Mode          : Enabled
IDE Primary Master PIO      : Auto
IDE Primary Slave  PIO      : Auto
IDE Secondary Master PIO    : Auto
IDE Secondary Slave  PIO    : Auto
On-Chip Primary    PCI IDE: Enabled
On-Chip Secondary PCI IDE: Enabled
PCI Slot IDE 2nd Channel    : Enabled

KBC input clock             : 8 MHz
Onboard FDC Controller      : Enabled
Onboard Serial Port 1       : 3F8/IRQ4
Onboard Serial Port 2       : 3F8/IRQ4
UR2 Mode                    : Sharp IR
Onboard Parallel Port       : 3BC/IRQ7
Parallel Port Mode          : ECP
ECP Mode Use DMA            : 1
USB Controller              : Enabled
USB Keyboard Support        : Enabled

ESC : Quit          ↑↓→← : Select Item
F1  : Help          PU/PD/+/- : Modify
F5  : Old Values    (Shift)F2 : Color
F6  : Load BIOS  Defaults
F7  : Load Setup Defaults
```

If you install a printer in Windows 95, you will have the option of giving an LPT port to the parallel port. Windows 95 doesn't use LPT ports; it just treats the printer like any other device with a separate I/O address, IRQ, and DMA. This makes a lot of technicians think that they don't need to deal with LPT ports. This is often true, but you still need to deal with the I/O address, IRQ, and DMA.

My printer will be set to I/O address 378, IRQ 7, and DMA 1, so let's add my parallel port to the list:

```
IRQ 2/9
IRQ 3
IRQ 4 (COM1, mouse)
IRQ 5
IRQ 6 (floppy drive, DMA 2)
IRQ 7 (LPT 1, printer, DMA 1)
IRQ 10
IRQ 11
IRQ 12
IRQ 14 (primary HDC, two drives)
IRQ 15 (secondary HDC, CD-ROM and ZIP drives)
```

Well, that's it for the obvious devices! The rest of the devices in the system will be determined through means other than just knowing the system and looking at CMOS. Let's take a look at the strategies and tools needed to determine system resources for the rest of the devices in the system.

The secret to determining system resources is understanding that, with any device, there is the device itself (hardware) and there is some program that configures the device (software). In older devices, a two-step process was used to address each of these areas. First you set jumpers or switches on the device, and then you ran an installation program. The installation program's job was to install drivers or applications, not to set up the device. At some point during the installation, you told the program what resources you used.

But even before PnP became popular, a lot of devices didn't use jumpers—they were known as "jumperless" installations and are still very popular today. The installation program not only loads drivers and applications, but also sets up the hardware—very convenient. These are not PnP, but they certainly act like it. For example, I have an old Creative Labs SoundBlaster sound card that I've installed under Windows 95. When this device was installed, it took I/O address 300, IRQ 5, and DMA 3. How could it know that those were available system resources? It must be PnP! No, it isn't. These were the default settings for the installation program. The SoundBlaster was preset to use those settings since the folks at Creative Labs know that most systems don't use them. Take a look at the I/O address map—what's at I/O address 300? Nothing. Look at the IRQ map. What's at IRQ 5? LPT2, right? How many people have a second printer using LPT2? So IRQ 5 is a good bet to be open. Same with the DMA channel 3, which is wide open by default. If you wanted to change the resources, you would have to rerun the installation program to make the changes.

Last are the PnP devices. From a software standpoint, PnP is virtually identical, except that the installation program automatically runs when you insert a device and restart the system. But once the device is installed, you still have a program that allows you to change system resources, just like a jumperless devices.

Be aware that some devices are combinations. My U.S. Robotics modem, for example, has jumpers that allow me to manually set the COM port and IRQ. However, if I remove all the jumpers, it is PnP. This is done to support the maximum number of systems—but it can also drive you crazy if you're not observant, or don't have the instruction book!

DEVICE MANAGER Assuming that you have Windows 95, the first, best place to determine system resources is through the Device Manager. The Device Manager allows you to see and edit all the devices in your PC (Figure 6.48). Just click on the computer icon to get a list of all devices organized by system resource—very handy! (See Figure 6.49.)

The only downside to the Device Manager is that it can see only devices under the control of Windows 95 drivers. If you have devices that use DOS or Win 3.*x* drivers, they won't show up in Device Manager. So if you're using Windows 3.*x* or DOS, you're going to need to poke around in

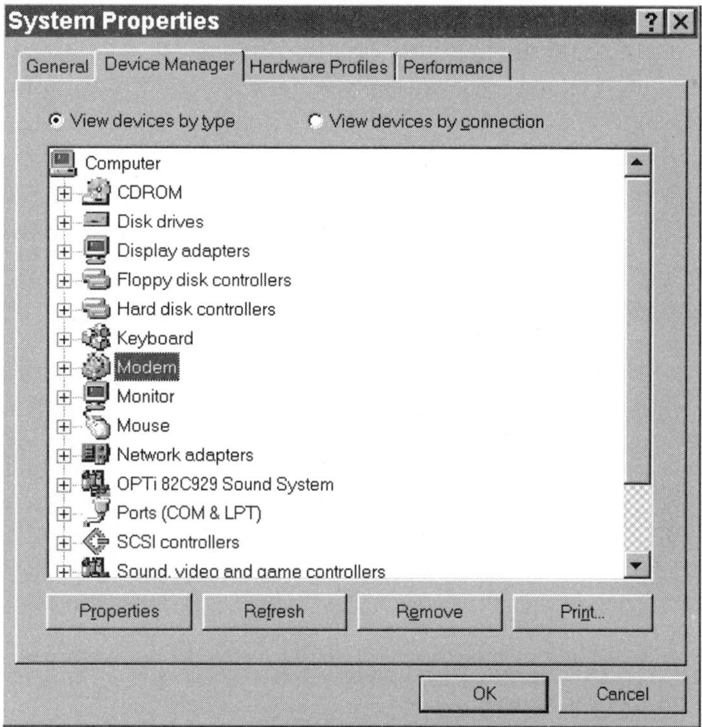

Figure 6.48
Windows 95 Device Manager

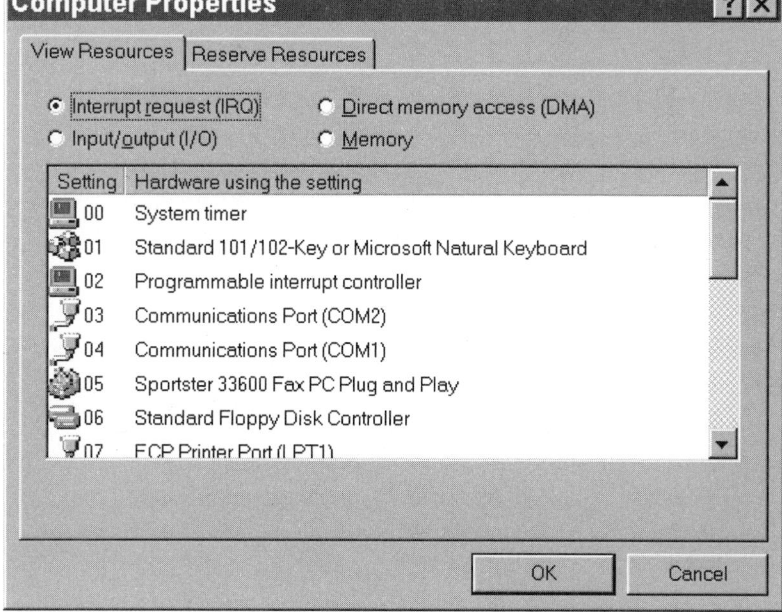

Figure 6.49
Sorted by resource

the SYSTEM.INI, CONFIG.SYS, and AUTOEXEC.BAT files. You'll also want a third-party "system information" program such as CheckIt Pro Analyst, from Touchstone. The Advisor function knows hundreds of peripheral cards and will help you select the best settings. It can also help in the documentation process. The best IRQ and I/O address tester is CheckIt Pro Sysinfo, also from Touchstone. This product, although imperfect, is the best at identifying the IRQ and I/O addresses currently in use.

CONFIGURATION FILES There's a little bit of art to looking in configuration files for resource use. The trick is knowing what you're looking for, even if you aren't sure what it looks like. Unlike the Device Manager in Windows 95, there is no rule as to how devices store their configuration information. The bottom line is that you're looking for something that implies system resources. Fortunately, these settings tend to be grouped together, so you can usually see them rather easily—how many different things could a line like IRQ=4, IO=220 mean? Let's look at some examples:

SYSTEM.INI The SYSTEM.INI file is the first place to look in Windows 3.*x*, and Windows 95 for backward compatibility. Most devices will have their own group with all the resource settings. Look for lines towards the end of the file such as these:

```
[mmstudio]
wav=220
midi=330
IRQ=5
LDMA=1
HDMA=5
```

By simply changing these settings, you can change the resources, although I prefer to rerun the installation/setup program that came with the device in case I missed anything.

CONFIG.SYS For pure DOS systems, CONFIG.SYS is always the first place to look. For other operating systems, it is also important—including Windows 95. Again, you need to be a bit of a detective, but the resource settings do tend to stand out. Here's an old proprietary CD-ROM driver from a system I worked on recently:

```
DEVICEHIGH=C:\PCD650S\PCD650S.SYS /B:340 /D:MSCD001
```

The /B:340 is the I/O base address for the CD-ROM.

AUTOEXEC.BAT AUTOEXEC.BAT is rarely used for resource settings, with one glaring exception: DOS-based sound cards. Try to find a setting that look like this:

```
SET BLASTER=A220 I10 D1 H5 P330 T6
```

IRQ/DMA CARDS When all else fails, use a card that can directly monitor the IRQ and DMA wires. There is an excellent diagnostic card on the market that can do this: the JDR-PDI card by JDR Microdevices. The JDR-PDI card also has a built-in POST card. The PDI card monitors the wires directly through the expansion slots, and whenever one of the IRQs or DMA channels is in use (has voltage on it), the card lights up a corresponding LED. To order a JDR-PDI card, call JDR Microdevices at 800-538-5000. Now that you have all the information, here's my completed inventory:

```
IRQ 2/9
IRQ 3 (COM2, modem)
IRQ 4 (COM1, mouse)
IRQ 5 (sound card, 220, DMA 5)
IRQ 6 (floppy drive, DMA 2)
IRQ 7 (LPT 1, printer, DMA 1)
IRQ 10 (scanner, 300)
IRQ 11
IRQ 12
IRQ 14 (primary HDC, two drives)
IRQ 15 (secondary HDC, CD-ROM and ZIP drives)
```

So what resources are available? Well, I can look at the list and see that IRQ 2/9, 11, and 12 are open. I can also refer back to the DMA map and by process of elimination see that DMA 3, 6, and 7 are good. But what about I/O addresses? Table 6.9 lists the classic areas that are used to add extra devices. Compare this list to either of the earlier IBM maps. The open areas are used only by convention—there is no rule or standard that requires them! Your machine might be different.

There are a lot of other open I/O addresses, but the ones I've highlighted are *by far* the most common places to install devices. Now that you know the available resources, you can begin the next step—installation.

Install

Installing a device in your PC usually means installing a card of some type into an expansion slot. Given this fact, I will concentrate on installing some type of card into a PC.

TABLE 6.9

Classic Open I/O Addresses

0170-0177	Secondary hard drive controller
0178-01EF	Open for use
01F0-01FF	Primary hard drive controller
0200-0207	Joystick
0210-0217	Reserved
0218-0277	Open for use, common soundcard
0278-027F	LPT2
0280-02AF	Open for use
02B0-02DF	Secondary EGA
02E8-02EF	COM4
02F8-02FF	COM2
0300-0377	Open for use, common network, sound
0378-037F	LPT`
03B0-03BF	Mono video

HANDLING CARDS Optimally, a card should be in one of two places: in a computer or in an antistatic bag. When inserting or removing a card, be careful to hold it only on its edges. Do not hold the card by the slot connectors or touch any of the components. (See Figure 6.50.)

Never insert or remove a card at an extreme angle. This could damage the card or wipe out the CMOS data. A slight angle, however, is acceptable,

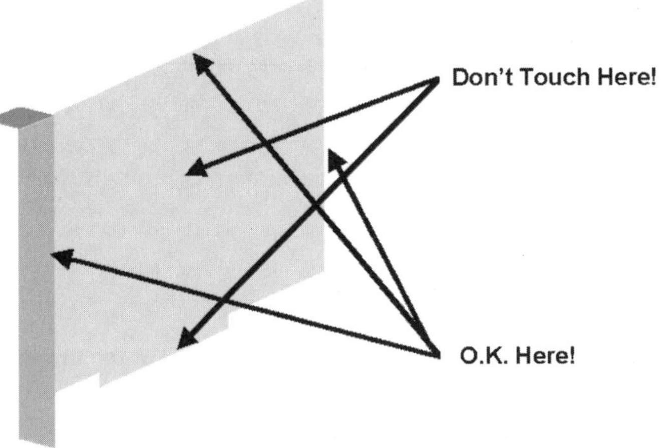

Figure 6.50
Where to handle a card

Figure 6.51
Always screw down all cards

even necessary, for removing a card. Cards should always be screwed to the box with their connection screw, which will keep them from slipping out and potentially shorting other cards (Figure 6.51). Also, many cards use the screw connection to ground the card to the box.

Many technicians have been told to clean the slot connectors if a particular card is not working. This is almost never necessary, and if done improperly it can cause damage. An installed card should never need the slots cleaned. Clean slot connectors only if they have a card that's been "on the shelf" for a while and the slot connectors are obviously dull. *Never use a pencil eraser.* Pencil erasers leave behind bits of residue that wedge between the card and slot connector, preventing contact and causing the card to fail. Use a "bright boy," available in any hobby shop.

INSTALLATION PROGRAMS So many installation programs, so little time! There's no way I can go through every aspect of all the different installation programs available today—and I don't need to. Most of the time, the only thing to do is run the installation program and enjoy the device. With many installation programs, you might have to accept resource conflicts in order to get the device to install, then rerun the setup program or use the Device Manager to set the device to a proper resource. This is particularly true with Windows 95. However, if you know your available resources—and you do—actually running an installation program is usually a no-brainer.

Tweak

If everything goes right with the installation step, this step is unnecessary. Just be sure to double-check the inventory for open resources. You might also find yourself with other system resources being used. Many devices, sound cards in particular, are notorious for using more than one I/O address, IRQ, and DMA!

If you have a conflict, don't worry, just fix it by rerunning software, editing configuration files, or changing PnP settings in the CMOS. If two devices share I/O addresses, the devices won't work, but you won't cause any damage to the hardware—just reference your inventory and try again.

IRQ and DMA conflicts are equally safe, but a lot more irritating. If you get a DMA or IRQ conflict, the system will lock up, requiring a hard boot to restart the system. Again, take your time and keep an active copy of the inventory handy.

Check and Final Inventory

Once you're comfortable that you have assigned the device to unique system resources, it's time to check it. Make the device do whatever it is supposed to do. If it's a network card, get on the network and transfer a file; if it's a sound card, play a tune or record your voice! You really need to be a little aggressive here and try to break the device. Finalize and stash that inventory sheet—you'll use it every time you install on this machine! Plus, this is also a fun time to play with any applications that came with the device. If you're smart enough to install it, then you must be an expert at using it too—right?

CHAPTER 7

Floppy Drives

In this chapter, you will:

- See how to install a floppy drive.
- Learn basic floppy-drive maintenance.

Floppy drives have the unique distinction of being the only component of a PC to contain basically the same technology as that of the original IBM PC. Certainly there have been tremendous gains from the first 160K, 5.25-inch, dual-sided, single-density drives to the 2.88MB, 3.5-inch, dual-sided, quad-density drives, but the cabling, configuration, and BIOS routines have remained the same as the floppy drives in the original IBM PC.

There are two basic types of floppy drive sizes: 5.25-inch and 3.5-inch. The 5.25-inch drives (Figure 7.1) can accept two different capacities of floppy diskettes. These sizes are the now obsolete 360K diskettes and the virtually obsolete 1.2MB diskettes. 3.5-inch drives (Figure 7.2) accept three different capacities. First are 720K disks, which are extremely rare. Second are the 1.44MB disks, which are by far the most common disks used today. The third and last type is a 2.88MB disk, which was virtually stillborn and basically doesn't exist. There is no way to tell the difference between any of these 3.5-inch disks by simple observation.

Figure 7.1
5¼" floppy drive

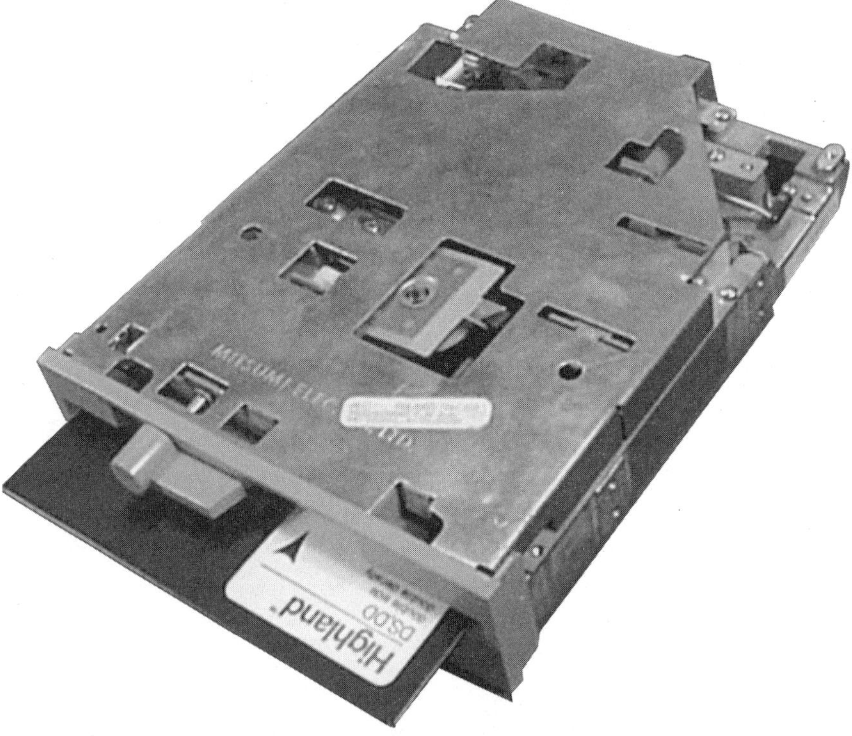

Figure 7.2
3½" floppy drive

DOS and Windows have reserved drive letters A: and B: for floppy drives. You cannot name them anything other than A: and B:. DOS and Windows are designed to look for a floppy drive called A: at boot, so if you have only one floppy drive, it should be called A:. The second floppy drive will then be called B:. See Figure 7.3.

Floppy drives are connected to the computer via a 34-pin cable (Figure 7.4). This cable has a seven-wire twist, which differentiates the A: and B: drives. The floppy-drive BIOS routines are designed to support no more than two floppy drives. Some of the older cables have connections only for the older 5.25-inch drives, but there are readily available conversion plugs that allow 3.5-inch drives to plug into them.

If the floppy drive is installed on the end connector, it is the A: drive; if the drive is installed on the middle connector, it is the B: drive.

Figure 7.5 shows a 5.25-inch connector, and Figure 7.6 shows a 3.5-inch connector. The power connection will be either the large molex-type connector for the 5.25-inch drive, or the smaller mini connector for the 3.5-inch drive (Figure 7.7).

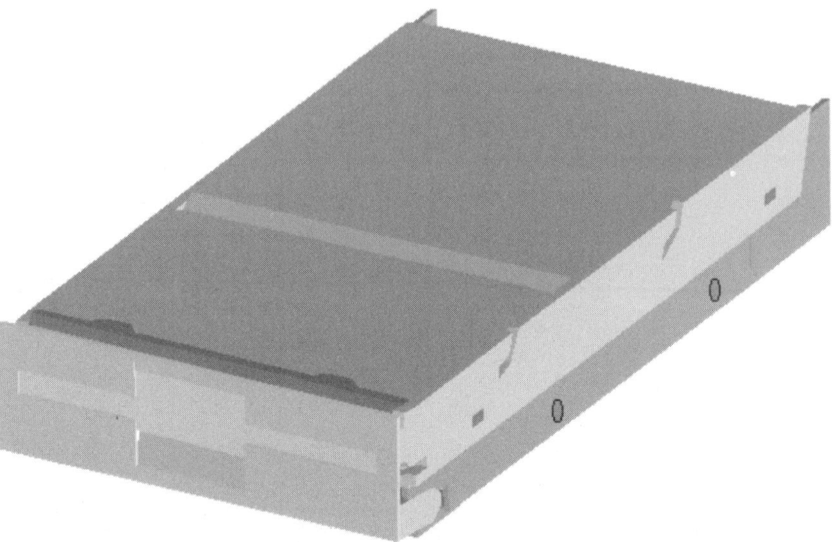
I can be A: or B: - that's it!

Figure 7.3
A floppy can only be A: or B:

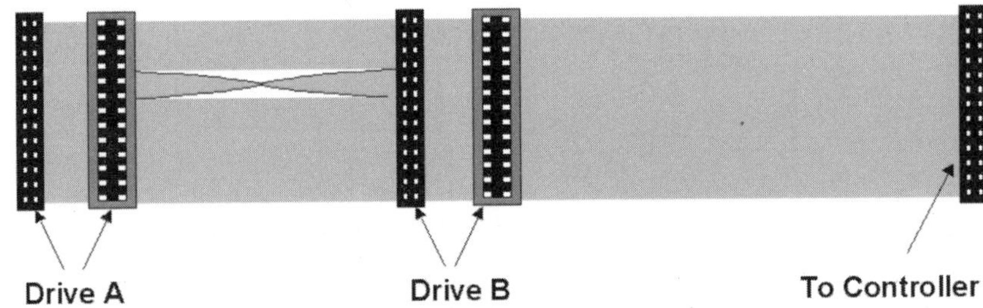
Drive A
Drive B
To Controller

Figure 7.4
Floppy drive cable

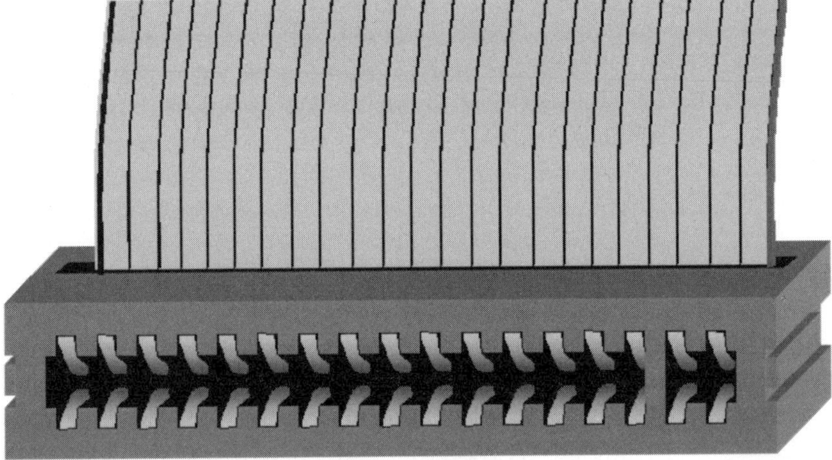

Figure 7.5
5¼" connector

Figure 7.6
3½" connector

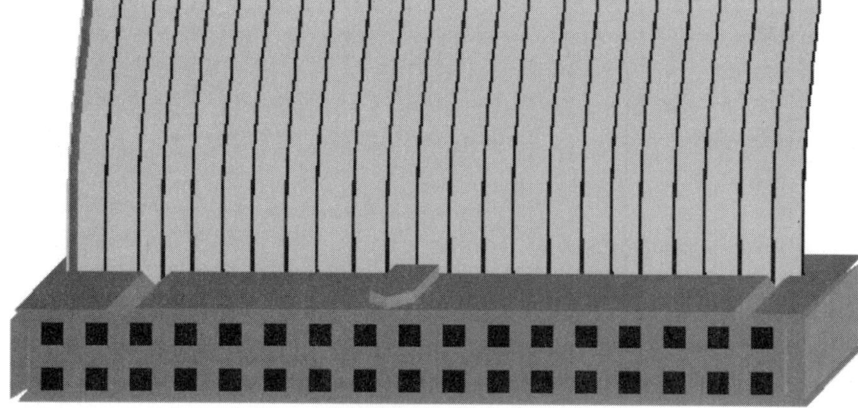

Figure 7.7
Properly inserted mini-connector

After the floppy drive is installed, the next step is configuring the CMOS settings, which must correspond to the capacities of the drives. Simply select the drive (A: or B:) and enter the correct capacity. (See Figures 7.8 and 7.9.)

Many older CMOSs will not contain settings for either 1.44MB or 2.88MB 3.5-inch floppies. There is enough space in the CMOS to accept these values. However, older CMOSes were developed before these drives and, as a result, were not able to provide the setup options for these drives. In other words, the CMOS can handle the values, but the CMOS setup isn't designed to provide the options. If one of these more advanced floppy drives is installed without CMOS support, there are many third-party utilities that will allow the CMOS to accept the necessary values to support the drives. One of many excellent third-party utilities is Checkit Pro by Touchstone Corp.

There are a few other interesting settings that can be seen in most of today's Pentium-class CMOSes. One of the most handy is the Swap Floppy Drive setting, which allows you to change the A: and the B: drives without moving the cables. The commonly-seen Boot Up Floppy Seek

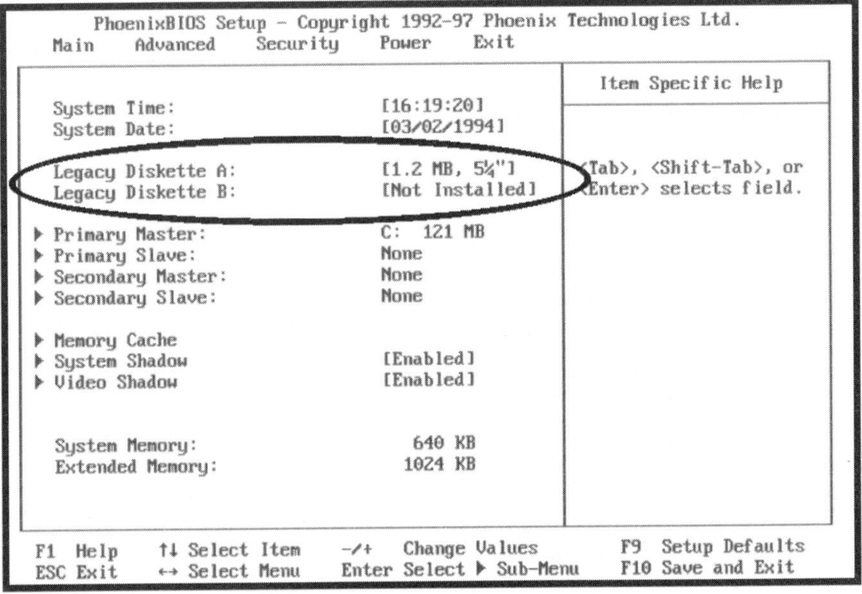

Figure 7.8 Phoenix CMOS showing floppy drive selection

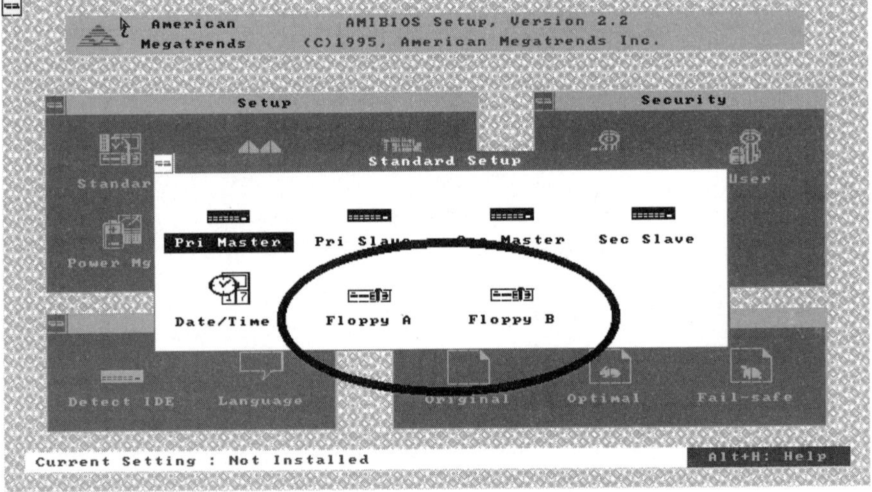

Figure 7.9 AMI WinBIOS giving floppy options

message tells the PC not to look for a floppy during the POST, which isn't very handy except for speeding up the boot process. Another popular option is the boot sequence, which allows the system to seek out the C: drive first and then look for a floppy drive. The boot sequence option is a powerful security tool, preventing would-be hackers from accessing a PC by loading a boot diskette. See Figure 7.10.

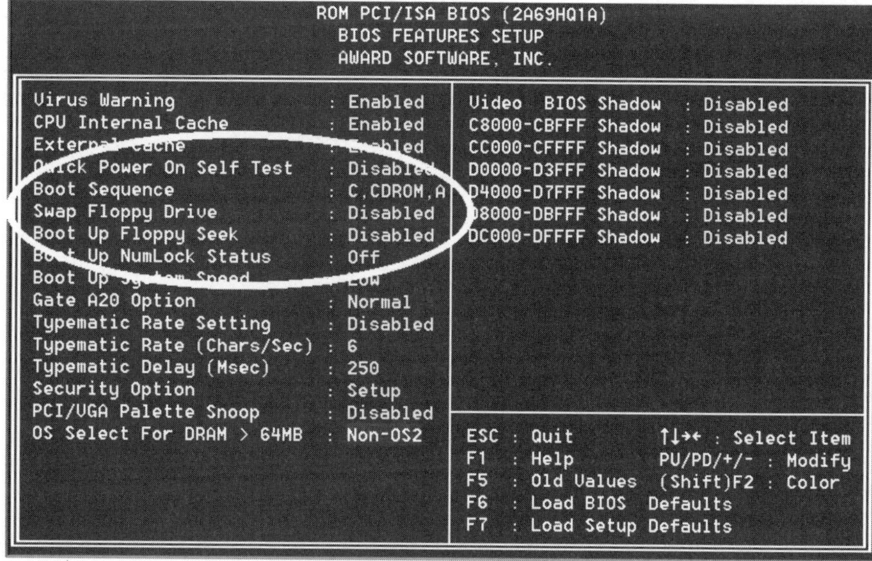

Figure 7.10 Common "extra" CMOS floppy options

Care and Feeding of Floppy Drives

There is no part of the computer that breaks more often than the floppy drives. They are the only component with their internals directly exposed to the outside environment. There is only a small door (or, in the case of 5.25-inch drive, not even a door) that divides the read/write heads from dust and grime. Floppy drives are also exposed to the threat of mechanical damage. Floppy drives are often the victims of inverted disks, paper clips, and other foreign objects.

As a result of this abuse, it is imperative that serious preventative maintenance be performed on all floppy drives. Above all, *keep the floppy drive clean!* Excellent cleaning kits are available everywhere, and should be used at least once a month to ensure the best possible performance from your floppy drives.

Repairing Floppy Drives

When a floppy drive dies, follow these steps to resolve the problem:

First, Blame the Floppy Disk

The vast majority of the time, when the floppy drive decides not to respond to reading the floppy disk, the bad guy is the floppy *disk*, not the floppy *drive*. When the disk can't be read, insert another disk. If a new diskette from a fresh box won't work, don't insert another one from the same box. Find another disk, preferably from another box, to retest. If two disks are unreadable, then you can start to consider the floppy drive as the problem.

Second, Check for Data Errors on the Disk

If other floppy disks work in the drive, it's the floppy disk. If a floppy disk is bad, the best thing to do is just throw it away. But often there is data on the disk that you need. Since other disks operate in the drive, the errors must be one of the ominous type that look like this:

```
Data error reading drive A:
Seek error writing drive B:
Sector not found reading drive A:
```

or any error that ends with one of these two happy little phrases:

```
Abort, Retry, Fail?
Abort, Retry, Fail, Ignore?
```

These are problems with the floppy disk, not the drive. The process for repairing floppy diskettes is *identical* to the process for repairing hard drives. Refer to the hard drive chapter to review the process of running the Norton's Disk Doctor/Spinrite combination for data repair.

Third, Check the CMOS Setting

CMOS settings for floppies rarely cause problems. The main reason for this is that most recent BIOS makers default the CMOS settings for the A: drive to 3.5-inch high density if the CMOS battery dies or if the CMOS is accidentally erased. So while an erased CMOS might keep everything else on your computer from running, at least the floppy will still work (assuming you have a 3.5-inch A: drive). The rare instances of a problem with CMOS can be dangerous, since technicians rarely look there. The following errors can point to the CMOS as a problem (but *not* exclusively):

```
Not ready error reading drive A:
General failure reading drive A:
Insert diskette for drive A: and press any key when ready . . .
```

So double-check the CMOS. A quick peek can save a lot of time!

Next, Blame the Floppy Controller

The floppy controller is extremely sensitive to static and trauma. It is common for floppy drives to fail after a move, after a few months in a high-static environment, or, most frustrating of all, when a new computer is first delivered (I'm convinced delivery people use boxes with computer parts for their lunch-time volleyball games).

If the data cable or power plug is loose, the POST will flag with either "FDD Controller Failure" or "Drive Not Ready" errors. At this point, open the machine and verify the connections. If the connections are good, remove and reseat the controller. If the same errors show up again, replace the controller.

It's impossible to find a floppy-drive controller card that is only a floppy-drive controller card. All floppy-drive controllers are welded onto I/O cards that invariably include some (and usually all) of the following:

- Hard-drive controllers
- Serial ports
- Parallel ports
- Joystick ports

Try to keep an extra I/O card around just to check floppies. I keep an old I/O card with a bad hard-drive controller to test systems. I made sure to turn off all the other devices on the card, *including* the bad controller.

Maybe It's the Cable

The 34th wire on the floppy-drive cable is called the *drive change signal* (or *diskette change signal*). When a floppy drive is inserted or removed, this wire is active. When DOS or Windows first reads a floppy drive, a copy of the directory is left in RAM and is not updated unless the drive change signal is activated. This is quite handy since the system doesn't constantly reread the very slow floppy drive unless it needs to be read. However, if the drive change signal is disconnected by a bent pin or bad cable, you will keep seeing the same directory, even if you change the diskette! This problem can almost always be traced back to a bad floppy cable, so replace it and retry.

Last, Replace the Floppy Drive

At this point, if the floppy drive isn't working, the only recourse is to replace the drive. Replace the bad drive and *throw it away.* Keeping a bad floppy drive is a study in frustration, since almost all bad floppy drives aren't "always bad"—just "sometimes bad." Technicians are often tempted to give a bad floppy drive "one more chance." They install the drive, and viola—it works! They're convinced they made a mistake and declare the drive "good." If the drive is reinstalled somewhere else, however, it will soon die again. Throw it away.

Floppy drives fail more than any other part of a computer system. Given any five PCs, at least one floppy drive will need to be replaced in a year. So keep floppy drives in stock. Purchase them in quantity, at least five at a time, so you'll receive a discount. Buying floppy drives one at a time is expensive and a waste of time.

CHAPTER 8

Hard Drives

In this chapter, you will:

- Understand the concept of geometry.
- See the different types of hard drives.
- Learn how to install hard drives.
- Understand partitioning and formatting.
- Fix most common hard-drive problems.

Of all the hardware on a PC, none gets more attention—or gives more anguish—than the hard drive. There's a good reason for this: if the hard drive breaks, you lose data. As we all know, when the data goes, you have to redo work or restore from backup—or worse. It's good to worry about data, since it's the data that runs the office, maintains the payrolls, and stores the e-mail. This level of concern is so strong that even the most neophyte PC user is exposed to terms like *backup, defragment,* and *scan disk*—even if they don't put the terms into practice!

More than anything else, the goal of this chapter is to give you the tools necessary to ensure the safety of the data stored on hard drives. You must have a strong understanding of how they work, how to install them, and how to troubleshoot them. That way you won't have to worry about the bad things that could happen.

Hard drives were not a part of the original IBM PC. When the first PC debuted in 1980, it was equipped with one floppy drive and support for an external cassette tape drive. There was no direct support for hard drives, although there were a few proprietary add-ons. It wasn't until the IBM AT computer in 1984 that we saw true hard-drive support in the form of a system BIOS that could talk to hard drives. Since then, there have been many improvements to hard drives. They have become much faster and can hold hundreds of times as much data as the first 5MB to 10MB drives. Drives are much smaller and much more dependable. They are inarguably the most important part of a computer.

This long string of improvements makes teaching hard drives a bit of a challenge. Where do you start—at the first generation of hard drives way back in the early '80s? Many concepts and technologies that started with the first drives are still valid today. But with the same token, many are gone—dead and meaningless. So should we drop the early stuff and just concentrate on the latest and greatest? Nope, I can't do that either. There are a *ton* of older drive technologies out there, and many ancient terms we must cover.

The best way to handle this dilemma is to start with the most common drive available today, called EIDE. It has been the standard drive in all systems for almost five years. Once you understand how EIDE works, I will describe some of the "oldies but goodies." Then you can understand some of the older terms and also recognize the old stuff when you see it. Let's get started!

Inside the Drive

All hard drives are alike in that each is composed of individual disks, or platters, with read/write heads on actuator arms controlled by a servo motor—all contained in a sealed case that prevents contamination by outside air (Figure 8.1). The platters are made of aluminum and are coated with a magnetic media, usually cobalt or ferro-ceramics. There are two tiny read/write heads for each platter, one to read the top and the other to read the bottom of the platter (Figure 8.2).

The coating on the platters is phenomenally smooth! It has to be as the read/write heads actually "float" on a cushion of air above the platters, which spin at between 3500 and 7200 rpm. The distance (flying height) between the heads and the disk surface is less than the thickness of a fingerprint. The closer the read/write heads are to the platter, the more densely the data can be packed onto the drive. This is why the platters can never be exposed to outside air. Even a tiny dust particle would be like a mountain in the way of the read/write heads, and would cause cata-

Figure 8.1
Inside of typical IDE drive

Figure 8.2
Closeup of read/write heads and armatures

strophic damage to the drive. All hard drives have a tiny aperture to keep the air pressure equalized between the interior and the exterior of the drive, but it comes with an air filter.

Data Encoding

While data is stored in binary form on the hard drive, it is not a simple matter of a magnetized spot representing a one, and a nonmagnetized spot representing a zero. Although there are magnetized and nonmagnetized positions on the hard drive, the ones and zeros of the binary code are stored in terms of *flux reversals,* which are the transitions between the magnetized and nonmagnetized positions on the hard drive. There are several methods for encoding and interpreting these flux reversals.

The first method used on hard drives was called *frequency modulation,* and used the time spent in a magnetized state to determine ones and zeros. FM depended on every one or zero to be preceded by a "timing bit" that took up significant disk space. FM was quickly supplanted by *modified frequency modulation* (MFM), which reduced the number of timing bits by more than 50 percent by using the preceding data bits to indicate whether the current bit was a one or a zero. MFM was the predominant way to encode data on hard drives for many years. Starting around 1991, however, hard drives began using a data encoding system known as *run length limited* (RLL). RLL is the only data encoding scheme used today.

RLL uses patterns of ones and zeros to represent longer patterns of ones and zeros. For example, 1000 in RLL represents 11. This would seem inefficient, but RLL eliminates the need for timing bits, and combinations of RLL patterns can represent long strings of ones and zeros.

Because of the overwhelming usage of RLL-type data encoding, unless you are working with older (pre-1989) equipment, it isn't important to know what type of data encoding is used by a hard drive. You're never going to have to deal with data encoding!

Moving the Arms

The read/write heads are moved across the platter on the ends of actuator arms. To move these arms quickly across the hard drive, hard drive manufacturers use two methods.

The *stepper motor*, the first method developed, moved the arm in fixed increments or steps. This early technology had several limitations. Because the interface between motor and actuator arm required minimal slippage in order to ensure precise and reproducible movements, over time the positioning of the arms became less precise. This physical deterioration caused data transfer errors. Another problem with stepper motors was heat deformation. Just as valve clearances in automobile engines change with operating temperature, the positioning accuracy changed as the PC operated and its various components got warmer. Although these changes were very small, it could make accessing the data, written while the hard drive was cold, difficult if the disk was warm. In addition, the read/write heads could damage the disk surface if not parked (set in a nondata area) when not in use.

Most hard drives made today employ a linear motor to move the actuator arms. The linear motor is also called a *voice coil motor* because its design is the same in principle as the voice coil found in an audio loudspeaker. A permanent magnet surrounds a coil on the actuator arm through which an electrical current passes, thus generating a magnetic field that moves the actuator arm. The direction of the actuator arm depends on the polarity of the electrical current through the coil. Because there is no mechanical interface used between the motor and the actuator, there is no degradation in positional accuracy over time. Another advantage is the use of the hard drive's controller to automatically park the heads when power to the disk is discontinued. It is meaningless to "park" a voice coil drive.

The one drawback of this type of motor is an inability to accurately predict the movement of the heads across the disk. For this purpose, you must reserve one side of one platter for navigational purposes. The voice coil moves the read/write head to its best guess about the correct position on the hard drive. The read/write heads then use the "map" on the platter side, reserved for navigational purposes, to determine its true position and make any necessary adjustments. This explains why, when reading a hard-drive specification list, you will find an odd number of heads—one head is used for positioning all the others and is thus not available for data storage.

"Parking" a drive is meaningless in today's PCs.

Geometry

If you want to work with hard drives, you must be familiar with *hard-drive geometry,* which is the internal electronic organization of the hard drive. Have you ever seen a cassette tape? If you look at the actual brown mylar tape, you will not see anything. However, you know something is on the tape. The magnetized lines on the tape define the music. You could say that the physical placement of those lines of magnetism is the tape's "geometry."

Geometry determines where the data is stored on the hard drive. Just like the cassette tape analogy, if you were to open up the hard drive, you would not be able to see the geometry. The geometry for a particular hard drive is described with five special numerical values referring to the *heads, cylinders, sectors per track, write precomp,* and *landing zone.* The following sections describe what each value means.

Keep in mind that *all hard drives have geometry.* You must know these five numbers if you want to install or reinstall a hard drive!

HEADS Heads are the total number of sides of all the platters used to store data. If a hard drive has four platters, it would have eight heads (Figure 8.3). Based on this description of heads, you would think that hard drives would always have an even number of heads, right? Wrong! Most hard drives reserve a head or two for their own use. Therefore, a hard drive can have either an even or an odd number of heads.

CYLINDERS Take a Campbell's soup can and open both ends of the can; it is no longer a soup can, but a geometric shape called a cylinder. Now take that soup can and sharpen one end—so sharp that it can pass through the hardest metal. Place the can concentrically over the hard drive and push it through the drive. The can will go in one side and out the other of each platter. Each circle transcribed by the can is where you store data on the drive, and is called a *track* (Figure 8.4).

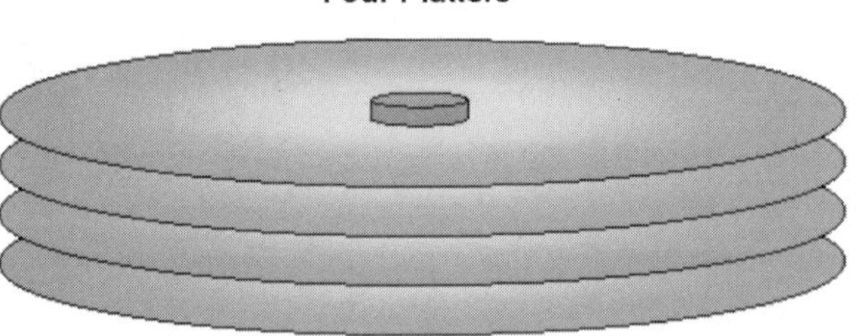

Figure 8.3
Heads

Figure 8.4
Tracks

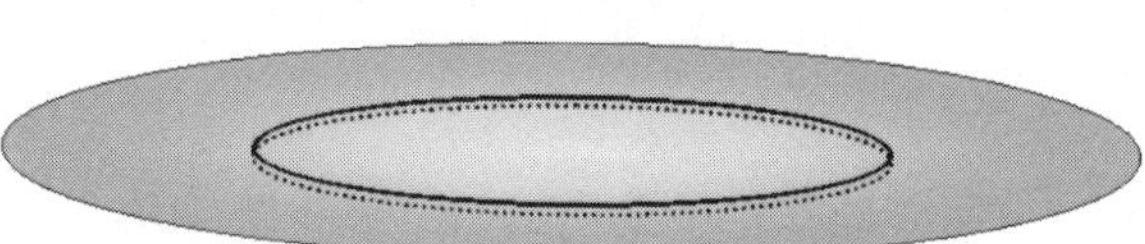
Two Tracks - One on Top and
another underneath

Every head has many hundreds
of tracks on each side

There are hundreds of tracks on each head. Interestingly enough, tracks themselves are not directly part of the drive geometry. What you are interested in is *all* the tracks of the same diameter, going all of the way through the drive. *That* is a geometry, and it is called a *cylinder*. One cylinder is the set of all tracks of the same diameter on every head of the hard drive. (See Figure 8.5.)

There's more than one cylinder! Go get yourself about a thousand more cans, each one a different diameter, and push them through the hard drive, too. Each of these is also one cylinder.

Figure 8.5
Cylinder

Campbell's
Soup
All Tracks of the same diameter
are called a Cylinder

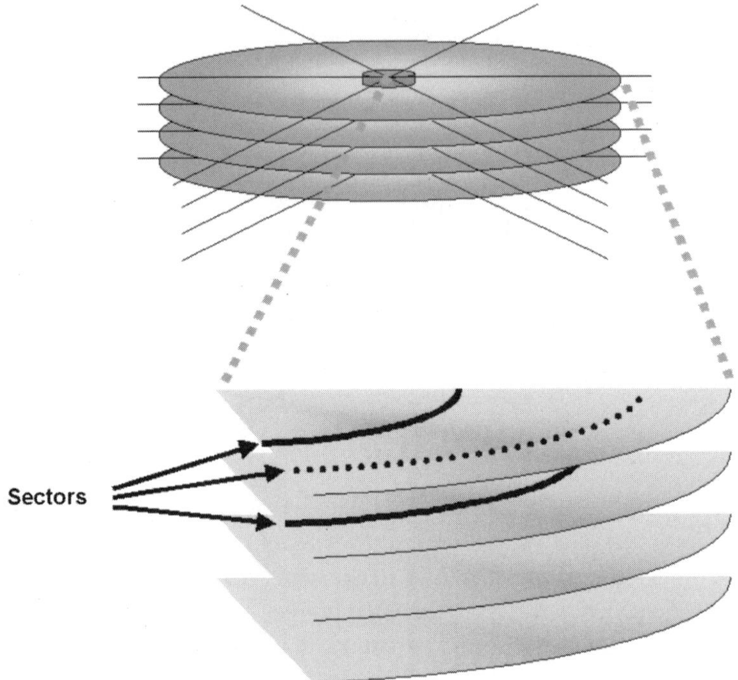

Figure 8.6
Sectors

SECTORS PER TRACK Imagine cutting the hard drive like a birthday cake, slicing all the tracks into tens of thousands of small slivers. Each sliver is called a *sector*, and each sector stores 512 bytes of data (Figure 8.6). The sector is the "atom" of all hard drives. You can't divide data into anything smaller than a sector. Although sectors are important, the number of sectors is not a geometry. The geometry value is called *sectors per track* and is written like this: *sectors/track*. The sectors/track value is the number of "slices" in the hard drive, and it describes the number of sectors in each track (Figure 8.7).

WRITE PRECOMPENSATION CYLINDER When data gets packed too closely together, you will get a slight shifting of the magnetism on the drive. This can be a real problem for the cylinders closest to the center of the drive. To handle this, an older drive would write data a little further apart once it got to a particular cylinder. This cylinder was called the *write precomp* cylinder, and the PC had to know which one it was. This is now handled internally by the drive, and the PC no longer needs to know.

The write precomp is obsolete.

Figure 8.7
Sectors/track

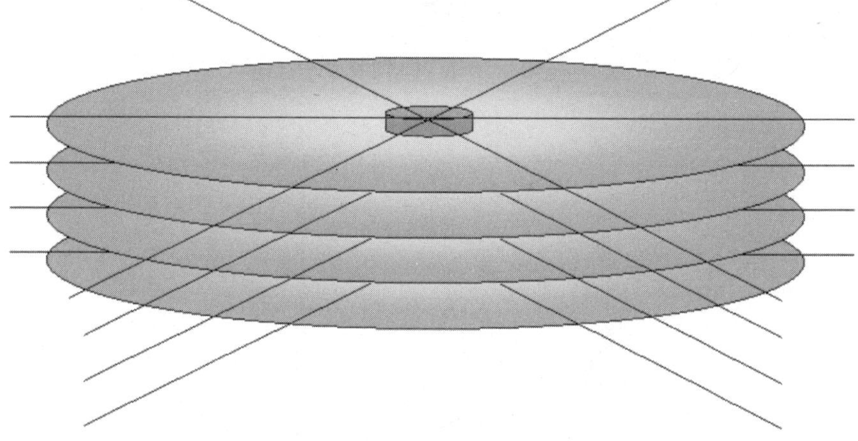

Six Sectors per Track (Sectors/Track)

LANDING ZONE On older hard drives with stepper motors, the *landing zone* value designated an unused cylinder as a "parking place" for the read/write head. It was important to park the heads on drives with stepper motors to avoid accidental damage when moving hard drives. There are special parking programs designed to park these older drives. Today's drives are all voice coil. Voice coil drives park themselves whenever they're not accessing data. The parking programs are simply ignored by voice-coil drives. As a result, the landing zone is no longer a necessary geometry.

The landing zone is obsolete.

TALKING THE TALK No one would say: "What are your cylinders, heads, and sectors/track?" when discussing geometry on a hard drive. You just say: "What's the CHS?" or "What's the geometry?" Also watch for abbreviations. A geometry like landing zone can be shortened to Lzone, LZ, Park—just about anything. Use your common sense and you'll be able to figure it out.

WHY GEOMETRY? The cylinders, heads, and sectors/track are very important. When you buy a hard drive, it has these three values printed on the drive. The system needs these numbers when the drive is installed. Plus, the capacity of a hard drive is defined by the geometry. Just multiply the cylinders by the heads by the sectors/track to get the number of sectors. Since every sector stores 512 bytes, just multiply the number of

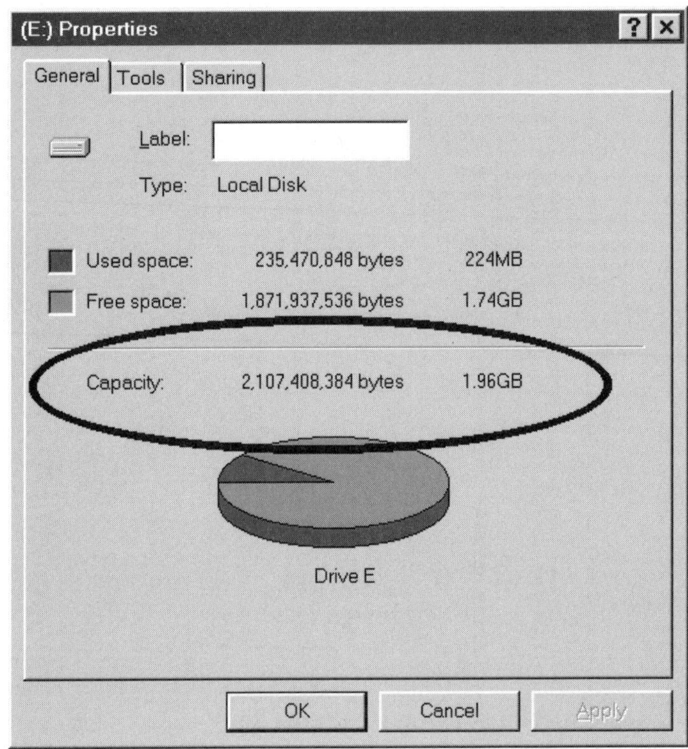

Figure 8.8
Win95 showing hard drive properties

sectors times 512 to get the capacity of a drive. Say you buy a hard drive with 1024 cylinders, 32 heads, and 63 sectors per track; the capacity of the drive would be: 1024 × 32 × 63 = 2,064,384 sectors × 512 bytes/sector = 1.056 billion bytes. A drive with 1024 cylinders, 32 heads, and 63 sectors/track is a 1.056-billion-byte drive.

This is *not* a 1.056 *gigabyte* drive! You have to be careful with capacities. When talking about capacities, you use the units of megabytes, or MB (1,048,576 bytes) and gigabytes, or GB (1,073,741,824 bytes). When a hard-drive manufacturer sells you a drive, they use the units of millions and billions of bytes. This unit difference makes people think that there is something wrong with the drive or that they have been "ripped off." Say you buy a 2.1GB hard drive. If you look on the label, the hard-drive maker says the capacity is 2100MB. That is 2100 million bytes, not megabytes! The manufacturer isn't lying, you're just reading wrong! So you install the drive and discover that the total capacity is shown as 1.96 gigabytes. It's as though you just lost 1.4 megabytes! No, it's just different units. Fortunately, Windows 95 reports both (see Figure 8.8).

IDE/EIDE

Since the early 1990s, the primary type of hard drive available has been the IDE drive type. The *IDE,* or Integrated Drive Electronics standard, uses the BIOS on the system ROM. Western Digital and Compaq developed the 40-pin IDE ISA pinout specification, and put this specification before the ANSI standards committees, which then put out the Common Access Method (CAM) AT interface in March of 1989. The term *IDE* is actually incorrect. The official name for these drives is *ATA,* which stands for *AT attachment.* Even though the proper name is ATA, however, everyone says IDE. In 1990, Western Digital forwarded a series of improvements to the IDE standard called *Enhanced IDE* (EIDE). Virtually all of today's hard drives and computers are EIDE (Figure 8.9). First I will discuss EIDE drives, and then take a short look back at IDE so you can understand the differences.

A lot of people use the term IDE when they mean EIDE.

Figure 8.9
Typical IDE/EIDE drive

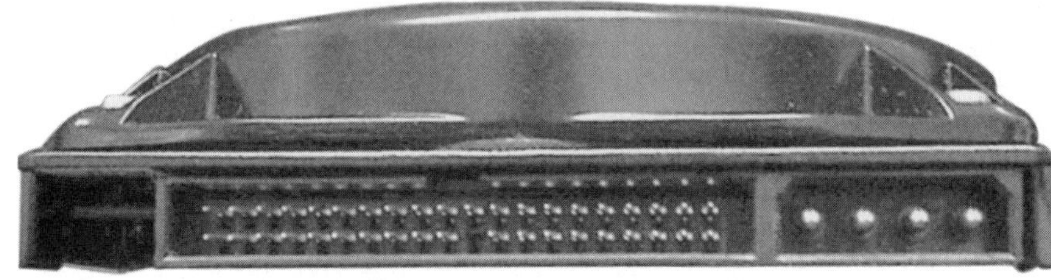

Figure 8.10
IDE drive connectors

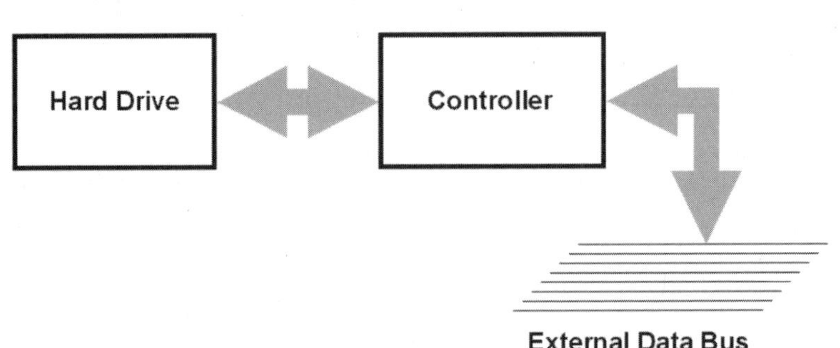

Figure 8.11
Relation of drive, controller and bus

Physical Connections

EIDE drives are connected to the computer via a 40-pin cable and a controller. Figure 8.10 shows the "business end" of an IDE drive, with the connectors for the controller and the power cable. The controller is the support circuitry that acts as the intermediary between the hard drive and the external data bus. Electronically, the setup looks like Figure 8.11.

There are usually two controllers in a system. Each controller can be connected to up to two hard drives, so the number of drives a PC can handle is limited to four. The controllers are usually on the motherboard (these are called *on-board controllers*) and manifest themselves as nothing more than two 40-pin male connectors. Older machines might have the controllers on a card that is snapped into the motherboard. Figure 8.12 shows some examples of EIDE controllers, both on cards and the more common on-board controller.

Although each controller is equal, the computer will look for one of the two when the system boots up. This is the *primary controller*. The other controller is the *secondary controller*. If you're going to use only one controller, it must be the primary one. Given this fact, it is important to be able to distinguish the primary controller from the secondary controller. First, you can read the motherboard book to tell you which is which. Second, you can look on the motherboard to see if some printing actually identifies the ports. Figure 8.13 is a close-up of a typical motherboard,

Figure 8.12
Typical EIDE controllers

A

B

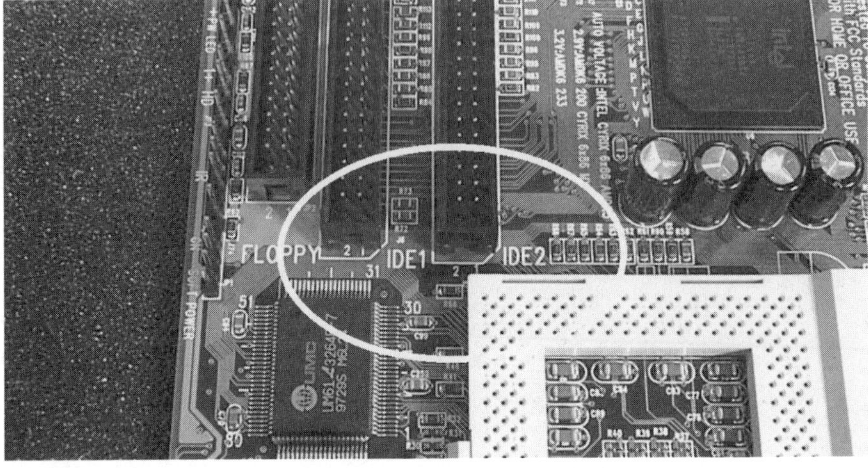

Figure 8.13
ID of primary and secondary controllers

showing the primary marked as "IDE1" and the secondary marked as "IDE2."

Cabling EIDE Drives

The EIDE drives are connected to the controllers via a simple 40-pin cable. There are no twists, although you might occasionally see a cable that has a split. A single cable can connect up to two hard drives (Figure 8.14).

Since there can be up to two drives connected to one controller via a single cable, you need to be able to identify each drive on the cable. The EIDE standard identifies the two different drives as *master* and *slave*. Moving jumpers on each hard drive performs these settings. If you have only one hard drive, set the drive's jumpers to master. If you have two drives, set one to master and the other to slave. Figure 8.15 is a close-up of an EIDE hard drive showing the jumpers.

At first glance, you might notice that the jumpers aren't actually labeled "master" and "slave." So how do you know how to properly set them? The easiest way is to simply read the front of the drive; most drives have a

Figure 8.14
IDE cable

Figure 8.15
Typical master/slave jumpers

nice diagram of the drive to explain how to properly set the jumpers. Figure 8.16 shows the front of one of these drives, so you can see how to set the drive to master or slave.

You should be aware of two important areas here. First, notice that there are a lot of jumpers that you don't use. This is normal on most hard drives. These other jumpers are used for diagnostics at the manufacturing plant or for special settings in other kinds of devices that use hard drives. Ignore them. They have no bearing in the PC world. Second, there is a third setting called "1 drive," which is used if there is only one drive. If you're observant, you have probably noticed that master and 1 drive are the same setting; this is quite common.

> Many hard drives have a third setting called "1 drive." Think of it as the "master of none" setting. If a single drive has only master and slave settings, set it to master.

Getting Jumper Information

If you don't have a label on the drive that tells you how to set the jumpers, you have several options. First, look for the drive maker's Web site. Every

Figure 8.16 Drive label showing master/slave settings

drive manufacturer lists their drive jumper setting on the Web, although it might take a while to get the information you're looking for. You can go to the Total Seminars Web site for handy links. Second, try phoning the hard-drive maker directly. Unlike many other PC parts manufacturers, hard-drive producers tend to stay in business for a longer period of time and have great technical support. For really fast information, your third choice is a powerful tool called the Microhouse Technical Library.

The Microhouse Technical library is an exhaustive compilation of data on every hard drive ever made. It is constantly updated and is distributed on CD-ROM. It will tell you everything you need to know about any hard drive. Figure 8.17 is a sample screen. Figure 8.18 shows a continuation of the same drive, showing the jumper settings. The Microhouse Technical Library also has information on motherboards, I/O cards, and network cards. It's a great tool, and can be found in most software stores.

Plugging It In

It doesn't matter where the master or slave drive is installed on the cable; just make sure you have the jumpers set properly or the computer won't be able to access the drives. Hard-drive cables also have a colored stripe that corresponds to the number-one pin on the connectors, just like on floppy drives. Failing to plug in the drive properly will also prevent the PC from recognizing the drive.

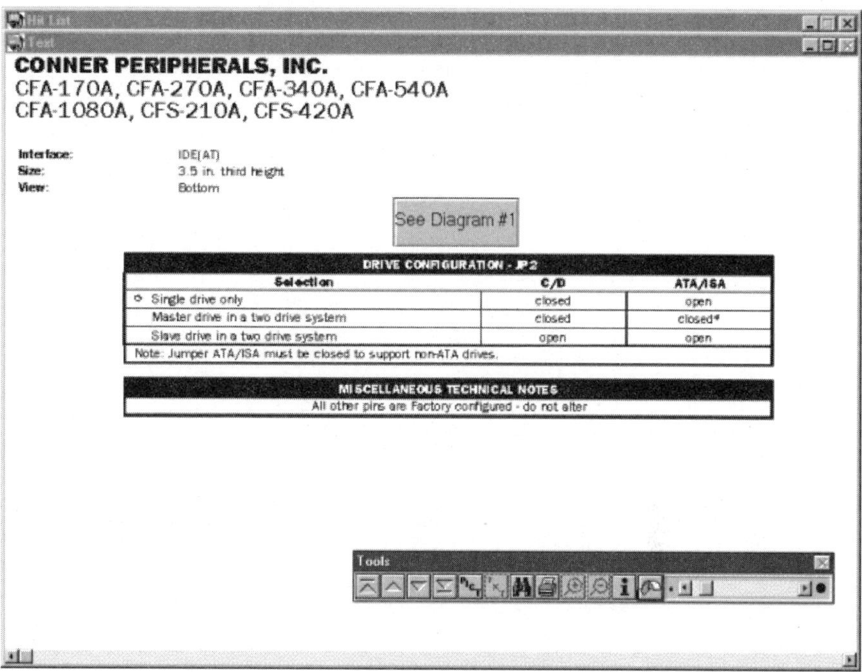

CONNER PERIPHERALS, INC.

CFA-170A, CFA-270A, CFA-340A, CFA-540A
CFA-1080A, CFS-210A, CFS-420A

Interface: IDE(AT)
Size: 3.5 in. third height
View: Bottom

See Diagram #1

DRIVE CONFIGURATION - JP2		
Selection	**C/D**	**ATA/ISA**
Single drive only	closed	open
Master drive in a two drive system	closed	closed*
Slave drive in a two drive system	open	open
Note: Jumper ATA/ISA must be closed to support non-ATA drives.		

MISCELLANEOUS TECHNICAL NOTES
All other pins are Factory configured - do not alter

Figure 8.17
Microhouse Technical Library

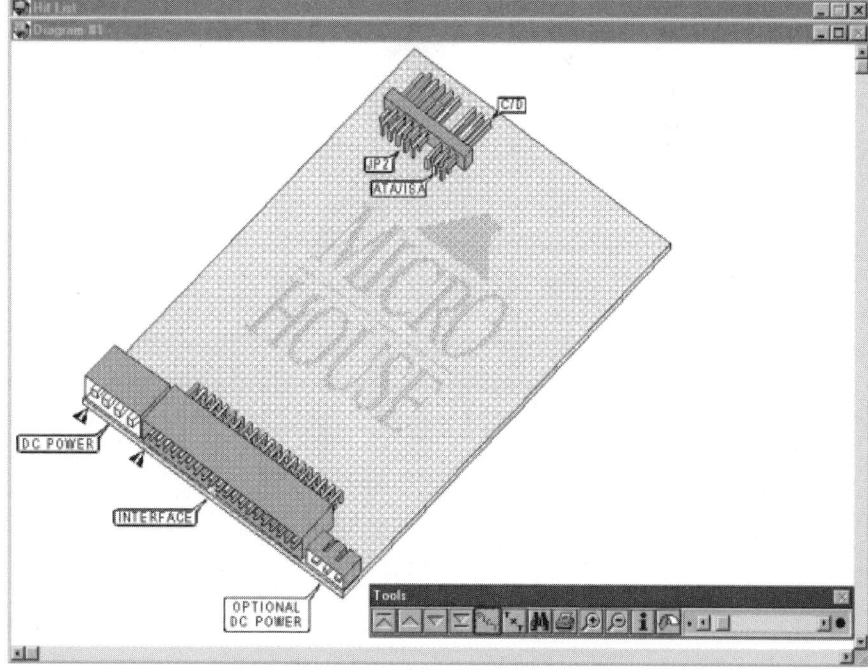

Figure 8.18
Microhouse Technical Library

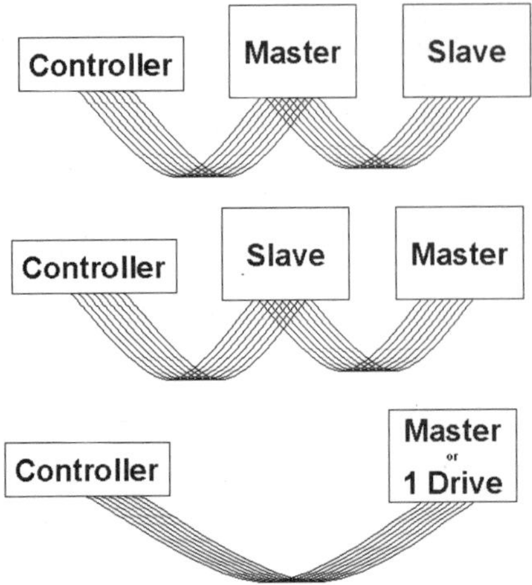

Figure 8.19 The three ways to connect to one controller

If you incorrectly set the master/slave jumpers or cable the hard drives, you won't break anything; it just won't work. There are only three ways you can install a hard drive to one controller (Figure 8.19).

CMOS

After physically installing the hard drive, its geometry must be entered into the CMOS through the CMOS setup program. Without this information, the hard drive will not work. Before IDE drives, you used to have to take the numbers from the drive and type in each value for the cylinders, heads, sectors/track, landing zone, and write precomp. IDE/EIDE drives can be queried through software, and they will simply tell the CMOS the correct settings. Figure 8.20 shows the hard-drive configuration information in a typical CMOS—in this case a CMOS from an older AWARD BIOS.

Note that there are settings for only two drives. In the days before EIDE, PCs could use only two drives. Why? Remember that the original CMOS in the first 286 could store only 64 bytes of data. The original IBM engineers allocated just enough space for two sets of drive information, so the standard allowed only two drives. Besides, who would ever need more than two hard drives?

Today's CMOSes are designed to handle up to four hard drives, and the days of typing in values are long gone. In fact, you can simply set the "type" to auto and the system will set up the hard drive's CMOS settings for you. Setting up the drive in CMOS is very easy on today's PCs. However, there are a few concepts here that I need to explain, starting with hard-drive *types*.

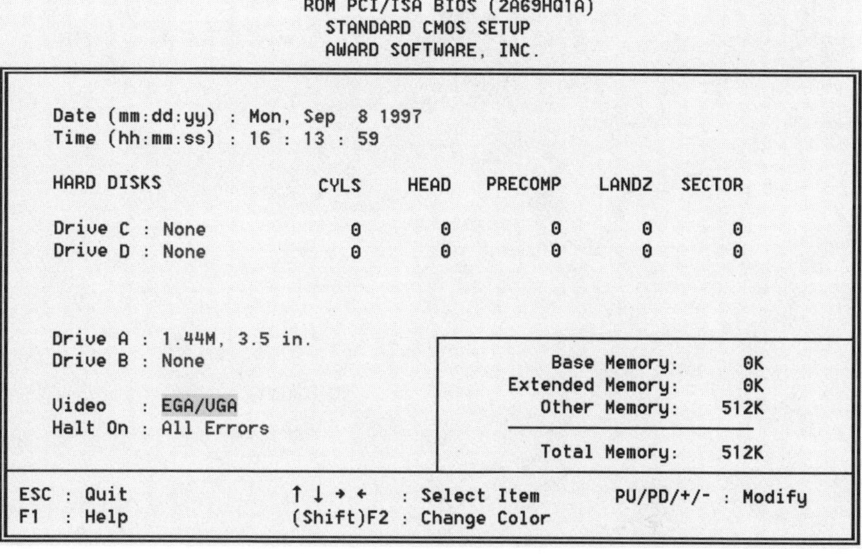
ROM PCI/ISA BIOS (2A69HQ1A)
STANDARD CMOS SETUP
AWARD SOFTWARE, INC.

Date (mm:dd:yy) : Mon, Sep 8 1997
Time (hh:mm:ss) : 16 : 13 : 59

HARD DISKS	CYLS	HEAD	PRECOMP	LANDZ	SECTOR
Drive C : None	0	0	0	0	0
Drive D : None	0	0	0	0	0

Drive A : 1.44M, 3.5 in.
Drive B : None

Video : EGA/VGA
Halt On : All Errors

Base Memory: 0K
Extended Memory: 0K
Other Memory: 512K

Total Memory: 512K

ESC : Quit ↑ ↓ → ← : Select Item PU/PD/+/- : Modify
F1 : Help (Shift)F2 : Change Color

Figure 8.20
Award standard

Hard-Drive Types

The number of heads, cylinders, sectors/track, write precomp, and landing zone determine how the hard-drive controller accesses the physical hard drive. Each number must be correct if the hard drive is to function properly. When IBM created the first CMOS on the 286 AT, they believed that the five different geometry numbers would be too complicated for normal users to configure. For simplicity, IBM established 15 preset combinations of hard-drive geometries, called *hard drive types* (see Table 8.1). So instead of worrying about five different variables, users could simply enter a hard-drive type into the CMOS. The concept of types did make entering geometry into the hard-drive CMOS configuration much easier.

Initially, this worked well, but a problem arose. Note the capacities of the original 15 hard-drive types. They are small. If a manufacturer came up with a new, larger hard-drive type, the list would have to be expanded. At first, IBM did exactly that, eventually expanding the list to 37 different types (see Table 8.2).

BIOS designers soon realized that adding to the list every time a manufacturer created a new hard-drive geometry was not practical, so IBM simply stopped using drives that required unique geometries (see ESDI drives) and stopped adding drive types. The other BIOS makers continued to add types until they got to around 45 different types (see Table 8.3). At that time, AMI created a new "user" type. With this type, instead of se-

TABLE 8.1

The Original Hard Drive Table for the IBM AT

Drive Type	Capacity (Meg)	Cylinders	Heads	Sectors	Write Precomp	Landing Zone
11	110	306	44	17	128	305
22	220	615	44	17	300	615
33	330	615	66	17	300	615
44	620	940	88	17	512	940
55	466	940	66	17	512	940
66	200	615	55	17	None	615
77	300	462	88	17	256	511
88	300	733	55	17	None	733
99	112	900	15	17	None	901
10	200	820	33	17	None	820
11	355	855	55	17	None	855
12	490	855	77	17	None	855
13	200	306	88	17	128	319
14	420	733	77	17	None	733
15		Reserved				

TABLE 8.2

The IBM Drive Geometry Table

Drive Type	Capacity (Meg)	Cylinders	Heads	Sectors	Write Precomp	Landing Zone
1	10	306	4	17	128	305
2	20	615	4	17	300	615
3	30	615	6	17	300	615
4	62	940	8	17	512	940
5	47	940	6	17	512	940
6	20	615	4	17	None	615
7	30	462	8	17	256	511
8	30	733	5	17	None	733
9	112	900	15	17	None	901
10	20	820	3	17	None	820
11	35	855	5	17	None	855

TABLE 8.2

The IBM Drive Geometry Table (Continued)

Drive Type	Capacity (Meg)	Cylinders	Heads	Sectors	Write Precomp	Landing Zone
12	50	855	7	17	None	855
13	20	306	8	17	128	319
14	42	733	7	17	None	733
15	Reserved					
16	20	612	4	17	None	633
17	40	977	5	17	300	977
18	57	977	7	17	None	977
19	60	1024	7	17	512	1023
20	30	733	5	17	300	732
21	42	733	7	17	300	732
22	30	733	5	17	300	733
23	10	306	4	17	None	336
24	20	612	4	17	305	663
25	10	306	4	17	None	340
26	20	612	4	17	None	670
27	40	698	7	17	300	732
28	40	976	5	17	488	977
29	10	306	4	17	None	340
30	20	611	4	17	306	663
31	42	732	7	17	300	732
32	42	1023	5	17	None	1023
33	30	614	4	25	None	663
34	20	775	2	27	None	900
35	30	921	2	33	None	1000
36	20	402	4	26	None	460
37	44	580	6	26	None	640

TABLE 8.3

IBM Drive Geometries

Type	Capacity	Cylinders	Heads	Sectors	Write Precomp	Landing Zone
1	10	306	4	17	128	305
2	20	615	4	17	300	615
3	31	615	6	17	300	615
4	62	940	8	17	512	940
5	47	940	6	17	512	940
6	20	615	4	17	None	615
7	31	462	8	17	256	511
8	30	733	5	17	None	733
9	112	900	15	17	None	901
10	20	820	3	17	None	820
11	36	855	5	17	None	855
12	50	855	7	17	None	855
13	20	306	8	17	128	319
14	43	733	7	17	None	733
15					Reserved	
16	20	612	4	17	0	633
17	41	977	5	17	300	977
18	29	697	5	17	None	697
19	60	1024	7	17	512	1023
20	40	965	5	17	None	965
21	80	965	10	17	None	965
22	65	733	7	26	None	733
23	101	3845	37	35	None	3845
24	31	612	4	26	None	612
25	104	1024	8	26	None	1024
26	65	1024	5	26	None	1024
27	42	1024	5	17	300	1024
28	102	855	7	35	None	855
29	100	776	8	33	None	776

TABLE 8.3

IBM Drive Geometries (Continued)

Type	Capacity	Cylinders	Heads	Sectors	Write Precomp	Landing Zone
30	20	611	4	17	306	663
31	42	732	7	17	None	732
32	42	1023	5	17	None	1023
33	30	614	4	25	None	663
34	20	775	2	27	None	900
35	30	921	2	33	None	1000
36	20	402	4	26	None	460
37	44	580	6	26	None	640

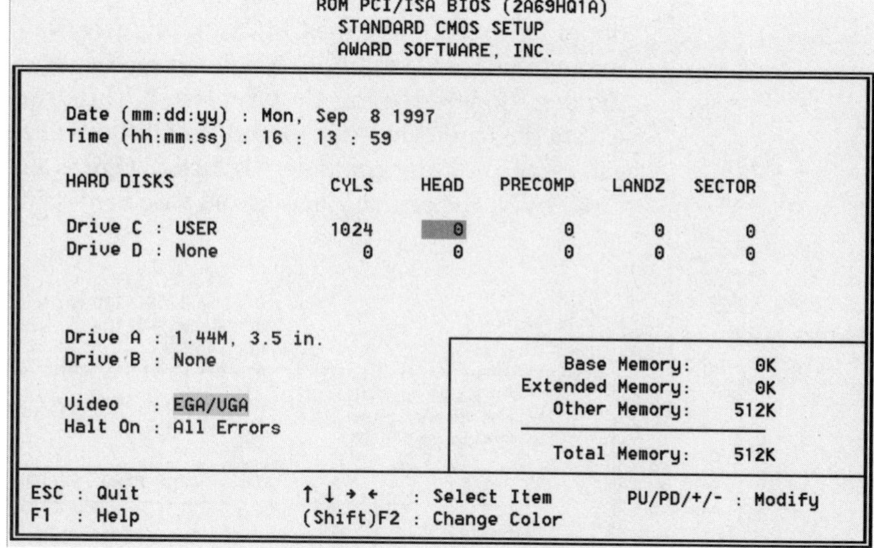

Figure 8.21
Award standard CMOS data entry screen set to user

lecting a special type, users could enter in the five geometry values manually. This provided more flexibility for hard-drive installation. Figure 8.21 shows that older Award BIOS with the CMOS being set to user and the CHS values being entered manually.

IDE/EIDE drives are very forgiving if you put incorrect information into the CMOS setup. If you install a 1020MB hard drive and set the

CMOS to make it a 200MB hard drive, the 1020MB will become a perfectly good 200MB hard drive! However, if you then reset the CMOS back to the proper settings to allow the drive to be 1020MB again, you'll lose all the data on your drive! Be careful and always keep a backup copy of your CMOS information, as described in the chapter on motherboards. The concept of hard-drive types is no longer crucial. On today's systems, just set the hard-drive type to auto or use the IDE autodetect function.

Autodetection

Before roughly 1994, you had to use the hard-drive type to install a hard drive. This manual installation process was always a bit of a problem. You had to have the proper CHS values, you might type them in wrong, and you had to store these values in case your CMOS was accidentally erased. Today, all PCs can set the CMOS properly by using autodetection. All IDE/EIDE drives have their CHS values stored inside of them. Autodetection simply means that the CMOS asks the drive for those stored values and automatically updates the CMOS. There are two common ways to perform autodetection. First, most CMOSes have a hard-drive type called "auto." By setting the hard-drive type to auto, the CMOS will automatically update itself every time the computer is started. Figure 8.22 is a typical modern CMOS with the primary master and slave hard-drive types set to auto.

Figure 8.22
AUTO configuration

```
                     ROM PCI/ISA BIOS (2A69HQ1A)
                        STANDARD CMOS SETUP
                        AWARD SOFTWARE, INC.

  Date (mm:dd:yy) : Mon, Sep  8 1997
  Time (hh:mm:ss) : 16 : 13 : 59

  HARD DISKS          TYPE    SIZE   CYLS HEAD PRECOMP LANDZ SECTOR  MODE

  Primary Master   : Auto       0      0    0       0     0      0  AUTO
  Primary Slave    : Auto       0      0    0       0     0      0  AUTO
  Secondary Master : None       0      0    0       0     0      0 ------
  Secondary Slave  : None       0      0    0       0     0      0 ------

  Drive A : 1.44M, 3.5 in.
  Drive B : None                                  Base Memory:      0K
                                              Extended Memory:      0K
  Video   : EGA/VGA                              Other Memory:    512K
  Halt On : All Errors
                                                 Total Memory:    512K

 ESC : Quit              ↑ ↓ → ←    : Select Item      PU/PD/+/- : Modify
 F1  : Help              (Shift)F2  : Change Color
```

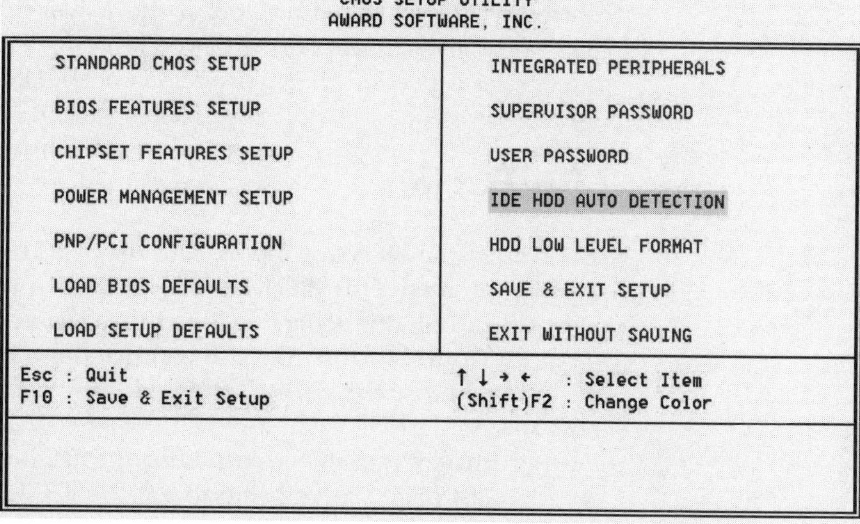

Figure 8.23
Autodetect selection

The second, slightly older way to perform autodetection is through the IDE Autodetection option. This is a separate option, usually accessed from the main CMOS screen, as shown in Figure 8.23. After selecting the Autodetection option, most CMOSes will look for any hard drive installed on the system. Figure 8.24 shows a typical autodetection.

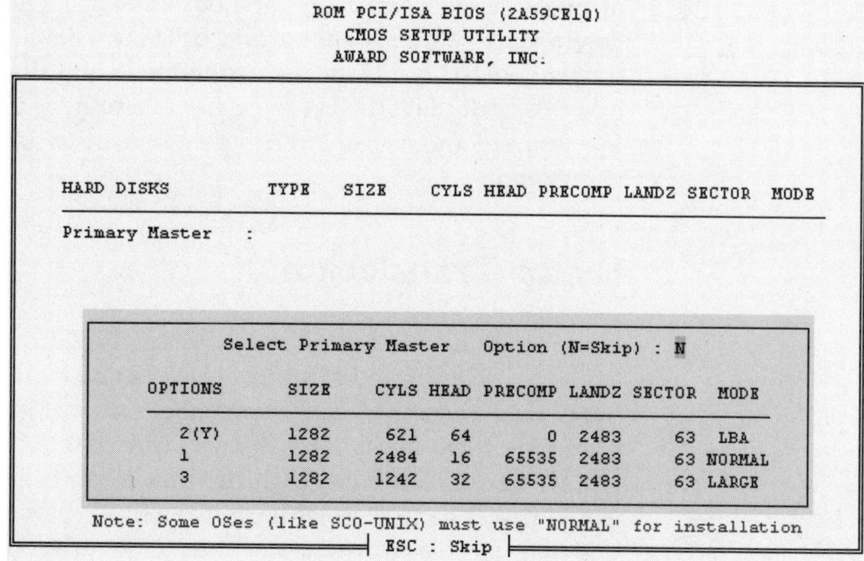

Figure 8.24
Successfully finding a drive with Autodetect

Wait a minute! This CMOS has found a master drive on the primary controller (a primary master), but it shows you three different CHS settings. What gives? To explain what you're seeing, I'll have to take a detour into one big aspect of EIDE drives: LBA and ECHS.

LBA/ECHS

IBM created the BIOS to support hard drives many years before IDE drives were invented. This BIOS was first shown in the IBM "AT" 286 computer. When IDE was being developed, the creators wanted IDE to be able to be run from the same AT BIOS command set. By providing this capability, you can use the same CMOS and BIOS routines to talk to a much more advanced drive.

Unfortunately, the BIOS routines for the original AT command set allowed a hard drive size only up to 528/504MB. The most cylinders you could have was 1024, the most heads was 16, and the most sectors/track was 63:

1024 cylinders × 16 heads × 63 sectors/track × 512 bytes/sector = 504MB

For years, this was no problem. But then when hard drives began to approach the 504MB barrier, the problem became clear—there needed to be a way of getting past 504MB. One of the differences between an IDE and an EIDE drive is that EIDE drives can be larger than 504MB via one of two different, competing methods known as LBA and ECHS. LBA was developed by Western Digital and ECHS was developed by Seagate. Since they are virtually identical in function, I will discuss both simultaneously. Basically, LBA/ECHS is the hard drive *lying* to the computer about its geometry, and is really nothing more than an advanced type of sector translation.

Sector Translation

Long before hard drives approached the 504MB limit, the limits of 1024 cylinders, 16 heads, and 63 sectors/track caused hard-drive makers fits. The big problem was the heads. Remember that every two heads is another platter, another physical disk that you have to squeeze into a hard drive. If you wanted a hard drive with the maximum number of 16 heads, you would have a hard drive with eight physical platters inside the drive! Nobody wanted that many heads: it made the drives too high, it took more

Figure 8.25
Too many heads!

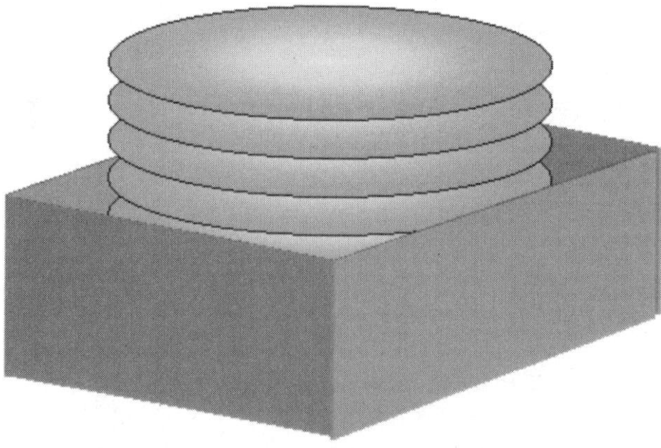

power to spin up the drive, and more parts cost more money (see Figure 8.25). There was no problem to make a hard drive that had *fewer* heads and *more* cylinders, but the stupid 1024/16/63 limit gets in the way.

Plus, there's a tremendous amount of wastage with sectors. The sectors toward the inside of the drive are much shorter than the sectors on the outside. The sectors on the outside don't need to be that long, but with the current geometry setup, hard-drive makers have no choice. You could really make a hard drive store a lot more information if hard drives could be made with more sectors/track on the outside tracks (Figure 8.26).

Figure 8.26
Multiple sectors/track

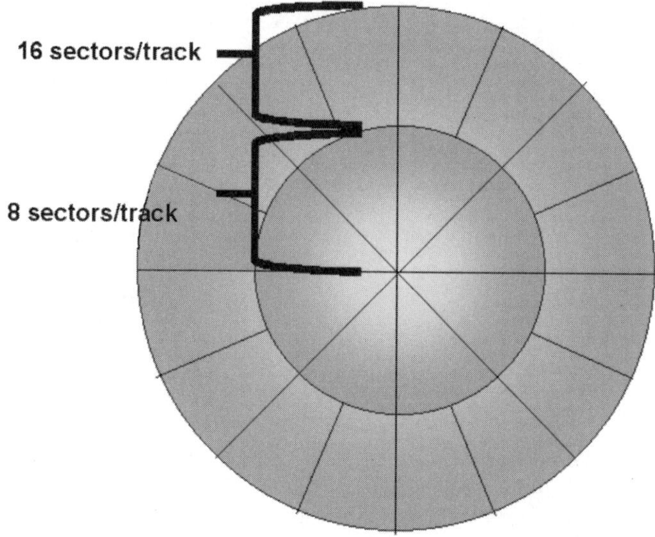

TABLE 8.4

Seagate's ST108 Drive Geometry

ST108 Physical		BIOS Limits	
Cylinders	2048 <- ***TOO BIG!***	Cylinders	1024
Heads	2	Heads	16
Sectors/Track	52	Sectors/Track	63
Total Capacity	108 Meg		

The IDE specification was designed to have two geometries: the *physical geometry* was the real layout of the CHS inside the drive, and the *logical geometry* is what the drive tells the CMOS. In other words, the IDE drive lies to the CMOS, thus allowing the physical drive to no longer be limited to the artificial limits of the BIOS. When data is being transferred to and from the drive, the on-board circuitry of the drive "translates" the logical geometry into the physical geometry. This function is called *sector translation.*

Let's look at a couple of hypothetical examples in action. First, pretend that Seagate came out with a new, very cheap, very fast hard drive called the ST108. However, to get the ST108 drive fast and cheap, Seagate had to use a rather strange geometry, shown in Table 8.4.

Notice that the cylinder number is greater than 1024. To overcome this problem, the IDE drive performs a "sector translation" that reports a geometry to the BIOS that is totally different from the true geometry of the drive. Table 8.5 shows the actual geometry and the "logical" geometry of our mythical ST108 drive. Notice that the logical geometry is now within the acceptable parameters of the BIOS limitations. Sector translation never changes the capacity of the drive; it only changes the geometry to stay within the BIOS limits.

Now let's watch how the advanced sector translation of LBA allows for hard drives greater than 528MB. This time we have the new Western Dig-

TABLE 8.5

Actual and Logical Geometry of the ST108 Drive

Physical		Logical	
Cylinders	2048	Cylinders	512
Heads	2	Heads	8
Sectors/Track	52	Sectors/Track	52
Total Capacity	108Meg	Total Capacity	108Meg

TABLE 8.6

Western Digital WD2160's Physical and Logical Geometries

Physical		Logical	
Cylinders	16384	Cylinders	1024
Heads	4	Heads	*64*
Sectors/Track	63	Sectors/Track	63
Total Capacity	2.1 GB	Total Capacity	2.1 GB

ital WD2160, a 2.1GB hard drive. Table 8.6 lists its physical and logical geometries. Note that, even with sector translation, the number of heads is greater than the allowed 16! So here's where the magic comes in. The WD2160 is capable of *logical block addressing*, or LBA. Now assuming that the BIOS is also capable of LBA, here's what happens. When the computer boots up, the BIOS queries the drives if they can perform LBA. If they say yes, the BIOS and the drive work together to slightly change the way they talk to each other. They can do this without conflicting with the original AT BIOS commands by taking advantage of unused commands to allow for using up to 256 heads.

Enhanced CHS (ECHS) is nothing more than a competitor to Western Digital's LBA. It works the same but comes up with different values than LBA. With LBA/ECHS, you can have 1024 cylinders, 256 heads, and 63 sectors/track for a maximum size of 8.4 gigabytes.

In order to have drives larger than 504MB, you must have a hard drive that has LBA/ECHS and a BIOS that supports LBA/ECHS. If you have an EIDE drive larger than 504MB, you can be sure the drive supports LBA and ECHS. Virtually all BIOSes support LBA and ECHS. Just run the autodetection utility. If the BIOS doesn't support LBA, all EIDE drives come with an installation utility such as On Track's Disk Manager software, which provides its own LBA support.

Whew! That was a lot of information! But now you can go back to the IDE Autodetect screen and understand why there are three different choices: LBA, Normal, and Large (Figure 8.27). LBA means the drive is capable of LBA, which is the most common setting for setting up a drive. Normal is the physical geometry, which is used only for operating systems that don't use the BIOS like Novell NetWare and UNIX. It is never used otherwise. Large shows that the drive is capable of ECHS. If you want, you can also set the drive to ECHS. (Windows 95 and Windows NT both use LBA and ECHS.)

I stay away from ECHS. It's not that there is anything wrong with it; it works perfectly. The problem is if I ever want to move the hard drive to

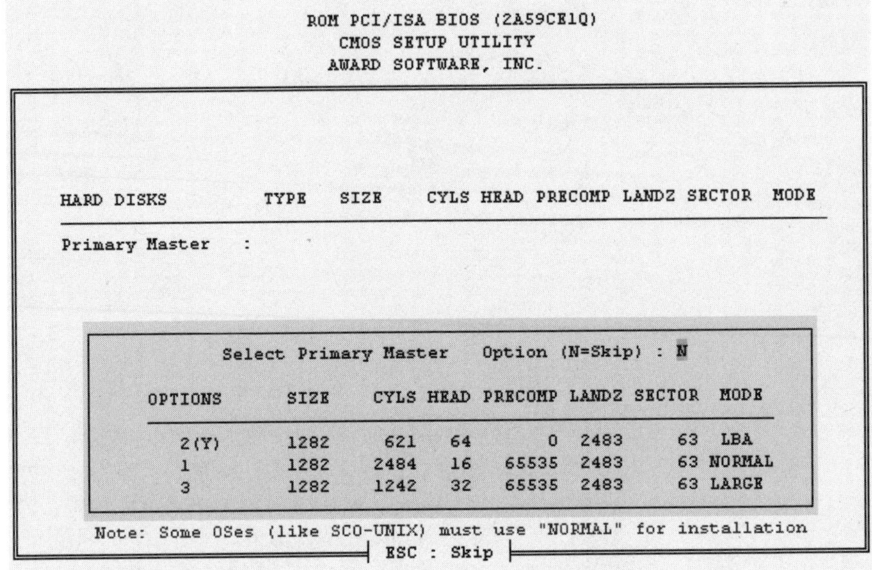

Figure 8.27 Autodetection revisited

another system, that other system also has to support ECHS. If it doesn't, I can install the drive under LBA, but *I will lose all the data on the drive*. Since all BIOSes support LBA, I never have to worry about that if I move the drive. Stick to LBA.

Autodetection has one other feature that makes it indispensable. When a drive doesn't work, the biggest question, especially during installation is: "Did I plug it in correctly?" With autodetection, the answer is simple; if it doesn't see the drives, there is something wrong with the hardware.

PIO Modes

ATA drives transfer data to and from the hard drive and memory via standardized protocols called PIO (programmable input/output) modes. Although the ATA drives could originally transfer data from the hard drive to RAM at a maximum rate of roughly 3.3 megabits per second (mbps), this speed was very quickly bumped up to 5.2 mbps, and then 8.3 mbps. The Small Forms Factor (SFF) standards committee defined these as PIO modes 0, 1, and 2. In the ATA world, all drives can use all three modes.

The SFF committee released a follow-up to the ATA standard that defined some new data throughput speeds. First, there were two new PIO speeds,

TABLE 8.7

PIO Speeds

PIO Mode	Cycle Time (NS)	Transfer Rate (MB/S)
0	600	3.3
1	383	5.2
2	240	8.3
3	180	11.1
4	120	16.6

called PIO 3 and PIO 4 (see Table 8.7). In order to get the best performance out of your hard drive, you must set the proper PIO mode for the drive.

Setting the PIO mode requires you to answer the following three questions: "What is the fastest mode the hard drive supports?" "What is the fastest mode the controller supports?" and "What is the fastest mode the BIOS or device driver will support?"

The fastest PIO mode you can set is limited by the weakest link. For example, if you have a hard drive capable of PIO mode 4, a controller capable of mode 2, and a BIOS capable of mode 4, the best you will get is mode 2. You should never try to use a mode faster than what is recommended by the drive manufacturer. While a faster mode will not damage your drive, it will most certainly damage your data.

To make it simple, most modern PCs will talk to the hard drive at boot and automatically set the proper PIO modes. It's easy to determine if the PC can perform this automatic negotiation. Go into the CMOS and look for something that says PIO, usually in the Advanced or Integrated Peripherals screens (see Figure 8.28). If the system has an Auto option, take it. This setting will query the drive for its top PIO mode and automatically set it up for you.

Sadly, there are still many older PCs out there using older-style hard-drive controller cards. In this case, there's a little more work required. You'll need to manually set the controller to the highest PIO mode that the hard drive can handle.

First, determine the highest PIO mode for the drive. There are no settings on the drive to set PIO modes. The hard drive's top PIO mode is preset. If the PIO mode isn't stated on the hard drive, call the manufacturer or guess. People don't like to see the word *guess* in print; it makes them uneasy. It shouldn't. The hard drive will lock up if the controller is too fast, then just move the controller to a slower mode. Most drives greater than 1GB or made after 1995 support mode 4.

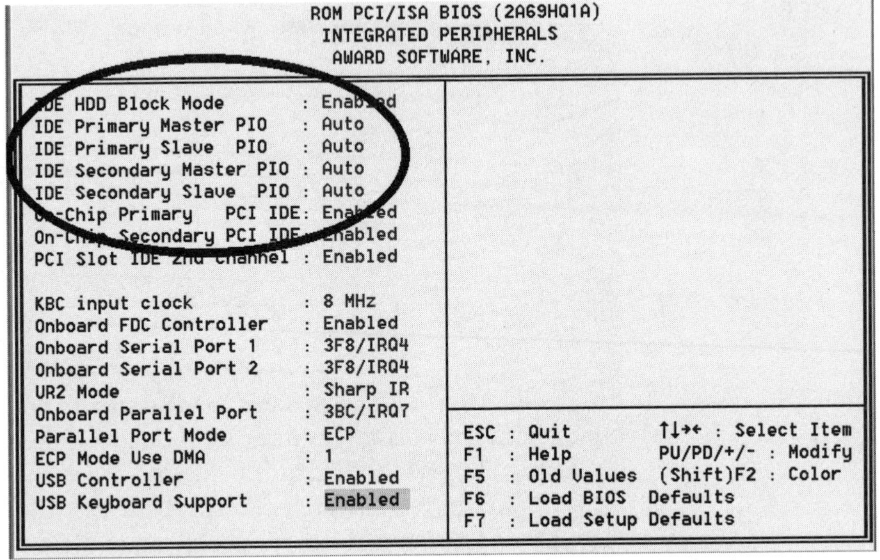

Figure 8.28
PIO mode settings in CMOS with onboard controller

Second, determine the fastest speed your controller can handle. All hard drives can at least support PIO mode 2. Therefore, the question is usually whether you want PIO mode 2, 3, or 4. If you're using an old ISA card, PIO mode 2 is the best you can get. The two fastest PIO modes, 3 and 4, must be run from either a VL-bus or a PCI controller. Many cards set their PIO mode by setting the cycle time and not the PIO mode (Figure 8.29).

Controllers capable of PIO modes 3 and 4 use a hardware flow control called IORDY (IO ready), also known as IOCHRDY. This setting allows the drive to slow down the data transfer as the head moves across the disk (Figure 8.30). If your drive does not support IORDY and you attempt to use your new EIDE controller and its software to force your old-style hard drive into PIO mode 3 or 4, data can be corrupted on the drive. So if a hard drive can't do PIO 3 or 4, don't try to force it. On older controllers, the IOCHRDY is usually a separate jumper setting that must set properly. Always enable IOCHRDY on older controllers.

DMA Modes

Direct memory access (DMA) is a data transfer method that is very different from a PIO mode. This method bypasses the CPU and transfers data directly into memory, leaving the CPU free to run programs. These transfers can function in one of two ways: by using the DMA controller on the

Figure 8.29
PIO settings on a typical controller

Figure 8.30
I/O CHRDY settings on typical controller

TABLE 8.8
DMA Speeds

DMA Mode Single Word (16-Bit)	Cycle Time (ns)	Transfer Rate (MB/s)
0	960	2.1
1	480	4.2
2	240	8.3

DMA Mode Double Word (16-Bit)	Cycle Time (ns)	Transfer Rate (MB/s)
0	480	4.2
1	150	13.3
2	120	16.6
"Ultra DMA"	60	33.3

ISA bus, which is slow and not done, or by using a bus-mastering controller that takes over the expansion bus and bypasses the built-in DMA controller. DMA data transfers can be either 16 bits (single word) or 32 bits (double word) wide. The transfer width depends on the data bus (ISA, EISA, PCI, or VLB) being used. Any type of DMA data transfer for ATA hard drives is extremely rare. For reference, the transfer rates for the various DMA modes are shown in Table 8.8.

Unlike PIO modes, most systems require special drivers to be installed to take advantage of DMA modes. A PC can use either DMA or PIO, not both. Fortunately, DMA drivers "turn off" PIO when they are used. DMA is faster than PIO modes, but a PC would have to be worked very hard in terms of data transfers to see a significant difference. Most desktop PCs won't show any improvement.

Drive Naming Conventions

If only one hard drive has been installed, it must be configured as the *primary master*. If another drive is installed, it must be installed as the *primary slave* or *secondary master*. Unfortunately, many older CMOS configurations like the examples here use the terms C: and D:. Simply remember that the master drive is C: and the slave drive is D:. This is only an issue on older systems whose BIOSes support only two drives. See Figures 8.31 and 8.32.

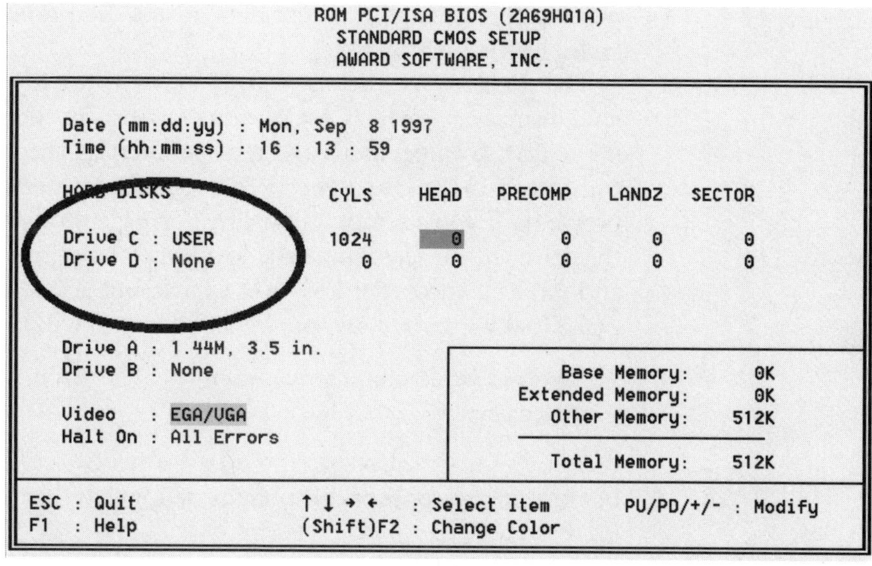

Figure 8.31
AWARD BIOS showing master as C: and slave as D:

Figure 8.32
Old AMI WinBIOS® showing master as C: and slave as D:

Low-Level Formatting

Once the CMOS has been updated with the hard-drive geometry, a program must be run to tell the controller to read the CMOS information and organize the hard drive. This is known as a *low-level format*. It performs three simultaneous functions: it creates and organizes the sectors, making them ready to accept data; it sets the proper interleave; and it establishes the boot sector.

The problem with sector translation is in the low-level format. All low-level formatters use the CMOS values to perform their low-level format, but if the CMOS values aren't the true geometries, they try to make the drive think that its logical geometry is its actual geometry—which could cause problems. If you attempt to low-level format a modern (post-1993) IDE drive, the drive will simply ignore the low-level format and the program will run and report a successful low-level format, but actually nothing would happen. However, most early (pre-1993) IDE drives will be destroyed!

Low-level formatting is done on only pre-IDE drives. All IDE/EIDE drives are low-level formatted at the factory.

Although low-level formatting is basically obsolete, it warrants discussion because many concepts and terms of low-level formatting are still being used today.

Sector Organization

In the earlier discussion of geometry, I stated that each sector contains 512 usable bytes of data. However, there are actually 574 bytes per sector on RLL, the additional bytes being reserved for organization of the 512 usable bytes of data. Table 8.9 shows the structure of a sector (I'll use an RLL

TABLE 8.9

Sector Structure

Area of Sector	Size (Bytes)	Function
SYNC	10	Allows drive electronics time to respond
IDAM	2	Warns of approach of sector ID
ID	4	Gives the sector number
ECC	4	Checks the first three values
GAP 2	5	Dead space for ECC calculation time
SYNC	11	Dead space for resync with hard drive electronics
DAM	2	Warns of approach of data area
DATA	512	Data area
ECC	4	Checks the data area
GAP 3	20	Signals end of sector

sector, since RLL is all that's used anymore, and the differences are unimportant to repair technicians).

Every hard drive comes from the factory with bad spots on the platters that are unacceptable for the placement of data. As the sectors are being created, the low-level format attempts to skip over the bad spots. Sometimes, however, it is impossible to skip over a spot, so the sector is marked as "bad" in the ID field.

Interleave

The second major aspect of low-level formatting is called *interleave*. To understand interleave, remember that when a file is retrieved from a hard drive, it doesn't magically move from the hard drive to RAM in one step. Files are chopped up into 512K chunks (sectors), so file retrieval is usually a matter of accessing many sectors in succession.

Data retrieved from (or saved to) a hard drive must pass through a buffer on the hard-drive controller. When writing data, the buffer stores the data until the hard drive can save it. When reading, the buffer stores the data until RAM needs it. This creates a problem with drives. If sectors are immediately next to each other, often the hard drive can't keep up with the spinning platters. As a result, if data is missed on a sector, you'd have to wait until the drive rotated back around before the data could be accessed. To eliminate this waste, you can number every other sector, every third sector, or even every eighth sector! That way the controller's buffer can be ready for the data and there is no waiting for the drive to spin back around to catch the next sector.

A drive can be anything from a 1-to-1 interleave up to as high as an 8 to-1 interleave. The interleave is determined by the program that performs the low-level format. The interleave can be entered manually during the low-level format, or the low-level format itself can automatically determine the best interleave. It is always best to let the program determine the best interleave.

There is no low-level formatting on IDE drives! All IDE drives use a special type of low-level formatting called *embedded servo*. This type of low-level formatting can be performed only by the manufacturer. Once the CMOS is set up on an IDE drive, you go straight to partitioning.

There are programs out today that supposedly allow you to low-level format IDE drives. These programs simply mark sectors good or bad in the hard drive's own internal error map. (Do not confuse this with the high-level format marking of bad clusters in the FAT!) These programs can be useful, and later, during a discussion of hard-drive repair, you'll look at them. However, these programs are not true low-level formatters; they are simply "bad sector mappers."

Many CMOSs have a Hard-Drive Utility option that allows users to low-level format their drives. These utilities are for pre-IDE drives exclusively. *Never use them on IDE or EIDE drives! You could destroy them!*

Bootable Floppy Disk

The next two sections will complete the process of setting up a new hard drive. Up to this point, everything has been done via hardware or CMOS. The next two steps, partitioning and high-level formatting, require special programs. The problem is that to complete these functions, you need a very important tool called a bootable diskette. Keep in mind that when you are installing a hard drive, you need to be able to boot an operating system and have the necessary programs to set up the drive. Refer to the chapters on DOS, Windows 3.*x*, and Windows 95 for instructions on making bootable floppies.

Partitioning

Assuming that you have an IDE/EIDE drive, which doesn't use low-level formatting, *partitioning* is the next step to prepare a drive. Partitions are logical divisions of a hard drive. They cannot be seen if a hard drive is opened. For example, a computer might have only one *physical* hard drive (called hard drive 0), but it could have anywhere from 1 to 24 *logical* drives, C: to Z:.

Partitions exist for two reasons. First, when DOS was initially designed to use hard drives, the largest hard drive that could be used was 32 megabytes because of the way DOS stored files on the hard drive. Partitioning was included in DOS 3.3 to allow larger physical hard drives by creating multiple logical drives, up to 32 megabytes each. Partitions today can reach up to 8.4 gigabytes. The second function of partitions is the ability to use more than one operating system (OS). One OS could be added to one partition and another OS could be added to another, allowing a computer to have more than one OS.

Within the DOS/Windows world, a hard drive can be divided into two types of partitions, *primary* and *extended.* The *primary* partition is where the operating system (DOS) is stored. If you want to boot from a hard drive, it must have a primary partition. Primary partitions are for storing the *boot sector,* which tells the computer where to find the operating system. The name of the primary partition is C:, and there is no way to change the name of the C: drive. The other type of partition is known as an *extended* partition, which is for a hard drive or part of a hard drive that does not have an operating system (again, DOS). The extended partition is not associated with a drive letter. Instead, the extended partition is further divided into "logical drives," starting with D: and progressing until drive letter Z: is created. DOS is limited by this alphabetic listing, so there can be only 24 logical drives on one system (remember that A: and B: are reserved for floppy drives).

Don't confuse a primary partition with the primary controller; they are totally different animals!

Partition Examples

These are an almost infinite number of possible combinations for physical hard drives and partitions, but Figure 8.33 shows the most common.

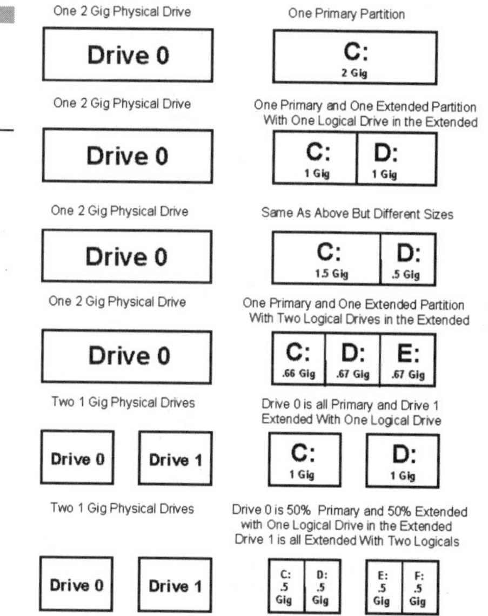

Figure 8.33 Examples of partitions

How to Partition

Assume that you have a 100MB hard drive installed, and you want to make it the C: drive. I'll walk you through partitioning the hard drive, and then provide an example of partitioning the drive into two partitions called C: and D:. You partition a drive using the utility FDISK utility that comes with DOS and Windows 95. Running FDISK will start the opening menu, which contains the following information:

```
Microsoft Windows 95
Fixed Disk Setup Program
Copyright Microsoft Corp. 1983-1995

FDISK Options

Current fixed disk drive: 1

Choose one of the following:

1. Create DOS partition or Logical DOS Drive
2. Set active partition
3. Delete partition or Logical DOS Drive
4. Display partition information

Enter choice: [1]
Press Esc to exit FDISK
```

By pressing the first selection, you can create a primary partition, an extended partition, or logical drives in an extended partition. The second selection lets you select the active partition. After the initial installation, this is used to switch between multiple operating systems. Selection 3 allows you to delete partitions and logical drives. Selection 4 displays current information. If you have more than one drive installed, FDISK adds a fifth option:

```
Microsoft Windows 95
Fixed Disk Setup Program
Copyright Microsoft Corp. 1983-1995

FDISK Options

Current fixed disk drive: 1

Choose one of the following:

1. Create DOS partition or Logical DOS Drive
2. Set active partition
3. Delete partition or Logical DOS Drive
4. Display partition information
5. Change current fixed disk drive
```

This fifth option simply allows you to choose the drive on which you want to work. Note that option 2 specifies setting the active partition, which is where BIOS looks for an operating system when you boot the computer. Many people confuse the primary and active partitions. *The primary partition is where the operating system is stored on the hard drive.* Other operating systems can exist on the extended partition.

Assume that you have DOS on the primary partition and OS/2 on the extended partition. There must be a mechanism to allow users to select the partition and therefore the operating system from which to boot. That's where the active partition comes into play. More advanced operating systems can create (if you tell them to) a special tiny partition called a *boot partition.* The boot partition is set to active. When a computer boots up, a menu appears that prompts users to pick which operating system they want to use. The boot manager then sets whichever partition you want to boot from as active, starting the operating system you want.

DOS and Windows 95 have a limitation not shared by any other operating system; they must be placed on the primary partition, and the name of that partition is always C:. This means that if you have two operating systems and one of them is DOS, then *DOS must be on drive C:.* More powerful operating systems such as OS/2, UNIX, and Windows NT can all boot from another drive letter, as well as from C:.

So the primary partition is where the DOS and Windows 95 boot files reside, and the active partition is where BIOS searches for the operating system to be booted. The active partition is an issue only when more than one operating system is to be installed on one hard drive; otherwise, always set the primary partition to be active.

The rest of this chapter assumes that you are comfortable with DOS commands. If you are not, you might want to jump to the DOS chapter before proceeding.

High-Level Formatting

The last step in preparing an IDE/EIDE drive is called the *high-level format,* although the term is almost never used. Instead, it is simply referred to as "formatting." The high-level format actually performs two major functions; creating and configuring the *file allocation tables* (FATs) and creating the *root directory.* The DOS root directory is the foundation structure upon which files and subdirectories are built. The primary partition, as well as every logical drive in the extended partition, must be formatted separately. To format a drive, the first step is to verify that the drive is already partitioned. From the A: prompt, run the FDISK command as follows: FDISK /STATUS. This will quickly allow you to see the partitions on the drive, for example:

```
Disk    Drv    Mbytes Free    Usage
1              1325           100%
         C     1325
```

In this example, the FDISK /STATUS command reports that there is only one partition, C:, and that it uses the entire drive. Every drive must then be formatted. To format, use the FORMAT command as follows: FORMAT *x*:, where *x* is replaced by the drive letter you want to format. So to format the C: drive, type FORMAT C:. To make the drive bootable, add the option /S, as follows: FORMAT C:/S.

The only drive that should ever receive the /S is the C: drive. If there are other partitions, they must also be formatted. The FORMAT command takes quite a while, based on the size of the drive. Let's look at the process of formatting and that very important "file cabinet of the drive," the FAT.

File Allocation Table (FAT)

The base storage area for hard drives is a sector, and each sector can store up to 512 bytes of data. If a file less than 512 bytes is stored in a sector, the rest of the sector is wasted. This waste is acceptable, however, since most files are far larger than 512 bytes. So what happens when a file larger than 512 bytes is stored? There must be a way to fill one sector, find another that's unused, and fill it—continuing to fill sectors until the file is completely stored. Also, it is important to remember which sectors a file is stored in should that file need to be retrieved.

In the DOS that first supported hard drives, MS-DOS version 2.1, a special data structure was created to keep track of where data is stored on the hard drive. This structure is called a *file allocation table,* better known as *FAT.* The FAT is nothing more than a "card catalog" that keeps track of which parts of a file are stored in which sectors. Each partition has two FATs stored near the beginning of the partition. These FATs, #1 and #2, are carbon copies of each other. It's nice to call a FAT a "data structure," but it is more like a two-column spreadsheet.

The left column gives each sector a number, from 0000 to FFFF (in hex, of course). This means there are 65536 (64K) sectors. (See Figure 8.34.) Notice that the left-hand side contains 16 bits. (Four hex characters make 16 bits, remember?) This FAT is called the *16-bit FAT* or *FAT 16.* Not only hard drives have FATs. Floppy drives also use FAT, but their FATs are only 12 bits since they store so much less data.

Figure 8.34
16-bit FAT

0000	
0001	
0002	
0003	
0004	
0005	
.	
.	
.	
.	
FFF0	
FFFA	
FFFB	
FFFC	
FFFD	
FFFE	
FFFF	

The right-hand side of the FAT contains information on the status of sectors. No hard drive is perfect. All hard drives have sectors that are not capable of storing data because of errors in construction. There must be a way to determine these bad sectors, mark them as unusable, and then prevent any files from being written to them. This mapping of bad sectors is one of the functions of high-level formatting. After the FATs are created, the format program proceeds through the partition, writing and attempting to read from each sector sequentially. If it finds a bad sector, a special status code (FFF7) is placed in the FAT, indicating that the sector is unavailable for use. Formatting also marks the good sectors as 0000.

Using the FAT to track sectors, however, creates a problem. The 16-bit FAT can address 64K (2^{16}) locations. Therefore, the size of a hard-drive partition should be limited to 64K × 512 bytes per sector, or 32MB. When FATs were first invented, that presented no problem since most hard drives were only 5MB to 10MB. As hard drives grew in size, FDISK was used to break them up into multiple partitions. For example, a 40MB hard drive would have been broken up into two partitions, each less than 32MB. But as hard drives started to become much larger, it was obvious that the 32MB limit for drives would be unacceptable. A new type of formatting had to be developed, one that would allow larger drives while still maintaining backward compatibility with the 16-bit FAT. This led to the

Figure 8.35 Cluster vs. sector

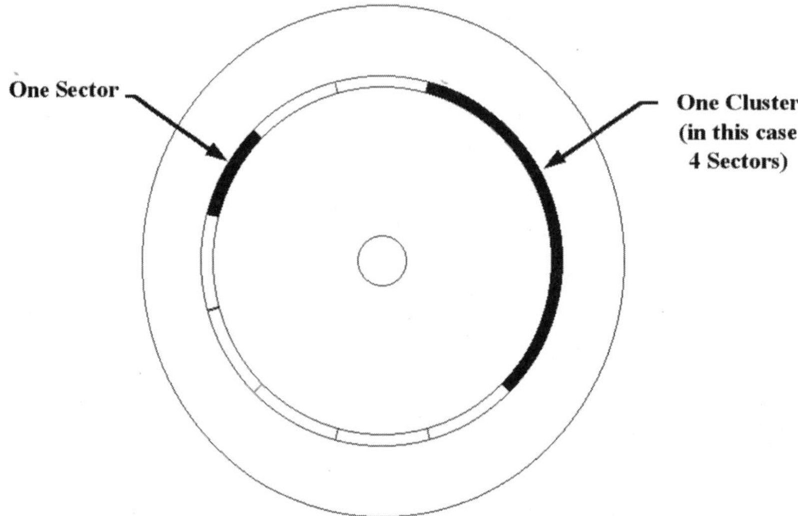

development of a more elegant method of handling larger hard drives, the one in use today, called *clustering*.

Clustering simply means to combine a set of contiguous sectors and treat them as a single unit in the FAT. These units are called *file allocation units* or *clusters*. Now each row of the FAT addresses a cluster instead of a sector. Unlike sectors, the size of a cluster is not fixed. The number of sectors in each cluster is determined by the size of the partition, so there are never more than 64K clusters. That way clustering is completely compatible with the 64K locations in the 16-bit FAT. The number of sectors in a cluster is calculated by FDISK when the partition is created. Figure 8.36 shows the number of sectors per cluster for FAT 16.

Sectors and Clusters

A sector is no longer the basic unit of storage; now it is a cluster. When saving a file of fewer than 512 bytes, the excess unused space in the sector was wasted. For example, saving a file of only 100 bytes left 412 bytes un-

Figure 8.36 Number of sectors/cluster by partition size for FAT-16

If FDISK makes a partition this big:	You'll get this many sectors/cluster
16 to 127.9 Meg	4 Sectors/Cluster
128 to 255.9 Meg	8 Sectors/Cluster
256 to 511.9 Meg	16 Sectors/Cluster
512 to 1023.9 Meg	32 Sectors/Cluster
1024 to 2048 Meg	64 Sectors/Cluster

used. Because files are usually much larger than sectors, the level of wasted storage was acceptable. For example, if you have a file with 15,000 bytes, you need 30 sectors to store it. The last sector will be only about 25 percent full, however, which produces about 3 percent waste.

This changed when clusters become the smallest storage area in a cluster. Let's say that same 15,000-byte file is stored on a 1200MB (1.2GB) partition. A partition of that size has 64 sectors/cluster, making each cluster 32,000 bytes. In this case, the 15,000-byte file will take one 32,000-byte cluster, leaving 17,000 bytes wasted. Storing the same file in clusters creates much greater waste due to the fact that clusters are so much larger.

To keep the waste as low as possible, partitions are kept as small as possible when using FAT 16. As a rule of thumb, keep your partitions at 1023.9MB or smaller if possible. A 1023.9MB partition will have 16K clusters, which keeps the level of wasted storage at an acceptable level. For example, a 1.2MB hard drive would be best partitioned into two partitions, each less than 1024MB.

If you are using Windows 95, you can also use a more powerful FAT, called FAT-32. As its name implies, FAT-32 uses 32 bits to describe each cluster. Since there are more bits to describe, you can have up to 8.4GB drive partitions. This is explained in more detail in the chapter on Windows 95.

The FAT in Action

When a file is saved, DOS starts at the beginning of the FAT, looks for the first space marked "open for use" (0000), and begins to write to that cluster. If the entire file can be saved within that one cluster, the code FFFF (last cluster) is placed on the cluster's status. The filename is added to the directory and the cluster number is placed with the filename. If the file takes more than one cluster, then DOS searches for the next open cluster and places the number of the next cluster in the status, filling and adding clusters until the file is saved. The last cluster then receives the end-of-file code (FFFF).

Let's do an example of this process, and start by selecting an arbitrary part of the FAT: from 3ABB to 3AC7. Assume you are saving a file, MOM.TXT. This file will take three clusters. The FAT before saving the file looks like Figure 8.37. DOS finds the first open cluster, 3ABB, and fills it. Needing more space, it must go through the FAT to find the next open cluster. It finds cluster 3ABC. Before filling 3ABC, the value 3ABC is placed in 3ABB's status (Figure 8.38). There is still more of the file to be saved, so DOS must find one more cluster. 3ABD has been marked FFF7 (bad cluster), so DOS skips over 3ABD, finding 3ABE (Figure 8.39).

Figure 8.37
Initial FAT

Cluster	Status
3ABB	0000
3ABC	0000
3ABD	FFF7
3ABE	0000
3ABF	0000
3AC0	0000
3AC1	0000
3AC2	0000
3AC3	0000
3AC4	0000
3AC5	0000
3AC6	0000
3AC7	0000

Figure 8.38
First cluster used

Cluster	Status
3ABB	**3ABC**
3ABC	0000
3ABD	FFF7
3ABE	0000
3ABF	0000
3AC0	0000
3AC1	0000
3AC2	0000
3AC3	0000
3AC4	0000
3AC5	0000
3AC6	0000
3AC7	0000

Before filling 3ABE, DOS enters the value 3ABE in 3ABC's status. 3ABE is not completely filled, but the remaining bytes are unavailable for use. DOS enters the value FFFF in 3ABE's status, indicating the end of file (Figure 8.40). After all the clusters are saved, DOS goes to the directory where

Figure 8.39
Second cluster used

Cluster	Status
3ABB	3ABC
3ABC	**3ABE**
3ABD	FFF7
3ABE	0000
3ABF	0000
3AC0	0000
3AC1	0000
3AC2	0000
3AC3	0000
3AC4	0000
3AC5	0000
3AC6	0000
3AC7	0000

Figure 8.40
Final cluster used

Cluster	Status
3ABB	3ABC
3ABC	3ABE
3ABD	FFF7
3ABE	**FFFF**
3ABF	0000
3AC0	0000
3AC1	0000
3AC2	0000
3AC3	0000
3AC4	0000
3AC5	0000
3AC6	0000
3AC7	0000

the file is to be saved (another cluster) and records the filename, size, date/time, and starting cluster, as such:

```
MOM.TXT 19234    05-19-96    2:04p    3ABB
```

That's how the FAT saves and retrieves files.

Fragmentation

Continuing with the example, let's save two more files: a letter to the IRS (IRS_ROB.DOC) and a letter to IBM (IBM_HELP.DOC). IRS_ROB.DOC will take the next three clusters—3ABF, 3AC0, and 3AC1—and IBM_HELP.DOC will take the two clusters—3AC2 and 3AC3. (See Figure 8.41.)

Now let's erase MOM.TXT. Although the cluster entries for MOM.TXT are not erased from the FAT, its directory entry is changed; the first letter is changed to the Greek symbol φ, so it does not show on a directory. It also tells DOS that its starting cluster is available for use (Figure 8.42).

Notice that all the data for MOM.TXT is intact. If you had some program that could change the φ back into another letter, you could get the document back. Programs such as Unerase in DOS or the Recycle Bin in Windows 95 work that way.

You are going to save one more file, TAXREC.XLS, a big spreadsheet that will take six clusters. As you save it, it overwrites the space that MOM.TXT was in, but it needs three more clusters. The next three available clusters are 3AC4, 3AC5, and 3AC6 (Figure 8.43).

Notice that TAXREC.XLS is in two pieces. Although this is an acceptable way to operate, it slows down the hard drive because it has to go to two different places to access the file. This file is *fragmented.* Although this example is fragmented into two pieces, in the "real world" a file could be fragmented into hundreds of pieces, forcing the read/write heads to travel

Figure 8.41
Three files saved

Cluster	Status
3ABB	3ABC
3ABC	3ABE
3ABD	FFF7
3ABE	FFFF
3ABF	3AC0
3AC0	3AC1
3AC1	FFFF
3AC2	3AC3
3AC3	FFFF
3AC4	0000
3AC5	0000
3AC6	0000
3AC7	0000

Figure 8.42
MOM.TXT erased

Cluster	Status
3ABB	3ABC
3ABC	3ABE
3ABD	FFF7
3ABE	FFFF
3ABF	3AC0
3AC0	3AC1
3AC1	FFFF
3AC2	3AC3
3AC3	FFFF
3AC4	0000
3AC5	0000
3AC6	0000
3AC7	0000

Figure 8.43
TAXREC.XLS fragmented

Cluster	Status
3ABB	**3ABC**
3ABC	**3ABD**
3ABD	3AC4
3ABE	FFFF
3ABF	3AC0
3AC0	3AC1
3AC1	FFFF
3AC2	3AC3
3AC3	FFFF
3AC4	**3AC5**
3AC5	**3AC6**
3AC6	**FFFF**
3AC7	0000

all over the hard drive to retrieve a single file. The speed of the hard drive can be improved dramatically by eliminating this fragmentation. Running a program to eliminate fragmentation is called *defragmenting* a drive. There are several programs designed to defragment hard drives, including DOS's Defrag and Norton Utilities' SpeeDisk (Figure 8.44).

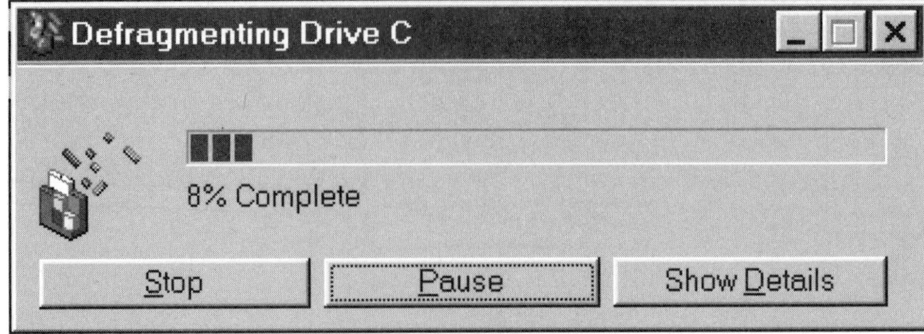

Figure 8.44 Defrag for Windows 95

Both Defrag and SpeeDisk support three levels of defragmentation. The first is file reordering, in which only the files are defragmented. The second is complete defragmentation, in which the subdirectories are also defragmented and all subdirectories are placed next to the root directory, allowing for quicker searches. The files are then defragmented. The third level is directory and/or file sorting. This simply puts the file and directory names in some order, usually alphabetical. This doesn't make file retrieval any faster, but it makes it easier to find a particular file or directory.

Defragmentation is crucial for ensuring the top performance of a hard drive. A good rule of thumb is to perform a file reordering once a week and a full defragmentation once a month. Refer to the DOS chapter for another view of the program Defrag.

The Finished Drive

Once the formatting has taken place, the drive has been set up and is ready to have more programs loaded. Let's review the steps:

1. Make the physical connection. Always use the primary controller first. There are two drives per chain, and every chain must have a master.
2. CMOS. Always use autodetection and LBA, if available. If the drive isn't detected, it points to a hardware problem.
3. Use FDISK to make the primary partition. Extended partitions are optional.
4. Use the FORMAT program, with the /S option to make it a bootable drive.

How to Fix Hard Drives

The following "Mike System of Hard-Drive Recovery" will work on all hard drives regardless of whether they are ST-506, ESDI, SCSI, or EIDE. In fact, this system will also work with floppy drives! Follow these rules to not only repair drives, but to recover data as well. Your hard-drive toolkit should contain the following:

- A backup copy of the hard drive's CMOS settings, partition table, and master boot record
- Norton's Disk Doctor, made by Symantec Corporation (part of Norton Utilities)
- Spinrite, by Gibson Research
- Drivepro, by Microhouse

Now the rules are very simple. You don't even need to know anything about hard drives, as long as you stick to the rules. In fact, if you know anything about hard drives, it won't help. Spin Doctor, Spinrite, and Drivepro are so automated that they do almost all the work for you!

Before the Drive Breaks

Perform good backups—I backup my critical data every day. Someone asked me once, "Mike, how often should I backup?" I replied, "How much of your work do you want to recreate?" You decide.

Use Drivepro to make a copy of your Boot Sector and Partition table and save it to a floppy. Some people like to use Norton's Image to make a backup. This is not a good idea unless you create a new Image file every day. The downside is based on the fact that IMAGE will also save a copy of the FAT tables. Unfortunately, an image file is only good until you change one file on the hard drive. If you can do an image file TO A FLOPPY at least once a day, then IMAGE can be helpful. Otherwise skip it.

When Good Drives Go Bad

I break up all drive errors into two groups: the group of errors that end with "Abort, Retry, Fail" or "Abort, Retry, Fail, Ignore" (I call them type one) and the group of errors that doesn't end with that phrase (type two). The following are examples of type-one errors:

```
Sector not found reading drive C:
Abort, Retry, Fail?

Data error reading drive C:
Abort, Retry, Fail, Ignore?

Read fault reading drive C:
Abort, Retry, Fail, Ignore?

Invalid media type reading drive C:
Abort, Retry, Fail?
```

And here are several examples of type-two errors:

```
No boot device available

Drive not found

No operating system present
```

The type of error you are getting, type one or type two, determines what you do next.

TYPE-ONE ERRORS The most common of hard-drive problems, type-one errors are the easiest to fix and can usually be attributed to a sector on the drive that has just decided to go bad. If you get a type-one error, run Norton's Disk Doctor or ScanDisk. These programs will will scan your drive, making sure that the drive structures are correct, the directories point to other directories, and the filenames are okay; then it will run a disk scan to verify that the bad clusters are all marked in the FAT tables. This marking of bad clusters is where Disk Doctor and ScanDisk do their best work. Before either program marks a sector bad, it attempts to move the data to a good cluster. They are often successful and can recover otherwise lost data.

If either utility finds a problem, they will prompt for the creation of an "undo" file, which allows you to undo whatever the program does to the drive. *Always make an undo file!* Almost all drives today will take advantage of built-in error correction code (ECC) that constantly checks the drive for bad sectors. If the ECC detects a bad sector, it will mark the drive's own internal error map. This is not to be confused with the FAT table. Therefore, if the ECC finds a bad sector, you will get a type-one error as the computer attempts to read the bad sector. Disk Doctor or ScanDisk will fix this problem most of the time.

However, many times the ECC can be wrong! In this case, you need a program that can go back into the drive and mark the sectors as good. That's where Spinrite comes into play. Spinrite can be considered a more thorough ECC. Spinrite marks sectors as bad or good more accurately than ECC. And if it finds a bad sector with data in it, Spinrite has powerful algorithms to recover the data! If you ran Disk Doctor or ScanDisk and it marked the cluster as bad, and then Spinrite fixed the sector, wouldn't you want to undo the work the first program performed? Good thing you created that undo file!

Whenever I run Disk Doctor or ScanDisk, the first thing I do after the program has run is to run it again. If either program is going to fix the problem, it will fix it the first time. If I run Disk Doctor or ScanDisk a second time and it gives a different error, I abort the process without saving a second undo file, and immediately run Spinrite.

TYPE-TWO ERRORS Type-two errors are created by a broad cross-section of problems. These can be broken down into four subgroups: CMOS, connectivity, lost partition or boot information, and dead drives.

CMOS

Losing the CMOS is one of the most common causes of type-two errors. It takes nothing to quickly check CMOS to verify that the drive's geometry is correct. Here are some of the more common errors that might point to CMOS problems:

- CMOS configuration mismatch
- No boot device available
- Drive not found
- Missing operating system

Connectivity

Connectivity means something isn't plugged in right or something has managed to unplug itself. These problems virtually always show themselves at boot time. Here are some classics:

- Hard-drive error
- No fixed disks present
- HDD controller failure
- No boot device available
- Drive not found

If you plug the cable in backwards for an IDE drive, the computer simply won't boot! It's a famous error and everyone who has ever installed a hard drive has done it. Just reinsert the cable and turn the machine back on.

You can usually conquer connectivity errors by carefully inspecting the entire connection system (including electricity) and finding the "silly" mistake (welcome to the club). Always remove and reseat the controller if you get an HDD controller failure, as they are prone to static build-up. I also keep an extra controller around to verify if the controller is good. Cables can go bad, but it is very rare unless the cable is obviously ripped or pinched. If your BIOS has an IDE autodetection function, use it! It will not function unless everything is installed correctly. It's a great, quick connectivity verifier.

Lost Boot and Partition Information

Your drive can lose partition information from time to time. The information is stored on sectors and, like any sector, one can go bad. If the partition table or boot sector is corrupted, the best tool for repairing it is a good copy of the partition table or boot sector. Examples of these errors are:

- Invalid partition table
- Corrupt boot sector
- Nonsystem disk or disk error
- Missing operating system

The tool for these errors is Drivepro by Microhouse. Drivepro will store the drive's boot sector and the partition table information on a floppy, so if you get an error like this, it can be quickly repaired. If you don't have a backup, Drivepro will attempt to rebuild the lost or corrupted information. Sometimes it can—but why take the risk? Just back up your drive information with Drivepro and you will always be able to rebuild.

Sticking to these rules will allow you to fix almost any drive *and* recover the data. However, understand that all hard drives will eventually die. The big clue is when Disk Doctor, Spinrite, or Drivepro fix a problem and it comes right back. In this case, the drive is dead and should be replaced.

ST506

Hard drives were not part of the original PC concept. They were supposed to use one, possibly two, floppy drives for permanent storage. Hard drives were in the realm of mainframe and minicomputers; normal PC users would never need the "massive" storage of the first hard drives (5 to 10 megabytes). As a result, the earliest hard drives (and their interfaces) were proprietary. There was no common cabling or command set—until ST506.

The ST506/412 interface was developed by Seagate Technologies around 1980 and originally appeared with the 5MB ST506 drive. The ST506 had a capacity of 5MB, an average access time on the order of 100 ms, and a price tag of around $3000. A year later, Seagate offered a 10MB drive with the ST412 interface; this was the hard drive first offered in the IBM PC XT. Since the ST506/412 was the only hard drive available for the IBM PC, it was the first to be supported by the ROM BIOS chip on the motherboard, starting with IBM PC AT.

The name *ST506* was poorly used. In common usage, ST506 referred to all hard drives that used the ST506 or compatible controller, and not simply to the ST506 itself. The name ST506 came to designate an entire class of hard drives. Another misleading name was "Winchester." Winchesters were a popular brand of ST506 controllers, but many used the term *Winchester* to mean *ST506*. Although incorrect, its widespread common use was accepted.

Cabling ST506 Drives

In the ST506 days, you could have no more that two hard drives in a computer. Whenever ST506 hard drives were installed into a computer, there

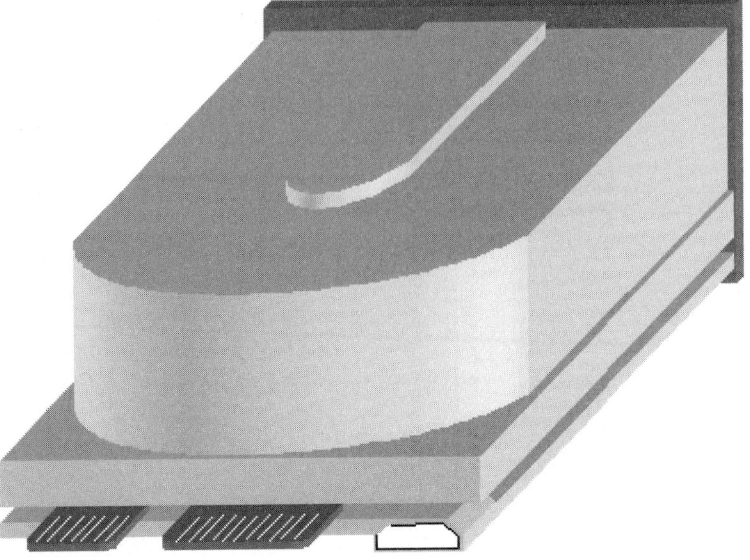

Figure 8.45
ST-506 drive

had to be a hardware setting on each drive (Figure 8.45). If you had just one hard drive in a computer, it was known as *hard drive 0* or the *master drive*. If you installed a second hard drive in a computer, it was known as *hard drive 1* or the *slave drive*. All hard drives had jumpers or DIPP switches to allow you to set them as drive 0/master or drive 1 /slave.

The cabling scheme for the ST506/412 was composed of two cables for a one-drive installation or three cables for a two-drive installation. These cables consisted of one 34-connector control cable that was daisy-chained for a dual drive configuration, and a 20-connector data cable for each drive (Figure 8.46).

Although ST506 drives had "drive select" jumpers that determined which drive was 0 and which was 1, these jumpers were rarely used. Instead, the 34-wire control cable usually had a twist in it for lines 25 through 29; this twist served to determine which hard drive was hard drive 0 and which was hard drive 1. If a ST506 was installed into the end connection, it was hard drive 0. If an ST506 drive was installed in the middle connection, then the drive was drive 1. There were some rare ST506 controller cables that had no twist. On these, the jumper on the first drive had to be set to indicate drive select 0, and if there was a second drive on the cable in the middle connector, it had its jumper set to drive select 1. See Figure 8.47.

In addition to a proper jumper setting on the hard drive, there was also another selectable device on the ST-506 hard drive, called the *terminating re-*

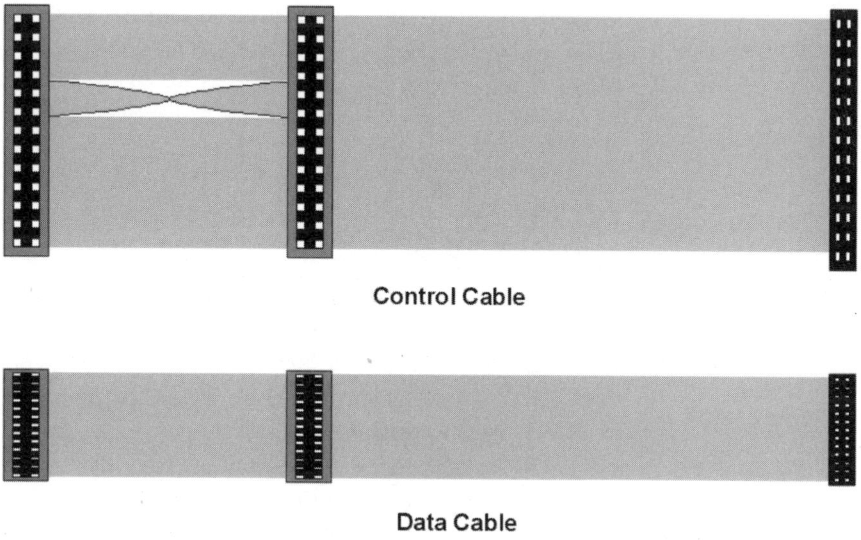

Figure 8.46
ST-506 cables

Control Cable

Data Cable

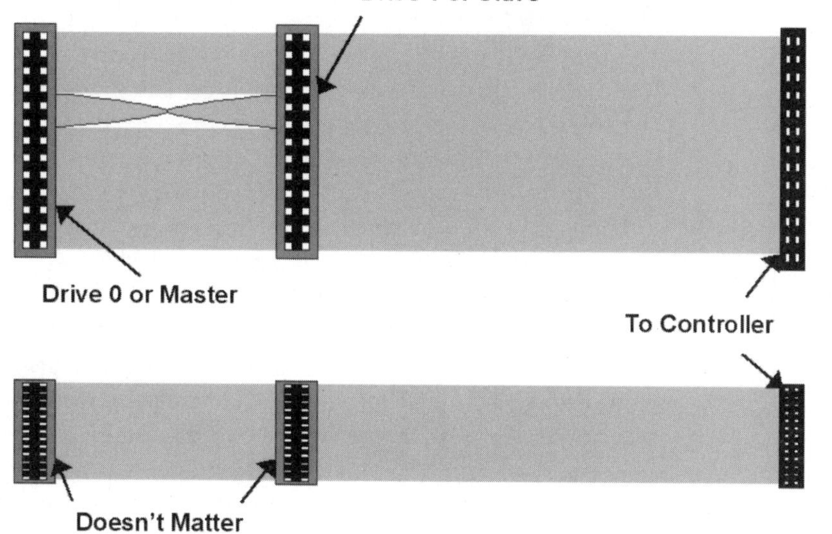

Figure 8.47
Function of ST-506 connectors

sistor. This resistor provided the proper electrical termination on the cable to prevent signal noise and data degradation, and also served to provide proper electrical impedance for the interface card. As shipped, the drives came with the terminating resistor installed; if you were installing a second drive on a system, you had to be sure to remove the terminating resistor.

Whenever you install any type of ribbon cable, be sure that the colored stripe points to the number-one pin on the connector. This is true for all ribbon cables—not just hard drives!

ESDI

The *ESDI* or *enhanced small device interface* was introduced in 1983 by the Maxtor Corporation, which led a consortium of other developers in adopting ESDI as the interface to succeed the underpowered ST506/412 design. The biggest change called for by ESDI was the incorporation of most of the controller functions directly onto the hard drive, which served to greatly improve data transfer speeds. Although the theoretical maximum transfer speed of an ESDI drive approached 25 mbps (millions of bits per second), most drives could sustain only between 10 and 15 mbps.

Some ESDI controllers offered enhanced command sets that supported having the motherboard's ROM BIOS setup automatically sense the drive's geometry. In other cases, it would be necessary to manually enter the data into the drive table. While the ST506/412 interface supported 17 to 26 sectors per track, ESDI supported, in most cases, 32 sectors per track, although as many as 80 sectors per track was possible. ESDI also supported an interleave of 1 to 1, which resulted in an even greater transfer rate.

The installation of ESDI drives was almost identical to the installation of ST-506 drives. The cabling, drive select jumper, and terminating resistor were all configured in the same manner as the ST506/412. The CMOS hard-drive type was almost always set to 1 (the ESDI drive would convert that geometry to something it could use). There was still the need to low-level format most ESDI drives, although some didn't it. If you had an ESDI drive that didn't need to be low-level formatted, the formatter would not allow you to perform the format. Partitioning and high-level formatting were identical to ST506. ESDI had one major disadvantage—it was extremely expensive. The high cost of ESDI drives made them obsolete by the early '90s (Figure 8.48).

Figure 8.48 ST506 and ESDI are dead

CHAPTER 9

SCSI

In this chapter, you will:

- Understand the concept and motivation for SCSI.
- Display SCSI chains, IDs and terminations.
- Show the different flavors of SCSI.
- See basic SCSI repair techniques.

Shugart systems introduced SCSI (Small Computer Systems Interface) in 1979 as a system independent means of mass storage. SCSI can be best described as a "miniature network" inside your PC. Any type of peripheral can be built as a SCSI device. Common SCSI devices include:

- Hard drives
- Tape backup units
- Removable hard drives
- Scanners
- CD-ROM drives
- Printers

SCSI has gone through a number of changes since its introduction. These different changes are based around a few industry standards that are identified by names like SCSI-1, SCSI-2, and Wide SCSI. Within these industry standards are some manufacturer-specific standards (e.g., Western Digital trying to push something new, but the industry hasn't yet adopted it) with names like Ultra SCSI. These different types of SCSI are often referred to as "flavors." Using SCSI-2 as a basis, this chapter will address the basic issues involved in implementing SCSI in a PC. Once you have a solid understanding of SCSI-2, I'll go into all the other types of SCSI so you can understand the differences between them.

SCSI manifests itself through a *SCSI chain,* which is a series of SCSI devices working together through a host adapter. The *host adapter* is the device that attaches the SCSI chain to the PC. Figure 9.1 shows a typical PCI host adapter. Note that there are three connections on this card. The first connector, at the left of the figure, is for devices on the outside (external) of the PC. The second and third connectors are at the top of the figure. These connectors are for inside (internal) SCSI connections. All SCSI chains are connected to the PC through the host adapter. Note that this particular host adapter is PCI. However, there are also ISA, EISA, and V-LB SCSI host adapters. Figure 9.2 shows a 16-bit ISA SCSI host adapter.

Figure 9.1
SCSI host adapter

Figure 9.2
ISA host adapter

SCSI Chains

All SCSI devices can be divided into two groups: internal and external. External devices stand alone and are hooked to the external connector of the host adapter. Figure 9.3 is an example of an external SCSI device. Internal SCSI devices are installed inside the PC and are connected to the host adapter through the internal connector. Figure 9.4 shows an internal SCSI device, in this case a CD-ROM drive.

All internal devices are connected to the host adapter and each other with a 50-pin ribbon cable. Figure 9.5 shows a common SCSI ribbon cable. Notice that internal 50-pin SCSI cables are very similar to 40-pin IDE cables (Figure 9.6). Use caution when installing SCSI devices. IDE devices, if they are plugged in wrong, just don't work. SCSI devices, when plugged in incorrectly (such as getting the cable backwards), can be damaged! Be careful to install it properly the first time!

Figure 9.3
Back of external SCSI device

Figure 9.4
Internal SCSI CD-ROM

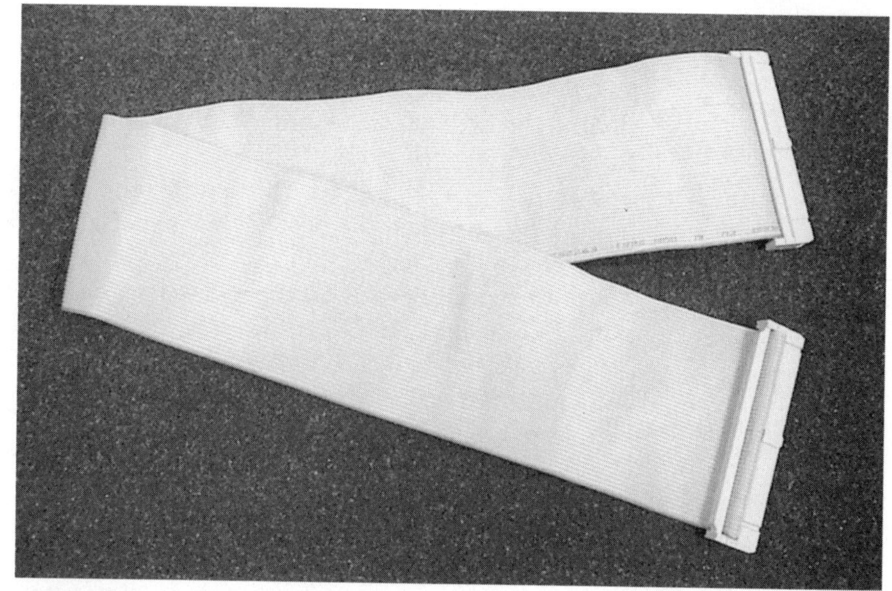

Figure 9.5
Typical 50-pin SCSI cable

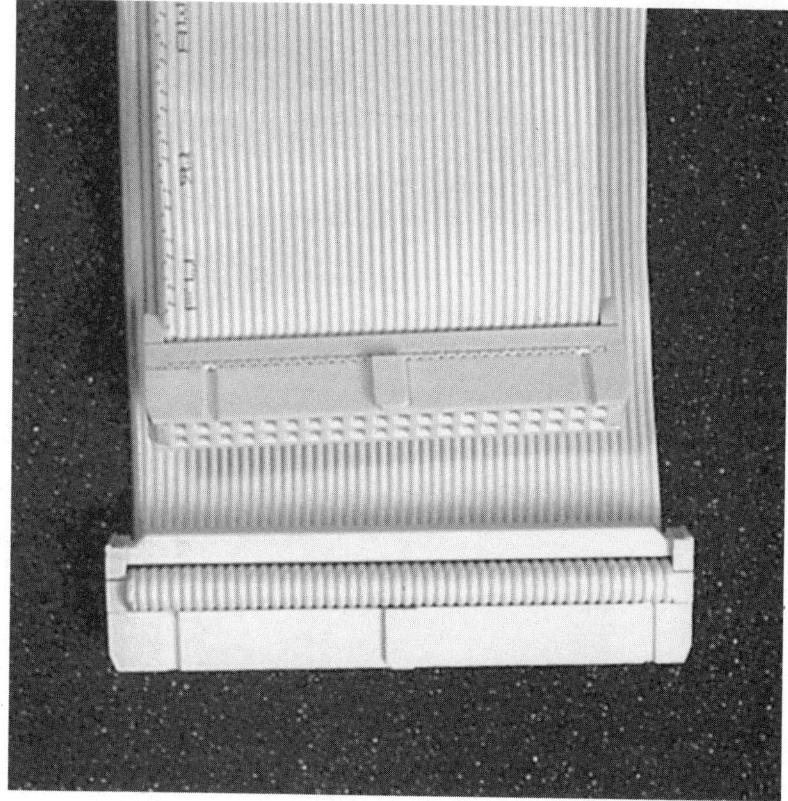

Figure 9.6
SCSI and IDE cables

Figure 9.7 illustrates an internal SCSI chain. Multiple internal devices can be connected together simply by using a cable with enough connectors. Figure 9.8 shows a cable that can take up to three SCSI devices, including the host adapter. Figure 9.9 shows two internal devices on a SCSI chain.

External SCSI devices are a little different. They are connected to the host adapter through the host adapter's special SCSI external connection. Some cheap host adapters do not have external connections, so you cannot put external devices on them. External devices all have two connections in the back, which allow you to daisy-chain multiple external devices together. Figure 9.10 shows a SCSI chain with an external device, and Figure 9.11 is a SCSI chain with two external devices. SCSI chains can be internal, external, or both (Figure 9.12). The maximum number of devices you can have on a SCSI chain, including the host adapter, is eight.

SCSI IDs

As mentioned earlier, the SCSI interface can simply be viewed as a miniature network within a desktop computer, and the individual components of this network each require a unique identifier—the ID number. The values for ID numbers range from 0 to 7. SCSI ID numbers are similar to many other hardware settings in a PC in that no two devices can share the same ID number. A SCSI device can have any SCSI ID, as long as no two devices share the same ID. See Figure 9.13.

Figure 9.7
Internal SCSI chain

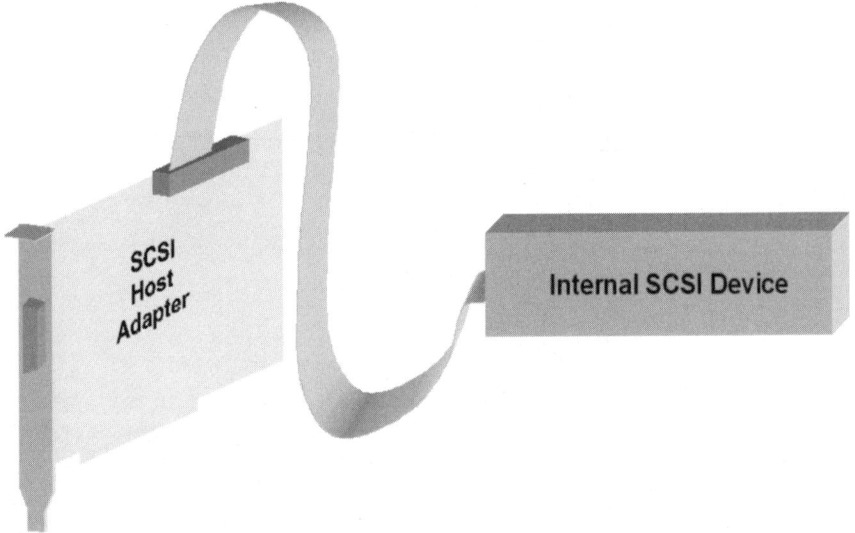

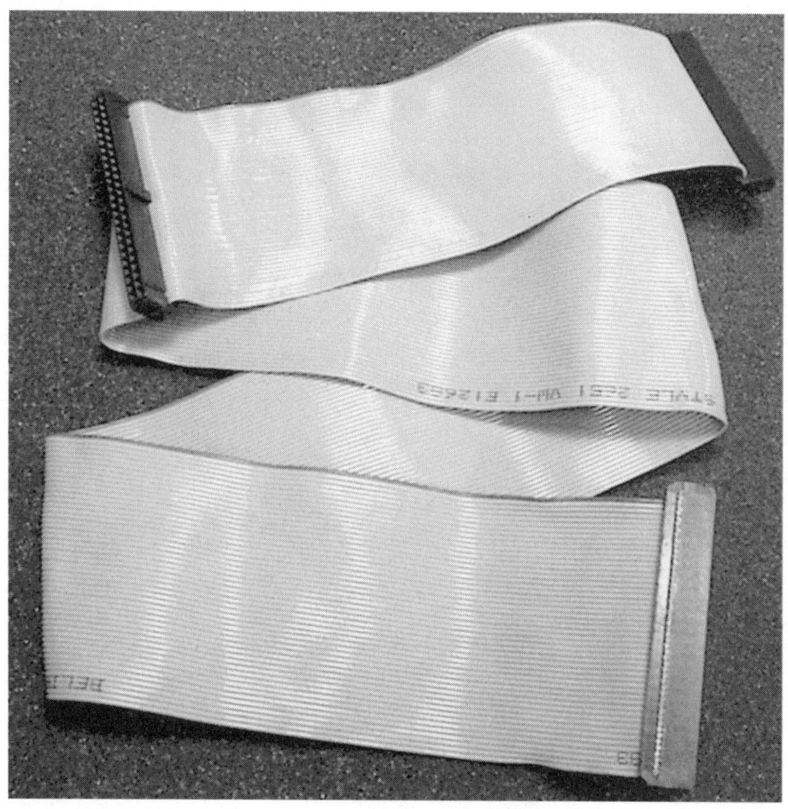

Figure 9.8
SCSI Cable with three connections

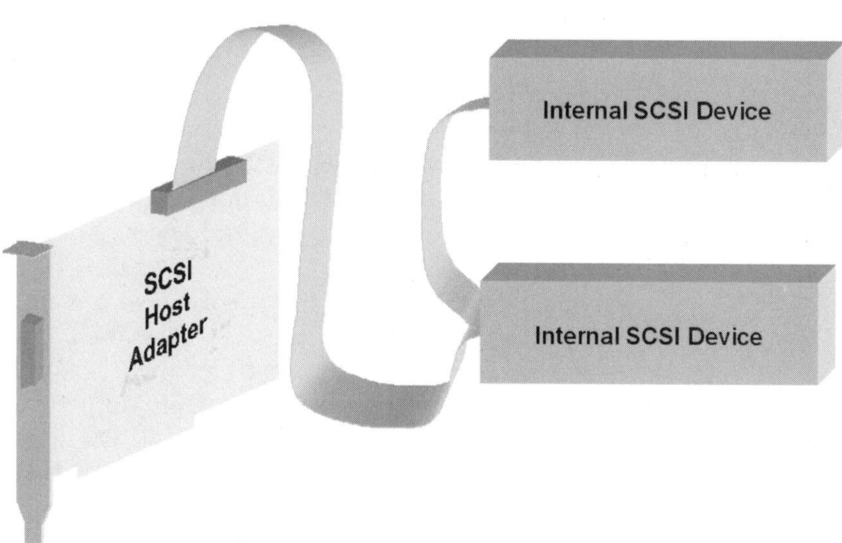

Figure 9.9
Internal SCSI chain with three devices

Figure 9.10
SCSI chain with external drive

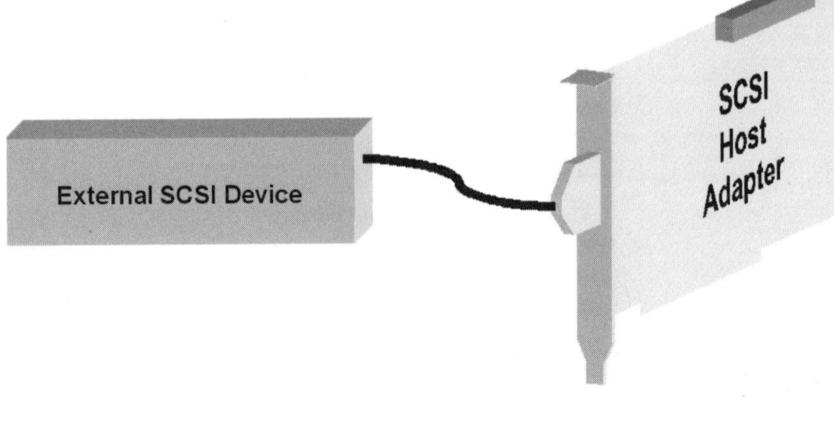

Figure 9.11
SCSI chain with two external drives

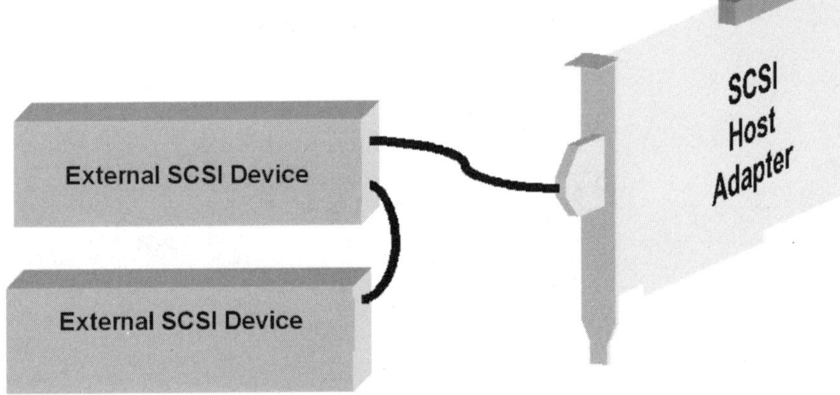

There are some conventions for SCSI IDs. Typically, most people set the host adapter to 7. While you can change this, there is nothing to gain by deviating from such a well-established tradition. Note that there is no order for the use of SCSI IDs. It does not matter which device gets which number, you can skip numbers, and any SCSI device can have any SCSI ID (Figure 9.14).

Setting a SCSI ID for a particular device is usually done with either jumpers or switches on the SCSI device itself. For example, all internal SCSI hard drives use jumpers to set their SCSI IDs. Figure 9.15 shows a SCSI hard drive that sets its ID through jumpers.

There is one exception to setting SCSI IDs. If you want a SCSI drive to be C: (which is required if you want to boot DOS off this drive), you must set that drive to the ID specified by the host adapter as the "bootable" SCSI ID (Figure 9.16). Most manufacturers of host adapters use SCSI ID 0

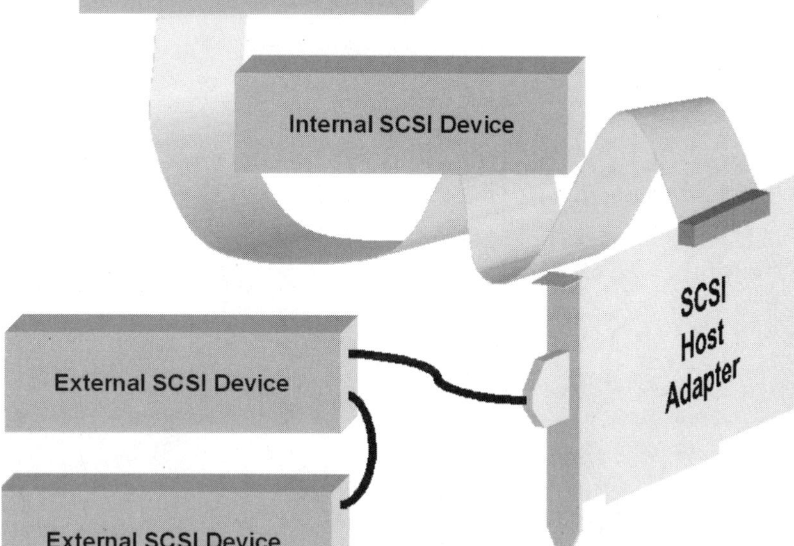

Figure 9.12
Internal and external devices on one SCSI chain

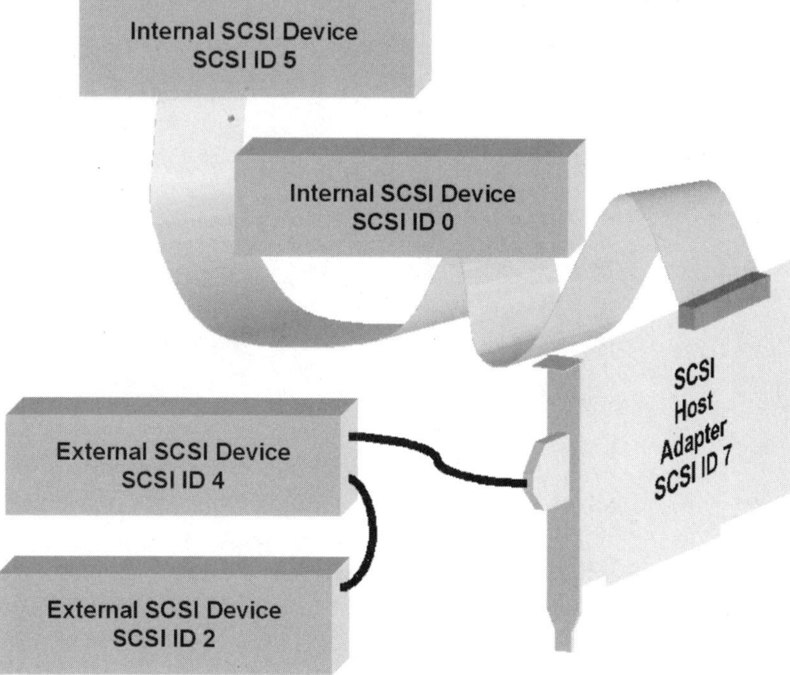

Figure 9.13
SCSI IDs

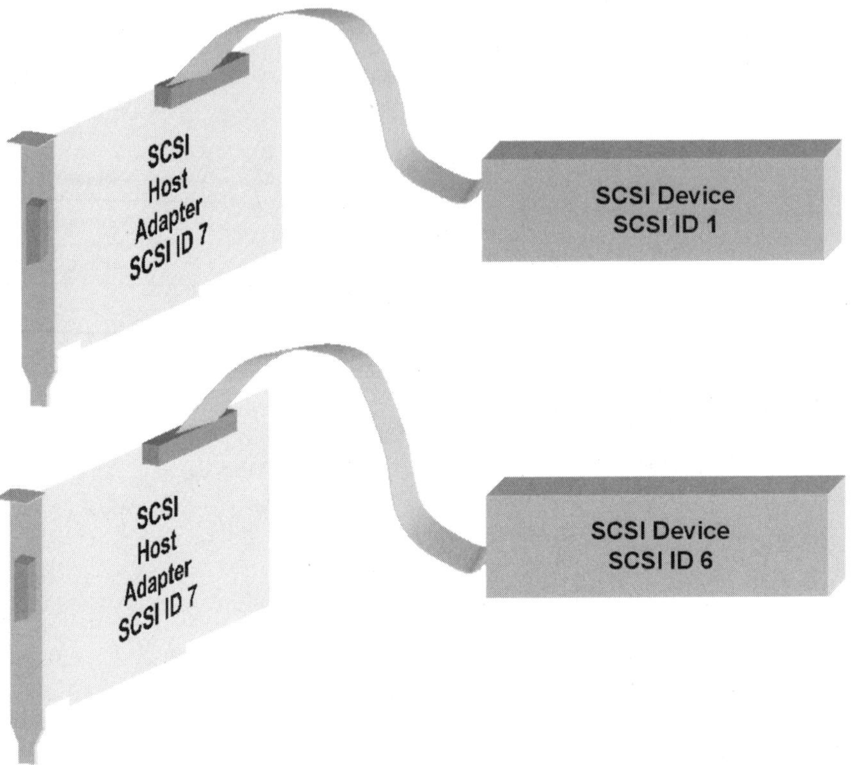

Figure 9.14
Any SCSI device can have any ID as long as no two match

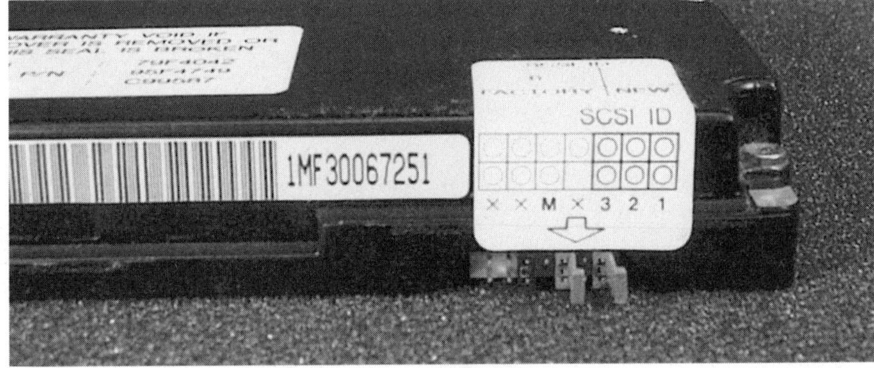

Figure 9.15
SCSI hard drive jumper settings

or 7, although a few older adapters often require SCSI ID 6. Read the host adapter information or guess; you will not break anything if you are wrong. Booting SCSI drives is discussed later in this chapter. Not all SCSI devices are designed to be set to every SCSI ID. For example, the ZIP drive in Figure 9.17 can be set only to SCSI ID 5 or 6. Work around it!

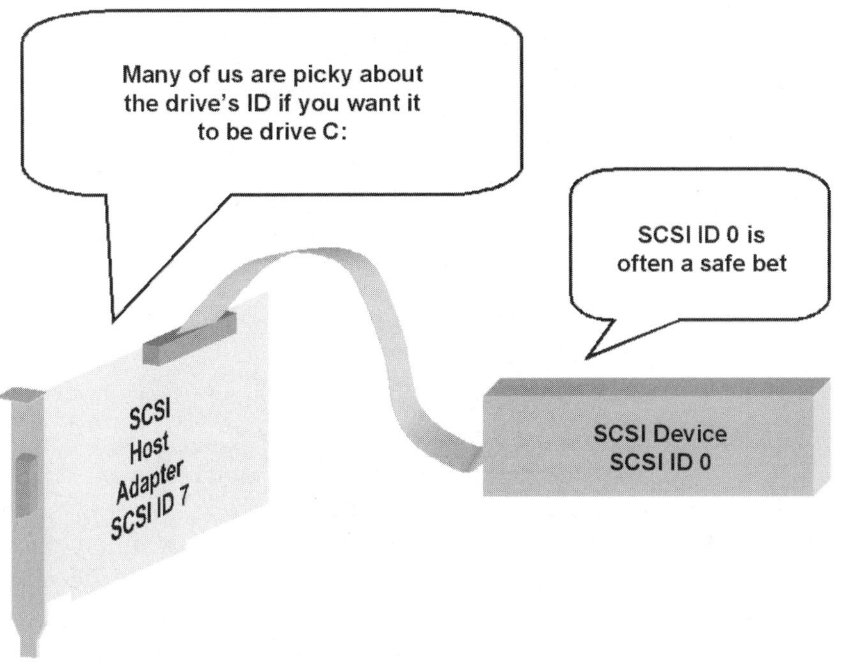

Figure 9.16
Proper setting of SCSI IDs for boot drive

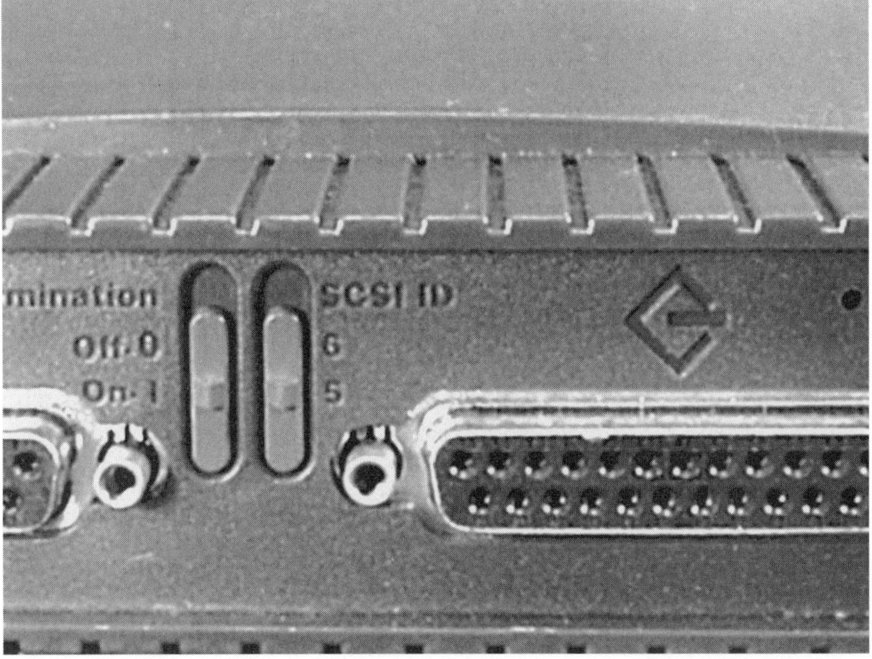

Figure 9.17
SCSI ZIP drive

Logical Unit Numbers (LUNs)

SCSI can also support more than one device per ID if you use *logical unit numbers* to provide a unique identifier for up to seven subunits per ID number. These are used primarily in hard-drive arrays, which create one large logical drive out of several smaller physical drives. LUNs are in the realm of network servers running NetWare, Windows NT, and UNIX that require highly specialized software. With the previous exceptions, LUNs are to be ignored.

Termination

Whenever you send a signal down a wire, some of that signal reflects back up the wire, creating an echo. It can cause tremendous confusion, and need to be prevented. *Termination* simply means putting something on the ends of the wire to prevent this echo. Terminators are usually "pull-down" resistors and can manifest themselves in many different ways. On most of the devices within a PC, the appropriate termination is built in. On other devices, including SCSI chains and some network cables, termination must be set during installation.

A SCSI chain is a number of devices linked by a cable, and this cable must be terminated on the ends. In a SCSI chain, the ends of the cables are the devices into which they are plugged. Therefore, in a SCSI chain, whatever devices are on the ends of the chain must be "terminated." Devices that are *not* on the ends do not need to be terminated. Since any SCSI device might be on the end of a chain, all SCSI devices can usually be terminated.

Figure 9.18 shows some examples of where to terminate SCSI devices. There are a large number of ways to set the termination. Figure 9.19 shows a hard drive that is terminated with a jumper setting. The hard drive in Figure 9.20 has terminating resistors that are inserted. They must be removed to "unterminate" the adapter. The ZIP drive in Figure 9.21 has a slide for termination.

The advanced host adapter's termination is set through software; Figure 9.22 shows how termination can be set through software. The ancient hard drive in Figure 9.23 is not capable of terminating itself. It needs a separate terminator piece. Some devices will detect that they are on the end of the SCSI chain and will automatically terminate themselves.

Be careful when you are terminating, since improper termination can cause damage to SCSI hard drives! Unlike setting SCSI IDs, termination

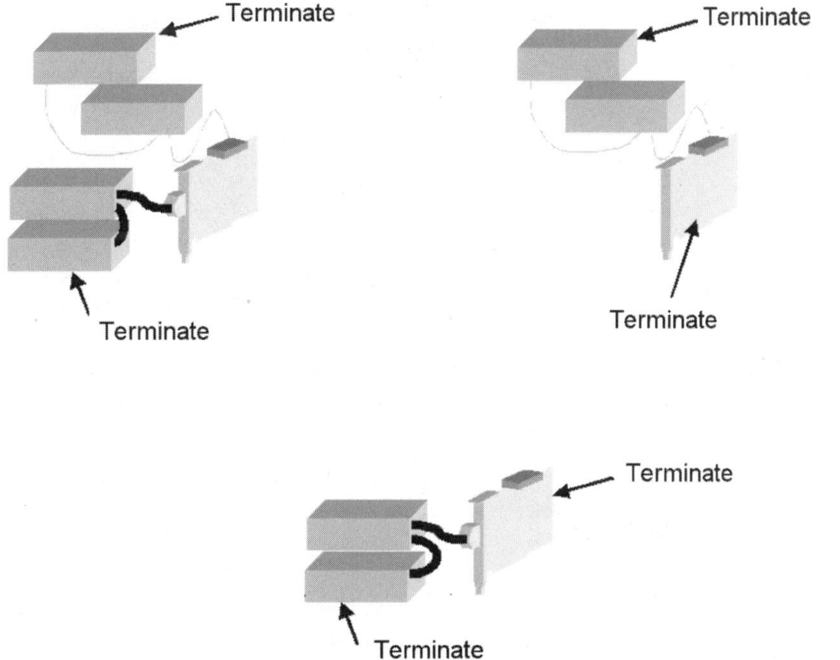

Figure 9.18
Location of the terminated devices

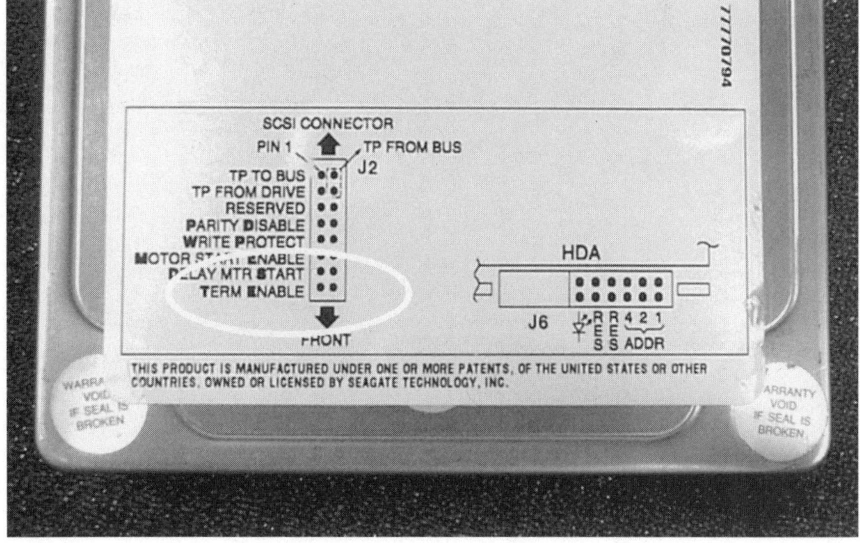

Figure 9.19
Setting termination

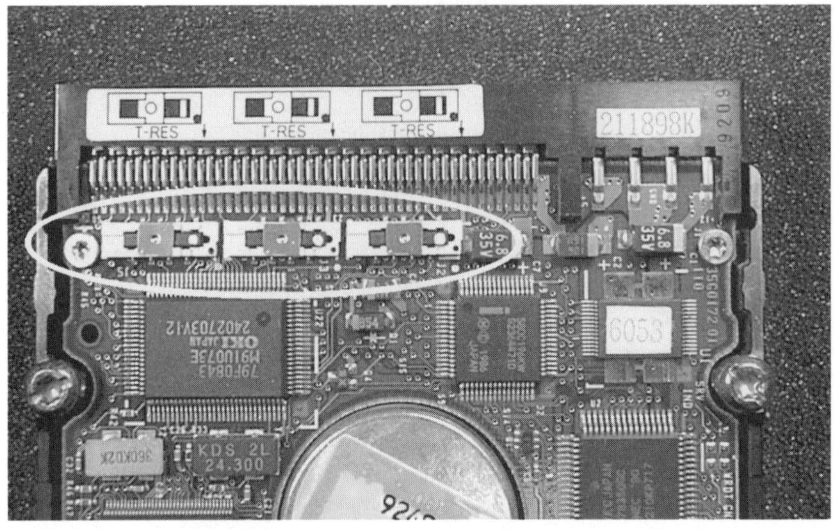

Figure 9.20 Hard drive with removable terminating resistors

Figure 9.21 Zip drive termination

```
        Adaptec AHA-2940/AHA-2940W SCSISelect(TM) Utility v1.11

              AHA-2940/AHA-2q4ow at Bus:Device 00:12h

                          CONFIGURATION

SCSI Bus Tnterface Definitions
 Host Adapter SCSI ID . . . . . . . . . . . . . . . . . . . . . . 7
 SCSI Parity Checking . . . . . . . . . . . . . . . . . . . . . . Enabled
 Host Adapter SCSI Termination  . . . . . . . . . . . . . . . . . Enabled

Additional Options
 SCSI Device Configuration  . . . . . . . . . . . . . . . .Press <Enter>
 Advanced Configuration Options . . . . . . . . . . . . . .Press <Enter>

           <F6>    Reset to Host Adapter Defaults

   Arrow keys to move cursor, <Enter> to select option, <Esc> to exit
```

Figure 9.22 Software termination setting

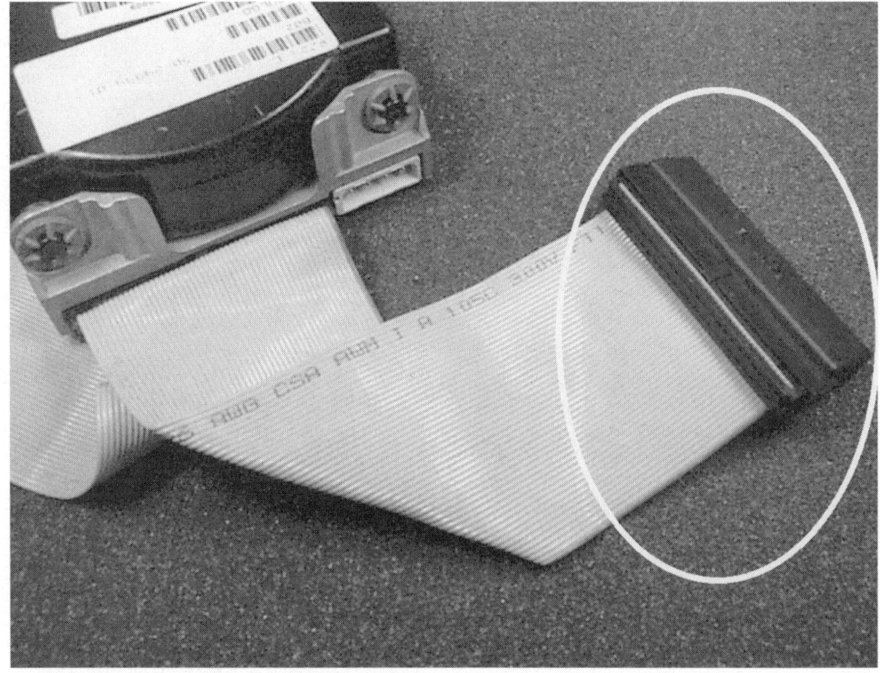

Figure 9.23
Old SCSI hard drive requires separate termination on the cable

can be a little tricky. But before we can discuss the different types of termination options, you must understand the different types of SCSI.

SCSI Flavors

Way back in 1979, Shugart Associates began work on an interface that would handle data transfers between devices regardless of the type of device. This interface would work at the logical or operating system level instead of the device level, creating a stable interface in a world faced with rapid device development. This new interface was called the Shugart Associates System Interface, or SASI, and was the precursor to SCSI. During 1980 and 1981, various committees from Shugart and NCR met to develop a draft proposal to present to ANSI. In April of 1982, the Accredited Standards Committee X3T9.2 met and drafted a formal proposal for the Small Computer System Interface (SCSI), which would be based on SASI. Between 1982 and 1986, the SCSI standard expanded to include more than just hard drives. In June of 1986, the first formal set of standards defining SCSI was approved as ANSI document X3.131-1986. This standard was known as SCSI-1.

Figure 9.24
Early SCSI-1 adapter

SCSI-1

The SCSI-1 standard defined an 8-bit, 5-MHz bus capable of supporting up to eight SCSI devices, but was very fuzzy in describing many aspects of SCSI. As a result, many manufacturers of SCSI devices had different opinions as to how to implement those standards. So SCSI-1 was really more of an opinion than a standard (Figure 9.24). In 1986, SCSI began to appear on IBM-compatible PC machines, and everyone seemed to have a proprietary SCSI device. The key word here is *proprietary* (meaning the device is supported only by the company that produced, designed, manufactured, and sold it). SCSI was being used in PCs for stand-alone devices such as hard drives, and each device came with its own host adapter. Makers of SCSI devices had no interest in chaining their particular device with anyone else's—primarily because they assumed (for the most part correctly) that their device was the only SCSI device in the PC. Each SCSI device had its own command set, and no two command sets were the same. Trying to get one vendor's SCSI hard drive to work with another vendor's SCSI adapter card was often impossible.

SCSI-1 devices transferred data only through an 8-bit parallel path, but did support up to seven devices on the chain. For most PCs using SCSI-1 devices, the 8-bit pathway was not much of a bottleneck. Although the devices themselves were not capable of high-speed data transfers, neither were the 80286-based machines of the time. SCSI-1 devices seemed fast in comparison. Plus, the only common hard-drive interface competition was the ST-506 controller, and 8-bit SCSI was far faster!

SCSI-2

By the time the SCSI-1 standard was adopted, a number of improvements were being adopted by manufacturers. As a result, the SCSI standards committee was put to work creating a new SCSI standard. Their work lasted from July 1986 to February 1989, when they sent their formal proposal (ASC X3T9.2) for SCSI-2 to ANSI. Formal adoption of SCSI-2 was not reached until July 1990.

The SCSI-2 standard was quite detailed, and addressed a large number of issues within SCSI. One of the more important parts of the SCSI-2 standard was the definition of 18 commands that have to be supported by any device labeled SCSI-2 compliant. This set of commands, called the *common command set* or *CCS*, made hooking up devices from various manufacturers less of a nightmare. The CCS also introduced commands to address other devices besides hard drives, including CD-ROM drives, tape drives, and scanners.

SCSI-2 also defined the types of connectors to be used. Before SCSI-2, there was no true standard for SCSI connectors, although a few types became de-facto standards. The new SCSI-2 connectors ensured that any two SCSI-2 compliant devices could be physically connected. SCSI-2 also more closely defined terminations.

The one area that creates the most confusion with SCSI-2 is the width of the data bus and the speeds. SCSI-2 defined two optional 16-bit and 32-bit buses called *wide* SCSI, and a new, optional 10-MHz speed called *fast* SCSI. SCSI-2 devices could now be 8-bit (narrow), 16-bit (wide), or 32-bit (wide), or they could be 5 MHz (slow, the standard) or 10 MHz (fast). This means six "subflavors" of SCSI-2 (we'll add SCSI-1 for comparison). See Table 9.1.

Even though SCSI-2 defined a 32-bit SCSI bus, it was almost completely ignored by the industry due to its high cost and a lack of demand. In reality, Wide SCSI means 16 bits wide.

Fast SCSI-2 transfers data in fast synchronous mode, meaning the SCSI device being talked to (the *target*) does not have to acknowledge (ack) every

TABLE 9.1

Standard SCSI vs. Fast SCSI

SCSI Type/Bit Width	5 MHz (Standard)	10 MHz (FAST)
SCSI-1: 8-bit	5 MB/S	NA
SCSI-2: 8-bit	5 MB/S	10 MB/S
SCSI-2: 16-bit (wide)	10 MB/S	20 MB/S
SCSI-2: 32-bit (wide)	20 MB/S	40 MB/S

individual request (req) for data from the host adapter (*initiator*). This allows for a doubling of transfer speed, from approximately 5 to 10 MBps. However, experience has shown that external fast SCSI devices will rarely provide "fast" performance unless the cable provides proper shielding and electrical impedance or load. Cables that do provide proper shielding and load are generally a bit more expensive, but are required to achieve true "fast" performance.

SCSI-1 devices were all *single-ended,* meaning they communicated through only one wire per bit of information. This one wire is measured or referenced against the common ground provided by the metal chassis and in turn by the power supply of the system. Noise is usually spread through either the electrical power cables or the data cable, and is called *common-mode noise.* A single-ended device is vulnerable to common-mode noise because it has no way of telling the difference between valid data and noise. When noise invades the data stream, the devices must resend the data. The amount of noise generated grows dramatically over the length of a SCSI cable, limiting the total length of a SCSI chain to only about six meters, depending on the type of SCSI.

To allow much longer SCSI chains, SCSI-2 offers an optional solution with *differential* devices. These devices employ two wires per bit of data—one wire for data and one for the inverse of this data. The inverse signal takes the place of the ground wire in the single-ended cable. By taking the difference of the two signals, the device can reject the common-mode noise in the data stream. This allows for much longer SCSI chains—up to 25 meters.

There is no obvious difference between single-ended and differential SCSI devices. The connectors and cabling seem to be identical. This is a bit of a problem as under no circumstances should you try to connect single-ended and differential devices on the same SCSI chain. At the very least, you will probably fry the single-ended device; if the differential device lacks a security circuit to detect your mistake, you will probably smoke it as well.

Don't panic! Although differential SCSI devices exist, they are rare. Single-ended SCSI still reigns. The makers of differential SCSI know the danger and will clearly label their devices.

There is a new type of differential SCSI that is becoming quite popular, called *low-voltage differential* (LVD). LVD SCSI uses less power and is compatible with existing single-ended SCSI. LVD devices can sense the type of SCSI and then work accordingly. If you plug an LVD device into a single-ended chain, it will act as a single-ended device. If you plug an LVD device into LVD, it will run as LVD. LVD SCSI chains can be up to 12 meters in length. The safety, ease of use, and low cost of LVD is making it quite popular in higher-end PCs and servers.

Beyond SCSI-2

SCSI technology has not stood still since the adoption of SCSI-2. Manufacturers have developed significant improvements in SCSI-2, particularly in increased speeds and easier configuration. There is no standard to reflect these improvements, though, so we currently live in a hodge-podge of confusing, proprietary terms, such as Ultra, Ultra-Wide, Ultra2, and SCSI-3. Let's take a minute to look at these.

There has been no standard since SCSI-2. The SCSI committees are working on a new standard, called SCSI-3, that will hopefully be adopted soon. The SCSI-3 standard is actually a group of standards, each defining a certain aspect of an improvement over SCSI-2. Any SCSI device that takes advantage of any of these options will be able to call itself SCSI-3. Many SCSI devices already do some SCSI-3 functions, so there are already quite a few available SCSI devices calling themselves SCSI-3. A more accurate term, however, might be "upcoming SCSI-3."

One of the more popular aspects to SCSI-3, and one that has already been widely adopted, is the ability for Wide SCSI to control up to 16 devices on one chain. Each device gets a number from 0 to 15, as opposed to just 0 through 7. This ability is often thought to be part of SCSI-2 because wide, 16-device control came out very quickly after the SCSI-2 standard was adopted.

The terms *Ultra* and *Fast-20* are used by many SCSI component manufacturers to define a high-speed 20-MHz bus speed. *Ultra2* and *Fast-40* define a 40-MHz speed, and *Ultra3* and *Fast-80* define an 80-MHz bus speed. There is still narrow and wide SCSI, look at the differences in Table 9-2.

Ultra SCSI is not a true ANSI standard, but it has been broadly accepted by all manufacturers and is therefore a de-facto standard. Not all Ultra speeds are yet available—for example, Ultra3 is not yet being pro-

TABLE 9.2

Narrow SCSI vs. Wide SCSI

SCSI Type/Bit Width	8-Bit (Narrow)	16-Bit (Wide)
Ultra SCSI (FAST20)	20 MB/S	40 MB/S
Ultra SCSI (FAST 40)	40 MB/S	80 MB/S
Ultra3 SCSI (FAST80)	80 MB/S	160 MB/S

TABLE 9.3

Upcoming Cabling Standards

Cabling	Speed	Number Devices	Max Bus Length
SSA	Up to 80 MB/S	128	25 meters
IEEE 1394	Up to 400 MB/S	63	72 meers
Fiber channel	Up to 400 MB/s	126	10 kilometers

duced. All speeds of Ultra SCSI will be incorporated into the SCSI-3 standard.

The upcoming SCSI-3 standard will also include optional *hot swap* capabilities. To *hot swap* means to be able to unplug a drive from the SCSI chain without rebooting or resetting the chain. Hot swapping is extremely helpful in laptops and servers, and is already becoming popular for high-end SCSI drives.

The last and most interesting function under the proposed SCSI-3 standard is serial SCSI. SCSI as we know it is a parallel interface; the SCSI bus consists of 8 or 16 parallel wires passing data. *Serial SCSI* means transferring SCSI commands over a single wire, as in classic serial communications. There are three main types of serial SCSI cabling: IEEE 1394 (firewire), fiber channel, and serial storage architecture (SSA). These new cabling systems are vying for predominance in the SCSI market, with fiber channel currently seeming to be the winner, although IEEE 1394 is also quite popular. SSA is not as widely used. These cabling systems offer long cable runs, hot swapping, and a low cost, which might make them quite popular (Table 9.3). Serial cabling systems also allow many more devices on one chain. Currently, they are most commonly seen in servers and some laptops. The SCSI-3 standards, or at least some of them, are now in the final stages of adoption.

Bus Mastering

Whenever you scan an image or search for a sector on a non-SCSI hard drive (IDE) system, the CPU transfers data for as long as it takes to complete the operation. SCSI allows devices to perform these functions independently by allowing them to disconnect through the SCSI bus. This provides other devices with an opportunity to perform their tasks faster and with less waiting. When backing up a hard drive to a tape drive in a typical non-SCSI PC, the CPU requests data from the hard drive, loads the data into its registers, and then writes the information to the tape drive, where the data is finally stored. During this entire process, which can last hours, the CPU must still try to handle your requests to run other types of software.

With a SCSI-equipped PC, however, the process is more efficient. The tape drive (SCSI) and hard drive (SCSI) usually communicate through the same host adapter. In this case, the host adapter remains in the circuit only long enough to arbitrate the connection between the hard drive and the tape unit. Once the data transfer is established, the host adapter drops off and lets the hard drive and tape unit communicate directly with each other while the backup is running. Once the backup is finished, or if the user interrupts the operation, the drives reestablish their presence on the SCSI chain. The great beauty of this lies in the lack of CPU and expansion bus usage. Once the connection is made, the two devices are, for all intents and purposes, no longer on the PC and not consuming any system resources.

The downside to bus-mastering devices is that they can seriously confuse a disk-caching program such as DOS's SmartDrive. A bus-mastering SCSI can change the address of data that might also be held in the cache, resulting in the disk cache causing really horrible corruption to your data. Whenever you install a new SCSI device to a PC, check the status of your SmartDrive. At a C: prompt, type SMARTDRV /S, and you will see the following:

```
Microsoft SMARTDrive Disk Cache version 5.0
Copyright 1991,1993 Microsoft Corp.

Room for 256 elements of 8,192 bytes each
There have been 44 cache hits
and 15 cache misses

Cache size: 2,097,152 bytes
Cache size while running Windows: 2,097,152 bytes

Disk Caching Status
drive read cache write cache buffering
----------------------
A: yes  no  no
C: yes  yes  -
D: yes  yes  yes

Write-behind data will be committed before command prompt returns.

For help, type "Smartdrv /?"
```

Under buffering, if you see either a dash or a yes, you need to add the following line:

```
device=c:\dos\smartdrv.exe /double_buffer
```

to the CONFIG.SYS file. This allows the disk cache to translate the addresses of the cached data on bus-mastered drives. This is only an issue with DOS disk caches! The Windows 3.*x* VCache and Windows 95/98 disk caches work perfectly with bus-mastering SCSIs.

SCSI Cabling and Connectors

There is no such thing as an official SCSI-1, SCSI-2, or Ultra SCSI cable. Although certain cables are designed for certain types of SCSI, there is a significant degree of overlap. The cable you need is based on whether the device is internal or external, what type of connectors are available, and the type of SCSI you're using.

The most common kind of SCSI cable is type A. It has 50 wires and is used for 8-bit data transfers in both the SCSI-1 and SCSI-2 standards. It is also used for 8-bit Fast SCSI-2. See Figure 9.25.

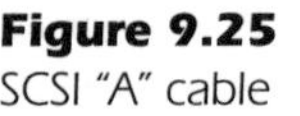

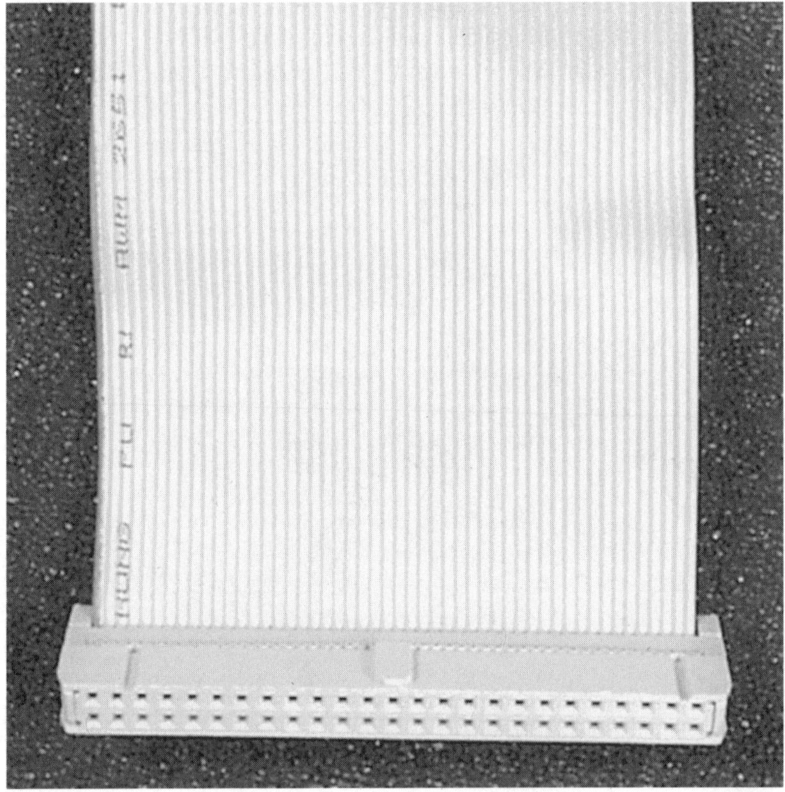

Figure 9.25
SCSI "A" cable

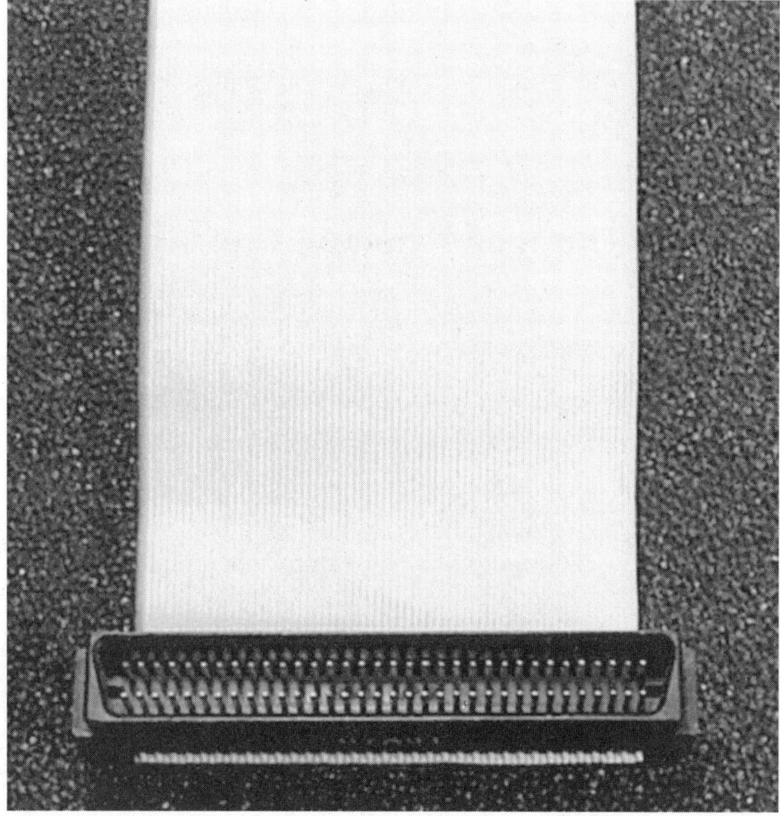

Figure 9.26
SCSI "P" cable

In the earliest days of SCSI-2, 16-bit data transfers required another cable: type B. It had 68 wires and was used in parallel with the 50-wire A cable (see Figure 9.26). Because the industry was so underwhelmed at the dual-cable concept, the B cable quietly and quickly disappeared, to be replaced by the P cable. Like its predecessor, this cable also had 68 wires; unlike the B cable, the P cable can be used alone.

Cable/Bus Lengths

There are strict limits as to the length of a SCSI cable/bus, which is the total distance from one terminator to the other. There are basically five lengths:

- SCSI-1 and SCSI-2 (5 MHz, single-ended): 6 meters
- SCSI-2 and up (10 MHz, single-ended, up to three devices): 3 meters

- SCSI-2 and up: (10 MHz, single-ended, more than three devices): 1.5 meters
- High-voltage differential SCSI bus: 25 meters
- Low-voltage differential SCSI bus: 12 meters

Types of External Connectors

All external connectors are female on the devices. The type of external connectors are as follows:

- 50-pin Centronics, obsolete SCSI-1 (Figure 9.27)
- 50-pin HD D-type, SCSI-2 (Figure 9.28)
- 68-pin HD D-type, wide SCSI-2 (Figure 9.29)
- 25-pin standard D-type (looks identical to parallel), SCSI-2, most commonly used on Macintoshes (Figure 9.30)

Figure 9.27 50-pin Centronics

Figure 9.28 50-pin HD "D"-type—SCSI-2

Figure 9.29
68-pin HD "D"-type—Wide SCSI-2

Figure 9.30
25-pin standard "D"-type

ASPI

Everything within your computer must have BIOS (basic input/output services). BIOS is nothing more than the software that allows the CPU to talk to the rest of the hardware. It can be hardwired into the motherboard (the system BIOS), it can be hardwired into the device (e.g., a ROM chip built into a video card), or it can be a device driver loaded off of the hard drive. The BIOS for SCSI devices can come from any of these sources.

If all your SCSI devices are hard drives, then the ROM chip on the SCSI host adapter provides all the BIOS you need. A program on the ROM chip runs during the boot process, detecting the SCSI hard drives and initializing the BIOS needed to communicate with them. Unfortunately, SCSI devices can be just about anything, not just hard drives. While the SCSI scan program will detect devices other than hard drives, it does not know how to talk to them. The ROM chips on SCSI host adapters, with rare exceptions, know how to talk only to hard drives. In order to get the BIOS for other SCSI devices, you will most likely need to load device drivers.

Unfortunately, not all device drivers play well together, and their incompatibility plagued early SCSI devices. Sometimes two device drivers simply could not be made to work together. Machines would lock up, reboot spontaneously, or simply give bizarre, seemingly unrelated errors because of incompatible device drivers. To solve this problem, a new standard evolved: *advanced SCSI programmer interface* (ASPI).

ASPI mandates a standard way to write BIOS device drivers for SCSI devices. The beauty of ASPI is that you can install a standardized matched set of device drivers for all your SCSI devices. Because they are all ASPI drivers, you can be confident that the drivers for a SCSI removable media drive and a SCSI scanner will work well together. Although there have been several "flavors" of ASPI, Adaptec's EZ SCSI is an excellent example.

With Adaptec's EZ SCSI, the host adapter requires its own device driver. Additional devices require additional EZ SCSI device drivers, although some devices can share a single device's drivers. For example, the EZ SCSI driver ASPIDSK.SYS supports both removable media drives (e.g., an Iomega ZIP drive) and traditional SCSI hard drives—as long as the ROM chip on the host adapter has been disabled. The ability to use a single device driver for more than one device makes ASPI products such as EZ SCSI extremely attractive from a memory-management perspective.

Windows 95 has a complete copy of protected-mode, built-in ASPI drivers. With Windows 95, as long as the physical connections are all correct, an ASPI-compliant device will automatically be recognized by the system.

If you are using ASPI drivers to support SCSI devices and you have an IDE drive to boot from, consider disabling the SCSI host adapter's ROM BIOS. A typical SCSI BIOS takes up about 16K of reserved memory, and the EZ SCSI ASPI drivers needed to support SCSI hard drives take up about 15K (9K for the host adapter driver and 6K for the ASPIDSK.SYS driver). While there is only a 1K difference, remember that the same ASPIDSK.SYS driver can also support removable media drives such as an Iomega ZIP drive. If you know that the device drivers can handle both, why not disable the SCSI ROM BIOS and let the ASPI drivers handle both devices? If all your SCSI devices are hard drives, there is no real advantage either way, but if you are using ASPI drivers to support your hard drives, disabling the ROM chip will free up 16K of UMB space in the reserved area.

Remember that you still need an IDE drive to boot from. Those device drivers have to be stored somewhere other than the boot drive. If you already have an IDE drive in your system, the primary DOS partition on it will already be drive C:. Because Windows 95 and DOS both require being booted off of either A: or C:, it will already be your bootable drive.

A special case arises in a minority of PCI systems that have BIOS support for SCSI hard drives. Some systems provide an NCR chipset, which will support a bootable SCSI drive without loading an ASPI device driver or having an active host adapter BIOS. Of course, ASPI drivers are still required for devices other than hard drives.

SCSI Performance

Which can move more cars more quickly—a 10-lane freeway or a four-lane city street? That sums up the effect of the expansion bus on SCSI performance. SCSI is a bus-mastering device, that is, it takes control of the expansion bus to transfer data from one device into memory or from one device to another device not on the SCSI host adapter. This is marvelous since it frees up the CPU to do more important things.

Unfortunately, if you plug a SCSI host adapter into an ISA slot, the best transfer speed you can obtain is approximately 5 MBps. Before you panic, remember that most advertised hard-drive speeds are actually for burst mode between the on-board disk cache and the host adapter, not internally to the hard drive itself. Most hard drives can sustain a transfer of only between 2.5 and 5.5 MBps.

If you really want to see things fly, then you need to consider an adapter for either the EISA, the VLB, or the PCI buses. These buses can support transfers at up to 33 MBps. Be aware that some PCI motherboards are available with NCR SCSI device management system support in the motherboard BIOS, which means you might be able to purchase a slightly cheaper host adapter with no on-board BIOS. This will allow you to install support for your SCSI devices directly from the motherboard—but you will still need to load an ASPI driver for the other SCSI devices!

Compatibility Among Flavors of SCSI

While it might seem unlikely that the various flavors of SCSI would be able to communicate through the same host adapter, that is exactly the case. Each device communicates at the maximum speed supported by that device.

Compatibility with IDE and Other Standards

The most important point to remember when it comes to compatibility is to make sure it works. You can mix IDE and SCSI, but if you have an IDE drive present on your system it will be the boot drive. All IDE drives installed in the system BIOS are assigned logical drive letters first.

There are a few permutations to this scenario because of EIDE. Briefly, EIDE allows support for up to four hard drives—two on the primary 40-pin IDE connection and two on the secondary connection. Device-driver support for at least the two primary hard drives will be present in the ROM BIOS, and support for the two secondary drives might be present in the ROM BIOS. So you might need a device driver in CONFIG.SYS to enable access to the secondary-port hard drives.

This provides at least two possible outcomes. First, with BIOS support for the secondary IDE connection, the IDE drives will get drive letters before any SCSI drives. Second, if the system BIOS provides support for only the primary IDE port, use of the secondary chain will require a device driver. With BIOS support for only the primary IDE port and a device driver required for the secondary port as well as the device driver (resident either in an on-board BIOS or a program file for the SCSI drives), the assigned drive letters will vary according to the device driver load order in CONFIG.SYS.

Repair and Troubleshooting

SCSI problems can be reduced to certain categories, some of which overlap and not all of which apply to every problem.

Power and Connectivity

In any PC repair scenario, confirm connectivity and power before going any further. Nothing will work if the devices do not have power and if they cannot access the external data bus and address bus. Fortunately, most SCSI host adapters provide an excellent utility for determining whether or not devices are properly powered and connected: SCSI Scan. As the host adapter initializes (provided that the host adapter's BIOS is active), a list of all the devices detected by the host adapter will be displayed on the screen. If one or more of your devices fails to appear, power or connectivity are the most likely problems. If the devices are not properly hooked up, they will not respond to the "identify yourself" commands sent out by the host adapter.

POWER What kinds of power problems could prevent a device from showing up? It's usually nothing more exotic than forgetting to plug it in. Make sure that both internal and external devices have power. Most SCSI devices, especially external ones, require power in order to provide termination, and all of them require power for operation.

CONNECTIVITY Make sure that the devices are properly installed. Is the termination set properly (one terminator at each end of the chain and none in between)? Does each device have its own unique SCSI ID? Are the cables seated correctly and firmly? You'll probably need documentation to double-check settings for termination and SCSI IDs.

Boot Firmware

If you do not see a SCSI scan during the boot process before you see "Starting DOS" or "Starting Windows 95," check to make sure that the ROM BIOS on the host adapter has not been disabled. In addition, other CMOS and SCSI ROM BIOS settings can cause problems. Is the ROM chip on the SCSI host adapter enabled or disabled? What IRQ, DMA, and I/O address is the card using? If you see an "HDD controller failure" or "HDD failure" message, is the CMOS set up to look for an IDE drive that is not present in the system?

Memory Chips

Problems with memory chips will usually cause problems with all the devices in a PC, not just the SCSI devices. Diagnose problems carefully. Does the symptom, whatever it happens to be, crop up only when using SCSI devices, or does it happen consistently with every device?

Storage

SCSI hard drives can have the same types of problems as any other hard drive. If you are using DOS or Windows 95, the partitions and FAT file system are no different than with IDE drives. In fact, except for the SCSI interface itself, IDE and SCSI drives are virtually identical. For the most part, the same repair and maintenance techniques apply. At a bare minimum, use ScanDisk and Defrag on a regular basis. For any error that ends in "Abort, retry, fail" or "Abort, retry, fail, ignore," use a program such as Norton's Disk Doctor or its equivalent. Use the SYS command and the FDISK /MBR command for boot problems. Treat SCSI hard-drive errors the same way you treat IDE hard-drive errors.

I/O

IRQ, DMA, and I/O address problems usually manifest themselves fairly quickly. Remember that if any of the IRQ, DMA, or I/O address settings are stored in a CMOS or EEPROM chip, power surges can reset them to their default settings. SCSI host adapters often store their settings in EEPROM chips. Do not assume that just because the user has not changed any settings that they have not changed. Many SCSI host adapters default to IRQ3, which would cause an IRQ lockup with any device using COM2 (often a modem or mouse).

Proper documentation of these settings for all your devices is the best way to avoid problems. If you don't have it, create your own. Use the F8 key to step through CONFIG.SYS and AUTOEXEC.BAT one line at a time. Many device drivers report their settings as they load. Look at jumper settings. Use a PDI or Discovery card to check for IRQ and DMA usage.

Device Drivers

If you have SCSI devices other than hard drives, they will require a device driver. Remember that some device drivers do not work well together. How do you determine if you have a conflict between two device drivers? Try loading only the device drivers for the SCSI devices. Does the symptom still occur? If not, then another device driver is causing the problem. Use the F8 key to determine which one. Once you know which device drivers are incompatible, you have several options. Look in the manuals or readme files of both devices. Your problem might be a known one with a solution. If the device driver is an executable, try running it with the /? option, which will usually show you a variety of command-line switches (e.g., MOUSE.EXE /?). Try a variety of switches and see if any of them solve the problem. If not, attempt to find an updated driver for one or both of the devices. If none of those solutions fix the problem, you might be forced to choose between the devices or go to a multiple boot configuration.

Memory Management

Remember that SCSI host adapters typically have their own ROM chips. Don't forget to put the appropriate X= statements in your EMM386.EXE line in CONFIG.SYS, and the appropriate EMMEXCLUDE= statement in your SYSTEM.INI file. A forgotten exclude statement often explains those "locking up every now and then" problems.

Cost and Benefits

SCSI is great for:

- File servers
- Workstations (both graphical and audio)
- Multitasking systems
- Any system moving large amounts of data among peripheral devices
- Any system with a large number of peripherals
- Any system requiring fault tolerance (mostly file servers)

Because the initial cost of SCSI is higher and the devices themselves are also more expensive, you must answer some questions to determine the need for SCSI:

- Is this a graphics/CAD workstation?
- Is this a network file server?
- Is this a stand-alone machine frequently running multitasking applications?

If the answer is "yes" to any of the above, then it will probably be worth the money to invest in a SCSI-based expansion bus. There are two reasons for this. First, a data-intensive application such as CAD/CAM design software, will benefit by the increased data throughput available with SCSI devices, especially hard drives and scanners. Second, SCSI is a bus-mastering device. In a multitasking environment, this leaves the CPU free to handle more important things, such as updating an Excel spreadsheet.

For systems supporting a data-intensive peripheral such as a full-page 24-bit color scanner, a 4GB Digital Audio tape backup drive, a Bernoulli removable-media disk drive, or multiple CD-ROM drives, SCSI is the best solution.

SCSI vs. EIDE

SCSI hard drives no longer have as large an advantage over IDE devices as they once did. For many years, SCSI hard drives were the only large hard drives available. Now EIDE drives are pushing into the sizes that once belonged exclusively to SCSI drives. Data throughput for EIDE has also increased to as fast as 33.3 MBps. While SCSI might support a transfer rate of up to 20 MBps, remember that except for the chipset on the disk controller card, IDE and SCSI hard drives are made the same—so the limitation in data transfer speeds comes from the hard-drive assembly, not necessarily the data bus. SCSI, with the potential for up to seven hard drives, made sense if you needed a large number of hard drives. Now that Enhanced IDE can support up to four devices, including CD-ROM drives and other mass storage devices, the SCSI advantage in number of devices has also shrunk.

While SCSI's advantages in some areas are not as pronounced as they once were, it still possesses a number of advantages that justify its higher cost. The bus-mastering capability makes SCSI ideal for data-intensive operations such as disk mirroring (see the next section). In addition, for external devices that are not hard drives, SCSI remains the high-performance interface of choice.

RAID

A way to ensure constant access to crucial data is through the use of disk arrays. Because SCSI buses use a bus-mastering DMA transfer, this echo process does not impose additional overhead to the CPU. If, for example, IDE were to be used in this way, the system would run much more slowly since IDE drives use programmed input/output (PIO) transfer modes that require CPU intervention.

RAID 0 combines two or more disks into one large logical drive through a process called *striping*. This process divides the data into 32K blocks, which are then divided between the two disks. This can lead to better performance since the mechanical access times are reduced.

RAID 1 is called *disk mirroring*, which provides a computer with instant online backups by echoing data writes to a second hard disk through a common host adapter. If the primary hard drive fails, the system will automatically transfer all reads and writes to the second drive. This transfer is transparent to the user and provides an excellent means of ensuring minimal downtime for mission-critical applications. Disk mirroring will typically slow down system performance because all disks must acknowledge write operations.

RAID 2 provides a greater degree of error detection by dedicating a drive for error correction information. RAID 2 also requires ECC error correction on all drives.

RAID 3 and 4 use at least two data drives and a dedicated ECC data drive. Again, data is striped between the drives with RAID 4, using larger data blocks or stripes, which provides a slight performance gain over RAID 3. Neither option is the best, since for every write operation the ECC data must be written to the dedicated ECC drive.

RAID 5 is the better choice among the RAID options because it distributes the ECC data among all the drives. This also has the side benefit of reducing ECC data redundancy to 25 percent.

RAID 6 is RAID 5 with the added capability of asynchronous and cached data transmission. RAID 6 is the last official level in the RAID specification, so any vendor advertising additional levels is probably pushing a proprietary RAID implementation.

Other Storage Options

Probably the oldest and most familiar storage device, at least to old-timers, is the Bernoulli disk. Bernoulli disks get their name from the Bernoulli effect, which states that between a fixed metal plate (the read/write head) and a rotating flexible medium (the disk surface) a highly compressed cushion of air will develop. This cushion maintains a very small distance between the head and the disk as long as the disk is rotating or the airflow between the head and the disk is uninterrupted. When the drive is shut down or the airflow is disrupted, the head jumps *away* from the disk surface. This is contrary to what you would expect from a hard drive, where the opposite has produced the traumatic term *head crash*. Bernoulli disks are a semiflexible removable storage medium ranging from as small as 20MB to 150MB on a disk.

Recently the hot topic in removable storage is the Iomega ZIP and JAZ drives. A ZIP drive is 100MB in size, with access times not much slower than conventional nonremovable hard drives. JAZ drives also use removable media, but hold either 540MB or 1GB.

Additional Facts from Adaptec's Technical Support Line

- Any Adaptec host adapter ending in the number 2 has a floppy controller.
- Some host adapters, such as the Adaptec AHA-274xAT and the AHA-274xW, can support more than seven SCSI devices.
- When using a SCSI hard drive as the boot device, always set its ID to 0.
- The floppy controller on a SCSI adapter will have a DMA and IRQ conflict with any other floppy controller present in the computer.
- The on-board BIOS should be disabled if the adapter does not support any hard drives.
- A hard drive set up on one manufacturer's SCSI adapter might not be seen with the same parameters when moved to another adapter, requiring repartitioning and reformatting.
- On a system with only a SCSI hard drive, the error message "HDD Controller Failure" indicates an improper CMOS setting for the SCSI drive. SCSI drives should be set to either "not installed" or SCSI.
- Some host adapters allow you to boot up from a removable media drive (AHA-2740/2W).
- Termination can be one of three flavors, depending on the type of SCSI chain: passive, active, or forced perfect termination.
- Passive termination is a holdover from the dinosaur days of the ST-506. The termination is nothing more than a network of resistors. The resistors are usually small, black and shiny, resembling very skinny black caterpillars. This type of termination is typically found only on plain-old ordinary narrow "8-bit" SCSI devices.
- For the quicker Fast/Wide SCSI, you have to maintain a tighter tolerance on the voltage and impedance of the SCSI chain. To do this, you must use active termination, which uses voltage regulators instead of resistors.

- Forced perfect termination (FPT) also maintains the correct voltage level on the bus, but does so to a finer tolerance by using diodes. These diodes function like a resistor in the passive termination, with one exception—a diode has a lower resistance in one direction, or orientation, than it does in the other. This is called *polarity.* The higher resistance in one direction helps to block current flow backward along the data cable much better than a plain resistor.

CHAPTER 10

Modems

In this chapter, you will:

- Understand the difference between analog and serial communication.
- Understand the function of modems and UARTs.
- See synchronous and asynchronous communication examples.
- Be able to define different speed, error correction, and data compression standards.
- Look at the AT commands for modems.
- Clarify IRQ and I/O issues with modems.

The term *modem* is an abbreviation of *mod*ulator/*dem*odulator. Modems are used in PCs primarily to allow computers to talk to each other via standard commercial telephone lines. Telephone wires transfer data via *analog signals,* which are continuously changing voltages on a wire. Figure 10.1 is an example of an analog signal.

Computers hate analog signals. Computers need *digital signals,* which are "on" or "off" voltages, meaning the wire has voltage present or it does not. Computers, being binary by nature, use only two states of voltage: zero volts and positive volts. Figure 10.2 is an example of a digital signal. Modems take analog signals from telephone lines and turn them into digital signals that your PC's COM ports can understand (Figure 10.3). Conversely, modems also take digital signals off the PC's COM ports and convert them into analog signals for the outgoing telephone line.

So modems convert signals from analog to digital and back to analog. However, this data is nothing more than a series of ones and zeros, which is why it's called *serial communication.* Your CPU needs to access data on the external data bus in discrete 8-bit chunks (Figure 10.4). The serial bits of data are converted into 8-bit "bytes" of data via the UART, which stands for *universal asynchronous receiver transmitter.* The UART chip converts the serial bits of analog data into 8-bit bytes that the PC can understand (Figure 10.5).

All COM ports are really little more than UARTs. A mouse is a serial device; it sends its data as a series of bits down one wire (the other wires are used for things other than sending data). If you have a mouse hooked to a COM port, the UART converts the serial information into the 8-bit-wide data that the external data bus can understand. There are many types of UARTs, each with different functions.

External modems only convert analog to digital and back, since they are connected to the COM port, which converts the data into 8-bit-wide data the CPU can understand (Figure 10.6). Internal modems come with their own COM port that handles the whole process (Figure 10.7).

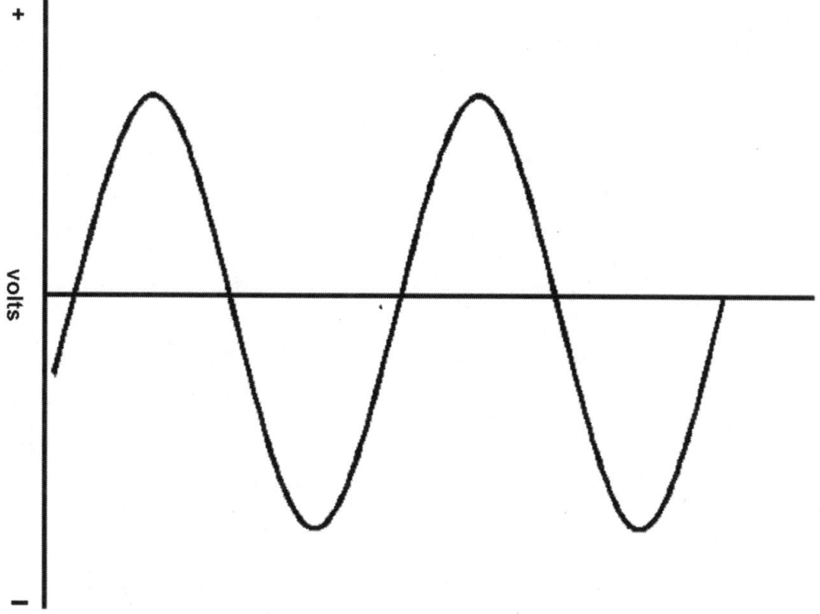

Figure 10.1
Diagram of analog waveform

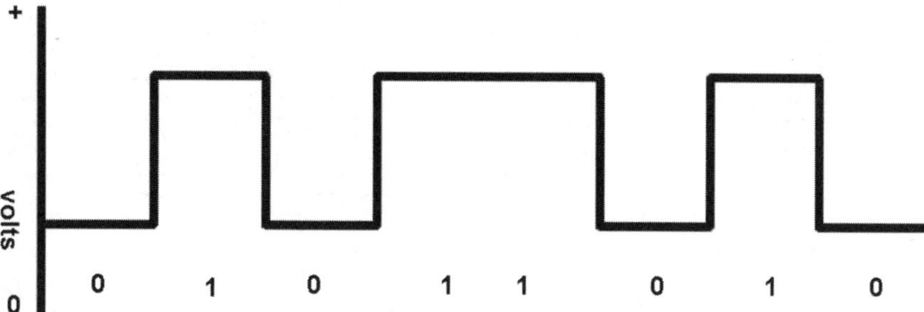

Figure 10.2
Diagram of digital waveform

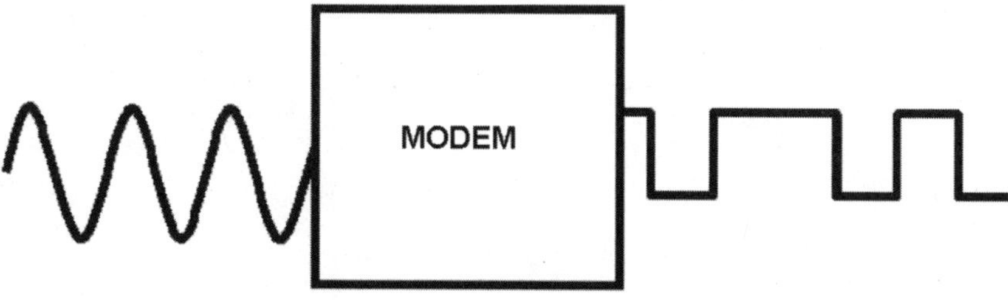

Figure 10.3
Modem converting analog to digital

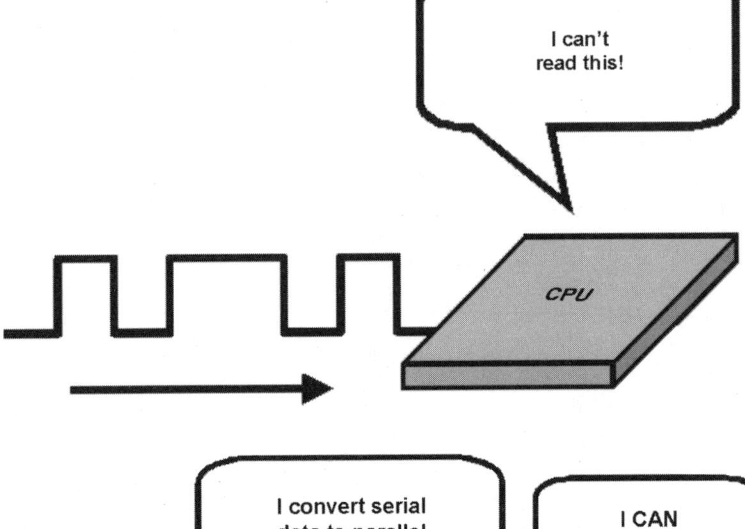

Figure 10.4
CPU can't read serial data

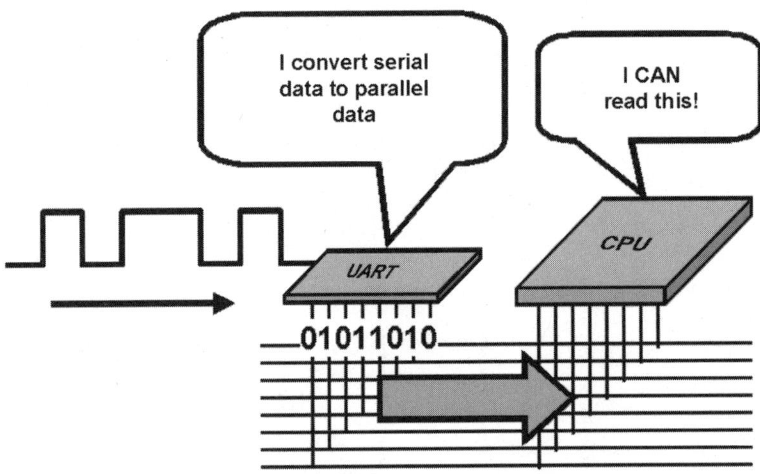

Figure 10.5
Serial to parallel data

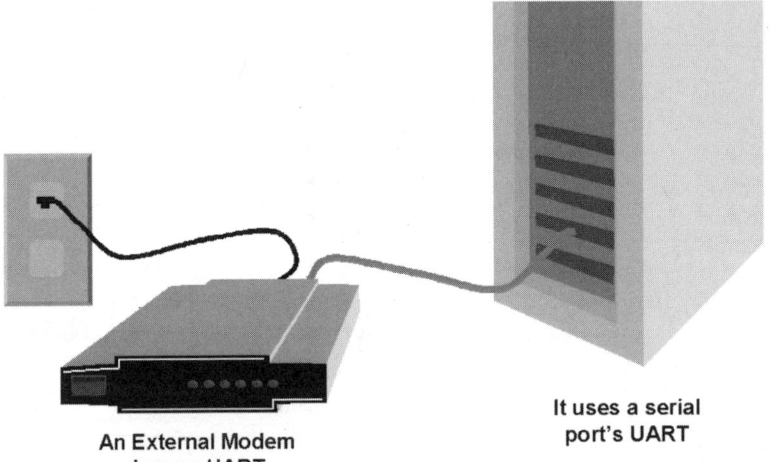

Figure 10.6
External modem connected to PC

Figure 10.7
Internal modem

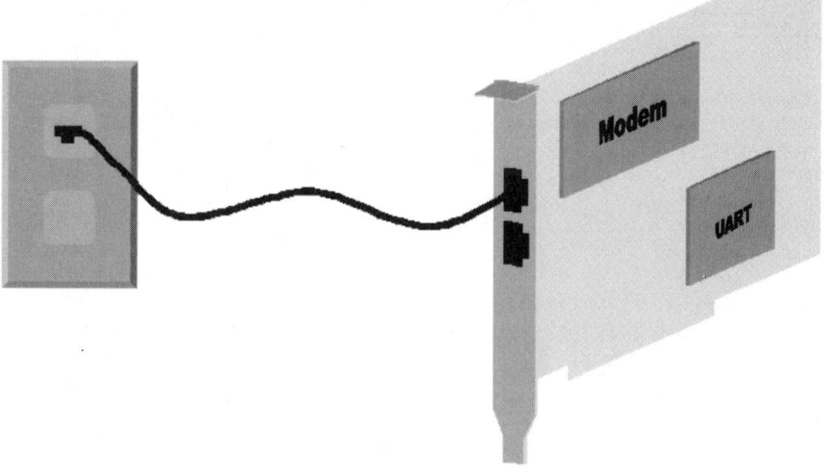

Converting Serial Data to PC Data

There's a problem with this picture. How does a port know how much information is data? Even if data was always 8 bits wide (it's not), where does one 8-bit burst stop and the next one start? There has to be some system that allows the port to "chop up" the incoming signal or to package the outgoing signal (Figure 10.8). There are two ways of organizing serial transmissions: *asynchronous* and *synchronous.*

Figure 10.8
Unorganized data

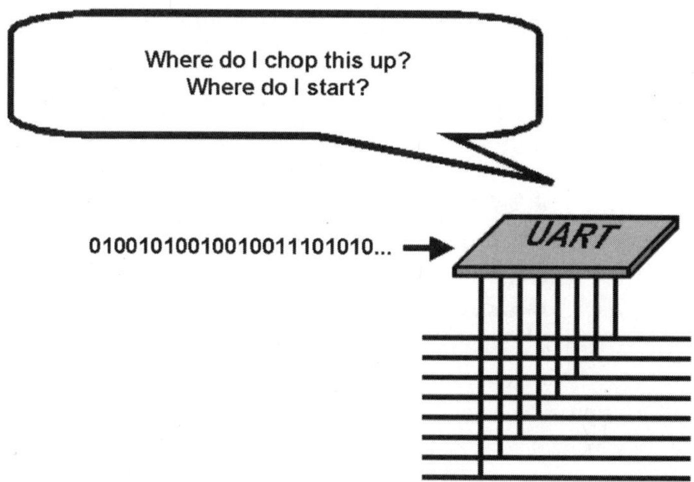

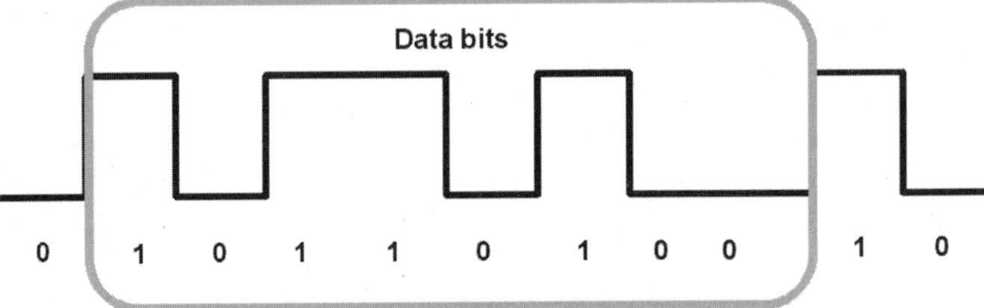

Figure 10.9
Eight-bit serial data

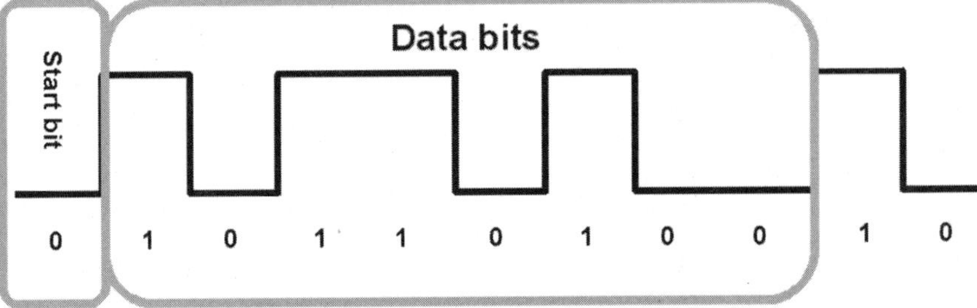

Figure 10.10
Start bit inserted at the beginning of the byte

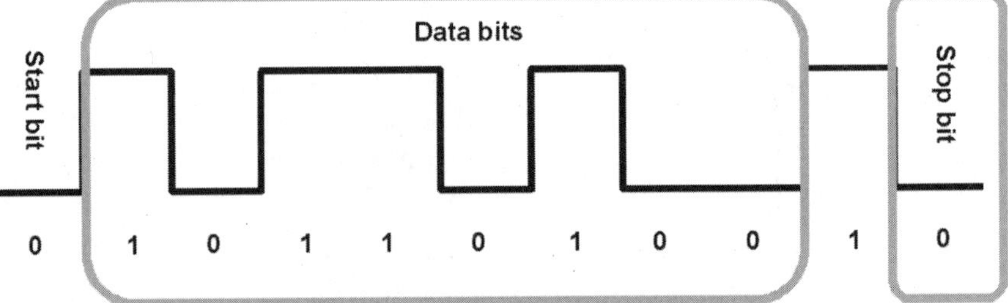

Figure 10.11
Stop bit added to the end of the byte

Asynchronous Organization

Asynchronous data transfers are the primary way in which two serial ports communicate. With this type of transfer, the data is chopped up into 7- or 8-bit packets. These are the bits that actually carry the data (Figure 10.9). Eight-bit data is the most common, although 7-bit data is still used occasionally. Each packet begins with a start bit to tell the receiving modem that it is the beginning of a piece of data (Figure 10.10). The start bit is always zero. Each data packet ends with a stop bit, to tell the receiver that the packet is over (Figure 10.11).

Asynchronous communication packets might also have an optional parity bit, which is used for error detection. The parity bit is sent by the sending port and then used by the receiving port to verify if the data is good or bad (Figure 10.12). There are two types of parity: even and odd (Figure 10.13). In even parity, the sending computer counts the ones in the data part of the packet; if the number is even, the parity bit is zero, which makes the total number of bits even. If the number of ones in the data part of the packet is odd, then the parity bit is set to one—again making the total number of bits even. The receiving port counts the data bits and compares its answer to the parity bit. Odd parity works in exactly the same way, except that the total number of bits is odd.

Parity bits are optional! In fact, almost no one uses parity bits anymore because modems are really good about reading data. It's usually no big deal if a character or two gets a little screwed up every now and then.

Asynchronous settings are group together like this: data bits, parity type, then stop bits. So if a system uses 8 data bits, no parity, and 1 stop bit,

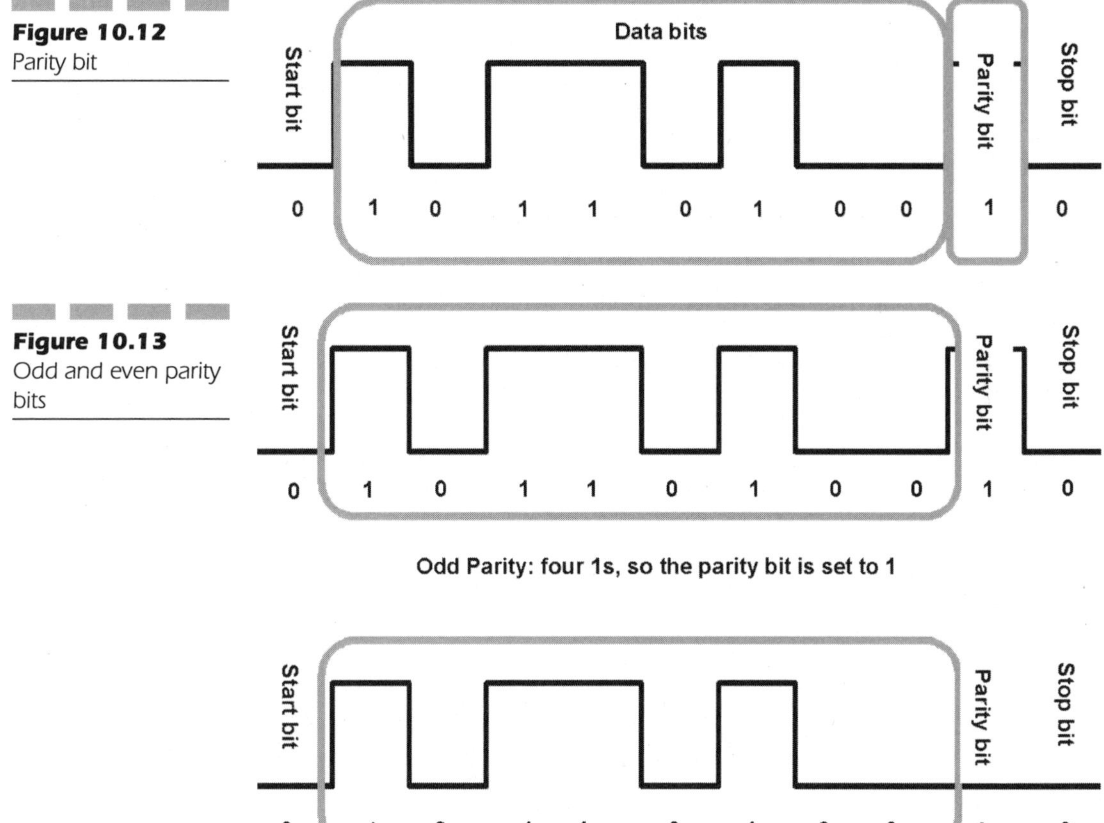

Figure 10.12 Parity bit

Figure 10.13 Odd and even parity bits

you'd say 8-N-1. If a system uses 7 data bits, even parity, and 1 stop bit, you'd say 7-E-1. Virtually everything uses 8-N-1 or 7-E-1 today.

Synchronous Organization

There is a time, however, when there can be no errors in data—when you're uploading or downloading a file to or from your computer. Even one incorrect bit in an .EXE or .COM file will probably make the file unusable. So when transferring files, you'll engage a completely different type of communication: *synchronous communication* (SC).

Although there are many types or "protocols" of synchronous communication, with names like Xmodem, Ymodem, and Zmodem, they all work in basically the same way. When a modem is about to send data via SC, it sends a series of standardized bytes called *sync* on the wire. The port on the other end receives the sync bytes, which tells the receiving port that it is receiving SC data and allows it to synchronize with the incoming data. (See Figure 10.14.) With most protocols, one side tells the communication software the type of protocol to send, while the other side tells the communication software the type of protocol to receive (Figure 10.15).

After the sync bytes, the sending modem adds an STX, or start-of-text character. Then the data bytes are sent. The data in a synchronous transmission is processed in "packets" or "blocks" of fixed length, depending on the protocol used. In order for a synchronous data transfer to occur, the incoming modem must know the protocol. That's why the protocols have to be set when the file transfer is initiated.

Figure 10.14 Synchronized handshaking

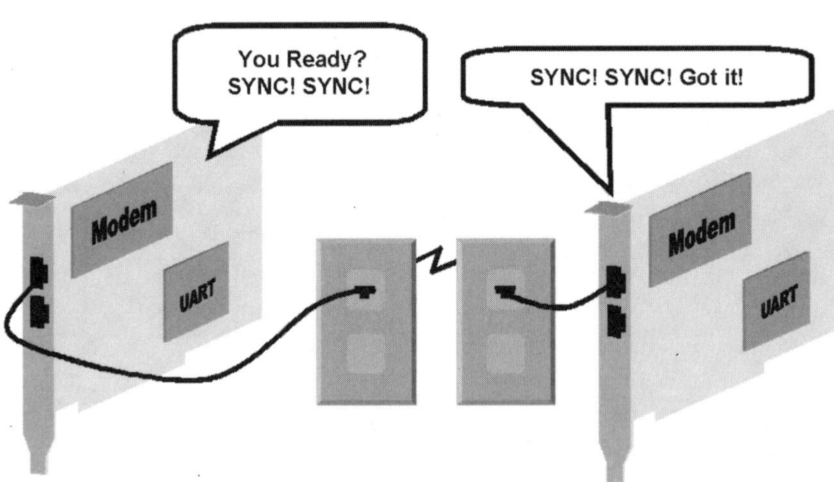

Figure 10.15
Selection screen for protocols

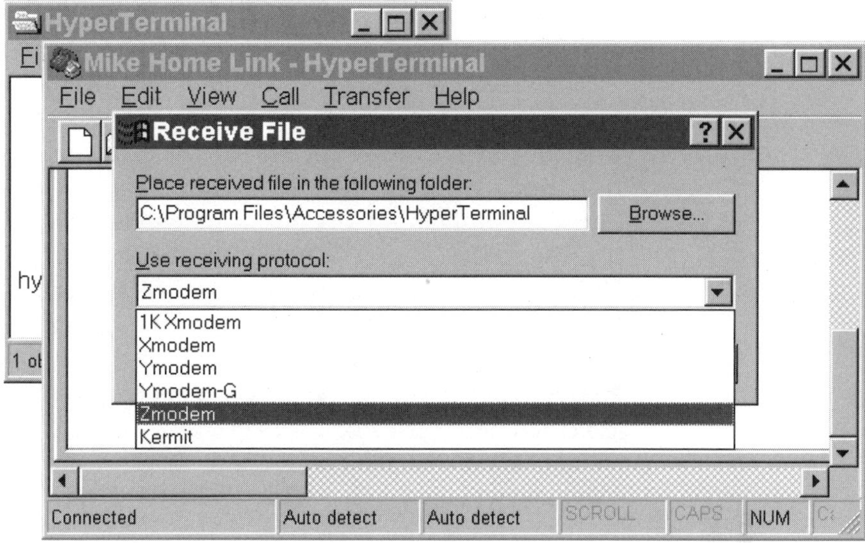

Figure 10.16
Synchronous data packet

Sync byte	Sync byte	STX byte	Data Packet	ETX byte	BCC ECC

After the data has been transferred, the packet ends with an ETX (end-of-text marker) and two error-checking characters called CRC and BCC. These characters use a clever algorithm to check the accuracy of the incoming data. The receiver then responds with an *ack* (acknowledge character) if the data is good, or a *nack* (no acknowledge) if the CRC reports an error (Figure 10.16). Note that in asynchronous communication, the receiving modem does not respond; it just reads the data and acts on it. In SC, the receiving modem must respond.

File Transfer Protocols

There are many commonly used file-transfer protocols in the PC world that allow you to download or upload to mainframes, minis, or other PCs. They should be included with the software that comes with your modem. Once you have established communications with a host, you can usually ask the host what type of protocol it uses, and select yours before you start transferring files.

ASCII This transfer protocol transmits each character as if it had come off the keyboard. This is not a good protocol for transferring program files. It has no error-checking features or compression.

XMODEM This protocol uses an error-detection method for transferring files. It transfers 128-byte blocks of data and one checksum character. The receiving computer calculates a new checksum and compares the two. If they are the same, it will transmit back an ack. If it is different, it will send back a nack and the transmitting computer will retransmit the same block.

YMODEM Ymodem transfers in 1024-byte blocks. Larger blocks means less time spent verifying data with acks and nacks. If you make an error-free connection, meaning your two modems are error-correcting, choose Ymodem.

ZMODEM Use this protocol whenever possible, because it includes all the features of Xmodem and Ymodem and adds a few new features, including crash recovery, automatic downloading, and a "streaming" file-transfer method.

KERMIT This was the first synchronous protocol used for uploading and downloading from a mainframe. It is considered very slow, and is virtually unused today.

Baud Rate

The *baud rate* is the basic cycle of time that a modem uses as its carrier frequency. For instance, a modem that is working at 300 baud means that the basic carrier frequency has 300 cycles per second. On a dial-up phone line, you can go up to 2400 cycles, known as a "baud rate of 2400" (Figure 10.17). Theoretically, if each cycle is one bit, then the fastest data you could transmit would be 2400 bits per second, but through different types of modulation, you can chop up the cycles to add more than one bit per cycle (Figure 10.18).

This is where you get the actual modem speed, measured in *bits per second* (bps). If your modem modulates one bit for each baud cycle, then your modem speed is 2400 bps. If your 2400-baud modem modulates two bits for one cycle of time, then your modem is said to have a speed of 4800 bps,

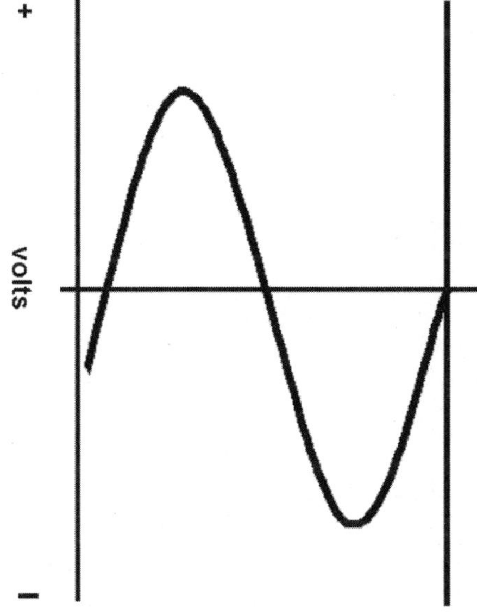

1 Cycle = 1 Baud

Figure 10.17
One cycle - one baud and one bit

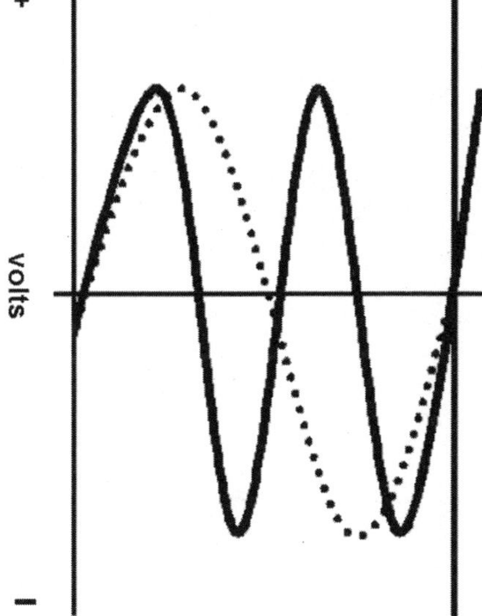

1 Cycle = 1 Baud

Figure 10.18
Two bits for each baud

not a baud rate of 4800. If four bits are modulated with one cycle time, then you have a modem speed of 9600 bps. Don't make the mistake of confusing bps with baud rate.

Flow Control (Handshaking)

Flow control, also known as *handshaking,* is the process by which two serial devices verify a conversation. Imagine people talking on a CB radio. When one finishes speaking, he will say "over." That way the person listening can be sure that the sender is finished speaking. The conversation is verified. The PC world has two distinct areas where conversations are taking place and where flow control is necessary: local and end-to-end (Figure 10.19).

The flow control between modems is handled by the modems themselves; you have no control over them. However, the local flow control between modem and COM port is very much within your control. In the PC world, there are two types of local flow control: hardware and software. Hardware flow control uses some of the extra wires in the serial connection between the modem and COM port to let the other device know that it is ready to send or receive data. These extra wires are called *RTS* (ready to send) and *CTS* (clear to send), so hardware handshaking is often called RTS/CTS. Software flow control uses a special character called XON to let the other device know that it is starting to send data, and another special character called XOFF to let it know when the data is finished, so software handshaking is often called XON/XOFF. XON/XOFF is very rarely used in modems anymore, since software handshaking is slower and not as dependable as hardware handshaking. Only some very old modems still use software handshaking. When in doubt, always use hardware flow control. See Figure 10.20.

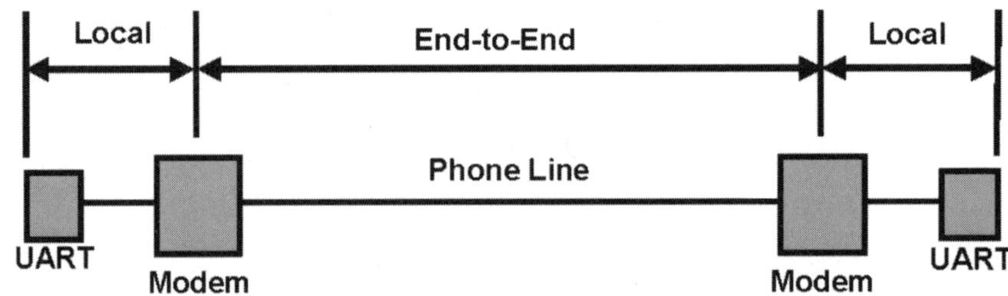

Figure 10.19 Example of local and end to end flow control

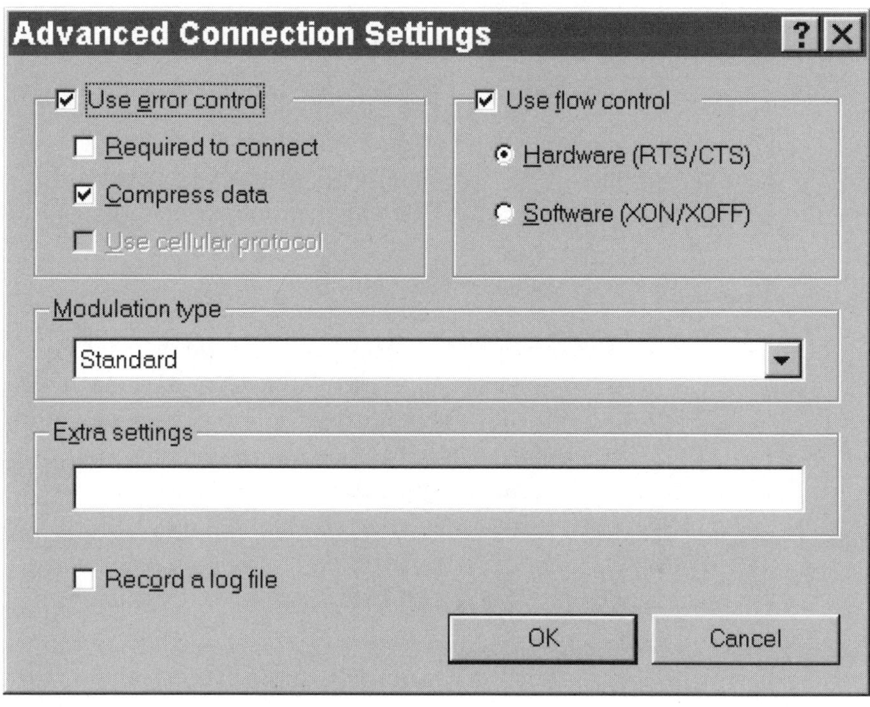

Figure 10.20
Flow control selection window

Error Detection

End-to-end error detection is usually the realm of the synchronous protocol software being used. However, some modems can provide a hardware-based error detection that is blindingly fast and invisible to the software itself. Both modems must each be able to perform this function in order to take advantage of error detection.

Data Compression

Some modems can perform on-the-fly data compression. These data compression algorithms are virtually identical to the ones used in ZIP files, and can significantly enhance the amount of data sent between modems. Of course, each modem must be able to understand each other's compression. Data compression was started by the modem maker Micron under their proprietary MNP5 standard. There are now industry standards for data compression.

Communication Standards

In the early days of modem communication, computers were restricted to the same type of modems on each side of the connection—e.g., an XYZ modem would have to talk to another identical XYZ modem. Most of the time, depending on the computer and modem, a technician would have to set up the operation using jumpers and specific cables. Compatibility was a great concern and proprietary modems were the norm.

These incompatibilities created a desperate need for industry standardization. There had to be a standard way for modems to query each other to determine each other's speed, error correction, and data compression. This standardization has come through two sources. First, certain companies released certain aspects of their modem functions to the public domain that other modem makers copied. Second, standards committees were formed to create standards, which all modem makers copied.

Bell 212A/103

The first really common modem standard was the Bell 212A/103. This modem could send data at either 1200 or 300 baud, depending on programming. The popularity of this modem made other modem makers want to copy the way the Bell 212A spoke to other Bell 212As. In other words, a Bell 212A could dial up a modem that was not a Bell 212A and speak to it because the other modem *emulated* a Bell 212A.

CCITT

After Bell 212A, modem standards came under the control of a United Nations agency, the Consultative Committee on International Telephony and Telegraphy (CCITT). This committee established what are known as V standards since each standard is specified by the letter V followed by a number. These standards include modem speed, data compression, error correction, and fax. They have equivalents to the Bell standards. The CCITT is now known as the International Telecommunication Union (ITU-T).

MNP

The Micron Company has released a series of standards for error detection and data compression to the public domain. These standards are known as the MNP (Micron network protocols) standards. Although still supported by most modem makers, they have been superseded by ITU-T standards.

Speed

Speed standards for modems are listed in Table 10.1.

Error Detection and Data Compression

Error detection and data compression protocols are listed in Table 10.2.

TABLE 10.1
Speed Standards

Standard	Baud	BPS	Comment
Bell 103	300	300	US & Can. Std.
Bell 212 A	600	1200	US & Can. Std.
V.21	300	300	Similar to Bell 103
V.22	600	1200	Incompatible with 212A
V.22bis	600	2400	World wide compatibility
V.23	1200	1200	
V.32	2400	9600	
V.32bis	2400	14400	
V.32terbo	2400	19200	
V.34	2400	28800 33600	
X2	2400	56K	US Robotics (3COM) Incompatible with Kflex
Kflex56	2400	56K	Lucent/Motorola Incompatible with X2
V90	2400	56K	

TABLE 10.2
Other Standards

Standard	Baud	BPS	Type	Comments
V.42	2400	2400 and up	Error correction	
MNP 1–4	2400	2400 and up	Error correction	
V.42BIS	2400	9600/38.4K	Data compression	V.42 must be present
MNP5	n/a	n/a	Both	

Modem Commands

Modems have many functions, and there must be a way to speak to a modem to tell it which function to perform (answer the phone, perform data compression, etc.). These commands are known collectively as the *modem command set.* You'd think that there would be a standard for modem commands, but there isn't. Modem commands vary from manufacturer to manufacturer, although there are a few front-runners that tend to control things. The number-one name in modem command sets is certainly Hayes. Hayes developed the famous AT command set in the early 80s, and released it to the public. All modem manufacturers follow the majority of these commands. AT commands are entered through the keyboard into the modem. Before you can use these commands, however, you have to make sure the communication software is loaded and that you are in either terminal mode or terminal screen. Unless your modem is set up to auto-connect, which is the *online mode,* it should be in *command mode,* which is where you use the AT commands. Although there are hundreds of these commands, Table 10.3 lists the ones that actually get used by technicians.

TABLE 10.3

Common AT Commands

AT	Your modem should respond with an OK, letting you know that your modem is plugged in and turned on.
ATE1	Echo your command on the screen.
ATE0	Turns off the echo to the screen. Some modems will not run correctly with the echo on, so make sure you turn it off when done with it.
ATH1	This is taking the phone off the hook. You should get a reply of OK or 0 back from the modem, a dial tone and an OH indicator on the modem, if it's an external modem.
ATM1	Turns the speaker on, this is for the dial tone. ATL0 is the lowest volume. ATL2 is the medium volume.
ATM0	Turns the speaker off.
ATD	This command will take the phone off the hook as ATH1 did. It will also dial a number if you include it with your command, i.e. ATDT222-2222. The T is for tone. Put a P in its place for a pulse phone. If you include a W (ATDTW), it will wait for a dial tone before dialing. If you include a (,) anywhere after the command, it will pause before continuing to dial. For instance, you may need a 9, for an outside line.
ATQ0	This enables result codes. This aids in troubleshooting problems. If you typed an ATV1 prior to this command, you will get back verbose result codes. (OK-BUSY-CONNECT 2400, 9600-COMPRESSION:V.42bis). If you type ATV, or ATV0, then you will get number or short codes: i.e. 0, 12, 10.
ATQ1	Disables result codes.
ATH,ATH0	Makes the modem hand up.
ATZ	This resets your modem to a predefined state. You can reconfigure your own profile for the modem for resetting. If it wasn't set previously, then it will reset to the factory's setting.

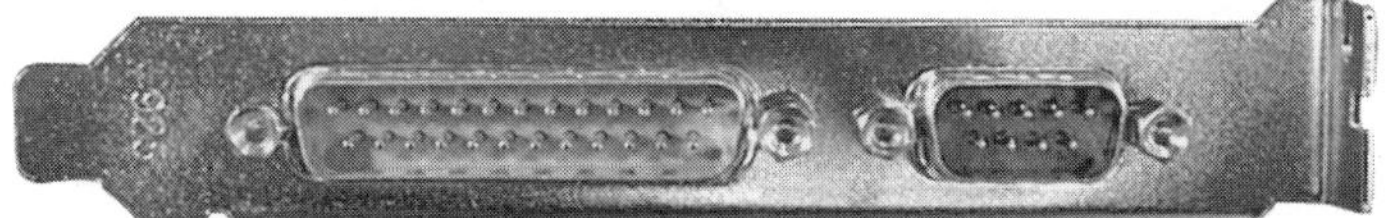

Figure 10.21
25-pin and 9-pin serial connectors

RS-232 Connector

External modems are physically connected by a serial port to a PC using the Electronic Industries Associations (EIA) standard RS-232. RS stands for *recommended standards,* and RS-232 is the revision that applies to serial ports. This standard in Europe is defined as V.24. RS-232 describes only signals, not the actual plug. RS-232 revision D specifies a 25-pin D-type connector. This 25-pin connector was mostly used for synchronous communications. Asynchronous communication can be handled with far less connectors. With PCs, the data transfer between serial ports and modems is always asynchronous. Therefore, starting with the 286-based AT, IBM invented their own proprietary 9-pin connector, which allowed them to use only asynchronous communication. See Figure 10.21.

Talking to Serial Ports

Serial-port gurus often use the terms DCE and DTE. DCE stands for *data communication equipment* and DTE stands for *data terminal equipment.* DCE is the device that sends data, and DTE is the device that receives data. The connection between the DCE and DTE is what is called the "handshake." It ensures that the DCE and DTE are in sync with each other for passing data that needs to be transmitted correctly and not lost. The signal ground and data signal rates are missing from the 9-pin norm. The signal names, direction, and purpose are listed in Table 10.4.

TABLE 10.4

RS-232 Pinouts

25 Pin	9 Pin	Signal	Direction	Description
1	—	—	—	Protective ground
2	3	TD	DTE->DCE	Transmitted data
3	2	RD	DCE->DTE	Received data
4	7	RTS	DTE->DCE	Request to send
5	8	CTS	DCE->DTE	Clear to send
6	6	DSR	DCE->DTE	Data set ready
7	5	—	—	Signal ground (common)
8	1	DCD	DCE->DTE	Data carrier detect
20	4	DTR	DTE->DCE	Data terminal ready
22	9	RI	DCE->DTE	Ring indicator
23	—	DSRD	DCE<->DTE	Data signal rate detector

Telephone Lines

Contrary to popular belief, telephone lines cannot be purchased or leased from the telephone company in different grades. There are only two types of "switched" phone lines (meaning you can dial different numbers). These two types are regular analog phone lines (often called POTS for "plain-old telephone service") and ISDN. There is no such thing as a "data-grade" phone line!

The good old phone line you use to talk to your mother every Sunday is an analog line. The basic analog phone line is guaranteed to handle speeds only up to 2400 baud. (Telephone companies think in terms of baud, not bps.) These lines are notorious for providing poor-quality transmissions. The problem is that your line is connected to the telephone company's main switch via a series of connections at smaller distribution switches. Each subswitch can cause degradation of phone quality by creating "noise" on the line. See Figure 10.22a.

A common trick to verify that you are getting the best quality is to call the phone company. Complain that you have a high-speed modem and the highest baud rate you can get is 1200 baud. If you complain that your 28,800-bps modem is working at only 14,400 bps, the phone company will tell you that you're getting 2400 baud and they won't do anything. However, if you complain that you're getting only 1200 baud, then the phone company has to fix the line. Most phone companies guarantee a minimum of 2400 baud telephone lines.

To improve your telephone lines, the phone company will first create a direct line between your line and the local switch. Then they will check your line to see if you have too much of a voltage drop. A phone line should run at approximately 48 volts. If the phone company feels that the voltage drop is too much (there's no definite number here, it's up to them), they will "condition" the line. Conditioning simply means adding a little voltage to the line to compensate for the voltage drop. See Figure 10.22b.

Figure 10.22A
Phone line routing

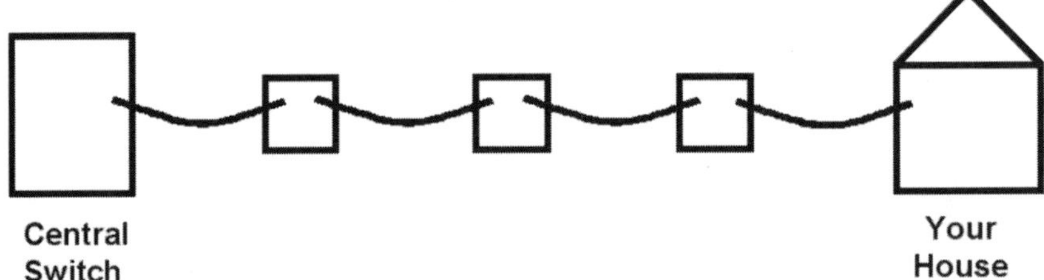

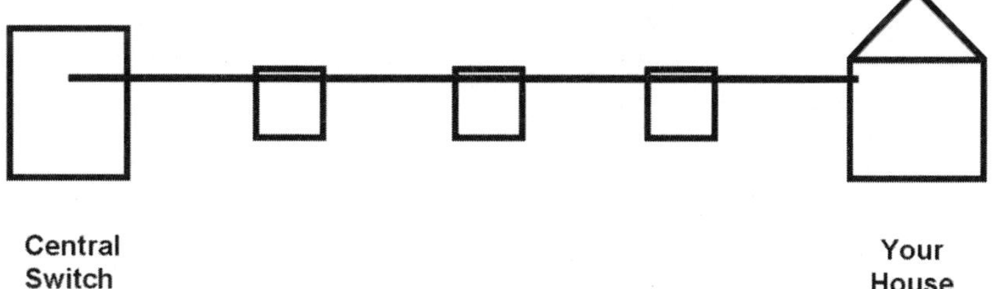

Figure 10.22B Improving the signal quality

Universal Asynchronous Receiver/Transmitter Chips (UARTs)

UARTs are the heart of many serial ports used in PCs and other computer applications. They take the parallel information off data buses and turn it into serial information to be sent out to a modem or another serial device. They can also receive serial information and turn it into parallel information to be put back on data buses for a computer's usage. They provide control signals for flow control to the serial devices. Table 10.5 shows the

TABLE 10.5

UARTs

Chip	Description
8250	This is the original chip selected by IBM for use in the PC. It had several bugs built into it, but IBM worked around them with built-in routines written in the PC and XT ROM BIOS.
8250A	This chip was developed to fix the bugs in the 8250, but in doing so, it would not work properly with the PC and XT BIOS. This chip would work with the AT BIOS. This chip does not work adequately at 9600 bps or above.
8250B	This chip was developed to fix the bugs in the previous chips, and also designed with the interrupt enable bug that was in the 8250 chip. This made it compatible with the PC/XT BIOS, and may work with the AT BIOS, but it still has problems with bps rates above 9600.
16450	This chip was initially picked by IBM for their AT systems. In fact it is a bare minimum for their OS/2 systems or the serial ports will not function properly. This chip has a higher throughput than the previous chips and has an added scratch register to aid in speed. The only drawback, is that it cannot be used with the PC/XT BIOS due to the interrupt bug being fixed.
16550	This chip was an improvement over the 16450, but cannot be used for FIFO (first in first out) buffering modes. It did allow programmers to use multiple DMA channels. This chip is not recommended for standard high speed communication use, and should be replaced by the 16550A, even though it has a higher throughput.
16550A	This chip as built-in FIFO registers for receive and transmit. It will increase your throughput without losing characters at higher rates of speed, due to the added registers. This is the only UART installed on today's systems.

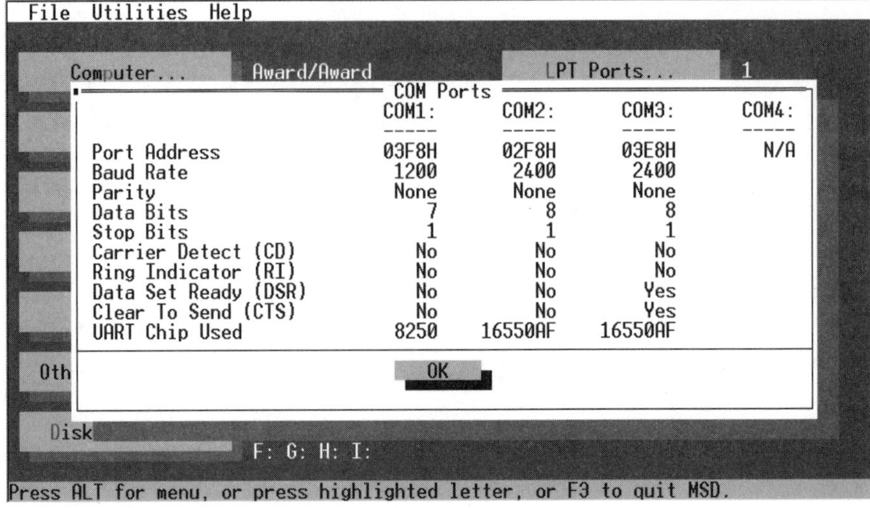

File Utilities Help
Computer...
Award/Award
LPT Ports...
1
COM Ports
COM1: COM2: COM3: COM4:
Port Address 03F8H 02F8H 03E8H N/A
Baud Rate 1200 2400 2400
Parity None None None
Data Bits 7 8 8
Stop Bits 1 1 1
Carrier Detect (CD) No No No
Ring Indicator (RI) No No No
Data Set Ready (DSR) No No Yes
Clear To Send (CTS) No No Yes
UART Chip Used 8250 16550AF 16550AF
Oth
OK
Disk
F: G: H: I:
Press ALT for menu, or press highlighted letter, or F3 to quit MSD.

Figure 10.23 MSD showing the serial ports assigned to the system

most popular and viable chips that are used for serial communications, and any defects that might have been built into them.

It's important to know what type of UART is in your COM ports. In order to ensure quality data communication at 9600 bps or better, you need a 16550A. You can easily determine this by using the MSD utility that comes with DOS, Windows 3.*x*, and Windows 95 (Figure 10.23).

Fax Modems

The technology for faxes was developed in 1842 by an inventor named Alexander Baine. He invented an electromechanical device that could translate wire-based signals into marks on a paper. There were no standards set and there were different types of facsimile standards, so CCITT, the European Standards Committee, adopted standards for the transmission of facsimile data in both the computer world and fax machines. Instead of transmitting bytes of data, the fax would transmit single dots represented by data bits, which could be converted into text files.

There are four different classes or groups of fax standards found in the PC environment. One advantage of PC faxes is that they can be used in the same format as picture reproduction, and they can also be converted to text files or graphics display.

TABLE 10.6

FAX Standards

Maximum Speed	Standard
300	V.21 channel 2
4800	V.27 ter
9600	V.29
14,400	V.17

Group 1 and 2 were used on 300-baud communication rates. They are analog devices, which don't include a modem. Although still supported by fax modems, they are rarely used. Group 1 transmitted one page in six minutes, and group 2 transmitted one page in three minutes.

Group 3 is digital, specified by standards set by CCITT. The same modem is used for data and fax. The difference is that a fax transmission could be at 9600 bps, while the data mode can operate at only 2400 bps. This means that some modems are not compatible with each other. You have to look at their V standards to make sure they can communicate with each other. There are several classes in this group because of the different speeds and methods of communicating. They can send information in binary and by different compression methods. The original group 3 was 200 × 200 dpi. The new class can produce 300 × 300 dpi, a resolution used by laser printers, scanners, and other fax machines. The newer compression rates can produce up to 400 × 400 dpi.

The original group 1 was set up by computer software. The newer group 2 is set up by CCITT, which means it can use hardware error correction and compression. It is also an advanced extension of the Hayes command standards. Table 10.6 lists the different fax-modem standards. Ensure that your fax-modem purchase has a group-3 or G3 fax-modem standard marked on the box or paperwork. Any good fax-modem software can run group 3. Group-4 modems will allow a higher resolution of 400 × 400 and up to 1200 × 1200 dpi. These will need to be used with the newer digital phone circuits (ISDN) or leased lines.

Modem Negotiations

Have you wondered about all the noise when your modem calls another modem? Those different tones—jokingly referred to as the "mating call"

TABLE 10.7

V.22 Calling V.22

Modem 1 (Transmitter)	Modem 2 (Receiver)
(1) Initiate call (dialing number)	(2) Detects a ring—goes off-hook, waits 2 seconds for billing purposes. (3) Transmit an answer tone of 2100 Hz for 3.3 sec to inform the originator that he has reached a modem and can go to data mode. This also disables echo suppressers so that transmission can be done in both directions. (4) Goes silent for 75 ±20 msec (this separates the answer tone from the signals that follow). (5) Transmit unscrambled binary 1s at 1200 bps(USB1). This is done at 2250 Hz and 2550 Hz
(6) Detects the USB1 signal in 155 ±10 ms. Goes silent for 456 ±3 ms. (7) Transmits double digit 00s and 11s @ 1200 bits (S1) for 100 ±3 ms>If this is a 1200 or V.22 modem, it won't transmit this signal. (8) Transmits scrambled 1s (SB1) @ 1200 bits to even out the bandwidth. This is known as White noise.	(6) Still transmitting (USB1) (7) Still transmitting (USB1). If it detects the (S1), it will then send 100 ms of (S1) signal to the caller to let it know that it is capable of going to 2400 bps. (8) Switches to sending SB1for 500 ms.
	(9) Switches to sending scrambled 1s at 2400 bps for 200 ms. Now it's ready to pass data.
(10) 600 ms after detecting SB1, it will transmit scrambled 1s for 200 ms, then it's ready to pass data.	

of modems—are actually a very standardized series of queries and responses between the two modems so they can determine optimal speeds, data compression, error detection, etc. Two examples of a modem performing a mating call are "V.22bis modem calling a V.22bis modem" (Table 10.7) and "V.32 modem calling a V.32 modem" (Table 10.8). As you can see, these procedures are quite complicated, and you do not need to know them to operate or troubleshoot a modem. I just wanted to give you an idea of what you might hear when a connection is being established.

TABLE 10.8

V.32 Calling V.32

Modem 1 (Transmitter)	Modem 2 (Receiver)
(1) Dials up number to receiver.	(2) Detects ring, goes off hook. Waits 2 seconds. Then transmits V.25 answer tone, but the signal is phase reversed every 450 ms which sounds like a clicking noise. This is done because it is V.32 to let the network know that the modems will do the echo cancellation themselves and to disable the network echo cancellors.
(3)After 1 second of the answer tone he transmits an 1800 Hz tone. This is known as AA in V.32 lingo. This lets the answering modem know that he is talking to another V.32 modem.	(4) If this modem heard the AA signal before the end of the answer tone (3.3 sec), it will try to connect as a 3.2 modem immediately. If it didn't see the AA, it will send a USB1 for 3 seconds, seeing if it can hook up as a V.22bis modem. (5) If there is one response to the USB1 signal, for one reason or another, it will try to reconnect as a V.32 modem by transmitting a 600 Hz signal with a 3000 Hz signal together for 1/2400 sec (64 symbol intervals). This means AC. It then reverses phase to send the signal CA.
(6) When this modem detects the phase reversal from the receiving modem, it reverses its phase, which changes its AA to CC.	(7) When this modem detects the phase reversal after 64 intervals, it reverses its signal to AC. Both modems are able to able to check the propagation time and round trip delays to cancel signal echoes. (8) Both modems then go into half-duplex of training signals to train the adaptive equalizers, test the quality of the phone lines, and agree on the data rate to be used. This modem transmits first from 650 ms to 3525 ms, then goes silent.
(9) This modem responds with a similar signal and leaves on the signal. (11) Both modems respond by sending scrambled binary ones for 128 symbol intervals, and then is ready to pass data.	(10) This modem responds one more time, establishing their data rate. (11) Both modems respond by sending scrambled binary ones for 128 symbol intervals, and then is ready to pass data.

TAPI

In order to allow a program to perform telephone functions such as dialing a number or receiving a call, the program must know how to "talk" like a telephone through the modem. For example, if a program wants to use the modem to call a particular number, it must be able to discern a dial tone before a call is made—and react properly if a dial tone is not present. In early communication software, this was handled by the program directly as there was no support for telephone functions built into DOS or Windows 3.X. This changed with Microsoft's introduction of TAPI (Telephony Application Programmers Interface). TAPI is a set of DLLs (Dynamic Link Libraries) that allow Windows 3.X and Windows 95 to separate programs from the modem. If a programmer wants to write a pro-

Figure 10.23A

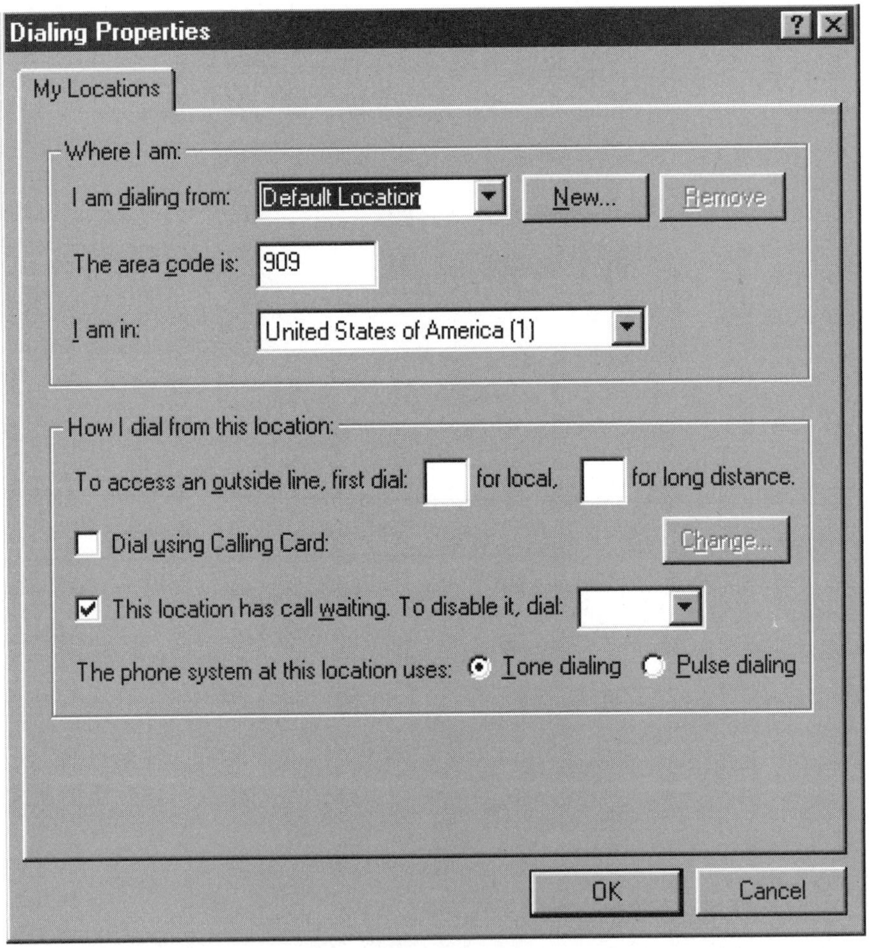

gram that can make a telephone call, they simply perform a call to the appropriate DLL with the phone number and the call is made.

TAPI makes the modem another resource. When a modem is installed, a good TAPI installation (the Modems control in the Control Panel is a good example) will configure the modem type, I/O address and IRQ, local phone number, long distance dialing codes, plus all of the other details needed by TAPI to allow it to use the modem.

Once TAPI is aware of the modem, any program can make calls to the TAPI DLL to handle telephone functions. Yet TAPI goes far beyond simply making telephone calls. A common TAPI use is for answering machines. A TAPI answering machine can link with the existing multimedia functions of Windows 3.X or Windows 95 and allow recording and playback of announcements and messages in standard WAV format. TAPI can allow voice mailboxes and even voice recognition. Finally, TAPI provides the ability to handle faxing, call forwarding, caller ID and paging.

Installation and Troubleshooting

Modems are extremely robust devices. The chances of a modem actually breaking, actually failing at a hardware level, are quite small. The majority of the time, modem problems are actually problems with the COM ports or with the way the communication software talks to the modem.

Set Up and Verify the COM Ports

The number-one reason that modems do not work is COM port and IRQ conflicts. Make sure you install non-conflicting I/O addresses and interrupts. To determine available I/O addresses for DOS and Windows 3.*x*, I use Touchstone's Checkit to verify the available ports (Figure 10.24).

Don't forget that COM3 and COM4 on most modems are preset to IRQ4 and IRQ3, respectively. If COM1 and COM2 are already in use, then they are almost certainly using IRQ3 and IRQ4. Be sure to set the modem's IRQ to something other than IRQ3 or 4. Use IRQ5, 7, or whatever the modem allows you to use (Figure 10.25).

After the COM ports and IRQs are set, make sure the software is aware of the modem. This will be handled differently depending on the type of operating system you are using. In DOS, the communications software itself has some type of utility to set the software to the modem's I/O address and IRQ (Figure 10.26).

In Windows 3.*x*, the modem should be automatically detected by the Windows communication software if it is set to COM1 or COM2. If you

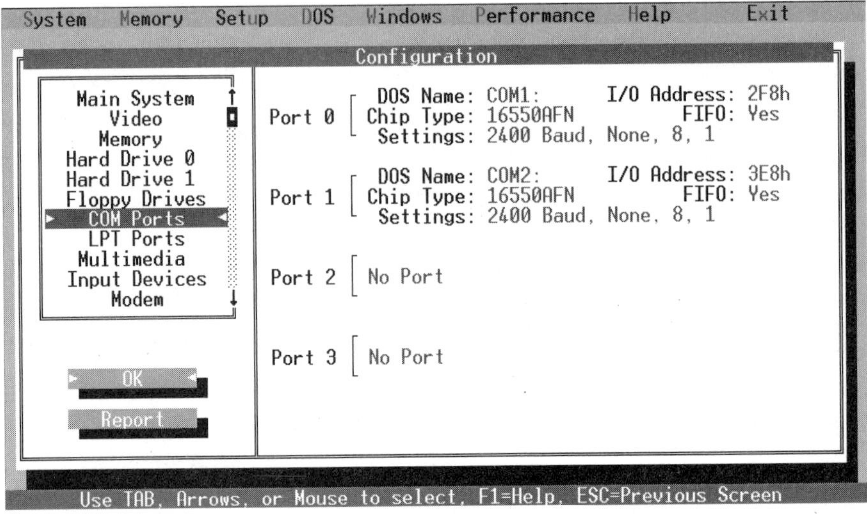

Figure 10.24 Checkit display for port assignments

Figure 10.25 Jumper settings for port and IRQ

Figure 10.26
Display of address assignments

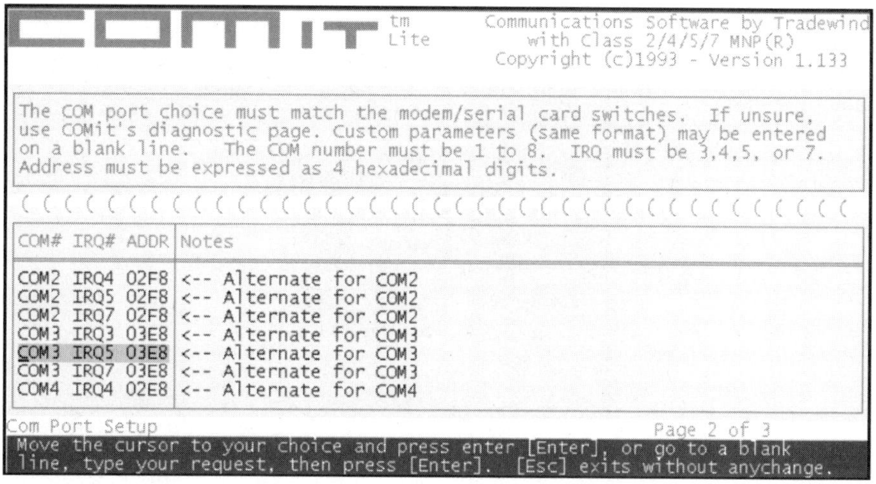

```
COMIT tm                 Communications Software by Tradewind
      Lite                   with Class 2/4/5/7 MNP(R)
                           Copyright (c)1993 - Version 1.133

The COM port choice must match the modem/serial card switches.  If unsure,
use COMit's diagnostic page. Custom parameters (same format) may be entered
on a blank line.   The COM number must be 1 to 8.  IRQ must be 3,4,5, or 7.
Address must be expressed as 4 hexadecimal digits.

COM# IRQ# ADDR Notes

COM2 IRQ4 02F8 <-- Alternate for COM2
COM2 IRQ5 02F8 <-- Alternate for COM2
COM2 IRQ7 02F8 <-- Alternate for COM2
COM3 IRQ3 03E8 <-- Alternate for COM3
COM3 IRQ5 03E8 <-- Alternate for COM3
COM3 IRQ7 03E8 <-- Alternate for COM3
COM4 IRQ4 02E8 <-- Alternate for COM4

Com Port Setup                                      Page 2 of 3
Move the cursor to your choice and press enter [Enter], or go to a blank
line, type your request, then press [Enter].  [Esc] exits without anychange.
```

decide to use COM3 or COM4, or if you decide to use a nonstandard IRQ on any COM port, you must edit the SYSTEM.INI file under the [386Enh] section. Assume that you've set up a modem to COM3 and IRQ5. You must add the following two lines:

```
COM3Irq=5
COM3Base=03E8
```

in order to make sure that Windows 3.*x* knows where the modem is located. If there is any trouble, set all the ports—including COM1 and COM2—in this section by typing:

```
COM1Irq=4
COM1Base=03F8
COM2Irq=3
COM2Base=02F8
COM3Irq=5
COM3Base=03E8
```

Once Windows is aware of the modem, the Windows communication software should find the modem automatically, or allow you to set it within the application (Figure 10.27).

The Windows 95 ability to handle Plug-n-Play modems makes most installations a true no-brainer—just make sure the modem is configured for PnP. Most PnP modems have a jumper to turn the PnP option on or off. If the modem is not PnP, the Add New Hardware Wizard will usually do an excellent job finding your modem (Figure 10.28). Unfortunately, the Add New Hardware Wizard will usually have trouble with uncommon IRQs. After running the Install Wizard, verify the port settings through

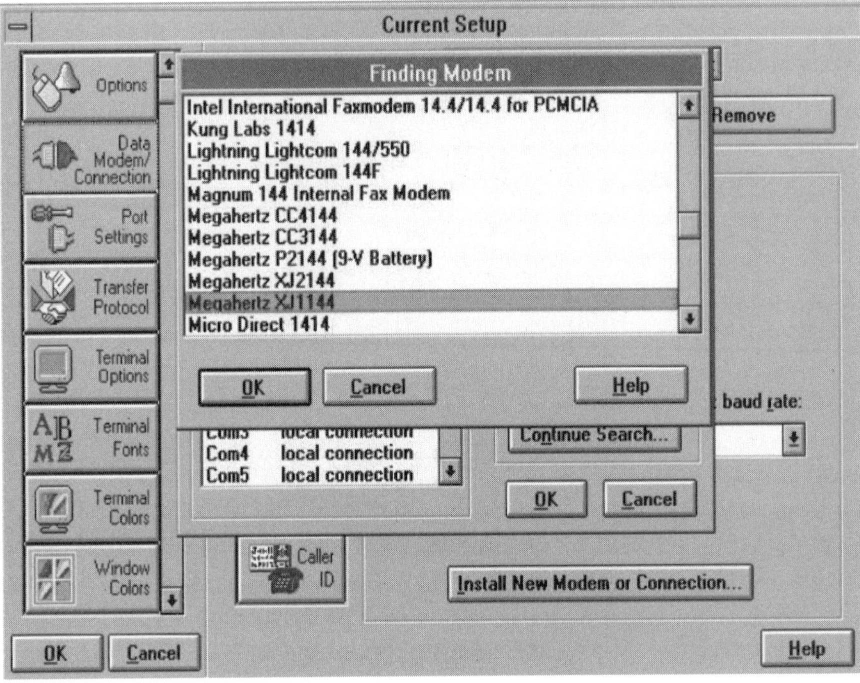

Figure 10.27 Windows 3.X communications program finding a modem

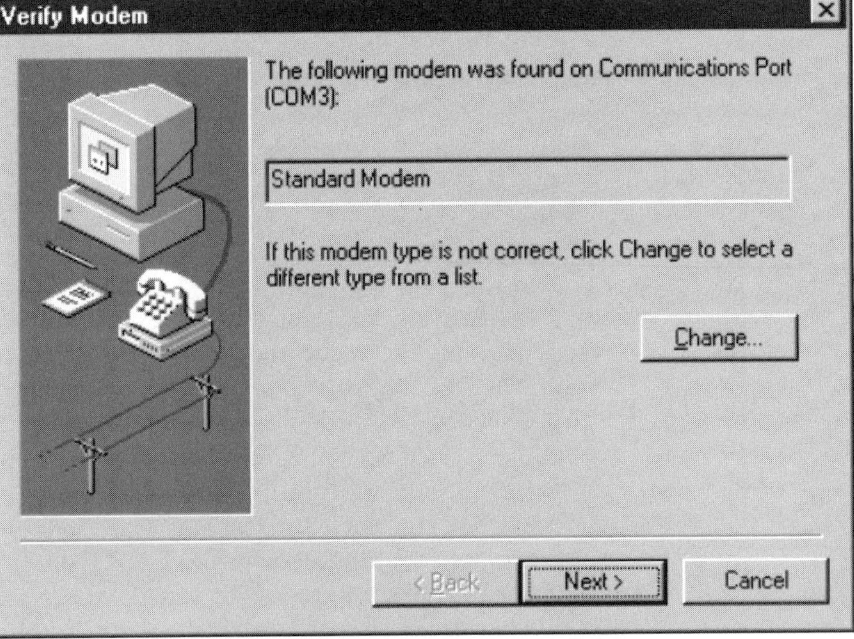

Figure 10.28 Win95 modem setup wizard

the Device Manager. If the settings are incorrect, manually change them and reboot.

Verify the Modem's BIOS

Today's modern modems all have on-board BIOS. Although the name BIOS is used, that is a bit of a misnomer. A better term might be *command set*—the ability to handle different commands from modem drivers or from other modems. This BIOS doesn't take up any DOS memory addresses, so there's no fear of memory-management problems, similar to those with other devices that have true on-board BIOS. This BIOS is usually manifested as a flash ROM on the modem, making it upgradeable through software—very convenient. As anticipated new technologies arise—the latest one being the 56K V.90 standard—modem makers can easily upgrade modems, giving customers confidence to purchase modems in the face of ongoing improvements. Upgrading is quite simple; you download a program from the Internet, AOL, CompuServe, a BBS, or whatever, and then run the program from a DOS prompt (although the actual upgrade process depends on the maker of the modem). The downside is that these can be corrupted quite easily, usually by something as simple as removing and reinserting the modem. There can also be many upgrades to the BIOS, so making sure you have the right version is important. Contact the modem's manufacturer to verify the version.

Set Up the Correct Command Set

Now that the modem's COM port is correct, you must make sure that the communication software knows the type of modem you have, so it will know how to give the correct AT commands.

DOS DOS-based communication software is reaching the end of its useful life. With the demise of ProComm for DOS, there is no longer a "universal" DOS communication software that can be reliably used with any modem. The problem is simply age; as soon as a new V standard comes out, the software becomes less useful. You can use an old copy of ProComm to run a modem, but if the software can only tell the modem to run at 2400 bps, your 28.8-Kbps modem will run only at 2400 bps. Also, DOS programs are bad at having preinstalled setup strings to allow different modems to run, forcing technicians to call manufacturers to manually install proper setup strings. There are still a lot of DOS communication packages available, but they usually come with the modem and are preconfigured to run only with that modem. Reconfiguration is often unsupported or undocumented. I avoid DOS communication programs.

WINDOWS 3.*x* Modern Windows 3.*x* programs are much more versatile. Programs like WinComm have configuration files that, if your modem is not listed, allow you to update it by downloading a free update from the modem manufacturer's Web site or CompuServe forum.

WINDOWS 95 Windows 95 communication programs do not need to know what type of modem you have installed, as this information is handled by Windows. Just make sure that you have the latest INF file for your modem to ensure seamless operation. The INF files that come with Windows 95 are almost certainly unacceptable, so call the manufacturer and check the modem's installation disk for the latest INF files. As a rule, always take a quick trip to the manufacturer's Web site to grab the latest INF file before you install.

If you just can't determine your modem type, guess. Try Hayes Compatible or Standard settings, if available. Try modems that sound like your modem. Look at your modem and see if you have a chipset name, then look for an option based on the chipset, not modem type. If you can't determine a chipset, try "Rockwell." It's very common and fairly generic. You can find one that will work—just keep trying!

When Modems Break

A modem that doesn't work is probably the most frustrating repair problem in the PC world. But by following these steps, you can make the problem much easier (I didn't say *easy*—just *easier*) to repair.

Do You Have a Non-Conflicting COM Port and IRQ?

To find out, I turn to a very powerful shareware program called Modem Doctor. This program is supplied with the accompanying CD-ROM and will query all your COM ports, looking for a modem (Figure 10.29). Modem Doctor is excellent for detecting COM ports and determining whether or not there is a modem at a particular COM port.

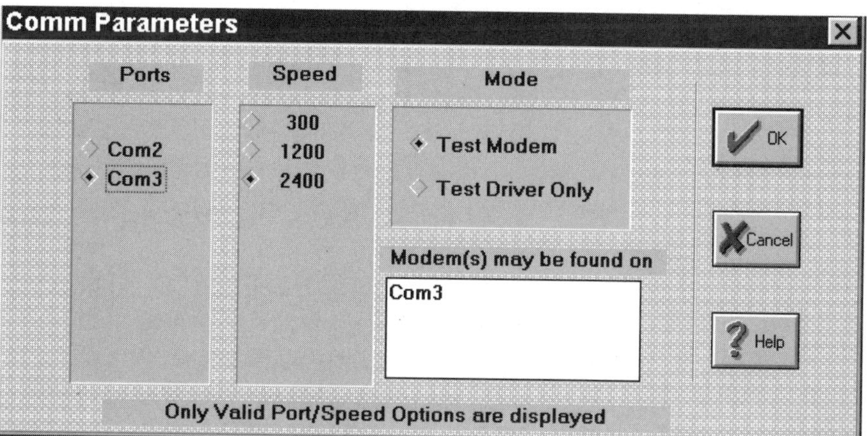

Figure 10.29
Modem Doctor

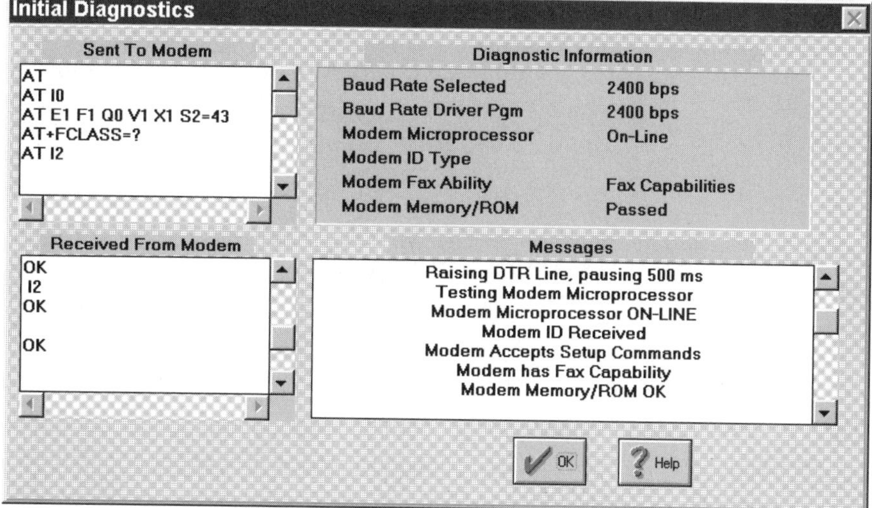

Figure 10.30
A diagnostic display of Modem Doctor

Many technicians make the mistake of not considering a COM port or IRQ conflict unless the modem or some other hardware has just been installed. Do not do that! Many different cards can be changed through software or corrupted files. Assume nothing!

Modem Doctor does far more than just verify COM ports. Many times a technician wants to know, "Is this modem still good?" That is where Modem Doctor shines. Modem Doctor will test your modem completely and give you a complete description of its quality. The one nice thing about modems is that they never get sick; they just die. Modem Doctor will let you know without a doubt if your modem is dead (see Figure 10.30).

If Modem Doctor says your modem is okay, then it's time to look at the software. At this point, you need to zero in on the type of problem.

Modem Doctor is contained on the CD-ROM in the following files: MODEMW10.ZIP for Windows and MODEMD70.ZIP for DOS.

The Software Says There's No Modem

Make sure the modem is looking at the right port, and make sure there's no conflict with another device. Reinstall the modem software and reconfigure to make sure you haven't corrupted a driver. If the modem is Plug-n-Play and you're using Windows 95/98, make sure the Device Manager shows the modem and that the modem is working properly.

The Modem Works Sporadically

Make sure you have the right modem installed or try another modem type. Check the phone lines in the house, or call the phone company and complain about the phone lines.

CHAPTER 11

Video

In this chapter, you will:

- Understand the different components that make video work.
- Explain refresh rates and how they affect monitors.
- Understand the concept of resolution.
- Learn how to fix basic monitor problems.

When the first IBM PC arrived, the choice in monitors was simple. You could choose which color—green or amber—that was it. Today the choices are not nearly as simple. You need to understand features such as dot pitch, resolution, convergence, refresh, interlaced vs. noninterlaced, multisync, pixels, color depth, and saving energy. And what about repairing a broken monitor?

This chapter will explain the basics of how video cards and monitors work. I will discuss what can be repaired, and what requires a more specialized expertise. Make no mistake—the interior of a monitor might appear similar to the interior of a PC because of the printed circuit boards and related components, but that is precisely where the similarity ends. No PC has voltages exceeding 15,000 to 30,000 volts, but most monitors do. So let's get one thing perfectly clear—*opening up a working monitor can be deadly!* Even when the power is disconnected, certain components retain a substantial voltage for an extended period of time. You can inadvertently short one of the components and fry yourself. Plus, monitors emit x-ray radiation. So there are certain aspects of monitor repair that you simply can't do, but I will show you how to safely address the problems you *can* fix.

Video consists of two devices that work as a team to get a picture in front of you: the *video card,* often called the *display adapter,* and the *monitor* (see Figure 11.1). The video card is like two devices on one card. One takes commands from the computer and updates its own on-board RAM, and the other scans RAM and sends the data to the monitor.

Let's separate these two devices for a moment and look at them individually. Having done that, I'll bring them back together as a team so you can understand the many nuances that make video so challenging.

Video Monitor Components

Before you can understand monitors, I'll need to take a moment and explain certain common elements of the monitor itself.

Figure 11.1
Typical video card and monitor

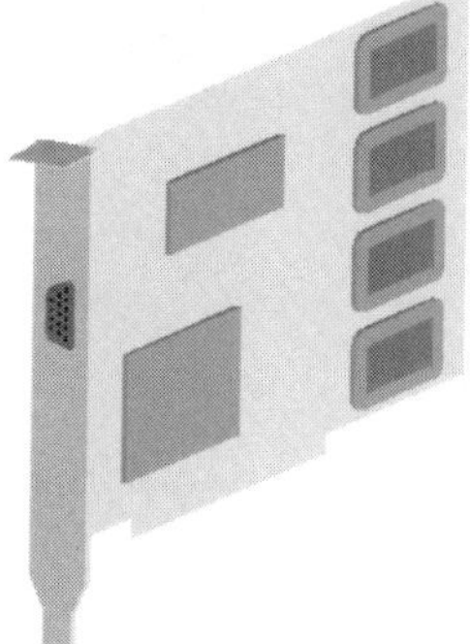

CRT

All monitors have a main vacuum tube called a *cathode ray tube* or *CRT*. One end of this tube is a very slender cylinder and contains three electron guns. The fatter, wide end of the CRT is the display screen with a phosphor coating. When power is applied to one or more of the electron guns, a stream of electrons shoots towards the display end of the CRT (Figure 11.2). Along the way, this stream is subjected to magnetic fields

Figure 11.2
Electron beam in CRT

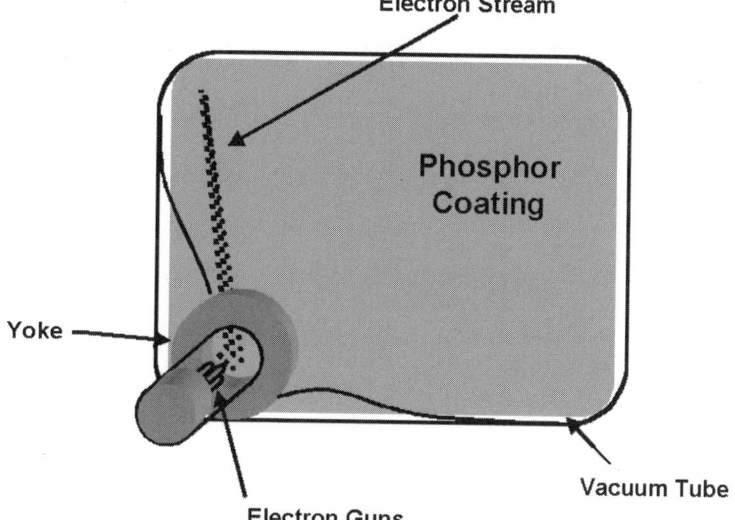

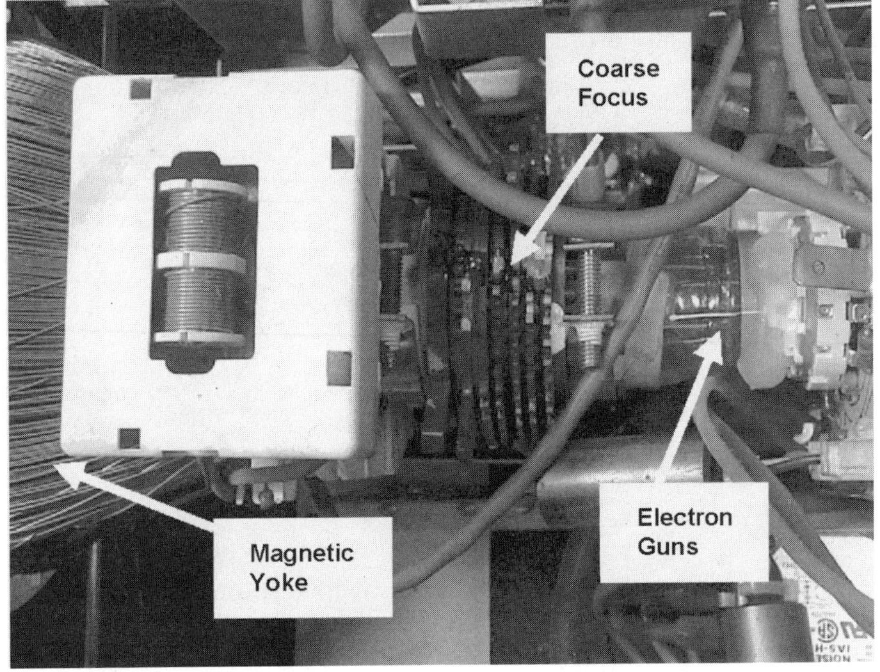

Figure 11.3 Components of electron gun

generated by a ring of electromagnets called a *yoke* that controls the electron beam's point of impact. When the phosphor coating is struck by the electron beam, it releases its energy as visible light. A picture of the electron gun and magnetic yoke assembly is shown in Figure 11.3.

This phosphorous energy release happens very quickly, too quickly for the human eye and brain connection to register. Fortunately for us, the phosphors on the display screen have a quality called *persistence,* which means the phosphors continue to glow after being struck by the electron beam. Too much persistence and the image is smeary; too little and the image appears to flicker.

Refresh Rate

Video data is displayed on the monitor as the electron guns make a series of horizontal sweeps across the display, energizing the appropriate areas of the phosphorous coating (Figure 11.4). The sweeps start at the upper left-hand corner of the monitor and move across and down to the lower right-hand corner. The screen is "painted" only in one direction, then the electron gun turns and retraces its path across the screen, to be ready for the next sweep. These sweeps are called *raster lines.*

The speed at which the electron beam moves across the screen is known as the *horizontal refresh rate* (HRR), as shown in Figure 11.5. The monitor draws a number of lines across the screen, eventually covering the screen with glowing phosphors. The number of lines is *not* fixed, unlike television screens, which all have a fixed number of lines. After the guns reach the lower right-hand corner of the screen, they all turn off and point back to the upper left-hand corner. The amount of time it takes to draw the entire screen and get the electron gun back up to the upper left-hand corner is called the *vertical refresh rate* (VRR), shown in Figure 11.6.

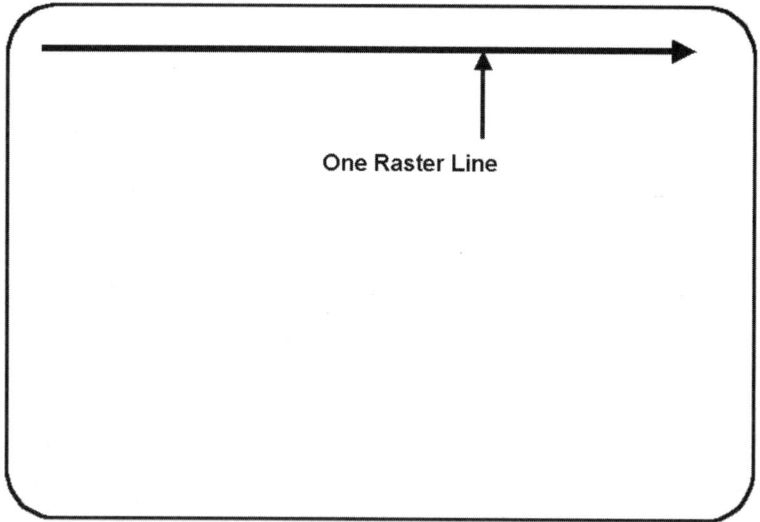

Figure 11.4
Screen traces on monitor

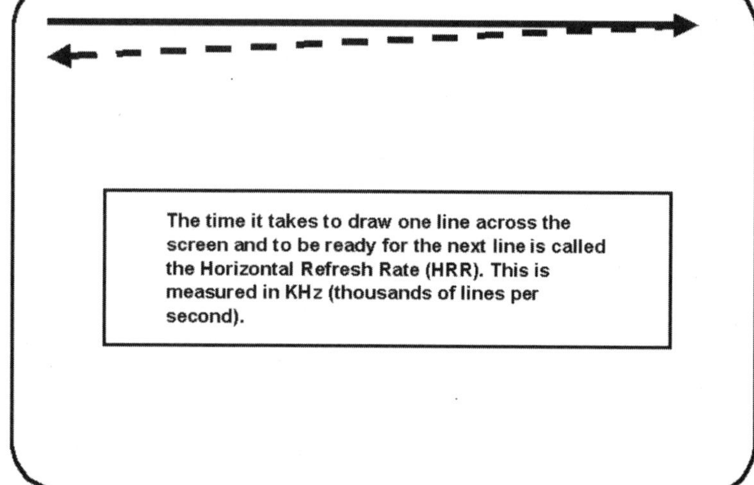

The time it takes to draw one line across the screen and to be ready for the next line is called the Horizontal Refresh Rate (HRR). This is measured in KHz (thousands of lines per second).

Figure 11.5
Horizontal refresh rate

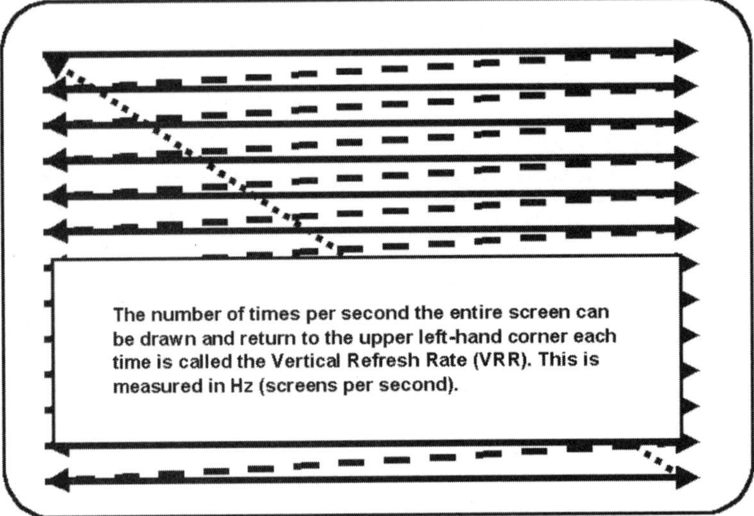

The number of times per second the entire screen can be drawn and return to the upper left-hand corner each time is called the Vertical Refresh Rate (VRR). This is measured in Hz (screens per second).

Figure 11.6
Vertical refresh rate

The action of the beam across the phosphors is called *sweeping,* and the number of times per second the electron beam sweeps across the phosphors is called the *refresh rate.* Too low a refresh rate results in a noticeable flicker, which can cause eye strain and headaches for users. Setting a refresh rate too high, however, can cause a definite distortion of the screen image and can damage or destroy the circuitry of the monitor. Up until the mid-1980s, monitors were limited to a fixed number of refresh rates, which had to be changed manually by users. Around 1986, NEC introduced the first monitor to support automatic selection of multiple refresh rates, called a *multiple-frequency monitor.* NEC coined the term *multisync* to describe its line of multiple-frequency monitors, but multisync refers to any monitor that can handle multiple refresh rates. Virtually all monitors used on PCs today are multisync.

Resolution

Most monitors contain dots of phosphorous or some other light-sensitive compound that will glow either red, green, or blue when an electron gun sweeps over them. Each dot is called a *phosphor.* These phosphors are evenly distributed across the front of the monitor (Figure 11.7).

The CRT has three electron guns: one to hit the red phosphors, one for the blue phosphors, and the last for the green phosphors. It is important to understand that the electron guns do not fire colored light; they simply fire electrons at different intensities, which then make the phosphors glow.

The higher the intensity, the brighter the color. Directly behind the phosphors is the *shadow mask*, a screen that allows only the proper electron gun to light the proper phosphors (Figure 11.8). This prevents, for example, the red electron beam from "bleeding over" and lighting neighboring blue and green dots.

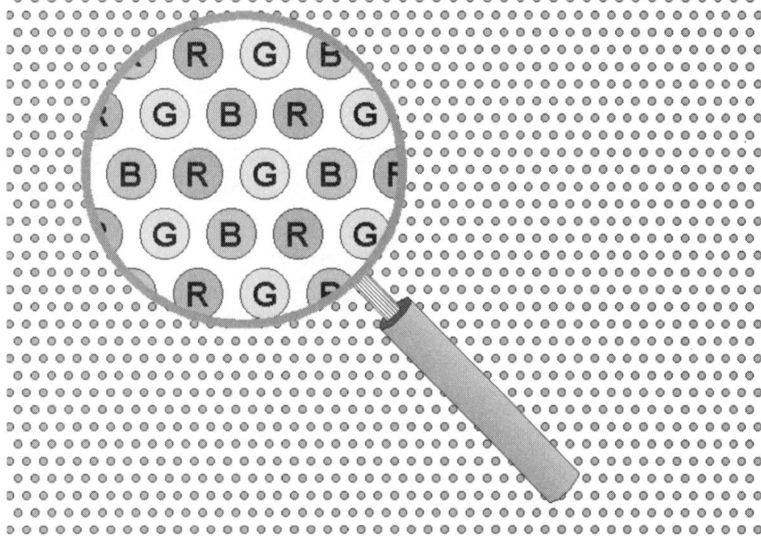

Figure 11.7 Graphic of phosphors

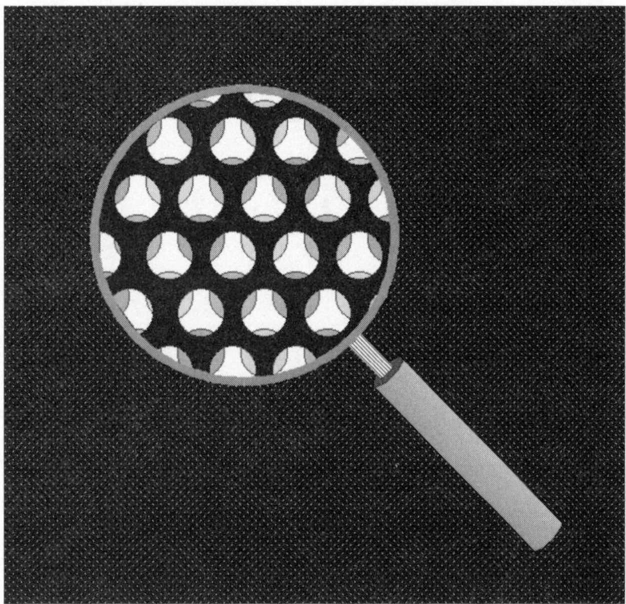

Figure 11.8 Shadow Mask

The electron guns sweep across the phosphors as a group, turning rapidly on and off as they move across the screen. When the group reaches the end of the screen, it moves to the next line. What is crucial to understand here is that turning the guns on and off, combined with moving the guns to new lines, creates a "mosaic" that is the image you see on the screen. The *number of times* the guns turn on and off, combined with the *number of lines* drawn on the screen, determines the number of mosaic pieces used to create the image. These individual "tiles" are called *pixels*, from the term *picture elements*. You can't hold a pixel in your hand; its just the area of phosphors lit at one instant when the group of guns is turned on. The size of pixels can change, depending on the number of times the group of guns is turned on and off and the number of lines drawn.

Monitor resolution is always shown as the number of horizontal pixels times the number of vertical pixels. A resolution of 640 × 480, therefore, indicates a horizontal resolution of 640 pixels and a vertical resolution of 480 pixels. If you multiply the values together, you can see how many pixels are on each screen: 640 × 480 = 307,200 pixels per screen. An example of resolution affecting the pixel size is shown in Figure 11.9.

Some common resolutions are 640 × 480, 800 × 600, 1024 × 768, 1280 × 1024, and 1600 × 1200. Notice that these resolutions match a 4:3 ratio. Most monitors are shaped like television screens, with a 4:3 (width to height) size, so most resolutions are designed to match—or at least be close to—that shape.

Figure 11.9 Resolution vs. pixel size

PIXEL PIXEL PIXEL PIXEL

Lower Resolution

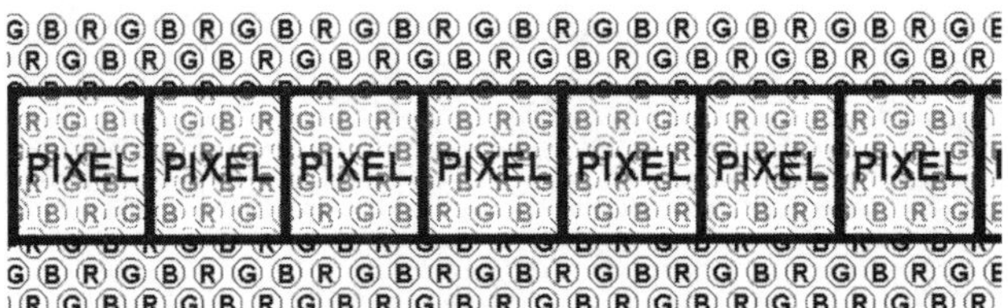

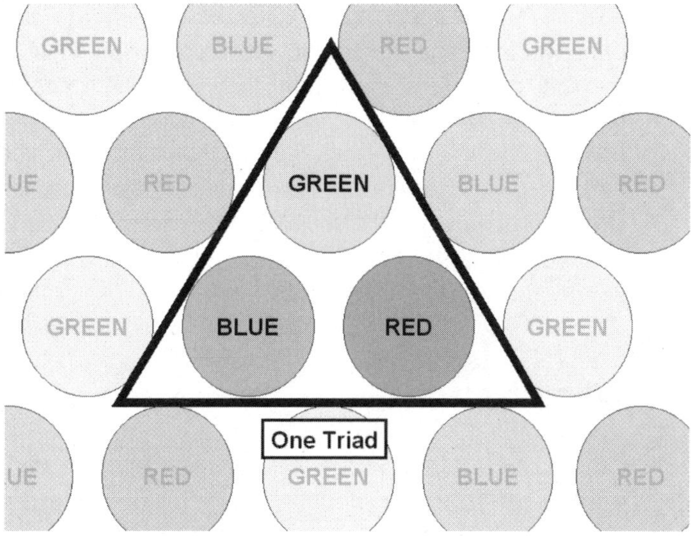

Figure 11.10
One triad

The last important issue is to determine the maximum possible resolution for a monitor. In other words, how small can one pixel be? Well, the answer lies in the phosphors. A pixel must be made up of at least one red, one green, and one blue phosphor to make any color, so the smallest possible pixel will be one group of red, green, and blue phosphors. This group is called a *triad* (Figure 11.10).

To review: each discrete dot of phosphorus is called a *phosphor dot,* each triangle of three phosphors (one red, one green, one blue) is called a *triad,* and each group of dots painted as the electron beam sweeps across the screen is called a *pixel.* Higher resolutions sweep a narrower beam with more pixels per row, and lower resolutions sweep a wider beam with less pixels per row.

As shown previously, the horizontal refresh rate (HRR) defines the speed at which the monitor can draw one line on the screen, while the vertical refresh rate (VRR) defines how many times per second the entire screen is redrawn. These values relate to the number of vertical resolution lines, as follows:

$$\text{HRR} = (\text{VRR}) \times (\text{number of lines}), \text{ so } (\text{number of lines}) = (\text{HRR}) \div (\text{VRR})$$

Given the HRR and VRR, you can determine the maximum number of lines of resolution a monitor can support. For example, given an HRR of 31.5 kHz (kHz = kiloHertz = thousands of cycles/second) and a VRR of 72Hz, what would be the maximum number of lines on the screen? Could you support 640 × 480? Take 31.5 kHz and divide it by 72 Hz: 31,500

÷ 72 = 437 lines. So no, with an HRR of only 31.5 kHz, you would have to either reduce the resolution or reduce the VRR and put up with increased screen flicker. By reducing the VRR to 60 Hz, the formula would be 31,500 ÷ 60 = 525 lines. Now your monitor could support 640 × 480 resolution.

Alternately, you could increase the HRR from 31.5 kHz to a value that allows 480 lines at a VRR of 72 Hz. If you used an HRR of 37.9 kHz and divided it by 72, you would have a maximum line value of 526, which would allow a 640 × 480 resolution.

Dot Pitch

The resolution of a monitor is defined by the maximum amount of detail the monitor can render. This resolution is ultimately limited by the dot pitch of the monitor. The *dot pitch* defines the diagonal distance between phosphorous dots of the same color, and is measured in millimeters. Because a lower dot pitch means more dots on the screen, it usually produces a sharper, more defined image. See Figure 11.11a. Dot pitch works in tandem with the maximum number of lines the monitor can support, to determine the greatest working resolution of the monitor. It might be possible to place an image at 1600 × 1200 on a 15-inch monitor with a dot pitch of .31 mm, but it would not be very readable.

The dot pitch can range from as high as .39 mm to as low as .25 mm. For most Windows-based applications on a 15-inch monitor, .31 mm is the maximum usable pitch. For most CAD/CAM applications, the maximum pitch is around .26 to .28 mm. Note: when comparing advertised prices, make a note of the monitor's dot pitch in the ad. Watch out for lower-priced monitors with an unacceptably high .39-mm dot pitch. By comparison, a mid-priced television has a dot pitch of around .35 mm.

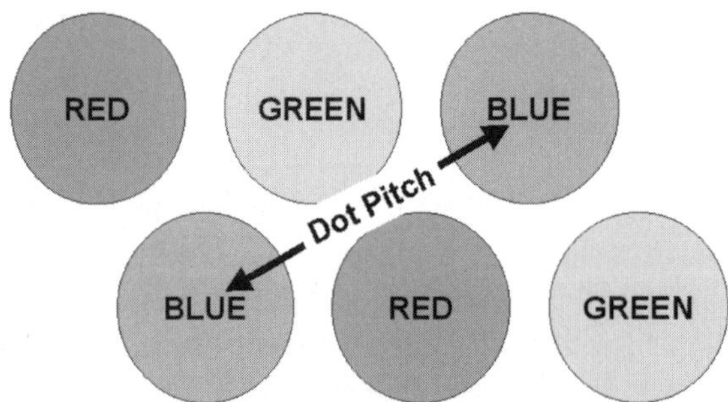

Figure 11.11a Measuring dot pitch

Figure 11.11b
Interlacing

Interlacing

Two Sweeps, One Screen

Interlacing

To keep costs down, some low-end monitors are available that produce interlaced images. This means that the monitor sweeps or refreshes alternate lines of pixels on the display. In other words, it takes two sweeps through the screen to make one image. In its first pass, the monitor covers all the odd lines, and on the next pass it covers the even lines (Figure 11.11b). Interlacing allows a low-end monitor to support faster refresh rates by giving it twice as much time to make a screen. But interlacing depends on the ability of the eye and brain to combine the two separate sets of lines into one stable image. Interlacing is another way of creating eyestrain and headaches, and should be avoided.

Bandwidth

Bandwidth is given in MegaHertz (MHz) and is the maximum number of times the electron gun can be turned on and off—in essence how fast can the monitor put an image on the screen. MegaHertz is millions of cycles per second, and is used because the number of on and off cycles is so large. A typical value for a high-resolution 17-inch color monitor would be around 100 MHz, which means that the electron beam can be turned on and off 100 million times per second. The value for a monitor's bandwidth will determine the maximum vertical refresh rate, as follows:

$$\text{maximum VRR} = \text{bandwidth} \div \text{pixels per page}$$

For example, what is the maximum vertical refresh rate (VRR) that a 17-inch monitor with bandwidth of 100 MHz and a resolution of 1024 × 768 can support? The answer is:

$$\text{maximum VRR} = 100{,}000{,}000 \div (1024 \times 768) = 127 \text{ Hz}$$

if the video card can go that high. At a resolution of 1200 × 1024, the vertical refresh would be:

$$100{,}000{,}000 \div (1200 \times 1024) = 81 \text{ Hz}$$

If you had a monitor with a bandwidth of only 75 MHz, the maximum vertical refresh rate (VRR) at a 1200 × 1024 resolution would be only 61 Hz.

Power Conservation

Approximately half the power required to run a desktop PC is consumed by the monitor. Monitors that meet the Video Electronics Standards Association (VESA) specification for display power-management signaling (DPMS) can reduce monitor power consumption by roughly 75 percent. This is accomplished by reducing or eliminating the signals sent by the video card to the monitor during idle periods. By eliminating these pulses, the monitor essentially takes catnaps. The advantage over simply shutting the monitor off is in the time it takes to restore the display. A typical monitor consumes in the neighborhood of 100 watts. During a catnap or power-down mode, the energy consumption is reduced to below 25 watts, while allowing the screen to return to use in less than 10 seconds. Full shutoff is accomplished by eliminating all clocking pulses to the monitor. While this reduces power consumption to below 15 watts, it also requires anywhere from 15 to 30 seconds to restore a usable display. Table 11.1 shows the various DPMS options.

Turning off the monitor with the power switch is the most basic form of power management. The downside to this is the wear and tear on the CRT. The CRT is the most expensive component of a monitor, and one of the most damaging things to a CRT is to turn it on and off frequently. When using a non-DPMS monitor or video card, it is best to turn the monitor on once during the day, and then turn it off only when you finished for the day. This on-off cycle must be balanced against the life of the

TABLE 11.1

DPMS Options

Monitor Status	Horz. Signal	Vert. Signal	Display State	DPMS Requirement	Power Savings	Recovery Time
On	Pulses	Pulses	Active	Mandatory	None	N/A
Stand-by	No Pulses	Pulses	Inactive	Optional	Fair	Short
Suspend	Pulses	No Pulses	Inactive	Mandatory	Good	Long
Off	No Pulses	No Pulses	Inactive	Mandatory	Excellent	Longest

CRT display phosphors. The typical monitor will lose about half its original brightness after roughly 10,000 to 15,000 hours of display time. Leaving the monitor on all the time will bring a noticeable decrease in brightness in just over a year (8,766 hours). The only way around this is enabling the DPMS features of the monitor or taking care to turn the monitor off.

Some monitors employ a form of power management known as *screen blanking*. Once the video signal from the video card ceases or the video cable comes loose, the monitor goes into a suspension mode. Technically speaking, this is not a DPMS mode, but it still reduces wear on the CRT while saving power. Before panicking over a "dead" display, make sure the cable is secure on both ends.

Adjusting the Image

Monitor adjustments range from the simplest—brightness and contrast—to the more sophisticated—pin cushioning and trapezoidal adjustments. For anything more than a simple gross adjustment of image appearance, you must have a program that can produce an image suitable for calibrating the monitor. An example of a calibrated image is shown in Figure 11.12a.

You'd use this particular image to adjust the aspect ratio of the display. An image with improper aspect would display the circles as ovals and the squares as rectangles. Usually the only possible adjustment is the height and width controls on the exterior of the monitor. Additional, finer adjustments require a trip inside the monitor.

As shipped, most monitors do not produce an image out to the limits of the screen because of poor convergence at the outer display edges. *Convergence* defines how closely the three colors can converge at a single point on the display. At the point of convergence, the three colors will combine to form a single white dot. With misconvergence, there will be a noticeable halo of one or more colors around the outside of the white point. The farther away from the center of the screen, the more likely the chance for mis-

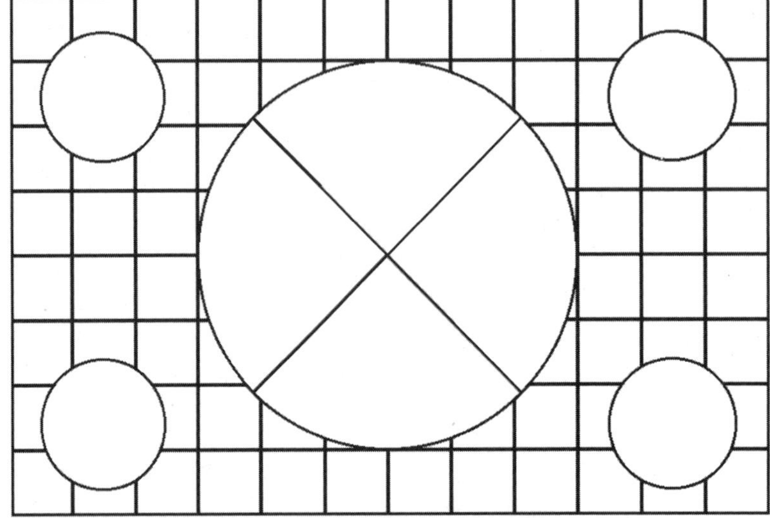

Figure 11.12a Example of aspect ratio calibration screen

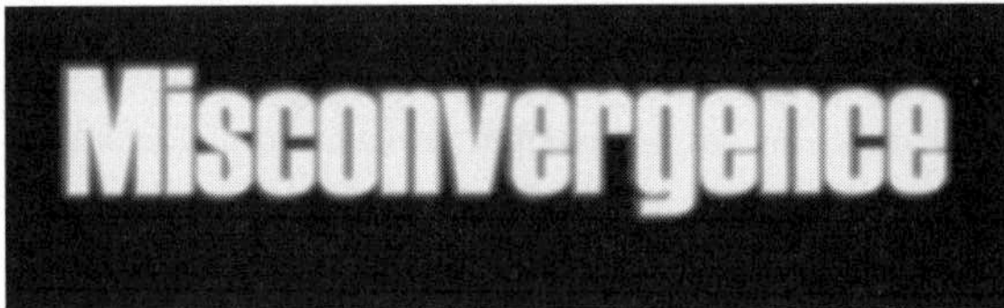

Figure 11.12b Example of misconvergence

convergence (Figure 11.12b). Low-end monitors are especially susceptible to this problem. While adjusting the convergence of a monitor is not difficult, it does require getting inside the monitor case and having a copy of the schematic, which shows the location of the variable resistors. For this reason, it is a good idea to leave this adjustment to a trained specialist.

Today's monitors have a large number of possible adjustments. They can be individual knobs or, in this case, an "up", "down", "minus," and "plus" key that allow users to manipulate the pop-up menu on the screen (Figure 11.13). The effect of each control is obvious and straightforward and, with the possible exception of the keystone and pincushion controls, can be found on almost all 15-inch color monitors today. Many 15-inch and virtually all 17-inch monitors will offer pincushion and keystone adjustments, which are often necessary when using higher resolutions combined with higher refresh rates. A higher refresh rate tends to pinch an image in the middle. These two controls work in tandem to allow users to properly "square up" the image. See the video drivers section in this chapter.

One other feature of 17-inch and larger monitors is the *degaussing* button. When the degaussing circuit is used, an alternating current is sent through a coil of wire surrounding the CRT, and this current generates

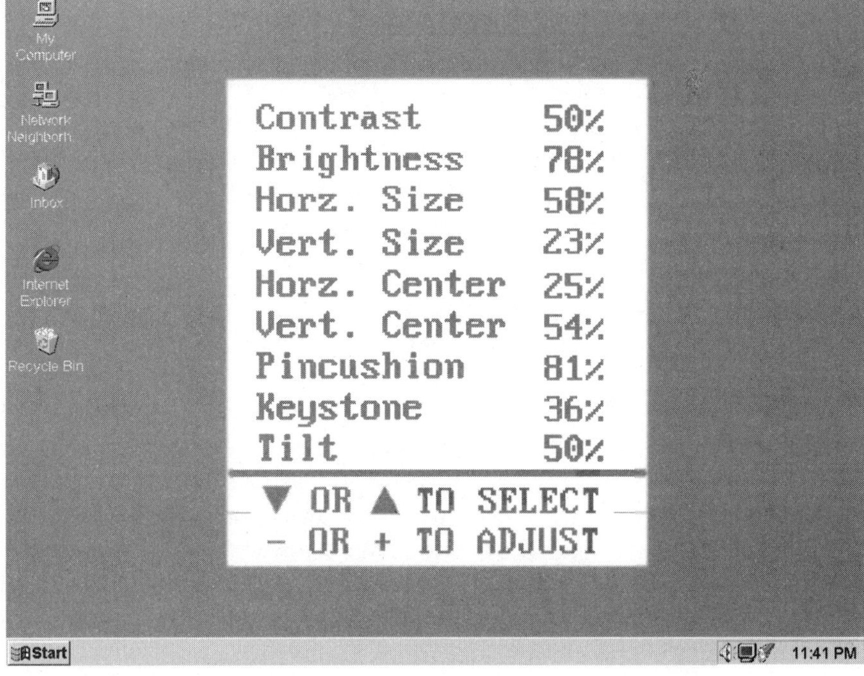

Figure 11.13 Common user controls on pop-up menus

an alternating magnetic field. The purpose of this field is to demagnetize the shadow mask, which over time can pick up a weak magnetic charge that can interfere with the focus of the electron beams. Degaussing randomizes this magnetic charge and keeps the colors purer and the dots more precisely defined.

Troubleshooting Monitors

First, keep your monitor clean. An occasional cleaning with a clean cloth and antistatic spray will do wonders for keeping down dust. Because of the inherent dangers of the high-frequency and high-voltage power required by monitors, and because proper adjustment requires specialized training, this section will concentrate on giving a support person the information necessary to decide whether or not a trouble call is warranted. Virtually no monitor manufacturers make schematics of their monitors available to the public because of liability issues regarding possible electrocution. To simplify troubleshooting, look at the process as two separate parts: external and internal adjustments.

External Adjustments

The external controls were shown previously in the chapter. They provide users with the opportunity to fine-tune the monitor's image for brightness and contrast. Some monitors allow you to fine-tune the image size and position; more sophisticated monitors allow you to fine-tune the geometric proportions to keep the image square.

Internal Adjustments

These controls are sometimes accessible without having to open the monitor. If this is the case, then the only thing to worry about is causing a bigger problem by tweaking the wrong control. The accessible controls are usually related to the focus of the onscreen image and the overall picture brightness. If the image seems a little blurry, you might be able to adjust the focus with this control. The brightness control might also provide a way of increasing image brightness in the event the front-panel brightness control is already set to maximum.

Controls that require you to remove the monitor case to make adjustments include those for convergence, gain for each of the color guns, and sometimes the focus control. Before proceeding further, however, refer to Figure 11.14.

A technician with either informal or formal training in component-level repair can usually figure out which controls do what. Balance the cost of repairing the monitor against the cost of death or serious injury—is it worth it? Finally, before making adjustments to the display image, especially with the internal controls, give the monitor at least 15 to 30 minutes of warm-up time. This is necessary for both the components on the printed circuit boards and for the CRT itself. The high-voltage anode on the CRT is shown in Figure 11.15, in relation to the yoke.

265V ~
This product includes critical mechanical and electrical parts which are essential for x-radiation safety. For continued safety replace critical components indicated in the service manual only with exact replacement parts given in the parts list. Operating high voltage for this product is 25kV at minimum brightness. Refer to service manual for measurement procedures and proper service adjustments.

Figure 11.14 Hey! That's 25,000 volts! BE CAREFUL!

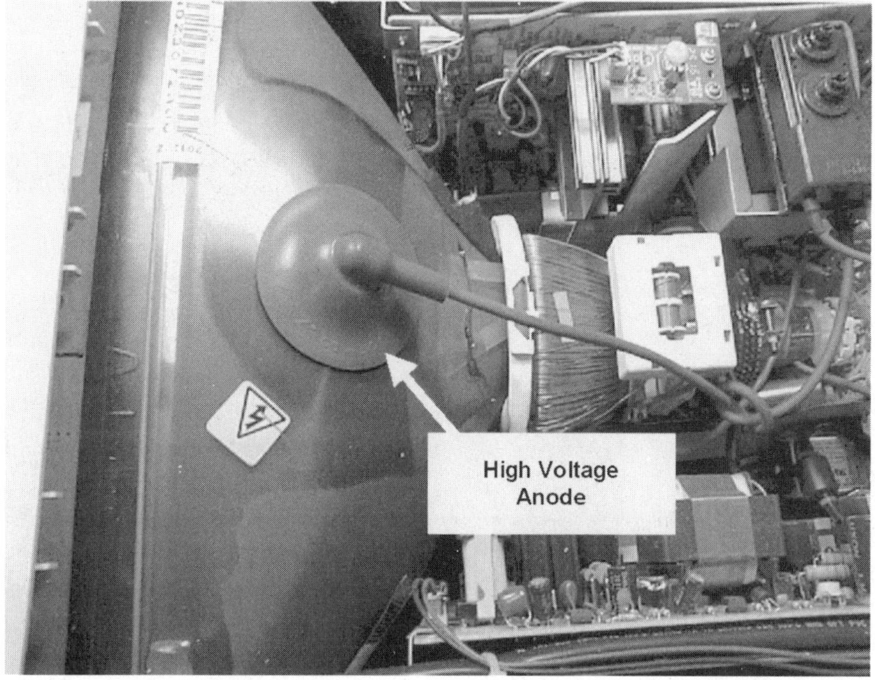

Figure 11.15
High voltage anode

Common Problems

- Ghosting, streaking, and/or fuzzy vertical edges: check the cable connections and the cable itself.
- One color is missing: check cables and, if present, check user controls for that color. If the color adjustment is already "maxed out," the monitor will require internal service.
- Brightness: as monitors age, they lose brightness. If the user-adjustable control is at maximum, the monitor will require internal adjustment. This is a good argument for power-management functions. *Don't* leave the monitor on with a picture on it, as this will reduce monitor life significantly. *Do* use the power-management options in Windows or your BIOS setup, or use the power switch.
- Focus adjustments might be external, but they are usually on the inside somewhere close to the flyback transformer. This is the transformer that provides high voltages to the CRT, so leave it alone. A picture of a typical flyback transformer is shown in Figure 11.16.

Figure 11.16 Typical flyback transformer & controls

- Hissing or sparking sounds are often indicative of an insulation rupture on the flyback transformer. This sound is usually accompanied by the smell of ozone. If your monitor has these symptoms, it definitely needs a qualified technician. Having replaced a flyback transformer once myself, I can say it is not worth the hassle and potential loss of life and limb.
- There are big color blotches on the display. This is an easy and cheap repair. Find the degaussing button and use it. If your monitor doesn't have a degaussing button, you can purchase a special tool called a *degaussing coil* at any electronics store.
- Bird-like chirping sounds occurring at regular intervals usually indicate a problem with the power supply.
- Say you got a good deal on a used 17-inch monitor, but the display is kind of dark, even though you have the brightness turned up all the way. This points to a dying CRT. So how about a CRT replacement? Forget it. Even if the monitor was free, it just isn't worth it, as a replacement tube runs in the hundreds of dollars. Nobody ever sold a monitor because it was too bright and too sharp. Save your money and buy a new monitor.

- The monitor displays only a single vertical line. This is probably a problem between the main circuit board and the yoke—or a blown yoke coil. This definitely requires a service call.
- The monitor displays only a single horizontal line. This is just like the previous one—take it in.
- A single white dot means the high-voltage flyback transformer is most likely shot. Take it in.

And here is a list of a few last dos and don'ts:

- Do keep the screen clean.
- Do keep the cables tightened.
- Do use quality cabling.
- Do use power-management features if available.
- Don't block the ventilation slots on the monitor.
- Don't use a refresh rate higher than recommended by the manufacturer.
- Don't leave the monitor on all the time, even with a screen saver.
- Don't place magnetic objects such as unshielded speakers close to the monitor. (This can cause color problems at best and could permanently magnetize the shadow mask at worst.)
- Be careful about disposing a dead monitor. Many local governments have laws regarding their safe disposal. Be sure to check with your local waste disposal entity or your company to verify proper disposal methods.

Video Cards

The video card, or display adapter, is the brain of the PC's video (see Figure 11.17). The video card is composed of two major pieces: the video RAM and the video processor circuitry. The video RAM is where the video image is stored. On the first video cards, this RAM was just good old DRAM, just like the RAM on the motherboard. The video processing circuitry takes the information on the video RAM and shoots it out to the monitor.

The trick to understanding video cards is to appreciate the beginnings and the evolution of video. Video output to computers has been around long before PCs were created. At the time PCs became popular, video was almost exclusively text-based. By text, I mean that the only image the video card could place on the monitor was one of the 256 ASCII charac-

Figure 11.17
Typical video card

ters. These characters were made up of patterns of pixels that were stored in the system BIOS. When a program wanted to make a character, it talked to DOS or to the BIOS, which stored the image of that character onto the video memory. The character then appeared on the screen.

The beauty of text video cards was that they were simple to use and cheap to make. The simplicity was based on the fact that there were only 256 characters, and there were no color choices—just monochrome text (Figure 11.18). You could, however, choose to make the character bright, dim, normal, underlined, or blinking. It was easy to position the characters, as there was space on the screen for only 80 characters per line and 24 lines.

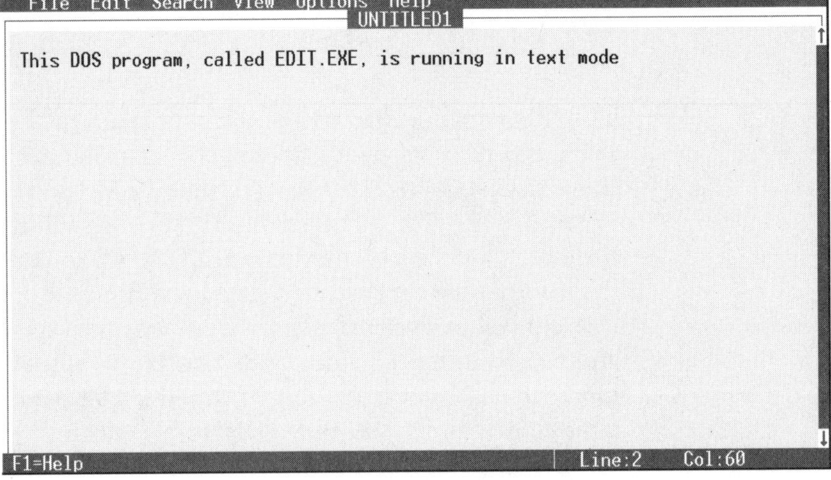

Figure 11.18
Text mode

Long ago, RAM was very expensive, so video-card makers were interested in using the absolute least amount of RAM possible. Making a monochrome text video card was a great way to keep down RAM costs. Let's consider this for a minute. First, the video RAM is where the contents of the screen are located. You need enough video RAM to hold all the necessary information for a completely full screen. Each ASCII character needs eight bits (by definition), so a monitor with 80 characters/line and 24 lines will need:

$$\frac{80 \text{ characters}}{\text{line} \times 24 \text{ lines}} = 1920 \text{ characters}$$

$$\frac{1920 \text{ characters} \times 8 \text{ bits}}{\text{characters}} = 15{,}360 \text{ bits or } 1920 \text{ bytes}$$

The video card would need less than 2000 bytes of memory, which isn't much, not even in 1981 when the PC first came out. Now be warned that I'm glossing over a few things—like where you store the information about underline, blinking, etc. The bottom line is that the tiny amount of necessary RAM kept monochrome text video cards cheap.

Very early on in the life of PCs, a new type of video, called a *graphics video card*, was invented. It was quite similar to a text card, but whereas the text card was limited to the 256 ASCII characters, a graphics video card allowed programs to turn any pixel on the screen on or off. It was still monochrome, but programs could access any individual pixel, allowing much more creative control of the screen. Of course, it took more video RAM. The first graphics cards ran at 320 × 200 pixels. One bit was needed for each pixel (on or off), so:

$$320 \times 200 = 64{,}000 \text{ bits or } 8000 \text{ bytes}$$

which is a lot more than what was needed for text, but it was still a pretty low amount of RAM. As resolutions increased, however, the amount of video RAM needed to store this information also increased.

Once monochrome video was invented, it was a relatively easy step to move into color for both text and graphics video cards. The only question was how to store color information for each character (text cards) or pixel (graphics cards). This was easy—just set aside a few more bits for each pixel or character. So now the question was "How many bits do you set aside?" Well, that depends on how many colors you want. The first color graphics video cards were limited to only four colors, and set aside only a few bits per pixel. Basically, the number of colors determines the number of bits. For example, if you wanted four colors, you'd need 22 bits (four bits per pixel). Then you could do something like this:

00 = black
01 = cyan (blue)
10 = magenta (reddish pink)
11 = white

So if you set aside two bits, you could get four colors. If you want 16 colors, you'd set aside four bits, which would make 16 different combinations. There are no common color depths for text beyond 16 colors, so let's start thinking in terms of graphics mode and pixels. To get 256 colors, each pixel would have to be represented with eight bits. In PCs, the number of colors is always a power of 2: 4, 16, 256, 64K, etc. Notice that as more colors are added, more video RAM is needed to store the information. Here are the most common color depths and the number of bits necessary to store the color information per pixel:

2 colors = 1 bit (mono)
4 colors = 2 bits
16 colors = 4 bits
256 colors = 8 bits
64K colors = 16 bits
16MB colors = 24 bits

Most technicians won't say things like "My video card can show 16 megabytes of colors." Instead, they'd say "I have a 24-bit card." Talk in terms of bits, not colors. It is assumed that you know the number of colors for any color depth.

Modes

Based on what you know so far, it would seem as though there were four different types of video cards: monochrome text, color text, monochrome graphics, and color graphics. Any PC might want to do more than one of these; you might want to start with a text mode and then switch into color graphics. So what are you going to do—keep two video cards in the PC and then switch the cable? Of course not. Instead, one video card can be all of the previously defined video cards in one. A modern video card can act as more than one type of card, displaying text or graphics, mono-

TABLE 11.2

MDA Modes

Mode	Type	Colors	Resolution/Characters
07h	Text	Mono	80 × 25

chrome or color, as needed. Each different level of operation is called a *mode*. First IBM and then the Video Electronics Standard Association (VESA) defined specific, uniform video modes for video cards. These video modes are given a hexadecimal value. For example, video mode 06h is defined as monochrome graphics at 640 × 200 pixels. As different types of video cards are discussed in the next few sections, I will list the modes associated with each type.

MDA

The first video card ever produced with the IBM PC was the text-only *monochrome display adapter* (MDA). An MDA is perfectly fine for DOS-based word-processing and spreadsheet programs. The MDA has a 9-pin female socket and is found only in the most ancient of PCs and landfills. Table 11.2 lists the available MDA modes.

CGA

The IBM PC offered the first-generation color monitor, the *color graphics adapter* (CGA) card, which supports colors but does so at a price: resolution. A four-color screen offered only 320 × 200 resolution. It was possible to support 640 × 200 resolution, but the number of available colors dropped to only two. Like its less-gifted older sibling, it also uses a 9-pin male connector. Refer to Table 11.3 for CGA's modes.

TABLE 11.3

CGA Modes

Mode	Type	Colors	Resolution/Characters
00h,01h	Text	16	40 × 25
02h,03h	Text	16	80 × 25
04h,05h	Graphics	4	320 × 200
06h	Graphics	2	640 × 200

TABLE 11.4

EGA Modes

Mode	Type	Colors	Resolution/Characters
00h,01h	Text	16	40 × 25
02h,03h	Text	16	80 × 25
07h	Text	Mono	80 × 25
0Dh	Graphics	16	320 × 200
0Eh	Graphics	16	640 × 200
0Fh	Graphics	4	640 × 350
10h	Graphics	16	640 × 350

EGA

The *enhanced graphics adapter* (EGA) was introduced in late 1984 as an improvement on the CGA standard (see Table 11.4). It could support a resolution of up to 640 × 350 with 16 colors in text mode, or 640 × 200 and two colors in graphics mode. Unfortunately, there were often problems with programs not working properly with an EGA card since the EGA standard was not fully backwards-compatible with CGA and MDA. EGA also used a nine-pin adapter, but also had a distinct DIP switch visible from the outside.

PGA

The *professional graphics adapter* (PGA) card was part of a package developed by IBM. Costing over $4000 and taking three ISA slots when fully configured, this system offered 3-D rotation and 60 frame/second animation. It was aimed at the engineering and scientific communities, but was dropped by IBM with the introduction of VGA in 1987. See Table 11.5.

VGA

With the introduction of the PS/2, IBM also introduced the *video graphics array* (VGA) standard (Table 11.6). This new standard offered 16 colors at a resolution of 640 × 480 pixels. One of the ways that VGA was able to offer more colors was by using an analog video signal instead of a digital one, as was the case prior to the VGA standard. A digital signal is either all on or all off. By using an analog signal, the VGA standard is able to provide 64 distinct levels for each color, providing 64^3 or 262,144 possible colors, although only 16 or 256 can be seen at a time. For most purposes, 640 × 480 and 16 colors defines VGA mode. This is typically the display resolution and color depth referred to on many software packages as a minimum display requirement.

TABLE 11.5

PGA Modes

Mode	Type	Colors	Resolution/Characters
00h,01h	Text	16	40 × 25
02h,03h	Text	16	80 × 25
04h,05h	Graphics	4	320 × 200
06h	Graphics	2	640 × 200
Special PGA only	Graphics	256	640 × 480

TABLE 11.6

VGA Modes

Mode	Type	Colors	Resolution/Characters
00h,01h	Text	16	40 × 25
02h,03h	Text	16	80 × 25
04h,05h	Graphics	4	320 × 200
06h	Graphics	2	640 × 200
07h	Text	Mono	80 × 25
0Dh	Graphics	16	320 × 200
0Eh	Graphics	16	640 × 200
0Fh	Graphics	4	640 × 350
10h	Graphics	16	640 × 350
11h	Graphics	2	640 × 480
12h	Graphics	16	640 × 480
13h	Graphics	256	320 × 200

TABLE 11.7

Some Simple Non-Standard Modes

Mode	Resolution/Characters	Colors	Maker
2Eh	256	640 × 480	Tseng
53h	256	640 × 480	Oak Tech
30h	256	640 × 480	Everex
5Fh	256	640 × 480	Paradise
67h	256	640 × 480	Video 7

SVGA

For years, *super video graphics array* was a lot like SCSI-1: more opinion than an established standard. Any video-card maker who made a video card with a resolution greater than 640 × 480 and 16 colors called themselves SGVA. Typically, the minimum requirement for SVGA compatibility is 640 × 480 and 256 colors. For many years, the lack of an SVGA standard created serious confusion. One manifestation of this confusion was the emergence of nonstandard modes, in essence extensions to the VGA modes (see Table 11.7). Each video-card maker would define their own modes, even for identical resolution and color depths.

The Video Electronic Standards Association has since established standards for SVGA resolutions, color depth, and video signal timings. Super VGA cards that follow the VESA standard are labeled VESA-compliant, and all video cards are VESA-compliant today (Table 11.8).

TABLE 11.8

Most Common SVGA Modes

Mode	Type	Colors	Resolution/Characters
100h	Graphics	256	640 × 400
101h	Graphics	256	640 × 480
102h	Graphics	16	800 × 600
103h	Graphics	256	800 × 600
104h	Graphics	16	1024 × 768
105h	Graphics	256	1024 × 768
106h	Graphics	16	1280 × 1024
107h	Graphics	256	1280 × 1024

TABLE 11.8

Most Common SVGA Modes (Continued)

Mode	Type	Colors	Resolution/Characters
108h	Text	16	80 × 60
109h	Text	16	132 × 25
10Ah	Text	16	132 × 43
10BH	Text	16	132 × 50
10Ch	Text	16	132 × 60
10Dh	Graphics	32K	320 × 200
10Eh	Graphics	64K	320 × 200
10Fh	Graphics	16.7M	320 × 200
110h	Graphics	32K	640 × 480
111h	Graphics	64K	640 × 480
112h	Graphics	16.7M	640 × 480
113h	Graphics	32K	800 × 600
114h	Graphics	64K	800 × 600
115h	Graphics	16.7M	800 × 600
116h	Graphics	32K	1024 × 768
117h	Graphics	64K	1024 × 768
118h	Graphics	16.7M	1024 × 768
119h	Graphics	32K	1280 × 1024
11Ah	Graphics	64K	1280 × 1024
11Bh	Graphics	16.7M	1280 × 1024

Resolution, Color Depth, and Memory Requirements

To determine the amount of video memory required at a given resolution and color depth, multiply the resolution (800 × 600) by the number of bytes of color depth. From the chapter on RAM, you know that memory on a PC is always in *byte*-sized units. Color depth on a 24-bit video card is referred to in *bits.* You know this is three bytes, so the equation is now 800

× 600 × 3 for the memory requirement in bytes. To convert this to megabytes, divide the result by 1,048,576:

$$800 \times 600 = 480{,}000 \text{ pixels per screen}$$
$$480{,}000 \times 3 = 1{,}440{,}000 \text{ bits of memory per screen}$$
$$1{,}440{,}000 \div 1{,}048{,}576 = 1.373\text{MB per screen}$$

This means that a video card with only 1MB of RAM cannot support a resolution higher than 640 × 480 and 16 million colors. Memory requirements for various resolutions and color depths are shown in Table 11.9. The amount of memory is given in megabytes because this is the usual increment for video memory.

Using more color depth slows down video functions. You've heard this time after time ever since Windows 3.0 came out—use 16 or 256 colors, because true (24-bit) color will slow you down to a crawl. Data moving from the video card to the display has to go through the video cards' memory chips and the expansion bus, and this can happen only so quickly. VL-bus and PCI both are limited to 32-bit transfers at roughly 33 MHz, yielding a maximum bandwidth of 132 MBps. It sounds like a lot until you start using higher resolutions, high color depths, and higher refresh rates.

For example, take a typical display at 800 × 600 with a fairly low refresh of 70 Hz. The 70 Hz means the display screen is being redrawn 70 times per *second*. If you use a reasonable color depth of 256 colors, which is 8 bits ($2^8 = 256$), you can multiply all the values together to see how much data per second has to be sent to the display:

$$800 \times 600 \times 1 \text{ byte} \times 70 = 33.6 \text{ MBps}$$

If you use the same example at 16 million (24-bit) colors, the figure jumps to 100.8 MBps. This obvious desire for bandwidth even higher than PCI can supply has been answered by Intel's new *advanced graphics port* (AGP), shown in Figure 11.19. AGP is derived from the 66-MHz, 32-bit PCI 2.1

TABLE 11.9

RAM Requirements for Various Resolutions/Color Depths

Resolution	16 Colors	256 Colors	64K Colors	16.7M Colors
640 × 480	0.15MB	0.29MB	0.59MB	0.88MB
800 × 600	0.23MB	0.46MB	0.92MB	1.37MB
1024 × 768	0.38MB	0.75MB	1.5MB	2.25MB
1200 × 1024	0.63MB	1.25MB	2.5MB	3.75MB
1600 × 1200	0.92MB	1.83MB	3.66MB	5.49MB

Figure 11.19
AGP port

specification, and is currently the fastest video available. AGP is a single, special port, similar to a PCI slot, which is dedicated to video. You will never see a motherboard with two AGP ports. AGP has a mind-boggling top speed of 533 MBps.

AGP has taken the video world by storm (Figure 11.20). While most systems still don't really need the speed of AGP, they would benefit by AGP's support for the slew of powerful games that are so popular in PCs.

Figure 11.20
AGP video card

Video Memory

The video memory is crucial to the operation of a PC. It is probably the hardest-working electronics on the PC, and is constantly being updated to reflect every change that takes place on the screen. The original video RAM was plain old DRAM, just like the DRAM on the motherboard. Unfortunately, DRAM has some significant limitations. As a result, a number of other types of RAM have been developed especially for video.

Memory produces two bottlenecks for data: access speed and data throughput. Typical low-cost video cards (usually $50 to $100) commonly use DRAM for data storage. There are a few aspects of DRAM that slow it down, making it a less than optimal choice for video RAM. One is the need to refresh DRAM memory approximately 18.5 times per second. During these refresh periods, the memory bits are unavailable to read. Another slowdown is the access/response time of DRAM. Even the fastest commonly available DRAM (50 ns) is too slow for the higher resolutions and color depths found on larger monitors. The final bottleneck for DRAM is physical. Its data lines are used both for writing data to the video port and receiving data from the CPU.

A way around this bottleneck comes from two directions. The first is reorganize the video display memory from the typical 32-bit-wide structure to 64, 128, or even 192 bits wide. This would not be of much benefit if it weren't for the fact that most video display cards are really coprocessor boards. Most of the graphics horsepower is generated on the card by the video processor chip. The main system simply provides the input data to the processor on the video card. By making the memory bus on the video card as much as six times wider than the standard 32-bit pathway (192 bits), data can be manipulated and then sent to the monitor much more quickly.

The first specialized video RAM option is dual-port memory or VRAM (video RAM). VRAM allows data to be written to video memory from the main system over the standard eight data lines in parallel, and provides a serial data line for data to the video port. Although faster, VRAM is more expensive, but economies of scale have lowered its price to where it is quite common.

WRAM (Windows RAM) is another dual-ported RAM that has seen success in video cards. WRAM is slightly faster than VRAM and costs about the same. The downside to WRAM is that it has not been as widely manufactured as some of the other specialized video RAMs.

TABLE 11.10

Need for DRAM and VRAM at Various Resolutions/Color Depths

32 Bit Wide Memory DRAM @ 75 Hz Resolution	No. of Colors 256	64K	16.8 Mill
640 × 480	Y	Y	Y
800 × 600	Y	Y	N
1024 × 768	Y	N	N
1280 × 1024	Y	N	N
1600 × 1200	N	N	N

64 Bit Wide Memory DRAM @ 75 Hz	No. of Colors 256	64K	16.8 Mill
640 × 480	Y	Y	Y
800 × 600	Y	Y	N
1024 × 768	Y	Y	N
1280 × 1024	Y	N	N
1600 × 1200	N	N	N

64 Bit Wide Memory VRAM @ 75 Hz Resolution	No. of Colors 256	64K	16.8 Mill
640 × 480	Y	Y	Y
800 × 600	Y	Y	Y
1024 × 768	Y	Y	Y
1280 × 1024	Y	Y	Y
1600 × 1200	Y	Y	N

SGRAM (synchronous graphics RAM) is the most popular specialized video RAM available. SGRAM is like SDRAM in that it is synchronized to the system clock. It is extremely fast and is capable of supporting video for the next few years—a veritable lifetime in the PC world!

While specialized video RAM offer substantial improvements in video speeds, it is also not necessary in the majority of office applications because the need for high data throughput is typically found only with high resolutions and high color depths. As you can see from Table 11.10, VRAM is simply an unnecessary expense until you need very high resolution (1280 × 1024 or better) and/or high color depth (64K or better), and thus higher bandwidth.

Video Drivers

A video driver is software that acts as an intermediary between a video card and the applications that need to put information on the screen. The single most important function of a video driver is to tell the video card to set itself to a particular mode. In DOS, the video mode can change many times a day as different programs, each with different modes, are loaded and unloaded. Video in Windows 3.X and Windows 95/98 usually are set to one mode at boot and tend to stay there unless a DOS program is run full screen. In addition to setting a video mode, most video drivers will also come with utilities that allow the mode to be changed on demand by the user. Let's take a quick look at video drivers from DOS and Windows 95 to appreciate how the video drivers perform their function.

DOS Video modes in DOS are a very basic affair. The vast majority of DOS applications run in a very limited number of modes. If a program wants to change the video mode, it must either use VERY standard modes (80 × 24 16-color text, 640 × 480 16-color graphics, etc.) or it must have its own built-in drivers. Since changing modes is up to the DOS application, the actual process of changing modes differs dramatically for every different program. The modes that a particular program can use are limited to the modes designed into it by the programmer who wrote the program.

DOS itself has a handy program called MODE that allows changing different text modes. Go to a DOS prompt (this also works in Windows 3.X and Windows 95) and type MODE CO40. This will change the text mode to color 40 columns. To return the text to the more normal 80 columns, type MODE CO80.

Windows 95 Windows 95, being a graphical program, is extremely interested in video modes. The interest is not based on required modes, as Windows applications will run in any graphical mode from 640 × 480—16 colors up to a theoretical maximum of 2048 × 2048 — 16.7 Million colors. Rather, the interest in modes is based on the users themselves. Different users will have different opinions as to what is the "best" video mode. In order to serve the general public, Windows 95 must be able to change the video mode to suit different users. This is accomplished through the Display properties in the Control Panel. Although the Display option can be accessed through the Control Panel, it is more commonly accessed by right-clicking on the desktop.

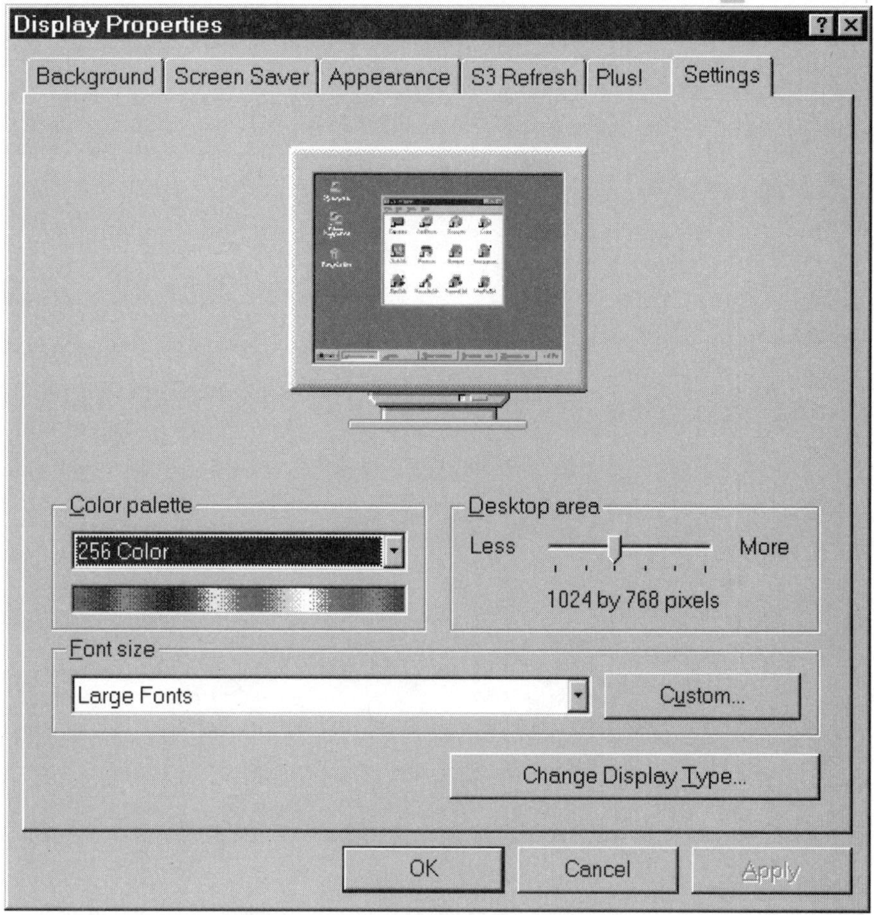

Figure 11.20a
Display properties

The number of resolutions and color depths that can be chosen are determined by the INF file settings for the video card and the monitor (see INF files in the Windows 95 chapter). A good video driver will also provide settings for changing the refresh rate of the video card.

Unfortunately, although Windows itself can readily change modes, the monitor may have problems with the changes. One of the problems with changing modes, especially in Windows 95, is that the amount of black space surrounding the screen will change. All CRTs will have some amount of black space where the screen is not being used.

While some black space is normal, changing modes or refresh rates will often make the black space unacceptably large, preventing the screen view from being as large as it could be. Plus, changing a video mode or refresh rate may cause the screen to shift up, down, left or right. The screen may also take on a "pincushion" or trapezoidal shape. In some cases, the screen may tilt one direction or another. These changes are annoying and counter-productive. There are a number of methods for adjusting the

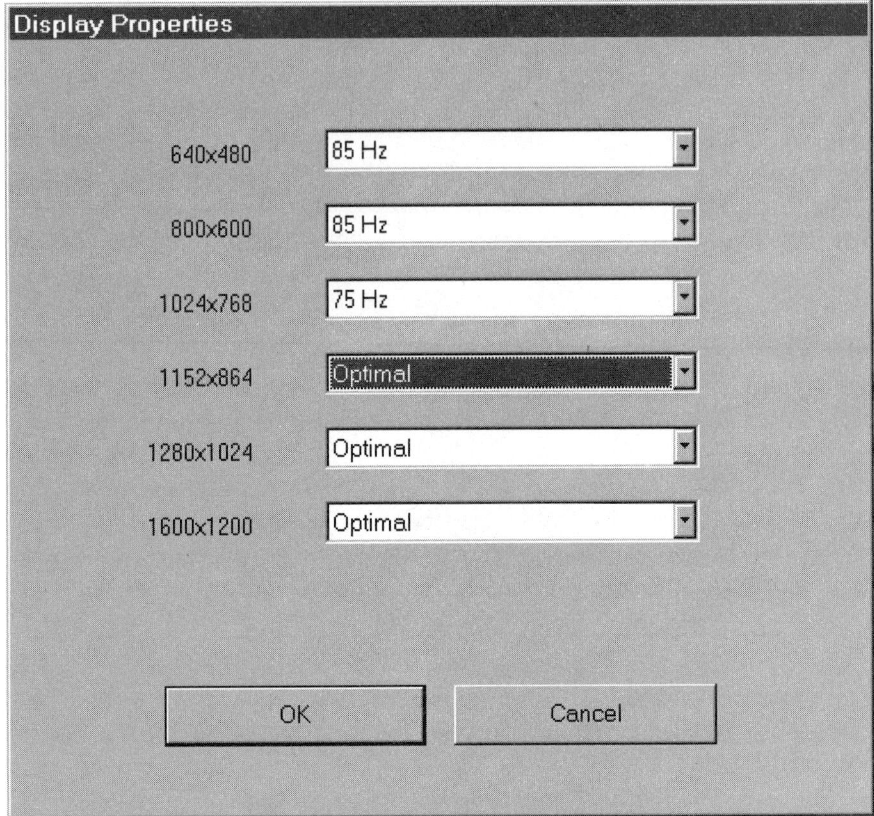

Figure 11.20b Typical refresh settings

screen to optimize the screen size. First, many monitors have adjustments that will allow the user to manually adjust the screen. The user sets a video mode then presses buttons on the monitor to adjust the screen. When the monitor has been adjusted, the settings are stored in the monitor itself. From then on, when the monitor detects a change in video mode or refresh rate, it retrieves these settings and readjusts itself. It is a common procedure when combining a video card and a monitor to take a few moments to adjust the screen.

Another important part of adjusting a monitor is to get the highest refresh rates possible. By setting the refresh rate higher, eyestrain is substantially reduced. Most people prefer a refresh rate of at least 72 Hz, although even higher (85 Hz or so) will make the screen much easier on the eyes. The downside to higher refresh rates is that it may limit the resolution and/or color depth. While a monitor may be able to handle easily an 800 × 600 — 64K color mode at 72 Hz, it may only be able to handle 1024 × 768 — 64K color at a refresh rate of 60 Hz. The choice is really up to the user.

Figure 11.20c
Black space

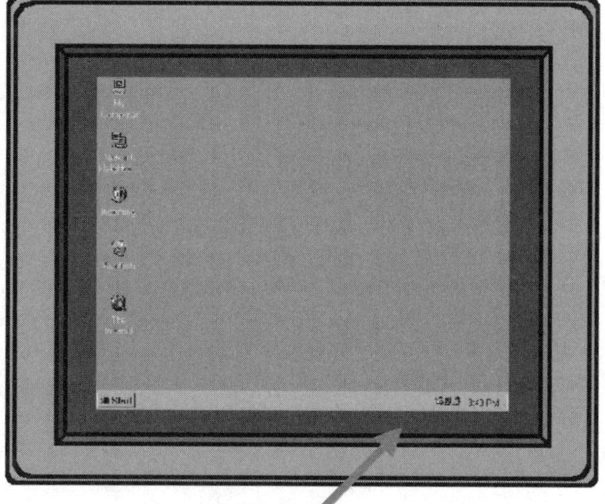

When Video Cards Go Bad

Fortunately, video cards rarely break. The majority of problems in video can be attributed to improper drivers, poor connections, and bad monitors. Unfortunately, when they do, invariably the only option is to throw them away. One area for possible repair is the video RAM. On the rare occasion where the video card is the problem, the usual culprit is the video RAM. Many video cards today have video RAM that is mounted in sockets, as opposed to being soldered directly to the video card. The reason video cards come with sockets is to allow one video card to be sold with varying amounts of RAM. However, sockets also allow the video RAM to be replaced when needed (Figure 11.21).

The trick is to recognize the classic signs of bad video RAM. The first is fixed speckles or spots on the screen. These spots can be any color, but are usually black. The important point to note here is that the speckles don't move; they are fixed in one location, although they might turn on and off a few times an hour. The second symptom is funny colors in Windows. We're not talking about a bad Windows color scheme here! This looks like a monitor covered with a colored film. The color is almost always complex. It won't be blue or red, but rather a "bluish-green with maybe a little purple" type of color. If you get this "filmy" look, boot the PC with VGA drivers (Safe Mode in Windows 95/98). If the filmy look is still there, the RAM is bad.

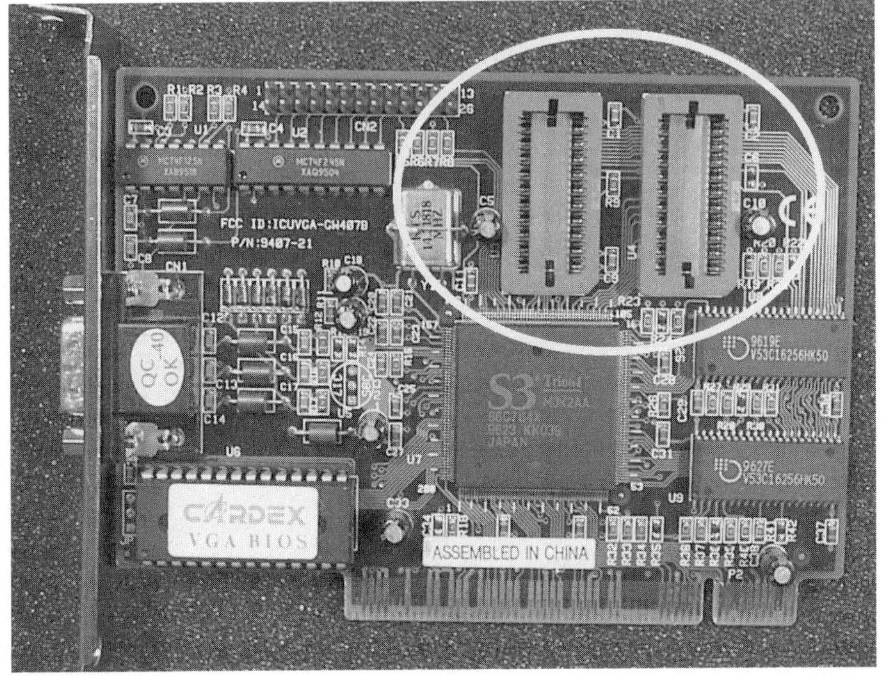

Figure 11.21 Replaceable video RAM

The last and the most common symptom of this uncommon problem is what I call "screen decay." Have you ever seen a movie where the film inside the projector suddenly melts? It usually starts with a small hole in the film and then quickly spreads throughout the film. Bad video RAM can cause this type of look. This is most common on video cards that have been upgraded and haven't been properly inserted into the sockets. The machine runs fine for a moment or two until the cards heat up, disconnecting the improperly inserted RAM.

CHAPTER 12

Printers

In this chapter, you will:

- Understand the different types of printers used today.
- Take a detailed tour of different laser printers.
- Learn to observe and repair basic printer errors.

Despite all of the talk about the "paperless office," printers continue to be a vital part of the typical PC system. In many cases, a PC will be used exclusively for the purpose of producing paper documents, but many people simply prefer dealing with "hard copy." Programmers cater to this preference by using metaphors such as page, workbook, and binder in their applications. The A+ certification strongly stresses the area of printing, and expects a high degree of technical knowledge of the function, components, maintenance, and repair of all types of printers.

Impact printers

Largely obsolete in today's office environment, impact printers leave an image on paper by physically striking an inked ribbon against the surface of the paper. Daisy-wheel printers (essentially an electric typewriter attached to the PC instead of directly to a keyboard) and dot-matrix printers are the two prominent examples of impact printers. Once the dominant printing technology, impact printers have largely disappeared from store shelves because of their inability to combine high quality and flexibility at a low cost. They still retain a niche market for two reasons: they have a large installed base and they can be used for multipart forms (carbons) because they actually strike the paper. Impact printers tend to be relatively slow and noisy, but when speed, flexibility, and print quality are not crucial, they provide acceptable results. PCs used for printing multipart forms, such as POS (point of sale) machines that need to print receipts with multiple copies, represent the major market for new impact printers, although many older dot-matrix and daisy-wheel printers remain in use.

Daisy-Wheel Printers

Daisy-wheel printers, while producing an acceptable quality of text, lack flexibility: you get only the single font on the daisy wheel in only one size. Daisy-wheel printers are completely obsolete today, although they are still employed in some situations where only a single font is needed or for multipart forms.

Dot-Matrix Printers

Dot-matrix printers offer far more flexibility than daisy-wheel printers, although their print quality tends to be inferior to that of daisy-wheel printers. Dot-matrix printers use an array of pins to strike an inked printer ribbon that produce images on paper (Figure 12.1). Using either 9 or 24 pins, dot-matrix printers treat each page as a raster image. The BIOS for the printer (either built into the printer or a printer driver) interprets the raster image in the same way a monitor does, "painting" the image dot by dot. Naturally, the more pins the higher the resolution.

One downside to dot-matrix technology is the need for ongoing maintenance. You must keep the platen (the roller or plate on which the pins impact) and the print head clean with denatured alcohol. Be sure to lubricate gears and pulleys based on the manufacturer's specifications. However, never lubricate the print head as the lubricant will smear and stain the paper. See Figure 12.2. The following sections list some common problems with dot-matrix printers.

WHITE BARS ON TEXT White bars going through the text point to a dirty or damaged print head. Try cleaning the print head with a little denatured alcohol. If the problem persists, replace the print head. They are available, for most printers, from the manufacturer.

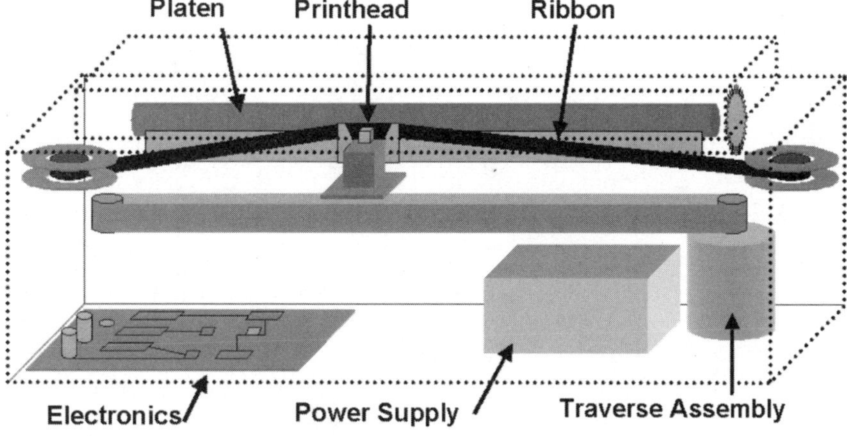

Figure 12.1 Inside a dot-matrix printer

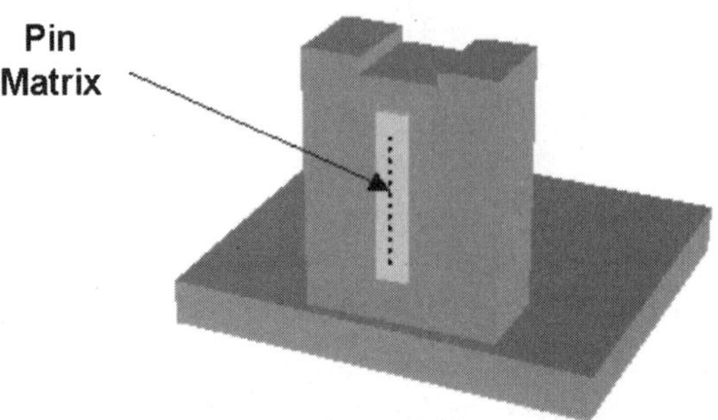

Figure 12.2
The dot-matrix print head

CHOPPED TEXT If the characters look chopped off at the top or bottom, the print head probably needs to be adjusted. Refer to the manufacturer's instructions for proper adjustment.

PEPPERED LOOK If the paper is covered with dots and small smudges, the platen is dirty. Clean the platen with denatured alcohol.

FADED IMAGE If the image is faded and you know the ribbon is good, try moving the print head closer to the platen.

LIGHT TO DARK If the image get gradually lighter on one side of the paper, the platen is out of adjustment. Platens are generally difficult to adjust, so send it to your local warranty center. The $30 to $50 bucks you'll spend is far cheaper than the frustration of trying to do it yourself.

Ink-Jet Printers

Inkjet printers work by ejecting ink through tiny tubes. The ink is ejected through the tubes by heating the ink with tiny resistors or plates that are at one end of each tube. These resistors literally boil the ink, creating a tiny air bubble that ejects a droplet of ink onto the paper, thus creating portions of the image.

Inkjet printers are relatively simple devices, consisting of the printhead mechanism, support elecronics, a transfer mechanism to move the printhead back and forth, and a paper feed component to grab, move and eject paper.

Inkjet printers have a tendency for the ink inside the jets to dry out when not used for a relatively short time. To counter this problem, all inkjet printers move the printhead to a special position that keeps the ink from drying. This area has many names, usually called the "park", "cleaning" or "maintenance" area.

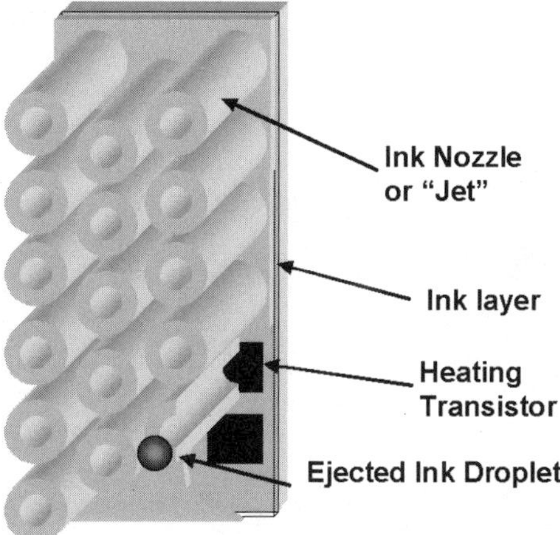

Figure 12.2a Detail of Inkjet printhead

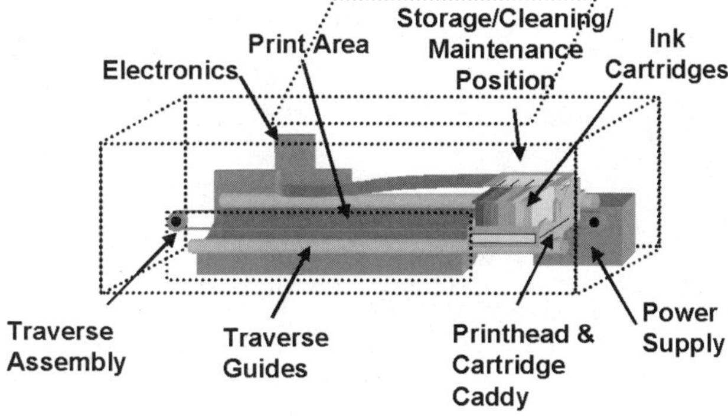

Figure 12.3a Inside an inkjet

Laser Printers

Laser printers have become the printer of choice for most applications. They produce high-quality and high-speed printing of both text and graphics (Figure 12.3b). Although more expensive than ink-jet or impact printers, their prices have steadily declined in recent years.

Laser printers rely on the *photoconductive* properties of certain organic compounds, meaning that when exposed to light, particles of these compounds conduct electricity. Laser printers use lasers as a light source because of their precision.

Parts

In order to reduce maintenance costs, many laser printer parts, including those that suffer the most wear and tear, have been incorporated into the

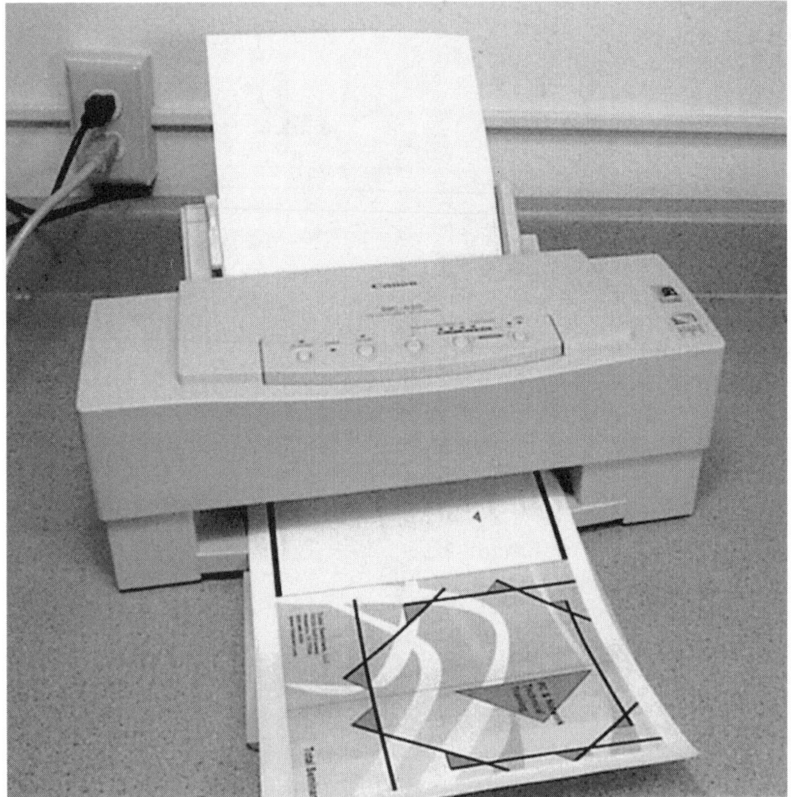

Figure 12.3b
An ink jet printer

toner cartridge (Figure 12.4). While this makes replacement of individual parts nearly impossible, it greatly reduces the need for replacement; those parts that are most likely to break are replaced every time you replace the toner cartridge. Unlike ink-jet printers, the relatively higher cost of laser printers makes their repair a common and popular option. A number of companies sell laser printer parts. My personal favorite is The Printer Works (800-225-6116), a large mail-order outfit with salespeople who are quite knowledgeable. Like an automobile parts store, they can often help you determine the problem and sell you the necessary part.

PHOTOSENSITIVE DRUM The photosensitive drum is an aluminum cylinder coated with particles of photosensitive compounds (Figure 12.5). The drum itself is grounded to the power supply, but the coating is not. When light hits the particles, whatever electrical charge they have drains out through the grounded cylinder. The drum, usually contained in the toner cartridge, can be wiped clean if it becomes dirty. However, *exercise extreme caution!* If the drum becomes scratched, the scratch will appear on every page printed from that point on. The only repair in the event of a scratch is replacing the toner cartridge.

Figure 12.4 Laser printer's toner cartridge

Figure 12.5 Toner cartridge with photo-sensitive drum exposed

ERASE LAMP The erase lamp exposes the entire surface of the photosensitive drum to light, making the photosensitive coating conductive. Any electrical charge present in the particles bleeds away into the grounded drum, leaving the surface particles electrically neutral.

PRIMARY CORONA The primary corona wire, located close to the photosensitive drum, never touches the drum. When charged with an extremely high voltage, an electric field (or corona) forms, allowing voltage to pass to the drum and charge the photosensitive particles on its surface. The *primary grid* regulates the transfer of voltage, ensuring that the surface of the drum receives a uniform negative voltage of between ˜600 and ˜1000 volts.

LASER The laser acts as the writing mechanism of the printer. Any particle on the drum that is struck by the laser becomes conductive, allowing its charge to be drained away into the grounded core of the drum. The entire surface of the drum has a uniform negative charge of between ˜600 and ˜1000 volts following its charging by the primary corona wire. When particles are struck by the laser, they are discharged and left with a ˜100 volt negative charge. Then the laser can "write" a positive image onto the drum.

TONER The toner in a laser printer is a fine powder made up of plastic particles bonded to iron particles. The *toner cylinder* charges the toner with a negative charge of between ˜200 and ˜500 volts. Because that charge falls between the photosensitive drum's original uniform negative charge (˜600 to ˜1000 volts) and the charge of the particles on the drum's surface hit by the laser (˜100 volts), particles of toner are attracted to the areas of the photosensitive drum that have been hit by the laser (i.e., areas that have a positive charge *relative* to the toner particles).

TRANSFER CORONA In order to transfer an image from the photosensitive drum to a piece of paper, the paper must be given a charge that will attract the toner particles off the drum and onto the paper. The transfer corona applies a positive charge to the paper, which draws the negatively charged toner particles to the paper. The paper, with its positive charge, is also attracted to the negatively charged drum. In order to prevent the paper from wrapping around the drum, a *static-charge eliminator* removes the charge from the paper.

FUSER The toner merely rests on top of the paper after the static charge eliminator has removed the paper's static charge. The toner must then be permanently attached to the paper to make the image permanent. Two rollers, a pressure roller and a heated roller, fuse the toner to the paper. The pressure roller presses against the bottom of the page and the heated roller presses down on the top of the page, melting the toner into the paper. The heated roller has a nonstick coating such as Teflon to prevent the toner from sticking to it.

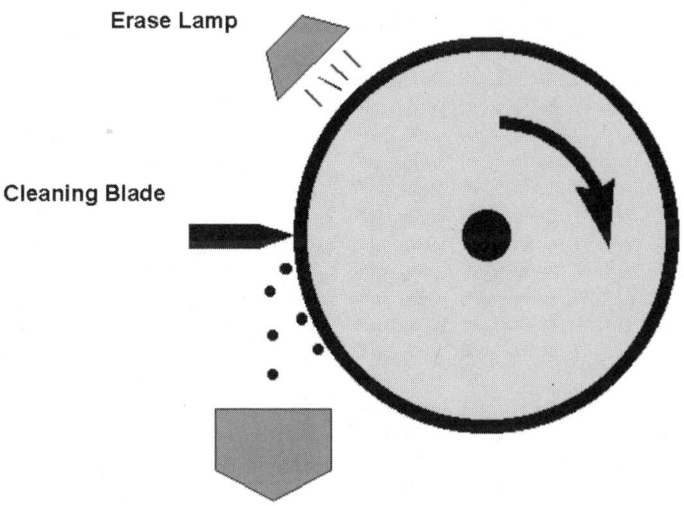

Figure 12.6
Cleaning and erasing the drum

The Physical Side of the Printing Process

CLEAN THE DRUM The printing process begins with both physically and electrically cleaning the photosensitive drum (Figure 12.6). Between printing each page, the drum must be returned to a clean, fresh condition. The printer must remove all residual toner left from printing each page, usually by scraping the surface of the drum with a rubber cleaning blade. If the residual particles remain on the drum, they will appear as random black spots and streaks on the next page. The physical cleaning mechanism either deposits the residual toner in a debris cavity or recycles it by returning it to the toner supply in the toner cartridge. The physical cleaning must be performed carefully. Damage to the drum will cause a permanent mark on every page that's printed.

The printer must also be electrically cleaned. One or more erase lamps bombard the surface of the drum with the appropriate wavelengths of light, causing the surface particles to completely discharge into the grounded drum. After the cleaning process, the drum should be completely free of toner and have a neutral charge.

CHARGE THE DRUM To make the drum receptive to new images, it must be charged (Figure 12.7). The corona wire applies a uniform negative charge to the entire surface of the drum (usually between ~600 and ~1000 volts).

WRITE THE IMAGE The laser writes a positive image on the surface of the drum (Figure 12.8). Every particle on the drum hit by the laser re-

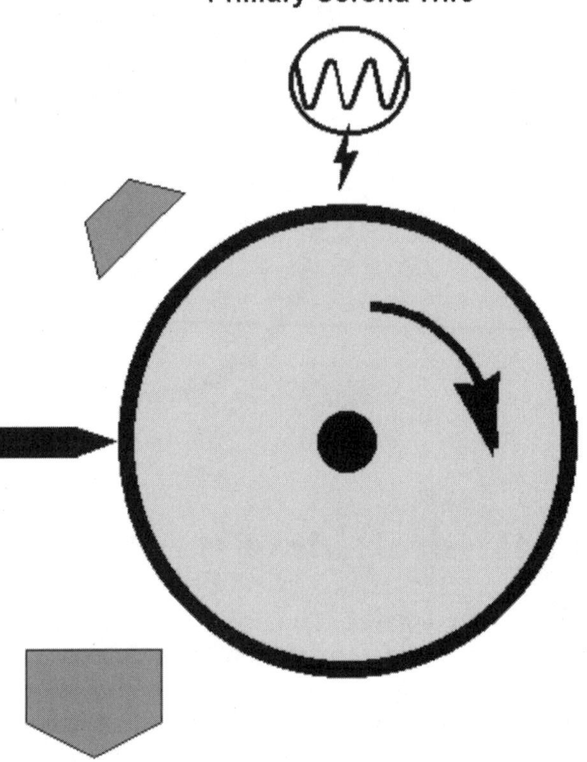

Figure 12.7
Charging the drum with a uniform negative charge

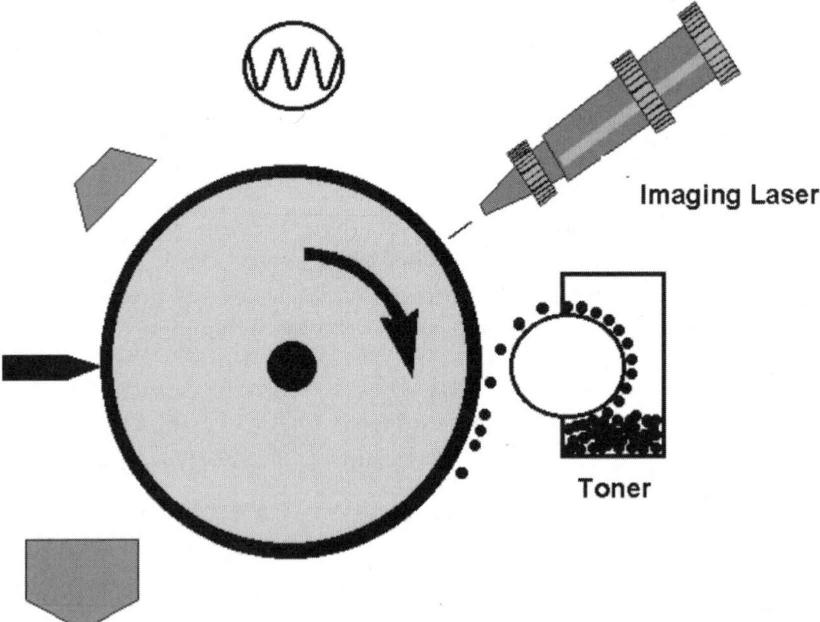

Figure 12.8
Writing the image

leases most of its negative charge into the drum. Those particles with a lesser negative charge are relatively positive to the toner particles, and will attract them.

TRANSFER THE IMAGE The printer must transfer the image from the drum onto the paper. Using the transfer corona, the paper is positively charged. Once the paper has a positive charge, the negatively charged toner particles leap from the drum to the paper. The paper's positive charge is removed by the static-charge eliminator. Once the charge is removed, the particles are merely resting on the paper. They must still be permanently affixed to the paper.

FIX THE IMAGE The particles must be fused to the paper (Figure 12.9). They have been attracted to the paper because of the positive charge given to the paper by the transfer corona, but if the process stopped there the toner particles would fall off the page as soon as it was removed from the printer. The toner particles are composed mostly of plastic, so they can be melted to the page. Two rollers, a heated roller coated with a non-stick material and a pressure roller, melt the toner to the paper, perma-

Figure 12.9
Fusing the image

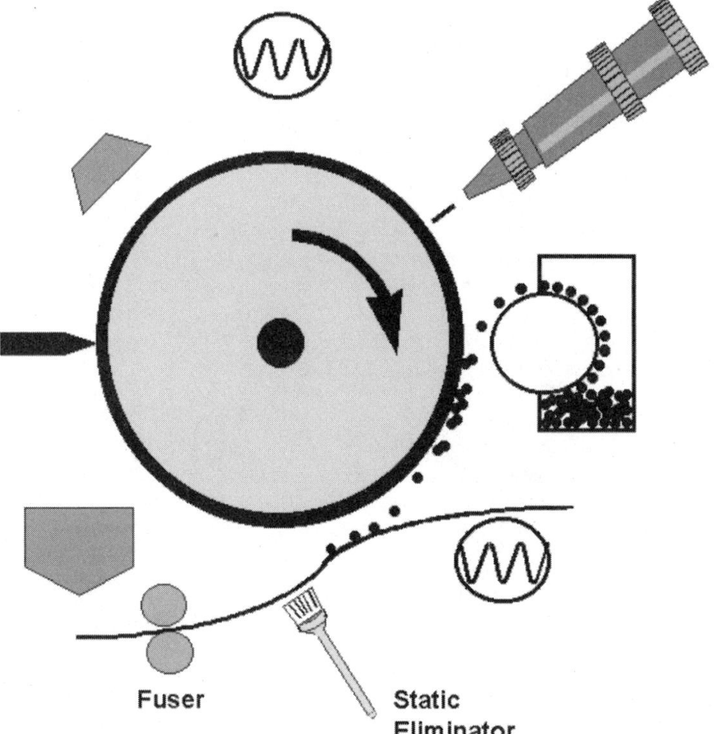

nently affixing it. The final printed copy is then ejected from the printer, and the process begins again with the physical and electrical cleaning of the printer.

The heated roller produces enough heat to melt some types of plastic media, particularly overhead transparency materials. *Never* use transparencies in a laser printer unless they are specifically designed for use in laser printers. Using nonapproved materials can seriously damage your laser printer and void your warranty.

And now for the rest of the laser printer—although the majority of the printing activity takes place within the toner cartridge, many other parts of the laser printer are hard at work outside the cartridge (see Figure 12.10a). In order to appreciate theses "other" components and their functions, you need to look at a regular print job and the many steps that are necessary to make the page appear on the paper.

POWER SUPPLIES All laser printers are distinguished by at least two separate power supplies. The first is called the *primary power supply* or sometimes just the *power supply*. This power supply, which might actually be more than one power supply, provides power to the motors that move the paper, the system electronics, the laser, and the transfer corona. The second, the *high-voltage power supply*, usually provides power only to the primary corona. The extremely high voltage of this power supply makes it one of the most dangerous devices in the world of PCs! It is imperative to always turn off a laser printer before you open it up, for anything other than just inserting a new toner cartridge!

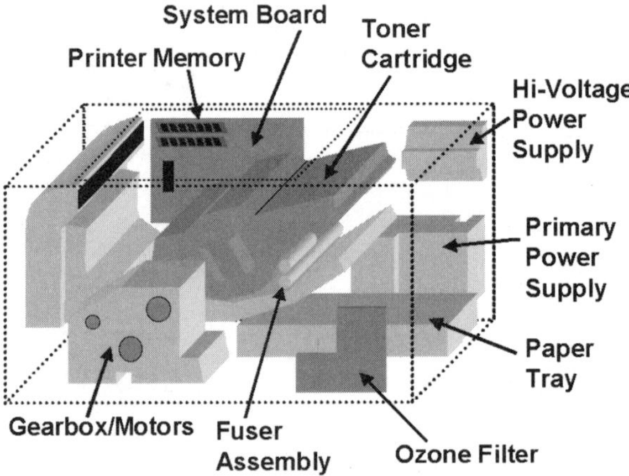

Figure 12.10a Inside a laser printer

TURNING GEARS A laser printer has many mechanical functions. First, the paper must be picked up, printed on, and kicked out of the printer. Second, the photosensitive roller must be turned and the laser, or a mirror, must be moved from left to right. Third, the toner must be evenly distributed and the fuser assembly needs to affix the toner to the paper. All these functions are served by complex gear systems. In most laser printers, these systems are invariably packed together in discrete units called *gear packs* or *gear boxes*. Most laser printers have two or three gear boxes that are relatively easy to remove in the rare case that one fails. Most gear boxes also have their own motor or solenoid to move the gears.

FUSING The fuser assembly is almost always separate from the toner cartridge. It is usually quite easy to locate, as it is close to the bottom of the toner cartridge and usually has two rollers to fuse the toner. Sometimes the fuser is relatively enclosed and is difficult to recognize because the rollers are hidden from view. Just think about the data path of the paper and the fact that fusing is the final step in printing to help you determine its location. In some laser printers, the transfer corona is also outside the toner cartridge. This is a thin wire, usually protected by other thin wires. The transfer corona is a particularly difficult part, as it is prone to building up dirt and must be cleaned, yet it is also quite fragile. Most printers with exposed transfer coronas provide a special tool for cleaning.

SYSTEM BOARD Every laser printer contains at least one electronic board. This board contains the main processor, the printer's ROM, and RAM (which stores the image before it is printed). Of particular importance is the printer RAM. One big problem with laser printers is when the printer doesn't have enough RAM to store the image before it prints, creating a memory overflow situation. Also, some printers store other information in RAM, including fonts and special commands. Adding RAM is usually a very simple job—just snapping in a SIMM stick or two—but getting the *right* RAM is important. Call the printer manufacturer and ask them for the type of RAM you need. Although most printer companies will sell you more of their expensive RAM, most printers can use generic DRAM like the kind you use in your PC. Many printers divide these functions among two or three boards dispersed around the PC. The printer might also have a ROM chip or a special slot in which to install a ROM chip. This is usually for special functions such as Postscript and special fonts.

OZONE FILTER The coronas inside the laser printer generate ozone (O_3). While not harmful to humans, the high concentrations of ozone will cause damage to printer components. To counter this problem, most laser printers have a special ozone filter that needs to be replaced periodically.

SENSORS AND SWITCHES Every laser printer has a large number of sensors and switches spread throughout the machine. The sensors are used to detect a broad range of functions such as jammed paper, empty paper trays, and low toner. Many of these sensors are really tiny switches that detect open doors, etc. Most of the time these sensors/switches work reliably, but they can become dirty or broken, sending a false signal to the printer. Simple inspection is usually sufficient to determine if the problem is real or just the result of a faulty sensor/switch.

The Electronic Side of the Printing Process

Now that you are comfortable with the many parts of a laser printer and its basic functions, let's delve into some of the electronic functions of laser printing.

RASTER IMAGES While impact printers transfer data to paper one character or one line at a time, laser printers transfer entire pages to paper. Laser printers deal with a raster image of the page, which represents what the final product should look like. A raster image is merely a pattern of dots. Laser printers use the same technique as video cards to produce images: they use a device (the laser in a laser printer or the electron gun in a CRT) to "paint" a raster image (on the photosensitive drum in a laser printer or on the phosphor coating on the inside of a CRT in a monitor). Because laser printers have to "paint" the entire surface of the photosensitive drum before they can begin to transfer the image to paper, they have to process the image one page at a time.

Laser printers use a chip called the *raster image processor* (RIP) to translate raster images into commands for the laser. The RIP needs memory (RAM) in order to store the data it must process. A laser printer must have enough memory to process the entire page. Some images that require high resolution also require more memory. Insufficient memory for processing an image will usually be indicated by a memory overflow error. The solution to this type of error is simply to add more RAM to the laser printer.

Do not assume that every error with the word "memory" in it can be fixed by simply adding more RAM to the printer. Just as adding more RAM chips will not solve conventional memory problems, adding more RAM will not solve every memory problem on laser printers. For example, on a HP LaserJet, the message "21 Error" indicates that "the printer is unable to process very complex data fast enough for the print engine." This indicates that the data is simply too complex for the RIP to handle. Adding more memory would *not* solve this problem; it would only make your wallet lighter. The only answer in this case is to reduce the complexity of the page image (fewer fonts, less formatting, reduced graphics resolution, etc.).

RESOLUTION Laser printers can print at different resolutions, just as monitors can display different resolutions. The maximum resolution a laser printer can handle is determined by its physical characteristics. Laser-printer resolutions are expressed in dpi (dots per inch). Common resolutions are 300 × 300 dpi or 600 × 600 dpi. The first number, the horizontal resolution, is determined by how fine a focus the laser can achieve. The second number is determined the smallest increment by which the EP drum can be turned. Higher resolutions produce higher print quality, but higher resolutions also require more memory. In some instances, complex images can be printed only at lower resolutions because of their high memory demands.

RESOLUTION ENHANCEMENT TECHNOLOGY (RET) Even printing at 300 dpi, laser printers produce far better quality than dot-matrix printers because of RET (resolution enhancement technology). RET allows a laser printer to insert smaller dots among the characters, smoothing out the jagged curves that are typical of printers that do not use RET (see Figure 12.10b).

Printer Languages

ASCII Most people think of ASCII (American Standard Code for Information Interchange) as nothing more than a standard set of characters, the basic alphabet in upper- and lowercase with a few strange symbols

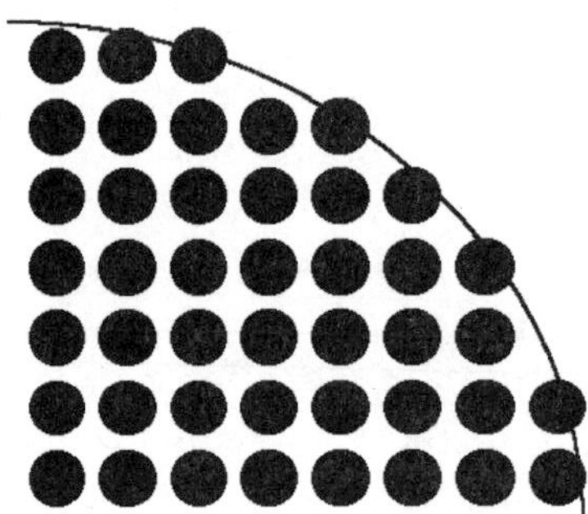

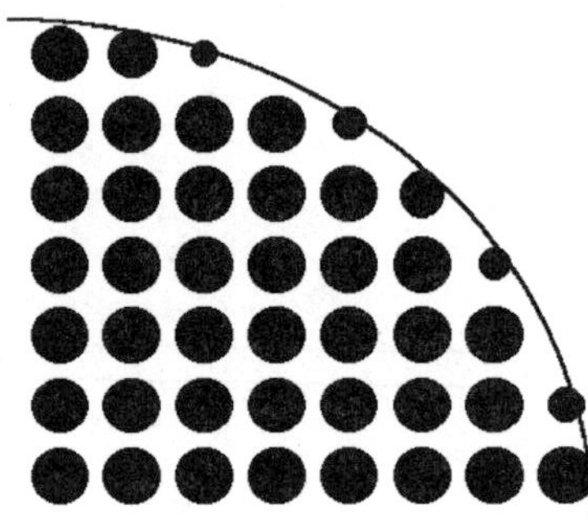

Figure 12.10b RET fills in gaps with smaller dots in order to smooth out jagged characters

thrown in. ASCII actually contains a variety of control codes for transferring data, some of which can be used to control printers. For example, ASCII code 10 (or 0A in hex) means "line feed," and ASCII code 12 (0C) means "form feed." These commands have been standard since before the creation of IBM PCs, and all printers respond to them. If they did not, the Print Screen key would not work with every printer. Being highly standardized has advantages, but the control codes are extremely limited. To use high-end graphics and a wide variety of fonts, more advanced languages are required.

PCL Hewlett Packard developed PCL (Hewlett-Packard printer control language) as a more advanced printer language. PCL features a greatly expanded set of printer commands, and was designed with text-based output in mind. It does not support advanced graphical functions. The most recent version of PCL, PCL5, features scalable fonts and additional line-drawing commands. However, unlike Postscript (see the following section), PCL is dependent on hardware. It is not a true page-description language in the sense that it uses a series of commands to define the characters on a page. These commands must be supported by the individual printer, and they do not define the page as a single raster image. PCL5 is limited to 300- and 600-dpi laser printers, and is not suitable for high-resolution graphics.

POSTSCRIPT Adobe systems developed Postscript PDL (page description language) in the early 1980s as a device-independent printer language capable of high-resolution graphics and scalable fonts. Postscript interpreters are embedded in the printing device. Because the Postscript language is understood by the printers at a hardware level, Postscript printers print faster (the majority of the image processing is done by the printer and not the CPU) and Postscript files are extremely portable. They can be created on one machine or platform and reliably printed out on another machine or platform (including high-end typesetters).

TABLE 12.1

CGA Modes

Product model (voltage)	Printer peak (Amps)	Peak duration (ms)	Fuser lamp on time (s)	Fuser lamp On/Off cycle times (s)	Printing Amps/ watts	Standby Amps/ watts
33440A (115)	20	10	2.0	8.2	7.6/170	.77/170
33440AB (220)	10	10	2.0	6.0	3.4/850	.42/170
33447A (115)	28	10	2.0	7.5	8.0/870	.78/170
33447AB (220)	13	10	2.0	6.1	4.0/890	.48/170
33471A (115)	15.5	10	1.5	6.3	4.8/550	.36/90
33471AB (220)	7.1	10	1.4	5.7	2.5/500	.20/90
33449A (115)	20	10	2.0	8.2	7.6/870	.77/170
33449AB (220)	10	10	2.0	6.0	3.4/850	.42/170
33459A (115)	28	10	2.0	7.5	8.0/870	.78/170
33459AB (220)	13	10	2.0	6.1	4.0/890	.48/170
33481A (115)	15.5	10	1.5	6.3	5.0/574	.36/44
33481AB (220)	7.1	10	1.4	5.7	2.3/507	.20/44
33491A (115)	21	10	2.0	6.9	9.4/1100	2.0/240
33491AB 92200	11	10	2.0	6.9	4.5/1100	1.0/240

Electricity

Laser printers draw considerably more power than other kinds of printers. When installing a laser printer, make sure that your circuit has adequate power to handle the printer's peak requirements. If your lights dim periodically when using the printer, this indicates that the current wiring is not sufficient for the printer and everything else running on the same circuit. Certain functions of the printer, such as powering the erase lamp and heating up the fusing roller, require relatively large amounts of power. Refer to the printer documentation for the peak power requirements of your particular model of printer, or refer to Table 12.1. In addition, the power requirements are usually listed on the back of the printer.

SWITCH BOXES If you want to use multiple printers hooked into the same parallel port, you have to use a switch box. Laser printers should never be used with mechanical switch boxes. Mechanical switch boxes create power surges that can damage your printer. If you must use a switch box, use a box that switches between printers electronically and has built-in surge protection.

REVERSE POWER UP Both laser printers and PCs require more power during their initial powering up than later (the POST on a PC and the warm-up on a laser printer). Hewlett Packard recommends a "reverse power up," which means turning on the laser printer first and allowing it to finish its warm-up before turning on the PC. This avoids having two devices drawing their peak loads simultaneously.

Maintaining and Troubleshooting Laser Printers

Unlike PCs, laser printer maintenance and troubleshooting is a fairly well-established procedure.

Keep It Clean

Laser printers are quite robust as a rule, but a good cleaning every time you replace the toner cartridge will help that printer last for many years. There are many cases of original HP LaserJets still running perfectly after 10 to 12 years of operation. The secret? They were kept immaculately clean.

There are generally only two items that will get your laser printer dirty. The first is excess toner. Toner is hard to see due to its black color, but it will slowly coat the entire printer. The second is paper dust, sometimes called "paper dander." This tends to build up where the paper is bent around rollers or where pickup rollers grab paper. Unlike toner, paper dust is easy to see and is usually a good test that a printer needs to be cleaned. Without being printer-specific, using a can of pressurized air to thoroughly blow out the printer is the best cleaning you can do. It's best to do this out of doors or you might end up looking like a chimney sweep from *Mary Poppins*!

Unfortunately, it's difficult to be specific, as every laser printer has its own unique cleaning method. However, one little area tends to be skipped in the cleaning instructions that come with your laser printer. Every laser printer has a number of rubber guide rollers on which the paper is run during the printing process. These little rollers tend to pick up paper dust and dirt over time, making them slip and jam paper. They can be easily cleaned with a little general-purpose cleaner or even just a bit of water. Also, remember to clean the corona wires if specified by the manufacturer. Most of these wires are quite fragile and require a special tool or a delicate touch—or both!

If you're ready to get specific, find your printer's service manual. Almost every printer manufacturer sells these and they are the main tool for keeping a printer clean and running. Sadly, not all printer manufacturers provide these. Call The Printer Works (800-225-6116) for most service manuals. While you're at it, see if the manufacturer has a Quick Reference Guide; these can be very handy for most printer problems.

Periodic Maintenance

While keeping the printer clean is critical, every laser printer will have certain components that need to be periodically replaced. While these parts vary between different models, there are some that are commonly replaced. Here's a quick list of possible parts.

Ozone Filter
Fuser Assembly
Transfer Corona
Paper guides/rollers
Thermal Fuse (used to keep the fuser from overheating)

Of cource, the ultimate source for determining the parts that need to be replaced (and when to replace them) is the printer manufacturer. Following the manufacturers maintenance guideline will ensure years of trouble-free, dependable printing from your laser printer.

Hewlett-Packard has maintenance kits for most of their laser printers. These contain replacement parts for the most commonly worn parts inside each particular type of HP LaserJet. Although not required for warranty, using these kits when specified by HP assures the ongoing reliability of your LaserJet printer.

The following several sections review what to do for common printer problems.

Ghosting

Ghost images sometimes appear at regular intervals on printed pages. They can be caused either because the EP drum has not fully discharged (and is picking up toner from a previous image) or because a previous image has used up so much toner that the supply of charged toner is either insufficient or has not been adequately charged.

A variety of problems can cause both light and dark ghosting, but the most common source of light ghosting is "developer starvation." If you ask a laser printer to print an extremely dark or complex image, it can use up so much toner that the toner cartridge cannot charge enough toner to print the next image. The proper solution is to use less toner (a.k.a. "don't do that any more!") by:

- Lowering the resolution of the page (print at 300 dpi instead of 600 dpi)
- Using a different pattern
- Avoiding 50 percent grayscale and "dot on/off patterns"
- Changing the layout so grayscale patterns do not follow black areas
- Making dark patterns lighter and light patterns darker
- Printing in landscape orientation
- Adjusting print density and RET (resolution enhancement technology) settings
- Printing a completely black page immediately prior to the page with the ghosting image, and as part of the same print job
- Changing the printer's environmental conditions (low temperature and low humidity can aggravate ghosting problems; check your users' manual for environmental recommendations)

Dark ghosting can sometimes be caused by a damaged EP drum, and can be fixed by replacing the toner cartridge. Light ghosting cannot be solved this way. Switching other components will not usually affect ghosting problems because they are a side-effect of the entire process.

Remember that most instances of light ghosting result from asking the printer to do too much: too complex an image, too dark an image, too high a resolution. Unfortunately, some problems are simply a result of limitations of the technology.

Vertical White Lines

These are usually due to clogged toner, which prevents the proper dispersion of toner on the drum. Try shaking the toner cartridge to dislodge the clog.

Blotchy Print

This is most commonly due to uneven dispersion of toner, especially if the cartridge is almost empty. Try shaking the toner from side to side and trying to print. Also be sure that the printer is level. Last, make sure the paper is not wet in spots. If the blotches are in a regular order, check the fusing rollers and photosensitive drum for any foreign objects.

Spotty Print

If the spots are at regular intervals, the drum might be damaged or some toner might be stuck to the fuser rollers. Try wiping off the fuser rollers and check the drum for damage. If the drum is damaged, get a new toner cartridge.

Emboss Effect

If your printouts have an embossed effect (like putting a penny under a piece of paper and rubbing it with a lead pencil), there is almost certainly a foreign object on a roller. Use a cleaner or regular water with a soft cloth to remove it. If the foreign object is on the photosensitive drum, you will probably have to get a new cartridge.

Incomplete Characters

Incompletely printed characters on laser-printed transparency can sometimes be corrected by adjusting the print density. Be extremely careful to use only materials approved for use in laser printers.

Creased Pages

Laser printers can have up to four rollers. In addition to the heated and pressure rollers of the fusing assembly, there are rollers designed to move the paper from the source tray to the output tray. These rollers will crease the paper in order to avoid curling it, which would cause paper jams in the printer. If the creases are noticeable, try using a different type of paper. Cotton-bond paper is usually more susceptible to noticeable creasing than other bonds. You might also try sending the output to the face-up tray, which circumvents one roller. There is no hardware solution to this problem. It is simply a side-effect of the physical printing process.

Warped, Overprinted, or Poorly Formed Characters

Poorly formed characters can indicate a problem with either the paper (or other media) or the hardware.

MEDIA Avoid paper that is too rough or too smooth. Paper that is too rough interferes with the fusing of characters and their initial definition. If the paper is too smooth (e.g., some coated papers), it might feed improperly, causing distorted or overwritten characters. While you can purchase paper made specifically for laser printers, all laser printers will run acceptably on standard photocopy paper. Try to keep the paper from becoming too wet. Don't open a ream of paper until it is loaded into the printer. Always fan the paper before loading it into the printer—especially if the paper has been left out for more than just a few days.

HARDWARE Most laser printers have a self-test function. This self-test shows whether the laser printer can properly develop an image without having to actually send print commands from the PC. The self-test is quite handy to verify those "Is it the printer or is it the computer?" questions." Run the self-test to check for connectivity and configuration problems. Some possible solutions are as follows:

- Replace the toner cartridge, especially if you hear popping noises.
- Check the cabling.
- Replace the data cable, especially if there are bends, crimps, or objects resting on the cable.
- If you have a front menu panel, turn off advanced functions and high-speed settings to determine if they are either not working properly or not supported by your current software configuration (check your manual for configuration information).
- If you are using Windows 3.*x*, go into the Control Panel, select Printers, and choose Connect. Change the port settings to LPT1.DOS and turn off (remove the × from) the Fast Printing Direct To Port box.

If these solutions do not work, the problem might not be user-serviceable. Contact an authorized service center.

HP Error Codes

Because Hewlett Packard commands a huge portion of the laser printer market, a discussion of their common error codes is warranted. Other brands will use different codes, but the range of errors will be similar.

41.3 ERROR This can be any of the following:

- Wrong size media in tray
- Two pieces of paper picked up and fed at once
- Incorrectly set up paper tray

To clear error message 41.3, hold down the Shift key on the printer control panel and press Continue.

FC (TOP, LEFT, RIGHT) The font cartridge was removed while the printer was online, and the cartridge contained buffered print data. Replace the cartridge and press Continue.

FE FONT CART ERR The font cartridge was removed while the printer was online. Turn the printer on and off to clear the message.

20 MEM OVERFLOW Too much data was sent. Simplify the print job or add memory. HP no longer offers upgrade memory boards for the HP LaserJet, LaserJet+, LaserJet 500, LaserJet Series II, or LaserJet IID printers. Third-party parts, however, might be available.

21 ERROR The printer is unable to process very complex data fast enough for the print engine. This can be caused by multiple addressing of single pixels, too many different fonts or characters on a page, too many cursor positioning requests per document, etc. Reduce the document's complexity by using fewer fonts or less formatting (bold, italics, shading, etc.), or by reducing the graphics resolution. Note: Adding memory will not solve the problem. It is a limitation of the print engine, usually the RIP (raster image processor).

22 ERROR This is caused by a serial buffer overflow or, if you are running parallel, a bad cable or printer interface. If the error occurs at startup, the serial printer cable is probably plugged into a parallel port. If the error appears only after data is sent, then it is probably a bad or loose cable or because you are using an incompatible handshaking protocol, usually XON/XOFF or DTR. Make sure the printer and PC are both using the same protocol. (See the chapter on modems for more information on XON/XOFF and DTR).

40 ERROR "Protocol error during the transfer of data from the PC to the printer."

This error can have several causes, including:

- Loose or damaged cable
- Loss of power to the computer while the printer is online
- Incompatible baud rate, parity, data bits, or stop bits settings
- The I/O being configured to serial and serial being set to RS-422 before a balun (matching transformer) is attached to the serial I/O on the printer and/or host system (on a LaserJet III or IIID)

For modular I/O cards, this means there was an abnormal connection break. Press Continue to clear the error message, and ensure that the printer and computer are configured for the same baud rate, typically 9600. Do not turn the power to the computer on or off when the printer is powered on. If the problem persists, repair might be required.

41 ERROR: HP LASERJET IIP Turn the printer off (data loss will occur), decrease the amount of paper in the MP tray or lower cassette, and do not refill the tray until empty. This error can be caused by adding paper while a print job is in progress.

51 ERROR: BEAM DETECT ERROR Press Continue and the printer will reprint the page. If the error reoccurs, replace the toner cartridge. If the printer has just been moved to a cold environment from a warm one, condensation might have formed inside the printer. Allow the printer to stand for up to six hours until the condensation has dissipated.

50 SERVICE ERROR OR 50 NEEDS SERVICE This can be caused by a malfunction in the fuser assembly. Turn the printer off for 10 to 15 minutes. If the problem persists, seek service.

79 SERVICE OR 79.*xxx* SERVICE This error indicates an "unexpected firmware error." Turn the printer off; remove any font cartridges, personality cartridges, or memory expansion cards; and turn the printer back on.

79 01BB ERROR ON HP LASERJET IIP+ PRINTER If the software gives you the option of manually entering the amount of printer memory, make sure that it is set up properly.

These are only a small sample of the most common error codes—refer to your printer's service manuals for a complete list of error codes!

All printers tend to generate a lot of trash. In today's environmentally sensitive world, there are many laws regarding proper disposal of most printer components. Be sure to check with the local sanitation department or disposal services company before throwing away any component. Of course, toner cartridges are never thrown away—there are companies that will PAY for used cartridges.

Parallel Communication

Parallel ports were included in the original IBM PC as a faster alternative to serial communication. The IBM engineers considered serial communication, limited to one bit at a time, to be too slow for the "high-speed" devices of the day (e.g., dot-matrix printers). Parallel is far faster than serial. Like so much of the technology used in today's PCs, the standard parallel port (sometimes referred to as the Centronics standard) has been kept around for backward compatibility despite several obvious weaknesses.

Speed has been a major concern with parallel ports. The speed of the standard parallel port has remained the same despite speed improvements in almost every other part of the PC (the maximum data-transfer rate of a standard parallel port is approximately 150 kilobytes per second). Standard parallel communication on the PC also relies heavily on software, eating up a considerable amount of CPU time that could be better used.

The second problem with the standard parallel port is that there is no standard. Although the phrase "Centronics standard" is widely used, there is no such animal. This lack of standardization remains a source of incompatibility problems for some parallel devices, although a very loose set of "standards" was adopted by manufacturers that reduced the number of incompatible parallel devices on the market. This lack of standards also applies to parallel cables. Because there are no standards for electromagnetic shielding on the cables, parallel cables longer than six feet are rare.

A lack of true bidirectional capability has also become a problem. While one-way communication for simple line printers and dot-matrix printers was acceptable, a wide range of external devices required two-way communication. While there are ways to get two-way communication out of a standard parallel port, the performance is not impressive. A new standard was needed.

IEEE 1284 standard

The IEEE 1284 standard attempts to deal with both problems (poor performance and lack of standardization) while maintaining backward compatibility. In 1991, a group of printer manufacturers proposed to the IEEE (Institute of Electrical and Electronics Engineers) that a standard be created for a backward-compatible, high-speed, bidirectional parallel port for the PC. The IEEE 1284 committee was formed. The IEEE 1284 standard requires:

- Support for all five modes of operation (compatibility mode, nibble mode, byte mode, EPP, and ECP).
- A standard method of negotiation for determining which modes are supported by both the host PC and by the peripheral device.
- Standard physical interface (e.g., the cables and connectors).
- Standard electrical interface (e.g., termination and impedance).

Because there is only one set of data wires, all data transfer modes included in the IEEE 1284 standard are half-duplex, meaning the data is transferred in only one direction at a time.

COMPATIBILITY/CENTRONICS MODE The standard parallel port used in the original IBM PC is often referred to as a "Centronics port." This connection normally manifests itself as a female DB25 (25-pin) connector on the PC and a corresponding male connector on the cable.

Eight wires are used as grounds: four for control signals, five for status signals, and eight for data signals going from the PC to the device. The control wires are used for control and handshaking signals going from the PC to the printer; the status wires are used for handshaking signals from the device to the PC and for standardized signals from the printer to the PC, such as "out of paper," "busy," and "offline." Only eight wires are used for passing data, and that data goes in only one direction—from the PC to the peripheral device. All of the IEEE 1284 transfer modes use this 25-pin cable for backward compatibility, although other types of connections are included in the standard.

The advantage of the "Centronics mode: is backward compatibility, but its disadvantages are clear. Data passes in only one direction, from the PC to the peripheral device (a.k.a. *forward direction only*). In addition, the CPU must constantly poll the status wires for error messages and handshaking signals, using a significant amount of CPU clock cycles. Standard/Centronics-mode transfers are limited to approximately 150 kilobytes per second.

Some manufacturers have included an enhanced form of Centronics mode that is not a part of the IEEE 1284 standard. It is referred to as *fast Centronics* or *parallel-port FIFO mode*, and devices that support this alternative mode add a hardwired FIFO (first in first out) buffer to the parallel port. Once the data reaches the buffer, the software that had been handling the data transfer assumes that the data has reached the printer and relinquishes control of the CPU to other programs. Once the data is in the buffer, any further handshaking is then handled by it. The buffer emulates the handshaking normally done by the software, allowing the fast Centronics mode to work with legacy peripheral devices that operate on the Centronics standard.

Using this nonstandard mode, some systems can achieve data-transfer rates of up to 500 kilobytes per second, a significant improvement. Remember that IEEE 1284 does *not* require support for this fast Centronics mode. However, for use with legacy devices such as older dot-matrix and laser printers that do not support the ECP or EPP modes, a fast Centronics parallel port actually provides superior performance to an IEEE 1284 parallel port. If possible, look for parallel ports that support both fast Centronics and the IEEE 1284 standard.

NIBBLE MODE Nibble mode is the simplest way to transfer data in "reverse direction," from the peripheral device to the PC. Nibble mode requires no special hardware, and can normally be used with any "standard" parallel port (i.e., it does not require an IEEE 1284 parallel port). All parallel ports have five status wires that are designed to send signals from the peripheral to the PC. Using four of these wires at a time, you can transfer a byte (eight bits) of data in two pieces, one nibble (four bits) at time. Nibble mode is even more software-intensive than compatibility/Centronics mode, eating up many CPU clock cycles. This intensive use of CPU time—combined with the limitation of passing data one nibble at a time—limits nibble-mode data transfers to approximately 50 kilobytes per second. However, nibble mode will work on any PC parallel port and, when used in concert with compatibility/Centronics mode, allows for a very limited form of bidirectional communication with any parallel port.

BYTE MODE/ENHANCED BIDIRECTIONAL PORT While a combination of compatible/Centronics and nibble-mode transfers could produce two-way communications, the resulting speed was not very satisfactory. As higher-performance external peripherals came to market, a more powerful means of two-way parallel communication was needed. A number of manufacturers (including IBM with the PS/2 parallel port) began to add a new data-transfer mode to their parallel ports—byte mode. Byte mode allows reverse-direction (peripheral to PC) parallel communication that uses all eight data wires. To accomplish this, extra hardware is added that handles the negotiation between the PC and the peripheral (remember that the original standard allowed the data wires to be used only for forward communication, from the PC to the peripheral). By using byte mode in conjunction with Centronics mode, two-way communication with eight bits in each direction became possible. With byte mode, two-way communication can achieve speeds approaching the speed of the one-way Centronics data transfers, approximately 150 kilobytes per second.

Parallel ports capable of byte-mode transfers are sometimes referred to as *enhanced bidirectional ports.* This terminology has led to some confusion between these early bidirectional ports and the more advanced parallel ports. The enhanced bidirectional port is far less capable, but is often supported on parallel ports and devices that do not support the entire IEEE 1284 standard.

EPP (ENHANCED PARALLEL PORT) For peripherals that require constant two-way communication with the PC, the *enhanced parallel port* (EPP) protocol offers high-speed, two-way data transfers with relatively little software overhead. Handshaking and synchronization between the peripheral device and the PC are handled by hardware. By removing the CPU from the handshaking process, an EPP port allows the CPU to transfer data to and from the port with a single command, saving a significant number of clock cycles.

Unlike ECP ports (see the following section), the EPP protocol calls for a close coupling between the program running the parallel port and the peripheral device—meaning that the program can monitor and control the flow of data at all times. This allows the program to change the direction of the communication easily, making EPP the ideal protocol for devices that frequently change from input to output and back again (e.g., external hard drives and tape backup units).

Because control of the handshaking and synchronization process is dependent on the hardware, manufacturers have considerable flexibility with regard to performance enhancements. As long as the device, whether a port or a peripheral, responds properly to the standardized EPP signals, manufacturers are free to implement any performance improvements they want to without violating the EPP standard. The end result is that data transfers using the EPP protocol can approach the speed of the ISA bus, transferring between 500 kilobytes and 2 megabytes per second.

The enhanced parallel port was developed before the creation of the IEEE 1284 committee. As a result, the early EPP protocol has a minor difference from the version adopted by the IEEE 1284 committee. Because of this difference, IEEE 1284 EPP parallel ports can fail to recognize that a pre-IEEE 1284 device is not ready to receive or send data. In that case, the device might fail to work properly. However, IEEE 1284 peripherals work just fine with the pre-IEEE 1284 parallel ports. These pre-IEEE 1284 ports and devices are sometimes referred to as *EPP 1.7* devices, referring to an earlier proposed standard.

ECP (EXTENDED CAPABILITY PORT) Microsoft and Hewlett-Packard proposed the *extended capability port* protocol as a response to the need for high-performance parallel communication for printers and scanners. ECP data transfers are loosely coupled, meaning that once the data transfer has begun, the software that initiated the transfer (e.g., a printer driver) cannot monitor the progress of the transfer. The software must wait for a signal that shows that the transfer has been completed. Even more than EPP, this reduces the number of clock cycles used by the transfer to a bare minimum. While it also reduces the amount of control that the software has over the process, not much control is needed. ECP is designed for operations that involve moving large chunks of data (e.g., a print job going out to a printer or an image coming in from a scanner). These types of data transfers do not require much monitoring.

ECP ports use a data-compression method called *run-length encoding* (RLE). With RLE, data can be compressed up to 64:1. This enhances performance significantly, because printers and scanners deal with raster images that tend to compress well. For RLE to work, both the device and the parallel port must support it. Note that RLE compression is not actually part of the IEEE 1284 standard, but is instead part of Microsoft's standard for implementing the ECP protocol.

The ECP protocol works especially well for multifunction devices such as combination scanner-printer-fax machines because of a feature called *channel addressing*. Using a Centronics or nibble-mode connection, if one device is busy, the other parts of the integrated device are inaccessible. For example, with a scanner-printer-fax device, you could not send a fax while a job was being sent to the printer. The parallel cable was essentially a party line, and only one device could use it at a time. With channel addressing, however, you can specify the part of the integrated device with which you want to talk. Without interrupting the print job, you can send a fax or even begin scanning a page (providing the device itself is capable of doing more than one thing at a time).

The ECP standard provides the same degree of flexibility to hardware manufacturers as EPP. As long as the parallel port and devices respond to the standardized ECP commands, manufacturers can enhance performance any way they want. Because the data transfers that use ECP do not require manipulation of the data, many manufacturers have added special capabilities to the ports, often with DMA or through programmable input/output (PIO). The capabilities of the port (or lack thereof) depend on the manufacturer.

SUPPORTING THE STANDARD Keep in mind that manufacturers do not always embrace the entire standard. On the peripheral side, this is not much of a problem. Some modes are more appropriate for some types of devices than others. ECP excels at handling large blocks of data, making it ideal for printers and scanners, but not so attractive for devices such as external CD-ROM drives. External devices that must frequently switch back and forth between read and write operations are better served by EPP, with its ability to change the direction of the data flow without additional handshaking and overhead. Many peripheral manufacturers do not support all five modes because it would be wasteful.

On the parallel port side, however, support for all five modes is vital. Because Centronics and nibble mode are controlled through software, any parallel port ever made for an IBM PC can do both. However, control for byte mode, ECP, and EPP resides in the hardware. Without the appropriate hardware support, expensive devices capable of high-speed communication must slow down to the speed of the parallel port.

NEGOTIATION The IEEE 1284 standard requires devices that operate in anything other than Centronics mode to respond to an identification command that determines which modes are supported by both the parallel port and the peripheral. To ensure backward compatibility, a failure to respond to that command is interpreted as meaning the device is capable of only Centronics mode (forward-only communication).

Connections, Cabling, and Electricity

Although no true standard exists, "standard parallel cable" usually refers to a printer cable with a male DB25 connector on one end and a 36-pin Centronics connector on the other (see Figures 12.11 and 12.12). The shielding (or lack thereof) for the internal wiring and other electrical characteristics is largely undefined except by custom. In practice, these standard cables are acceptable for transferring data at 10 kilobytes per second and for distances under six feet, but they would be dangerously unreliable for ECP or EPP operations.

While the specific electrical characteristics are not particularly important for individuals unless they want to build their own cables from scratch, the mere existence of a standard is a tremendous boon to consumers. All cables manufactured to IEEE 1284 specifications are marked as being "IEEE Std 1284-1994 Compliant." When using cables with that marking, end users can be confident that the cable will support the high data

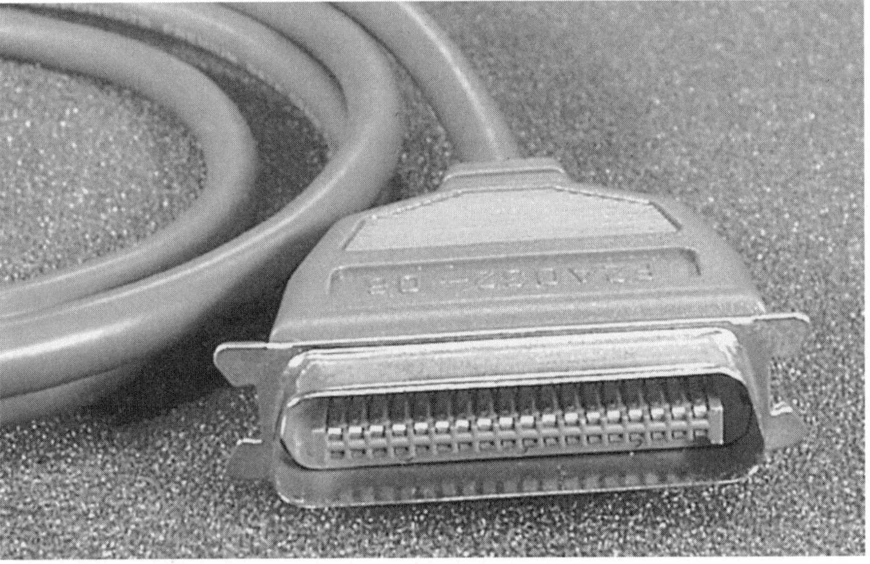

Figure 12.11 36-pin Centronics connector

Figure 12.12
DB25 connector

throughput of ECP and EPP, and work reliably at lengths of up to 10 meters. Generally, the DB25 and 36-pin Champ connectors have been retained. Some important reminders:

- Fast Centronics is not a part of the IEEE 1284 standard, although it can be useful for legacy hardware.
- An *enhanced bidirectional port* is only a port that's capable of byte mode. Do not confuse it with an *enhanced parallel port* (EPP).
- IEEE 1284 devices that use EPP might not work with EPP parallel ports produced before the IEEE 1284 standard.
- Just because a device supports some of the IEEE 1284 modes of operation, does not mean that it complies with all aspects of the standard.

CHAPTER 13

DOS

In this chapter, you will:

- Understand the concept of an operating system.
- Observe the history of DOS.
- See how DOS stores, manipulates, and retrieves data and programs.
- Learn several DOS commands and functions.

This section is a lot easier with a PC. That way, you can follow along with the explanations and try exploring around your machine. If you are running Windows 3 (the old Windows), just exit Windows to get to DOS. Although it would be best with true DOS, a computer running Windows 95/98 will also work acceptably. If you are running Windows 95/98, click on Start, then Run. Type command and then click OK (or use the MS-DOS prompt). You will be at a Windows 95/98 equivalent of DOS. Just be aware that the Windows 95/98 "DOS" is slightly different from true DOS. Even though all the DOS commands discussed in this chapter will work in Windows 95/98, many of the screens will look a little different.

Today's world is the world of Microsoft Windows. The overwhelming majority of people reading this book will have fairly good experience with some version of Windows. You understand how to create and delete folders, and how to copy, move, and delete files. Nevertheless, many people don't know DOS—and if they do, their experience is very limited. As a result of this I've included this chapter in the book to describe many of the basic DOS commands.

Just as in Windows, most of the DOS commands can be executed several ways. Unfortunately, to try to show every way would take a huge amount of time and be counter-productive to the goals of this book. Therefore, only one method will be used for each command. This method might not be the fastest or easiest, but it will be the one that most clearly explains the command and the command's effect on the system.

Every Computer Needs an Operating System

A computer exists only to perform one function—to run programs. No doubt the CPU inside your PC can run programs extremely well. Unfortunately, that CPU needs all the programs to be handed to it in a high-speed binary format. Even if you have a hard drive full of programs ready to run on that CPU, there are a number of functions that must take place before, during, and after a CPU runs a program. For example, users need some way to "feed" the desired program to the CPU and then deal with the data generated by that program. We all know that programs and data are stored in a hard, floppy, or CD-ROM drive, but how can the hundreds of discrete pieces of programs and data be kept separate, and how can they be organized so you can select a program and then tell the CPU to run that program? If a program is run many times and generates different data each time, how can users keep each piece of data separate? How can that data be organized so the users can later recall a certain piece of data? How can programs and data be moved, deleted, copied, and organized? All these functions, and many more, need to be in existence before a computer can do its job. And oh, by the way, these functions should be performed in such way that they make sense to normal, nontechnical people.

What is needed is an *operating system* or OS. An operating system is a program that performs four basic functions. First, it must communicate, or at least provide a method for other programs to communicate, with the hardware of the PC. It's up to the OS to access the hard drives, respond to the keyboard, and output data to the monitor. Second, the OS must create a *user interface*, which is a sort of representation of the computer, usually on the monitor, that makes sense to the people using the computer. The OS must also take advantage of standard input devices, such as mice and keyboards, to allow users to manipulate the user interface and thereby make changes to the computer. Third, the OS, via the user interface, must allow users to determine the available installed programs and run, use, and shut down the program of their choice. Fourth, the OS should allow users to add, move, and delete the installed programs and data.

All operating systems have definite traits that set them apart from regular programs. The first is that an OS is tied to a particular type of processor. The PC world is heavily dominated by the Intel-type CPUs, but there are many other CPUs in use today. Two examples would be the DEC Alpha, used by many UNIX systems, and the Power PC, the CPU inside most Macintosh computers. The OS must understand important aspects of the CPU, such as the amount of memory the CPU can handle, what modes of operation it is capable of performing, and the commands needed to perform any operation. Certain operating systems, such as Windows NT, claim to be able to run on more than one processor. This is not really true, however, due to the fact that Windows NT must have major parts of the OS changed for different CPUs.

The next trait specific to an OS is that it always starts running immediately after the PC has finished its POST, then takes control of the PC. The OS continues running until the PC is rebooted or turned off. There

TABLE 13.1

Operating Systems and Applications

PC operating systems	PC applications
DOS	Microsoft Word
Windows 95	Lotus 123
Windows NT	CorelDraw
UNIX	Netscape Communicator
	Adobe Acrobat
	Symantec ACT!
	Plus thousands more!

is no way to turn off the OS, unless you also turn off the PC. Another trait is that *application* programs such as word processors, spreadsheets, and Web browsers cannot run on a PC without an operating system. Therefore, application programs must be written so they can be controlled by the OS. Whoever makes an OS always provides a "rule book" that tells programmers how to write programs for a particular OS. These rule books are known as *application programmer interfaces* (APIs). Last, an OS must be flexible and have some facility for using new software and/or hardware that might be installed. Refer to Table 13.1.

Communicating with Hardware

From earlier chapters, you should understand that the system BIOS, stored on the NVRAM (ROM or flash) on the motherboard, has programs that know how to talk to the most basic and important parts of the computer. These include the hard drives, floppy drives, keyboard, and basic video. The operating system should be able to work with the system BIOS to deal with these devices. If users want to access the hard drive to retrieve a program, the OS should take the request and pass it to the appropriate hard-drive BIOS instruction that tells the drive to send the program to RAM. Plus, if for some compelling reason the BIOS is incapable of sufficiently performing its function, the OS should bypass the BIOS and talk to the piece of hardware directly. The OS talking directly to hardware and skipping BIOS has become very common in recent operating systems.

If the OS is going to take control of a new piece of hardware, then there must be some way for it to communicate with that hardware. Therefore, there must be a way to add the programming necessary to talk to that device. Since new devices can be added or removed, the method of adding more programming must be simple and flexible. Most OSes use *device drivers* to add this necessary code. An OS tells hardware makers how to create these programs and also creates a method of adding the device driver to the OS code. Since it's usually up to the makers of a particular hardware to supply the device driver with the hardware, it can be jokingly, although accurately, thought of as BYOB (bring your own BIOS).

Since the OS handles communicating with hardware, it should provide some type of error handling or at least error notification. If someone attempts to use a piece of hardware that isn't working properly, the OS should either try to fix the problem or at least attempt to communicate with the device a few more times. If the device continues to fail to work, the OS should provide an error screen to notify users of the problem.

Creating a User Interface

Most users are interested in being able to perform only a few simple functions with their PCs. First, they want to be able to know what applications are available; second, they want to be able to easily access those programs; and third, they want to be able to save the results of an application (data) and be able to label that discrete piece of data in such a way that it can be recognized later.

A shoe store is a good analogy of a user interface. The front of the shoe store is filled with attractive displays of shoes, organized and grouped by gender (men's and women's), age (adult and children), function (dress or sports), and style. This is done to allow consumers to see everything that's available and to be able to select the shoes they want to purchase. However, if a customer wants to buy a pair of shoes, what does he do? He hollers at a salesperson and shows him the the shoes he wants. The salesperson looks at the inside of the shoe and disappears through a small door. As the salesperson goes, the customer might wonder why the salesperson looked in the shoe. Have you ever seen the back of a shoe store? It's scary. All the shoes are organized, not by style, color, gender, or age, but by inventory code. Inside of every shoe is an inventory code to tell the salesperson where to look for that shoe. Without understanding the code, a customer would have no idea where to search for a pair of shoes, but it's the absolute best way to organize an inventory of 25,000 pairs of shoes. What a customer sees in the store is not all the shoes as they really are in the back, but a "user interface" of what's available. A computer's user interface performs the same function by providing a "display" to the user of the programs and data on the PC. The customers (users) can look at the display (the user interface) and tell the salesperson (the OS) what they want, without ever really knowing how all the shoes (programs and data) are really organized.

Finishing the analogy, the shoe store's displays are not written in stone. New displays can be added and old displays can be removed. Men's shoes can be switched with women's shoes relatively easily. Like the shoe store, a user interface should also be flexible and scalable, depending on the system in which it is installed.

Accessing and Supporting Programs

This is a simple but important concept. An OS must allow users to start a program. When a program is started, the user interface must disappear and allow the application to take over the screen. If the OS is still visible, it must move away from the main part of the screen and set itself to the top, bottom, or sides. While the application is running, the OS must still provide access to hardware: changing the screen, saving data, printing—whatever the application needs. If a program loses control, the OS should have some way of stopping it or at least being aware that it *is* out of control and hopefully generating an error message. And the OS should instantly return when the application is shut down, so users can then choose another application.

Organizing and Manipulating Programs and Data

A PC can store data and programs on floppies, hard drives, and CD-ROMs. One PC can have hundreds of programs and thousands of discrete pieces of data. Simply making all the programs and data visible would be like taking all the shoes in the shoe store and setting them neatly on the floor. It would be an overly complicated mess.

First, the OS needs to give a label or name to each program and each discrete piece of data, and this label or name must allow users to identify each item as either a program or data. If it's data, there must be some method of identifying what type of program uses that particular data. Then the OS must provide a naming system for all the drives. Each floppy, hard, and CD-ROM drive needs some sort of identifier. It can be as simple as a letter of the alphabet or as complex as a fully descriptive phrase. These names are usually determined when the device is first installed, and is not changed. Each drive also needs to be able to create distinct groupings of data and programs, and the OS's user interface must be able to individually inspect these groupings. Users must be able to "open" and "close" these groups via the user interface, as desired. There also needs to be a method of copying, moving, and deleting programs and data. The user interface must be established in such a way that users can perform these functions clearly and, especially with deletions, be able to ensure that the manipulations are done only to the desired programs and data.

There were operating systems long before PCs were invented. Methods for all of the previous functions were performed on mainframes and minicomputers with a high degree of refinement. By the late '70s, a few companies were already selling operating systems for the first-generation microcomputer market. When IBM invented the PC, they began to search for a company that could provide them with an OS for this new computer called the PC. After asking and being rejected by a company called Digital Research, they went to a tiny company that had invented a popular new programming language called BASIC. They asked the president if his company could make an OS for the IBM PC. This company had never written an OS before, but the man brazenly said "Sure!" That man was Bill Gates, and the tiny company was Microsoft.

In the Beginning, There Was DOS

After shaking hands with the IBM representatives, Bill Gates hurriedly began to search for an operating system based on the Intel 8086 processor. He found a very primitive OS called QDOS (Quick-and-Dirty Operating System), written by a one-man shop, and purchased it for a few thousand dollars. After a few minor changes, Microsoft released it as MS-DOS (Microsoft Disk Operating System), version 1.1. Although primitive by today's standards, MS-DOS 1.1 could provide all the necessary functions needed for an operating system. Over the years, MS-DOS went through version after version (see Table 13.2) until the last Microsoft version, MS-DOS 6.22, was released in 1994. Microsoft licensed MS-DOS to PC makers. They could add their own changes and then rename the system to something else, such as IBM's PC-DOS. This chapter will focus on MS-DOS 6.22.

Here's an interesting tidbit. Until MS-DOS version 5.0, you couldn't buy DOS off the shelf! Microsoft set up a deal where PC makers could provide DOS only with a PC. When you bought your new PC, it would already have DOS installed. Of course, you would also be provided with installation diskettes if for some reason you needed them.

TABLE 13.2 Common DOS versions

MS-DOS 1.0	First version, very primitive
MS-DOS 1.1	Supported 320K floppy drives
MS-DOS 2.0	Hard drive and subdirectory support
MS-DOS 2.11	International code page support
MS-DOS 3.0	1.2 MB floppy support
MS-DOS 3.3	3½″ floppies, multiple partitions
MS-DOS 4.0	504 MB partitions, very buggy
MS-DOS 4.01	Patch to 4.0
MS-DOS 5.0	Memory management, improved utilities (EDIT, MEM, DOSSHELL, Help utility)
MS-DOS 6.0	MEMMAKER added
MS-DOS 6.2	Doublespace disk compression, safer utilities
MS-DOS 6.21	Disk compression removed
MS-DOS 6.22	Drivespace disk compression

Let's look at several major DOS concepts that are important to understand, especially for Windows users. First, DOS was designed to run on an 8086 processor. DOS was never truly upgraded to take advantage of the more advanced Intel processor's protected mode. Therefore, DOS is a single-tasking operating system. Sure, you can run DOS on a Pentium II, but DOS can't take advantage of any protected-mode functions. All you really have is an extremely fast 8086! Second, DOS is text-based. Everything is done with a text-based screen, although applications can be graphical. All text is uppercase. If a lowercase letter is typed, it is automatically changed to uppercase. Third, DOS doesn't support mice, although it supports applications that use them.

DOS is completely case-insensitive.

Files

DOS manifests every separate program and piece of data as individual *files*. Each file has a name stored with the file on the drive. Names are broken down into the *filename* and the *extension*. The filename can be no longer than eight characters. The extension, which is optional, can be up to three characters long. There can be no spaces in the filename or extension, nor can any "illegal" character (/ \ [ ] ¦ < > + = ; , * ?) be used. The filename and extension are separated by a period. This is known as the "eight dot three" (written as "8.3") filename limit. Here are some examples of DOS filenames:

FRED.EXE
SYSTEM.INI
FILE1.DOC
DRIVER3.SYS
JANET
CODE33.H

and here are some unacceptable DOS filenames:

FRED.EXEC
WAYTOOLONG.F
BAD>CHAR.BAT
.NO

Windows 95/98 does not have the 8.3 limit. Files can be up to 255 characters. However, like DOS, Windows cannot use the same illegal characters.

The extension defines the function of the file. Program files end with either an .EXE or a .COM extension. All other files contain some form of data to support programs. Different programs use different types of data files. The extension shows which program uses the particular data file. For example, Microsoft Word for DOS (Yes, there is a Microsoft Word for DOS) creates files with the extension DOC. Therefore, files with the .DOC extension are *associated* with Word. You can change the extension of any data file and it would be a perfectly good file, but without the proper extension, it is difficult to know which program uses it.

Of course, all files are stored on the hard drive in binary format, but every program has its own way of reading and writing this binary data. Each unique binary organization is called a *format.* As a result, one program cannot read another program's files unless it has some conversion capability to turn the other program's format into its own format. In the very early days of DOS, no programs were capable of performing this type of conversion. Yet people wanted to exchange files. They wanted some type of "common" format that any program could read. The answer was a special format called *ASCII* (American Standard Code for Information Interchange). The ASCII standard defines 256 eight-bit characters. These characters include all the letters of the alphabet (upper- and lowercase), numbers, punctuation, many foreign characters, box-drawing char-

Figure 13.1 ASCII characters

000 <nul>	032 sp	064 @	096 `	128 Ç	160 á	192 └	224 α
001 ☺ <soh>	033 !	065 A	097 a	129 ü	161 í	193 ┴	225 β
002 ☻ <stx>	034 "	066 B	098 b	130 é	162 ó	194 ┬	226 Γ
003 ♥ <etx>	035 #	067 C	099 c	131 â	163 ú	195 ├	227 π
004 ♦ <eot>	036 $	068 D	100 d	132 ä	164 ñ	196 ─	228 Σ
005 ♣ <enq>	037 %	069 E	101 e	133 à	165 Ñ	197 ┼	229 σ
006 ♠ <ack>	038 &	070 F	102 f	134 å	166 ª	198 ╞	230 µ
007 • <bel>	039 '	071 G	103 g	135 ç	167 º	199 ╟	231 τ
008 ◘ <bs>	040 (	072 H	104 h	136 ê	168 ¿	200 ╚	232 Φ
009 <tab>	041)	073 I	105 i	137 ë	169 ⌐	201 ╔	233 Θ
010 <lf>	042 *	074 J	106 j	138 è	170 ¬	202 ╩	234 Ω
011 ♂ <vt>	043 +	075 K	107 k	139 ï	171 ½	203 ╦	235 δ
012 ♀ <np>	044 ,	076 L	108 l	140 î	172 ¼	204 ╠	236 ∞
013 <cr>	045 -	077 M	109 m	141 ì	173 ¡	205 ═	237 φ
014 ♫ <so>	046 .	078 N	110 n	142 Ä	174 «	206 ╬	238 ε
015 ☼ <si>	047 /	079 O	111 o	143 Å	175 »	207 ╧	239 ∩
016 ► <dle>	048 0	080 P	112 p	144 É	176 ░	208 ╨	240 ≡
017 ◄ <dc1>	049 1	081 Q	113 q	145 æ	177 ▒	209 ╤	241 ±
018 ↕ <dc2>	050 2	082 R	114 r	146 Æ	178 ▓	210 ╥	242 ≥
019 ‼ <dc3>	051 3	083 S	115 s	147 ô	179 │	211 ╙	243 ≤
020 ¶ <dc4>	052 4	084 T	116 t	148 ö	180 ┤	212 ╘	244 ⌠
021 § <nak>	053 5	085 U	117 u	149 ò	181 ╡	213 ╒	245 ⌡
022 ▬ <syn>	054 6	086 V	118 v	150 û	182 ╢	214 ╓	246 ÷
023 ↨ <etb>	055 7	087 W	119 w	151 ù	183 ╖	215 ╫	247 ≈
024 ↑ <can>	056 8	088 X	120 x	152 ÿ	184 ╕	216 ╪	248 °
025 ↓ <em>	057 9	089 Y	121 y	153 Ö	185 ╣	217 ┘	249 ∙
026 <eof>	058 :	090 Z	122 z	154 Ü	186 ║	218 ┌	250 ·
027 ← <esc>	059 ;	091 [	123 {	155 ¢	187 ╗	219 █	251 √
028 ∟ <fs>	060 <	092 \	124 ¦	156 £	188 ╝	220 ▄	252 ^{n}
029 ↔ <gs>	061 =	093]	125 }	157 ¥	189 ╜	221 ▌	253 ^{2}
030 ▲ <rs>	062 >	094 ^	126 ~	158 ₧	190 ╛	222 ▐	254 ■
031 ▼ <us>	063 ?	095 _	127 ⌂	159 ƒ	191 ┐	223 ▀	255

acters, and a series of special characters for commands such as a carriage return, bell, and end of file (Figure 13.1). The ASCII standard, however, is for more than just files. For example, the keyboard sends the letters you press, in ASCII code, to the PC. Even the monitor outputs in ASCII when you are running DOS. ASCII files, more commonly known as *text* files, store all data in ASCII format.

ASCII was the first universal file format. Virtually every type of program—word processors, spreadsheets, database, presentation programs—can all read and write text files. However, text files have severe limitations. A text file can't store important information such as shapes, colors, margins, bold, underline, and font. Therefore, even though text files are fairly universal, they are also limited to only the 256 ASCII characters.

Even in the most basic text, there is a need to perform a number of actions that are not simple characters. For example, how does the program reading the text file know when to start a new line? This is where the first 32 ASCII values come into play. These first 32 characters are very special commands, although some of them are both commands and characters. For example, the ASCII value 7 can be either a large dot or a command to play a note (bell) on the PC speaker. ASCII value 9 is a tab. ASCII value 27 is an escape. How these first 32 values are treated depends on the program that reads them. As a rule, DOS treats the first 32 ASCII values as commands.

DOS makes heavy use of text files for system configuration and optimization. A technician who uses DOS must be comfortable accessing and editing text files with a special program called a *text editor.* DOS comes with a text editor called EDIT that allows technicians to manipulate text files. You'll see more of EDIT later in this chapter.

Drives and Directories

Each drive in DOS is assigned a drive letter. The first floppy drive is called A: and the second, if installed, is called B:. DOS cannot support more than two floppy drives, because it supports the original IBM PC, which was designed for only two drives. Hard drives start with the letter C: and can continue to Z: if necessary. CD-ROM drives are usually given the next drive letter after the last hard drive. These letters are defined by DOS and cannot be changed. DOS, like almost every other OS, uses a "hierarchical directory tree" to organize floppies and hard drives. These groups are called *directories.* Windows calls them *folders.* Files don't have to be in a directory. Any file that is not in a directory is said to be in the *root directory.* A system can have directories inside directories. A directory inside a directory is called a *subdirectory.* Any directory can have multiple subdirectories. There can be two or more files of the same name in different directories in a PC, but two files in the same directory cannot have the same name. Equally, no two subdirectories under the same directory can have the same name, but two subdirectories under different directories can have the same name.

When describing a drive, you use its letter. For example, the hard drive would be represented by C:. To describe the root directory, put a backslash (\) after the C:, so C:\. To describe a particular directory, add the name of the directory and another backslash. For example, if a PC had a directory called TEST, it would be C:\TEST.

Subdirectories in a directory are displayed by additional backslashes and names. If the TEST directory had a subdirectory called SYSTEM, it would be shown like this: C:\TEST\SYSTEM. This naming convention allows a complete description of the location and name of any file. If the C:\TEST\SYSTEM directory had a file called TEST2.TXT, it would be C:\TEST\SYSTEM\TEST2.TXT.

The exact location of a file is called its *path.* The path for the TEST2.TXT file is C:\TEST\SYSTEM. Here are some examples of possible paths:

C:\DOS
F:\FRUSCH3\CLEAR

A:\REPORTS
D:\

Directories are not required by any law of man or nature—or DOS. A computer will work even if every file is dumped in the root directory. However, directories make the organization of files much easier. Generally, when a DOS program is installed, it is given its own directory. However, unlike drive letters, directories are not permanent. Users can create and delete any directory, even one that holds files. It is common for users to create directories and subdirectories to store their own personal data files.

Structure: Three Main Files

The DOS operating system is composed of three main files, accompanied by roughly 80 support files. The three primary files are *IO.SYS*, *MSDOS.SYS*, and *COMMAND.COM*. These files must be on the C: drive or the computer will not boot. IO.SYS handles talking to the BIOS and hardware, MSDOS.SYS is the primary DOS code, often called the "kernel," and COMMAND.COM actually interprets commands typed into the computer, and passes that information to MSDOS.SYS. COMMAND.COM is also called the *command interpreter*. IBM's PC-DOS calls their IO.SYS version IBMBIO.SYS, and their MSDOS.SYS version IBMDOS.SYS. Despite the slightly different names, they perform the same function.

The core part of DOS is composed of these three files, but there are also a large number of files that are part of DOS. These are separate programs that are usually stored in a directory called C:\DOS (the Windows 95 equivalents are stored in a directory called C:\WINDOWS\COMMAND). These are the very important *external* programs.

Different versions of DOS are for the most part incompatible. Let's say two PCs are running MS-DOS 5.0 and MS-DOS 6.2. Although they both have the three files IO.SYS, MSDOS.SYS, and COMMAND.COM, the files are different and not interchangeable. It is important to know the version of DOS for each machine being supported and not mix them up. Later in this chapter you will learn how to determine the version of DOS on a particular PC.

The DOS User Interface

The text-based DOS user interface might seem primitive when compared to the attractive, colorful interfaces (like Windows) used by many systems to-

Figure 13.2
The DOS prompt

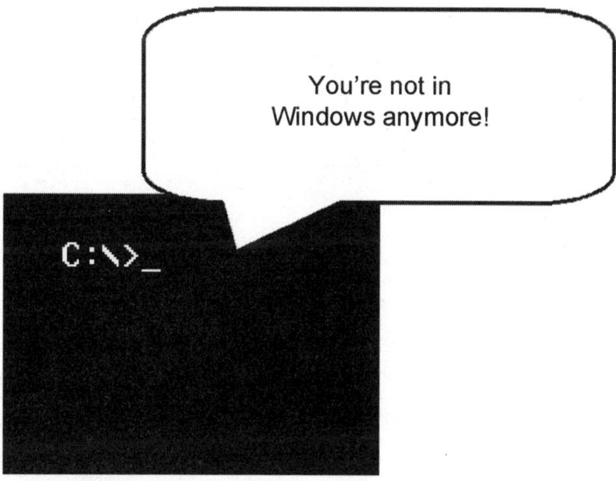

day, but it is actually quite fast and powerful. An experienced user can perform many equivalent jobs faster in DOS than in Windows 95. But the interface is picky and unforgiving: the result of one missed keystroke can be either nothing happening at all or wiping out crucial data with no warning.

The DOS Prompt

The DOS user interface is centered on the *prompt,* which is a path followed by a greater-than sign (>) and a flashing cursor. When you see the prompt, DOS is telling you "I'm ready to take your commands!" See Figure 13.2.

DOS is always "focused" on a directory, and any commands you issue are performed on the directory on which DOS is focused. The prompt shows you which directory currently has DOS's focus. For example, if you see a prompt that looks like C:\>, you know that DOS is focused on the root directory of the C: drive. If you see a prompt that looks like C:\DBASE\>, then you know that DOS is focused on the DBASE directory of the C: drive. The trick to using DOS is remembering to first get DOS to focus on the drive and directory where you want to work. Let's put this idea to practice with the DIR command.

The *DIR* command shows you the contents of the directory that currently has the focus of DOS. Assuming that the DOS prompt is focused on the root directory of C:, the prompt will look like C:\>. By typing in DIR and then pressing the Enter key (you must always press Enter after every command in DOS), you will see something like this:

```
C:\>DIR

 Volume in Drive C is
```

```
 Volume Serial Number is 1734-3234
 Directory of C:\

DOS                <DIR>          09-03-96    9:34a
COMMAND   COM              34222  04-01-94    4:33p
AUTOEXEC  BAT              14     09-03-96   11:55a
WINDOWS            <DIR>          11-07-97    1:34a
CONFIG    SYS              34     09-03-96    4:36p
QUAKE              <DIR>          09-03-97    8:15a
JUNK      DOC              55677  04-03-98   10:03a
COMMAND   COM              23222  09-03-96    4:33p

9 file(s)          72233    bytes
                18288834    bytes free
```

If you are following along on a PC, remember that different computers contain different files and different programs, so you will absolutely see something different! If a lot of text scrolls quickly down the screen, try typing DIR/P (pause) or DIR/W (wide). Don't forget to hit Enter. After you type the command, you will see some entries that look like this:

```
CONFIG   SYS      34      09-03-96       4:36p
```

These are files. DIR lists the filename, extension, creation date, and size of the file in bytes. What you need to find are entries that look like this:

```
DOS            <DIR>         09-03-96     9:34a
WINDOWS        <DIR>         11-07-97     11:34a
```

If you type DIR/W, they might look like this:

```
[DOS]
[WINDOWS]
```

These are directories. The *CD* (or *CHDIR*) command allows you to change the focus of DOS to another directory. To use the CD command, simply type the name of the directory to which you want to change the focus. To go to the C:\DOS directory, type either CD C:\DOS or just CD\DOS, and then hit Enter. If the system has a DOS directory, the prompt will change to C:\DOS>. If there is no DOS directory, the system will report that it can't find it and the prompt will remain the same. To return to the root directory, just type CD\. You can use the CD command to point DOS to any directory. For example, you could type CD\FRED\BACKUP\TEST and the prompt would change to C:\FRED\BACKUP\TEST>.

Once the prompt has changed, try typing DIR again. You should see a different list of files and directories. Every directory holds different files and subdirectories; as DOS points to different directories, the DIR command shows the contents of the directories.

One very important shortcut when using the CD\ command is the ability to use a space instead of a backslash. Go to the root directory by typing CD\. Then you could move the focus to the C:\WINDOWS directory by typing CD WINDOWS. This works, however, to move the focus only one directory level. The command CD FRED\BACKUP\TEST wouldn't work, but the following three commands, one after the other, would (shown here with the prompts):

```
C:\>CD FRED
C:\FRED\>CD BACKUP
C:\FRED\BACKUP>CD TEST
```

Take some time to move the DOS focus around the directories of your PC using the CD and DIR commands. Use DIR to find directories, and CD to move the focus. Remember, CD\ will always get you back to the root directory!

The CD command isn't used to move between drives! To get DOS to point to another drive, just type the drive letter and a colon. If DOS is pointing at the C:\DOS directory and you want to see what is on the floppy (A:) drive, just type A: and DOS will point to the floppy drive. You'll see the following on the screen:

```
C:\DOS>A:
A:\>
```

To return to the C: drive, just type C: and you'll see:

```
A:\>C:
C:\DOS>
```

Note that you return back to the same directory that you left.

To create a directory, use the *MD* (or *MKDIR*) command. To create a directory called QUAKE from the root directory of C:, for example, first ensure that you are in the root directory by typing CD\. It should be C:\>. Now that DOS is pointing to the root directory, type MD QUAKE. There will be no response from DOS; you must use the DIR command to see the new directory.

> DOS almost never does anything to tell you that a command has been performed successfully. But be assured it will complain when you do something wrong! The old adage is: "DOS never pats you on the back, but it will slap you in the head!"

To create a subdirectory of the QUAKE directory, called FILES, first get DOS to point to the QUAKE directory with the CD\ command: CD\QUAKE, then run the MD command to make the FILES directory: MD FILES. The trick is to first be sure that DOS is pointing to the directory where you want to make the new subdirectory before you run the MD command.

Removing subdirectories is exactly like making them. First, get to the directory that contains the subdirectory you want to delete, and then run the *RD* (or *RMDIR*) command. In this example, let's delete the FILES subdirectory in the C:\QUAKE directory. First get to where the FILES directory is located—C:\QUAKE—by typing CD\QUAKE. Then type RD FILES. Nothing happened? Good. That means you probably did it right! Type DIR and the FILES subdirectory should be gone.

DOS will not delete a directory that contains files or subdirectories. If you want to delete a directory that contains files or subdirectories, go into that directory and use the DEL (for files) or RD (for directories) commands. You can also use the *DELTREE* command. DELTREE will delete the directory as well as all files and subdirectories. DELTREE is handy but dangerous, since it's easy to delete more than you want. Use the maxim "check twice and delete once." Let's delete the QUAKE and FILES directories with DELTREE. Since the QUAKE directory is in the root directory, point DOS to the root directory with CD\. Then run the DELTREE command: DELTREE C:\QUAKE. DOS will respond with the following:

```
Delete directory "C:\QUAKE" and all its subdirectories? [y/n]
```

Press the Y key and both C:\QUAKE and C:\QUAKE\FILES will be eliminated.

Running a Program

To run a DOS program, simply change DOS's focus to the directory where the program is located, and type the name of the program. To try this, go to the C:\DOS directory using the CD command. If you're using Windows 95/98, go to the C:\WINDOWS\COMMAND directory. Type DIR/W to see the files in the wide format. You will see a file called MEM.EXE. As mentioned earlier, all files with the extensions .EXE and .COM are programs, so MEM.EXE is a program. To run the MEM.EXE program, just type the filename, MEM (and hit Enter). Congratulations, you have just run your first DOS program!

Fun with Files

This section will deal with basic file manipulation. You'll learn how to look at, copy, move, and delete files. I'll assume that you have a C: root directory with the following files and directories:

```
C:\>DIR

 Volume in Drive C is
 Volume Serial Number is 1734-3234
 Directory of C:\

DOS                <DIR>            09-03-96    9:34a
COMMAND   COM             34222     04-01-94    4:33p
AUTOEXEC  BAT             44        09-03-97    11:55a
WINDOWS            <DIR>            11-07-97    1:34a
OLD_DOS            <DIR>            09-03-97    11:55a
BACKUP             <DIR>            09-04-96    6:42p
SPINRITE  COM             144654    11-02-96    8:00a
CONFIG    BAK             34        02-03-98    4:36a
CONFIG    NU              32        11-07-97    3:30p
AUTOEXEC  OLD             31        09-02-97    12:04a
VIRUS     COM             81222     04-01-97    5:29p
AUTOEXEC  1ST             21        09-03-96    11:14a
CONFIG    SYS             34        02-03-98    4:36p
QUAKE              <DIR>            09-03-97    8:15a
JUNK      DOC             15677     04-03-98    10:03a
AUTOEXEC  NU              32        11-07-97    3:30p

18 file(s)    3542233     bytes
              182888343   bytes free
```

Attributes

All files have four special values, or *attributes*, which determine how the file will act in special situations. These attributes can be set through software. The first attribute is called *hidden*. If a file is hidden, it will not be displayed when the DIR command is performed. Next is the *read-only* attribute. When a file is read-only, it can't be modified or deleted. Third is the *system* attribute, which is used only for system files such as IO.SYS and MSDOS.SYS. In reality, it does nothing more than provide an easy identifier to these files. Fourth is the *archive* attribute, which is used by backup software to identify files that have been changed since their last backup.

ATTRIB.EXE is an external DOS program that allows for the inspection and changing of file attributes. To see all of a file's attributes, enter the ATTRIB command followed by the name of the file. To determine the attributes of COMMAND.COM, type ATTRIB COMMAND.COM. The results would be:

```
A      COMMAND.COM
```

To show that the only marked attribute for COMMAND.COM is the archive attribute. The letter A stands for archive, R is read-only, H is hidden, and S is system. To add an attribute, use the plus sign (+). To delete an attribute, use the minus sign (–). To add the read-only attribute to COM-

MAND.COM, type ATTRIB +R COMMAND.COM. To remove the archive attribute, type ATTRIB -A COMMAND.COM. Multiple attributes can be added or removed in one command. Here's an example of removing three attributes from the IO.SYS file: ATTRIB -R -S -H IO.SYS.

Wildcards

Visualize having 273 files in one directory that need a number of changes to their attributes. Some of the files need to be hidden, some read-only, and some archive. Oh boy, this could take a while! If only there was some way to run the ATTRIB command on more than one file at a time, some way to select groups of files in a directory! The answer is *wildcards*.

Wildcards are two special characters, * and ?, that can be used in place of all or part of a filename in DOS commands so the commands act on more than one file at a time. Wildcards work with *all* DOS commands that take filenames. A great example is the DIR command. When you use just DIR, it shows all the files and folders in the specified directory. You could type the command DIR COMMAND.COM, however, and and get the following result:

```
 Volume in Drive C is
 Volume Serial Number is 1734-3234
 Directory of C:\

COMMAND   COM      34222       04-01-94   4:33p

1 file(s)     34222        bytes
              182888343    bytes free
```

Not very useful, but it works. What if you wanted to see all the files with the extension .COM? In this case, you'd use the * wildcard, like this: *DIR *.COM*. A good way to think of the * wildcard is "I don't care." Replace the part of the filename that you don't care about with *. The result of *DIR *.COM* would be:

```
 Volume in Drive C is
 Volume Serial Number is 1734-3234
 Directory of C:\

COMMAND     COM     34222          04-01-94      4:33p
NDOS        COM     76248          04-01-95      6:13p
SPINRITE    COM     144654         11-02-96      8:00a
VIRUS       COM     81222          04-01-97      5:29p

4 file(s)       206338      bytes
                182888343   bytes free
```

Wildcards also work with extensions:

```
C:\>DIR CONFIG.*
```

```
 Volume in Drive C is
 Volume Serial Number is 1734-3234
 Directory of C:\

CONFIG    BAK     34       02-03-98       4:36a
CONFIG    NU      32       11-07-97       3:30p
CONFIG    SYS     34       02-03-98       4:36p

3 file(s)      100          bytes
               182888343    bytes free
```

and partial filenames. Here, the DIR command finds every file that starts with the letter C:

```
C:\>DIR C*.*
 Volume in Drive C is
 Volume Serial Number is 1734-3234
 Directory of C:\
COMMAND    COM      34222      04-01-94     4:33p
CONFIG     BAK      34         02-03-98     4:36a
CONFIG     NU       32         11-07-97     4:30p
CONFIG     SYS      34         02-03-98     4:36p
4 file(s)       34322        bytes
                182888343    bytes free
```

The ? wildcard replaces any one character, which can be handy when you're looking for filenames with a particular number of characters. To find all of the files with a four-character filename ending with COM, you would type:

```
C:\>DIR ????.COM

 Volume in Drive C is
 Volume Serial Number is 1734-3234
 Directory of C:\

NDOS     COM        76248      04-01-95    6:13p

1 file(s)       76240        bytes
                182888343    bytes free
```

Deleting Files

File deletion is performed with the *DEL* or *ERASE* command. DEL and ERASE are identical commands and can be used interchangeably. Deleting files is very simple, maybe too simple. Once a file has been erased, it can be recovered only with a recovery utility such as UNERASE. DOS doesn't have anything like the Windows Recycle Bin. Again, the rule here is "check twice and delete once."

To delete a single file, type the DEL command followed by the name of the file to delete. To delete the file AUTOEXEC.BAK, for example, type DEL AUTOEXEC.BAK. Although nothing will happen on the screen, the file is gone. You have to use the DIR command to see that the AUTOEXEC.BAK file is no longer listed.

You can also use wildcards with DEL and ERASE in order to delete multiple files. To delete all files in a directory with the extension COM, you would type DEL *.COM. To delete all files in a directory with the filename CONFIG, type DEL CONFIG.*. To delete all files in a directory, you can use the popular *.* wildcard (often pronounced "star-dot-star" or "splat-dot-splat"), like this: DEL *.*. This is one of the few DOS commands that will elicit a response from DOS. Upon receiving the DEL *.* command, DOS will respond with "Are you sure? (Y/N)" to which you respond with a Y or N. Every file will be erased, so be careful with *.*!

Don't confuse erasing files with erasing directories. DEL erases files, but it will not erase directories. Use RD or DELTREE to erase directories.

Copying and Moving Files

The ability to copy and move files in DOS is crucial to all technicians. Due to its finicky nature and myriad of options, it is also rather painful to learn, especially if you're used to simply dragging icons in Windows. The following tried and true five-step process will make it easier, but the real secret is to get in front of a C: prompt and just copy and move files around until you're comfortable. Keep in mind that the only difference between copying and moving is whether the original is left behind (copy) or not (move).

1. Point DOS to the directory where the files to be copied/moved are located.
2. Type COPY or MOVE and a space.
3. Type the name of the file(s) to be copied/moved (with or without wildcards) and a space.
4. Type the path of the new location for the files.
5. Press Enter.

Let's try an example. The directory C:\QUAKE contains the file README.TXT. We'll copy this file to the floppy drive (A:).

1. Type CD\QUAKE to point DOS to the QUAKE directory.
2. Type COPY and a space.

3. Type README.TXT and a space.
4. Type A:\.
5. Hit Enter.

The entire command and response would look like this:

```
C:\QUAKE>COPY README.TXT A:\
1 file(s) copied
```

If you point DOS to the A: drive and type DIR, the README.TXT file will be visible. Let's try another example. Say there are over 100 files in the C:\DOCS directory, and about 30 have the extension .DOC. Now say you want to move these files to the C:\QUAKE directory.

1. Type CD\DOCS to point DOS to the DOCS directory.
2. Type MOVE and a space.
3. Type *.DOC and a space.
4. Type C:\ QUAKE.
5. Hit Enter.

The entire command and response would look like this:

```
C:\DOCS>MOVE *.DOC C:\QUAKE
30 file(s) copied
```

Communicating with Hardware

DOS can talk to a wide variety of PC hardware. The simplest way for DOS to talk to hardware is via the system BIOS. Every time the COPY command is run, DOS talks to the PC's system BIOS, which in turn talks to the drives in order to move data. These BIOS-level "calls" are completely built into DOS and are transparent to users. DOS uses the system BIOS for all basic functions: drives, floppies, monitor, and keyboard. For these devices, there is nothing to do other than to be sure that they are properly connected and, if necessary, configured in CMOS. DOS will automatically know they are there and respond to them.

When Microsoft invented DOS, they knew that devices would be invented in the future. Since IBM had already invented the very flexible PC, DOS had to be equally flexible to access and use any future device. As you know from previous chapters, all hardware needs BIOS. If a new device is snapped into an expansion slot, where is its BIOS? The system BIOS can't help, since it knows how to talk to only the most basic parts of the PC.

Therefore, it is up DOS to provide more programming, to add extra BIOS for new devices.

DOS provides two vehicles for adding control to new hardware: *device drivers* via CONFIG.SYS and *TSRs* via AUTOEXEC.BAT. Let's look at each of these important files in detail and understand what they are.

Device Drivers and CONFIG.SYS

The most common way to add BIOS is through special files called *device drivers*. A device driver is little more than all the programming necessary to talk to a new device. Device drivers usually come from the same company that makes the new hardware. If you buy a sound card or network card, it will come with a diskette or CD-ROM containing the necessary file(s). Even DOS comes with a few device drivers. Some examples of DOS device drivers are DRIVER.SYS, 3C509.SYS, and CLTV3.SYS.

As mentioned in the chapters on motherboards and BIOS, device drivers are loaded through a special file called CONFIG.SYS, a text file that must be in the root directory of the C: drive. Although CONFIG.SYS has some secondary functions, the best way to describe it is as the "DOS BYOB (bring your own BIOS) loader." The most common way to add device drivers in DOS is to first copy the device driver onto the C: drive (either manually using the COPY command to copy the driver from the floppy drive or CD-ROM to the hard drive, or automatically by running an installation program that does the copying for you). Either way, the result is a device driver on the C: drive, usually in its own directory. Once the device driver is copied to the C: drive, a line is added to the CONFIG.SYS file. This line starts with DEVICE= or DEVICEHIGH=, followed by the name and the path to the device driver.

Windows 95/98 doesn't need a CONFIG.SYS file, but most PCs running Windows 95/98 have a CONFIG.SYS to support DOS programs and device drivers. See if you have a CONFIG.SYS in the root directory of your C: drive. If you do, you can see the contents of the CONFIG.SYS file by typing TYPE CONFIG.SYS. Here are some typical device driver lines in CONFIG.SYS:

- DEVICE=C:\DOS\ANSI.SYS (DOS device driver)
- DEVICE=D:\CR_ATAPI.SYS /D:MSCD000 /Q (CD-ROM driver)
- DEVICEhigh=C:\VIBRA16\DRV\VIBRA16.SYS /BLASTER=A:220 I:5 D:1 H:5 (sound-card driver)

Before you go any further into CONFIG.SYS, there are some rules you need to understand:

- You need a text editor to edit CONFIG.SYS. Try using DOS's built-in text editor, the EDIT program. EDIT is fine, but it takes a little time to be comfortable with it—especially if you're used to Windows. Take the time to become familiar with opening and saving files, and exiting the EDIT program *before* you start messing around with crucial text files.
- Don't make changes to CONFIG.SYS without first making a backup! The best backup is to copy CONFIG.SYS to another directory. Make a directory called \BACKUP and copy CONFIG.SYS into it. This way, if you really mess it up, you can put a good copy back.
- Always do a "safe delete." If you think a line is unnecessary, put a semicolon (;) in front of the line, like this: ;DEVICE=C:\DOS\JUNK.SYS. The semicolon tells DOS to ignore the line. Then if you suddenly discover that you still need the line, just remove the semicolon. If the PC is still running properly after a couple of days, you can delete the line.
- Having unfamiliar lines isn't necessarily bad. It's common to just leave such lines alone.
- If a change is made to CONFIG.SYS, the change will not be reflected by the system until the computer is rebooted.

DOS comes with many device drivers, most of which are so terribly obsolete that they weren't used even when DOS was the only game in town. Of the DOS drivers that are still useful, most are discussed later. However, there are a few device drivers that warrant covering here:

SETVER.EXE The first driver is called SETVER.EXE. A few DOS application programs, especially those for networks, were designed to run on a certain version of DOS. If you attempt to run one of these programs on a version of DOS other than the one for which it was designed, it will return an error or lock up the computer. You can load the SETVER.EXE program as a device driver to tell DOS to report whatever version of DOS you want to any program. It is usually the first line in CONFIG.SYS, such as this one: DEVICE=C:\DOS\SETVER.EXE. Unless you are running some really old software, odds are good that you won't need this line.

ANSI.SYS The ANSI.SYS driver allows you to add color and features to the prompt. It also allows you to remap the keyboard. You don't *need*

ANSI.SYS; you *want* ANSI.SYS. ANSI.SYS wasn't always an optional item. Very early communication software programs would often require ANSI.SYS so DOS could emulate different terminals, like this: *DEVICE =C:\DOS\ANSI.SYS.* You can use ANSI.SYS with the PROMPT command to change the prompt and the keyboard.

There are many other device drivers that come with DOS, but to understand their function, you must first have a stronger understanding of the hardware they support. Once you understand memory management and disk caching, we'll return to CONFIG.SYS and the specialized drivers used by DOS to perform these functions.

CONFIG.SYS is not used only to load device drivers. There are a large number of "configuration commands" that are used by DOS to set up or optimize devices. This section will cover the most common configuration commands. Although not an exhaustive list, these are the only ones used on a regular basis.

BUFFERS During disk I/O, DOS needs some memory as an "assembly/disassembly area" for incoming and outgoing files, known as the *buffer space.* The BUFFERS statement defines the size of the space as follows: buffers=*nn,m,* where *nn* is the number of buffers, with a range of 6<99, and *m* is the number of buffers in the "look-ahead" buffer, with a range of 0<8 (optional). Here are some common BUFFERS= lines:

```
BUFFERS=20
BUFFERS=15,3
```

If you leave out the BUFFERS statement, you will get 15 buffers, which should be plenty. Leave out the BUFFERS statement unless you receive an error that contains the word "buffers." The look-ahead value is essentially a very early form of disk caching that is now obsolete.

STACKS A CPU uses its registers to run a program. Let's say you are running program X, so the registers inside your CPU are full of program X code. When a device like a mouse hits its IRQ, the CPU must run the mouse driver to act on the mouse IRQ. In order to run the mouse driver, the CPU must use the registers. But the CPU would like to return to program X when it's done with running the mouse driver. In order to do this, DOS sets aside some memory to temporarily store the register information. This memory area is called the stack. The register values for program X are stored in the stack, the mouse driver is run, and the register values for program X are restored to the registers.

The command's syntax is STACKS=*nn,mmm,* where *nn* is the number of stacks, with a range of 0, 8<64, and *mmm* is the size of each stack (0, 32<512). Some common STACKS= lines are:

```
STACKS=9,256
STACKS=32,128
```

The STACKS statement is rarely needed in CONFIG.SYS. By default, DOS sets STACKS=9,128. In the rare situation where you need a STACKS statement, you'll know since the machine will give you some nasty error such as "Stack Overflow." If you get an error like this, try increasing the size of each stack. If that doesn't help, reduce the stack size and increase the number of stacks. Last, try increasing both. Stack errors are particularly a problem where you have in-house programmers who write bad code. Resolve stack problems in this case by talking to the programmer, not by increasing the STACKS= statement.

FILES DOS needs to keep track of all files on the hard drive that are being used. A part of memory is set aside to store this information. Each area of memory used to store the information for one file is called a *file handle.* The FILES= statement tells DOS how many file handles are to be used. Its syntax is FILES=*nnn,* where *nnn* is the number of files, with a range of 8<255. Some common FILES= lines are:

```
FILES=15
FILES=99
```

You need a FILES= statement. The default value of eight files is insufficient for most PCs. Set the files to FILES=20 for stand-alone PCs and FILES=99 for networked PCs. If you need more file handles, you'll get an error like "Insufficient file handles." Increase the value by tens until it goes away.

FCBS DOS uses file handles to track open files, but an ancient operating system called CPM used something called *file control blocks.* When DOS first came out, Microsoft wanted people to be able to use their CPM programs on DOS PCs with as little change to the code as possible. As a result, DOS supports file control blocks. The command's syntax is FCBS=*nnn,mmm,* where *nnn* is the maximum number of open files, with a range of 1<255, and *mmm* is the maximum number of files that will never close, with a range of 1<255 (obsolete after DOS 4). Some common FCBS= lines are:

```
FCBS=4,0
FCBS=8
```

This line is obsolete. Unless you are running some ancient DOS program (before 1988), there is absolutely no way you need this line. Delete it.

SHELL COMMAND.COM is known as the "command interpreter" because it interprets commands like DIR /W and then tells MSDOS.SYS that the user wants to see a directory in the wide format. However, COMMAND.COM also defines what DOS looks like. COMMAND.COM produces the C:\> prompt and the paths you see when you're working in DOS. In addition, it saves a small amount of memory for what are known as *environment variables,* which store information that is available to any program.

So COMMAND.COM is many things: a command interpreter, a holder of environment variables, and a "front end" that manifests the operating system. Collectively, this is known as the *shell.* By default, the shell that you use in the root directory of the C: drive is COMMAND.COM. You don't have to use this COMMAND.COM, however; you can use another shell. The SHELL= statement defines which shell. SHELL's syntax is a bit more complex:

```
SHELL=path_to_shell/P/E:nnnnlocation_of_transient_shell
```

where `path_to_shell` is the location of COMMAND.COM or another shell, /P is the permanent switch (you won't be able to exit this command interpreter), /E:*nnnnn* is the size of environment space in bytes, with a range of 160<32768, and `location_of_transient_shell` tells where to find the transient shell if its overwritten. Some common SHELL= lines are:

```
SHELL=C:\DOS\COMMAND.COM /P /E:512
SHELL=C:\COMMAND.COM /P C:\COMMAND.COM
```

The quick answer is you probably don't need the SHELL= statement. If you don't have one, the shell will be the COMMAND.COM in the root directory. The SHELL statement is usually needed for its options. For example, /E:*nnnn* increases the DOS environment (see AUTOEXEC.BAT and SET, later in this chapter). The DOS environment holds options like PATH, PROMPT, and TEMP. If you look in the AUTOEXEC.BAT, you will see options like:

```
SET TEMP=C:\WINDOWS\TEMP
SET BLASTER=A220 I7 D1
```

If you have more than 256 bytes of information in SET statements (including the PATH and PROMPT statement, which are really SET statements in disguise), you'll get the nasty error "Not Enough Environment Space" and your system will lock up. The /E:*nnnn* option adds environment space beyond the default 256 bytes to correct this error. Start with

/E:512 and keep adding until the error goes away. The /P option prevents you from using the Exit command to stop the current COMMAND.COM. This option is usually needed only by programs that take control or replace COMMAND.COM, like QEMM or some programs in Norton Utilities. If you don't use a SHELL= statement, the default is as though there was a /P. Therefore, if you use a SHELL= statement, always add the /P option since that most closely mimics the DOS default.

The last option, transient shell, is a little weird but you'll probably need it from time to time. COMMAND.COM is broken into two pieces: permanent and transient. The permanent part is loaded into conventional memory and is the part you see when you use the MEM /C/P command. This is also the part you can load into the HMA using the DOS=HIGH command. The transient part is loaded into the top of conventional memory and can be written over by programs that need the memory. If a program overwrites the transient part of COMMAND.COM, the transient part must be restored when the program ends. This setting specifies where to find the COMMAND.COM that has a copy of the transient area. The COMMAND.COM that has a copy of the transient area is invariably the main COMMAND.COM. For example:

```
SHELL=C:\DOS\COMMAND.COM /E:512 /P C:\DOS\COMMAND.COM
```

is the most common way to do this. You don't add the transient portion to the SHELL statement unless a program won't return to the DOS prompt after it ends.

TSRs and AUTOEXEC.BAT

The second way to add support for devices is through a *TSR* (terminate and stay resident) program. TSRs are less common than CONFIG.SYS device drivers, but they can work equally well. You run a TSR like any other program, by typing its name at the prompt. Unlike other programs, however, a TSR will immediately return you to a DOS prompt (terminate), but will still be in RAM (stay resident). One of the most common TSRs is for mice. Most mice come with a diskette that includes a TSR so you can use it in DOS. These TSR programs usually have a catchy name like MOUSE.COM. When you run the program, you'll see something like this:

```
C:\>MOUSE

Mouse driver version 8.20
Copyright (c) 1991-1993
```

```
All rights reserved
1993-11-09

Mouse driver installed

C:\>
```

It seems as though nothing has happened, but it has. The MOUSE program is still in memory and is ready to support DOS programs that use a mouse. Try running the EDIT program and move your mouse. Tada! You have a mouse cursor! That's a classic use of a TSR. Windows 95/98 has a built-in mouse TSR, although you'll almost never need it.

There are relatively few devices that use TSRs in DOS; most use device drivers in CONFIG.SYS. However, DOS itself uses quite a few TSRs. Many have special functions that are covered in other sections of this book, but there are three that should be discussed here:

DOSKEY One very popular TSR used in DOS is DOSKEY.COM, which is a handy program that keeps track of commands you have typed, creates keyboard "macros," and adds extra power to the function keys for typing commands. The ability to store previously used commands is very helpful. Let's say you've been copying a lot of files from different directories. It might be very handy to be able to bring back a command you entered two or three commands ago. If you have DOSKEY running, you can retrieve old commands just by pressing the up arrow. You can also create a macro. In DOSKEY, a *macro* is a way to assign a series of keystrokes to one key combination like Ctrl<I. You can use DOSKEY for practical jokes, such as assigning the display "No directory today" to DIR. Try it. Type this command:

```
DOSKEY DIR=echo No directory today
```

The echo means to output to the screen, not to run a program. When you type DIR, you'll get

```
C:\>DIR
No directory today
```

Now type *DOSKEY DIR=* to erase the macro. Use your imagination for more practical examples. How about a macro that will automatically delete all files with the extension TMP from the C:\TEMP directory?

MODE The MODE.COM program is rarely used, but quite powerful. It can change the look of the monitor and allow you to redirect output from ports, as well as a number of other, less used features. Go to a prompt and type MODE CO40. You'll get wide letters! Then type MODE CO80 to put it back. When a screen mysteriously goes blank in DOS,

MODE CO80 will often correct the problem. The MODE command is also handy for configuring and redirecting ports, although this is rarely done anymore. For example, to set COM1 to 9600 baud, no parity, eight data bits, and one stop bit, type MODE COM1:9600,8,n,1. This should be done only if an application tells you to do so. Another somewhat popular MODE command to redirect output from an LPT port to a COM port is MODE LPT1=COM1, which will redirect all data from LPT1 and output it to COM1. Like the other MODE command, this isn't done unless specified by an application.

SHARE The SHARE command is still quite common on DOS PCs. When a DOS program uses a file on a network, it is possible for another program to try to use the same file. This can cause file corruption, which isn't good. To prevent this, the SHARE program is installed to create "file locking" so while one program is using a file, no other program can try to open it again until the first program closes the file. So SHARE should actually be called ANTISHARE. SHARE's syntax is SHARE /F:*xxxx* /L:*yyy*, where *xxxx* is the maximum amount of RAM to use for sharing information (default of 2048), and *yyy* is the number of files to lock (default of 20). Some common SHARE lines are:

```
SHARE
SHARE /F:4096 /L;500
```

SHARE should be used only when specified by an application.

Now let's say that you decide you like DOSKEY and you are going to use a mouse. Every time you reboot, you will have to enter DOSKEY.COM and MOUSE.COM before you start working. Wouldn't it be great if you could tell DOS to just start certain TSRs automatically? Well, that's the job of AUTOEXEC.BAT. AUTOEXEC.BAT is a text file that resides in the root directory of the C: drive, just like CONFIG.SYS. Using the EDIT program, you can create a text file with two lines:

```
DOSKEY
MOUSE
```

and save it with the name AUTOEXEC.BAT—be sure to put it in the root directory of C:! Now, every time you boot the PC, DOSKEY and MOUSE will start automatically. You can add any command that can be typed at the prompt to AUTOEXEC.BAT. If you added CD\DOS:

```
DOSKEY
MOUSE
CD\DOS
```

DOS would run DOSKEY and MOUSE, and then point to the C:\DOS directory every time it booted. There are a number of commands you might like to run every time the PC boots. Let's take a look at these and see why:

SET The SET command creates *environment variables,* which are values that can be stored so any DOS program, including DOS itself, can read them. The SET command is commonly used with sound cards. Most sound cards create a special environment variable to inform any DOS program that wants to use it that it is present and what it can do. Here's a common SET statement for a sound card:

```
SET BLASTER=A240 D3 I5 H5 T1 MIDI=D330 D1
```

All DOS programs that use sound cards look for an environment variable called BLASTER, which tells the program all the I/O information and the type of sound card. If you have DOS games that use sound cards, you'll want the BLASTER environment variable. Here are some other common SET statements:

```
SET TEMP=C:\WINDOWS\TEMP
SET CTCM=C:\CTCM
SET BACK=C:\BACKUP
```

Any program can make and use environment variables. There are hundreds of different SET statements and they are quite common. Two more environment variables that are created and used by DOS, PATH and PROMPT, are a little involved and warrant a more detailed inspection.

PATH The PATH environment specifies where to look for programs if they aren't in the current directory. Go to the C:\> directory, type DIR, and verify that the EDIT program is not there. Now type EDIT. The program runs! If you'll remember from an earlier discussion, you need to be *in the directory* where a program is located in order for it to work. So what gives? Type SET. You'll see something like this:

```
PATH=C:\;C:\DOS;C:\WINDOWS;
PROMPT=$P$G
BLASTER= A240 D3 I5 H5 T1 MIDI=D330 D1
TEMP=C:\WINDOWS\TEMP
```

The SET statement shows all the environment variables. Look at the PATH= line. Do you see C:\DOS? That's why EDIT works! The PATH environment variable says: "Look, if the program you're trying to run isn't in the current directory, look in these directories in the order listed." You can erase the PATH by typing PATH=. Now try running EDIT:

```
C:\>EDIT
Bad command or file name
C:\>
```

Replace the PATH, using semicolons between each directory, by typing PATH=C:\;C:\DOS; and you should be able to run EDIT again. Clearly, the PATH is something you'll want to run every time the PC starts, so let's add it to the AUTOEXEC.BAT (make it the first line):

```
PATH=C:\;C:\DOS;C:\WINDOWS;
DOSKEY
MOUSE
CD\DOS
```

The very last versions of DOS automatically added C:\DOS to the PATH. You had to add anything else. The PATH line in AUTOEXEC.BAT can look different. It's really an environment variable, so it might look like SET PATH=C:\;C:\DOS; or it might not have the = sign, like this: PATH C:\;C:\DOS;. They all work equally well.

PROMPT The PROMPT command defines how the prompt looks. Go to the C:\> prompt, type PROMPT=*, and watch what happens. Hmmm, where's the prompt? It's an asterisk. Now type CD\DOS. No change, but you are in the C:\DOS directory. If you type DIR, you will see the contents of that directory. The PROMPT command takes some special commands—here's a partial list:

$P = path
$G = greater-than sign
$D = date
$T = time
$$ = dollar sign
$V = DOS version
$L = less-than sign
$E = escape

To change the prompt back to the way you're used to seeing it, type PROMPT PG. The prompt command can be used to make quite an impressive, colorful prompt if you have ANSI.SYS loaded. You need to use $E to do it. Try typing this (pay attention to which letters are upper- and lowercase):

```
C:\>PROMPT $E[1;34;40m$P$G$E[0;37;40m
```

My, what a pretty prompt! For the $E[X;Y;Zm part of the command, X = brightness, Y = foreground, and Z = background. Replace the letters with

TABLE 13.3

Prompt Color Codes

Brightness	Foreground	Background
0 for normal display	30 black foreground	40 black background
1 bold on	31 red foreground	41 red background
4 underline (mono only)	32 green foreground	42 green background
5 blink on	33 yellow foreground	43 yellow background
7 reverse video on	34 blue foreground	44 blue background
8 invisible	35 magenta foreground	45 magenta background
	36 cyan foreground	46 cyan background
	37 white foreground	47 white background

the numbers for the colors and attributes (see Table 13.3). The command PROMPT $E[0;31;47$pgE[0;37;40m will make a red-on-white prompt.

The PROMPT command goes way beyond even these settings. Check your DOS book for details on moving the cursor and remapping your keyboard. DOS defaults to PROMPT PG if no other prompt is specified. Now put all of this together in the AUTOEXEC.BAT file:

```
PATH=C:\;C:\DOS;C:\WINDOWS;
PROMPT $P$G
DOSKEY
MOUSE
```

Startup Options

One of the big problems with CONFIG.SYS and AUTOEXEC.BAT is when they go wrong. Say you go to the local computer store and buy the new Acme GerbilMan 2.01 for DOS. The program comes with an interface card that you install. It also comes with a "drivers disk." You snap the drivers disk into the A: drive, type A: and then DIR. There's a program called INSTALL.EXE, so you run it. The INSTALL program creates a directory called C:\GERBIL and copies the application program. It then goes into your CONFIG.SYS and adds the following line:

```
DEVICE=C:\GERBIL\GBLDRV.SYS /FEED:YES /CLEAN:NO
```

You don't see any of this happening. All you see is a stupid "percent done" bar. Eventually, the installation stops and says: "Installation Complete. To run GerbilMan, reboot and type GERBIL from the C: Prompt."

Great! an easy installation. You reboot the PC, but unbeknownst to you, six weeks earlier an assembly-line worker at ACME software was in kind of a hurry while packing the box containing the GerbilMan you ended up buying. Instead of putting in the correct driver disk (version 2.00.12/A), he threw in an old copy (version 2.00.06/F).

Well, it just so happens that if you run driver version 2.00.06/F on a GerbilMan 2.01 card, it will lock up like a stone the moment the device driver runs from CONFIG.SYS. This is clearly documented, if you had used the ACME fax-back service and requested fax document G32342 *or* taken the time to go to http:\\www.acme.com\techsupp\gerbil\drivers\download\latest *or* called the per-incident line and paid $35 *or* read the tiny slip of paper called "latest developments" shoved into the User Manual between pages G-43 and G-44.

So lucky you, the PC boots up, makes the usual noises, says "Starting MS-DOS," and then locks up like a stone. If the PC locks up at this point, the problem is in one of the DOS system files (IO.SYS, MSDOS.SYS, or COMMAND.COM) or either of the startup files (CONFIG.SYS or AUTOEXEC.BAT). The only thing that has changed since the machine ran properly was updating CONFIG.SYS—but you can't look at CONFIG.SYS since the computer locks up every time you reboot.

This is a classic problem for DOS. To help, the latest versions of DOS have two new uses for function keys F5 and F8: overriding and stepping through the CONFIG.SYS and AUTOEXEC.BAT files, respectively. When the computer shows "Starting MS-DOS" while booting, you have two seconds to press F5 or F8. If you press F5, you'll get: "MS-DOS is bypassing your CONFIG.SYS and AUTOEXEC.BAT files."

So you have completely skipped both startup files and are sitting at the C:\> prompt. Good. Now you know the problem is in either CONFIG.SYS or AUTOEXEC.BAT. Reboot again, and this time use the F8 key. MS-DOS will prompt you to confirm each CONFIG.SYS command. Each line of the CONFIG.SYS will be displayed individually, with the option to run or not. Press Y to run the line and N to skip it:

```
DEVICE=C:\DOS\SETVER.EXE? [y/n] Y
DEVICE=C:\GERBIL\GBLDRV.SYS /FEED:YES /CLEAN:NO [y/n] Y
```

When you lock up, you've found the problem! Another handy startup option for CONFIG.SYS device drivers is a question mark in the DEVICE= or DEVICEHIGH= statement, like this:

```
DEVICE?=C:\GERBIL\GBLDRV.SYS /FEED:YES /CLEAN:NO
```

This will act as though you pressed F8 just for that line, which is handy for checking device drivers.

Working with Drives

I've already touched on using DOS to work with drives, in the chapter on hard drives. There I reviewed using FDISK and FORMAT to prepare drives for use. You also saw how the PC boots and used a bootable disk to set up a drive. In this section, you'll see some of the other programs that come with DOS that you can use to work with drives.

One of the most important items in your toolbox is a bootable floppy diskette. It has many uses—in particular booting up a system when the hard drive isn't working properly. You can make a bootable floppy from any properly operating PC. Don't wait to make one until you need it; you might not have a properly operating PC available. Make sure you have a bootable floppy for every version of DOS. To verify the version of DOS, type VER from any prompt. After you have verified the version, insert a blank floppy and use the SYS command to make it bootable. Then copy the following files onto the floppy:

- FDISK.EXE or FDISK.COM (depends on the version of DOS)
- FORMAT.EXE or FORMAT.COM (depends on the version of DOS)
- SYS.COM
- EDIT.COM (from Windows 95, but also works with old DOS)
- HIMEM.SYS
- EMM386.EXE
- SMARTDRV.EXE
- MSD.EXE or MSD.COM
- MSCDEX.EXE
- MEM.EXE
- ATTRIB.EXE
- DEFRAG.EXE
- DELTREE.EXE
- EXPAND.COM
- LABEL.COM
- SCANDISK.EXE
- SHARE.EXE

These files just barely fit on a 3.5-inch floppy. Add or subtract from this list as you get more comfortable. Remember that there are many versions of DOS. Be prepared! This works equally well for Windows 95/98, but it's much easier to tell Windows to make a startup disk. See the chapter on Windows 95.

VOL

Every drive letter has a *volume label,* which is roughly equivalent to a sign placed in front of a building. Like a sign, it tells the function of the drive—whereas the drive letter is really no more than an address. The idea behind a volume label is to allow users to create a more personal, more descriptive name for their drives. The volume label can be up to eleven characters and can include spaces. It is displayed every time you run the DIR command.

```
C:\>DIR C*.*

Volume in Drive C is Mikes PC
Volume Serial Number is 1734-3234
Directory of C:\

COMMAND COM     34222    04-01-94    4:33p
CONFIG  BAK     34       02-03-98    4:36a
CONFIG  NU      32       11-07-97    3:30p
CONFIG  SYS     34       02-03-98    4:36p

4 file(s)    34322       bytes
             182888343   bytes free
```

You can also use the VOL command to see the volume label:

```
C:\>VOL
Volume in Drive C is Mikes PC
Volume Serial Number is 1734-3234
```

You can create or delete a volume label with the *LABEL* command:

```
C:\>label
Volume in drive C is Mikes PC
Volume Serial Number is 1734-3234
Volume label (ENTER for none)?
```

The volume label is not required, not used by any applications, and is considered obsolete. However, there is one point where the volume label can be crucial. In FDISK, when you are deleting a primary partition, the FDISK program will ask for the volume label. If you don't type in the correct volume label, you won't be able to delete the partition. Many technicians purposely add a volume label just to keep users from accidentally trashing a partition.

SYS

The SYS command copies the three DOS system files to a partition, making it bootable. In the chapter on hard drives, you saw how to use the FORMAT command with the /S option to format a drive and copy the system files. Sometimes you don't want to reformat a drive; you just want to add or replace the system files. To do this, run the SYS command followed by the letter of the drive we want to make bootable. This command is very handy for making preformatted floppy diskettes bootable. The SYS command looks like this:

```
C:\>SYS A:
System transferred
```

The SYS command works equally well to replace a suspect system file on a hard drive. Whenever you lock up on boot after the POST, a quick SYS C: is a handy way to verify that the system files are intact.

LASTDRIVE

The LASTDRIVE= command allows you to allocate memory for the drive letters of storage devices other than local hard drives. Non-hard-drive storage devices include CD-ROM, ZIP, and network drives—anything other than a local hard drive that uses a drive letter. DOS allocates only enough space for two extra drive letters beyond C: for these devices. For example, if you had a hard drive that was C:, then you could add only two CD-ROM drives before you would get the error "Not enough drive letters available."

To tell DOS to allocate more space for drive letters, add the command LASTDRIVE=x to the CONFIG.SYS, where *x* is the highest drive letter you'll need. LASTDRIVE= is almost always set to Z (LASTDRIVE=Z) to provide space for all the possible drive letters. LASTDRIVE is very commonly used in a DOS PC's CONFIG.SYS file.

Checking Drives

The D in DOS stands for *disk*, since DOS was one of the first operating systems that took a "disk-centric approach" to the PC. The greatest representation of this idea is the prompt itself, which always points to a drive and a directory. With DOS, you get the feeling of moving around inside of drives (CD\) and looking around (DIR). This feeling is so prevalent that it is common for a person to say "I'm in the FRED directory on my C: drive" or "Go to the FRED directory and delete all the files."

Clearly, a disk-centric OS like DOS is going to be interested in the general health and welfare of both hard and floppy drives. To help ensure that the drives are in good working order, DOS comes with a number of utilities to inspect, optimize, and repair drives. Some of these utilities were discussed earlier in the book, but now we'll look at them in more detail.

CHKDSK

The CHKDSK program was the first disk utility to be included as a part of DOS. CHKDSK identifies and repairs lost cluster chains. It will also identify, but cannot repair, cross-linked files. In the chapter on hard drives, you learned that a lost cluster chain is a series to clusters that has no filename, while cross-linked files are two files trying to claim the same cluster. CHKDSK repairs a lost chain by giving it a filename called FILE*xxxx*.CHK, where *xxxx* starts with 0000 and increments for each lost chain CHKDSK locates. These files are then placed in the root directory of the drive that is being checked. For example, if you run CHKDSK and it finds three lost chains, it will give those chains the names FILE0000.CHK, FILE0001.CHK, and FILE0002.CHK. These files are usually just deleted, thereby recovering the disk space for use by other files. CHKDSK must be run with the /F option to repair lost chains. Otherwise it will simply report their existence without repairing them. If you use CHKDSK, use the /F option:

```
C:\>CHKDSK /F

Volume Serial Number is 306D-1CDA

 2,111,537,152 bytes total disk space
    61,702,144 bytes in 113 hidden files
    11,272,192 bytes in 344 directories
   628,555,776 bytes in 6,256 user files
 1,410,007,040 bytes available on disk

 32,768 bytes in each allocation unit
 64,439 total allocation units on disk
 43,030 available allocation units on disk

 655,360 total bytes memory
 590,560 bytes free
```

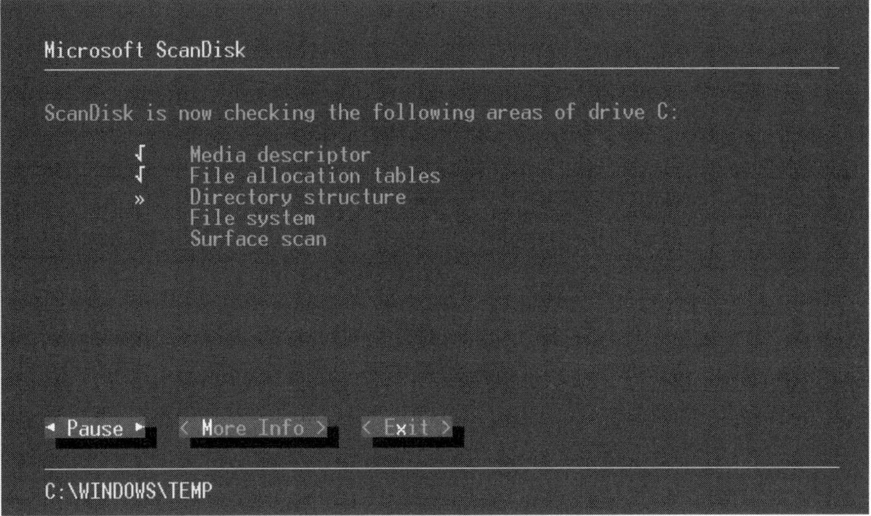

Figure 13.3a
Scandisk

Instead of using CHKDSK, try using SCANDISK. SCANDISK can reliably detect and fix a much wider range of disk problems. DOS now comes with the SCANDISK program. As the warning says, SCANDISK can detect and repair a far greater range of disk problems. If the version of DOS you are using comes with SCANDISK, there is no reason to use CHKDSK /F.

SCANDISK

The SCANDISK program is a significant improvement over CHKDSK. SCANDISK is a highly flexible, relatively safe, and very powerful disk-repair utility (Figure 13.3a). Where CHKDSK can fix only lost clusters, SCANDISK can repair lost clusters, cross-linked files, directory and file structures, file allocation tables, even volume labels. SCANDISK will also rescan all the clusters on a drive to verify their proper working order and FAT status. The best thing to say about SCANDISK is that there is so little *to* say. Its safety and ease of use make it the first line of defense in drive maintenance and troubleshooting.

DEFRAG

As discussed earlier in the book, hard drives need to be defragmented about once a week. DOS's DEFRAG program is a simple defragmentation program that does an admirable job of clearing up file fragmentation without any user intervention (Figure 13.3b).

However, DEFRAG has a few interesting, and for the most part ignored, options. First is the optimization method, which is either Full or Files Only. Full optimization copies all directories to the front of the drive, increasing access speed, while the Files Only options does as it says—optimizing only files (Figure 13.4).

It's hard to find a file in a directory with more than 20 files. DEFRAG has a handy option that allows you to sort the files and directories on a drive. You can choose the sort criteria by filename, extension, date, and size (Figure 13.5).

Figure 13.3b
Defrag

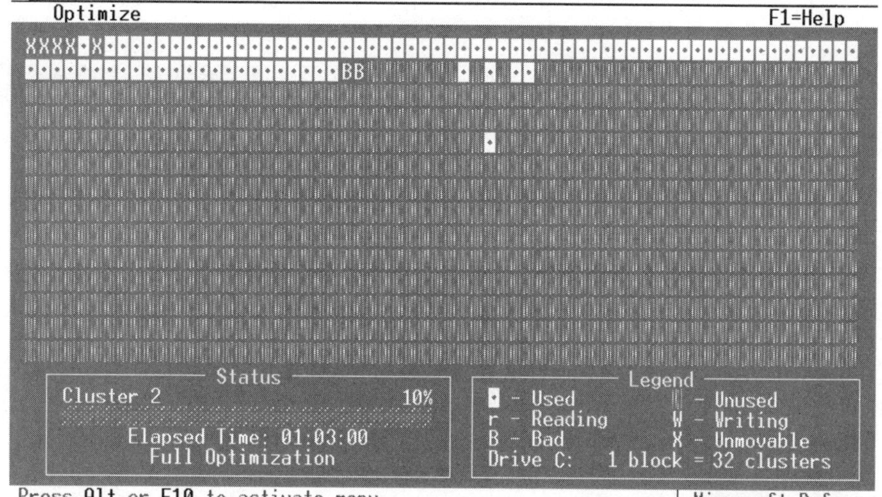

Figure 13.4
Optimization method

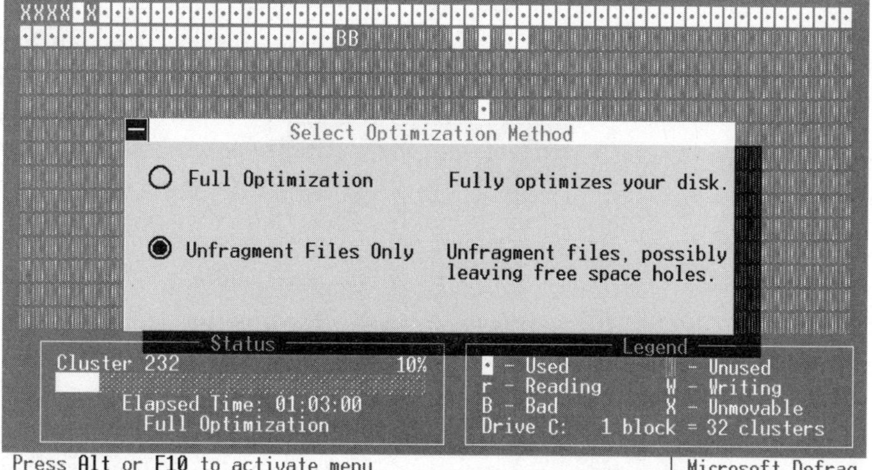

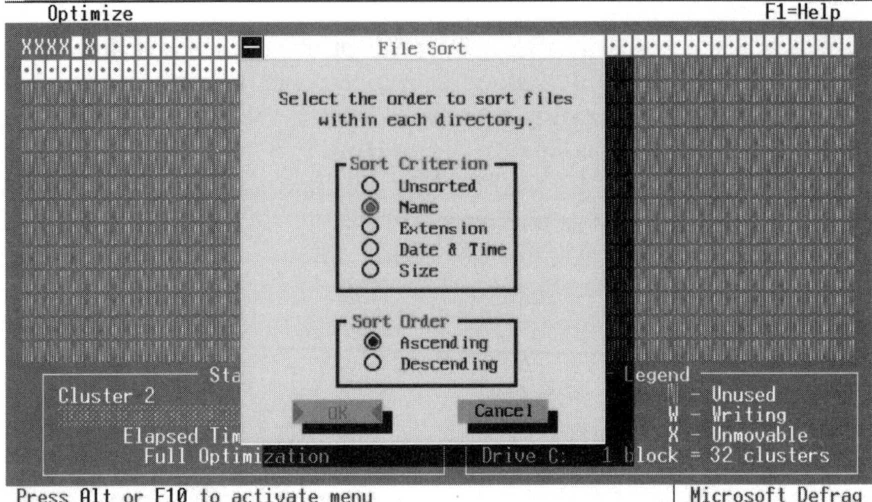

Figure 13.5 Sort criteria

Disk Caching

Whenever someone asks "What is the most important thing I can do to make my PC faster?" the first answer should always be "Make sure your disk cache is enabled!" A disk cache is crucial to the performance of your PC. I want to take a moment to explain the function of a disk cache, and then you can look at the venerable DOS disk cache SMARTDRV (smart-drive) and see some "tweaks" to ensure good performance.

Have you ever listened to your hard drive or watched your hard drive light while you're working on your PC? Have you noticed that there is quite a bit of activity on the drives, even when you're doing work that has nothing to do with the drive? You see, the system constantly accesses the hard drive, not just when you start a program. When you start most DOS application programs—let's use Microsoft Word for DOS as an example—you aren't loading the entire program. Any good program will have only the part of its code necessary to do the business at hand in RAM. If you're not spell-checking, why load the spell-checker code and data, and lose precious RAM that could be used for something else? Every program accesses many subroutines stored in files to perform many different functions, like making margins, accessing menus, and importing graphics. These extra files are loaded on an as-needed basis (Figure 13.6a) and are then unloaded from RAM when their job is done (Figure 13.6b).

Not only do programs constantly access the hard drive, they constantly access the *same files* over and over again! (See Figure 13.7.) As you know, accessing a hard drive is a very slow process when compared to accessing

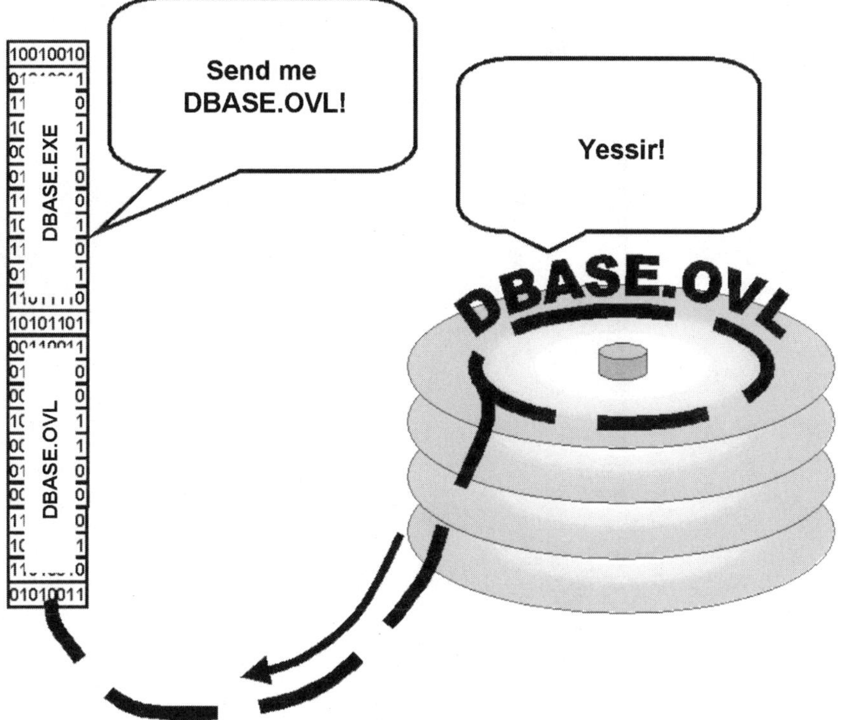

Figure 13.6a
Programs constantly access the hard drive

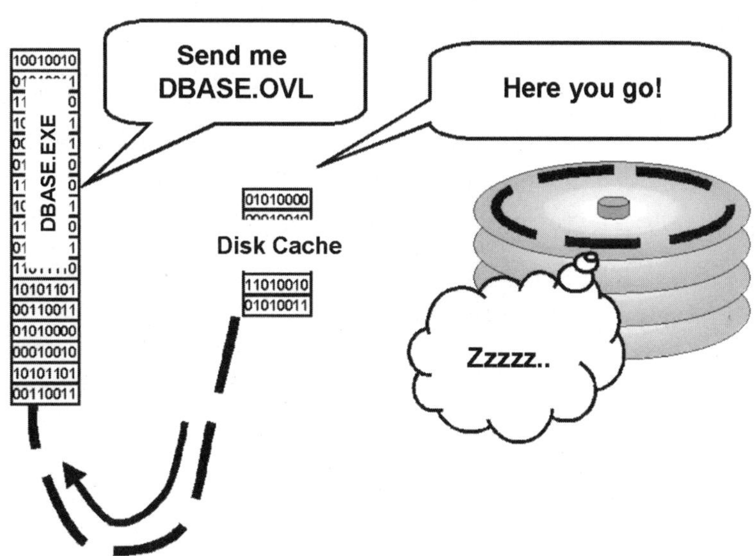

Figure 13.6b
Unneeded programs are erased from RAM

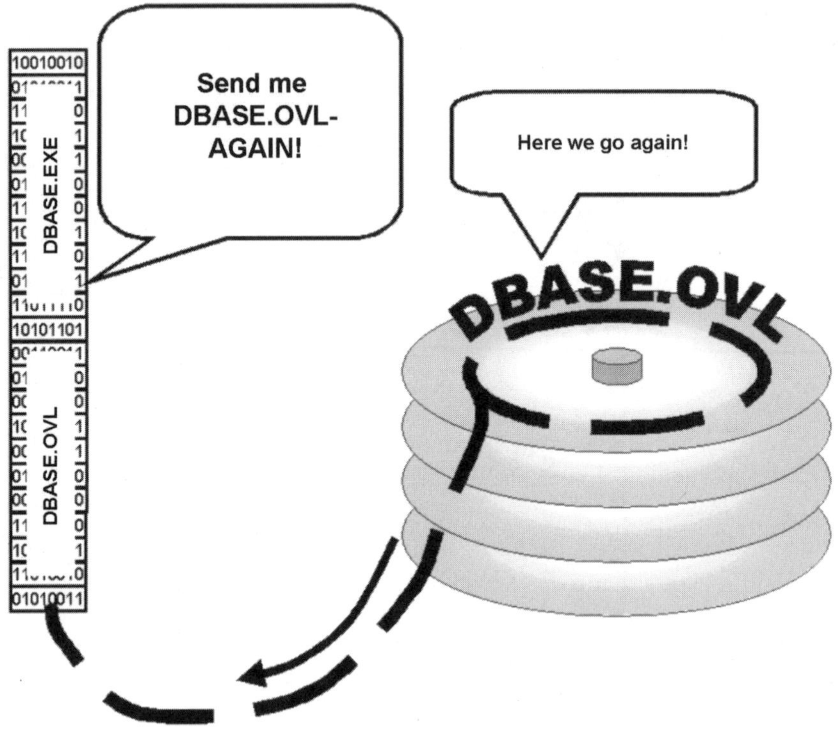

Figure 13.7 Calling a file many times

RAM. What is needed is some kind of "fast storage area" to place copies of files that the main program constantly needs to access. That way, when the program calls them, they're in something faster than the hard drive, ready to be used.

There are special hardware devices and software programs that set aside a part of RAM to be used as a *disk cache*, which is actually composed of two separate items: a RAM "holding pen" that stores data from the hard drive, and a program that monitors drive accesses. I'll call the program "the cache" and the RAM that holds the data "the holding pen."

The disk cache monitors all access to the drive, keeping a copy of accessed data in its holding area (Figure 13.8a). Whenever a program needs to get something from RAM, the cache first checks its holding pen to see if the data is there. If the data is present, the cache passes the data to RAM, thus avoiding any need to access the relatively slow hard drive and making the system much faster.

There are many ways to make a disk cache. One way is to have special hard-drive controller cards that are populated with RAM (Figure 13-8b). These controllers store bits of hard drive data on RAM, on a sector-by-sector basis. When the computer asks for a particular sector, special pro-

Figure 13.8a
The disk cache monitoring drive access

Figure 13.8b
Hardware disk cache

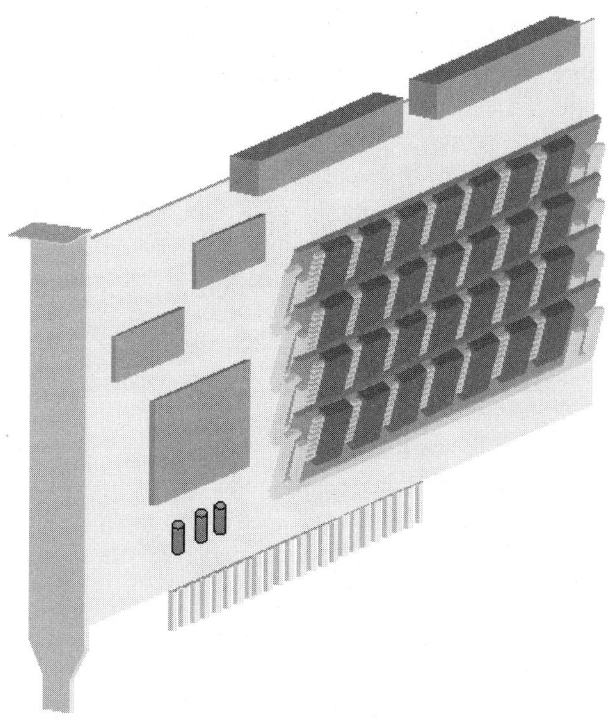

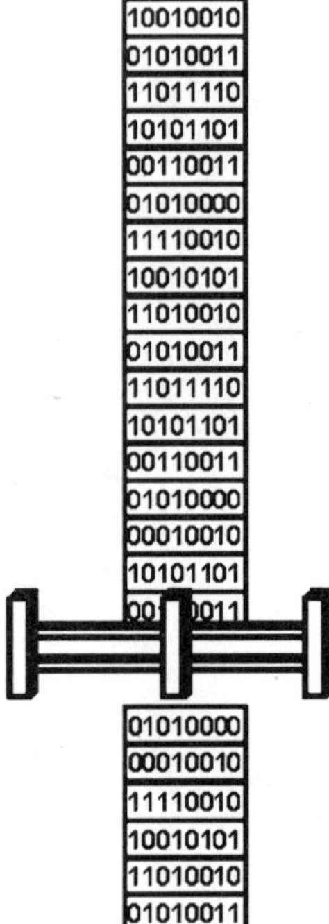

A Software Disk Cache sets aside some of the system DRAM as a cache

Figure 13-9 Setting RAM aside

grams on the controller search the on-board RAM to see if that sector is in the cache. If it is, the data is immediately sent to the system. If not, the sectors are taken off the drive, a copy is stored on the on-board RAM, and then it is sent to the system. If the system asks for that sector, the data is in the cache, ready to go. These are called *caching controllers*.

Caching controllers are generally expensive and rare. Instead, most systems use a software caching method. Software caching is cheap—often free—and for most users it is just as good as a caching controller card. In software caching, a portion of the computer's DRAM is electronically set aside to be used as the cache, while the caching program resides in RAM (Figure 13.9).

Unlike hardware-based disk caches, software caches tend to look at the drive in clusters, but otherwise they work in exactly the same way. By far the most popular software disk cache in DOS computers is the famous SMARTDRV, which comes bundled free as a part of DOS.

SMARTDRV SMARTDRV is initiated from the AUTOEXEC.BAT file with a line like SMARTDRV.EXE. Simply adding this line provides an excellent disk cache. However, is it good enough? There are ways to measure the quality of the disk cache. The ultimate unit is called the *hit rate,* which is measured with the formula:

hit rate = (number of times data is in cache/number of data requests × 100%

So the hit rate means "What percentage of all the times the system goes to the hard drive for data is the data already in the cache?" A good hit rate is in the area of 75 to 90 percent! Amazing! That means a good disk cache will eliminate the need to use the slowest part of your computer, the hard drive, around 80 percent of the time. Measuring the hit rate is the tool you use to optimize the disk cache. You can determine the hit rate by typing:

```
C:\>SMARTDRV /S

Microsoft SMARTDrive Disk Cache version 5.0
Copyright 1991,1993 Microsoft Corp.

Room for 16 elements of 8,192 bytes each
There have been 997 cache hits
and 291 cache misses
```

After SMARTDRV is running, it can be run from the C:\> prompt to perform certain functions. For example, you can type SMARTDRV /S at a C:\> prompt to determine the hit rate:

hit rate = 997 hits /(291 misses + 997 hits) × 100% = 77% (could be better)

Although SMARTDRV will run if you add the line SMARTDRV to the AUTOEXEC.BAT file, you can increase the hit rate substantially by special tweaks to the line. Here's a good SMARTDRV line:

```
SMARTDRV a- b- 1024 /B:32
```

where a- and b- tell SMARTDRV to not cache floppy drives. The whole idea behind caching is loading the cache with files that you're going to ask for again. Files on floppies aren't called repeatedly. Think about it. What is on a floppy? Usually something temporary that you work with and then dump. Don't waste cache space by loading files you won't call again. Turn off disk caching to the floppy drives.

The number, in this case 1024, is the cache size. This is the size of the cache's "holding area." The rule for SMARTDRV's cache size is to make the cache one-quarter of the size of the total RAM, up to 2MB (see Table 13.4). Never make a SMARTDRV cache larger than 2MB. Please note that these limits are only for SMARTDRV! The more advanced disk caches used by Windows 3.11 and Windows 95/98 are not subject to these limits.

TABLE 13.4

Optimal SMARTDRV Cache Sizes for DOS

Total RAM	Cache Size
< 1MB	None
1 MB	256K
2 MB	512K
4 MB	1 MB
8 MB	2 MB
16 MB	2 MB
> 16 MG	2MB

The /B:32 takes a little explaining. If you promise to defragment the hard drive, you can increase the look-ahead buffer. If there is room in the cache, SMARTDRV will grab extra clusters of data when it accesses the drive. The number of clusters to grab is the look-ahead buffer. Without the /B option, SMARTDRV will by default set the look-ahead buffer to 16K. A well-defragmented drive will benefit from increasing the buffer to 32K. Here are some other SMARTDRV options:

/X (turn off lazy writing) Lazy writing is when data is written to the hard drive. A lazy writing disk cache will store saved data in the cache, waiting until the system has slowed down before writing to the disk. In other words, you might click on File, Save but the file isn't really saved! It's still in the cache! What if you turn off the computer before the cache decides to write the data to the drive? Sound dangerous? It can be. The nice part is that you won't see a C:\> prompt until everything in the cache is "flushed" (written to the hard drive). So if you can train people to *never* turn off the computer until they see a C:> prompt, then lazy writing is great. And it's faster than no lazy writing.

/L (load low) SMARTDRV loads high by default. The /L setting will make it load low.

/N (don't wait for C:> prompt on lazy writes) This is the ultimate risk. You will get a C:> prompt when the cache is not yet flushed—too much risk for almost no return. Don't use it.

/U (don't load the CD-ROM cache) If SMARTDRV sees MSCDEX, the CD-ROM utility, it will cache the CD-ROM drive (if you have DOS 6.0 or later).

/U prevents the CD-ROM part of SMARTDRV from loading. It's a pretty useless option.

/E (element size) This option changes the number of bytes processed by SMARTDRV at a time. Leave it alone. It's a waste of time.

/Q (quiet mode) This specifies that when SMARTDRV loads, it doesn't show anything on the screen.

/V (verbose mode) This shows all SMARTDRV parameters on the screen when starting.

/C (immediate flush) You can type SMARTDRV /C to force an immediate flush of all lazy write data still in the cache. Many users will type this command immediately before turning off the computer as a safety function.

/R (flush and restart) First it writes all lazy data to the drive, then it erases everything in the cache. This one's also pretty much useless.

Double buffering If you look in the CONFIG.SYS file, you might notice a line that looks like this:

```
DEVICE=C:\DOS\SMARTDRV.EXE /DOUBLE_BUFFER
```

This must be entered when bus-mastering controllers (drive controllers that do their own DMA transfers) are in the computer. Bus-mastering controllers conflict with SMARTDRV, and this line is necessary to tell SMARTDRV to run a special second buffer to prevent conflicts. In AUTOEXEC.BAT, you must load the MSCDEX driver before you load SMARTDRV. If you load MSCDEX after SMARTDRV, it won't know there is a CD-ROM drive to cache!

You probably won't use SMARTDRV with Windows 3.*x*, and you definitely won't use it with Windows 95/98! Each has its own, more powerful disk-caching functions (VCACHE in Windows 3.*x* and disk caching in Windows 95/98).

RAM DRIVE Don't confuse a RAM drive with SMARTDRV! A disk-cache program like SMARTDRV uses extended memory as a dedicated cache. Users have no access to this RAM; it is totally under the control of SMARTDRV. The operation of a disk cache is invisible to users; they just

Figure 13.10
"I'm the D: drive"

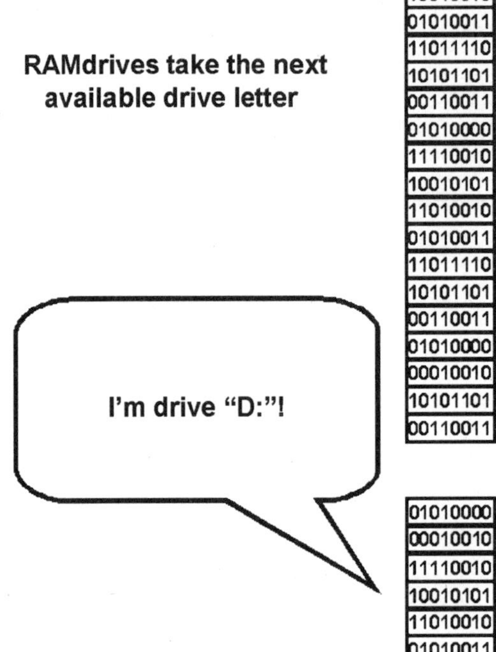

enjoy a faster computer. A RAM drive is RAM that thinks it's a hard drive. Unlike a disk cache, users have total control over what is stored in a RAM drive. A RAM drive actually has a new drive letter assigned to it, and users can read, write, copy, and delete to a RAM drive as if it were a hard drive. RAM drives can be handy on a DOS machine as a place to store files that are often called by the system. RAM drives were particularly popular with DOS before SMARTDRV was introduced. See Figure 13.10.

DOS comes with the device driver that's necessary to create a RAM drive: RAMDRIVE.SYS. You can install a RAM drive by adding the following line to your CONFIG.SYS file:

```
device=c:\dos\ramdrive.sys 1024
```

The number at the end is the amount of RAM to set aside as a RAM drive. This RAM will no longer be used as regular RAM. Instead, it will be given the next available drive letter after the last real drive. The onset of SMARTDRV made RAM drives virtually obsolete. Why create a fixed RAM drive for programs that are often called when the disk cache will probably have the same information?

The Computer Virus

Although computer viruses are not limited to DOS, this chapter provides a number of concepts that are necessary to understand the function of computer viruses. Since these concepts are still "fresh", this is a good point to learn about viruses and their prevention/removal.

The words "I think your machine has a virus" can send shudders down the back of even the most competent PC technicians. The thought of megabytes of critical data being wiped away by the work of some evil programmer is at the least annoying—and at worst a serious financial disaster. No doubt viruses are a serious problem but unlike human viruses, a few well-established tools and procedures can prevent them from invading a PC.

The secret to avoiding viruses is to understand how a virus works. A virus is a program that has two functions: 1) proliferate (make more copies of itself) and 2) activate (at some signal, count, date, etc. do something—usually something bad like delete the boot sector). A virus does not have to do damage to be a virus. Some of the first viruses written were harmless and downright amusing. Without going into overly gritty detail, there are basically only four types of viruses.

Boot Sector These viruses change the code in the Master Boot Record (MBR) of the hard drive. Once the machine is booted, they reside in memory, attempting to infect the MFRs of other drives such as floppy drives, connected network machines or removable media and creating whatever havoc they are designed to do by the programmer.

Executable These viruses reside in executable files. They are literally extensions of executables and are unable to exist by themselves. Once the infected executable file is run, the virus loads into memory, adding copies of itself to other EXEs that are subsequently run and again doing whatever evil that it was designed to do.

Macro Macro viruses are specially written application macros. Although they are not truly programs, they perform the exact same functions of regular viruses. These viruses will autostart when the particular application is run and will then attempt to make more copies of itself—some will even try to find other copies of the same application across a network to propagate.

Trojan Trojans are true, freestanding programs that do something other than what the person who runs the program thinks they will do.

An example of a trojan would be a program that a person thinks is a game but is really a CMOS eraser. Some trojan are quite sophisticated. It might be a game that works perfectly well but when the user quits the game, it causes some type of damage.

Bimodal/Bipartite A virus that uses both boot-sector and executable functions. Anti virus programs use certain methods to detect and destroy viruses. Anti-virus programs work in two ways. First is the scan method. These programs scan the boot sector and files, looking for viruses. Second, they can monitor programs as they are run, detecting and killing viruses as they attempt to start. These are often called virus shields. They detect boot sector viruses by simpling comparing the drive's boot sector to a standard. Most boot sectors are basically the same as there is only the OS default and the occasional Drive overlay (review the hard drive chapter if any of these terms are confusing). Some anti-virus programs will make a copy of the boot sector and place that copy back if a virus is detected. Executable viruses are a little more difficult as they can be on any file in the drive. To detect executable viruses, the anti-virus program stores a library of "signatures". A signature is a code pattern of a known virus. The anti-virus program looks at an executable file and compares it to its library of signatures. While effective, there have been instances where a perfectly clean program coincidentally held a signature—usually causing the anti-virus maker to quickly provide a patch to prevent further alarms. Macro viruses are detected through signatures or by recognizing certain macro commands that indicate a known macro virus.

Now that we understand the types of viruses and how anti-virus programs try to remove them, there are a few terms that are often used when describing certain traits of viruses.

Polymorphics/Polymorphs A polymorph will attempt to change its signature to prevent detection from anti-virus programs. Usually they have a bit of useless code that is continually being scrambled. Fortunately, the scrambling code can be recognized and used as the signature—but only after the anti-virus makers become aware of the virus. One trick that is sometimes done to counter unknwn polymorphs is to have the anti-virus program create a checksum on every file in the drive. These checksums are created differently by different anti-virus programs (they are also usually secret as the anti-virus makers don't want the virus makers to be able to come up with ways to beat them). The anti-virus program then stays in memory and as a program is run, a new checksum is calculated and compared to the earlier calculation. If the checksums are different, it is a sure sign of a virus.

Stealth The term stealth is more of a concept than an actual function of a virus program. Most stealth programs are boot sector viruses that hide from anti-virus software through various methods. One popular stealth virus will hook a little known (but often used) software interrupt and only run when that interrupt is run. Others make copies of innocent-looking files.

The secret to preventing virus attacks is to prevent getting one in the first place. All good anti-virus software includes some type of virus shield that will automatically scan floppies, downloads, etc. Use them. It is also a good idea to scan a PC daily for possible virus attacks. Again, all anti-virus programs include TSRs that will run every time the PC is booted. Last, know where software has come from before it is loaded. Whereas the chance of commercial, shrink-wrapped software having a virus is virtually nil (although there have been a couple of well-publicized exceptions), the illegal copy of Tomb Raider II borrowed from a local hacker definitely needs to be carefully inspected.

Get into the habit of keeping around an anti-virus floppy disk. An anti-virus disk will be a bootable, copy-protected floppy with a copy of an anti-virus program. If a virus is suspected, even if a PC has an anti-virus program that say it eliminated the virus, the anti-virus diskette should be used. Turn off the PC and boot it up with the anti-virus diskette. Run the most comprehensive check the anti-virus program provides to be sure the virus is removed. After the virus is removed, check all the removable media that has been exposed to the system. Then check any other machine that may have received a disk or is linked on the network to the cleaned machine. Remember, a virus can often go for months before anyone knows of its presence.

Why Mess with DOS?

This can be a tough chapter to get motivated to study, especially if you are a tried and true Windows user. What could possibly be the use of all of these DOS commands? DOS is dead, right? Wrong. Although DOS might be going, going, (gone?), Windows 95/98 still needs its equivalent of the DOS prompt. For example, you need a DOS command just to install

Windows. A new installation of Windows requires that you edit CONFIG.SYS, add a DOS CD-ROM driver, edit AUTOEXEC.BAT to add the MSCDEX program, reboot, access the CD-ROM drive, and use the CD\ command to find the Windows 95/98 startup program!

Need another example? A brand-new hard drive doesn't have Windows, so how are you going to make it bootable? You better have a bootable floppy with at least FDISK and FORMAT. Even though DOS might be going, the legacy of DOS commands is alive and well in Windows. It's a wise move to be comfortable with DOS.

CHAPTER 14

Windows 3.*x*

In this chapter, you will:

- Review protected mode and learn how it relates to Windows 3.*x*.
- Understand virtual memory.
- Learn how to optimize Windows 3.*x*.
- Learn basic Windows troubleshooting.

I began the DOS chapter with the assumption that you had little or no DOS experience. This chapter, however, assumes that you have a very basic understanding of Windows 3.*x* or Windows 95/98. You should be comfortable using a mouse, clicking and dragging, resizing and moving windows, and using menus. You should be familiar with file manipulations using File Manager in Windows 3.*x* or Windows Explorer in Windows 95. Plus, you should be comfortable using File Manager or Explorer to locate and start programs.

Graphical or Not?

On first glimpse, it might seem safe to describe Microsoft Windows as a *graphical user interface* (GUI). Instead of using a character-based interface like DOS and memorizing a large number of commands to run programs and administer files, you "see" programs, files, and directory structures as tiny graphics called *icons*. You use a mouse to manipulate icons, start programs, and manipulate files.

Because so many people use Windows, they assume that it is also an operating system. A GUI, however, is not necessarily an operating system! It does nothing more than translate the manipulation of icons into commands that are understandable to the operating system. The operating system actually does the work. Application programs must be written "from the ground up" in order to take advantage of the concept of GUI.

GUIs are implemented in many different ways. Some operating systems like Apple's System 8 have GUIs built into them as an integral part of the operating system. In other words, there is no C:\> prompt on any Apple computer that uses System 8. No Macintosh user needs to understand the concept of a prompt since everything, from starting programs to installing hard drives, is done from the built-in GUI. System 8 is a completely graphical operating system.

UNIX, Windows NT, OS/2, Windows 3.*x*, and Windows 95 are character-based applications that come with an optional GUI to make life easier. The GUI is not required, but the operating system usually installs it automatically and activates it on startup, giving the impression that it is part of the operating system, like a Macintosh. It is not.

DOS is a character-based operating system that does not come with a GUI. DOS is further hampered by the fact that it is designed to run on the Intel 8086 processor. If DOS is run on a 286 or better processor, the machine will not run at its full capacity; it will run as if it was an 8086 processor (a very fast one, but an 8086 nonetheless).

In the mid-'80s, Microsoft and IBM were working hard on OS/2, and it was assumed that when OS/2 was released DOS would be obsolete. Microsoft Windows was originally designed as nothing more than a third-party DOS add-on GUI that ran on top of DOS. Microsoft used the first versions of Windows as little more than "test beds" for OS/2 GUI concepts. (This was in the days when Microsoft was in IBM's lap—a long time ago). OS/2 was designed to take advantage of the protected-mode functions of the 80286 and later (much later) machines, and was redesigned to take advantage of the 80386 protected-mode and virtual-8086-mode functions. This gave Microsoft a good understanding of these advanced functions. As they had done before, Microsoft used Windows as a test bed for these functions. Before the GUI was loaded, a few drivers were run to place Windows in protected mode. Running programs to engage protected mode made Windows more than just a GUI. Windows was now performing functions like an operating system. Later versions of Windows took on more and more aspects of an operating system. With the arrival of the Windows version 3.11, almost all operating-system functions had been taken over by Windows.

The first generation of Microsoft Windows came in the following five versions:

- Windows 3.0
- Windows 3.1
- Windows for Workgroups 3.1
- Windows 3.11
- Windows for Workgroups 3.11

This entire first generation of Windows is referred to as Windows 3.*x*, which still needs to run on top of DOS. After the computer has booted to DOS, you start Windows 3.*x* by typing the command WIN. When Windows 3.*x* is started, the user is confronted with the cornerstone of Windows 3.*x*—the Program Manager (see Figure 14.1).

The Program Manager will seem extremely limited when compared to a more advanced GUI such as Windows 95 or Windows 98. There is no

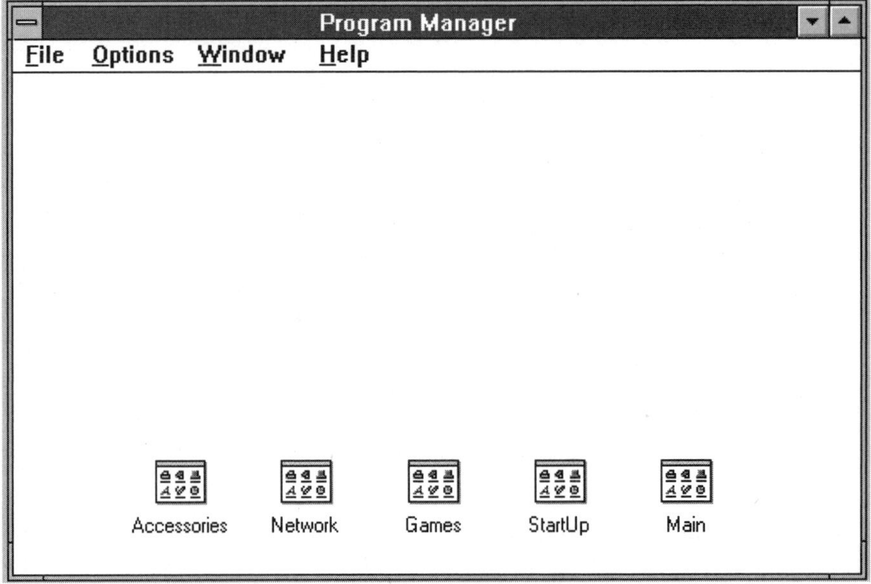

Figure 14.1
Program manager

task bar and no start button with the handy listing of all installed programs. Instead, Windows 3.*x* uses a special icon called a *group* into which icon pointers to programs are inserted.

Microsoft Windows has been around in one way or another since 1984. Given this long lifespan, Windows has continually changed to take advantage of the latest CPUs. This has resulted in Windows 3.*x* being able to operate in different modes, matching the Intel CPU modes.

Real Mode

Microsoft Windows was originally conceived as a DOS-based GUI. The first version of Windows did not have any memory-management functions and was not capable of multitasking. It was only for starting programs and managing files. This version of Windows ran in the DOS limit of 1MB of RAM. As later versions of Windows were released they began to move outside this limit, but they continued to support the DOS mode, called *real mode,* until version 3.11. Later version of Windows 3.*x* cannot operate in real mode, which is now obsolete. See Figure 14.2.

Standard Mode

The first versions of Windows to break out of the DOS 1MB barrier did so by engaging the 286-level protected mode (Windows 2.0). By engaging protected mode, Windows could address up to 16MB of RAM. Unfortunately, DOS programs could run in only the first megabyte of memory, so specialized programs had to be written that would run in (and only in) the extended memory controlled by Windows. Since these programs could be run only while Windows was active, Microsoft decided to expand the concept of Windows even further by adding support for standardized graphics, fonts, I/O devices, and memory mapping (together known as *resources*). Windows already had built-in resources, and was therefore an extremely easy environment for writing programs. When Windows broke the DOS barrier by engaging the 286 protected mode and began to take control of many hardware functions, Windows was said to be running in *standard mode* (Figure 14.3).

One of the disadvantages to 286 protected mode was the inability to return easily to real mode. DOS (and therefore DOS programs) runs only in real mode. In order to run in real mode, Windows stored a 50K stub of data in conventional memory and reset the CPU. This was like a Ctrl<Alt<Del or pressing the reset button; only the CPU was reset and everything else stayed the same. The DOS program could then be loaded and would automatically transfer the DOS program to the hard drive when you switched back to Windows. In standard mode, Windows could run only one DOS program at a time. This mode was supported by Win-

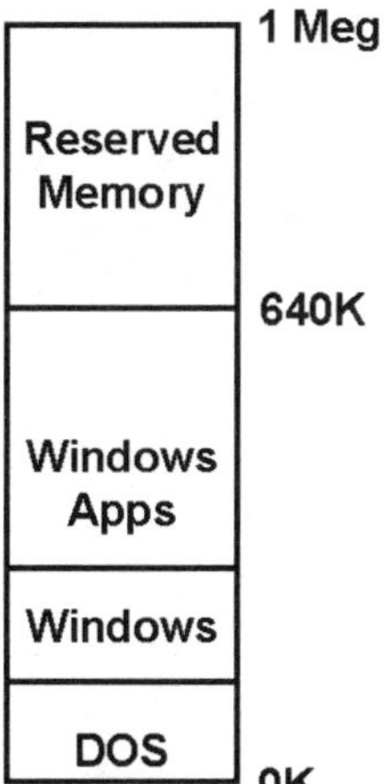

Figure 14.2
Real-mode Windows

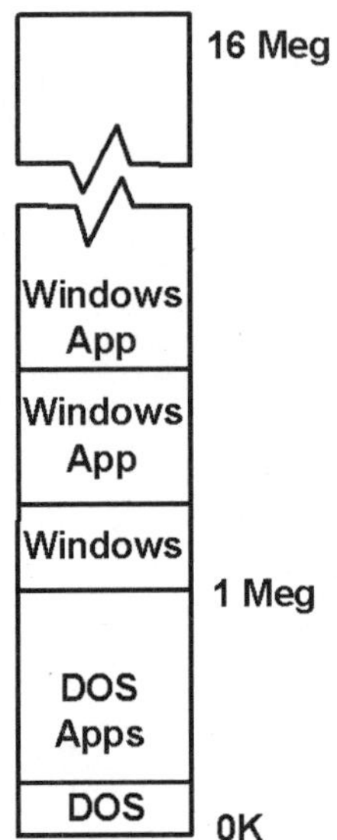

Figure 14.3 Standard-mode memory map

dows up to Windows for Workgroups 3.11, when it was dropped in favor of the current mode: 386 enhanced.

In order for Windows to operate in standard mode or 386 enhanced mode, the CONFIG.SYS file should have the HIMEM.SYS device driver loaded. This is the only required device driver.

386 Enhanced Mode

Windows 386 became the first version of Windows to take advantage of the 386's protected mode. This was quickly followed with Windows 3.0, Windows 3.1, and Windows 95. Windows in 386 protected mode can address up to 4 gigabytes of memory, supports virtual memory, and allows multiple DOS programs to run simultaneously (see Figure 14.4). Starting with Windows for Workgroups 3.11, only 386 enhanced mode is allowed in Windows. To understand how Windows uses 386 enhanced mode, we need to understand how Windows works.

Windows looks at everything in the computer as a selection of resources: memory, video, serial ports, sound, etc. (everything that your computer has, or at least that Windows sees). All resources are presented to Windows through device drivers. Some device drivers are built into Windows and some are separate files. Almost all device drivers are stored in the \WINDOWS\SYSTEM directory and almost always end with either a .DRV or .386 extension.

The Windows 3.*x* core consists of three files: KRNL386.EXE, USER.EXE, and GDI.EXE. These three files are programs that allocate and keep track

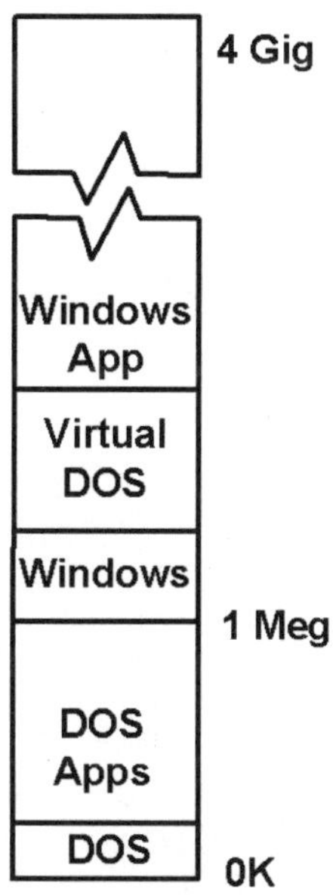

Figure 14.4
Windows memory map in 386 enhanced mode

of all system resources requested by applications. They use a number of 64K storage areas of extended memory (called *heaps*) to keep track of which application is using which resource. They also have some ability to take away resources (mainly RAM).

Applications themselves are little more than requesters of resources. The resources are requested via very standardized subroutines, called the *application programmers interface* (API). A program can speak to the Windows core directly or through a special file called a *dynamic link library* (DLL). A DLL acts as a storage house of subroutines that either come with the compiler that creates the application or are made by the programmer. DLL files are distinctive in that they always end with the extension .DLL.

When a program starts in Windows, it first loads a small piece in conventional memory called a *stub*. The stub asks for RAM from KRNL386.EXE. KRNL386.EXE allocates the amount of RAM needed by the application. This area of RAM is known as a *segment* and its location is stored in a heap. After the program has loaded itself in memory, it then begins asking for whatever other resources it needs—video and a mouse, as well as anything else it needs to run. As long as there are resources to give, the Windows core will give them. Figure 14.5 shows a model of Windows in 386 enhanced mode.

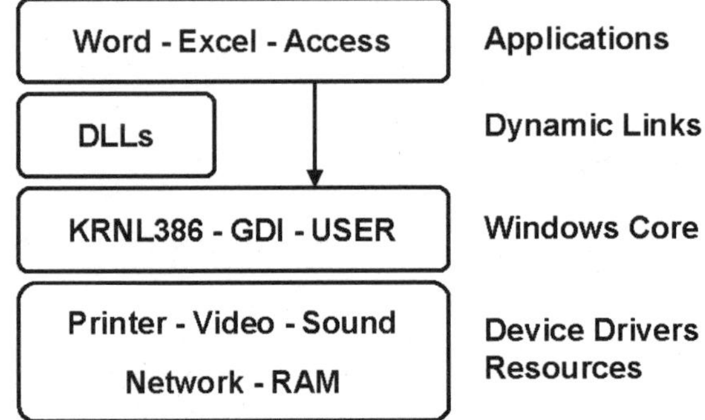

Figure 14.5 Model of Windows in 386 enhanced mode

Swap Files

Since Windows 3.*x* runs in 386 protected mode, it can take advantage of virtual memory. As explained in Chapter 1, virtual memory is an advanced function of 386 protected mode that lets the CPU allow mass storage (hard drives) to act like RAM. Virtual memory manifests itself through a special, hidden *swap file,* which is the part of the hard drive that thinks it is RAM. The swap file is very useful in Windows 3.*x,* due to the large amount of RAM used by the operating system and applications.

Let's assume you have a PC with 16MB of RAM. Figure 14.6 shows the system RAM as a thermometer, with gradients from zero to 16MB. As programs load, they take up RAM (Figure 14.7), and as more and more programs are loaded, more RAM is used (Figure 14.8).

There is a certain point at which you won't have enough RAM to run more programs (Figure 14.9). Sure, you could close one or more programs to make room for yet another program (D), but you can't keep all the programs running simultaneously. This is where Windows 3.*x* virtual memory comes into play. Windows 3.*x* virtual memory creates a swap file called 386SPART.PAR, which resides somewhere on your hard drive (see Figure 14.10).

The swap file is like a temporary storage box (Figure 14.11). Windows uses the swap file to remove running programs temporarily from RAM

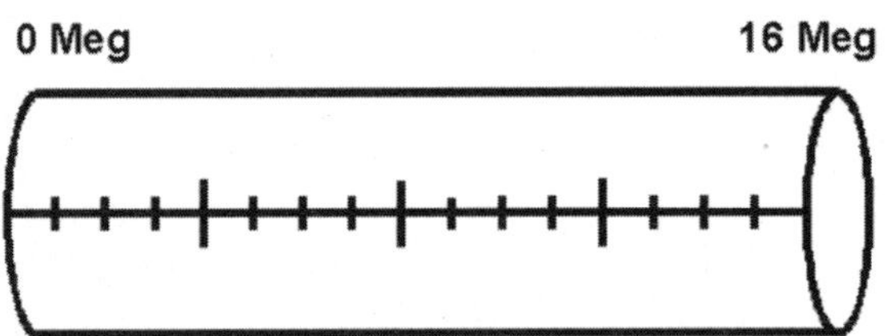

Figure 14.6 A RAM thermometer

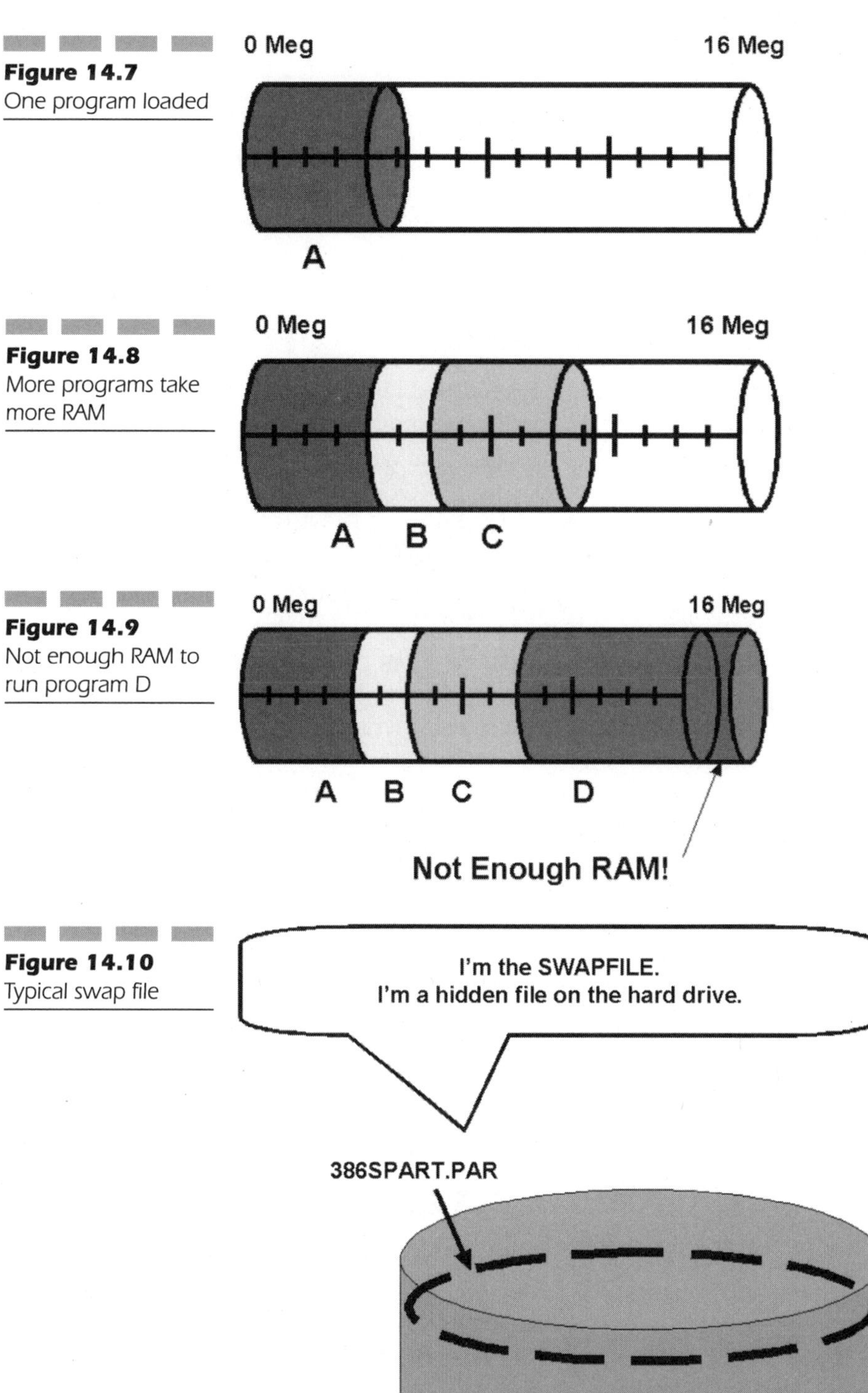

Figure 14.7
One program loaded

Figure 14.8
More programs take more RAM

Figure 14.9
Not enough RAM to run program D

Figure 14.10
Typical swap file

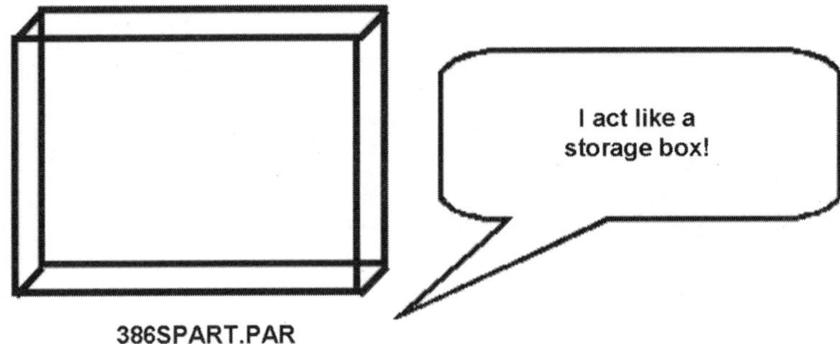

Figure 14.11 The swap file is like a storage box

so other programs can be loaded and run. A swap file is used only when you run out of RAM. If you have enough RAM to run all your programs, there is no need to use the swap file. Windows brings the swap file into place only when there isn't enough RAM to run all open programs.

In order to load program D, you need to have enough RAM so it can load. Clearly, some program (or programs) must be unloaded from RAM—without actually closing the program(s). Windows looks at all running programs, in this case A, B, and C, and decides which program is the least used. That program is then cut out of or "swapped" from RAM and copied into the swap file. In this case, Windows has chosen program B (Figure 14.12). Unloading program B from RAM provides enough RAM to load program D (Figure 14.13).

It is important to understand that none of this activity is visible on the screen! Program B's window is still visible along with all the other programs that are running. There is nothing to tell users that program B is no longer in RAM (Figure 14.14).

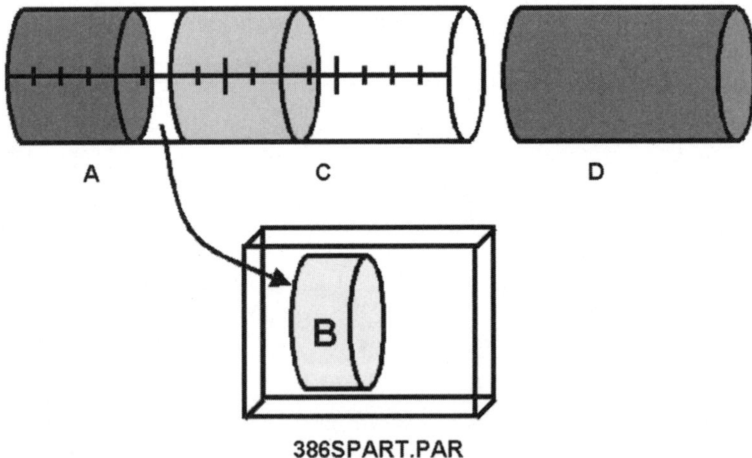

Figure 14.12 Program B being unloaded from memory

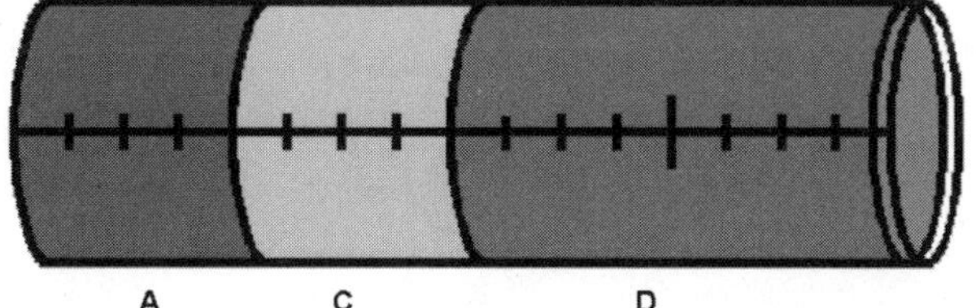

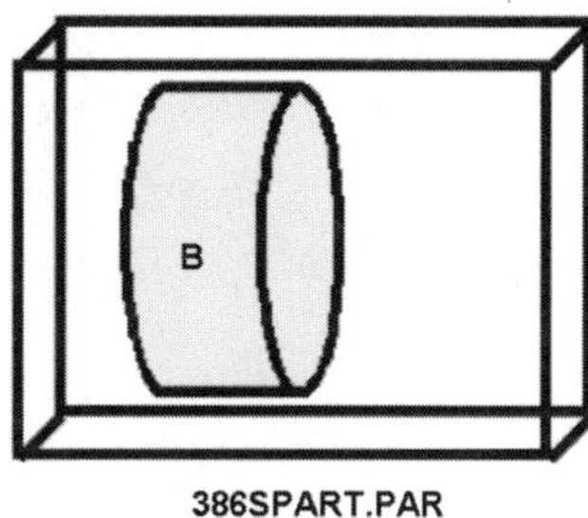

Figure 14.13
Program B stored in the swap file—room for program D

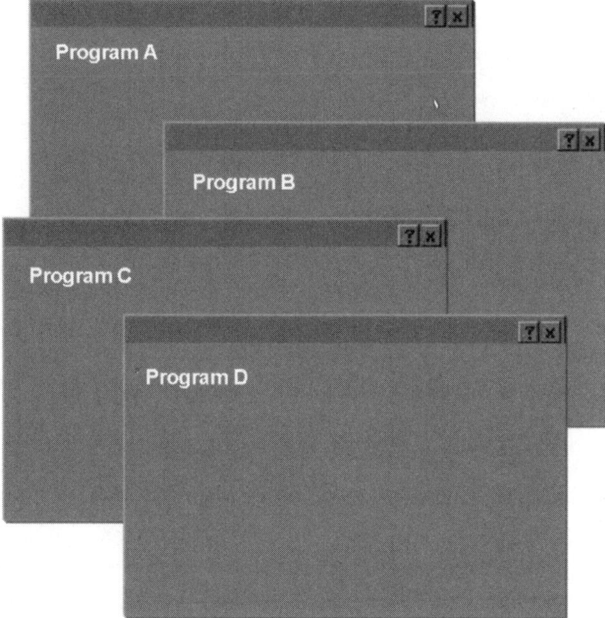

Figure 14.14
You can't tell if a program is swapped or not

So what happens if you click on program B? Well, the program can't actually run from the swap file. It must be reloaded back into RAM. First, Windows decides which program must be removed from RAM, and this time Windows chooses Program C (Figure 14.15). Then program B is loaded into RAM (Figure 14.16).

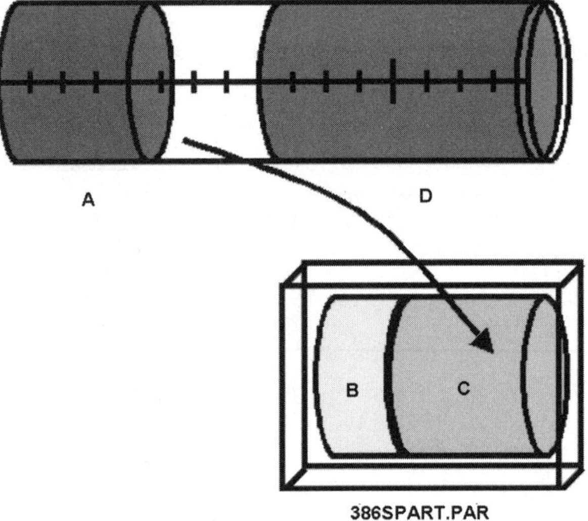

Figure 14.15 Program C is swapped to the swap file

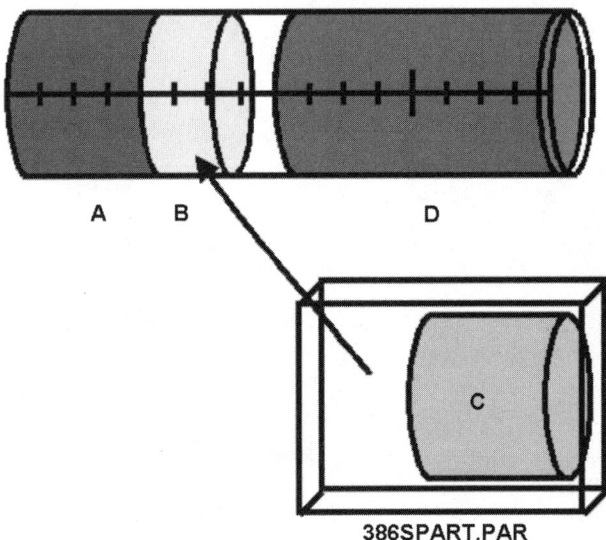

Figure 14.16 Program B is swapped back into RAM

Swapping programs to and from the swap file and RAM takes time. Although there are no visual clues that a swap is taking place, the machine will slow down quite noticeably as the swaps are performed. However, the alternative (Figure 14.17) is far less acceptable. Swap files are a crucial aspect of Windows 3.*x* operation. Later in this chapter you will see how to properly install and optimize a swap file.

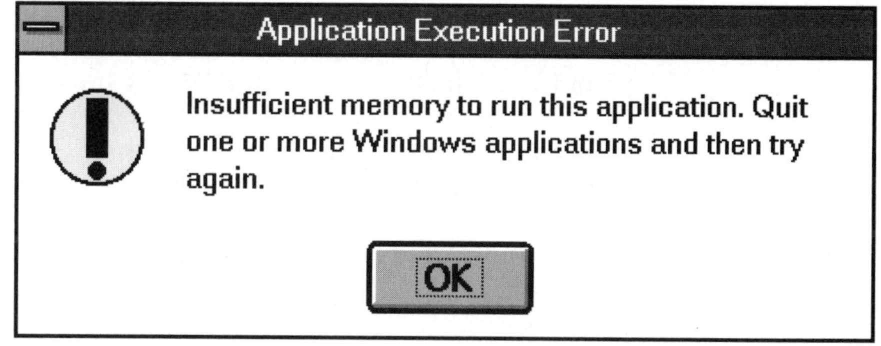

Figure 14.17
The alternative to swap files

Initialization Files: *.INI

Text files with the extension .INI are used by Windows to initialize just about everything in Windows, from device drivers to Windows itself to applications. Any Windows computer will have at least three but usually dozens of these files stored in the \WINDOWS directory (Figure 14.18). Initialization files are created by both Windows and Windows applications. Knowing how to edit and what to edit in these files is crucial to repairing PCs.

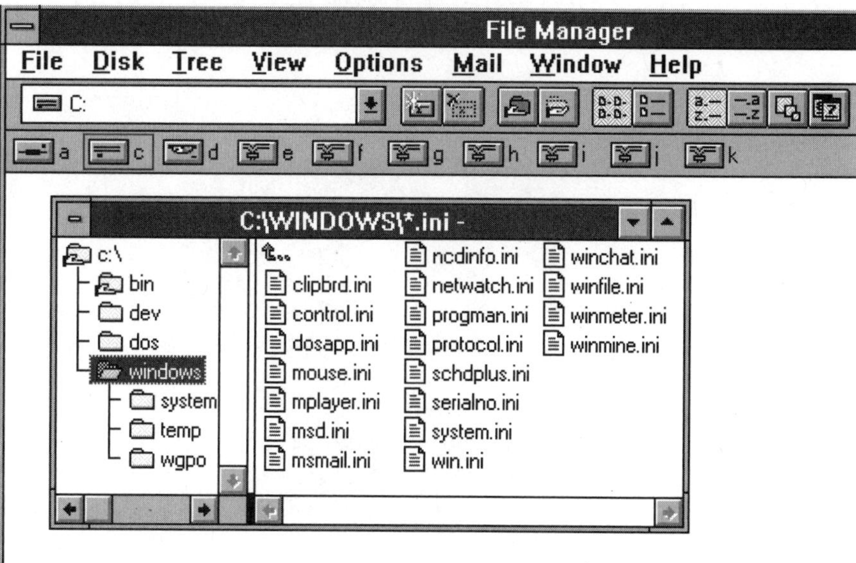

Figure 14.18
I have a lot of INI files!

All .INI files are text files, and can be edited with any text editor. You don't have to have Windows running; you can edit these files from a DOS prompt using EDIT or any other DOS-based word processor. Windows 3.x comes with a handy GUI text editor called Notepad. Figure 14.19 shows Notepad being used to show the contents of SERIALNO.INI, a typical .INI file. SERIALNO.INI registers the copy of Windows and is thus contained in all Windows computers.

Note that all .INI files (including SERIALNO.INI) are broken up into logical areas called *groups*. Each group starts with a word or words in square brackets, called a *group header*—for instance, [GroupHeader]. All .INI files are broken into these groups. Following each group header are the settings for that group. They are organized with the syntax *item=settings*.

Even though .INI files can be edited with a text editor, special configuration menus are more often used to make changes to them. Windows 3.*x* comes with two major setup screens, Control Panel and Windows Setup. The PROTOCOL.INI file, for example, has a line for the IRQ of the network card (Figure 14.20a). You can edit the IRQ here, but it is safer to do it from Windows Setup\Options\Change Network Settings (Figure 14.20b).

Although there can be a large number of .INI files, the following are found on almost all Windows 3.*x* machines:

CONTROL.INI Used to set colors and background patterns. It's rarely touched.

MOUSE.INI This controls mouse hardware settings. It's never touched.

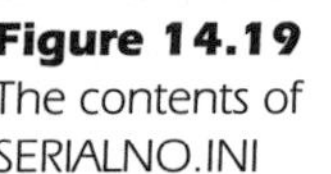

Figure 14.19 The contents of SERIALNO.INI

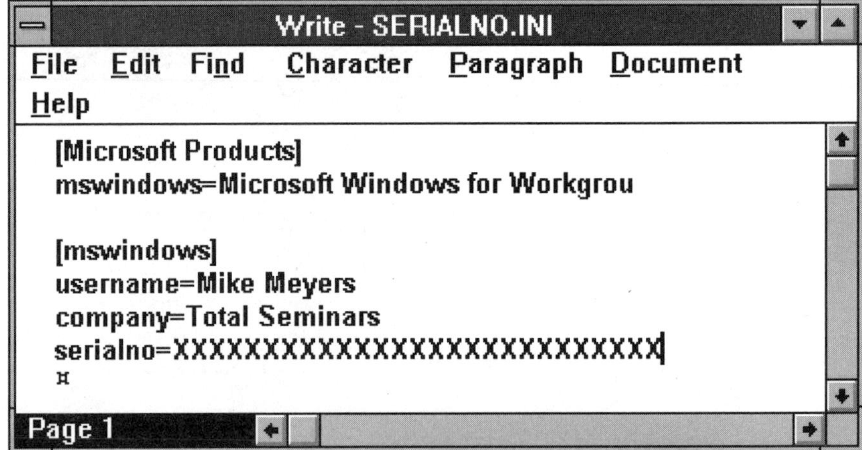

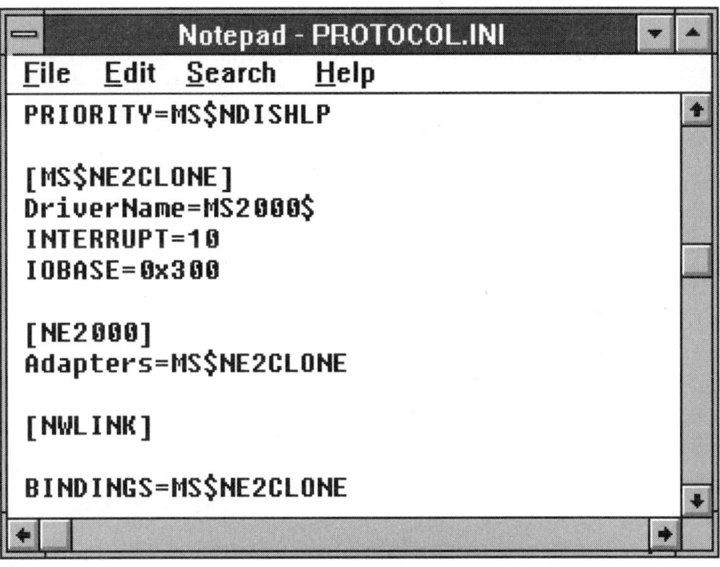

Figure 14.20a IRQ setting in PROTOCOL.INI

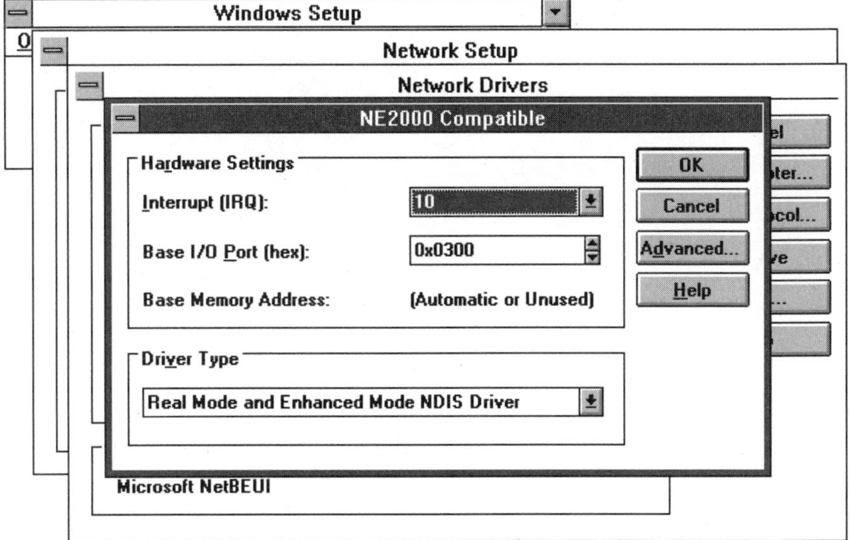

Figure 14.20b Changing IRQ using menus

PROGMAN.INI By default, PROGMAN.INI defines what groups are in the Program Manager and their relative positions. However, this .INI file has a number of settings to restrict user access. For example, you can add a setting to prevent users from exiting Windows. Very handy! It's often manually edited.

PROTOCOL.INI The PROTOCOL.INI file defines all the details necessary for the PC to exist on a network. Included is the language of the network, the network card driver, and any special settings that are unique to the network. This file is never touched; it's for use with Windows for Workgroups only.

SYSTEM.INI SYSTEM.INI is the CONFIG.SYS of Windows. All the resources are initialized there, as well as a number of global settings that define how rescues are to be used. This is often manually edited.

WIN.INI WIN.INI is like the AUTOEXEC.BAT of Windows. It defines all the "personalizations" of Windows, such as screen savers and colors, fonts, associations, and how resources interact with applications. WIN.INI is also the dumping ground for settings that do not seem to have a home anywhere else. This file is often manually edited.

SYSTEM.INI Groups and Settings

SYSTEM.INI is the most used (and abused) of all the .INI files. To know SYSTEM.INI is to understand Windows. Let's take a look at the main groups of SYSTEM.INI:

[**boot**] This has the most basic drivers needed by Windows to boot. Leave it alone.

[**boot.description**] This contains text descriptions of the [boot] section. It is used in Windows setup. Leave it alone.

[**keyboard**] This is the keyboard driver and a few optional settings. Yet again, it's a good idea to leave this group alone.

[**386Enh**] This is the most important section of the SYSTEM.INI file. It is explored in more detail following this listing of groups.

[**NonWindowsApp**] This group contains information about DOS applications. It's virtually unused; leave it alone.

[**vcache**] This is a special 32-bit file access setting. Leave it alone.

[**mci**] This group contain media control interface drivers. Leave it alone.

[**drivers**] This is a generic driver names section. Application are supposed to put names here, but often ignore this section and add the information in their own sections. Again, leave it alone.

[**Network**] This section is sometimes manually updated, but only by a network person. It's for use with Windows for Workgroups only.

Almost all the sections in SYSTEM.INI are created properly when Windows is installed and should never be changed. However, the [386Enh] section is *very* important and warrants a closer inspection because it stores all the values for 386 enhanced mode. Most of the problems associated with Windows itself (as opposed to Windows applications) can be directly attributed to problems with this section. Here are the more important settings:

32BitDiskAccess=On¦Off If, after you decide to try 32-bit disk access, you find that you can't start Windows, try starting Windows with the command WIN /D:C. This special option allows you to start Windows without 32-bit disk access. If the computer runs okay, then you can turn the option off through the Virtual Memory/Change Menu in the Control Panel/386 Enhanced Menu, or just change the On to an Off.

ComXIrq=Number Many of today's serial devices use nonstandard COM ports—for example, my modem uses COM2, but not the default COM2. Instead, it uses I/O address 2F8 (default), but also uses IRQ5, which is not the default IRQ for COM2. Since I use a Windows-based communications program, it will look on IRQ 3 (the default), unless I tell it otherwise. I set my line like this: Com2Irq=5.

EMMExclude=XXXX-XXXX Anytime you have an *x*=XXXX-XXXX line in your EMM386 line in your CONFIG.SYS file, you will also need an equivalent EMMExclude statement in the [386Enh] section. Even if you don't use EMM386, you'll still need these statements in this section. Read about excluding memory addresses in chapter on DOS memory management.

EMMInclude=XXXX-XXXX This is the same as EMMExclude, except it tells Windows where to include spaces it might not otherwise see. See the chapter on DOS memory management.

MaxBps=768 Many intermittent general protection faults (GPFs) that take place in Windows happen because there aren't enough break points. This line is usually not even in [386Enh]. Add it. I find a setting of 768 is a good balance between the need for enough break points and an excessive use of memory.

WIN.INI

WIN.INI is not nearly as important as SYSTEM.INI. In fact, you can erase all the .INI files on the computer *except* SYSTEM.INI and Windows will still run. However, WIN.INI has "problem areas" that can cause trouble: LOAD= and RUN=. These lines automatically load programs when Windows starts, acting like a hidden Startup Group. If some program keeps running and you don't have a Startup Group, it's being loaded here.

Configuring Windows

Although Windows will do a solid job with its own basic installation, you can perform a number of tweaks to substantially improve its reliability and throughput.

Using a Disk Cache

If a disk cache is handy in DOS, it is absolutely imperative under Windows! Windows performs constant, aggressive drive accesses, which will cause the computer to run slowly unless a disk cache is used. Drive caches, therefore, aren't really optional; rather, the question is which one to use. Unless you have Windows or Windows for Workgroups 3.11, you will have to use good old SMARTDRV. It can be used exactly as described in the DOS chapter, with one exception. Note the second number here: SMARTDRV 1024 256.

The 256 is called the *Wincache*. To understand what it is, you must remember that the SMARTDRV cache is taken from extended memory. Windows applications also use extended memory. What if there isn't enough RAM to load the programs currently running? In that case, SMARTDRV is actually counter-productive. Why take up space for clusters you might call again when you don't have enough RAM to run the programs you need now?

Windows is designed to shrink the disk cache in order to give programs the extra RAM they need. That's where the Wincache setting comes in. It tells Windows how small it can shrink the SMARTDRV cache. The preceding example had a Wincache setting of 256, which tells Windows not to shrink the cache to less than 256K. The Wincache size is a number you can set. Start at 256K and build up until the hit rate flattens or begins to shrink.

In AUTOEXEC.BAT, you must load the MSCDEX driver before you load SMARTDRV. If you load the MSCDEX after SMARTDRV, it won't know there is a CD-ROM drive to cache! If you have Windows 3.11 or Windows for Workgroups 3.11, there is a powerful replacement for SMARTDRV called VCACHE. See the *32-Bit File Access* section for details.

32-Bit Disk Access

Even though Windows runs on top of DOS, it takes control of about every piece of hardware on your computer except the hard drive. Every time a file is retrieved from or saved to the hard drive, Windows starts a DOS session, DOS talks to the BIOS, the BIOS talks to the hard drive, and then the whole process is reversed. This is a slow, resource-consuming process. If Windows could skip the BIOS or DOS, it would definitely improve the speed of disk accesses.

32-bit disk access or *fast disk* is a fancy name for Windows skipping the BIOS on hard-drive accesses. Windows still needs to start a DOS session, but DOS talks directly to the Windows driver while in protected mode, eliminating some of the bottleneck. Actually, the only reason a DOS session is opened is to allow for updating the FAT. If your drive is compatible with a Western Digital WD1003 controller, you can use 32-bit disk access. Almost all ST-506 and a few older IDE drives are compatible. If your system is less than four years old, you'll need special drivers since computers with power-down modes are not WD1003-compatible. IDE drives using multisector reads and EIDE drives using greater than PIO mode-2 transfers are likewise not WD1003 compatible. All these drives require you to install special drivers in the Windows SYSTEM.INI file in order to take advantage of 32-bit disk access. These special drivers come with new hard drives or can be downloaded from hard-drive manufacturers' Web sites.

Here's how to engage 32-bit disk access. Go into the Control Panel and the 386 Enhanced section (Figure 14.21), Access Virtual Memory (Figure 14.22), and you'll see your current setup. Now click on Change (Figure 14.23). The next menu is for Windows 3.11 or Windows for Workgroups 3.11. If you are still using Windows 3.1, you won't have the options for 32-bit file access. Just click on the Use 32 Bit Disk Access option at the bottom and you've got 32-bit disk access!

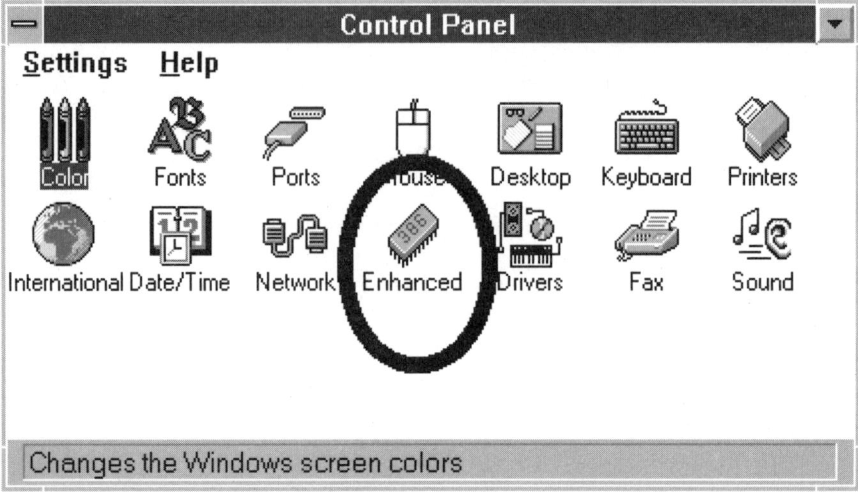

Figure 14.21
Control Panel

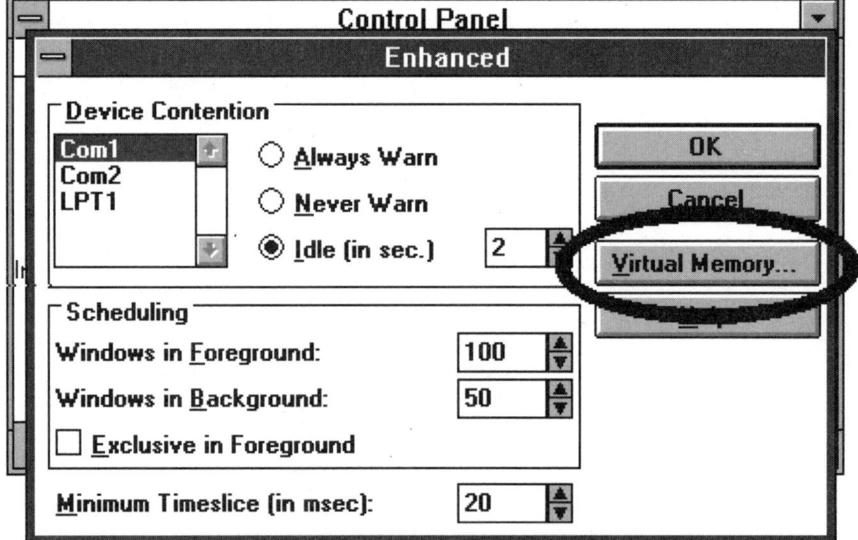

Figure 14.22
Accessing virtual memory

32-Bit File Access

If you have Windows for Workgroups or Windows version 3.11, you can enable 32-bit file access to make Windows even faster. 32-bit file access removes DOS from the process of accessing your hard drive. Let's look at the earlier example where you engaged 32-bit disk access. With 32-bit file access, the DOS part of the hard drive access is intercepted by Windows, which means a DOS session—a Virtual Machine (VM)—doesn't need to

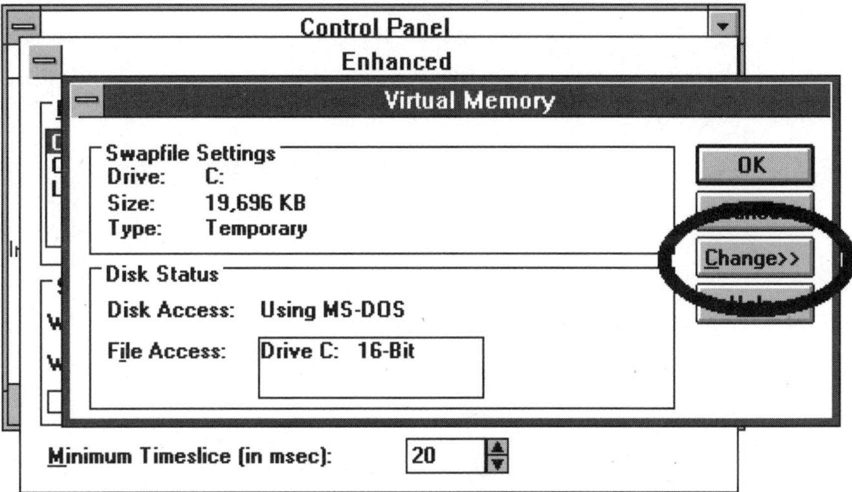

Figure 14.23
Changing virtual memory

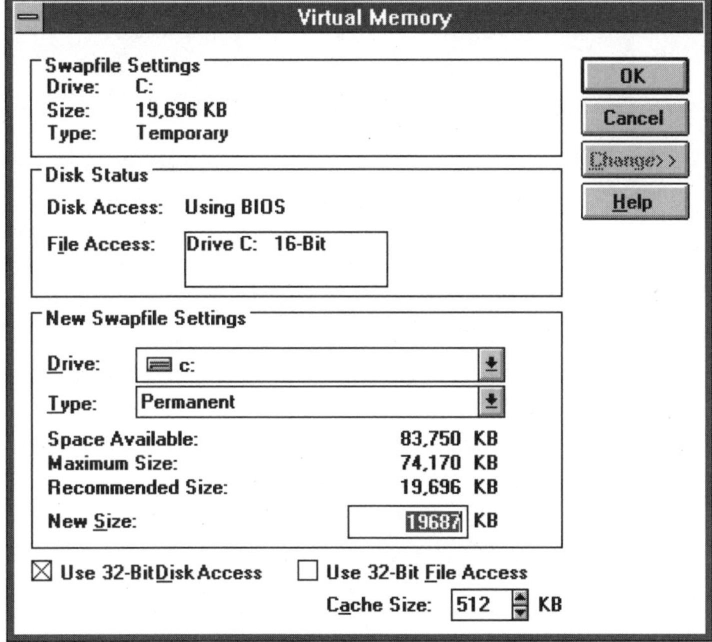

Figure 14.24a
Accessing a 32-bit disk

be opened whenever the drive is accessed (Figure 14.24a). 32-bit file access is not hardware-sensitive and will often run even when 32-bit disk access won't. 32-bit file access is often known by the name of the device driver that starts the 32-bit file access: VFAT. You can see a file called VFAT.386 in the initialization files for Windows. The best combination by far is to run

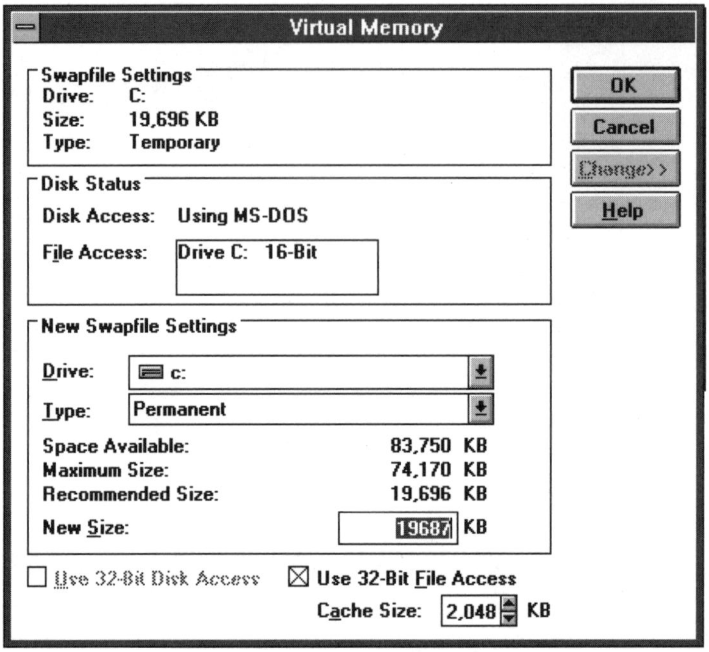

Figure 14.24b Accessing a 32-bit file and V cache

both 32-bit disk and 32-bit file access simultaneously. This will prevent all creation of DOS VMs and will speed up the computer dramatically.

While adding 32-bit file access, you might notice another option directly underneath, called Cache Size. This is an extra bonus you get when 32-bit file access is enabled—*Vcache* (see Figure 14.24b). Vcache is a superior, protected-mode disk cache that replaces the relatively slow, real-mode SMARTDRV. Although performance varies from machine to machine, Vcache usually increases overall caching performance by a factor of eight over SMARTDRV. Vcache is automatically set to roughly one-quarter the available RAM, and, unlike SMARTDRV, Vcache has no limits as to total cache size. The only drawback to using Vcache is that it cannot cache a CD-ROM drive, therefore SMARTDRV is still necessary for machines using a CD-ROM drive in Windows 3.*x*. Thus the question: "Don't SMARTDRV and Vcache conflict with each other?" The answer is no; Vcache is designed to work around SMARTDRV, even using the same cache space!

Permanent Swap File

Earlier, you saw the importance of swap files in providing virtual memory in Windows. However, there are two different types of swap files: temporary and permanent. *Temporary swap files* are only in existence while Windows is running. When you exit Windows, the temporary swap file is erased. *Permanent swap files,* on the other hand, are never erased. So why use permanent swap files? Permanent swap files have the advantage of "preaddressing" every cluster within Windows. This is necessary for 32-bit file access to run. In other words, if you want 32-bit file access (and you do) you'll need a permanent swap file. Permanent swap files are also permanently defragmented, allowing for faster file access. So you want a permanent swap file. When Windows is installed, you are automatically given a temporary swap file, so you'll have to make it permanent.

First, exit Windows and defragment your hard drive using Norton SpeeDisk or DOS's Defrag. When installing a permanent swap file, DOS tries to take one-quarter of the largest contiguous (defragmented) part of the specified drive—up to about 25 megabytes. Swap files are very large, and you need a lot of defragmented hard-drive space to get a large enough swap file to make it worth your while.

Second, go to the Virtual Memory-Change Window, just as if you were setting up 32-bit disk or file access. Pull down the Type Menu under New Swap File Settings and select Permanent (Figure 14.25). Watch the size! Unless you have applications like Corel Draw or AutoCAD, which demand

Figure 14.25 Selecting a permanent swap file

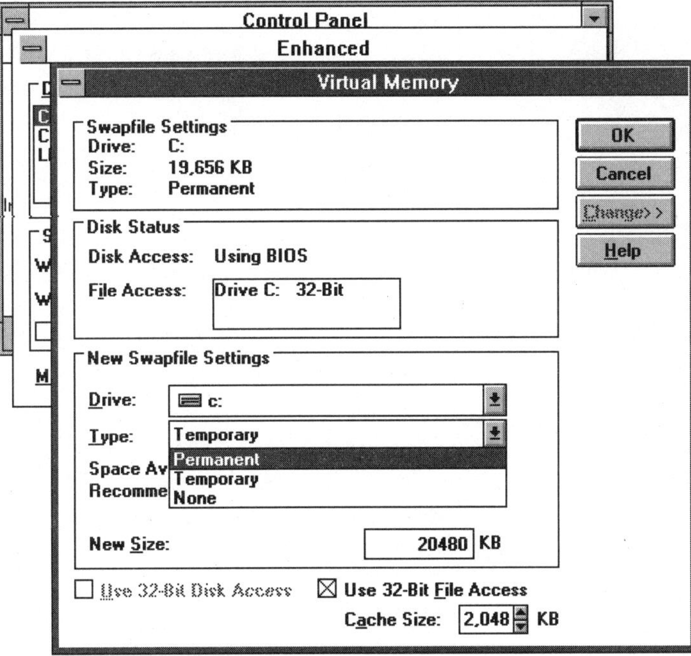

huge swap files, most people find that 8 megabytes (or less) is plenty. You might want to try 12MB if you have only 4MB of RAM. The swap-file size is inversely proportional to the amount of RAM. The more RAM you have, the smaller swap file you need. Start at around 8MB. If that's too small, you'll get a "not enough memory" error. You can always change it.

TEMP Files and RAM Drives

Many applications need to store data temporarily on the hard drive. For example, print spoolers such as Print Manager often write print jobs to the hard drive, and applications like Word create backup files (files that exist for only a short time and are then erased). There can be a number of temporary files open at any given moment. They always end with a .TMP extension.

Temporary files are stored in one directory. This can be any directory, and is defined in the AUTOEXEC.BAT file with the statement SET TEMP=*path*. My SET TEMP line is SET TEMP=C:\WINDOWS\TEMP. All applications that create temporary files send those files to the directory determined by the SET TEMP variable.

Every time a TEMP file is created, read, or erased, a hard-drive access is required. This slows down the PC. 32-bit disk access and file access help, but there is something else you might be able to do. You can install a RAM drive and tell the computer to save the TEMP files to the RAM drive instead of to the hard drive. If you have 16MB or more of memory, add the following line to CONFIG.SYS:

```
device=c:\dos\ramdrive 1024
```

This will make a new drive letter—in this example E::—depending on your last real drive letter and whether a CD-ROM drive is installed. Now add these lines to AUTOEXEC.BAT:

```
md E:\temp
SET TEMP=E:\temp
```

All temporary files will now be written to the RAM drive instead of the hard drive, speeding up whatever process uses them. There are two down sides to doing this, however. First, creating a RAM drive takes up extended memory that Windows needs, so it is not smart to make a RAM drive unless you have at least 16MB of memory. Second, many applications make very large TEMP files, requiring a very large RAM drive. It's best to make a RAM drive at least 4MB, and 8MB is better.

Memory Configuration

Memory configuration is important in Windows. Most intermittent lockups, Windows startup failures, and GPFs can be blamed on poor DOS memory management. Assuming your DOS memory management is correct, you should get substantially fewer lockups and GPFs. There are a few memory-management functions that need to be dealt with within Windows.

EMMExclude and EMMInclude If you have exclude or include statements in your CONFIG.SYS file, they need to have corresponding EMMExclude and EMMInclude lines in your SYSTEM.INI file under the [386Enh] section. If your EMM386.EXE line has x= and/or i= options like this:

```
device=c:\dos\emm386.exe ram x=c800-c9ff x=da00-dd00 i=e000-e7ff
```

be sure to add lines like these to the SYSTEM.INI file in the [386Enh] section:

```
EMMExclude=C800-C9FF
EMMExclude=DA00-DD00
EMMInclude=E000-E7FF
```

These lines can be placed anywhere in the [386Enh] section.

Translation Buffers Windows needs UMB space for what are known as *translation buffers*. These are small storage areas of RAM that are used to support DOS applications and networks. Windows needs to have some UMB space reserved for its own use. If you are loading many devices into UMBs, add WIN= statements to the EMM386 line of CONFIG.SYS, as follows:

```
DEVICE=C:\DOS\EMM386.EXE RAM WIN=C800-C9FF
```

Also, if you "include" the monotext area, you can use that area for Windows with this line:

```
DEVICE=C:\DOS\EMM386.EXE RAM INCLUDE=B000-B7FF WIN=B000-B7FF
```

Be sure to add EMMInclude=B000-B7FF to the [386Enh] section of SYSTEM.INI. Some older SVGA cards will cause bizarre problems when you do this. That's because these cards use the monochrome area for its own needs. If you see strange images and text on the screen after using the monochrome area, remove the changes.

Printing Configuration

When installing Windows, be sure to never use the printer drivers supplied with the installation diskettes. These drivers have only minimal functions, are notoriously slow, and are usually obsolete. New print drivers are available from printer manufacturers, as well as on CompuServe and the Internet.

Get rid of the Print Manager. It is horribly slow and is often worse than not having a print manager at all. Try a third-party replacement like PC-Kwik by Multisoft or SuperQueue by eSoft. Both of these print spoolers are available at all major software dealers. They usually cost between $35 and $50 per machine, but are worth the cost.

PIF Files If you run DOS applications in Windows, you should make a PIF (program information file). A PIF is a binary file that tells Windows how to create a DOS virtual machine (VM). The PIF directs the amount of memory resource given to the DOS application. This memory resource is divided into video, conventional, expanded, and extended areas. The PIF also helps the DOS application by limiting swapping to the disk and reserving keystrokes. The VM that the PIF defines can be as small or as large as is needed by the DOS application. If you don't make a PIF for DOS applications, a file will be provided for you—_DEFAULT.PIF—which is de-

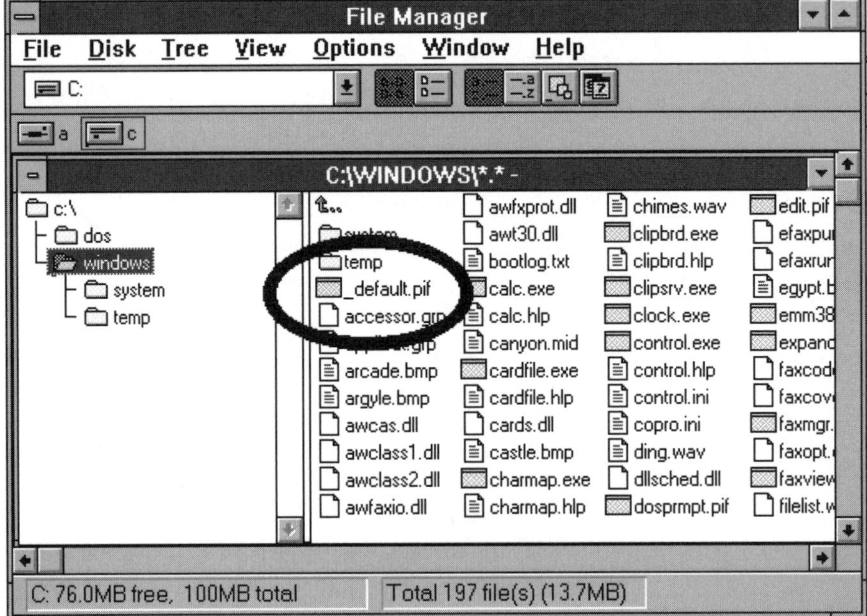

Figure 14.26 The bad guy—DEFAULT.PIF

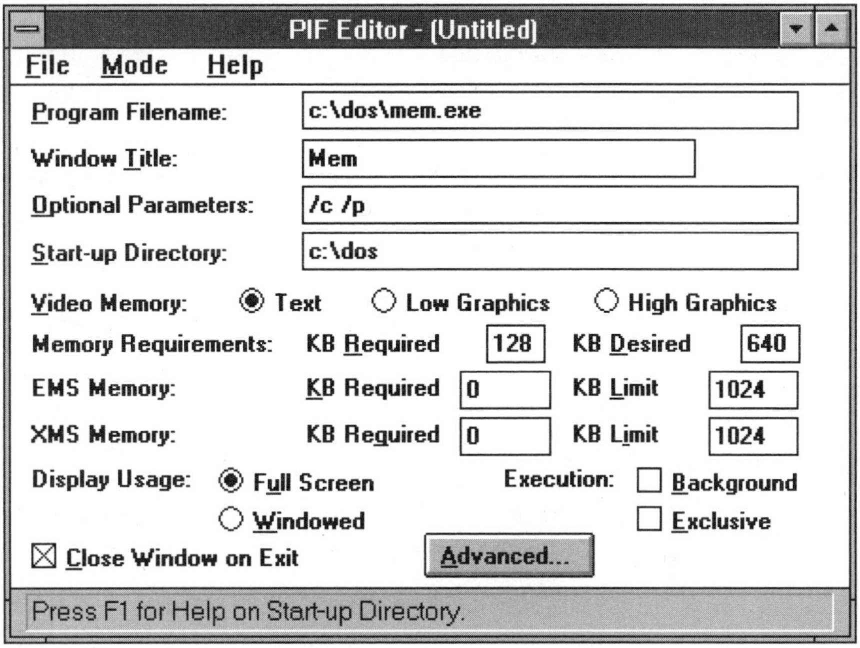

Figure 14.27
Windows PIF editor

signed to create a VM that runs with as many DOS applications as possible. So it creates a huge, horrible VM that takes almost 1MB of memory. This is a phenomenal waste of memory in almost all cases.

To make a good PIF, use the PIF editor that comes with Windows; it is usually located in the Main directory (Figure 14.27). Let's look at how to make a good PIF:

PROGRAM FILENAME This is the name and path of the DOS program to run. If the DOS program is in the path, you don't need a path, but I still put one in to play it safe.

WINDOWS TITLE This is what the program says at the top of the menu. Put anything you want.

OPTIONAL PARAMETERS Many DOS programs can run with switches after the program name. For example, you could type EDIT CONFIG.SYS to run the EDIT program and load the CONFIG.SYS simultaneously.

START-UP DIRECTORY Some DOS programs are sensitive to the directory in which they start. For example, dBASE III and WordPerfect 5.1

will look for their data files in the directory that you start them in. Lotus 2.*x* must be started in its \123 directory or it will lock up. The Start-Up Directory option allows these programs to run in a specified directory.

VIDEO This option specifies how much memory is reserved for video. Text will allow 16K, Low Graphics gives 32K, and High Graphics gets a whopping 128K. If you are running a dedicated text program, you can save 122K of memory by setting this to Text.

MEMORY REQUIREMENTS This is probably the most important line in the PIF file. The first setting, KB Required, is the minimum amount of conventional memory needed by the program to run. KB Desired is the amount of conventional memory Windows will give if it is available. The number to watch here is KB Desired, which can be reduced substantially for small DOS applications like EDIT, saving as much as 384K of memory! Check the minimum requirements to determine the smallest possible setting.

EMS AND XMS MEMORY This is the same as Memory Requirements, but for expanded and extended memory.

DISPLAY USAGE This setting lets the DOS application run in a window or full screen. Press Alt<Esc to toggle between window and full screen.

EXECUTION Background allows the DOS application to run in the background. This is a good setting to select, because DOS applications by default get only a tiny amount of background time, causing them to run slowly when in the background. The Background option allocates more time to the program dynamically, taking back the time when the program is idle. Exclusive means that when the DOS application is in the foreground, everything else, including DOS and Windows, stops. The Exclusive option is rarely used.

CLOSE WINDOWS ON EXIT Why did Microsoft add this option? It's checked by default, which is how it should be left. If you unselect it, when you close the DOS application, you'll get a stupid blank window—useless! Leave this option at its default and move on.

ADVANCED Very few programs require changes to the Advanced options (Figure 14.28). Let's look at them so you'll know why:

MULTITASKING OPTIONS Multitasking options are almost useless because Windows always gives precedence to a DOS application in the foreground. Leave these options alone.

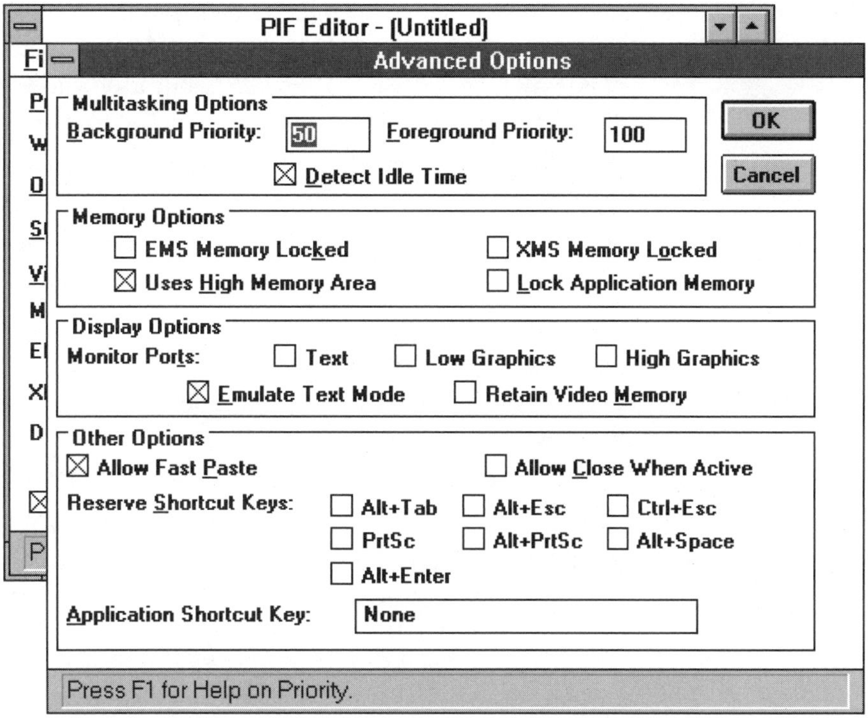

Figure 14.28
PIF advanced options

EMS MEMORY LOCKED AND XMS MEMORY LOCKED This prevents Windows from swapping expanded or extended memory used by DOS programs—again useless. Ignore them!

LOCK APPLICATION MEMORY These options prevent any conventional memory from being swapped. It allows the application to run faster, but everything else is crippled. Leave it alone.

USES HIGH MEMORY AREA This reserves HMA space for DOS applications, but no DOS applications use the HMA. Leave it selected or turn it off.

MONITOR PORTS This is only for EGA monitors. EGA monitors can't report their current video mode and have to be actively monitored so Windows knows how to resolute the screen. If you don't have an EGA monitor, leave it alone. If you still have an EGA monitor, upgrade!

EMULATE TEXT MODE Windows can emulate most text characters, but some applications don't like Windows doing that. Turning off this option forces Windows to use the characters on the video BIOS. It's almost never used.

RETAIN VIDEO MEMORY Remember the Video Memory option? If you select High Graphics and the DOS application doesn't use it, Windows will take it back! If the DOS application suddenly decides it needs it back, Windows will return it—*if* it has the memory to spare. This option prevents Windows from taking the memory.

ALLOW FAST PASTE Some DOS applications can't handle the speed of Windows cutting and pasting. If you lose characters between DOS applications, turn this setting off. Windows will add a few milliseconds between characters.

ALLOW CLOSE WHEN ACTIVE This allows a DOS application to be closed with either Alt<F4 or the File Close menu, which is handy when you're trying to debug a new PIF file. It can be dangerous, however, if you're using applications that hold open data files like dBASE, since files can be corrupted.

RESERVE SHORTCUT KEYS Certain programs like the IBM mainframe communication program PC3270 use Windows keys to perform certain functions. If you run PC3270 from DOS and press Alt<Esc, you will switch between mainframe sessions. But if you run it in Windows and press Alt<Esc, you will toggle among all active Windows programs. Selecting the Alt+Esc box tells Windows to leave PC3270 alone; when you type Alt<Esc, you will again toggle through the mainframe sessions.

APPLICATION SHORTCUT KEY This allows an application to be started by a key combination such as Alt<S.

Troubleshooting Windows 3.x

Windows 3.*x* problems can be divided into three distinct groups. The first are lockups, which is when the PC locks up without any errors—the machine simply refuses to operate. Next are GPFs (general protection faults), which are the famous errors that come up when one program writes over another. The last are "erratics," which is strange behavior by programs or devices that don't actually lock up the machine or generate errors.

Lockups

Lockups are simple. The machine no longer responds to input, but doesn't display any errors: the mouse pointer doesn't move, keyboard controls don't work, and the machine seems to be frozen solid. Lockups tend to point towards fairly serious hardware problems, and need to be dealt with aggressively, since there is a risk of data corruption and loss. Let's look at the following problem areas:

POWER SUPPLY Power supplies tend to create lockups. System lockups will happen for no apparent reason, and no one application, function, or time seems to cause the problem. If the power supply is the problem, the errors will continue in DOS, Windows, or any other operating systems you use. Turn off the machine, turn it back on, and walk away for 20 minutes. If you come back to your computer and it has locked up, it is the power supply. See the *Power Supplies* chapter for more complete repair techniques.

CORRUPTED FILES Lockups can be caused by two types of corrupted files. The first are files that have been corrupted due to bad hard, floppy, or CD-ROM drives. The second type are corrupted by a software problem: bad writes during copy, during defragmentation, or your computer shutting down unexpectedly. Files can also be corrupted through no fault of your (or your hardware's) own. Problems during download, for example, can corrupt files. Files can even come corrupted straight from the software producers.

The major symptom of a corrupted file is that the lockup happens consistently, at the exact same time. For example, every time you start an application, it reaches a certain point and then locks up. To correct the lockup, try running Norton Utilities or ScanDisk to determine if the problem lies with the hard disk. If this doesn't correct the problem, try reinstalling the application in another directory, so it will not write on the same area of the hard disk. Refer to the *Hard Drives* chapter for a more detailed explanation.

BAD RAM Lockups due to bad RAM chips look a lot like a power-supply problem because they seem to happen at different times. Fortunately, bad RAM lockups can be easily detected; if a RAM chip is so bad that it causes a lockup in Windows, the HIMEM.SYS file will detect it and scream at boot time. Reboot the computer and watch HIMEM.SYS while it's loading—use the F8 key if necessary. If the RAM is bad, it will say something like:

```
HIMEM has detected unreliable XMS memory at xxxx:xxxxxxxx
```

Use a third-party utility like Allmicro's Troubleshooter to verify that the RAM is bad. See the chapter on *RAM* for a detailed description of RAM problems and repair scenarios. Note that most RAM problems show up as errors or GPFs.

CORRUPTED SWAP FILE Corrupted swap files can also cause lockups, although this is rather rare. These lockups tend to show themselves when you first start Windows or when you exit Windows. Turn off the swap files and try starting Windows again. If you can get into Windows, find the 386SPART.PAR file and erase it. Windows will give you an error on startup, but it *will* start up. Defragment the drive and recreate the swap file.

IRQ AND DMA CONFLICTS Lockups generated by IRQ and DMA conflicts are created when the two devices begin to speak at the same time, but not all IRQ and DMA conflicts manifest themselves as lockups. Remember that these conflicts don't happen on machines that were "working fine before." Invariably, they happen on computers where a device has just been added or changed.

INCORRECT DRIVERS Improper drivers can sometimes lead to lockups. Make sure that your video, hard drive, sound card, etc., are using the proper drivers. When updating drivers, keep the old copy handy in case you have problems; at least you can go back to a working machine if the new driver locks up your machine.

General Protection Faults

There are three broad categories of general protection faults (GPFs): memory-management problems showing up as a GPF in KRNL386.EXE; GDI or USER errors, which indicate a resource heap overflow; and application-specific errors. Last, and also fitting into the RAM category, is a GPF that occurs over and over again at a specific memory address—which usually points to a problem with a RAM chip.

Memory management is typically an issue on machines that run DOS applications and have been configured by a technician (not you, of course) with an incorrect or incomplete understanding of proper memory-management techniques. Pay particular attention to proper use of exclude statements in the EMM386.EXE line.

A GPF caused by a GDI (graphical device interface) heap overflow can be visually exciting. They occur on machines with an animated screen saver running along with some minimized high-powered applications such as PowerPoint or Excel. Usually the animated part of the screen saver will disappear. When you deactivate the screen saver, often all the icons will turn into white squares or parts of the desktop will disappear. This is caused by the GDI heap losing all the data describing the attributes of each icon. With resource heap overflows, the only sure-fire cure is to quit trying to do so many things at once—either that or upgrade to Windows 95 or Windows NT, whose resource heaps aren't limited to 64K.

Application-specific errors are the most frustrating because there is nothing you can do to make them go away. In order to truly fix these errors, you must repair the application software at the source. The best you can hope to accomplish is to identify the specific instances (other programs running, usually) that cause the problem, and avoid those situations in the future. When you get these errors, call the company that makes that particular software; you'll probably find that there is some type of "patch" to repair the problem.

Backing Up

Backing up Windows 3.*x* is crucial. The trick is to determine which files to backup. The easiest backup is to just back up everything—all files in the \WINDOWS directory and its subdirectories. The total size is less than 100MB on most systems, making an easy fit on tape backups or any removable media disk.

Maybe you want to perform a new installation, but you'd like the new installation to look exactly like the old one. You want your colors, groups, and window positions just as they were before. In that case, make a backup of the GRP files as well as PROGMAN.INI—most technicians just copy all the .INI files. When Windows 3.*x* is installed, copy PROGMAN.INI as well as the GRP files to the Windows directory.

CHAPTER 15

Windows 95

In this chapter, you will:

- Understand how Windows 95 operates.
- Look at disk caching.
- Inspect the Windows registry.
- Understand PIF files.
- Learn basic Windows troubleshooting.

Supporting Windows 95 is a daunting task. So many aspects of these operating systems are changing at such a rapid rate that it is imperative for a good technician to keep up with the nonstop rush of updates and patches that are constantly being produced by Microsoft, hardware and software companies, and a large number of independent technical groups.

Internet Resources

The only way for a technician to "keep up" is via the Internet. I spend an average of one hour a day accessing certain resources on the Net to keep myself informed of the "goings on" with Windows. This section describes some of the main places I check from time to time to keep informed.

Microsoft's Web Site

The Microsoft Web site is a great source for information on Windows. Of particular help is the popular Microsoft KnowledgeBase at www.microsoft.com/support/. This Web site has all of Microsoft's answers to the majority of problems that can take place within Windows. Unfortunately, due to the vast amount of information, searching can be a little painful, and you must phrase your searches carefully.

Other Web Sites

There are a large number of Web sites geared to Windows support. Here are a few of my favorites:

- http://www.sns-access.com/~netpro/win95.htm
- http://www.conitech.com/windows/
- http://www.interaccess.net/~denyse/win95upd.html

Each of these Web sites have excellent links to other sites that you might find helpful.

Newsgroups

Usenet newsgroups are a great place for information. They are also super for asking questions; you can almost always get an answer to a technical problem, assuming that you pick the correct newsgroup and provide fairly detailed information. Here are a few good Windows newsgroups:

- Comp.os.ms-windows.win95
- Comp.os.ms-windows.setup.win95
- Comp.os.ms-windows.apps.utilities.win95

And there are many, many more! Basically, try any or all groups under Comp.sys.ibm-pc and Comp.os.ms-windows.

Be patient with newsgroups. Unlike Web sites, you are dealing directly with a fellow human being. When you first get started, take a few days scouring through each newsgroup to get a "feel" for the topic and the people answering the questions before you jump in with a question of your own. Be aware that not every question will be the right one, and don't be afraid to question an answer that you don't agree with—politely, of course. See if you can find the FAQ (frequently asked questions) for the newsgroup. Not all newsgroups have a FAQ, but they can be quite helpful.

How Windows 95 Works

Windows 95 is really two products: a DPMI (DOS protected-mode interface) and a protected-mode GUI. The improved "DOS" part of Windows 95 looks and acts pretty much exactly like good old DOS, but it is DPMI-compliant, so it can support the use of extended memory even though it cannot multitask. Windows 95 first starts DPMI and then fires up the GUI. This means that you do not have to use the GUI to boot to Windows 95! This is important as a lot of PC repair functions, particularly for the hard drive, are handled at a C: prompt. Do not confuse booting Windows 95 without the GUI with a DOS window inside Windows 95! They are completely different! I'll begin the discussion of Windows 95 by looking at DPMI. For simplicity's sake (and to make Microsoft mad), I'll call this new and improved product DOS 7 (see Figure 15.1).

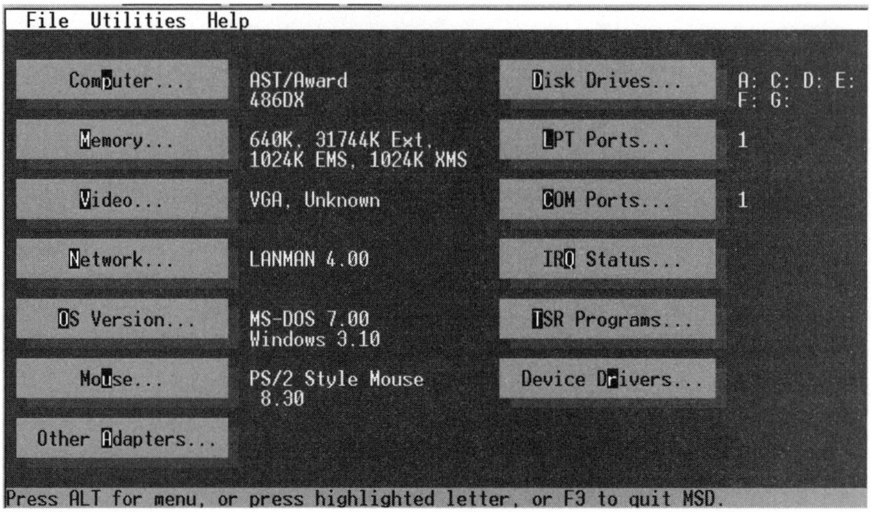

Figure 15.1
"DOS 7"

```
File  Utilities  Help

Computer...          AST/Award                Disk Drives...     A: C: D: E:
                     486DX                                       F: G:
Memory...            640K, 31744K Ext,        LPT Ports...       1
                     1024K EMS, 1024K XMS
Video...             VGA, Unknown             COM Ports...       1
Network...           LANMAN 4.00              IRQ Status...
OS Version...        MS-DOS 7.00              TSR Programs...
                     Windows 3.10
Mouse...             PS/2 Style Mouse         Device Drivers...
                      8.30
Other Adapters...

Press ALT for menu, or press highlighted letter, or F3 to quit MSD.
```

DOS 7

Remember IO.SYS and MSDOS.SYS from older versions of DOS? Well, they are still in Windows 95, but all their functions have been combined together into IO.SYS. MSDOS.SYS has been turned into a hidden, read-only text file in the root directory of the boot drive. MSDOS.SYS is used as a startup options file. COMMAND.COM is still there and still performs the same basic function of the old COMMAND.COM—providing the prompt. COMMAND.COM is no longer required if the system will always run in the GUI mode. But if a C:\> is ever needed, or if the system needs to use an AUTOEXEC.BAT file, COMMAND.COM must be present in the root directory. When the computer boots up and says "Starting Windows 95," press the F8 key and select "Command Prompt Only." You will be at a DOS 7 prompt. Type ver and you'll see "Windows 95."

MSDOS.SYS is no longer the DOS kernel as it was before DOS 7. It is now considered a replacement for many of the AUTOEXEC.BAT and CONFIG.SYS functions that are still needed before the GUI kicks in. MSDOS.SYS is the information file that tells DOS 7 how to boot up and where to do it. All the options must be placed under the [Options] group. Each example shows the default setting, but other settings are listed. Learn all the following options, because they will help you time and time again:

BOOTCONFIG=1 Allows to boot up a particular hardware configuration—for example, BootConfig=2 would start configuration 2.

DISABLELOG=1 Enables the BOOTLOG.TXT file (0 = disable).

SYSTEMREG=1 Loads the system registry (0 = don't load).

BOOTSAFE=0 This option does not force the machine to boot in safe mode (1 = safe mode).

DRVSPACE=1 or DBLSPACE=1 loads Doublespace or Drivespace drivers (0 = don't load).

BOOTWIN=1 Boots Windows 95 (0 = DOS).

BOOTWARN=1 Shows the "You Are in Safe Mode" warning message (0 = don't show).

BOOTKEYS=1 Specifies using the function keys at boot (0 = no keys).

BOOTGUI=1 Specifies booting the Windows 95 GUI (0 = DOS prompt only).

NETWORK=1 Shows boot in safe mode, with a networking menu option available (0 = don't show).

BOOTMENU=0 Does not load boot menu (1 = show menu).

BOOTMENUDEFAULT=1 Shows the default boot menu option if you don't pick one:

1 = Normal
2 = Logged to Bootlog.txt
3 = Safe mode
4 = Safe mode with network support (if network is installed)
4 or 5 = Step by step
5 or 6 = Command prompt
6 or 7 = Safe mode command prompt
7 or 8 = Previous version of MS-DOS (if bootmulti = 1)

DOUBLEBUFFER=1 Loads VFAT's double buffer (0 = don't load).

BOOTMULTI=0 Will not prompt for previous version of MS-DOS in boot menu (must have BootMenu = 1).

LOGO=1 Shows an animated logo (0 = don't show).

LOADTOP=1 Loads COMMAND.COM at the top of 640K (0 = load normally).

BOOTDELAY=X Specifies how long the computer waits, in seconds, after showing "Starting Windows 95."

All the following options must show under the [Paths] group:

UNINSTALLDIR=C: This specifies where to find the Windows 95 uninstall file.

WINDIR=C:\WINDOWS This lists the Windows GUI files.

WINBOOTDIR=C:\WINDOWS This specifies the support windows files needed to boot.

HOSTWINBOOTDRV=C This is always the C: drive.

The GUI

The magic of Windows 95 starts when the GUI starts, which is a protected-mode overlay of the DOS 7 shell (Figure 15.2). The GUI loads its own device drivers for *everything*. Assuming a Windows 95 device driver

Figure 15.2 The Windows 95 GUI shell

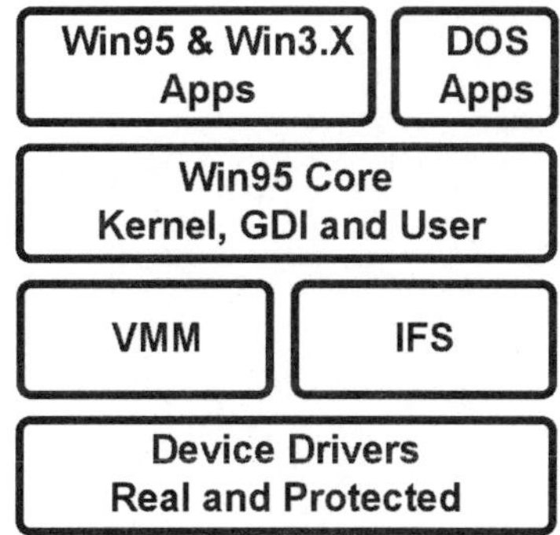

Figure 15.3
GUI architecture

is available, this means you don't need CONFIG.SYS to load device drivers anymore. Windows 95 also supports FILES, BUFFERS, DOS=UMB, and just about everything else CONFIG.SYS does. So, again assuming Windows 95 drivers are available, you do not need CONFIG.SYS. In addition, the GUI loads protected-mode MSCDEX for most CD-ROM drives, and protected-mode mouse support for Windows 95, Windows 3.*x*, and DOS applications, so you probably don't need AUTOEXEC.BAT either. Figure 15.3 shows how the GUI is organized.

The lowest levels of Windows 95 are the device drivers—either real-mode drivers loaded at CONFIG.SYS or AUTOEXEC.BAT, or protected-mode drivers loaded with the GUI (Figure 15.4). After the device drivers is the virtual memory manager (VMM), which supports memory usage at both the DOS 7 and GUI levels. At the DOS 7 level, VMM does little more than load a simple DOS. When the GUI is loaded, VMM takes advantage of the power of 386 and better protected mode to create virtual machines (VM), one for Windows 95 and one for any DOS programs running in Windows 95. Along with the VMM is the installable file system (IFS), which provides support for hard, CD-ROM, and network drives. The IFS

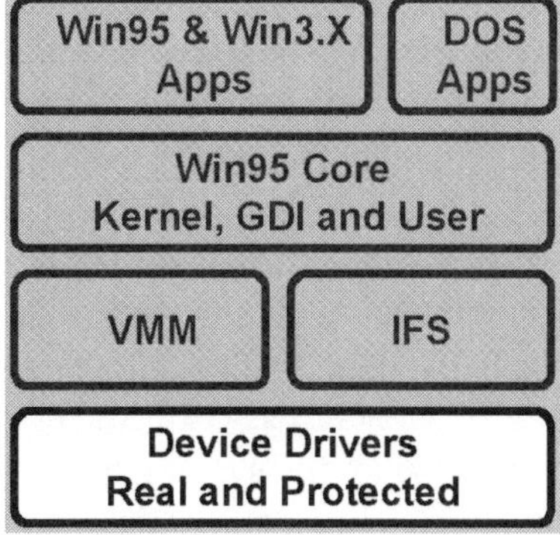

Figure 15.4
Device drivers

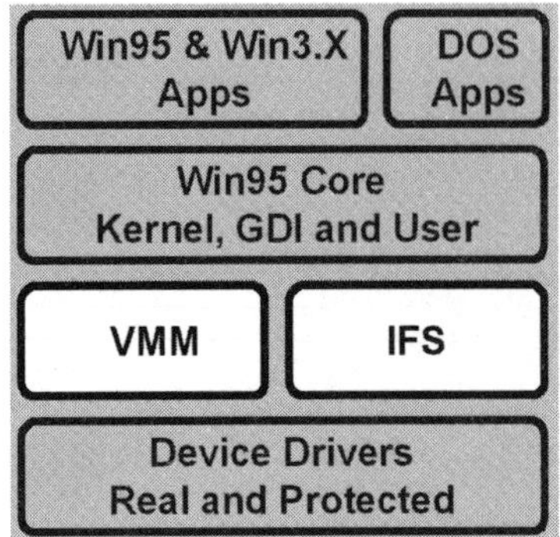

Figure 15.5
VMM and IFS

also provides the support for long filenames. The IFS runs for DOS 7 as well as the GUI. See Figure 15.5.

When the GUI is running, the main functions of Windows 95 are handled by the kernel, user, and graphical device interface (GDI) modules. Windows 95 applications look at the operating system as a pool of resources: memory, modem, video, whatever the system has is offered up to applications by these three components as a "resource." Programs or DLLs call these three whenever they need to place something on the screen, check the status of the mouse, use some memory, or anything else. This is similar to the way Windows 3.*x* works, but with some big improvements. First, most of these functions run in full 32-bit protected mode, whereas in Windows 3.*x* most functions run in 16-bit real mode. Second, Windows 95 runs as a preemptive multitasker. This means that Windows 95 allocates time to each program. Windows 3.*x* is a cooperative multitasker, which means that it's up to the programs themselves to take and release time as they see fit.

In Windows 3.*x*, the GDI and user have fixed memory areas called "heaps" to keep track of all resources. These heaps are 64K in size. When Windows 3.*x* was made, it was thought that 64K was plenty of space. It was not, however, especially with screen savers sapping the GDI heap, and these fixed heaps caused a lot of trouble in Windows 3.*x*. Windows 95 heaps are variable in size and are no longer subject to this problem. See Figure 15.6.

At the top of the Windows 95 architecture is the user interface (Figure 15.7), which is what you actually *see* on the screen: the icons, windows, and toolbars. Windows 95 can use the default interface, the Windows 3.*x* interface, or even other shells. The GUI also allows for the use of older Windows 3.*x* applications and DOS applications run within the GUI.

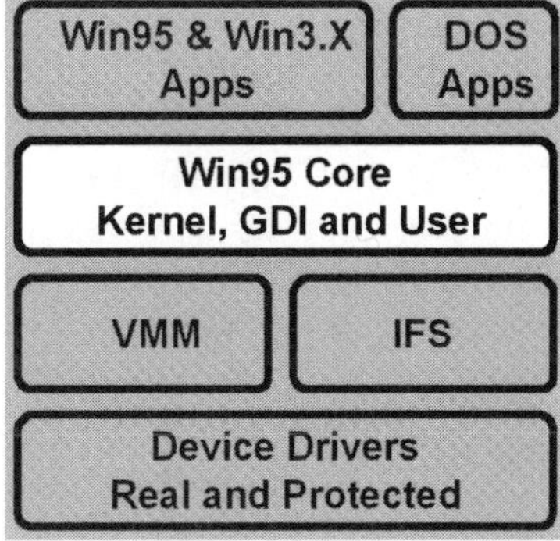

Figure 15.6
The Windows core

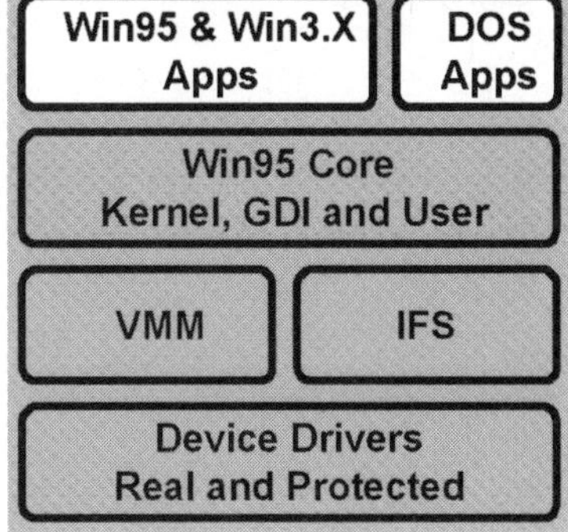

Figure 15.7
The user interface

The Registry

Windows 3.*x*'s use of .INI files creates a bit of a problem in that you can have settings for a number of different aspects of the computer scattered among tens, possibly hundreds of .INI files across your computer. There is no standard format for .INI files and no standard location, which makes updates and uninstalling problematic at best. Realizing this, Microsoft created a new way to store system information for Windows 95: the registry. The registry is composed of two binary files called SYSTEM.DAT and USER.DAT, which are located in the \WINDOWS directory. These two files store all the information about your PC, as well as information on all the hardware in the PC, network information, user preferences, file types, and virtually anything else you might run into with Windows 95. Backups of the Registry files are created every time Windows starts. These files are also stored in the \Windows directory and are distinct by the extension "DA0". The idea of the registry is to have one common database for the entire PC.

In a perfect world, the registry replaces CONFIG.SYS, AUTOEXEC.BAT, and every .INI file. Windows 95 will, however, still read all .INI files at boot time for backward compatibility with Windows 3.*x* programs that use them, and it will also read CONFIG.SYS and AUTOEXEC.BAT if they are present.

The registry is almost never directly accessed; it should work in the background, and be updated by only a few menus and installation programs, quietly storing all necessary data for the system. Unfortunately, the reality is that a technician will need to manipulate the registry from time to time. Therefore, let's take some time so you can become comfortable with accessing and changing the registry.

Accessing the Registry

The main way to access the registry is through the Control Panel (Figure 15.8). The only function of the Control Panel is to update the registry, just as the Control Panel in Windows 3.*x* was used to update the SYSTEM.INI file.

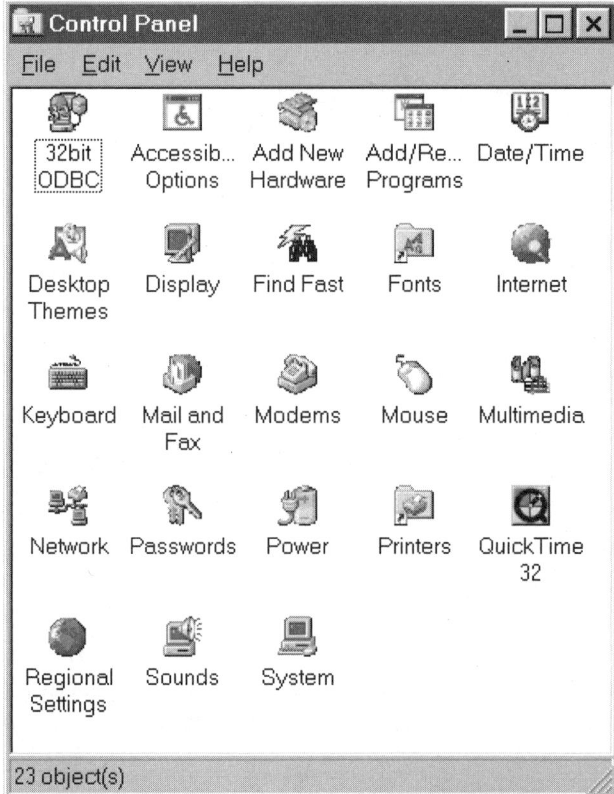

Figure 15.8
The Control Panel

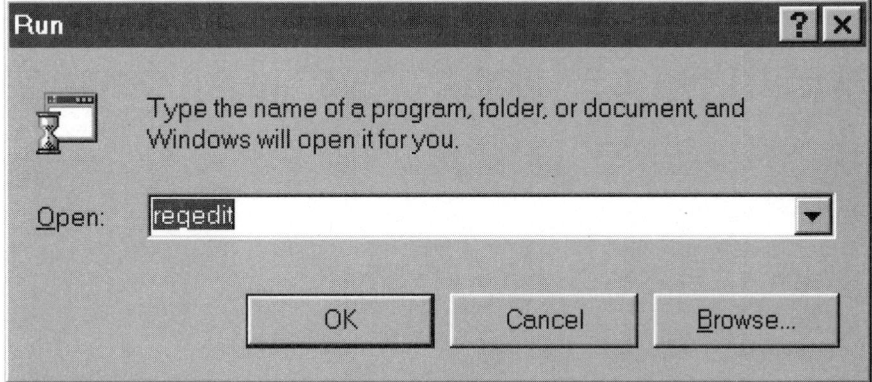

Figure 15.9
Starting the Registry Editor

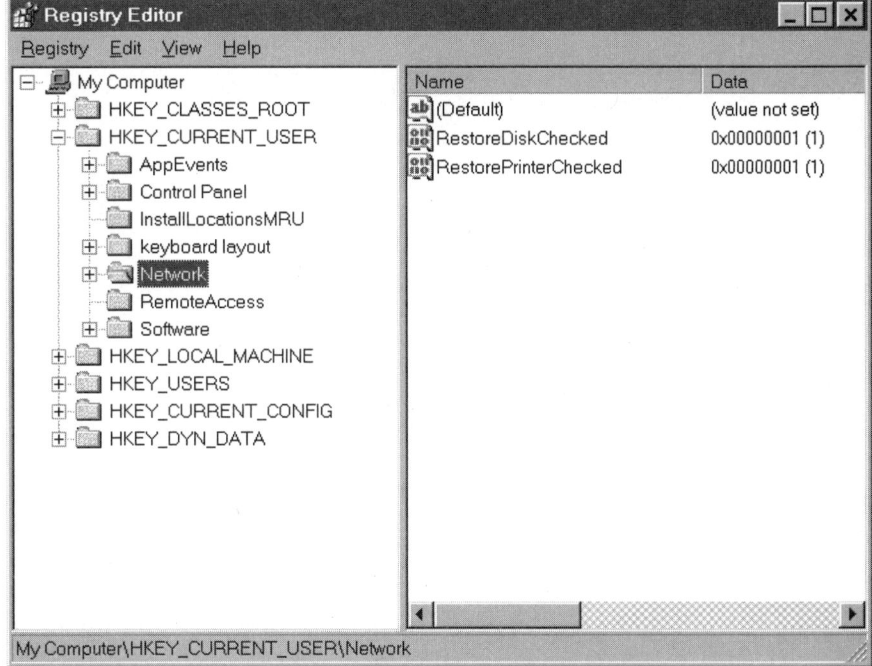

Figure 15.10a
The Registry Editor

In Windows 3.*x*, many necessary options are unavailable in the Control Panel, forcing you to open the SYSTEM.INI file directly to make changes. So far, this is basically untrue in Windows 95. Everything necessary to configure the system so it works can be handled from the new Control Panel. However, there are times when you might want to access the registry directly. To do this, you must use the Registry Editor. Start the Registry Editor by using the RUN command from the Start button, and typing regedit (Figure 15.9). This will start the Registry Editor (Figure 15.10). Remember that the registry is a binary file! You cannot edit it with

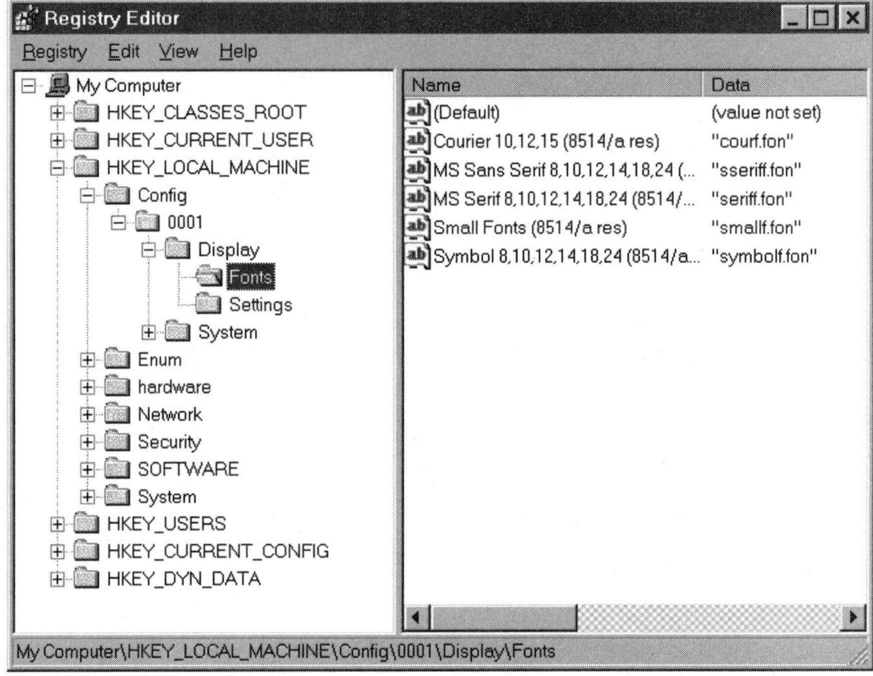

Figure 15.10b Typical keys and values

EDIT or any other text editor like you could with SYSTEM.INI. You must use REGEDIT.

Registry Components

The registry is organized in the same tree structure as directories in the PC. Once REGEDIT is open, there are six main subgroups or *keys*: HKEY_CLASSES_ROOT, HKEY_CURRENT_USER, HKEY_LOCAL_MACHINE, HKEY_USERS, HKEY_CURRENT_CONFIG, and HKEY_DYN_DATA. Try opening one of these keys, and note that there are more subkeys underneath them. A subkey also has other subkeys and/or *values*. Figure 15.10b is an example of a subkey with some values. Notice that REGEDIT shows keys on the left and values on the right, just as Windows Explorer shows directories on the left and files on the right.

When writing about keys and values, I'll use the expression *key = value*. The key to understanding the registry is to first understand the function of the six main keys. Each of these subgroups has a specific function, so let's take a look at each of the keys:

HKEY_CLASSES_ROOT This key defines the standard class objects used by Windows 95. A class object is a named group of functions. Pretty much everything that has to do with files on the system is defined by a class object. For example, a MIDI sound file can be defined with two class objects. First is the class object that defines the association of the .MID file extension with the name "midfile" (Figure 15.10c).

So the next question is "What is a midfile?" That's what the HKEY_CLASSES_ROOT key is designed to handle. Continuing to move through this section, the midfile key can be located. Figure 15.10d lists the values for midfile.

As you can see, this key tells the system everything that needs to be known about a particular software item. It's here that the file associations are defined, icons are shown, and options are displayed when an item is right-clicked. Although it is possible to change these settings via REGEDIT, the normal way is to use the \VIEW\OPTIONS menu from Windows Explorer (Figure 15.10e).

HKEY_USERS AND HKEY_CURRENT_USER Windows 95 can be configured to support more than one user on the same PC, storing per-

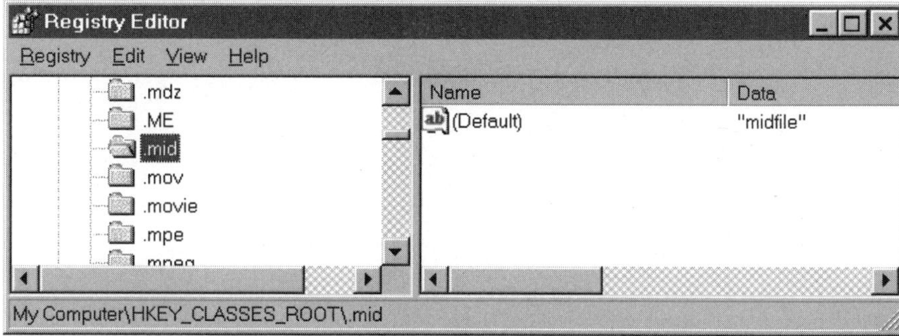

Figure 15-10c Association of .mid to midi files

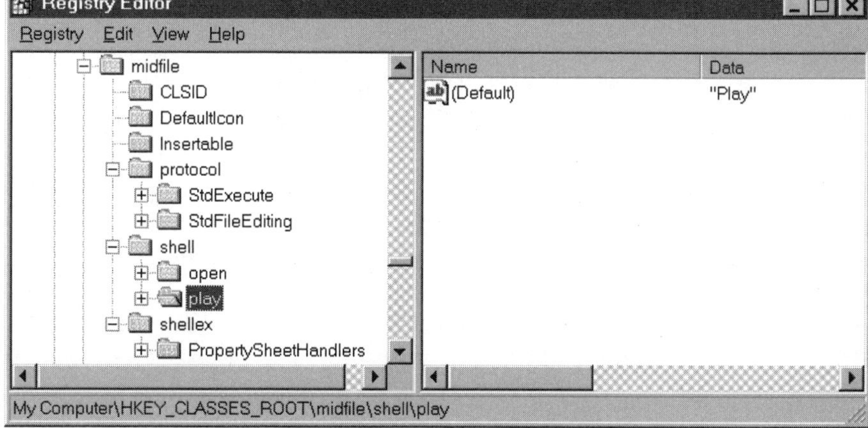

Figure 15.10d Midfile settings

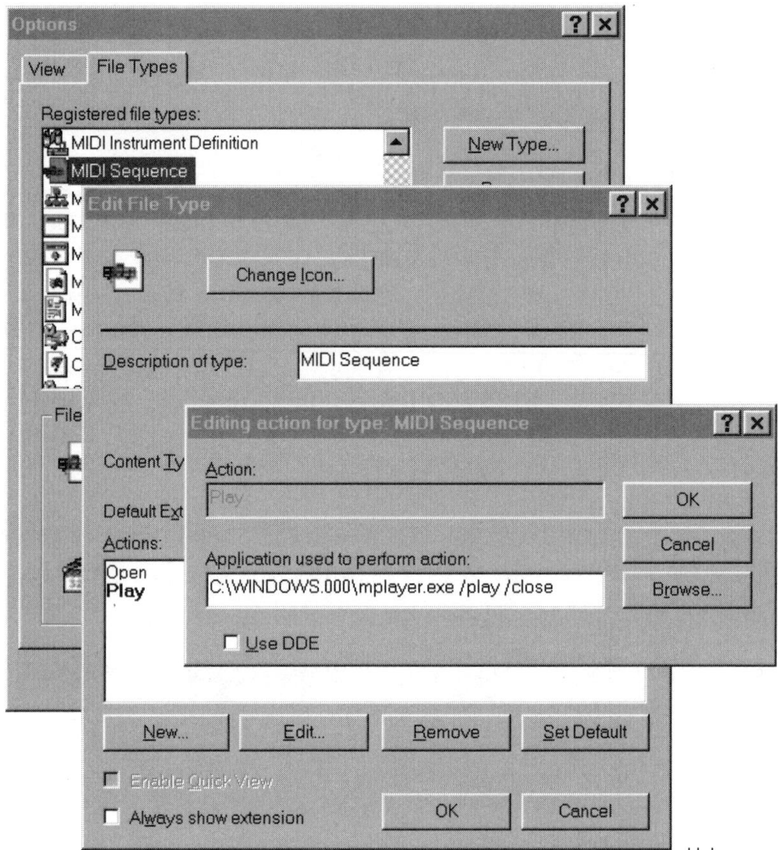

Figure 15.10e Changing association options

sonalized information such as colors, screen savers, and the contents of the desktop. HKEY_USERS stores all of the personalization information for all of users on a PC. The HKEY_CURRENT_USER key stores the current user settings, which is a good place to fix personalizations like fonts, some icons, and colors on systems that are set up to support multiple users.

HKEY_LOCAL_MACHINE This contains all the data for a system's non-user-specific configurations. This includes every device in your PC, including devices that you removed. For example, Figure 15.11 shows the description of a SCSI ZIP drive. You'll be seeing more of HKEY_LOCAL_MACHINE in the discussion of configuration and repairing hardware in Windows 95 later in this chapter.

HKEY_CURRENT_CONFIG If there are values in HKEY_LOCAL_MACHINE that have more than one option, such as two different moni-

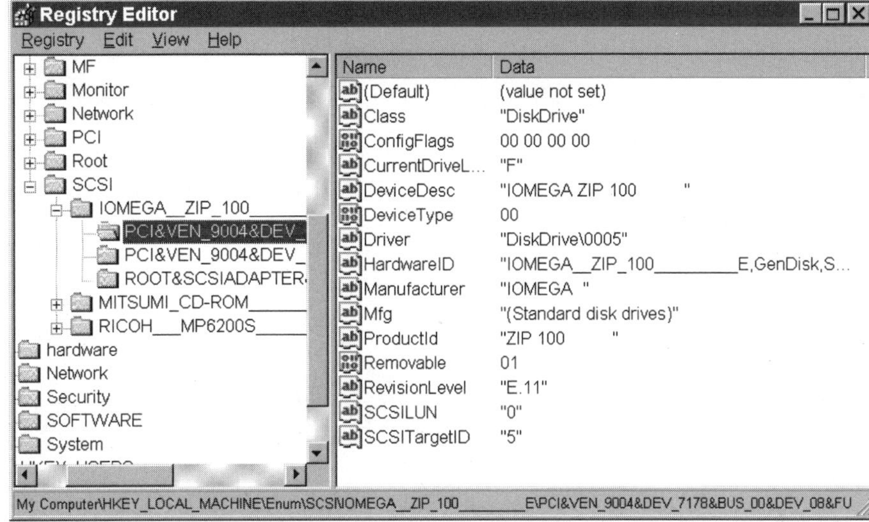

Figure 15.11 Registry information for a SCSI ZIP drive

tors, this defines which one is currently being used. Since most people have only one type of monitor and similar equipment, this area is almost never touched.

HKEY_DYN_DATA This is registry data stored in RAM to speed up system configuration. A snapshot of all hardware in use is stored here. It is updated at bootup and when any changes are made in the system configuration file.

Windows 95 File Structure

A major improvement in Windows 95 over Windows 3.*x* is long filenames (LFN). LFNs remove the old 8.3 filename limitation of older versions of DOS. LFN support works whether you are using the DOS 7 or GUI shell. In a regular DOS 8.3 directory, all file records are stored in 32-byte records. Ten of these 32 bytes are "reserved," which means Microsoft has said not to use them. The other 22 bytes are used to store information on starting clusters, creation date, and creation time. LFNs exist on FAT partitions because the filename is chopped into 12-byte chunks (LFNs steal one of the "reserved" bytes) and allows up to 13 chunks, which creates a filename limit of 255 characters. Table 15.1 is an example of an old DOS filename stored on a hard drive.

TABLE 15.1

Long File Name Structure

Function	Size in bytes	Example
First	8	MULTI
Extension	3	DOC
Attribute	1	0h
Reserved	10	???????
Creation time	2	8:00 AM
Creation date	2	2/15/96
Starting cluster	2	2343
File length	4	231

TABLE 15.2

Storage of Long File Name in Directory

First	Extension	Attribute	Reserved
think.doc		HSRV	
don't you		HSRV	<space>
ng file nam		HSRV	e
heck of a l		HSRV	o
This is one		HSRV	<space>
THISIS~1	DOC	A	

When an LFN is saved, the system first creates a short name that fits to the 8.3 standard, so the data of the following long filename:

```
This is one heck of a long file name, don't you think.doc
```

will be saved to an 8.3 filename (THISIS~1.DOC). Then each 12 characters is cut off and stored in its own directory section, as shown in Table 15.2.

The directory entries that make up a long filename are called *LFN entries*. This is great, but it must be backwardly compatible to DOS programs and to DOS itself. To make LFNs compatible really means to make sure that DOS ignores the LFN entries in the directory structure. This is achieved by giving LFN entries the bizarre attribute combination of hidden, read-only, system, and volume label. There are no instruction in DOS code for dealing with this combination of attributes, so DOS will not mess with them.

Unfortunately, older disk utilities will try to erase the LFN entries. It is crucial that any disk utility that tries to diagnose the directory structure (Norton Utilities 8.0 or older Scandisk for DOS) should never be run on a computer with LFNs. The ScanDisk that comes with Windows 95 and the latest version of Norton Utilities are all compatible with LFNs.

Windows 95 has also added some great new bits of file information, the best one being a "last accessed" date value that tells you when a particular file was last used. This includes executables, dynamic link libraries, and other nonuser data files like font files. This is very handy for asking questions such as "When was the last time you used Excel on this machine?"

FAT 32

Until recently, Windows 95 disk structures were nothing new. Partitions and formats were good old DOS FAT 16, identical to DOS, and you still needed FDISK and FORMAT to set up hard drives. A hard drive that was formatted with an older version of DOS was identical to a drive formatted with Windows 95. This changed in 1996 with the inclusion of a new format—FAT 32.

First, FAT 32 is optional. You don't have to use it if you don't want to, because FAT 16 runs just fine. Second, you can't buy Windows 95 with FAT 32 off the shelf. It is sold only with new systems under Windows 95 version OSR2. It's easy to tell if you have OSR2. Just right-click on the My Computer icon and select Properties. Under the General tab, locate the version of Microsoft Windows. If you have OSR2, you will see version 4.00.950B—and you have the capability to use FAT 32.

FAT 32 has some great advantages over FAT 16. First is the reduced cluster size. As you'll remember from the chapter on hard drives, one of the big downsides to FAT 16 is the way clusters are used by the system. A cluster is composed of sectors, each sector is 512 bytes, and the size of each cluster is determined by the size of the partition. For example, if a partition is between 512MB and 1GB, there are 32 sectors/cluster. If a partition is between 1 and 2GB, there are 64 sectors/cluster. The cluster is the single smallest unit of storage on a hard drive, so if you create a one-byte text file and save it in a 1.5GB partition, that one byte file will use one 64-sector cluster. That 64-sector cluster is 32K large, resulting in a dramatic loss of disk space. FAT 32 clusters are only 4K in size, and seriously reduce the amount of wasted cluster space.

Secondly, FAT 32 has no limit to the number of root directory entries. With FAT 16, the root directory is a fixed structure and you can only insert 255 entries in a root directory. With FAT 32, the root directory is treated like any other directory and can have an unlimited number of entries. Last, FAT 32 is more redundant. With FAT 16, you have only one boot sector. If the boot sector is damaged, you can't boot up the system. FAT 32 stores two copies of the boot sector, so if one boot sector is damaged, you can recover from the backup.

FAT 32 is completely compatible with all DOS and Windows applications, but you must never use any disk utilities unless they are designed for FAT 32!

You set up and install FAT 32 the same way you install FAT 16—by using FDISK and FORMAT. When you run the OSR2 FDISK, it asks you if you want "support for large disks." If you answer "yes," everything you do in FDISK will be FAT 32. If you say "no," everything will be FAT 16. When you run OSR2 FORMAT, it reads what type of partition is made and formats accordingly—very simple.

Device Drivers in Windows 95

Microsoft's goal for Windows 95 is to make all device drivers run in protected mode. Windows 95 comes with protected-mode versions of almost every device in your CONFIG.SYS and AUTOEXEC.BAT. HIMEM.SYS, double-buffering, SMARTDRV.EXE, SETVER, and IFSHLP.SYS are all loaded from within IO.SYS. Also, Microsoft provides protected-mode drivers for a broad cross-section of peripherals.

When Windows 95 installs over DOS/Windows 3.*x*, it looks for real-mode drivers in CONFIG.SYS and AUTOEXEC.BAT that it can replace. The list of device drivers that can be safely replaced is stored in a text file called IOS.INI that is located in the \WINDOWS directory. Figure 15.12 shows part of the IOS.INI file.

There are roughly 300 device drivers that Windows 95 can replace. That means that there are about 300,000 device drivers that Windows 95 has never heard about—especially in older devices. These real-mode drivers must run in order for the device they support to operate, which is why you still need CONFIG.SYS, SYSTEM.INI, and AUTOEXEC.BAT.

Unfortunately, Windows 95 must still support DOS programs and DOS device drivers, which still eat up conventional memory. Windows 95 must also support Windows 3.*x* applications that also use conventional mem-

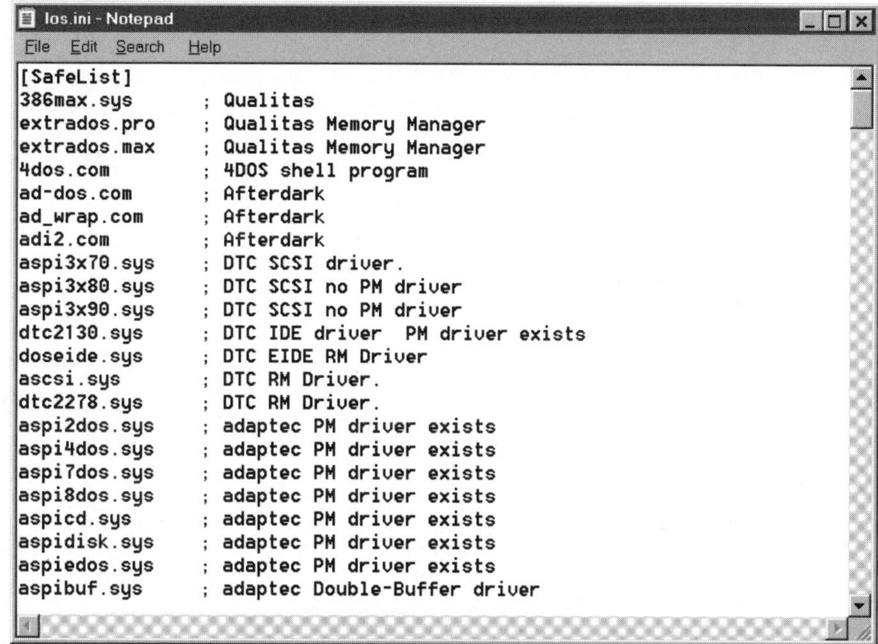


```
[SafeList]
386max.sys      ; Qualitas
extrados.pro    ; Qualitas Memory Manager
extrados.max    ; Qualitas Memory Manager
4dos.com        ; 4DOS shell program
ad-dos.com      ; Afterdark
ad_wrap.com     ; Afterdark
adi2.com        ; Afterdark
aspi3x70.sys    ; DTC SCSI driver.
aspi3x80.sys    ; DTC SCSI no PM driver
aspi3x90.sys    ; DTC SCSI no PM driver
dtc2130.sys     ; DTC IDE driver  PM driver exists
doseide.sys     ; DTC EIDE RM Driver
ascsi.sys       ; DTC RM Driver.
dtc2278.sys     ; DTC RM Driver.
aspi2dos.sys    ; adaptec PM driver exists
aspi4dos.sys    ; adaptec PM driver exists
aspi7dos.sys    ; adaptec PM driver exists
aspi8dos.sys    ; adaptec PM driver exists
aspicd.sys      ; adaptec PM driver exists
aspidisk.sys    ; adaptec PM driver exists
aspiedos.sys    ; adaptec PM driver exists
aspibuf.sys     ; adaptec Double-Buffer driver
```

Figure 15.12
The IOS.INI file

ory. Although the need for memory management is reduced, it is still there.

Configuring Windows 95

Unlike Windows 3.*x*, Windows 95 can be run fairly successfully without any tweaking. However, like Windows 3.*x*, the longer you have used Windows 95, the more often smaller problems come to light that need to be addressed. Let's look at some of these issues, paralleling some of the same areas covered in Windows 3.*x* and adding a few new ones.

Windows Updates

Windows has gone through a number of evolutionary changes in its short life. Since its inception, Windows 95 has had a number of patches and upgrades to correct or improve a broad cross-section of problems. There are three different ways to update Windows 95: patches, service packs, and new versions.

Figure 15.13 Patching Windows 95

Patches are .EXE files that you get from Microsoft to fix a specific problem. You run these programs and they do whatever they're supposed to do—updating DLLs, reconfiguring registry settings, or whatever else they need to do to fix a particular problem. For example, Figure 15.13 is a patch to fix a problem Windows had with extended partitions on LBA drives.

What is a TSD Virtual Device? Who cares? What is important is that these patches are required to keep Windows running properly. This does not mean that Windows 95 requires every patch produced. Ignore the patches that have nothing to do with what you do or fix a problem that you don't have. There are roughly 25–50 patches for Windows 95, and the majority of them are extremely important.

Sometimes a patch might not totally fix a particular problem or might cause other problems. In that case, you'll need a "patch for a patch." Also, some patches need to be installed before another patch can be used. This creates a unique situation where the patch order is quite important.

The order in which you install patches can be crucial!

When Windows 95 first was released, a long series of patches followed over the next few months, fixing everything from password problems to memory leaks. Microsoft packaged these together into a single .EXE file that would perform the patches simultaneously. This grouping of patches is called a *service pack*. There is currently only one service pack, predictably called Service Pack 1. If you have an original version of Windows 95, you'll need this patch.

Microsoft eventually sold Windows 95 with Service Pack 1 already installed. This version was called OSR 1 (OEM service release 1). After OSR 1, more patches were created, and so roughly a year later, another set of patches were combined into OSR 2. There has been only one significant patch since OSR 2.

Be aware that service packs/OSRs are usually far more than just fixes of problems in Windows 95. For example, the OSR 2 release adds powerful new functions, such as FAT 32. Although these additions can be very handy, this section focuses on fixes of known bugs and skips all the "toys" provided by these service packs and OSRs.

There are currently some 30 to 40 different patches, and three distinct versions of Windows 95. Each patch and version has its own unique features and problems, which makes it absolutely necessary for you to be able to identify which version you're using.

You need to be able to answer the question "Which version of Windows 95 do I have, and what patches should I install?"

Identifying your version is relatively easy. Go to My Computer/Properties, and the version is named there. Each Windows 95 version and service pack has a unique identification number, for instance: 4.00.950 for original Windows 95, 4.00.950a for OSR 1 or Original Windows patched with Service Pack 1, and 4.00.950B for OSR 2. For example, the system in Figure 15.14 uses original Windows 95 patched with Service Pack 1.

Identifying patches is a little tougher. The best way to determine the patches currently loaded on your system is to use Microsoft's QFECHECK (Figure 15.15). QFECHECK can be downloaded from the Microsoft Web site, and gives a detailed list of all patches performed on your machine. Note that the patches can be expanded to show the details of the files that were updated. In this case, a file called SHELL32.DLL was updated to version 4.71.1712.3.

Remember that service packs and OSRs are compilations of patches. When you install a service pack or purchase a machine with an OSR, QFECHECK will show *all* the patches performed by the service pack or OSR. In Figure 15.15, only Service Pack 1 and two patches have been in-

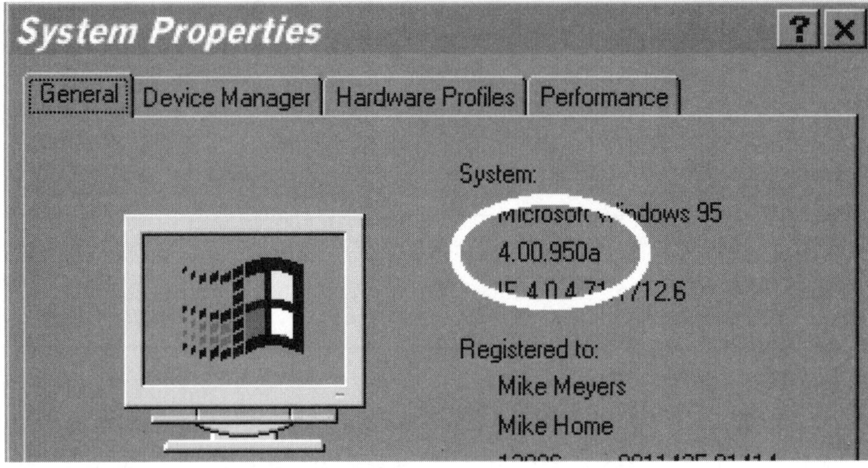

Figure 15.14 Reading the version of Windows

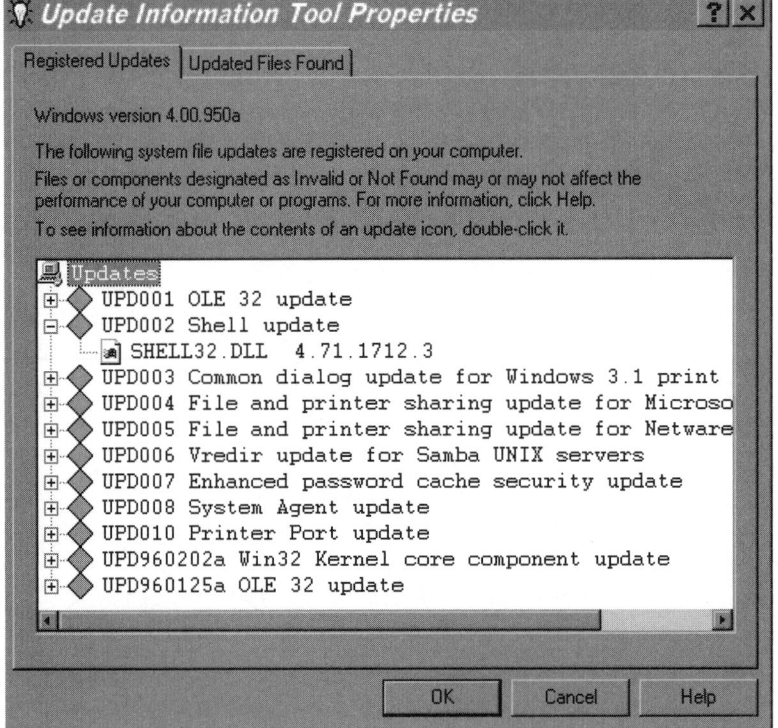

Figure 15.15 QFECHECK in action

stalled. But Windows breaks down all the patches in Service Pack 1 as separate patches in QFECHECK.

As mentioned earlier, the order of patching is crucial. To ensure that you are patching correctly, follow these steps. The version of each patch is provided. The following patches are part of Service Pack 1:

OLE32 Update This fixes a problem with Office applications (Word, Excel, and PowerPoint). Files created in these applications retain deleted information. This information can be read if the file is loaded into a text editor, creating a serious safety concern.

OLE32.DLL, 2.10.35.37 (Shell32 Update) This fixes a nasty bug in which a file that is copied onto itself will occasionally reduce to a zero-length file. It also adds some extra support for NetWare 4 printers.

SHELL32.DLL, 4.71.1112.3 (Common Dialog Printing Update) This fixes problems with Windows 95 applications that try to print from Windows 3.*x* drivers.

COMDLG32.DLL, 4.0.0.951 (Vserver Update) This fixes a file and print-sharing problem when working with Samba UNIX clients on a network.

VSERVER.VXD, 4.0.0.952 (Nwserver Update) This fixes a security problem with Windows 95 under Novell networks.

NWSERVER.VXD, 4.0.0.951 (Vredir Update) This fixes a filename bug when Windows 95 PCs access a Samba UNIX server.

VREDIR.VXD, 4.0.0.955 (Password List Update) This makes it more difficult to break into encrypted password files.

MSPWL32.DLL, 4.0.0.951 and NET.EXE, 4.00.951 (SAGE Update) This fixes a bug with the Microsoft Plus SAGE.DLL and floating-point calculations.

SAGE.DLL, 4.40.0.311 (ECP Port Update) This adds true ECP support for Windows 95.

LPT.VXD, 4.0.0.951 (Driver Updates) This is a broad cross-section of device drivers not found in the original Windows 95.

Service Pack 1/OSR 1 Patches If you own OSR2, you already have these patches!

Kernel 32 Update This fixes memory problems with systems that use Windows sockets.

KERNEL32.DLL, 4.0.0.951 (Part 2 of the OLE32 Update) This is a patch of a patch; it improves the Service Pack 1 OLE32 update.

OLETHK32.DLL, 4.71.1120.0 (Password Cache Update) This is a patch of a patch; it fixes a few bugs with the Service Pack 1 patch (files having the same numbers as earlier files).

NET.EXE, 4.00.951 (LBA Drive Update) This fixes a bug when using LBA drives with extended partitions.

Service Pack 2/OSR 2 Patches The only significant patch since Service Pack 2 is a rather large patch for encrypting passwords stored in memory. This is a three-part patch; which part you use depends on the version/service pack already installed. If you have Service Pack/OSR 1, it will contain:

- Mprserv.dll, 4.00.955
- Nwnet32.dll, 4.00.951
- Nwredir.vxd, 4.00.960
- Pppmac.vxd, 4.00.954
- Vredir.vxd, 4.00.1114
- Vnetsup.vxd, 4.00.1112
- Rasapi32.dll, 4.00.954

If you have Service Pack 2/OSR 2, these files will be on the patch:

- Mprserv.dll, 4.00.955
- Nwnet32.dll, 4.00.951
- Nwredir.vxd, 4.00.960
- Pppmac.vxd, 4.00.954
- Vredir.vxd, 4.00.1114
- Vnetsup.vxd, 4.00.1112
- Rasapi32.dll, 4.00.1113

If you are using a Microsoft NetWare client, add the file Nwredir.vxd, 4.00.975. All patches can be found on the Microsoft Web site at www.microsoft.com.

Configuring Virtual Memory

Windows 95 requires the use of virtual memory, of mapping a portion of the hard drive with memory addresses to mimic RAM. Windows 95, just like Windows 3.x, creates a swap file that allows it to have more programs

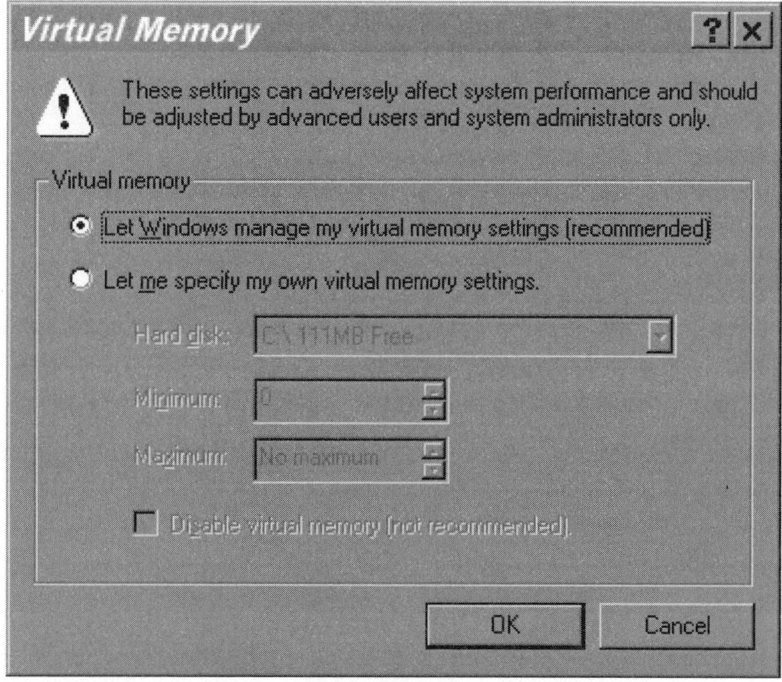

Figure 15.16 Performance window/virtual memory settings

open on the screen than it could normally hold in real RAM. (See the Windows 3.x chapter for a detailed discussion of virtual memory and swap files.) Unlike Windows 3.x, the swap file is always called WIN386.SWP. The initial size of the swap file in Windows 95 is set automatically by Windows according to how much free space is available on the C: drive. While this automatic setting works fairly well, we can easily optimize Windows' use of that swap file with a few judicious alterations. The swap file is configured in the Device Manager under the Performance Tab/Virtual Memory button (Figure 15.16).

One of the most common reasons for changing the default swap file is to move it to some other drive than C:. Many systems tend to fill up the C: drive, so there's little or no room left for the swap file. The swap file can use only the unused space on the drive; when the space is filled, the swap file won't get any larger, resulting in the nasty "Not Enough Memory" error. This necessitates moving the swap file to another drive.

The most common reason for getting the "Not Enough Memory" error in Windows is not having enough free drive space for the swap file. To move the file, click on the "Let me specify my own virtual memory settings" radio button and select another drive (Figure 15.17). Notice the minimum and maximum swap-file sizes (Figure 15.18). Windows will set these at zero and the size of the free space on the drive, respectively.

Figure 15.17 Selecting a different drive letter

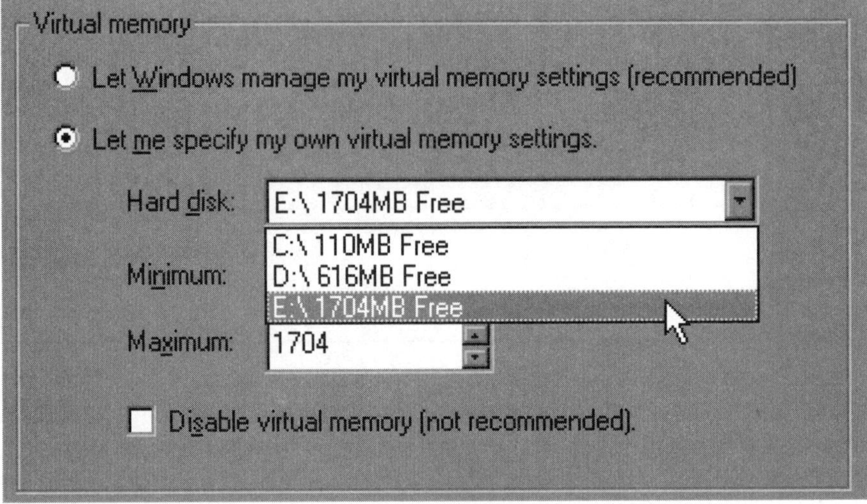

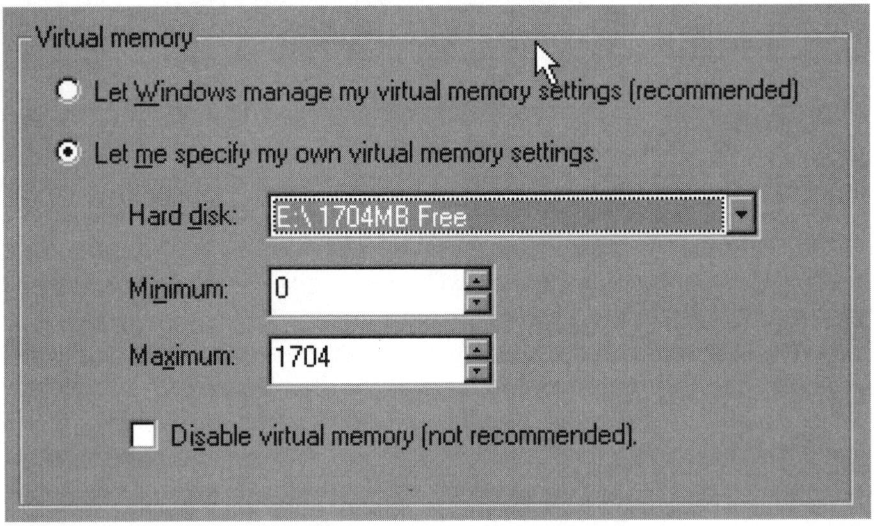

Figure 15.18 Large default swap file

Experimentation has shown that leaving these settings at their defaults can create *enormous* swap files, far larger than you really need. The current consensus is to reduce the swap-file size down to around two or three times the amount of RAM (Figure 15.19), meaning a system with 32MB of RAM is going to have its swap file set to around 64 to 96MB. Set both the minimum and maximum to the same number.

Certain programs demand large swap files. If you use programs like CorelDraw, you will find that the "two to three times" rule won't work.

Gradually increase these settings until the "Not Enough Memory" errors go away.

From time to time, you might need to turn virtual memory off, due maybe to corrupted swap files or the need to XCOPY from a DOS prompt within Windows. If you try to XCOPY within the directory that stores a swap file, the swap file will be copied, but it will take forever. In these rare occasions, simply click the Disable Virtual Memory checkbox and reboot your computer (Figure 15.20). Remember to turn virtual memory back on when you are finished!

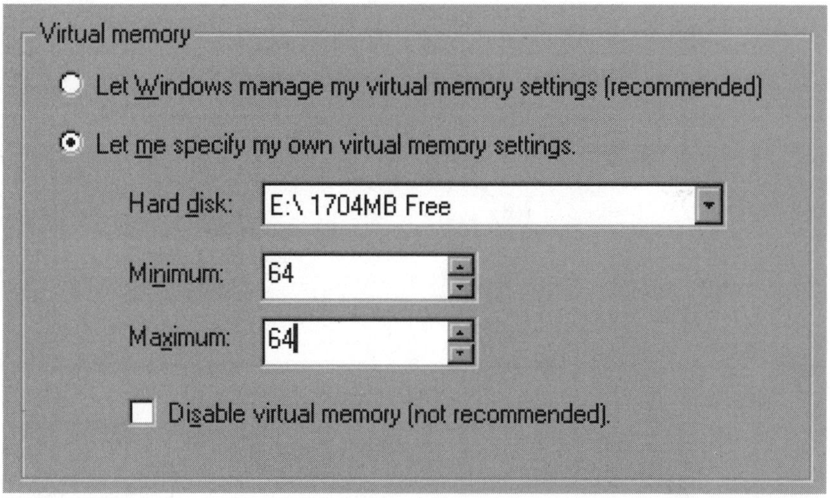

Figure 15.19
Manually setting the swap-file sizes

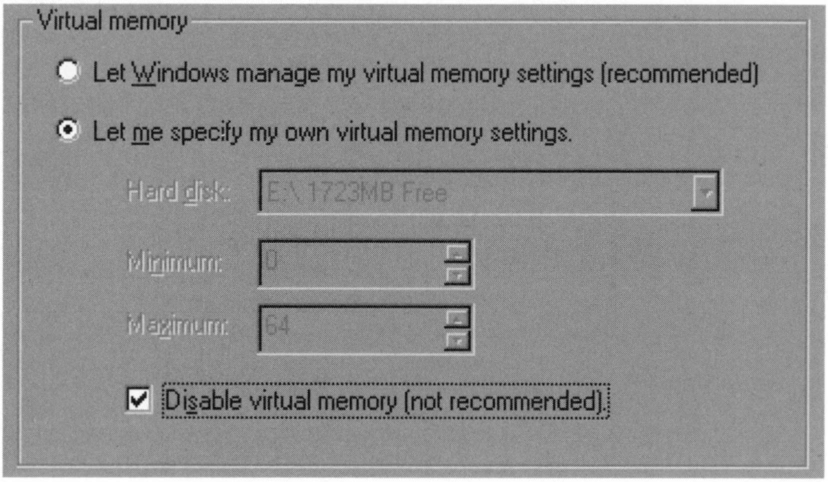

Figure 15.20
Disabling virtual memory

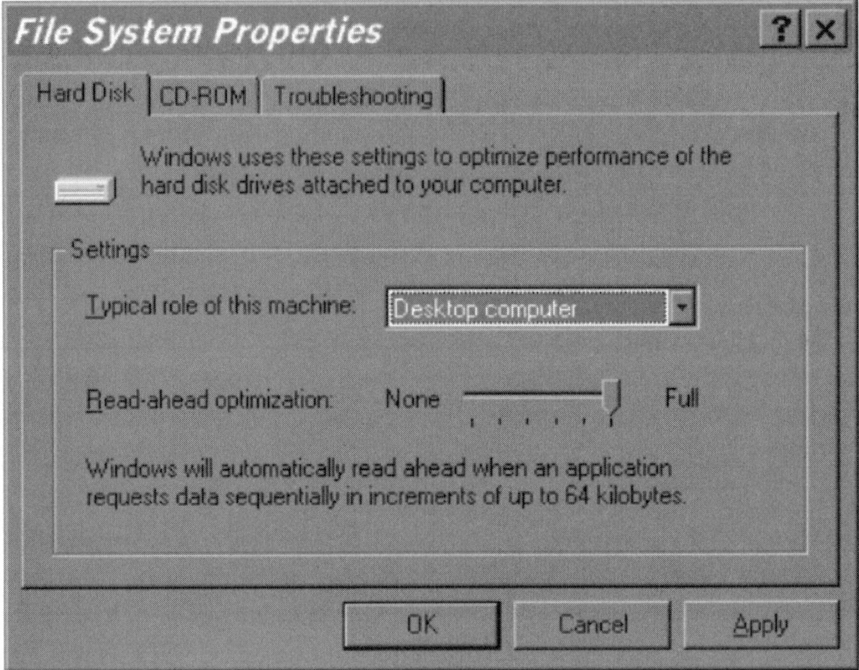

Figure 15.21
File system window

Disk Caches

The disk caching that comes with Windows 95 installs automatically and is virtually maintenance-free. The size of the disk cache is roughly one-fourth the total size of the RAM. Windows automatically sets the size of the "holding pen" based on settings that are given at setup. You can change these settings by accessing the Device Manager/Performance Tab/File System button (see Figure 15.21).

There are two settings for changing the disk cache: Typical Role of This Machine and Read-Ahead Optimization. The Typical Role button determines how much RAM to set aside for the disk cache holding pen. Setting this to Network Server can give a big performance boost. Before you do this, be aware of a nasty bug in Windows 95 before the OSR2 patch. You need to go into the registry (use REGEDIT) and find:

```
HKEY_LOCAL_MACHINE\SOFTWARE\Microsoft\Windows\CurrentVersion\FS
Templates\Server
```

When you open this branch, you'll see the three options shown in Figure 15.22. Make sure that NameCache and PathCache read as follows:

```
NameCache 40 00 00 00
PathCache a9 0a 00 00
```

They should look exactly like the example. Read-Ahead Optimization determines how much to read ahead when the system goes to the hard drive. Think about this for a minute. The disk cache doesn't think in terms of files; it thinks in terms of clusters. When the hard drive asks for data, it's actually asking for a number of clusters, because files tend to span many clusters. So if the system asks for one cluster, what are the chances that it will come back in a few milliseconds and ask for the next cluster? Pretty good, it seems. So why not have the disk cache grab a few more clusters, in hopes that the program will ask for them? This is called the *read-ahead* (Figure 15.23). You can adjust the read-ahead using a sliding bar (Figure 15.24). It should always be set to Full. This allows the disk cache to read-ahead 64K worth of clusters, or two to four clusters ahead on most systems.

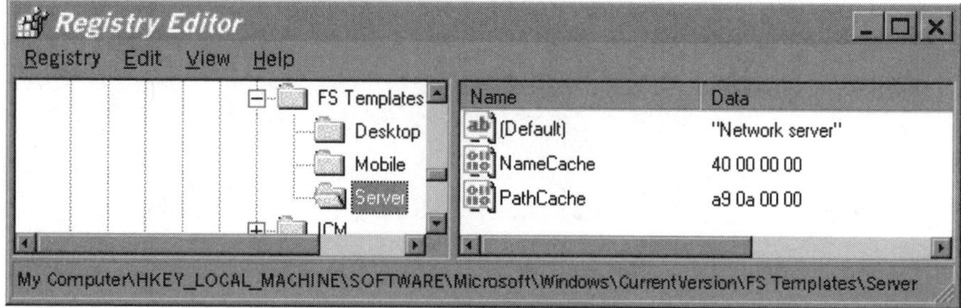

Figure 15.22 Registry settings for a server cache

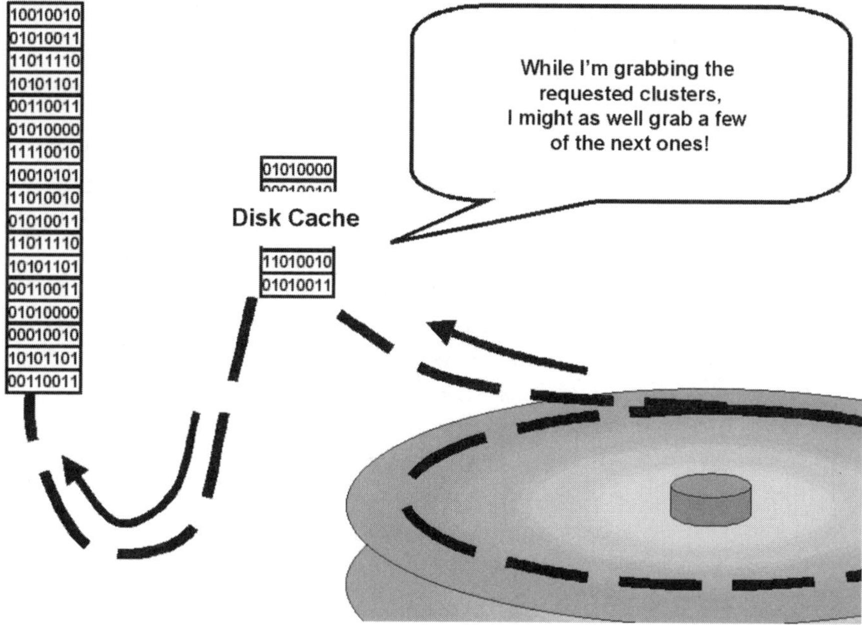

Figure 15.23 The read-ahead in action

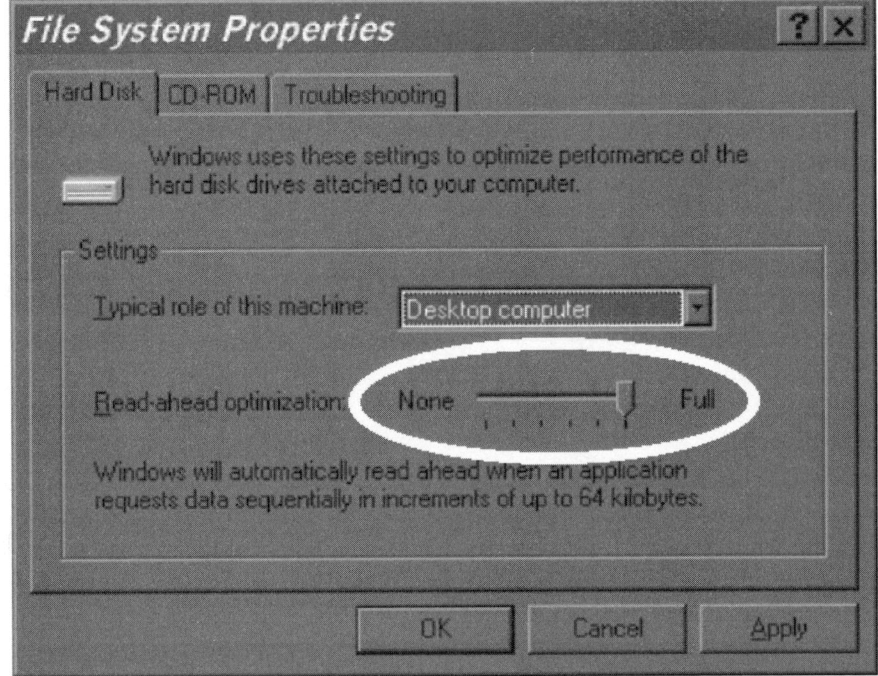

Figure 15.24 Adjusting the read-ahead

DOS Memory

DOS is alive and well in your Windows 95 PC. In fact, there are many situations when DOS programs will actually run better in Windows 95 than they could ever hope to do under DOS itself. The trick is to understand the versatility and power of Windows 95's support of DOS applications. You can run DOS three different ways: as a previous version of MS-DOS, by using PIF files, or in MS-DOS mode. Let's look at all three.

If you just want your old DOS back, reboot the system and press F8 when you see "Starting Windows 95." If you see an option that says: "Previous version of MS-DOS," select it and you will be sent back to your old DOS (assuming that you installed over an old version of DOS). Warning! Do not do this if you are running Windows 95 OSR 2. OSR 2 cannot boot to Previous Version of MSDOS and back. Your system will lock up.

The most common way to run DOS programs in Windows is to use PIF files. PIF files take advantage of the virtual 8086 abilities of Windows to allow DOS programs to run within Windows itself. This is far better than having to reboot the system to go to the previous version of MS-DOS or dealing with MS-DOS mode. A PIF file is a binary file that stores all the settings to tweak the virtual 8086 machine for each DOS program. PIF files allow you to configure special requirements for a particular DOS program, like access to extended memory, expanded memory, and a number of other settings. PIF files reside in the same directory as the DOS program they support, and are distinguished by the PIF extension. Windows calls them "shortcuts to MS-DOS programs."

Don't confuse DOS shortcuts with Windows shortcuts! DOS shortcuts are .PIF files and Windows shortcuts are .LNK files. Same name, different animals.

To create a PIF, just select the DOS program you want, right-click, and select Properties. You'll see the screen shown in Figure 15.25. Although most of these options are obvious (such as full screen/window), some options are worth clarification. Click on the Program Tab (see Figure 15.26).

Cmd Line The path and name of the program you want to run.

Working The directory in which you want the program to start.

Batch file You can have a batch file run before the program, which is handy if you need to start a TSR (maybe a special mouse driver) whenever the program is run.

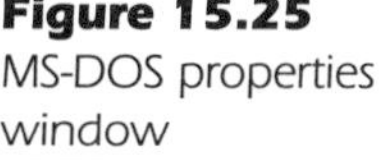

Figure 15.25
MS-DOS properties window

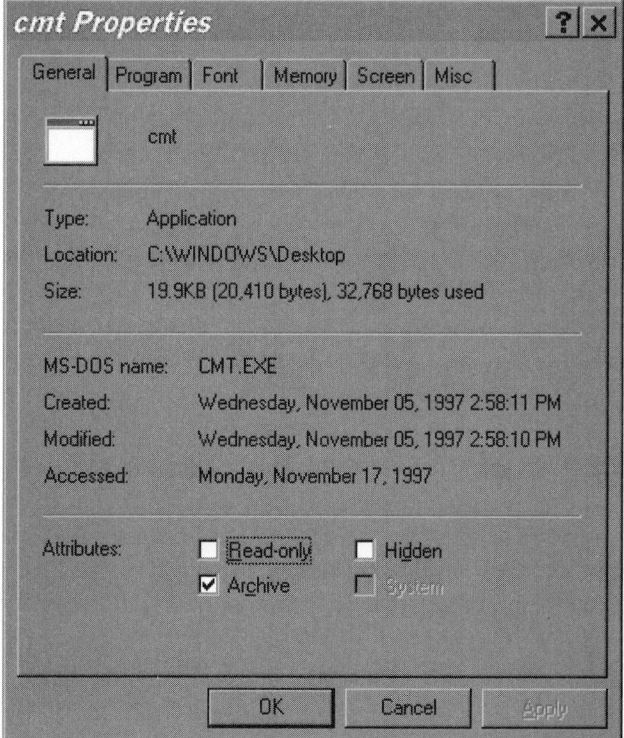

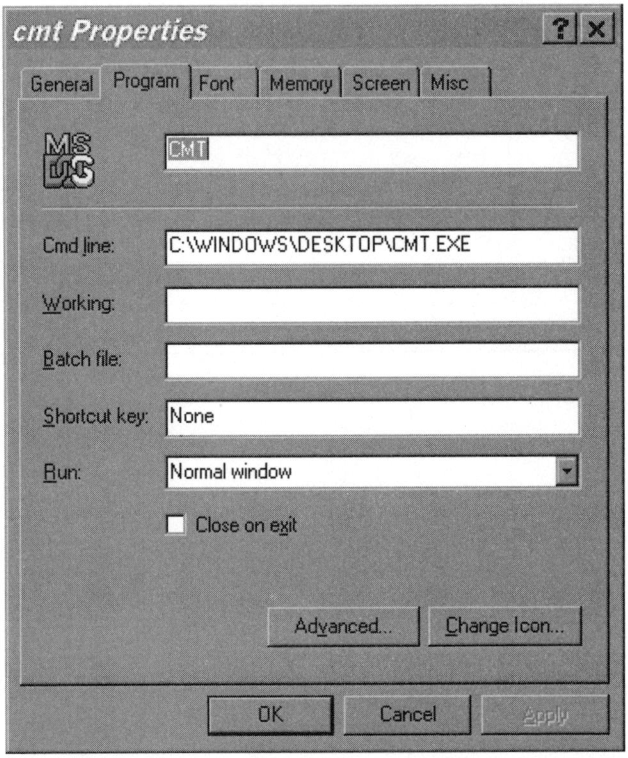

Figure 15.26
Program window

Shortcut key You can set a shortcut key to start this program.

Run Minimized, maximized, or normal window.

Advanced MS-DOS mode is described a bit later in this section.

The Memory window holds some of the more powerful settings for PIF files (Figure 15.27). These settings are most commonly used to minimize the amount of RAM used by DOS programs, while still providing all the memory they need. Here are the selections under the Memory tab:

Conventional Memory The amount of conventional memory needed. Auto means "give them what they want." Many DOS programs use very little conventional memory. The initial environment is the DOS environment, which is handy for programs that use a lot of environment space. Protected protects the system from the DOS program, and vice versa.

Expanded Memory It's usually best to put a limit on this value based on what the program needs. The Auto setting tends to confuse many programs.

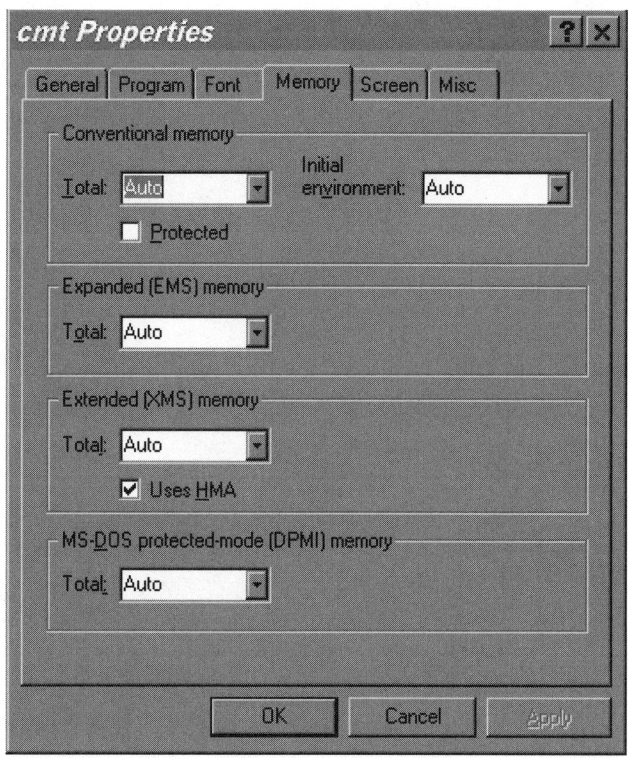

Figure 15.27
Memory window

Extended Memory No DOS program known uses plain extended memory, so ignore it.

DPMI Memory This is for DOS programs that use DPMI memory. A good example is Doom. Leave it on the Auto setting.

When you are done making the changes for your program, click on OK and a new file will appear, like the one in Figure 15.28.

You can click on either icon and the PIF will engage. No matter how hard you try, some DOS programs just hate to be run under Windows. To get these programs to run, Windows has a special type of DOS called *MS-DOS mode,* which allows a DOS program to run without Windows and allows the DOS program to have its own AUTOEXEC.BAT and CONFIG.SYS files. You engage MS-DOS mode by selecting the Advanced option under the PIF file's Program settings (Figure 15.29).

When you click on the MS-DOS Mode checkbox, you can choose to either use the default CONFIG.SYS and AUTOEXEC.BAT or enter your own, as shown in Figure 15.30. Windows will also automatically load some of the more common DOS utilities when you click the Configuration

Figure 15.28
DOS program and PIF together

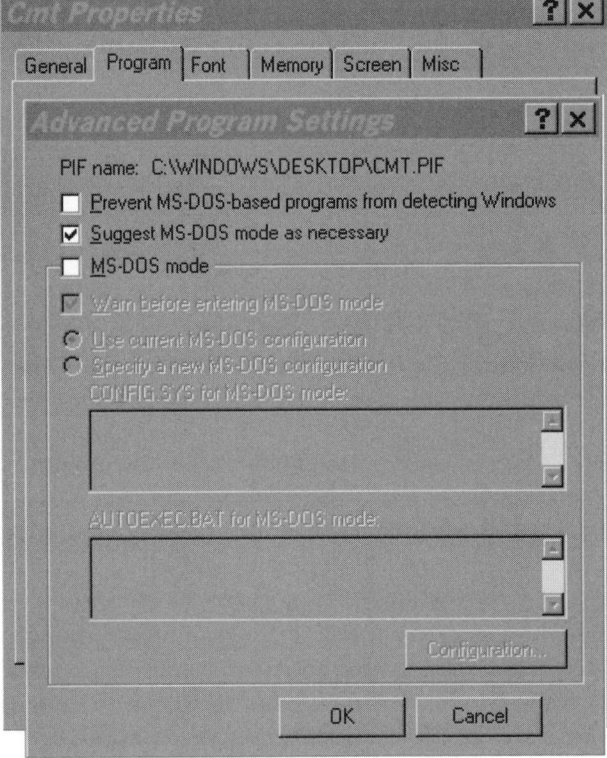

Figure 15-29
Advanced setting (MS-DOS mode)

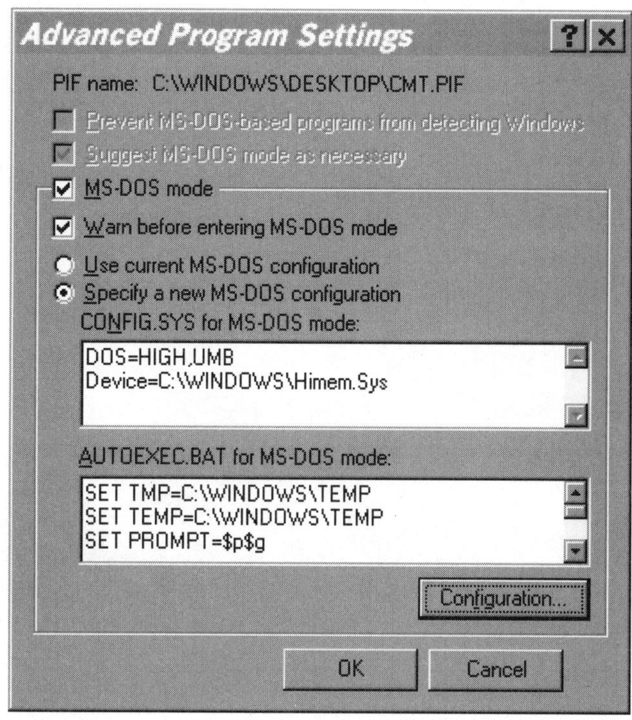

Figure 15.30 Settings for CONFIG.SYS and AUTOEXEC.BAT

button (Figure 15.31). Here you can tell Windows to load EMM386, DOSKEY, and the DOS disk cache SMARTDRV. You can also let the DOS program directly access the drive, as opposed to using Windows 95.

MS-DOS mode has one serious drawback. When you click on a PIF file set to run MS-DOS mode, the program will reboot the computer. This is necessary to run the custom CONFIG.SYS and to remove as much of Windows 95 as possible. Windows will keep a small "stub" of information in memory so that it can reboot back to Windows when you close the DOS program.

Troubleshooting Windows 95

Like Windows 3.*x*, most Windows 95 problems can be divided into the same three distinct groups: lockups, page faults (called GPFs in Windows 3.*x*) and erratic problems. Although the fixes are similar, there are also a few changes. Most importantly, you must know how to boot the computer for a technician's startup. The Windows 95 startup can be performed in a number of ways to help you diagnose a PC. Let's look at these:

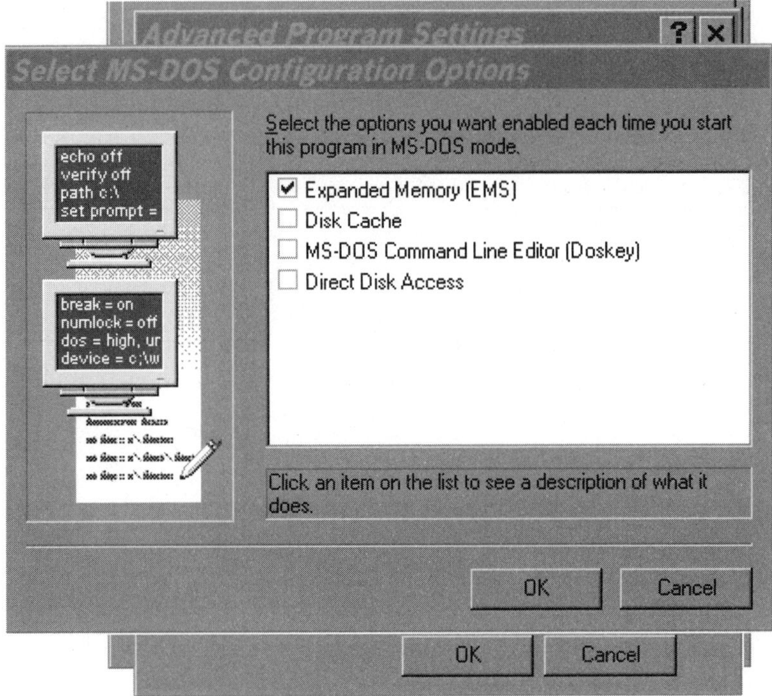

Figure 15.31 Advanced configuration options

Skip Startup

To skip any programs that are set to automatically start at boot, hold down the left-shift key while booting.

Safe Mode

To access safe mode, Reboot and press the F5 key when the PC says "Starting Windows 95." You can also access safe mode by pressing F8 when the PC boots to get the Startup menu. You can then select Safe Mode.

Stepping Through

This is virtually identical to the old DOS F8 option. However, instead of allowing a step-through of only CONFIG.SYS and AUTOEXEC.BAT, this step-through allows you to choose whether to autoload HIMEM.SYS, SETVER, and doublespace drivers. It will also allow you to load the registry and start the GUI. Very handy!

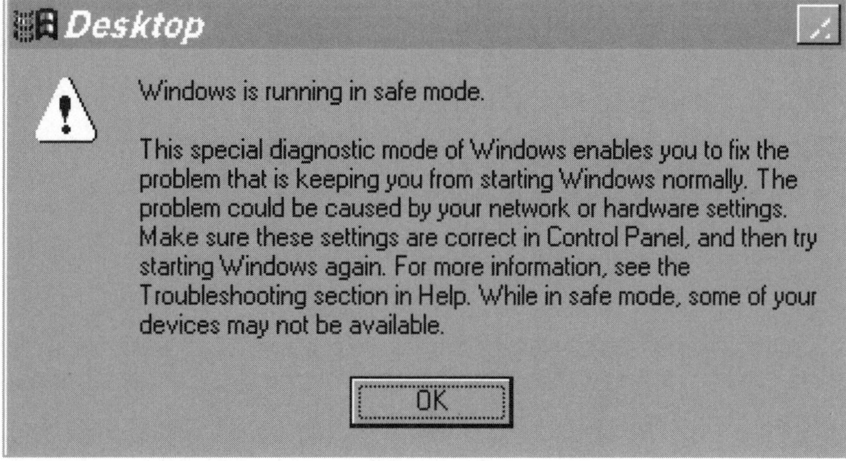

Figure 15.32 Startup screen for safe mode

Command Prompt Only

This is identical to the DOS F5 option. There's no CONFIG.SYS, no AUTOEXEC.BAT, no registry, no GUI—nothing but the C: prompt.

Lockups

All the reasons for lockups in Windows 3.*x* also apply to Windows 95. One major difference, however, is the patches that were discussed earlier—so keep your patches current! Corrupted files can be extremely difficult to diagnose. The best thing to do if you suspect a corrupted file is to try to uninstall and then reinstall the application into a directory different than the one into which it was installed previously. This eliminates the possibility of a bad spot on the hard drive.

One of the most powerful tools available for diagnosing page faults is Windows' safe mode (Figure 15.32). Safe mode is well named as it starts Windows in an extremely safe way. All advanced disk-access functions such as virtual memory are disabled, the video driver is set to basic VGA, and a number of other functions are shut down or reduced in such a way as to allow the system to start with as little overhead as possible. You can start safe mode by selecting it from the Start menu, or Windows might start it if it was not properly shut down.

Safe mode is usually the first place to start for most Windows problems. Lockups and page faults will usually force Windows into safe mode. You usually just boot into safe mode and then simply shut the machine down and reboot again. You'd be amazed how often this simple process will fix many problems!

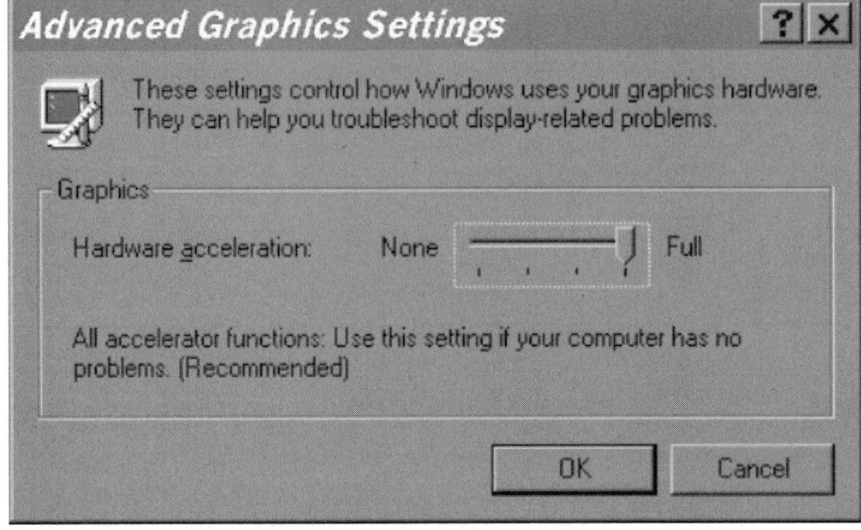

Figure 15.33 Advanced graphics window

Most erratic behavior problems can be attributed to bad or outdated drivers. When cruising around for patches, keep an eye out for updated drivers. Here are a few other tricks that might also be helpful:

- If the video looks weird (ghosted images, windows that won't go away, bizarre color bars), go into the Device Manager/Performance tab and select Graphics (Figure 15.33). This is the video accelerator. Most video cards can handle the Full acceleration option, but some older and/or cheaper cards will give these strange errors. Try changing it to None and see if the problem goes away.
- Make sure the motherboard is set for the proper CPU. Windows works your RAM caches hard, and any configuration error can cause strange, intermittent problems.
- Buy RAM, lots of RAM. Even 16 megabytes isn't enough—especially if you have the audacity to use active desktops (Internet Explorer/Windows 98) or have heavyweight programs like Microsoft Office, CorelDraw, or any serious graphics package.
- Shut off the network functions by starting Windows with the /N option. Corruption in the network software can cause some strange problems. If the system works fine without the network, delete the network settings and reinstall.

Making Backups

Now that Windows 95 can be called a mature operating system, you can count on a stable, solid machine as long as you keep your patches current, your drivers up to date, and your hard drive scanned and defragmented. But problems can and will happen. Keep yourself covered with two powerful tools: a startup disk and a backup of all of your important files.

It's easy to make a boot disk. Just go into Control Panel/Add Remove Programs/Startup Disk (Figure 15.34). A startup disk is simply a bootable disk with all the important files you'll need to rebuild a system like FDISK, FORMAT, SYS, and EDIT (Figure 15.34). It also includes programs that aren't much good, like REGEDIT. (If you're using a boot diskette, it's too late for REGEDIT!) Add MSCDEX from the WINDOWS\COMMAND directory and a real-mode CD-ROM driver so you can access your CD-ROM drive if you need to reinstall Windows 95 from scratch.

One of the big downsides to a Startup disk is that it doesn't keep a copy of the Registry. Fortunately, Microsft provides a powerful tool for backing up the Registry files.

This tool is called the Emergency Recovery Utility (ERU.EXE) and is on every Windows 95 CD-ROM. This handy little program will save all the crucial Windows files and allow you to save them to a floppy disk. It comes with a handy program (ERD.EXE) to restore all these files in case of a system crash (Figure 15.35).

Figure 15.34
Making a startup disk

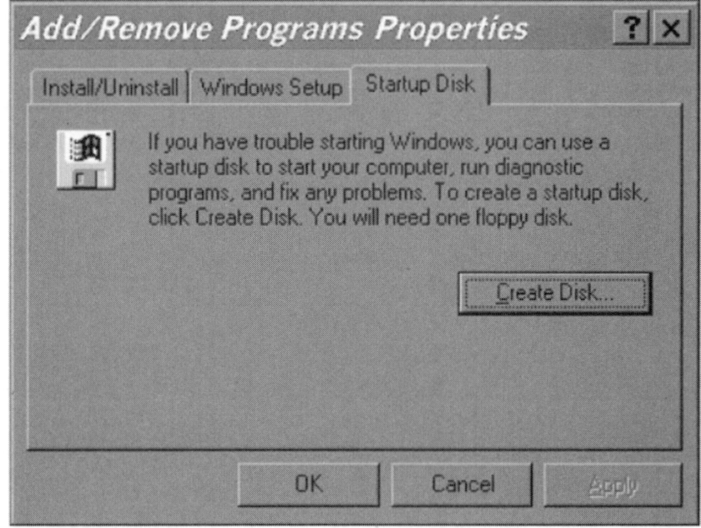

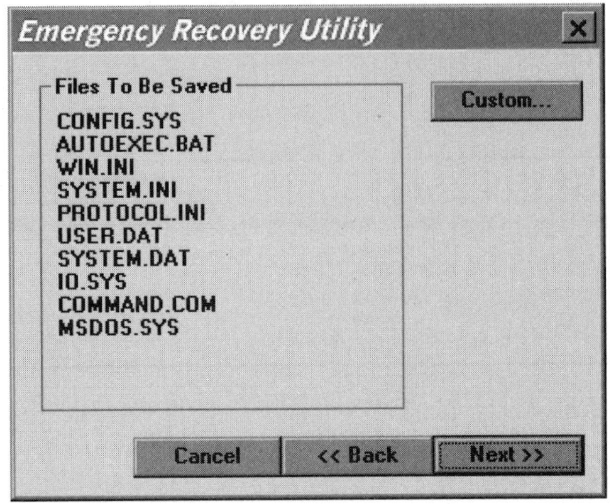

Figure 15.35
ERU saving important files

CHAPTER 16

DOS Memory Management

In this chapter, you will:

- Understand the concept of memory.
- Understand the relationship of RAM to memory.
- Learn how the first megabyte of memory is organized.
- See how to reduce conventional memory use.
- Take a detailed tour through CONFIG.SYS and AUTOEXEC.BAT.

Whether you have an old 386SX running DOS 3.3 or a Pentium II running Windows 95 OSR 2, DOS is still alive and well, happily humming under the hood of your PC. So until that final far-away day when we all get to collectively throw out COMMAND.COM for good and load up that next-generation NT-UNIX-OS/2-Next operating system, the nasty specter of DOS-based memory management still looms large in the eyes of PC technicians.

The BOOT Process

When your PC boots, a series of programs are loaded into conventional memory, starting at location 00000 and building up from there (Figure 16.1). By the time you get to a C: prompt, a significant amount of conventional memory has been used. Let's look at the lowest part of conventional memory in detail.

Figure 16.1 DOS loading

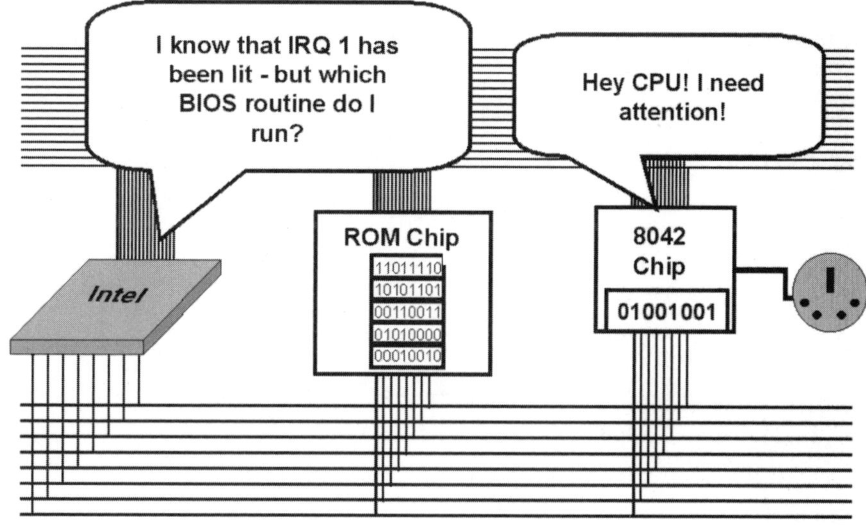

Figure 16.2 Which BIOS routine should be run?

Interrupt Vector Table (IVT)

If a program or a hardware device wants to get the CPU to do something, it must interrupt the CPU. There are two types of interrupts: hardware and software. An example of a *hardware interrupt* would be the mouse moving and setting off its IRQ; an example of a *software interrupt* would be a program setting the PC into protected mode. The interrupt vector table is a data structure used by the system to handle both hardware and software interrupts.

The trick to understanding the IVT is to understand that when a device or a program sends an interrupt to the CPU, the CPU needs to know what program to run in order to do whatever the interrupting device wants the CPU to do. For example, if the mouse (set to COM1) hits IRQ4, how does the CPU know where the mouse programming is located so it can run that program? If a game program tells the CPU to check the current status of the joystick, how does the CPU know the memory location of the joystick BIOS so it can find out if the joystick is moved or if a button is pressed?

Let's use the keyboard as an example. Say someone presses a key and the keyboard sends its IRQ2 to the CPU. How does the CPU know which of the hundreds of BIOS routines on the system ROM to run? (See Figure 16.2.) This is the function of the IVT, which takes the first 1024 bytes of conventional memory—from 00000 to 003FF (Figure 16.3). The IVT is broken up into four-byte chunks called *pointers* or *interrupts*. Interrupts are designated with the name *INT*, so INT 0 is at memory location 00000, INT 1 is at memory location 00004, and INT 2 is at memory location 0008.

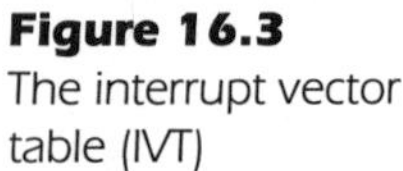

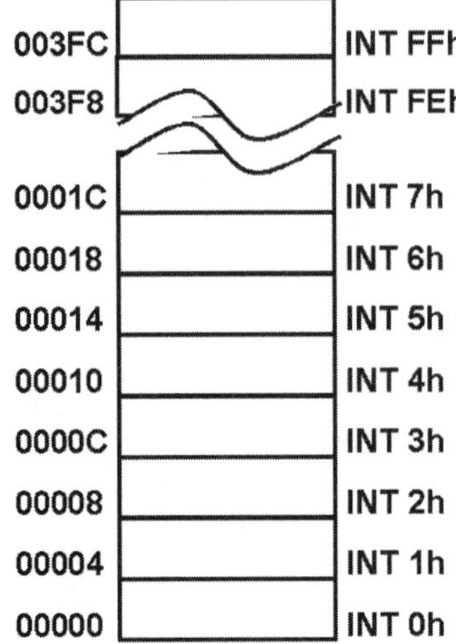

Figure 16.3 The interrupt vector table (IVT)

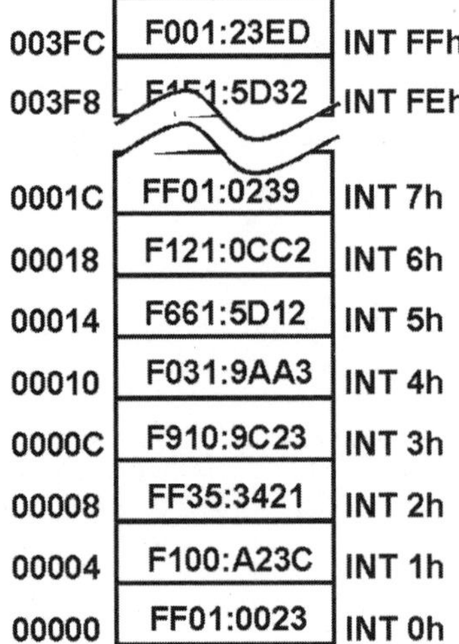

Figure 16.4 The IVT showing memory locations

Every address in the IVT is dedicated to a particular function, which is locked in stone and cannot be changed. For example, INT 10h is for video and INT 76h is for the primary hard-drive controller. There are software interrupts, such as INT 20h for terminating a program. Each interrupt stores the memory location of the program that needs to deal with whatever is assigned to that interrupt (Figure 16.4).

Now I need to take a short tangent. In case you're not aware, DOS doesn't think in terms of five hex values for memory addresses. Instead, DOS uses a segment/offset concept of two 16-bit addresses to make one 20-bit address. When you see an address, it is given a nomenclature of *seg-*

ment:offset, where each value is a 16-bit address. When you see the *xxxx:xxxx* memory address, you can convert it to a 20-bit address.

For example, let's take the value 1000:3ABC and convert it to a five-digit hex value. First, take the segment value and multiply it by 10h. Remember this is hex. What do you do with a regular number (base 10) when you multiply it by 10? You add a zero to the end. So guess what happens when you multiply a hex number by 10h? You put a zero on the end:

$$1000h \times 10h = 10000h$$

Then you add the offset value to get the five-digit value:

$$10000h + 3ABCh = 13ABCh$$

So 1000:3ABC = 13ABCh! Now that you understand the segment:offset convention, let's return to the IVT. The CPU first creates the IVT itself. The IVT is *not* a DOS function and *not* a Windows 95 function; it is a CPU function created by Intel. However, the CPU fills in only a few interrupts. When the BIOS loads, it adds some functions, and then DOS adds a few. In fact, any program that wants to gain control of some aspect of the PC can edit the IVT.

The big question here is why do you do it this way? Why don't you just lock all the BIOS routines into certain memory locations and let the programs themselves point to the proper locations? That way you could dump the IVT completely! Well, you could—it would work fine. However, there are two flaws with that concept. First, it doesn't allow for a flexible BIOS. Every BIOS on every PC would have to be identical, never allowing for new or more powerful functions. Second, it doesn't allow programs to take over INTs. I'll explain this by continuing the keyboard example. Let's look again at INT 9h, the keyboard interrupt (see Figure 16.5).

When the system boots, the BIOS puts the memory address of the BIOS routine to handle keyboard requests F121:0CC2 into the INT 9h position, as shown in Figure 16.5. But let's say you want to make a cool program that will reboot the system after every 250 keystrokes—can you say *virus*? You would need some way to monitor the keystrokes without interference, until you get to keystroke number 250, of course. To do this, when you load your "evil program," it overwrites the BIOS address and instead points to itself. This is called "hooking an interrupt" (Figure 16.6).

00024 | F121:0CC2 | INT 9h

Figure 16.5
INT 9h—the keyboard interrupt

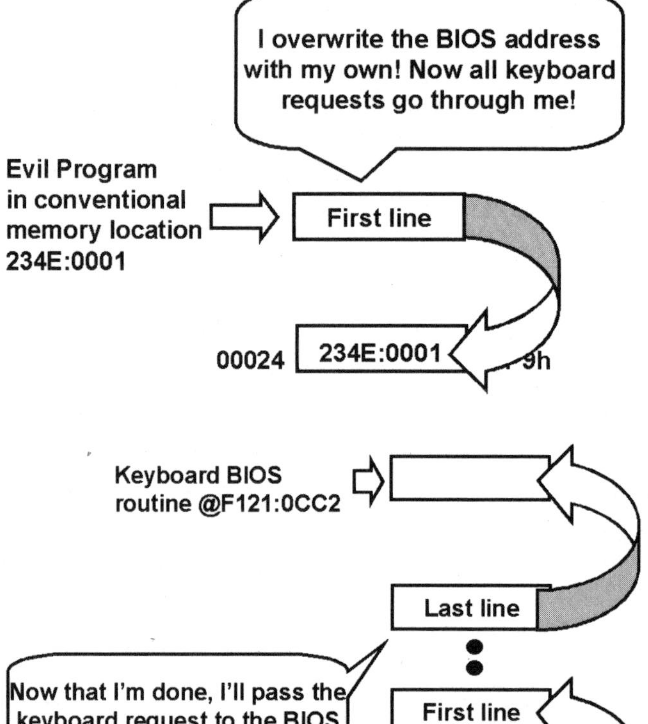

Figure 16.6 Evil program "hooking" the interrupt

Figure 16.7 Evil program passing the interrupt

The evil program doesn't want to handle the keyboard request; it only wants to know that a key has been pressed. So as soon as it has updated the counter (on its way to 250), the program sends the request to the BIOS routine (Figure 16.7). Clearly, the IVT is crucial to operating a PC. Let's move to the next loaded item(s), device drivers.

Device Drivers

The BIOS knows how to handle quite a few different hardware components on your PC. It can control your floppy and hard drives and some basic video, which is how IBM designed it a long time ago. But as you know, technology has improved since then. There are many new types of hardware, such as sound cards, CD-ROM drives, and ZIP drives. The BIOS isn't designed to support these devices, so they need to be able to "bring their own BIOS" (BYOB). PCs can store the necessary BIOS in special files on the hard drive called *device drivers*. When the machine boots, it reads a special text file called CONFIG.SYS to load the files, using the convention:

```
DEVICE=driver_name
```

to load these device drivers. Here are a few device driver lines in a typical CONFIG.SYS file:

```
Device=c:\dos\emm386.exe ram
Device=c:\tri\tricd.sys /d:msc000
```

Each device driver takes up some conventional memory, which, in a classic DOS machine, can be quite large. But without these drivers, the device won't work.

DOS Kernel

Next is the DOS kernel, comprised of IO.SYS and MSDOS.SYS. Together, these programs really *are* DOS. This is where your internal commands like DIR and COPY are processed. You must have IO.SYS and MSDOS.SYS in the root directory of the C: drive in order for DOS to boot. They take up a relatively small amount of conventional memory. The DOS environment interacts directly with the kernel and provides RAM space for a number of data structures needed by DOS, such as buffers and files.

TSRs

Terminate and stay resident programs (TSRs) run and are then terminated like any other programs, but with one big difference. A TSR stays in memory and acts like a device driver. TSRs are quite popular for CD-ROM and mouse drivers in DOS. Although a TSR can be run from a C: prompt like any other program, they are usually run from a special text file called AUTOEXEC.BAT. Here are a few lines of TSRs being loaded from AUTOEXEC.BAT:

```
C:\msmouse\mouse.com
C:\dos\MSCDEX.EXE /D:MSC000
```

Saving Conventional Memory

The great bane of DOS memory is the fact that there is only 640K of space in which to run programs. As you add more and more devices to a DOS computer, you can find that DOS, the device drivers, and TSRs take up so much memory that it becomes impossible to run a program. A number of methods and products have been designed to help reduce the amount of conventional memory used while still allowing the system to run all the necessary drivers and TSRs to support the hardware on a PC. This is called *DOS memory management.* My goal in this chapter is to outline the issues and tools involved with DOS memory management, and detail the more advanced issues.

Hexadecimal

Sorry, but before I go any further, I'm going to have to review hexadecimal numbers. I know this was covered in the chapter on the expansion bus, but if you're going to perform memory management, you have to know how to talk "the dreaded hex!" If this section is starting to look familiar, it should. It is very similar to the hex section in the expansion bus chapter.

First of all, *don't panic.* Hex is really almost trivial once you understand the secret. Hexadecimal, also known as base-16 mathematics, is a complete numbering system based on 16 instead of 10 digits. You can add, subtract, or do trigonometry with hex, but the only part of hex you need to know is how it is used in the PC world. To help you understand hex, I will use the address bus.

As you know, the 8086 had a 20-wire "address line." These wires could have either voltage or no voltage on them. A wire with voltage could be represented by a one, and a wire with no voltage by a zero. This equals 1,048,576 different combinations of ones and zeros, from: 00000000000000000000 to 11111111111111111111.

Each combination of charged and uncharged wires represents one memory location. IBM declared that each memory location should be 8 bits long. Since 8 bits = 1 byte, you can address 1,048,576 different one-byte memory locations with an 8086. This number is 1 megabyte or 1MB, so the address bus can access 1MB.

Can you imagine what a pain it would be to try to keep track of these locations? The microprocessor would have no problem, but imagine saying something like "Where in memory are you?" or "I'm at location

TABLE 16.1

Sixteen Different Permutations for Four Wires

0000	All wires off	1	1000	Only 1st wire on	9
0001	Only 4th wire on	2	1001	1st and 4th on	10
0010	Only 3rd wire on	3	1010	1st and 3rd on	11
0011	3rd and 4th on	4	1011	Only 2nd off	12
0100	Only 2nd wire on	5	1100	1st and 2nd on	13
0101	2nd and 4th wire on	6	1101	Only 3rd off	14
0110	2nd and 3rd wire on	7	1110	Only 4th off	15
0111	Only 1st wire off	8	1111	All wires on	16

00101001000101000111O." There has to be an easier way to describe the state of a bunch of wires at any given moment! That is where hexadecimal becomes very useful. You can use hex as a shorthand description of the state of wires. Pretend you have a computer with a four-wire address bus. How many memory locations can you address? All the possibilities are listed in Table 16.1.

So there are 16 different possibilities. There are no computers with only a four-wire address bus, but just about every processor ever built has an address bus with a multiple of four wires (8, 16, 20, 24, 32), so you can use this to create a shorthand. You can represent any combination of four ones and zeros with a single character. Since there are 16 different combinations, the 16 unique characters of the base-16 numbering system called hexadecimal were the natural choice. So when you talk about a particular memory location, you don't say 10110110011000101101 or 10110110011000101101.

First, you mentally break the 20 digits into five sets of four: 1011, 0110, 0110, 0010, and 1101. Then give each four-character set its hex shorthand: 1011 (B), 0110 (6), 0110 (6), 0010 (2), and 1101 (D). So instead of a bunch of ones and zeros, you'd have something like B662D. To represent all the possible addresses for the 20-bit address bus, you'll always have five digits, from all zeros (which equal 0) to all ones (which equal F). All the possible memory locations for an Intel 8088 can be represented by five-digit hexadecimal values, starting at 00000 and ending at FFFFF.

Memory Space vs. Memory

Understand that the Intel 8086 CPU can "see" up to 1MB of memory. All these combinations are collectively called the *memory address space*. However, just because you have a 1 megabyte of memory address space, that doesn't mean that you use all of it. In order to place code at a certain memory location, you need some type of chip at the location that can store the byte of code. You need RAM or ROM chips at every memory location you want to use. Do not confuse the memory address space with the actual memory.

When some people think of a memory address, they hear the word *address* and think in terms of the U.S. Post Office, visualizing the addresses as physical locations. Memory addresses are *not* physical locations. When you hear *memory address,* think of phone numbers instead. If one person has the address 515 Main St., Houston TX 77007 and another person has the address 516 Main St., Houston TX 77007, you would agree that these two people almost certainly live right across the street from each other. However, if one person has the phone number (713) 520-0784 and another person's phone number is (713) 520-0785, the fact that their phone numbers are sequential has no bearing on whether they live next door to each other. Memory addresses work exactly the same way. Two sequential memory addresses might not be physically next to each other.

The DOS Memory Map

There are special phone books you can buy, called "reverse directories." They sort phone numbers not by name, but by phone number. They look something like this:

```
201-228-0277 SOUTH ORANGE PAVING CO 12 FELDSTONE PL, CALDWELL, NJ
201-228-0278 UNUSED
201-228-0279 RUBIN GOERTZ & CO CPA 101 EISENHOWER PKY, ROSELAND, NJ
201-228-0380 UNUSED
201-228-0381 DEVCO ENGINEERING INC 36 PIER LN, FAIRFIELD, NJ
201-228-0382 GRAND VARIETY 371 BLOOMFIELD AVE, CALDWELL, NJ
201-228-0383 RULLO & GLEESON 127 ROSELAND AVE, CALDWELL, NJ
201-228-0384 UNUSED
201-228-0385 DONALD PLUMBING & HTG 69 DEERFIELD RD, CALDWELL, NJ
```

In order to look at the entire range of addressable memory for DOS, you have to make a reverse directory of all the possible memory addresses, from 00000 to FFFFF. You don't know what any of these addresses will be for, so they're all unused:

```
00000 UNUSED
00001 UNUSED
00002 UNUSED
00003 UNUSED
00004 UNUSED
```

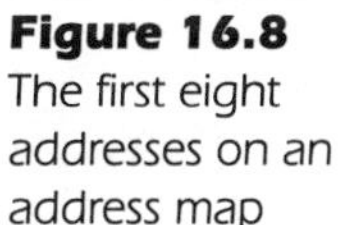

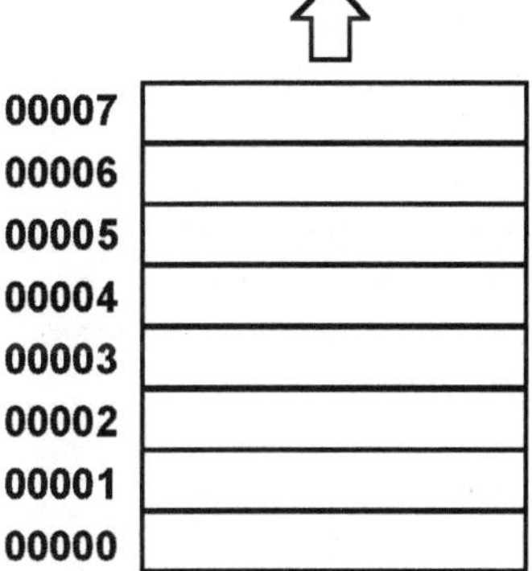

Figure 16.8
The first eight addresses on an address map

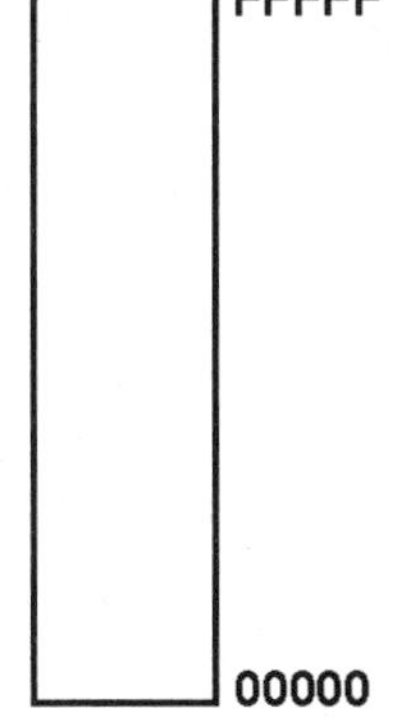

Figure 16.9
Real memory map

```
00005 UNUSED
00006 UNUSED
00007 UNUSED
00008 UNUSED
00009 UNUSED
0000A UNUSED
0000B UNUSED
0000C UNUSED
```

Wait a minute. This list is going to be kind of long, isn't it? You're going to need about 1,048,576 spaces to list every address space. So for convenience, just represent all the addresses by drawing a bar to represent all the address spaces. We will also start at the bottom of the page and then build the bar up from the bottom. The first eight addresses are shown in Figure 16.8, and the completed "address map" looks like Figure 16.9.

***NOTE:** Please do not confuse this memory map, this phone book, with memory chips. This is just a list of different permutations of address bus wires being turned on and off. At this point, there are no chips to correspond to any memory locations.*

Assigning Addresses

When IBM built the PC, the company decided to specify how the memory in the IBM PC was to be used. The PC had an 8088 CPU, so the most addresses it could see were one megabyte's worth. The main function of these addresses was for plain old RAM. However, there were also chips like the system ROM, which held the BIOS, other ROMs from optional devices, and special RAM on the video card. All these chips needed to be seen by the CPU, so they had to take up some of the addresses. To keep things organized, IBM decided to dedicate all the addresses from 00000 to 9FFFF to the exclusive use of regular memory (RAM). The rest of the addresses, from A0000 to FFFFF, would be "reserved" for the exclusive use of chips other than regular memory (RAM). Let's look at this in some detail.

Conventional and Reserved Memory

The one megabyte of memory locations available to the DOS PC can be broken into two distinct areas. The area from 0 to 640K (00000h to 9FFFFh) is called *conventional memory* (Figure 16.10). Conventional memory contains all the memory addresses that are set aside for RAM to run programs. All the addresses from A0000 to FFFFF are set aside for everything else: ROMs and specialized RAMs. This memory is called *reserved memory* (Figure 16.11). Conventional memory has 655,360 memory locations (640K), and reserved memory has 393,216 memory locations (384K), for a total of 1,048,576 memory locations (1024K or 1MB). Figure 16.12 shows a map of the 1MB, showing both the conventional and reserved area.

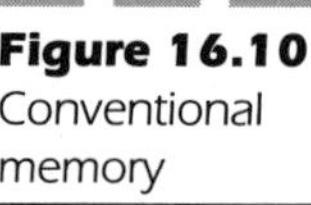

Figure 16.10 Conventional memory

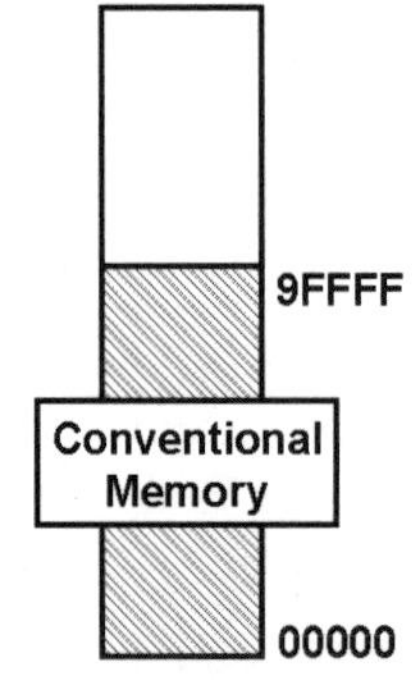

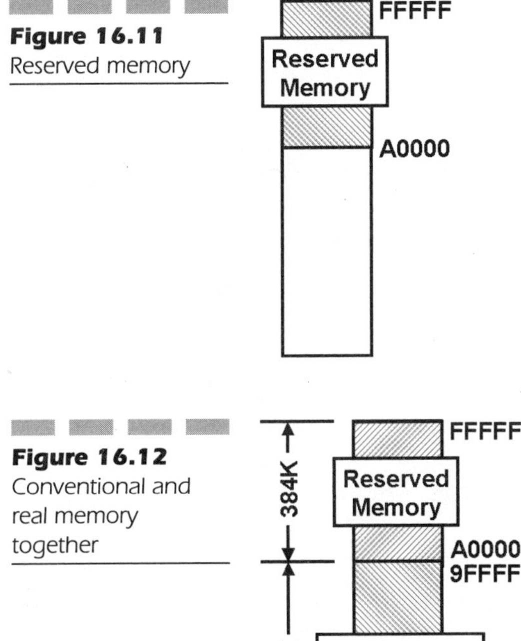

Figure 16.11
Reserved memory

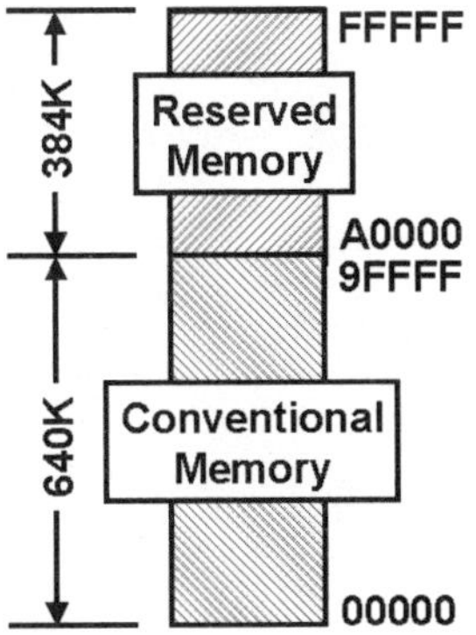

Figure 16.12
Conventional and real memory together

The Reserved Area

The reserved area is a rather complex compilation of different ROMs and RAMs that use memory. Most of these devices have very distinct memory locations, either determined by IBM long ago or by a de-facto process of clone makers and device manufacturers "taking over" certain memory locations. By far the most important device in the reserved area is the System BIOS. Although there can be some variation, it is classically located in the memory locations from F0000 to FFFFF.

All programs take up a *range* of memory locations. For example, the System BIOS takes the memory locations from F0000 to FFFFF (see Figure 16.13). To clarify this, I put the starting location on the left of the chart and the ending location on the right.

Video cards all have RAM that is mapped into the reserved area in three different areas (Figure 16.14). When your video card is in a color text mode (like in DOS), its RAM uses the memory locations B7FFF-BFFFF. When the video card is in graphics mode, its RAM is mapped to A0000-

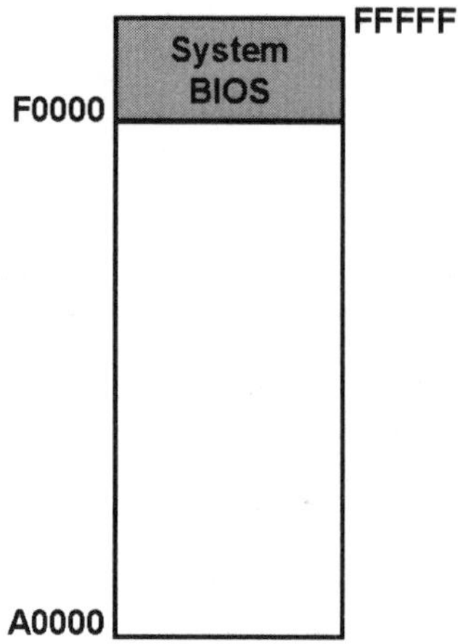

Figure 16.13
The system BIOS

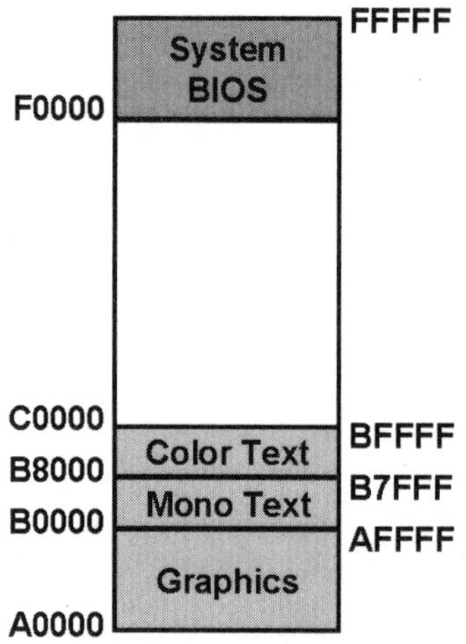

Figure 16.14
Video RAM memory locations

B0000. The first generations of video cards were monochrome text. Their video RAM was mapped to B0000-B7FFF. Monochrome video cards are obsolete, and this memory area is unused today.

None of the reserved memory addresses from C0000 to EFFFF are dedicated to any particular device. They are for optional ROMs and RAMs that peripheral makers might install on their cards (Figure 16.15). Different types of cards can come with ROMs or RAMs, although there is no hard and fast rule. There is one device, found in every PC, that carries an optional ROM: the video card. The video card's ROM uses the memory range from C0000 to C7FFF (Figure 16.16).

Although all memory addresses from C0000 to EFFFF are available, every video card has a ROM and that ROM takes the memory range from C0000 to C7FFF. So this range is *not* available for option ROMs.

The Conventional Area

When IBM was developing the PC in the late '70s, 640K of memory addresses seemed a massive amount of RAM. The maximum amount of memory anybody was using in competing microcomputers was around 64K. Like these machines, IBM also put 64K into their PC. IBM was confident that they had provided plenty of room for upgrades, but no one anticipated the growth in complexity of DOS and applications.

As users became more sophisticated and more comfortable with PCs, they demanded more powerful applications. Programs like Lotus 1-2-3 were notorious for growing larger as they grew in sophistication to match user demands for more features. Users also demanded more data: larger spreadsheets and documents. As the size of programs and data grew, users

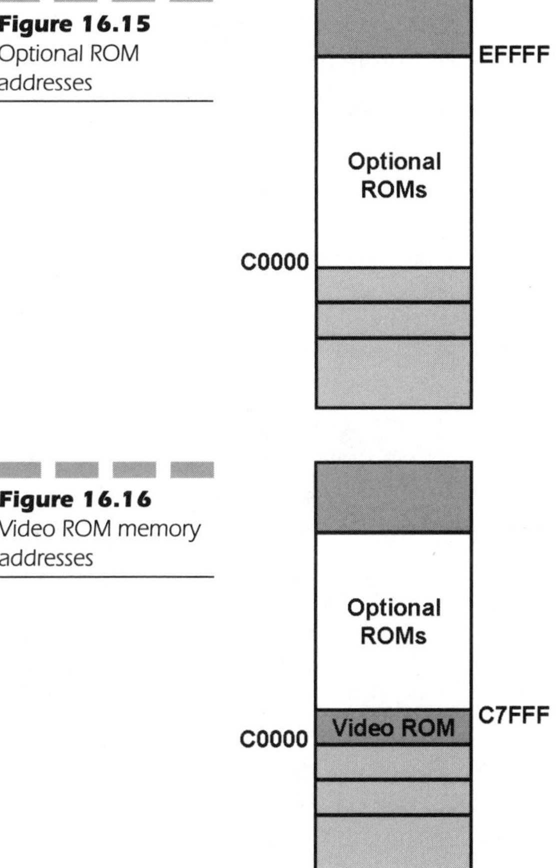

Figure 16.15 Optional ROM addresses

Figure 16.16 Video ROM memory addresses

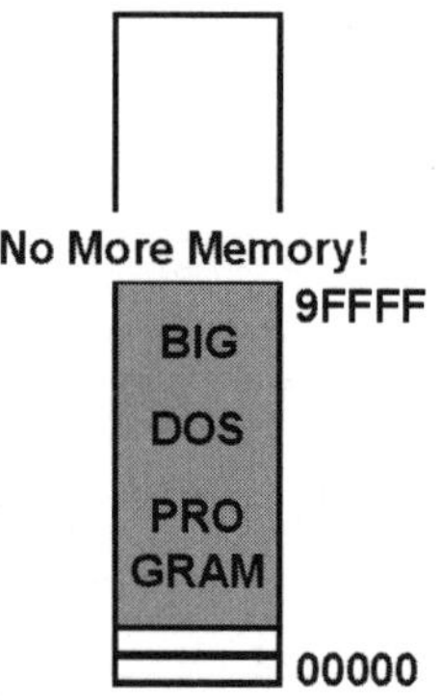

Figure 16.17a
No more memory!

added more RAM chips to computers, which grew from 64K to 128K to 256K to 512K to 640K. As a result, within the first few years of the existence of IBM PCs, 640K of RAM became the standard. 640K of RAM, which was supposed to last until the year 1990, was installed in most PCs in 1984. Even at 640K, however, it became obvious that still *more* RAM was needed. Unfortunately, 640K was the limit. You could no longer simply add memory chips. See Figure 16.17a.

Expanded Memory

There were no more memory addresses. Of the 1 megabyte of memory addresses, the first 640K of addresses were occupied with RAM chips, and the rest were "reserved" for ROMs and video RAM. If a computer did not have optional BIOSes, however, there were relatively large gaps of unused memory addresses in the reserved area. Knowing this, an industry group led by Lotus, Intel, and Microsoft got together in 1984. They came up with a way to put more memory into a computer while staying within the 1MB limit. The answer was *expanded memory.*

Expanded memory was originally an expansion card full of RAM chips (Figure 16.17b). The chips on the card were divided into 16K chunks called *pages.* A card could have from 4 to 512 pages. You could even have multiple cards, as long as the total number of pages was 512 or less (512 pages × 16K bytes/page = a maximum of 8 megabytes of memory. Each page was labeled electronically with page numbers (Figure 16.17c).

In order to access this card of RAM chips, you need two things: a device driver to access the card and applications that know how to talk to the device driver to get work done with the card.

The device driver was called EMM.SYS (which would eventually evolve into EMM386.EXE). Basically, EMM.SYS electronically readdressed the chips on the expanded memory board. When EMM.SYS initialized, it took the expanded memory card's first four 16K pages and addresses and changed them into one, unused, 64K area in the reserved area. This 64K area was known as the *EMS page frame* (Figure 16.18). EMM.SYS decided where to put the EMS page frame and, once established, the page frame was (and still is) immovable. In almost all machines, that address range was from D0000 to DFFFF or E0000 to EFFFF.

Programs ask EMM.SYS to move different pages into this 64K area, so you can load large amounts of data onto the EMS card while using only

Figure 16.17b Expanded memory card

Figure 16.17c EMS pages on card

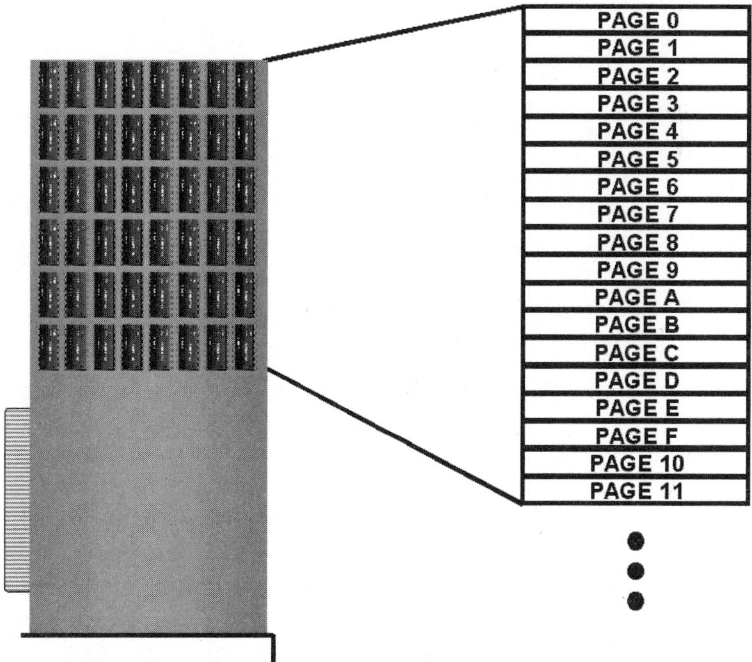

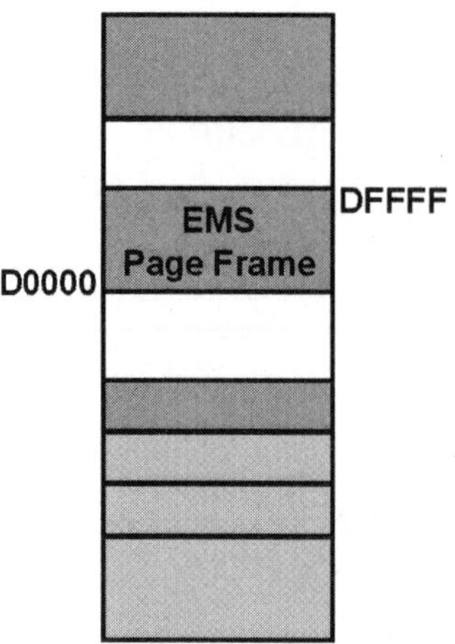

Figure 16.18
EMS page frame

64K of memory! Of course, the downside is that programs have to keep track of the page on which a certain piece of data resides. Therefore, applications must be written to use expanded memory.

In order for a program to use EMS memory, it had to be specifically written to do so, and virtually every commercial DOS program ever made could. When an EMS-aware program ran, it loaded the first four 16K pages into the 64K page frame—in essence, those first four pages temporarily took the memory addresses (Figure 16.19). The program would then load its data into those pages instead of using conventional memory. As those pages filled, the program would then tell the EMS card to swap out a filled page with an empty one (Figure 16.20).

Only DOS programs use expanded memory. Windows will use expanded memory, but only for backward compatibility. Windows programs use extended memory (discussed later in this chapter). It should also be mentioned that expanded memory cards are obsolete. Instead, systems can take extended memory and electronically turn it into expanded memory through specialized software programs. This process is called "limulation" and will be discussed in detail later.

The term "limulation" comes from the Lotus-Intel-Microsoft (LIM) standard that defines expanded memory. The terms *LIM, EMS,* and *expanded memory* are interchangeable.

Only DOS programs need expanded memory, so how many DOS programs have been compiled to use expanded memory? It is easier to ask "What programs have *not* been compiled to use expanded memory?" The answer is "Of the major DOS applications, only dBase does not use EMS memory. All other DOS applications use EMS."

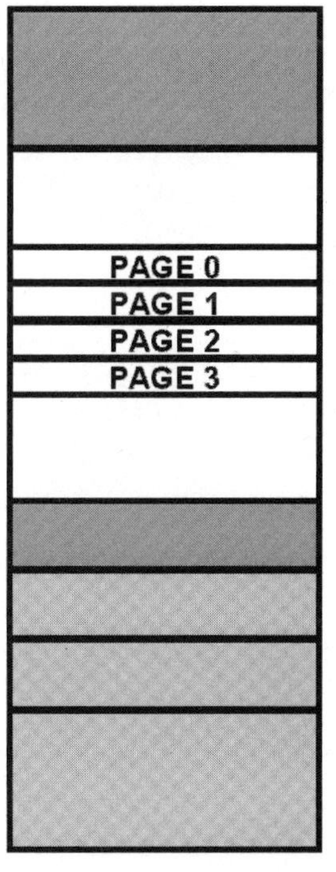

Figure 16.19
Model of Windows in 386 enhanced mode

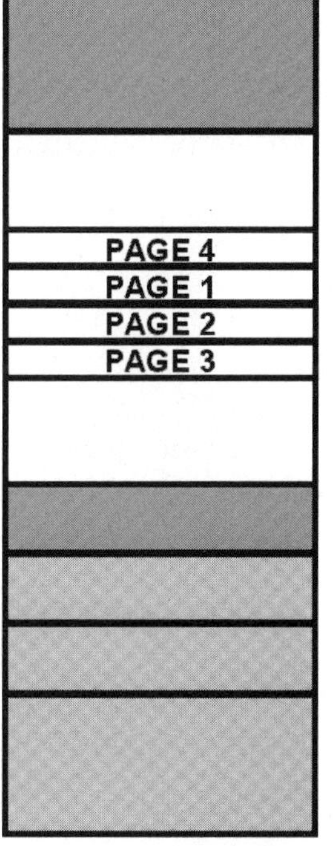

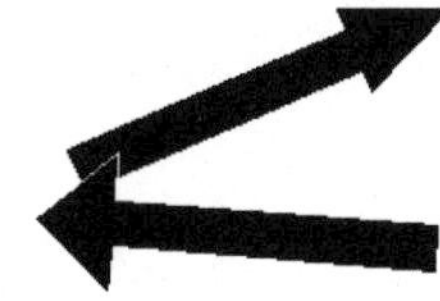

Figure 16.20
Swapping a filled page for a new empty page

Only data can be stored on EMS cards; programs must exist in the conventional memory area. In other words, your spreadsheet file can be stored in expanded memory, but Lotus itself (the program) must be in conventional memory. Also, once a program detects EMM.SYS, it starts using EMS memory automatically. You do not have to do anything to make it happen. Some programs (like WordPerfect) allow you to configure them to not use EMS memory, which can be handy for troubleshooting.

Remember that this type of memory was invented by Lotus, Intel, and Microsoft. They wrote a book called the *LIM 3.2 Standard.* (Why was the first version 3.2? There were actually earlier versions, but 3.2 was the most widely accepted.) This is why expanded memory is often called *LIM memory.*

LIM 3.2 Standard Expanded Memory

Expanded (EMS) memory is exclusively the domain of DOS programs. Although Windows and Windows programs can use expanded memory, they would rather not. Expanded memory allows the creation of larger pieces of data: bigger spreadsheets, documents, and databases.

- Expanded memory is divided into 16K chunks called *pages.*
- EMM.SYS electronically changes the addresses of the EMS frames to fit within the EMS page frame.
- The EMS page frame must be 64K.
- Applications must be written to use EMS memory.

LIM Standard 4.0 Memory

A consortium of AST, Quarterdeck, and Ashton-Tate created an advanced version of LIM 3.2 called EEMS (Extended Expanded Memory System). First, EEMS was 100 percent compatible with the LIM 3.2 standard. If you purchased an EEMS card, EMM.SYS would see it as a regular EMS 3.2 card. EEMS could take up to 32MB of EMS memory. EEMS had some very impressive features. First, you could have more than one page frame. Second, the page frame(s) could be sizes other than 64K. Third, page frames could be in conventional memory. Note that, although *page frames* were now very flexible, the *pages* themselves were still 16K.

Flexible page frames allow something fascinating to take place. Imagine the following scenario. You start with an old XT computer with 640K of RAM, and remove about 512K. You add some amount of EEMS memory, let's say 1024K (the more EEMS memory, the better). Then you set the page frame (which is flexible in EEMS, so you need to set it up) to fill the memory addresses of the RAM chips you removed. So, instead of a 64K page frame in the reserved area, there is now a 512K page frame *in conventional memory*. This is known as *backfilling*.

Since backfilling creates conventional memory from EEMS memory, programs can be loaded into EEMS memory. A program can be loaded into EEMS memory and then swapped out of the page frame, and another program can be loaded into the page frame. The programs are swapped back and forth very fast. Guess what? You are now multitasking on an old IBM XT! Pretty neat!

The LIM group incorporated EEMS into EMS with a new version, the LIM 4.0 standard, in 1985. Although LIM 4.0 hardware and software were backward compatible with the LIM 3.2 standard, none of the old LIM 3.2 standard hardware or software could be used with LIM 4.0. You needed a new type of memory card, a new EMM.SYS. Applications had to be rewritten to be able to understand the new hardware and device driver. Unlike LIM 3.2, LIM 4.0 was very complicated and expensive. As a result, LIM 4.0 devices were not as popular as LIM 3.2. Very few developers rewrote their applications to use LIM 4.0. However, the worst aspect of LIM 4.0 was that EMS card makers would not stick to the standard. For example, a card might support multiple page frames, but not conventional memory page frames. As a result, LIM 4.0 was not supported nearly as widely.

Extended Memory

Extended memory is simply all memory above 1 megabyte (Figure 16.21). If you have a PC with 32MB of RAM, it has 31MB of extended memory. Extended memory cannot be directly used by DOS, although there is a new functionality called DPMI (DOS protected-mode interface), which allows the most modern DOS versions to make limited use of extended memory. Since DOS doesn't directly use extended memory, it's not really part of DOS memory management, with the exception of the high memory area (HMA).

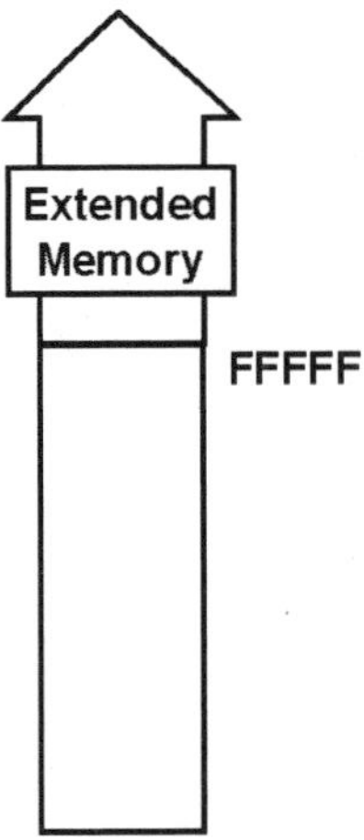

Figure 16.21
All memory above 1MB is extended memory

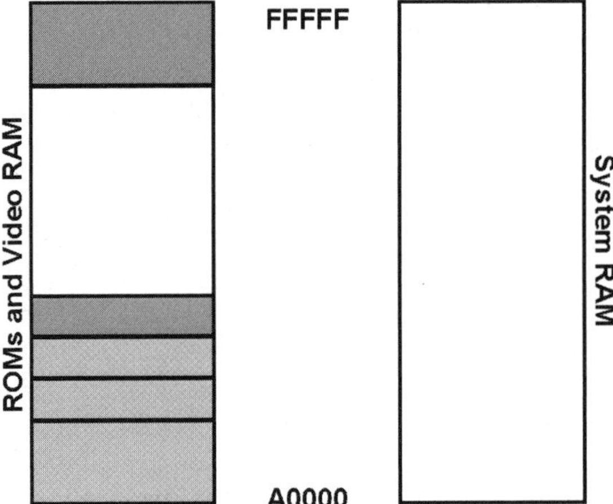

Figure 16.22
RAM and BIOS at the same memory location

Shadowing

The idea of masking this 384K off or moving it into extended memory left many motherboard manufacturers unhappy. They came up with an excellent idea. They left the RAM at the same memory locations as the reserved area (Figure 16.22).

Now, no two chips can share the same memory location. Having two or more chips with the same memory location is like having two telephones with the same phone number. If the CPU dials one address, then code at both locations will be placed on the external data bus and the PC will lock up.

How can we avoid locking up at this point? Well, what is BIOS? BIOS is software that is stored on ROM so certain important information is still there when you turn off the computer. The biggest problem with ROM is that it is very slow compared to the computer's RAM. RAM is much faster than ROM. Remember that every time you want to talk to the keyboard, you have to access the BIOS routine stored on the ROM chip, which is slow.

What if you were to copy the BIOS routines from the ROM over to the RAM at the same address, and then turned off the ROM? Then every time the CPU needed a BIOS routine, it could access the routine from RAM, not ROM. This process is called *shadowing*, which allows for a much faster response from BIOS routines since they are on fast RAM and not slow ROM. Of course, once the PC is turned off or rebooted, all the BIOS routines on RAM are erased. Therefore, shadowing must be redone every time the PC is turned on or rebooted. Figure 16.23 shows a shadowing diagram. Note that the video BIOS is shadowed, but not the video RAM. Video RAM is fast RAM already, and would not benefit from shadowing.

The best way to shadow your BIOS is through the CMOS setup. Figure 16.24 shows a classic CMOS setup screen. Note that there are options for video BIOS and System BIOS, as well as a large number of optional BIOS locations. To shadow, simply enable the address range for whatever you want to shadow. Shadowing is safe and easy. In fact, System BIOS is automatically shadowed on almost all systems today. If your CMOS does not give the option to shadow System BIOS, don't worry; it is already being shadowed.

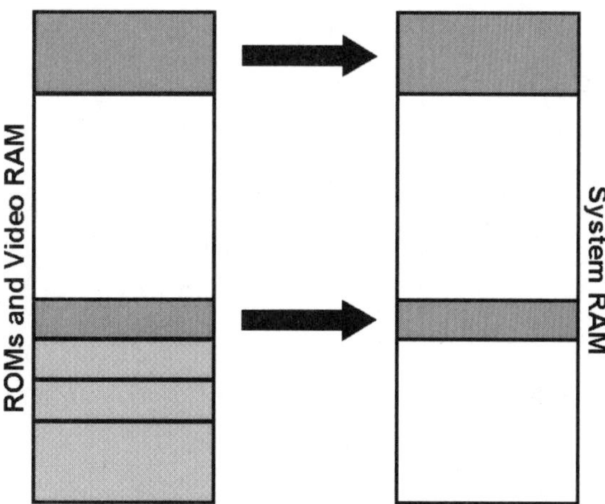

Figure 16.23 Shadowing system and video BIOS

Figure 16.24
CMOS setup screen

```
                    ROM PCI/ISA BIOS (2A69HQ1A)
                       BIOS FEATURES SETUP
                       AWARD SOFTWARE, INC.

Virus Warning                : Enabled     Video  BIOS Shadow   : Disabled
CPU Internal Cache           : Enabled     C8000-CBFFF Shadow   : Disabled
External Cache               : Enabled     CC000-CFFFF Shadow   : Disabled
Quick Power On Self Test     : Disabled    D0000-D3FFF Shadow   : Disabled
Boot Sequence                : C,CDROM,A   D4000-D7FFF Shadow   : Disabled
Swap Floppy Drive            : Disabled    D8000-DBFFF Shadow   : Disabled
Boot Up Floppy Seek          : Disabled    DC000-DFFFF Shadow   : Disabled
Boot Up NumLock Status       : Off
Boot Up System Speed         : Low
Gate A20 Option              : Normal
Typematic Rate Setting       : Disabled
Typematic Rate (Chars/Sec)   : 6
Typematic Delay (Msec)       : 250
Security Option              : Setup
PCI/VGA Palette Snoop        : Disabled
OS Select For DRAM > 64MB    : Non-OS2     ESC : Quit        ↑↓→← : Select Item
                                           F1  : Help        PU/PD/+/- : Modify
                                           F5  : Old Values  (Shift)F2 : Color
                                           F6  : Load BIOS  Defaults
                                           F7  : Load Setup Defaults
```

HIMEM.SYS

Programs use the two 16-bit CS and IP registers to create a 20-bit memory address. Let's see how a program can access a particular memory address. First, you place a value in CS: 0001001001001100 (binary) and 124C (hex). Then you place a value in IP: 0000101011100111 (binary) and 0AE7 (hex). The CS value is shifted left four binary places (124C0), then they are added together (124C0 + 0AE8 = 12FA8), giving you the memory address. No problem, right?

First, place a value in CS: FFFF (all ones, a legitimate value), then place a value in IP: FFFF. The CS value is shifted left four binary places—FFFF0—and they are then added together—FFFF0 + FFFF = 10FFEF—which is six digits, not just five!

The old 8088 would have a real problem if you accidentally addressed a little too high. In fact, if the 8088 tried to write to address 10FFEF, it would instead write to 0FFEF, or somewhere in the first 64K of memory, a phenomenon called *wrap-around*. The CPU cannot see the first 1, because it does not have enough address wires to go beyond FFFFF! How many address wires would you need for six hex characters? Go back to the description of the 286 processor in Chapter 1 and see the size of address bus that was on the 286.

When the 286 was in the final stages of development, Intel discovered that the 286 could address slightly more than 1MB while running in 8086

Figure 16.25
The HMA

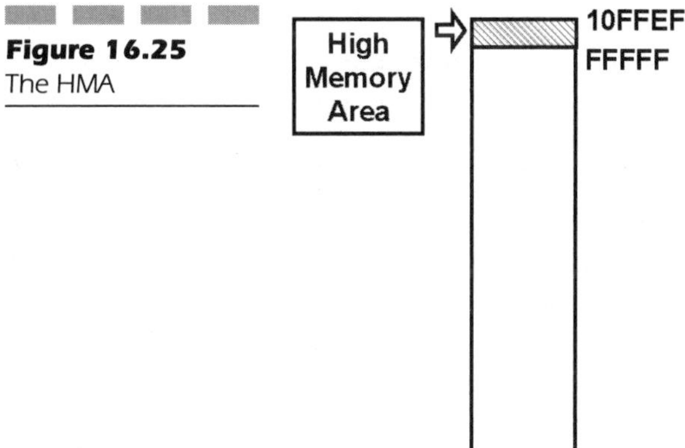

mode. Recall that the 286 could see up to 16MB, but only if it was running in protected mode. We're still using good old DOS, so we're still in real mode. The 286 could see more than one megabyte because of the wrap-around effect of using two 16-bit registers to represent one 20-bit address bus.

Intel wanted the 286 to be 100 percent compatible with the 8088, so they "masked off" everything higher than 1MB of RAM, so the 286 couldn't "see" it. Someone at Intel or Microsoft discovered that if you ran a certain BIOS routine through the 8042 (keyboard) chip, you could "unmask" the 21st address wire (A20) and see more memory. This extra 64K minus 16 bytes of memory—is called the *high memory area*, or the *HMA* (Figure 16.25).

Remember that the HMA is just more memory addresses; in order to use them, ships must populating the addresses above FFFFF. There must be extended memory. You must also run the special BIOS routine to activate it. When the HMA was discovered, it was considered academically fascinating.

Crowded Extended Memory

By the late 80s, manufacturers began to ship a large number of PCs with installed extended memory. IBM was pushing OS/2 and telling everyone who would listen: "You better buy a PC with one or two megabytes of extended memory! OS/2 is going to take over and you'll be sorry if you don't buy PCs now with the memory you'll need!" When the early versions of OS/2 came out, everyone hated them and no one used them. A significant percentage of all machines installed had extended memory and no operating system to use it with. Some programs would take advantage of extended memory, though—the VDISK.EXE program that came with DOS version 3.3 would take your extended memory and turn it into a tiny but very fast hard drive, complete with a drive letter!

All this unusable memory drove software developers crazy. Tired of being told to wait for the latest OS/2, they wanted to use extended memory. Companies like Lotus, AutoDesk, and Xerox began developing software applications that would take over some operating system functions—in particular extended memory access. Programs that ran on top of DOS but then went beyond its capabilities were called *DOS extenders*. In addition, a powerful cottage industry turned extended memory into expanded memory, creating "limulators" that allowed 386 or better PCs to no longer need expanded memory cards.

So around 1989, everyone was using extended memory in their own proprietary way. Guess what showed up in 1990? Windows 3.0. Guess what kind of memory Windows 3.0 wanted? Extended memory. But by the way things were going, there were going to be some serious lockups between any two programs that wanted to use the same memory locations in extended memory. Plus, remember the HMA? If you had extended memory, you could access the HMA—but there was no standard method to access it for all PCs.

Microsoft to the Rescue

Microsoft provided a new device driver with both Windows and DOS: HIMEM.SYS. This program performed two functions. First, it unmasked the 21st address wire (the A20 wire) and created the HMA. Second, it in essence "stood at the gate" of extended memory and forced all applications to sign in—creating a way for applications to know where in extended memory they could and could not go. Any programs that use extended memory today must have HIMEM.SYS running or they will not run. By the way, any extended memory under the control of HIMEM.SYS is called *XMS memory*.

Setting HIMEM.SYS

The overwhelming majority of people install HIMEM.SYS the same way. The first line in your CONFIG.SYS file will look like this:

```
DEVICE=C:\DOS\HIMEM.SYS or DEVICE=C:\WINDOWS\HIMEM.SYS
```

depending on whether your version of DOS or Windows is newer. Always use the most recent version of HIMEM.SYS. Just check the date when you type DIR. Most of these switches were designed to allow HIMEM.SYS to work with later 286 and early 386 models. Chances are you will never need any of these options:

/A20CONTROL:ON|OFF (COMPLETELY OBSOLETE) Tells HIMEM .SYS to take control of A20 even if another program has control. The default setting is /A20CONTROL:ON. Some early 386 computers had a CMOS option that handled limulation. This setting kept HIMEM.SYS from corrupting the system while allowing it to create XMS memory.

CPUCLOCK:ON|OFF (COMPLETELY OBSOLETE) The official story is that, on some late 286 and early 386 systems, running HIMEM.SYS would affect the clock speed—sometimes speeding it up and sometimes slowing it down. If your computer's clock speed changed when you installed HIMEM, specifying /CPUCLOCK:ON sometimes corrected the problem. The default setting is /CPUCLOCK:OFF. Even Microsoft has problems explaining this option. My best guess is that somebody's chipset got all screwed up when HIMEM.SYS was loaded, forcing a clock slowdown. I've never used this option.

/EISA (STILL NEEDED, BUT RARELY) Tells HIMEM that this is an EISA machine, so it can access memory above 16 megabytes. This switch is necessary only on an EISA (Extended Industry Standard Architecture) computer with more than 16MB of memory. You will need this option only for some EISA machines with more than 16MB of RAM. Even most EISA machines do not require this option, but it never hurts to add it to the HIMEM.SYS line.

/HMAMIN=*n* (NEVER USED) Back when HIMEM.SYS was first invented, Microsoft thought that other programs other than DOS would want to use the HMA. Since only one program can use the HMA at a time, this feature was designed to keep programs out that wouldn't use the HMA efficiently.

/NUMHANDLES=*n* (NEVER USED) Quoting Microsoft, this setting "specifies the maximum number of extended-memory block (EMB) handles that can be used simultaneously. You can specify a value from 1 to 128; the default value is 32. Each additional handle requires an additional 6 bytes of memory."

/INT15=*xxxx* (OBSOLETE) When HIMEM.SYS is used, it turns all your extended memory into XMS memory. Some old programs used extended memory on their own and wouldn't play with HIMEM.SYS unless some extended memory was left under the control of BIOS. This setting kept some of the XMS memory as regular extended memory. You can specify a value from 64 to 65535 (K). If you specify a value less than 64, the value becomes 0. The default value is 0.

/MACHINE:*xxxx* (OBSOLETE) When HIMEM.SYS came out, some PC chipsets had weird ways of unmasking the A20 wire and accessing the HMA. As a result, HIMEM had special settings for those PCs. See Table 16.2.

TABLE 16.2

Special HIMEM Settings

Code	Number	Computer type
at	1	IBM AT or 100% compatible
ps2	2	IBM PS/2
ptlcascade	3	Phoenix Cascade BIOS
hpvectra	4	HP ectra (A & A+)
att6300plus	5	AT&T 300 Plus
acer1100	6	Acer 1100
toshiba	7	Toshiba 1600 & 1200XE
wyse	8	Wyse 12.5 MHz 286
tulip	9	Tulip SX
zenith	10	Zenith ZBIOS
at1	11	IBM PC/AT (alternative delay)
at2	12	IBM PC/AT (altenative delay)
css	12	CSS Labs
at3	13	IBM PC/AT (alternative delay)
philips	13	Philips
fasthp	14	HP Vectra
ibm7552	15	IBM 7552 Industrial Computer
bullmicral	16	Bull Micral 60
dell	17	Dell XBIOS

/SHADOWRAM:ONOFF (USELESS) HIMEM.SYS can turn off shadowing. This setting specifies whether to disable shadow RAM. HIMEM.SYS will try to turn shadowing off to get more memory. A few systems would let their shadowing be turned off, but only a very few. The overwhelming majority of PCs ignore this setting, which defaults to /SHADOWRAM:OFF.

/TESTMEM:ON¦OFF (USEFUL IF YOU'RE IN A HURRY) HIMEM performs a nice little RAM test every time you turn on the PC, but it can be a little slow. Adding /TESTMEM:OFF turns this RAM test off. You can also use /TEST:OFF.

/VERBOSE (USEFUL IF YOU LIKE TO WATCH) Tells HIMEM to put a bunch of useless junk on the screen while it loads. You can also hold the Alt key while HIMEM starts and loads.

HIMEM.SYS and DOS=HIGH

If you have a 286 or better and some extended memory, be sure to add the line DOS=HIGH anywhere in your CONFIG.SYS file. This option moves most of the COMMAND.COM file from conventional memory into the HMA. This option will save you about 30 kilobytes of conventional memory.

All memory addresses are five hex digits, but when people talk about memory locations, almost no one uses five digits—they're rounded off to four. So instead of talking about the memory range D0000-DFFFF, you round off to the nearest four digits: D000-DFFF.

We usually only use four characters when discussing memory locations. So instead of saying all five characters, like C7FFF, just drop the last character and say C7FF.

Upper Memory Blocks (UMB)

The last type of memory you should be aware of is *upper memory blocks*, or UMBs. They are unused memory addresses in the reserved area (Figure 16.26).

You can have more than one UMB in a system. As mentioned earlier, almost no PCs today use a monochrome text video card, so that unused area is also a UMB. This creates a situation where there is more than one UMB,

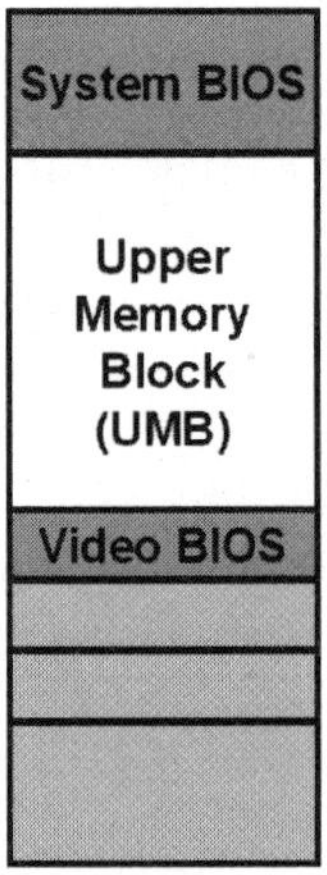

Figure 16.26
An upper memory block (UMB)

System BIOS
Upper Memory Block (UMB)
Video BIOS

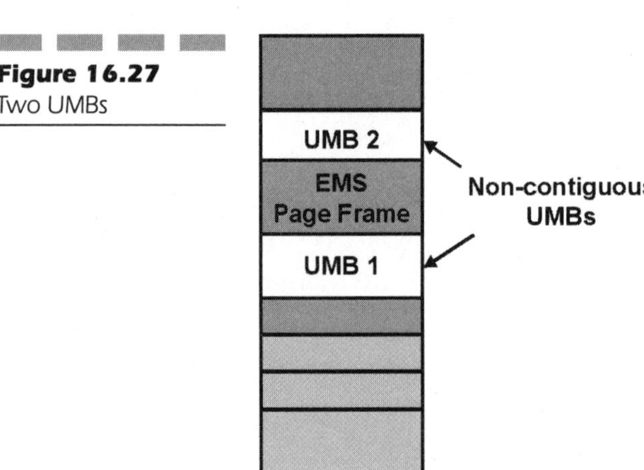

Figure 16.27
Two UMBs

as shown in Figure 16.27. By convention, UMBs are numbered from top to bottom. Adding ROM or EMS can create even more UMBs. Figure 16.28 is a system with an EMS page frame, creating a total of three UMBs. As you will soon see, UMBs play a crucial role in DOS memory management.

Reducing Conventional Memory Use

The secret to reducing conventional memory use is to find some unused memory in which to store programs. Basically, there are two places where you can move device drivers and TSRs. One is the HMA and the other is a UMB. Special programs, generically called *memory-management software,*

are used to move device drivers and TSRs out of conventional memory and into the HMA and UMBs. This process is called *loading high.*

Our goal in DOS memory management is to reduce the amount of conventional memory used so DOS programs can run. This begs the question "How much conventional memory do I need?" Well, that depends on what programs you are running. If the only program you use is EDIT, you only need about 350K of conventional memory—but how many people only run EDIT? A good rule of thumb is to try to have 600K of conventional memory open, which will allow virtually any DOS program to run comfortably.

UMB Gateway

By default, UMBs are completely unused and wasted—that is, unless you have a UMB gateway. With a UMB gateway, you can load CONFIG.SYS's device drivers (all those device=statements) into these UMBs and free up conventional memory (loading high).

UMB gateways also allow you to load AUTOEXEC.BAT's TSRs (like DOSKEY or MOUSE.COM) into UMBs, again saving precious conventional memory. Many third-party companies have made their fortunes from UMB gateways such as Quarterdeck's QEMM and Qualitas' 386MAX. Even DOS has a UMB gateway (EMM386.EXE).

TSR stands for "terminate and stay resident." A TSR is a DOS program that runs and then terminates, but stays in RAM. This is handy for hardware support (like mice and CD-ROM drives) in DOS.

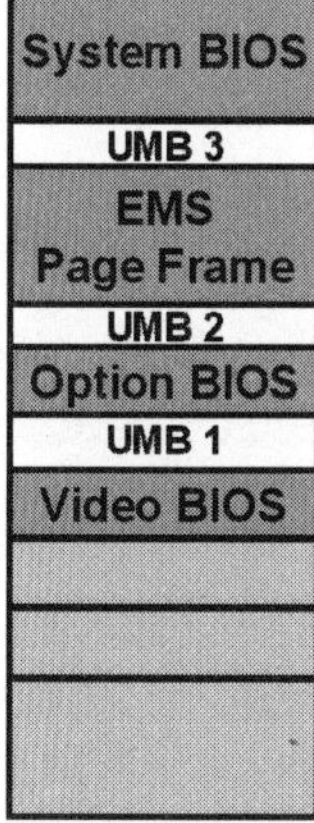

Figure 16.28
Three UMBs

Loading high is not loading into extended memory or the HMA; it is really loading into the UMB. Simply loading programs into UMBs can be deadly. For example, what if you have an EMS card? The EMS page frame takes up 64K of UMB space! What would happen if you tried to load some device driver into the same addresses as the EMS page frame? Every time you tried to access that driver or EMS memory, the computer would lock up. A good UMB gateway should be able to inspect the entire reserved area and steer clear of ROMs, Video RAM, and EMS page frames. This is known as *memory management*. Every UMB gateway program is also a memory manager. As a result, nobody uses the term *UMB gateway*. Instead they use the term *memory manager*. EMM386.EXE is DOS's memory manager.

NOTE *: Memory managers only prepare the UMB for device drivers and programs. They never do the actual loading into the UMB. The actual loading is carried out by special commands that are recognized by the memory manager. With EMM386.EXE, there are two different ways to load something high, depending on whether it is a device driver in CONFIG.SYS or a TSR in the AUTOEXEC.BAT. In CONFIG.SYS, you simply change any device= line to devicehigh=. For programs in AUTOEXEC.BAT, insert the command Loadhigh or LH in front of the command you want loaded into the UMB.*

EMM386.EXE

EMM386 does two jobs in one package: limulation and memory management. EMM386 can perform both functions or just one, depending on how you set it up. Remember that you must have a 386SX or better with 1MB of RAM before you can use EMM386.

Limulation

If you have a 386 or better with extended memory, you do not have to buy an expensive EMS card. You can make some or all of the extended memory behave identically to EMS memory. This emulation of the LIM standard, discussed earlier, is known as "limulation." In order to limulate, you need a device driver that can access extended memory and convert it to EMS memory. These programs are known as "limulators." Limulators are usually expanded-memory device drivers that replace EMM.SYS. EMM386.EXE is DOS's built-in limulator. Installing EMM386.EXE into the CONFIG.SYS file automatically turns some or all of your extended memory into EMS 3.2

and 4.0 compatible memory. By default, you get a 64K EMS page frame in the reserved area, but EMM386.EXE is highly customizable to take advantage of the more advanced features of LIM 3.2 and LIM 4.0. In order to turn some or all of your extended memory into expanded memory, all you have to do is to add the following line: (caps are not necessary):

```
DEVICE=C:\DOS\EMM386.EXE
```

to your CONFIG.SYS file. The only rule is that you must have the line:

```
DEVICE=C:\DOS\HIMEM.SYS
```

before it. It's that simple. If you have a computer with 4MB of memory, you will now have a computer with 640K of conventional memory, 384K of UMB, and 3072K (3MB) of expanded memory. You will have a page frame established in the UMB, and if you run a program that uses EMS memory, such as Lotus 1-2-3, you will be able to make huge spreadsheets before running out of memory. You can limit the amount of extended memory that is turned into EMS memory by specifying this with a number. For example:

```
DEVICE=C:\DOS\EMM386.EXE 1024
```

would convert 1MB of extended memory into EMS memory, the rest staying as regular extended memory. So on a 4MB system, this command would give you 640K of conventional memory + 386K of UMB + 1024K of EMS + 2048K of extended memory, equaling 4MB. Remember when you limulate, you create a page frame, usually at D000-DFFF. Starting with DOS 6.0, you never give a value to the amount of EMS memory you want to limulate. By not adding a number to the EMM386 line, EMM386 will take all the memory and dynamically allocate it as EMS or XMS for programs that need it.

Preparing to Load High

In order to let EMM386 know that you want to load high, you must add a few commands. First, add the line DOS=UMB anywhere in the CONFIG.SYS file. This tells DOS that you will be loading high. You can combine the DOS=UMB command with the DOS=HIGH command discussed earlier. All of the following are acceptable: DOS=HIGH,UMB *or* DOS=UMB,HIGH *or* DOS=HIGH and DOS=UMB *or* DOS=UMB and DOS=HIGH.

The next item informs EMM386.EXE what you want to do. Remember that EMM386 allows you to load high and limulate. What do you want to do? A dedicated Windows machine that runs only Windows programs doesn't need to limulate. Limulation is only for DOS programs. Say you want to load high, but not limulate. Place the word *NOEMS* here:

```
DEVICE=C:\DOS\EMM386.EXE NOEMS
```

A PC that runs Windows and also supports DOS applications that use expanded memory will need the word *RAM*:

```
DEVICE=C:\DOS\EMM386.EXE RAM
```

To limulate but *not* load high, as you did in the earlier discussion of limulation, don't add anything:

```
DEVICE=C:\DOS\EMM386.EXE
```

If you don't want to do either, do not use EMM386! Now you're ready to add DEVICEHIGH= statements in CONFIG.SYS as well as LOADHIGH statements in AUTOEXEC.BAT.

Loading High

After you have prepared everything properly, the last and easiest step is to load your devices into the UMB. I often add DEVICEHIGH= statements to the all device= lines in my CONFIG.SYS, and then LH to all the TSRs in my AUTOEXEC.BAT. The problem is that there is only so much UMB space. The trick is to load as much into that space as possible. The order in which devices load is crucial in determining how much gets loaded into UMB space. To handle these problems, I usually use MEMMAKER. The MEMMAKER utility automatically loads as many devices as possible high. Once you have prepared the UMBs, you can let MEMMAKER do the rest.

MEMMAKER

Be careful with MEMMAKER; this program will cause trouble if placed in the wrong hands. Many technicians hate MEMMAKER because they say it does a poor job, which is untrue. MEMMAKER does one thing well; it will fit as much stuff as possible into the available UMB space.

The most important aspect to using MEMMAKER is to never use the Express Setup; always use the Custom Setup. When you run the Custom Setup, you have more control over how MEMMAKER works. Be aware that MEMMAKER edits the CONFIG.SYS and AUTOEXEC.BAT files, nothing more. MEMMAKER does nothing that you cannot do or undo manually, but it does it faster.

After you select Custom Setup, MEMMAKER brings up two screens that help determine the correct setup of the EMM386.EXE line in CONFIG.SYS. The first screen simply asks whether you have programs that use expanded memory. If you have DOS programs that need expanded memory, choose yes; otherwise choose no. Based on what you select here, MEMMAKER will put either RAM or NOEMS in the EMM386.EXE line.

The next screen, Advanced Options, causes most of the problems in the Custom Setup. The Advanced Options screen asks six yes/no questions:

SPECIFY WHICH DRIVERS AND TSRS TO INCLUDE IN OPTIMIZATION? The answer is always no—at first. There are a very few devices that will make the computer lock up if they're loaded high. Unfortunately, the only way to find out is to try everything and see if you lock up. If you lock up during boot, use the F8 step to see which device is locking up. Then reboot and use F8 to not load that device.

SCAN THE UPPER MEMORY AREA AGGRESSIVELY? Yes, but you should understand why. MEMMAKER wants to add HIGHSCAN, which is EMM386's super ROM finder. It's an automatic X= (Exclude) and I= (Include) maker. Exclude and Include will be discussed in detail under the EMM386 Options in a few pages. It does a pretty good job, but you've already taken care of all this by adding your own X= and I= statements. Why put in X= and I= if HIGHSCAN takes care of all of this? Because MEMMAKER is not perfect. If I'm in a hurry, I will skip the manual X= and I= lines and just run MEMMAKER. Sometimes it will work.

OPTIMIZE UPPER MEMORY FOR USE WITH WINDOWS? Yes, if you run Windows. MEMMAKER wants to add one or two WIN= entries to the EMM386 line. WIN= excludes UMB space from being loaded with device drivers, reserving it exclusively for Windows. Windows needs at least 16K of UMB space in order to run. You can actually prevent Windows from running by loading too many devices and not giving it enough UMB space. Let MEMMAKER take some UMB space for Windows by adding one or two WIN= statements.

USE MONOCHROME REGION (B000-B7FF) FOR RUNNING PROGRAMS? Maybe. If you have no monochrome video card, the address from B000 to B7FF is unused. You can load devices into this region by adding an I=B000-B7FF line to the EMM386.EXE line. This will work fine with VGA cards, but SVGA is questionable. If the video card is VESA-compliant, go for it! You will get an extra 32K of memory. If you are unsure, try it. If it doesn't work, your screen will show bizarre information and probably, although not always, lock up. If you're using Windows 3.*x*, be sure to add:

```
DEVICE=C:\DOS\MONOUMB.386
```

to the [386Enh] section of your SYSTEM.INI file.

KEEP CURRENT EMM386 MEMORY EXCLUSIONS AND INCLUSIONS? Yes. You spent 30 minutes adding all these X= and I= lines to your EMM386 line. Do not let them be erased.

MOVE EXTENDED BIOS DATA AREA FROM CONVENTIONAL TO UPPER MEMORY? Yes. Some computers have an extended BIOS data area (EBDA) that loads in the top of conventional memory. EMM386 will load the EDBA into an available UMB space.

The MEM Command

DOS has a very handy program for a quick check of upper memory, called MEM. The MEM program provides great answers to questions like "I just changed my device= line for my scanner to devicehigh=; did it actually load into a UMB?" You can enter the MEM command by itself to determine the amount of conventional and UMB space used and available:

```
Memory Type      Total  =   Used +    Free
------------     --------   ------    -------
Conventional     640K        50K      590K
Upper            87K        35K       51K
Reserved         384K        384K     0K
Extended (XMS)   2,985K      1,241K   1,744K
------------     -------    ------    --------
Total memory     4,096K      1,711K   2,385K

Total under 1 MB 727K        86K      641K

Largest executable program size       589K (603,600 bytes)
Largest free upper memory block        27K  (27,856 bytes)
MS-DOS is resident in the high memory area.
```

However, the best way to use MEM is with the /C option. Here's what you can learn from the MEM /C command:

```
Modules using memory below 1 MB:

Name       Total  =          Conventional  +    Upper Memory
-------    -------           --------------     --------------
MSDOS      19,501   (19K)    19,501   (19K)     0          (0K)
HIMEM      1,120    (1K)     1,120    (1K)      0          (0K)
EMM386     4,144    (4K)     4,144    (4K)      0          (0K)
COMMAND    2,976    (3K)     2,976    (3K)      0          (0K)
JMOUSE     23,760   (23K)    23,760   (23K)     0          (0K)
POWER      4,672    (5K)     0        (0K)      4,672   (5K)
SMARTDRV   27,488   (27K)    0        (0K)      27,488 (27K)
DOSKEY     4,144    (4K)     0        (0K)      4,144   (4K)
Free       656,288 (641K)    603,696 (590K)     52,592 (51K)

Memory Summary:

Type of Memory  Total = Used + Free
--------------                 ---------   ---------   ---------
Conventional                   655,360     51,664      603,696
Upper                          88,896      36,304      52,592
Reserved                       393,216     393,216     0
Extended (XMS)                 3,056,832   1,270,976   1,785,856
--------------                 ---------   ---------   ---------
Total memory                   4,194,304   1,752,160   2,442,144

Total under 1 MB               744,256     87,968      656,288

Largest executable program size   603,600    (589K)
Largest free upper memory block   27,856     (27K)
MS-DOS is resident in the high memory area.
```

Inspecting each line individually:

MSDOS The total amount of memory used by the two hidden DOS files, MSDOS.SYS and IO.SYS, as well as the DOS environment space. This is always in conventional memory.

HIMEM HIMEM.SYS, also always in conventional memory.

EMM386 Notice how small (roughly 4K) it is. EMM386 is actually much larger, but loads mostly into a UMB. EMM386 does this automatically, so you never have to add devicehigh= to the EMM386 line. If it loads high, why does nothing show up in the Upper Memory column? Beats me; go ask Microsoft.

COMMAND If you used DOS=HIGH, this is the part of COMMAND.COM that stays in low memory—always in conventional memory.

JMOUSE, POWER, SMARTDRV, and DOSKEY These are devices in my CONFIG.SYS, as well as TSRs in my AUTOEXEC.BAT. All these devices are loaded high except JMOUSE. These will differ from PC to PC, depending on what drivers are loaded in your CONFIG.SYS.

FREE This tells us how much free conventional and upper memory is available. In this system, I have 590K conventional and 51K upper memory free.

MEMORY SUMMARY This breaks memory down into four parts:

CONVENTIONAL Tells you that you have 655,360 (640K) of conventional memory, of which 51,664 bytes are used, leaving 603,696 bytes free.

UPPER Tells you that you have 88,896 bytes of UMB space, 36,304 bytes used by devices loaded high, leaving 52,592 bytes free. The total upper memory is determined by the following equation: 393,216 (384K) – all shadowed memory • video memory – excluded areas (X=) + included areas (I=), which in this case equals 88,896 bytes.

RESERVED This means you have a reserved area of 384K. Ignore this useless line.

EXTENDED (XMS) Shows you have a total of 3,056,832 bytes of extended memory, of which 1,270,976 bytes are being used by something called SMARTDRV (see the chapter on Windows), leaving 1,785,856 bytes free.

TOTAL UNDER 1 MB Adds conventional and upper memory.

LARGEST EXECUTABLE PROGRAM SIZE The largest single amount of open conventional memory available. This is almost always slightly smaller than free conventional memory.

LARGEST FREE UPPER MEMORY BLOCK The largest open UMB. If the free upper memory block in Type of Memory is the same as this number, you have only one UMB. As you can see, I have 52,592 bytes of free upper memory, but the largest block is 27,856 bytes. Therefore, I have more than one UMB.

MS-DOS IS RESIDENT IN THE HIGH MEMORY AREA This tells you that DOS=HIGH is in the CONFIG.SYS file.

Another handy switch for the MEM command is /F. MEM /F tells you if you have more than one UMB. Here's an example of the MEM /F command from the same computer:

```
Segment  Total
-------  ---------------
007D3    96        (0K)
01DF8    603,600   (589K)

Total Free: 603,696  (590K)

Free Upper Memory:

Region   Largest Free       Total Free      Total Size
------   -------------      -------------   -------------
1        24,736   (22K)     24,736   (22K)  24,736   (22K)
2        27,856   (27K)     27,856   (27K)  27,856   (27K)
```

You can see that there are two UMBs.

EMM386 Options

The vast majority of these options are for older 386 computers and no longer have any function. They are discussed here for historical sake only:

[ON¦OFF¦AUTO] (OBSOLETE) Activates the EMM386 device driver (if set on), suspends the EMM386 device driver (if set off), or places the EMM386 device driver in auto mode (if set to auto). Auto mode enables expanded-memory support and upper memory block support only when a program calls for it. The default value is on. This was used for early systems that needed multiple memory managers.

MEMORY (OBSOLETE AFTER DOS 5.0) Sets the maximum amount of extended memory (in kilobytes) that you want EMM386 to provide as expanded (LIM) memory. You can put any number between 64 to 32,768, up to the total amount of extended memory on your system. EMM386 after DOS 5.0 uses DPMI and allocates expanded memory from extended, as needed.

MIN=*size* (OBSOLETE AFTER DOS 5.0) Sets the minimum amount of extended memory (in kilobytes) that you want when EMM386 provides expanded (LIM) memory. EMM386 after DOS 5.0 can allocate expanded memory as needed, so this value is no longer needed.

W=ON¦W=OFF (VIRTUALLY OBSOLETE) The Weitek coprocessor was a special math coprocessor that was popular for a short time in the late 1980s. It needed a special PGA socket, was very expensive, and was completely incompatible with regular math coprocessors. If by some rare chance you have a Weitek coprocessor, you need this option.

M*x* (UNNEEDED, USE FRAME) There are three different ways to set a page frame, and here's one that no one uses—using the M*x* option, with a number from 1 to 14. The following list shows each value and the base address that value represents:

1	C000h	8	DC00h
2	C400h	9	E000h
3	C800h	10	8000h
4	CC00h	11	8400h
5	D000h	12	8800h
6	D400h	13	8C00h
7	D800h	14	9000h

The FRAME option does the exact same thing. Use this if you like to confuse your fellow technicians.

FRAME=*address* This is the right way to set an EMS page frame. You can use any hex value from 9000h up to E000h, in increments of 400h. To provide expanded memory and disable the page frame, you can specify FRAME=NONE, but this emulates the LIM 4.0 expanded memory standard. Programs that require LIM 3.2 expanded memory (almost all expanded memory programs) will lock up.

/P*mmmm* (UNNEEDED, USE FRAME) Another way to set page frames. The *mmmm* is just the hex value, the same as with the FRAME statement. The FRAME option does the same thing.

P*n*=*address* (OBSOLETE) This is only for programs that support LIM 4.0 expanded memory. You can actually split the page frame into four discontiguous pieces. The last popular program to do this was Lotus 1-2-3, ver. 3.0. Leave this one alone!

X=*mmmm-nnnn* (STILL NEEDED) Prevents EMM386 from using a particular range of segment addresses for an EMS page or UMBs. Valid values for *mmmm* and *nnnn* are in the range A000h through FFFFh, and are rounded down to the nearest four-kilobyte boundary. The X switch takes precedence over the I switch if the two ranges overlap. Let MEMMAKER do it.

I=*mmmm-nnnn* (HANDY) Specifies a range of segment addresses to be used (included) for an EMS page or UMBs. Valid values for *mmmm* and *nnnn* are in the range A000h through FFFFh, and are rounded down to the nearest four-kilobyte boundary. The X switch takes precedence over the I switch if the two ranges overlap. Again, let MEMMAKER do it.

B=*address* (OBSOLETE) Only for backward compatibility with ancient memory managers/environments like Desqview. Even the more recent versions of Desqview don't need it.

L=MINXMS (OBSOLETE AFTER DOS 5.0) Reserves a little extended memory after EMM386 is loaded. Ignore this line.

A=*altregs* (OBSOLETE) Specifies how many fast alternate register sets (used for multitasking) you want to allocate to EMM386. Valid values are in the range 0 through 254, and the default value is 7. Every alternate register set adds about 200 bytes to the memory size of EMM386. Versions of Windows before 3.0 needed this, but today it is ignored.

H=*handles* (VERY RARELY USED) Specifies how many handles EMM386 can use. Valid values are in the range 2 through 255. The default value is 64, which is plenty unless you can load more than 30 devices high.

D=*nnn* (VERY RARELY USED) Specifies how many kilobytes of memory should be reserved for buffered direct memory access (DMA). Discounting floppy-disk DMA, this value should reflect the largest DMA transfer that can occur while EMM386 is active. Valid values for *nnn* are in the range 16 through 256. The default value is 32. If you have multiple devices using DMA channels and are getting strange DMA errors, changing this value to something like 64 might help, but it eats memory.

RAM=*mmmm-nnnn* (UNNECESSARY, USE X= AND I=) Specifies a range of segment addresses to be used for UMBs, and also enables EMS support. If you do not specify a range, EMM386 will use all available adapter space to create UMBs and a page frame for EMS. RAM tells EMM386 where are the upper and lower boundaries for UMBs are. By default, EMM386 assumes that all memory from C800 to F000 is available. Use X= and I= to modify this.

NOEMS (COMMONLY USED) Provides access to the upper memory area, but prevents access to expanded memory.

HIGHSCAN (SOMETIMES HANDY) Specifies that EMM386 uses an additional check to determine the availability of upper memory for use as

UMBs. On some computers, specifying this switch will have no effect; on others, it will cause EMM386 to identify upper memory areas as available when they are not. As a result, your computer might stop responding.

VERBOSE (UNNECESSARY, BUT PRETTY) Directs EMM386 to display status and error messages while loading. By default, EMM386 displays messages only if it encounters an error condition. You can abbreviate VERBOSE as V. (To display status messages without adding the VERBOSE switch, press and hold the Alt key while EMM386 starts and loads.)

WIN=*mmm-nnnn* Reserves a specified range of segment addresses for Windows instead of for EMM386. Valid values for *mmmm* and *nnnn* are in the range A000h through FFFFh, and are rounded down to the nearest four-kilobyte boundary. The X switch takes precedence over the WIN switch if the two ranges overlap. The WIN switch takes precedence over the RAM, ROM, and I switches if their ranges overlap.

NOHI (USELESS) Prevents EMM386 from loading into the upper memory area. A portion of EMM386 is normally loaded into upper memory. Specifying this switch decreases available conventional memory and increases the upper memory area available for UMBs. Adding it takes away about 30K of conventional memory.

ROM=*mmmm-nnnn* (RARELY USED) Specifies a range of segment addresses that EMM386 uses for shadow RAM and random-access memory used for read-only memory (ROM). Valid values for *mmmm* and *nnnn* are in the range A000h through FFFFh, and are rounded down to the nearest four-kilobyte boundary. Specifying this switch might speed up your system if it does not already have shadow RAM. If your BIOS doesn't support shadowing, you can shadow your BIOS this way.

NOMOVEXBDA (SEE SECTION ON MEMMAKER) Prevents EMM386 from moving the extended BIOS data from conventional memory to upper memory.

ALTBOOT (I HAVE NEVER USED THIS) Specifies that EMM386 use an alternate handler to restart your computer when you press Ctrl< Alt–Del. Use this switch only if your computer stops responding or exhibits other unusual behavior when EMM386 is loaded and you press Ctrl–Alt–Del.

Memory-Management Procedures

The main reason computers lock up is that two programs try to occupy the same UMB addresses at the same time. This happens because of a failure to properly prepare the UMB. Before loading high, you must inform EMM386 there are programs that might occupy UMB space, primarily ROM BIOSes from cards. There are also devices like PCMCIA slots, which take UMB RAM for their own programs and data and do not report doing so. Any attempt to load high without special commands to inform EMM386 of the presence of these programs will result in the computer locking up. The lockups attributable to memory conflicts are those frustrating "every now and then" type. When someone says they have an "intermittent" problem, it is usually due to improperly preparing the UMB.

The number-one rule to loading high is "Before loading high, prepare the UMB!"

Rules for Preparing the UMB

- Keep it contiguous.
- Find the ROM BIOSes.
- Find the sneaky programs that steal UMB space.

KEEP IT CONTIGUOUS Pretend you have a nice plain Pentium desktop computer with 32MB or more of RAM and no optional BIOSes other than the video card. The reserved area would look something like Figure 16.29. Now say you have some DOS programs you want to run that use expanded memory, so you want to limulate. You set up your CONFIG.SYS with the following lines:

```
DEVICE=C:\DOS\HIMEM.SYS
DEVICE=C:\DOS\EMM386.EXE RAM
```

The reserved area would now look like Figure 16.30a. Instead of one contiguous UMB, you have two little ones. Your UMB is no longer contiguous. This is bad as it wastes potential UMB space. Let's see why. Say you have a scanner and you want to load the scanner driver high. You set up your CONFIG.SYS with these lines:

```
DEVICE=C:\DOS\HIMEM.SYS
DEVICE=C:\DOS\EMM386.EXE RAM
DOS=HIGH,UMB
DEVICEHIGH=C:\SCANGAL\SCANDRV.SYS
```

Figure 16.29 Typical reserved area

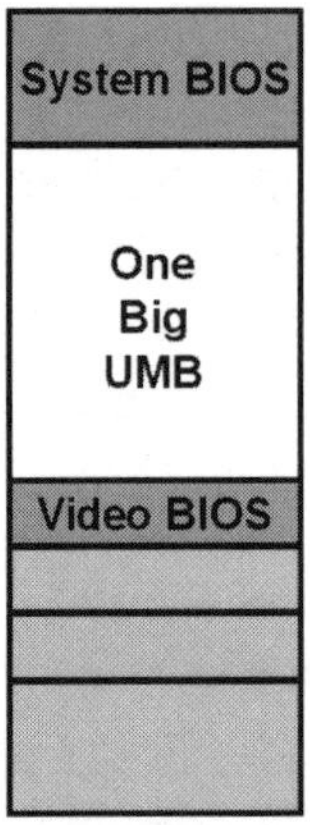

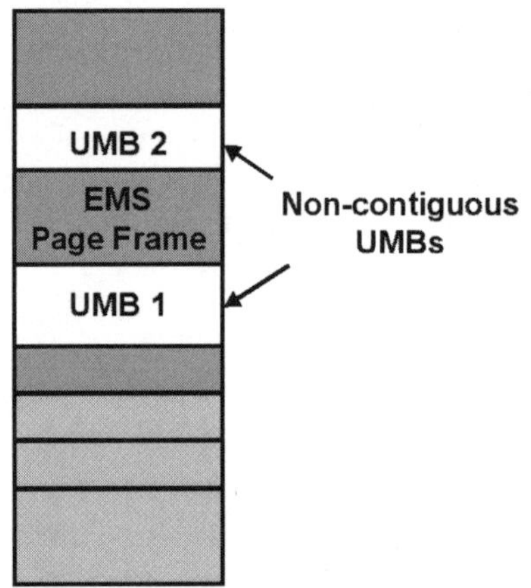

Figure 16.30a Noncontiguous UMBs

If you reboot the computer, the scanner driver might not load high. What went wrong? To discover the answer, use the DOS MEM /C/P command to look at the size of SCANDRV.SYS. You will see that it is 34,324 bytes. The rule of loading high is that DOS will start looking at the bottom of the UMB for a contiguous space large enough for the designated device driver. If there is not enough room, then the device will not load. The area from C8000 to CFFFF is 32K. There was not enough room to load.

What about the space from E0000 to EFFFF? Why won't it load in there? Because DOS will not let any device drivers load into this space until you fill the space from C8000 to CFFFF, though there are exceptions to this based on DOS versions. If you have DOS 6.0 or later, you put the command /L:2 in the DEVICEHIGH line to force the scanner to try to load in the larger area, as follows:

```
DEVICEHIGH /L:2=C:\SCANGAL\SCANDRV.SYS
```

The scanner will now successfully load in the second area. If you have DOS 6.2 or later (including 6.2, 6.21, 6.22, and Windows 95), then the device will always load into the largest space automatically. But sometimes loading into the largest UMB can be bad. For example, what if I had two UMBs, the first 27K and the next 45K? If I had two devices, one 26K and the other 40K, where would the 40K driver load if I loaded the 26K driver first and it went into the 45K UMB? There would be no room for the 40K device. In order for both devices to load, I would have to be sure to load the 40K driver first and then the 27K driver—what a hassle.

If you can keep the UMB contiguous, this entire conversation is moot. You wouldn't need to worry about which version of DOS you had, nor about using commands like /L:2 to move device drivers, nor about a device having enough room to load. You also wouldn't need to worry (much) about the order of loading. Virtually anything that goes into the UMB is movable to help you keep the UMB contiguous. In this case, you would have to move the EMS page frame. The command FRAME=C800 will move the EMS page frame down to the top of the video BIOS:

```
DEVICE=C:\DOS\HIMEM.SYS
DEVICE=C:\DOS\EMM386.EXE RAM FRAME=C800
DOS=UMB,HIGH
DEVICEHIGH=C:\SCANGAL\SCANDRV.SYS
```

Figure 16.30b shows the result of moving the page frame: one big, contiguous UMB.

FIND THE ROM BIOSES The reason to find the ROM BIOSes is so EMM386 will not try to load devices high into the same addresses occu-

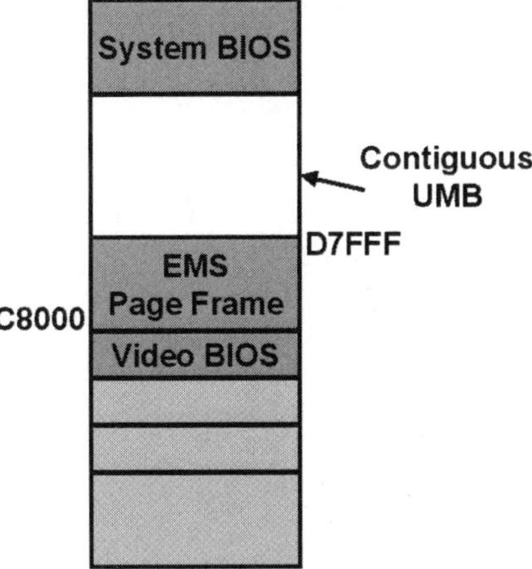

Figure 16.30b Creating contiguous UMBs by moving page frame

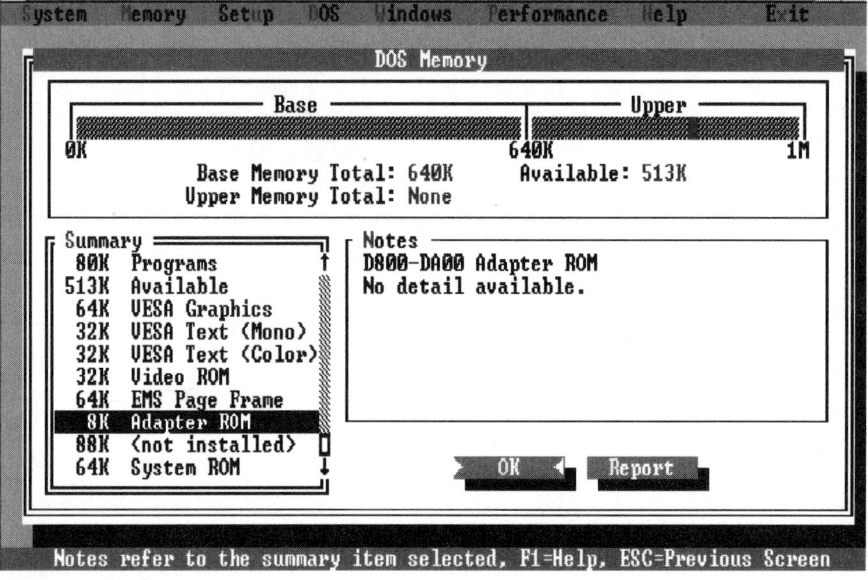

Figure 16.31 SYSINFO finds an optional ROM

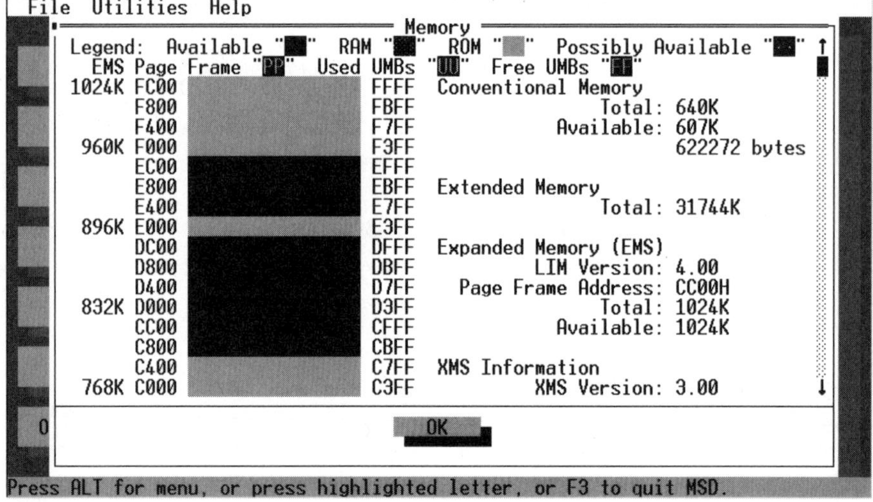

Figure 16.32 Detail from MSD showing optional ROM

pied by ROM BIOSes. EMM386 attempts to automatically detect optional BIOSes, but is notorious for failing to detect them, especially with versions of EMM386s before DOS 6.2. The best BIOS finder in existence today is the SYSINFO utility, enclosed with every copy of Touchstone's CheckIt (Figure 16.31). If you do not have SYSINFO, the next best choice is the free MSD utility that comes with DOS (Figure 16.32). It is a little hard to read, but it is better than a lot of system information programs that cost extra.

Be sure to always run from a clean boot when looking for ROMs.

Whenever you find BIOSes, first make sure that they keep the UMB contiguous. If a particular device does not allow the UMB to be contiguous, refer to the installation program for that device to determine how to move the BIOS.

EXCLUDING (X=) After locating a ROM chip, add the command X= to inform EMM386 that it should not attempt to load into that BIOS's addresses. Referring back to Figure 16.31, you run SYSINFO and see that there is an optional BIOS at location C800-C9FF. Go to the CONFIG.SYS file and add the X= statement to the EMM386.EXE line, as follows:

```
DEVICE=C:\DOS\HIMEM.SYS
DEVICE=C:\DOS\EMM386.EXE RAM FRAME=C800 X=C800-C9FF
DOS=UMB,HIGH
```

Notice that there's an EMS page frame set at C800 that overlaps the excluded area! What do you do with the page frame? You'll have to move it as well. Change the FRAME= statement to CA00, right above the excluded area:

```
DEVICE=C:\DOS\HIMEM.SYS
DEVICE=C:\DOS\EMM386.EXE RAM FRAME=CA00 X=C800-C9FF
DOS=UMB,HIGH
```

Add all the X= statements that you need to the EMM386 line. Here is a computer with three X= statements:

```
DEVICE=C:\DOS\HIMEM.SYS
DEVICE=C:\DOS\EMM386.EXE NOEMS X=C000-C7FF X=E000-E3FF X=D200-D7FF
DOS=UMB,HIGH
```

EMM386 assumes that you have a system ROM at F000-FFFF and a video BIOS at C000-C7FF. Anything else should be excluded.

INCLUDE (I=) Look at a screen from SYSINFO, shown in Figure 16.33. Note that the System BIOS is only 48K, from F400 to FFFF (SYSINFO calls the top of memory 10000). EMM386 assumes that the System BIOS is from F000 to FFFF. There is an extra 12K of memory, F000-F3FF, that you can

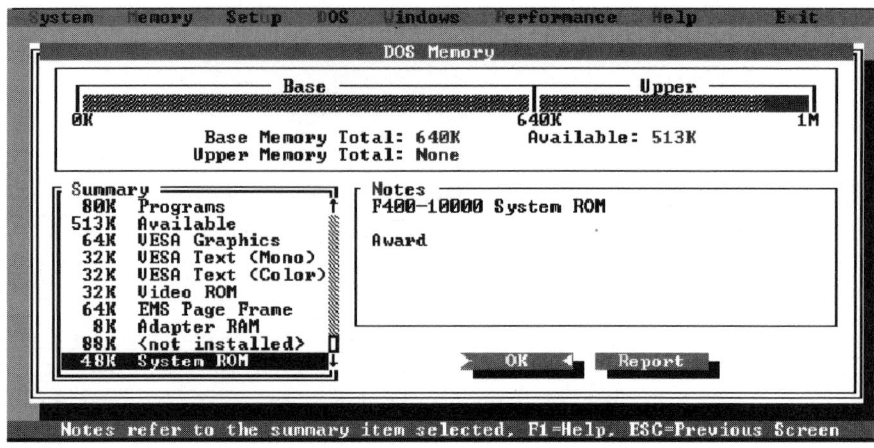

Figure 16.33
SYSINFO screen

use if you tell EMM386 to include it by adding the line I= to the EMM386 line:

```
DEVICE=C:\DOS\HIMEM.SYS
DEVICE=C:\DOS\EMM386.EXE RAM FRAME=CA01 X=C800-CA00 I=F000-F3FF
DOS=UMB,HIGH
```

FIND THE SNEAKY PROGRAMS THAT STEAL UMB SPACE Many programs will load themselves high without the help of Devicehigh= or LH statements. Two programs that do this are most mouse drivers and the SMARTDRV.EXE disk cache that comes with DOS. These programs are well behaved and report their presence to the memory manager so it knows what addresses they use and will not try to load anything high into their addresses. Many programs that load themselves (or at least part of themselves) high, however, that are not well behaved. They are notorious for locking up systems. Some scanners, PC cards, and SCSI device drivers do this. Unfortunately, the memory-management software currently available can rarely detect them. So here is a list of potentially dangerous devices. If you see one of these, read the documentation carefully to find memory areas you need to exclude:

- Token-ring network cards
- ATM and 100BaseT network cards
- All hand scanners
- Flatbed scanners
- SCSI host adapters that bus-master
- All PC cards (PCMCIA)
- Caching controller cards

Loading High

Once you have installed all of the necessary include and exclude statements, just dive into CONFIG.SYS and AUTOEXEC.BAT and start loading high. If you're lucky, you'll get a MEM /C/P that looks like this:

```
Name          Total =            Conventional +  Upper Memory
--------    ---------------    --------------  ------------
MSDOS         16,989  (17K)       16,989 (17K)          0 (0K)
HIMEM          1,168  (1K)         1,168 (1K)           0 (0K)
EMM386         3,120  (3K)         3,120 (3K)           0 (0K)
COMMAND        2,992  (3K)         2,992 (3K)           0 (0K)
ANSI           4,208  (4K)             0 (0K)       4,208 (4K)
CR_ATAPI      12,784  (12K)            0 (0K)      12,784 (12K)
VIBRA16       21,504  (21K)            0 (0K)      21,504 (21K)
CTMMSYS        8,160  (8K)             0 (0K)       8,160 (8K)
MOUSE         14,176  (14K)            0 (0K)      14,176 (14K)
MSCDEX        46,544  (45K)            0 (0K)      46,544 (45K)
SMARTDRV      30,368  (30K)            0 (0K)      30,368 (30K)
Free         651,808  (637K)     630,928 (616K)    20,880 (20K)
```

616K to 620K is about the best it can be. You will always have MSDOS, HIMEM, EMM386 and COMMAND in conventional memory. That's okay, because they have actually loaded themselves high and what you see in conventional memory are small "stubs" that link them to the parts that are loaded high. This brings to mind an important point—some stuff just isn't supposed to be loaded high. Never attempt to load the following device drivers high:

- SETVER.EXE
- HIMEM.SYS
- EMM386.EXE
- Any Plug-n-Play configuration manager, like CTCM.EXE

Any attempt to load these fellows high will result in either their not loading or locking up the system. Also be aware that some device drivers—really old ones—might lock up the system if you try to load them high. If you keep locking up, use the F8 key in DOS or the step-by-step menu option in Windows 95 to walk through CONFIG.SYS. You'll quickly find which device driver doesn't like being loaded high.

Another problem that can drive you crazy is device drivers that should load high, but never load into UMBs. You run MEM /C/P and see that there is plenty of room in the UMB—the size of the program is smaller than the free UMB space—but no luck. This can be due to one of two reasons. First, many device drivers (and TSRs) have their own .INI or .CFG file that tells them whether they can load high or not. All the LHs and

DEVICEHIGHs in the world won't get them to load if their .INI says no. Look for .INI files and open them up. See if you can find a line that says Mem=low. It doesn't take a lot of skill to figure out that this line is the problem. Unfortunately, there are no standards on what to put in these files, so check the documentation or guess.

The second problem is that some device drivers/TSRs take a *lot* of RAM while loading and then shrink down. This is okay—if only you knew how big they would get. Amazingly, the best tool to determine this is good old MEMMAKER. Just run MEMMAKER and when it asks you if your system is running properly, say no. MEMMAKER will erase all its work, but will leave behind a little jewel of a text file called MEMMAKER.STS. As part of the configuration process, MEMMAKER runs a handy little program called Sizer, which measures how big and how small a device loads into memory. Here's a snippet from a MEMMAKER.STS file:

```
Command=D:\CR_ATAPI.SYS /D:MSCD000 /Q
Line=8
FinalSize=12832
MaxSize=20528
FinalUpperSizes=0
MaxUpperSizes=0
ProgramType=DEVICE
```

MaxSize is how large the device gets while loading, and FinalSize is what you see in MEM /C/P. In this example, there is almost a 7K difference. I've seen devices that take 70K to load and then shrink down to 14K! By the way, always try to load these first while there is still lots of UMB space.

You've been given a lot of tools in this section. But one tool is more important than any other—making sure to take your time with memory management. Be patient. When I'm performing memory management on a PC, I feel lucky if I can do it in 30 minutes and have to reboot the PC only 12 times!

Always make backup copies of CONFIG.SYS, AUTOEXEC.BAT, and SYSTEM.INI before you start!

CONFIG.SYS Memory Hogs

When people think of memory management, they tend to concentrate on loading high. Granted loading high is crucial, but there are a few other items in CONFIG.SYS and AUTOEXEC.BAT that warrant a little inspection. Many of the BUFFERS= options can be real memory hogs. This section looks at some of the most common CONFIG.SYS options and discusses their effect on memory use.

Only a few of the settings in CONFIG.SYS and AUTOEXEC.BAT have significant effects on memory. I've listed the biggest memory hogs and most noteworthy ones here.

BUFFERS

```
BUFFERS=20
BUFFERS=15,3
```

Each buffer takes 532 bytes, and each look-ahead buffer takes 512 bytes. The BUFFERS= statement can be a huge memory hog. Plus, if you are running a disk cache like SMARTDRV, you almost certainly won't need the BUFFERS statement. If you leave out the BUFFERS statement, you will get 15 buffers, which should be plenty. You can save a little memory by setting BUFFERS to 6. I leave out the BUFFERS statement unless I receive an error statement that contains the word *buffers*.

Under DOS 5.0 and later, if HIMEM.SYS is running, DOS stores all buffers into unused space in the HMA, saving conventional memory. After loading part of MS-DOS into the HMA with the DOS=HIGH command, there is usually space for 40 to 44 buffers. If your BUFFERS= statement asks for more buffers than the HMA can handle, *all* buffers will be stored in conventional memory. The look-ahead value is essentially a very early form of disk caching. This value is obsolete.

STACKS

```
STACKS=9,256
STACKS=32,128
(the number of stacks × the size of each stack × 2 = the approxi-
mate memory usage (9,256 = 9 × 256 × 2 = 4608 bytes memory used)
```

The STACKS statement is rarely needed in today's PCs. If you don't have a STACKS statement, you get STACKS=9,128, which takes roughly 2K. You can get that memory back by using the line STACKS=0,0.

FILES

```
FILES=15
FILES=99
```

The first eight file handles take a total of 192 bytes. Each file handle, after the first eight, takes approximately 40 to 64 bytes, depending on the DOS version. Windows 3.*x* really likes to have file handles for DOS applications. You can add file handles for DOS applications without using the FILES= statement. Go to the SYSTEM.INI file, the [386Enh] section, and add the line PerVMFilesxx, where *xx* is the number of file handles you want for DOS programs. Be careful—if you run out of file handles in Windows, you will get an unrecoverable application error (UAE). Whenever I get a UAE in Windows, the first thing I check is the FILES= or PerVMFiles= statements.

FCBS

```
FCBS=4,0
FCBS=8
```

Each open file takes 60 bytes. The maximum number of open files has no effect on memory.

SHELL

```
SHELL=C:\DOS\COMMAND.COM /P /E:512
SHELL=C:\COMMAND.COM /P C:\COMMAND.COM
```

Because you always have a copy of COMMAND.COM running, the SHELL= statement doesn't take any more memory than not having one. The /E:*nnnnn* statement adds its size to low memory minus 256 bytes. For example, a setting of /E:512 takes (512 - 256 = 256) bytes of memory.

RAMDRIVE.SYS

```
DEVICE=C:\DOS\RAMDRIVE.SYS 2048
```

The 2048K is the amount of extended memory that is to be turned into the RAM drive. You can use as little as 64K and as much as 16,384K (16MB) for a RAM drive. Although RAMDRIVE.SYS uses relatively little conventional memory, by definition it takes away large chunks of extended memory.

Windows 3.*x* and 95 still support RAMDRIVE.SYS. Just for fun, add a RAM drive to your system and watch everyone go crazy trying to figure out what the heck that tiny hard drive is doing in Windows Explorer! Then take it out and never use it again.

DOS Mouse Drivers

DOS mouse drivers are possibly the single largest memory hogs in the AUTOEXEC.BAT file. They are also notorious for expanding to a huge size while loading, then shrinking down to a lower size. This can make it tough to load a mouse driver high. Let's say you have 30K of UMB space to load a mouse driver. When you run MEM /C/P, it will look like this:

```
Name     Total =          Conventional +     Upper Memory
-----    ------------     --------------     ------------
MOUSE    23,760 (23K)     23,760 (23K)       0 (0K)
```

So there should be plenty of room in UMB to load this driver, right? Well, you add the LH to the front of the MOUSE line in AUOTEXEC.BAT (LH MOUSE), you reboot, run MEM /C/P, and the mouse driver is still in low memory! This is because the mouse driver is bigger than 30K while loading, then shrinks down to 23K after it is loaded. You can't do anything about this.

If you knew how big the mouse driver would be while loading, then maybe you could make enough temporary space for it. The secret here is to run MEMMAKER. Just run MEMMAKER—you can even use the Express Setup option. The last question MEMMAKER asks after rebooting your PC a few times is: "Does your computer seem to be running properly?" Say no. MEMMAKER will then abort everything it did and restore the original CONFIG.SYS and AUTOEXEC.BAT files. However, MEMMAKER will leave you the text file MEMMAKER.STS. Look for it in your C:\DOS directory. As mentioned earlier in the chapter, MEMMAKER.STS is created by MEMMAKER and stores all the information on every driver in the CONFIG.SYS and AUTOEXEC.BAT. Here's the entry for the MOUSE driver in MEMMAKER.STS:

```
Command=d:\mouse\mouse.exe
Line=7
FinalSize=24096
MaxSize=58480
FinalUpperSizes=24096
MaxUpperSizes=24096
ProgramType=PROGRAM
```

Note that MaxSize and FinalSize are different. MaxSize is the memory required while the driver is loading, and FinalSize is the amount of memory required after loading. Anytime you have a device that won't load high—and you know there is enough space to load it—use MEM-MAKER.STS to check its load and final sizes.

MSCDEX

MSCDEX, which you can use to give your CD-ROM drive a drive letter, is another nasty in the "takes a lot of memory" department. There are a few tricks you can do to reduce its memory usage. Normally, MSCDEX looks something like this:

```
MSCDEX /D:ATAPI_000
```

When MSCDEX loads into memory, it loads two different pieces: the program and the buffer. The program is MSCDEX himself, and the buffer is the part of MSCDEX that, like the DOS BUFFERS= command, stores files being read from the CD-ROM drive. You can't see the separation between the program and the buffers as they load together, but if there isn't enough UMB space for both the program and the buffer, the buffer will be loaded high and the program will be loaded low. This can look rather strange when you run MEM /C/P:

```
Name     Total =        Conventional +  Upper Memory
------   ------------   --------------  ------------
MSCDEX   27,936 (27K)   12,948 (13K)     14,188 (14K)
```

The 13K in low memory is the program, and the 14K in UMB is the buffer. On most systems, if you are running SMARTDRV.EXE—and you should be—you can set the buffers part of your MSCDEX to a small value by using the /M:*xxxx* switch. Each buffer is roughly 2100 bytes. By default, the buffer's size is 6, for a total size of 12,618 bytes. So if the default is 6, how low can you go? Unfortunately, 0 won't work, and neither will 1. The smallest value for this setting is 4, which means that, at about 2100 bytes per buffer, you can save over 4K of valuable UMB space by reducing the value to 6. So a MSCDEX setting should look like this:

```
MSCDEX /D:ATAPI_000 /M:4
```

If, for some strange reason, you have no desire to use a disk cache, you will need to increase the number of buffers beyond 6. It is entirely possible to set the number of buffers to an astronomical value, such as 200, but this will require over 400K of conventional memory, which is counterproductive. In order to minimize the hit on memory, you can load the buffers into expanded memory with the /E option. Of course, you must first create expanded memory out of extended memory, but this is no problem since everybody has too much RAM on their computers anyway. Do you see how silly this is? Just use SMARTDRV to cache the CD-ROM drive and be done with it.

SMARTDRIVE

The SMARTDRV disk cache can take a fair amount of conventional memory (24K), but as soon as UMBs are created it automatically loads high, thus freeing conventional memory. In fact, SMARTDRV will load into noncontiguous UMBs if necessary.

Settings for SMARTDRV allow users to specify how much extended memory is allocated for the disk cache in either DOS or Windows 3.1. Why Windows 3.1 and not 3.11 or Windows for Workgroups? Because these two versions of Windows provide a protected-mode replacement for SMARTDRV called VCACHE. (See the Windows chapter for more information regarding setting up VCACHE, and setting up SMARTDRV under VCACHE). For non-VCACHE use, the command line for SMARTDRV is relatively straightforward:

```
c:\dos\smartdrv.exe 2048 2048
```

Place this line into AUTOEXEC.BAT after MSCDEX.EXE (if present) in order to provide disk caching for the CD-ROM drive. The amount of memory set aside for the disk cache can be any value, up to the limit of available extended (XMS) memory. Making the cache larger, however, won't necessarily increase the performance. With a cache size of 2MB (2048K), most users will find a cache "hit" rate of between 80 and 90 percent. By doubling the cache size, you might see a 3 to 7 percent performance improvement as measured by the cache hit rate, but the *overall* system performance will, on a system with 16MB of RAM or less, actually *decrease*. This is because the total system memory available to Windows has been reduced by the increased size of the SMARTDRV cache, this in turn forces Windows to use more virtual memory, and virtual memory is on the slow hard drive—which you want to use as seldom as possible! So in this case, more is definitely not better.

So how can you tell where SMARTDRV is loaded and how much memory it occupies? Again, you can rely on the command MEM /C/P run from the DOS prompt:

```
Modules using memory below 1 MB:

Name       Total =         Conventional +   Upper Memory
--------   -------------   --------------   --------------
MSDOS       12,989 (13K)   12,989    (13K)     0       (0K)
HIMEM        1,168 (1K)       1,168 (1K)       0       (0K)
EMM386       3,128 (3K)       3,128 (3K)       0       (0K)
COMMAND      2,928 (3K)       2,928 (3K)       0       (0K)
SMARTDRV    27,936 (24K)     12,948 (13K)   14,188   (14K)
Free       764,608 (747K)  635,072 (620K)  120,536   (127K)

Memory Summary:

Type of Memory    Total =     Used +       Free
--------------   ---------   ---------   ---------
Conventional       655,360      20,288     635,072
Upper              158,560      29,024     129,536
Reserved           393,216     393,21            0
Extended (XMS)   7,181,472   2,323,616   4,857,856
--------------   ---------   ---------   ---------
Total memory     8,388,608   2,766,144   5,622,464

Total under 1 MB   813,920      49,312     764,608

Press any key to continue. . . .

Largest executable program size         634,976    (620K)
Largest free upper memory block         129,480    (126K)
MS-DOS is resident in the high memory area
```

By looking at the chart under the heading "Modules using memory below 1 MB," you can see that yes, SMARTDRV is loaded on this system. If you look further down, we can see that some XMS memory is also being used. But how much is used by SMARTDRV for a disk cache? To determine this, you need to use another command from the DOS prompt: SMARTDRV /S. This will give the following information:

```
Microsoft SMARTDrive Disk Cache version 5.01
Copyright 1991,1993 Microsoft Corp.

Room for 256 elements of 8,192 bytes each
There have been 3 cache hits
and 10 cache misses

Cache size: 2,097,152 bytes
Cache size while running Windows: 2,97,152 bytes

Disk Caching Status
drive   read cache  write cache  buffering
------------------------------------------
A:      yes         no           no
B:      yes         no           no
C:      yes         no           no

Write behind data will be committed before command prompt returns,

For help, type Smartdrv /?
```

But wait, there's more! Notice that each of the 256 elements or "chunks" of data is 8192 bytes in size. Disk caching works under the "If I needed it once, I'll probably need it again" rule, which also says "If I need a piece of a file, I'll probably need more of the same file soon." You can tell SMART-DRV to grab extra data from the disk with a simple addition to the SMARTDRV command line in AUTOEXEC.BAT.

Adding the /b: switch to the end of SMARTDRV will tell SMARTDRV to load additional data from the disk into its read-ahead buffers by increasing the size of these buffers. But remember there is no such thing as a free lunch. The increase in buffer size comes at the expense of additional memory required by SMARTDRV. By doubling the size from the default of 16KB to 32K with the /b:32000 switch, you will find that SMARTDRV also requires an additional 16K of memory. If it can find this memory in UMBs, great; if not, then it must take up some conventional memory instead.

CHAPTER 17

Testing Power

In this chapter, you will:

- Understand basic electrical theory.
- See how household circuits work.
- Learn how to use a voltmeter to test power and power supplies.
- Understand the function of different electrical components and their symbols.
- Understand how a PC power supply works.

This chapter goes into great detail about electrical power and power supplies. In fact, this is—as far as I'm aware—the first attempt to discuss such a topic in detail for PC repair. In today's "board swap" world, many fellow technicians might wonder about the necessity of this level of depth. I feel that the small investment of time learning electrical power and how your PC uses it is well worth it. However, there are two good arguments—possibly opinions—I must address before beginning this chapter.

> Argument #1: Power supplies are cheap; if it's bad, just throw it away!

I agree with this *most* of the time, but how do you know a power supply is bad? Because the PC won't turn on? There is so much more to a power supply than just that! In this chapter, I will describe the myriad of problems that take place within the power supply—problems where a PC runs, but receives poor or incorrect power. These are problems that destroy data and the hard drives that store data, problems that make a PC reboot, problems that create bizarre CMOS errors, and other so called "intermittent" problems that distract you from the real problem: the power supply. So I would argue that understanding the power supply is important in determining that the power supply is bad.

> Argument #2: Once I know that the power supply is bad, I can't believe it's cost-effective to replace individual components.

But sometimes it *is* cost-effective. A decent power supply costs about $60 to $100. If you can locate a bad component and replace it in about 30 minutes, it's well worth it! But you have to invest in one aspect of training that this chapter doesn't cover; you have to learn how to solder. Go to an electronics store, get a $25 soldering kit, and sweet-talk an electrician buddy to show you how! It's not hard, but it takes a little practice. If you can solder, then this chapter will be that much more helpful.

Understanding Electricity

Electricity is simply a flow of negatively charged particles, called electrons, through matter. All matter allows the flow of electrons to some extent. Materials in which electrons move freely are called *conductors*. As you can probably guess, metallic wire is a very good conductor. The amount of electrons moving past a certain point on a wire is called the *current*, which is measured in units called *amperes* (abbreviated *amps* or *A*). The "pressure" of the electrons through the wire is called *voltage* and is measured in units called *volts* (V). Electricity comes in two flavors: *direct current* (DC), where the electrons flow in one direction around a continuous circuit, and *alternating current* (AC), where the flow of electrons alternates direction back and forth in a circuit (Figure 17.1).

Your PC uses DC voltage. The voltage supplied by the local power company is AC. You have to convert the AC to DC, which is done by the power supply. The power supply in a computer is designed to convert 115 V AC power to both 5 V and 12 V DC power (Figure 17.2). If the AC voltage going into the power supply is not correct, then the output DC voltage will be intolerable to the PC circuits, and the PC will function improperly or not at all.

PCs need steady, reliable power to their components. A technician must be able to test the entire power system (power supply and distribution), which means testing the AC supply coming to the computer as well as the DC power supply going to the PC circuits. Testing AC verifies that the electricity coming from the power company and into the power supply is correct, and testing DC means that the power coming from the

Figure 17.1 Alternating current (AC) vs. direct current (DC)

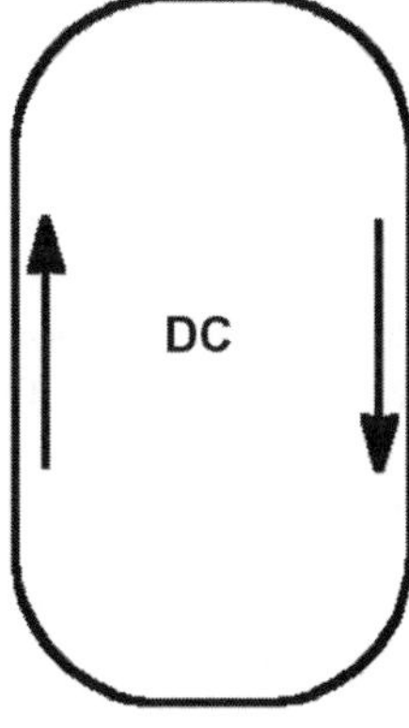

Constant voltage in one direction

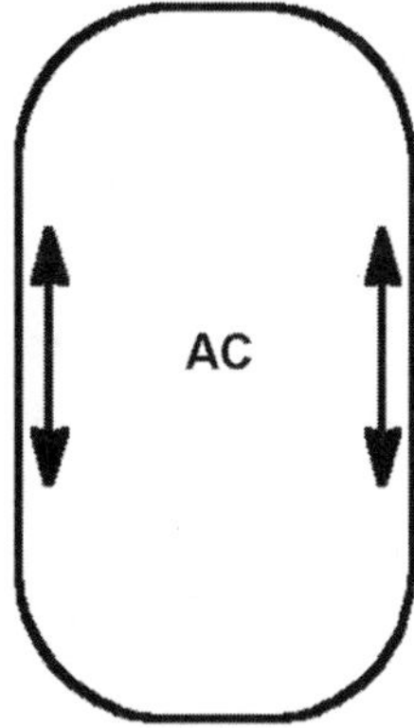

Voltage in both directions, constantly switching back and forth

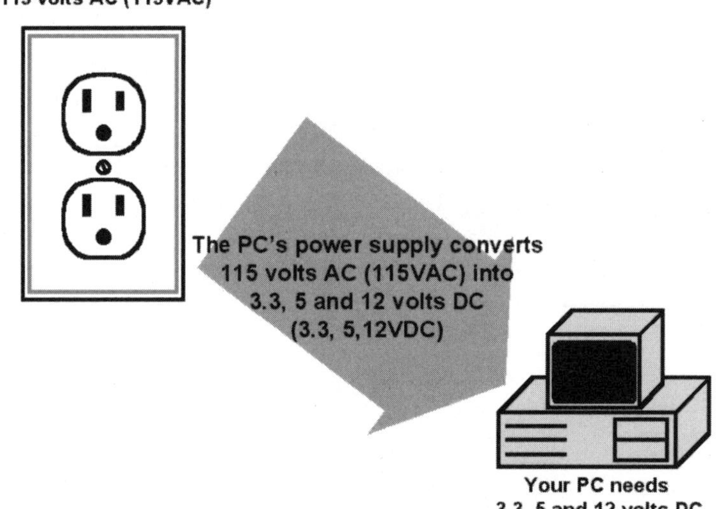

Figure 17.2 The power supply's job

power supply into the PC components is correct. Let's look at AC and DC testing separately.

AC Power

AC power means that the flow of electrons "alternates" direction in the wires. It is a much more efficient way to transport power over long distances, and is used in more types of electrical equipment. The frequency that the flow of electricity alternates in an AC power supply is measured in cycles per second, or Hertz (Hz).

All standard electrical power in the U.S. is AC, approximately 115 volts and 60 Hz (Figure 17.3). The outlets into which you plug toasters, TVs, and computers provide access to the power supplied by the power company. These outlets are usually three-prong connections. The smaller rectangular hole is called the *hot,* the larger rectangular hole is called the *neutral,* and the small round hole is called the *ground.* The combination of hot and neutral wires supplies the path for the alternating current; they can be traced all the way back to the generator at the power station. Two black wires, each providing 115 volts AC, are run into your fuse box from the power pole. The neutral is the return wire, which runs from the plug, out to your fuse box, and along its own wire back to the power company. It's the bare wire that runs from your fuse box to the power pole. Some equipment, such as electric stoves, clothes dryers, and water heaters, might occasionally need 230 V. This is done by combining the two 115 V lines to a special outlet.

As the neutral returns to the power company, a series of safety connections called *grounds* are placed at certain intervals. Grounds are simply connections between the neutral and the earth. These connections are at your fuse box and every power pole. They are sort of like an emergency dump. In a short circuit, a large flow (amps) of electricity is discharged all at once. This short will burn out circuits unless it can be "dumped" somewhere fast. See Figure 17.4.

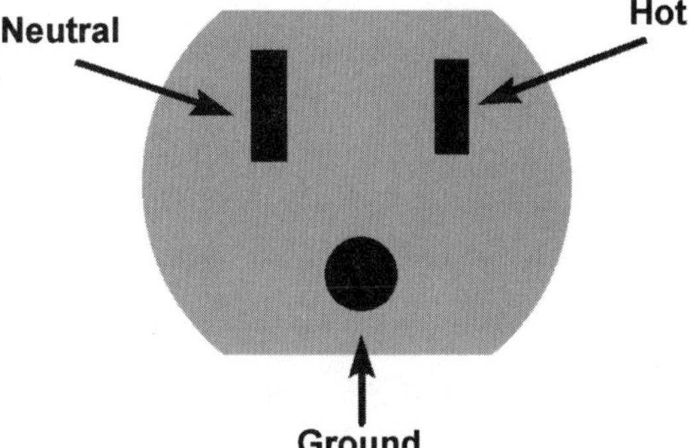

Figure 17.3 Household 115-volt outlet

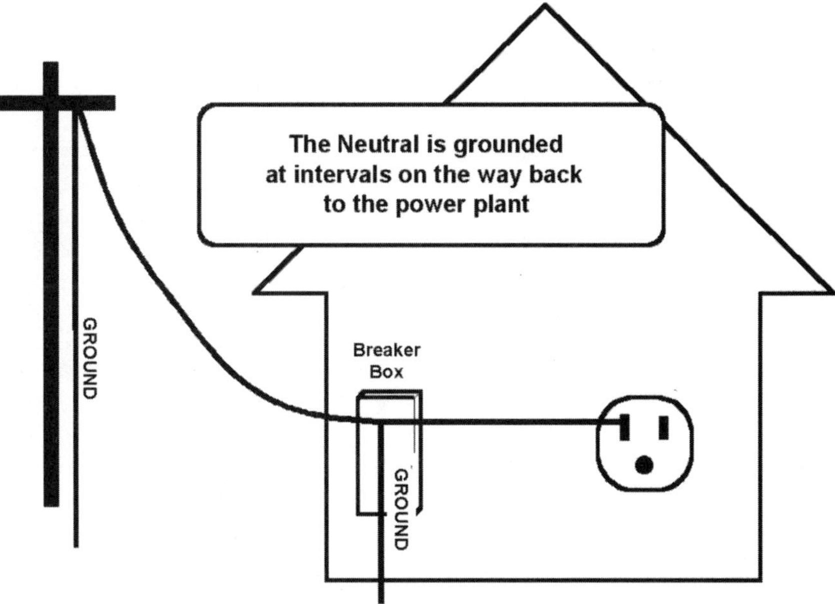

Figure 17.4 Neutral's job

So if the neutrals are connected to ground, what is the ground plug for? Imagine a short circuit, where the current seeks the path of least resistance back to its voltage source. For example, if the hot supply comes directly in contact with a case or cover that doesn't have a ground connected, it will sit there like a storm searching for something to hit. As a storm seeks a path of least resistance, so do electrons to a voltage source. If anything—or anyone—comes in contact with the case, it becomes a path for the current to travel from ground to the source, which is the hot supply.

This current flow can cause physical damage to both equipment and people. It can cause fires, component damage, permanent disability, even death. The ground plug is a direct connection to the earth. If the case is tied to one of the ground leads, then the current seeks the path of least resistance and will travel to earth without any harm to equipment or people in contact with it. See Figure 17.5.

Ground is a kind of safety circuit when an electrical device has a short (Figure 17.6). The ground wire is where the surge of electricity is dumped when a short circuit occurs. It also ensures that all the connected equipment is at the same potential (0 V). This is very important, especially on networks. It also serves as a direct line to discharge static electricity when servicing equipment.

Nongrounded plugs—plugs without the third ground wire—are *unacceptable* for use in PCs! Don't use them! This includes extension cords!

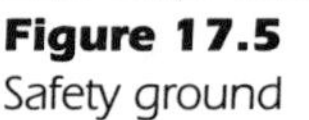

Figure 17.5
Safety ground

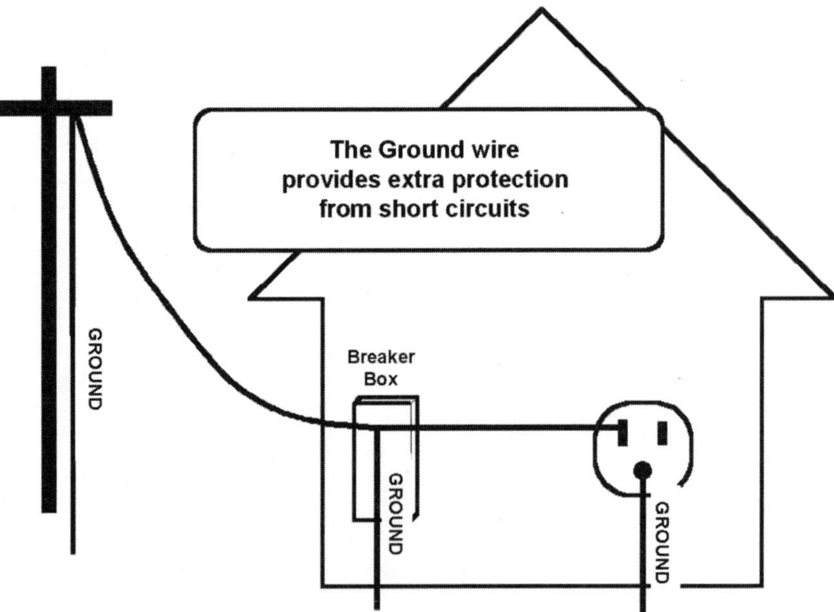

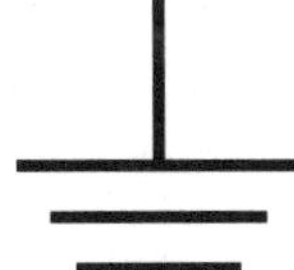

Figure 17.6
Electronic symbol for ground

Failure to properly test AC outlets will result in inoperable or destroyed equipment, as well as possible electrocution. Check all customer AC input voltages in all the equipment of any new installation. Don't assume that if you checked one socket, all the other inputs are wired correctly. When testing AC power, you want to check for three things: that the hot is outputting approximately 115 V, that the neutral is connected to ground, and that the ground is connected to ground. There are two ways to perform these three tests: with a multimeter or with special equipment.

I want to take a moment to explain multimeters. They are sensor devices that are used to measure aspects of electrical currents. All multimeters are designed to provide at least four major measurements: AC voltage, DC voltage, continuity, and resistance. A multimeter consists of two probes, an analog or digital meter, and a dial to set the type of test you want to perform. Refer to Figure 17.7 to become familiar with the different components of the multimeter.

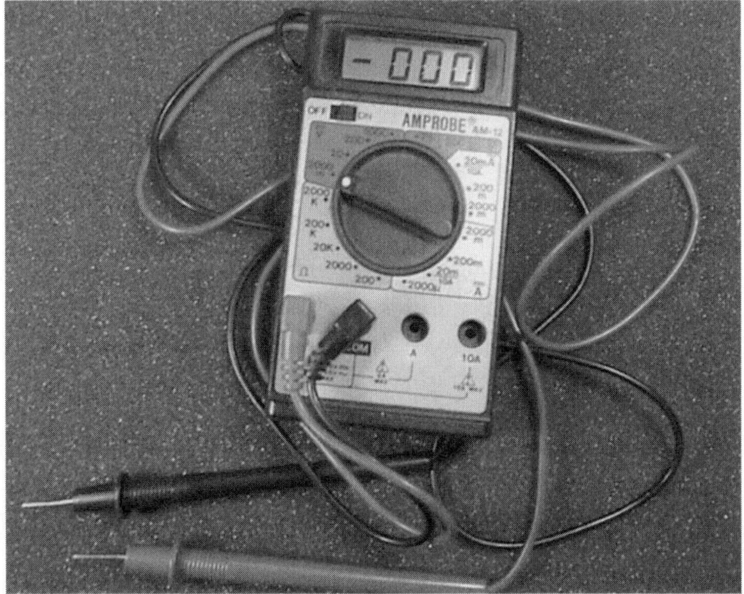

Figure 17.7
Digital volt-ohmmeter

The concept of measuring AC and DC voltage should be clear. The last two, however—continuity and resistance—might not be. I want to take a moment to make sure you understand these two important settings.

Continuity

Continuity is simply whether or not there is a connection. It determines breaks in wires and components (Figure 17.8). A multimeter will determine continuity by lights or beeps. If you don't have a continuity setting, use the resistance setting (explained in the next section). If the multimeter shows infinite resistance, then there is *no* continuity (see Figure 17.9); if the multimeter shows no resistance, then there *is* continuity.

Resistance

Resistance is the measure of how much a wire or component "resists" the flow of current. Resistance is measured in units called *ohms,* and the symbol for an ohm is Ω. The resistance measurement will be discussed in detail later in this chapter. Now that you have somewhat of an understanding of how a multimeter works, let's use one to test an AC electrical outlet.

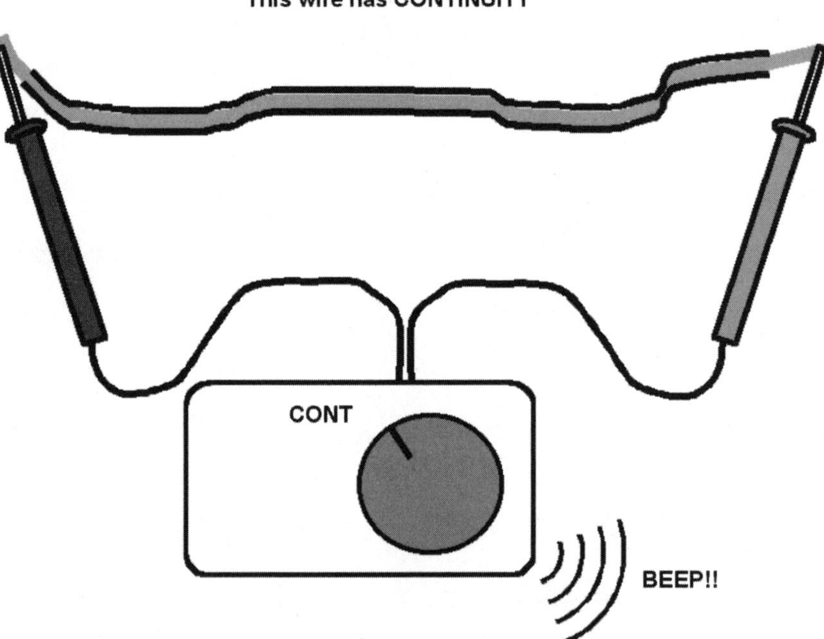
This wire has CONTINUITY
CONT
BEEP!!

Figure 17.8 Continuity

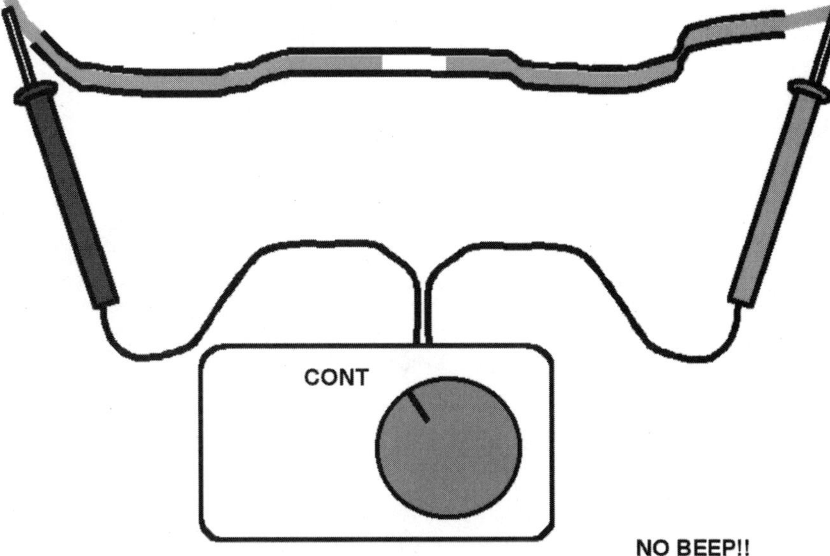
This wire DOES NOT have CONTINUITY
CONT
NO BEEP!!

Figure 17.9
No continuity

Using a Multimeter to Test AC Outlets

To set up the meter, follow these steps:

1. Place the black lead in the common (-) hole. If the black lead is permanently attached, ignore this step.
2. Place the red lead in the V-Ohm-A (+) hole. If the red lead is permanently attached, ignore this step.
3. Move the selector switch to the AC V (usually red). If there are multiple selections, put it to the first scale higher than 120 volts (usually 200 V). "Auto-range" meters set their own range; they don't need any selection except AC volts. See Figure 17.10.

Now, to read the meter:

1. Put either lead in hot, the other in neutral. You should read 110 to 120 volts AC.
2. Put either lead in hot, the other in ground. You should read 110 to 120 volts AC.
3. Put either lead in neutral, the other in ground. You should read 0 volts AC.

If any of these readings are different from what was described, it's time to call an electrician.

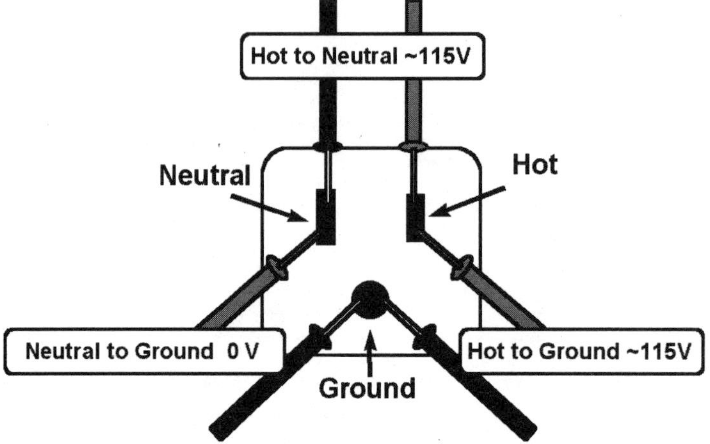

Figure 17.10
Outlet voltages

Using Special Equipment to Test AC Voltage

There are a number of good AC testers available (Figure 17.11). Simply by inserting these testers, all voltages for all combinations can be tested at the same time. Be sure to test all outlets the system uses: PC, external devices, and monitor. Although convenient, these devices aren't as accurate as a multimeter. My favorite tester is CAT #12200101, made by Radio Shack. This handy device provides three LEDs that describe everything that can go wrong with a plug. I use it heavily.

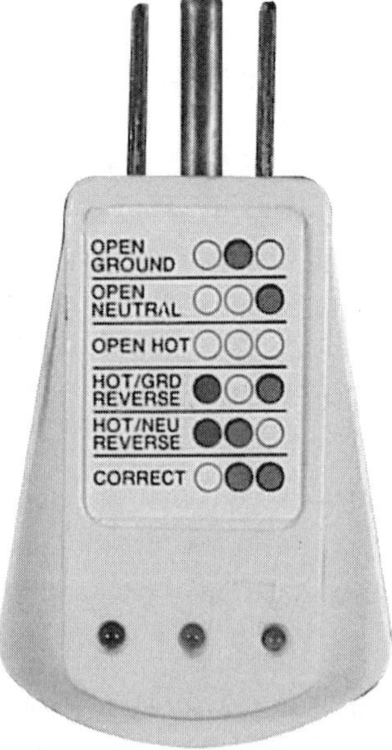

Figure 17.11
Circuit tester

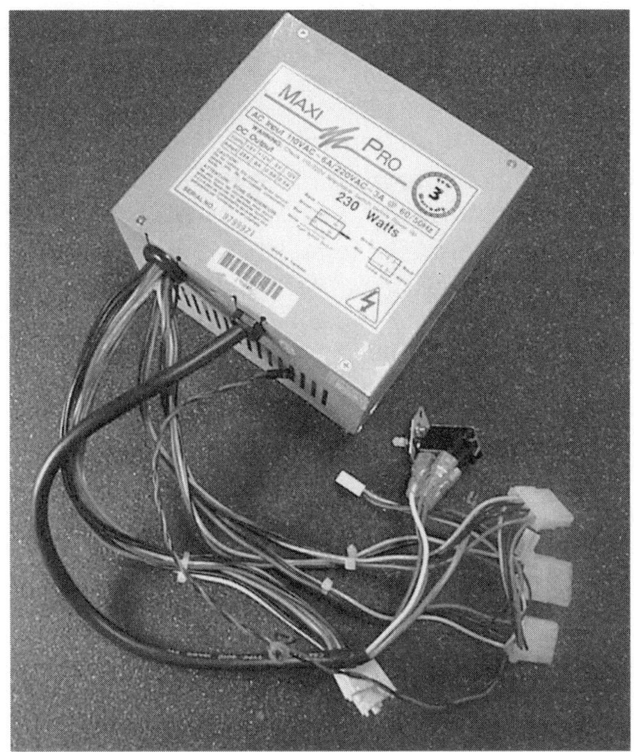

Figure 17.12
Power supply

DC Power

DC power is far simpler in concept than AC power. DC power is what comes out of your power supply and is used by the PC. In reality, your power supply does nothing more than turn 115 volts AC into 3.3, 5 and 12 volts DC (Figure 17.12). Your power supply is really an AC/DC converter or step-down transformer in one unit. Another example of this type of converting power supply is the small "sealed" AC unit that supplies power to small appliances like radios and electric shavers. The difference here is you can open the PC power supply and repair it.

Since DC flows in only one direction, the circuits have a distinct polarity, which points to the direction of the flow. There are the + and – you see when installing batteries in flashlights or radios (Figure 17.13).

Virtually all PC power supplies use the famous P8 and P9 (Figure 17.14) or P1 type connectors (Figure 17.15) to provide both positive and negative voltages. AC also has polarity, but it's not as great an issue because it changes direction 60 times a second.

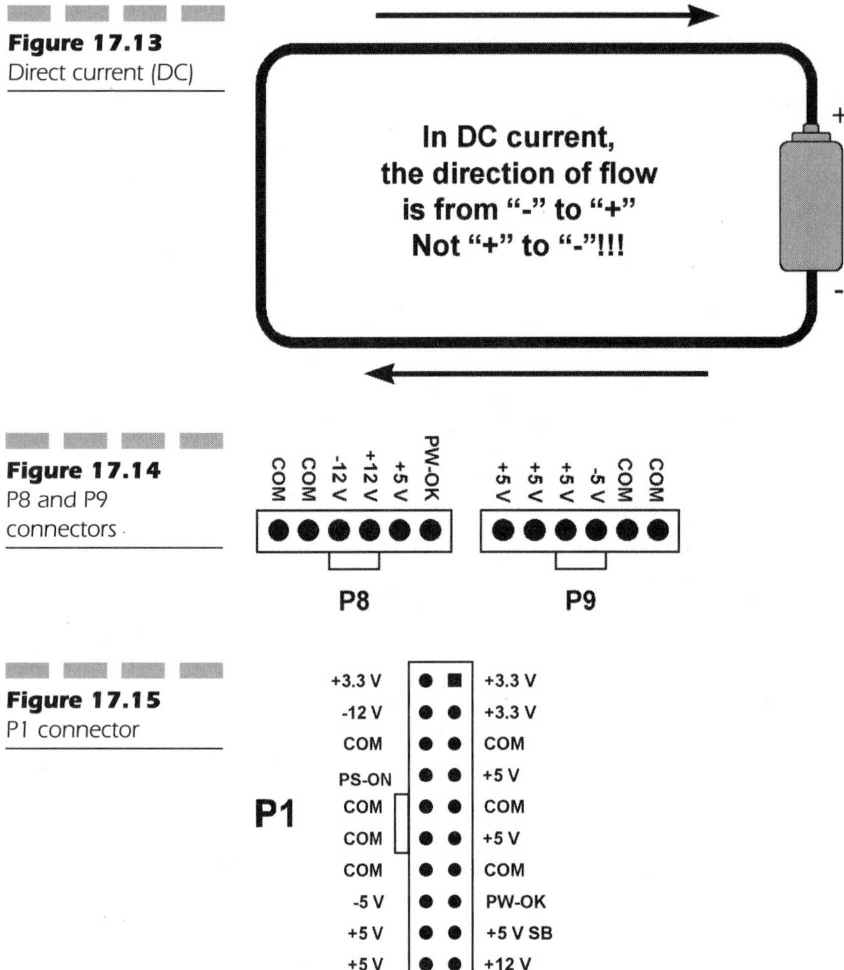

Figure 17.13 Direct current (DC)

Figure 17.14 P8 and P9 connectors

Figure 17.15 P1 connector

Testing DC

Probably a quarter of all PC problems can be traced to the power supply either directly or indirectly. A bad power supply can cause intermittent lockups and reboots, as well as intermittent boot-up difficulties. Bad power supplies can erase CMOS information and sometimes even destroy data on mass storage devices. I test a power supply at two levels, basic and advanced. A basic test just verifies voltages. An advanced test requires opening the power supply and performing component-level searches.

BASIC TEST The basic test simply verifies voltages. Most power supplies that are slowly dying begin to show their age by a reduction in voltage. Although this voltage drop shows up in the 3.3-volt, 5-volt and 12-volt outputs, it is more pronounced on the 12-volt side. Therefore, I concentrate all my testing there. Here's how to test for proper voltage using a multimeter:

1. Set the meter leads the same way as was done for AC testing. Turn the selector knob to DC-V, observing the scale if the multimeter doesn't auto-range. Most multimeters have a 15-volt DC range that's perfect for PC voltages.
2. Test voltages at the P8/P9 connectors. As shown in Figure 17.16, put the multimeter's black (ground) lead onto the black wire connection, and the red (positive) lead on the yellow +12-volt connection and read the voltages. A good voltage is between 11 and 13 volts. Between 10 and 11, you need a new power supply. Less than 10 volts, and you know why your PC won't boot!
3. When checking voltages with an analog meter, be sure you reverse the leads when checking negative voltages. The digital meter can remain the same, except it will show you a negative sign with the reading.

Make sure to isolate the problem when no voltage is present. Hook up your meter leads as described above, turn off the ac power, disconnect all

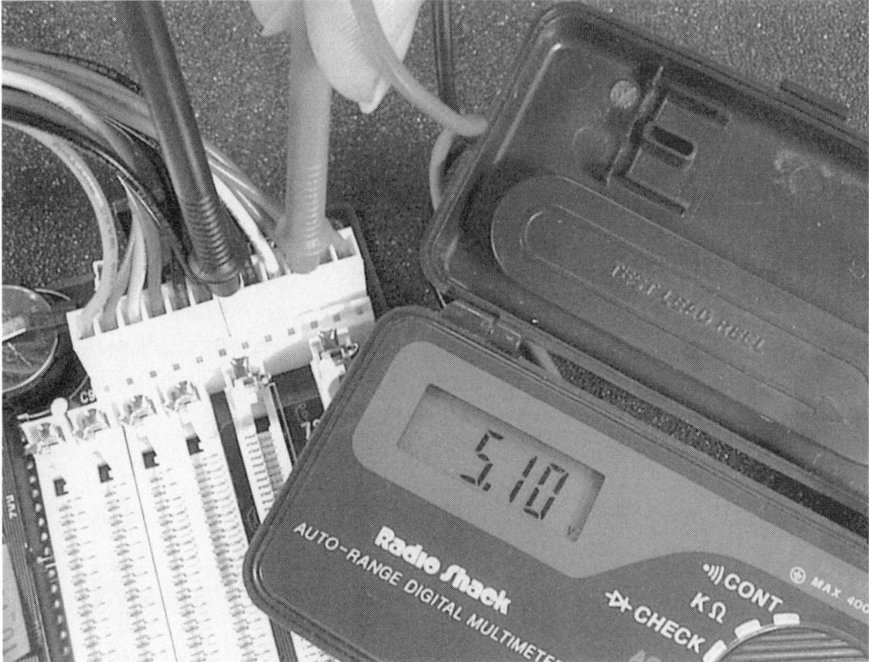

Figure 17.16
Testing voltage

the Molex plugs from the devices, and turn the power back on. If power is present on the motherboard, then one of the devices is bad and has caused the power supply to shut down. It is now a simple matter of reconnecting each Molex plug until the guilty device is found. If no voltages are present, turn the power back off and reconnect all Molex plugs, then remove P8 and P9 from the motherboard. Turn the power back on (still checking the wires in P8 and P9) and, if the voltage is now present, there is a motherboard problem.

If the power supply stopped working when you added a new device, such as a CD-ROM drive, it might not be the power supply's problem. It might just be too small. Most PC's today come equipped with a 230-watt rated power supply, which is usually more than ample. But if you have an unusual setup, for instance two to three CD-ROM drives, four to five hard drives, or any device that draws more current than your power supply can deliver, you will have to replace it with a larger one. A rule of thumb is "Start with 200 watts. Then, for every two drives, increase your power supply by 50 watts."

ADVANCED TEST The basic test is designed as a quick test. However, many other problems can cause failures. The single biggest symptom pointing to a more serious problem is intermittent rebooting. Also, if you check all output voltages using the basic testing methods and one or all voltages are missing, you must remove the cover to troubleshoot. This advanced procedure is a serious kind of "Is this power supply worth saving or not?" type of test.

Before beginning the advanced test, however, you must understand how a power supply really works. A power supply consists of three major areas: the switching network, the transformer, and the voltage regulator (Figure 17.17).

SWITCHING NETWORK Ac power coming from the power company is imperfect at best. It can have sudden increases in voltage called "spikes" and decreases in voltage called "sags." Significant long-term increases in voltage (more than a few seconds) are called *amplitude increases*. The cycles per second can vary wildly. While these problems might not bother a

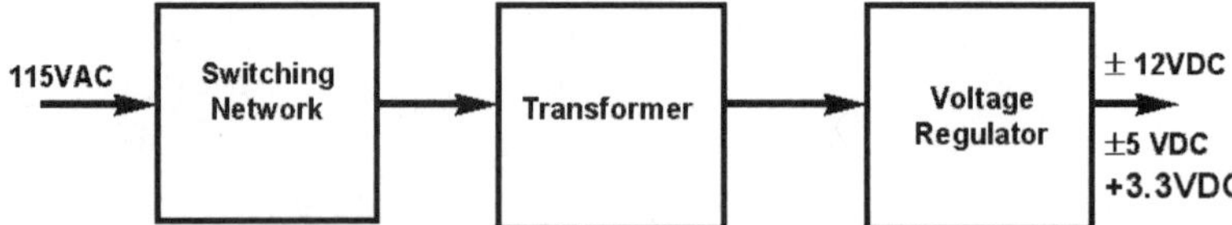

Figure 17.17 Main units of a switching power supply

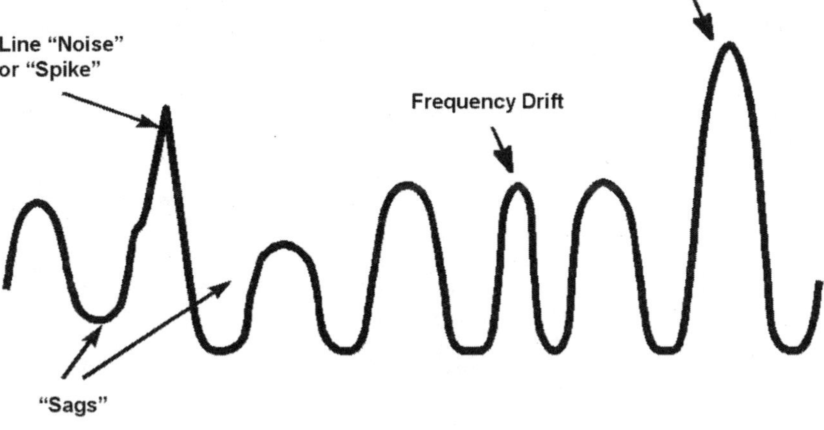

Figure 17.18 Problems with AC voltage

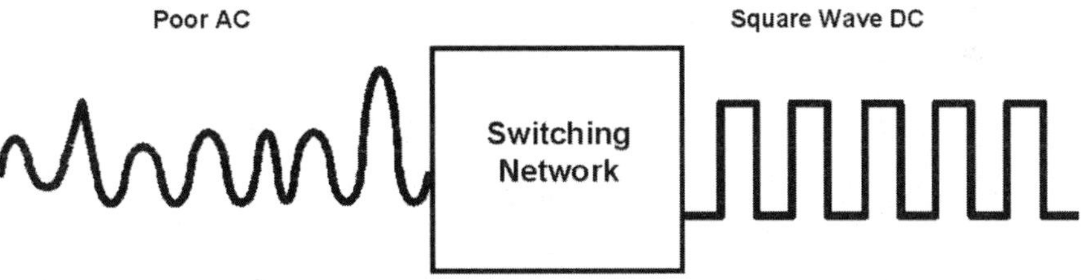

Figure 17.19 Switching network

toaster or washing machine, they can cause havoc to a power supply. See Figure 17.18.

The switching network first cleans and converts the input ac by using a rectifier to change AC into DC (Figure 17.19). This removes spikes, sags, and noise. The dc is converted into a very special *square-wave DC*. This type of DC is very dependable compared to the AC coming from the outlet, and is much easier for the rest of the power supply to modify into pure, regulated DC. The term "switching power supply" comes from the way the switching network converts the AC to DC and back to AC.

TRANSFORMER The transformer has a very simple function. It reduces the voltage of the square-wave DC into separate 12-volt and 5-volt square-wave AC circuits. See Figure 17.20.

VOLTAGE REGULATOR The voltage regulator section performs three functions. First, it converts the AC output of the transformer into +12, –12, and +5 volts DC by using three separate rectifiers; second, it "regulates" the voltage to a constant output level; and third, it monitors the amount of current being used by the computer circuits (Figure 17.21). The

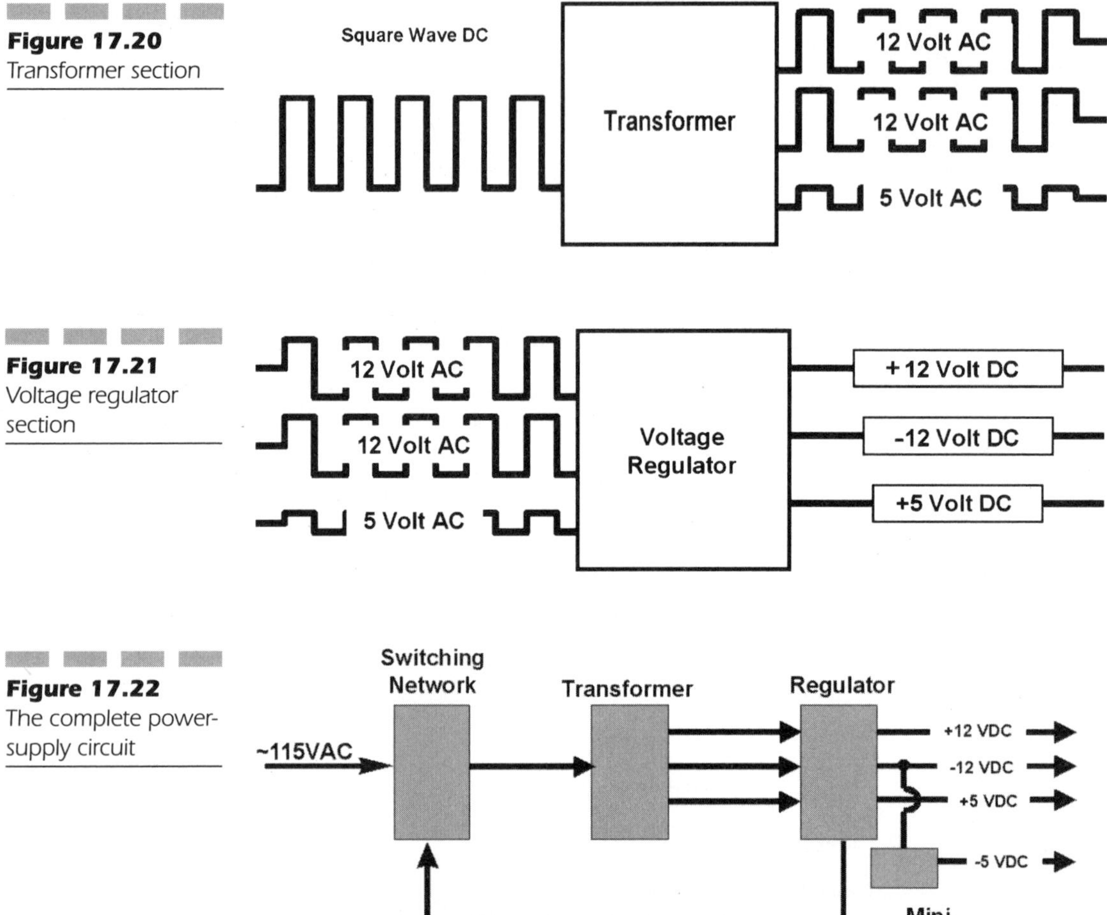

Figure 17.20 Transformer section

Figure 17.21 Voltage regulator section

Figure 17.22 The complete power-supply circuit

regulating output stage is in constant touch with the switching network via a special *feedback circuit*.

There is one other voltage (–5 volts) used by ancient RAM cards, ancient PC and XT floppy controllers, some POST cards, and—as far a I can tell—nothing else. So even if you have some bizarre device that actually uses –5 volts, it will take a trivial amount of current. However, power-supply makers want to be backwardly compatible, so they continue to provide –5-volt current. Power-supply manufacturers known that you won't need much –5-volt current, so they simply add a mini-voltage regulator off the –12 volts (see Figure 17.22). Now look at the "big picture" of a switching power supply (Figure 17.23). As you can see, all

Figure 17.23
Power supply, an internal view

the components are soldered to a single board. This "component board" is held to the case of the power supply by a few screws, and can easily be removed.

Do not open the power supply while it is plugged in! Do not open the power supply until you have discharged it!

DISCHARGING A POWER SUPPLY Early power supplies needed to be discharged (Figure 17.24). Although I haven't seen a power supply that needs to be discharged in a long time, I still do it every time I need to work on it. Use a screwdriver to discharge the power supply before you open it! Place a regular screwdriver between the ground and either pole in the outside male AC connector plug to discharge it.

Armed with a solid conceptual knowledge of how a power supply works, let's inspect each of the three major parts in detail in order to understand how they work and how to test them. Zeroing in on the component board (Figure 17.25), you can see the different components that create the three functional groups of the power supply.

Figure 17.24 Discharging a power supply

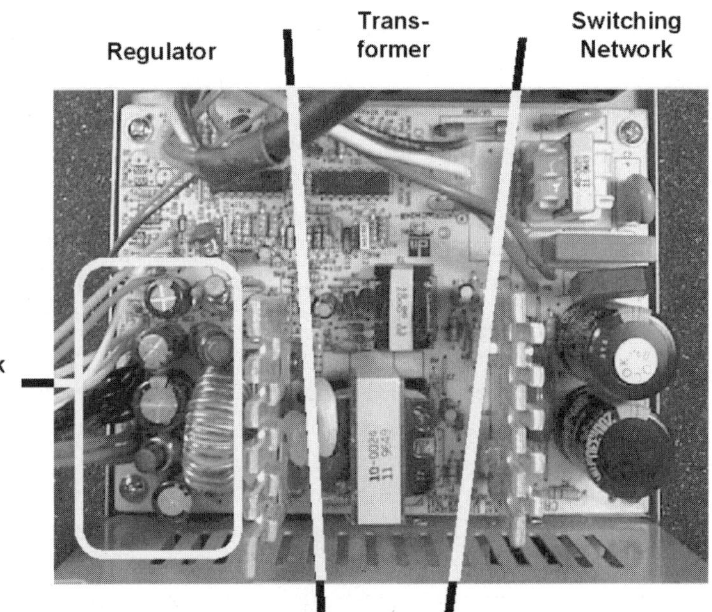

Figure 17.25 View of all sections

Switching Network

As described earlier, the switching network receives the ac power from the outlet via the power cord. The main responsibility of this section is to:

- Filter out spurious electrical noise (spikes, sags).
- Eliminate frequency changes (make sure it stays at a constant 60 cycles).
- Convert the AC sine-wave signals to square-wave AC signals.

The main components in this section (Figure 17.26) are as follows:

- Fuses
- Capacitors
- Rectifiers
- Switching transistors

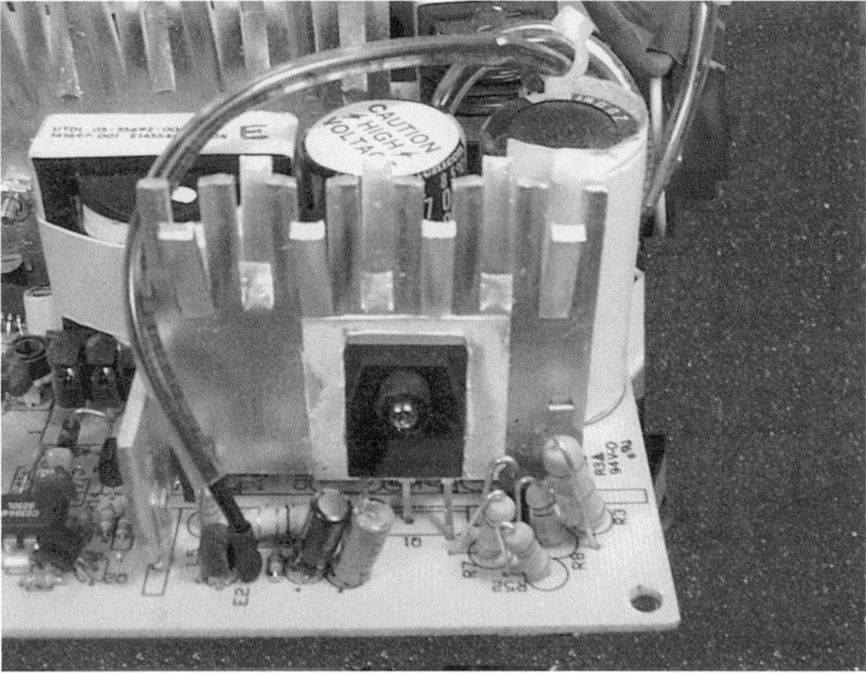

Figure 17.26
View of capacitors and switching transistors

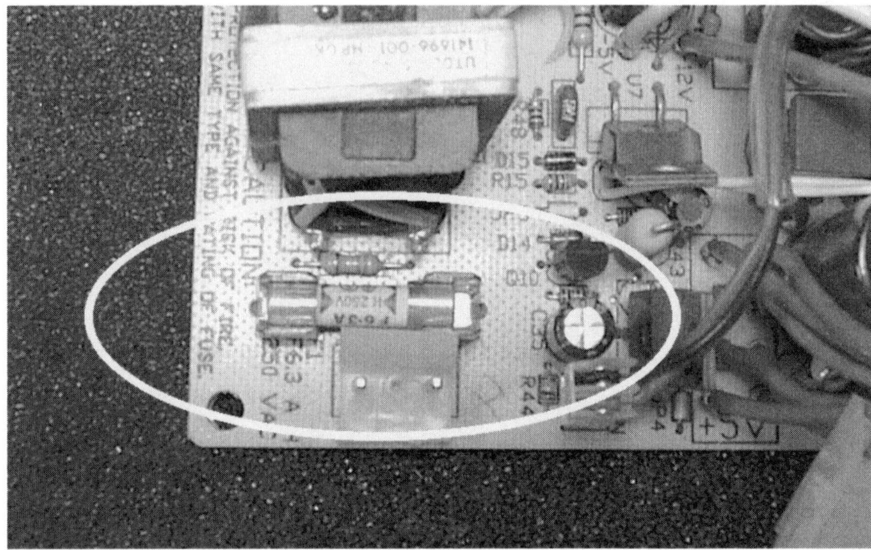

Figure 17.27
Close-up of fuse

Figure 17.28
Electronic symbol for fuse

Fuses

A *fuse* is a small piece of wire, usually stored inside a clear glass tube, that is designed to "melt" (burn) open if more than a certain amount of current flows through it (Figures 17.27 and 17.28). Therefore, all fuses have an amperage (A) rating. Almost all input voltage regulator fuses carry a 15A rating. Look on the metal ends to check the amperage rating for your fuse.

If a fuse is bad, the PC won't power up. A bad fuse is often obvious—the wire inside the tube will be broken or there will be a black residue inside the tube. To test, simply perform a continuity or resistance test, as described earlier in this chapter.

Capacitors

Capacitors are like rechargeable batteries and are used to even-out current flows. The switching circuit uses two to four big cylindrical ones to control sags and spikes (they also have other uses, as you'll see later). The unit of measurement is a microfarad (µF)—see Figure 17.29. This determines the size of the capacitor, and is marked on the capacitor along with a voltage. This is the largest amount of charge that can be applied before the capacitor breaks. Putting too much charge on a capacitor will cause it to short-circuit—a very common source of power-supply problems.

Although there are many types of capacitors, the big ones you're about to test are called *electrolytic capacitors*. They have a distinct polarity (– and +) to their two leads. Before you test a capacitor, make sure to discharge the power supply!

Capacitors rarely fail, but if they do and you suspect one of them, I can show you a quick way to test them with a meter. Put the black lead in the common (–) socket and the red lead in the multiple (+) socket, and turn the selector knob to resistance ohms or continuity. Make sure the power is turned off on the machine or board being tested. Put the black lead of the multimeter on the negative capacitor lead and the red lead of the multimeter on the other lead of the capacitor. See Figure 17.30.

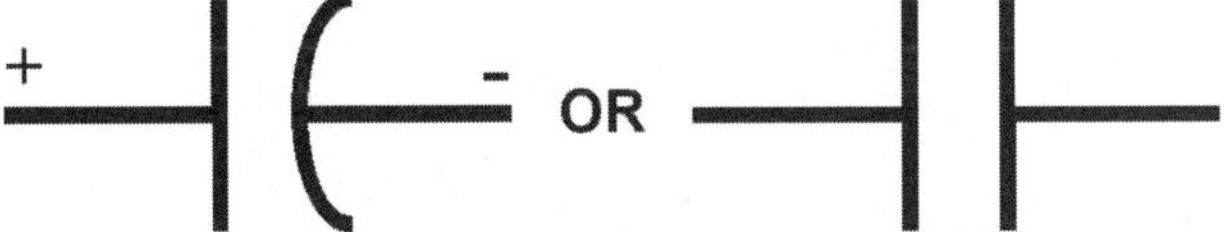

Figure 17.29 Electronic symbol for capacitor

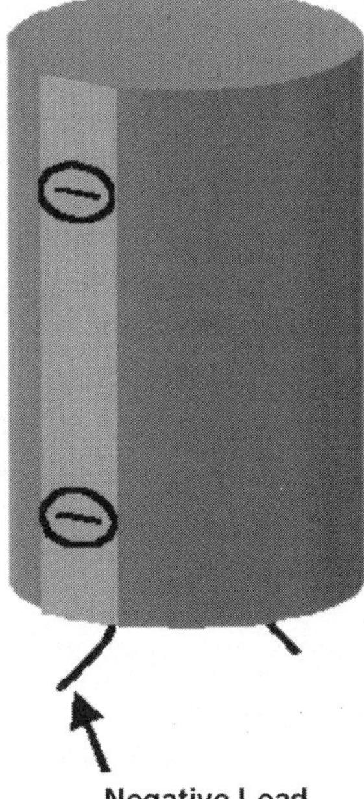

Figure 17.30 Capacitor

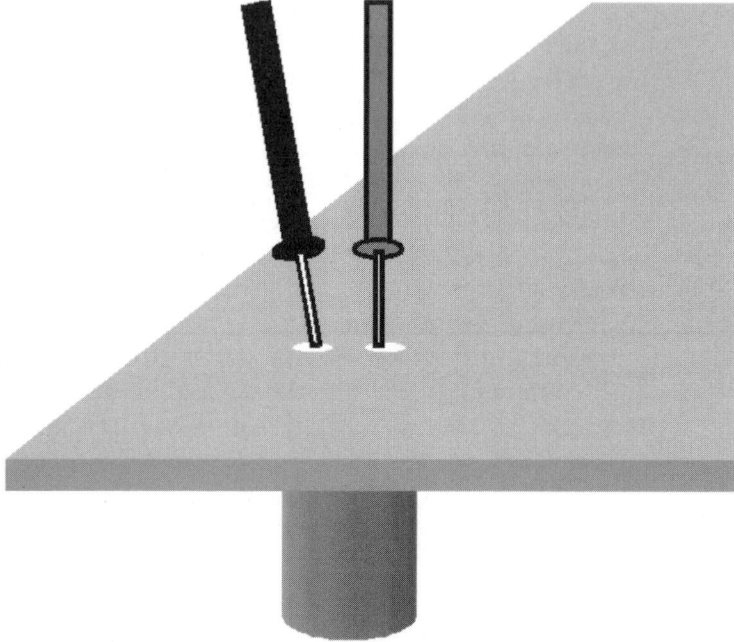

Figure 17.31
Testing a capacitor

If the indicator shows a zero resistance or a tone from the continuity setting, the capacitor is shorted and needs to be replaced. If the indicator shows infinite or overload, it indicates that it is not shorted and is probably good, especially on a small capacitor. If the capacitor is large enough, the indicator will show an increasing reading until it stops. This shows that the capacitor is charging up to the voltage applied to it. After it stops, change your function knob to DC volts. The scale should now display the amount equal to or some amount less than your meter voltage. These two tests will confirm a good capacitor (Figure 17.31).

Diodes and Rectifiers

In order to understand these devices, let's start with the diode, which is an "electrical one-way valve." It allows current to pass though it in only one direction. So when the AC current is flowing in one direction, for example negative to positive (see Figure 17.32), the current will pass through. When the AC current reverses direction, say positive back to negative, the diode will "block" the current flow. See Figure 17.33. Therefore, on every cycle of AC, you pass only half of the signal (called *half-wave rectification*).

Rectifiers are mini-circuits made up of two or four diodes placed in parallel to change the AC current to pulsating DC current. Two diodes produce half-wave rectification (Figure 17.34a), and four diodes produce full-wave rectification, sometimes called a *bridge network* (Figure 17.34b).

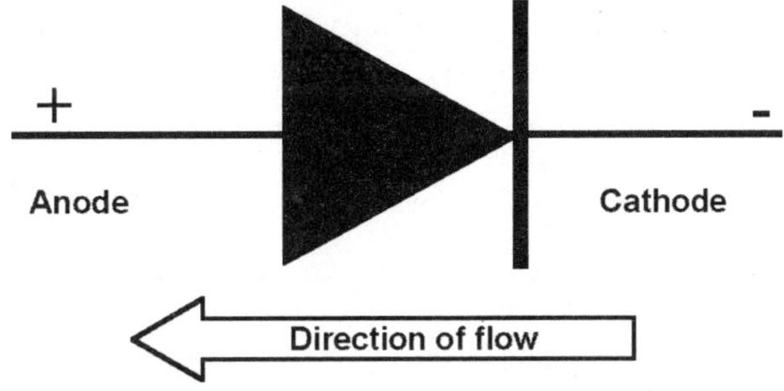

Figure 17.32
Diode changes the signal

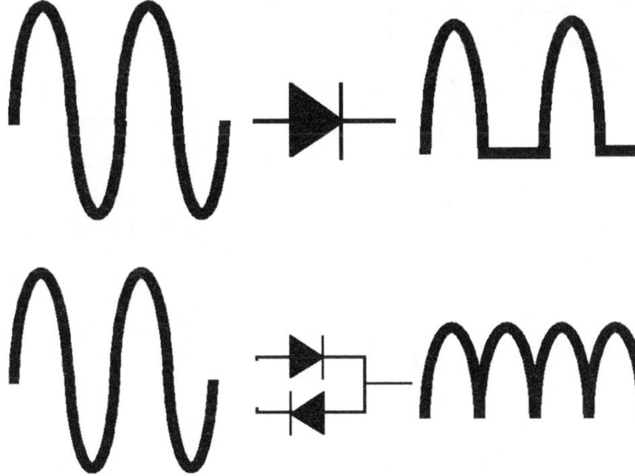

Figure 17.33
Converting AC to DC

Figure 17.34a
Full-wave rectification

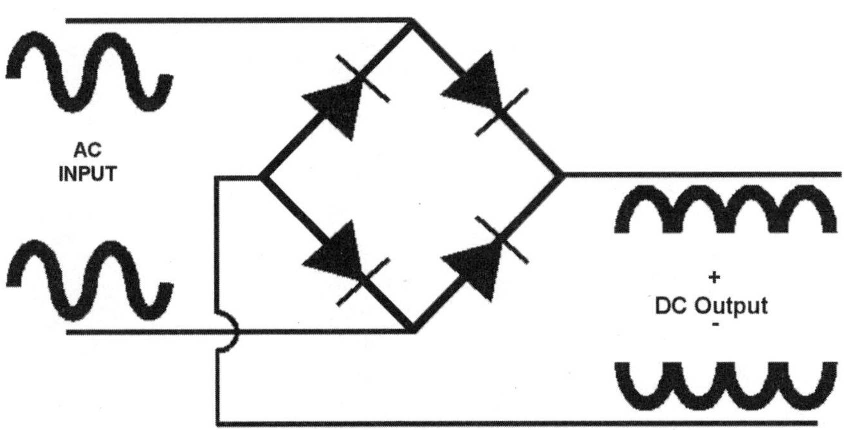

Figure 17.34b
Full-wave rectification

Transistors

Transistors are electrical components that can best be described as two diodes in series with an on-off switch between them (Figures 17.35 and 17.36). The input and output terminals are labeled E (emitter) and C (collector), respectively. The switch is called the B (base). Varying a voltage on the base will "switch" the transistor on or off to pass current. The two switching transistors convert the pulsating DC voltage into the square-wave dc needed by the transformer.

Transformer

The transformer section consists of exactly one device: a transformer. A *transformer* is nothing more than two wire-wrapped coils separated by a metallic core (Figures 17.37 and 17.38). Current is passed from one coil to the other via induction to pass alternating current. One coil has more wire wrapped around it than the other, which creates a difference in voltage.

Transformers reduce the current coming from the switching network down to the 5 and 12 volts needed by PCs. Since the voltage is being re-

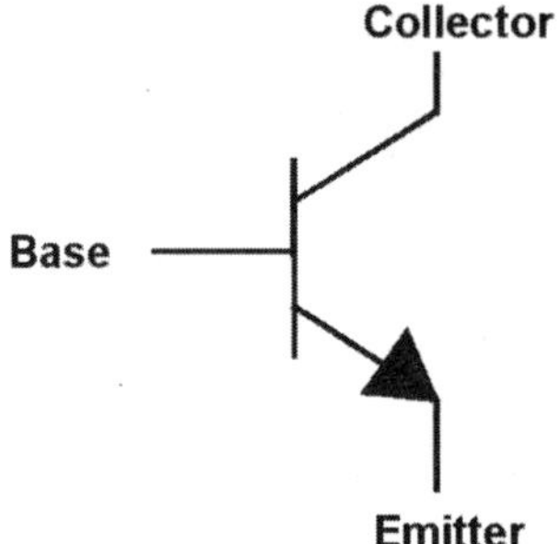

Figure 17.35 Transistor symbol

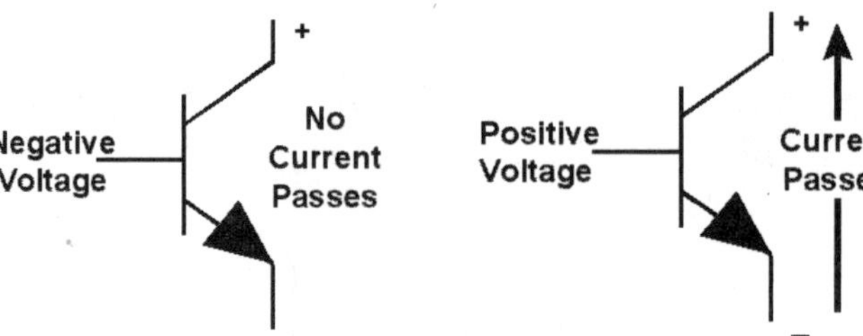

Figure 17.36 Function of a transistor

Figure 17.37
Transformer

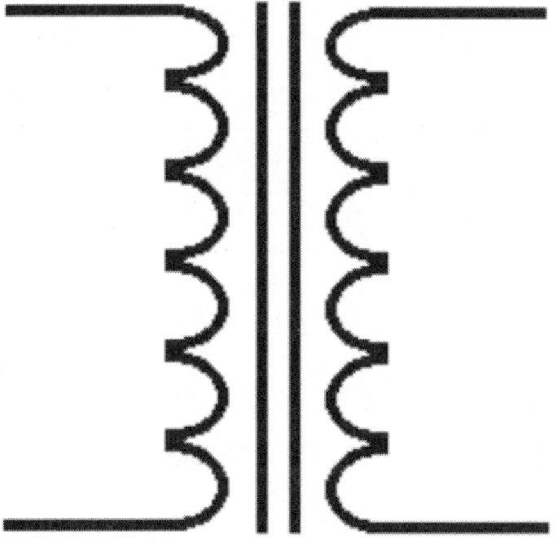

Figure 17.38
Transformer symbol

duced, the transformer is called a *step-down transformer.* The input wires of the transformer are collectively called the transformer's *primary,* and the output side is called the *secondary.*

The transformer in your PC usually has one primary and three secondaries (Figure 17.39a). The three secondaries output the voltages your PC

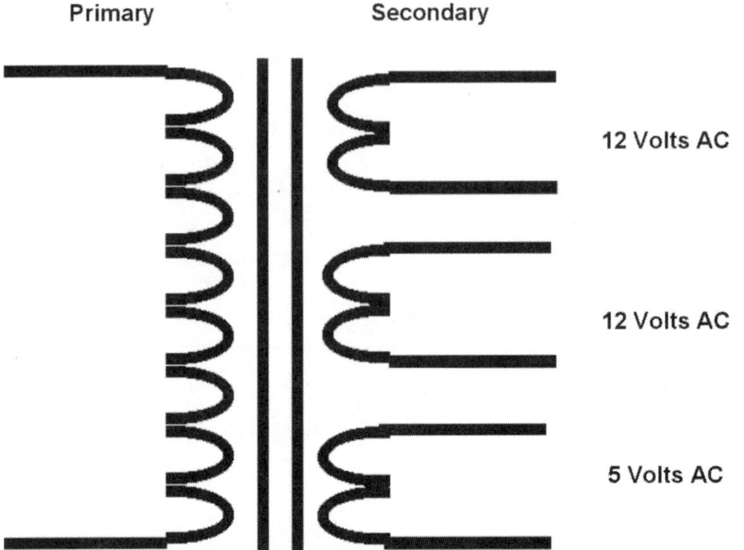

Figure 17.39a Transformer with three secondaries

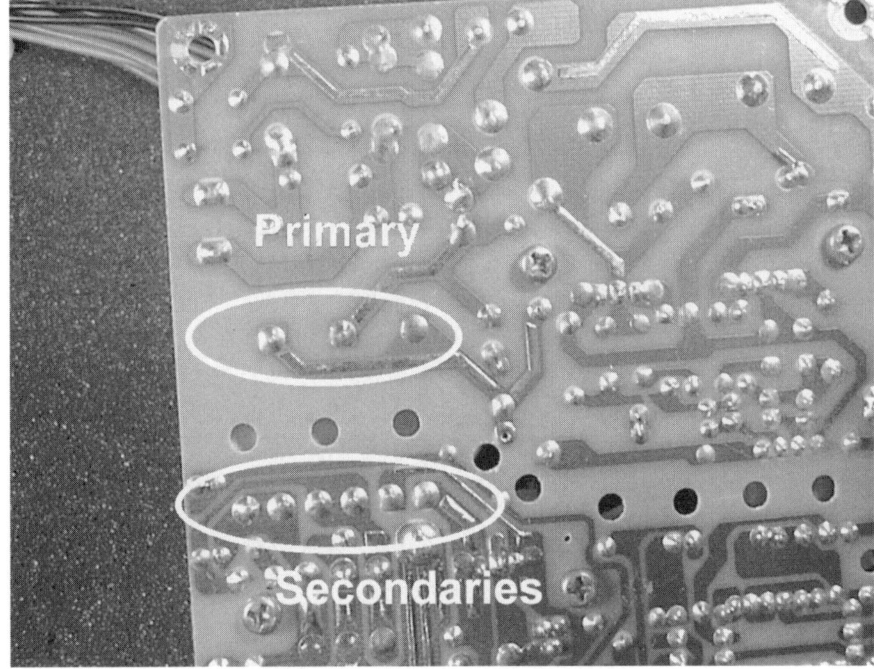

Figure 17.39b Underside of transformers

needs into two 12-volt and one 5-volt outputs. You can see this by looking at the underside of the transformer (Figure 17.39b).

To test a transformer, since it is nothing more than a coil of wire, use the ohm scale on your meter. Look at the underside of the power supply's motherboard. The primary pair and secondary pairs are clearly together, as shown in the previous figure. Be sure power is disconnected and the capacitors are discharged. Touch each lead of your multimeter to one of the pairs of contacts. You should see a reading of low resistance. An ultra-high reading could indicate that one of the coils is broken.

Regulator

The *voltage regulator area* receives the low-voltage ac outputs of the transformer and converts them to clean dc (Figure 17.40). It uses rectifiers (diodes) to convert the alternating cycles to a straight-line output (some ripple is still present); it has capacitors to remove any ripples that are present; and it regulates the output to pure dc. The main components in this section are rectifiers, capacitors, and coils.

Rectifiers

Figure 17.41 shows the rectifiers, capacitors, and coils of the regulator section. The rectifiers in this section work exactly like the rectifiers in the

Figure 17.40
Regulator section

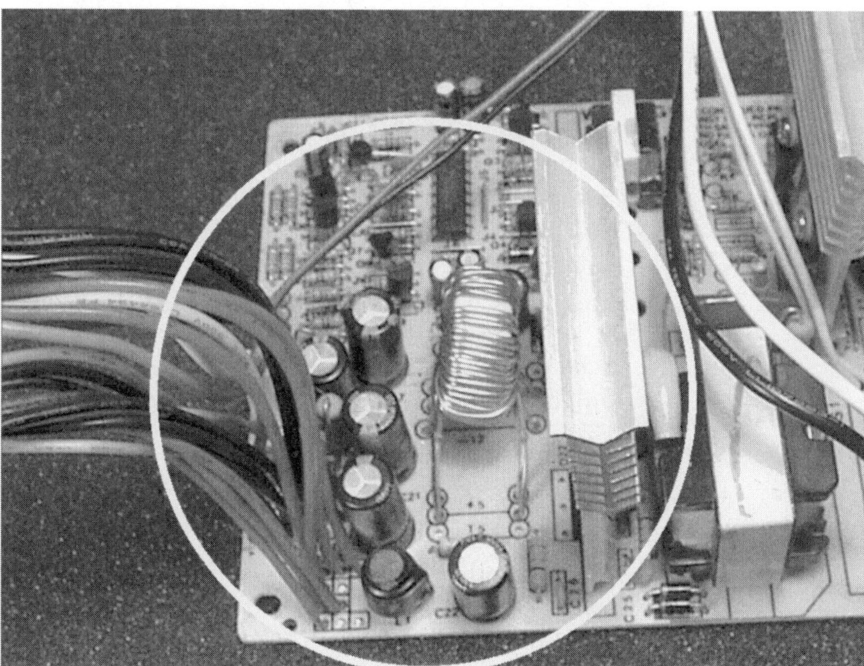

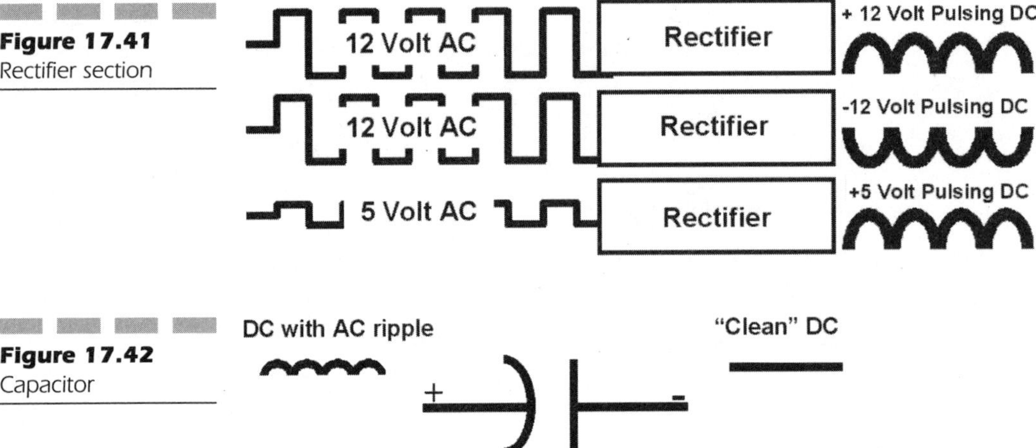

Figure 17.41 Rectifier section

Figure 17.42 Capacitor

switching network; they take the AC voltage and turn it into DC voltage. Refer back to the switching network section to review how they work. Although they convert the AC back to DC, notice the "ripple" of the pulsating current. This *AC ripple* is unacceptable to the circuitry of the PC, so you need to smooth it out with coils and a capacitor.

Capacitors

In the switching network section, you saw that the large capacitors filtered out the sags and spike from the incoming electrical service. In the regulator section, a number of smaller capacitors perform a different function. These capacitors smooth out the AC ripples in the dc current (Figure 17.42).

Capacitors are second only to fuses as the part of your power supply most likely to fail. As a capacitor begins to fail, more and more AC ripple begins to slip through. If your capacitors are beginning to fail, test for noise or AC ripple riding on a DC voltage with your meter. Set it up for an AC reading, connect a .1 ufd capacitor, and attach it to the red lead. With the power on, test the DC voltage; if there is any ripple, the meter will display the amount of AC ripple as a voltage.

Coils

A coil or inductor is the component that opposes any change in current flow (Figures 17.43 and 17.44). It will not offer much opposition to DC current, but will have a large reactance to AC current. The inductor is con-

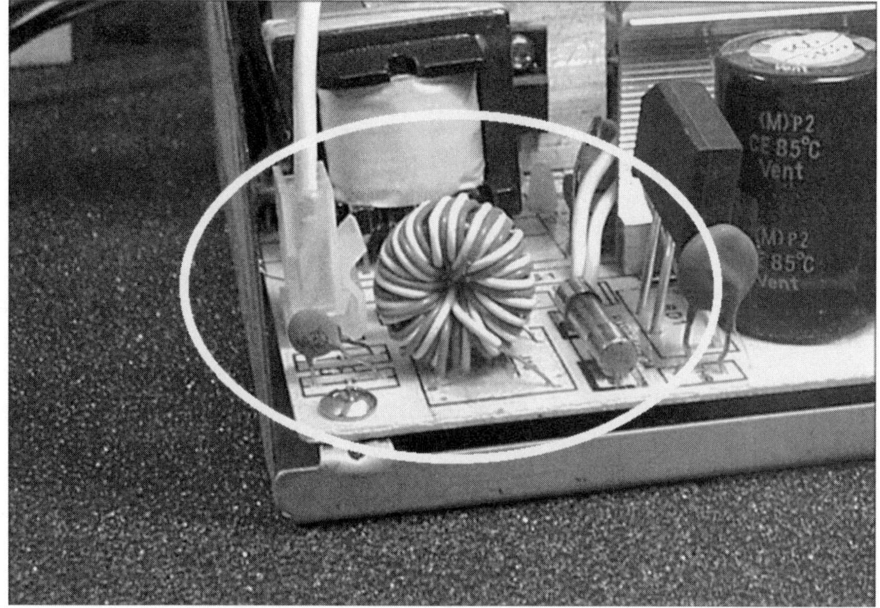

Figure 17.43
Coil

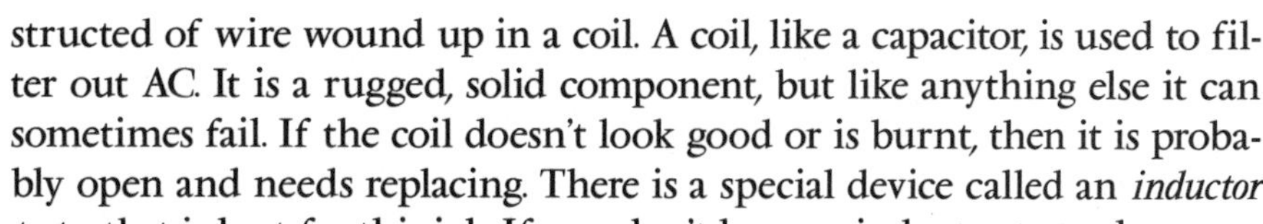

Figure 17.44
Coil symbol

structed of wire wound up in a coil. A coil, like a capacitor, is used to filter out AC. It is a rugged, solid component, but like anything else it can sometimes fail. If the coil doesn't look good or is burnt, then it is probably open and needs replacing. There is a special device called an *inductor tester* that is best for this job. If you don't have an inductor tester, however, you can use the multimeter for a simple test.

Set the meter as discussed for a capacitance or resistance check. Make sure the power is off, disconnect one end of the inductor, and proceed with testing. Put the leads across the coil and look at the readout. It should be 0 or a very low reading. This shows that it is not open, and possibly not shorted. If the meter indicates an infinite reading, the coil is open and should be replaced. Remember, if the coil is particularly large, the meter might indicate a larger resistance. You cannot simulate its true reactance without special equipment, because it needs a changing current to show its true reactance.

As the final step of the switching power supply, each set of rectifiers supplies the desired DC voltage to the system. This voltage is split within the power-supply box to supply current to P8 and P9 as well as the Molex and mini-connectors.

Electrostatic Discharge (ESD)

In its purest term, static electricity is an "electrical charge at rest." If *electricity* is the continuing flow of electrons through a conductor, then *static electricity* is the build-up of electrons in a conductor (or insulator) waiting for a path to allow a flow of current. See Figure 17.45.

Static electricity is caused by creating friction along with a sudden separation of two dissimilar materials. Friction causes heat that excites the molecular particles. When the two materials are separated, electrons from one material might transfer to the other, causing a charge to build up on both. One becomes positive while the other becomes more negative. Electrostatic discharge (ESD) is when static electricity stops resting and moves toward a ground (Figure 17.46).

Lightning is perhaps the most common event displaying static discharge. Most people have experienced walking across carpeting and, upon touching a doorknob, receiving a shock. And everyone has occasionally experienced the "static cling" caused by the rubbing of different fabrics like wool and silk.

The amount of static electricity generated depends on the materials in contact with each other, the amount of friction, the relative humidity, and the speed of separation. Common plastic will generally create the greatest static charge. Low humidity and buildings using dry heated air in the winter promote the generation of static charges. Materials that easily transfer charges between atoms are called *conductors* and have "free" elec-

Figure 17.45
Static electricity

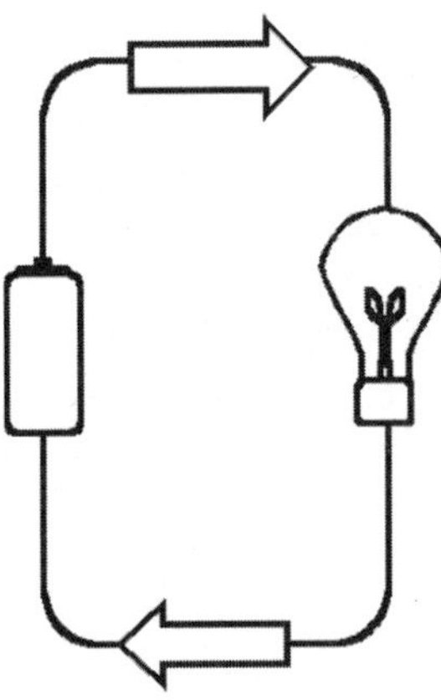
"Regular" electricity
is moving - kinetic

Static electricity
is not moving

Figure 17.46 ESD is charge moving towards ground

trons in their molecular construction. Good conductors are metals, carbon, and the human body's sweat layer. Materials that do not easily transfer charges are called *insulators*. The best known insulators are common plastics, glass, and air.

Both conductors and insulators can become charged with static potential. Conductors will discharge more rapidly than insulators, but insulators will discharge nonetheless.

Typical Electrostatic Voltages

Humans can accumulate potentials well over 25,000 volts. Although we might experience a shock or other sensation when the charge is dissipated, it is a very quick, low-current flow that is not harmful. But as little as 10 volts can destroy some of today's more sophisticated integrated chips, so daily activities can generate static charges on your body that are potentially harmful to sensitive electronic components. Consider the following:

Walking across carpet: 1500 to 25,000 volts
Walking over untreated vinyl floor: 250 to 12,000 volts
Picking up a common plastic bag: 1200 to 20,000 volts
Working at a bench: 700 to 6000 volts
Handling a vinyl envelope: 600 to 7000 volts

Costly Effects of ESD

When you experience a static shock, the discharge is a minimum of 3000 volts of electricity. This "shock" is known as *electrostatic discharge* or *ESD*, and could have been responsible for damaging many of the "questionable" components you handled and could not find a problem with, so you returned them as bad. While you can feel an ESD of 3000 volts, you can't feel smaller charges, and these charges can still damage semiconductor devices. Many of the CMOS technology components can be destroyed by less than 1000 volts.

Technology is advancing and components are getting smaller. The microscopic spacing of insulators and circuits within chips is increasing the sensitivity to ESD. Proper ESD protection is a must!

Most of today's circuits are made using metal-oxide semiconductors. These are very low-voltage devices with microscopic spacing of conductors and insulators. Some 486DX, Pentium, and Pentium Pro CPUs are now running at 3.3 volts. Memory SIMMs are plugged onto motherboards that supply 5 volts. The construction of these devices allow millions of transistors to be contained in a relatively small footprint, so the sensitivity to high voltages is greatly enhanced.

Types of ESD Damage

The damage caused by ESD can take on three forms: upset failures, latent catastrophic failure, and direct catastrophic failure.

Upset failures occur when an ESD is small enough to cause minor gate leakage and is intermittent in nature. This type of damage might not be detected by quality control or end-user test programs, but it will show up as an unexplained loss of data. These are the most embarrassing to technicians because they might have caused this condition by mishandling parts. The embarrassment manifests itself as repeated calls or, worst yet, installing more RAM and the system displays random-memory errors during POST. The cost of repair is very high.

Latent failures occur when the ESD damage causes the transistor junction to become weakened; these are known as "zings." This transistor might pass all tests, but over a period of time will react with poorer system performance and eventually complete failure. Because latent failures show up well after installation, the cause of the system crash is "unknown," which is costly to troubleshoot and repair.

Direct catastrophic failures, known as "zaps," are the best if you consider the alternatives. They are final, and usually occur with ESD shock of more than 3000 volts. They are the easiest to find because they will show up during testing. TIFs (technician-induced failures) are always costly to fix, but are the ones you can eliminate through proper handling of the plug-in boards and integrated circuit chips. ESD damage in a computer is hard to detect. Think of it as a virus.

Severe loss of data or unexplained system crashes can occur. The best defense is preventing ESD damage. Without a good ESD procedure in place, you are prone to many intermittent problems, which could significantly reduce your company's profitability.

Preventing ESD Events and ESD Damage

Once you understand that you can damage a semiconductor device just by handling it before it is plugged in, you are well on your way to preventing ESD problems.

ESD problems can happen anywhere, anytime. Have you ever watched jet planes be refueled at an airport? First, they hook up a "static" strap to equalize the charges between the plane and the refueling truck. The truck is then connected to a "ground" strap, which is connected to a ground rod in the concrete apron to dissipate any stray currents. Or have you driven your car on a major toll road and seen a "static" wire just in front of the toll booth to discharge the static from the car so the toll takers aren't shocked as you hand them the money? These two are just examples of how a "strap" is used to dissipate static to a safe place. PC technicians can also use a wrist strap in the same manner.

You can purchase an ESD kit from any good electronics store. It contains an antistatic mat, wristband, static strap, and ground wire. Place the antistatic mat on the work surface next to the PC, connect the ground wire to the mat and frame of the PC, and connect the strap to the wristband and put the wristband on (Figure 17.47). Be sure the other end of the strap is connected to the antistatic mat. By placing the removed components on the mat, you protect them from stray static stored in vinyl coverings, plastic boxes, and other unapproved surfaces.

Please be careful; AC voltage can kill. Never disconnect and remove boards from a PC with power applied. While you are connected to a "live" PC via the wrist strap, there is a 1-megaohm resister in the strap to protect you in case of an accident. Also never, never, never work on a monitor

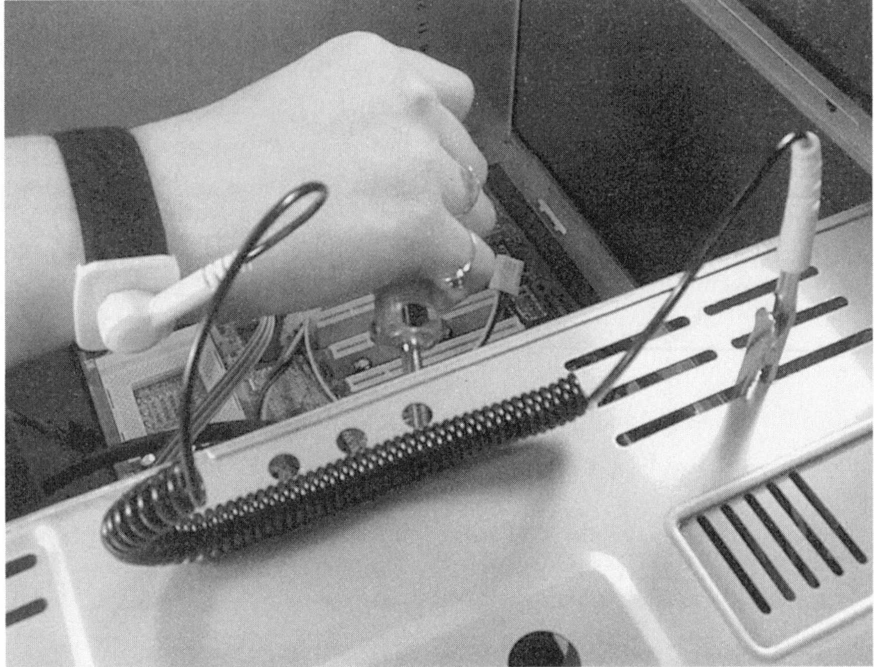

Figure 17.47 ESD wrist strap in action

with the cabinet removed, power applied, and your wrist strap on. If you accidentally reach over the CRT assembly and the wrist strap comes in contact with the high-voltage wire (30,000 volts), you will most likely die.

Get in a good habit of "grounding" yourself to the PC chassis, since sometimes it is not practical nor convenient to put on a ground strap. As long as you touch a part of the metal chassis before removing devices and you do not move around a lot, it is okay to occasionally not put on an antistatic strap. The following are guidelines:

- Do not be careless.
- Make sure you use good grounding practices.
- Do not place boards on metal or foil. They might have batteries installed.
- While working at a bench, wear the wristband.
- Try not to wear synthetic clothing when working on PCs.
- Store parts in antistatic bags. Styrofoam cups waved over a board can cause damage.
- Keep chips in protective foam while not in use, which keeps the pins straight and equal potential on all of them.

- Never place unprotected boards or components in plastic containers.
- Always touch the metal chassis before handling parts.
- Handle boards by the metal brackets.
- Use antistatic sprays for cleaning. Detergents can build up charges.
- Vacuum cleaners are bad! The crevice tool made of plastic will build up a massive charge from the dust it picks up.
- Do not use erasers. Not only are they abrasive, but the rubbing builds up static.

Finally, everyone in your company should know about ESD, from the president to all notice PC users. Remember that *prevention is the best defense!*

Uninterruptible Power Supplies (UPS)

Uninterruptible Power Supplies are designed to protect your computer (and, more importantly, your data) in the event of a power dip (brownout) or power outage (blackout). A UPS essentially contains a big battery that will provide AC power to your computer, regardless of the condition of the AC outlet. There are two basic types of UPS: Online (properly UPS) and Stand-by (SPS).

An Online UPS is a true uninterruptible power supply. A UPS converts AC power from the outlet and charges the battery. The battery in turn provides power for the computer. The UPS battery is always "online," protecting your data against accidental loss from power outages. An added benefit of the UPS is *power conditioning*. The AC power is filtered through the battery, thus giving your computer's power supply a very smooth AC current. Though not the budget choice, an Online UPS is clearly the best choice for the PC: data is protected and the computer runs better.

A Stand-by UPS removes the battery from the AC circuit until the AC power drops below 80–90 volts. An SPS will then engage the battery and (hopefully) save your data. Although a less expensive solution than a true UPS, the SPS has two potential liabilities. Most obviously, removing the battery from the regular AC power also removes the AC conditioning. Data is not actually protected until the AC drops well below the standard 110–120 volts and neither are the fragile electrical components of the computer. Second, if the battery dies at some point, you might not know until the SPS simply fails one day and your data is lost. An SPS provides fairly good protection from power outages at a reasonable price, but does not protect against poor or fluctuating AC from your electric company.

All UPSes are measured in Watts, in the amount of power they are capable of supplying in the event of a power outage. You can spend a lot of time and mental energy figuring precisely how much wattage your computer, monitor, drives, etc. require in order to get the proper UPS for your system. A quicker method, however, is to look on the box provided by the manufacturer. Most manufacturers will list how many minutes the UPS will last with a certain voltage. Cut the number of minutes in half and that will give you a good conservative estimate of that UPS's abilities.

Although a true or "Online" UPS provides far better protection than an SPS, almost all "UPSes" sold today are actually SPSes. Regardless, any UPS will give protection for your data and for your equipment and should be considered a necessary part of a complete computer system today.

CHAPTER 18

Portable PCs

Figure 18.1 Getting a PC to "go mobile" was a daunting task

From the moment that PCs first began to appear in the early 1980s, people have wanted to be able to move them from one location to another, and the PC's ability to hold and process data led eventually to a way to transform static desktop PCs into mobile devices designed to serve an increasingly mobile business environment. The advantage of mobile PCs was the promise of increased efficiency and profitability; the disadvantage was that desktop PCs, as envisioned by IBM, were an absolute nightmare to make mobile for a number of reasons (Figure 18.1).

The biggest problem was power. The first desktop PCs were designed to run from standard 120-volt AC with big switching power supplies to convert to multiple voltages of DC. At least the low dc demands of PCs made batteries, and therefore truly mobile PCs, possible.

One interesting item is that there was an early push at IBM to go for voltages higher higher than 12 volts for some aspects of PCs. If that had been successful, mobile PCs might have been substantially delayed. But even running at 12 volts or less, a first-generation PC with a hard drive could have quickly drained any of the smaller, inexpensive batteries of the early eighties.

The first generation of mobile computers got around the power problem quite elegantly; they simply didn't have batteries. If you wanted to move a PC, you had to turn it off, unplug it, physically move it to the next location (the first ones were heavy), plug it back in, and turn it back on to start using it again. This was fine for someone moving from office to office, but what about a person working in a car, plane, or some other place where a power outlet wasn't available? Batteries, and the power they provided, quickly became very important to mobile computing.

This demand for more power and for PC components that use less power has created an entire family of products that are functionally identical to their desktop equivalents, but use much less power. Low-power monitors, CPUs, chipsets, hard drives, and CD-ROM drives are now the de-facto standards for laptops. And many of these low-power components, or at least the technologies that created them, have made strong penetrations back into the desktop market.

The second big challenge was to ensure reliability. Desktop hard and floppy drives were never designed to be used in the back of a bouncing pickup truck or inside a turbulent airplane. The read/write heads would bounce around, never properly accessing the data, or, worse, destroying it. This was countered by new methods of drive design that compensated for missed data, and methods to help prevent the heads from crashing into the drive. These technologies eventually became standard even on desktop PCs. In addition, there was a need to make the entire PC more robust. Many first-generation mobile PCs actually had small shock absorbers to help compensate for shocks and to make the PC generally more robust than its desktop equivalent.

The last challenge was functionality. Mobile PCs needed to be able to mimic the functions of their desktop brothers. This functionality ranges from the need to keep up with a mobile version of whatever "latest and greatest" device is on desktops to the human factors of trying to make desktop devices smaller and lighter, while still being functional for average users. A great example of this quandary is the mouse. Even though the first mobile PCs could handle a mouse, the standard desktop rodent would hardly serve someone packed into the middle seat of a 737 or a busy duty nurse making the rounds in a hospital ward. The demand for a mobile mouse spawned a series of new, innovative pointing devices, from trackballs to touchpads.

The challenges of power, reliability, and functionality continue to challenge mobile computing. We continue to demand longer-running, more reliable PCs while expecting the same convenience, firepower, and speed that we enjoy on desktop computers. Unfortunately, the ability to conquer one challenge usually creates new problems in another. As improvements in batteries and power management continue to increase available power, there are demands for new devices. As new devices become available, demands for reliability begin to surface. The cycle is unending. See Figure 18.2.

Figure 18.2 The demand for more functionality

Background

Trying to point to the first mobile computer is guaranteed to produce a fight between any two computer historians, so it might be easier to simply discuss the first computers that were widely marketed and available to the public. This crown can arguably be given to the famous Osborne One from the late '70s (Figure 18.3). Although not truly a PC (it didn't use IBM's BIOS and couldn't interchange parts with the PC), the Osborne One de-

Figure 18.3 The Osborne (Photo courtesy of Obsolete Computer Museum)

fined a series of technologies that helped define how the first generation of portable computers would look and operate. In particular, the Osborne defined the concept of the "suitcase luggable." The Osborne One was organized with a small screen, 5.25-inch floppy drives, and a keyboard that acted as a cover during transport.

Due to its proprietary design, the Osborne cannot be officially listed as the first mobile PC clone. (Remember that only IBM can make a PC and everyone else makes clones, but the term *PC* now envelopes all IBM and IBM clones.) That moniker would have to be given to the mobile PCs developed by Compaq in the early '80s (Figure 18.4). Not only were these the first mobile PC clones, but they were the first PC clones of any type! Before Compaq, only IBM made PCs. Compaq started the entire clone concept, and Compaq mobiles were the first clones. They were, however, quickly followed by a succession of similar machines, including a genuine IBM luggable.

The luggables were all AC powered, so there were no battery problems. They ran on 8086 CPUs or equivalent, and all ran the exact same DOS as their desktop cousins. Therefore, they could easily exchange data and programs with those machines. These mobile PC-compatible computers made a tremendous impact on many industries, substantially changing the way they did business.

Figure 18.4 The Compaq portable (Photo courtesy of Obsolete Computer Museum)

Figure 18.5
A luggable isn't a laptop!

Of all the industries affected by portable PCs, public accounting was probably the most so. First-generation luggables, combined with early spreadsheet programs such as Lotus 1-2-3, literally transformed the way accounting firms conducted their day-to-day business. Public accounting firms like Coopers & Lybrand or Arthur Andersen are hired by companies to do their auditing. As any new CPA will tell you, the life of a young auditor is a highly mobile affair, flying from one client's location to another, diving through records, and running around collecting financial information for audits. The combination of luggables and spreadsheets was the perfect tool for this industry. So public accounting firms were major purchasers of early mobile computers.

The first generation of suitcase luggable PCs, although highly functional, were seriously limited (Figure 18.5). First, they were very heavy, some in excess of 40 pounds. The high weight made the system's mobility a function of brawn more than convenience. Second, they had tiny screens due to the limited frontal area. Third, they were bulky. They needed to be placed on top of a stout platform in order to work safely. You couldn't put them on a flimsy table, a cardboard box, or—heaven forbid—a person's lap!

Laptops

As 286 CPUs began to dominate the desktop market, two separate technologies simultaneously came to fruition, or at least became cheap enough, to allow PCs to at last become truly portable. The first was the portable battery. Obviously, batteries have been around for quite a while, but regular batteries, such as the D cells in a common flashlight, are unacceptable for usage in PCs because of the voltage. When a new set of batteries is placed into a flashlight, the light is quite bright. But over time, the batteries begin to wear down and the light dims and then eventually goes out (Figure 18.6). The reason is simple. As the batteries begin to lose power, the voltage output drops correspondingly. While this voltage drop is no big deal with a flashlight, it is absolutely unacceptable with a computer. PCs need a continuous, steady voltage in order to properly operate, or they will lock up (Figure 18.7).

The need for continuous voltage led to the invention of Nickel-Cadmium (Ni-Cd) batteries. This was the first of a series of battery technologies that would provide the necessary constant voltage that mobile PCs needed to operate.

The second technology that allowed PCs to move from luggable to truly mobile was the liquid-crystal display (LCD). The CRT displays of the first generation of mobile PCs were usually very small, no bigger than four to six inches diagonally. They couldn't be any larger or they wouldn't fit inside the luggable, and the extra weight would make the already overweight portables even heavier. Clearly there was a need for a lighter and larger display.

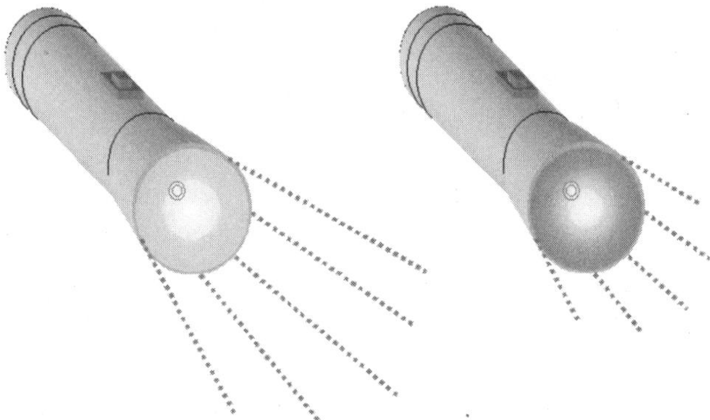

Flashlights can run on lower voltages, they just get dimmer

Figure 18.6 Flashlights can go dim

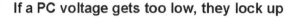

If a PC voltage gets too low, they lock up

Figure 18.7
PCs need constant voltage

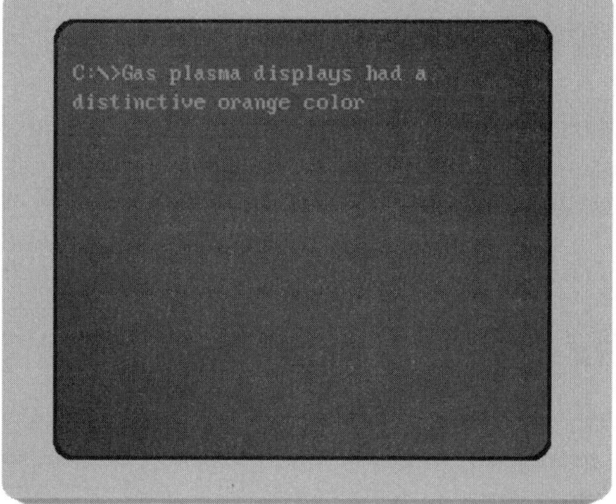

Figure 18.8
A gas plasma display

The first common replacement for CRTs was called gas plasma (Figure 18.8), which was a flat-panel display, as opposed to the elongated tube sticking out of the back of the typical CRT. Gas Plasma panels were filled with a gas, usually neon, that would glow when exposed to an electrical charge. The monitor was covered with a grid of wires. If the computer selected the proper X and Y wire, a corresponding spot on the screen would glow. Gas Plasma displays were quite popular, but they used large amounts of power and were limited to monochrome. They were quite easily distinguished by their orange-red characters on a black background.

Gas plasma displays were quickly overshadowed by LCDs, which used a special fluid, a liquid crystal, to selectively allow the passage of light through the display. Unlike CRTs, LCDs don't emit light; they can only prevent light from passing through them. The liquid crystals most commonly used in PC displays have molecules that normally allow the passage of light, but when they are exposed to an electrical charge, the molecules "line up" in a fashion that prevents light from passing through. LCDs had been around for some time and have been heavily used in watches and calculators since the early 1970s, but the early LCDs were too slow to keep up with the constantly changing PC screens. This changed with a new technology called *super twist nematic* (STN), which became the cornerstone of all LCD displays. The technology of LCDs continues to improve even today.

Zenith (although some say it was Data General) first combined a Ni-Cd battery and LCD display with a mobile computer, massively reducing the overall size and taking a marginally mobile, heavy, awkward device and turning it into the prototypical mobile device we know today. These new mobile PCs (Figure 18.9) could run anywhere due to their batteries and relatively light weight. In fact, the most common place for these new mobile PCs was on the user's lap, hence the common name *laptop*. The first lap-

Figure 18.9 Zenith laptops (Photo courtesy of the Obsolete Computer Museum)

tops did away with the old suitcase concept, and were the same basic shape: the clam-shell, keyboard-on-the-bottom, screen-at-the-top design used for all mobile PCs today.

As mobile computing, led by laptop PCs, continued to grow as an overall percentage of all PCs, users began to demand something even smaller and lighter. The problem with laptops was that they were still large enough to demand their own carrying case, and even the lightest laptops still approached 15 pounds, making cross-town and cross-country trips a rather daunting task for all but the most hearty laptop-hauling users. The dream was to reduce the size of the laptop so it could fit in an briefcase. The laptop would then be roughly the size of a notebook—thus the name *notebook* was given to all mobile PCs in the new, smaller size (see Figure 18.10).

Today's mobile PCs are still notebook size. It seems that this is just about the most optimal size for a mobile computer. Although the tech-

Figure 18.10
My notebook

nology exists for much smaller PCs, human factors such as keyboard and display size keep the notebook form as the standard today. Interestingly, mobile PCs might actually be getting larger instead of smaller, due to a number of reasons. First, the concept of throwing a PC in a briefcase hasn't really come to pass. Today's notebooks usually travel in their own specialized travel cases, so the idea of a little extra size no longer bothers most users. Second, the extra size can allow for larger screens and keyboards—two areas that have always been too small for most people. Third, the extra size doesn't include significant extra weight, and it provides users with virtually all the amenities and peripherals that they can get on their desktops—which is the holy grail of mobile computing.

Yet even since the earliest mobile computers, there has been a demand for very small, reduced-function PCs. These devices might not use the same operating systems as their desktop brethren, but they should be able to interface with them. They don't need all the firepower, but they should be able to handle the demands of on-the-go executives and sales people. These devices should at the very least be able to store names, addresses, and phone numbers, track appointments and meetings, and provide to-do lists. Preferably, they should handle faxes, e-mail—maybe even pagers and Internet access! Generically, these devices are called *palmtops* or *personal digital assistants* (PDAs). PDAs are definitely niche players, but they have been around since the first mobile computer and they continue to grow in popularity. Figure 18.11 shows one of the first PDAs: the Poqet PC. The Poqet had 640K RAM and an 8086 CPU. It ran DOS and all of the popular DOS programs of the day. It even had the first type of PC card!

A PDA should fit into a shirt or pants pocket and weigh as little as possible. With this in mind, PDAs over the years have made great strides in removing superfluous equipment—in particular the keyboard. Many of today's PDAs use a combination of handwriting recognition and modified mouse functions, usually in the form of pen-based computing. One of the modern PDAs is the popular Palm Pilot from 3COM (Figure 18.12).

I want to take a moment to clear up the often misunderstood variety of names for the different mobile PC layouts, such as *suitcase, laptop, notebook,* and *palmtop.* The broad use of these terms implies that there are clear definitions for each layout. There are no such definitions, however; these are marketing terms that have moved into mainstream usage. As a result, many devices fit more than one layout. For example, an extra-large notebook might just as easily be described as a small laptop. A more full-featured PDA might just as easily be considered by someone else as a small notebook. This overlap or gray area is perfectly acceptable, but easily understood.

Figure 18.11
A Poqet PC

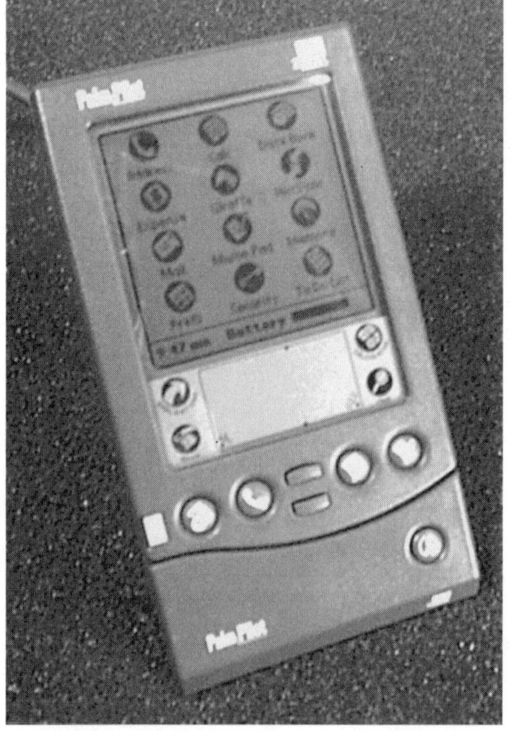

Figure 18.12
3COM Palm Pilot

Batteries

Of all of the many technologies unique to mobile PCs, the usage, care, and troubleshooting of batteries is probably the most frustrating but most easily supported. The secret to understanding batteries is understanding the types of batteries and appreciating each of their special needs and quirks. The symptoms that point to battery problems are *usually* obvious and easily remedied. First of all, there are only three types of batteries commonly used in mobile PCs: Nickel-Cadmium (Ni-Cd), Nickel-Metal Hydride (Ni-MH), and Lithium-Ion (Li-Ion). Let's look at each of these types.

Nickel-Cadmium

Ni-Cds were the first batteries commonly used in mobile PCs (Figure 18.13). As previously mentioned, PCs, unlike flashlights or Walkmans, must have a steady voltage. Before Ni-Cd, there wasn't a cheap battery technology that provided that necessary steady voltage. Ni-Cd, being the first of its type, was also full of little problems. Probably the most irritating was a little thing called "battery memory," which was the tendency of a Ni-Cd battery that was repeatedly charged without being totally discharged to lose a significant amount of its rechargeability. In essence, a battery that originally kept a laptop running for two hours would eventually keep that same laptop going for only 30 minutes or less. In order to prevent memory problems, a Ni-Cd battery had to be completely discharged before each recharging. Also, a Ni-Cd could not be overcharged. Overcharging was sometimes difficult to determine as there was no way

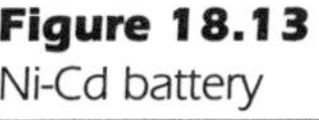

Figure 18.13
Ni-Cd battery

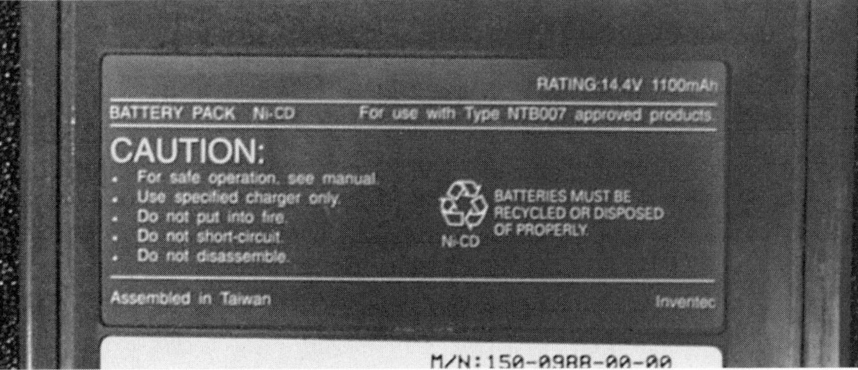

to verify when the battery was totally charged, unless you purchased an expensive charging machine. As a result, most Ni-Cd batteries lasted an extremely short time and were then replaced.

Unfortunately, many people ignored this problem because the fixes allowed batteries to last three to four times longer. Another quick fix was to purchase a conditioning charger. These chargers would first totally discharge a Ni-Cd battery, then provide a special "reverse" current that "cleaned" internal parts of the Ni-Cd to allow it to be recharged more often and to run longer on each recharge.

Ni-Cd batteries would at best last for 1000 charges, although with poor treatment they would last far less. Ni-Cds were extremely susceptible to heat and would self-discharge over time if not used. Leaving a Ni-Cd in the car in the summer was the equivalent to throwing it in the garbage. But Ni-Cd batteries didn't stop causing trouble even after they died. The highly toxic metals inside the battery made it unacceptable to simply throw them in the trash. Ni-Cd batteries needed to be disposed of via specialized disposal companies. This is very important! Even though Ni-Cd batteries aren't used in PCs very often anymore, many devices, such as cellular and cordless phones, still use them. Don't trash the environment by tossing Ni-Cds in a landfill. Turn them in to the closest special disposal site—most recycling centers are glad to take them. Also, many battery manufacturers and distributors will take them.

Nickel Metal Hydride

Ni-MH batteries were the next generation of mobile PC batteries, and are still quite common today (Figure 18.14). Basically, Ni-MH batteries are Ni-Cd batteries without most of the headaches. Ni-MHs aren't nearly as susceptible to memory problems, can take overcharging somewhat better, take more recharging, and last longer between recharging. Like a Ni-Cds, Ni-MH batteries are still susceptible to heat, but at least they are considered nontoxic to the environment—although it's still a good idea to do a special disposable. Unlike Ni-Cd, it's usually better to recharge a Ni-MH with shallow recharges as opposed to a complete discharge/recharge. Ni-MHs are a popular replacement battery for Ni-Cd systems.

Lithium Ion

The most common battery used today is the Lithium-Ion (Figure 18.15). Lithium-Ion batteries are completely immune to memory problems, are

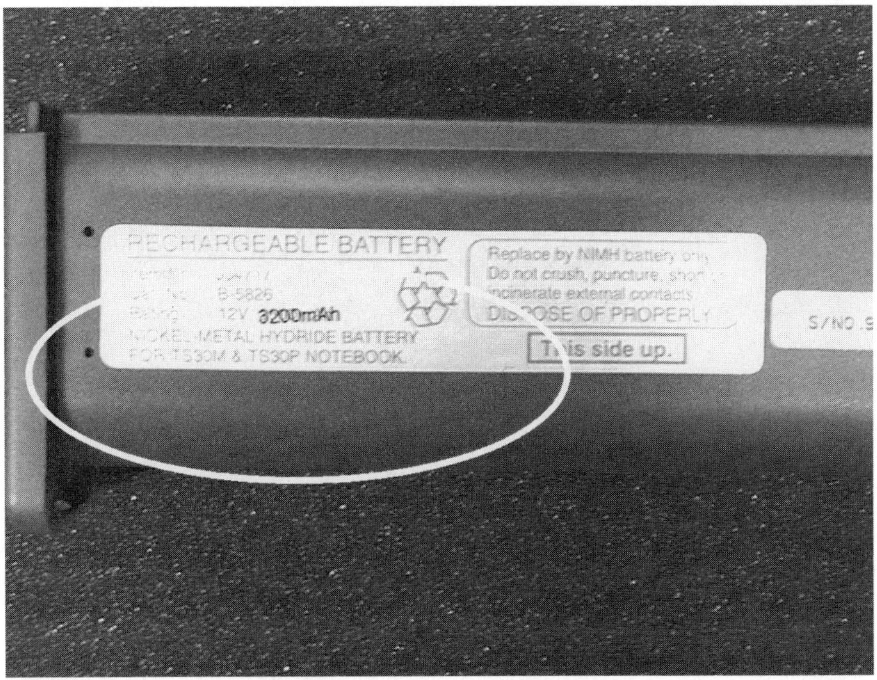

Figure 18.14
Ni-MH battery

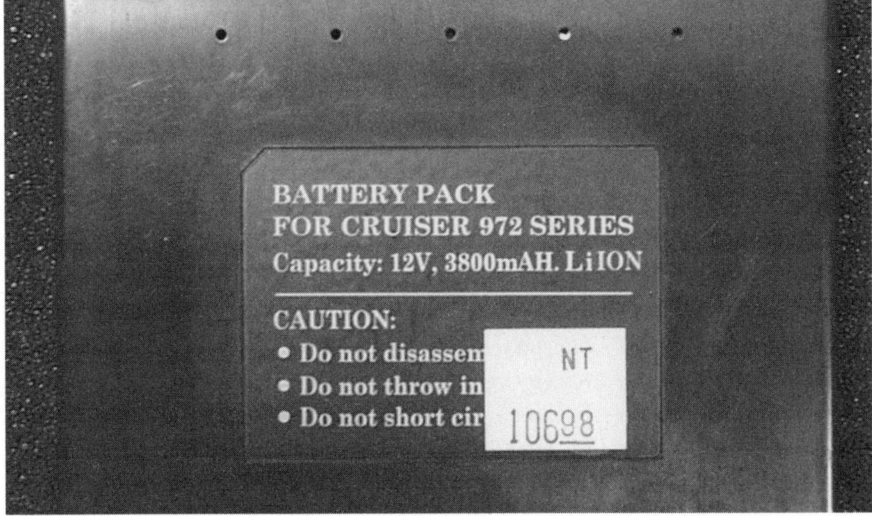

Figure 18.15
Li-Ion battery

very powerful, and last at least twice as long as a comparable Ni-MH battery on one charge. Sadly, they can't handle as many charges as Ni-MH, but today's users are usually more than glad to trade a shorter total battery lifespan for longer periods between charges. Lithium-Ion batteries simply can't be overcharged—they will explode—so all Lithium-Ion batteries sold with PCs have built-in circuitry to prevent accidental overcharging. Therefore, Lithium-Ion batteries are also completely immune to overcharging. They can be used only on systems designed to use them. They can't be used as replacement batteries.

Smart Batteries

In an attempt to provide better maintenance for laptop batteries, manufacturers have developed a new type of battery called a *smart battery.* Just now becoming known, it can tell a computer when it needs to be charged, conditioned, or replaced.

Keep in mind a few caveats when using any kind of portable-computer battery. First, always store the batteries in a cool place. Although a freezer is in concept an excellent storage place, moisture, metal racks, and food make it a bad idea. Second, condition Ni-Cd and Ni-MH batteries; they'll last longer. Third, keep battery contacts clean with a little alcohol or just a dry cloth. Fourth, never handle a battery that has ruptured or broken; the chemicals are very dangerous. Last, always recycle old batteries.

LCDs

While batteries can often cause angst for troubleshooting, LCDs (liquid crystal displays) cause the most angst *before* the computer is purchased due to the high cost and vast selection. The cost of the LCD is usually 50 to 75 percent of the total cost of the laptop, so you want to make sure to purchase the proper LCD.

The secret to understanding LCD panels is to understand the concept of polarity in light. Everyone knows that light travels in waves. In fact, the wavelength of light is what determines its color. What we don't appreciate is the fact that the orientation of the waves is three-dimensional. To visualize this, think of light coming from a flashlight, as shown in Figure 18.16. Now think of the light from that flashlight as if someone were shaking a jump rope (Figure 18.17)—but not a rhythmic shaking back and forth or up and down, more as if someone were shaking it up, down, left, and right, constantly changing the speed.

That's how light really acts. The different speeds create wavelengths, from very short to very long. When light comes into your eyes at many

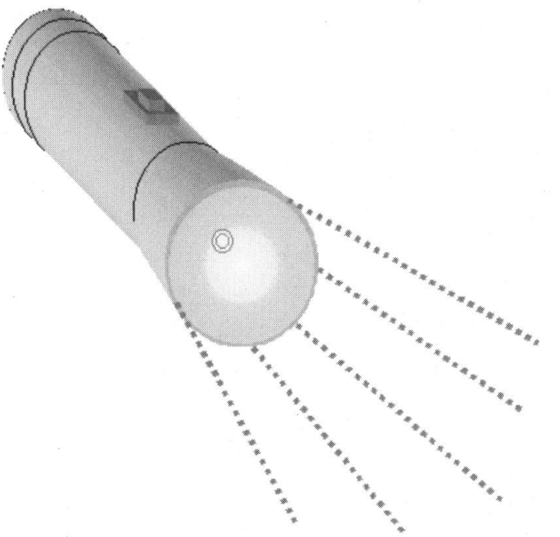

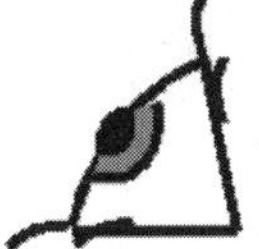

Figure 18.16
Light coming from a flashlight

Figure 18.17
Light waves are like someone shaking a jump rope

Figure 18.18
Waves of similar orientation

Figure 18.19
Effect of polarization

different wavelengths, you see white light. If the light comes in only one wavelength, you will see only that color.

A polarizing filter is like putting a picket fence between you and the person shaking the rope. You see all the wavelengths, but only the waves of similar orientation (see Figure 18.18). We would still see all of the colors, just less of them, making the image darker (Figure 18.19). That's why many sunglasses use polarizing filters.

Now what would happen if you added another picket fence, but put the slats in a horizontal direction, as shown in Figure 18.20? This would effectively cancel out all the waves, which is what happens when two polarizing filters are combined at a 90-degree angle—no light passes through (see Figure 18.21).

Now what would happen if you added a third fence between the two fences, with the slats at a 45-degree angle? It would "twist" some of the shakes in the rope so they could get through (Figure 18.22). This is what happens with polarizing filters. The third filter twists some of the light so it gets through (Figure 18.23).

Liquid crystals are composed of long, thin molecules that like to orient themselves in the same direction (Figure 18.24). When these molecules are placed in contact with a grooved surface, they attempt to line up with the

Figure 18.20
Two sets of slats, at 90 degrees to each other, allow no waves to pass

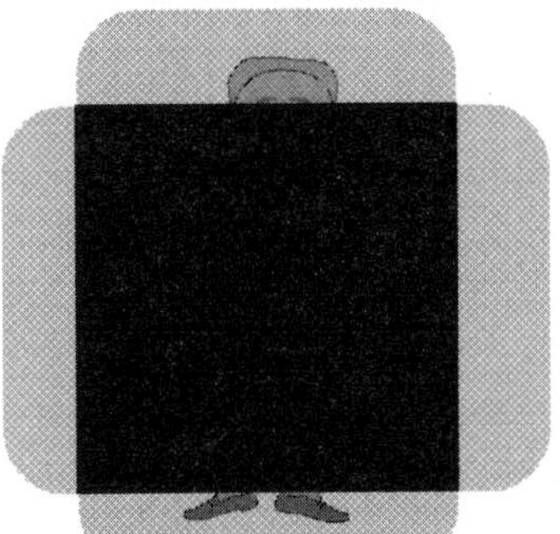

Regular Image

Image viewed through two polarized lens at 90 degrees relative rotation

Figure 18.21
Two polarizing filters, through which no light passes

Figure 18.22 Three sets of slats, which allow waves to get through

Figure 18.23 Three polarizing filters, where lights gets through

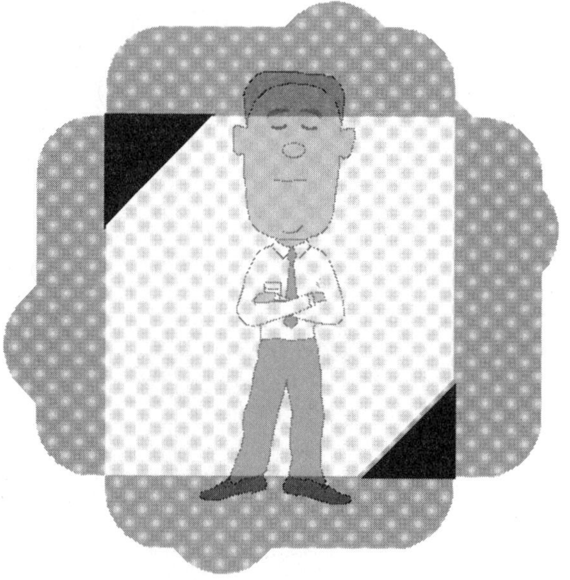

Image viewed through two polarized lens at 90° relative rotation with a third 45° lens in between

Figure 18.24 Liquid crystal molecules

grooves in the surface (Figure 18.25). If another grooved surface is placed opposite of the first one, the molecules in contact with that side attempt to line up with it. The molecules in between, in trying to line up with both sides, will immediately line up in a nice twist (Figure 18.26).

So if two perpendicular polarizing filters are placed on either side of the liquid crystal, the liquid crystal will twist the light and allow it to pass (Figure 18.27). But if the liquid crystal is exposed to an electrical potential, the crystals change their orientation, the twist goes away, and no light passes through (Figure 18.28).

So how do you charge the right spot? In the first LCDs, each piece of whatever you wanted to view was marked out and filled with liquid crystal. To darken an area, it was charged (Figure 18.29), called *static charging*. This is still quite popular in numeric displays such as calculators and cellular phones.

The static method would not work in PCs due to its inherent inflexibility. Instead, the screen was crossed with a matrix of wires (Figure 18.30). The vertical Y wires were on one side of the liquid crystal, and the horizontal X wires were on the other side. By lighting any X and Y wire, a small part of the display could be charged, cutting off light transfer.

If you want color, you have three matrices that intersect very close together. Above the intersections, the glass is painted with tiny red, green, and blue dots. The amount of voltage would allow different levels of red, green, and blue, creating colors (Figure 18.31). This is called *passive matrix*

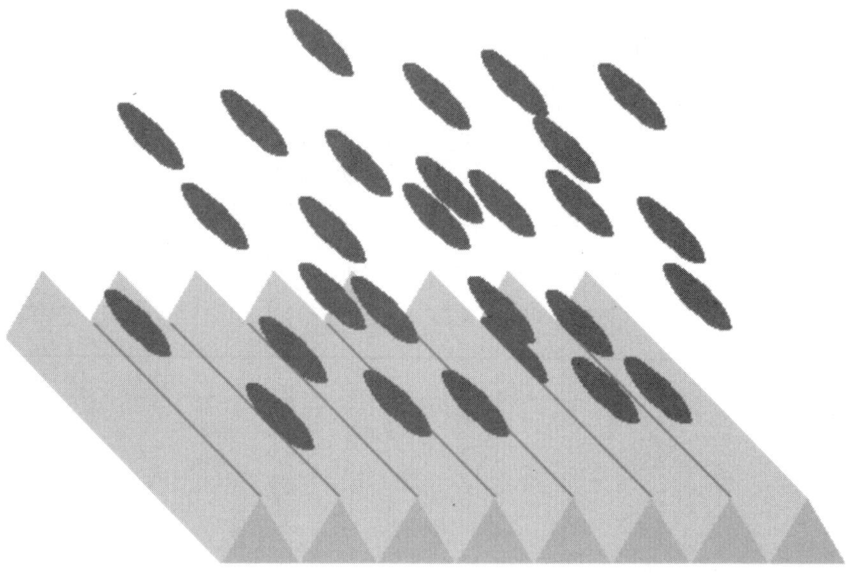

Figure 18.25 Liquid crystal molecules tend to line up together

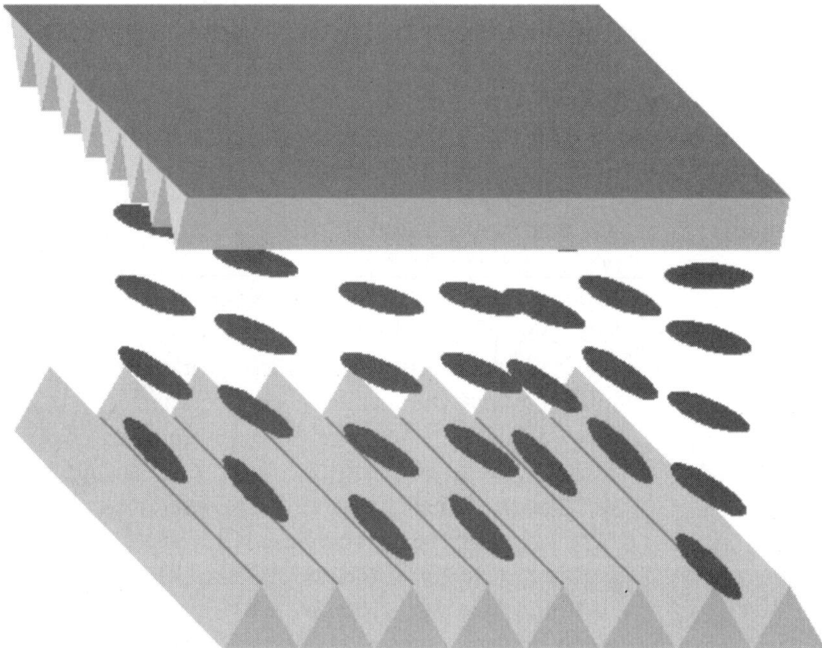

Figure 18.26 Liquid crystal molecules twisting

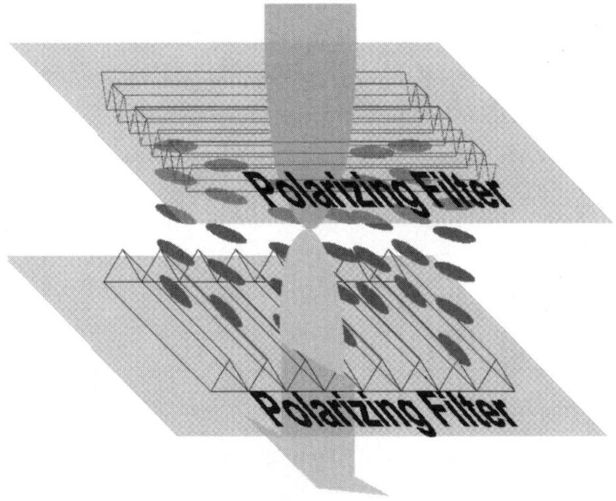

Figure 18.27
No charge, allowing light to pass

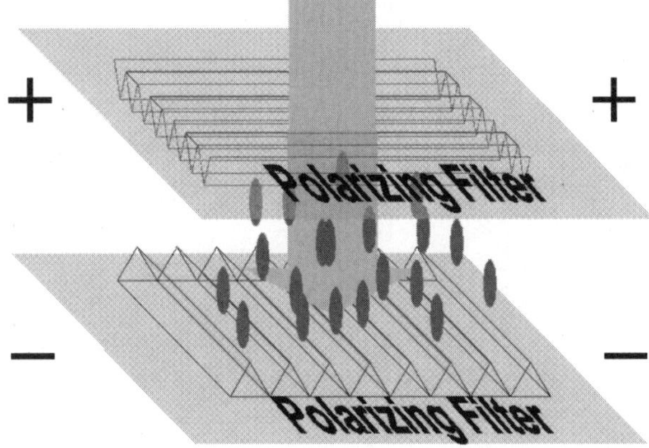

Figure 18.28
Electrical charge, allowing no light to pass

and was the only way to create color on a PC's LCD for many years. Unfortunately, passive matrix is slow and tends to create a little overlap. The speed was improved by allowing the screen to be refreshed two lines at a time, called *dual-scan passive matrix,* which is the most common low-end way to create color LCDs panels.

A vast improvement over dual scan is *active matrix.* Instead of using X and Y lines, each color dot is controlled by its own tiny transistor, providing faster refresh and much tighter color control. Active matrix is the LCD of choice today, even though it is much more expensive than passive matrix (Figure 18.32).

Active matrix displays have many advantages over passive matrix displays. First, they are brighter and have better contrast. Second, they can handle far more colors. The passive's slow speed keeps it at a practical

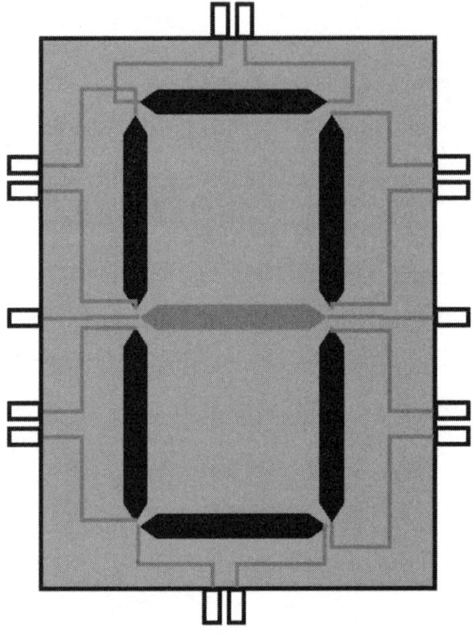

Figure 18.29 Single character for static LCD numeric display

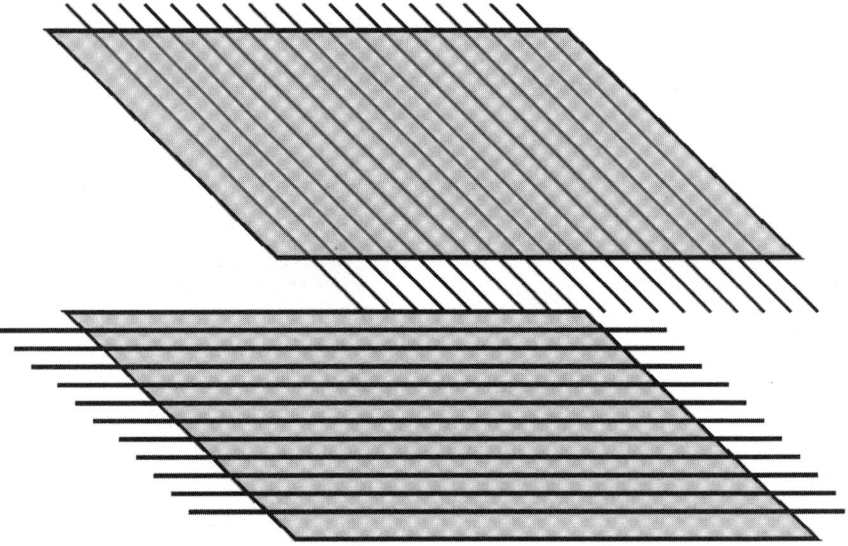

Figure 18.30 Matrix LCD

limit of no more than 256 colors (8 bits), while the latest active matrix displays can display up to 16.7 million colors (24 bits). Third, active matrix displays have a much wider viewing area (Figure 18.33). Where passive matrix displays are rarely more than 45 degrees, active matrix displays are closer to 100 degrees!

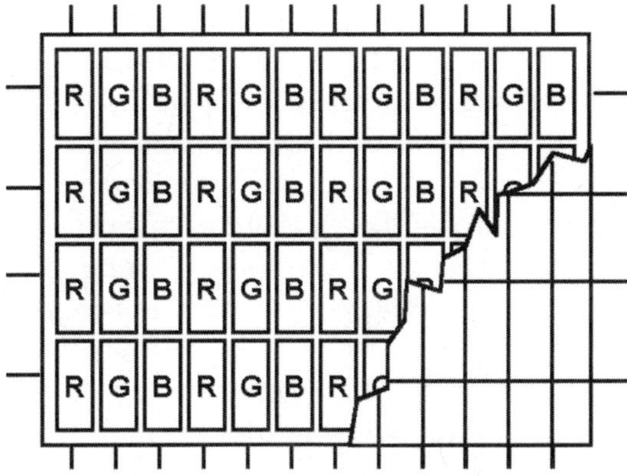

Figure 18.31
Color matrix LCD

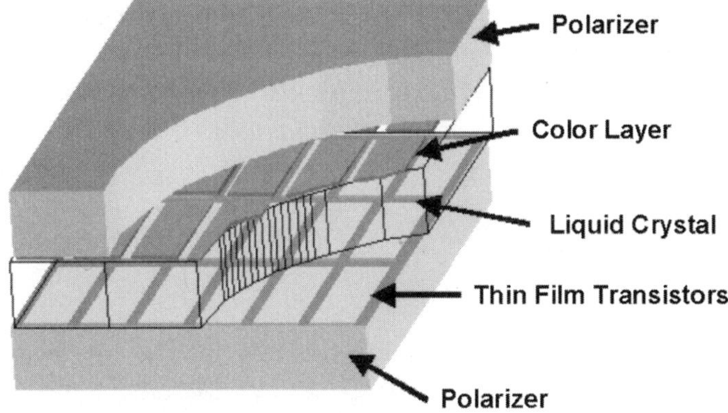

Figure 18.32
Active matrix cutaway

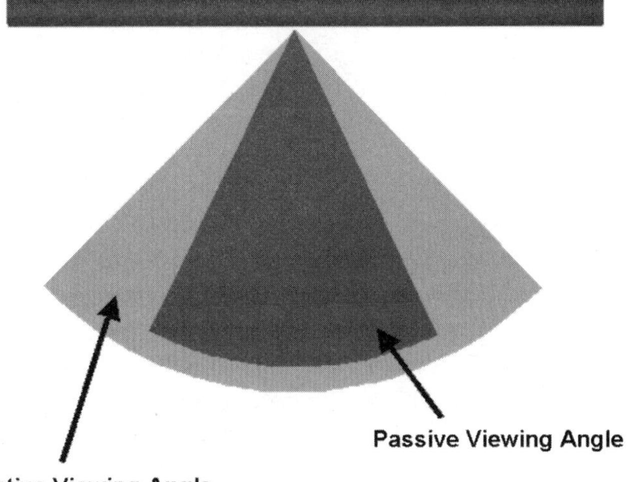

Figure 18.33
Viewing angle for active and passive matrix

Although LCD technology is vastly different from that of CRT, the daily support of LCD panels is quite similar to the support for CRTs. LCDs have a bandwidth, just like CRTs, although it is often referred as the *dot rate.* If you go past the dot rate, you create the same problems as when you push the refresh rate on a CRT. Fortunately, since the video is almost always a permanent part of the system, this is handled by the PC's manufacturer. This leads to a bigger problem—video drivers on laptops.

As discussed in the chapter on video, it is common, even necessary, to constantly update video drivers and tweak CRT refresh rates on desktop systems. The reverse is true for laptops. Since laptop makers don't anticipate users replacing or tweaking their video drivers, many continue to place ancient, bizarre device drivers in CONFIG.SYS, AUTOEXEC.BAT, SYSTEM.INI, and WIN.INI. Most of these drivers are simply to support DOS applications, but they can also be for video refresh or screen remapping (to get rid of excess blank space on the monitor in different modes). When dealing with laptop video drivers, stick to the manufacturer's settings unless you absolutely have to do otherwise.

PC Cards

PC cards, still commonly known by the older term PCMCIAs, which stands for the Personal Computer Memory Card International Association, are as standard on today's mobile computers as the hard drive. They are credit-card-sized, hot-swappable devices that can and do perform virtually every PC function (Figure 18.34). Although originally visualized as a memory card, today there are PC card hard drives, modems, network cards, sound cards, SCSI drives . . . the list continues almost indefinitely. PC cards are easy to use, inexpensive, and convenient.

Unfortunately, it is this same convenience and ease of use that makes PC cards a real challenge to configure and troubleshoot. Like so many other parts of the PC, the secret to understanding the individual components of PC cards is recognizing symptoms when they happen. The place to start is recognizing that there are three different physical sizes of PC cards, as determined by the PCMCIA committee: Type I, Type II, and Type III (see Table 18.1). While PCMCIA doesn't require that certain sizes perform certain functions, most PC cards follow their recommendations.

The only difference between the three types is the thickness of the card. All PC cards share the same 68-pin interface; as long as the slot that accepts the card is high enough, any PC card will work in that slot. Type

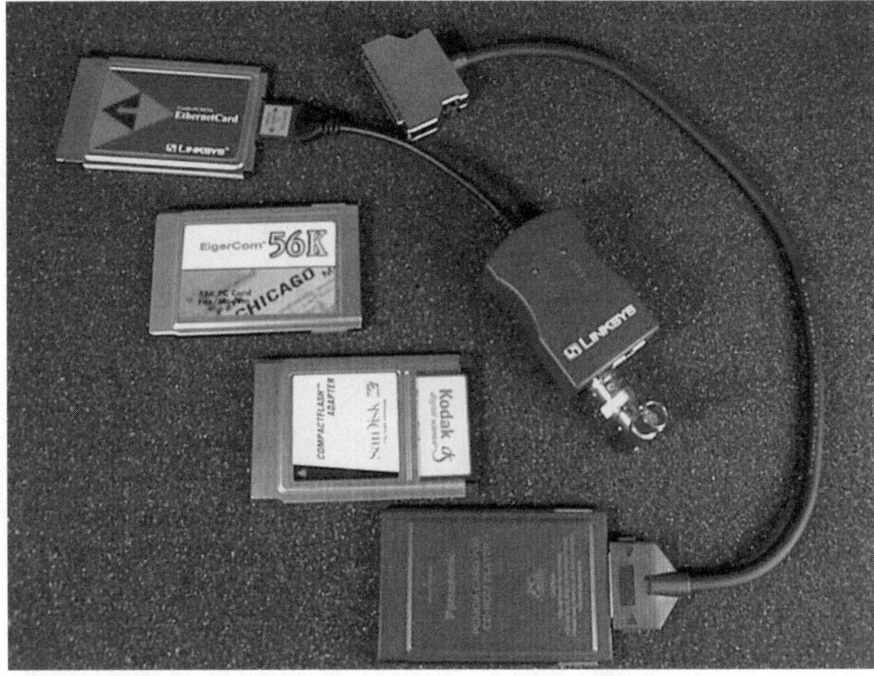

Figure 18.34
Assorted PC cards

TABLE 18.1

Type I, Type II, and Type III PC Cards

Length	Width	Thickness	Recommended Use	
Type I	85.6 mm	54.0 mm	3.3 mm	Flash memory
Type II	85.6 mm	54.0 mm	5.0 mm	I/O (modem, LAN, etc.)
Type III	85.6 mm	54.0 mm	10.5 mm	Hard drives

II cards are by far the most common, so most laptops will have two Type II slots, one above the other, to allow the computer to accept two Type I or II cards or one Type III card (Figure 18.35).

The PCMCIA standard defines two levels of software drivers to support PC cards. The first, lower level is known as *socket services*, which are device drivers that support the PC card socket, allowing the system to detect when a PC card has been inserted or removed, and providing the necessary I/O to the device. The second, higher level is known as *card services*, which recognizes the function of the card and provides the specialized drivers necessary to make a particular PC card work. When PC cards were first used back in the days of DOS and Windows 3.*x*, card and socket services were manifested through device drivers in CONFIG.SYS, AU-

Figure 18.35 Two PC cards in a laptop

TOEXEC.BAT, and SYSTEM.INI. Here's a hypothetical example from an old laptop that runs only DOS:

```
DEVICE=C:\SERVICES\PCMCIA2.SYS /M=D000-DFFF /L
DEVICE=C:\SERVICES\TOSCS.SYS
```

The early days of PCMCIA put most of the responsibility of making PC cards work in the hands of the individual laptop manufacturers, so if you wanted to be sure a PC card worked, you had to purchase it from the same place you got the laptop. This problem continued until Windows 95 and modern laptop chipsets arrived on the scene. In today's laptops, the socket services are standardized and handled by the system BIOS. Windows 95 itself handles all card services and has a large preinstalled base of PC card device drivers, although most PC cards come with their own drivers. The Windows 95 card services can be accessed via the PCMCIA option in the Control Panel. See Figure 18.36a.

Many PC card makers advertise a Type IV slot. It is not part of the PCMCIA standard and is used to describe any PC card thicker than Type III. The newest type of PC card is called *cardbus,* which is nothing more than a special 32-bit PC card type and special slot. The cardbus has some major advantages over regular PC cards. It is 32 bits rather than 16 bits, it

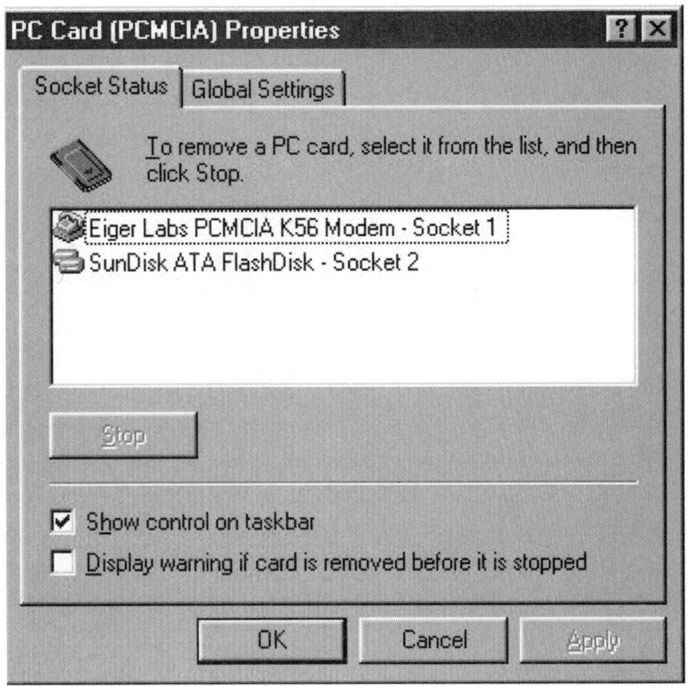

Figure 18.36a
PC card settings

can handle PCI bus mastering since it is really an extension of PCI, and it allows for single cards to have up to eight functions. Regular PC cards can have a maximum of only two functions. An example of a two-function PC card is a modem/network card. Well, don't be surprised to find you can purchase a modem/network/ISDN/sound/SCSI card! A cardbus PC card is identical to a regular PC card, comes in the same types, and has the exact same pinout. This allows regular PC cards to work in a cardbus slot. Unfortunately, a Cardbus card will not work in a regular PC card socket. In fact, a cardbus uses 3.3-volt power instead of the regular 5-volt PC card power, so a cardbus has special keying that won't allow you to accidentally plug it into a regular PC card socket. The cardbus has become the PC card of the future, and is standard equipment on most new laptops. Finally, in order for a cardbus to operate, the laptop should be running Windows 95 OSR2 or later.

Power Management

There are a lot of different parts to the typical laptop, and each part of that laptop uses power. The problem with early laptops was that every one of these parts used power, whether the system needed that device or not. For example, the hard drive continued to spin whether or not it was being accessed, and the LCD would continue to display, even when the user walked away from the machine.

The optimal situation is a system where the user could instruct the PC to selectively shut off unused devices, preferably by defining an amount of time of inactivity that, if reached, would shut down a particular device. Longer periods of inactivity would allow the entire system to eventually shut even itself down, leaving crucial information loaded in RAM, ready to restart the system in the event of a "wake-up" action, such as pressing a key or moving the mouse. This type of system would have to be sensitive to potential hazards, such as shutting down in the middle of writing to a drive, and could not add significantly to the cost of the PC. Clearly, a machine that could perform these functions would need specialized hardware, BIOS, and an operating system to allow proper operation. This process of cooperation between hardware, BIOS, and the OS to reduce power use is known generically as *power management*.

SMM

Intel began the process of power management in a series of new features built into the 386SX CPU. These new features allowed the CPU to slow down or stop its clock without erasing the register information, and a number of other features dealt with power saving in peripherals. These collective features were called *System Management Mode* (SMM). From the humble beginnings of the 386SX, SMM slowly started to appear in, and is a now common addition to, all PC CPUs. Although a power-saving CPU was okay, the power management was relegated to little more than special "sleep" or "doze" buttons that would stop the CPU and all the peripherals on the laptop. In order to really take advantage of SMM, the system required a specialized BIOS and OS to go with the SMM CPU. To this end, Intel forwarded the *Advanced Power Management* (APM) specification in 1992.

APM

APM requires several items in order to function fully. First on the list is an SMM-capable CPU. As virtually all CPUs are SMM-capable, this is easy. The second is an APM-compliant BIOS, which allows the CPU to send the necessary commands to shut off peripherals when desired. The third requirement is that it must have peripherals that will accept being shut off. These are usually called Energy Star devices to show their compliance with the EPA's Energy Star rating. To be an Energy Star device, a peripheral must be able to be shut down without actually being turned off. Last, the system's OS must know how to shut down particular devices, and either slow down or stop the CPU's clock.

APM defines five different operating levels of power usage for a system, which are intentionally "fuzzy" to allow manufacturers considerable leeway in their use. The only real difference between them is the amount of time for each power usage level to return to normal usage. The levels are:

FULL ON Everything in the system is running full power, with no power management.

APM ENABLED The CPU and RAM are running at full power, with power management enabled. An unused device might be shut down.

APM STANDBY The CPU is stopped, RAM still stores all programs, all peripherals are shut down, and configuration options are stored (in other words, to get back to APM enabled, you don't have to reinitialize the devices).

APM SUSPEND Everything in the PC is shut down or in their lowest power-consumption settings. Many systems use a special type of suspension called "hibernation" where crucial configuration information is written to the hard drive. Upon a wake up event, the system is reinitialized and the data is read from the drive to return the system to the APM enabled mode. Clearly, the recovery time from suspend to enable modes is much longer than the time from standby to enable modes.

The APM BIOS can be configured via CMOS settings (Figure 18.36b) or through the OS. Generally, OS settings will override CMOS settings. Even though the APM standards allow a great deal of flexibility, and therefore some confusion between different implementations, there are certain settings for all CMOSes. First is the ability to initialize power management, which allows a system to enter the APM enabled mode. Many CMOSes will then provide time frames for entering standby and suspend modes, as well as determining which events take place in each of these modes. Finally, many CMOSes will provide settings to determine wake-up events. An example might be the ability for a system to monitor a modem or a particular IRQ.

Figure 18.36b CMOS power settings

```
                    ROM PCI/ISA BIOS (2A69HQ1A)
                      POWER MANAGEMENT SETUP
                       AWARD SOFTWARE, INC.

Power Management       : Disable        ** Power Down & Resume Events **
PM Control by APM      : No             IRQ3  (COM 2)         : OFF
Video Off Method       : Blank Screen   IRQ4  (COM 1)         : OFF
MODEM Use IRQ          : 4              IRQ5  (LPT 2)         : OFF
                                        IRQ6  (Floppy Disk)   : OFF
Doze Mode              : Disable        IRQ7  (LPT 1)         : OFF
Standby Mode           : Disable        IRQ8  (RTC Alarm)     : OFF
Suspend Mode           : Disable        IRQ9  (IRQ2 Redir)    : OFF
HDD Power Down         : Disable        IRQ10 (Reserved)      : OFF
                                        IRQ11 (Reserved)      : OFF
** Wake Up Events In Doze & Standby **  IRQ12 (PS/2 Mouse)    : OFF
IRQ3  (Wake-Up Event): OFF              IRQ13 (Coprocessor)   : OFF
IRQ4  (Wake-Up Event): OFF              IRQ14 (Hard Disk)     : OFF
IRQ8  (Wake-Up Event): OFF              IRQ15 (Reserved)      : OFF
IRQ12 (Wake-Up Event): OFF
                                        ESC : Quit        ↑↓→← : Select Item
                                        F1  : Help        PU/PD/+/- : Modify
                                        F5  : Old Values  (Shift)F2 : Color
                                        F6  : Load BIOS  Defaults
                                        F7  : Load Setup Defaults
```

Configuring an OS for power management is a highly progressive process, dating from the early DOS-based systems, through Windows 3.*x*, and ending with the highly integrated functions of Windows 95/98.

In DOS, the only real tool was the POWER.EXE program, which gave DOS the ability to handle power management. Depending on the version, POWER.EXE was also capable of a broad cross-section of settings for most APM functions. Interestingly, most users simply added POWER.EXE to the CONFIG.SYS and AUTOEXEC.BAT file, and accepted the default settings. As Windows 3.*x* became more common, many laptop makers began to add special applications that would either add configurations to POWER.EXE or add their own protected-mode APM tools. Either way, the lack of any standard interface made power management a rather interesting experience, since each manufacturer had their own opinion as to what constituted power management!

APM in Windows 95 and later has greatly simplified the process of power management, primarily by creating a standard interface. Power management shows itself in two areas. The first area is the Monitor settings in the Control Panel. These settings can also be accessed by right-clicking on the desktop. Since the monitor is one of the biggest power users, this is a great place to start the power-management configuration process (Figure 18.37).

Windows 95/98 hides the APM concept of standby and suspend, with the exception of adding the Suspend option to the Start button. Instead,

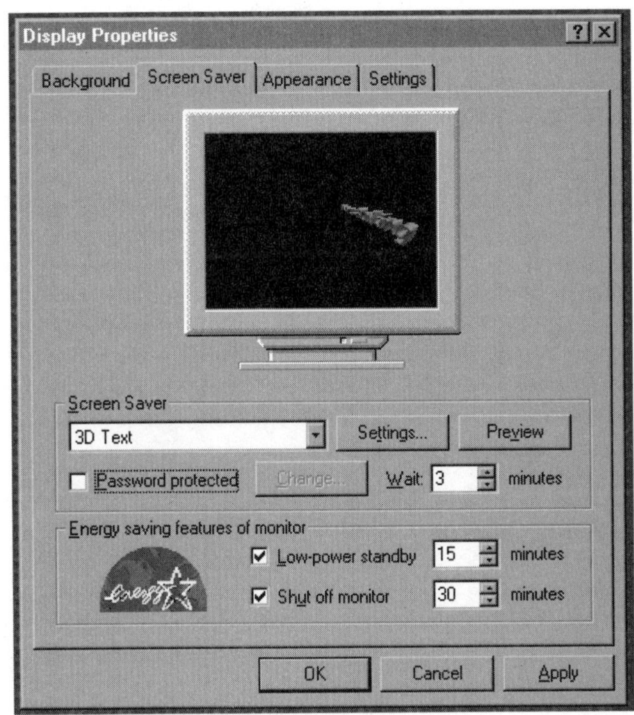

Figure 18.37 Monitor power settings

Windows tries to provide individual control for the big power eaters—monitors, PC cards, and hard drives—and makes its own assumptions for everything else in the PC. These controls can be found in the Power section of the Control Panel (Figure 18.38).

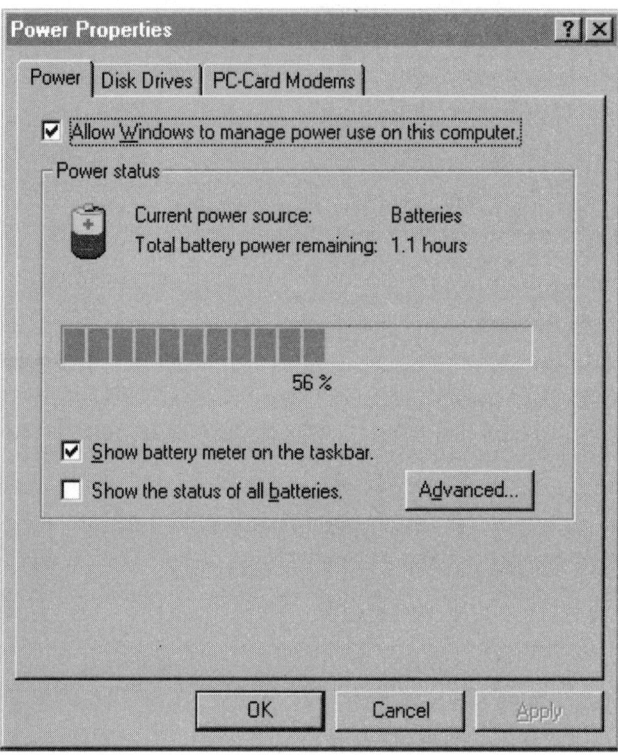

Figure 18.38
Power settings

CHAPTER 19

Networks

Early on in the life of the personal computer, it became obvious that there was a need for separate PCs to be able to share data and peripherals. Certainly, any PC can read another's data by way of floppy disks. But moving data to a floppy, physically transporting the data to another machine, inserting the floppy, and accessing the data requires time. Although functional, it was very slow; and for certain types of data, it was completely useless. In particular, the PC world likes many users to be able to access simultaneously the same information. This type of data could be a list of customers, inventories, students, etc. The examples of this type of data, better known as a *database*, are endless. Next, there is a great demand for sharing devices. Why give everyone in a company a laser printer when a single laser printer that everyone can access would be sufficient?

Clearly, there was a strong motivation to create a grouping of PCs, a *network,* that can share data and peripherals. The big question was how. It's easy to say, "Just run a wire between them!" Although most networks do manifest themselves via some type of cable, this barely touches the thousands of questions that come into play here. Here are a few of the big questions:

- How will each computer be identified? If two or more computers want to talk at the same time, how can you ensure that all conversations are understood?
- What kind of wire? What gauge? How many wires in the cable? What do all of the wires do? How long can the cable be? What type of connectors?
- If more than one PC is accessing the same file, how can they be prevented from destroying each other's changes to that file?
- How can access to data and peripherals be controlled?

Clearly, there is a lot more to making a network than just "stringing up some cable." The standard PC network can be broken up into four major areas: hardware, protocols, sharing resources, and accessing shared resources. This chapter, for the most part, is broken down into these four categories and will discuss each one in great detail. Let's take a quick look at the categories so you'll know what to expect:

HARDWARE The hardware is probably the most self-explanatory of all four of the categories. This section will cover the many different ways data can be moved from one PC to another, as well as the different types of cabling (or lack thereof if the network is wireless). This section also explains how network cards are installed and tested. The hardware category hits on all those interesting boxes to which all of the wires in a network run (hubs, switches, and repeaters). Finally, this section will explain all the hardware terms, such as *Ethernet, 10BaseT,* and *topology.*

PROTOCOLS Protocols are the language of networks. They have interesting names such as NetBEUI, IPX/SPX, and the ever-popular TCP/IP. A protocol is a highly standardized language that handles most of the "invisible" functions on a network, such as determining which computer is "Server 1" and disassembling/reassembling data passed over the network. In early computer networks, there was only one protocol. Today it is common for the same network to run more than one protocol, primarily to allow that network to connect to other networks. This section will cover the most common protocols used today and will show how they are installed, configured, and repaired.

SHARING RESOURCES Once the hardware is installed and the protocol is determined, the next step is to decide what resources will be shared and how the sharing will manifest itself. In this section, the concepts of client/server and peer-to-peer will be clarified. Also, if a drive, directory, or file is to be shared, that item must be named so the network can display it to other PCs as being available for sharing. The rules for naming shared resources are known as *naming conventions.* A good example is a system that offers its D:\FRED directory for sharing. This D:\FRED directory needs a network name, such as SERVE_FRED. This network name is displayed to all the devices on the network. The process of creating shared resource names will be covered in this section. A network also needs to control access to resources. A laser printer, for example, might be available for sharing, but best used solely by the Accounting department, excluding other departments. This section describes in detail how networks make resources available and control access to those resources.

ACCESSING SHARED RESOURCES Individual systems need to be able to access shared resources. There needs to be a process by which a PC can look at the network and see what is available. Having found those available resources, the PC then needs to be able to treat them as though they were local resources. For example, say another computer has offered a shared resource called SERVE_FRED. The local machine might want to create a phony drive called H:, which is really the SERVE_FRED resource. The process of taking network resources and making them act like local resources is popularly called *redirecting.*

Hardware

The most obvious item shared by all networks is the need for hardware. There must be some way to get the bits of data between computers. For the overwhelming majority of networks, this means all the PCs are linked together through some type of cabling. Invariably, all the cables from all the PCs come together in some mysterious box called a *hub*. Even though most networks share the same basic "look and feel," the way the data moves around inside those wires might be quite different from one network to the next. The term *topology* describes these different configurations.

Packets/Frames

Before we dive into the concept of topology, you need to understand that data is moved from one PC to another in discrete chunks called *packets* or *frames*. These terms are interchangeable. Every network card (commonly called a *network interface card* or *NIC*) in the world has a built-in identifier called a media access control (MAC) address, a binary address that is unique for every network card. That's right—every network card in the world has a unique MAC address. The MAC address is 48 bits long, which provides for over 281 trillion MAC addresses, so there are plenty to go around (Figure 19.1).

Later you will see that there are many different types of frames, but there are certain aspects that all frames have in common (Figure 19.2). First, packets contain the MAC address of the network card to which data is sent. Second, they have the MAC address of the network card that sends the data. Third is the data itself, which can be different sizes depending on the type of frame. Last, there is some type of data check to allow the receiving network card to verify if the data was received in good order.

Topology

The layout of the cabling between computers on a network is the network's *topology*. Since the first networks were invented over 30 years ago, many types of topologies have been invented. However, there are only two types commonly used in today's networks: bus and ring topologies. Each has its advantages and disadvantages. The best topology for a specific situ-

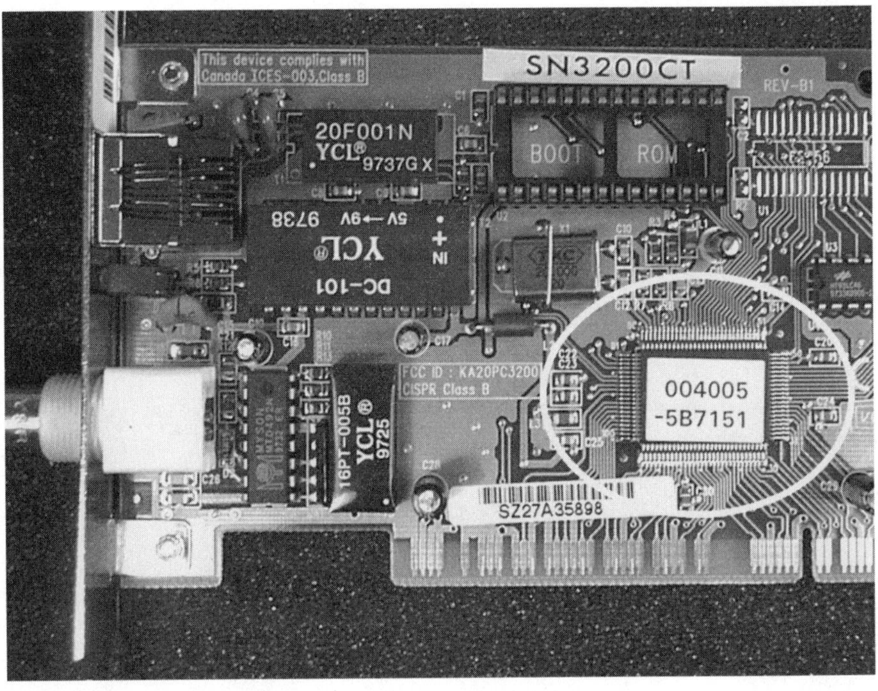

Figure 19.1 Some NICs have their MAC address on the card

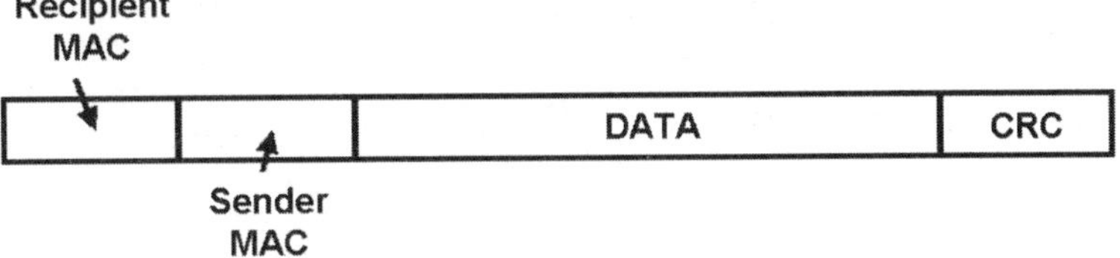

Figure 19.2 Generic frame/packet

ation depends on a variety of factors, including ease of installation, physical position of the PCs, number of PCs in the network, cost, and speed.

BUS TOPOLOGY The first type of topology was the bus topology, which means that all the PCs are connected via a single cable that runs to all the PCs. Although a bus topology looks like Figure 19.3, for simplicity, they are drawn as shown in Figure 19.4.

Although it was the first topology ever invented, the bus topology is still quite popular. In fact, most networks use it. A bus topology works like a big telephone party line; all devices must first listen to see if anyone else is sending packets before they can send a packet (Figure 19.5). If the cable is not being used, then the device sends its packet on the line. Every network card on the bus sees and reads the packet. This is called CSMA/CD (Carrier Sense Multiple Access/Collision Detection).

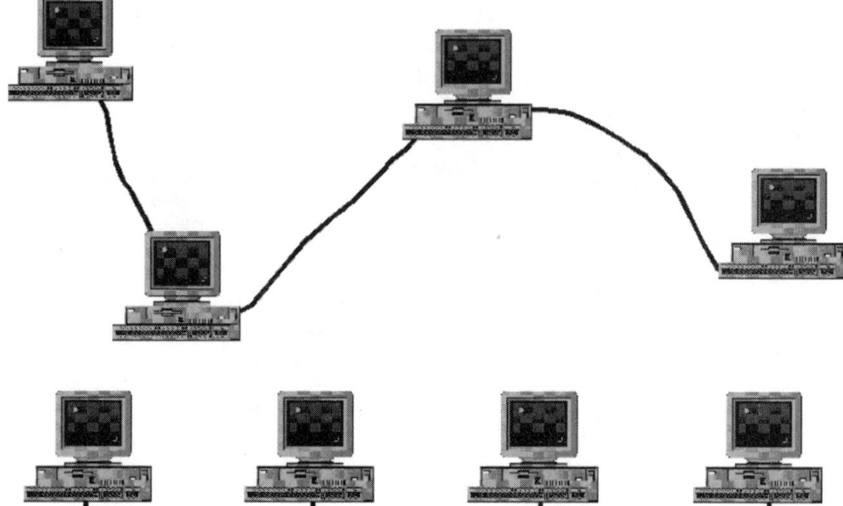

Figure 19.3 True wire path in a common bus topology

Figure 19.4 Topology schematic

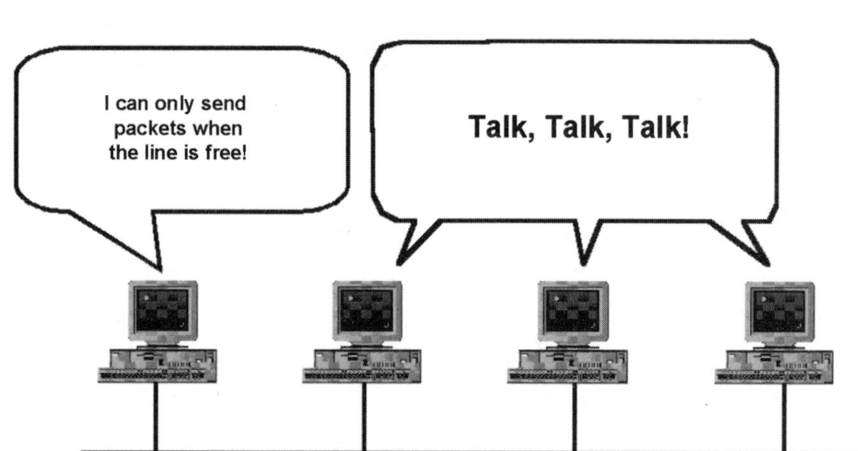

Figure 19.5 You can send packets only when the line is free!

Sometimes two cards do talk at the same time. This is called a *collision* and the cards themselves arbitrate to see who gets to resend their frames first (see Figure 19.6).

REFLECTION AND TERMINATION The ends of the bus topology present a bit of a problem: the signal. Any time voltages are being sent down a wire, some voltage will bounce back or "reflect" when it reaches the end of the wire (Figure 19.7). Network cables are no exception. Based on what we know so far, the packets would uselessly reflect back and forth, making the cards that want to send data wait for no reason. After a short while, the bus would be so full of reflecting packets that no other card could send data.

To prevent the packets from being reflected, a device called a *terminator* must be plugged into the end of the bus cable. A terminator is nothing more than a "pull-down" resistor that absorbs the signal, thus preventing reflection (Figure 19.8). This need for termination is a weak spot in bus topology; if the cable breaks anywhere, a packet storm is instantly created, and no device can send data, even if the break is not between the devices exchanging data (Figure 19.9).

RING TOPOLOGY Ring topology is more recent than bus topology (although that does not make it more popular). A ring topology connects all the PCs together on a single cable much like bus topology. However, as the name implies, the bus is shaped like a ring (Figure 19.10).

Oops! Pardon Me!
Excuse Me!

Figure 19.6
Packet collision

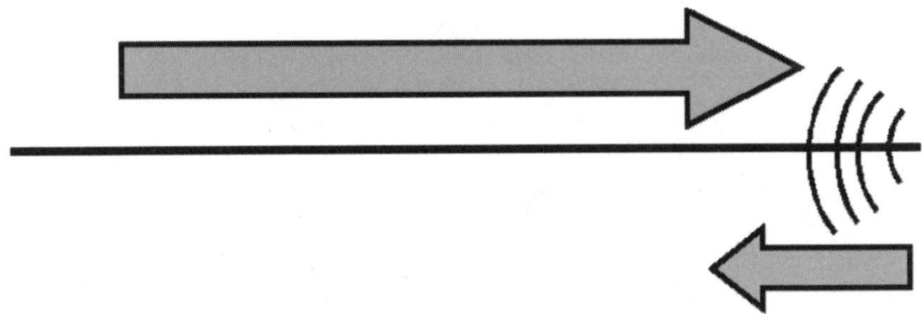
When an electrical signal
reaches the end of a wire ...
some of the signal
is reflected back

Figure 19.7
Reflection

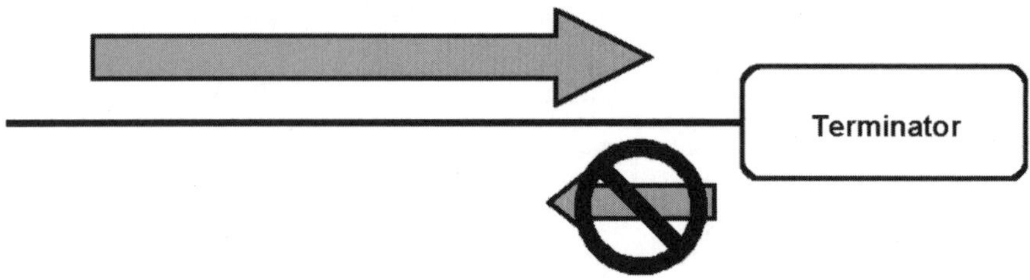
When an electrical signal
reaches the end of a terminated wire ...
Terminator
There is no reflection

Figure 19.8
Termination

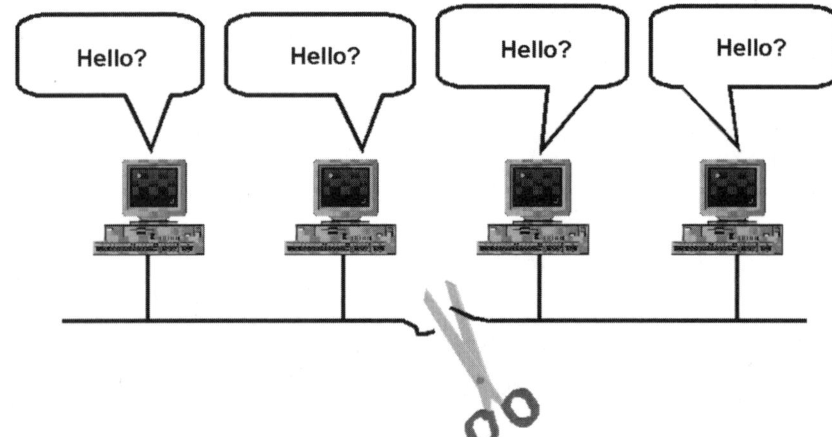
Hello?
Hello?
Hello?
Hello?

Figure 19.9
The network is down!

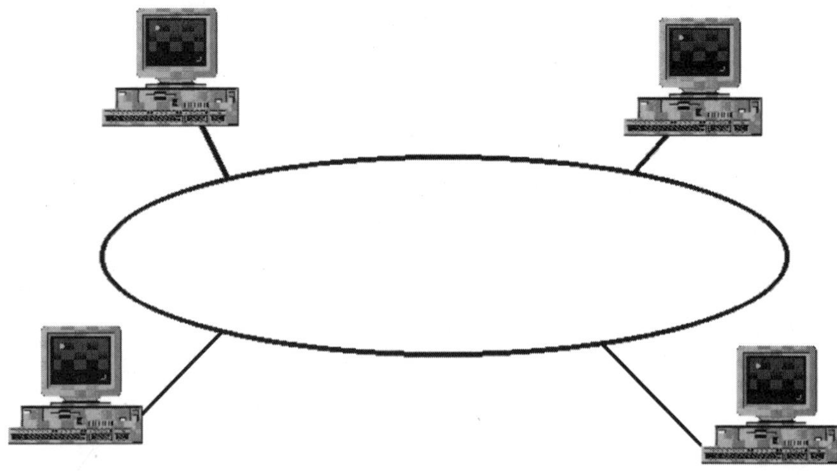

Figure 19.10
Ring topology

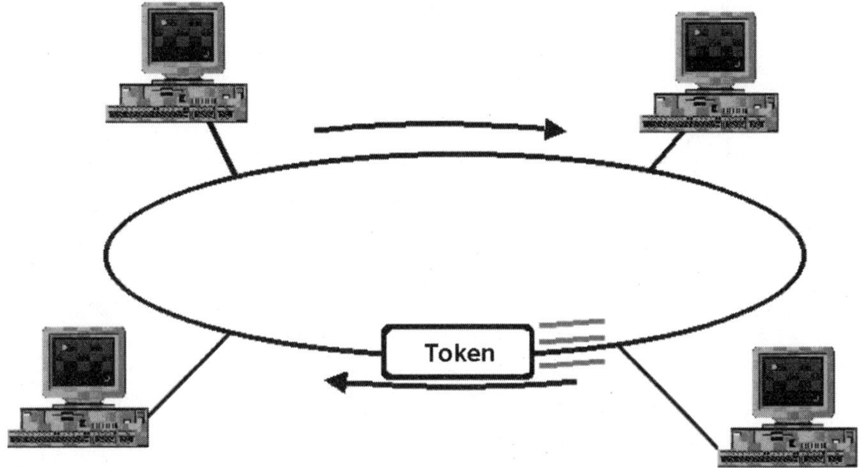

Figure 19.11
Token passing

Ring topologies use a transmission method called "token passing" in which a miniature packet called a *token* is constantly being passed from one card to the next in one direction (Figure 19.11). If one PC wants to talk to another, it must wait until it gets the token. The packet is then attached to the token and sent back out the ring. If another PC wants to send data, it must wait until a "free" token (one that doesn't have an attached packet) comes around.

Since ring topologies use token passing, the term *token-ring* is often used when describing ring networks. There were once a few instances of a ring topology using features other than token passing, but they are all long gone. If it is a ring topology, it is token-ring.

STAR RING The token-ring topology was perfected and packaged (though not invented) by IBM. Token-ring actually uses a topology called *star ring*. Instead of running a ring of cable all around the LAN, the cabling scheme is as shown in Figure 19.12. The ring is stored inside a special box called an MSAU or MAU (Multi-Station Access Unit), shown in Figure 19.13. It's often called just a *hub*, although most token-ring technicians would have a heart attack if you said it in earshot of them! Although token-ring is a ring, it looks more like a star.

Token-ring is slowly losing market share to bus-type topologies, because it was proprietary IBM technology and was more expensive than bus topology. However, it is still heavily used in hundreds of thousands of networks. Because token-ring normally uses a more robust type of cabling, it is also still very popular in areas where there is a lot of electrical interference. For example, many military vehicles like tanks and aircraft that need to link many computers within the vehicle use a modified form of token-ring.

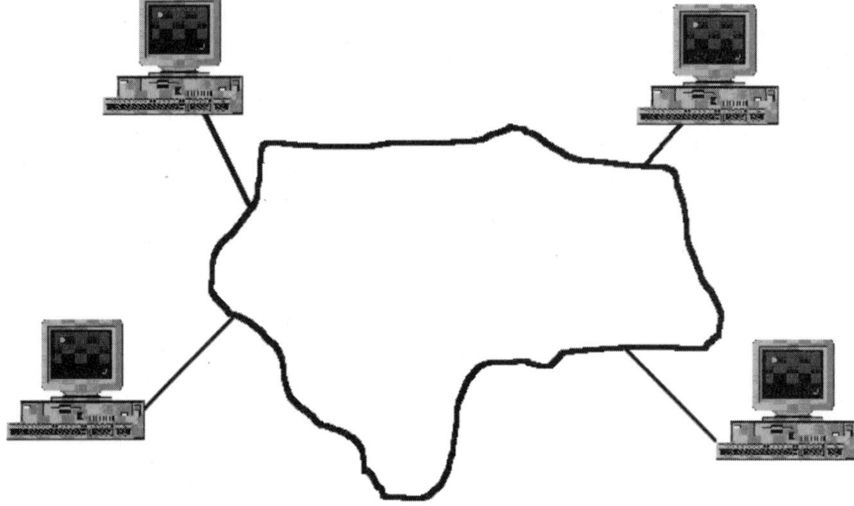

Figure 19-12 True wire path in a ring topology

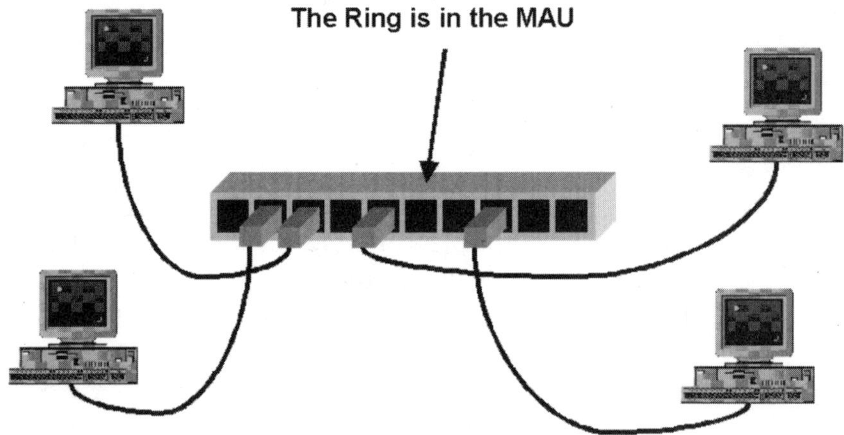

Figure 19.13 Token-ring with MSAU

STAR BUS The star configuration used in token-ring made it very dependable and easy to expand, which led to a variation of the bus topology called *star bus* (Figure 19.14). Both star and bus topologies have significant advantages and disadvantages.

Imagine if you had a bus network and shrank the bus down small enough to fit into a hub. The bus topology would sure look a lot like a star, wouldn't it? This type of topology, called a *star bus,* is the single most popular topology today. Cheap and centralized, a star bus network does not go down if a cable breaks. True, the network would go down if the hub itself failed, but that is very rare. Even if a hub were to fail, replacing a hub in a closet is much easier than following the bus running through walls and ceilings trying to find a break!

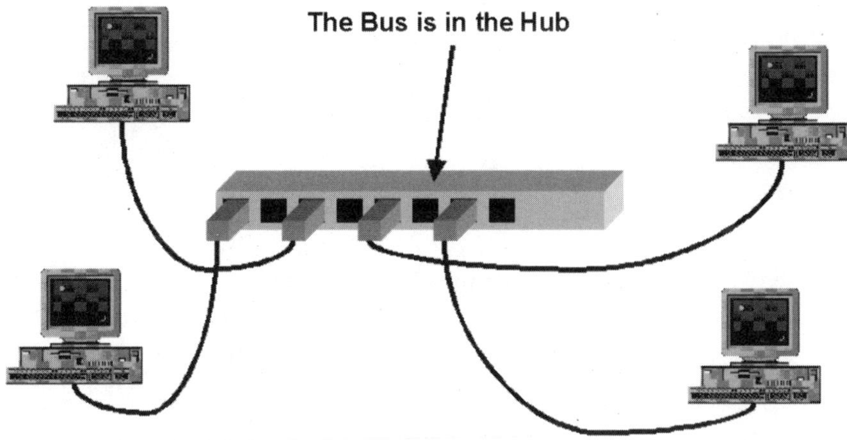

Figure 19.14
Star bus topology

Hardware Protocols

The next big question is: "What are the different types of frames?" The problem in answering this question is that it encompasses many items. When the first networks were being created, everything (frames, connectors, type of cable, etc.), had to be invented from scratch. A consortium of companies centered on Digital, Intel, and Xerox invented the first network in the mid-'70s. More than just creating a network, they wrote a series of standards that defined everything necessary to get data from one computer to another. This series of standards was called *Ethernet* and is the most dominant standard in today's networks.

Ethernet

The Ethernet standard is quite broad, based on a CSMA/CD bus topology. Ethernet standards were released to the IEEE (Institute of Electrical and Electronic Engineers) standards body, which still controls it today. The IEEE committee designated to handle the Ethernet standard was formed in February of 1980 and was given the name 802. The 802 Committee is still the primary body for changes and enhancements to the Ethernet standard, as well as other network standards.

COAXIAL CABLE Coaxial type is the oldest of all network cabling, but it is still widely used and supported. With a few exceptions, coaxial (coax) cable is used exclusively in bus topologies. By definition, coax cable is a cable within a cable; it contains two cables that share the same center or axis.

Coax consists of a center cable (core) surrounded by insulation, which is, in turn, covered with a "shield" of braided cable. The inner core actually carries the signal, and the shield effectively eliminates outside interference. The entire cable is then surrounded by a protective insulating cover.

THICK ETHERNET The original Xerox Ethernet specification defined a very specific type of cabling for the first Ethernet networks. This type of cable is called *Thick Ethernet* (Figure 19.15) and could handle data transfers of up to 10 megabits per second. Also known as *thicknet,* it is a very thick coaxial cable (about a half-inch in diameter) that is manufactured under the Belden 9580 standard. (Belden is a BIG cable manufacturer, and their internal part number for thick Ethernet is a very popular way to define thicknet.) The cable to which a PC is connected is called the *segment.* Thicknet can have up to 100 devices hooked to one segment. The maximum length of one segment is 500 meters.

Thicknet is clearly marked every 2.5 meters, which is where to connect devices to the cable (Figure 19.16). All devices on thicknet must be connected at these marks, which assures that all devices are some multiple of 2.5 meters apart. This spacing is required to reduce noise due to oscillations in the signal.

Devices are connected to thicknet with a "vampire connector," which pierces the cable, creating the connection. The vampire connector is also a transceiver, a device that both receives and sends data. The transceiver is the device that allows connections between devices and the common cable. Transceivers also detect when collisions take place. Actually, all networks use transceivers, but thicknet uses an external transceiver (Figure 19.17). The cable from the vampire connector/transceiver to the device must be no more than 50 meters.

Thick Ethernet uses a bus topology, so it needs terminators. There is a very specific terminator made just for thicknet, a 50-Ohm terminator that

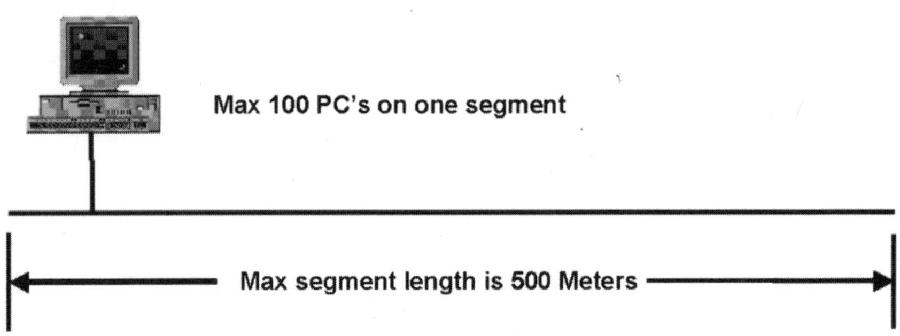
10BASE-5
Max 100 PC's on one segment
Max segment length is 500 Meters

Figure 19.15
Thick Ethernet

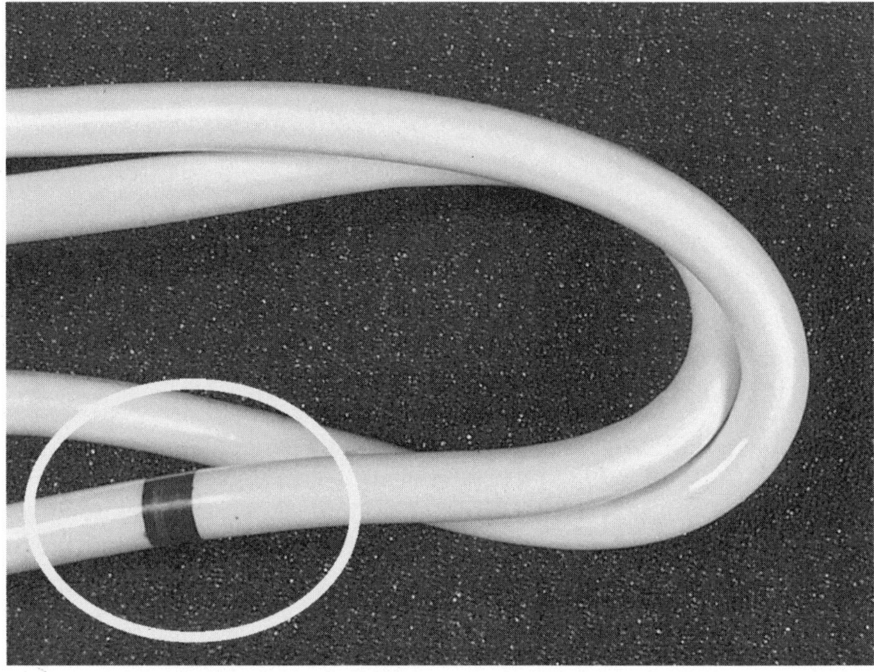

Figure 19.16 Spacing mark on thicknet

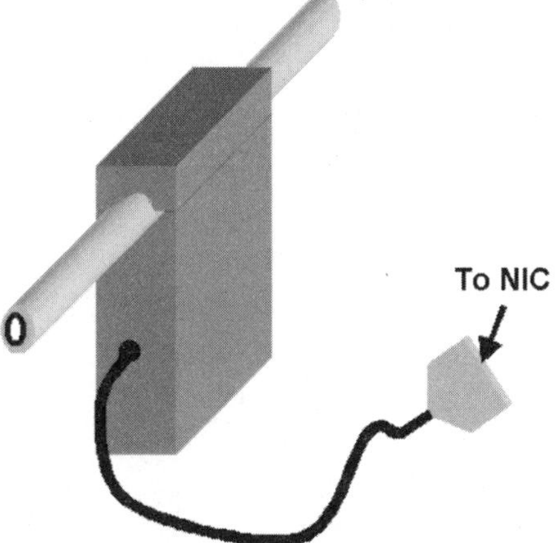

Figure 19.17 Drawing of a thicknet transceiver

must be placed on each end of the segment. Thicknet connects to the PC's network card via a 15-pin male connector. This connector is called the AUI or sometimes the DIX (Digital, Intel, Xerox) connector (Figure 19.18).

Thick Ethernet is on the way out. Bus topologies are always risky. One break on the cable will cause the entire network to fail. In addition, thicknet is hard to work with and expensive. The cable, transceivers, and terminators cost far more than in any other network. Thick Ethernet has a

Figure 19.18 Photo of a thicknet connector

substantial installed base and it is still actively used, especially where longer distances and/or heavy shielding are needed.

THIN ETHERNET Thin Ethernet, also known as *thinnet* or *cheapernet,* was invented as a less expensive alternate to thicknet. Thinnet is much easier to handle than thicknet, and is the preferred type of cabling for small networks.

Thinnet uses a specific type of coax called RG-58 (Figure 19.19). RG stands for *radio grade,* and it is an industry standard for measuring coax cables. This type of coax looks exactly like the coax used by your cable television, but it is quite different. A television cable is RG-6. If you attempt to use an RG-6 cable on your computer, the network will work poorly or not at all. The RG rating should be clearly marked on the cable. If it is not, it will specify something like "thinnet" or "802.3" to let you know you have the right cable.

While thin Ethernet also runs at 10 megabits/second, it has several considerable limitations not shared by thick Ethernet. Thin Ethernet can

Figure 19.19 Thin Ethernet coax

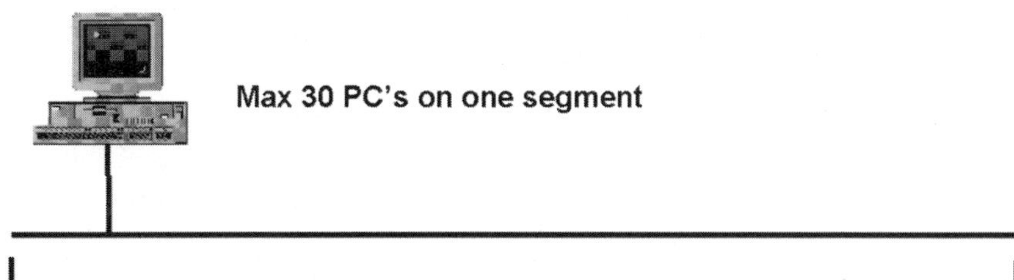
10BASE-2
Max 30 PC's on one segment
Max segment length is 185 Meters

Figure 19.20
Thin Ethernet

Figure 19.21
T connector

have only 30 devices per segment, and each segment can be only 185 meters long. However, cabling with thinnet is a snap compared to thicknet (Figure 19.20). The cable is much thinner and more flexible than thicknet. In addition, the transceiver is built into the thinnet network card, so thinnet does not require an external transceiver. Each thinnet network card is simply connected to the bus cable with a T connector (Figure 19.21).

The thinnet cable has twist-on BNC connectors that attach to the T connector, forming the network. Termination is handled by twisting on small, specialized terminators to the unused end of the T connector on the machines at the ends of the chain.

When installing thinnet, it is important to ground one of the terminators. There are special terminators that can be grounded to the case of the PC. Just be sure the PC is also grounded! You *must* use a T connector! Connecting the cable as shown in Figure 19.22 will not work. Figure 19.23 shows some examples of complete thinnet networks.

To add another PC to the network, simply remove the terminator from the last PC, and add another piece of cable with another T connector and terminator on the end. It is also very easy to add a PC between two systems by unhooking one side of a T connector and adding another PC and cable in between.

Thicknet and thinnet both use CSMA/CD and Ethernet packets. This means that, although the cable media is different, they "speak the same language." Consequently, many Ethernet network cards are designed to handle both thicknet and thinnet. These are usually called "combo cards." You can even purchase special converters that allow you to connect a thinnet network card to a thicknet cable and vice versa. However, this is rarely done. The "combo cards" are usually much cheaper than the converters.

Thinnet is very popular for SOHO (small office / home office) networks. However, given its relatively short maximum segment lengths and small number of devices per segment, thinnet is totally unacceptable for larger networks.

10BaseT

Probably the most popular of all networks today is Ethernet 10BaseT. This is Ethernet running on unshielded twisted-pair (UTP) wire, at 10 megabits/second in a star bus topology. Unlike other Ethernet flavors, 10BaseT does not use coaxial cable. Instead, 10BaseT is designed to work with unshielded twisted-pair cable.

UNSHIELDED TWISTED-PAIR Twisted-pair cabling is the defined cabling for 10BaseT, and is the predominant cabling system used today. There are many different types of twisted-pair cabling available, depending on the needs of the network. Twisted-pair cabling consists of AWG 22- to 26-gauge wire twisted together into color-coded pairs, loosely encased in a common insulation (Figure 19.24).

CAT LEVELS UTP cables come in categories that define the maximum speed at which data can be transferred (also called the *bandwidth*). The five major categories (CATs) are:

CAT 1: Standard phone lines
CAT 2: Data speeds up to 4 megabits/second, ISDN and T1 lines
CAT 3: Data speeds up to 16 megabits/second
CAT 4: Data speeds up to 20 megabits/second
CAT 5: Data speeds up to 100 megabits/second

Figure 19.22
Improper connection

Figure 19.23
Thinnet examples

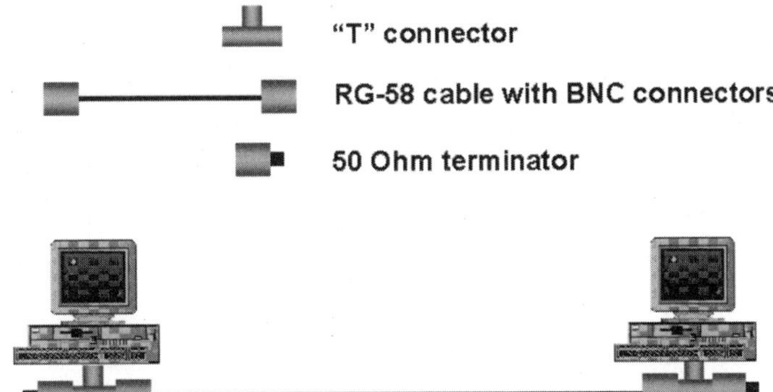

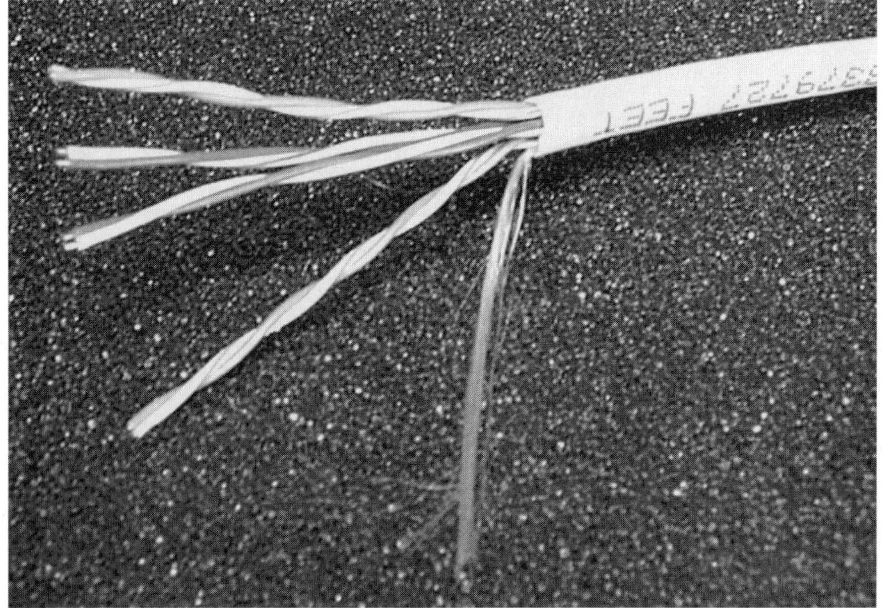

Figure 19.24 Unshielded twisted pair

The CAT level should be clearly marked on the cable, as shown in Figure 19.25. These categories are established by the TIA/EIA (Telecommunication Industry Association/Electronics Industry Association), and are under the EIA-568 specification. Currently, most installers use CAT 5 cable if they can afford it (CAT 5 is about 30 percent more expensive than CAT 3). Although most networks run at either 10 or 16 megabits/second, there is an entire new group of fast networks that are designed to run at up to 100 megabits/second! Since only CAT 5 can handle these speeds, just about everyone is installing CAT 5, even if they are running at speeds where CAT 3 or CAT 4 would do. Consequently, it is becoming harder to get anything but CAT 5 cable.

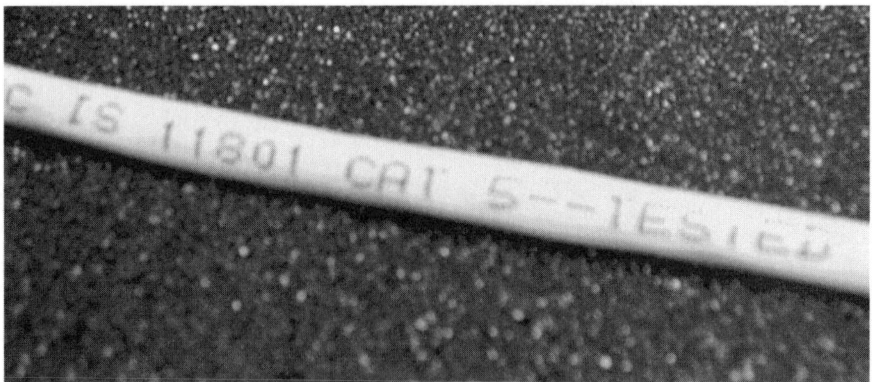

Figure 19.25 CAT level on a cable

There are also different numbers of pairs. Currently, two- and four-pair cable are the most popular. Virtually everyone is buying four-pair UTP and using only two of the pairs. The reason for this is simple—fear of the future. No one knows what type of network speeds will be common in the future or how many pairs will be needed, so just about everyone is playing it safe and installing four-pair, CAT 5 UTP. You should also.

There are a number of wire makers that are pushing UTP with even higher ratings. A good example is Belden Wire and Cable's Datatwist 350 cable, designated to run as fast as 350 megabits/second! These new cables tend to get names like CAT 6, but as of now there are no official levels above CAT 5.

10BaseT cabling uses two pairs of wires, two for sending and two for receiving. 10BaseT runs on CAT 3, CAT 4, and CAT 5 cable. These cables use a special connector called RJ-45. The RJ designation was invented by Ma Bell years ago and is still used today. Currently, you will see only two types of RJ connectors: RJ-11 and RJ-45 (Figure 19.26).

RJ-11 is the connector that hooks your telephone to the telephone jack. It can be used for up to two pair of wires, although most phone lines use only one pair. The other pair is for supporting a second phone line. RJ-11 connectors are not used in any common network installation, although a few weird (and out-of-business) "network in a box" type companies used them.

RJ-45 is the standard in UTP connectors. It has connections for up to four pairs and is clearly much wider than RJ-11. Use the diagram in Figure 19.27 to determine the #1 pin on an RJ-45 jack. Also, see Table 19.1.

Figure 19.26 RJ-11 and RJ-45 connectors

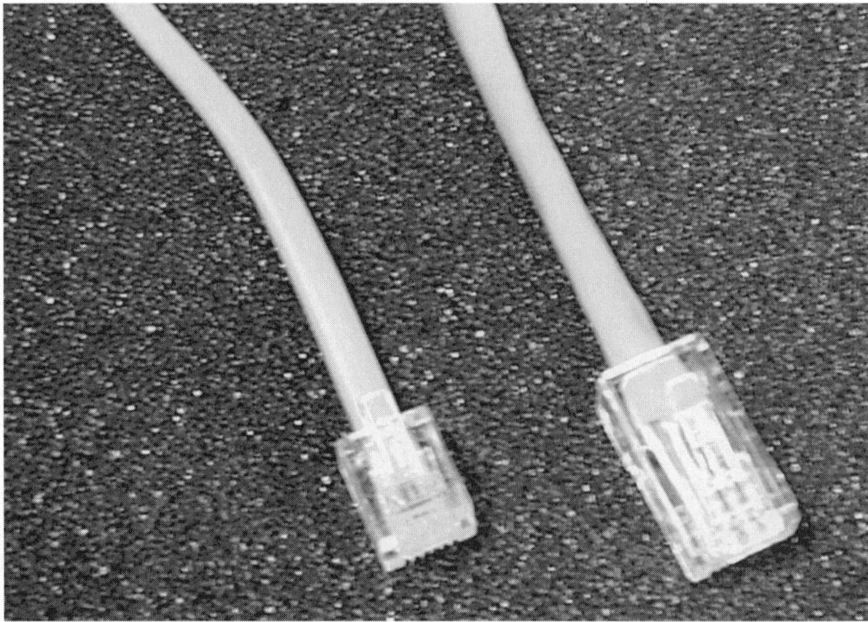

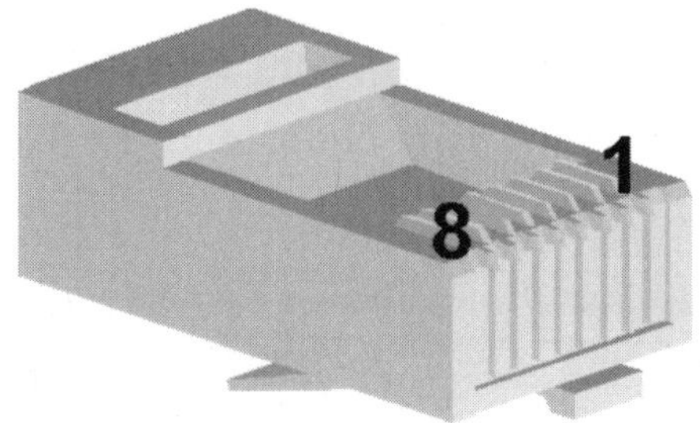

Figure 19.27 RJ-45 pin numbers

TABLE 19.1 RJ-45 connector

Pin Functions
Pin 1 - Transmit Data (+)
Pin 2 - Transmit Data (–)
Pin 3 - Receive Data (+)
Pin 4 - Unused
Pin 5 - Unused
Pin 6 - Receive Data (–)
Pin 7 - Unused
Pin 8 - Unused

The good news is that there are standards for color coding the wires to match these pins. These standards were established by the EIA/TIA (Electronics Industries Association/Telecommunications Industry Association). The bad news is that there are two standards—EIA/TIA 568A and 568B—and both are acceptable. You do not have to follow any standard as long as you use the same pairings on each end of the cable, but it's much easier to choose a standard. Make sure that all of your cabling uses the same standard, and you will save a great deal of work in the end. Most importantly, keep records!

The wires in UTP are numbered, but there are no actual numbers on each wire. Instead, each wire has a standardized color. Table 19.2 is the official EIA/TIA standard color chart for UTP. Since 10BaseT uses the same language as 10Base2 or 10Base5, you can find Ethernet combo network cards that support two or even three different types of connections (Figure 19.28).

HUBS In a 10BaseT network, each PC is connected to a 10baseT hub (Figure 19.29). These hubs have multiple connections, called *ports*—one for each device. To add a device to the network, simply plug another cable

TABLE 19.2

EIA/TIA Standard Color Chart for UTP

Pin #	EIA/TIA 568A	EIA/TIA 568B
1	White/Green	White/Orange
2	Green	Orange
3	White/Orange	White/Green
4	Blue	Blue
5	White/Blue	White/Blue
6	Orange	Green
7	White/Brown	White/Brown
8	Brown	Brown

Figure 19.28
Example combo cards

Figure 19.29
10Base-T hub

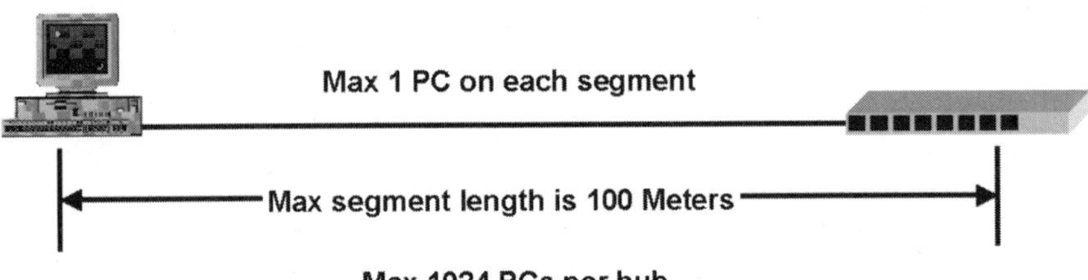
10BASE-T
Max 1 PC on each segment
Max segment length is 100 Meters
Max 1024 PCs per hub

Figure 19.30
10Base-T Ethernet

into the hub. Remember that 10BaseT uses the star bus topology. The hub holds the actual bus and allows access to the bus through the ports. Using a star bus topology creates a robust network: the failure of a single node will not bring down the entire network (Figure 19.30).

The maximum distance from the hub to any device is 100 meters. No more than one PC can be hooked to each segment, and the maximum number of PCs hooked to any one hub is 1024, although you will be hard pressed to find a hub with that many connectors. Most hubs come with 4, 8, 16, 32, or 64 ports. 10BaseT hubs act as repeaters, amplifying the signals between devices hooked into the network. They need power to provide this amplification, so make sure that the hubs are plugged into a good power source.

You can actually hook two 10BaseT network cards together without a hub! Just connect the two PCs together with a crossover cable. Crossover cables are a great quick way to network two PCs. You can make a crossover cable by making one end TIA586A and the other TIA568B.

Combining Different Types of Ethernet

Many 10BaseT hubs have a thinnet BNC connector or a thicknet AUI connector in the back, allowing the hubs to be directly connected to either a thinnet or thicknet backbone. These are great for connecting to an existing thicknet or thinnet network, or for connecting multiple hubs (Figure 19.31).

A *repeater* is an electronic device that amplifies the signal on a line. Repeaters are used to extend the length of a segment beyond its specified maximum. In networks, a repeater can be one of two different types. First, there is a dedicated box that is used to take input from one segment, amplify it, then pass it to another segment. A diagram of a common repeater for 10Base2 is shown in Figure 19.32. Using a repeater like this, you can link together two 10Base2 segments (Figure 19.33), which would allow you to get past the 185-meter maximum length. The second type of repeaters are 10BaseT hubs (Figure 19.34). As mentioned earlier, hubs are also re-

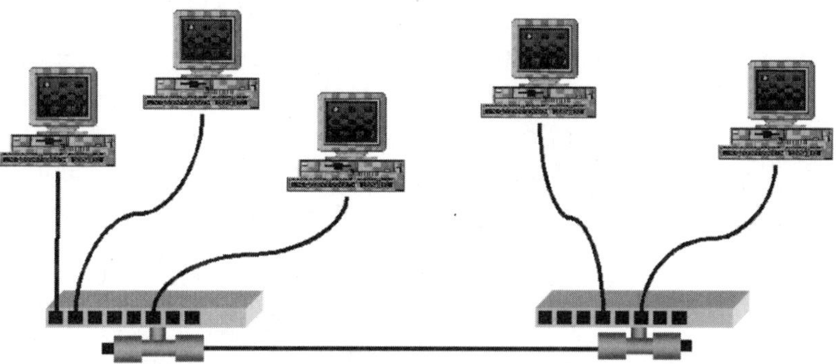

Figure 19.31 Combining Ethernet networks

Figure 19.32 Repeater

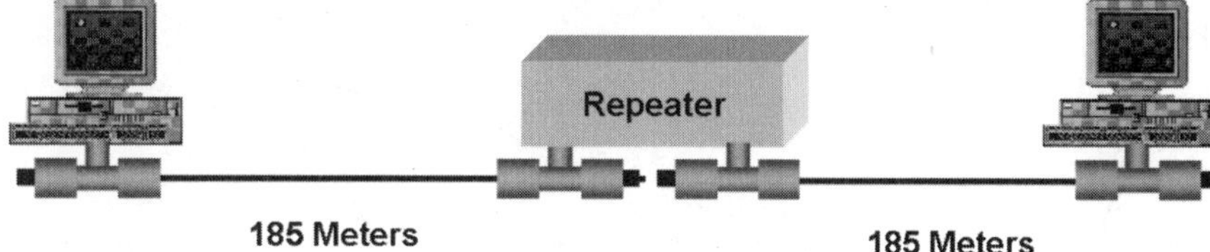

Figure 19.33 Using repeaters in 10Base-2

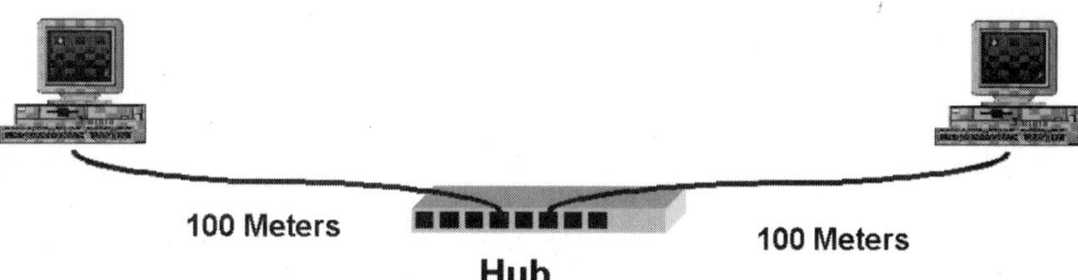

Figure 19.34 Using repeaters in 10Base-T

peaters, allowing a maximum separation of 200 meters between PCs on a 10BaseT network.

Fast Ethernet

There is a strong move today towards even faster Ethernet networks. The biggest push is towards a 100 megabit/second or 100BaseT Ethernet. Unfortunately, there is not a single 100BaseT standard. The two most common types of 100BaseT are 100BaseT4 and 100BaseTX. 100BaseT4 requires four-pair CAT 3 or better UTP, while 100BaseTX requires only two-pair CAT 5. In either case, these high-speed Ethernets need their own 100BaseT4 or 100BaseTX network cards and hubs. They are incompatible with each other, although most 100Base hubs and cards will support 10BaseT.

Fiberoptic Ethernet

Fiberoptic cable is a very attractive way to transmit network packets. First, since it uses light instead of electricity, fiberoptic cable is immune to electrical problems like lightning, shorts, and static. Second, fiberoptic signals travel much further, usually 2000 meters (compared to 100 meters for 10 or 100Base-T). There are two standards for using fiberoptic cable with Ethernet (Figure 19.35). In either case, the cabling is the same: "62.5/125 multi-mode" fiberoptic. All fiberoptic Ethernets need two of these cables.

The two fiberoptic standards are called 10BaseFL and 100BaseFX. As you can guess by the names, the only real difference is the speed of the network. Unfortunately, fiberoptic cabling is delicate, expensive, and diffi-

Figure 19.35
Fiberoptic cables: ST and SC connectors

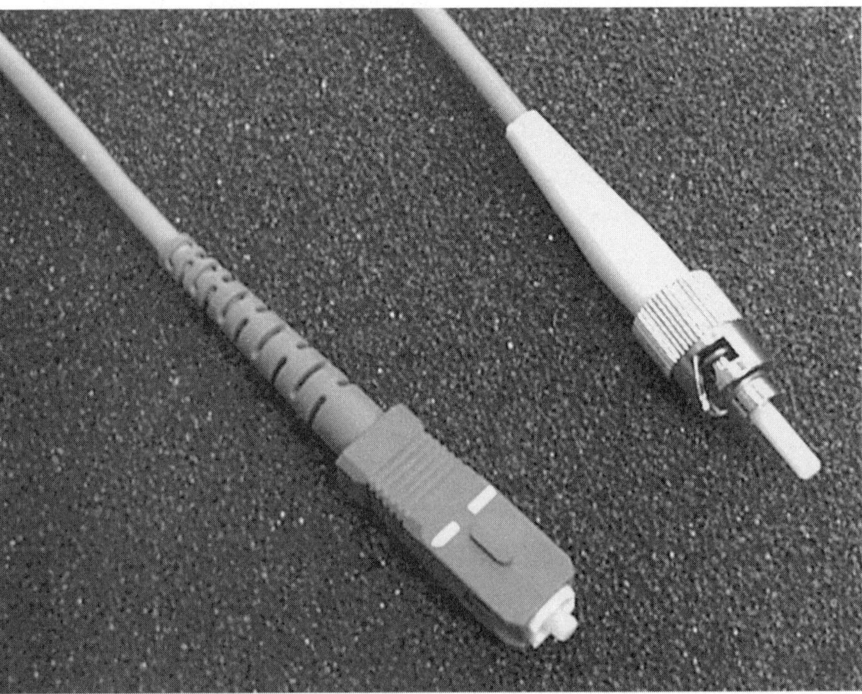

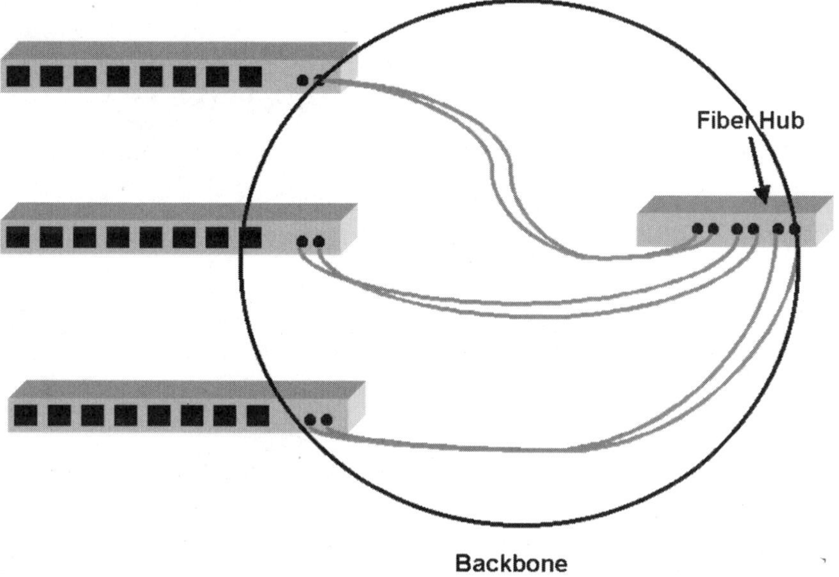

Figure 19.36 Concept of a backbone

cult to use, so it is usually relegated to "backbone" situations. A *backbone* is the main piece of Ethernet to which all other hubs are connected. Figure 19.36 shows an example.

Token-Ring

Token-ring is a confusing term. The problem is that it is really two related but different items. First, token-ring is a topology; second, it is a set of network standards developed by IBM that define a complete network system. Token-ring is completely incompatible with Ethernet, and is considered a direct competitor. Token-ring runs at either 4 or 16 megabits/second, depending on the type of token-ring network cards you buy. Token-ring was originally based around the IBM type-1 cable. Type-1 cable is a two-pair, shielded twisted-pair (STP) cable that is designed to handle speeds up to 20 megabits/second (Figure 19.37). Today, Token-ring can use either STP or UTP.

STP TYPES STP cables also have certain categories, called "types," which are defined by IBM. The most common types are listed in Table 19.3.

TOKEN-RING CONNECTORS Type-1 token-ring connectors are not RJ-45s; instead, IBM designed a unique "hermaphrodidic" connector (Fig-

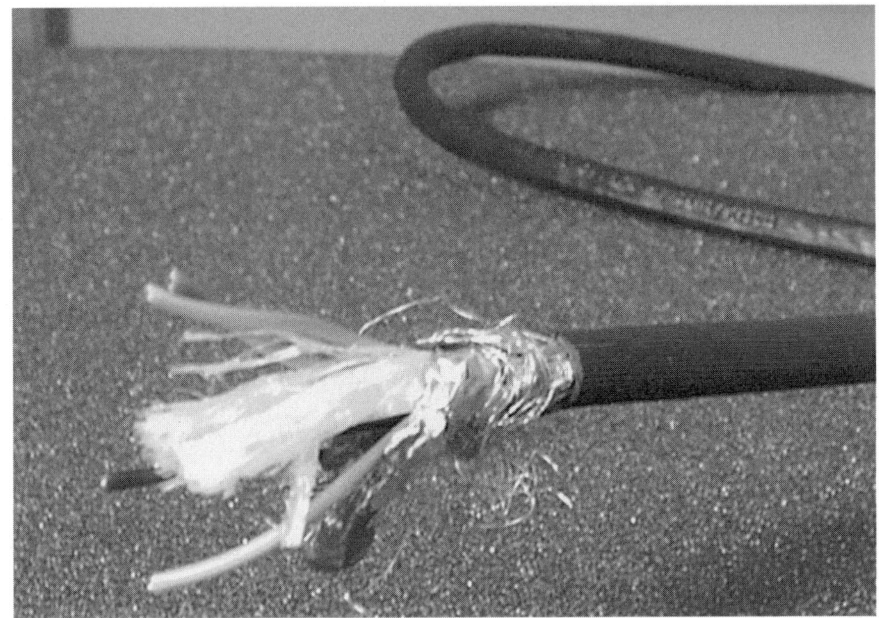

Figure 19.37
Type-1 STP cable

TABLE 19.3
Types of STP Cable

Types of STP Cable
Type 1 - Standard STP with 2 pairs—the most common STP cable
Type 2 - Standard STP plus two pair of voice wires
Type 3 - Standard STP with 4 pairs
Type 6 - Patch cable—used for connecting hubs
Type 8 - Flat STP for under carpets
Type 9 - STP with 2 pairs—Plenum grade

ure 19.38). These connectors are neither male nor female; they are designed to plug into each other. Token ring network cards use a nine-pin female connector. A standard token-ring cable has a hermaphrodidic connector on one end and a nine-pin connector on the other.

Token-ring can also use CAT 3, 4, or 5 UTP. When combined with UTP, token-ring uses an RJ-45 connector, so, from a cabling standpoint, token-ring UTP and Ethernet UTP look the same. Many token-ring network cards are combo cards, meaning they come with both a nine-pin connection for STP and an RJ-45 connection for UTP.

As discussed earlier, token-ring uses a star-ring topology, so it uses a hub (Figure 19.39). A token-ring hub is not interchangeable with an Ethernet hub. IBM has a special name for its hubs: either MAUs or MSAUs (mul-

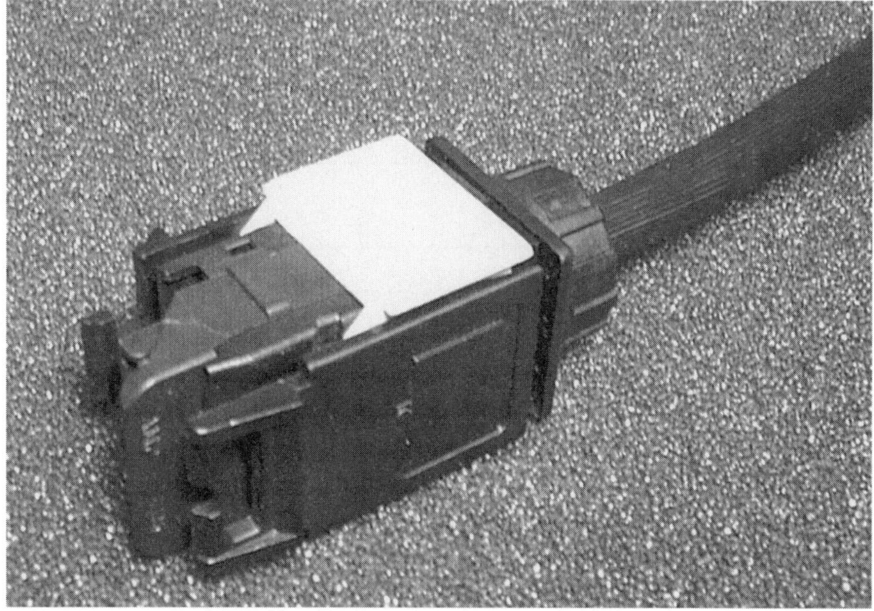

Figure 19.38 Token-ring type-1 connector

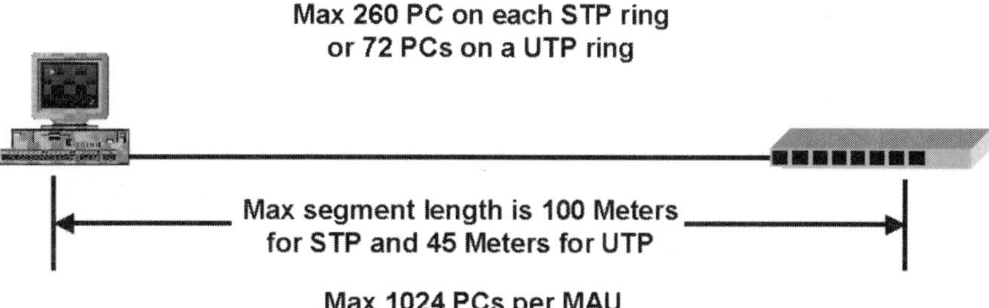
Token Ring
Max 260 PC on each STP ring
or 72 PCs on a UTP ring
Max segment length is 100 Meters
for STP and 45 Meters for UTP
Max 1024 PCs per MAU

Figure 19.39 The rules of token-ring

tiple-station access units). Unfortunately, they are sometimes called just *hubs* (usually by Ethernet people who do not know any better).

Token-ring can support up to 260 PCs using STP and up to 72 computers using UTP. Using UTP, the maximum distance from any MAU to a PC is 45 meters. Using STP, the maximum distance from any MAU to a PC is 100 meters. Token-ring also uses repeaters. Token-ring repeaters can be used only between MAUs. With a repeater, the distance between two MAUs is increased to 360 meters with UTP and 720 meters using STP.

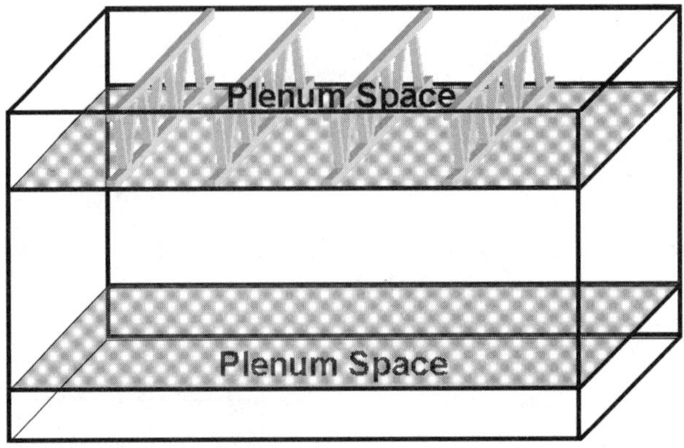

Figure 19.40
Location of plenum

Plenum vs. PVC

All cabling comes with one of two types of insulation: plenum or PVC. The *plenum* is the space between the real ceiling and the drop ceiling of a room, and also the space between a real floor and a raised floor. Plenum-grade insulation is designed to reduce the fire hazards from cable strung in the walls (or plenum area) of a building. In a fire, regular PVC (polyvinyl chloride) cable will emit noxious fumes. Plenum-grade cable emits only a small amount when compared to PVC. Plenum- grade cable is required by almost all building codes, but is usually two or three times more expensive than equivalent PVC. See Figure 19.40.

Protocols

Just moving data from one machine to another hardly makes for a complete network; there are many other functions that need to be handled. For example, if a file is being copied from one machine to another, who or what keeps track of all the packets so the file can be properly reassembled? If many machines are talking to the same machine at once, how does that machine keep track of which packets should be sent to or received from all the other PCs? Also, what happens if one of the machines in the network has its network card replaced? Up to this point, the only way to distinguish one machine from another was by the MAC address on the card. Each machine needs a name, an identifier for the network, that is "above" the MAC address. Each machine, or at least one machine, needs to keep a list of all the MAC addresses on the network and the name of the system, so packets and names can be correlated. That way, if a network card is replaced, the network, after some special queries, can update that record to show the new network card's MAC address to the name associated to that PC.

The protocol is the software that takes data from the network card, keeps it organized, sends it to the correct program that needs the data, and then hands the card data to be sent out. All networks have a protocol. Although many different protocols exist, the top three—IPX/SPX from Novell, NetBEUI from Microsoft, and TCP/IP from UNIX/Internet—hold a virtual lock on the market.

IPX/SPX

Novell invented the Internetwork Packet Exchange/Sequenced Packet Exchange protocol (IPX/SPX), and built all versions of NetWare around it. The IPX/SPX protocol offers speed, works well with routers, and takes up relatively little RAM when loaded.

NetBEUI

During the 1980s, IBM developed the NetBEUI (NetBIOS Extended User Interface), the default protocol for Windows for Workgroups, LANtastic, and Windows 95. NetBEUI offers small size and a relatively high speed, but cannot be used for routing. Its inability to handle routing limits NetBEUI to networks smaller than approximately 200 nodes.

TCP/IP

Terminal Control Protocol/Internet Protocol (TCP/IP) was originally developed for the predecessor to the Internet, ARPANET. In 1983, TCP/IP became the built-in protocol for the popular BSD UNIX, and other flavors of UNIX quickly adopted it as well. TCP/IP is becoming a preferred protocol for larger (greater than 200 node) networks. The biggest network of all, the Internet, uses TCP/IP as its default protocol. Windows NT also uses TCP/IP as its default protocol. TCP/IP lacks speed and takes up a large amount of memory when loaded (especially in real mode), but it is robust, well understood, and universally supported.

AppleTalk

AppleTalk is the proprietary Apple protocol. Similar to IPX, it is small and relatively fast. The only reason to use an AppleTalk protocol is to communicate to Apple computers on the network.

Client/Server vs. Peer-to-Peer

A network operating system (NOS) is the program that makes a network function. All network operating systems can be broken into two basic organizational groups: client/server NOSes and peer-to-peer NOSes.

How do you share resources across a network? Can everyone share their hard drives with everyone else? Can you place limits on sharing? If everyone needs access to a particular file, where will it be stored? What about security? Can anyone access the file? What if someone erases it accidentally? How are backups to be handled? Client/server and peer-to-peer networks answer these questions differently.

Client/Server

A client-server network dedicates one machine as a resource to be shared over the network, with a dedicated NOS optimized for sharing files. This special operating system includes powerful caching software that allows for high-speed file access. It also has extremely high levels of protection and organization that allow for tremendous control of data. This machine is called a *dedicated server*. All the other machines that use the data are called *clients* or *workstations*.

Client/server machines do not run DOS or Windows 95. They use highly sophisticated and expensive NOSes that are optimized for the sharing and administration of network resources. There are currently two major competitors in the client/server arena: Novell NetWare and Microsoft's NT Server. Currently, Novell NetWare is the overwhelmingly dominant client/server NOS available, installed in about 50 percent of all client/server networks. However, NT Server is slowly becoming more popular, holding roughly 35 percent of the market.

A machine running Novell NetWare or NT Server is not running DOS! DOS is a terrible operating system for dedicated servers. Not only is it clueless about networking, but it is a real-mode, single-tasking operating system. NetWare and NT can both multitask while running in protected mode.

A server is not directly used by anyone. It just serves. It does not, or at least it would prefer not to, run programs like Excel or CorelDraw. Many network administrators remove the keyboard and monitor from a server to keep people from using it.

Servers require significantly more hardware than a regular PC. For starters, the amount of RAM should be at least 32MB for Novell and NT, although 64, 128, and even 256 is not uncommon. The need for RAM increases as the amount of data being shared and the number of users grow. Servers also require high-speed hard drives and fast network cards. Simply put, dedicated servers need power.

Peer-to-Peer

Some NOSes do not require dedicated servers. In these networks, every computer acts as both a server and a client. Peer-to-peer networks are much cheaper than client/server networks since the software costs less and does not require a high-end machine to be used as a dedicated server. The most popular peer-to-peer NOS today is Windows 95/98. However, there are many peer-to-peer NOSes, some of which have special features that make them attractive in niche markets.

A peer-to-peer network allows any or all machines on the network to act as a server. As long as the total numbers of machines on the network stays relatively low, this is no problem. As the number of machines begins to go past 20 or 30, however, the entire network begins to slow down. If one file is being shared heavily, even five or six machines can bring the entire system to a crawl. Security is the other big weakness of peer-to-peer networks. Password protection and data backup is limited.

However, peer-to-peer networking remains very popular. The price (usually free) combined with the tremendous ease of use make peer-to-peer the NOS of choice for smaller networks that do not need the high level of protection and high speed provided by client/server NOSes.

Windows 95

Windows 95 is the culmination of the long-fought melding of a standalone OS and a NOS. In the first days of networks, the NOS was a separate program that ran with or under DOS and early versions of Windows. Starting in 1994, a new version of Windows called Windows for Workgroups was created. This was Windows 3.1 with a built-in, peer-to-peer NOS. Although a little buggy and a little challenging to use, Windows for Workgroups was extremely popular. Windows 95 is the result of learning from Windows for Workgroups. All network functions are seamless and easy to configure, making Windows 95 the OS and NOS leader in PCs today.

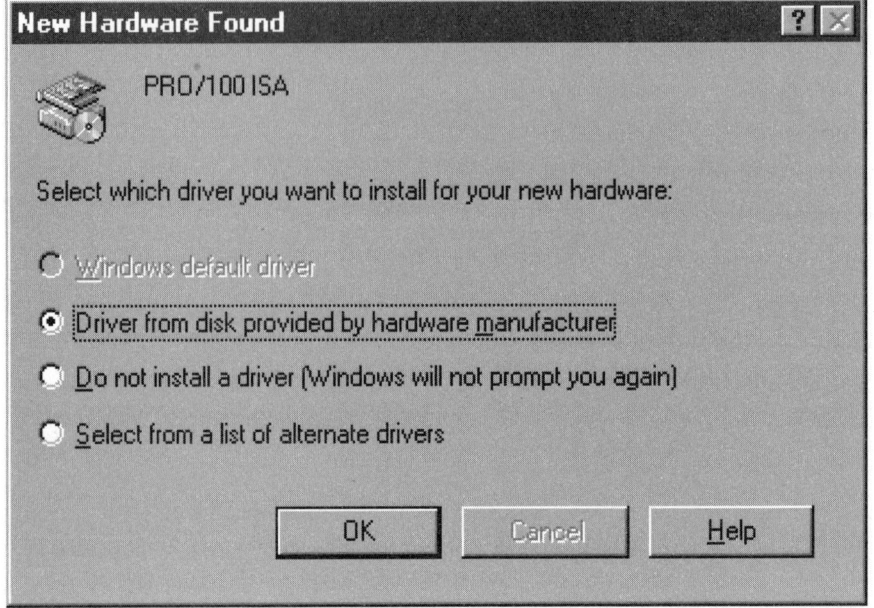

Figure 19.41 Plug-n-Play prompting for drivers

Installing NICs

Installing a NIC into Windows 95 is usually a no-brainer, as most NICs today are completely Plug-n-Play (Figure 19.41). For the most part, it is simply a matter of turning off the PC, installing the card, and turning the system back on. The only trick is to remember that you should use the disk that comes with the NIC, even if Windows offers its own drivers.

Cards, however, might still need to be installed manually. As with all cards in a PC, NICs will definitely use an I/O address and IRQ. Some will even use memory locations and/or DMA channels. It is important to remember that with legacy (non-PnP) NICs, the card needs to be configured, and then Windows 95 needs to be told what resources the card is using. Although some cards still use jumpers, most NICs use a software-based resource setting that is manifested by a setup or install program on an accompanying floppy disk. Figure 19.42 is a screen shot from such a program.

These programs should be run only from MS-DOS mode or a bootable floppy, as Windows will invariably interfere with them. After the card has been set up, be sure to save the information on the card (some do this automatically) and then write down the information so Windows 95 can be properly configured to talk to the card.

After the card has been installed, you can manually install the drivers. Fire up the "install new hardware" icon in the Control Panel. Although Windows will often find the card automatically, it's usually faster to perform a manual installation. Select Network Adapters and the Have Disk button to tell Windows where to locate the driver (Figure 19.43).

If the NIC did not come with a diskette, see if Windows has a driver. If Windows doesn't have the driver, contact the company where you purchased the card or try the manufacturer's Web site. Keep in mind many no-name Ethernet cards will use a NE2000-compatible driver. Most of the time, the card will install itself with a series of preset (and always incorrect) resources (see Figure 19.44). You must then reboot the system, and manually change the resources in the Device Manager (Figure 19.45). After setting the proper resources, restart Windows one more time and reopen the Device Manager. Verify that the network card is operating properly.

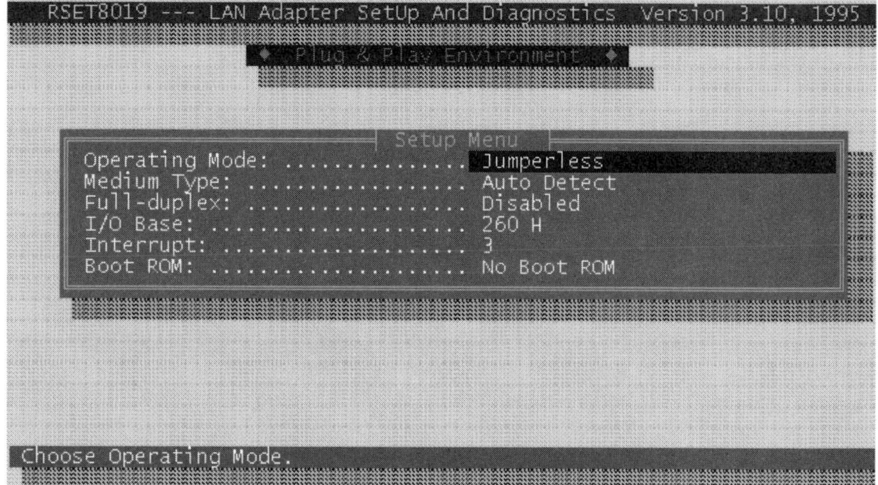

Figure 19.42 Typical NIC setup program

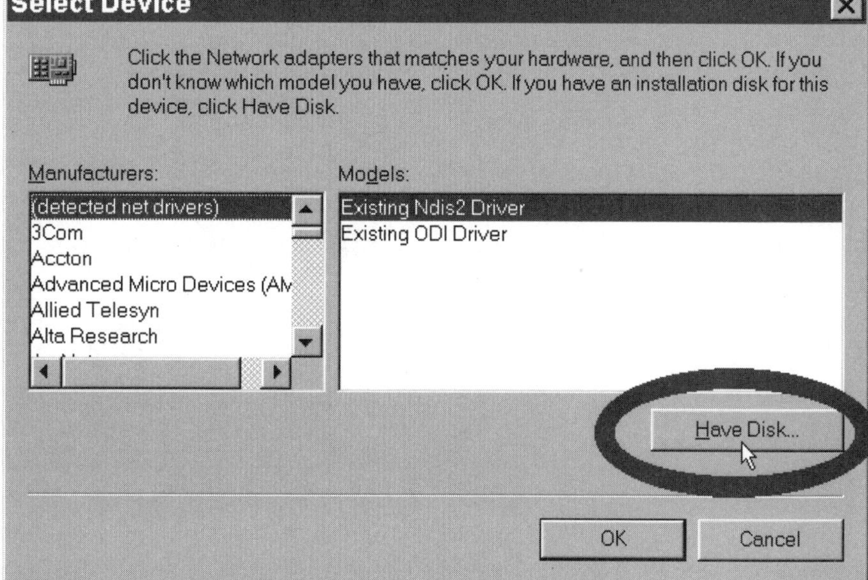

Figure 19.43 Manually adding a driver

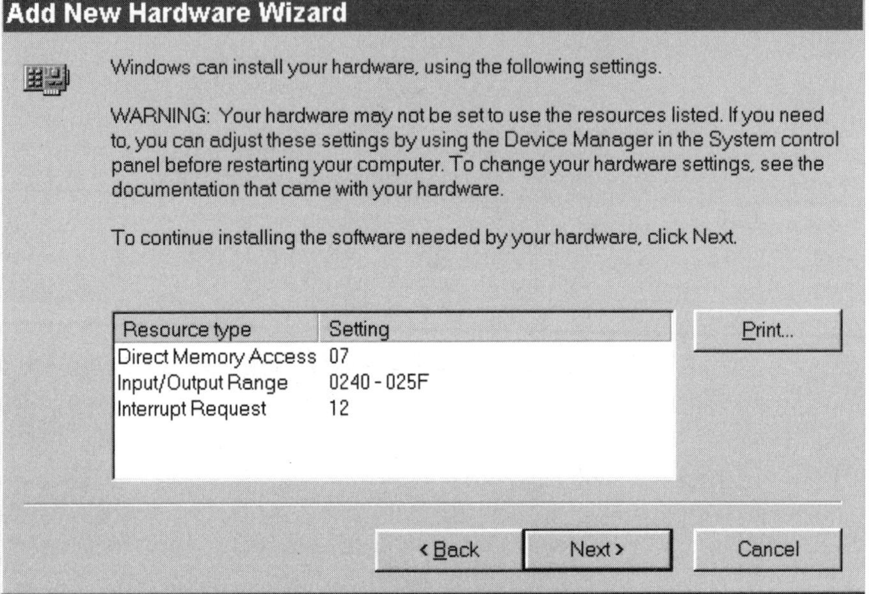

Figure 19.44 Default resources

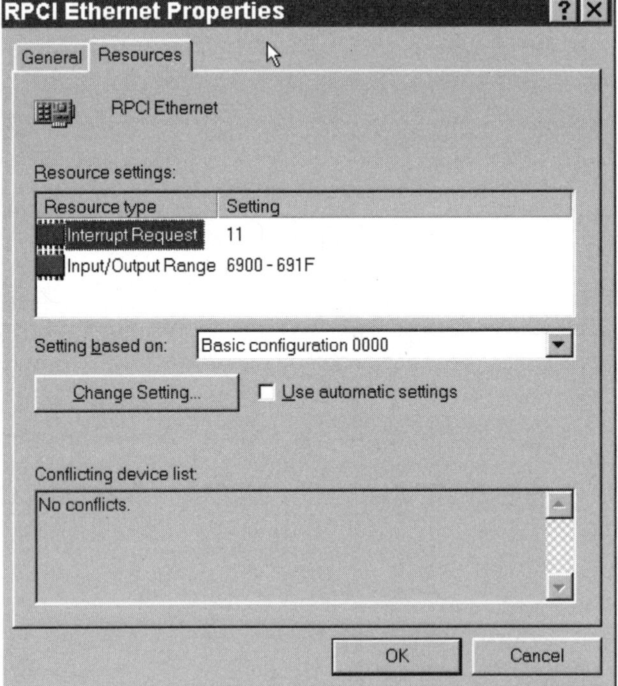

Figure 19.45 Manually setting resources

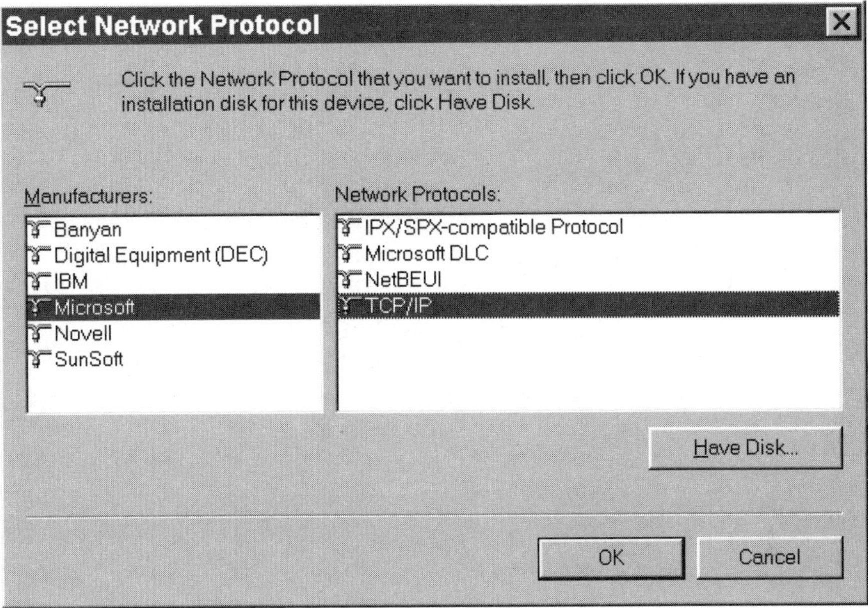

Figure 19.46 Installing a protocol

Installing Protocols

Windows 95 will automatically install both its own IPX and NetBEUI protocols whenever a network adapter is installed. If the PC is going to need to access other Windows 95 machines, keep the NetBEUI. If the PC is going to link into a Novell NetWare server, keep the IPX/SPX. If the PC is part of a larger network, you'll probably be told which protocols to install. Unlike NIC drivers, most networks never need to install their own protocols. Windows 95 comes with enough protocols to link to most networks. To install a protocol, go to the Network window in the Control Panel, select Add/Protocol, and choose the protocol you want to install (Figure 19.46).

In many networks, it is common to have a number of installed protocols. My machine links to a Novell server (IPX/SPX), other Windows 95 systems (NetBEUI), and the Internet (TCP/IP). TCP/IP will be discussed later in this chapter.

Sharing

Since Windows 95 is a peer-to-peer NOS, any PC can be a server or workstation. By default, all machines are workstations. In order to make a PC a server, some extra software called a "service" must be added. There is a special service that allows the PC to share its printers, its hard drives, or both. Once again, open the network features, this time from the Network button in the Control Panel. Again click on Add, but this time select Services. Locate File and Print Sharing. You can select Files or Printers (Figure 19.47).

Just because a machine has been set up as a printer, this does not mean it is ready to share. Installing file and print sharing simply gives the machine the *ability* to share. To actually *start* sharing requires that you decide what is to be shared and how it is to be shared, and that you give it a share name. Let's do this for both a directory and a printer.

Windows 95 can share drives and directories, and both are shared in basically the same manner. Simply right-click on any drive or folder and select Sharing. The menu shown in Figure 19.48 will appear. By clicking on the Shared As radio button, you can add a share name (Figure 19.49). This is the name that all of the other workstations will see when they are looking for resources to access. The trick here is to give it a name that clearly describes the resource. For example, if the goal is to share a machine's local C: drive, naming the resource C: would be confusing be-

Figure 19.47
Adding printer and file sharing

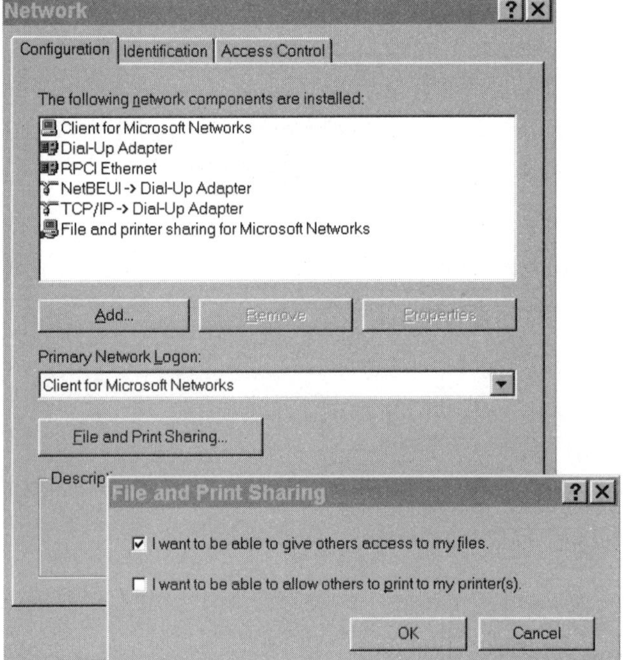

Figure 19.48
Sharing Windows

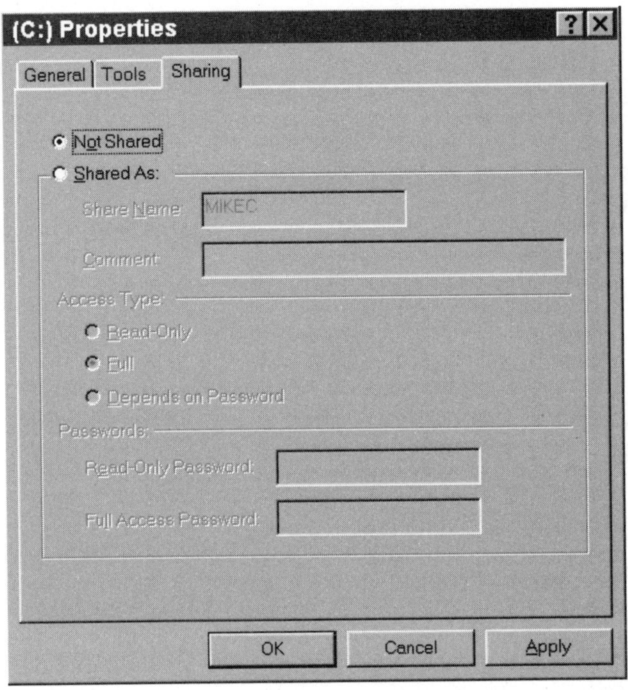

cause the name doesn't specify *which* C: drive it is—and there are a lot of other ones in the network. Instead, try a more detailed name like FREDC or SALES3C. As a rule, try to keep the name short and without spaces.

After establishing the share name, note that you can determine how it is to be shared. The options are simple: Full Access, Read-Only, and Depends on Password. This is one of the major limitations of peer-to-peer networks. In a client/server network like Windows NT or Novell NetWare, the access controls are much more powerful. In Novell NetWare 3, the choices would be:

- Write (write to a file)
- Read (read a file)
- Modify (modify a file)
- File Scan (see the contents of a directory)
- Access Rights (change other users' access)
- Create (create new files or directories)

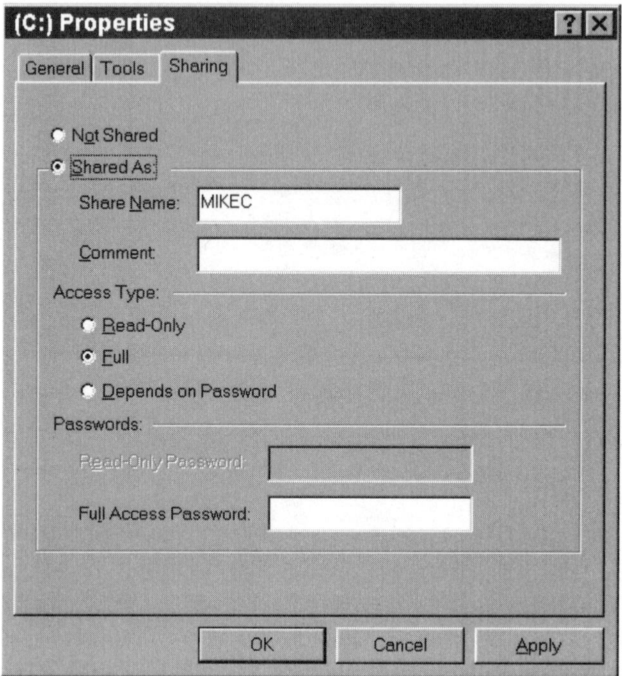

Figure 19.49 Setting up a share name

- Erase (erase files of directories)
- Supervisory (total control)

Windows NT has roughly similar rights. Note that this level of access allows much better control. Also, in a client/server NOS, these rights can be applied to any one user or group of users, where in peer-to-peer it can be applied only to the drive or directory itself. If you need a measure of control, the network needs to be client/server.

Back to Windows 95—after selecting the network name and access, click the OK button and a little hand will appear to show that the network resource is being shared (Figure 19.50).

Accessing Shared Drives/Directories

Once a drive or directory has been set up to be shared, the final step of networking is to access that shared drive/directory from another machine. In Windows 95, the shared devices can be accessed through the Network Neighborhood (Figure 19.51).

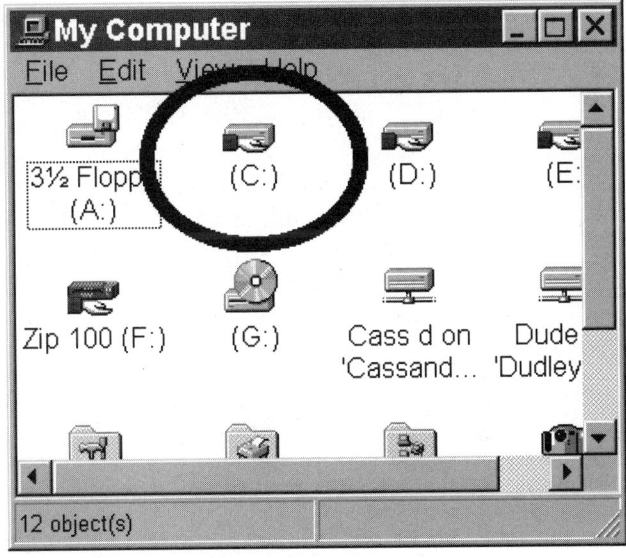

Figure 19.50
A shared drive

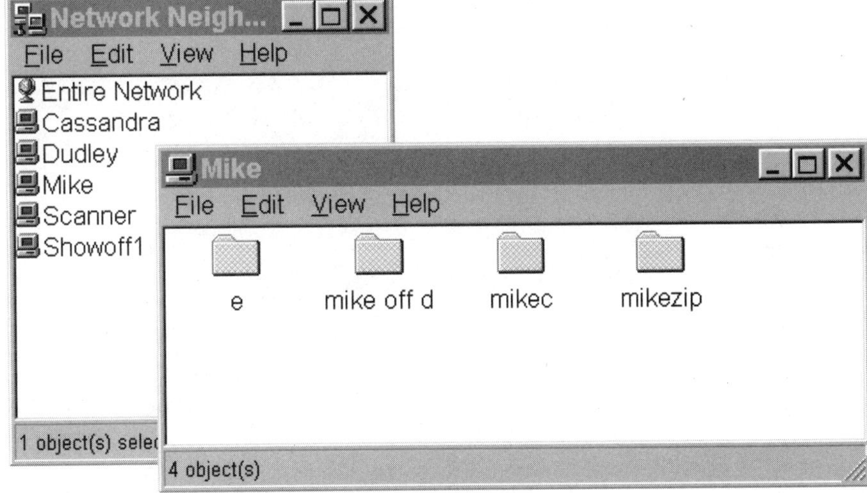

Figure 19.51
Shared drives on Mike's PC

Network resources can also be "mapped" to a local resource name. For example, you can map FREDC to be a local hard drive such as E: or F: either from Windows Explorer or by right-clicking on the Network Neighborhood under Map Network Drive. Mapping is usually done either for a permanent connection or to support older programs that might have trouble accessing a drive called FREDC.

All computers that share have a network name, and all the shared resources have a network name. You can describe any resource on the network by combining the name of the sharing system and the resource being shared. If a machine called SERVER1 is sharing its C: drive as FREDC, the complete name would be \\SERVER1\FREDC. This is called the Universal Naming Convention or UNC. The UNC is distinguished by the use of the double backslashes to describe the sharing system, with a single backslash to describe the shared resource.

Sharing Printers

Sharing printers in Windows 95 is just as easy as sharing drives and directories. Assuming that the system has loaded printer sharing services, you just go to the Printers folder in the Control Panel and right-click on the printer you want to share. Select Properties, go to the Sharing tab, clicked on Shared As, and give it a name (Figure 19.52).

To access a shared printer, simply click on the "add printer" icon in the Printers folder. When asked if the printer is local or network, select Net-

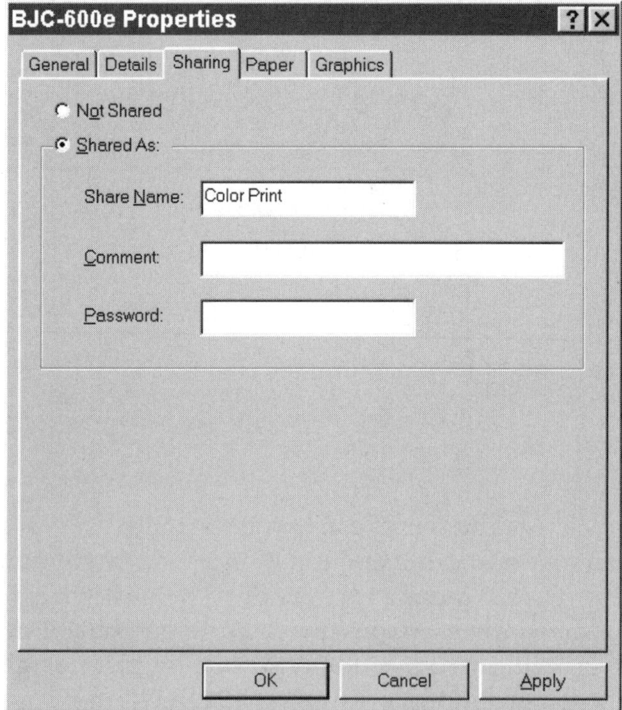

Figure 19.52 Sharing a printer

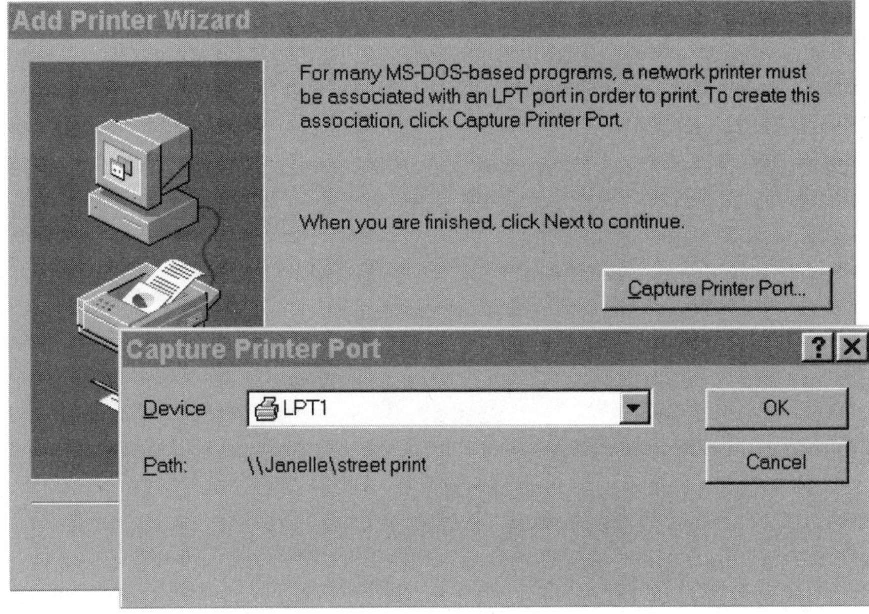

Figure 19.53 Redirecting an LPT port

work, browse the network for the printer you want to access, and Windows 95 will take care of the rest! In most cases, Windows will copy the printer driver from the sharing machine. This was a big hassle in the older versions of Windows since you had to install the drivers on every PC and *then* tell the system where you wanted the output to go.

Before Windows 95, most network printing was done by redirecting an LPT port. A printer would be installed and an unused LPT port, like LPT2 or LPT3, would take all the print information. This redirected LPT would then send the print job over the network to the proper network printer (Figure 19.53). Although today this is usually unnecessary, Windows 95 still provides the option to support older applications.

TCP/IP and the Internet

This final section on networking covers the Internet and TCP/IP. TCP/IP (or, to be more correct, IP) is the primary protocol of the Internet. If a PC wants to access the Internet, it must have the TCP/IP protocol loaded. TCP/IP can be added via Add/Protocol in the Networks section of the Control Panel (Figure 19.54).

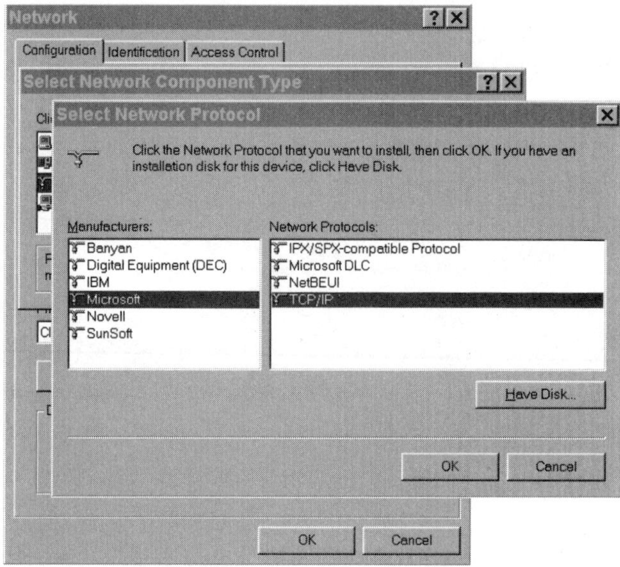

Figure 19.54 Adding the TCP/IP protocol

This is a big improvement over the "old days" of Windows 3.*x*, where all the TCP/IP software had to be loaded via a special program that was incorrectly but commonly called a *socket.* They had names like Trumpet Winsock, and contained all the programming needed to talk to the Internet. Today, Windows 95 has all of these sockets built into the NOS.

In a TCP/IP network, the systems don't have names. Instead, they use four sets of eight binary numbers (octets) separated by a period. So instead of a computer being called SERVER1, it gets a name like 202.34.16.11. Remember there are 256 different permutations that an eight-bit binary number can have, from eight zeroes (00000000) to eight ones (11111111). So instead of writing an address like this:

```
11110010.00000101.00000000.00001010
```

The TCP/IP folks decided to write the decimal equivalents, so 00000000 –0, 00000001 – 1, 00000010 –2, and so on, up to 11111111 –255, for a total of 256 different octets. So in theory there are a lot of IP addresses (from 0.0.0.0 to 255.255.255.255). Unfortunately, there are rules in the TCP/IP world that make many IP addresses unusable. For example, no address should use all zeroes or all ones, making addresses like 207.255.43.167 illegal (255 is 11111111 in binary and is not allowed). The significant reduction in IP addresses, combined with the explosion of new systems on the Internet, has actually placed a serious strain on the number of available IP addresses. This shortage of IP addresses has led to the creation of a method that allows systems to share IP addresses. (See DHCP later in this chapter.)

TCP/IP is very different from a Windows 95 peer-to-peer network. While TCP/IP can share printers and files, it is done quite differently than in other NOSes. And TCP/IP comes with many other services. For example, you can access one machine as though you were actually at that machine, called *telnet*. TCP/IP has file transfer protocol (FTP), which allows a user to move files from one machine to another. All machines with TCP/IP come with a handy utility called Ping. Ping allows one machine to check wither it can communicate with another machine. Here is an example of a ping:

```
C:\>ping 10.203.55.64

Pinging flash.net [10.203.55.64] with 32 bytes of data:

Reply from 10.203.55.64: bytes=32 time=164ms TTL=251
Reply from 10.203.55.64: bytes=32 time=174ms TTL=251
Reply from 10.203.55.64: bytes=32 time=168ms TTL=251
Reply from 10.203.55.64: bytes=32 time=194ms TTL=251
```

In a regular network setting, ping is a fine way to find another machine. Ping over the Internet, on the other hand, is often futile because the ping will time out before returning a signal. If you cannot ping a machine in Beijing, it does not necessarily mean that machine is off line, simply that the distances are too great.

TCP/IP also has newsgroups, which are really nothing more than electronic bulletin boards. Last, but probably most important, it has the World Wide Web. Of course, TCP/IP also provides many other less-used services that are either obsolete or little used today.

So the goal of TCP/IP is to link together multiple networks (called local-area networks or LANs) to make an entire wide-area network (WAN), as shown in Figure 19.55. The LANs are usually linked together via some

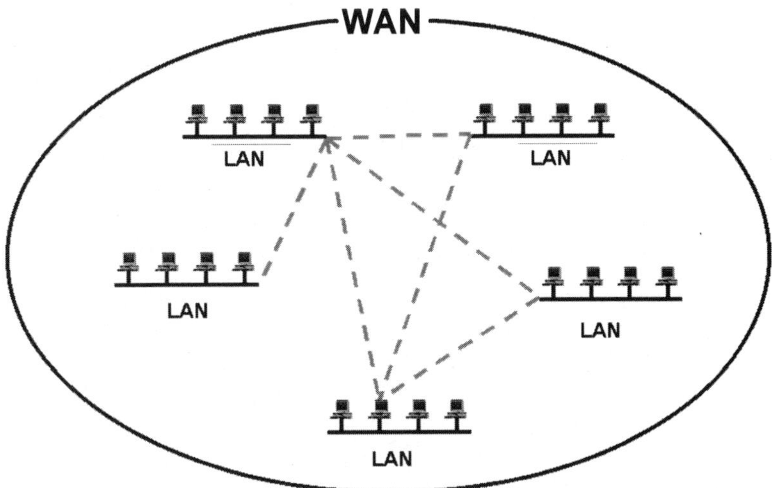

Figure 19.55
Concept of a WAN

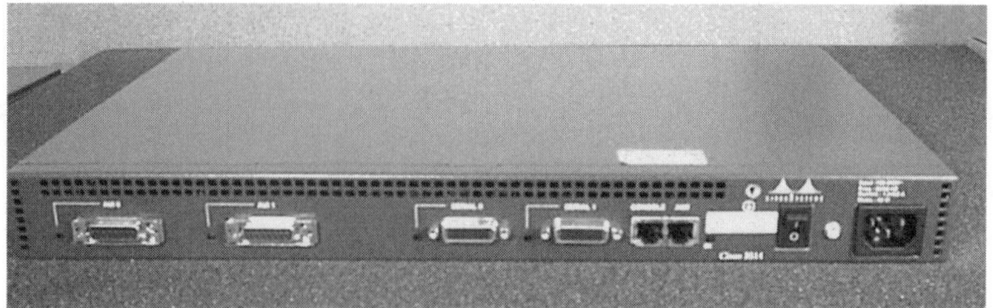

Figure 19.56
A router

type of telephone service, from basic dial-ups to dedicated, high-speed, and expensive data lines.

The goal is to make a WAN that generates as little traffic as possible on the expensive links. Machines that are linked to the phone lines and to each LAN are specialized computers called routers (Figure 19.56). To reduce traffic, each router reads the information from all packets on the LAN and decides if they should go out to the WAN. The router makes these decisions based on the IP addresses.

TCP/IP Settings

TCP/IP has a number of unique settings that are required for proper network functionality. Unfortunately, these settings can be quite confusing as there are quite a few of them and not all settings are used for every type of TCP/IP network. The location of these settings can also be a little strange. For the most part, there are two locations for TCP/IP settings. For computers that use a modem to access the Internet, the selection Dial-Up Networking, under My Computer, is the place to start. Right-click on an existing setup and select Properties, Server Type, and then TCP/IP Settings to access the TCP/IP settings for the dial-up adapter (Figure 19.57). The other place for TCP/IP settings is under the Control Panel: Networks, TCP/IP, and the Properties box (Figure 19.58). Now let's discuss some of the more common TCP/IP settings.

Default Gateway

If a computer wants to send data to another machine on the WAN, it can't keep track of all the IP addresses of all the computers on the Internet. Instead, IP machines have the name of one computer to send all data that is not for the LAN. This machine is called the *default gateway* and is usually the IP address for the local router. You can set the default gateway by selecting Properties for the TCP/IP protocol (Figure 19.59).

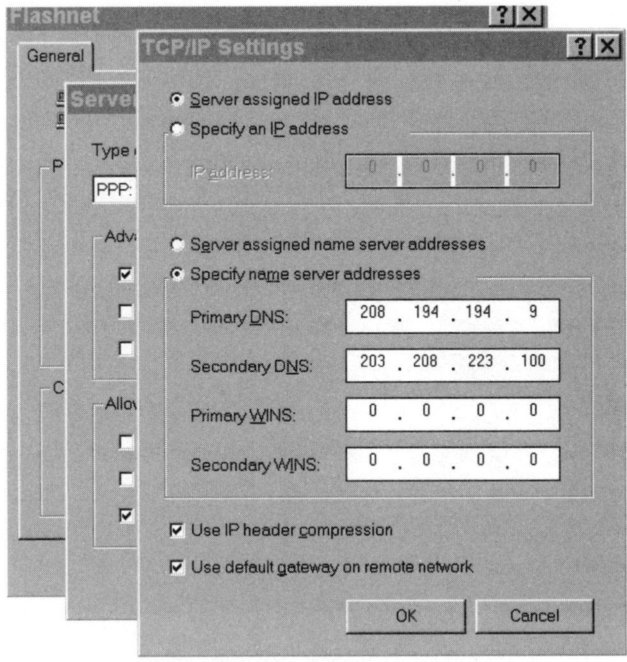

Figure 19.57
TCP/IP setting under Dial-Up Adapter

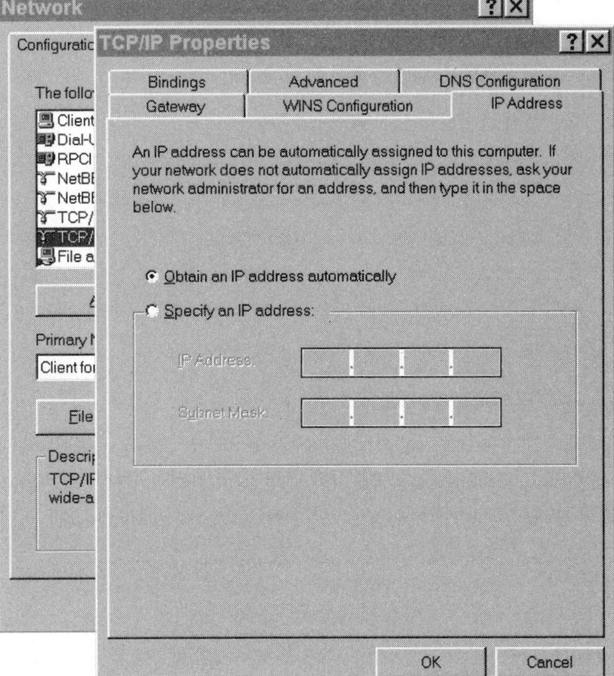

Figure 19.58
TCP/IP properties under Network

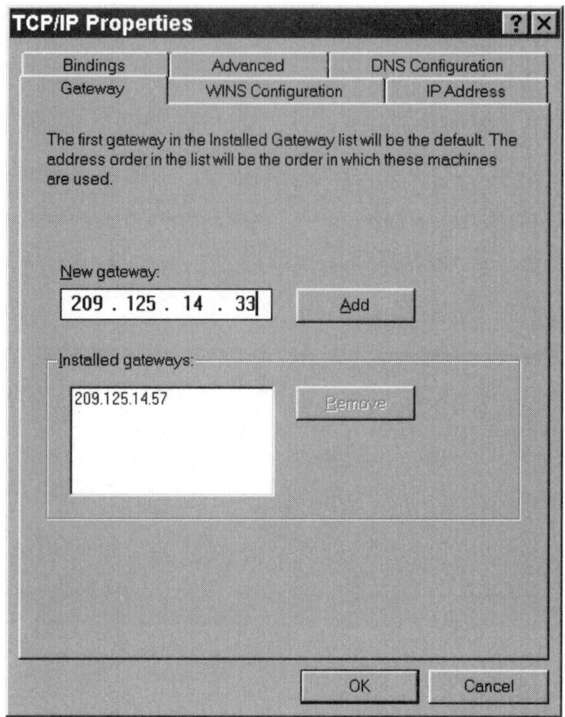

Figure 19.59 Setting up the gateway

Domain Name Service

Keeping track of a lot of IP addresses is basically impossible. How can you tell users that they need to access a directory to FTP a file? Instead, special computers called *domain name servers* (DNSs) keep track of special domain names. A user could call his machine TOTAL.SEMINAR1, and update the local DNS to correlate the IP address to his new domain name. Virtually all TCP/IP networks require the setup of DNS. Like the default gateway, these settings are in the TCP/IP Properties of the Network menu (Figure 19.60).

DHCP/WINS

The last items that most TCP/IP networks require are a dynamic host configuration protocol (DHCP) and Windows Internet name service (WINS). These are most often seen when Windows NT is being used on servers. To understand DHCP, first remember that every machine must have an IP address. In many systems, this is manually added to each machine in the TCP/IP Properties menu. A permanent IP address assigned to a machine is known as a *static IP address* (Figure 19.61).

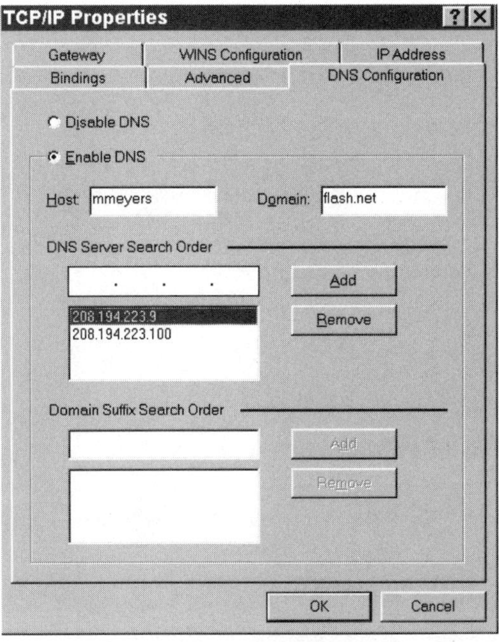

Figure 19.60
Setting up DNS

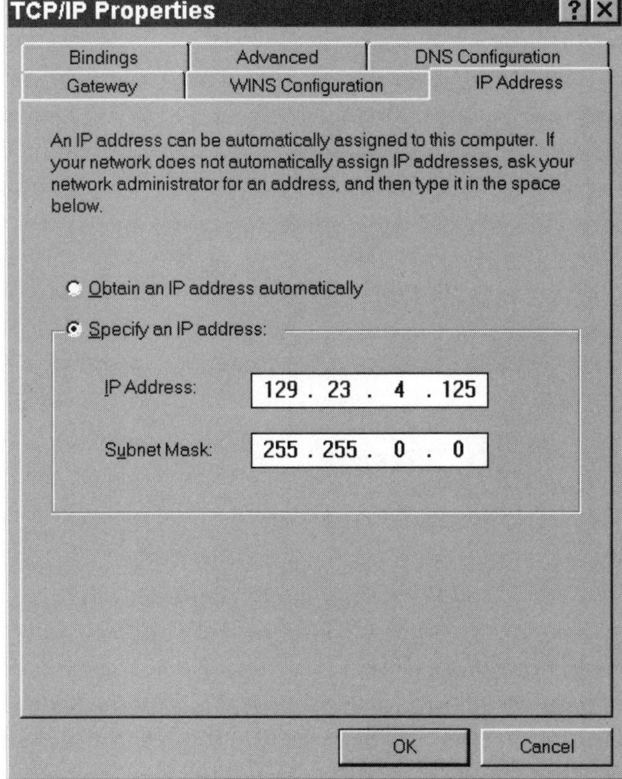

Figure 19.61
Setting up a static IP address

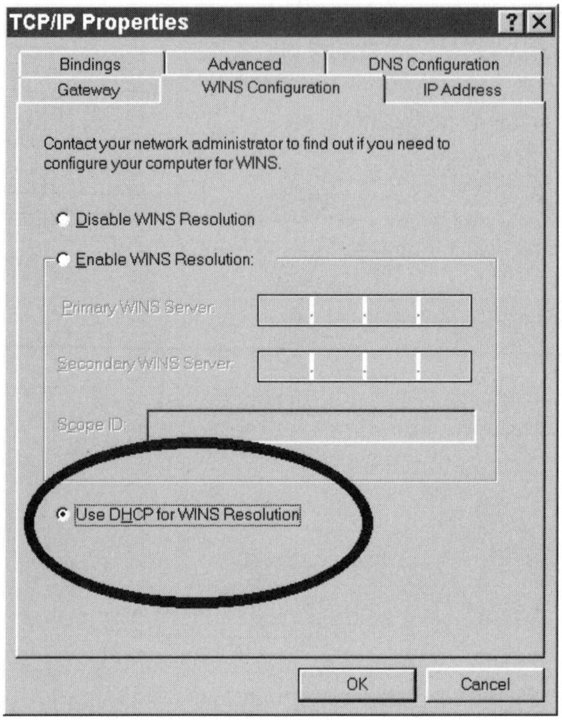

Figure 19.62
DHCP/WINS option

DHCP allows for a "pool" of IP address to be given to machines when they need it, and taken away when no longer needed. DHCP is especially handy for networks that have a lot of dial-in systems. Why give a machine that is only on for a few minutes a day a static IP address—especially if IP addresses are becoming more and more difficult to obtain? For that reason, DHCP is quite popular. WINS allows Windows network names like SERVER1 to be correlated to IP addresses, like DNS, but with Windows network names instead of TCP/IP domain names (Figure 19.62).

Dial-in and PPP

Dial-in links to the Internet have their own special hardware protocol called *point-to-point protocol* (PPP). PPP is a streaming protocol developed especially for dial-up Internet access. To Windows 95, a modem is nothing more than a special type of network adapter that has its own network settings (Figure 19.63).

As mentioned earlier, modems also have a second set of settings under Dial-Up Networking Settings and Properties. These properties are divided into the main Properties window, the Server Type window (Figure 19.64),

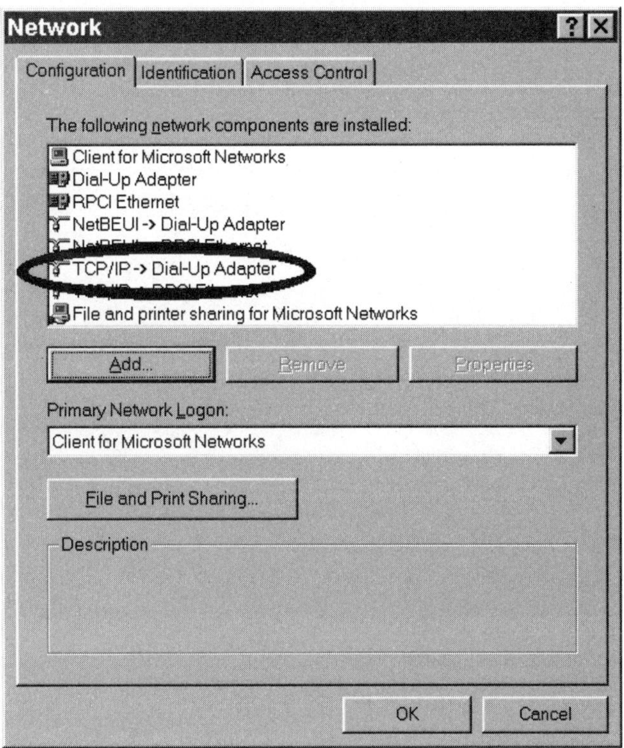

Figure 19.63 Windows 95 treats a modem like a NIC

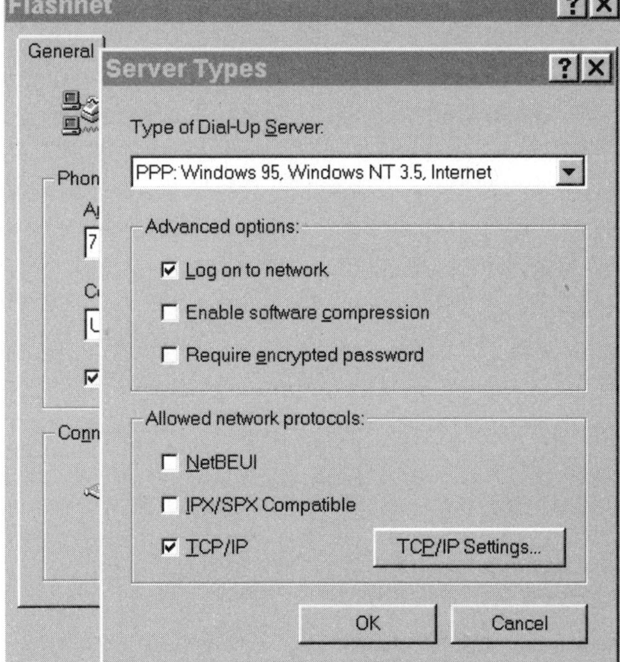

Figure 19.64 Server type window

and the TCP/IP Settings window. Notice that many of these are the same as settings in the Network Settings window (Figure 19.65). They are needed in both places to allow the broadest number of dial-up systems to link to Windows.

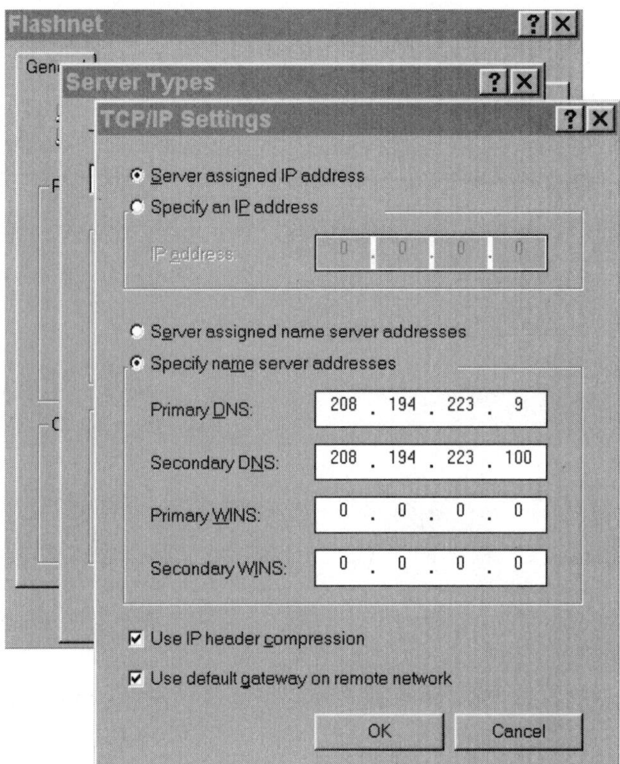

Figure 19.65 Network settings windows

CHAPTER 20

Multimedia

Multimedia is a generic term used to describe a PC's ability to provide graphics, sound, and video in simultaneous display in order to impart information better than any one media alone could. To a PC technician, multimedia might be better described as two separate processes. The first process is sound, which includes the hardware to create and play sounds (soundcards, speakers, and microphones), as well as the drivers, applications, and data formats to make any sound demanded by users. The second process is video, which again includes the hardware (video cards and CD-ROM drives), as well as the drivers, applications, and data formats to allow video or animated graphics on the screen. The goal is to have all of this hardware and software work in simultaneous harmony in the system, but it is often hard to achieve.

The biggest problem in achieving the multimedia goal is the constant change in hardware and software technologies. In an industry famous for its ability to constantly change, multimedia stands heads above any other aspect of the PC business for its ability to create technologies and standards that move from cutting edge to total obsolescence almost instantly. Knowing this, this chapter will concentrate on two pieces of hardware that form the cornerstone of multimedia: sound cards and CD-ROM drives. From there, I will build a basic foundation of software and hardware technologies and standards, ignoring the obsolete, the weird, and the "not yet ready for prime time" aspects of this fascinating area of the PC world.

CD-ROM Drives

A CD-ROM drive, at one time a unique "extra" for high-end PC systems, is now as standard a piece of computer equipment as a keyboard or a monitor. This technology of high-capacity, tough, easy-to-make discs has helped move the world forward from relatively small, floppy-installed applications to the much larger-scale applications available today. It is interesting to speculate on the path of application software if CD-ROM drives and CD-ROMs hadn't come along when they did; would we still be using 1.44MB floppies? Would we need hundreds of floppies to install the software that can so beautifully be held on only one CD-ROM? At the very least, software complexity would have not approached its current levels without the cheap, large-capacity CD-ROM.

As most of us know, CD-ROMs didn't begin their life in computers. They were first developed by Phillips and Sony in the late seventies, and were unveiled in 1980 as a replacement for LP records. These CD-ROMs can store up to 74 minutes of high-quality sound, and their high-data density, random access (you can jump to any spot easily), small size, and great sound has made them the most popular way to store music.

How CD-ROMs Work

A CD-ROM (compact disc, read-only memory) stores data in microscopic pits that are burned into the disc with a powerful laser. Once a master is created, copies can be made using a process similar to that for making vinyl records. The copies are coated with aluminum, and then more plastic for protection. Interestingly, the data on a CD-ROM is near the "top" of the disc, where the label is located (Figure 20-1).

Many people believe that if a CD-ROM is scratched on the bottom, it is unreadable. This is untrue. If a CD-ROM is scratched on the bottom (the shiny side), these scratches can be polished out (assuming that they aren't too deep), allowing the disc to be read. Scratches on the top of the disk, however, can wreak havoc on a CD-ROM! For that reason, avoid writing on the top of a disc with anything other than a soft pen—and certainly don't scratch the top!

To read a CD-ROM, a CD-ROM drive uses a laser and mirrors to read the data. The aluminum covering on the CD-ROM makes a highly reflective surface. The pits don't allow reflection, creating binary ones, and the nonpitted spots make binary zeros. It's actually a little more complicated than this, but you get the idea! These pits are densely packed on the CD-

Figure 20.1 Cutaway of CD-ROM showing the location of data tracks

ROM, allowing for the storage of a vast amount of data. A CD-ROM can hold 5.2 billion bits, or 650 million bytes of data.

CD-ROM Formats

The first data CD-ROMs, and all music CD-ROMs still sold today, organize their information in a special format called CD-DA (compact disc, digital audio). Although it's an excellent way to store music, CD-DA is a terrible way to store data because there is no error-checking. Sure, your Rolling Stones CD can miss a few bits and you'd probably never even know it, but try copying an .EXE file from a CD and missing a few bits—the system will lock up.

Storing data on a CD-ROM required error-checking, which generated the next CD-ROM format: ISO-9660. This format is also called High Sierra, or simply CD-ROM. This is the format used by the vast majority of data CD-ROMs and CD-ROM drives.

The CD-ROM drives installed into PCs are designed to read either type of format. Most have enough hardware to even play regular audio CDs. These CD-ROM drives have an earphone jack and controls right on the front of the drive (Figure 20-2). However, PCs need device drivers in order to access a digital CD-ROM (this will be addressed in a moment).

Figure 20.2
Speaker jack and volume control for analog CD-ROMS

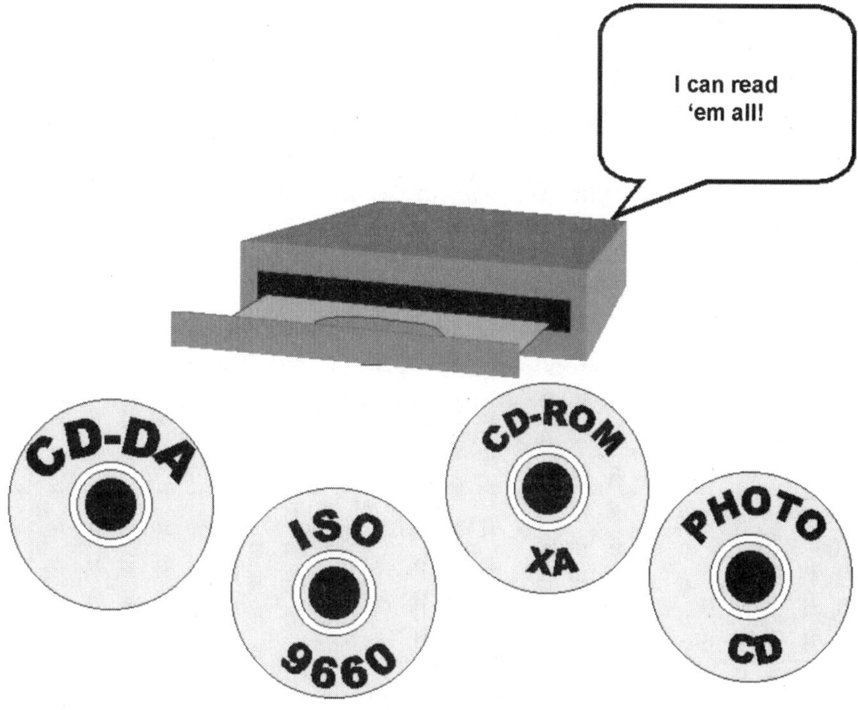

Figure 20.3
I can read 'em all!

Although not very popular, a few other formats can be read by most CD-ROM drives. The first is CD-I (compact disc, interactive), which was developed to allow a CD to store sound and video, and also allow simultaneous playback. The idea behind CD-I is that a machine—a CD-I "player"—had all the necessary electronics to play the disc. It was a small step to develop PCs that could also play CD-Is.

A second format is CD-ROM/XA, which is little more than a specialized format that takes most of the interesting aspects of CD-I. Like CD-I, most CD-ROM drives support CD-ROM/XA, even though few CD-ROMs use the format.

The last format is Kodak's Photo-CD. Kodak sees the CD-ROM as a replacement for paper photographs for a broad section of existing computer users. The Photo-CD format is a compressed format that stores many photos on one CD-ROM. Kodak envisioned people purchasing a Photo-CD reader, just as they would a CD-I reader. However, most CD-ROM drives can also read the Photo-CD format, assuming that the proper software is loaded (Figure 20-3).

Speeds

The first CD-ROM drives processed data at roughly 150,000 bits per second, or 150 kilobits per second (150 kbps), roughly the minimum amount of speed necessary to output high-quality sound. While this speed is excellent for listening to music, it is much too slow for smooth video output. Even if you are simply using a CD-ROM drive to install programs, transferring files off a CD-ROM at 150 kbps is like crawling. Since the day the first CD-ROM drives for PCs hit the market, there has been a desire to speed them up. Each increase in speed is measured in multiples of the original 150-kbps drives, and are given an × and number to show their relative speed over the first (1×) drives. Here is a list of the more common CD-ROM drive speeds:

Drive	Speed
1×	150 kbps
2×	300 kbps
3×	450 kbps
4×	600 kbps
6×	900 kbps
10×	1500 kbps
12×	1800 kbps
16×	2400 kbps
32×	4800 kbps

Keep in mind that these speeds are maximums and are rarely met in real-life operation. Most programs are written to run on 4× CD-ROM drives, so there is little benefit in purchasing higher-speed CD-ROM drives for programs. However, as high-speed CD-ROM drives are so inexpensive, many people buy them anyway so installations will be faster!

Connections

A CD-ROM drive needs to be connected to a PC in order to operate. Since their inception, CD-ROM drives in PCs have gone through a fascinating series of controllers and connections, leading to the fast yet simple connections used today. Let's look at these, starting with the first, proprietary connectors.

PROPRIETARY When the first CD-ROM drives began to appear in the early nineties, there was no standard connection to make them work

Figure 20.4 Creative Labs Multi-CD showing proprietary CD-ROM connectors

in a PC. Early CD-ROM drive makers were compelled to provide their own controllers. The first generation of CD-ROM controllers could be broken down into three groups: Panasonic (also called Creative or MKE), Sony, and Mitsumi. Although these controllers operated acceptably well, the fact that they were proprietary—combined with the fact they looked extremely similar—made them difficult to use and change. One early adopter of CD-ROM controllers was Creative Labs. Creative Labs saw CD-ROMs and CD-ROM drives as a natural complement to their sound cards. To that end, they began to sell sound cards with CD- ROM controllers built into them. One measure of the frustration of the time was the Creative Labs Multi-CD sound card, which had three separate CD-ROM controllers—one of each proprietary type (Figure 20-4). So no matter what CD-ROM drive was used, the sound card could communicate with it.

ATAPI The onset of the ATAPI standard virtually ended all the proprietary drivers overnight. Instead of dedicated connectors and unique drivers, ATAPI allowed a CD-ROM drive to be treated exactly as though it were an EIDE drive. ATAPI CD-ROM drives have 40-pin connectors and master/slave jumpers, and can be installed as just another drive. Unlike a hard drive, there is no reason to go into CMOS. The device drivers handle everything. Just plug in the drive and it's ready.

Like any EIDE drive, ATAPI CD-ROM drives must be properly jumpered in order to operate. They can act as a master or slave and can be run on either the primary or secondary controller, although you don't want to boot to a CD-ROM drive. (Yes, there is a way to make a CD-ROM drive bootable, but that fits under the "weird" group that this chapter is avoiding.) Classically, CD-ROM drives are installed as secondary slaves or primary master in systems with one hard drive. Figure 20-5 shows one running as a slave, with a hard drive on the system's primary IDE controller.

SCSI SCSI (small computer systems interface—see Chapter 9) predates ATAPI and, although not quite as common, it is in many ways a superior way to use CD-ROM drives. A SCSI chain allows many CD-ROM drives to be installed on one machine, which is a handy way for networks to access many CD-ROM drives. SCSI CD-ROM drives have all the same features of any other SCSI device. As a rule, SCSI CD-ROM drives are slow and narrow SCSI, given that the relative speeds of the CD-ROM drive aren't conducive to wide or fast SCSI. Some of the newest CD-ROM drives, however, have moved to narrow, fast SCSI.

Like all SCSI devices, SCSI CD-ROM drives need a unique SCSI ID and must be terminated on the end of a SCSI chain. Figure 20-6 shows an internal SCSI CD-ROM drive with an attached internal cable. SCSI CD-ROM

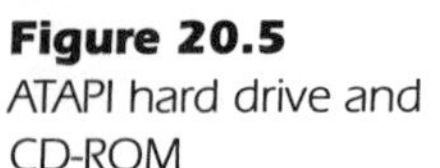

Figure 20.5
ATAPI hard drive and CD-ROM

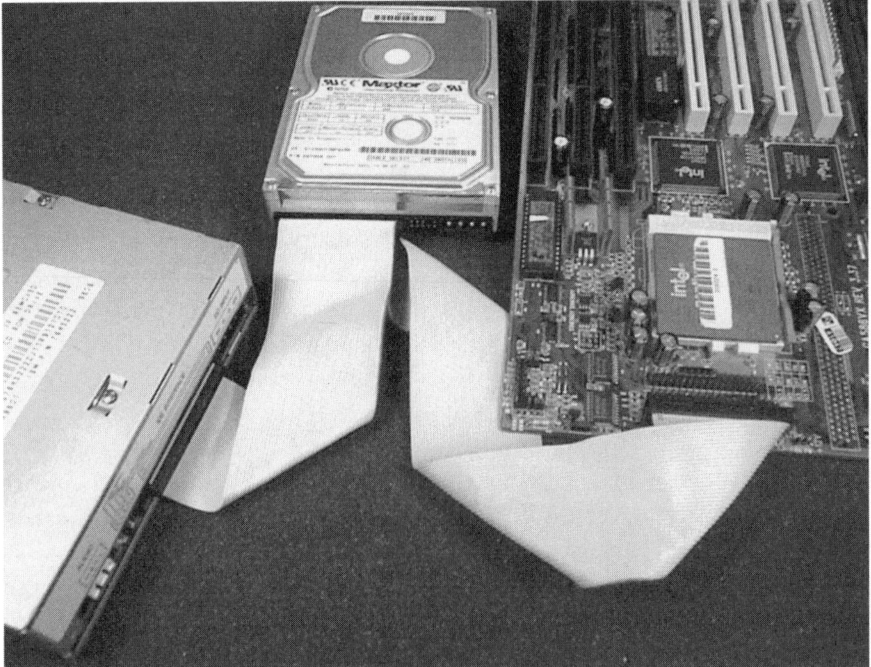

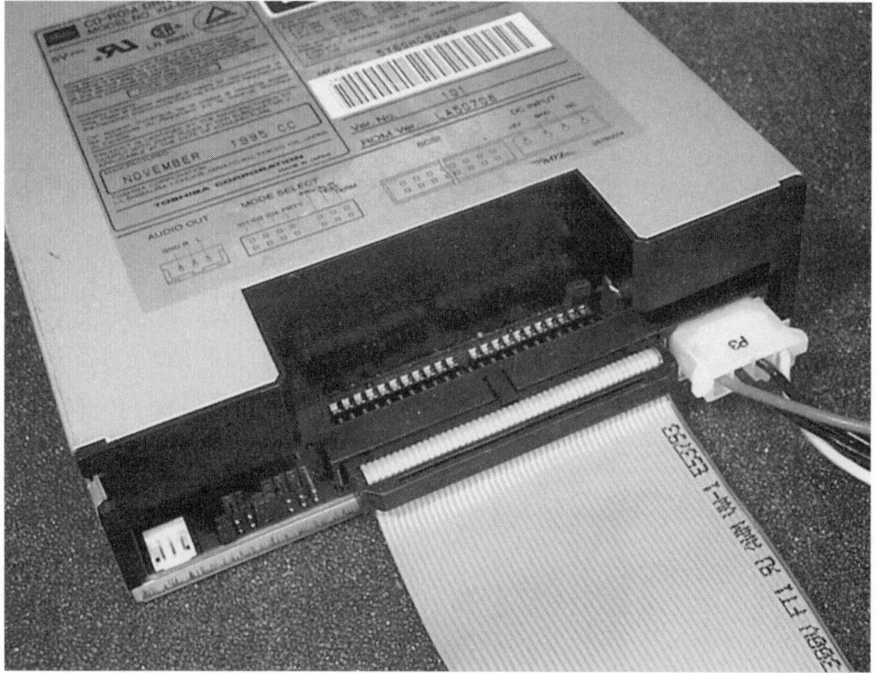

Figure 20.6 SCSI CD-ROM on SCSI chain

drives are one of the most common external SCSI devices. Figure 20-7 shows the connections for an external SCSI CD-ROM drive. Note the external terminator.

The SCSI ASPI standards includes device drivers for SCSI CD-ROM drives for both DOS and Windows 3.*x*. Windows 95/98 has complete, built-in ASPI support. Once the CD-ROM drive is physically installed and the required jumpers are set correctly, it's time to install device drivers and support software to make the drive work.

Device Drivers and Software

CD-ROM drives, like anything else in a PC, need device drivers in order to operate (see Figure 20-8). A CD-ROM drive is a mass storage device like a hard drive. In PCs, the goal of CD-ROM use is to make a CD-ROM drive look like any other storage device—in particular, to make it look and act as though it were just another hard drive, although a read-only hard drive. Basically, the goal is to give the CD-ROM drive a letter that can be accessed by the operating system.

The process of turning a CD-ROM drive into a device with a drive letter that is visible to the system varies, based on the type of connection

Figure 20.7 Typical SCSI CD-ROM connections

Figure 20.8 I need a drive letter!

and the computer's operating system. Let's take a look at the device drivers and other programs used by DOS, Windows 3.1, and Windows 95/98 to make a CD-ROM drive visible to a computer.

DOS DOS was the predominant operating system when CD-ROMs and CD-ROM drives were first developed for use with PCs. This has led to certain methods of software usage that are still being used today. In particular, a two-step process was developed in which a hardware-specific device driver is installed to create an interface to the CD-ROM drive, and then a higher-level, totally hardware nonspecific program is run to actually give the CD-ROM drive a letter. In DOS, this is done by a device driver, usually written by the CD-ROM drive manufacturer, with CONFIG.SYS, and with a special TSR called MSCDEX.EXE, which was written by Microsoft and is placed in AUTOEXEC.BAT.

The installation of the device driver depends on the connection and the manufacturer. Here is a device driver for any early proprietary connection:

```
DEVICE=C:\CDROM\CLSBDV.SYS /A:220 /I:5 /D:MSCD001
```

Before Plug-n-Play, devices would have their I/O addresses and IRQs set with jumpers on the card. The settings were then placed, via options, in the device driver's line in the CONFIG.SYS file. The previous line illustrates a common way this was done. These exact settings will not exist in other CD-ROM drivers (although they tend to look fairly similar), but note the /D: option. This is required in all CD-ROM DOS device drivers. The name after /D:, however (in this example, /D:MSCD001), is the name of the device. The MSCDEX program will use this information to determine the CD-ROM drive's letter. You can use any name as long as it doesn't include any punctuation marks. Underscores and hyphens are the only exceptions.

SCSI CD-ROM drives usually used the popular DOS ASPI driver ASPICD.SYS. Note that, although there is no IRQ or I/O address information (remember that SCSI devices other than the host adapter don't need them), the required /D: option is present:

```
DEVICE=C:\SCSI\ASPICD.SYS /D:ASPICD
```

ATAPI CD-ROM drives don't enjoy the high level of driver standardization that is present in SCSI CD-ROM drives. Here is a sampling from many different manufacturers. Note that, while they might look different, they all still contain the crucial /D: option:

```
DEVICE=C:\DEV\ATATPI.SYS /D:SONY_000
DEVICE=C:\NEC_IDE.SYS /D:MSCD001
DEVICE=C:\CDD\WCD.SYS /D:WD_CD-ROM
DEVICE=C:\TSY\TSYCDROM.SYS /D:TSYCD1 /P:SM
DEVICE=C:\DEV\HIT-IDE.SYS /D:MSCD005
DEVICE=C:\MTM\MTMCDAI.SYS /D:MSCD001
DEVICE=C:\TORISAN\TORISAN.SYS /D:TSYCD3 /P:SM
DEVICE=C:\CDD\WCD.SYS /D:WP_CDROM
```

There is no standard option other than /D. Most DOS CD-ROM drivers did not use any other options. Manufacturer often made their own options (note the /P option in two of the examples). Check the documentation or contact the CD-ROM drive manufacturer for details on other options.

MSCDEX Once the driver is installed into the CONFIG.SYS file, Microsoft's MSCDEX.EXE program is then placed into the AUTOEXEC.BAT file. MSCDEX, short for "Microsoft CD-ROM extensions," takes the device name that is set in the CD-ROM drive's device driver line and assigns it a drive letter. Although there are many options with MSCDEX, the only required one is /D:, to match the /D: name set in CONFIG.SYS. So if a device driver line looked like this:

```
DEVICE=C:\DEV\HIT-IDE.SYS /D:MSCD005
```

the MSCDEX line in AUTOEXEC.BAT would look like this:

```
MSCDEX /D:MSCD005
```

Again, there is no significance to the /D: names as long as the ones in the driver and MSCDEX match. A CONFIG.SYS like this would work equally well:

```
DEVICE=C:\DEV\HIT-IDE.SYS /D:FRED
```

as well as the following MSCDEX line in AUTOEXEC.BAT:

```
MSCDEX /D:FRED
```

Along with the /D: option, MSCDEX has a few options that might be useful.

/M:XXX (BUFFERS) The /M: option sets the number of buffers, which are like the assembly area for files coming from the CD-ROM drive. By default, there are six buffers. The /M: option is not often used, unless a particular CD-ROM drive or application asks for it to be changed. There is no practical reason to set it above 20. The /M:10 and /M:15 options are fairly common:

```
DEVICE=C:\DOS\MSCDEX.EXE /D:MSCD001 /M:10
```

/V (VERBOSE) Gives a lot of extra information, particularly on memory use. Here's an example:

```
MSCDEX Version 2.25
Copyright (C) Microsoft Corp. 1986-1995. All rights reserved.
Drive F: = Driver FRED unit 0561552 bytes free memory
```

```
0       bytes expanded memory
13030   bytes CODE
2112    bytes static DATA
20882   bytes dynamic DATA
36288   bytes used
```

/L (DRIVE LETTER) By default, MSCDEX gives the CD-ROM drive the next available drive letter, which can be highly unattractive in some situations. For example, a network might want to use those drive letters for networked drives. The /L option allows you to change the CD-ROM drive's letter to anything, from the next available drive letter all the way to Z:. The following would give the CD-ROM drive the letter S:

```
MSCDEX /D:SDC001 /L:S
```

DOS is highly limited in the number of drive letters that are available, due to the way it uses memory to store them. You can add more memory for drive letters by using the LASTDRIVE= line in CONFIG.SYS (see Chapter 8 for details).

WINDOWS 3.*X* Windows 3.*x* was designed to work with the DOS drivers and MSCDEX. In Windows 3.*x*, the system boots up in DOS, reading CONFIG.SYS and AUTOEXEC.BAT. Once the CD-ROM drive is established, the system then starts Windows. All Windows functions recognize the drive, including File Manager. Although this system worked acceptably, there was one rather large problem area—caching the CD-ROM drive (see Chapter 13). The old SMARTDRV.EXE program could easily cache CD-ROM drives, but it was a DOS- based program. Windows 3.*x*'s newer VCACHE was a fantastic caching program, but it could cache only hard drives; it was useless for CD-ROM drives. As a result, Windows 3.*x* systems will often run both SMARTDRV and VCACHE—SMARTDRV for the CD-ROM drive and VCACHE for the hard drives. This created a significant amount of problems due to wasted memory, redundant programs, and dependence on real-mode device drivers. The solution would have to wait until Windows 95.

WINDOWS 95/98 Windows 95 has eliminated the inefficiencies of the CD-ROM usage in DOS and Windows 3.*x*. In particular, MSCDEX has been replaced with the protected-mode CD File System (CDFS) driver. Not only is CDFS protected-mode, but it is part of the Windows 95 Installable File System (IFS) family of cooperative drivers for storage devices. IFS drivers allow tighter integration of different types of storage devices, creating more flexible caching, cooperation with networked drives, and storage in other operating systems. Finally, CDFS, like all protected-mode drivers, doesn't use conventional memory. Another big advantage of Windows 95 is that it has built-in drivers for most types of CD-ROM drives. For most systems, CD-ROM drives are automatically recognized and assigned a drive letter. Very easy.

When a new Windows 95/98 system is installed or a new CD-ROM drive is added to an existing system, the first thing most people want to know is, "Will Windows 95 recognize my CD-ROM drive? You can quickly determine this by opening the My Computer icon and verifying whether or not a CD-ROM drive is present (Figure 20-9).

The Control Panel/System Profile/Device Manager contains most of the information about the CD-ROM drive. The General tab informs you of its current status, basically whether or not the device is working properly—rather useless information compared to actually trying the device (Figure 20-10).

More useful are the Settings and Driver tabs. The Driver tab lets you update drivers (Figure 20-11). Since CD-ROM drives use the CDFS, you shouldn't need a driver. This is reflected by the system.

Figure 20.9
My computer

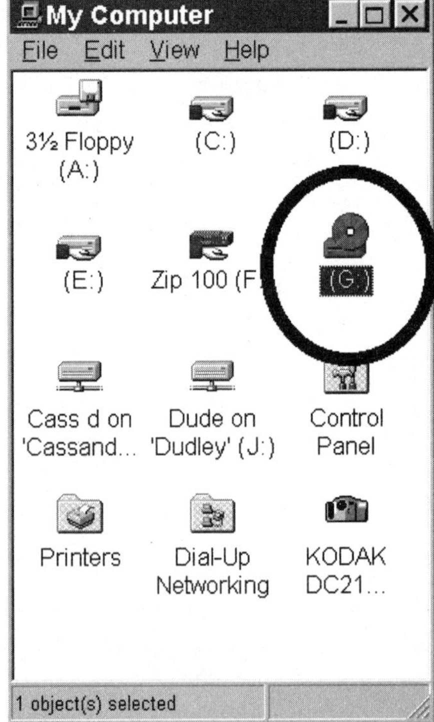

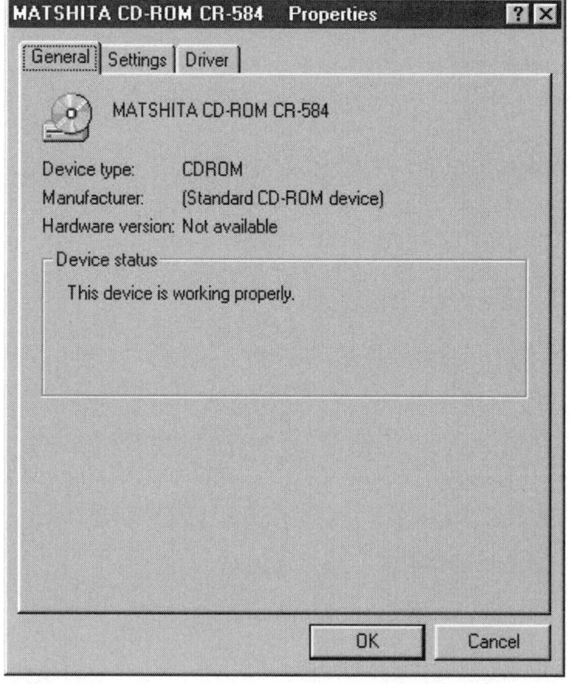

Figure 20.10 CD-ROM properties/general tab

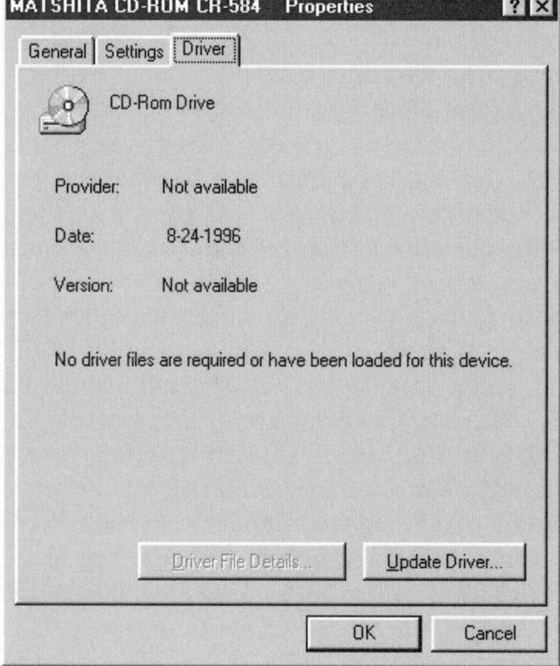

Figure 20.11 CD-ROM properties/driver tab

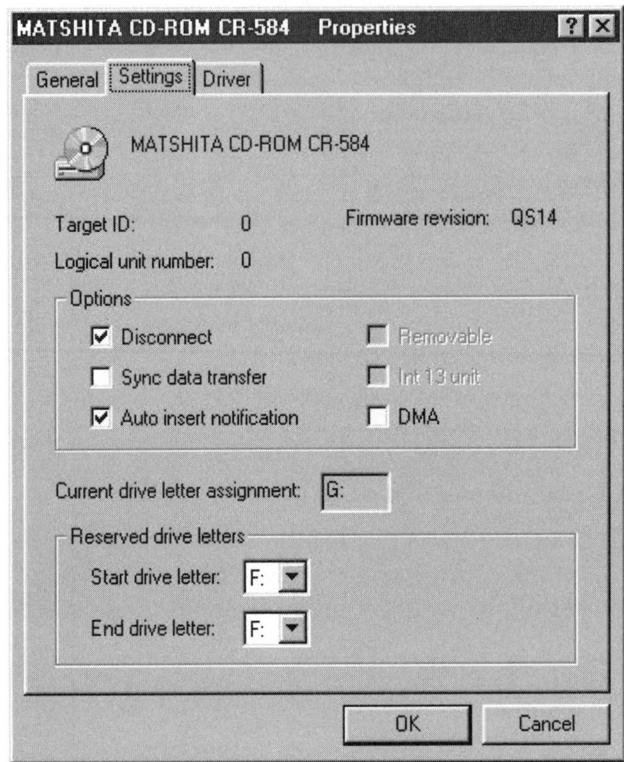

Figure 20-12 CD-ROM properties/settings tab

The Settings tab contains the bulk of the noteworthy CD-ROM drive settings (Figure 20-12). First is the drive letter setting. Like the /L: option in MSCDEX, here is where the drive letter is determined. You can't directly assign a particular drive letter to a CD-ROM drive. Instead, you must select a range of reserved drive letters. In essence, then, you can select a particular drive letter by assigning the same beginning and ending letter.

Another setting of note is Auto Insert Notification. Windows 95/98 automatically detects the presence of audio or data CD-ROMs. If a CD-ROM is inserted, Windows 95/98 will automatically begin to play it. If the CD-ROM is audio, track 1 plays automatically. If the CD-ROM is data, Windows searches the CD-ROM's root directory for a special text file called AUTORUN.INF. Although handy, this option can sometimes be annoying and unproductive. By unchecking the Auto Insert Notification box, you can specify that Windows does not automatically run CD-ROMs.

By default, Windows 95/98 does a pretty good job of setting up a CD-ROM drive for the most optimal settings. However, the Control Panel/System Properties/File System/CD-ROM options allows you to control the CD-ROM cache (Figure 20-13). When Windows 95 first came out, most

PCs were still running in the 4-, 8-, and 16-megabyte range. CD-ROM drive settings are configured to allow users to optimize their system based on the amount of RAM and the speed of the CD-ROM drive. Given that the vast majority of PCs today have 16MB of RAM and quad-speed CD-ROM drives at the very least, these outdated settings are invariably pushed to the maximum.

Troubleshooting

A CD-ROM drive is one of the most reliable and durable components in a PC; however, there are times when that reliable and durable device decides to turn into an unreliable, nondurable pile of plastic and metal frustration. This section covers a few of the more common problems with CD-ROM drives and how to fix them.

The single biggest problem with CD-ROM drives, especially in a new installation, has to do with its connections—meaning it hasn't been properly installed in some way. A few other common problems are forgetting to plug in a power connector, inserting a cable backwards, or misconfiguring jumpers and switches. Although knowing the type of

Figure 20.13 CD-ROM cache settings

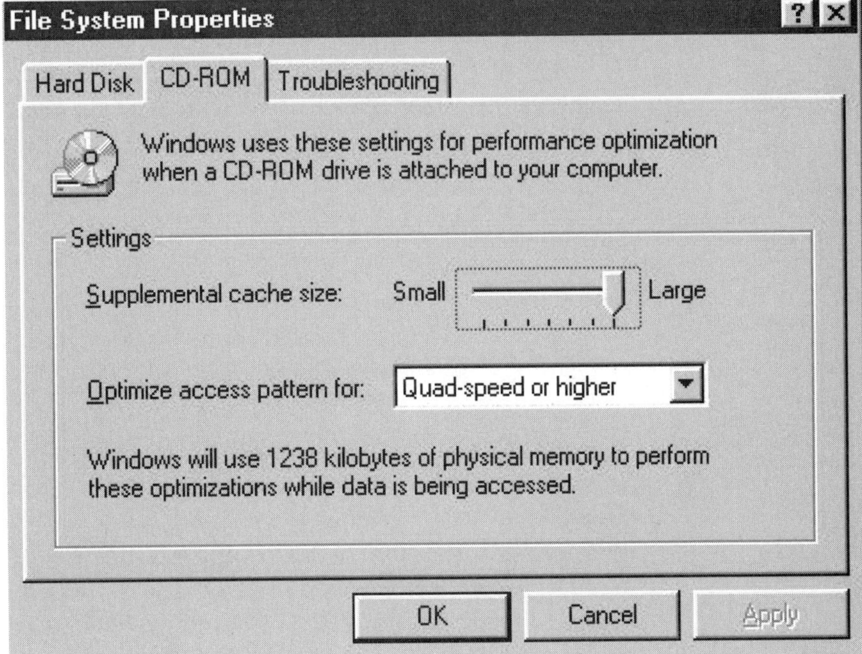

CD-ROM drive (ATAPI, SCSI, or proprietary) is necessary, testing for an improper physical connection is always the same—using BIOS or DOS-level device drivers to see if the system can see the CD-ROM drive.

Using BIOS really depends on the system. Most CD-ROM drives used today are the ATAPI type. Knowing this, most BIOS makers have created intelligent BIOSes that can see an installed CD-ROM drive. Here's a more modern Award Software, Inc. BIOS recognizing an ATAPI CD-ROM drive during startup:

```
Award Plug and Play BIOS Extension v1.0A
Copyright (C) 1996, Award Software, Inc.
   Detecting HDD Primary Master  ... WDC AC22500L
Found CDROM : MATSHITA CR-584
```

These type of messages tend to move by rather quickly during bootup, so a good eye and/or a fast press on the Pause key might help. Now, not all BIOSes can immediately recognize a CD-ROM drive, nor will even the most advanced BIOS see a proprietary or SCSI CD-ROM drive. There is one BIOS, however, that might "see" a SCSI CD-ROM drive. If the system has a better adapter, an Adaptec 2940 perhaps, there will usually be some text at boot that says something like:

```
Press Ctrl-A for SCSI Select
```

which allows you to access configuration options. The goal here is to make the host adapter scan the SCSI bus and return a list of devices on the bus. If the SCSI CD-ROM drive doesn't appear, there is a problem with the hardware. Look for options like Scan SCSI Bus or Diagnostic. The function is given different names by different SCSI host adapter makers, but the result will be a screen that looks like this:

```
SCSI ID 0       Seagate ST4302
SCSI ID 1       No Device Detected
SCSI ID 2       No Device Detected
SCSI ID 3       No Device Detected
SCSI ID 4       No Device Detected
SCSI ID 5       IOMEGA ZIP100
SCSI ID 6       HITACHI CD20032
SCSI ID 7       ADAPTEC 2940
```

If a SCSI CD-ROM drive is visible to the computer, it has a valid SCSI ID, is properly connected and powered, and the SCSI chain is properly terminated.

Without some type of BIOS support, the only other option is to boot to a DOS-level device driver. For DOS and Windows 3.*x* systems, the driver should already be installed. For Windows 95/98, a DOS driver needs to be temporarily loaded into CONFIG.SYS. Step-through the boot process

(Press F8 in DOS, press F8, and select Step by Step in Windows 95/98) and run the CD-ROM driver. Here's a successful boot from Windows 95:

```
Process your startup device drivers (CONFIG.SYS) [Enter=Y,Esc=N]?Y
DEVICE=C:\DOS\TRICD.SYS /D:MSCD001 [Enter=Y,Esc=N]?Y
Triones ATAPI CD-ROM Device Driver, Version 3.6
Copyright (c) 1994-1997 Triones Technologies, Inc. All rights re-
served.
Secondary/Master: MATSHITACD-ROM CR-584    , Multi-word DMA 1
ATAPI CD-ROM Device Driver installed.
```

Here's the same boot with the data cable intentionally inverted:

```
Process your startup device drivers (CONFIG.SYS) [Enter=Y,Esc=N]?Y
DEVICE=C:\DOS\TRICD.SYS /D:MSCD001 [Enter=Y,Esc=N]?Y
Triones ATAPI CD-ROM Device Driver, Version 3.6
Copyright (c) 1994-1997 Triones Technologies, Inc. All rights re-
served.
Error: No CDROM detected.
```

Of course, be sure to have the correct DOS driver for the CD-ROM drive that is being tested! If the device is detected, yet can't read a CD-ROM, the first thing to try is another CD-ROM. CD-ROMs that are badly scratched will not be able to be read by the CD-ROM drive. There's not much use in attempting to clean CD-ROM drives since there is no contact between the read head and the CD-ROM, and therefore little opportunity for dirt build-up. From time to time, however, an extremely dirty CD-ROM drive can be recovered with a commercial CD-ROM drive cleaning kit.

Cleaning CD-ROM drives might not be a very useful task, but cleaning the CD-ROMs themselves is quite common and very useful. While there are a number of fine CD-ROM cleaning kits, most CD-ROMs can be cleaned quite well with nothing more than a damp soft cloth. Occasionally, a mild detergent can be added. A common "old tech's tale" about cleaning CD-ROMs is that they can be washed in a dishwasher! Although this might seem laughable, the tale has become so common that it requires a serious response. This is not true for two reasons. First, the water in most dishwashers is too hot and can cause the CD-ROMs to warp. Second, the CD-ROMs can be pushed around, hitting other objects and getting scratched. Don't do it!

Sound

The evolution of PCs has been very exciting from the very beginning. It's probably safe to say that there has never been a two-month period since the early eighties where a new computer technology hasn't been unveiled. Granted, most of these technologies have become obsolete (ESDI hard drives, for instance) or for one reason or another just didn't catch on (such as light pens). While there have been many technologies, a few have literally become milestones—where the rest of the computer industry is described in terms of "before" and "after" the technology existed. Certainly, the addition of sound via sound cards is one of those milestones. While sound is now taken for granted, very few technicians really understand the sound process and how it affects the system. This section will delve into sound, and help to clarify and separate the many different functions of the average sound card.

Types of sound

How can a computer, capable of nothing more than processing a bunch of ones and zeroes, play Handel's *Messiah*? How does a sound card create the dynamic hum of a race car speeding by at 180 mph? Before understanding how a sound card works, let's take a moment to understand how a sound card records, stores, and recreates the sounds that make PCs so much more useful and fun than they were "before."

WAV Basically, there are only two ways to make sounds on PCs. The first is to generate waveforms—in essence a tape recording (Figure 20-14). Referring back to fourth-grade science, sounds travel in waves. Higher-frequency waves make higher- pitched tones, and lower-frequency waves make lower-pitched tones. You can visualize sound as a constantly changing series of frequencies entering the ear over time.

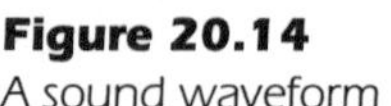

Figure 20.14
A sound waveform

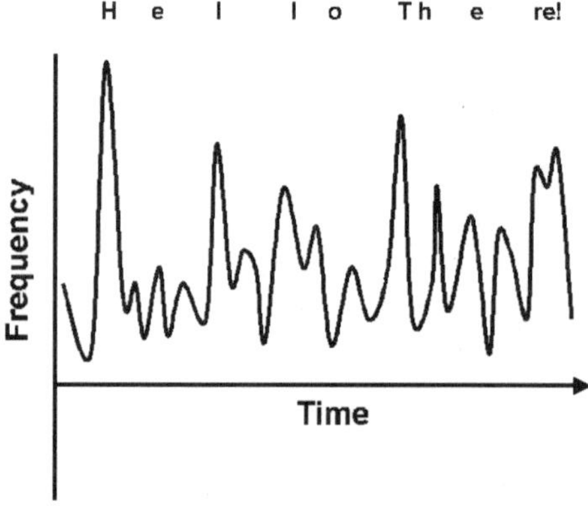

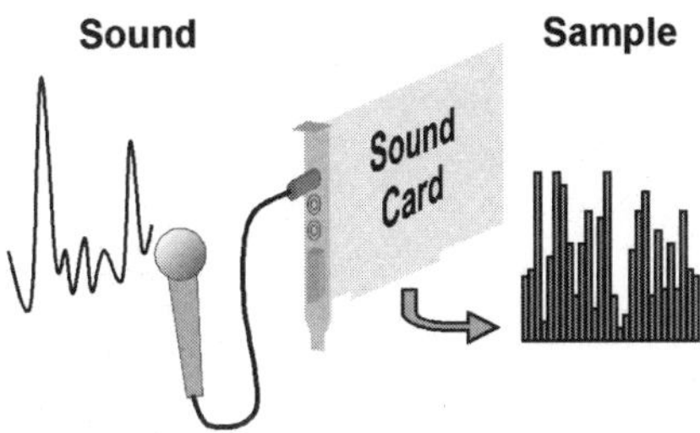

Figure 20.15a
Sound being sampled

This waveform can be stored digitally in "samples" taken at regular intervals (Figure 20-15a). The quality of the recorded sound is based on the number of bits used for each sample and how often the sound is sampled. The number of bits per sample is usually either 8 or 16. An 8-bit sample allows 256 different frequencies, which is acceptable for only the most basic of sounds, like a telephone conversation. A 16-bit sound allows up to 65,536 different frequencies, covering roughly all the frequencies that can be detected by the human ear. The sampling rate is measured in kiloHertz (kHz), and usually varies from about 11 to 44 kHz. Last, waveforms are sampled in either mono or stereo. Waveforms are therefore recorded at different bits, samplings, and either mono or stereo for different qualities. As can be imagined, a waveform tends to be a rather large file. A high-quality waveform recording can use over 100 kilobytes per second!

In the first years of waveforms, there were many types of file formats, each requiring its own separate player/recorder application. During the era of Windows 3.*x*, Microsoft adopted a new type of file format, WAV for Windows. Microsoft then began to add free WAV files and free WAV file applications to later versions of Windows 3.*x*, making WAV the de-facto waveform standard. Today, WAV files continue to be the most popular waveform format.

MIDI MIDI, or Musical Instrument Digital Interface, is the second most popular type of PC sound. MIDI was not designed for the PC; it was created for musicians, to allow them to create, store, and play a broad cross-section of instruments, including those invented on synthesizers. MIDI starts with a sound card that has built-in recordings of real musical instruments. The number of instruments stored and the quality of the recordings are what separates a cheaper sound card from a more expensive one. A MIDI file can be best described as "electronic sheet music." It contains a series of commands that specify the instrument (labeled by number, not type), the note to play, and how long to play it. The number of different instruments a sound card can play simultaneously is called its *polyphony*, and each instrument is called a *voice*. Most sound cards today have at least a 32-voice polyphony. The way musical instruments are stored on a sound card is primarily "FM synthesis" or "wave-table synthesis." Wave-table is much higher quality than FM, creating a much more realistic sound.

Given the fact that MIDI files store only the notes, they are tiny compared to WAV files. However, MIDI is limited only to instruments. You can't save a human voice or the sound of an explosion. But when a game needs a musical soundtrack or a user wants to listen to some classical music, MIDI can't be beat.

Waveforms and MIDI are completely different methods of creating and reproducing sounds. For a sound card to support both waveforms and MIDI, it must contain two completely separate sets of soldered components. In essence, a sound card can be better thought of as two devices on one card. As will be seen later in the chapter, this usually means providing separate resources (I/O addresses, IRQ, DMA, drivers) for each type of sound.

Sound-card Connections

The cornerstone of PC sound is the sound card. The average sound card should have the hardware to allow the following functions, assuming that the system has the necessary software: recording and playing waveform files, recording and playing MIDI files, recording via a microphone or auxiliary input (recording from an analog CD player, vinyl record, or tape), and playing analog CD-ROMs from the CD-ROM drive.

Keep in mind that these are average functions! Different sound cards will provide different functions. To support these functions, there must be physical connectors to allow the sound card to interface with devices such as microphones and speakers (Figure 20-15b). Let's look at the common connections on a sound card and discuss their functions.

SPEAKER The speaker connection allows the sounds to be output to speakers. While this connection is quite simple, it is the source of many of the "I can't hear any sounds!" complaints. The problem is usually the speakers themselves. The sound card has only a minimal amount of amplification, so most speakers come with their own built-in amplifiers. These amplifiers need power, so speakers will need to be powered with either batteries or an AC adapter (Figure 20-16a). In addition, most speakers will have a power switch and a volume knob. It is important to be sure that the speakers are properly powered, are turned on, and have the vol-

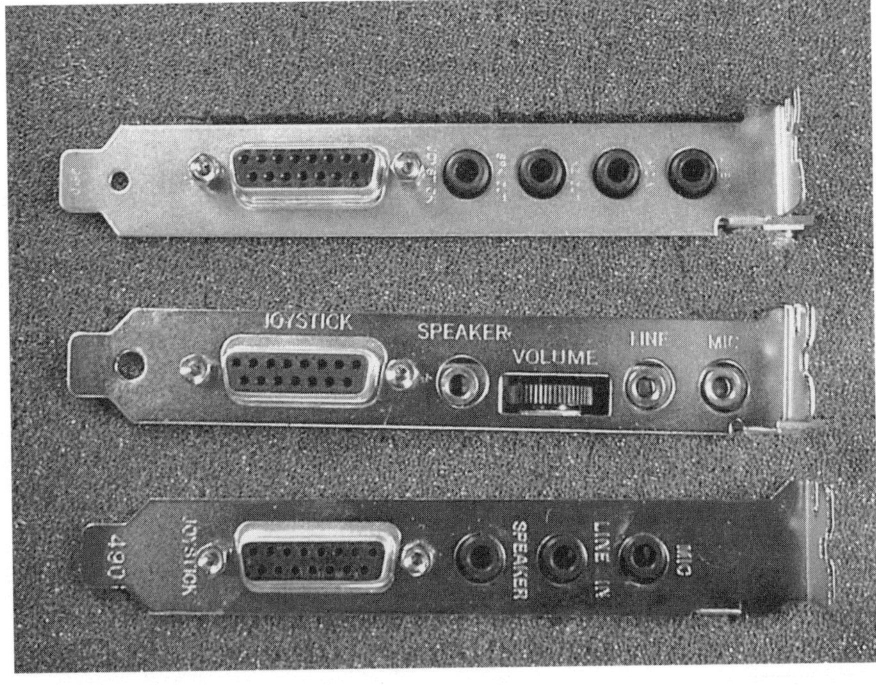

Figure 20.15b
Typical external sound-card connections

Figure 20.16a
These speakers use AC or batteries

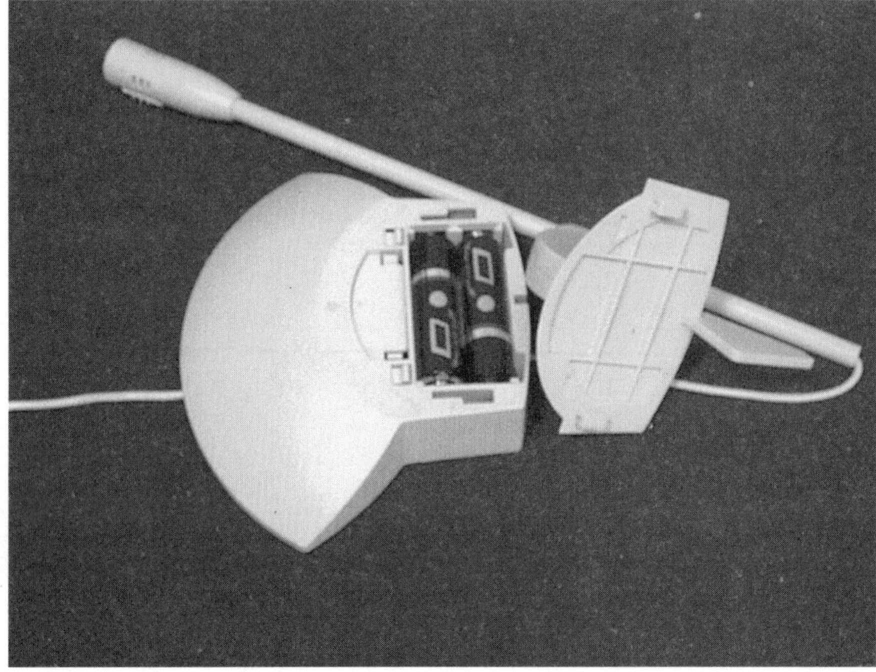

Figure 20.16b
Microphone batteries

ume turned up to ensure that the sound can be heard. Many of the "no sound" problems can be fixed by simply pressing an "on" button or replacing dead batteries.

Speakers don't necessarily need to be powered. If they aren't, then they have no amplification and simply play the relatively weak signal coming from the sound card. This is acceptable, but these unpowered speakers will not be able to provide the louder, better-quality, more robust sound that games and other sound applications need. Last, most powered speakers can create acceptable output without batteries or AC power, as long as the power switch on the speaker is also turned off.

MICROPHONE The microphone connection is as simple as the speaker connection. Just like the speaker connection, the problem lies not in the connection, but in the part to which it is connected. Microphones often have batteries and, unlike speakers, these batteries must be good for the microphone to work (Figure 20-16b). Also, microphones invariably have an on/off switch that must be turned on to allow the microphone to do its job. Don't let the simple stuff fool you!

LINE IN AND LINE OUT The line in / line out connectors allow input from and output to other devices than a microphone or speaker. Classically, the line in connector runs to a line out or auxiliary connector on the back of a stereo receiver system. This way, the sound card can take input from an audio CD player, radio, or whatever else is connected to the stereo system. The line out is also often added to a stereo system, primarily to output to big speakers or to allow tape recording.

CD-ROM CONNECTION CD-ROM drives and sound cards can be physically connected in three different ways. First, many sound cards continue to provide support for an ATAPI CD-ROM drive. Note that this ATAPI link is usually a totally separate I/O address and IRQ from the EIDE primary and secondary controllers, allowing the system to actually support a fifth IDE device. This connection has nothing to do with sound, and is provided only to ensure that there is a place to connect the CD-ROM drive. This connection usually requires a separate device driver, so most systems don't use it and simply install the CD-ROM drive on one of the EIDE connectors for the sake of simplicity. (Figure 20.17.)

The second way is the expansion bus itself. If there is a sound file on a CD-ROM, the program that wants to play the sound takes it from the CD-ROM drive via the expansion bus, loads it in RAM, and then outputs the sound, again via the expansion bus, to the sound card. This connection works as long as each device's resources (I/O addresses, IRQ and DMA) are properly configured.

The third connection is the CD-ROM drive's audio connection (Figure 20-18). The CD-ROM drive can play audio CDs by itself, but it must use

Figure 20.17
CD-ROM connection

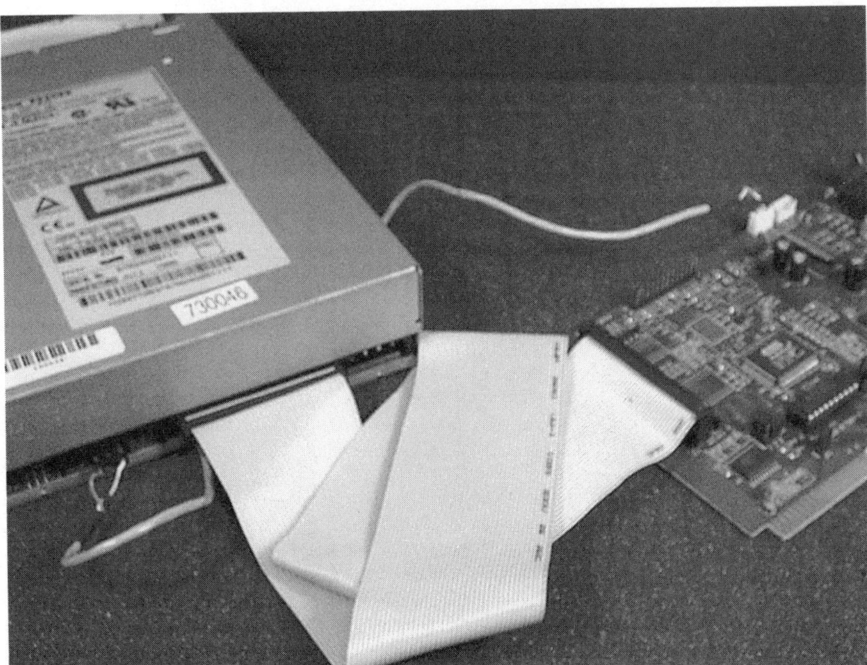

the CD-ROM's speaker jack. As most folks don't have a second set of speakers, sound cards have a special CD audio connector that directly links the sound card to the CD-ROM drive. Clearly, a CD-ROM drive also has a corresponding connector, and if you add a special wire between the devices, you can play audio CD-ROMs and output the sound to the sound card speakers. This connector must be installed to allow Window 95/98 to play audio CD-ROMs.

MIDI/JOYSTICK The beauty of MIDI is the ability to connect to other MIDI devices. To allow a MIDI-capable sound card to connect to other MIDI devices, it needs a 15-pin, female, DB-type connector. This is an excellent connector, but there are two drawbacks. First, very few people use it. Second, it is identical to a game (joystick) port. To make the port more functional and to prevent people from accidentally plugging in their joysticks and calling the sound card manufacturer, this connector can also act as a game port (Figure 20-18). Most sound cards autodetect the presence of a joystick and properly configure the port, but some older cards require moving a jumper or switch to tell the port whether it's being used for MIDI or a joystick.

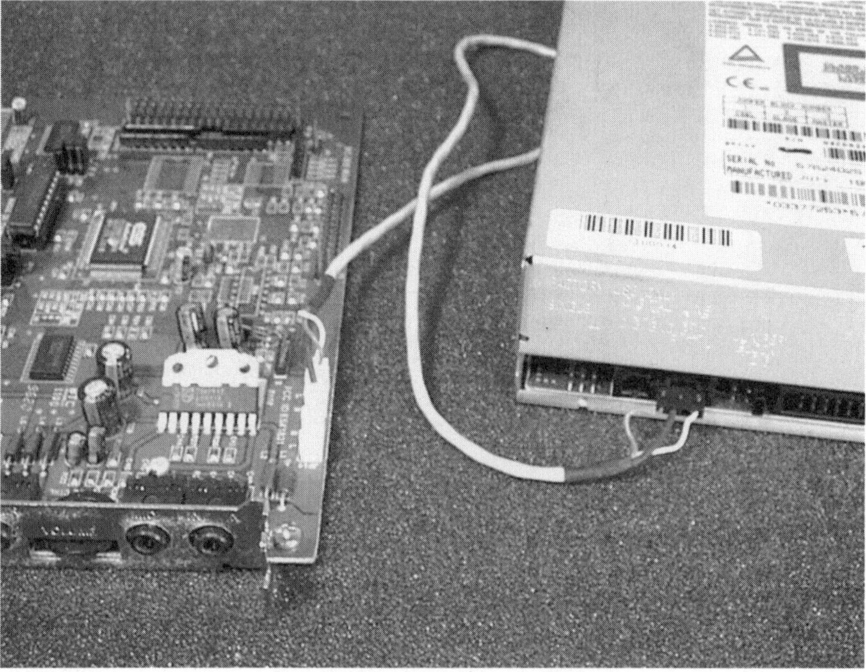

Figure 20.18 CD audio connector

Device Drivers

Sound cards are notorious for having complicated device drivers, due mainly to their multiple functions of waveform, MIDI, and possibly CD-ROM input. This problem is particularly difficult with computers running DOS, although Windows 3.*x* and Windows 95/98 are also challenging. The trick to understanding sound-card device drivers is to remember this multiple-function aspect and to treat each function as though it were a separate device requiring its own device driver. Instead of thinking "sound-card driver," think "waveform driver," "MIDI driver," and "CD-ROM controller driver"—based on the what features are contained in the individual sound card.

DOS DOS has no clue about sound cards. As a result, if a sound card is to be used in a DOS system, there are a lot of device drivers to talk to the card, and a lot of TSRs for items such as volume and application support. Plus, each DOS application that wants to use the sound card must have built-in support for the particular sound card installed in the machine. Running a sound-card installation program on a DOS machine usually adds a minimum of five to seven lines to the CONFIG.SYS, and two to three lines to AUTOEXEC.BAT. To illustrate, I'll show example CONFIG.SYS and AUTO EXEC.BAT lines from some popular sound cards. Keep in mind that different brands of sound cards have different drivers and different options, but they generally work pretty much the same.

All sound cards have a "primary" driver that provides the main link to the sound card. The sound cards that were first used with DOS predated Plug-n-Play, so I/O addresses, IRQs, and DMAs had to be set manually. In the very earliest cards, these values were set with jumpers on the card itself. The primary driver was then run with special options to inform the driver of those resources. Later, but still non-Plug-n-Play sound cards, called "jumperless" cards, would require that the I/O address, IRQ, and DMA be set from the driver itself. Either way, the driver would look basically the same. This driver could be in either CONFIG.SYS or AUTOEXEC.BAT. Here are two examples of drivers loaded from CONFIG.SYS:

```
DEVICE=C:\SB16\DRV\CTSB16.SYS /blaster=a:220 i:5 d:1 h:5
```

This one has an I/O address of 220 and an IRQ 5. It also uses two DMA channels—1 and 5.

```
DEVICE=C:\SOUND\ES668.COM /a:220 /i:7 /d:1
```

This one has an I/O address of 220, an IRQ of 7, and a DMA of 1.

```
DEVICE=C:\MEDVSN\pa3d.sys a220 d1 h7 m320 q2
```

And this one has an I/O address of 220, an IRQ of 7, and a DMA of 1 and 7. The MIDI is treated as a separate device with I/O address 320 and IRQ 2. Now here's a rare sound card with the primary driver loaded in AUTOEXEC.BAT:

```
LH C:\FMDRV\SNDCFG.EXE /A:220 /I:5 /D:1 /B:330 /Q:2
```

The /B:330 and /Q:2 are for the MIDI. Along with the primary driver, there might be a number of other device drivers for specialized applications. If you didn't use the applications, they weren't needed.

```
DEVICE=C:\SB16\drv\CTMMSYS.SYS
DEVICE=C:\SB16\DRV\CSP.SYS /unit=0 /blaster=a:220
```

There were often settings for volume, usually in AUTOEXEC.BAT. Here are two examples:

```
C:\SB16\sb16set.exe /m:220 /fm:220 /cd:220 /mic:220 /line:220
C:\ESS\ESSVOL.EXE /v:8 /l:8 /w:8 /m:8
```

Most of these volume settings are self-explanatory (clue: /fm is for waveform files), but the numbers varied depending on the manufacturers. A silent sound card could often be fixed with a higher sound setting.

Last were CD-ROM drivers. These drivers were like the other CD-ROM drivers shown earlier, but because they were lumped together with sound-card drivers, they were often mistaken for something to do with sound.

The following card uses two drivers for the same card: one for the sounds and another for the CD-ROM drive. Note how the sound-card driver and the CD-ROM driver look very similar:

```
C:\DIASND\DIASSND.SYS /A:220 /I:5 /D:1 /MID:330 /Q:9
C:\DISSND\DIASCD.SYS /A:320 /I:10 /D:MSC001
```

There are a few more settings, but before I can explain them, you must understand a very important DOS environment variable, called SET BLASTER.

In the days of DOS, as today, there were many different brands of sound cards on the market. There were also many different DOS programs that used sound. When a DOS program that used sound was installed, at some point the user was asked to pick a sound card out of a list (Figure 20-19).

Figure 20.19 DOS game prompting for a sound card

What if a manufacturer wasn't on the list? How could a DOS game support an unlisted card? The answer was provided by Creative Labs, the company that started the sound-card craze with its now famous SoundBlaster card. Creative Labs is to sound what Hewlett Packard is to laser printers. They were the first to come out with a major new technology, and they continue to be the sound card to match. Just as competing laser printer manufacturers will produce a laser printer that emulate's HP's LaserJet, so competing sound-card makers will make their cards act like a SoundBlaster. Creative Labs made this easy by creating a DOS environment setting called SET BLASTER. Like all DOS environment settings, this was placed in AUTOEXEC.BAT:

```
SET BLASTER=a220 i5 d1 h5 p330 t6
```

where p330 is the MIDI I/O address, and t6 is the type of SoundBlaster card:

1 for an original (old) SoundBlaster
2 for an original (old) SoundBlaster Pro
3 for a newer SoundBlaster 2.0 (SoundBlaster deluxe edition)

4 for a newer SoundBlaster Pro (SB Pro 2.0)
5 for a MicroChannel Sound Blaster (IBM PS/2 MCA- bus systems only)
6 for a Sound Blaster 16, Vibra 16, or AWE32

A competing card could read the SET BLASTER statement and then take the same settings. The sound-card installation would look for the SET BLASTER statement and set the driver settings to match. This way, users could say the card was a SoundBlaster of some type and the card would work. This became so popular that even Creative Labs began to do the same thing with its own drivers. Many device drivers were replaced with a TSR that simply read the SET BLASTER statement. Clearly, these TSRs had to be loaded after the SET BLASTER statement. Here's an example from an AUTOEXEC.BAT:

```
SET SOUND=C:\sb16
SET BLASTER=a220 i5 d1 h5 p330 t6
SET MIDI=synth:1 map:e
C:\SB16\diagnose /s
```

The DIAGNOSE program was just for certain Creative Labs SoundBlaster cards. It read the SET BLASTER statement and configured the card to match. The SET BLASTER statement continues to be important, primarily to support the many DOS games still being produced.

When configuring sound cards in DOS, you must consider three items. First, what does the application need: a wave table, MIDI, or both? Make sure the card supports what the application needs. Second, determine unused I/O address, IRQ, and DMA, keeping in mind that the card might need more than one of any of those resources. Install the card with those settings. Third, install/configure the application to see the card with the resource settings the card is using. Refer to the Chapter 6 for card installation issues.

DOS was never designed to support sound, and neither did Windows when it was first released. Fortunately, Windows' ability to treat hardware as one resource that all applications can use removed the nasty DOS aspect of setting up the sound card for each application.

WINDOWS 3.1 Although all versions of Windows 3.*x* would support DOS sound-card drivers, by the time Windows 3.1 became popular, device drivers and applications quickly moved from the real-mode CONFIG.SYS and AUTOEXEC.BAT files to the protected-mode SYSTEM.INI files. The cornerstone of Windows 3.*x* support was based on a software layer called the Media Control Interface (MCI). The MCI was broken down into subgroups to support different standard devices. These standard devices had names like WAVE (waveforms), MIDI (MIDI files), and MIXER (sound control). Windows programmers could simply make program calls to the MCI interface, and it would handle the details of playing and recording multimedia files. The MCI interface supported both sound and video. The MCI drivers, or really pointers to the drivers, were listed under the [drivers] section of SYSTEM.INI. The location of the sound drivers could be anywhere in SYSTEM.INI, and they would look any way the sound-card manufacturer wanted. Here are pieces of a typical SYSTEM.INI of the day, showing the line for the sound-card drivers:

```
[drivers]timer=timer.drvmidimapper=midimap.drvWAVE=es1688wn.drvMIDI
= es1688wn.drvAUX=es1688wn.drvMIXER=es1688wn.drv
```

The [drivers] section is in every SYSTEM.INI and defines the different sound-card drivers. The following [es1688wn.drv] section is unique to this particular manufacturer. Note that it performs the exact same functions as a DOS sound- card driver.

```
[es1688wn.drv]
mpu401=yes
AudioDrive=ES1688
port=220
int=5
dmachannel=1
portMPU401=330
intMPU401=2
VolumeMaster=32768
VolumeWave=32768
VolumeSynth=32768
VolumeLine=32768
VolumeMic=32768
VolumeCD=32768
VolumeAuxB=32768
```

These settings are created from an installation program (see Figure 20-20). Once installed, they are usually changed through the Control Panel and Drivers (Figure 20-21). From Drivers, select the device whose resources need to be changed (Figure 20-22) and change it (Figure 20-23).

Windows 3.*x* applications don't need to know the resources used by an application. They simply make calls to Windows for WAV, MIDI, etc. and Windows handles the rest. Windows 3.*x* itself came with only a primitive application called Media Player, but sound cards always carry a broad cross-section of applications.

Before Windows 3.*x*, there were many different file formats for both waveforms and MIDI sounds. While Microsoft didn't prevent any of these formats from working under Windows, the strong support for WAV and MIDI formats under MCI has made them predominant. In the next

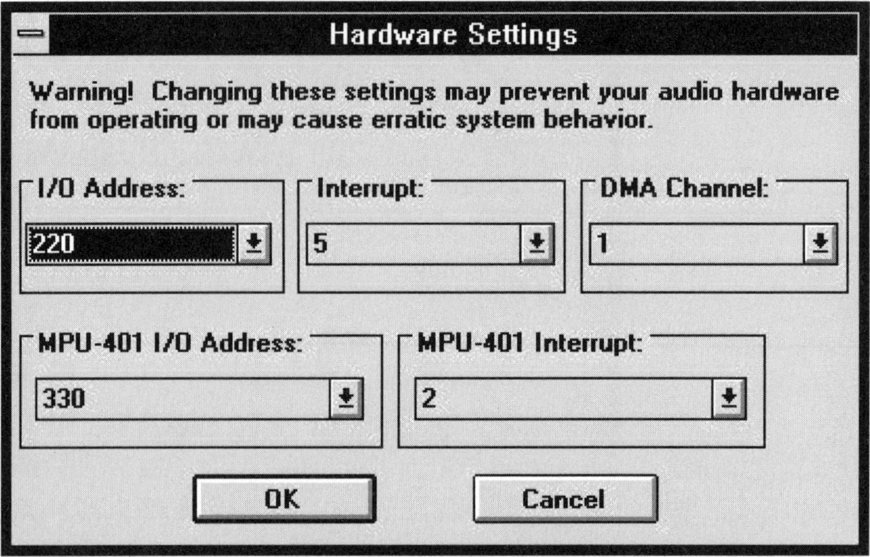

Figure 20.20 Typical Windows 3.x installation program

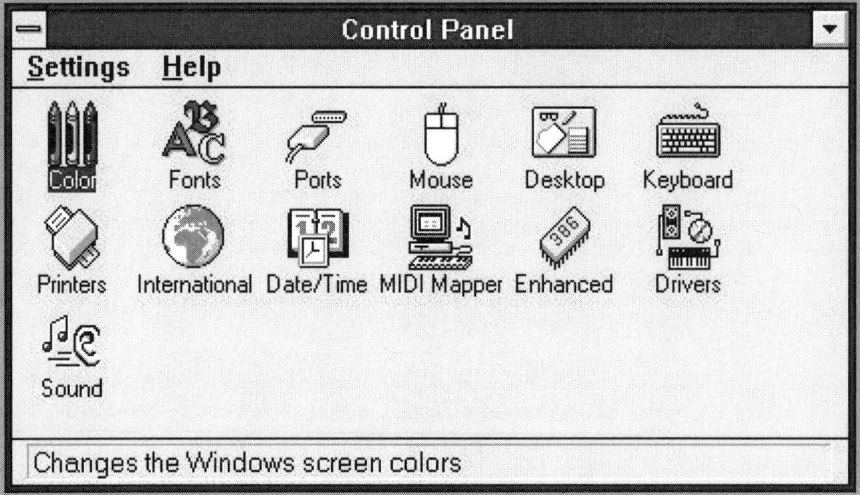

Figure 20.21 Windows 3.x control panel

section, you will see the return of a number of different file formats, in particular compression formats or CODECs (compressor/decompressors), due to the broad support of Windows 95/98.

WINDOWS 95/98 Windows 95/98 draws upon the experience gained by using sound cards in DOS and Windows 3.*x* to make sound-card installation, configuration, and use almost trivial. The resource allocation problems of DOS and Windows 3.*x* are basically gone, as Windows 95/98's use

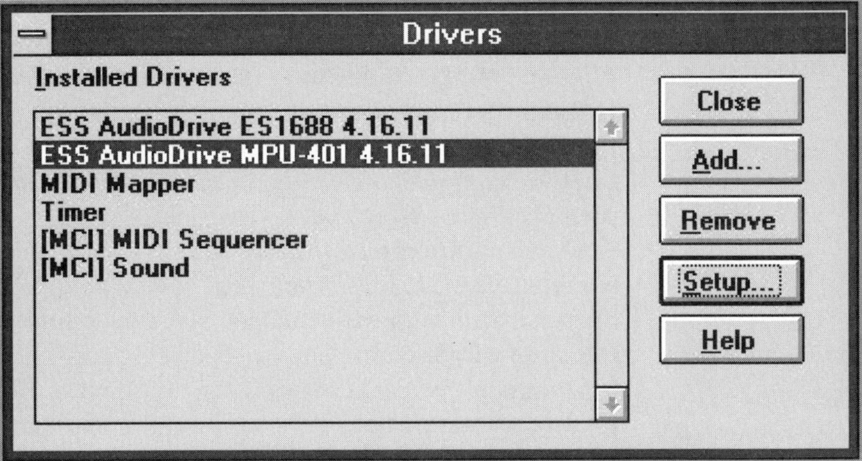

Figure 20.22
Drivers screen

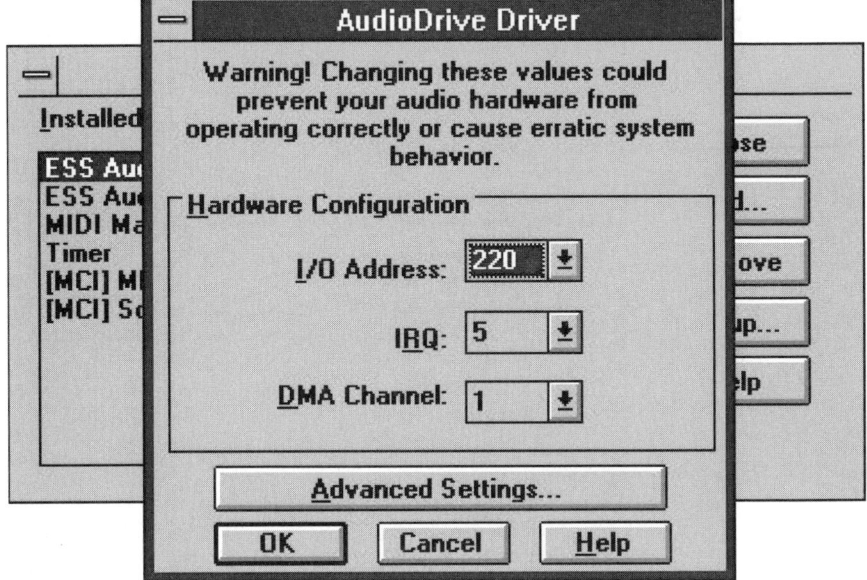

Figure 20.23
Changing resources for a sound card in Windows 3.x

of Plug-n-Play has made non-Plug-n-Play sound cards completely obsolete. Device-driver installation has been reduced to inserting a floppy or CD-ROM with the proper INF file—on the rare chance that Windows doesn't already have the necessary sound card. Windows now includes a basic, but complete, set of applications that allow the playing and recording of WAV files, playing of MIDI files and CD-ROMs, and a handy volume control applet that sits on the taskbar. Still, with all the conveniences provided by Windows 95/98, a good technician should be aware of a few nuances.

DEVICE MANAGER The first stop for understanding sound cards is the Device Manager; like any other piece of hardware, a device recognized by Windows 95/98 will be found here. Like DOS and Windows 3.*x*, Windows 95/98 looks at the separate functions of the sound card as separate devices. In the Device Manager, you'll see a sound card as a waveform player and a MIDI player (OPL3 is a type of MIDI device that this sound card emulates). See Figure 20-24.

System resources rarely need to be changed, especially if the sound card is Plug-n-Play. However, even Plug-n-Play devices can sometimes create unanticipated resource conflicts. You can change resources for each device simply by selecting properties for that particular device (Figure 20-25).

One problem that is particularly tough with sound cards is an "invisible, but working device." When Windows 95/98 is installed over DOS or Windows 3.*x*, it tries to replace all the DOS and Windows 3.*x* device drivers with Windows 95/98 drivers. Occasionally, Windows can't recognize a particular sound card; in this case, it leaves the CONFIG.SYS/AUTOEXEC.BAT/SYSTEM.INI settings intact and simply uses the existing drivers. The result is sound without a sound card listed in the Device Manager. You can usually fix this by locating the sound-card manufacturer for the proper Windows 95/98 drivers.

Figure 20.24 MIDI settings in Windows 95/98

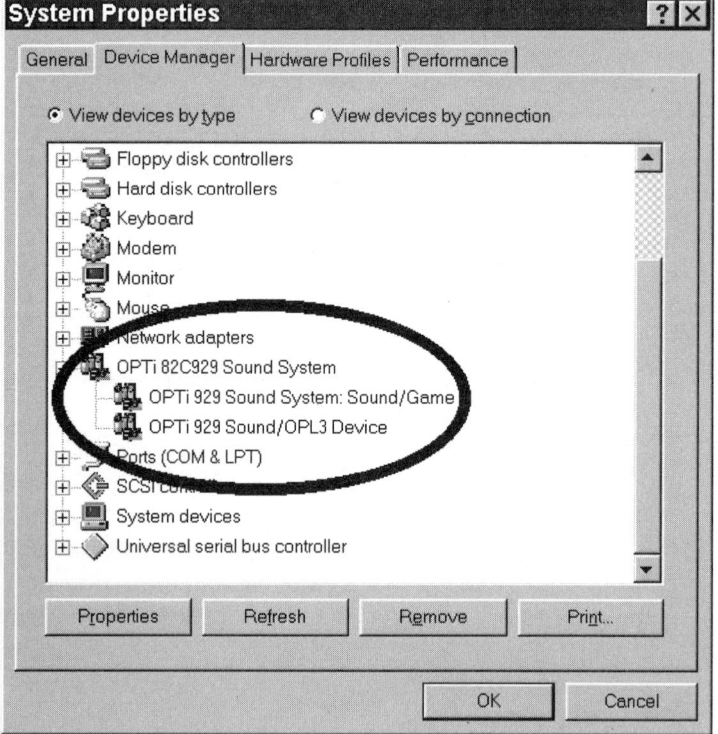

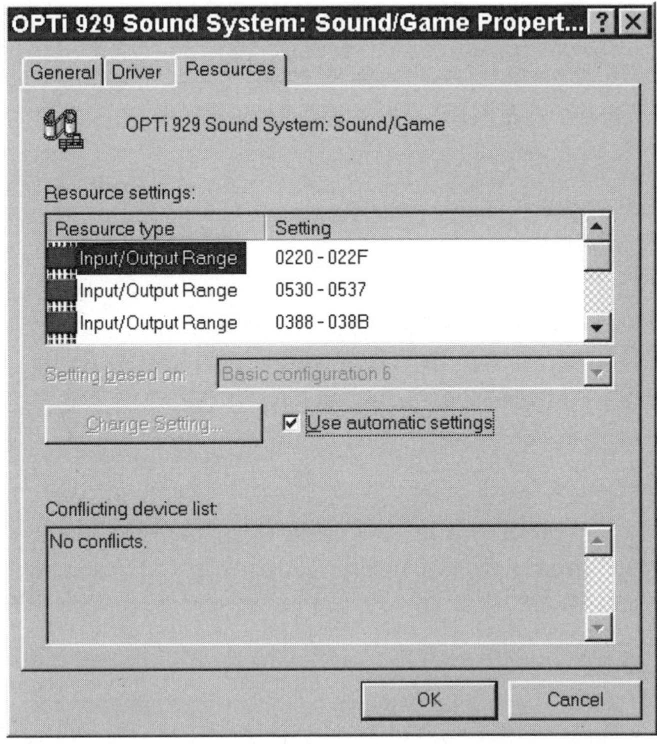

Figure 20.25 Resource settings in Windows 95's device manager

Once Windows 95/98 recognizes the card and it is displayed in the Device Manager without exclamations, it should work. This assumes that the speaker cables are properly inserted, the speakers are on if necessary, and the volume is set loud enough to be heard.

MULTIMEDIA The Multimedia section in the Control Panel is rarely used, but can be a handy place for determining some crucial information in the PC (Figure 20-26). This menu is broken up into five tabs: Audio, Video, MIDI, CD Audio, and Advanced. The Audio screen allows you to set playback and recording volumes and set recording quality. As most applications have these settings, this screen is almost never used. The Video screen is for setting the size of video playback. The MIDI screen is for setting the MIDI outputs, which is useless unless you're going to hook up MIDI devices. CD Audio displays the drive letter for the CD-ROM drive to play audio files, and sets the volume for audio CD-ROM output. The last tab, Advanced, is the most useful. This is a list of all the drivers and software loaded in the machine to support multimedia.

The most important part of this screen are the audio compression and video compression CODECs. A CODEC (compressor/decompressor) is a support program that, as its name implies, compresses and decompresses audio or video files. As mentioned earlier, there is only one type of waveform, Microsoft's WAV format. In order to reduce the size of a WAV file, a number of compression formats can be used (Figure 20-27). Different compression formats meet different needs. Some CODECs do a better job of compression, but lose some of the sound quality. Others keep all the quality, but might not compress as well. So even if you have a WAV file, if it doesn't have the proper CODEC, it won't play. The same is true for video. In video, if you don't have the proper CODEC, you'll see something that tells you you're missing the CODEC. Unfortunately, in audio files, you usually get no more than an "Invalid File Format" error. When receiving a multimedia file, it is common to ask about both the file format and the CODEC to ensure that the file can be played.

Clearly, the process of providing device drivers for sound has moved from the incredibly complicated DOS world to the almost boring world of Windows 95/98. Yet the process of making a sound card "do its thing" remains basically the same in ensuring correct connections, valid resource usage, and proper loading of device drivers. By following these steps, multimedia configuration will be a basic, although sometimes tedious, process.

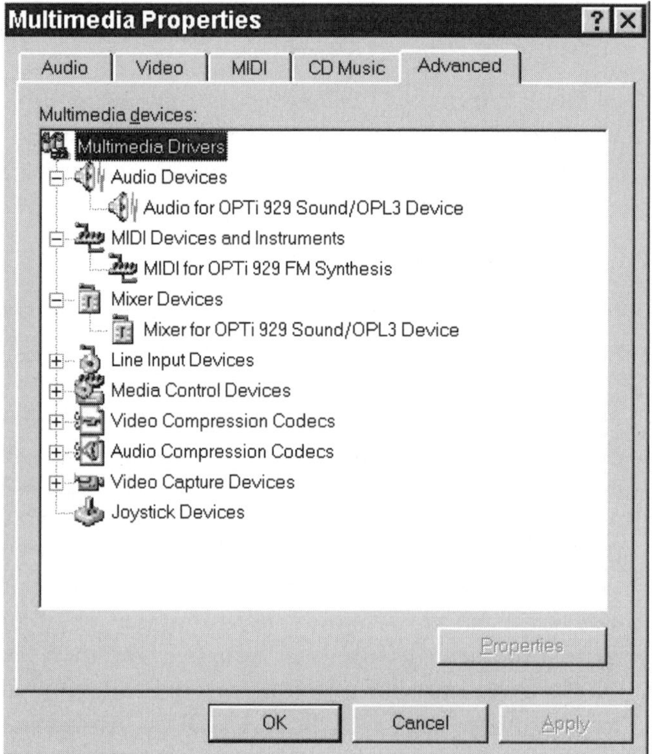

Figure 20.26 Advanced settings in Windows 95's multimedia

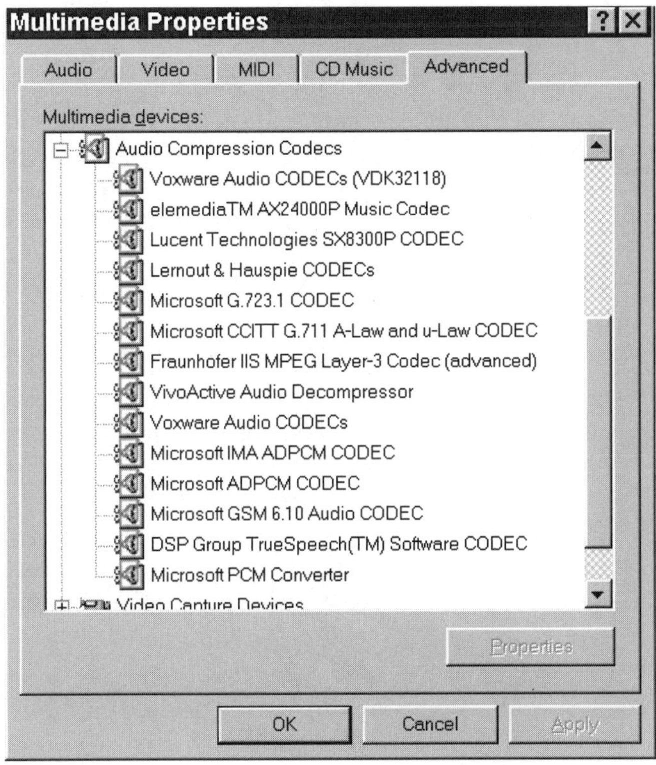

Figure 20.27 Typical CODECs installed in Windows 95

Troubleshooting

Whether sound is on an old DOS machine or the most recent version of Windows 98, when something goes wrong, certain areas point to the problem. The trick is to appreciate that all sound problems can be broken down into three groups: physical, resource, and driver.

PHYSICAL ERRORS Simply stated, this means that something isn't turned on, plugged in, or turned up. Of all problems with sound cards, these are probably the easiest, most common, and also most overlooked. Fortunately, they are easy to diagnose—the software says everything is great, but no sound comes out (or, in the case of a microphone, no sound goes in). A good triple-check is important here to verify that all connections are good and to make sure that devices that need power are getting it.

Be careful with volume controls. There can be up to four places to change volume, and if any of these are turned down, the system will have no sound. Many speakers have a volume control, and a few of the older sound cards will have a volume control wheel on the card itself. In the software world, individual applications have a volume control, and the operating system itself might also have a volume control.

Last, remember that speaker and microphone wires are exposed to all the abuse that shoes, chairs, and vacuum cleaners can provide. Most of the time, wires fray on the inside and slowly come apart without anything noticeable happening to the outside jacket. Listen for cracking sounds coming from the speakers and in recordings made by the microphone. This usually points to bad wires.

RESOURCES All sound cards need I/O addresses, IRQs, and DMA channels; even PCI sound cards will map an IRQ to the ISA bus. It is imperative to properly configure sound-card resources to get the card to work. Generally, the two big clues to resource errors are: applications and device drivers giving errors saying they can't find the card or the card is not working properly, and system lockups.

In DOS, this is usually seen at boot. As the device drivers load, they spout off error codes such as "Error: sound card not found or not working!" or "SND002: No sound device found at I/O address 220." These errors sometime move by quickly; use the F8 key to step through the driver so you can see the errors. Then it's time to check jumpers, rerun installations, and use diagnostic software to properly set up the card and the device driver. Once they are properly configured, write the settings down.

Windows 3.*x* is very good at providing clues to problems. First, DOS drivers give errors as they boot. Second, as Windows 3.*x* loads, any device driver that can't find its hardware will give an error (Figure 20-28). The only trick is in knowing what device is giving the error. Since most resources errors occur during installation, however, it's usually obvious.

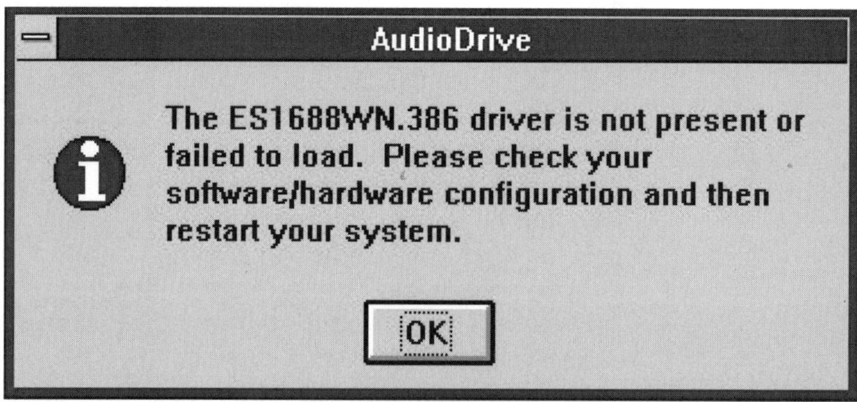

Figure 20.28 Sound-card error in Windows 3.x

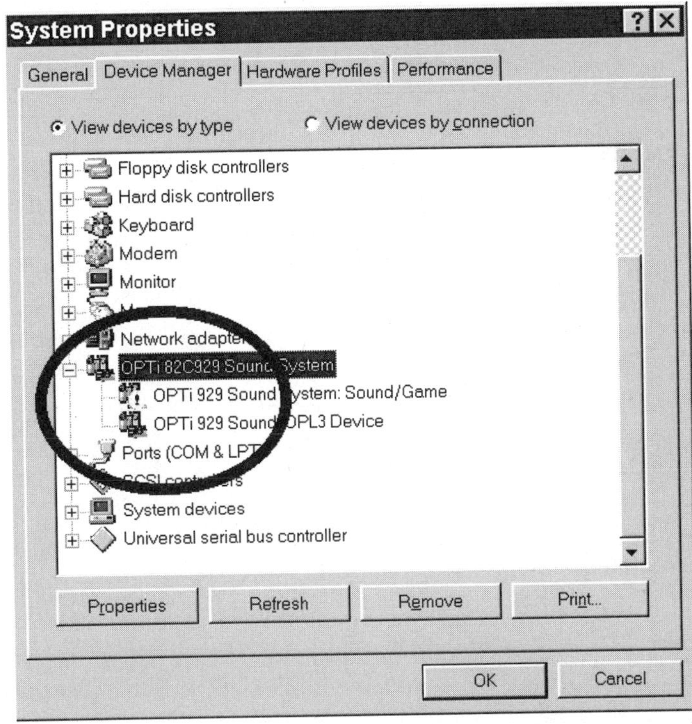

Figure 20.29 Sound-card error in Windows 95

Check the card again and rerun installation programs. Additionally, make sure that you need the DOS drivers by checking the sound-card documentation. If the system makes sounds only in Windows, these drivers can often be removed. If the DOS drivers are required, make sure that the resources for the DOS drivers match the resources for the Windows drivers.

Windows 95/98 is the easiest of all, assuming that it sees the card (it almost always does). Not only does the system give a boot error, but it also generates an exclamation in the Device Manager, showing that the device is not working properly (Figure 20-29).

Since resource errors are relatively rare in a Plug-n-Play world, the problem is usually due to incorrect Plug-n-Play settings in CMOS and the card not finding an open IRQ. Make sure that the PnP is set to Automatic or the PnP operating system is present. If other cards force the system's PnP to be set manually, make sure that the card can access one of its IRQs. Look in the sound-card properties in the Device Manager or open its INF file to determine what IRQs the card can use. Here's part of a sound card's IRQ settings from its INF file:

```
[OPT0929.LC0_0_1]
ConfigPriority=NORMAL
```

```
IOConfig=201-201                        ; 00 JOYSTICK
IOConfig=530-537, 604-60B, E80-E87, F40-F47
IOConfig=388-38B
IOConfig=F8D-F93
IOConfig=300-301 , 310-311 , 320-321 , 330-331
IRQConfig=9, 11
IRQConfig=10, 9, 7, 5
DMAConfig=0, 1, 3
DMAConfig=0, 1, 3
```

In this case, the card can choose from many IRQs. Make sure that at least one is available *before* the card is installed. Don't forget that sound cards might require separate I/O addresses, IRQs, or DMAs. If the systems plays WAVs but not MIDI files, or MIDIs but not WAVs, make sure that each type of necessary device has the proper resources.

DOS and Windows 3.*x* systems are very susceptible to lockups due to IRQ and DMA conflicts. The lockups might be somewhat deceptive, as most sound cards don't use the IRQs and DMAs constantly. For example, a sound card often won't use IRQs when playing WAV files, but it will when recording. As this is different for different cards, there is no one solid answer other than to try to recreate the lockup situation. If the lockup can be recreated, that's a sure sign of IRQ/DMA conflict.

Be aware that a damaged sound card looks just like a resource problem. Some sound cards come with a diagnostic to allow them to be tested without any type of installed drivers, but many sound cards don't have such a diagnostic. If the proper drivers are installed, all jumpers/switches and setup programs are properly run, the resources are known to be available, and the card still refuses to work, then the card is physically damaged and it is time to replace the card.

DRIVERS All sound cards come with drivers. You can count on a sound card to have Windows 95/98 and Windows 3.*x* drivers, although many cards no longer provide DOS drivers. Windows 95/98 also comes with drivers to support a vast majority of sound cards. The problem is that, as quickly as a device comes out, new drivers are written to replace the existing drivers. These new drivers are written to correct discovered conflicts, fix errors or inefficiencies in the original drivers, or take advantage of new technologies such as CODECs. This means that the driver that comes with a sound card or is supplied with Windows 95/98 is often obsolete before it even gets a chance to be used. It's a good idea to poke around the manufacturer Web sites before installing a new card, and then again every few months to see if a driver has been updated.

Incorrect or corrupted drivers usually manifest themselves with lockups, general protection faults (in Windows 3.*x*), and page faults (in Windows 95/98). The fix is to uninstall/reinstall the drivers. As most corrupted drivers get that way due to bad hard drives, be sure to thoroughly check out the drive—SCANDISK at the very least—before reinstalling. If possible, get the replacement drivers from another source other than the original installation, as you might just be recreating the problem.

INDEX

Illustrations are indicated in **boldface**.

D

I

N

O

P

Q

R

T

About the Author

Michael Meyers is president of Total Seminars, LLC, a major provider of PC and network repair seminars for individuals, corporate clients, and governmental agencies throughout the United States.

ENCLOSED CD-ROM

The attached CD contains:

4 FREE A+ Practice Exams, 2 core and 2 DOS/Win exams

Each test can be taken in two ways: Exam or Practice mode. Exam mode emulates the actual exam, giving you a final score at the end of the exam. Practice mode gives you book references for each question to look up before you answer.

At the end of each exam you get your score and can print a list of the questions you missed with an explanation of the correct answer and a book reference for further study.

Access to 500 Additional Test Questions

Contained on the CD are 5 Core exams and 5 DOS/WIN exams that are "locked." Key codes to "unlock" these exams can be purchased from Softlock by phone, email or over the Internet with a secure web browser. The cost for a key code to access the additional questions is $79. The CD contains a utility to walk you through this process.

Shareware/Freeware

On the CD is a \UTILS directory that holds freeware and shareware referenced in the book. Read the programs README files for instruction as to their proper use. These programs are not the property of McGraw-Hill or Total Seminars. You must abide by each program's software license agreement before use.

By opening the enclosed CD package, you are agreeing to be bound by the following agreement:

This software product is copyrighted, and all rights are reserved by Total Seminars, LLC or the licensers of the software. You are licensed to use this software on a single computer. You may copy and/or modify the software as needed to facilitate your use of it on a single computer. Making copies of the software for any other purpose is a violation of the United States copyright laws.

This software is sold as is without warranty of any kind, expressed or implied, including but not limited to the implied warranties of merchantability and fitness for a particular purpose. Neither the author, publisher nor its dealers for distributors assume any liability for any alleged or actual damages arising from the use of these programs. (Some states do not allow for the exclusion of implied warranties, so the exclusion may not apply to you.)

SOFTWARE AND INFORMATION LICENSE

The software and information on this diskette (collectively referred to as the "Product") are the property of The McGraw-Hill Companies, Inc. ("McGraw-Hill") and are protected by both United States copyright law and international copyright treaty provision. You must treat this Product just like a book, except that you may copy it into a computer to be used and you may make archival copies of the Products for the sole purpose of backing up our software and protecting your investment from loss.

By saying "just like a book," McGraw-Hill means, for example, that the Product may be used by any number of people and may be freely moved from one computer location to another, so long as there is no possibility of the Product (or any part of the Product) being used at one location or on one computer while it is being used at another. Just as a book cannot be read by two different people in two different places at the same time, neither can the Product be used by two different people in two different places at the same time (unless, of course, McGraw-Hill's rights are being violated).

McGraw-Hill reserves the right to alter or modify the contents of the Product at any time.

This agreement is effective until terminated. The Agreement will terminate automatically without notice if you fail to comply with any provisions of this Agreement. In the event of termination by reason of your breach, you will destroy or erase all copies of the Product installed on any computer system or made for backup purposes and shall expunge the Product from your data storage facilities.

LIMITED WARRANTY

McGraw-Hill warrants the physical diskette(s) enclosed herein to be free of defects in materials and workmanship for a period of sixty days from the purchase date. If McGraw-Hill receives written notification within the warranty period of defects in materials or workmanship, and such notification is determined by McGraw-Hill to be correct, McGraw-Hill will replace the defective diskette(s). Send request to:

Customer Service
McGraw-Hill
Gahanna Industrial Park
860 Taylor Station Road
Blacklick, OH 43004-9615

The entire and exclusive liability and remedy for breach of this Limited Warranty shall be limited to replacement of defective diskette(s) and shall not include or extend to any claim for or right to cover any other damages, including but not limited to, loss of profit, data, or use of the software, or special, incidental, or consequential damages or other similar claims, even if McGraw-Hill has been specifically advised as to the possibility of such damages. In no event will McGraw-Hill's liability for any damages to you or any other person ever exceed the lower of suggested list price or actual price paid for the license to use the Product, regardless of any form of the claim.

THE McGRAW-HILL COMPANIES, INC. SPECIFICALLY DISCLAIMS ALL OTHER WARRANTIES, EXPRESS OR IMPLIED, INCLUDING BUT NOT LIMITED TO, ANY IMPLIED WARRANTY OF MERCHANTABILITY OR FITNESS FOR A PARTICULAR PURPOSE. Specifically, McGraw-Hill makes no representation or warranty that the Product is fit for any particular purpose and any implied warranty of merchantability is limited to the sixty day duration of the Limited Warranty covering the physical diskette(s) only (and not the software or in-formation) and is otherwise expressly and specifically disclaimed.

This Limited Warranty gives you specific legal rights; you may have others which may vary from state to state. Some states do not allow the exclusion of incidental or consequential damages, or the limitation on how long an implied warranty lasts, so some of the above may not apply to you.

This Agreement constitutes the entire agreement between the parties relating to use of the Product. The terms of any purchase order shall have no effect on the terms of this Agreement. Failure of McGraw-Hill to insist at any time on strict compliance with this Agreement shall not constitute a waiver of any rights under this Agreement. This Agreement shall be construed and governed in accordance with the laws of New York. If any provision of this Agreement is held to be contrary to law, that provision will be enforced to the maximum extent permissible and the remaining provisions will remain in force and effect.